D1831267

# THE LIFE AND LETTERS
# OF
# THE RIGHT HONOURABLE
# FRIEDRICH MAX MULLER

F. Max Müller.

Aged 41

# THE LIFE AND LETTERS
# OF
# THE RIGHT HONOURABLE
# FRIEDRICH MAX MULLER

EDITED BY HIS WIFE

IN TWO VOLUMES

VOL. I

WITH PORTRAITS AND OTHER ILLUSTRATIONS

GYAN

*Published by*

Gyan Publishing House
5, Ansari Road
Daryaganj, New Delhi-110002
Phone: 011-47034999, 9811692060
E-mail: books@gyanbooks.com

*Distribution Network*
gyanbooks.com
India, USA, Canada, UK, Australia, France

**© Publisher**

All rights reserved. No part of this work may be reproduced, stored, adapted, or transmitted in any form or by any means, electronic, mechanical, photocopying, micro-filming, recording or otherwise, or translated in any language, without the prior written permission of the copyright owner and the publisher.

ISBN : 978-81-212-3707-9 (Set)
ISBN : 978-81-212-4845-7 (PB)
First Published, 1903

2nd Impression 2020

*Printed at:* Gyan Press, Delhi.

The book is sold subject to the condition that it shall not, by way of trade or otherwise, be lent, resold, hired out, or otherwise circulated without the prior publisher's written consent.

**The Life and Letters**
**of**
**The Right Honourable Friedrich Max Muller**
Edited by: Mrs. Friedrich Max Muller

# THE LIFE AND LETTERS

OF

THE RIGHT HONOURABLE

# FRIEDRICH MAX MULLER

EDITED BY HIS WIFE

'Blessed is he who has found his work: let him ask no other blessedness'

CARLYLE

IN TWO VOLUMES: VOL. I

WITH PORTRAITS AND OTHER ILLUSTRATIONS

LONGMANS, GREEN, AND CO.
39 PATERNOSTER ROW, LONDON
NEW YORK AND BOMBAY
1902

DEDICATED

TO THE

BELOVED MEMORY

OF A

GREAT AND GOOD MAN

# PREFACE

It may be thought that the publication of these volumes is superfluous after the two works *Auld Lang Syne* and the *Autobiography*, written by Max Müller himself. But it seemed that something more was wanted to show the innermost character of the real man; for *Auld Lang Syne* gave recollections of his friends only, 'a small portion of the panorama of life that passed before' his eyes; and the *Autobiography* is but a fragment, bringing us little beyond the threshold of his career. The plan pursued throughout these volumes has been to let Max Müller's letters and the testimony of friends to his mind and character speak for themselves, whilst the whole is connected by a slight thread of necessary narrative. The selection from the letters has been made with a view to bring the man rather than the scholar before the world. His innumerable works, covering a period of nearly sixty years, have made known the scholar; the object of this book is to show 'the elevation of soul and enlargement of mental outlook which was revealed more and more as his life's work opened up before him[1]'—that work which he carried on to within ten days of his death.

It is a matter of regret that much valuable correspondence has been destroyed. In America no letters have been preserved to Emerson or Oliver

[1] Funeral Sermon.—Rev. H. J. Bidder.

Wendell Holmes, and only one to Lowell. In England the letters to Carlyle, Sellar, Froude, Sir A. Grant, and other intimate friends have been burnt. In Germany all to Humboldt are gone, and all except a few trifling notes to the brothers Curtius, to Carrière, Mommsen, and others. In France none have been found to Stanislas Julien, to Regnier, or Barthélemy-St.-Hilaire. From Italy, too, no letters have been recovered. The corresponding letters from these distinguished men show how much of deep interest to the public has been lost.

I here desire to express my grateful thanks to many friends and relatives who have helped me in my task, especially to Mrs. Rowland Corbet and Miss Mabel Peach, who have translated and copied innumerable letters for me; to the many known and unknown in all quarters of the globe who responded to my petition for letters; and I am also greatly indebted to Messrs. Hills and Saunders for the use of the Photographs which illustrate the work.

If at times I have found the labour almost beyond my powers, it has been a labour of love, bringing strength and solace to many lonely hours. As Mr. Mozoomdar writes to me, 'The most heavenly relation here is the relation between the living and the dear dead. We cannot draw them down to us, but they continually draw us to them.'

GEORGINA MAX MÜLLER.

IGHTHAM MOTE,
*September*, 1902.

# CONTENTS

## LIST OF ILLUSTRATIONS

# CHAPTER I

## 1823–1841

Parentage. Father's death. Dessau. Musical training. School. Poetical tendencies. Nicolai School, Leipzig. Dr. Carus. Music. Letters to his mother. Examination at Zerbst.

FRIEDRICH MAX MÜLLER was born at Dessau, the capital of the Duchy of Anhalt Dessau, on December 6, 1823. His father was the popular lyric poet, Wilhelm Müller, Librarian to the Duke of Dessau, and master at the Gymnasium (chief school) in that place; a man of great cultivation, of most genial disposition, a general favourite, keenly alive to the enjoyments of life, in every way of noble and forcible character.

Max Müller's mother was Adelheid, elder daughter of President von Basedow, Prime Minister of the Duchy of Dessau. She was very small, but very beautiful, clever and lively, and had a fine contralto voice; and it was from her that Max Müller inherited his intense love of music. Frau Hofräthin Müller was a highly cultivated woman, understanding English, French, and Italian perfectly. She was a woman of an eager, even passionate temperament, and her children evidently suffered early from this, as Wilhelm Müller's letters are full of warnings to her not to punish too severely, and not to expect too much from her children (babies of four and five when their father died). Her father, President von Basedow, was himself the son of a man famous in Germany in his day, the pedagogue Basedow, the forerunner of Pestalozzi and Fröbel.

Friedrich Max was named after his mother's elder brother,

who later on succeeded his own father as President of the Duchy, and after Max in the *Freischütz*, an opera which had then just appeared; Carl Maria von Weber being an intimate friend of his parents and Max's godfather. Soon after he finally settled in England he used Max as part of his surname, Müller alone, as he always said, being as distinctive a name as Smith without any prefix in England. His only sister was nearly two years older than himself, and he never had any brother. Max Müller had but a vague memory of his first home, the Librarian's house in Dessau, with its pretty garden—a memory founded more on visits to the house in subsequent years than on any clear remembrance of his life there. His recollections of his father, too, were very dim, as he was not quite four at the time of his death. Such as they were they are recorded in the *Autobiography*.

'Wilhelm Müller's life in Dessau was a very happy one,' wrote his friend, the poet Gustav Schwab; 'he was valued by his Duke and Duchess . . . devotedly loved by his pupils, and a favourite with all who had once recognized his character and nature; he had a clever, attractive wife, and healthy, handsome children, to whom he was a most devoted father, and with whom he would play for hours like a merry child himself.' Though only thirty-three when he died, he had achieved a considerable amount of work, and evidently possessed the power of working rapidly, a power inherited by his son. The end to this happy life came with frightful suddenness. Wilhelm Müller had been to Oranienbaum, a park near Dessau, to see the Duke, and returned late, in high spirits. In the night his young wife woke to find him dead by her side! The awful shock is supposed to have brought on the deafness from which she soon began to suffer, and which became total many years before her death. Adelheid Müller, who had only a small pension as the widow of a civil servant, went for a time with her two children to live in her father's house, the house she had left but a few years before as a brilliant, happy bride.

But Wilhelm Müller's widow had not been forgotten by his friend and patron, and shortly after his death she received the following letter from the Duke of Dessau:—

*Translation.*

'Whilst I wish again to express my sincere sympathy in the great loss you have sustained, I am anxious in some degree to lessen the cares which the education of your children must bring, and I therefore grant you, as long as you remain a widow, the yearly sum of 100 thalers[1] till your son has completed his twenty-first year, and then for your life the sum of fifty thalers, to begin from the first of this month. I beg to assure you of the continuance of my true esteem.
LEOPOLD.

'*Nov.* 30, 1827.'

Max Müller tells us in his *Autobiography* of the gloom cast over his whole childhood by his father's death. Happily he had inherited much of that father's joyous temperament, so that the almost daily visits to the grave 'where the young mother stood and sobbed and cried' whilst her two children looked on, had less effect on him than might be expected; and the constant intercourse with various friends and relations brightened what would otherwise have been a time of dark memory for his whole life. The few left who remember those early days agree in describing Max Müller as brimful of fun and mischief, and his mother's old servant Hanna, who lived to a great age and was never tired of asking for news of her former torment, used in those early days to call him *Dieser infame Junge*, 'this terrible boy.'

After some years, Hofräthin Müller left her father's home and settled herself and her two children on the ground floor of a very small house. This house, though altered and improved, is still standing, a type of the old style of Dessau houses, consisting of a ground floor and one story above, with a loft under the high-pitched brown roof. The house looks into the churchyard of the Johannis Kirche, the church mentioned in *Deutsche Liebe*, where the effect of the Easter hymn on the musical child is so vividly described:—

*Translation.*

'On this Easter Day . . . the old church, with its grey slate roof, and the high windows, and the tower with the golden cross, shone with marvellous brightness. Suddenly the light which streamed through the high windows began to wave and seem alive. But it

[1] £15.

was far too bright to look at; and as I shut my eyes, the light still came into my soul, and everything seemed to shine and be fragrant, and to sing and sound. I felt as if a new life began in me, as if I had become another being—and when I asked my mother what it was, she said it was an Easter hymn, which they were singing in the church. I have never been able to discover what was the pure holy song which then sank into my soul. . . . I have never heard it again. But now when I hear an adagio of Beethoven, or a psalm of Marcello, or a chorus of Händel . . . I feel as if the lofty church windows were again sparkling, as if the organ notes rang through my soul and a new world opened to me.'

It is needless to repeat all that Max Müller has told us in *Auld Lang Syne* and the *Autobiography* of the life at Dessau, and the appearance of the little *Residenz-Stadt* (capital) at that time, still walled in, and with gates shut every night, its night watchman, and the oil lamps swinging across the streets. The night watchman and the oil lamps existed till late in the century. And yet with these primitive arrangements and simple life the little town was a centre of intellectual interest and cultivation. Music, such as one hears now only in a great capital; a first-rate theatre, as far as the acting and opera were concerned; real intellectual society, which hardly exists in our hurried modern life—were all to be found at Dessau, and enjoyed at so modest a cost that they were within reach of all.

Those who remember Max Müller's pianoforte playing when he first came to England will not be surprised to hear that his musical training began very early, and before he went to any school. A young musician who lived next door taught him to play, as a surprise to his mother. They had made friends over the hedge that divided their gardens, and after the musician had discovered the little fellow's genuine love of music he lifted him daily over the hedge, and gave him his lesson. For months the child kept the secret, till at last one day he sat down before several friends and played his first piece. There are easy sonatas of Beethoven with his name on them and the date, showing that he was only six years old when he learnt them. At fourteen he played brilliantly, and took part in concerts at Dessau and Leipzig, and when at home for the holidays was often sent for by the Duchess of

Dessau, who was herself a fine musician, to play duets with her on the piano. Whilst still quite a child he was invited to any good music that was given in Dessau. One note written by a Dr. Otta, about the year 1831, runs thus:—

*Translation.*

'In the hopes of giving you pleasure, I take the liberty of inviting you to hear the quintette to be played to-night at my house. I trust your mother will kindly give you permission.'

The note is addressed to—

The distinguished Musician
Master Max Müller.

When Max was only six years old Mendelssohn visited Dessau, and taking the child into the large church set him on his lap at the organ and made him play the keys, whilst he himself managed the pedals, which the little boy could not reach.

Many of Wilhelm Müller's old friends took an interest in his lively attractive boy.

There is a charming letter dated Saturday, July 31, 1830, from M. Gathy, to whose friendship Max Müller owed a good deal in later years in Paris:—

*Translation.*

'As I could not, my good Max, have you, as I wished, last Sunday for a long visit, I keep you to your promise and invite you and your dear little sister to have breakfast with me to-morrow at half-past eight, hoping that you will both receive permission to do so. If you paid me a visit in Hamburg, I could show you many beautiful things—toys of every sort, and particularly the most beautiful coloured tin soldiers, which would delight you. But I have left them all at home, and the hobby-horse and dolls and toys I have here would not amuse you. Toys are delightful—are they not, Max?—when one receives them from one's loved parents; but other things, that one must be busy with, for other reasons, when one is older, are not nearly so pretty, or so nice to play with. Besides my brave tin soldiers, I had three beautiful collections of pictures, and flowers and butterflies. But one cannot always keep, my good Max, what one has, and, alas! everything does not last as one would wish. Everything is perishable, everything changes, and that is a great pity. Now, I still have all the pictures. I carry them about with me, yet I cannot show them to you; but the flowers are all withered, and mostly turned to dust, and my lovely coloured butterflies turn at last into crickets [1], which do not look so pretty or so pleasant. So it is with my toys, my good Max. But it does not matter; I will be like my little soldiers, which were always my greatest delight. They stood up firmly, without knowing why, and let themselves be seized and pushed about on every side, and fought bravely and never complained. And when evening came they were gathered together and placed quietly in the dark cupboard, and there was peace. But don't be frightened, Max: come here and bring your fine sword with you; we will play and talk with each other, and from the window nod to your dear mother, as I always like to do, as she goes by to church, to pray the good God that you may always be a courteous, kind, good boy, and learn diligently and thrive to your own good, and her pleasure. Adieu, dear Max; you are expected then by your friend GATHY.'

It is doubtful whether, inborn poet as he was, Max Müller could at six and a half have understood the beauty and pathos of this letter from the little deformed Jew.

Max entered the Gymnasium or High School at Dessau at six years old, and remained there till he was past twelve. His school reports were not remarkable, and certainly at that time he gave little evidence of the power that was in him. 'Writing bad' was the almost invariable report, and in later years he often lamented the small pains taken by the writing-master to improve it. An old schoolfellow, still living at Dessau, writes that all the other boys considered him a clever boy. 'He was full of life and much loved by all his schoolfellows.'

To our ideas the life led by the little Max was one of considerable hardship. Thinly clad and poorly fed, not from want of care and love, but from sheer poverty, his breath in winter frozen into a sheet of ice on his bed from the absence of fire, suffering from constant headaches, which may have originated from want of full nourishment such as a growing child needs, and yet nothing seems to have clouded his naturally sunny, joyous temperament. He tells us: 'As a little boy, when I could not have the same toys which other boys possessed I could fully enjoy what they enjoyed, as if they had been my own. It was not the result of teaching,

[1] A play on the word *Grillen*, which means crickets, and worries.

still less of reasoning—it was a sentiment given me, and which certainly did not leave me till much later in life.'

He remembered how constantly he was enjoined to take care of his clothes and make them last: and when he and his sister returned from school the boots that cost so much were put away and replaced by shoes made for them by the careful mother. It was this frugal training, this life of constant self-denial and careful thought for every trifle, that gave Max Müller in after life the feeling of thankfulness, and the power of rejoicing in every little luxury and pleasure which he could afford himself. To the very last 'the child's pure delight in little things' gave a constant zest to his life, and made it easy for others to give him pleasure. Through his whole life he took every good thing, every honour that he received, as a gift he had not deserved. Some of his critics, who never knew him personally, speak of his vanity, because he dwelt with pleasure and gratitude on the honours and successes that came to him in later life. Any really vain man would have shrunk from showing his enjoyment of the good things that fell to him, for fear of being thought vain. One who knew him well mentions his entire freedom from vanity as a prominent point in his character. There is a mock humility more akin to vanity than the grateful rejoicing in all blessings (his own talents included) which was a characteristic of Max Müller's whole life. It is true that he greatly valued and even desired the love and approbation so largely accorded him, but this arose from his loving nature, which craved for sympathy, and not from vanity.

One more glimpse is given us of the early life in a letter from his von Basedow grandmother. His mother had gone in the early summer of 1835 with some friends to Heligoland; and she took her daughter with her, leaving Max at his grandfather's to go to his school. The Frau Präsident writes to her absent daughter:—

*Translation.*

'6 a.m. MY DEAR ADELHEID,—The father is out riding, Max is having his music lesson, Julie is still asleep, and I am sitting in the garden, in the summer-house, where we breakfast every morning. I think that I cannot employ my time better than in writing to you, to give you an account of us all, for Max now belongs to us. We are all, down to the youngest, quite well, thank God. Max is very good and diligent, and has given no occasion for punishment. He bathes regularly, either with Fritz or our servant, but never alone. I am much too nervous to allow that. Just now he goes with Julie, who bathes every other day in the Mulde. We shall miss him very much when he leaves us, he has become quite one of us. You would be amused if you saw him smoking a pipe with his grandfather. He can also take a pinch of snuff, and he does not refuse a taste of liqueur. The father has a very quiet horse on which he can ride alone, so you will find him quite a grown-up man in all the finer arts. His trousers indeed have a very variegated appearance from cherries, bilberries, and ink, but a young man does not think much of that.'

We have spoken of Max Müller as an inborn poet, and in later life he told a friend he had all his life tried not to be a poet. From the early age of nine he began to write verses, all of which were carefully kept by his devoted mother. They are verses written for Christmas, or family birthdays, but one on the beautiful God's Acre at Dessau attempts a higher flight.

'It is a beautiful and restful place,' he says in the *Autobiography*, 'covered with old acacia trees.' It was probably this association that gave Max Müller a peculiar love for acacia trees, and it was a real grief to him when one that stood in the Parks close to his house in Norham Gardens withered and died. He tells us that the inscription over the gateway of the God's Acre was a puzzle to his young mind: 'Death is not death, 'tis but the ennobling of man's nature.' It may have been the echo of these words in his mind that made him in 1884, in writing to one of his Buddhist pupils, speak of 'looking forward to a better life—I mean a life in which *we* shall be better.' When at school at Leipzig he constantly wrote poems in the letters he sent his mother, and there were three occasions at his school at Leipzig where he had to recite publicly verses of his own writing. There is a whole book full of manuscript sonnets and poems written during his University career, some of which were published at the time in journals and papers, and brought in a little money, most acceptable to the poor student. During the hard battle with life in Paris and London, the muse seems to have been silent. A few beautiful sonnets exist, written later under the pressure of great sorrow, but his life was too full of other work, to which he was pledged to devote his time, for him to indulge in poetry, and except two sonnets to the Emperor Frederick (1871 and 1888), and an ode on the death of the Duke of Albany, nothing exists written in later years but a few birthday couplets. Max Müller never published any of his poems, except in his University days.

After his grandfather's death Max was sent, at Easter, 1836, to the famous Nicolai School at Leipzig. He lived in the house of Dr. Carus, an old family friend, whose only son, Victor, was of the same age. 'Max was taken as a friend,' writes Professor Victor Carus, 'and was treated entirely as a son of the family. Aunt Müller, as his mother was called by all of us, never paid anything, as my parents were intimate friends of hers. We went together to the Nicolai School, we slept in the same room, worked together, and had, in fact, everything in common.' Max was placed in Quarta, which answers to Remove at Eton. The education was almost entirely classical, and before he left the school, five years later, he could speak Latin with perfect ease. He was able to hear a great deal of good music at Leipzig, Frau Carus herself being very musical, with a fine voice, and she and Dr. Carus delighted in collecting the best musicians at their house. Victor Carus was a good violinist, and when the two young friends, Victor and Max, were about fifteen years old, they astonished Dr. Carus on his birthday by playing the whole Kreutzer Sonata by heart.

There had long been an intimate friendship between the Mendelssohns and Max Müller's parents, therefore he naturally saw much of Felix Mendelssohn, who was conductor of the Gewandhaus Concerts at Leipzig from 1835 to 1843. He thus describes his first musical evening to his mother :—

*Translation.*

'I went on Friday to Mendelssohn's, and already on the staircase heard the lovely music. I went in bravely[1], and was received in the

[1] He was little over thirteen.

most friendly manner. I found Felix, David, Dreischock, and Mendelssohn's sister Fanny. Hensel was very kind, so was she; both spoke of you, and Hensel of my father too, whom he admired immensely. Mendelssohn stood close to the piano, and I sat where I could watch Dreischock with great comfort. He is still the first of pianists, and quite a young man. He played here last winter and was taken for Thalberg. He played really marvellously, so that Mendelssohn wondered at his skill, though he (Felix) immediately afterwards played an imitation of his composition. I must say, I much prefer Mendelssohn, even if the other has more skill, particularly in octave playing, in which he is decidedly the first of artists. Then Hensel told me a delightful story. They had already last Wednesday sent here for me, but Sophie did not understand the maid, and sent her to Dr. Müller, who lives behind this in the Garden house. And so he went in the evening, beautifully got up, and nobody knew him, or what to say to him. That was funny.'

Later, he writes thus of Thalberg:—

*Translation.*

'Now I have seen and heard Thalberg. It was yesterday evening. It is indescribable. I am still perfectly enchanted by it; there can be nothing else like it. He is quite young, handsome, and very distinguished looking, beautiful hands and such skill, execution, and power.'

From the time he went to Leipzig, Max Müller began the correspondence with his passionately loved mother, which continued till the year of her death, 1883. Almost every letter has been kept, and the whole forms a complete journal of his doings when not with her. With his ardent affection for her, he felt the separation keenly, and writes on the first birthday on which he was not with her, as follows:—

*Translation.* *Oct.* 10, 1836.

'MY DEAR GOOD MOTHER,—To-day, for the first time, I have to be far away from you on your birthday, and you can fancy how sorry I am. I think it grieves you too, little mother, for I know your love for me. Oh, how I long to be with you, only for a moment, only to press you in my arms, only to tell you how I love you: but it can't be. Your birthday is always doubly dear to me, first because it is your birthday, and then because it was the first day that you roused yourself again from your sorrow [1], to which just in these weeks of the year you

[1] W. Müller died Oct. 1; her birthday was Oct. 12.

gave way more than usually. You were right to grieve, and it would not have been proper to try to console and amuse you. You must have sorrowed this year more than usual, as the birthday of our good grandfather was this week. But I will not write more about this; it will but renew your sorrow. I will only say that God has replaced something of what you have lost, in giving you two beings who love you as no others do. You best know whom I mean.

'Your Max.'

These early letters to his mother show a maturity of thought and earnestness of purpose that are very unusual in so young a boy; and as life went on the relations of mother and son seem changed, and it is the son who takes the guiding and protecting tone towards the mother.

In March, 1839, Dr. Carus lost his wife, who had watched over Max with the same motherly care she gave to her own boy. His grief at the time, and his later letters, prove how sorely he missed her. In one letter he gives his mother an account of his day, which would probably have been laid out more wisely had the kind *Tante* (aunt) been still there to watch over him.

*Translation.*

'You will be surprised to hear that I have arranged everything for certain fixed hours, but I am very glad to have settled it so that I am not interrupted. I get up at five, or even earlier, and work till seven, go to school, play the violoncello at eleven, the piano at twelve, then dinner, then school again, then coffee and gymnastic exercises, then work again till I can get fresh air in the garden, which is impossible in this heat, during the day. I seem quite changed to myself, and you know that such punctual arrangements were not at all in my line. I eat only a roll from five in the morning till one o'clock, and drink no coffee early, and I often feel rather faint. Then for the last week I have had constant headaches, but I am getting quite accustomed to them, and I lead a very happy life.'

In the last years of his school life he seems to have read a good deal for himself, and discusses the books he reads with his mother.

*Translation.*

'I had already said to myself that you would not be pleased that I had read *Wilhelm Meister*, and in some respects you are quite right; not that it can exactly hurt me, but that it might occupy my thoughts too much. On the evil influence of reading or other temptations, I could not point out any better passage than the Latin verse in *Faust* which Mephistopheles repeats to the student, that God is holy and good just because He knows what evil is. This is very true if only further explained, i. e. because He knows evil, but never commits it. If we could imagine that God did not know what sin and temptation are, we could not call Him God, for we should have an imperfect God. . . . The more dangerous things I read, the stronger I become, if I am not mistaken, to wage war with them. And yet again what you say is true, for how foolhardy it would be to throw oneself into temptations without thoroughly knowing oneself, and how far one could stand firm. So a *desire* for dangerous reading is in itself a crime.'

And again—

*Translation.*

'I have had a great deal of pleasure from Bettina von Arnim's letters and diary. It is full of beautiful feeling and well expressed, though towards the end it is weaker, for there it becomes laboured; at first it just bubbles up of its own accord.'

Though Max Müller tells us he had little chance of travelling during his school days, there is a journal of three days spent at Dresden and in a walking tour through Saxon Switzerland at Whitsuntide, 1839, when he was fifteen and a half years old. This visit gave him his first sight of really great works of art, for though there are some choice pieces of sculpture and a few good pictures at Dessau, the little capital naturally possesses nothing quite of the first rank. 'It was perfect enchantment,' he says, 'to step into the Raphael room, where the great Madonna standing on the globe shines down upon us, a picture that far exceeds all one's imagination, and stands there, the crown of all pictures.' The same feeling animated him in 1857, when he wrote in *Deutsche Liebe*: 'To stand before the Madonna di San Sisto in Dresden, and to allow all the thoughts to wake in us, which year after year the unfathomable look of the child has created in us.'

From reasons of economy he was not always able to spend his holidays at Dessau with his mother and sister, as we see from the following little note dated 'Silvester Evening,' that is December 31, probably 1839:—

*Translation.*

'How often I wish that I were so far advanced that I could myself earn something to make your life easier—you who deprive yourself of everything and spare everything to make us happy. But I will try to be more and more diligent, and better, that, as far as I can, I may give you pleasure, which is the only possible return for all your love and care.'

Max Müller had to pass his abiturienten examination in the early spring of 1841 at Zerbst, in order to gain a Dessau scholarship for the University. This examination was more scientific than classical, but he passed easily, taking a first class, and gained his scholarship, such as it was—£6—a mere trifle to English ideas, but an important help to him. Before the examination, Dr. Nobbe, the head master of the Nicolai School, wrote thus of him to his mother:—

*Translation.*

'I rejoice that I can see him leave this school with testimonials of moral excellence not often found in one of his years, possessed of knowledge first rate in more than one subject, and with intellectual capacities excellent throughout. May this young mind develop more and more, and may the fruits of his labours be hereafter a comfort to his mother for the sorrows and cares of the past.'

For months before leaving school, though only seventeen, the thought of the future weighed heavily on him, and he seems, almost to the time of entering the University, to have felt uncertain as to the special line of life he should adopt. Poor and without influence, it was necessary that he should be in a position to keep himself as soon as he left the University. The following letter shows how carefully he weighed and considered the question:—

To his Mother.

*Translation.*

'I recognized blindly that a free, unfettered life is the best, but did not reflect sufficiently on the results that might arise. . . .

'It would be indeed delightful, and my greatest wish, to be engaged actively as a philologist, and make a career at the University. But who can be certain that I shall distinguish myself? and where there is only mediocrity, this life as a philologist is miserable. Many struggle on their whole lives here as tutors (Privatdocent) and never arrive at being full Professors. Such a life costs a great deal, and how miserable I should feel, for there is something so uncertain in it, and one's success depends on how one pleases others by one's writings and lectures, and a risk of this kind in my circumstances seems too great. It is quite certain that I must have an assured support. On the grounds of prudence I consider philology *alone* as too uncertain a foundation, but that I wish to work in philology and philosophy is true. Remember the many works on these subjects by theologians and doctors. Think of distinguished philologists who have studied law. This influences me to look round for a certain position, that I may not attempt to erect an airy building, on a yet more airy foundation. Medicine is disagreeable to me; I am physically unfit for it. I like theology, but it is too unsettled and occupies too much time. There remains the law, which is certainly very dry and pedantic; but it may lead to more lively studies, and it also leaves time for other intellectual employments. One must begin everywhere in a small way. If other subjects of culture are added to the knowledge of law, that helps not a little—so one can lay the foundations of a satisfying life, for on good fortune or rather on God's will most things depend. If we do not forsake Him, He guides us at last to where we should be, however we may choose paths where we should like to walk. I have so far settled to choose my way, but if another road must be followed I shall not make myself unhappy. So do not be anxious about this.'

At Easter, 1841, Dr. Nobbe, in his farewell address to the boys who were leaving the Nicolai School, thus parted with Max Müller:—

*Translation.*

'I must also mention F. Max Müller from Dessau, a highly talented youth, who has just passed the final examination in his own Duchy, and who, with far from common endowments, joins the University, where he will study philology.'

On November 26, 1900, at the gathering always held in memory of the old members of the Nicolai School who have passed away in the year, the Director thus ended his mention of Max Müller, 'He was without any doubt, next to Leibniz, one of the greatest of our pupils.'

Before leaving the house of Dr. Carus, Max writes to his mother:—

*Translation.*

'When I remember the time that I first sent you my birthday greetings from Leipzig, and now see that this period of life is nearly over, I must gratefully acknowledge how good God has been to us in various ways, and has given us many compensations. But above all, how grateful we should be that God has preserved you, our dear mother, to us, to sweeten for us all that is bitter, to reward all effort. How I rejoice over next year, in which a new existence opens for me, a higher aim in life floats before me, and I shall have you both [1] with me. I cannot tell you how I rejoice at the thought of this time, when I must take another step forwards, and shall again, at all events for a time, be with my own people.'

Max Müller's old friend, Victor Carus, thus sums up his recollections of these school days :—

'Our chief recreations were pretty regular walks on Sundays during the summer, and skating in winter. There was no fencing during our school life, it was not allowed. It began at the University; if I remember, Max went to the "Fechtboden," the official fencing-lessons of the University. On the whole there was not much free time left to us, and we were happy when my parents had some music in the evening, or when we might amuse ourselves with my father's pensionnaires. Max was a handsome boy, but not so strikingly so as in later years. He was rather thin, and gave the impression of a delicate boy, but he was strong, and not once seriously ill.'

[1] His mother and sister.

# CHAPTER II

## 1841–1844

University life at Leipzig. Studies. Sanskrit. Friends. University life at Berlin. Friends. Lectures. Hagedorn. Humboldt. Bunsen.

MAX MÜLLER joined the University of Leipzig in the Summer Term, 1841; his mother and sister left Dessau and moved to Leipzig to make a home for him and lessen expenses. They occupied an apartment on the third floor of a house in Reichel's Garden, then on the very outskirts of the town, now entirely surrounded with houses. The arrangement was a very happy one; his clever, agreeable mother and pretty sister made his home bright and pleasant to his many student friends, whilst the mother wisely did not attempt to interfere with his perfect liberty. Of his studies and the immense variety of lectures he attended during his first term, Max Müller has given a full account in the *Autobiography*. He attended twelve separate courses of lectures, of which the subjects, except Greek and Latin, were totally new to him, yet he really worked hard at all these various subjects, took copious notes, some of which still exist, and read the books the Professors advised. He had no one to direct his studies, no father or older friend on whose advice he could rely. Later on, when he was elected to Hermann's Seminary and Haupt's Latin Society, these Professors gave him valuable help and guidance in his classical studies, and he did some work for them. It was probably the keen personal interest taken in him by Brockhaus, that led him eventually to turn his attention exclusively to Sanskrit. He entered the University as a philologist, and in the Winter Term of 1841–2 he began to study Sanskrit under the then newly appointed Professor, partly compelled, he says, by the charm of studying something which his friends and fellow students did not know. It was only in his last term at Leipzig that he first approached the subject he was to make so peculiarly his own, the Hymns of the *Rig-veda*.

During his time at the University, Max saw but little of his old friend Victor Carus. Dr. Carus had married again, and his house was in a part of Leipzig distant from that where Max Müller lived, and as the friends were studying totally different subjects they never met in the lecture-rooms. Professor Carus writes: 'I cannot tell you anything of Max's life as a student; the difference of our studies led us to different occupations, friendships, and ways.' Max Müller's chief friends were Theodore Fontane, so well known later as a novel writer, and Prowe, afterwards a master at the chief school at Thorn, with whom he formed an intimate friendship. Fontane gives an interesting account of a literary society which they frequented; it was a society of Leipzig poets, and to it belonged, among others, Fontane himself, Prowe, Wolfssohn, and Max Müller.

*Translation.*

'All made themselves a name in the small or great world. In the really great world, indeed, only one, the last named. Wolfssohn on certain points gave the tone to our society. We others were all young people of average attainments; Wolfssohn, on the contrary, was a refined man of the world. But the great feature of our club, of course from what he became afterwards, was Max Müller. He could have rivalled Wolfssohn on his own ground, that of social distinction, perhaps even beaten him, had he not been too young, only seventeen years of age. Feeling this, he kept himself in the background, and confined himself chiefly to following with the shrewd bright face of a squirrel our rodomontades on freedom, relative to our plans "pour culbuter toute l'Europe." Only now and then he himself shot off a small arrow. When the Journal for the Elegant World, which we always called for short "The Elegant," changed its editor, and appointed Heinrich Laube in the place of Gustav Kühne, Müller said, good-humouredly,

Was sich Kühne nicht erkühnt,
Wird sich Laube nicht erlauben[1].

'On the whole he went his own way, both in small and great matters. He was very much loved and respected in our circle, and

[1] Impossible to translate, from the play on the names.

that not only because, as we all knew, he had been a pattern scholar at school, but more especially as the son of his distinguished father. That he would in the eyes of the world far surpass his father, we naturally never dreamt in those days.'

Fontane seems to have left Leipzig for Dresden in 1842, and a few of Max Müller's letters to him are still extant.

*Translation.*

'As dumb as a fish, dear Fontane. To what purpose does the Leipzig Railway go daily, when you won't even take the trouble to send me a few lines, especially as lately you have had so much that you might have imparted to me? For some time it has not been wise to mention your name to me, and yet there was so much in my heart that I wanted to say to you. I hope you have not been idle, but will soon give us something good and new. How would it be if we wrote a novel together? There are many such. The other partner must alter nothing, and it is of the utmost importance to carry on the mutual thoughts adroitly. I have written a great deal lately, but only prose. My new name is Max Dessauer, under which name you will find several things in The Planet, i. e. several very poor things, for I must not give much of my time to them.'

Max Müller speaks here of 'writing a great deal.' Various small papers of the day published in Leipzig, *The Comet*, *The Planet*, *The Shooting Star*, &c., contain small tales by Max Dessauer, decidedly sentimental, and giving little promise of his future power of description and clearness of expression. There is, however, one set of papers written in 1843, *Camera Obscura from Berlin*, which are far in advance of the tales, and are full of clever, sarcastic remarks on Berlin ways and manners, and the frivolous life of the Berlin people of that time, always amusing themselves and always full of chatter and gossip.

In the *Autobiography* Max Müller tells us of three duels he fought during his three years at the University of Leipzig, and justifies these affairs as the only means of keeping the rougher elements found in every German University in order. He was greatly surprised in after years, when he first visited Oxford, to hear that duels were as unknown there as they were unnecessary.

On September 1, 1843, Max Müller passed his examination

for the degree of Phil. Doc. He did not tell his mother that he meant to offer himself for examination so soon, for fear of disappointing her by failure. Too poor to buy the necessary dress coat for the occasion, he borrowed one. He passed with ease, and his mother must have felt rewarded for all her efforts and cares, when her son, still three months under twenty, laid his card, *Dr. Max Müller*, in her lap. Among her papers after her death the following was found copied from some English book: 'The tie of mother and son, of widowed mother and only son, the tie unlike all others in the world, not only in its blessedness, but in its divine compensation.' It would seem from the following letters written just afterwards that he had been far from well all the summer, probably overworked:—

*Translation.* *September*, 1843.

'DEAR FONTANE,—I can well imagine that you have often cursed me not a little as I gave no sign of life for such a long time; but *Morbus excusat hominem*, and I will add, *Nisi homo excusat morbum!* I hope you have carried on your Latin studies so far as to comprehend the deep meaning of these words; and if a human heart still beats in your breast, you must pity me, poor wretch, for having spent nearly the whole vacation in a nervous fever, so that I must stay almost the whole of next term here in Leipzig. It is ill-luck, you will agree. Well, one could almost despair, but where's the good of it? I have quietly unpacked my books and things again, and sit in Reichel's Garden, up three flights, up which I have to climb with many gasps. I am in Leipzig *incognito*, for I had already paid my farewell visits everywhere, and altogether feel no inclination for society.'

TO THE SAME.

*Translation.* *January* 4, 1844.

'Just lately I have been busy with a new edition of the *Griechenlieder*[1], and I wrote a preface to it, as I have included the hitherto unpublished poems and the hymn to Raphael Riego. I was very much annoyed that the preface could not be printed, as what I thought of most in the new edition was to excite a feeling of contempt for those who by their policy of friendship brought the struggles of a whole people for liberty to an end: or at least to invite sympathy for a betrayed country. But if the reader welcomes the poems, as belonging to the past, no reference to the present would find favour in his eyes, and I must satisfy myself

[1] The first edition of his father's poems in which he was personally concerned.

with giving a simple literary notice. You see there is nothing left but to avoid all living subjective topics, and take refuge in the objective past. So I have picked out a work from hoary antiquity and my first *Opus* will soon appear, a German translation of the oldest Indian collection of fables. You will find many acquaintances of childhood's days, from Gellert, La Fontaine, &c., and the interesting thing is that one can follow the wanderings of these fables, through twenty different languages, from the oldest to the most recent times, a work which I am reserving for another time. Wolfssohn has quite disappeared, and of Schauenburg I know little except that he is closely watched in Berlin.'

The translation of the *Hitopadesa* was brought out in March, 1844; the book is dedicated to Brockhaus. Towards the end of his University career at Leipzig, Prince Wilhelm of Dessau, who had in 1840 married Emilie, his mother's cousin, expressed a wish to adopt Max Müller, and put him into the Austrian Diplomatic Service. 'I at once said no,' he tells us in the *Autobiography*; 'it seemed to interfere with my freedom, with my studies, with my ideal of a career in life.'

Max had long felt an ardent wish to go for a year to Berlin to study Sanskrit under Bopp, but more especially Philosophy under Schelling. He wanted also to examine the collection of Sanskrit MSS. which the King of Prussia had just bought in England from the executors of Robert Chambers. His sister had been married in February of this year to a young physician, Dr. Krug, and had removed to Chemnitz; and it was settled that the mother should live there with the young couple, rather than with her son at Berlin. Max Müller had his scholarship for one year more, but it was only forty thalers (£6), and in this year (December, 1844) he would come of age, and the pension of a hundred thalers (£15), granted to his mother at the time of his father's death, would be reduced to half. How Max Müller, when away from his mother, was able to live, is certainly a puzzle, but living then in Germany was extraordinarily cheap; during a hard winter the firing for the family cost about twopence a day, and everything else was in proportion. So in March, 1844, the little home in Reichel's Garden was broken up, and the mother started for Chemnitz. On his last evening at Leipzig, which had been his home, more or less, since 1836, Max Müller writes to his mother:—

*Translation.* LEIPZIG, *March*, 1844.

'MY DEAR LITTLE MOTHER,—I had meant to write to you first from Berlin, when I had settled myself there, but I know you will be glad to get a letter from me sooner. How often we two [M. M. and Prowe] thought of and pitied you! I am sure it was an uncomfortable journey. We were very tired, but yet went late to bed. From the post-house we went to Reichel's Garden. We went up into the old rooms, where we had passed many happy hours all together. It looked very desolate, and we went home, where we had tea, and were much better for it, and talked till past eleven. I was glad when I woke early to think of you three happy and comfortable together in Chemnitz. I am full of delight at the thought of Berlin, and there I shall find a letter from my dear mother. Take good care of yourself, and do not do too much. Prowe sends many affectionate messages. Write soon to 'YOUR MAX.'

The following letter was written soon after he arrived in Berlin:—

TO HIS MOTHER.

*Translation.* BERLIN, *April* 15, 1844.

'You have no doubt been expecting a letter from me sooner, and will have thought I was long ago settled in Berlin. But you know how it is in Dessau, how one is kept day after day, and so I only got here a few days ago, and have as yet done nothing but hunt for lodgings. Everything was very pleasant at Dessau, but it took some time before I found the various people at home. I went first to the Chamberlain, from whom I hoped to hear something definite as to the Leopold Stipendium [1]. Unfortunately he gave me no hope, nor did Bernhorst or Morgenstern. They were all very kind, and accepted the *Hitopadesa*. Bernhorst had told the Duke I was in Dessau, and came himself to tell me the Duke would see me. So on Wednesday early I went to the Pater Patriae, who talked to me a long time, but of the Stipendium or of other arrangements not a syllable. Then I went to Fräulein Rath, who told me I was to see the Duchess the next day. She too was most gracious and kind, asked me why I did not go to England, and I told her everything most openly, but it produced no result. When I went to Advocate Richter, I could not but tell him my position after the next, that is the last, payment of my scholarship. You see, dear mother, I have spared no pains. I must see now how I can help myself. I drew fifty thalers from my savings bank. I left Dessau at

[1] A Stipendium founded by the Duke for poor scholars, and which Max Müller hoped he might have when his scholarship ceased.

two o'clock, and arrived in Berlin about seven. Uncle and Aunt Hake said at once I was to stay with them as long as I liked, whilst I looked for a really nice room. I have done that most conscientiously, for to-day and yesterday I have seen at least forty. I am very tired with all this running about, and long for a quiet, settled life. I shall not pay any visits till I am settled, but when will that be?'

*Translation.* *April 17.*

'I have found a room, a few yards from Unter den Linden. The house is clean and light, and I like my room very much. I give for it and service and cleaning boots, six thalers (18*s.*) a month. It is nicely furnished, and the people of the house are clean and respectable.

'Your MAX.'

It is evident from his letters to his mother and his Diary that the early part of his time at Berlin was most agreeable. He went into society more than he had done at Leipzig, and was fortunate in having the *entrée* of several very pleasant houses, chief among which was the house of Hensel the artist, married to Mendelssohn's favourite sister Fanny. The Krügers, connexions of his own (he was also an artist), were very kind to the young student, and he dined there every Sunday, unless he had any other invitation. His aunt, Julie Hake, also had him to dinner every week. At Berlin, Max Müller began keeping a journal, and continued it fairly regularly till August. He seems to have dined, when not asked out, at a restaurant, where he paid sixpence for his dinner, which he reports as good. He matriculated as a theologian! Soon after, he writes: 'Worked early, but could not concentrate myself'; and adds the same evening, 'Dreaming, and a little poetry, and a very little work. I must work more in future.' A few days later he paid his first visit to the Library in search of Sanskrit MSS., which he seems to have been unable to see owing to the absence of the head librarian.

Towards the end of April he met Fontane as an Imperial Grenadier at Kosch's, where he dined. 'He came to me at five, and we talked of many things, and finally of the Divine and Human. He is a fine fellow, and has to submit to a good deal.' Fontane writes of these times:—

*Translation.*

'I had a strong affection for Müller from the first at Leipzig, but we only became really intimate three years later, when we were both for a time in Berlin, he at his Sanskrit studies, I as a Kaiser Franz Grenadier. He lived then on the third floor of a corner house, close to the Werder'sche Kirche, where he, greatly to his own satisfaction, lodged with a shoemaker. If only the workshop had not been next his room! The beating of leather went on the whole day long, and Müller would have lost all patience, but for the wonderful view. The whole town lay like a panorama before him, especially the royal palace with its beautiful gardens. To look at this was a real solace, and he held out against the noise. He already gave promise of becoming some one, and rejoiced in being in especial favour with Friedrich Rückert, who in these years, yielding to the King's wish, gave lectures at the University. Max Müller was then translating, among other works, Kâlidâsa's *Cloud Messenger*. If I owe all I know of Russian Literature to Wolfssohn, I owe to Müller what little I learnt about Sanskrit poetry. He still showed the same, not ironical, but kindly, mischievous temperament which he already possessed in Leipzig.'

Max Müller had expected great things from Schelling, and in a letter to his mother thus describes his first visit to the great philosopher:—

*Translation.*

'I went to announce myself. He receives people at four o'clock. I had not expected much, for I had heard how he had dismissed Jellinick, but I was more fortunate. I asked him if he would continue to lecture next term on the Philosophy of Revelation. He said he could not decide yet, therefore probably only a private lecture again. Then I spoke to him of my time in Leipzig, of Weiss and Brockhaus, and then we came round to Indian Philosophy. Here he allowed me to tell him a good deal. I especially dwelt on the likeness between Sankhya and his own system, and remarked how an inclination to the Vedânta showed itself. He asked what we must understand by Vedânta, how the existence of God was proved, how God created the world, whether it had reality. He has been much occupied with Colebrooke's *Essays*, and he seemed to wish to learn more, as he asked me if I could explain a text. Then he asked where I was living, knew my father as Greek poet and a worker on Homer, and at last dismissed me with "Come again soon," offering to do anything he could for me.'

The following letters give his mother a pleasant account of his life:—

*Translation.* *May*, 1844.

'Hensel's house is a delightful resort to me, and she is especially friendly. I go there oftener than I can really spare the time; they are always sending me invitations. I was there last Saturday, and they asked me to dinner the next day. I went at twelve, for a large musical matinée; they sang the choruses of the *Antigone*. Then I stayed in the garden with the tutor, and we played with Hensel a sort of ninepins; then came dinner, and they asked me to return in the evening, as Oehlenschläger, the German poet, was coming to them, so I spent nearly the whole day there. I have not played there yet, as she has not asked me to do so, but when I told her I wanted to hire a piano, cheap but not bad, she offered to lend me an English one, on which she used to play. He too is most friendly, and has given himself a great deal of trouble to get leave from the Minister for me to have the MSS. to use in my own room, which I hope will soon be granted. The Hakes too are very kind, and I can always dine there, Mondays and Thursdays. I have called besides on Bopp; Professor Höfer, who will review my *Hitopadesa*; Dr. Kuhn, another Sanskritist, to whom Brockhaus recommended me; Professor Petermann, whose lectures on the history of Oriental Literature I attend; Professor Schott, with whom I learn Persian; and I think everything will go well. I am also going to Schelling, from which my purse suffers. I have not had time to call again on "Bettina." As friends I have Vogel and Fontane, whom I seldom see except at dinner. At home I only have bread and butter. I drink coffee without milk or sugar. I have just received ten copies of the *Griechenlieder*; they are very well printed. So you see I do very well here, and nothing is wanting but my dear little mother. Now write soon, but don't say again you do not like Chemnitz; a contented spirit is happy anywhere. In the *Hitopadesa* it says, "To the man who has leather shoes on, the whole world is covered with leather."'

*Translation.* *May* 22.

'Four days in the week I have lectures at eight; the woman cleans my room, then I stay at home till 1.30, and then dine close here. Then some days I have a lecture at four o'clock, and I am very glad to be living so close to the University, and shall be more so when the real Berlin heat begins.'

*Translation.* *May* 28.

'I have just come from Hensel's. As you see, I am a pretty constant guest. They are really so good to me, and it is the only house where I feel "you would *like* to go there"; generally one feels "you *must* go there." You say, you are glad that I don't work so hard; I can't quite understand that, for I often don't know what I should begin first, when I think of the future and on so much which I still have to do before I can take any rest. . . . I do not often see any papers, as the public reading-rooms are so dear; in this respect you are better off in Chemnitz.'

Max Müller seems soon to have found out the expense of the life at Berlin, and the old doubts whether he could afford the life of a scholar revived. On June 26 he writes to his mother:—

*Translation.*

'I must make the most of my time in Berlin, as I cannot stay here more than a year, unless I can find some chance of lessening my expenses. Where I am to go next Easter is not at all certain. I hesitate between Paris, Vienna, and Bonn. I am attracted to Vienna by the thought of studying Persian and Turkish, for which there are better means than in Paris, and they are certainly necessary should I ever have the chance of employment in the East. You can fancy that these plans often disturb me, as for the nearest future I have no certain prospect; and the University course is so expensive and wearisome, that I cannot reckon on it, as generally for the first three years, that is six years after leaving school, one is not admitted to anything. Well, one must console oneself with the lilies of the field!'

Two days later he writes in his Diary: 'I *cannot* give up Sanskrit, though it holds out no prospect for me.' Over and over again come the entries in his Diary: 'All day at home'—'no dinner'—'dinner of stirred eggs' (which he prepared himself)—'work till 3 a.m.'

At this time he began Bengali, 'which may perhaps be useful to me later, and is now for comparison with the low Indian dialects. I attend Schelling's course more diligently and with great interest; his philosophy has something Oriental about it. I am translating the *Kathâka Upanishad* for him with great diligence.'

The term at Berlin which had begun so cheerily was now drawing to an end. Max Müller had not found pupils or sufficient employment in copying Sanskrit MSS. to eke out his small stipend, and just before returning to Chemnitz he wrote almost despairingly to his mother:—

*Translation.* *Aug.* 19.

'I am longing to be away from Berlin, to get a thorough change of thought, as I really think I had every chance here of becoming a confirmed hypochondriac. This is no mere transitory feeling, but it is founded on my circumstances, which have cost me many sad thoughts latterly. I acknowledge that the plan of life I had formed is not to be realized; that it is difficult for me to part with all these favourite ideas you can well imagine. And yet I see that it would be folly in my circumstances to attempt a University career. You tell me that I still have 800 thalers[1] (£120), but this would only just last till I had settled where to live, and that I should then have the prospect of living for five years as a tutor (Privatdocent) without any stipend from Government. I should therefore in this way study on to starve, just in order not to give up an idea which I had taken up for my own pleasure, and to which I had sacrificed much money and time. Had I more courage or only anywhere a firm point to cling to, I could perhaps still try my chance, but as it is, nothing remains for me but to become a sensible schoolmaster, which at all events gives one bread and butter. You will feel that a certain amount of resignation is needed for such a decision, and therefore I rejoice all the more at the thought of the next few weeks, which will repay me for many sad hours.'

He spent the vacation at Chemnitz, where the society of his mother and sister cheered and encouraged him. It is not clear how he found funds to finish his course at Berlin, but he probably used part of the small patrimony already alluded to.

He returned to Berlin early in October, and soon after his return received the pleasant news that, in answer to an appeal from his mother for a prolongation of the full pension for a time, the Duke had granted it for another five years. The Duke's letter was an encouragement to the young scholar to persevere in his chosen path :—

*Translation.*

'According to your petition of the twenty-eighth of last month I have ordered that the pension granted you of a hundred thalers shall be continued in full for the next five years, till 1849 inclusive. I hope that your promising son may continue to give you as much cause for joy as hitherto, and I gladly take this opportunity to assure you of my special good wishes.' LEOPOLD.

'DESSAU, *Oct.* 10, 1844.'

He writes to his mother again on October 24 :—

[1] Some money left by W. Müller, and religiously guarded by his mother to start him in life.

*Translation.* BERLIN.

'I hope you make yourself as happy in the backstream of life as I do. As I sit here in my garret and for days together see no one I know, I fancy myself as a bird alone in its nest on a tall tree, and Leipzig, Chemnitz, and Dessau appear perfect Eldorados. But I am quite happy and amuse myself, by myself, as far as possible. But I must tell you how I kept your birthday. I thought the Hakes would have invited me that we might drink your health together; but as they did not, I invited Fontane for the evening, who brought a friend, and we brewed punch, set your picture on the table, and drank your health right joyously. I have heard from Dessau that I cannot have the scholarship for a seventh term. Well, I have enough for the present, and I think of the birds in the sky; they have no fire, yet they don't freeze, but I do freeze.'

This term Max Müller does not seem to have attended many lectures, but worked in his room on Pâli and Hindûstânî and on translations from the Sanskrit. He finished his translation of the *Meghadûta*, and submitted it both to Rückert and Brockhaus. His MS., with Rückert's notes in pencil, still exists; and Brockhaus wrote to him as follows:—

*Translation.*

'I have read your translation with the greatest delight. You have conquered a great difficulty, and reproduced this peculiar artificial poetry in intelligible, and at the same time poetic, language. You have wisely omitted many isolated traits in order to preserve the principal picture, and to give the reader not accustomed to such pictures a clear idea of the whole. Your idea appears to me almost everywhere the right one. In a few places, I should take a different view, but you have been able to use explanatory materials with which I am not acquainted, and which, no doubt, justify you in many points.'

Towards the end of November the old family friend, Baron Hagedorn, suddenly appeared in Berlin, and invited Max Müller to stay with him in Paris, to carry on his Sanskrit work. Baron Hagedorn was born near Dessau in the house of a forester, where his mother left him and never returned. It was evident that his parents were wealthy, as a large sum was yearly paid by a banker in Frankfort for his maintenance. As a schoolboy he had been boarded with Frau Klausnitzer, the mother of the Cousin Emilie so often mentioned in

Max Müller's letters, and thus became the intimate friend of the family.

Max writes on his twenty-first birthday to tell his mother of his unexpected happiness :—

*Translation.* *Dec.* 6.

'MY DEARLY LOVED MOTHER,—As I am sitting here quite alone on my birthday (the twenty-first) I must give myself at least the delight of writing to those who love me so, and whom I dearly love. And first of all comes my darling little mother. My best thanks for your love and goodness, which in many things are far too great. I wrote to Frau Rath to ask for a letter of introduction from the Duchess to Alexander von Humboldt. Very soon after, Frau Rath wrote in the most friendly way, sending me the Duchess's letter. I left this with my card for Humboldt. The other day I passed half an hour with him, and a few days later came a letter from him saying I should have the Sanskrit MSS. at home, which ever since Easter I had begged for in vain from the Minister. As to my *Meghadûta*, it has been a long time with Professor Brockhaus in Leipzig, who at last returned it. I then gave it to Rückert, with whom I am learning Persian, and who remembers my father with great affection. He has given me many valuable hints with regard to versification, and even improved several of the verses himself. I shall send it in a few days to Mayer Wigand, as I should like to see it printed before I leave for Paris. I wish I could see you, darling mother, and talk over all the unexpected and undeserved kindness that has been shown me. I went Thursday early to Hagedorn, and we talked over everything; and the result is he has asked me to go to Paris with him, to live with him there and work. So in about four weeks from to-day I shall be in Paris. Hagedorn will tell you all this himself more fully. The only thing to settle is, shall I come for a few days to Chemnitz before I start? As you can fancy, I should like to do so very much, only I am afraid it would give us more pain than pleasure.'

During the short time Max Müller still passed in Berlin after receiving the letter of introduction from the Duchess of Dessau, he must have seen Humboldt often enough to impress the great man most favourably; for on November 27, 1844, Chevalier Bunsen, then Prussian Minister in London, wrote to his friend Archdeacon Hare :—

'I have received from a highly respected quarter [1] a very strong

[1] i. e. Humboldt, and also Baroness Stolzenberg, who herself wrote to Bunsen about her young cousin.

recommendation of a young man of twenty-two (*sic*) years of age, much thought of by Schelling. He has made himself known by a new edition of the *Hitopadesa* from the Sanskrit, and is a general scholar altogether distinguished. He desires to live some years in England. He is the son of the celebrated poet and philologer Wilhelm Müller (author of the *Griechenlieder* and *Römische Ritornellen*), of high moral character, and as far as I know of serious convictions.'

In quoting this letter in the *Life* of her distinguished husband, Baroness Bunsen adds:—

'This is the first indication of an important event in the life of Bunsen, the acquaintance which at once became warm friendship with Dr. Max Müller, now Professor at Oxford; and his approach is hailed as the rising of a beneficent luminary on the horizon. The kindred mind, their sympathy of heart, the unity in highest aspirations, a congeniality in principle, a fellowship in the pursuit of favourite objects which attracted and bound Bunsen to his young friend, rendered this connexion one of the happiest of his life.'

But nearly two years were to pass before Max Müller met this friend, patron, and benefactor; whose kindly influence was to alter the course of his whole life.

# CHAPTER III

## 1845–1846

Paris. Lonely, struggling life. Gathy. Burnouf. *Rig-veda.* Rachel. Dvarkanath Tagore. Boehtlingk.

ARCHDEACON HARE lost no time in responding to the letter of November 27 from Chevalier Bunsen, for we find a note from Max Müller to the Chevalier dated 'Chemnitz, January 1, 1845,' which implies that one, if not more letters had already passed between them as to a tutorship in an English family, suggested by the Archdeacon. But we will leave Max to tell his own further story in his Diary.

*Translation.* BONN, *March* 6, 1845.

'Once more a new change in my life, and once more an attempt at something definite. My stay in Berlin is over; I have made many and influential friends there—Schelling, Rückert, Humboldt, Bopp, Jacobi, Mendelssohn. My views of life become clearer and more sensible, my inner life more active and more independent of outward circumstances. There was not much to be gained in knowledge in Berlin; the learned men are too learned, too reserved, and do not attempt to gain any influence; and even the treasures of the Library were long closed to me, till a word from Humboldt put an end to the constant refusals of the librarian Pertz and the Minister. In December Hagedorn came to Berlin and asked me to stay with him in Paris, and just then I received an offer to go as a tutor to London. Great indecision. At length decided on Paris and its pleasant independence, though at the same time I did not refuse all other possible offers. I had a longing for Paris, and I soon went to Chemnitz, saw Hagedorn in Dessau, where he was dawdling. I was some time in Chemnitz and had a good deal of society, balls, sledge-parties, &c., but not a word from Hagedorn. So I started at last for Dessau, not feeling much confidence in Hagedorn. When we met we got on very well and settled everything. On February 26 I started for Paris. In Cöthen the train was stopped by the snow, and we returned by extra post to Dessau. Here Hagedorn found business letters which kept him. At last, March 3, I started alone for Hanover. The 4th to Elberfeld; at night by post to Deutz, arriving early in Cologne; railway to Bonn. Table d'hote in Hotel de Trèves; two English families, whom I could not understand; very cross. Afternoon to Lassen, not very interesting talk; five o'clock, lecture by Dahlmann on Publicity, Coming of Age, Jury, &c.; very remarkable, quiet, no gesticulations, irrefutable, convincing, a skilful man. In Bonn the old topics still going on—Catholicism, the Holy Coat, and Protestantism.

PARIS, *March* 15.

'My journey is happily over. I left Bonn on the 6th for Cologne, and started on the 8th for Brussels; here I found myself already in the midst of French, which I found very troublesome. I stayed the night. On the 9th I started at three o'clock by train. On the way difficulties with the douane and my passport; the 10th at three o'clock I arrived in Paris.'

Max Müller has himself given us an amusing account of his difficulties on his arrival in Paris, owing to Hagedorn having failed either to write or appear; and though he stayed in Paris till June, 1846, as Hagedorn never came he lived at his own expense in Hagedorn's rooms, instead of being his friend's guest as was at first arranged. If he found economy necessary in Berlin, it was far more so in Paris, where soon after his arrival he says, 'I am spending a lot of money'; though in his carefully kept accounts there are very few entries but for dinner—for which, unless he went 'hors la barrière,' he had to pay two francs—and copying paper, the amount of which shows how hard he was working. His life was very lonely; he at first knew hardly any one but some of the employés at the Library, and he says, March 17, 'I feel very lonely and forsaken, and of Paris I see nothing'; and again, 'Great inertia and fatigue, and out of spirits, no inclination for work'; and yet he writes cheerily to his mother not to distress her:—

*Translation.* PARIS, *April* 10, 1845.

'Of course I have heard nothing from Hagedorn, and therefore do not expect to see him very soon. But it is well I did not further postpone my journey, for Humboldt being here has been of the greatest use to me, and he goes away now very soon. He is kindness itself, and is even thought more of in Paris than in Berlin. It is very difficult to get leave here to take out MSS. to work at at home, and the Prussian Minister, under whose protection I am here—for in Paris no one has heard of such a land as Anhalt Dessau—is so stupid that he has never given his guarantee for such a purpose, whilst all other Ambassadors, even the Turkish, are constantly doing so. Humboldt knew this, but told me he thought I should find his own guarantee considered quite satisfactory; and it is quite true. I soon had the MSS. in my hands, and was treated in so friendly a way by all the employés, that I was quite astonished, till at last I was told, "Vous êtes si vivement recommandé par M. Humboldt, il n'y a pas une meilleure recommandation." As to the printed books, I have not yet got the permit, but hope soon to do so, though this is more difficult; leave is seldom given, and all Paris, learned and unlearned, sit in the reading-room, packed like herrings, and read there. I have been now for some time in full swing of work, and only wish there were more strength in the machine, for there is endless work to be done here. You will wish for a description of my life; that is soon given. I get up early, have breakfast, i.e. bread and butter, no coffee. I stay at home and work till seven, go out and have dinner, come back in an hour, and stay at home and work till I go to bed. So you see I know nothing of Paris but from my appetite, which has got over its first astonishment at the excellence of everything, and now rather wonders that the Paris restaurants are so renowned. But one thing I have seen, that is, that everything in Paris is terribly expensive. With 12,000 francs a year one could live here nicely; I am afraid I shall hardly work my income up to that. I am on the whole well, though I must live most economically and avoid every expense not actually necessary. The free lodging is an immense help, for unless one lives in a perfect hole, one must pay 50 or 60 francs a month and 10 francs for service, 60 francs dinner, 30 francs breakfast; this makes 160 francs a month without light and fire, or washing and clothes, nearly 2,000 francs a year. Theatres, cafés, &c., are very dear, particularly for foreigners, who don't know how to manage; so I have not been to any theatre, except one evening, when I had to pay 2 francs for a cup of chocolate. I thought, "Never again." But don't think I have nothing to amuse me. I can only say, one walk on the Boulevards is far better than two evenings at the Chemnitz theatre. It is a strange feeling to be so entirely strange among the thousands of faces that pass by one, and for interesting observation there is no place like this. How often I say to myself, "Oh, if mother were only here." Yesterday and to-day are called in the serious world Holy Thursday and Good Friday; here they are called Longchamps, and all Paris is driving out through the Champs Élysées in their finest clothes, but looking miserable in this cold. The hero of the day is General Tom Thumb; the Rue Richelieu is blocked the days he receives; the aristocracy vie with each other in running after him, and of course Louis Philippe at their head. I have seen both heroes without paying—Tom Thumb in his carriage, which is about as big as a child's go-cart, and the King to-day for the first time when I crossed the Place du Carrousel just as they were on parade, and the old King was riding round bare-headed with all his suite. I was only twenty paces from him; he has a very characteristic face, full, with thick grey curly hair, but in spite of his dignity something cunning and crafty in his eyes. I see his likeness but too often, that is whenever I have to pay away a five-franc piece, which, alas! happens frequently. By-the-by I have just paid 50 francs for books; what do you say to that? Gathy[1] sent me one day a ticket for a concert, where I saw the *beau monde* of Paris; he is most friendly to me. Twice a week I go to lectures at the Collège de France. It is some way off; but they are very good, and I pay nothing and I hear French spoken, for which otherwise I have hardly any opportunity. But enough of my life here, which, if on the whole very simple, keeps me in good spirits as you see, and at all events does not as yet interfere with my work. But you can fancy that in this utterly strange land I sometimes feel lonely and forsaken, and would gladly find myself for a few hours in Chemnitz with you all. But the best cure for such thoughts is continuous work, and that I have. And then when I think of you all I feel I am not so far from you; I know all you would say to me if I were sitting with you, and all that you are often in your thoughts saying to me. Separation loses its bitterness when we have faith in each other and in God. Faith in each other keeps us close together in life, and faith in God keeps us together in eternity. But I see I am talking Sanskrit philosophy instead of simply telling you not to be unhappy, not to make yourself and others uneasy, but try to enjoy life in this lovely spring weather, whether in Chemnitz or Dresden. How gladly I would have put something in the letter for Auguste's birthday from the Paris shops, for the sight of the splendid and tastefully arranged windows is most tempting. But, alas! my purse suffers from chronic consumption; you know this family complaint, which has followed me to Paris.'

Max Müller's first visit to Burnouf was paid on March 20, and was the beginning of a friendship to which he looked

[1] His childhood's friend. See p. 5.

back with affectionate gratitude to the last year of his life.

DIARY.

*Translation.*

'Went to Burnouf. Spiritual, amiable, thoroughly French. He received me in the most friendly way, talked a great deal, and all he said valuable, not on ordinary topics but on special. I managed better in French than I expected. "I am a Brâhman, a Buddhist, a Zoroastrian; I hate the Jesuits"—that is the sort of man. I am looking forward to his lectures.'

Max Müller describes his teacher as

'Small, his face decidedly German, only lighted up with a constant sparkle which is distinctively French. I must have seemed very stupid to him when I tried to explain what I really wanted to do in Paris. He told me afterwards that he could not make me out at first. His lectures were on the *Rig-veda*, and opened a new world to me. He explained to us his own researches, he showed us new MSS. which he had received from India, in fact he did all he could to make us fellow workers.'

In Burnouf's select class Max Müller met men who, many of them, remained his firm friends through life, as Barthélemy-St.-Hilaire, the Abbé Bardelli, Thomas Goldstücker, and a few others. Max Müller survived them all. When he was in Paris for the Centenary of the Institute in 1895 he paid a long visit to Barthélemy-St.-Hilaire, finding him, as had been his custom for years, sitting by lamplight with the daylight carefully excluded. The old man, then ninety years of age, died soon after, and his friend wrote an eloquent and appreciative account of his life and work in the *Times* of November 29, 1895.

Max Müller recalls also a visit to Humboldt, whom he found at the Collège de France: 'His friendliness and true kindness make me feel quite shy; I hardly know what to say. "If you were only a little more practical in your views," he said, which startled me. He then wrote a long letter to Reinaud and gave me his *Cosmos* to read, and left me with reiterated assurances of his wish to help me.'

Max seems to have gone through a good deal of drudgery in mastering French, and often took refuge with Gathy, 'to make up by talking German the tortures I suffer in talking French.' Another day he says, 'I did hardly anything but study this abominable language; how much time I have wasted on it! yet it is necessary that I should get some fluency in expressing myself.' Gathy occasionally gave him a concert ticket, and he speaks of amusing himself by making walks of discovery about Paris: 'and people look at me, and I know no one; it seems as if I hardly belong to the genus of *animaux sociables.*'

He appears to have found it difficult at first to decide on the distinctive work he should take up; 'the same life, which has almost become unbearable; I long for work to occupy my mind.' He read a good deal of French. Balzac: 'all his works that I know treat of the analysis, the anatomy of love, before and after marriage; he knows married life and dissects it with artistic skill.' Paul de Kock: 'colourless babyish reading, often droll, some characters well conceived.' It was the influence of Burnouf that decided him to take up the Hymns of the *Rig-veda*, with the great native commentary of Sâyana, as his distinctive work. 'Either study Indian philosophy or study Indian religion and copy the Hymns and Sâyana,' said Burnouf. To the youth of only twenty-one, knowing hardly half a dozen people, living alone up five flights of stairs, often not speaking to a soul for twenty-four hours round, life may well have seemed dreary; and yet he never for one moment really regretted the choice he had made, and his old master, Professor Brockhaus, gave him constant encouragement. Brockhaus writes from Leipzig:—

*Translation.* *June* 4, 1845.

'You have delighted me very much by the few lines you have sent me from Paris, from which I see with what active interest you pursue your study of Sanskrit. It is very natural that you should turn to the Vedas with decided preference; one becomes more and more attached to these old monuments the more one studies them, and when once one can survey them as a whole, they make a much more powerful impression than one would expect from isolated fragments.'

He never allowed his letters to his mother to show the fierce struggle it was to live.

To his Mother.

*Translation.* Paris, *May* 5.

'One's money runs away here, one does not know how, and though of course it costs one more in the beginning, the daily wants do not lessen. That I am as saving as possible you may be sure, for it is my greatest wish to stay here as long as possible, where I have found so much necessary to my studies. On amusements I have really spent nothing, and have not yet been to Versailles, or other places round, though I am often tempted when I see the great placards on the walls; but that is easily set aside if I can attain my other object. I shall not order any summer things, for I need not make myself smart, that is one advantage of being unknown.'

TO THE SAME.

*Translation.* PARIS, *June* 11, 1845.

'Have I already told you that I am collecting here the materials for an edition of the oldest *Veda*, and gather together everything I can find? This is the oldest and most important book in India, perhaps the oldest book that exists. The Commentary written in Sanskrit fills four folios, each of a thousand pages, which must all be copied out and compared with other MSS., and this is the most important and necessary work. Now I must see what I can do—only health and money, that is the question. I have lately met a Sanskrit scholar here who has been three years in Paris, and has just come back from London. We have worked a great deal together, and I have for some weeks been with him day and night, which my portier takes very ill, and I certainly could not make him understand that I had been doing nothing but work; altogether there are odd rumours about Monsieur Max, as I am called, who drinks no coffee early, eats till evening only two dry rolls (the butter is knocked off), and writes *Hebrew* the whole day.'

When copying MSS. for others his plan was to work the whole night through, and the second night only sleep two hours on his bed without undressing, the third night to go to bed and then begin again. He had told his mother nothing of what he calls in his Diary an abominable time from April 26 to May 4, when he suffered frightfully and without intermission from toothache. 'I could do nothing, neither write, nor eat, nor go out. I felt abandoned by every one, no one to pity me or take care of me.' At length he crawled to Gathy, who sent him to a dentist. 'I went home quite exhausted; the portier and his daughter took endless care of me when they saw how weak and suffering I was, and brought me broth and chocolate. It was a black week.'

All this time no news came from his uncertain friend Hagedorn, and his want of money soon began to cause him great anxiety. 'It was indeed a hard struggle, far harder than those who have known me in later life would believe. It was a hard fight, and cannot have been very good for me physically, but I do not regret it now; often did I go without my dinner, being quite satisfied with boiled eggs and bread and butter.' He had chosen his own line, and instead of settling down in Germany as a teacher in some school with a fixed salary, as most of his friends wished, or going as tutor to England, he had taken the tiny patrimony still left him after the expenses of the University, and had determined to carry on his beloved Sanskrit studies. 'It was in my own hands whether I should sink or swim.' There is a passage in an American novel, *The Increasing Purpose*, by J. A. Allen, which exactly applies to Max Müller's struggles in Paris and London, and the effect on his whole character for life. One could almost fancy Mr. Allen had known him. Speaking of a man choosing his work in life, Allen says:—

> 'Yet happy ye, whether the waiting be for short time or long time, if only it bring on meanwhile the struggle. One sure reward you have then, though there may be none other, just the struggle, and the marshalling to the front of rightful forces, with effort, endurance, devotion, the putting resolutely back of forces wrongful, the hardening of all that is soft within, the softening of all that is hard; until out of the hardening and the softening result the better tempering of the soul's metal, and higher development of those two qualities which are best in man, and best in his ideal of his Maker, strength and kindness, power and mercy. Real struggling is itself real living, and no ennobling thing of this earth is ever to be had by man on any other terms; . . . a divine end is to be reached, through divine means, a great work requires a great preparation.'

The four years Max Müller spent after leaving his mother at Leipzig were this time of preparation, by means of a great struggle, for the brilliant success of his after-life.

It is pleasant to read of a little variety in a life of such incessant work, when in October, 1845, a friend took him one night to the Théâtre Français, where he saw Rachel in *Phèdre*.

To his Mother.

*Translation.*

'She is a wonderful actress in her own style, but the part of Phèdre is so horrible, that though one must admire the perfection of representation, one has no real enjoyment from it. Then from the beginning to the end Rachel was nothing but a pale shadow whose only life is passion and despair, but passion which fails in all tragic effect because it has no influence on one's own feelings. It is a crude and painful passion with which she is possessed, and in which there is nothing to awake our sympathy. It is a tragedy which, on the Greek stage only, could represent men in their struggle with fate, with blind unalterable fate, which avenges the sin of the father in the sex of Phèdre; if this one moral motive is wanting, as on the French stage, the whole loses its deep meaning, and nothing remains but the sensual longing, which is neither great nor elevating. Then Rachel stood alone; the other actors were but foils to her. After that—so characteristic of the French, who like to see everything without feeling anything—came a comedy of Molière, *Le Médecin malgré lui*, which was very well played.'

One most interesting acquaintance Max Müller made in Paris, Dvarkanath Tagore, a rich Hindoo, who, though no student of ancient Sanskrit himself, took a lively interest in the young scholar presented to him by Burnouf at the Institut de France. He invited Max Müller to his house, and they spent many an hour together talking or enjoying music, for the Hindoo was a good musician, had a fine voice, and had been fairly well taught. He liked Max Müller to accompany him when singing either Italian or French music. After a time he was persuaded to sing Persian and real Indian music, and when his hearer confessed that he saw no beauty in it, neither melody, rhythm, nor harmony, his Indian friend lectured him on the prejudices of Western nations, who turn away from all that is strange and unpleasing to them. Max pacified him by assuring him that he knew that India possessed a remarkable science of music founded on mathematics. He was present at the great party given by Dvarkanath Tagore to Louis Philippe, when the room was hung with Indian shawls, afterwards distributed among the most distinguished guests. It was at this time also that Max Müller saw a good deal of Baron d'Eckstein, who employed him frequently in copying MSS. for him.

All this while Max Müller was working hard in preparing a correct text of the Hymns of the *Rig-veda*, together with a perfect text of Sâyana's Commentary, and the work was so far advanced that the question of a publisher had to be considered. It required a large capital to print and publish a work of six thousand pages quarto, and at the same time pay the editor enough to live on. The idea of publication by a publisher at Königsberg, with the help of subscriptions, which is mentioned in the letters to his mother, and for which a prospectus was actually printed and circulated from London, was abandoned, when in the spring of 1847 the East India Company undertook the task. The following letter to his mother gives an account of his plans and prospects to the close of 1845 :—

To his Mother.

*Translation.* Paris, *Dec.* 23, 1845.

'You know on the whole a great deal about my work, but less on the plans that depend on it. As the printing of the *Veda* could not be undertaken by any publisher on account of the cost and length of the work, I was obliged, though there is no chance of printing for the next two or three years, to apply to several Governments and Academies, to find out how such a work could best be carried out. I therefore made inquiries through friends in London and St. Petersburg, and received tolerably reassuring answers from both places. In London, Wilson, the father of Sanskrit literature, declared himself ready to get the work undertaken by the University of Oxford; but only on condition that he should publish the text of the *Rig-veda*, and I, in conjunction with other young Sanskrit students, the text of the Commentary, which is really the most important work, and fills about eight thousand pages. This, as far as it went, was very well and a great honour; but as the two other students were leaving London, one for Petersburg, the other for Tübingen, it was necessary I should settle in London, and for that I have no money. At the same time Herr Boehtlingk wrote from Petersburg that he could persuade the Academy to print the work, but with a condition that I worked with him, and gave up the publication of the text to him. As the publication of the text is, as I said, of little scientific importance, only for the credit of being the first to publish the full text of the *Veda*, I wrote that I was ready to accept the offer if a sum of money were promised me, to recoup me for the expense of copying this enormous Commentary, and other books necessary for reference, or that a place should be found for me in Petersburg, where I should have to live, which would enable me in a few years to put by enough to repay myself. To this I have had no answer. At the same time I thought of Berlin, and wrote to Humboldt and Bopp, and sent them a detailed prospectus of my work, and asked if any of the rich funds there could be applied to printing the Commentary. Humboldt soon sent me a very kind letter, in which indeed he gave no definite results, but said he thought it was impossible in Prussia, and urged me emphatically to accept the invitation from London or from Petersburg. This was the state of things, when within the last few days I received from Hase, one of the sub-librarians of the Bibliothèque Royale, a suggestion to go as tutor with the Bavarian Minister, Baron von Cetto, to London. Unexpected as the idea was, I at once resolved to do everything I could to obtain the post, and for the last few days have been in communication with the Baron, who is in Paris. Everything seemed arranged, when this morning, at the last visit, I discovered that the post was impossible for me, as he required me to promise, in writing, that I would never be away from the children for an hour, never go anywhere without them; in fact I should have led a monastic life. Strongly as I felt it was my duty to do all that was in my power to secure a post in which I could gain my own living, and deeply as the feeling has weighed on me, more especially of late, of being a burden to others, and well as I knew that to many of my relations such a post would appear most advantageous, such regulations seemed to me so degrading and foolish that I told his Excellency so, and took my leave. I was quite ready, though I dislike teaching, to take the post. It was a good one, all expenses paid and 3,000 francs; and then I should be in London, which however necessary for my work seemed unattainable in any other way, and before everything else it was a certain substantial position, which would free me from many disagreeables, and in which, instead of taking money from you, my dearest mother, I could have given you some little pleasure. But it was impossible, unless I sacrificed my whole future, and wasted the little I have already done; and I hope that as I feel I have little to reproach myself with, I shall not be blamed by others. I shall work on till I hear something definite from London or Petersburg; if neither negotiation leads to definite results, I must return next spring to Germany, and settle down in Berlin, or more probably in Königsberg. That I have not thought much of myself in all this you will see, as I was ready to go into exile for four or five years, without any chance of seeing you, my dearest mother, or seeing or speaking to any creature belonging to me. They have been trying days through which I have lately lived, and trying nights too, in which I struggled to subdue my heart and intellect, with all my inclinations and ambitions, that I might do what really seemed my duty; and even now, when I can breathe freely,

I feel the pressure, for I have learnt that life is difficult, and why? because of that cursed money, which so many throw away, which makes thousands miserable, and very few happy; yes, there must be a curse on money that is not won by honest toil. But enough of these lamentations, which are of no use, least of all in Paris. Melancholy and frivolity are the two scales in which men here go up and down; happy he who sits in the middle quiet and observant as an Indian Muni. Now for Paris. In the first place, I have moved now and lost my beautiful view and look into the court. The rooms are good, fifth floor; changing was very tiresome and very dear, and I have had many difficulties, caused by Hagedorn's silence, and had to arrange about his furniture and everything. As he never writes, I have again had to get 200 francs from Lederhose, and with the money you have just sent shall manage till January or February. I have sent away my piano, for it cost too much. I can well fancy that you think life here very expensive. I have been told it is dearer in Berlin, but in Berlin one can manage economies better than here; it is the actual necessaries of life that cost so much in Paris. My birthday went by very quietly. Gathy came early to see me, and I fetched some cakes and a bottle of wine which was in Hagedorn's cellar, which, *bon gré, mal gré*, he had to contribute as a birthday present, and we drank my health. My Christmas will be very quiet and lonely, for it is not a *festa* here. I think I shall go to bed at six o'clock and dream. This old year has gone faster than any before, and I was really amazed when I said to myself, I am twenty-two years old. My wish for the New Year is a speedy joyful meeting.'

The letter from Humboldt mentioned above runs thus:—

*Translation.* BERLIN, *December* 8, 1845.

I hasten—though only in a few lines, for I am harassed by many duties—to thank you, dear doctor, for your kind keepsake[1]. I seriously advise you to accept the offer made to you from England or Russia. After all my inquiries, and knowing what I do about the amount of contribution which may be expected from the Government here, it does not seem to me in the least likely that even Bopp and Lassen, Professors of different Universities and personally devoted to this special work, could send you means to print a thousand pages of the *Veda*. Life here is so much more prosaic, and it is inadvisable to raise misgivings or qualms . . . and your well-considered and well-written prospectus contains hints of spoliation. Here one is so cosmopolitan that one does not care *where* the *Veda* may appear, whether in Germany, Oxford, Paris, or St. Petersburg.

[1] M. M.'s translation of the *Hitôpadêsa*.

I know many of your promising writings, and as I am proud of possessing warm German national feelings, I am sorry that I cannot send you a more satisfactory answer to your request. With kind regards, yours A. V. HUMBOLDT.

Just after the last letter to his mother, Max Müller was taken ill with influenza and rheumatism, and for a whole month was unable to work or do anything. He explains his further plans to his mother in the following letter:—

TO HIS MOTHER.

*Translation.* *February* 17, 1846.

'I have been quite ill. I got a bad chill early in January (chiefly by being up in the cold nights hunting fleas), and the whole month had so much rheumatism in my head and back that I had at last to go to bed, and there for several days I was very feverish. The worst is that I have lost a whole month's work, for I got so weak I could not hold a pen. And imagine all that time, the swarms of fleas which would have driven a strong man almost mad. As soon as I was a little better, I sent for the landlord, and told him I would give up the rooms at once, if the whole were not properly cleaned out. This has been done, the wooden panels taken down and the walls behind washed with aqua fortis, every room fresh papered and varnished; the worst was I had to go to an hotel, for the smell was so strong. It is still like autumn here, no snow, no frost, but sitting still at work I use a good deal of wood. I have put up a stove, for the open fire is only for ornament. The season is nearly at an end, I have been out a good deal, as I have made many acquaintances; one goes at nine and is home by eleven, unless there is dancing, when one is home at one o'clock. It is not very amusing, and there is nothing to eat, only tea and cake and a little coloured water, and it does not pay for one's gloves. I did not have a doctor when I was ill, or any servant, though many days I was almost starved, for if I wanted anything I had to go out and fetch it myself. I have lately made friends with an Indian here, with whom I practise talking English and Bengali. I had already studied the latter, and have prepared a Bengali Grammar in French, but as yet I have not found a publisher. As to my plans, they are pretty nearly settled. For London and Berlin I have not money enough, and I had a most friendly letter from Bopp, in which he openly said that all he might be able to do for me in Berlin was to find money enough to publish *extracts* from the great Commentary. Then came a letter from Boehtlingk from Petersburg, requiring a definite answer to lay before the Academy. I should find there the means to print with Boehtlingk the text and Commentary. He writes that if I first took a post as private tutor, which he had found a good plan, some place under Government might be found for me. The Academy had sent for MSS. from India for the work; in fact everything, with one or two exceptions, seems so promising that I have decided to go there. I shall find six Sanskritists in Petersburg, of whom I know two, who write to me that they lead a very pleasant and busy life there. I have asked (for Russians are not to be trusted) for a written transcript of the decree of the Academy, and shall not start until I have received it. I don't know how much longer I shall be in Paris. But I must know how my money matters stand; I don't know how much money I have left. If the Petersburg plan succeeds I need trouble no one, but if I return to Berlin, which Bopp advised, I must borrow some money and start as a tutor (Privatdocent). I cannot say how I long to go to London, but I cannot manage it. When the Petersburg plan is settled I will write to the Duchess[1] for introductions, for they are of great use in Russia. I went to the Theatre the other night and saw an operetta, the *Domino Noir*; then, on Emilie's recommendation, I went to the Masked Ball at the Opera House; it was odious, vulgar people, wretched dresses, noise, tumult, and horrible atmosphere, and at the end every one was drunk. I shall never go again. The music was excellent. I am busy learning Italian with my Italian Sanskritist, an Abbé, who is longing to convert me. Burnouf I see often, and he is very good to me. I wonder where I shall pitch my tent.'

To the Same.

*Translation.* PARIS, *Easter*, 1846.

'Now I must tell you about Petersburg. I received another letter (they each cost five francs), to say that the cost of printing was provided for, and enclosing a copy of the *procès-verbal* of the Meeting of the Academy. It ran thus: "Monsieur Boehtlingk, Member of the Academy, will publish *conjointly* with Monsieur Müller of Paris the *Veda*," &c. At the same time I was asked if I would take a place in the Museum of the Academy, rooms and firing, and 1,200 francs a year pay; of course I had to decide at once, and had many points to consider. First, I did not approve of *conjointly*, and I was afraid from what I was told of St. Petersburg, that if I was once there *conjointly* would turn out to be something very different. Boehtlingk has again quarrelled with Bopp, and does not seem dependable, so that Burnouf and all other Sanskritists advised me to give it up. As

[1] Of Anhalt Dessau.

to the place at the Museum, Boehtlingk had already written to me that I could not live on the pay, and must give private lessons, so that a great deal of time must be sacrificed to earning my bread. And after all one goes to Russia if one *must*, but then one must sell oneself as dear as possible, and I could see that a long stay there would in itself cut me off from a return to Germany. If one has the good luck to be born in Germany, or any other civilized country, one ought not lightly to throw away this blessing, and the satisfying quiet life of a German Professor outweighs with me a Russian Privy Councillorship, with all its orders and titles. So I wrote I could not take such a post, and that as far as printing the *Veda* was concerned, I kept to my earlier written conditions, the acceptance of which the Academy must send direct to me in writing, using my own words. I am pretty certain this will not be done, but that is no matter, for I have *just* had a letter from a bookseller, Samter in Königsberg, who has set up a Sanskrit printing office, and who will print my whole work, and if possible pay me something for it. This must depend upon subscriptions, which he would open, so that I should gain my point in Germany. And now I will honestly confess I long for quiet and for home; and a life in Russia, so forsaken of God and man, would be a terrible sacrifice on my part, which one must be ready to make for science and personal usefulness, but which one need not exactly seek out.'

It was necessary to give these letters *in extenso*, as in 1891 Boehtlingk attacked Max Müller and accused him of having behaved at this time discourteously towards (*d'avoir brusqué*) the Academy of St. Petersburg. From the first, Burnouf and Goldstücker warned Max Müller against accepting any offer from Boehtlingk, but, despairing of other means of getting the *Veda* printed, he was ready to close with the offer on condition that some provision was secured for him whilst he was working with Boehtlingk. The latter seems to have first proposed to the Academy that they should buy the MSS. and materials which Max Müller had collected for his Vedic work, *after* they had been sent to St. Petersburg for inspection, and that the post of Assistant Keeper of the St. Petersburg Museum should be given him; but Boehtlingk says his colleagues demurred, and kindly adds the reason, 'because so young and unknown a person could not be safely trusted with the custody of the treasures of the Museum.' One cannot but wonder with what sort of men they had lived! All the correspondence carried on was with Boehtlingk, not with the Academy, which *never* made Max Müller a definite offer. How then could he have been discourteous to the Academy? The conditions he made were that the Academy should give him in writing an undertaking to complete the work of bringing out the *Rig-veda.* No doubt this condition was suggested by the distrust which Burnouf and others felt about the whole matter. The Academy would not accept this condition, and there the matter broke off. One fails to see why Boehtlingk was so angry with Max Müller for not telling him he had received an offer from a German bookseller to publish the *Rig-veda* by subscription, *after* he had stated to the Academy the conditions on which he could join Boehtlingk, and which the Academy rejected. As in his subsequent attack (*Max Müller als Mythen-Dichter*), Boehtlingk is most anxious to prove that 'under the Petersburg Academy *only* the representative of Sanskrit in the Academy could be meant'; one could understand his feeling personally disappointed, but one fails again to see any insult to the Academy in proposing the conditions named above. Is it not rather the other way? The Academy, according to Boehtlingk, refused to place in the Museum a man trusted and admired by Humboldt, Bopp, Brockhaus, and Burnouf. If 'the Academy' meant 'only the representative of Sanskrit in that body,' Max Müller, after this curious refusal, was right to follow the advice of Burnouf and Goldstücker, and have nothing more to do with him. 'Burnouf repeatedly warned me against Boehtlingk, and promised if I would only stay in Paris to give me his support with Guizot,' says the *Autobiography.* Boehtlingk boasts in his attack on Max Müller that he had prevented his ever being made a Correspondent of the Academy of St. Petersburg, and it has the distinction of being the only Society of real note throughout Europe where his name does not appear. When Boehtlingk's attack came out in 1891 Max Müller wrote to the Secretary of the Academy giving an explanation. The Secretary wrote the following answer:—

'N'ayant pu porter à la connaissance de la Conférence de l'Académie que lors de la réouverture de ses séances votre honorée lettre et votre mémorandum, qui me sont parvenus en été, je suis chargé par la Conférence de vous informer, Monsieur, que la brochure de Mr. Böhtlingk a été publiée personnellement par lui sans le concours de l'Académie en quoi que cela soit, et l'auteur n'a même fait aucune communication à l'Académie par rapport à cette publication, ni avant, ni après son impression, de sorte que l'Académie ne se trouve en rien solidaire avec les opinions émises par Mr. Böhtlingk. D'autre part, l'Académie, n'ayant à son grand regret jamais eu l'occasion d'entrer en relations directes avec vous, honoré Monsieur, il ne peut même pas être question de mésentendu entre la Conférence de l'Académie et l'illustre sanscritologue, que notre Académie apprécie à sa juste valeur.

'Veuillez agréer, honoré Monsieur, l'assurance de mes sentiments les plus distingués. LE SECRÉTAIRE PERPÉTUEL.'

The whole of this affair is well summed up by an Englishman, a good German scholar, who has carefully examined all Boehtlingk's letters. 'It is clear that Max Müller had come to no agreement with Boehtlingk. The risks incurred by a young scholar going to St. Petersburg without some assured means of livelihood were obviously considerable, and Max Müller evidently regarded these as a last resource. After the warnings he had received, he was certainly not to be blamed for asking Boehtlingk, before he agreed to go, for a guarantee that the edition should be completed. This quite reasonable request was refused, and the project consequently came to an end. During the negotiations Max Müller was perfectly justified in continuing to look out for a publisher in Germany, or England, who would offer him more advantageous conditions. Boehtlingk's assumption that his own plan would be carried out was premature, and he had begun collating MSS. of the text of the *Rig-veda* before any bargain had been concluded with Max Müller. Boehtlingk had not originally meant to edit the *Rig-veda*, but after he had taken the matter in hand, he was evidently annoyed at having gone so far himself when the negotiations came to an end, representing the request for a guarantee of completion as a slight to the Academy. It was only natural that Max Müller should have wished to publish the whole work himself, if he could obtain the means of doing so. He entertained the idea of collaboration only because compelled to do so by circumstances.' Dr. Boehtlingk made his attack in 1891 when he was in friendly correspondence with Professor Max Müller, and did not even send him a copy of his pamphlet. He had destroyed all Max Müller's letters in 1868, his own letters exist, and by no means bear out Boehtlingk's version of the whole affair, which was drawn from an unsound and somewhat tainted memory.

A month later than the last letter to his mother, Max Müller found that he had saved enough money for a short visit to England, and the next letter speaks of his happy prospects.

To his Mother.

*Translation.* Paris, *May* 24.

'My prospects in London are good, and everything well arranged. I cannot state when I go, as I expect a letter from Hagedorn about his rooms, which should arrive on the 7th. Then I go straight to London. Baron von Cetto has written to me three times from there with new proposals. Perhaps I shall give private lessons, but am sure to make a little money by Sanskrit commissions. The prospectus for my work will be published in London in five languages, German, English, French, Bengali, and Sanskrit. It will be printed in Königsberg. A few days ago I received offers of support from the German Oriental Society, of which I am a member, as well as from the Société Asiatique in Paris. They offered money towards printing, and as this is no longer needed, I hope to have something for myself. I have written to Humboldt. Burnouf has done so too, and Dr. Goldstücker hopes to see him about it in Berlin. I am rejoiced at going to London, and shall stay as long as I can. But whatever happens I will not stay away another whole year without once seeing you, were it but for an hour. In all that I think and do I remember you always, my dear mother, and it is my greatest joy to be any pleasure to you. I need only patience and courage! One must bend or break, and perhaps we shall find a pleasanter corner than St. Petersburg in which to spend the next twenty-five years. Your Max.'

He went for three weeks, and lived in England above fifty-four years.

# CHAPTER IV

## 1846–1847

London. W. H. Russell. Bunsen. Visit to Germany. East India Company and the *Rig-veda.* British Association.

*Translation.* 46, ESSEX STREET, STRAND, LONDON, *June* 13, 1846.

'MY DEAR MOTHER,—Here I am really in London; but I hardly know how to write, my heart is so full of all I have heard and seen. So I will only say, I arrived safe without being swallowed up by the world-encompassing ocean. I left Paris on the 9th, at 5 p.m., by diligence. I had met with such kindness on all sides, and had so many invitations, that it was difficult to get away. My neighbours at table gave me a dinner, so did the Marrins, Burnouf, Countess Berthöer, whom I do not think I have mentioned to you. She is a young and very agreeable woman, whose husband was killed eight months ago in Algiers. She was for some time in India, and is very musical, and we have played and smoked a great deal together. Many friends came with me to the post-house, and I drove away with rather a heavy heart. I had many expenses those last days, and I am all the more grateful for the thirty thalers you put up with the shirts; the orange sugar was confiscated on the frontier—which will make you very angry, as it made me. So I left Paris, travelled the whole night, and arrived at 11 a.m. in Boulogne. At last from far off I saw the dancing, widespread sea, and I had hardly patience to get down at the hotel, but set off at once for a walk along the shore. *You* know that no words can describe its wondrous beauty. I wandered about for five hours, till I was forced to return to the hotel from sheer hunger. At ten at night I went on board a ship, bound direct for London. It was almost full moon, and the sea was smooth and beautiful, and except for a short time of misery I really enjoyed it. We got into the Thames early in the morning; and you can have no idea of the life and traffic. The river was alive with ships, among them huge three-masted vessels. Thus we reached the Custom House, where all my books and papers were turned out. I took a cab, and looked for lodgings, which I soon found in a pleasant, respectable street. I have a room on the first floor, looking on the street, for which I pay 10*s.* a week. The house belongs to a tailor, and as yet I am fairly comfortable. In the morning I make my tea, and dine at four or five o'clock for 1*s.* 6*d.* I have been running about paying visits, but found hardly any one at home. To-morrow I shall call at Bunsen's and on Baron von Cetto. To-day I went to the East India House, where Wilson was very kind, and invited me to dinner. I have been to the British Museum, and made some pleasant acquaintances. Now I have my MSS. at home, and am happily settled in quiet to work. I shall do all I can to give private lessons, for German money does not go far here. I always hope for the best, and I shall manage. Only think that I am in London, that I have seen Hyde Park, St. James's Palace, St. Paul's, Westminster, and the Tower! It seems to me impossible, and I am most fortunate; how well all goes with me, how far beyond all I deserve! Write to me soon; that is the one thing left to wish for. Life here is very wonderful, and so different from Paris. I find the language very difficult, but I shall soon manage it. Yesterday evening I spent with an Englishman, a reporter for the *Times*, whose acquaintance I have made, and who has already been most helpful and kind to me. I am so tired with running about that I am nearly asleep, and don't know whether you can read my scrawl.

'Your M.'

It will be seen by the above letter that Max Müller did not enter into all details in writing to his mother. The life was so different to anything to which she was accustomed, and required so much explanation, that we often find him passing over things well known to his friends on the spot. He does not recount above his first meeting with his kind friend and benefactor, the famous *Times* correspondent, Dr. now Sir William Russell, whose own pen shall describe the event:—

202, Cromwell Road, S.W.,
*October* 8, 1901.

'Dear Mrs. Max Müller,—My daughter is writing for me; I have to use her pen, conscious that I have too long delayed fulfilling the promise I made to recall the incidents connected with my first acquaintance with my ever dear friend, your husband.

'Early in June, 1846, I was in France, and was summoned back to take charge of the Parliamentary Committee on Railway Bills. I took my passage on board a steamer which went direct from Boulogne to London, landing passengers at the Custom House above Blackwall. I distinctly remember the interest I took in a young man, a little younger than myself, who was very anxious to ascertain the names of the places on the river which the steamer passed on her way from the Downs up to the Docks. He was evidently a foreigner, and had some difficulty in making himself understood by the mate, who appeared to have him in charge. I had observed him during a rather rough passage seated on the deck and holding on by one of the stays, evidently engaged in a contest with the advanced posts of *mal de mer*, but he resisted stoutly, and by the time we entered smooth water he was conqueror. He was neatly and carefully dressed in a suit which showed his erect, slight, but well-built figure to advantage; the expression of his face was most engaging, regular features, fine intelligent eyes, no trace of whiskers, beard, or moustache, but thick dark hair under his felt hat; an alert air and penetrating looks. Some casual question which he addressed to one of the passengers produced a very misleading answer, and I ventured to give the true explanation of the vessels which were moored in the Downs, waiting for favourable wind or tide. The melancholy look which had attracted my attention when we were in mid-channel as he sat holding on to a rope had vanished; there was something to look at and to inquire about. Soon we became on good terms, and he told me that he was going to England to pursue his labours in Oriental literature; whilst I informed him that I was a law student residing in the Middle Temple. At the Custom House there was, I remember, some trouble about passports, and my companion produced a paper in which his name was set forth as Max Müller—an official document which satisfied the authorities. But he was soon in much distress; his portmanteau could not be found; he told me it contained all his worldly goods, with his letters and papers, and that it would be ruin to him if it were not forthcoming. All the passengers' luggage was overhauled, and still not a trace of the missing trunk. My newly made friend was in serious anxiety, and I felt for him deeply. What could he do? an utter stranger with very little money about him, almost all he possessed being in the unfortunate box that could not be found. The Custom House people having cleared all the baggage, were anxious to clear us out; so I told my young friend that I had chambers where I would be most happy to give him a shake-down for the night, and on the following day he could go back to the Custom House and see if the missing box had been landed. He was very much moved, and accepted my proposal with a charming cordiality. We drove together to the Temple, and despite his anxiety the strange new sights filled him with the greatest interest. We dined at Anderton's in Fleet Street, and when we got back to the Temple we found that the laundress had arranged a comfortable couch for him, and had laid out a sleeping-suit for the stranger. Next day we made a journey to the Custom House, and to his inexpressible joy Max Müller was shown his treasured portmanteau, which he opened for examination, and then saw passed, with the traditional chalk-mark on it, to the cab and carried to my rooms. I think it was that day that I went out with him, at his request, and found a decent bedroom in Essex Street, close by, of which he became the tenant, and where he had his breakfast every morning. Max Müller had letters for Professors at King's College, the Prussian Embassy, &c., and he was soon in communication with some of them; but I saw him every day I should think for two or three months, and every hour I did so increased my regard for him—so simple, so straight, and so learned; kindly and grave, but with a keen sense of humour, and a most bright and joyous disposition. In those days gentlemen of the press were more in favour with the dramatic world than they are at present. I could always obtain free admissions to concerts and theatres, and so we went together night after night to Drury Lane, Her Majesty's, the Haymarket, Adelphi, and so forth; and Max's enjoyment of the Opera was intense and delightful. It was the custom at that time for students after dining in hall (at the Temple) to go off to their rooms with a friend or two, and others dropped in. Max Müller was always the most welcome guest at mine, and he provided strange and wonderful entertainment for the company. For the first time the Temple was enlivened by the strains of "Edite, bibite, conviviales," "Crambambuli," and other Studenten-Lieder. One *morceau* of surpassing excellence, as we all thought, we always encored, and Max smilingly complied[1]. It was an imitation of a whole orchestra—trumpets, drums, bassoons, and goodness knows what besides!—delivered with the greatest precision. Those of the company who had rooms in the Temple were eager to secure a special right for this diversion. There are, as far as I know, none of these now alive. At last Max went away, but whether back to Germany or to Oxford I cannot remember. In the winter I was dispatched on a special commission in relation to the famine in Ireland, and whilst there I received a letter from Max, written in a hand I could not read then, but which I made out later, in which he told me of his projects;

[1] 'O Tannenbaum! o Tannenbaum!'

but I did not see him again till I visited Oxford in 1848. He had established himself at Oxford, and had already gained the position there due to his character and acquirements. Then came the revolutions in Europe, ample employment for me in all quarters, so that for a good many years there could be but very short and accidental snatches of intercourse between us; but I heard of his rising fame with great satisfaction. After the Crimean War I delivered a series of lectures at various towns in England, and a visit to Oxford enabled me to renew an acquaintance always delightful and dear to me; and after I returned from India in 1859 we met several times, and engaged in correspondence concerning my experience of a country in which he was deeply interested. And now I think I may make a jump to 1870 and the war with France, when as soon as I came home we had frequent meetings; and the only cloud that ever obscured the warmth and brightness of our intercourse arose from a discussion caused by an intemperate objection I made to the opinions he expressed about the great Bismarck, then the god of the people who worshipped success all over the world. You know what happiness it was to me to make a descent upon Oxford, and spend a few days under your roof at 7, Norham Gardens, and how my wife entered fully into the great repose and comfort we enjoyed there. I shall say no more, except that I reckon your husband's friendship one of my greatest treasures, and that I shall lament his loss as long as I live.

'I am sorry to send you such a bald account, but my memory of late has melted—it is without form and void.

'Yours very truly and with great regard,

'W. H. RUSSELL.'

Max Müller had been in correspondence whilst in Paris with Professor Wilson, the Librarian of the East India House, so there was no difficulty about borrowing MSS. and beginning work at once. The following letter to his mother mentions the momentous visit to Bunsen which determined the whole course of his life:—

*Translation.* 3, WARDROBE PLACE, DOCTORS' COMMONS,
*July* 13, 1846.

'I have only time to tell you that all goes well with me here, that Bunsen has received me in the most friendly way as the son of his friend, and has promised me his fatherly support in every way possible. I have therefore explained my exact position to him, that my work, which interests him very much, makes a long stay in London absolutely necessary, and he assures me I have found a friend in him, who will care for me as a father for his son. I stayed two days in the country with him. His family are very pleasant and cultivated. One evening I went to a party where were the Archbishop of Canterbury, the Bishop of Jerusalem, and others of the *haute volée*. He is himself a very clever man, and a great favourite here, and perhaps he may find something for me. I do my best too with Wilson, but I can't do much, for I must first master the language. I have already changed my room, because it was not clean and so hot. I am not satisfied here, and must pay 10*s*. weekly. I have signed the contract with my publisher; the prospectus will be out November 1, and then also the *Meghadûta*, and I hope at Easter a thick volume of Sanskrit.'

Of Max Müller's first visit to the Prussian Legation Mme. Ernest de Bunsen writes:—

'I remember the Professor on the morning of his arrival when he joined the family party at No. 4, Carlton Terrace. The Legation was then in full swing, and Baron Bunsen and the Professor were absorbed in one another independently of our home party. I value my vivid remembrance of his first appearance, for we were astonished at his youth and cheerfulness, and immediately he gained a place amongst us.'

Max Müller had not been long in London before he wrote to acquaint his friend and teacher Burnouf with his prospects. After thanking him for his friendly counsel and encouragement, and the loan of his valuable MSS., which had helped him to continue his work when he was almost in despair, a work which he now hoped to be able to carry through and make of use to science, he adds:—

*Translation.*

'I never can forget all I owe to you. As to my stay in London, I am on the whole thoroughly satisfied with it. The MSS. are splendid, but in such masses that to copy all that concerns the *Veda* and my work would take at least two or three years of merely mechanical labour. So I must stay in England, and with the MSS. at hand bring out the *Veda* and its Commentary. I shall do this if I can possibly, by private lessons and copying MSS., make enough to face the great expense of life here. I hope that in this way it will be possible for me to carry out the work in a shorter time than I at first expected. I do not deny that it is perhaps foolish to make such a sacrifice, and lead this anxious life for another five years without doing anything that can secure a settled post; but as I have once begun the work it must be finished, and I see no other way of doing it. Professor Wilson is most friendly, and I meet him constantly either at his own house or in the Library of the East India House.'

Burnouf replied that he thought his plans excellent, and that those who understood the magnitude of the task Max Müller had undertaken and the wealth of materials for it in London, would consider that he must work very fast, if he only stayed four years. 'Mr. Wilson will indirectly render a great service to Indian letters, if, with the benevolent liberality with which he meets all those who ask his support, he makes it possible for you to stay in London as long as the task of publishing your *Rig-veda* with its commentaries and indispensable indices may require.'

To his mother he writes:—

*Translation.* LONDON, *August* 3, 1846.

'I had meant to write sooner, but I have been so busy. I am between two fires, or rather Ministers, for the Bavarian Minister, Baron von Cetto, has made fresh offers to me which are tolerably advantageous—1,000 thalers a year and free board; so that I could have put by 600 thalers, and later he would recommend me for some place in Bavaria. On the other hand Bunsen advised me strongly to decline this offer, taking on himself all the responsibility, and told me to trust myself absolutely to him. He is really marvellously kind to me, and I am constantly in his house, early, late, and to dinner. I have not quite decided, and want to postpone a decision. Bunsen is so much interested in the publication of the *Veda*, which falls in with his own studies, and he urges me first to print some of it. I shall do so as soon as I can, but have still a great deal to do to it. Wilson too is very helpful, and promises to do all he can to get me some place in England, which is the height of my ambition; but that may take years, and meantime how shall I eat and drink? Bunsen sent me an article from the *Augsburger Zeitung* with the heading "Max Müller"; if you have not seen it, get it, and I think even you will be satisfied! Of London I can tell you little, except that last Saturday I saw its full splendour. A friend took me to the Italian Opera, which I had not yet seen either here or in Paris. It was wonderful. A larger house than I have ever seen, and every one in full dress. The boxes filled with the nobility, and I saw Queen Victoria and Prince Albert, the Duke of Cambridge, &c. The music absolutely perfect; *Anna Bolena*, sung by Grisi, Mario, and Lablache; all the highest artistic perfection. And then a ballet to which there can be nothing equal, the *Jugement de Paris* with Taglioni, Grahn, and Cerito as the three goddesses. The decorations were beautiful. The stalls cost 7*s.* 6*d.* The same friend asked me to go with him to Scotland as his guest, but I cannot, gladly as I would do so. So you see your son is still afloat, and everywhere friendly hands are stretched out to help him on his way. 'Your MAX.'

*Translation.* *August* 28.

'DEAREST MOTHER,—I have been able to arrange that your letters [1] may come by messenger. They leave Berlin every Tuesday, and you must send them to the Ministry of Foreign Affairs under Bunsen's address. The letters leave here to-day and reach Berlin in five days, and Chemnitz therefore in six.'

TO THE SAME.

*Translation.* *August* 25, 1846.

'All goes tolerably well with me. My work gets on. Bunsen is wonderfully good to me. I dine there once or twice every week, and he always gives me fresh courage and hope. When my first volume is out he hopes to get a salary for me from the Prussian Government. I must stay in England till the whole work is finished, and that will be five years. If I should then return to Germany is the question, for I am so delighted with this country. I could willingly live here always, if only a place could be found for me. But those are future plans which do not trouble me much now; at all events I feel nearer my haven here, if only my pilot holds out! To-morrow I am again invited to Bunsen's for his birthday. Professor Lepsius from Berlin is now staying at Bunsen's with his young wife; he owes everything to Bunsen. He got him a Stipendium to study, then to go to Italy, France, and England, and at last to Egypt; and now he is Professor at Berlin, with 1,500 thalers a year. I have become acquainted with Archdeacon Hare, and dined with him. He is a very kind old man, and I am on most happy terms with him. I am still in Wardrobe Place, and more comfortable, as I can dine in the house with one of the other lodgers; very good, and only 1*s.* He is a young German bookseller, married to an Englishwoman, with whom I can talk English, which is already much easier to me. I have not seen much more of London; the city is less interesting than the people and the life. I am well and don't feel anything of the spleen to which I am

[1] He had to pay 1*s.* 6*d.* in England for letters on which his mother had already paid something.

naturally inclined. I read the *Times* every day with great interest, while I drink my tea and smoke a pipe, and then to work. The one thing I long for is quiet and a certainty, and a pleasant home life with my dear mother. But as often as I think it is near at hand it goes again, and who knows when I may at last gain it? My work is full of interest, and keeps me straight; but sometimes one longs for more in life than this everlasting struggle. Now only quiet and content!'

In September Max Müller issued a prospectus of the *Rig-veda* to be published, as has been seen, by subscription by Samter of Königsberg. This plan was given up when the East India Company undertook the publication of the *Rig-veda*. The prospectus contains a proposal for a German translation, and sets forth clearly the importance of the *Rig-veda* for the history of human thought. Soon after, he heard of the very alarming illness of his mother, and his ever faithful friend Bunsen sent him with dispatches to Berlin, to enable him to see her. Such was his anxiety to reach his mother, that he insisted on crossing, though it was a frightful storm and he was the only passenger. It took nearly six hours to get to Calais! He was able to spend several weeks with her, and returned by Berlin.

To his Mother.

*Translation.* Berlin, *October* 27.

'Your letter which I got yesterday was a great pleasure, though it made me sad, when I saw how my leaving you had excited and weakened you. Now I hope, if you really love me, you will think of your health, and spare yourself as much as possible. Remember the distance is not so very great, and that we can reach each other now so easily; think too that it is of great importance and use to me, and that in after years we shall find a rich reward for it. There is not much to tell you of my journey. . . . I arrived early in Leipzig, and went straight to Victor Carus. I went also to Brockhaus, with whom I had much to talk over, and then on to Dessau. Here they were all very well, and glad to get a better account of you. That evening I had to go with them to the theatre, and there the Duchess saw me, and the next morning commanded me to the Schloss. She was exceedingly friendly, and kept me nearly an hour. . . . She then gave me a letter of introduction to Prince Waldemar in Berlin. I have been to Bopp and Lepsius, and have still to call on Humboldt, Schelling, &c. . . . There was a large party here last night . . . where I met many interesting people. I shall be glad when I am quietly back in London.

'Your MAX.'

TO THE SAME.

*Translation.* BERLIN, *November* 11.

'You will be surprised at getting another letter from Berlin, when I hoped to be already in London. But there was so much to do of real importance concerning my work and prospects that I was obliged to put off my journey, and cannot even now fix the day. The worst is I have had no rest the whole time, always running about, paying visits to Geheimräthe and Ministers. Humboldt has again been most good to me, and done all he could to support the publication of the *Veda*, in such a way that I should gain something by it. He gave my prospectus to the King, who had it read out to him, and spoke most graciously about it, and sent me word through Humboldt I should write him a letter regarding the religious importance of the *Veda*. I had to do this at once, and you know how much care and time such a thing takes. The King is unfortunately not in Berlin, but has received my letter, and already promised a considerable sum towards the undertaking. Then there was much to arrange about the Sanskrit types, which belong to the Academy, but I am in great hopes that my plans will be successful, and that I can return to London in good spirits. . . . I dined with Prince Waldemar, who is a remarkably charming and cultivated man. After dinner we had coffee in an Indian tent, with fine carpets and tiger-skins, everything Indian, even to the long pipes and tobacco.'

Soon after his return to London the negotiations with the East India Company for printing and publishing the *Rig-veda* began. The success of his plan of publishing the *Veda* in Königsberg depended on the support of the East India Company—who were asked to subscribe for 100 copies, the King of Prussia and the French Government having already promised to take a large number. But when, as advised by Bunsen and Wilson, Max Müller called on the various Directors on the subject, they declared themselves averse to supporting a work carried out by a foreign country. Bunsen was ready to seize the opportunity, for he saw at once that the East India Company was the proper body to undertake the whole work.

'It was not an easy task,' says the *Autobiography*, 'to persuade the Board of Directors, all strictly practical men, to authorize so considerable an expenditure, merely to edit and print an old book that none of them could understand, and many of them had never even heard of. Bunsen pointed out what a disgrace it would be if some other country than England published this edition of the Sacred Books of the Brâhmans.'

Professor Wilson, the Librarian of the India House, who had long been preparing a translation of the *Rig-veda* and often found himself hampered from want of a perfectly correct text, added his powerful advocacy, and though months of uncertainty were yet to try the young scholar, everything was finally arranged by April, 1847.

To his Mother.

*Translation.* London, *December* 25.

'I put off writing, for I hoped to give you news of employment, about which I have been busy ever since the end of November, and in constant hopes of a favourable decision, but I am still without any definite information. I can hardly tell you how uncomfortable such a position is, such uncertainty makes me unfit for anything. I can truly say I have lost the whole of December, as I could do nothing but write official letters to the Honourable Court of Directors of the East India Company, and pay official visits, &c. But if it succeeds, I shall have £150 a year, and nothing to do but bring out a Sanskrit work for the Company. You can imagine how delightful such a position would be, and can picture to yourself my intense anxiety as to yes or no! Bunsen and Wilson have done all in their power, and Bunsen especially has taken the liveliest interest in the whole affair, but such arrangements cannot be made in a hurry, and so I must be patient. My birthday passed by quietly, with no one who knew it. I dined at Bunsen's. The whole month has gone in hopes, expectations, disappointments, and rejoicings, and though it is possible I might hear to-day that all is settled, it may dawdle on into next year, and even fail entirely. So do not talk about it, and do not paint my future to yourself in rosy colours, for it may first be very grey! I feel sure I can depend on Bunsen under all circumstances. How I have deserved his kindness, I know not, for he has done me so many kindnesses, not only where his position made it easy for him, but even when it was disagreeable to him, and required great self-restraint. I was there for Christmas Eve. The whole family were together, children and children's children—in all thirty people, and then all the servants. A huge Christmas tree, and two large rooms lighted up and decorated, and presents for every one. I had a beautiful writing portfolio fitted up with everything; I was as happy as one can be when obliged to be away from home. We have been waiting five days for the courier, who comes by Hamburg, and is probably frozen in! From January 1, a letter to Germany will only cost one shilling. To-day I dine with Wilson—a large party. The English keep Christmas by eating enormously, but one needs an English appetite for it! . . . I have forgotten to send my New Year's wishes—you know how I wish you all with all my heart a very happy year—and no year will be happier for me than the one when I find myself able, if only in the smallest degree, to add to your comfort!—MAX.'

His life all these months had been one of very hard work and constant self-denial, and but for Bunsen's substantial help he could not have lived on in England. He tells us how he walked to and from the India House every day, his arms full of books and papers. One day he left his spectacles, which he had broken, to be mended at a shop in the Strand, and on calling to fetch them, he laid down a sovereign to pay for them. The shopman returned him change for half a sovereign, and persisted that Max Müller had only given him ten shillings. It was in vain to remonstrate, the man only became abusive to the unmistakable foreigner in a well-worn coat, and Max left the shop, sadly aware that the missing ten shillings represented several dinners, which he must give up. Some days passed, dinnerless, when one evening the man rushed out of the same shop as Max was passing it, with ten shillings in his hand, which he held out to him—'Oh, sir,' he said, 'I have watched for you several days. You were right; I found I had ten shillings too much when I counted up my money that evening, and I have longed to get it back to you,' adding, 'for you look as if you wanted it.'

Meantime he was making friends in England. He had stayed more than once in the country at Totteridge with Bunsen, and with him had visited Archdeacon Hare. Mr. Vaux of the British Museum had become a fast friend, an intimacy which lasted till Mr. Vaux's death. Max Müller constantly attended the suppers given by his friend, where the invitation cards were adorned with pictures of Nineveh bulls and hawk-headed deities, and where clouds of not over-good tobacco smoke filled the air. 'Billy Russell,' as we know, constantly sent him tickets for concerts and theatres, so that, notwithstanding his hard work, and the uncertainty about the *Veda*, his early London life was far more enjoyable than the first year of his stay in Paris. There were several young German Sanskritists at work in England, and with these and the colony of German merchants, living chiefly at Denmark Hill, and the members of the German Consulate he was in constant intercourse.

Early in 1847 he went for a short time to Oxford to copy Sanskrit MSS.—his first sight of his future home. About the same time he made acquaintance by letter with Benfey, the great Sanskrit scholar at Göttingen, an acquaintance that soon ripened into a true friendship. Benfey was then engaged on his edition of the *Sâma-veda*, and many letters passed between the friends on points of Vedic grammar.

To his Mother.

*Translation.* London, *February* 12, 1847.

'Still in great uncertainty. I have only just returned to London, for I have been staying at Oxford, working in the Library there, and have thus seen the most interesting and beautiful city in Europe. The whole town is of the Middle Ages, and consists almost entirely of churches, monasteries (now Colleges), castles, and towers, all in old English or Gothic, and the whole life is of the Middle Ages. All students in black and white gowns and black caps, and so are the Professors, &c. And then the wealth and easy life in the Universities (*sic*), which are more High Schools than Universities.'

Not long after Max Müller's return from Oxford he was able to write to his mother:—

*Translation.* 5, Newman's Row, Lincoln's Inn Fields,
*April* 15, 1847.

'At last the long conflict is decided, and I have carried off, so to speak, the prize! I can yet hardly believe that I have at last got what I have struggled for so long, entire independence, and I am filled with the thought of how much more I have gained than I deserve. . . . I am to hand over to the Company, ready for press, fifty sheets each year—the same I had promised to Samter in Germany; for this I have asked £200 a year, £4 a sheet. They have been considering the matter since December, and it was only yesterday that it was officially settled. I have to read the corrections, and shall have plenty of time left to devote to my studies. . . . As the work will be above 400 sheets, I have a certain position for the next eight years, and the work is really so light I could take another post with it. This in fact has been already offered me, i.e. a place as Librarian at the British Museum, with £150 a year. But on Bunsen's advice I have refused this, as I would rather be free the first years to study, till something more suitable presents itself, of which there is little doubt in time. And now what do you say, dearest mother? Is it not more than I could have ever expected? And have I not been right throughout to hold out to the very last, and devote all my time and strength and money to one aim, and pursue that to the last gasp? But only think that I had not a penny left, and that in spite of every effort to make a little money, I should have had to return to Germany had not Bunsen stood by me and helped me by word and *deed*. It has been a bad time, and now that it is over I may say so. I saw that the turning-point of my life had come, and that after all the uncertainty I was only a few steps from the goal, and yet I was not in a position to wait longer, but should be forced to return to Germany, to give up my favourite studies, if not entirely, yet mostly, in order to gain a scanty living at a school or by private lessons. I knew that none of my relations and friends agreed with me; on the contrary, that they all thought my plans foolish and exaggerated, and I had no one from whom I could expect support—I mean, who would have lent me a small sum for a few years. In fact, all my time, money, and work, indeed my whole life perhaps, would have been sacrificed and lost, had not Bunsen, who had once been in the same position, without my saying anything to him, stood by me, and in this way made it possible for me to struggle on with joyful confidence and firm faith towards the goal I had set before me. I do not know whether I should thank God more that I have at last attained my long-desired and long-sought object, or that I have gained the friendship of so noble and distinguished a man as Bunsen. It is in these last weeks that I have learned to know and value him so thoroughly. Archdeacon Hare invited Bunsen and me to spend Easter with him in the country, and so I spent the whole time in constant intercourse and conversation with these two men and Sir John Herschell, the famous astronomer, who was there on a visit, and thus I forgot all my troubles. In fact, I spent a delightful time, and when I reached London yesterday I found all settled, and I could say and feel, Thank God! Now I must at once send my thanks, and set to work to earn the first £100. Till then Bunsen will lend me some money, which will not be necessary later on, as one can live here comfortably on £150, and at first my expenses will be small. We will not make any plans yet for the future. When my work is once arranged I can easily spend a month or two each year in Germany, and when I have put by a little you might try if you could live comfortably in England. But at first, patience! My rooms here are small, but very nice—sitting- and bed-room—with a beautiful view over an old park and Gothic buildings. I pay, however, nearly £45, and that is cheap. As soon as I have earned a little money, my first purchase will be a piano—hiring is almost as dear as buying a second-hand one, which is always easy to find. What did you think of my *Meghadûta?* I am well and happy.'

This summer Max mentions hearing Mendelssohn several times, both in public and at Bunsen's. It was his last intercourse with the friend of his childhood, boyhood, and youth; for at the close of the year he writes:—

TO HIS MOTHER.

*Translation.* 1, GARDEN PLACE, *December* 11.

'The death of Mendelssohn was a great shock to me, and yet is not his lot to be envied? and if to live is to work, has he not lived longer than many? What comes from God is right and good. How beautifully Jean Paul speaks of comfort, but how much more beautiful and elevating is another book, which unhappily through man's unreason and man's wisdom is so spoilt for us from childhood, that we can only slowly and by degrees read and live into it again. Here the general sympathy has been expressed in so many different ways. Elijah was twice performed, all in mourning, no applause, and at the beginning the Dead March in Saul. I could not go, it was too much for me. I could not at first touch the piano. Now there is a collection for a monument, probably in Westminster, where you know Handel is buried.'

To return to his daily life, now given up to the preparation of the text and Commentary of the *Rig-veda*. The MS. of the first volume was rapidly approaching completion. 'I get up at five every morning,' he says (May 10), 'for I have a great deal to do, and the evenings are generally wasted in society. Summer is beginning, and there is more green each morning on the great trees before my window.'

For nearly four years Max Müller had been copying and collating the MSS. of the *Rig-veda* in order to publish a correct text, but this was by no means the most difficult part of his task, though it is the part that has been best understood and appreciated by the public. Real Sanskrit scholars know that his knowledge of Sanskrit was tested and shown in the critical edition of Sâyana's Commentary. This work involved enormous labour, and he was often urged to work faster and less critically, but he kept to his first resolution, to publish the whole text of the Commentary, making it as perfect as possible. At the time he began his edition, many of the Sanskrit works quoted by Sâyana were still unedited, whilst the references were brief, presupposing an intimate acquaintance with the works quoted. Max Müller had to trace these references, to copy the MSS. where they occur, and make full and careful indices. This he did, though often delayed by some obscure reference to Pânini's Grammar or Yâska's Glossary. All these references had to be found, and their meaning ascertained, before any printing could be begun. They are now given in his edition of the *Veda*. He tells us he was often driven to despair by some obscure reference which neither Burnouf nor Wilson, the greatest Sanskrit scholars of the day, could help him to discover. 'It often took me whole days—nay, weeks—before I saw light. In the purely mechanical part other scholars could, and did, help me; but whenever any real difficulty arose, I had to face it by myself, though after a time I gladly acknowledge that here too their advice was often valuable to me.'

Bunsen was determined, as his young friend would live in England, at all events for several years to come, that he should make the acquaintance of influential and distinguished people, not only in London society, but in scientific and literary circles, and therefore insisted on his attending, under his guidance, the meeting of the British Association, which in 1847 was held at Oxford. He not only attended, but prepared and read a paper in English on the relation of Bengali to the Aryan and aboriginal languages of India. He had been but a year in England, and though he had completely mastered English, and wrote and expressed himself correctly and forcibly, his pronunciation was still very foreign, and it was with no little trepidation that he stood up for the first time before a large and critical English audience. His subject was one entirely new to most of his hearers, but it excited great interest, and gave rise to a keen discussion, in which the young scholar was ably and chivalrously defended by Dr. Prichard, President of the Section, against the attacks and objections of certain members who thought that no good thing could come out of Germany. Though Max Müller never reprinted this paper separately, and considered it as the crude production of a very young man (he was not twenty-four), he received, as late as 1892, a letter from a gentleman engaged in like studies with this allusion to his early essay: 'It seems to me that you have stated far more clearly than I have seen elsewhere the main facts of Bengali agglutination, and it is astonishing to me how wonderfully you have grasped them without visiting Bengal.'

It was on this occasion that Max Müller first came into personal contact with Prince Albert, for whom he ever afterwards felt the strongest admiration and sympathy. They met from time to time at public dinners, or whenever the Prince Consort visited Oxford, but both were aware that, strongly as they felt drawn to each other by common interests and national sympathies, more constant intercourse would not be wise for either of them, both being, in their different spheres of work, jealously watched as foreigners by suspicious John Bull.

After Max Müller's return to London he tells his mother that he was 'feeling mentally and physically exhausted, as the various discussions in English tried him rather.' Still, he speaks of this meeting as a delightful time, and he felt sure it would be of use to him.

TO HIS MOTHER.

*Translation.* *July*, 1847.

'The suggestion came, of course, again from Bunsen, who is determined to push me in the world. He continues just the same to me, and his friendship and affection make my life very happy here. Yesterday there was a great Egyptian dinner at Bunsen's. I was there; for, after long indecision, I too have joined the hieroglyphists. The printing goes on very slowly, as new letters have to be made, and it will be a whole year before the first volume is ready: but when everything is in order, I shall make £3 or £4 a week. As yet Bunsen is still my banker, but my credit stands high with him! The death of Fanny Hensel has grieved me very much. I have not heard Jenny Lind yet, it is too expensive. How gladly would I have a quiet fortnight with you; one gets no rest here.'

To the Same.

*Translation.* London, *July* 13.

'London is really unbearable from heat and dust, and I am longing so for the country that I shall try and find a little room, if possible, at the seaside, which I know will do me good. If only England were not so very dear, especially when one wants to amuse oneself. Prince Waldemar is here, and I have seen him several times and had several good dinners with him. I enclose the menu of the largest dinner, given by the Directors of the East India Company. Each cover cost £5. It is impossible to describe it, and I assure you I had rather eat potatoes in Chemnitz! Lord John Russell was there, and the *élite* of society. Bunsen again did little else but introduce me to people who would be useful to me. But running about in society, eating, drinking, and talking, tires one out, and I shall get away as soon as I can.'

The printing of the *Veda* had now begun in real earnest, and on July 13, 1847, he was able to send to Burnouf in Paris the first two sheets of Volume I. 'How willingly,' he says, 'would I have visited Paris this summer to seek advice and information on many points from you, but I am chained here. When my first volume is ready I shall take a holiday, that I may present it to you in person. I rejoice in the prospect, for I cannot repeat often enough that I owe it to your advice and friendly sympathy alone that I am now realizing the plans I formed in my youth.'

In August he writes to his mother from 1, Garden Place, Lincoln's Inn:—

*Translation.*

'As you see I have changed my rooms once more, as there was a bad smell in the other house in this heat, and I thought it was not healthy. I am quite away from the street, and live as in a garden. I have in fact two houses, for all day long I am in the India House, where I have my own room, all surrounded by books and MSS. I have a long way to walk there and back every day, which is very good for me. My printing goes on well, so that I am quite happy and satisfied. I had to give up my stay in the country, or at the seaside, as I had neither money nor time for it. Instead, I have hired a piano, which is a great delight. How often I have thought of you lately, and your pleasant life at Dresden. Yes, however good the life here is for the brain and soul, one's heart often longs for something else, and if I had not Bunsen and his family, life here would often be very sad to me. But I will not complain, I am determined to be as happy as I can be, for how much brighter has my whole life turned out, than I ventured to expect or hope. My life in London now is so quiet and uniform that I have nothing to tell you. The Bunsens are going into the country, where he will rest after the long season. He does a great deal of literary work, and I read or hear it all, and we often have sharp discussions, as you may imagine, as I cannot help speaking out plainly, and he also wields a sharp sword. But he is delightful, and we always remain good friends.'

To THE SAME.

*Translation.* *September* 1.

'My rooms in London are delightful, and my piano a real joy. In the same house lives Dr. Trithen, an Orientalist, whom I knew in Paris, and who was once employed in the Office for Foreign Affairs in St. Petersburg. Then there are a great many other Orientalists in London, who are mostly living near me, and we form an Oriental colony from all parts of the world. Dr. Bergstedt, a Swede; Köllgren, a Finn; Abbé Bardelli, an Italian; Dr. Dillmann from Suabia; Dr. Spiegel from Bavaria; Dr. Weber from Berlin. When we are all together, it sounds like a perfect Babel, and we have a good deal of fun at our cosmopolitan tea-evenings.'

By the middle of October, Max Müller was able to send the first sheet of Sâyana's Commentary to M. Burnouf. He says in a letter dated '1, Garden Place, Oct. 18':—

*Translation.*

'This first sheet has cost me much time and trouble, as they had not sufficient types at Oxford, which caused endless delay. Now that they have founded the accented letters, I hope to get on faster, but I send this first sheet because if you have any serious objections to the general plan I have adopted, conformably with my position here in London, I could still make necessary alterations. I often feel that the *Rig-veda* and Commentary ought to have fallen into worthier hands, but I will do all that I possibly can. I count on your indulgence, but shall, at the same time, be most grateful if you will point out any mistakes.'

To this Burnouf replied :—

*Translation.* *November* 9.

'MY DEAR FRIEND,—I thank you for having sent me the sheets of your grand edition of the *Rig-veda.* I use the word grand, not to avoid saying excellent, because I consider it both grand and excellent, but because I must express my admiration of Professor Wilson's fine and vigorous Devanâgarî type. I have examined your sheets, and I must own that I am astonished that in so short a time you have been able to master the mass of materials at hand. One has a right to demand of an editor a correct list, a suitable division of the words, an indication of the Hindu divisions according to the two systems, the text so far separated from the Commentary that they can never be mistaken the one for the other, a reproduction of the Pada MS. and position of the accents according to the copies of the Rishis. You have given all this with exemplary care and completeness. But you have given us much more, and here I cannot praise you too highly. You indicate the quotations, and trace them not only to works that are accessible, but to many that are still entirely unedited. I congratulate you with all my heart on your *début*, and I venture to say on your success, for your success is secured. You know me well enough, I hope, to feel the sincerity of my congratulations. We older men, who came too early to embark on the great enterprises which younger men can undertake, we have only the duty of clapping our hands to show the public what they ought to honour and esteem. Believe me, I shall not fail in doing this; and it is a great delight to do it for a man whose knowledge I admire and whose character I love. And I think I may be allowed to reflect with pleasure on any effort I may have made to encourage you to march on in entire independence, avoiding all collaborations. This is the only thing on which I can pride myself, and it again is entirely to your honour, because it only proves that I recognized all that science might expect from you. Believe me that I am more than ever filled with this sentiment, and continue to reckon me among those who follow your success with the greatest delight. 'E. BURNOUF.'

TO HIS MOTHER.

*Translation.* *November* 9.

'My time is entirely occupied with the *Veda* ... but my work is delightful, and I feel sure that in six or seven years it will bring in plenty, and I am quite independent, and that is worth more than anything else. But the idea of marrying is absurd, and happily as yet love has left me tolerably alone, for I have other things to fill my head and heart. I have just had an offer to go to Benares, and print the *Veda* there, which I have refused. I correspond with the Brâhmans there, and the Indian papers often mention Dr. M. M., but that is of no help.'

To Burnouf he writes:—

*Translation.* 1, GARDEN PLACE, *December* 5, 1847.

'Your last letter gave me the greatest pleasure, and I thank you warmly. I know well that you are full of indulgence and kindness, such as I must not expect from the severe critics of Russia and Germany, but I own that your favourable opinion, and that of Wilson, Lassen, and Bopp, are the most delightful reward, and the only one I wish for, and that it gives me new courage to persevere in a task that would otherwise often seem dry and distasteful. The news that I have received through M. d'Eckstein that you have successfully deciphered the Nineveh inscriptions would have astonished me, had one not been accustomed to such happy surprises from the successor of Champollion. I consider this discovery the grandest and most important of the century; it must throw light on many fundamental questions of ancient ethnography. Up to now, I have not found anything really solid and satisfactory in all the conjectures on the so-called Indian, Babylonian, and Assyrian inscriptions. I hear that Dr. Hincks sent yesterday to the Asiatic Society a complete translation of the inscriptions of Van, made by means of an Indo-germanic language. But I must examine it myself. Rawlinson has at last managed to copy a part of the third inscription at Behistun, and he writes that he now for the first time touches solid ground. Incredulous as I have been about all these promises and experiments, I am now convinced that under your guidance a new region will be opened to science, and I await the signal impatiently.'

This important year of Max's life was drawing to a close. His success had justified his perseverance in a career which had at one time seemed utterly hopeless, and he was rewarded at last for the long struggle, for the bitter self-denials of his early years.

For the first time we find a mention in his Christmas letter of a gift of money to the mother to whose unceasing care and self-forgetfulness he owed everything. This he never forgot to the last hour of her life, and it was his constant delight from this time onwards to add to her comforts and pleasures.

To his Mother.

*Translation.* 1, Garden Place, Lincoln's Inn,
*December* 11, 1847.

'... I must now give you some commissions. Take the enclosed £5 note and change it at a banker's, and with half of it buy something very nice for Frau Hofräthin Müller; with the other half something pretty for Frau Dr. Krug, and some toys for the two little Krugs.

'Your Max.'

# CHAPTER V

## 1848

**Visit to Paris. Revolution. Settles at Oxford. Friends there. Letters to Burnouf and Bunsen.**

THE year 1848 began gaily for the young stranger. He had moved to King William Street, Strand, to be a little nearer to the Prussian Legation, though he already began to recognize the disadvantage of being so far from his printers, now that the first volume of the *Rig-veda* was passing through the Press. No London firm could have undertaken the work, from want of the proper types, whilst the Oxford University Press, with the help of Professor Wilson, had secured the finest Devanâgarî types then known. Of his gaieties he writes to his mother:—

*Translation.* 5, KING WILLIAM STREET, STRAND, *January* 27, 1848.

'Last week I went to two balls in English families to whom I have been introduced. It was a beautiful sight, and the balls lasted till four. I have not treated myself to a new evening coat—my old one does fairly well, and I danced away in it. The young girls in England are very beautiful and very pleasant; one hardly sees a single ugly face in a ball-room—which one cannot say in either France or Germany—and so one spends a very pleasant evening. The Bunsens do not give balls, but most agreeable parties with good music. But my chief employment is my work at the East India House, and I hope this year to finish the first volume of about 600 pages.'

In February he found it necessary to visit Paris, to look at some MSS. in the Bibliothèque Royale, and was still there when the Revolution broke out. In the *Autobiography* he has described his difficulty in getting back to England, but says little of what he actually saw in Paris, and the letter he wrote to his mother immediately after his escape, for it was really that, is full of interesting details.

*Translation.* LONDON, *Monday, March* 1, 1848.

'I went for a fortnight to Paris, partly to see Hagedorn, partly to finish some work at the Bibliothèque Royale. You will have seen from the papers what a fearful time I had there, and I thanked God when I stood safe again on English ground. I am still so excited that I can hardly describe all I have seen and done. Since Tuesday last, I have had sleepless nights from fighting, the roar of cannon, burning of houses, fall of buildings, &c., men murdered by hundreds or simply shot down in the streets. No one's life was safe, for there was neither Government, police, nor soldiers. The man in the blouse was lord of all, and blood ran in the streets, which were filled with barricades. Women on horseback, ruffians on the finest officers' chargers paraded the streets, carrying Louis Philippe's throne in triumph. The only brave soldiers were the Municipal Guards, and I saw them cut down and hacked in pieces by the mob. One could see all that went on from Hagedorn's windows; the bullets whistled on every side, and yet ladies went out on foot *pour voir la Révolution*. We did the same, and were more than once pursued by the cavalry. I saw barricades built up of omnibuses, tables, and pianos, attacked and taken, and again built up, till at last the soldiers fraternized with the people, gave up their weapons, and finally withdrew. There was nothing grand in it. The French journals have no authority, for they are written by and for the victors, who proclaimed liberty of the Press, but against whom the Press dare not assert its liberty. It might have been worse, that is the only thing one can say for the mob. The Garde Nationale were cowards, never appeared at all the first day, from fear of the Minister. The second day everything seemed over and quiet, and one rejoiced that without any loss of life a blinded Ministry had fallen, and the people had carried their point in a constitutional way. But those who had made the demonstration the first two days were not yet satisfied; the Republicans and Communists tried to profit by the public excitement to stir the people up again. On the other side the friends of Thiers intrigued, especially Bugeaud, who was Commandant of Paris, and who on the evening of the second day could still have re-established order, had he not connived with his troops to place the Ministry in Thiers' hands by letting the revolution have its own way a little. But when this was effected, it was too late; the people and the troops fraternized and streamed together to the Tuileries: the people armed, but not the military. Louis Philippe, the King of the barricades, fled from the barricades, and from the people who trusted their rights to him, and whose interests he had sacrificed in his selfish plans for his own dynasty. No resistance was then possible; the Republicans had no opposition to fear; the Duchess of Orleans with her sons was insulted, and the Republic proclaimed. The railways were already broken up, only the one to Havre had been forgotten, so over the barricades, and with shots on all sides, I got to the station at ten at night on Thursday. Next morning I reached Havre, and by six on Saturday evening, after a very bad passage, arrived in London. I am glad to have seen what I did, but seeing it was terrible. I was at one time quite close to the mob, and escaped by some side steps from the Boulevard des Capucins, where Guizot's house stands, into the Rue Basse des Remparts. In one instant came a shot, then a fusillade, and from that moment the fighting and flying never ceased, till Louis Philippe was gone and the Republic proclaimed. I could do little work, and am thankful to be back and in safety with my *Veda*. In spite of all this turmoil I am much better, and so my work will get on faster.'

It was Max Müller who brought Lord Palmerston the first certain news of Louis Philippe's flight.

To his friend Dr. Pauli, the Anglo-Saxon scholar, at this time settled in England, and whom he had first met in Paris, he wrote: 'It was terrible, but one learns history by it.'

On March 23 he writes again to his mother:—

*Translation.*

'You must not trouble yourself too much with these bad times, and their reforms and revolutions. They are developments which are unavoidable in history, and such crises are necessary to get rid of all the poison that has long been collecting in society. One must not imagine that a few men who are at the head of affairs *make* these revolutions. Such events are not *made*; they *happen*, through a higher Will, though the tools employed do not always seem the most worthy. When one sees the beginning of a revolution, with all its details and apparent accidents, as I saw it in Paris, one quickly perceives that it is in no one's power to reckon on these movements, where often one look, one resolution, one cry, determines the fate of hundreds and thousands. In such moments a man feels his true weakness, he realizes what he is; during the quiet course of a peaceful life a man becomes so self-confident and so certain of his own wisdom, that such shocks are necessary to bring him again to himself. These lessons are specially good for the wise diplomatists who imagine they can direct mankind according to their own prudent and self-seeking calculations, and for the sovereigns who imagine mankind is only made for them. Now is the time for all to learn that nothing lasts or gives us power but what is right, and the consciousness of having desired the welfare of others and not of our own selves. I hoped this movement would pass over more quietly in Germany than elsewhere. I trusted our kings as having a more upright judgement, and higher desires, more love for their people, and a more self-sacrificing spirit. Instead of this, everywhere, either cowardice or miserable blindness and self-confidence. The punishment for this will not be wanting, and it is sad that bad teeth can only be extracted with loss of blood and much suffering of the whole body. If all those gentlemen could be sent to England to the Universities, they might learn what are the conditions which alone make a king possible in these days. Would to God they might learn the lesson! The longer they hesitate, the greater will be the demands, the more terrible the conflict. The German people are good-tempered, but can be roused by deceit, distrust, and selfishness. Here in England all is quiet, and the means exist here for making revolutions in a peaceful, lawful, and constitutional way. I am only afraid they may summon Bunsen to Berlin. He might do much good there, but it would be a terrible loss to me, and I hardly think I could endure life here without him. He is the sort of diplomatist they all should be, a true man, simple and good, desiring and striving for what is right, and leaving the rest to Providence. For this the wise Metternich pronounces him to be no diplomatist. We shall see who stands firmest. In spite of the great excitement in which one lives, I can collect myself enough to work hard—and that quiets one. I am much better since I was in Paris, and have got rid of my cough. I really feel quite well, so there is no cause for you to be anxious. Your last letter arrived some time after I had sent mine off, for the post everywhere is most irregular now. If the weather is fine, I may spend part of the summer in Oxford to be nearer my printers. The Governors of the East India House wish to see something for their money; but I have only two arms—not a thousand like Vishnu.'

During his whole life in England, Max Müller found the variable climate, and especially the damp winters, a great trial to his strength, and in his two first winters passed in London he was so constantly laid up with severe colds and headaches, and unable to do his work, that his mother was seriously anxious about him. He always maintained that the severe cold of a German winter was less trying to the constitution than the fogs, and damp, and bitter east winds of England. Early in May he went for change to Oxford, intending only to stay through the bright summer months in a place which, from his first visit in June, 1847, cast the glamour of its beauty over him, and which was to be his home for above fifty-two years. He settled himself in two small rooms in Walton Place, as being near the Press, and soon after his arrival he writes to his valued patron and friend the first of many letters:—

*Translation.* 17, WALTON PLACE, OXFORD,
*May* 18, 1848.

'YOUR EXCELLENCY,—Beautiful and pleasant as Oxford is at this season, and happy and contented as I feel in this *sedes Musarum*, it is difficult, at least on a day like this, the opening day of the Reichstag in Frankfort, to subdue the longing for one's German home; and so I hope you will allow me, at all events for a short time, to feel as if I were in my native surroundings, by writing to you. The delightful hours which you allowed me to spend with you in London are indeed the only thing that I miss here in Oxford, and that make me long sometimes to be back in old London. I therefore hope you will allow me from time to time to recall in writing those happy hours, and if my letters arrive like inopportune visitors in the midst of dispatches and diplomatic notes, please lay them aside, just as you so often used to say in your friendly way, "Now, make haste and go." It is delightful that you have chosen Schleswig, and Schleswig has chosen you. It is indeed no usual object of ambition to sit on the same bench with master butchers and cobblers, but it is a sacrifice which in these days the true Aryan is willing to make for the Fatherland, when he has the right and opportunity to do so. In this indistinguishable chaos the necessary thing is to find men who can form a party, and attract a majority to them. In Germans, however, personal opinion and conviction are so supreme and unruly, that we need men who will seize the German John Bull, not, as is usual, by the horns, but in a friendly way, by his soft and weak points. No doubt there will be many good men of the State there, but few good statesmen. Everything in Frankfort will depend on how the first majority is formed, but I don't believe that any party in Germany, be it what it may, would have any prospect of influence, if, when finding itself in a minority, it resorts to violence. Modern history accustoms itself to look on majorities which have arisen naturally in the same way as the old world must have originally looked upon their "Judgement of God," but with this difference, that for the Christian world the Godlike has assumed the form of humanity and freedom, by the side of that of nature and necessity. Life here in Oxford is remarkably pleasant; the place is so beautiful, and everybody so friendly and good, many people very superior and interesting. I have not seen much of Stanley, as he is very much occupied; but I know many of the Fellows, who pursue the same objects, and with even more *understanding* and determination. From many different sides one hears of a wish for reforms in the life of the University, but they are afraid of the Government; and that if they once give it the opportunity it will interfere far more than they desire. They particularly dread the tendencies of the Cheap Government, which might involve them in Cheap Education, and therefore they would rather remain quiet and keep their own. I have given your pamphlet on Schleswig to Stanley, Dr. Jacobson, Dr. Plumptre, and Dr. Acland, and I hear that Dr. Twiss means to write an answer; the same man who wrote on the Oregon question. One hopes it may come *post factum*, like King Oscar's troops, though I must own that it would be wonderful if they could persuade the Holger Danske to listen to reason and act accordingly.'

To his mother he describes his new life thus:—

*Translation.* 17, WALTON PLACE, *May* 21.

'Here I am at last settled in Oxford. I have already told you how beautiful it is, and now in spring it is perfect; the finest gardens I have ever seen, the old trees and the green velvety turf such as one only sees in England. I am enjoying the spring here as I have not enjoyed it for years, and feel better than I ever felt in hot, dirty, noisy London. I like the people here very much, and my work gets on much faster, which will delight you. Forty large sheets already printed, and £160 already spent! But I can live more cheaply here, and save a little, which as yet I have not been able to do. I have not had a piano for a long time; now I have hired one for 30*s*. a month. I find my music very useful in society, for they like to hear it, though few people play. Of course I miss Bunsen very much, but who can say how long he will stay in London? and in these busy times I have seen but little of him. My speech at Oxford is published under the title, "Three Linguistic Dissertations read at the Meeting of the British Association in Oxford, by Chevalier Bunsen, Dr. Meyer, and Dr. Max Müller." I find it a good visiting card here. It is difficult to say when my first volume will be ready, as the printing is sometimes easy and sometimes very difficult; but be sure I work as hard as I can, for it is most important for me to get the first part published.'

To the Same.

*Translation.* Oxford, *June* 28.

'I live here so quietly that I often wish I had you all here, safe out of the trouble and turmoil in Germany. It is the greatest delight to walk in these gardens, where the old gables and towers peep through the green trees on all sides. I am asked to dinner nearly every day—this is at five o'clock in one of the old Colleges. After dinner we have coffee and tea in the gardens on the grass, and smoke our cigars. We have a great deal of music, and I get on very well with all these reverend sirs.'

Peaceful as his life in Oxford was, Max Müller was too patriotic not to be deeply occupied with the events in his native country, and he writes to Dr. Pauli :—

*Translation.* *June* 27, 1848.

'One needs earnest and difficult work to keep one quiet. I suppose in time one will get accustomed to this new world, but up to now I have not had courage or power even to talk about it : in time the sea-sickness will leave one, and then one can watch the storm carefully and wonder at it. You ought to come to Oxford ; it is the most beautiful city I have ever seen, and one must have seen it to know England. Living is tolerably cheap, and the libraries rich in manuscript treasures. I shall stay here till October, then publish a volume and go to Germany.'

Max Müller became almost immediately on intimate terms with a number of undergraduates, as well as many younger dons, whilst several of the heads of houses and Professors showed great kindness to the man whom they remembered as reading a paper but the year before at the British Association, on a subject quite unknown to most of them, but which had provoked interesting and important discussions. Dr. Gaisford was particularly condescending to the young scholar, who often mentioned with pleasure the real courtesy of the Dean, as being the only head of a house who thought it necessary to call before sending him an invitation to dinner.

He has given an amusing account of that visit, and the attack made on the Dean by his Scotch terrier, Belle. To the few who still remember those days the name of Belle will recall many a happy hour. She was a small terrier, by no means a great beauty, and had belonged to Robert Morier, who willingly passed her on to his friend, to avoid the trouble of looking after her. She lived to a great age, and gave her new master a good deal of occupation in taking care of her and her innumerable puppies. Her devotion made her very jealous, and when some years after a beautiful Skye puppy was given him by a much-loved friend, Belle ill-treated it so, that he had to part with it to save its life! Max Müller was always devoted to dogs, and his friends will recollect his great deerhound Oscar, Musk, a Skye terrier, and in later years his well-known dachshunds, Waldmann and Männerl, and at the very last, Longbow and Big Ben.

Among Max's intimate friends at this time were Morier, afterwards Sir Robert Morier, who died Ambassador at St. Petersburg; William Sellar, later on Professor of Latin at Edinburgh; Palgrave, to whose advice he owed a great deal when he first began to write English books; William Spottiswoode; Alexander Grant, who, after many years in India, became Principal of the University of Edinburgh; Theodore Walrond, afterwards his brother-in-law, and whom for many years he used to call his English conscience; Earle, later Professor of Anglo-Saxon; Church, afterwards Dean of St. Paul's; George Butler; ffolliott, who in the last letter he wrote to Max Müller says, 'Your friendship has been one of the happiest elements of my life'; Thomson, of Queen's, who became Archbishop of York; Story-Maskelyne, later Professor of Mineralogy; Clough, the poet; Dr. Stanley, then Tutor of University; Dr. Acland; Manuel Johnson, the Radcliffe Observer; Professor Donkin, drawn to him by their common love of music; 'Bodley' Coxe; Jowett, then the popular young Tutor of Balliol; and J. A. Froude, of Exeter. To the two last Max Müller was a staunch friend, standing by them when their opinions exposed them to a good deal of obloquy and closed many doors against them. Most of these men remained Max Müller's devoted and intimate friends through life; from others, from circumstances of residence and occupation, he was more or less separated, though when they met there was always a hearty recollection of the 'merry days when they were young,' and enjoyed many a joke and many a discussion in their various rooms, whether in College or in lodgings. The very few left who remember quite the early years when Max Müller first settled in Oxford, recall his great powers of attraction, his lively conversation, even though in still rather quaint English, his fun, his power of repartee, above all his kindly lovable nature, to which a singularly beautiful countenance bore witness, his brilliant pianoforte-playing, and behind all this a seriousness of purpose, a loftiness of aim, with an amount of general culture seldom met with in a man of little more than twenty-four; whilst the almost entire ignorance of the great subject to which he was devoting his life only added to their wonder and interest.

Mr. Tuckwell in his delightful Reminiscences says: 'I recall the black-haired, slight young foreigner in 1846[1] or thereabouts, known first as a pianist in Oxford drawing-rooms, whose inmates ceased their chatter at his brilliant touch.'

To Chevalier Bunsen.

*Translation.* 17, Walton Place, *June* 13, 1848.

''Tis hard to carry a full cup even. Oxford is most beautiful, but one longs for German Professors, for Greek societies and seminars! My *Veda* gets on; forty-five sheets are printed. I have good news from India. The Pundits, to whom I sent proof-sheets, are delighted with the plan and the way it is being carried out. As it does not seem likely that the Prussian Government will at this moment grant any money for MSS. from India, I shall apply to the East India Company. The expense is very small, 1,000 lines of thirty-two syllables for eight shillings. I think of staying here till my first volume is ready, which it cannot be before the end of the year, and then I shall go to Germany. But I must find some further occupation here, for Sanskrit alone does not yield enough to live on. It is delightful to reconstruct a chapter in the historical consciousness of mankind, especially one that is so ancient and so important for the intellectual migrations of the Aryans as is the Vedic epoch. But when mankind is at work it requires people who can wield the hammer in order to forge a new link in the chain of humanity. Only I don't know with what hammer I should try to work, but it seems to me pretty certain that for the next thirty years the *Veda* and such literary ruins will find few friends and explorers. For what we now see is but the prelude to wake and shake the mind, to bring it into the necessary condition, "corruptos hominum mores bellis emendare atque conterere."'

[1] 1848 it should be.

In the following letter to his mother he describes his first Commemoration, little imagining how many more he was to see, till his own children were enjoying them from thirty to forty years later:—

*Translation.* *July* 11.

'There were great festivities for the end of term. Guizot was here, two sons of Metternich, Baron von Hügel, and many of the best English families, and a crowd of such beautiful women as I have never before seen. The festivities lasted from early dawn till night; the gardens lighted up, with music and singing, were enchanting. There were good concerts, the *Messiah*, the *Creation*, in which Birch, Tadolinée, and Lablache sang; in fact it was magnificent, and champagne and hock flowed in streams. Now every place is empty. I have the beautiful gardens to myself, and that is delightful, where I take a walk of an evening and smoke my cigar; but it would be yet better on the Terrace at Dresden! "However——" as the English say, and I do my best to acquire an Englishman's patience and indifference.'

The summer was spent quietly in Oxford, working at the *Veda* and the long Introduction, or Prolegomena, of which we hear more in the following year.

To his Mother.

*Translation.* Oxford, *August* 8.

'The times are not suited for *quiet* enjoyment, and who knows when this struggle of the discontented masses will cease? But when one remembers all the suffering and sorrow, the thousands who are perishing from war, disease, and famine, one ought to be contented oneself, and thank God if we escape with a few inconveniences. It sometimes seems to me wrong to be sitting and working here so peacefully in Oxford, whilst so many in Germany are torn away from their scientific employments and must share all the dangers of war. One is not better than all those who die by thousands in battle or of cholera, or who see all their prospects for life ruined in a moment. And yet, surely, all this want and calamity must do some good, by teaching men that they are placed on the earth not for enjoyment but for a struggle and trial: in quieter times one forgets too easily the real earnest task of life, and the true man in us perishes. Now every one must stand fast and be ready for anything. If we do our duty and have a good conscience and trust in God, this little world cannot do us much harm. I lead a most pleasant life here in Oxford. Many of my friends come to see me, and live in the same house—Dr. Köllgren from Helsingfors, Dr. Pauli from Berlin. Then of course I do not get through so much work—we take long walks, bathe, &c.; but when they are gone I shall be able to work hard again till the first volume is ready. That will not be till Easter, as the first volume will have 1,000 pages, and only 500 are now printed. Everything seems to have quieted down in Dessau: they had not a large aristocracy to put down! I should like to see for myself how things are, for here one can form but little idea about it.'

The next letter tells of the spread of the revolutionary spirit to Chemnitz, where his mother still lived, though no longer in her daughter's house.

To his Mother.

*Translation.* Oxford, *October* 3.

'You can imagine my anxiety about you when I read in the papers of the insurrection of the workpeople in Chemnitz, of barricades and fighting in the streets, and remembered how far from strong Auguste is. From day to day I looked for a letter, and at last heard from you that you had escaped all danger. We must not complain of small deprivations, but thank God, who has watched over us hitherto with fatherly care. If I know that you are well in Chemnitz, and have always a sure refuge with Krug, and if you know that I am happy and well in Oxford, even if we do not see each other often, we can think of each other with perfect satisfaction; and how few can say that in these times. One cannot expect things to settle down in Germany for many years. I cannot wish to be back in Germany, however much I long for German life, for one would only be drawn into all these party conflicts, without power to effect any good. I often think it might be well to settle down entirely in England. I think one might be quite at home and happy here. If I go to Germany next year, I must look about and see what can be done there, and if any prospects open for me; if not, I must look out for some career that later on would settle me here. I like Oxford so much better than London, that I shall remain here. Life is cheaper here, and I had already saved £20, but have spent it on MSS. from India, which I need for my work. Dr. Pauli is still living here, which is very pleasant, and gives me some one to talk to. Dessau seems to set an example to the world with its liberal institutions. What does Stockmarr[1] say to it all? Uncle Fritz, doubtless, is much amused. I should like to see it with my own eyes; it sounds a little fabulous!'

Max Müller seems to have been so much absorbed in the

[1] An old and very conservative General, married to the sister of Max Müller's aunt, Frau Präsident von Basedow. The old man lived to keep his Iron Wedding (sixty-five years), and died a few days after, as did his wife, and they were buried the same day.

*Veda* as to let a long time pass without any communication with his revered master, Burnouf, who sent him the following gentle reminder, which shows how even the life of a quiet student was upset by the political disorders of the times:—

*Translation.* PARIS, *October* 7, 1848.

'MY DEAR FRIEND,—It is a long time since I heard anything of you, and enough has happened here to make me forget any one to whom I was less attached than I am to you. But I have heard of you indirectly. I received a few days ago a sign of your remembrance of me, which touched me much; and I have read your *mémoire* with delight, and have learnt from it many curious facts of the way in which Bengali has used for its own analytic purposes concrete words borrowed from Sanskrit. The work is well done, and I have observed with great satisfaction, among other things, a virtuous attack on the modernizers of Brâhmanism in the interests of Buddhism, which has nothing to gain by outraging history and good sense. I venture to assert that, notwithstanding their pretensions, the dilettante authors of these heteroclite hypotheses understand neither Brâhmanism nor Buddhism. I am now working at the second volume of my Introduction to Buddhism, having been obliged to set aside the work I had begun on the Nineveh inscriptions. These researches cannot be carried on usefully in a time of political disturbance, such as the present; the tempest in the streets distracts the mind. . . . Under these circumstances, I am devoting myself to Buddhism, to occupy my mind; it is the only one of my labours for which I do not need State aid. Yours heartily, 'E. BURNOUF.'

To this Max Müller replied:—

9, PARK PLACE, *November* 1, 1848.

'MY HONOURED MASTER AND FRIEND,—. . . I was very sorry to learn that the political agitation in France has disturbed your literary work. Every one felt that the only hope of a successful and scientific deciphering of the Nineveh inscriptions lay with you, for you stand alone in such work. Yet the second volume of Buddhism will be a welcome gift to many, to some perhaps not welcome, as it will destroy their last heteroclite hypotheses. Unfortunately things look very black for literature in Germany too, and I am glad that I can give my time here in England quietly to the *Veda*. The first Ashtaka, with a long introduction, will appear at Easter. I am now writing the latter, and I often wish I could go to you for advice, for here in England there is really no one who takes much interest in real Indian antiquity. Wilson has finished his *History of British India*, which is very much liked, and is at work now on a lexicon of modern Indian names for measures, weights, and other words in daily use between Indians and Englishmen. Besides that he is preparing a catalogue of the MSS. of the East India House, as well as a translation of the *Rig-veda*. It is wonderful how busy he is, though one often wishes he would devote his valuable time and powers more exclusively to Indian antiquity. . . . I have heard nothing of Baron d'Eckstein since the Revolution, and would gladly hear how he is. . . . My time is so taken up with printing the *Rig-veda*, which has reached page 608, that I have no time for any other work; for this I am very sorry, for the Commentary is terribly wearisome, and yet full of small difficulties, for which I often miss the help of MSS. from other parts of India. I have therefore ordered for myself a copy from Poonah, where your own valuable MS. was copied, and must await its arrival before I begin the second Ashtaka, as I have no collation of your MS. for that, and the MSS. here of the second Ashtaka are very imperfect. The East India Company has declared itself ready to buy Vedic MSS. if they can get them, so I hope for much new help from India.'

The following letter to Bunsen is the only allusion to a scheme which Max Müller can hardly have contemplated seriously, though a Pass Degree would have been child's play to him, and no doubt a life in College such as that led by many of his friends must have appeared more attractive than his solitary lodgings:—

*Translation.* 17, WALTON PLACE, *October* 8, 1848.

'I think of going to London for a few days early next week to do some work at the East India House. It would be a great delight to me if I could see you for a few minutes, to ask your advice in a matter which occupies me a good deal. The revolutions in Germany have laid such hold on all the circumstances of life, and have so undermined the foundations of society, that one loses all courage to build one's future on such a soil. Unless one feels the strength and power to take an active part in initiating and settling matters, but wishes to find one's ideal of life in the narrow quiet circle of science, one has the right, I think, to seek shelter there, where science, if not patronized and aided, is at least tolerated and let alone. With all my love of the past, and with a full belief in the future of Germany, I feel more drawn at present to English than to German soil. My work will keep me in England for the next few years; and as Oxford is a very pleasant place of residence, I have an idea of entering one of the

Colleges as an undergraduate, keeping my twelve terms, and then taking my degree. I should hope to defray the expense by my own work, and the competition in the Oriental market is so small, that my prospects later on would probably not be bad. It is, of course, difficult to resolve to take such a backward step, and begin again from the beginning, when my friends and contemporaries have already found their spheres of activity as teachers and Professors. My own studies would meet with many interruptions, but when one sees that the path one has hewn for oneself does not lead to the goal, it is better to turn round than to pursue the wrong road till no return is possible. My work goes on merrily; seventy-two sheets are printed, and I am writing the preface, which often overwhelms me; but I have time till Easter, when the first two volumes and the preface will appear. Dr. Pauli is still living with me, but he has a good chance of being appointed to the Advocates' Library in Edinburgh. In the hope of soon having the happiness of seeing you, I am, with my whole heart, yours obediently.'

We hear no more of the undergraduate scheme, and on his return from London he moved to pleasanter lodgings, No. 9, Park Place, now 18, Banbury Road, where he remained till January, 1856. Here he occupied the front floor, and some other German generally lodged in the same house.

To his Mother.

*Translation.* 9, Park Place, *November* 5.

'I have been staying with Bunsen in London and the country for a week. I was in his house, and we had long talks together, and I came back to my work with fresh courage. He is a delightful, excellent man, so that it is a real refreshment to see him. He is so quiet, so contented, and so confident, although living in the very midst of all the troubles; he trusts mainly to Frankfort, and his whole soul is with Germany. When I returned to Oxford I changed my lodgings. If I could afford it I should take riding lessons. Every morning crowds of students pass by in their red coats and jockey caps going out hunting; but that is very dear, so I never think of it, but work on quietly at the *Veda*, and when Volume I is finished, I shall pack up and be off; 620 pages are finished. It has been a hard piece of work. I have no desire to join the Dessau militia. I would rather become a naturalized Englishman. The news from Vienna is terrible, one can hardly believe it, and in Berlin it is fermenting and seething as if for something of the same sort.'

On his birthday he writes to her again:—

*Translation.* OXFORD, *December* 6, 1848.

'Twenty-five years, an age that might make one sad, but we are all well and happy; though my life in a foreign country often seems too long, and I should like to get away; but it can't be helped, one must work to live, and work where one finds work. I am quite content with mine. Of course, if one could find work in Germany instead of here, and live at one of the Universities on the Rhine, at Bonn or Heidelberg, one might enjoy life more. That will come some day, and then we can live happily together and drink a good glass of Rhine wine. Hurrah! If only the *Veda* were not so long! The old Indians 3,000 years ago might have written less; 1,000 quarto pages. But work agrees with me, and I take long walks, and the life is, on the whole, very pleasant, and yet one feels as if one hardly belonged to it; people are too polite for one to feel quite at one's ease. Do you know I would willingly take the post of Librarian at Dessau if it were free? I could carry on my work there, and in these troublous times, the more retired one's life, the safer and happier for one. But those are only plans, and one must be satisfied to be independent and able to earn one's daily bread; and it is better in these days to be a bachelor, in spite of all the good advice you give me from time to time—rich heiresses are not so plentiful, even in England. Last week Jenny Lind sang here in a concert. I had never heard her, and paid my ten shillings, which I do not regret. She sings wonderfully, has a full, strong, rich voice, but there was a want of softness. She sang Italian songs, and Weber's *Und ob die Wolke*, which she sang most beautifully, and showed a real love of her art. Her Swedish songs are lovely, so original. I longed to hear her sing some of Mendelssohn's songs; but she had to think of her public, and the John Bulls have little knowledge of music. She said afterwards to a friend of mine, that she considered Mendelssohn's *Suleika* the most beautiful song she knew, and she loved to sing it. The people here were wild about her, perfectly enchanted; but when Beethoven's *Septette* was played as a finale, they mostly went away; perfect barbarians! And yet they are good honest people, with whom it is easy to live when one understands them. I get on very well with John Bull, and he does not mind when I sometimes take him by the horns and shake him.'

To Bunsen he writes the same day:—

*Translation.* *December* 6, 1848.

'You will have perhaps already seen in the paper the delightful news of Trithen's appointment as Professor here. I am as pleased as if I had got it myself, for it was perhaps the only way of making a good useful man of him, after all the disappointments which of late weighed more and more on him. Though I had myself thought of this place, and had perhaps better chances than Trithen, I feel I have acted rightly, perhaps calculated rightly; for had Trithen divided votes with me, most probably a third candidate would have appeared, whereas now Trithen was almost unanimously elected. I hope something of the same sort may be found for Pauli, for I have begged Trithen to do all he can to get the Secretaryship of the Geographical Society for him, which Trithen must give up. So one helps another, and if one only desires what is right, one feels happy and at home in that united and ever-mysterious concatenation of results and circumstances which constitute human life. Twenty-five years of this life lie behind me to-day, and one feels involuntarily in a more earnest and solemn frame of mind at such a moment. I look back with gratitude on the first half of my life, which, notwithstanding many sad moments, leaves me with the memory of a happy youth, and which at the same time, after many struggles, has given me a firm faith in a Divine Providence, trust in mankind and peace in myself, and cheerful courage to begin the second half of my life. If it is hard to give up all the plans and hopes which might have been realized in better times, still life is worth living, be it but a life of duty. God will help me further. Only continue your sympathy and kindness to me. It will be my endeavour to show myself worthy of them.'

To this Bunsen sent the following beautiful answer, which is the first of the letters printed by permission of Baroness Bunsen in *Chips*, Vol. III, first edition. Being out of print it is given here:—

*Translation.* LONDON, *December* 7, 1848.

'MY DEAR M.,—I have this moment received your affectionate note of yesterday, and feel as if I must respond to it directly, as one would respond to a friend's shake of the hand. . . . And now, my very dear M., I congratulate you on the courageous frame of mind which this event causes you to evince[1]. It is exactly that which, as a friend, I wish for you for the whole of life, and which I perceived and loved in you from the very first moment. It delights me especially at this time, when *your* contemporaries are even more dark and confused than *mine* are sluggish and old-fashioned. The reality of life, as we enter the period of full manhood, destroys the first dream of youth; but with moral earnestness, and genuine faith in eternal Providence, and in

[1] Trithen's election to Taylorian Professorship.

the sacredness of human destiny in that government of the world which exists for all human souls that honestly seek after good—with these feelings the dream of youth is more than realized. You have undertaken a great work, and have been rescued from the whirlpool and landed on this peaceful island that you might carry it on undisturbed, which you could not have done in the Fatherland. This is the first consideration, but not less highly do I rate the circumstances which have kept you here, and have given you an opportunity of seeing English life in its real strength, with the consistency and stability, and with all the energy and simplicity that are its distinguishing features. I have known what it is to receive this complement of German life in the years of my training and apprenticeship. When rightly estimated this knowledge and love of the English element only strengthens the love of the German Fatherland, the home of genius and poetry. I will only add that I am longing to see you amongst us; you must come to us before long. Meanwhile think of me with as much affection as I shall always think of you.'

Max Müller spent Christmas with his kind friends at Totteridge, but the large and merry family party did not quite make up for the distance from his own relations, and when sending his mother a little money, which he exhorts her to spend and not hoard up, he adds, 'The day will come that we shall again be all together—only patience—in time all will come right.'

# CHAPTER VI

## 1849

Death of sister's children. Froude. Visit to Lakes. Prix Volney. Publication of first volume of *Rig-veda*. Carus. Visit to Germany.

MAX MÜLLER returned from his Christmas at Totteridge and three days alone in London with Bunsen with renewed health and courage for his work, resolved that, whatever effort it cost him, this year should see the publication of the first volume of the *Rig-veda*. Not only the East India Company, but Sanskrit scholars abroad were getting impatient for a first instalment of his great work; all but Burnouf forgetting the labour and time involved in contending single-handed with such a task. His old master, Brockhaus, wrote to him from Leipzig, urging him to publish some part at once: 'You must have printed a good deal; why leave us so long in suspense? Pending your edition, all Vedic studies remain vague and unsettled.' But unmoved by such complaints Max Müller pursued his own course, determined that his work should not be injured by hurry or carelessness. He tells his mother that he hardly gives himself the time to write her his usual monthly letter, 'I do nothing but work at the *Veda*.'

On his return Max found his old Paris friend, Dr. Pauli, who later on became Bunsen's private secretary, settled in Oxford, in the same house in which he himself lodged; so that although it was vacation, and Oxford was nearly empty, he had pleasant companionship. A very intimate friendship sprung up between the two, and their letters show on what easy terms they were with each other; and though their different lines of study drew them apart, they had the deepest affection for each other to the last. Dr. Pauli died in 1882.

At this time, Max Müller made an attempt to take up his Diary again, in which he had written nothing for four years. This attempt lasted about a week, and the habit was never resumed, except for a short time in 1857.

DIARY, 1849.

*Translation.* *January* 6.

'What a pause! By mere chance I found this book to-day, and as I read it can hardly believe I wrote it! Four years are gone, perhaps the most important of my life; well I remember them, though I have not written them down. But such short notices are interesting in later years, and so I will begin again. I conquered Hagedorn, have learnt of Goldstücker and Trithen, and stand well with Bunsen; 688 pages of the *Veda* are printed, and my way tolerably clear. To-day I received the news of G. Hermann's death; Letronne, too, died lately; where are their successors? I would gladly have seen old Hermann again; he was so brave, and noble, and free—a real Greek, and yet a German, with his small bright eyes. He has not lived in vain! Now for politics, but where to begin? In Germany all is tottering, and only kept up by bayonets. The King is frightened at the Imperial Crown. If Bunsen only stays quietly in England! He is to-day with the Queen; one hopes it is not to take leave. Stockmar, too, is there; I have seen his picture, quiet and clever; he influences Bunsen, who, however, makes use of him. Now vacation in Oxford. I worked bravely since I spent Christmas with Bunsen. This evening at a horrible party with —— in —— College. Ugly men and women, bad music; escaped with Pauli and Sellar, and smoked cigars in Balliol with Weatherly.'

*January* 7.

'A real English Sunday, which produces a certain dullness even in one's work. Read proof-sheets, and studied Lepsius's (Egyptian) *Chronology* without much effect. There are no clear results there as yet, though many clever hypotheses and difficulties. There is so little in Egypt to warm one! Walked with Sellar, dined with Weatherly, who had an evening party; on the whole pleasant, but not remarkable, so that men took to horse-play; that seldom happens in Germany. Bunsen has gone to Berlin, ostensibly to be instructed on the German question, but one hopes that his letters, which he let me read in Totteridge, have had an effect, and his presence may do more—unfortunately only for the moment—in the highest circles: may he come back safely! Pity that he is a diplomatist, or that the world wants such clever men.'

To Bunsen he writes on January 24:—

*Translation.*

'If you are really going to exchange beautiful Totteridge for the dusty Wilhelmstrasse, I am sure England will soon become strange to me. You may laugh, but pray believe that the thought of you is so closely united with my whole thoughts and wishes, however seldom I venture to intrude upon you, that I cannot accustom myself to the idea of living so entirely separated from you.'

On January 29 we find Max Müller writing to Burnouf to inquire about the Prix Volney, a prize founded by Volney for the best work on language, written in any language during the year, and sent in for competition. He asks if his paper on the relation of Bengali to the other Indian languages, read before the British Association, was of sufficient importance to have any chance of winning the prize. Burnouf had noticed the little article very favourably in the *Journal Asiatique*. Max Müller ends his letter thus:—

'The printing of the *Rig-veda* goes on very slowly, and yet I give up nearly all the day to it, and often the night also. Ninety sheets are printed, up to half of the sixth Adhyâya, but I have undertaken a little too much, and I find I have not much time to study for myself, and arrange in some sort the results of my researches. I shall have to be content with presenting only the materials to the learned world, and all I wish is that they may find the text of my edition correct according to the MSS., and that others who are more worthy, and more skilful than I am for discoveries in the highest philology, may draw the inferences. In any case the mines of the *Rig-veda* are not the mines of California; the grains of gold are not to be found so near the surface that the pipîlakâs[1] can find them without any effort. It is for me to act as miner and for others to sift the ore; for it is given to few persons to do both, as you have done for the Zend-Avesta.'

But occupied as he was with his work, his longing for home and German life is constantly shown in his letters to his mother; and in one of them, in utter weariness of spirit, he writes of Oxford as 'the most tedious place in the whole of tedious England.' One pleasant prospect he had this summer; he had found occupation for his old friend Victor Carus as

[1] Gold-finding ants in the *Mahâbhârata*.

assistant to Dr. Acland, and the letters to his mother are full of happy anticipations of his arrival.

On February 9 Burnouf answered Max Müller's inquiries about the Volney Prize. On consideration his honoured master evidently thought the treatise too short for the Volney competition, and that being printed with Bunsen's and Meyer's much longer papers might also be a disadvantage. 'Men are so made,' says Burnouf, 'that size and bulk impose even on the most enlightened people. You have plenty of time to decide, and I hope you are convinced that if you compete your work will find a zealous advocate in me. I am so occupied with all the troubles in which we live, that I have become sadly and uselessly idle, and my health suffers. I owe the Revolution a disease of the heart. Receive the assurance of my lasting friendship.'

This year began Max Müller's great intimacy with J. A. Froude, which continued till the death of the latter in the autumn of 1894. On the publication of the *Nemesis of Faith* early in this year, and the consequent loss of his Fellowship, Max Müller was one of the few people in Oxford who stood by Mr. Froude and took a deep and active interest in his future plans of life. A remarkable letter from Bunsen on the subject will be found in the third volume of *Chips* (first edition). The following letter is in response to this:—

*Translation.* 9, PARK PLACE, *May* 9, 1849.

'Froude has asked me to tell you that he will be in London in the course of a few days, and that his great wish is to see and talk with you. It would be very sad if talents such as Froude's fell into the hands of English Radicals, Chartists, and Unitarians, who are already opening their arms for him. You will see that Froude, on the contrary, has all the best elements of the High Church party in him, that the unity of the Christian Church is his ideal, for which he would sacrifice as much as a German for the unity of Germany. I am quite convinced that the regeneration of the English Church can only come from the High Church party. It alone has influence, and the respect of the English people, and possesses the best intellectual power. Newmanism is now taking a direction of which formerly one had no idea, and which with all its bad motives must produce, *nolens volens*, the finest effect. In order to prove the necessity of belief in authority, men forget, to a certain degree, the danger of the use of the sacred writings, their contradictions and difficulties with regard to chronology, astronomy, and geology. "Give me the Bible," said Socinius, "and I will prove all my heresies." Ewald's name is constantly mentioned here; he has proved as a grammarian that the five books of Moses were not written by Moses, thus destroying the theory of inspiration, and faith demands new guarantees. This the old Fathers foresaw, and therefore kept the Bible from the people. . . . Whence then come all the difficult passages in the Bible? Because with your idiotic theological grammarians, you cannot enter into the language of the Bible. Where is there anything in the Bible of your inspiration *à la Houdin*[1]? It is not the language, but the spirit of the Bible which has become strange to us. . . . Newmanism was originally natural and honest in the English Church. The soil and air spoils it and inclines it to Romanism, but even this spoiling must work for good, and bring the English Church into a state of fermentation out of which she will come purified and reformed. Mere transference and translating of German works would never have any influence in England, but if men like Froude, who know the English nation, could show the practical results of German investigations and give them to the people not as a foreign, but as a native product, it might be possible for England to complete its reformation. There are people who believe as little in English mental power as in German marine power, but I have seen so many excellent gunboats launched here, and think that one might risk an Eckenförde[2]. Froude is already more of a little steamship, that need not fear the salt water, but he wants more ballast, and that he must fetch from Germany, or he will suffer shipwreck. *Visé* his passport for a German port, where, spite of all storms, there is less danger than on the Dead Sea.'

Whilst working hard and almost entirely absorbed in the *Veda*, his thoughts were unexpectedly turned into another channel by the almost sudden death of two of his sister's children within three weeks of each other. The devoted young mother never really recovered from this sorrow.

TO HIS MOTHER.

*Translation.* OXFORD, *April* 4, 1849.

'The news of the death of my little godson was wholly unexpected, and filled me with sorrow, especially for poor Auguste, who, doubtless, feels this first loss deeply; but if the poor little fellow was so weakly, it is a blessing that God called him back so quickly to Himself.

[1] A great conjurer.
[2] An engagement in the Danish-Prussian War, 1849.

I know that it is useless to look for comfort in such thoughts, or that they lessen the grief and pain. Nor should they, for sorrow is necessary and good for men; one learns to understand that each joy must be indemnified by suffering, that each new tie which knits our hearts to this life must be loosed again, and the tighter and the closer it was knit, the keener the pain of loosening it. Should we then attach our hearts to nothing, and pass quietly and unsympathetically through this world, as if we had nothing to do with it? We neither could nor ought to act so. Nature itself knits the first tie between parents and children, and new ties through our whole life. We are not here for reward, for the enjoyment of undisturbed peace, or from mere accident, but for trial, for improvement, perhaps for punishment; for the only union which can ensure the happiness of men, the union between our self and God's self, is broken, or at least obscured, by our birth, and the highest object of our life is to find this bond again, to remain ever conscious of it, and hold fast to it in life and in death. This rediscovery of the eternal union between God and man constitutes true religion among all people: religion means binding together again. The impression made on me by the look of a child who is not yet conscious of himself and of the world round him, is that of still undisturbed godliness. Only when self-consciousness wakes little by little, through pleasure or pain, when the spirit accustoms itself to its bodily covering, when man begins to say *I*, and the world to call things *his*, then the full separation of the human self from the Divine begins, and it is only after long struggles that the light of *true* self-consciousness sooner or later breaks through the clouds of earthly semblances, and makes us again like the little children "of whom is the kingdom of heaven." In God we live and move and have our being—that is the sum of all human wisdom, and he who does not find it here will find it in another life. All else that we learn on earth, be it the history of nature or of mankind, is for this end alone, to show us everywhere the presence of a Divine Providence and to lead us through the knowledge of the history of the human spirit to the knowledge of ourselves, and through the knowledge of the laws of nature to the understanding of that human nature to which we are subjected in life. The death of a child is as if the flash of the Divine eye had turned quickly away from the mirror of this world, before the human consciousness woke up and thought it recognized itself in the mirror, often only to perceive for a moment, just as it closes its eyes for the last time, that that which it took for itself was the shadow or reflection of its eternal self. All this is not written in the Bible, but enough to guide the thoughtful Christian. It cannot be given to men, but each must find it for himself, and many paths lead to the same goal. If you think differently, there is no harm, for the difference lies only in the form, in names and words; on the whole we agree, and if a difference of life and occupation, if especially the powerful impressions of the moment bring greater joy or greater sorrow, and often lead to excitement, to doubts, one recovers oneself and finds that the doubts and difficulties lie where we ourselves have made and seek them! Each one must help himself, for it is difficult to discuss such things! A good conscience is better than all knowledge; that alone gives the peace we so sorely need. It is not enough to believe and pray, we must work and try to make ourselves useful. With a firm, upright will one can conquer everything. A good sailor is as self-possessed in a storm as in fine weather, for he knows no wave can rise higher than God wills. Those are the best statesmen in the present crisis who do their duty according to their conscience, unheeding party strife and noise. There is no rule of statesman's craft like "Do right and fear no one." Instead of this the wise diplomatists believe that they can do better with their tricks and stratagems, on which they place more reliance than on the eternal law of universal history, that what is good bears good, what is evil, evil fruit. And what applies to statesmen applies to every individual, and this everlasting vacillation and hesitation in Germany and elsewhere are more the result of infidelity, selfishness, and vanity than of anything else, and must naturally meet with their reward. I consider myself most fortunate in not being drawn into this whirlpool, and as little as I should hide my convictions, if so circumstanced that they might produce some good, so little would I exchange my study for a club (political) and my *Veda* for newspaper-writing, from ambition, passion, or sloth. These are the three powerful levers of our modern statecraft. Buy something for me for Auguste's birthday and give me credit till I come, which will be some time yet. But I won't grumble; I know this first volume of the *Veda* is of the greatest importance for me, and that I must do everything in my power to make it as good and perfect as possible. I will not tell you how much I long for home, but I should not enjoy it, if I had neglected anything in my work, for when I come I mean to enjoy myself; but spring, summer, and autumn may pass first, though I work as hard as I can without hurting my health. Bunsen has invited me several times to stay with them, but gladly as I would do so, I have always refused, so as not to waste time. I expect Victor Carus in August, so that I can myself introduce and settle him here. I shall be glad to have him, and he seems very much pleased with the post, though he only gets £100 a year.'

The following letter is interesting, as containing a mention of Tennyson, whose poems Max had learnt to admire from Palgrave, who gave him the earlier volumes:—

9, Park Place, *April* 27.

'My dear Palgrave,—When I went to London a fortnight ago, I hoped to see you there, but all my plans were upset, and instead of staying in town three days (this was all the furlough I could get from myself), I was there only for about six hours, and spent the rest of my time near London. London is certainly not the place to see one's friends, but Oxford is, and I hope you will keep your promise as soon as your duties as Ministre de l'Instruction Publique will allow you. Although I can offer you no lotus, you will find a good weed, which, you may tell Tennyson, does just as well. I can quite imagine how you must rejoice in his acquaintance, and I am afraid you will soon look down from the poetical height of the Tennysonian Olympus pitying that unhappy set of mortals who through their philosophical spectacles see only forms and shadows, while you, a poet amongst poets, enjoy life and light. However, you read old Goethe—he is more than a poet, and more than a philosopher, he is a full man, a whole humanity in himself. I wish I could read him with you for my own sake, not for yours, for you are not the man to misunderstand him. Did it not strike you in Froude's *Nemesis* how the death of the child is a beautiful echo from the *Wahlverwandtschaften?* Oxford is flourishing again. Stanley, Jowett, &c., are up. Old Froude, however, has left a blank, and if you saw how they have pulled down your house, and how the fireplace where we smoked so many a jolly cigar is exposed to the eyes of the *vulgus profanum*, you would find it a subject not unworthy an elegy. Plans for the summer I have made none, but think that my work will keep me till September. Then I shall go to pay homage to the German Emperor, or to the President of the German Republic, an alternative which will be decided in a very few days. Bye, bye, old fellow. Don't forget Oxford and the old set, who send you their love.'

To Dr. Pauli, who had settled in London, he writes:—

*Translation.* Oxford, *May* 14.

'My printer rides me nearly to death. I must soon unseat the fellow and go to grass. You would do better if, instead of working till you are weary and worn, you were to come here to us, where you would amuse yourself thoroughly.'

After all the sorrow that his sister had passed through, her mother had taken her for a few days' change to Dresden.

They had hardly arrived before the Revolution of 1849 broke out. Max Müller saw in the papers the serious aspect of affairs, and for days had no letter from his mother. He writes to her:—

*Translation.* 9, PARK PLACE, *May* 22.

'I can hardly tell you the anxiety with which I awaited your last letter. I never had a line for more than a month, and was afraid that you were ill from all the sorrow; and then came the terrible days in Dresden, and I read each day in the papers of the fighting and destruction spreading more and more towards the part of the town where I knew you were. Thank God that you escaped! but when you write that cannon-balls flew right over you, you cannot wonder that I am terrified. If this goes on in Germany I cannot leave you there without protection, and I am really thinking of giving up my work here, and going to you. In times like this all other considerations must give way, and many plans be given up. Why should one live on here in peace and quiet whilst others have to make such sacrifices? If I could only have you here with me! I have been thinking it over day and night, not the cost only, but if you could bear it here, so entirely alone, I all day at the Library or busy at home, and you with no one you could understand. I do not urge you to come, I only suggest it, and if you come I will gladly give up my plans for travelling when Vol. I is out. Your account of little Agnes' death[1] was heartrending. I cannot tell you how hard it is to hear all this from far away, and then not to have a moment's rest from the incessant pressure of work and care and sorrow. Wherever one looks all is black and hopeless: I am so out of spirits that for weeks I have been nowhere, and find no peace unless I forget myself in work. If I could do anything to give you a pleasure, that is the only happiness I wish for.'

Some time before this he had written to Dr. Pauli:—

*Translation.* PARK PLACE, 1849.

'MY DEAR PAULI,—I expect every day to receive marching orders, or else be denounced as a deserter and unworthy son of my Dessau Fatherland! The young Dessauers have marched; the old Dessauers, such as the old Fritzes, are, alas! no longer to be found in our days. It seems hardly possible to avoid a civil war; folly has grown to madness, and one shudders in thinking of the consequences. Well, for the present, I shall stay quiet with my *Veda*, notwithstanding all Dessau Prime Ministers. One lives from day to day, till the real

[1] She died three weeks after her baby brother, aged four years.

marching order comes. If you see the Minister Pulski, tell him that in the old Tory University of Oxford, at the last debate at the Union, a vote of sympathy with Hungary was carried by a large majority.'

To his Mother.

*Translation.* Oxford, *June* 15.

'As I opened your last letter the little lock of Agnes's hair fell out; dear little child, how much you have lost in her, especially as she seemed so devoted to you, and was already so useful to you. I own that my hopes for a speedy solution of the difficulties in Germany disappear more and more, and though I still trust my later life will be spent there, I shall now begin to look about for a settled position in England. I am convinced that after a time it would not be difficult to find a settled and remunerative occupation, where I could give you a pleasanter life than in this student's housekeeping. The great advantage of my present post is, that for the next six or eight years, I can live decently and am not forced to accept the first appointment that turns up. God will help further, and, notwithstanding the loneliness and the strange climate in which I have now lived so long, I recognize with deep thankfulness how much better off I am than many of my friends, though I have not deserved it. I lately received such a kind invitation from Bunsen for a party, that I went to London, and stayed with him two days. He lives in another house, a very fine one, one of the best in London. They had asked 750 people—the whole *Corps Diplomatique*, and the *élite* of English society. The whole house was like a garden, the balconies covered with awnings from which one had a splendid view over London, the garden of the house illuminated, beautiful music, German songs with a full chorus, from the German Opera now in London. I cannot describe the diamonds and the dresses, but I have never seen such a crowd of beautiful women and girls together. Guizot was there, and Palmerston; in fact, all the lions and lionesses of the season. The next evening I was invited to Lord Ellesmere's, one of the richest men here, whose collection of pictures is famous. Only think of looking round in the middle of a conversation and seeing on all sides Raphaels, Titians, Murillos, Carlo Dolces—all originals! This sort of thing only exists in England. Bunsen is unchanged in his affection; in spite of all he has to do, I always get a few lines from him as soon as anything of interest happens. He always hopes for the best, though prepared for the worst.'

After telling his mother she is wrong in entirely shutting herself up, he ends with these words:—

'Every one carries a grave of lost hope in his soul, but he covers it over with cold marble, or with green boughs. On sad days one likes to go alone to this God's acre of the soul, and weep there, but only in order to return full of comfort and hope to those who are left to us.'

Knowing the general ignorance in England at that time as to the value and meaning of the *Rig-veda*, Max Müller had been busy in writing a full and explanatory preface to the first volume. This, when finished, he gave to Wilson, who corrected and praised it, and had nothing to object to, but when Max Müller on June 1 showed him a letter he had written on the subject to the Directors, he suddenly turned round and seemed determined it should not be printed, and also told Max that he, Wilson, would never hear of his returning to live in Germany till the whole of the *Rig-veda* was finished. Though Max Müller had kept to his bargain and prepared his fifty sheets a year, Wilson, whose translation depended on his edition, scolded him like a schoolboy, telling him he might do more if he chose. The next day Wilson seemed to repent of his ill humour, and said he would like to see the preface printed as a separate work, not with the *Veda*. Max Müller concludes his account of the whole scene with these words, 'I cannot make that old man out. He is honest and straightforward, of great power and energy, but nothing to grease the wheels.'

In his letter to the Court of Directors Max Müller mentions that in this preface, which consisted of 300 pages quarto, he had given for the first time an account of the Vedic literature and its three distinguishable periods, and had explained the relation of the Vedic to the rest of Sanskrit literature. He had evidently discussed the matter with Bunsen, for in a letter written about the middle of June he says, 'I have at once copied again the letter which you were so good as to correct, and for which you have personally secured a good reception, and enclose it, begging you, if all is right, to post it,' and in September he writes to Bunsen:—

*Translation.* PARK PLACE, 1849.

'The news of the success of my petition was a complete surprise—therefore all the more joyful, and all the more so that I again owe the success to your friendly services. Your proposal, which the Directors accept, gives me far more than I asked. Of course I shall print and publish it in England, but first I shall go to Germany, and spend the winter there. Are three months of holiday really too much after three years' work and absence from home?'

After the pleasant visit to Bunsen in June, he writes to him:—

*Translation.*

'I have returned safely to my Isola Bella, as though after a fairy voyage. The awaking after such a beautiful dream is not always pleasant, and so I will employ the first moments of my solitude here, whilst my Sanskrit does not yet attract me, in thanking you for the refreshing hours which your kind invitation secured me. . . . "Nil desperandum Teucro duce et auspice Teucro!" But what would have become of me had not such a Teucer taken me up? Now I do not despair of finding a new Salamis, wherever it may be! If the wind improves, then up with the sail; if it is against one, then "pull away," and perhaps at last one will reach a safer and German port. Oxford is so beautiful just now, I wish I could show it to you. . . .'

It was not long before his unremitting work began to tell on him. He says in a letter at this time, 'I am writing all day,' and worse almost than this was the constant worry of trying to hurry on the printers. At length he acknowledges that 'the English will not be driven, one must take them as they are.' His headaches became almost incessant, and his doctor at last insisted on his taking some rest, so Morier carried him off to the Lakes to join a reading party under Jowett, Froude being also in the neighbourhood. He writes from there to Burnouf:—

*July* 26, 1849.

'The reason I have left your last friendly letter so long unanswered is that I wished to send you an essay for the Prix Volney. I have followed your kind advice, and instead of sending in the printed essay, I have put together a special one for this purpose from my Collectaneum. It treats of the history of the civilization of the Aryan nations before the fifteenth century B. C., as far as one can construct it from the researches of comparative philology. I was very much grieved to hear that your health has suffered of late, and that your work has been therefore interrupted. I hope you are now feeling better, and are able to carry on your important investigations with renewed vigour. I have been ill again and had to leave Oxford to recruit here at the Westmoreland Lakes. I hope soon to be so far better as to be able to finish the first Ashtaka. Rawlinson will soon come to England, and has promised the explanation of the

Babylonian inscriptions. Wilson is busy with an English translation of the *Rig-veda*; he does not consider the translation of Langlois literal enough. I hope soon to go to Germany, as I cannot stand the climate of England; incessant headaches make any fatiguing work impossible.'

Two days later he writes to his mother:—

*Translation.* GRANGE, DERWENTWATER, *July* 28.

'I have been for a fortnight in this beautiful country, with two great friends, who were going to spend their holidays here, and asked me to go with them. We take long walks every day on the mountains, or row on the lakes, or ride, which we enjoy very much. I was knocked up with incessant work, but I feel perfectly well since I came here, and hope soon to be able to return to Oxford. The beauty of England is so great that one cannot understand why the English always go to the Continent in search of beautiful scenery. There is nothing so beautiful as being alone with nature: one sees how God's will is fulfilled in each bud and leaf that blooms and withers, and one learns to recognize how deeply rooted in one is this thirst for nature. In living with men, one is only too easily torn from this real home; then one's own plans and wishes and hopes and fears spring up; then we fancy we can perfect something for ourselves alone, and think that everything must serve for our ends and enjoyments, until the influence of nature in life or the hand of God arouses us, and warns us that we live and flourish, not for enjoyment, nor for undisturbed quiet, but to bear fruit in another life. When one stands amid the grandeur of nature, with one's own little murmurs and sufferings, and looks deep into this dumb soul, much becomes clear to one, and one is astounded at the false ideas one has formed of this life. It is but a short journey, and on a journey one can do without many things which generally seem necessary to us. Yes, one can do without even what is dearest to our hearts, in this world, if we know that after the journey which we have to endure we shall find again those who have arrived at the goal quicker and more easily than we have done. Now if life were looked upon as a journey for refreshment or amusement, which it ought not to be, we might feel sad, if we have to make our way alone; but if we treat it as a serious business-journey, then we know we have hard and unpleasant work before us, and enjoy all the more the beautiful resting-places which God's love has provided for each of us in life. We have all of us, in these last years, had such a long rest, and enjoyed life so quietly, that now, when we have to fight on again, we have quite forgotten that our power for fighting was meant for something more than parades and reviews.

Look how the true soldier rejoices when a real battle is at hand, and so the true man should rejoice, when God calls him to an earnest life struggle; and when the last friends fall right and left, one goes into the conflict with yet more determined courage to gain that object which is set before each of us. You may think this too serious a view of life: I assure you it is this view of life which has given me my cheerful spirit, and helps to keep it up, and which makes it possible for me with firm faith to contemplate fearlessly the struggles of life that are still before me. The one thing I desire and hope is that God will give me strength to maintain my independence by unremitting work, so that I may always pursue that way in life which according to my convictions appears the right one. If God gives me more, and it is granted me to lead a quiet and happy life with you, it is more than I deserve But courage—nothing *can* happen to us in life, but what is really the best for us. And now for my plans. I have about 100 pages more to print, which may be ready in six weeks. Then I shall go to Germany and spend the winter with you, wherever you like. I shall look about in Germany, to see if I can find a place in any University, preferably at Bonn, and see if it would be possible to prepare my MS. in Germany, and to come over every year for a short time to England for the printing. That would be delightful—but I won't build any castles in the air, as there is much to consider. If this does not answer I would return to England, and you could come and visit me. Then I should alter my plans and build my hopes on England and on finding a post here, where you could be quite comfortable, and live with me and keep house. The longer one lives in England, the more one longs to be back in Germany. A stormy is better than a dead sea! The English grow more like the Chinese with each year, and nature herself has built a Chinese wall round their lovely country. But if one makes oneself into a Chinaman, one gets on well with them.'

He writes to Dr. Pauli from Borrowdale:—

*Translation.*

'The neighbourhood here is glorious, and we are just in from a walk with old Morier. We can jump out of our windows into the water, we fish for trout, and smoke a weed. Then there are boats, ponies, carts, and no living soul except dogs and sheep, and an old farmer's family with a lingo which is difficult to understand. I shall stay some time, and wish you could come here, for it is really unique, and whilst I write I hear the sound of waterfalls on all sides, for they are swollen by late rains. Froude lives close by, and I am going to stay with him. Mary Barton, Miss Martineau, and other literary swells live about here—and the *Veda* may see how it can do without me.'

Whilst at the Lakes Max Müller copied out his treatise on the 'Results of the Investigations of Language as to Ancient History,' forming part of the Prolegomena to the *Veda*, which he sent to M. Burnouf for the competition for the Prix Volney. In writing to acknowledge the safe arrival of the MS., Burnouf says:—

*Translation.*

'We shall need all the forces at our disposal, for the number of competitors is large, and from what I hear powerful, and many of these will be supported by very active friends. I have been entrusted with the first examination of your Essay, and shall receive it to-day. But if we must fight, we will fight—you know we French do not fear blows, we like them, alas! only too much. Good-bye, my dear friend. Take care of your health. I am very sorry to hear that it has suffered from overwork. But to work, one must live.'

To Dr. Pauli he writes after leaving the Lakes:—

*Translation.* *August* 24, 1849.

'I have at last finished my holiday, and yet, long as it was, did not get to Scotland. But we amused ourselves to the last day. I was a fortnight with Froude, boating, and fishing, and whatever other amusements there are, whereby we grow older but not wiser. Morier and Jowett are gone to the Isle of Man, but my old love, the *Veda*, drew me back to Oxford.'

On returning to Oxford he found his friend Dr. Acland contending almost single-handed with a serious outbreak of cholera. It was the depth of Long Vacation, the members of the University were away, and most of the medical men taking their summer holiday. Max Müller put himself at his friend's disposal, and worked with him in tracing out cases, attending to the sick and giving relief, till he himself nearly succumbed to a sharp attack, and Dr. Acland would not allow him to do any more visiting. On recovering he writes to Bunsen:—

*Translation.*

'I enclose a letter from M. Reinaud for you to read. I think I can now feel pretty confident of receiving the prize. I am delighted at the result, and feel how much more good comes to me than I have ever deserved. But I will now begin again to work in all earnest, if God gives me health, which has again in these last weeks lost me much time, and German air will, I hope, prove better medicine than all I have been swallowing here.'

In September his old friend Victor Carus arrived, and settled in the same house with Max Müller. They breakfasted together, and then separated for their work, Carus working at Christ Church, and they dined together, when not asked to dine out. Carus finally left Oxford at Easter, 1851, but he had been absent for many months of the time, working in the Scilly Isles, and the last few months of his stay in Oxford he lived in Dr. Acland's house, so that the friends were really less together than they had expected.

Early in October came the welcome news that he had gained the Prix Volney. Burnouf writes:—

*Translation.* PARIS, *October* 5, 1849.

'MY DEAR FRIEND,—I hasten to announce to you, that on my report, the Commission of the Institute, who have to adjudge the annual prize founded by M. de Volney, has accorded you the first prize of 1,200 francs. A second prize of 1,000 francs has been awarded to another work, curious in fact, but not sufficiently serious in form. I held that the first prize must be adjudged you, as much for the merit of your work, as for the dignity of those great studies, of which, in a very short time, you will be one of the chief ornaments. No one can feel greater pleasure than I do in announcing your success to you. Everybody entertained the kindest feelings towards you. Remember, you are not to mention your success before the 25th, as it is not till that day that the prizes are announced at the public *séance*. Your devoted friend, 'E. B.'

And now, after four years of labour in collecting the materials, the first volume of the Hymns of the *Rig-veda*, with Sâyana's Commentary, was printed and nearly ready for publication. The text had been prepared from MSS. in the Bibliothèque Royale of Paris, the East India House, and the Bodleian Library, for in the whole of Germany no MSS. were to be found, except some very old and imperfect copies of the text and a few worm-eaten fragments of Sâyana at Berlin. The MSS. in France and England had been collated and copied by Max Müller's own hand, entirely without help. The MSS. of Sâyana were most imperfect, made by copyists who did not understand their subject, and were therefore full of mistakes, which had all to be rectified to produce a correct text. It abounds moreover in obscure quotations, and many of the works quoted had not been edited at this time, and yet every quotation had to be verified and explained. It was a gigantic undertaking for so young a scholar, and in his preface he gratefully acknowledges the constant encouragement he had received from men like Burnouf and Wilson, and the readiness with which the librarians of the public libraries in Paris, London, and Oxford spread their treasures before him, whilst Burnouf and Dr. Mill generously placed their private collection of MSS. at his service, and Dr. Rieu, Sub-Librarian of the British Museum, aided in the correction of the proof-sheets of this volume.

So after three years of absence he was able to hurry off to his own family, with the restful feeling that he had well earned his longed-for holiday. He thus takes leave of Bunsen :—

*Translation.* LONDON, *October* 20, 1849.

'In the hurry of my journey it is not possible to answer your kind letter, which is very precious to me. Your confidence in me gives me fresh courage, and an earnest resolution to work on bravely; but do not expect too much from me, that I may not fall too far short of your expectations. The love of science and desire of distinction are often too weak to overcome the *vis inertiae* and the longing for rest and retirement, especially in these days of barbarism, of mental poverty and godlessness, where one finds no hearing for research, let alone the hope of starting anything useful. I owe you much, very much, were it only that the thought of you keeps alive in me the love of duty, and the desire to win the approbation of good men.'

Immediately on his arrival in Berlin Max Müller sought out his friend and patron, Alexander von Humboldt, who continued to the end to take a deep interest in the scholar whom he remembered from his Berlin student-days. Unfortunately all the letters from Max Müller to Humboldt have disappeared, but permission has been given to use one or two of Humboldt's notes to Max, though there is nothing of special interest in them, as showing his friendly feelings towards the young Sanskritist.

*Translation.* POTSDAM, *November* 2, 1849.

'It is with the greatest joy that I greet again on German soil so talented and industrious a scholar as Dr. Max Müller. An unforeseen absence from home robbed me the other day of the joy of your visit. I expect you, therefore, the day after to-morrow, Friday, between 1 and 2 o'clock, if that suits you. The Prolegomena to the *Veda* will be of the greatest interest to me, and I shall hand it to the public with pleasure, if you wish me to do so. With kindest regards, yours, 'A. v. HUMBOLDT.'

From Berlin Max Müller writes to his friend and master Burnouf:—

9, SCHADOW STRASSE, BERLIN, *November* 8.

'DEAR SIR,—My best thanks for your kind letter. You can imagine how happy I am, after having received from the French Academy this unexpected distinction, but what gives to this distinction its highest value is that this honour has been bestowed on my essay on your recommendation. I knew very well your kind intentions towards me, and was persuaded that I should find in you a kind judge. But I was also too well acquainted with your character, to expect that your kindness for me could exercise any influence on those principles on which you act. Having received therefore this prize through you, I think I have solid reason to feel happy about it, and to consider it as a good omen for my future studies. The first volume of the *Rig-veda* has at last appeared. I left it finished before I went to Germany, and though I am afraid there will be some delay by the bookbinder, bookseller, &c., I hope you will soon receive a copy of it at Paris. I have not yet given up my plan of coming to Paris, before I return to England. There are many things connected with the *Veda*, which I have treated in my Prolegomena to the *Veda*, on which I should like very much to hear your opinion before it is printed. I hope no other Revolution will come between it, as the last time when I came to Paris, for I see also here at Berlin that revolutions leave the minds of men not in a favourable disposition for discussing questions connected with the history of bygone nations. I hope your health will soon be entirely restored, and I shall find you again at your morning upanishads, animated by the same lively interest, and with the same warmth of discussion and conversation, as three or four years ago.

'Believe me, dear sir,

'Yours very gratefully and faithfully,

'M. MÜLLER.'

From Berlin he writes again to Bunsen:—

*Translation.* BERLIN, *November* 12, 1849.

'After spending a short time in Dresden and Leipzig, I have come to Berlin, and my mother with me, and shall stay here till Christmas. I have found many of my old friends here, and satiated with politics the interest in scientific pursuits seems to be slowly reviving. The feeling of dejection in Prussia and Germany is great, and the good see with dismay that the pendulum of the State machinery, which in March was swung too far to the left, now, with the same want of caution, is swung too far to the right. That from that point there will again be a reaction every one seems to forget. They fancy they can hold the pendulum fast to the right, forgetting that either the clockwork must break, or the weight must fall back with the same force. Yesterday, I received a letter from Oxford, in which I am told that my Oxford friends are taking pains to secure me a place in the British Museum, and have written to you about it. It is the place of Keeper of the Oriental MSS., with £450 income. I shall not stand for the place: the tastes of the late librarian led him to collect a wealth of Arabic, Syriac, and Persian MSS., but Indian and Old Persian were totally neglected. I should not suit the place, but might not Rieu get it? His knowledge exactly fits him for it, and this appointment would assure his whole future and be a great advantage to science. Lepsius is very well, and is just going to bring out another volume, chiefly drawings. Lepsia, too, and Lepsiuncula are well. Bopp is just the same, unchanged; but one cannot expect anything more from him for Sanskrit. It is to be hoped that Weber by his work will soon gain a Professorship, not only in his own interest, but also for the sake of his work. I have not yet seen Humboldt; he is in Potsdam, and I will wait till I have received the copies of the *Rig-veda.* I am going to-day to the Chamber for the first time. The seats in the Chamber are already getting empty, and ennui will do more service than a state of siege. To see men like Dahlmann[1] taking a part in these transactions is really sad. He is too good an historian to be a politician. I occupy myself here with the revision of my Prolegomena; I cannot alter it much more. Yours in true devotion.'

[1] Died 1860.

# CHAPTER VII

## 1850–1851

Dinner at Potsdam. Morier's illness. Return to Oxford. Rauch. Waagen. Appointed to lecture at Oxford. Letters from Professors Cowell and Story-Maskelyne. Visit to Froude. Article in *Edinburgh Review*. Made Deputy Professor and Honorary M.A.

AFTER a pleasant Christmas at Chemnitz with his mother and sister, where also his friend Morier joined him, Max Müller, with Morier, returned to Berlin, where the latter meant to spend some months studying German. Max writes to his mother from Berlin:—

*Translation.* BERLIN, *Jan.* 30.

'I am very comfortable with Goldstücker, but I am tired of being idle, and am longing to be back in Oxford now I am no longer with you. I have been visiting old friends, Bettina von Arnim and Varnhagen; they have both become red republicans.'

He had met Humboldt, who told him that the King had expressed a wish to see him before he returned to England, and soon after brought him a command to dine at Potsdam. He sends his mother a lively account of the dinner:—

*Translation.* BERLIN, *Feb.* 2, 1850.

'DEAREST MOTHER,—I must tell you all about my visit to the King. Early Friday came a messenger from the palace to invite me to dinner at Charlottenburg, and at 2.30 Humboldt came in his carriage to take me there. He told me it would be quite a small party, but when we arrived we found about thirty people already assembled, and we all waited for the King. Humboldt introduced me to various people, and the ladies and gentlemen of the Court were evidently much surprised at my presence, as I was the only man without epaulets and about ten Orders. At last came the King and Queen. I was again the only person who had not yet been presented. So I was taken through all the ladies and gentlemen and presented to His Majesty. "Brahma is great, but fear not!" I thought, as I looked at the King, only separated from me by his mountainous *embonpoint*. He asked me where I was born, and told me that in the Dessau library he had seen the poet Müller. Then he talked of the Duchess, and at last asked how I liked England, and then saying "Wünsche Ihnen guten Appetit" (I wish you a good appetite), bowed and dismissed me. Then the Queen came up to me, and was asking me about the Duchess, when the King hurried up to her, gave her his arm, saying as Berlin wit, "Monsieur, s'il vous plaît, dinner is served." Then we went into the next room. I sat between two officers, and enjoyed my dinner, which was a very good one. I took the liberty of letting my knife and fork go with each course, till I remarked that the servants looked askance, and then I saw to my great surprise that the ladies and gentlemen round me eat everything with the same knife and fork! What to do? to imitate them? No, I went quietly on to the last dish, and let the footmen and my neighbours and *vis-à-vis* think of me what they pleased; but I was amused. After dinner we had coffee in quite a small room. The King came up to me again, and asked if I knew English, and other kindly questions, and then joined the Queen. I had some talk with some of the Gentlemen in Waiting, Count Pückler, &c.; then their Majesties went away, and I drove home with Humboldt. He was very sorry that the party had been so large, but said the King was so much occupied it was difficult to see him alone. It amused me very much to have this peep into the royal circle, and it may be useful to me later on. Humboldt was delightful. I have been busy for him on the names of the Dogstar in Sanskrit, which he will mention in *Cosmos*. That is better than dining with the King, but I knew you would want me to describe it all, but you must not repeat it to everybody. I am often afraid on this account of telling you everything when I write. There was no talk of an Order, which would do me more harm than good.'

Max Müller had arranged to leave Berlin directly after the dinner at Potsdam, but his friend Morier was taken suddenly ill with quinsy, and he was obliged to stay on and nurse him through a most alarming attack, and it was not till quite the end of February that he was able to start for Paris, where he received his 1,200 frs. for the Prix Volney and saw Burnouf and many of his old French friends.

Meantime Professor Wilson—always a cold, hard man, unable

to enter readily into the difficulties and engagements of other people where they were contrary to his own views—became very impatient for his return, and wrote to him as follows :—

OXFORD, *Feb.* 26, 1850.

'MY DEAR MÜLLER,—I had hoped to have seen you in Oxford on the occasion of my visit there, but it is now drawing to a close, and I understand there is no prospect of your early arrival. I regret this much, as unless we can proceed a little quicker than we have done with the printing of the *Rig-veda*, I fear I shall scarcely live to see it finished, in time at least to finish the translation; unless I do as Langlois has done, and go to work upon the MSS. only. In that case I should have to walk off with all the India House copies, and leave you to the Bodleian alone. The only other expedient I can think of is to summon some other Vaidik—Roth, for instance—to your help; but seriously I wish you would soon resume your labours. It is high time to put a stop to all the wild fancies that a partial knowledge of the light and a reliance upon such equivocal guides as the Brâhmanas and Sûtras seem likely to engender. I want you also to help in the distribution of the copies. I have the Court's sanction to the presentation of above 100 copies to different public bodies and eminent individuals both here and abroad. If I cannot expect your assistance in carrying this sanction into effect, I must do as well as I can without it, but it is a task that will give me some trouble. I have finished the translation, and printed about half of it. It will be completed, I hope, in about six weeks. Trithen and your other Oxford friends are all well, and will be glad to see you again amongst them. Yours sincerely, 'H. H. WILSON.'

Max Müller had written from Paris to his mother :—

*March* 8.

'It was an unfortunate thing being kept in Berlin, but I have the happy feeling that I was doing what was right, and so I must be satisfied.'

He was scarcely settled in Oxford before he writes to Bunsen :—

*Translation.* *March*, 1850.

'My best thanks for your friendly welcome to England. I hope your health has not suffered from the various efforts and excitements of your journey to Germany. I have seen with great interest in the publication of the Prussian Circular Note the realization of the ideas to which you gave expression before the end of last year. And so, suddenly, the Gordian knot of the Austrian diplomatic tow-rope is cut to pieces, and Prussia at last appears as *primus inter pares*. That the idea of an Emperor is put down as a possible impossibility is sad, but as it had become a subject of scandal it was better to give it up. Should the thunder-clouds of civil war really burst over Germany, the German Emperor would come, not from Schmerling or Gagern, but by the grace of God. How much I wish to see you, how many questions I would gladly have answered! But your invitation now in the midst of all your business is too much for me to accept, though I cannot be certain that a strong influence may not drive me to London for a few hours. I am expecting a lot of MSS. from India, which I have bought for myself, as I did not think that the Berlin Library would receive permission for such things at this moment. I am in direct correspondence with the Asiatic Society in Calcutta. My old *Veda* is a real comfort to me, despite all the wearisomeness of the difficult and yet mechanical work of revision, but it will require much time and labour before the end is possible. Mr. Langlois, Professor of Rhetoric, has made the task much easier to himself. Without commentary, and, as he proudly says, without philological considerations, he has translated the *Veda* straight away very *cavalièrement*: the two first books have just appeared at Didot's. One cannot enter into discussion with a man of this sort, and yet it is provoking, for the book is easy to read, and from the first page will give ideas of the *Veda* which will afterwards cost much trouble to remove, just as people now use and quote the translation of the *Ezour-veda* by Voltaire. An approximate translation of the *Veda* can be made, and I believe that even Wilson's English translation will only be approximate. And yet if I had to wait ten years, I would not translate a single line till the whole Vedic antiquity with its wealth of thought lay clearly before me. If you take a hymn from the last book of the *Rig-veda* interesting for social considerations and moral ideas, as a whole it is clear, but the sequence of ideas is very difficult. Forgive this long scrawl. You need not read it all, and to-morrow is Ash Wednesday, when all diplomatists must do special penance for last year. The poor Pope must cover his head with ashes, and the new Roman Commonwealth will be a common misery. Gioberti seems to have had his day of Damascus, and wishes to make himself an Italian Gagern. The worst are always the best when once the scales fall from their eyes. They won't believe this in Berlin, but Messrs. Brandenburg, &c., are really *too* good for these bad times.'

Max Müller devoted nearly all the year after his return from Germany to the *Veda*, and only gave himself a few days' rest from time to time, as he continued to find the Oxford climate very trying. He writes to his mother:—

*Translation.* OXFORD, *April* 26, 1850.

'One thing is necessary above all things in order to live peaceably with people, that is in Latin *humanitas*, German *Menschlichkeit.* It is difficult to describe, but it is to claim as little as possible from others, neither an obliging temper nor gratitude, and yet to do all one can to please others, yet without expecting them always to find it out. As men are made up of contradictions, they are the more grateful and friendly the less they see that we expect gratitude and friendliness. Even the least cultivated people have their good points, and it is not only far better, but far more interesting if one takes trouble to find out the best side and motives of people, rather than the worst and most selfish. I write to you what I have often said to myself when I was brought in contact with strangers, and because I find that on the whole I get on well with them. This may appear very artificial, but life is an art, and more difficult than Sanskrit or anything else. A kindly nature can win us by taking pains, but an unkind nature fails, notwithstanding all art and cunning. I am so busy that one day goes after another. I hardly see any one; then I have caught cold, and have constant toothache and headache. But one must *faire bonne mine à mauvais jeu*, and if we have no one to pour out our ills to, we must get on as well as we can. I meant to write sooner, but I have been out of sorts the whole time.'

To Bunsen, who had begged him to go 'with bag and baggage to 9, Carlton Terrace, to one who longs to see' him, he writes:—

*Translation.* OXFORD, *May* 17, 1850.

'How gladly would I accept your kind invitation; the hours I am allowed to spend with you are not only the happiest, but the most instructive and most remunerative; but I have sold my freedom and made myself a day labourer, so at all events I must not leave the cart sticking fast as long as it is in human power to move it. I have a section of MS. ready, which I can print with a good conscience. What will happen later I don't yet know myself, but hope for an *interim fit aliquid.* I hope, however, to make myself free for a couple of days as soon as I can—that is, as soon as Wilson leaves; he comes next week to Oxford for his lectures. I have heard nothing of Froude for a long time, except that he is very happily married. I don't believe he is the author of any "red and raw" articles, and as far as I can discover he has only written *one* literary article for the

*Leader*, but I cannot answer for this, as I don't know the paper. I cannot get Rawlinson's treatise. His brother says he told him that you are the only person in London with whom he can talk about Babylon.'

A little later we find Max Müller paying a visit to Morier's father and mother at Bath. He was delighted with the place, and still more with the affection shown by the old people to one to whose devoted nursing their only son owed his life—a debt of gratitude never forgotten by any member of the family, who all remained his faithful friends till called away before him one after another.

To F. Palgrave, Esq.

9, Park Place, Oxford, *June* 18, 1850.

'My dear Palgrave,—I hope I shall be able to get away from Oxford about the end of this week, so if you can give me a bed I should like to come to Kneller Hall on Friday or Saturday. I am thoroughly tired of Oxford, and hope I shall feel jollier again when we sit together on your tower and smoke a weed; but no *In Memoriam*, rather something about airy, fairy Lilians and other sweet creatures without a soul. However, I do not mean to say that Tennyson's last poems are not very beautiful, yet I do not like those open graves of sorrow and despair, and wish our poets would imitate the good Christian fashion of covering them with flowers, or a stone with a short inscription on it.'

From Kneller Hall Max Müller went for a week to Bunsen, from whom he always gathered fresh courage for his hard work and more or less lonely life. Of this visit Max Müller tells his mother:—

*Translation.* Oxford, *July* 22, 1850.

'I met Rauch the sculptor in London, who was staying at Bunsen's: a really delightful old man, who lives only for the beautiful, and has no eyes for anything else. He came to Oxford with me, and was quite enchanted with it, and I enjoyed it more than ever with him. He was quite ill with the wealth of the buildings, monuments, churches, halls and pictures, and the beauty of the scenery, and really when seeing the most striking things he seemed hardly able to control himself. One day I went with him to Blenheim. . . . Later on I had a visit from Professor Waagen, the Director of the Berlin Museum, and one of the best German connoisseurs of art; I had to show him about. Then came Professor Ennemoser from Munich, and lastly

George Bunsen, who only left me yesterday. He sings beautifully, and we had a great deal of music.'

From the following letter it is evident that his Vedic studies were beginning to attract general attention, and that an article on the subject was desired for one of the great Quarterly Reviews:—

TO CHEVALIER BUNSEN.

*Translation.* 9, PARK PLACE, OXFORD, *July*, 1850.

'YOUR EXCELLENCY,—I feel much refreshed spiritually by having been in your presence, which always acts like fresh spring rain on dusty fields; physically I feel better, though I cannot say well yet, and though the body ought to be subject to the spirit, still the spirit has only too often to follow the lead of the body.

With regard to Empson's and Dr. Wilson's letters, it is difficult to advise. I have no doubt whatever, that something can be written about the *Veda* which would reach even the dullest ears. Whether Dr. Wilson can undertake that task is another question. You know the dry hard shell in which the *Veda* is presented to us, and which seems still harder and more wooden in the English translation. Nevertheless *I* of course shall be glad if the *Rig-veda* is dealt with in the *Edinburgh Review*, and if Wilson would write from the standpoint of a missionary, and would show how the knowledge and bringing into light of the *Veda* would upset the whole existing system of Indian theology, it might become of real interest.'

Only a few days after writing the above, Max Müller heard from Bunsen that Eastwick, the translator of Bopp's *Comparative Grammar*, wished for a review of it in the *Quarterly*, and urging him to undertake it. This is the first mention of the article which appeared ultimately in the *Edinburgh Review* in October, 1851, and which was the first of several articles written by Max Müller for that periodical.

TO CHEVALIER BUNSEN.

*Translation.* OXFORD, *July* 14, 1850.

'I accept with pleasure the proposal with regard to an article on Bopp's *Comparative Grammar*, translated by Eastwick, and thank you for it. I must ask you to be good enough to assure Mr. Lockhart of my readiness. I do not think that a short review will cost much time and labour, and if you will allow me, next week, when I shall be in London for a few days, I will call and get some directions and hints from you. God help Schleswig-Holstein, and not punish Prussia in His wrath. If the Schleswig-Holsteiners are conquered and annihilated, they have fought for their rights and have fallen gloriously on the field of honour, after the will of history. But if a power, to which all Europe has offered the leading position, allows itself to be intimidated by the threats of the Danes and Russians, and withdraws a given promise, that is worse than a retreat before a battle.'

Two days later he writes to Palgrave :—

9, PARK PLACE, OXFORD, *July* 16, 1850.

'MY DEAR PALGRAVE,—If you have ever amused yourself in spending a whole Long Vacation in Oxford—of which I do not think you have ever been guilty—you would know that it is more like purgatory than anything else. Yet here I am, and I cannot get away on account of one miserable MS. which I must go and look at every day while I am carrying my *Rig-veda* through the Press. I should have liked very much to spend a few weeks with you and Froude, and I have tried everything to accomplish my plan, but it was impossible without stopping my work altogether, which for many reasons I could not do. I shall be tied to Oxford for a month or two longer—a pleasant prospect, as then the fine season will be over, and no chance left for refreshing one's soul except in the cold weather. However, it is no use writing *epistolae ex Ponto!* I am glad to hear that Froude gets on so well, and that his choice has been such a happy one. Johnson is back, and looks very joyful, as well as his bride. Professor Waagen is staying with him, and I am sure you would enjoy their conversation. I can only admire their skill in admiring the most ugly, stiff and out of joint pictures: however, such is art.'

From the very moment that his own position became tolerably settled by the patronage bestowed on his *Rig-veda* by the East India Company, Max Müller was always trying to help others in some respects less fortunate than himself. A long correspondence exists as to the place of German teacher at Rugby, which he tried in 1849 to secure for Dr. Pauli. Soon after the latter became private secretary to Bunsen, Max heard of a place vacant at the University of Berlin, and writes to Pauli :—

*Translation.*

'If Bunsen is interested about it, he should not forget Weber. He is older than ——, and has done more, and then has a wife and child. Please do not forget to mention this.'

And in the following letter, whilst presenting his father's

poems to Bunsen, he tries to do another friend a good turn:—

*Translation.* OXFORD, *October* 9, 1850.

'I am sending the new edition of my father's poems which I brought out during my German "Winter-journey." There are many new things in it, and I trust the work will help to keep alive the memory of the poet who died so early! You have spoken of him to me so often, and in a manner so grateful to my feelings, that it is a great pleasure to be allowed to send you this new edition. Then I wish to ask your advice. I visited Froude this week to make the acquaintance of his wife and *daughter*. He is thinking of an article on German poetry since Goethe. He has collected some good material, especially very successful translations from Uhland, Heine, and a few poems of my father's. Do you think that the *Quarterly* would open its columns to an article on Uhland, Müller, Heine, Lenau, &c., and is it too much to ask you to persuade Lockhart to take such an article? It is quite understood that the subject would be treated purely from the historical and aesthetic point of view.'

Towards the end of this year, after an almost continuous summer of labour at the *Veda*, Max Müller was seized with a sudden feeling of utter weariness of England and his life here, and writes to Bunsen:—

*Translation.* OXFORD, *November*, 1850.

'As soon as I received your letter I wrote to Froude. I do not think that he can write as comprehensive an article as you describe. What he could best write would be a small *genre* picture of German lyric poetry since Goethe, the time when the old man tripped over the roots of the trees he had himself planted; an estimate of the (compared with Goethe) *poetae mediocres* to whom with Horace one willingly denies all right to existence, because they have never, like Homer, Dante, Goethe, and Byron, visited the devil in hell. If Froude once left this sphere to sketch a picture of the mental and religious struggles of the Fatherland since Goethe, he would from want of accurate knowledge fall into extremes; and the *Edinburgh*, which is not far behind the *Quarterly* in anti-German feeling, would be closed against him. The prospects for Germans in England get steadily worse: happy he who can live in his own land. Things look very grey. The conferences in Bregenz and Warsaw have made a new revolution a duty for every German, and those who are by nature inclined to a *bouleversement modéré* rub their hands. But a stormy sea also is splendid, and shows who are true men. We must expect that some of our stately steersmen will be seasick, but there are men who fear neither wind nor weather, and who do not think that Germany's peace is too dear to buy at any price. I am thinking of writing to Lassen to ask him whether he can employ me in Bonn. I am heartily tired of England, and if there is nothing in Germany I will try India. My work is entirely at a standstill, my MSS. from India lost for the *second time* by the shipwreck of the *Manchester*. I must therefore come to a decision. The problem of the Egyptian language occupies me very much, but it is difficult to find guiding principles when the comparison depends on the mere mass, not on the organization of the language. Benfey's researches prove the Semitic character of the Egyptian grammar beyond all doubt, and much will become simpler and clearer by the old Egyptian grammar. But in the comparison of words with the Indo-European, we expose ourselves to many dangers, especially as long as a sufficient number of Indo-European, or rather *common* roots in Semitic also, are not authenticated. To-morrow Wilson comes to Oxford, with whom I have a good deal to discuss; then a decision must be made as to beginning a new life.'

Bunsen's answer came by return of post: 'Your letter has frightened me by what you tell me of your strong impulse to go to Bonn or Benares. This is the very worst moment for Bonn. . . . The crisis in our country disturbs everything,' and ends by urging him to go up to London at once and stay at the Legation. To this Max replied:—

*Translation.* OXFORD, *November* 5, 1850.

'How willingly would I have accepted your invitation to London, were I not kept by two lectures which take up my whole time, one on astronomy by Professor Donkin, and another by Wilson to learn Hindûstânî. An interruption would throw me out too much, especially in the astronomy, which I can only follow by the closest attention. I have spoken to Wilson; he advises me to stay in England, or to go to India, but I do not think he would make difficulties if I had a definite purpose in Germany, that is if I could tell him that I really expected a position in a University. Therefore I think it is best first to hear Lassen's views, to know whether he would recommend the faculty in Bonn to give me an appointment, or whether he would rather keep Sanskrit to himself. I am quite ready to stay another year here, to print my Introduction, but I should like to have a certain prospect and not live on at random. My early Oxford friends, with whom I felt at home, leave this one after another, and it is not worth

I 2

while to make new acquaintances. And then in spite of all disorders and crises I am drawn back towards Germany, or if I must live in a foreign country, I would rather go to the Antipodes than live in suspense in England. That I am not in my right place here, I know and feel more each day. So away, and the sooner the better, and God will help me further.

'Wilson received a letter from Benares the other day, which says that the learned Brâhmans there shook their heads mightily at first, but now, after having received and read a specimen of 200 pages, they are highly pleased with the edition of the *Veda*. They have settled among themselves, and it is common talk in Benares, that a colony of Germans will come and settle there, and turn Brâhmans. So if all my plans fail, I may perhaps find a refuge there.'

It was in the very midst of all this uncertainty that he was asked by the Curators of the Taylor Institution to undertake two courses of lectures as deputy for his friend Trithen, who had suddenly fallen into a state of melancholia, quite incapacitating him from work. He tells his mother on December 14:—

*Translation.*

'I received for my birthday a quite unexpected present, a letter from the University asking me to lecture in the place of Trithen, who is very ill. He lectures on modern literature and languages. I cannot say I care very much for it, as it must break into my other work, but as my Oxford friends and also Bunsen were very anxious I should undertake it, I wrote to accept. The first course will be on the History and Origin of Modern Languages, and the second on the *Nibelungen*. If they make me a Professor, I shall not object to it, though I should prefer a German Professorship. Well, we shall see.'

Though wishing Max Müller to accept the offer to lecture in Oxford, Bunsen had written to him on December 18, urging him to pay a flying visit to Bonn before Christmas to see what the prospects there were, adding: 'As a friend of many years' standing, you will forgive me if I say, if the journey to Bonn is not financially convenient to you just now, I *depend* on your thinking of me.'

To this letter Max replied:—

*Translation.* OXFORD, *December* 13, 1850.

'Many thanks for the kind sympathy which, even in the storm and stress of these evil times, you, an always faithful friend, have shown me. I quite acknowledge how well it would have been had I been able myself to reconnoitre the position at Bonn. But before I received George's answer, I had written to Lassen, to ask his advice in this affair. So I could not change things; the first impression had been made, and could hardly be altered by my cursory presence. I will now quietly await what he writes, and have meantime accepted the Oxford invitation to give two courses of lectures. I only hope they won't cost too much time, for if I go to Bonn at Michaelmas, and wish first to finish the second volume of the *Rig-veda*, and the Prolegomena in which a Latin catalogue of the Bodleian MSS. is to appear, I have my hands full. If Lassen makes difficulties I must decide to stay in England, till a kindly fate leads me out of the Oxford hermit's cell, into free German air, or into a forest solitude in India. Here is the review to which you were good enough to promise your powerful recommendation. I should be very glad if the *Edinburgh* would take it, but I am afraid I have hardly hit off the right tone, though I tried hard in writing it to think of ladies uninterruptedly. The advice "think of a lady whilst you are writing" does not come direct from Lockhart, whom I never saw, but from Eastwick, whom Lockhart taught.'

Among the references which the Taylorian Curators received before they appointed Max Müller as a deputy for Trithen, the following was sent in by Wilson. Though it in no way guarantees Max's gifts as a lecturer on Modern European Languages, it shows what Wilson, the Nestor of Sanskritists as he has been called, thought of his young friend as a Sanskrit scholar:—

*November*, 1850.

'His knowledge of the Sanskrit language I regard as most comprehensive and critical, and displaying a more than usual familiarity with the principles of its structure as established by native grammarians. I consider him also as extensively conversant with the general literature of the Hindus, especially with that part which relates to their traditions, institutes, and laws, and I look upon him as *without an equal* in that interesting and important department of it to which he has particularly devoted his attention, the Literature of the *Vedas*, the study of their ancient texts, and of the many voluminous and difficult subsidiary compositions which are indispensable for their elucidation.'

Of Max Müller's position at Oxford, even in these early days, Canon Farrar gives an interesting account:—

'The first time when I met him, was at dinner in the Hall at Balliol about 1850. At that time, before society in Oxford was broken up into sets during the transitionary period of University reform, there were hardly any private dinners. Certain days each week were assigned in each College for inviting graduate friends from other Colleges to the high table. On the night in question I was dining with Jowett, and Max Müller with Walrond. Though the talk during dinner was not strictly literary, some point of literature turned up, and Müller's opinion on it was asked across the table by Walrond. Instantly there was silence among the twenty men at table. All listened to this stripling (as he appeared). Stanley, who was sitting next to me, and who had been discussing the memoir of Sterling, stopped and listened attentively. Müller replied to the question with great modesty, though with self-possession, and with a brevity which allowed conversation to flow back soon into its previous course. I instantly asked Jowett who he was, and learnt that he was a young German of great promise who had been in Oxford for about two years and was employed in editing the oldest Sanskrit literature. I name this as a sign of the profound respect which at so early a period was shown to him in an *élite* society like that of Balliol.'

Christmas of this year was spent in Oxford, though Bunsen had invited his young friend again to Totteridge, but Max had already promised Victor Carus that they should spend it together; and he tells his mother they had a tree, and gave each other many presents, and with Belle's assistance passed as happy an evening as they could with their thoughts far away in their German homes.

The year 1851 was the determining point of Max Müller's future life. Forced to continue his stay at Oxford, to print the *Rig-veda*, he found it necessary to have some other means of support than the *Veda* alone, in order to live the rather expensive life of a young man in Oxford society. This was found for him in the invitation to lecture in his friend Trithen's place. At first he was only asked to give two courses of lectures, but they were so well attended and made such an impression, that he was invited to continue his task, and was appointed Deputy Professor as soon as it became apparent that Trithen was hopelessly ill, and on his death was elected to succeed him in the Taylorian Professorship. The close of this year too saw his first connexion with the *Edinburgh Review*, and from this time on he added to his income by constant contributions to various periodicals in England and Germany, and some years later in America also.

About his article for the *Edinburgh* he writes to Bunsen :—

*Translation.* OXFORD, *January* 27, 1851.

'I have been waiting for Stanley's return, to talk to him about the article for the *Edinburgh*. He tells me he can write neither a head nor a tail to it: he thinks it wants no head, though a tail might perhaps be useful. Jowett and Morier have promised me to provide the perhaps needed additions; I think Stanley is too busy and has no time for it. If you agree to this, and will show me the friendly service of sending my MS. to Empson with a few words, the thing can perhaps be carried through, and I believe it will be of great use to me here in Oxford. My lectures are written, and your kindly advice as far as possible followed. Jowett is now Select Preacher, and preached an excellent sermon last Sunday. I hope he will publish it with the others. Even the heathen acknowledge it was beautiful language. Sir R. Inglis was present, but seemed little edified.'

To his mother he wrote the same day :—

*Translation.* OXFORD, *January* 27, 1851.

'I went to London lately to a party at Bunsen's, most interesting, where I met Macaulay, the historian and former Minister, Lord Mahon, Radowitz, and many other celebrities. Old Bunsen is always cheerful, and studies Egyptian and Chinese to drive politics out of his head. In a fortnight my lectures begin. I have only undertaken them for six months, but Bunsen persuades me strongly to remain, and I am thinking it over carefully. If I undertake it entirely I should have £400 a year for giving twenty-four lectures, and more than half the year vacation. I could go on with the *Veda*, and should have an income of about £600, with which one can live well in Oxford, and then you could come and pay me a visit for as long as you liked. But do not talk about it—it is all still uncertain, and I have not myself determined to take it, but would far rather be a Professor in Germany, if I could only at the same time carry on printing the *Veda*, for that is still my chief business. At all events, my prospects are not bad, and God will help me further. I have hired a piano again, though I have not much time for music, but my Oxford friends expect it, for they all like to listen, though few of them play.'

Of these early days and first lectures, Professor Cowell

(now Professor of Sanskrit at Cambridge) writes, December 24, 1900:—

'MY DEAR MRS. MAX MÜLLER,—It has occurred to me that I could not better illustrate Max Müller's influence on his contemporaries than by briefly describing his influence on my own career.

'I went up to Oxford as a married undergraduate in January, 1851. I had previously studied the classical Sanskrit poetry by myself, and I eagerly embraced the opportunity of reading with the Boden Professor. I used to go to his lodgings at the end of the High Street. It was on one of these afternoons that the Professor suddenly stopped our reading and said, "Dr. Max Müller is going to deliver his first lecture on Comparative Philology at two o'clock to-day; let us walk up to the Taylor Buildings and hear it." The lecture was a written one, and was delivered to a large and attentive audience, and to most of those present, as well as myself, it was an introduction to the new world of Comparative Philology. It was the first of a series of such lectures, all of which I carefully attended. After the lecture, Professor Wilson introduced me to the lecturer, who kindly invited me to take tea with him that evening. We soon became fast friends, and I found in him the very guide and counsellor that I needed. He was especially suited to inspire a younger student with enthusiasm. He soon discovered that I was fairly acquainted with the classical Sanskrit and its literature, but knew nothing of the grammarians, the commentators, or the *Rig-veda*; and he read with me some of the first volume, then just published, of his great edition of the *Rig-veda*.

'During the six years of my life at Oxford, Max Müller was my constant guide in my Sanskrit studies; he taught me to read Sâyana's Commentary and some of the philosophical works, but, above all, he imbued me with his own enthusiasm for Indian literature and his deep sympathy with the Hindu mind. When I went out to Calcutta in 1856 I tried to carry out many of his suggestions, and devoted my spare time to further studies on the lines which he had first pointed out to me; and my Brâhman pandits only carried on the work which he had commenced for me in Oxford.'

Mr. Tuckwell may again be quoted:—'I remember that Sir Thomas (then Mr.) Acland and I went together to Max Müller's opening lecture. Acland was disturbed, fidgeted, bit his nails—"It frightens one," he said. . . . I attended Müller's stimulating philological lectures, learning from his lips the novel doctrine of the Aryan migrations, and the rationale of Greek myths; the charm of his delivery heightened by a few Germanisms of pronunciation and terminology.' Mr. Story-Maskelyne writes of these early Oxford days:—

BASSET DOWN HOUSE, SWINDON, *October* 13, 1901.

'DEAR MRS. MAX MÜLLER,—In reply to your letter, I regret to tell you that I cannot put my hand on letters from Max. My acquaintance with him began almost immediately after my being called to Oxford to take the duties of one of the Chairs held by Dr. Buckland, at the time when his genial and energetic nature was clouded by mental failure. Max was summoned—I think in the same term as myself, in 1851—to fulfil the duties of the Chair of another Professor under a similar eclipse. My impression is that I first made his acquaintance at the house of Donkin, the Professor of Astronomy, a fine mathematician and scholar as well as musician; one, indeed, like Henry Smith, of those men of refined and beautiful nature that one meets only occasionally in the world, and who leave it too soon. There Max was at home. In that congenial atmosphere there also moved Carus, a physiologist and friend of Max. Often would he, a master of the violin, accompany Max, under whose hands the piano became a poem in music. I am no musician, but even to-day I can remember with enjoyment the dual music that Max and Carus used to produce; occasionally, too, in my own queer little rooms under the Ashmolean, where I retained a piano that would suggest this use of it.

'You know that Max and I were nearly of the same age, and I am now seventy-eight, with a memory, alas! no longer quick and vivid. The figure of Max is, however, never dimmed in my vision. Though near my age, I never looked on him as less than ten years older than myself, in wisdom, tact, experience of life, and knowledge of men. "Klug" was the term Bunsen applied to him, and though he seems from the beginning to have lived with the Olympians, whether intellectual or social, it was they who sought him rather, I think, than he who climbed into their company.

'He lived in those days in a little lodging in a terrace in the Banbury Road, with a little companion, Belle his dog. Many and many were the walks—*Oxonicè*, constitutionals—which we three had together in those years, 1851–7, and many of the interests of my later life had their germs planted then.

'Johnson, the Radcliffe Observer, was one of his Oxford friends. Frank Palgrave, Froude (of course), Morier were among the contemporaries outside of Oxford whom one met with him.

'Well do I remember his lectures. I think his first course[1] was on

[1] It was his second course.

the *Nibelungen-Lied.* They were given in the Taylor Building, and were remarkable in various ways. It was a new star in the Oxford firmament. Probably not half a dozen of his audience knew anything of the old epic or its history. Before the best of the men from the Common Rooms—a considerable gathering—stood the young German Professor, and the weird old tale, or redaction of old tales, he illuminated with side-lights from sagas and myths gathered from the folk-lore of Iceland and of Gamle Norge; and through the whole ran the sad refrain so often recurring in the rugged music of the poem. But for pure, terse English and luminous exposition I do not think any Oxford man—unless it was Church of Oriel (afterwards Dean of St. Paul's)—could have given such a course of lectures. It was a new light, a new idea of literature and lecture, that Max imported into the grey old walls of beautiful Oxford. Mr. Philip Pusey rode over all the way from his place near Faringdon with his boy-son to hear each lecture, an early homage to the rising fame of the redactor of the *Rig-veda.* I had to sit at the back of the audience, and to offer faithful criticism on idiomatic expression and on pronunciation. I had little to offer, though of course now and then Max's fine English touched an inexact note, more particularly in the latter difficulty. He received such criticisms with great kindness. But, in truth, the lectures were too interesting to allow of one's thinking of such very slight and by no means unpicturesque foils to them. Natural Science was not in high vogue then at Oxford, but the leaves on the trees were beginning to stir, so that when Max proclaimed his thesis that Comparative Philology and the historical development of language should rank with the Natural Sciences, there was a little rustle of scepticism, though in fact he was anticipating the assertion of evolution being the key to Natural Science.

'I should be tiring you—perhaps I may say any one *but* you—were I to continue reeling off these phonographs of a somewhat clouded memory. But these shadows of the past, as they seem to grow into images and visions, call for my pen to record them as they flit across my memory. Yours very truly,

'N. STORY-MASKELYNE.'

Max Müller's first course was on 'The History of Modern Languages,' in the Lent Term of 1851; his second on 'The Home of the Nibelungen'; and the third, in the Autumn Term, on 'The Origin of the Romance Languages.' The Science of Comparative Philology was then little known in England, and these lectures of the young foreigner struck a new, almost strange note, amid the classical studies of the old University, opening out a dim vista of life far older than the times of the Greeks and Romans, and of a language more perfect than Hebrew, and with which, as the elder sister of the Teutonic tongues, Englishmen ought to become better acquainted.

To HIS MOTHER.

*Translation.* OXFORD, *March* 13, 1851.

'My lectures are nearly at an end, and did very well. I had an audience of from fifty to seventy people, mostly Professors and tutors, and a number of ladies. I must prepare my course for next term, and I get no rest and the *Veda* gets on very slowly, and so my finances suffer. I have not yet decided whether I shall stay here. My friends persuade me to do so, but it has its difficulties and disagreeables, as no foreigner can have the position an Englishman would have. I shall quietly wait what comes, and if they make me a good offer take it; at all events, for the near future.'

The next day Max Müller writes to Bunsen:—

*Translation.* *March* 14, 1851.

'For some days I have been intending to write to you, to thank you warmly for your friendly recommendation of my article to Empson. I should like, as there is so much time, that Empson should return me the MS. to look through again, before it is printed. During my lectures some jokes have occurred to me, which appear to amuse John Bull, and which I should like to add. The lectures are nearly over; to-day is the last but one. They went off better than I expected. Many people took real interest in them.'

The same day Bunsen writes:—

*Translation.* LONDON.

'It is such a delight to be able at last to write to you, to tell you that few events this year have given me such great pleasure as your noble success in Oxford. The English have shown how gladly they will listen to something good and new, if any one will lay it before them in their own halls. Morier has faithfully reported everything, and my whole family sympathize in your triumph, as if it concerned ourselves.'

Through this vacation, Max Müller stayed quietly in Oxford to prepare his next lectures, and seems to have been far from well, suffering, as usual, from the Oxford climate. He writes to Dr. Pauli:—

*Translation.* *April*, 1851.

'I have long wanted to write to you, but I have been so unwell the whole time, that I could not manage it. Cold, cough, headache, and toothache are a quartette that makes one quite miserable; now I only have the solo of toothache, but that is enough to spoil life. I would willingly have gone to London, but I cannot now. I have lectures to write, &c. Have you got any treatise on the *Nibelungen* you can lend me?'

To CHEVALIER BUNSEN.

*Translation.* *April*, 1851.

'After the end of next term I hope to go to London, and there are many things that I wish to tell you, and consult about with you.

'I shall lecture this term on the *Nibelungen*, chiefly with reference to the Homeric question. For the relation of the poetical order to the legendary material I take *Firdusi*; for the fact of preservation in the memory, the *Mahâbhârata*; for the loss and historizing of the legend, Niebuhr's *Rome*; for the changing and misunderstanding of epic songs, the *Nibelungen* compared with the *Edda*. The whole is to be a continuation of comparative philology, brought about by the transition into the Epos, in its three grades of legends of Gods, Heroes, and Men.'

Yet, notwithstanding his hard work, Max Müller could write to Dr. Pauli:—

*Translation.* *May* 9.

'In spite of wind and weather we are very jolly, and play Beethoven trios, duets, and solos every evening, and two little singing birds from London have settled here, and so we *Mendelssohn* a good deal.'

To HIS MOTHER.

*Translation.* *June* 1.

'I am glad my lectures will soon be over, and that I shall then return to my regular work. I have again had a good audience, and people have shown great interest. How it will be later I do not know, and trouble myself but little about it. If the Professorship were definitely offered me, I would take it for five years. It is a pleasant position, and independent, and affairs in Germany are such, that I don't desire any Government appointment. But I shall not carry on the lectures provisionally, as they hinder me so much from my other work, and I can earn much more money by the *Veda*. If I could only send you something from time to time, that you might make your life a more comfortable one, but I have myself to be so very careful to manage to live here in Oxford, that I don't think I can take a journey in the vacation. I shall go to London when term is over, as Bunsen has invited me to his house, but I shall probably stay with Morier, where one feels freer. I have been up for the day to see the Exhibition, but it is quite impossible to give you the least idea of the impression this house of glass makes on one. I had lately a visit from the young Prince of Prussia [1], who came to Oxford, and I had to take him about the whole day. He seems to me very clever, very natural, has the greatest admiration for England, and is evidently in good hands. I do not envy him his future; he will have a difficult life, however happy and free from care it may now appear as he looks on. In the evening we dined together, and I accompanied him to the railway, where he took leave of me in the most hearty manner.'

In July Max Müller went to London to Morier, and tells his mother that he has been asked to continue his lectures with a higher salary as Deputy Professor, and that he has accepted. His health at this time was better, and his headaches less frequent, owing to a plan of treatment his doctor had adopted, so that he could work on with less interruptions. 'How much time would have been saved had I known of this medicine sooner!' He tried to persuade his mother to visit England this year to see the Exhibition, and assured her, if she would do so, he would be able in a year's time to repay her her expenses, though just at the moment he had no spare money.

From London Max Müller returned to Oxford, and then went to Wales to the Froudes', and from there writes to his mother:—

*Translation.* PLAS GWYNANT, *August* 21.

'I am staying with a friend whom I knew earlier in Oxford, Mr. Froude, a very gifted writer. He has written some novels which have made a great sensation in England. He has been married nearly two years; his wife is very highly educated and agreeable, and here they live among the mountains, and he enjoys the *dolce far niente*, fishing, shooting, riding, and writing. The situation of the house is perfect. . . . I shall stay here a fortnight. The only thing I miss is my beautiful piano, which I bought in London. It is a grand square by Collard, and by Neukomm's help, who is a great musician, I got

[1] The Emperor Frederick.

it for £50. It is in splendid tone, but is so large it could not be got up the staircase, but with great difficulty was hoisted through the window. You may now address me as Professor if you like, but not Professor and Doctor together.'

He says later: 'The time in Wales was delightful, and I was idle, which set me up.'

TO DR. PAULI.

*Translation.* OXFORD, *September*, 1851.

'A few days ago I found at the Bodleian the copy of *Alfred*[1] you sent there for me. My best thanks for it. I have only read a little of it, which interested me very much, especially the critique on Asser's *Gesta*. Do you really think that Asser wrote for his countrymen? If so, they must have been different fellows to the present Welsh, who really are more like Wallachians. I made acquaintance with them at Froude's, where they broke into the house at night, and we had to sleep with loaded pistols to make our lives safe. But notwithstanding I enjoyed myself there thoroughly. I bathed every morning in the waterfall, and all day long we walked, and fished, and shot. Snowdon is beautiful, and the lakes beyond description. When I have finished *Alfred* I shall send it to Froude, who will be delighted with it. He has, as you know, written the life of St. Neot in the *Lives of the Saints*, and does not trust Asser. He may be able to write a readable review on it. He is very happy with his wife and baby, and I would gladly have stayed longer, but it was so beautiful I could do no work. So here I am again in Oxford, busy with the *Veda* and lectures.'

On returning to Oxford he put the last touches to his review of Bopp's *Comparative Grammar*, which appeared in the October number of the *Edinburgh*. It excited considerable interest at the time, and many were the guesses made at the authorship, though probably there are not many now alive who remember reading it. Bunsen and Stanley and other valued friends wrote to congratulate. Bunsen says: 'Early this morning I read it through at last, and joyfully and heartily utter my *macte virtute*. Your examples and particularly your notes will help and please the English reader. The introduction is as excellent (*ad hominem* and yet dignified) as the end.' The end is perhaps one of the

[1] *Life of Alfred*, 1851.

most melodious paragraphs that Max Müller ever wrote. The article has never been reprinted. It ends thus:—

'And now that generations after generations have passed away, with their languages—adoring and worshipping the name of God—preaching and dying in the name of God—thinking and meditating on the name of God—there the old word stands still, breathing to us the pure air of the dawn of humanity, carrying with it all the thoughts and sighs, the doubts and tears, of our bygone brethren, and still rising up to heaven with the same sound from the basilicas of Rome and the temples of Benares, as if embracing by its simple spell millions and millions of hearts in their longing desire to give utterance to the unutterable, to express the inexpressible.'

In October Max Müller received a visit from Dr. Bernays, the eminent philologist, later Professor at Bonn, 'a very capable and delightful man,' and a very close friendship, as we shall see later from their constant correspondence, sprang up between the devout Jew and the young Professor.

To his Mother.

*Translation.* Oxford, *November* 16.

'My dear Mother,—I am well accustomed to decipher MSS., but still it is not a little labour to read your letters, especially when, like the last, they are written with more water than ink. If I could send you a bottle of good English ink, I would gladly do so. But I think if you look about in Dresden, you will be able to get some decent material for about a penny.

'I am not worrying my head with plans for the future, but let it go as it best may. I have not at all made up my mind to spend the rest of my life in Oxford, though I quite see it would be folly to turn away from the prospects opening for me here. But one misses a good deal here that one has in Germany, especially pleasant intercourse with learned men: for there is little talk here of literary work. If all is quiet, I thought of going in the vacation not only to Germany but to Italy—but this will be only if I continue to lecture in Oxford. If I do so, I must learn to talk Italian, and this one can only do in the country. But these plans are all vague—and who knows what may happen first? . . . We stand every moment in God's hands, and He knows best what is for our real welfare.

'Trust in God is the only happiness on earth: without that our whole life is but anxiety and care. . . . I send you £5 to buy Christmas presents for yourself and the Krugs.'

On December 4 Max Müller was made honorary M.A., and a member of Christ Church. He writes at once to tell his friend Dr. Pauli, and through him the Bunsens:

*Translation.* *December*, 1851.

'To-day I have been made member of a college, no less than Christ Church, where the Common Room is now the most agreeable. The old Dean performed the ceremony in the pleasantest way, and feels free from all scruples, because he has found a precedent in Graevius, who was made a member of Christ Church some hundreds of years ago. Without that he would hardly have given his consent! Happy old England! . . . I can hardly help laughing when the black gown flaps about my legs. But one gets accustomed to everything, and with each year one is older and more *middle-aged*—that is sad—but one cannot escape it here in Oxford.'

Of Max Müller's associates in Christ Church Common Room in the early fifties very few are left. Mr. Prout recalls Max's freshness and originality, which made him a very popular member of Common Room, and the genuine regret of the other members when the time came for him to leave, on his election as a Fellow of All Souls. And Dean Kitchin remembers how much he enlivened the party, and how he was 'always brimming over with good things.' The Dean had, however, known him earlier in his career in Oxford, and says: 'Max Müller left on me an enduring picture of himself—the young eager student, with his handsome face and sympathetic manner and bright, expressive eyes. He was then seeing his *Veda* through the Press. I remember how I with my German sympathies was attracted by his clever pianoforte playing—the Sanskrit I took for granted.'

# CHAPTER VIII

## 1852–1853

Member of Bavarian Academy. Summer in Germany. The Butlers. Arrival and baptism of Dr. Aufrecht. Essay on Turanian Languages for Bunsen. Visit to Scotland. First meeting with future wife. Missionary Alphabet.

ON February 2, 1852, Max Müller writes to his mother that he has just had the most agreeable surprise, having been elected a member of the Royal Bavarian Academy at the same time as Bunsen and Macaulay. Max had only just completed his twenty-eighth year, and to be elected with two such *confrères*, men whose names had been before the world when he was a mere student, was no slight compliment. He writes to Dr. Pauli:—

*Translation.* OXFORD, 1852.

'DEAR PAULI,—The Diploma from Munich has arrived safely; as I knew nothing about it, I was very much surprised. It must have been Bunsen's recommendation: I should like to know this that I may thank him. The news of Eliot Warburton's death touched me deeply, as we had seen him so lately, and well and happy.

His lectures during the first two terms of the year were on the 'History of German Literature in the Seventeenth Century,' and were well attended. These early lectures and his influence over his audience were described many years later by one of his hearers:—

'There has seldom been any one less like the typical German workman than Professor Max Müller. He is a marvellous example of how a foreigner may use the English tongue with more fluency and elegance than even the ordinary cultivated native; and how a man trained in other than English conditions may be all the better qualified to stimulate and instruct the English mind when he speaks its own familiar language. It is now more than half a century since he began to act as a fertilizing agency in what was then the rather arid field of English scholarship. His quick and sensitive intellect, so easily touched, so rapidly assimilative, had been moved on the philological side by men like Burnouf, on the philosophical by Schelling, and on the religious by Bunsen. And this combination of masters saved him from falling into the detached specialism which has been the note of so many German workmen, and supplied the sort of co-ordinating idealism which has been the mark of all his work. He had thus the instincts and training of the scholar, and also, in a rarer degree, the genius of the popular expositor. The quick and sensitive and assimilative qualities of his mind made him, especially in the earlier part of his career, all the more stimulative a teacher. He was a kind of prophet of the dawn, while as yet it was dark—i. e. he interpreted to the slow-paced English mind things especially touching language and religion which had never entered into its heart to conceive, but which had been exercising the higher scholarship and the newer philosophy of both Germany and France.'

One of the great pleasures of this year was the return of his old friend Mr. George Butler with his brilliant young wife to live in Oxford. Mrs. Butler was a very good musician, and the possessor of a fine grand pianoforte, and for the next five years, till the Butlers left Oxford, Max Müller was on the most intimate terms with them. Mrs. Butler recalls his gaiety, his readiness of repartee, his brilliant powers of conversation, his fresh, almost boyish enjoyment of everything: whilst the common bond of music drew them much together. Numerous were the excursions and picnics in which Max Müller took part with his friends, whose house was constantly full of young guests, sisters or other relatives of the Butlers. With the exception of Professor Donkin's family, and the Observer Manuel Johnson, there was no house in those days where Max felt so completely at home, or was so welcomed and liked by all the inmates.

Some years later Mrs. Méricoffre, Mrs. Butler's sister, wrote:—

'I recall one afternoon, a few days before the old Duke of Wellington's funeral, when we hunted Max Müller out of his Sanskrit den, and made him take a long walk with us. He bought some fresh eggs at a farm-house, and put them in the tail pockets of his coat. On returning we climbed some fences, and we sat upon some stiles, and on reaching home Müller found an extensive omelet in his pocket.'

But agreeable and bright as his life was at this time, which he fully recognized, the old longing for Germany constantly breaks out. 'I long so often to be back in Germany,' he writes to his mother, 'that if any sort of favourable prospect offered, I would willingly exchange my pleasant life in Oxford for a simple German *ménage*.'

To F. Palgrave, Esq.

9, Park Place, *March* 21, 1852.

'I was at your gate on Saturday afternoon as I had written to you the day before. I was very sorry to have missed you, and still more when I heard the sad reason[1] which kept you at home. It is the hardest trial which we have to go through, I think—at least there is nothing which I dread so much. I feel for you and with you more than I can say; however, nothing strengthens our hope of meeting again as much as the loss of those we love. Oxford has been very quiet, and I have been hard at work on the *Veda* as my lectures did not give me much trouble. The English book has been stopped, but it will be finished before the Long. In summer I hope to go to Germany, but I have a good deal to do before I go. . . . Jowett is hard at work, and has finished the Romans. Stanley lives with Conington, and writes reports in the tower at University. Whenever you are back at Kneller Hall, I hope to pay you a visit, unless you prefer to come to Oxford.'

Max allowed himself only a day or two of holiday in the Easter Vacation. 'I feel that every day I waste now, I lose a day of my summer holiday,' and as his headaches were less frequent and also less severe when he did have them, he could work on vigorously. He tells his mother that he means to be thoroughly idle in Germany and amuse himself. He will not visit either Leipzig or Berlin. He writes:—

*Translation.* *April* 18, 1852.

'I am nowhere so happy as in Dessau. You will laugh at this, but had you been living for six or seven years among strangers you would understand how delightful it is to see well-known faces and well-known streets and houses round one. If I had independent means, I would live in Dessau, and by choice in my grandfather's house with the garden, where I know every tree. If we stay some time there in the vacation, I had rather not stay the whole time with my uncle. Perhaps we could take some rooms, or live in the hotel?'

[1] His mother's dangerous illness.

In June he writes like a schoolboy expecting his holidays: 'the joy of meeting makes up for the long separation, and, as old Goethe says, it is not necessary to be always together to remain united.' He had to take his part in the Grand Commemoration of that year, and a few pages of *Veda* to finish, and then he was free. On June 14 he writes to his mother:—

*Translation.*

'You will have heard the sad news of Burnouf's death. In him I have lost a good friend, and the loss to literature is irreparable. Many of his books remain unfinished, and as there is no good Sanskrit scholar in Paris, I have half promised his friends to go there to advise with them about his library and MSS. It may be this will only be later, when the Will is known. He leaves a widow and four daughters. But I should only have to spend a day or two there, and should be glad if it could be on my return journey.'

Early in July, Max Müller left England, joined his mother at Dresden, where his friend Palgrave met him for a time but was summoned back to England by his mother's increased illness, and after a visit to his sister at Chemnitz took his mother to Carlsbad, and from there he made an excursion to Munich and the beautiful scenery of the Salzkammergut. From Munich, after many hours in the Pinakothek, he writes to his mother:—

*Translation.*

'I am more than ever convinced that the Italian, Spanish, and French schools together are not so fine, and true, and strengthening, as the old German and Dutch schools. J. van Eyck, Hans Hemling, Rembrandt, Dürer, even Holbein and Cranach, were very fine. The Raphaels, Andrea del Sarto, Palma Vecchio, Perugino, . . . Leonardo, &c., are also wonderful, but they make so much parade of their art, and they are more bent on showing how beautifully they can paint, whilst the Germans just paint away because their heart is in it.'

He had plenty of time to visit all the beauties of Munich, as he was detained there several days through some difficulty about his passport for Austria, as he intended to visit the Tyrol. It must have been during this visit to the Tyrol that he found himself in great danger. After a long lonely day on foot he arrived late at a most forbidding-looking little inn, but it was too late to go further. The people of the inn were rude and evil-looking, and he was thankful to be able to barricade his door with a heavy piece of furniture. The door was twice attempted in the night. In the morning he found that the only guide to be had over a lonely road was a surly-looking man, but he made the guide keep in front of him the whole way, and was himself armed with a strong walking-stick. He always said that had he shown the least fear the man would have attacked him. It must be remembered that in 1852 the Tyrol was less explored and known than it is now.

On rejoining his mother they spent some happy weeks together, and Max returned to Oxford by Leipzig and Berlin, visiting many old friends. He tells his mother on his arrival in Oxford:—

*Translation.*

'One cannot always have such a happy time as I spent this summer. I cannot tell you how comfortable I was this time at home, but I will not complain, but only hope that it will be so again another time, if God wills. We owe to Him all the good that befalls us, and what He orders is best. Take care of yourself, and don't be unhappy, all goes with us so much better than we deserve, and than with many others. The recollection of all the happiness is a comfort too, and never has the recollection of our time together been so bright and undisturbed as this time. You were so good to me, my dear mother. I would willingly live in Dresden, but as that cannot be, you must come to Oxford when the weather is fine.'

To F. Palgrave, Esq.

9, Park Place, *October* 22, 1852.

'I need not tell you how I felt your loss. I should like to shake your hand—but these losses must be borne in silence. Do come to Oxford if you can, and let us talk about our little expedition to Dresden. I had such a pleasant journey afterwards to Carlsbad, the Tyrol, Salzburg, Munich—how I wished you had been with me. As to art, Munich beats everything, and the people are so much nicer, much more genial than at Berlin. Their beer is excellent, and it makes them good-natured. And such pictures, particularly from the German school . . . you must go there next year, I am sure you will be delighted. That old king was after all a great genius, whatever Lola may say of him, and however bad his poems and his prose may be. Walrond is going away; Conybeare going to be married; Morier going to Australia: so one begins to feel alone, and that is bad, and the only thing to be done is to work. Please remember me kindly to Temple.'

His lectures this term were on the 'Classification of Languages,' but he had hardly began them before he was again laid up from Oxford fogs and damp.

*November*, 1852.

'Dear Mrs. Butler,—It is very kind of you to cheer me up from time to time with kind inquiries, good admonitions, dear messages, and other how-do-you-do varieties. I wish I could return thanks myself, but in this weather the doctor tells me I must not go out for a week. I am quite resigned to my fate, and begin to understand what it means that you are nowhere freer than in prison. I read and write, and get a good deal of work done, which has been weighing heavily on my conscience for some time. I need not go out and eat many dinners, or make many calls. I can smoke without fear of detection. I get my friends one by one to see me and talk to me, which is so much better than if you have them all at once. I need not deliver lectures; altogether I am as happy as mortal man can be with November fogs and earthquakes all around him, not to mention gout, rheumatism, sore throats, and divers kinds of diseases to plague him. . . . Thomson asks me to write him an article on Indian Logic for the third edition of his *Laws of Thought*, which I am doing just now;—and here I was interrupted by Miss Grey's visit, and could not even go downstairs to speak to her, for I am so thoroughly Germanized in appearance that I must not show myself to any lady, and here a visit, so I must give it up for to-day, and remain yours truly, M. M.'

This attack of illness determined him to follow the advice Bunsen had long given him, and take an assistant for the more mechanical part of his Vedic work. Bunsen seems to have mentioned Dr. Aufrecht from Berlin to him. Max Müller entered into negotiations with Dr. Aufrecht, who arrived in Oxford in December. Early in that month Max writes to Bunsen:—

'. . . I expect Aufrecht daily. You have always advised me to seek help, and I could no longer get through my work alone, with the many interruptions caused by my health. Aufrecht is a very conscientious scholar, and as far as the rest goes that will all be right.'

Max Müller writes to his mother telling her of the new arrangement:—

*Translation.* *December* 19.

'Dr. Aufrecht is a very clever man, a Sanskritist, &c. We work together, and he helps me at my *Veda*, for which I pay him enough to live here. We shall try the plan at first for six months, and I hope it will all go well. It is very pleasant for me to have some one with whom I can talk about literary things, and my time is so filled up that I am very glad to have some one to whom I can leave part of my work: but I must wait awhile to see how it works, and whether it brings me in as much as it costs. I must spend Christmas in Oxford, as I cannot well leave him alone. The weather is dreadful, and I have constant headaches, mostly from severe colds. Otherwise I have got quite accustomed again to the English way of living, and if I would often rather find myself in Germany, you know it is not my way to grumble. We must take life as God sends it, and it would be ungrateful did I not acknowledge the many comforts I have here, and only dwelt on what I miss.'

Aufrecht lived in the same house with his employer.

The following letter alludes to the book known as Church's *Essays and Reviews*, a title that had not then become notorious:—

9, PARK PLACE, *December* 22, 1852.

'MY DEAR PALGRAVE,—I thought you would be sure to come to Oxford for the Exeter College election, else I should have written to you before this, and asked whether you would put your name to a testimonial which we intend to present to Church. You know he is going to leave Oxford, and take a small living to marry. Some of his friends are going to ask him to allow them to print a selection of his articles—not theological—and to make him a present of the whole edition. We have already a large subscription, about forty names. The subscription will be £3. Please tell me whether you wish your name to be added. Acland, Donkin, Butler, Marriott, &c., take great interest in the matter, but until the whole expense is secured by subscription, it must not be talked about. If you can get some of your friends to join, please write to them. Grant and Sellar have been written to, and have sent their subscriptions. You know probably that Sewell is going to leave Oxford. Why do you never write? Have you heard from Froude? He is staying at his father's, and very happy.'

The early part of this Christmas Vacation was spent by Max Müller in Oxford, in order to initiate his secretary Aufrecht in the work he had to do. The great floods of 1852 had left the place in a very unhealthy state, and before his lectures began again his friends the George Butlers, who were spending the vacation with their father Dean Butler at

Dover, asked him to pay them a visit there. On his return he writes:—

To Mrs. Butler.

9, Park Place, *January*, 1853.

'I have not had a quiet minute since I came back; there was a friend from Germany waiting to be lionized all over Oxford: then all sorts of people who came to vote, and at the same time to walk and talk: then Aufrecht with lots of questions: then dinner-parties again: and letters to answer, and proofs to correct. I really wish I could sport my oak like an undergraduate, and have done with the world altogether, at least for an hour or two, that I might be able to tell you how much I enjoyed my trip to Dover, and how happy I felt among people who seemed all to be so very happy themselves. Please to translate into as good English as possible my best thanks to the Dean and Mrs. Butler. I am glad to hear that you have had a few fine days; the weather is getting better at Oxford also. As to the floods, they will not be gone before March, but the late storms have made the atmosphere quite healthy again. I do not know anything about the election; in fact, I have not seen a paper since I came back. Belle is in the most flourishing condition, so Oxford cannot be such an unhealthy place after all.'

To his Mother.

*Translation.* Oxford, *January* 30, 1853.

'... My lectures begin next week, and give me a good deal of work; and then I was away for a week at Dover. Dover was beautiful, especially in the storms. The waves almost beat on my windows. From the *land* a stormy sea looks grand. I would willingly have stayed on, but I could not leave my house companion longer alone. He is a capable man, but a little difficult to get on with. At present he takes up a good deal of my time, as I must tell and explain everything to him; but I think later he will be an advantage. I must give more time to my lectures, for England expects every man to do his duty. I do not worry about money, and would rather live more economically than let my work suffer. ... I often feel now how much time I lost from my work during my long holiday last year—that must not happen again, life is not long enough for such pauses—and yet when I am with you I always think, "You can make up the time afterwards in your work; enjoy the time together as long as you can." ... We have had a great business here with the Parliamentary election. Gladstone, who was elected, and is now Chancellor of the Exchequer, was here on a visit a few days ago. I have seen and talked with him several times; he is an interesting man, and a very good speaker.'

To Chevalier Bunsen.

*Translation.* 9, Park Place, *February* 2, 1853.

'I get on better with Aufrecht, but not so very well yet. He decidedly desires to be baptized, but he does not feel inclined to talk to others on this point or anything connected with it.

'It is possible that when he has once taken this step he may get to feel more inner satisfaction and confidence in friends, which is prevented now by morbid impressions and imaginations. I am convinced he is a true and honest soul, but he is unsympathetic. His knowledge is thoroughly sound and comprehensive. He works well, and he seems to like his position, as he desires to stay in England. But there can be no question about working *together*, for as soon as one presses him a little hard he draws his head into his shell like a tortoise, and one must then leave him alone. But I still hope that in time things will take a better shape, as they are already far better than they were at first.'

The Deputy Professor was to lecture this term on 'Declension,' and so popular were his lectures, that he had a large proportion of ladies among his audience, a greater proportion than was convenient in a small lecture-room, and on being asked by a rather pompous Don what the title of his lectures meant exactly, he was ungallant enough to reply, 'I wish it might mean that I decline ladies!' This must have got abroad, to judge from the next letter to Bunsen:

*Translation.* 9, Park Place, *February* 19, 1853?

'... I am very well now and very happy. Aufrecht begins to "thaw." My time is almost entirely taken up with my lectures, which for the first time give me great pleasure. I have fifty hearers, all undergraduates, and many of them capable and industrious men. I write nothing, but speak extempore to them, and I feel that I can be really useful to them. My former hearers were mostly curious and suspicious Dons, and I got tired of writing rhetorical essays to be read to them. Now everything gets into much better shape, and I only hope that next term I may receive my definite appointment. I have now got to the old Latin inscriptions, *Columna Rostrata*, &c., and it is incredible how little one can rely upon copies; in almost every edition you find inaccuracies and variations. If only somebody would at last give exact facsimiles.'

A day or two later he writes again to Bunsen, in answer to a letter advising him to give a course of lectures on Greek Literature :—

*Translation.*

'I shall have finished my lectures in about a fortnight. The holidays will only last three weeks, then lectures begin again. I dare hardly venture to undertake a course on Greek literature, for my subject must always be more or less in connexion with modern languages. This is possible with titles like "declension," "conjugation," &c., including a few words about modern formations, and then concentrating on Greek, Latin, and Sanskrit. But "history of Greek literature" would hardly fit into anything. I shall hope to continue next term my lectures on Declension, and to prepare lectures on Italian Ethnology. One has to read up what is fit for the examination; and the population of Italy according to Livy and Niebuhr belongs to the standing questions. I am getting on better and better with Aufrecht, and I hope in time we shall get on capitally.'

To his Mother.

*Translation.* Oxford, *March* 5, 1853.

'The uncertain weather we are having in Oxford is very unhealthy. And yet I feel better than I have felt for a long time, and my work gets on well. I do not know what the papers have been saying again about me. My position has not as yet changed in the least, but I hope to get my full salary in October. The uncertainty is unpleasant, but I shall not starve, and everything else can be borne! My assistant costs a good deal, but that will in time be repaid, and his company, at least for literary discussion, is very useful. Of course there are many difficulties, but in time they will be set right. I correspond pretty regularly with Bunsen; he writes one book after another, but writes too much and too quickly. The events in Milan are terrible. But how can the Austrians imagine that England will interfere? That England will never give up a political refugee is well understood. England has always been a refuge for dethroned kings and popular leaders, and the English would rather go to war than give up their right.'

In accordance with Dr. Aufrecht's own wishes about his baptism, Bunsen suggested that his eldest son, the Rev. Henry Bunsen, Rector of Lilleshall, should receive him, and perform the ceremony in his own parish church. This scheme was carried out. On his return Max Müller writes:—

*Translation.* 9, Park Place, *April* 3, 1853.

'Your Excellency,—We have passed the Easter holidays most agreeably at Lilleshall, and I, as well as Aufrecht, am most grateful to you for the great help you have given us in this somewhat difficult matter. Nowhere could the act have been performed so simply, so solemnly, and so undisturbedly as by your son at Lilleshall. The friendly welcome we received has not missed its impression upon Aufrecht, and I hope that in future matters will improve with him more and more . . .'

To his mother he writes:—

*Translation.* *April.*

'I would gladly go with you to Carlsbad, but after careful consideration I see that it is impossible for me to leave my work this year for the whole summer. I have begun several things which have been on my conscience for several years, and I owe it to myself to finish them; and this I can only do here in England, and in the Long Vacation. And now I am busy with my lectures, and the decision as to my full salary occupies my time too. I have indeed a fair prospect that there will be no opposition; but of course there is a prejudice against a foreigner, and I must do my best to keep all straight.'

On May 12 Bunsen wrote to urge Max Müller to join him at St. Leonards, but the Taylorian Professorship was vacant, and it was necessary to be on the spot.

To Chevalier Bunsen.

*Translation.* 9, Park Place, *May* 15, 1853.

'The business is more complicated than I expected, and the steering more difficult the nearer one approaches the harbour. I am prepared for disappointment, but do not give up hope. The new difficulties arise from the fact that the Curators are intending to raise the salary considerably: this would be delightful, if I already had the appointment, but now it brings other interests into play, and entices others to stand as candidates. But still my prospects are good, and my opponents have but one card to play, that they are Englishmen, I not. In Oxford the tables won't dance. I have wasted some hours in trying my hand at it, but the whole thing seems perfectly useless, especially as it is purely mechanical.

'Aufrecht is going on all right—he does not wish to return to Germany.'

Bunsen wrote cheerily in reply, and says he had written to his 'brotherly friend Pusey' (the squire) to help in the canvass. 'I know few men so able to give good advice; besides, he is very much attached to you.'

To the Same.

*Translation.* 9, Park Place, *May* 28, 1853.

'Contrary to my expectations, my affairs get more hopeless and involved. The Curators have at last had a meeting, and settled to postpone the election till after the Long Vacation. It is a hard trial of one's patience, especially as it is still uncertain whether my election may not after all be opposed, and I should then have lost four years' time and work. For three years I have laid all aside, and given my whole time to this office. I felt *Spartam nactus es, hanc exorna*, and if I had thus provided for my material wants for the rest of my life, I could well be satisfied, and should have had time and leisure to make up what I had lost. Now I really don't know what to do, and whether it is not best to return to Germany and finish up and publish what I have already done on the *Veda*. My friends advise me to stay on here, and they assure me Convocation would veto the election of any one else, if the Curators attempted it. For myself, I am almost indifferent. I shall probably have another year of this uncertainty, of which I have had enough in the past three years. However, such is the world, says John Bull, and tries to console himself. I am doing my best to follow his good advice.'

To this Bunsen replied :—

*Translation.* *May* 30.

'It is a great trial of patience, but *be* patient, that is *wise*. One must never allow the toilsome labour of years of quiet reflection and of utmost exertion for the attainment of one's aim to be destroyed by an unpropitious event. It is most probably the best for you that the affair should not now be hurried through. Your claims are stronger every quarter, and will certainly become more so in the eyes of the English through good temper and patience under trying circumstances. I don't for a moment doubt that you will be elected. Germany would suit you now as little as it would suit me, and we both should not suit Germany. So patience, my dear friend, and with a good will.'

Early in May, Bunsen had written to Max Müller asking his help in the work then occupying all his leisure time and thoughts, 'The Philosophy of Universal History applied to Language and Religion,' being Volumes III and IV of *Christianity and Mankind*. Bunsen says :—

'In working over the historical part I put aside a chapter, "The Primitive Languages in India," but find out, just as I intended to make you the *heros eponymus*, that you only dealt in your lecture (before the British Association) with Bengali. . . . Could you not write a little article on this for my book? The original language in India *must* have been Turanian, not Semitic; but we are bound in honour to prove it.'

This invitation led to the pamphlet *On the Turanian Languages*, which is now out of print as a separate publication, but it forms, under the title, 'Last Results of the Turanian Researches,' the second half of the third volume of Bunsen's *Christianity and Mankind*, and though not published till 1854, owing to incessant delays in printing, was almost entirely written in 1853, and involved a constant correspondence with Bunsen through the rest of this year. It is many years since Max Müller gave up most of the views enunciated in his essay on the Turanian languages of India, views which were disproved as these languages were more fully known and studied. The concluding paragraph is perhaps worth quoting as applicable to all linguistic studies :—

'And now, if we gaze from our native shores over that vast ocean of human speech, with its waves rolling on from continent to continent, rising under the fresh breezes of the morning of history, and slowly heaving in our own more sultry atmosphere, with sails gliding over its surface, and many an oar ploughing through its surf, and the flags of all nations waving joyously together, with its rocks and wrecks, its storms and battles, yet reflecting serenely all that is beneath and above and around it; if we gaze and hearken to the strange sounds rushing past our ears in unbroken strains, it seems no longer a wild tumult, but we feel as if placed within some ancient cathedral, listening to a chorus of innumerable voices; and the more intensely we listen, the more all discords melt away into higher harmonies, till at last we hear but one majestic trichord, or a mighty unison, as at the end of a sacred symphony.

'Such visions will float through the study of the grammarian, and in the midst of toilsome researches his heart will suddenly beat, as he feels the conviction growing upon him, that men are brethren in the simplest sense of the word—the children of the same father—whatever their country, their colour, their language, and their faith.'

This was the year of Lord Derby's installation as Chancellor of the University, and Max Müller resolved to take refuge from all the gaieties with Bunsen, who had long been pressing him to come to Carlton Terrace.

Besides the treatise on the Turanian or nomadic languages of India, Bunsen asked his help in tracing the relationship of the Vedic language with Zend, urging him to gather the results of his investigations into a separate chapter.

TO CHEVALIER BUNSEN.

*Translation.* 9, PARK PLACE, *July* 3, 1853.

'When you spoke to me in London about printing your work on Egypt, you told me that you expected my contribution in September. I therefore began at once to arrange and carry out the part with regard to the comparison of Egyptian and Aryan roots. The work requires great care, and if the essay is to be printed just as I write it, and under my responsibility, I cannot really promise its completion *before* September. The relation between Egyptian and Aryan is much like that which would exist between Sanskrit and French, did we not possess the connecting links. *Mère*, *père*, *frère*, and *sœur*, set against *mâtar*, *pâtar*, *bhrâtar*, and *svastar*, show a systematic parallelism and a common origin. But if one had to compare Sanskrit *aśru* with *larme*, how could one prove their identity without the connecting links? Well, I will try, but it is quite impossible for me to solve the problem so quickly. Also in the matter of the relation of the Zend and Vedic peoples I will gladly formulate and prove the conclusions at which I have arrived, but I am a slow coach, and fear accidents in an express train. I hope, especially if there is no war, that you may have so many diplomatic occupations, that I may be ready before *Egypt* comes to be printed. I work every day at the Bodleian from nine till four, at the catalogue of the Sanskrit MSS.; then I am printing the preface to the second volume of the *Veda*, which is ready: then I am writing a treatise on the burning of bodies in the *Veda*, which is nearly ready (widows were not burnt). Then comes the essay for Lepsius on the Indian alphabet. Then the first volume of the Prolegomena must be printed before the end of the vacation; and lastly comes a course of lectures for next term. Where am I to find time without robbery? Professor Stenzler, of Breslau, is now here, a very capable man of the last generation, but who advances with modern progress, and has taken refuge from Alexander's *India* in Vedic antiquity. He is Weber's teacher.'

TO CHEVALIER BUNSEN.

*Translation.* PARK PLACE, *July* 7, 1853.

'I am sorry that I must again trouble you for an explanation as to the extent, as well as the sort of essay, on the original inhabitants of India and the Zend emigrants. You write that it is for your philosophical work. Is that "The Prophets" which I saw when I was in London, or is it an addition to the philosophical Aphorisms of Hippolytus? If it is for the Aphorisms, it ought to fill a couple of pages at most; but if it is for the great work on the "History of the World," it must be much more diffuse. Or is it another book at which you are working?'

It is not surprising that Max Müller was puzzled by the multiplicity of Bunsen's works, for nearly all of which he asked for help from his young friend. At this time he was expecting immediately three separate papers from Max Müller—on the *Zend Avesta*, the *Rig-veda*, and the Turanian languages of India, and later in the year Bunsen hoped for a linguistic chapter for his work on Egypt.

On July 11 Max Müller sent Bunsen the chapter on Persian Researches which will be found on p. 110 of Volume III, *Christianity and Mankind*, and which was reprinted in the original edition of *Chips*, Volume I, but was omitted in the last edition as 'not up to date.' On July 13 Bunsen writes:—

'"What one desired in youth one obtains in old age." I felt this as I read your chapter yesterday. It is exactly what I first wished to know myself in order to tell it to my readers. You have done it after my own heart—only a little too briefly, for a concluding sentence on the connexion of the language of the Achaemenian Inscriptions with Zend is wanting.'

On July 30 he writes to his mother:—

*Translation.*

'Sunday is my best day for letter-writing. During the week work goes on from early till late, and my head is so full of Sanskrit I feel quite stupified. I am very glad I stayed here this summer. I had so many books to read and work through, for which I have no time in my lectures, and yet one must keep up with literature, or one would have to sing, like the Austrian militiamen, "Immer langsam voran." That it was hard to give up my plans for travelling, you can believe; but one must remember the duties as well as the enjoyments of life, and so we will look forward to next year, when, please God, we shall be together. I am very well, and the harder I work the better I feel.'

At this time, when his old friend Carus was about to be married, he writes to his mother, who was always exhorting him to follow so good an example, 'I have not yet any plans of the sort. I think one has trouble enough in making one's own way through the world. If such a thing presents itself—well; but I have no wish to take much trouble in looking about.'

Max Müller writes to Bunsen for his birthday:—

*Translation.* 9, PARK PLACE, *August* 24.

'First of all I wish you joy of this day with all my heart. May this day often return to you in the midst of all your dear ones, and in the full tide of all your work and labour. If to grow a year older means to have completed a new work, we can stand the growing older very well—it is not then a growing older; but it is growing, working, and getting young again, and our strength grows with every year that has been made use of, and with every work that has been completed. A fresh and powerful Senatus is after all the real strength of a country, the real support of the *res publica* in politics as well as in spirit. The Juventus is too much occupied with itself, and youth is often more hindering than useful when it comes to losing sight of oneself as much as possible. Allow me to continue to find courage and counsel with you, and have patience with a passenger who would like best to sit still in the carriage corner, and though not asleep would fain close his eyes till he has arrived at the last station.'

The sad tone of the last sentence is fully accounted for in the next letter to Bunsen, written the end of August:—

*Translation.* *August* 28.

'I feel what the English call knocked up, and I must get some fresh air before I can get to work again. You shall receive an essay on Vedic Antiquity from Wales, where I go to-morrow. It is possible that there may be, among the Persians, people or even races whose forefathers were Turanian or Semitic, but they acquired Persian just as the Normans acquired Saxon, and the Persian language has always remained the same. If it comes to classification of languages, it does not depend on who *speaks* the languages, just as little as a botanist troubles himself to know whether a potato has grown in Europe or America. I always use the term Aryan instead of Indo-European, Iranian only for Persian and Median. Both together I take as the South-Aryan branch, in contrast to all the rest of the Aryans who turned to the north-west. The collection of Hymns of the *Rig-veda* was completed towards 1000 B.C. That cannot of course be proved like $2+2=4$, but it is as sure as all our knowledge of these times can be. I enclose a sample translation which is to find a place in the *Veda* article: do you know of a poet who could Miltonize it a little more? He must add nothing however, for so far the translation is literal, as far as this is possible with the old thoughts.'

Max Müller went to the Froudes' in Wales, but his enjoyment of this visit was spoilt by the weather. He tells his mother it rained day and night, and the mountains were too wet for any expeditions. On his return to Oxford he writes to Bunsen:—

*Translation.* OXFORD, *September* 21, 1853.

'I returned yesterday. My holiday was longer than I expected, and I hasten to send you the introduction to the Aryan chapter. I went first to Wales to Froude, who is very well, and hard at work. He has just published an article on John Knox in the *Westminster*. In the next number there will be an article on Job, and in the *Edinburgh* one on Spinoza. From Wales I went to Glasgow, where I stayed in Calder Park near the city with my friend Walrond. With him I made excursions to Oban and Ardtornish, then to Inverary, Loch Lomond, the Trossachs, and back to Glasgow, then to Edinburgh. The scenery was beautiful, and the fine air very enjoyable, and I hope my work will go on all the better for it.'

The expedition to Ardtornish, to stay with the parents of their old friend W. Sellar, nearly proved fatal to Max Müller and Theodore Walrond. They crossed from Oban, and a sudden storm coming up, the row-boat in which they were was in great danger. The crew, who only spoke Gaelic, to quiet their fears, imbibed so much whisky that they seemed incapable of managing the boat, and both Max and his friend had to lend a hand at the oars. But they were well repaid on their arrival by the beauty of the scenery round Ardtornish, and the next morning, the sea being calm, Max Müller, who was all his life a good swimmer, ran down to the beach for a dip. Putting his things, as he thought, in safety under some stones, he enjoyed his bath to the full. But he had not calculated on the force of the wind, and on emerging from the waves he found his clothes scattered far and wide, and some gone for ever. The stony beach was covered with a sort of prickly growth, probably a sea-holly, and the search was long and painful, and resulted in the recovery of only a few necessary garments. In this guise he had to make his way back to the house, the hall of which was used for breakfast, and where the family were already assembling. He used to say, in recounting the story, that the horror of the moment always came back upon him in full force.

On September 24 Bunsen writes:—

'You have sent me the most beautiful thing you have yet written. I read your *Veda* essay yesterday, first to myself and then to my family circle, including Lady Raffles your great friend *in petto*, and we were all enchanted with both matter and form.'

The article of which Bunsen speaks will be found on p. 128 of Volume III, *Christianity and Mankind*, and was republished in *Chips*, Volume I, original edition, but like the Persian chapter was omitted in the last edition. In diction it well deserves the praise bestowed on it by Bunsen.

We constantly at this time, in his letters to Bunsen, find Max Müller complaining of the dilatoriness and carelessness of even the best London printers, as compared with the University Press at Oxford. In the latter years of his life he would consent to print nowhere else.

The lectures this term were on 'The Origin of the Romance Languages,' and he tells Bunsen his 'audience is larger than ever.' How he managed to get through all his work is a marvel, for besides his lectures, his Vedic work, the Turanian article for Bunsen, and a new work forced on him by his indefatigable friend, of which we shall hear presently, he was collecting testimonials for the Curators of the Taylor Institution, who had definitely fixed the election to the Professorship for the beginning of the January Term. Meantime they had been so satisfied with the result of the lectures, that, as he tells his mother, he is already receiving this quarter the full salary. The testimonials, the originals of which must ever be a precious treasure for his children, are from Humboldt, Bunsen, Bopp, Lepsius, Canon Jacobson (later Bishop of Chester), W. Thomson (later Archbishop of York), Mr. Jowett, Professors Wilson and Donkin. Mr. Jowett says of him, 'There are few persons in whom so much judgement is combined with so much imagination. It would be unnecessary to add, except to those who do not know him, that, during his stay at Oxford, he has been universally beloved and respected.' Mr. Donkin says, 'He can be elementary without being (in the bad sense) popular, and scientific without ceasing to be intelligible and interesting to beginners.'

And now we come to an event that was to alter and influence the whole remainder of Max Müller's life, though for several years to come the outer tenor of it may have seemed unchanged, and only one or two intimate friends knew the influence at work within him. On November 26 Max and his future wife met for the first time at her father's house. Mr. Froude, her uncle by marriage, had often spoken of his clever young German friend, and his brother-in-law asked him to bring Max Müller for a Saturday to Monday visit. Years after, he told her that as soon as he saw her, he felt, 'That is my fate.' The party assembled at Ray Lodge was a pleasant one, and he at once fascinated all present by his brilliant, lively conversation and exquisite music. He was very dark, with regular features, fine bright eyes, and a beautiful countenance full of animation, and it was difficult to reconcile his youthful appearance with his already great reputation. Two days later they met again, this time at Oxford, where the family from Ray Lodge went for a meeting of the leading Church choirs of the Diocese. Max Müller was their constant guide, and Magdalen, Merton, Christ Church, the Bodleian, &c., were visited in his company. He was asked to spend Christmas at Ray Lodge, but fealty to Bunsen and the work he was engaged in for him kept him at Oxford.

To Chevalier Bunsen.

*Translation.* Oxford, *December* 9, 1853.

'I gladly accept your invitation for next Tuesday (to meet Kingsley), and I hope by then the first half of my essay will be printed. Aufrecht is very busy. A week ago he left this house and has taken a lodging for himself. He feels more independent, and I too feel more free. I wish one could find a secure place for him. He has been a year here, and I have never seen a man so totally changed, and certainly only for the better.'

It was almost at the close of the year that Bunsen asked Max Müller to help him in a scheme which was occupying his own mind a good deal, i.e. a Uniform Alphabet to be used by missionaries in reducing languages to writing for the first time. Lepsius had been occupied with this problem for some time, but his alphabet seemed too complicated for cheap printing. Max Müller at once took up the subject, and so hard did he work that his pamphlet, *Proposals for a Uniform Missionary Alphabet*, was ready to lay before the first conference held on the subject at Bunsen's house early in January, 1854. Max Müller's alphabet was very simple, employing italics for the modifications of the usual alphabet, whereas Lepsius's plans represented these modifications by signs, in some cases as many as three, over each letter. In one letter to Bunsen, Max Müller says, 'If we come to a common understanding with regard to the thirty-five definable consonants, and the twelve to fourteen vowels, let us thank God.' And again, 'If conferences are first to be held, I think it would be best I should not appear, but ask you to play the part of pleader. I have spoilt so many things through undue eagerness, that I prefer managing everything by writing. But I await your orders. If my proposals are not likely to be accepted, it is not worth the trouble of printing. If it is accepted, I am ready to publish them in golden letters on parchment! I promise Lepsius that if his alphabet is accepted, I will not print a word but in that, even if each letter has three accents.' So carefully and thoroughly did Max Müller go into the whole question, that he spent several days dissecting throats with Dr. Acland. 'I could give the whole alphabet anatomically drawn,' he says.

In the *Life of Baron Bunsen* we find some extracts from the diary of one of his daughters:—

'To breakfast came Sir C. Trevelyan, Sir J. Herschell, Mr. Arthur, Professor Owen, afterwards Mr. Venn and several missionaries and men of learning, to take part in the long-planned conference on the comparative merits of two systems of transcription for all alphabets. According to that of Max Müller, *italics* would take the place of all accents, lines, dots, used by Lepsius. The conference lasted uninterruptedly till half-past one o'clock.

'Bishop Thirlwall dined with us, and the conversation was animated between him and Lepsius (who arrived on the 27th) and Max Müller and my father. The alphabetical conferences take place every day.

'Lepsius has returned to Berlin. The last conference to-day leaves the matter undecided.'

And so it remained, after all the labour and time Bunsen and Max Müller had expended. The English missionary societies now mostly follow a system used by the Bible Society, but there is not entire unanimity.

# CHAPTER IX

## 1854–1855

Professor of Modern Languages. Second volume of *Rig-veda*. Death of Burnouf. Crimean War. *Languages of the Seat of War*. Bunsen's resignation. Nehemiah Goreh. Visit to Germany. Froude. Kingsley. Macaulay. Visit to Malvern. Indian Civil Service Examinations. Paris. Dresden. M.A. by decree. Renan.

THE year opened darkly with rumours of war. Writing to Bunsen for the New Year, Max Müller says:—

*Translation.* 9, PARK PLACE, *January* 1.

'Above all, my best congratulations for the New Year: may it be a calm and blessed one for you and yours; and may it above all things teach the Russians and the Russophiles, that Europe will not be Cossacked nor Kossuthed, and that she would prefer to see the Crescent at Petersburg to the Russian Cross at Constantinople.

'My best thanks for your kind testimonial, which arrived just at the right time; I hope it will have had its good effect in about a fortnight or three weeks' time; if not, I am just as ready to go to India as Böttícher is.'

TO HIS MOTHER.

*Translation.* OXFORD, *January* 26, 1854.

'Since Christmas I have not had a quiet moment, though it is our vacation. . . . I have had to go constantly to London to talk to missionaries and others. The alphabet is now printed, and yesterday we had a general conference at Bunsen's, where all missionary societies were represented. There are many difficulties, and I am tired of the whole thing, for it takes up so much of my time, and it is difficult to fit all missionaries with the same cap! I was quite alone here in Oxford at Christmas, to write my treatise on the alphabet, which had to be printed before the New Year. Since then I have been living between Oxford and London, and have thus met many interesting people, which is always a good thing. Bunsen now begins to believe in war, but always says, if the Russians can find a back door, they will yield. But England begins to feel it has had enough, and when they once begin war here, diplomacy can do nothing; for it is the people that make war here, not the sovereign and ministers. It was very cold early in January and I had some skating. How curious that you should just have been at Jessnitz when the old grandmother died! One need not lament her death, for her soul must have longed to be free from its old body. No doubt the soul must find it difficult in childhood to accustom itself to the human body, and it takes many years before it is quite at home. Then for a time all goes well, and the soul hardly knows it is hidden in a strange garment, till the body begins to be weakly, and can no longer do all the soul wishes, and presses it everywhere, so that the soul appears to lose all outward freedom and movement. Then one can well understand that we long to be gone, and death is a true deliverance. God always knows best, when the right time comes. I have just been reading Rückert's poems; they are very beautiful in spite of a certain weakness, and his latest home poems are full of natural feeling.'

Though much time and thought had been given to the missionary alphabet, Max Müller's real interest was with the second volume of the *Rig-veda*, which was published early in this year. The preface is dated Christmas, 1853, and the printing had been finished by that date, but there was always some delay about the binding and publishing, which were not in Max Müller's hands. With the text of the Hymns in this volume there had not been much difficulty, but the MSS. of Sâyana's Commentary were most defective. Max Müller, before finishing the first volume, had written to India to obtain, at his own expense, new MSS. for the second. After long delay he heard that the MSS. which Dr. Roer had secured for him in Calcutta had been lost by shipwreck. Fortunately, Professor Wilson received just at this time a complete copy of the Commentary from Benares, the most ancient copy of Sâyana that had then come to Europe. This he generously gave to his young friend. It contained many emendations and corrections, which greatly simplified the editor's labour. The task had been further lightened by the work of other Vedic scholars, who, since Max Müller had begun his edition, had published many of the works alluded to by Sâyana, which, for his first volume, Max had had to copy and collate for himself, before he could verify the innumerable quotations. The *Sâma-veda* had been published by Benfey, and the *Yajur-veda* by Weber, whilst Stenzler, Roth, and Whitney had all been active in this field of Sanskrit literature. To all these writers Max Müller acknowledges his indebtedness, and also gratefully mentions the assistance and active co-operation of his secretary, Dr. Aufrecht, in the latter part of Vol. II—'my learned friend,' as he calls him, and adds, 'The benefit of his services cannot be too highly valued.' The preface ends with an eloquent tribute to his master and friend, Eugène Burnouf, whose death in 1852 had been an almost irreparable personal loss to Max Müller, as well as to all Sanskrit students:—

'In losing Burnouf we have lost, not only an indefatigable fellow labourer, not only a disinterested teacher, but a most respected judge; in his approval valued by all, in his censure feared, in his verdict distinguished unfailingly by fairness and by truth. . . . When I heard of his death I felt—and I believe that many engaged in similar studies shared the feeling—as if our work had lost much of its charm and its purpose. "What will Burnouf say?" was my earliest thought on completing the first volume of the *Rig-veda*. And now as I finish the second, in its turn submitted to the judgement of so many scholars whose friendship I value, and whose learning I admire, my thoughts turn again to him who is no longer among us, and I think, not without sadness, of what his judgement would have been.'

Early in February the long uncertainty about the Taylorian Professorship was brought to a close by Max Müller's nomination by the Curators, confirmed by Convocation on February 21. The Vice-Chancellor, Dr. Cotton, in writing to announce the unanimous election by the Curators, adds, 'I feel great satisfaction in the consideration that so eminent and talented a Professor has been elected.' He hastens to announce his success:—

To F. Palgrave, Esq.

*February* 8, 1854.

'The Professorship has been settled at last, and I got it. I cannot tell you how happy I feel, after the long suspense, to have at last a ποῦ στῶ for the rest of this life, and to be able to look on quietly till the moving panorama comes to an end. I feel now more than ever that it is owing to the kindness of those who first received me at Oxford that I owe my further success and my present position—ce n'est que le premier pas qui coûte, and after I was once in the right boat, I was sure to get into harbour sooner or later. I shall write to old Joe. I wish we could all meet again and have a jolly party, as we used to have five or six years ago, when I little thought of what was looming in the future. I hope we shall manage a little gathering after Froude is able to come. He has taken a cottage at Babbicombe for the next year. I was in London for a week, kept from day to day by alphabetic conferences, where I had to act as secretary and to write generally till 3 o'clock in the morning. I had not an hour to myself, and after it was over I had to go to Oxford in order to see that all was going right about the ship. Now it is launched, and I hope to have a pleasant cruise in it.

'Ever yours, M. M.'

Bunsen wrote at once to congratulate:—

*Translation.* *February* 8.

'. . . Your position in life now rests on a firm foundation, . . . and that in this heaven-blest, secure, free island, and at a moment when it is hard to say whether the thrones of princes or the freedom of nations is in greatest danger. With true affection, yours.'

TO HIS MOTHER.

*Translation.* OXFORD, *March* 10.

'I am living in such a turmoil that I can settle to nothing, and have hardly time to write a letter. I have been made full Professor this term, and so there have been endless invitations and parties of all sorts. I am rather tired of it all, and wish I lived some miles out of Oxford, so as to have my time to myself. You can imagine I was not a little pleased when everything was definitely settled, but when one waits so long for a thing it does not give one the same pleasure as when it comes unexpectedly. But I heartily thank God that my future is now entirely secured, as far as food and raiment are concerned! At present I shall stay where I am, and I shall be very sorry to leave, but I know I must take a larger house in time. I shall stay here till the Summer Vacation, and then when I come back I will furnish a small house, in which you can perhaps help me. Or perhaps you will pay me a visit in the vacation here, instead of my going to Dresden? I have still a good deal of correspondence with missionaries, who are not always easy to deal with. Aufrecht is still working for me, but he lives in another house for himself, and gives private lessons. He is happy here, and very useful to me, but it is rather expensive. I shall not want for money, when I think with how little I managed once. I enclose a little proof of my Professorship; you will know what use to make of it. If you want to buy a book,

I would recommend Tauler's *Sermons*; they are very beautiful, but you must get an edition in modernized German. We already begin to feel the war. Everything is dearer, and the taxes will be doubled. It can't be helped, and there is no doubt as to the result.'

On March 21, three days before war was declared against Russia, Max Müller received a letter from Sir Charles Trevelyan, then Assistant-Secretary to the Treasury, begging officially for his help in directing the officers proceeding to the East how to study the languages of the northern division of the Turkish Empire and the adjoining provinces of Russia. Some private letters had already passed between Sir Charles and the Professor of Modern European Languages, and Max Müller had written:

'That corner of Europe between the North of Italy and Turkey and along the Danube is a real linguistic rookery. All the lost daughters of the European families of languages have taken refuge there; and they exhibit, each, the lowest degradation and corruption of grammar that can be imagined. In the Albanian we recognize the noble features of Greek; in Wallachian, those of Latin; in Bulgarian, those of the Old Slavonic language; but all sadly distorted and disfigured. Very little has been done toward a literary culture of these dialects, and even grammars are scarce; there are certainly none in English, as far as I am aware.'

He had prepared a list of elementary grammars and a few simple instructions, which Sir Charles had imparted to all the commissariat officers. But the letter, dated March 20, states that something more than this should be attempted, and adds, 'If you agree with me in this, you will at once feel that there is a call upon you to help in this good work'; and Sir Charles entreats Max Müller to prepare at once a treatise, showing what languages are spoken in that part of the world, their general structure, and the alphabets used, and what would be the most useful books on the respective languages. Sir Charles concludes thus: 'I have only two further suggestions to make. (1) That whatever you do should be done quickly. Every part of this great effort is under war pressure. (2) That you should tell us *at once* what you know *now*, leaving the rest to be perfected hereafter.' So heartily did Max Müller respond to the call, that by May 16 he was able to send Sir Charles his *Suggestions for the Assistance of Officers in learning the Languages of the Seat of War in the East.* A second edition was required within a year.

In his introductory letter to Sir Charles he first called attention to a subject that continued to occupy his thoughts almost to the end of his life. He writes:—

'It is undoubtedly high time that something should be done to encourage the study of Oriental languages in England. At the very outset of this war, it has been felt how much this branch of studies—in emergencies like the present so requisite—has been neglected in the system of our education. In all other countries which have any political, commercial, or religious connexions with the East, provision has been made, by Government or otherwise, to encourage young men to devote themselves to this branch of studies. Russia has always been a most liberal patron of Oriental philology. In the Academy of St. Petersburg there is a chair for every branch of Oriental literature. The French Government has founded a school, 'L'école pour les langues orientales vivantes.' At Vienna there is an Oriental seminary. Prussia finds it expedient to give encouragement to young Oriental scholars, employed afterwards with advantage as consuls and interpreters. In England alone, where the most vital interests are involved in a free intercourse with the East, hardly anything is done to foster Oriental studies.'

Just before the publication of his book, Max writes to Bunsen:—

*Translation.* PARK PLACE, 1854.

'I am busy with my lectures, and am printing my book on the Languages of the Seat of War, 100 pages, with a very fine map by Petermann, so that I never get to bed before 2 a.m.'

To his mother he writes:—

*Translation.* PARK PLACE, *April* 11.

'I am so engrossed with work, that I have hardly a free minute, and that will go on till vacation. I cannot feel certain about my plans for travelling. I must spend part of the vacation in Paris, as I must work at a MS. in the library there. The only thing that draws me to Germany is Auguste, who cannot well leave Chemnitz, otherwise life in Dresden or Dessau is not very attractive, and we might all meet nicely in Paris, if Emilia would come there. Time becomes more precious every year, and a quarter of a year is now as important to one as a year was formerly. This shows one is no longer young. One becomes economical with one's time, and life is so serious just now, one has no right to think of pleasure, when so many men are suffering. And yet it is a war that could not be avoided. The Russian lust of conquest and the whole influence of Russia in Europe, especially in Germany, must be thrown back on its own borders, or we should have to fight the battles which are now being fought on the Danube, on the Elbe or Rhine. It will be a terrible war, but one cannot doubt the issue, for England, when war once begins, puts forth her whole strength, and the feeling that you are fighting for a just cause keeps up the courage even in disaster.'

But whilst realizing the necessity of the war, Max Müller was to be indirectly one of the many sufferers from it. His friend and patron, Bunsen, could not approve the attitude of Prussia, and it was widely known that his recall from England was imminent. George Bunsen, Max Müller's most intimate friend of all Bunsen's sons, writes to him:

CARLTON TERRACE, *April* 14.

'DEAREST FRIEND,—So it is. My father has not up to this moment received a recall. On the other hand, we expect to-morrow the reply to an answer sent by my father to a renewed and very impetuous offer of leave of absence. In this answer my father made his accepting leave of absence dependent on certain conditions guaranteeing his political honour. If the reply to-morrow does not contain those conditions, nothing remains but for my father to send in his resignation.'

TO F. PALGRAVE, ESQ.

9, PARK PLACE, *April* 18, 1854.

'... I should like to have seen you when you heard of Scott's appointment. I am afraid you did not use quite parliamentary language on the occasion; I neither, particularly as, up to the last, Jowett's chances seemed as clear and certain as could be, without downright bargaining. I am sorry to see that Jowett feels it very much, and I think just now some testimonial from his friends, like the one you contemplated some time ago, would be very opportune. Could you persuade Richmond to do his portrait? I think it might be done for about £100, and I am sure we could get as much from his friends. What do you say? Vacation is nearly over, and I have not yet been away, though I intended to go to the seaside and get fresh air. But I have to do some work for the Government, and have been at it day and night, working against time. I hope we shall hear something from the Black Sea soon. The slowness of these people is intolerable; they are always a day too late. I congratulate Bunsen on having got out of the claws of the Black Eagle. I dare say he will get the next vacant seat on the Episcopal bench in England!

'Ever yours, M. M.'

Besides the work for the Government, Max Müller was busy in printing his essay on the Turanian languages for Bunsen's book, which had grown under his hands, and had had to be put aside whilst the missionary alphabet was printing. The dilatoriness of the printers in London caused him and Bunsen much trouble, as the work had to be finished before Bunsen left England, and though Max Müller worked through half the night whenever a proof-sheet appeared, his letters are full of despair. Bunsen writes on May 10, 'The work presses,' but did not seem to realize that the delay was not with Max nor in Oxford. In the same letter the Minister, writing for the last time from Carlton Terrace, says, 'The house is deserted, but the heart rejoices, and the soul already spreads its wings.'

To his Mother.

*Translation.* OXFORD, *May* 12.

'Bunsen's resignation is a real loss to me. I saw him in London—the house is now empty. Yet one can only congratulate him on having saved his good name, at the right moment. His leaving gave me a great deal of work and disturbance. He is just bringing out a new book in seven volumes. I had various things to write for him, and as it had to be ready by the twentieth, I never got to bed before two. Now I have undertaken a work for Government, which is just printed. Then came the lectures, and the *Veda* above all, so that I really have not a moment to think of or do anything else, and can say nothing about my plans for summer.'

To Chevalier Bunsen.

*Translation.* OXFORD, *May* 22.

'I cannot believe that you think of leaving England. Surely the Prussian crisis cannot last much longer, and when it is over, you will have to return to Carlton Terrace. Whilst writing the word *believe*, I think of a question I meant to ask. *To believe*, as far as I know, means "to be"—*lieben*; Lat. *libere* and *lubere*.'

To the Same.

*Translation.* OXFORD, *June* 8.

'Are you really leaving as soon as Acland tells me? If this is so, I must go to London on Saturday or Sunday, the only days I can get away, as I am giving my lectures. I still wait, and still hope, a new Prussia will arise, which cannot do without you here in England. England begins to feel like a strange land to me, when I think that you are really going. Will you not wait till *Hippolytus* is out? The printer does not seem in any hurry.'

On June 12 Bunsen, writing to his wife, who had gone to Heidelberg to settle his future home, mentions that he had had 'a delightful day with Max Müller.' Five days later, this faithful friend left England, and Max felt as if stranded in a foreign land. Too much occupied at this time with his work to write more than very short letters to his mother, in all of them he expresses his sense of loss. Bunsen's house in London had been a second home to him, where he was always sure of a welcome, always sure of encouragement and sympathy, of intellectual intercourse, and of that intelligent interest in his work and the far-reaching problems which it unfolded, which he missed so sorely in his daily life in Oxford, where hardly any one understood the work on which he was engaged, or took a real interest in it, or were capable of discussing it with him scientifically.

'In all my researches,' he writes in the *Autobiography*, 'no one took a livelier interest or encouraged me more than Bunsen. When some of my translations of the Vedic Hymns seemed fairly satisfactory, I used to take them to him, and he was always delighted at seeing a little more of that ancient Aryan torso, though . . . he was more especially interested in Egyptian chronology and archaeology. Often when I was alone with him, we discussed the chronological and psychological dates of Egyptian and Aryan antiquity.'

The last left of the daughters of that large and happy family writes:—

To Mrs. Max Müller.

Carlsruhe, *December* 13, 1901.

'My memory now only recalls *impressions* of your dear husband. The charm of his whole being, his beautiful, almost Greek profile, his wonderful playing, specially of Mendelssohn and Chopin, and delightful power of interesting and fascinating one by his conversation, all that is still very clear and warm in my recollection; and we girls all fully understood my father's admiration, and fatherly love, and interest in him. . . . He did not live in Carlton Terrace with us, only came in and out, and of course was chiefly closeted with my father in his library below; and we only saw him at meals, or when he had time to look us up in the drawing-rooms, and there, I well remember, we tried as soon as possible to get him to sit at the pianoforte and play to us. 'Very truly yours,

'EMILIA VON BUNSEN.'

It was soon after the parting with his friend and patron that Max Müller heard from Sir Charles Trevelyan that he was thoroughly satisfied with his treatise: 'I cannot bestow higher praise upon it than by saying that it appears to me completely to answer the important object for which it was written.' Bunsen, too, wrote: 'I read your book . . . with real delight and sincere admiration.'

The following letter from Dr. John Muir, the editor of *Original Sanskrit Texts, or the Origin and History of the People of India*, and later the munificent founder of the Sanskrit Professorship in Edinburgh, then just returned from twenty-five years' service in India, contains the first mention of a man of whom Max Müller always spoke with reverential affection:—

33, SUSSEX GARDENS, *June* 26, 1854.

'MY DEAR SIR,—It may interest you to know that there is at present in London a Pundit from Benares, though he has become a Christian. He has come to England with the Maharaja Duleep Singh, as a sort of tutor or companion to His Highness. His name is Nehemiah Nilkanth, the former appellative having been adopted by him according to his own wish on the occasion of his baptism. He was not a professed Pundit in the sense of being a teacher of Sanskrit Grammar, or of any of the Six Darsanas or any other branch, but he is a Sanskrit scholar, being able to write the language accurately and fluently, and having a general knowledge of the philosophical schools. At the commencement of his inquiries into Christianity, he wrote an answer to one of my tracts (a former edition of the *Mataparikshâ*), composed in Sanskrit verse. After long and painful inquiries and struggles, he became convinced of the truth of Christianity, which he accordingly embraced. He has latterly been employed as a catechist; and when Dr. Login (who has charge of the Maharaja) was leaving India, he brought Nilkanth along with him.

'If, therefore, you are curious to see a specimen of a Pundit without going beyond London, your wish can be gratified, and if you desire it, I shall be glad to go with you to Dr. Login at Mivart's in Brook Street, if you are likely to be soon in London. Nilkanth, since his conversion, has written a tract in Hindoo against the *Vedánta*, which is interesting as an exposition of what he considers the doctrine of that school. He knew some English when I last saw him, and is probably improved in his knowledge of it now.

'Believe me, yours very faithfully,

'John Muir.'

Nehemiah Goreh came to Oxford to see Max Müller, and they became, after a short time, very intimate. Nehemiah had suffered cruelly for his change of religion, and on his return to India his mind seems to have lost its balance, and after some years of asceticism and complete renunciation of the world, he joined the branch of the Cowley Fathers established in India. Up to that time, he had written to and heard from Max Müller from time to time. When he revisited England and Oxford many years later, he was so completely under the discipline of the Brotherhood, that it was only the very day that he left Oxford, where he had spent many weeks, that he was allowed to visit his old friend for a few moments, and the visit gave little pleasure to either. 'He was steeped in the Christianity of the Church,' which Max always distinguished from 'the Christianity of Christ.'

In July Max Müller went to Germany, and with his mother revisited his sister and many other relations.

To Chevalier Bunsen.

*Translation.* Chemnitz, *July* 30, 1854.

'I received your last friendly letter from Heidelberg, just as I had struck my tent in Oxford, and was on my way to Germany. Since then I have been always on the move from place to place, and never had any rest or a moment for writing. Now I have finished my visits, and am going on a few longer expeditions, and your kind invitation draws me westward to Heidelberg, and thence I hope to go to Switzerland, North Italy, Venice, and Vienna. My plan is to start in a few days with my mother, to pay a few visits on the way, to see Rückert and reach Heidelberg about the middle of August. I hope to stay there with my mother for a fortnight, and as it is not so far from Heidelberg to your house as from the City to the West End, I hope to renew the happy hours which, only a short time ago,

I could spend with you in Carlton Terrace. I do not know Heidelberg, and your account has made me long to see the Academia Nicorina. Then I hope we shall be reconciled about Aryans or Iranians, about which I do not care to speak from Chemnitz, as no philological wind blows here. The middle of August I expect some friends in Heidelberg, perhaps Jowett, and we may go on together to Italy and Vienna. Unfortunately I must be back by October 1, as the Election takes place then. I have not yet heard whether the Bill has been sent back to the Commons, and what changes have been made in it, but I fear I must be at my post by the beginning of term. The parties are nearly equal, and each vote tells. Dissenters are admitted, but Gladstone has done much harm, and the Commissioners are very much restricted in carrying out the needed reforms, at least in what concerns the colleges. The advance of public opinion in Oxford is remarkable, when one thinks how quickly it has come.'

After a pleasant time in Heidelberg, where he was able to introduce to his friends his dearly loved mother, of whom Bunsen writes later as 'your remarkable mother,' Max Müller joined his old friend Baron Hagedorn, and with him visited Worms, Speyer, Baden-Baden, and the Black Forest, and went on alone to spend a week at Vienna with his friend Robert Morier, then secretary at the English Embassy. Italy had to be given up on account of cholera. From Vienna he went again for a time to his mother in Dresden, and finally returned to Oxford early in October, where he tells his mother he had a rapturous welcome from his little dog Belle. He writes on his return that he is feeling so very well that he has no qualms of conscience over his three months' idleness, and adds, 'If we can be together three months in the year, free from all cares, we can bear the other nine months, and if the parting is always very painful, it is made up for by the joy of meeting.'

During the summer, Max Müller received from time to time, through Sir Charles Trevelyan, letters from officers, consuls, and others on his *Languages of the Seat of War*, many of them containing valuable corrections which he embodied in the second edition. The consul at Mitylene wrote, 'I have received Müller's admirable memoir, and must thank him for the pleasure and instruction it has afforded me. It is like letting in broad daylight on a subject which had been hitherto explored by a farthing rushlight.'

To his Mother.

*Translation.* *November* 11, 1854.

'I tried on your birthday to play a little, but I have no time now for such things. I have a great deal of work in prospect, and however great the delight I feel in music and art, my work comes before everything else. My free time I must give to walking, which is most necessary; and to get stronger exercise I play racquets, which makes one perspire even more than camomile tea. When one is nearly thirty-one, one must be economical of one's time, and give up many things that are a pleasure, but for which one's time is too precious. How many things I would like to read, but there is no time, and I must be content. One's delight in music always lasts, and I owe the old instrument so much—not only the enjoyment one has had, and the use my music has been as an introduction in a foreign place, but also the happy frame of mind which music unconsciously produces in one, and it smooths many little roughnesses which one often sees in those who have no taste for music. People who cannot sing are almost as badly off as people who cannot cry, but one does not always want to cry, nor always to sing; if we know that we can, it is enough.'

In this same letter he mentions that the cholera had been so bad in Oxford—worse than anywhere else in England—that the lectures had, many of them, been postponed.

To the Same.

*Translation.* Oxford, *December* 10.

'I must thank you for all your love, which is the best of birthday gifts. As I took up your birthday letter, I wondered where the smell of violets came from, and when I opened it and found them, the scent was as fresh as if they were just picked; and even now, as your letter lies on my table, they have not lost it. Your letter too is full of love and goodness, which remains ever fresh. But I must tell you I was not in Oxford on my birthday, but in Bideford. I was first with Froude, who lives at Torquay, and then I went with him to Bideford to stay with Kingsley. He is a well-known writer, and his last novel *Hypatia* has made a great sensation. He is married to a sister of Froude's wife, and they are both charming. I played to them on my birthday, and thought of you. . . . I shall probably be quietly in Oxford at Christmas, unless I go to George Bunsen's wedding; he is engaged to an English lady. . . . Here one hears of nothing but the war . . . the losses are very great. Taxes are very high, six per cent. now, and we are to be prepared for ten per cent.'

To THE SAME.

*Translation.* OXFORD, *December* 28.

'I spent Christmas quietly here, for I had wasted so much time that it was high time to begin my work again. On Monday, as I was drinking my coffee, came your letter, and soon after I received your picture, which I like very much. . . . I made acquaintance this time in London with Macaulay, and had a long conversation with him on the teaching necessary for the young men who are sent out to India. He is very clear headed, and extraordinarily eloquent.'

This must be the interview so humorously described in *Auld Lang Syne*, where the young Professor, primed with every possible argument in favour of Oriental studies, had to sit silent for an hour whilst the historian poured forth his diametrically opposite views, and then dismissed his visitor, who had tried in vain to utter a single word. 'I went back to Oxford,' says Max Müller, 'a sadder, and, I hope, a wiser man.'

The New Year found Max Müller quietly at work in Oxford. He had been to London, intending to accompany his friend George Bunsen to Norfolk for his wedding, but serious illness in the bride's family prevented any but the nearest relatives from being present. Max's mother had been urging him to follow his friend's example—a favourite theme with her—and she amused herself from time to time in recommending him a wife.

To HIS MOTHER.

*Translation.* OXFORD, *January.*

'That you are so anxious to find me a wife is very good of you! But I am afraid there are difficulties, and in such things we must take life as God sends it. A happy marriage must be a great blessing, but how few marriages are happy. I have no opportunity of really knowing and observing young girls, as one can if one lives at home, and where families know each other, and live much together. I should not fall in love with a merely pretty face, and for a *mariage de convenance* there is plenty of time. Elise, who delighted you so much in Carlsbad, seemed to me pleasant enough; but, as I had no opportunity of knowing her better, I have never thought more about her. If you are writing, greet her kindly, but don't make any proposals for her hand! Perhaps if Krug sends you this year to Carlsbad, you can tell me if she is the sort of daughter-in-law you would like.

Sunday is my best day for writing letters, as I get up early, and go at eight o'clock to our chapel, and have the whole day then to myself. Getting up so early at this time of the year is not pleasant; but the chapels here in the colleges are so beautiful, so warm, and so well arranged that one is far more comfortable in them than in our large cold churches.'

Bunsen had written to him earlier in the month to express his pleasure that Max Müller 'would undertake to bring the last sevenfold child of my English love' (*Christianity and Mankind*, in seven volumes) 'into public notice. You know better than any one what is the unity of the seven volumes, and what is the aim and result. Your own is certainly an important and independent part of it. But you have, with old affection, worked and thought yourself into the whole, even when the particulars were of less interest to you.' To this the following answer was sent:—

*Translation.* 9, PARK PLACE, OXFORD, *January* 14, 1855.

'Philip Pusey seems quite unexpectedly better. Acland had very little hope, but thinks it quite possible now that his life will be spared. He is living still with his brother in Oxford, and as I have had little intercourse with the latter, I cannot call there to inquire. His brother has engaged a tutor for Sidney, who now reads with him, but his chief studies are Pusey's folios, the *Patres* and the *Haeretici*. Oxford is in a sad condition; the reform has done nothing, and we are worse off than before. Balliol has declared that Dissenters will not be admitted; but the minority has appealed to the Bishop of Lincoln, who has cancelled the resolution. Gladstone's Bill has introduced a complicated and impractical system, which suffocates all proposals for the better. There is only one chance of salvation for Oxford—fellowships open to all and no clerical restrictions. If this were done we should have a very different Oxford in about twenty years. At present lay-fellows are only admitted as fellows for a certain period—if they are admitted to an open fellowship at all. What remains therefore is nothing but the coffee-grounds which nobody desires to have—clergymen without a parish and scholars without scholarships! I often long to get away. I cannot, especially as a German, take part in these things; my old friends leave, and I have no wish to make new ones, and so the MSS. of the *Veda* are my one consolation.

'I have written a review on the philological part of your work; I told Dasent[1] about it a fortnight ago, but I have had no answer so far.

[1] Editor of the *Times*.

'Aufrecht has at last made up his mind to go to London. I have written to Dr. Jelf, who may probably secure for him the Sanskrit Professorship at King's College. I shall look out for somebody later on, who will do the mechanical work of copying and compiling, so that I shall only have the constructing of the text to do. Aufrecht was too good for this mechanical work. I do hope he will succeed better in London than here. . . . I think of going to Paris in the summer, to study there, and to get acquainted with the people, if only there were no Exhibition. And what about the war?—I hope there will be no peace till Sebastopol has fallen.'

. . . . . . . . .

(Continuation on *Monday*.)

'I received your letter this morning, which made me reflect, *Alea iacta est*, but where and how? The old Prussia is lost, and a new one can only rise from a Protestant, constitutional Germany. The hour for that must soon be at hand, for I do not believe in the peace negotiations. If once the struggle becomes widespread, it will be the voice of the people that will secure the welfare of the Fatherland. In war and in peace, in death and in life, the people must have a voice, and it could never wait for the word of command to emanate from one family. Peace now would be a great disaster.

'I wish the notice of your book had fallen into better hands. Dasent told me that the second part of his review of the first edition had not passed the censor[1], and so had never been printed. After hearing this, I did what I could, i.e. I explained the connexion of the whole—but it is for the *Times*, and the times are bad!'

It will be observed that in the beginning of this letter Max Müller speaks of having had little intercourse with Dr. Pusey. When he was made an M.A. of Christ Church, he attended chapel regularly, and Dr. Pusey at once announced that he would never administer the Holy Communion to him, as he had only been confirmed in the Lutheran Church—not by a bishop! The Dean, Dr. Gaisford, at once said that he had no scruples of the sort. This, of course, made a feeling of estrangement for some years between Dr. Pusey and the young Professor; but it passed away gradually, and in 1860, at the time of the election to the Sanskrit Professorship, it is well known that Max Müller had no warmer supporter or more energetic canvasser than Dr. Pusey, who sat up

[1] Mr. Walter, proprietor of the *Times*, saw almost all articles that touched on religious subjects.

many nights writing letters in his favour. Max always remembered and alluded to this with gratitude. His feelings about Pusey form some of the most interesting passages in the *Autobiography*. Their religious views were far asunder. Max Müller, who, as he tells us, had learnt his practical religion from his mother, which remained unshaken amidst all storms, could not sympathize with the utter terror with which Dr. Pusey looked back on his own religious difficulties, as if they were in themselves a crime. Max always felt that 'religion, in order to be *real* religion, a man's own religion, must be searched for, must be discovered, must be conquered. If it is simply inherited, or accepted as a matter of course, it often happens that in later years it falls away, and has either to be reconquered, or to be replaced by another religion.'

How completely all distrust of Max Müller had passed from Dr. Pusey's mind, is shown by the following extract from a letter from his daughter, Mrs. Brine:—

'. . . I remember well the happy walks my father and I used to have through the Parks up to your house, when he wanted to consult Professor Max Müller on some abstruse questions. You know the very high esteem in which my father held the Professor.'

In February Bunsen writes to Max Müller:—

*Translation.*

'I am delighted to hear that your *Veda* gets on. If you would only not allow yourself to be frightened from the attempt to let others work for you in *mere handicraft*. You have now fixed your impress on the work, and any one with the *will*, and with the necessary knowledge of the tools, could not go far wrong under your eye. I should so like to see you free for other work. Only do not leave Oxford. You would not like Germany, and Germany could offer you no sphere of activity that could be compared ever so distantly with your present position. So do not be low-spirited, my dear M., or impatient. It is not so much the fault of England, as of yourself, that you do not feel settled and at home. You have now as good a position as a young man of intellect, and with a future before him, could possibly have anywhere, either in England or Germany. Make a home for yourself. Since I saw your remarkable mother, I have been convinced that, unlike many mothers, she would not stand in the way of your domestic happiness, even were it contrary to her own views.'

To his Mother.

*Translation.* *February* 25, 1855.

'There has not been such a winter in England for twenty years—even the Thames is frozen over, and here in Oxford the cold was unbearable, for the open fires are not as warm as a German stove. The one pleasure is the skating, which one generally gets for a couple of days only—this frost has lasted for weeks. You must have felt the cold, if you have carried out your stove-economies, and used a lamp instead of fire. I am very busy with my lectures, and am printing a second edition of my *Languages of the Seat of War*, and there are many other things which fill up my time. The war becomes more complicated, but we must hope that they will not make peace hurriedly, so that the victims will have fallen in vain. Here people are very much excited, chiefly from the constant change of Ministers and the incapacity of the highest officials. It is a real revolution, only such crises pass over quietly here, but the effect is the same. The aristocratic party must yield before it comes to street fighting. I have made no plans for the summer. I must stay here during vacation, unless I go to Paris for work. If you have really meanwhile found a wife for me, that may make a difference, but I am not at all inclined for one!'

In March, Max Müller tells his mother of a visit to London, where he had made acquaintance with Lord Ashburton, 'one of the richest peers in England, and a patron of literature.' He stayed with his friend George Bunsen, and laments that his pleasant, amiable, and rich wife has no sister to take the place of Elise of Carlsbad, who was going to be married, much to his mother's disappointment! True to his determination to spare his mother all anxiety, he never betrayed what his real feelings were.

To Chevalier Bunsen.

*Translation.* 9, Park Place, Oxford, *April* 15, 1855.

'... I chiefly work at the *Veda* now, and have just sent an essay on Vedic burials to the *German Oriental Journal.* It is always the same story with Aufrecht, and, alas, no position seems to turn up for him. Jowett has been in London for the whole term; his *Commentary* is printed and is to appear soon. I expect few facts, but free and open treatment of the matter. Tischendorff appeared here in Oxford with all his various Orders and MSS. I hope to get the latter accepted by the Bodleian. Are they really worth £800 after having been collated and edited?'

On April 17 Bunsen wrote to thank Max Müller for an article on his *Outlines*:—

*Translation.*

'You have so thoroughly adopted the English disguise that it will not be easy for any one to suspect you of having written this "curious article." It especially delights me to see how ingeniously you contrive to say what you announce you do not wish to discuss, i.e. the purport of the theology. In short, we are all of opinion that your cousin was right when she said of you in Paris to Neukomm, that you ought to be in the diplomatic service!'

The letter goes on to sketch out a new work in which Bunsen was anxious for Max Müller's co-operation, *The Kosmos of Language*, in four volumes—the second and fourth volumes to be entirely the work of Max Müller, and half of volume three—and Bunsen asks his friend to Heidelberg, or to Nice in the winter, to discuss the whole scheme.

*Translation.* 9, PARK PLACE, OXFORD, *April* 26, 1855.

'Alas! I cannot send any definite answer to your kind proposals. My news from home are bad. My mother has been very ill and her recovery is very slow. She is ordered to go to Carlsbad in the summer, and wishes me to go with her, and this seems almost impossible. Last year even I meant to go to Paris to study there, and to occupy myself with the collation and copying of various MSS. I have been hindered for several years in concluding and finishing various works of mine by not knowing these said MSS. My plan therefore is to spend the summer in Paris, and to give some years entirely to the close study of the *Veda*, and therefore meanwhile to let the *Science of Language* alone. The second part of the review in the *Times* has after all appeared amidst cries and wailing. Nobody seems to know in the least who is the writer of the article, and I have already assisted in various Common Rooms to abuse it, without betraying myself by the movement of a muscle. The gloom here is widespread. As it was said of France in 1847, "La France s'ennuie," so it may be said here now, John Bull is sulky. He has still thought it possible that men like Aberdeen, Clarendon, Palmerston, &c., could at least have brought Austria round. But as he sees that even that could not be managed, he turns disagreeable. Parliament will have to be dissolved, and a numerous national party will choose statesmen like Layard, Lowe, Bright, Cobden, &c. Whigs and Tories are done for.'

It was in this spring that Max Müller joined in a delightful geological excursion to Malvern, which he often mentioned later with unfeigned delight. The following account is from one of the party, Canon Farrar:—

'It was in 1855 that I had the opportunity of knowing Max Müller more closely, and seeing his mind employed on a new subject, Geology, in an interesting excursion to the Malvern Hills under the guidance of Professor Phillips, who wisely proposed to utilize the three days' vacation which at that time separated the two summer terms at Whitsuntide, by taking a party to visit the igneous formations of the Malvern Hills. The party was of graduates, except one gentleman commoner. The only survivor besides myself is the Rev. H. F. Tozer. We hired a country hotel at Malvern Wells, and thence made excursions under the Professor's guidance. Müller was one of the party. He had only lately taken up the subject of Geology; the practical application of it in field work was new to him, and therefore he afforded unintentionally to us the means of watching the workings of his mind, both in observation and reflection. I recall at the interval of forty-six years his looks of surprise and of intelligent delight. He was amazed by the mineralogical transformations, but what struck him most was the odd fragments which were indications of obliterated rock formations. He was fascinated by the inferences which Phillips drew. I cannot but suspect that there was in his mind the perception of the close analogy offered by his own favourite study of the history of language. These fragments of early strata were parallel to the presence of roots or old forms of words embedded in later linguistic strata. The second day of our stay was Sunday: most of the party gave themselves a holiday, and did not go to church. But Phillips and Müller accompanied me and some others to the Abbey Church of Great Malvern. I hope that I am not lifting indelicately the veil from sacred acts, if I say that it being Whit-Sunday, and there being Communion, to my surprise both Müller and Phillips stopped to partake of the Communion. I name this, for the reason that I suppose that in Oxford it would have been thought that the two men just named were, though Christians in life, most indefinite in their religious views, and probably suspected of excessive broadness. The sight of these two laymen, whose stay at the Eucharist must of course have been prompted solely by sincere religious principle, impressed me much; it was a rebuke to many of us clergymen, and led me to a life-long conviction that a depth of Christian purpose without formal profession exists in many a heart, undiscovered by man, and I often thought of this occurrence, when Müller, at the time of his rejection for the Sanskrit chair, was unfairly charged with the irrelevant question of Rationalism. After the service, our small party mounted to the top of the hills and listened to Phillips pointing out not only the physical and topographical geography of the vast panorama, but explaining the reasons by which he reproduced the probable configuration of the country, of land and sea, at the distant period of the elevation of the hills. This again seemed to impress Müller deeply. While he revelled in the beauty of the scene, he had never before heard physical geography in a large landscape connected with geology, with the extinct flora and fauna made to live again in Phillips' description. Our next day, Monday, was spent in a fatiguing walk along the southern half of the hills. Here Müller had for the first time the opportunity of seeing two British camps; one of them, the Herefordshire beacon, of gigantic size and remarkable construction, to which ancient German camps offer hardly any parallel. Müller showed an equal interest in archaeological as in geological history.'

For the May Term of this year Max Müller announced for the first time a course of reading and working lectures, 'sine ulla solennitate,' and from this time onwards gave one such course each year. This first class was for reading extracts from German classics to illustrate the history of German literature. His lectures continued to be well attended; there are above seventy names of undergraduates in one term for certificates of attendance, and the more private classes were also very popular. The wide range of investigation which Max Müller contrived to bring within the scope of modern languages and literature and the vivacity and picturesqueness with which every subject was treated were totally unlike the usual professorial lecture, and he continued to attract large audiences till tutorial teaching gradually destroyed the attendance at Professors' lectures.

Early in June, Max Müller was placed on the commission for the examination of the candidates for the Civil Service of India, and appointed examiner in Sanskrit. The preliminary meetings he found very interesting, and the constant visits to London gave him opportunities of seeing many old friends. He was busy with the examination in July, and was then asked to undertake the German and French examinations for commissions in the Engineers and Artillery, which included the history and literature as well as the grammar of both languages.

The middle of August Max Müller settled himself in Paris, glad to have the change from England and all the work he had been doing. He found Gathy and other old friends there, and began to work at collating and copying the MSS. he had specially come to see. His mother, however, when she knew that the sea no longer separated them, became impatient to see him, and the end of the month he started for Dresden, where he stayed a fortnight.

On his return from Dresden he found Paris so full for the Exhibition that it was with difficulty he secured a room for himself, and an apartment for his cousin Emilie and her husband Prince Wilhelm. Princess Friedrich of Anhalt-Dessau and her two daughters were also in Paris, and, as Max Müller soon found, he was expected to act as cicerone to the whole party; so he gave up all idea of work, and spent the short time that remained before his return to England in a round of amusements. He tells his mother he was never quiet from morning till night, and that he had explored Paris again from end to end. There were delightful excursions to Fontainebleau and Versailles, constant visits to the Exhibition, whilst almost every evening was spent at the theatre. The princesses, accustomed to a stiff little German court, were delighted with the freedom of the life, the dinners at the cafés, and the gaiety of the city, and were very pleasant and amused at everything. Max Müller, however, was not sorry when the arrival of the old family friend, Baron Hagedorn, set him free to return to his busy, yet quiet, life in England.

To his mother he writes before leaving Paris :—

*Translation.*

'It is tiresome, though, that my plans for work were all upset, but it can't be helped; one must take life as it comes, and do one's duty by others, when it is necessary. The summer has been a happy one, and I am quite satisfied. *We* had a happy time together in Dresden —happier than I had dared to hope for.'

On his return home, Max Müller found himself involved in a controversy on the examinations for the Indian Civil Service. He entirely agreed that the first examination should be a test of that liberal education which can be obtained at our schools and universities, and that a small number of marks should then be given for Arabic or Sanskrit. But in the second examination he was anxious that high marks should be given for Sanskrit as the origin of nearly all the spoken languages of India, and that the vernaculars should be studied in India, when a man knew in which presidency his life would be passed, and which vernaculars he would really require. In Mr. Lowe's reconstruction of Macaulay's scheme, Sanskrit had been set aside in favour of vernaculars. Max Müller wished to see 1,000 marks for Oriental languages divided into 800 for Sanskrit and 200 for one vernacular.

The lectures this term were on 'The History of the Languages of Europe,' with again a good attendance. Great part of the term was spent in looking for a house, as the lodgings where he had lived since the autumn of 1848 were now too small for his rapidly growing library, though it had not yet attained the dimensions of later years, some 13,000 volumes. The choice of houses was very limited in those days: none of those to the north of St. Giles' Church then existed, except some half-dozen in Park Town, which was considered an impossible distance from Oxford for a Professor!

To his Mother.

*Translation.* Oxford, *November* 9.

'Everything goes on again as usual. Lectures, work, parties, and one day follows another without anything special to mark it. But a holiday does one good, and one's work goes on all the better after a time of thorough idleness. Only think, my poor Belle has been very ill ever since I came home, and cannot die; she is a perfect skeleton. The people say I ought to give her poison, but I can't do it, though she is hopelessly ill.... I have long had fires, and the weather is cold and disagreeable, just like England, and then every night I must make myself wretched with a heavy English dinner, whilst in Paris one never felt one had eaten anything. Yet Emilie will tell you we did not live so badly there!'

The end of November his faithful little companion for seven years, little Belle the terrier, so well known to his old friends, died. Max tells his mother that it had made him very unhappy, and he missed the little creature terribly.

Max Müller, who had been made an honorary M.A., as we

have seen, in December, 1851, was made M.A. by Decree of Convocation on December 13 of this year.

To his Mother.

*Translation.* 9, Park Place, *December* 28.

'There is little to tell you about my Christmas. Oxford is nearly empty in the vacation, so one does not see much festivity. But the week before Christmas I enjoyed myself very much. I went to a friend (Augustus Vansittart) in Cambridge, which I had not yet seen, and most beautiful it is, in some points more beautiful than Oxford, which is saying a great deal. Everybody was very hospitable, and for a whole week I had to eat four dinners daily, for breakfast, luncheon, dinner, and supper were all like a gala dinner in Germany. Four times a day roast pheasant, and never in bed before 2 o'clock. It was real feasting, and I am only surprised that I could eat my way through without headaches. I came back through London, and dined with one of the Ministers, where I met . . . Sir Colin Campbell, the English general from the Crimea; and then I went to the Latin Play by the scholars of Westminster School. So you see one can amuse oneself here, if not *at* Christmas, but beforehand.'

Towards the close of this year Renan wrote a sharp attack on Max Müller's Turanian article in Bunsen's *Christianity and Mankind*. The attack appeared in Renan's *Histoire générale des langues sémitiques.* Max Müller complained bitterly of the passage in a letter to Stanislas Julien, which he, with childlike innocence, showed to Renan, who wrote a long explanatory letter to Max Müller, in which he repeated the very point that was really the cause of offence, i. e. that in that essay Max had been under the influence of Bunsen, and had written it more to command than from conviction. Owing to the indiscretion of Stanislas Julien, the quarrel threatened to become serious, as Max Müller could not but feel that his honour as a writer had been called in question. He wrote a review of Renan's *Grammaire Sémitique* which amounted to a fierce attack upon the book. Bunsen wrote to Max Müller:—

*Translation.* *December* 2, 1855.

'I send you these lines . . . to stop if possible your wrath against Renan. He confesses in his letter "Ma plume m'a trahi"; he has partly said what he thinks, and partly said what he does not think. . . . But his note is not that of an enemy. You must deal gently with him. You will do it, will you not, for my sake?'

Renan, too, wrote: 'Pardonnez-moi. Je n'ai pas compris ce que vous vouliez dire.' On this Max Müller suppressed the pamphlet, though already printed, and they gradually became great friends.

To Chevalier Bunsen.

*Translation.* *December* 25, 1855.

'... Your next work, *God in History*, will be a joy to read, for the beginning of the God-consciousness in the *Veda* has much occupied me of late, and has made me enter into depths of human consciousness hitherto unknown to me. The *Veda* alone of all works I know treats of a genesis of God-consciousness, compared to which the Theogony of Hesiod is like a worn-out creature. We see it grow slowly and gradually with all its contradictions, its sudden terrors, its amazements, and its triumphs. As God reveals His Being in nature, in her order, her wisdom, her indestructibility, in the eternal victory of light over darkness, of spring over winter, in the eternally returning course of the sun and the stars, so man has gradually spelt out of nature the Being of God, and after trying a thousand names for God in vain, we find him in the *Veda* already saying: They call Him Indra, Mitra, Varun*a*; then they call Him the Heavenly, the bird with beautiful wings;—that which is One they call in various ways; they call it Agni, Sama, Mâtarisvan. The belief in Immortality is only the other side as it were of the God-consciousness, and both are originally natural to the Aryan race. "As the sun sets, yet never dies, but returns," says the old Aryan, "neither shall I go into non-existence, but I shall live with the sun." The non-existence he denies as often as he can, and in the *Veda* the a sat is the night of nature, which is nothing, though it frightens man and torments him, but just on account of that very thing makes him most sensitive to belief in and to hope of the ever-returning light. The *Veda* is inexhaustible, and the more I long to get to a close, the more I feel how much there remains still to be done, and yet I feel it a great blessing that such work has been given to me to do as the daily occupation of my life—and then everything seems to become indifferent, even if Monsieur Renan reviles me!

'In Oxford everything proceeds slowly but well. Liddell has been made Dean; he has a difficult position, but he is surely planted, and nobody will succeed in moving him away again. It is said that the Prince of Wales will be with him, but that may only be a report. Secondly, Jowett is established, and Pusey gets angry about him, and is sure to accuse him of heresy, and so secure him much greater influence. Pusey is very dangerous, and his influence is again on the increase. He seems to have designs on me, and I am on my guard. Then there is Thomson, Provost of Queen's, honest and friendly. Vaughan is also to come to Oxford. Brodie has been made Professor without signing the Articles, my own case preceding his, but he had a stronger case, being an Englishman. Everything was tried against him, even secret surprises at the voting, after making it known that no contest would take place. Everybody was afraid of a sudden attack at nightfall; the guards were called out, and the ambuscade found itself confronted by a picket which towered above them. Everything cannot go exactly as we wish, but the avalanche rolls in the right direction.

'What a beautiful speech Prince Albert made in Birmingham! He ought not to show his cards too readily; he has to play the Brutus with the English, or else he will be treated as was Aristides. Excuse this long letter, but it is so rarely that one can speak to anybody about one's thoughts and feelings, that when I write to you my pen runs away with me.'

Bunsen later thanked Max Müller for his just, but sharply expressed and *nobly* suppressed, essay against Renan.

# CHAPTER X

## 1856–1857

Comparative Mythology. Commemoration. His mother in England. Volume III of *Veda*. Curator of Bodleian. Christmas at Glasgow. *Deutsche Liebe*. Buddhist pilgrims. Examination at Exeter. Visit to Froude. Germany. Manchester Exhibition.

IN the last days of the old year, Max Müller had found a house, 55, St. John's Street, and so hard did he work that he was settled before term began, as the notice of his lectures is dated from his new house. His course was on the 'History of the German Language, and its relation to Greek and Latin.' He writes to tell his mother how comfortably he is settled, and how much he hopes she will visit him in the summer, to see his home and life in England, though at the same time he cautions her not to expect much amusement, as he is far too busy to travel about with her, or give up much time to her, as he has daily work at the Bodleian, besides all his work at home. To Bunsen he writes:—

*Translation.* 55, ST. JOHN'S STREET, *March* 14.

'Everything progresses well in Oxford; it seems to me there is no other country in the world so pliable as England. At the right time we shall get everything in Oxford that we wished for, and the whole academical phraseology changes visibly. Of course Jowett is preached against every Sunday; it does not hurt him in the least, however, and he is occupied with a second edition[1]. The essay in the *Quarterly* is by Conybeare; I have not read it, for that sort of thing does not matter. When we grow older here in England we leave the talking and writing to others, and we occupy ourselves with the "doing"; and as I am now a member of Convocation and Congregation the committee-work and report-writing begin to occupy all my time. So I retire as

[1] *Commentary on the Thessalonians*, &c.

much as possible and rejoice when something is really accomplished. It looks disgraceful in Prussia; the whole morality begins to be bankrupt.

'I am so glad to know that your great work[1] is to be concluded before the great war breaks out. I should have liked to send you my little contribution about the *Veda*, but Easter approaches, and till then I am actually glued to my table day after day, as I have promised Brockhaus, by contract, to hand over to him the MS. at the end of March. I am sending him a Vedic grammar as introduction to the first volume of the German edition of the *Rig-veda*. The text was printed some time ago, and therefore he presses me to send him the preface. So you see it is absolutely impossible to answer your questions now.

'The Flood-legend does not occur in the Hymns of the *Veda*, but in the Brâhmanas. Burnouf considers it borrowed, and he may be right, as it only occurs in a modern Brâhmana. The Fall is hinted at, not morally but only metaphysically. . . . The keynote which runs through the whole always is: We do not know; who looked on when God made the world? To whom did he mention it? I mean to stay here for the summer, and expect my mother to pay me a visit.'

### TO HIS MOTHER.

*Translation.* OXFORD, *March* 23.

'You must lead a very quiet life, and not anger and excite yourself. The things that annoy us in life are after all very trifling things, if we always bear in mind for what purpose we are here. And even in the heavier trials, one knows, or one should know, that all is sent by a higher Power, and in the end must be for our best interests. It is true we cannot understand it, but we can understand that God rules in the world in the smallest and in the largest events, and he who keeps that ever in mind has the peace of God, and enjoys his life as long as it lasts. I am sure that a quiet, contented mind is better than all medicine and Carlsbad. I dare say a change of air will be good for you, and life in England is very healthy, if you will live quietly. We cannot travel about much, for it is too expensive and requires younger legs, but Oxford itself is sure to please you, and you will see what my life here is.'

This spring Max Müller's article on Comparative Mythology appeared in the *Oxford Essays*. It has been reprinted in both editions of the *Chips*. A contemporary writer speaks of the 'great impression made by Max Müller's essay on

[1] *Egypt.*

Comparative Mythology, published in the *Oxford Essays*, in which he applied the rules of comparative philology to the elucidation of Aryan myths, in a manner at once scientific and popular.' 'Max Müller,' says Professor Macdonell in his obituary notice in the *Journal of the Royal Asiatic Society*,

'was a pioneer in this country of the Science of Comparative Mythology, founded by Adalbert Kuhn. . . . Beginning with his essay on Comparative Mythology, which appeared in 1856, he wrote a number of papers on mythological subjects. . . . His mythological method, based on linguistic equations, has but few adherents in the present day, for most of his identifications . . . have been rejected owing to the more stringent application of phonetic laws which now prevails in Comparative Philology. . . . Nevertheless, his writings have proved valuable in this field also by stimulating mythological investigations even beyond the range of Aryan-speaking nations.'

Of this essay a friend wrote many years later to Max Müller:—

'When I was young I remember you were my ideal hero—the magician who admitted me into a gorgeous fairy-land. I can remember as if it were yesterday, in the early sixties, how I read *the* Oxford essay in the British Museum, and walked home to Clapham westward facing a glorious sunset, hardly conscious that I was a creature of this planet! And later on a new book of yours was an event in my life!'

Bunsen was busying himself at this time with questions of Indian chronology, in which Max Müller could not sympathize, feeling the ground too insecure for any real historical treatment. In one letter he says:—

*Translation.* *April*, 1856.

'I only recognize one chronology for India, the four literary periods of the *Veda*, which bring us to at least 1500 B.C., and even at that time show us a formulated system of divinities and even priestcraft. Before this time the schism of Brâhmans and Zoroastrians had taken place. And long before this, even, the schism between the Aryans tracking north-eastward and those tracking southwards took place; and before the nomadic Greeks separated from the nomadic Indians, centuries must have passed. There seems no doubt that the South Aryans (later on divided into Indians and Zoroastrians) had settled together in Bactria. . . . The *alphabet* on the Aryan coins in the north of India is no doubt Semitic. The Sanskrit alphabet has its origin from elsewhere, and I believe I shall be able to trace it to the Himyaritic. *When* it reached India is the great question, and that I am unable to answer. "Ophir" proves how old the commerce between India and Phoenicia must have been; for "Ophir" is Abhíva on the Indus. So you see the *oldest* date of the name Ophir occurring in the Bible is the *latest* time in which the Aryans were already settled by the sea, and at the time of the *Veda* they had not yet settled there. Could it be proved that Solomon knew the name Ophir, it would of course be a *terminus a quo*. His lion-throne made of ivory reminds one of the Sanskrit lion-seat, i.e. throne. Lassen has established the Sanskrit etymology of the products of Ophir. I am now printing my old Vedic grammar—just think that 400 B.C. each syllable of the *Rig-veda* had been counted, each lengthened syllable had been carefully marked, and each metrical inaccuracy had been carefully registered. But it is an awful work, and I long to return to my mythology.'

This letter crossed one from Bunsen, in which he tells Max Müller, 'It would be a great pleasure to you, my dear friend, if you could see the enthusiasm of my reawakened love for India, which possessed me in 1811–4, and which now daily overpowers me.' The letter ends, 'Send me a letter, only without "Your Excellency." I beg you will always write to me as friend to friend.'

To this friendly invitation Max Müller replies:—

*Translation.* 55, ST. JOHN STREET, OXFORD, *April* 25, 1856.

'YOUR EXCELLENCY,—Allow me to continue to call you so; it is an old habit, and reminds me of the time when first I entered your study to have my passport to Germany *visé'd*, in a despairing mood as I was then, without an aim, without means to carry out the one scheme which I had clearly planned for myself! How much has happened since then! Oh, when I think how I have to thank you, your encouragement, your sympathy, for the whole turn of my fate, if I consider that, I know of no other word which would better express my veneration for you, my love and my gratitude, than the one by which I addressed you with German awkwardness at the first visit I paid you, a word which, like many another one, has been much misused, but has nevertheless not yet lost its true meaning!

'With regard to Megasthenes[1], I do not know how I can help you. As far as I have occupied myself with the chronological question,

[1] Greek envoy from Seleucus Nicator (306–298 B.C.) to Chandra-gupta (Sandrocottus). He wrote a work on India.

which has never been a passion with me, I do not see in the least how Megasthenes *could* know more than Wilford or Sir W. Jones. Megasthenes could not know anything but what we know, for though we know nothing of Indian history, we know the history of Indian literature sufficiently well to be able to ascertain that no annals have ever been lost, simply because none ever existed. We have the most distinct traces in the *Rig-veda* of the schism between the Brâhmans and the followers of the *Zend-Avesta*.

'I intend very soon to publish something about this, perhaps in the Long Vacation, when Mrs. Liddell, &c., will have no more music parties, when there are no more examinations in London and no more lectures in Oxford, and when the third volume of the *Veda* has been published. Now I feel so hunted that I can accomplish nothing. I have so many claims on my time during term, that I often have to do the most necessary work in the middle of the night. Froude's *History* is out; I have devoured the first volume, and have put the second on one side for later on. It seems to me very good. Jowett has not yet been burnt; instead of that he thinks of publishing Plato's *Republic*. Examinations, education, are the *ordre du jour*; in a very short time all positions will be open for competition. What a social revolution that is! It would have drawn blood in other lands. Much of it is due to Trevelyan. Gladstone made a manful speech last night—how much that means. Ever yours.'

To his Mother.

*Translation.* Oxford, *May* 6.

'I have been in London again for a week and have made many interesting acquaintances. Life in England is so grand, and I wish you could see me at such a dinner as lately at Lord Denbigh's—such pictures all round the room! I am in no want of work to do, and with all the interruptions here, I can hardly get on. . . . I hear occasionally from Bunsen. I do not believe he means to return to England. As to your journey here, you must inquire whether any acquaintances are coming to England. I shall certainly stay in Oxford this summer, as I have a good deal of work before me. Oxford in summer during the vacation is delightful. In a fortnight I must go again to London. I shall be staying with friends in one of the best houses—very pleasant, and cheap. Then I shall hear Jenny Lind, and in a month she is coming to Oxford to give two concerts, and we shall have grand festivities; Peace festival, &c.'

To Chevalier Bunsen.

*Translation.* 55, St. John Street, Oxford, *May* 4, 1856.

'Your Excellency,—Your last letter awaited me in Oxford, as

I spent all last week in London to examine there. The more I see how deeply you penetrate into Indian chronology, the more I regret that I cannot follow you as I did formerly. It would indeed be a great work if you could find a secure historical foundation for the Indian traditions. I am still at the previous question—i. e. *Could* Megasthenes make any discovery besides that which we have made from Sanskrit literature? This question must be answered, and there I am afraid Megasthenes with his total ignorance of Sanskrit will have the worst of it, as compared with Manetho and his knowledge of hieroglyphics, and Berosus with his knowledge of cuneiform. However, I am ignorant, and therefore unprejudiced, and I am willing to learn and to believe. My passion is now Mythology; and I see you cannot serve two masters, for at present I cannot get away from it, though so many other things claim my attention. I long for the Long Vacation, and I expect a visit from my mother, and therefore I shall not go to Germany. I hope to write something more about Mythology. I find that John Bull has taken a bite and asks for more. At present I am working at my grammar, and I am also working at a German Historical Reader, which I could not refuse on account of my Professorship. Forgive me, therefore, that I do not throw myself into Indian chronology, but I can do nothing unless I can do it with all my heart. Confident of your kind indulgence, I always remain, much honoured friend, master and benefactor, your faithful M.M.'

In April of this year Max Müller had again met his future wife, and during six weeks they saw each other constantly at her home, and in London, and at the Grand Commemoration and Peace festivities in Oxford; little foreseeing the painful three years of total silence and separation that they had to go through before their marriage was allowed. In the first days of July Max's mother arrived, accompanied by Emilie von Stolzenberg, and the faithful family friend Baron Hagedorn. They spent two or three weeks in London, seeing all the sights, going to the Opera, dining at Richmond. The mother, cousin, and Hagedorn went from London to the Isle of Wight without Max, who returned to Oxford. After the visit to the Isle of Wight, Hagedorn returned to Germany, the mother and cousin going to Oxford. From there the Baroness visited Scotland, and the whole party then returned to London, and devoted themselves to sight-seeing, till Emilie went to Germany towards the end of August, leaving the mother to enjoy her son to herself for two months longer.

On July 17 Bunsen writes to congratulate Max Müller on the visit of his mother and cousin:—

*Translation.*

'You know it was a letter of the *latter* which first told me *of you*, and made me wish to see you. And then you came *yourself*, and all that I prophesied of you after the first conversation in London, and your first visit to us in the country, has been richly fulfilled—yes, beyond my boldest hopes. You have won an honourable position in the first English University, not only for yourself, but for the Fatherland, and you have richly returned the love which I felt for you from the first moment, and have faithfully reciprocated a friendship which constitutes an essential portion of my happiness.'

On August 25 Max Müller sent his usual birthday congratulations to Bunsen. It must be remembered that birthdays are much more observed in Germany than in England, hence the constant references in Max Müller's letters to his own birthday or those of his mother and sister. In after-years the birthdays in his own home circle were specially marked and joyful days.

To Chevalier Bunsen.

*Translation.* 55, St. John Street, Oxford, *August* 25, 1856.

'I have thought of you with much feeling to-day, and send forth my hearty congratulations, as I think of the beautiful old age, vigorous in mind and body, with which Heaven has blest you. May this day return many a time, and find you surrounded by all dear to you; and may your life, perfect as it has been, be a pattern and comfort to the world at large. I am looking forward to the concluding part of *Egypt*, especially to the mythological part of it. I can well imagine that you have found a more comprehensive form of mythological consciousness. I had only just knocked at the door with my essay. I intended to prove that the mythical form was unavoidable. In the great regions of God-consciousness we ourselves still think and feel mythically, that is, language runs away with our thoughts. My essay has called forth some opposition, which makes me glad; for I thought the matter so evident, that nothing further could be said about it; instead of which I perceive that not only has a hole to be made through the wall, but that the whole wall has to be pulled down and each barricade to be got rid of. Whether *I* shall be able to do this is doubtful, for with all my love for antiquity and the past, my dreams for the future return again and again, and I feel somewhat drawn to India—a desire difficult to resist in the end. Only I do not know *how* to get there; but my life here seems so aimless and unfruitful that I shall not be able to bear it for very much longer. I thought the other day whether I could not manage to go to India with the Maharajah Dhulip Singh. He is very well spoken of, and he returns next year after having learnt in England what good things he may do some day for his Fatherland in India. It seems to me it would form the natural nucleus of a small Indo-Christian colony, and it is only necessary to create such a centre in order to exercise one's power of attraction on all sides. After the last annexation the territorial conquest of India ceases—what follows next is the struggle in the realm of religion and of spirit, in which, of course, centres the interests of the nations. India is much riper for Christianity than Rome or Greece were at the time of St. Paul. The rotten tree has for some time had artificial supports, because its fall would have been inconvenient for the Government. But if the Englishman comes to see that the tree *must* fall, sooner or later, then the thing is done, and he will mind no sacrifice either of blood or of land. For the good of this struggle I should like to lay down my life, or at least to lend my hand to bring about this struggle. Dhulip Singh is much at Court, and is evidently destined to play a political part in India. I wish I could get in touch with him in some quite natural way. Could it be managed with the help of Prince Albert, or would you help me to it? I do not at all like to go to India as a missionary, that makes one dependent on the parsons; nor do I care to go as a Civil Servant, as that would make me dependent on the Government. I should like to live for ten years quite quietly and learn the language, try to make friends, and then see whether I was fit to take part in a work, by means of which the old mischief of Indian priestcraft could be overthrown and the way opened for the entrance of simple Christian teaching, that entrance which this teaching finds into every human heart, which is freed from the ensnaring powers of priests and from the obscuring influence of philosophers. Whatever finds root in India soon overshadows the whole of Asia, and nowhere could the vital power of Christianity more gloriously realize itself than if the world saw it spring up there for a second time, in a very different form from that in the West, but still essentially the same.

'Much more could be said about this; a wide world opens before one, for which it is well worth while to give one's life. And what is to be done here? here in England? here in Oxford?—nothing but to help polish up a few ornaments on a cathedral which is rotten at the base. But enough for to-day! My mother and my cousin have been with me for about eight weeks, and some other friends. With the exception of my mother, who is going to stay on with me, they left a few days ago, and I have set to work again; my work was interrupted for so long. I long for Germany; and how I should like to come to you to Heidelberg, but that is impossible this year, and next year I hope to see you in England. In faithful friendship, yours.'

The poor mother who in her Diary speaks of the quiet time in Oxford alone with her son as 'unclouded happiness,' had little idea of all these thoughts poured out to his fatherly friend!

Meantime the third volume of the *Rig-veda* had been published, the last volume that was brought out under the auspices of the old East India Company, and dedicated to them. There had been in the previous year some doubt whether it would be possible to finish this great work. The first calculation of the extent of the work, and therefore of its cost, had been based on defective MSS., consequently when the third volume was ready for printing, it was found that this only completed half of the work, whilst exhausting a great deal more than half of the money voted for the whole, and it was with some difficulty and after many anxious months that, owing to the influence which Professor Wilson possessed over the Board of Directors, the additional funds were voted. The preface to this volume therefore ends with an expression of the editor's gratitude to the Directors 'for having sanctioned the continuation of the work and granted funds necessary for its completion; an act of enlightened liberality which will be applauded by all persons interested in the history of India, and in the history of mankind, and by which one of the most important monuments of antiquity will be rescued from oblivion and restored in its integrity.' Max Müller was able in his preface to speak of the growing interest the work was exciting among scholars, as being—

'found to shed the most unexpected light on the darkest periods in the history of the most prominent nations of antiquity. Thus, though not yet known in its completeness, the *Veda* has assumed an importance which no other literary production of India could ever have claimed; and we may rest convinced that as long as a man cherishes the records of his family, in the widest sense of the word, these simple songs will maintain their place among the most natural annals of ancient history. One class of readers may have been disappointed [in the *Veda*]: men who study ancient literature less on account of its historical than its practical value. But the true historian values facts ancient and genuine, and a corroded copper As of the Roman Republic is of greater value to him than an imperial gold medal of the most exquisite workmanship. . . . I must confess that I could have wished that the ancient poets of the *Veda* and their Indian commentators had been less diffuse; for though I believe that no edition of any author in Sanskrit, or any other language, for which MSS. had first to be copied, others to be collated, innumerable references to be verified, and an index to be made of every word, has ever been brought out so rapidly as this edition of the *Rig-veda*; yet I feel that ten years of my life are gone, and I know not whether I shall have sufficient time left to finish a work which I once undertook perhaps with too much confidence. Yet even if I should not see the completion of this work, I should not be sorry for the time I have spent on it; and nothing will ever induce me to change the principles which I have hitherto followed, and to give a hasty copy of a MS. instead of a critical edition of the text and commentary of the *Rig-veda*.'

Max Müller again acknowledges the valuable assistance of his learned friend Dr. Aufrecht, and his sincere 'regret that he should no longer[1] enjoy this advantage, as much of the correctness and accuracy of the last volumes was due to his conscientious co-operation.'

The lectures this term were on 'The History of German Civilization and Literature, from the earliest times to the reign of Charlemagne.'

On October 30 Max parted with his mother, who left under care of a friend, going by boat from London to Antwerp, and so to Chemnitz to her daughter.

That afternoon Max writes to his mother:—

*Translation.*

'Our happy time is over, and the winter will not bring me much pleasure. But I beg you to enjoy your time in Chemnitz, . . . and you must tell them how happy we have been here together. I cannot thank God enough for the happiness that I had in your visit, even if I did not talk much about it. You know that one feels most when one says least.'

In several of his letters to Bunsen, Max Müller refers to Mr. Jowett, whose orthodoxy was at this time suspected by

[1] See p. 164.

many of the leading people in Oxford, and his intimacy with whom brought Max himself into ill odour with several of his more narrow-minded friends. He received early in the autumn a letter from a friend whose good opinion and affection he highly valued—a letter questioning the orthodoxy of his religious views. He answered it thus:—

To ——.

55, ST. JOHN STREET, *October* 4, 1856.

'Your letter has been in my hands for some time, and I have thought about it many times, and I have tried to make it clear to myself why you should have written that letter—but at last I felt convinced that, though you must have known that it would give me much pain, you wrote it from the kindest motives, and with that anxiety which we feel for a friend only. I see clearly that in your own heart you do not believe the charge which somebody unknown to me has brought against me. For if you did, you would not have written to me, you would not have asked me. For how *can* I defend myself against such a charge, except by telling you it is not true, and if you believe in me, do not believe it? If I have said or written anything that has given offence to your friend, let me know it, and I shall then be able to defend myself. But if some one, without giving any proof, without giving even his name, tells you that I am an unbeliever, that I do not believe in the Bible, that I do not believe in Christ our Lord and Saviour, I need not fear him. I know that there are not a few who treat our faith as such a light matter that they think nothing of charging a man with infidelity, though they would shrink from charging him with dishonesty. And some of them are honourable men, who act from pure and high motives, and whose only fault is too much confidence in themselves and too little confidence in others. But, I say again, I need not fear them. I have many friends who know me, and know my religious convictions; and though I have always avoided theological controversy, I have never avoided expressing my faith in the doctrines of Christianity, when I felt called upon to do so. I am not a theologian, and though I have been occupied for many years with the study of the ancient forms of religion, and though I have followed with a deep interest the history of our own Church from the earliest times, I do not feel competent to lay down the law, or even to express an opinion on all points, where even the best and wisest have stumbled, because they endeavoured to fathom with their human reason the depths of a Divine mystery. If you read the history of the Church, you will find that this has been the source of all heresy, and that all divisions and persecutions in the Church have arisen from the attempts of theologians to substitute their own thoughts and their own expressions for the simple language in which Christianity has been revealed to us in the Bible. And if we know the dangers of religious controversy, if we see how it is opposed to the very spirit of Christianity, how it appeals to the worst passions and destroys every feeling of charity, we ought to pity the priest or theologian who, like a physician, must enter into this pest-house; but surely we have a right to refuse to follow him, and to be dragged into it against our will. And if he tells us that we are ourselves infected with heresy, it is a serious charge indeed, but we may appeal to our friends and to a higher tribunal, and we may at least remind our accuser of one of the last commandments; nay, we may tell him that at a time when Christianity was a crime, Roman Emperors who had no scruple in making martyrs of all who professed the name of Christ, thought it fair to pass a law by which informers who could not substantiate their charge of Christianity against a Roman citizen were liable to a severe, even capital, punishment. I must say no more, for I do not wish to offend you by saying anything harsh against one who is your friend, and who may have been induced by a feeling of kindness towards you to disregard a duty which, as Christians, we owe to all men, even to a mere stranger. . . . Whatever our hearts may feel, and whatever our fleeting passions may say against it, there is no true, no lasting love, unless it has its source and life in God. . . . Through my whole life I have learnt this one lesson, that nothing can happen to us unless it be the will of God, and this I believe now more than ever. My life has been a happy one, and seeing that all I wanted, and much more, was given me, I began to think that there could be no disappointment in life. I have learnt better, and yet I feel again that there can be no disappointment in life, if we but learn to submit our will to the will of God. . . . We ought to remember also that our faith is not our faith, but that, like everything else, it is given us. Therefore we should not glory in our faith, or look down upon others whom we think poor in faith, or who may seem to differ from us. Let us wait for a little while—and to those whose eyes are turned to God and eternity the longest life is but a little while—let us wait then in faith, hope, and charity; these three abide, but the greatest of these is charity.'

Soon after his mother had left him, Max Müller was cheered by a visit from his old friend Fontane, who had been wandering about England, collecting materials for two works which he afterwards published under the titles, *England, Studies in English Art, &c.*, and *Beyond the Tweed.* Fontane writes of this visit :—

*Translation.*

'In the autumn of 1856 I paid a visit to Müller. I wanted to see the "heart of England," the midland counties, . . . and Oxford was to be my first halting-place. I was with him for two days, and count these days among the pleasantest in my memory, for the sake of Müller and the place itself. I have seen a large number of the cities of Western Europe, but none have made so powerful, so enchanting an impression on me. It is difficult to say in what the superiority of Oxford consists. It is not merely its architecture. . . . But in a peculiar mingling . . . of beautiful architecture, beautiful landscape, and rich historical recollections it stands alone. Since the day I left Oxford I have not seen Müller again in England.'

To his Mother.

*Translation.* London, *December* 6.

'I cannot write much to-day, as I am not quietly at home, but am staying with Walrond, and I have but a minute to tell you that I have entered my new year well, and of good courage. God has helped me hitherto, and will surely further help me and all of us, and whatever happens to us is always the best for us, even if we do not at once understand and perceive it.'

Max Müller was appointed a Curator of the Bodleian in this year, and always took great interest in the Curators' meetings. He was a keen advocate for more liberal arrangements in lending out MSS. under proper precautions, a privilege accorded by so many of the leading foreign libraries.

Christmas was spent at Calder Park, near Glasgow, with the parents of his friend Walrond. Max Müller writes from there to thank his mother for her beautiful Christmas gift, the fine bust of Goethe, which his friends will remember always stood on the top of the bookcase opposite the writing-table at which he spent so many hours of his life, and he would often look up at it as if to imbibe fresh courage for his work from the strong and noble features of the mighty master.

The year 1857 was devoted by Max Müller to the *Rig-veda*, and to the preparation of his *German Classics*. He was far from well the whole year, and out of spirits, and though forced to enter into society by his many kind friends, it is evident from his Diary, resumed this year, that it was mere weariness to him, and he buried himself as much as possible in his work. The correspondence with Bunsen was not very constant, and his general correspondence not as voluminous as usual throughout this year.

TO CHEVALIER BUNSEN.

*Translation.* 55, ST. JOHN STREET, *January* 24, 1857.

'I have through this week been in such constant intercourse with you, have heard and learnt so much from you, and have so often thought of the happy time when your real presence made a home for me in a strange land, that although I have nothing to tell you, or to complain of, I must at least thank you for the mental enjoyment your book *God in History* has brought me. Your book is a fact, and as such must produce an effect, if there is any life left in mankind, if the retrospective look does not blind the spirit, and the eyes of the present generation are not obstinately closed to all glimpses into the future. You have said afresh what is old, unveiled what is hidden, and made dead things live. You have placed the Bible within the focus of history, so that men can perceive its real greatness, whilst to most people this book stands so close they cannot see it, or so far they cannot reach it. I can form no judgement on many single points, and I am glad of this for the present, as the whole has therefore a greater effect on me. But if I find that my strength lasts out, I too must enter on this study, when my other work is finished, which I have undertaken, and must carry out. But in that too lies many a problem, which must be solved, and I cannot reconcile it to myself, to draw the limits of God-inspired mankind so narrowly as you do in many passages in your last work. The men in India were not forsaken by God, and if we cannot join in their prayers, the fault is ours. The heart is too narrow, the spirit too proud. I do not yet despair of discovering the chord by which the dissonance of the *Veda* and *Zend-Avesta* and the Chinese *Kings* will be brought into unison with the key-note of the Bible. There can be nothing accidental, nothing inharmonious on earth and in history; the unresolved discords in the East must find their solution, and we dare not leave off till we have discovered the why and the wherefore. You will come to treat of this in your second volume, where the Greek dissonance resolves itself in the Apostle of the Gentiles, and it is a pity your completed work has not appeared at once. This must at all events be the case in England. I had already read the book before I received the copy you have yourself sent me, and for which I send my warmest thanks. Of my useless life here I have nothing to tell you. I am weary and worn out, perhaps things may yet go better. I remain, in true affection and gratitude, yours ever, 'M. M.'

To this his fatherly friend replied:—

*Translation.* *January* 29.

'I am not at all easy at what you tell me about yourself and your feelings. But why are you unhappy? You have gained for yourself a delightful position in life. You are getting on with your gigantic work. You (like me) have won a Fatherland in England without losing your German home, the ever excellent. You have a beautiful future before you. You can at any moment give yourself a comfortable and soul-satisfying family circle. If many around you are *philistines*, you know that already; still they are worth something in *their* own line. Only step boldly forward into life.'

Max Müller seems to have given more time again to music this year, and he tells his mother early in February, 'The two Miss Jelfs are here, and we have had a great deal of music, and have studied and sung Mendelssohn's *Forty-second Psalm* with chorus. It went very well, but I had a good deal to do in practising the choir. We were sixteen voices.' Mrs. Thomson[1] writes of these parties:—

'Your husband kindly conducted my concerts in the Hall at Queen's, where we got up the *Lobgesang* and the *Forty-second Psalm* by Mendelssohn, sung by amateurs. Thanks to his kindness, they were a very great success, and sounded so well in the Hall, which was furnished as a drawing-room, with palms and sofas and rugs. He seemed much pleased with the result.'

There is a photograph taken by Professor Maskelyne and Dr. Thomson of Max Müller and several members of his choir; all gone now, except Mrs. Thomson and one other friend. Max Müller tells us in the *Autobiography* that Mendelssohn's music was still despised by some of the old school, and that one evening Dr. Elwes, the old organist of New College, who had been listening to the *Hymn of Praise*, 'walked up to me—to thank me, as I thought—but no, he burst out into a torrent of real and somewhat coarse abuse of me for venturing to introduce such flimsy music into Oxford.'

It was in the February of this year that *Deutsche Liebe* was published by Brockhaus in Leipzig. It had been written in the autumn, whilst Max Müller's mother was still with him. So much has been written and said about this prose idyll, so many people have declared it to be autobiographical, that it is perhaps well once for all to say that it is pure fiction

[1] Her husband was then Provost of Queen's.

as far as the characters and circumstances are concerned. It was written as a relief to his own feelings, and Max Müller thought by making an invalid princess the object of those feelings no one would easily guess the author, or the reason why it was written. That the Schloss and scenery described resemble Dessau was but natural, seeing how little else Max had seen in his own country. The book came out anonymously, and for two or three editions the secret was well kept. Only to Bunsen did Max Müller acknowledge himself as author. Of his English friends, Froude alone from the first guessed the authorship, and in a review of the book in the *Saturday Review* says:—

'One of our first impulses on seeing the general character of this work was to turn to the "Bekenntnisse einer schönen Seele" in *Wilhelm Meister*, and to refresh our recollection of that remarkable production. It was not without feelings of satisfaction that we laid down the volume of the great master and took up the one before us, reflecting how much half a century had done to elevate and purify the tone of society. . . . It is due to the author to say that it is truly gratifying to find, in a book which touches at so many points on the domain of religion, not one expression which can offend, in the slightest degree, any reasonable and right-minded person.'

The book is now in its twelfth edition in Germany, where after forty-five years it still commands a steady sale, whilst an unauthorized translation in America, under the title of *Memories*, has had an enormous circulation, and continues to be a general favourite there. Miss Winkworth published a translation in English as soon as the book appeared, by leave of the publisher, and twenty years later Max Müller brought out a translation by his wife, made many years previously, which has been through several editions. One review spoke of *Deutsche Liebe* as a book 'full of tender grace, touching sympathy, noble compassion, impressing love. With a delicate hand the author places before us the deeper depths of a true soul. It is a humanizing, refining, chastening volume, and is worthy of the widest circulation.' Another paper says: 'These recollections touch with much delicacy of feeling upon some of the most sacred emotions and hopes. Whoever the original author or authors may be, the papers reveal a very deep and sympathetic insight into man's nature; and many notable things are said of happiness, love, loss, gain, and suffering, as they constantly affect and impinge upon the human soul.' It was pronounced by Bunsen to be one of the most perfect specimens of German writing he had ever read.

To his Mother.

*Translation.* *February* 24, 1857.

'I wanted a short time ago to send you a book, written by a very intimate friend of mine, and published by Brockhaus. It is called *Deutsche Liebe.* The author does not wish his name to be known. If you have any spare money, buy a copy, and tell me how you like it, but do not tell any one that I know the author. I was very sorry to hear of Krüger's[1] death, though I never really saw much of him. He lived in quite another world, and his art did not appeal much to me. But he had won a good position by his work alone, and that was greatly to his credit, and one always rejoices when merit like his is recognized by a man's contemporaries. I wish I had a picture of you by him. Find out how much a good oil picture costs in Dresden, but it must be *good*, by Hübner or some other good artist.'

Max Müller's course of lectures this term was on 'Epic Poetry.'

To his Mother.

*Translation.* London, *March* 26.

'I was not at all well: bad colds and toothache had made me quite ill, and I needed a change and amusement. I am staying with Walrond, you know where that is, and I visit old friends. I hoped to find Morier, but he has not yet arrived, though he has left Vienna. I must tell you, and Emilie also, that I am quite innocent as to *Deutsche Liebe.* I know the author, but have promised not to mention his name, as he makes a point of it. He only published the book because he thought that here and there it might do some good, and might cure young people of the epidemic of so-called unfortunate love. The book contains the antidote to *Werther's Leiden*, and in so far is interesting; but it ought to have been more fully worked out to have much influence. I entirely agree with the spirit of the book, and am glad you like it. I do not care much for the plan of the story; it is too sketchy, and is wanting in repose and unity.'

It was in the *Times* of April 17 and 20 of this year that a review appeared by Max Müller of Stanislas Julien's *Voyages des Pèlerins Bouddhistes.* It was afterwards published as

[1] The artist.

a pamphlet, together with a letter on Nirvâna called forth by a protest printed in the *Times* of April 24, against Max Müller's view of Nirvâna as *utter annihilation*, whereas the writer of the protest maintained that Nirvâna meant *union and communion with God.* Max Müller's opponent appealed to the works of Mander and Creuzer, who were neither of them Oriental scholars, and who wrote before the canonical books of the Buddhists had been brought to Europe. In his answer Max explains the etymology of the word, which means *blowing out.* 'The human soul, when it arrives at its perfection, is blown out, like a lamp, as the Buddhists say, not absorbed, as the Brâhmans say, like a drop in the ocean.' He shows also 'that Nirvâna, as taught in the metaphysics of Kâsyapa, a friend and pupil of Buddha himself, is annihilation, and there is no earlier document from which we can form an opinion as to Buddha's original teaching.' 'Buddhism, therefore, if tested by its own canonical books, cannot be freed from the charge of Nihilism, whatever may have been its character in the mind of its founder, and whatever changes it may have undergone in later times, and among races less inured to metaphysical discussions than the Hindus.' 'Buddha himself, however, though perhaps not a Nihilist, was certainly an Atheist. He does not deny distinctly either the existence of gods, or that of God; but he ignores the former, and is ignorant of the latter. Therefore if Nirvâna in his mind was not yet complete annihilation, still less could it have been absorption into a Divine Essence.' In 1869 Max Müller gave an address at Kiel on Buddhist Nihilism, before the Association of German Philologists, in which these words occur: 'No person who reads with attention the metaphysical speculations on the Nirvâna contained in the Buddhist Canon, can arrive at any other conviction than that expressed by Burnouf, i. e. that Nirvâna, the highest aim, the *summum bonum* of Buddhism, is the absolute nothing.' Those among Max Müller's friends who know his own strong convictions as to the immortality of the soul, may perhaps feel surprised at the increasing interest he took in Buddhism as years went on. For at Kiel he declared, 'Buddhist Nihilism has always been much more incomprehensible than Atheism. A kind of religion is still conceivable, when there is something firm somewhere, when a something eternal and self-dependent is recognized, if not *without* and *above* man, at least *within* him. But if, as Buddhism teaches, the soul after having passed through all the phases of existence, all the worlds of the gods and the higher spirits, attains finally Nirvâna as its highest aim and last reward, i. e. becomes quite extinct, then religion is not any more what it ought to be—a bridge from the finite to the infinite, but a trap-bridge hurling man into the abyss, at the very moment when he thought he had arrived at the stronghold of the Eternal.' But even from his address at Kiel, it may be gathered that by that time Max Müller had convinced himself that the third part of the Buddhist Canon, in which alone the doctrine of Nirvâna in its crude form is to be found, was not 'pronounced by Buddha,' and that passages are to be found in the first and second parts of the Canon which contradict this crude Nihilism. Max Müller asks pertinently, 'Where Buddha speaks of Nirvâna as the highest happiness, can he mean annihilation?' It was when preparing a translation of the *Dhammapada* in 1870, afterwards revised and published as Volume X of the Sacred Books of the East, that the extreme moral beauty of Buddha's teaching powerfully attracted Max Müller's sympathy for Buddhism, and this was further increased when two years later he came in contact with living Buddhists, his pupils Bunyiu Nanjio and Kenjiu Kasawara, and still later Professor Takakusu, and saw the purity of their character, their true and gentle dispositions, and entire devotion to duty. The article on Stanislas Julien's book was almost Max Müller's first introduction to Buddhism. Pâli he had studied at Berlin.

After several months of silence Max Müller writes again to his old friend Chevalier Bunsen:—

*Translation.* 55, St. John Street, *May* 1.

'One may fight against physical illness, though it is difficult with persistent colds, which attack the head to-day, the teeth to-morrow, to keep up one's good-natured warmth and communicativeness; but if the cold once takes possession of the mind and the spirits, it is really the best thing to shut oneself up for a time. I have felt like this this winter. I felt I was not myself, and I did not wish to be a burden to others with my worries and blue devils. You will laugh at me and scold me, for no one has any sympathy with mental illness till it takes the worst form. But I can assure you that I have suffered a great deal, and am still suffering in spite of the approach of spring. I cannot sympathize with the fancy of most people always to appear happy. But when I feel miserable, I will at all events not be a burden to others, and so I shut myself up, and write no letters. So forgive my long silence, and have patience with me, who have so much that I must bear patiently. I received the three volumes of *Egypt* but recently, and I cannot find that you wrote to me that you wished for any supplement or remarks for your English edition. I have read your work here and there, and have followed with great delight your Herculean labours in the Augean stable of Indian history. But as my present work lies in quite a different direction, I have postponed the careful reading of your book to Long Vacation, and hope then to be able to say something more definite about it. It will interest you to find in the journal of the Chinese traveller Hiouen-thsang, therefore in the seventh century A.D., quotations in several places from native Indian historical works, of which we till now knew nothing, and whose existence even in the seventh century appeared to me till now very problematical. The work is full of interest, and I have written a long review on it in the *Times* of April 17 and 20. I have also given there the translation of a Vedic hymn, which would interest you. I have had to give up and waste my time lately on German literature. The University raised my salary, and I felt I must work for it, and so I am printing a chronologically arranged Reading Book, extracted from Wackernagel, &c. It is a sad waste of my time, for I could do better and more important work, but I cannot help myself. . . . I consider Roth's conception of Yama as entirely mistaken. Yama is the setting, dying sun, thus the Beyond, the eternal life, or personified, the Lord of those who are gone, of the kingdom of death. What we call death was to the Hindus always a passage; later they called it a setting free, a word that suits us better than death. . . . You are really unjust to Froude. Even if his idea of Henry VIII is mistaken, his picture of English life is not affected by that. There are chapters in his work that are really masterly—the Irish rebellion, the Charterhouse monks; and he has described the secret workings of the Reformation among the common people with genuine feeling and sympathy. Froude's idea of Henry VIII seems to me too problematical. But at all events Henry was one of the most popular of kings, and has his admirers not only in Froude but in his people, and in such historians as Sharon Turner, and such philosophers as Carlyle. I have a great affection for Froude, for I know him with all his faults, and know that he prays and works. Kingsley is a more brilliant nature, but his relation to Froude has never been that of a teacher; on the contrary, that of an admirer. *Le roman ne vaut pas l'histoire.* How people came to look on the *Saturday* as Kingsley's and my organ I cannot imagine. I met the editor once in London, and have sent him a few articles. The paper is *politically* in the hands of decayed Peelites; in *literature* it is independent and active. I remember one gross attack on you in the political part of the paper, but I should have felt it unworthy of your name to take any notice of such an attack. Woe to the man who has no enemies in England—you will never want for them, but they help far more than they hurt. I have to fight my way bravely, and here in Oxford the battle never ceases. I sit on the same board with Pusey, and know the man. He will soon attack me, but I am armed. Stanley is now coming to Oxford. Liddell is better, and comes back next month from Madeira. Jowett is indefatigable, and they have not conquered him. He is printing his second edition [1]. Vaughan is married, and comes very seldom to Oxford. Pattison is as reserved as ever, and trusts no one. It is a deep secret that he writes the article in the *Westminster* [2]. I live chiefly alone, and see no one but Jowett. My mother left me in October. She was not strong enough to stand an English November; but I hope to have her here again this summer. And now I have written really too much, and must again beg you to have patience with a poor melancholy invalid. Begging you to remember me most heartily to all your party, I remain as ever, yours in true reverence and devotion.'

With this letter Max Müller sent his pamphlet on *Buddhist Pilgrims* to Bunsen.

On May 8 Bunsen writes:—

*Translation.*

'I must thank you, and express my delight at your letter and article. The *letter* confirms my fears in the highest degree, namely that *you are not well*, not to say that you begin to be a hypochondriacal old bachelor. But that is such a natural consequence of your retired sulky Don's life, and of your spleen, that I can only wonder how you fight so bravely against it. . . . You will soon see how nearly we agree together, although I cannot say so much of the humanizing influence of Buddhism. . . . You have represented the whole as with a magic wand. We really *edified* ourselves yesterday evening with it, Francis read aloud and we listened.'

[1] *Commentary on Thessalonians.*

[2] On Bunsen's *God in History.*

This term Max Müller read the *Nibelungen* with his class.

To his Mother.

*Translation.* Oxford, *May* 24.

'How beautiful it must be in Carlsbad . . . how gladly would I find myself there for a couple of weeks! But I am up to my ears in work, and then just now I have so many interruptions—parties, picnics, business in London, examinations, &c. We have just begun our musical practisings again. The Jelfs are here, and other ladies who sing very well, and this time we are studying Mendelssohn's *Lobgesang*. There are difficulties, and it is not easy to keep twenty voices together and conduct them. And I must not swear like old Schneider! I have so much to do I shall probably take no holiday. If I do get to Germany I must go to Leipzig, where I have to print a book. But it must first be written. . . . The gardens are so lovely here now—even my little garden looks nice, and your ivy begins to grow. The heat is beginning, and what that is in these small rooms you know. In about three weeks I am going to Froude to the seaside, and to another friend who lives near Exeter, a brother of Dr. Acland.'

To Chevalier Bunsen.

*Translation.* 55, St. John Street, *May* 24.

'It really does one good to be thoroughly scolded and abused. Here no one takes the trouble to do it, and I have done it myself so long without any result that I give the Oxford Don his own way, till at last of his own accord he becomes German again. But I cannot tell you how much one has to bear in this promised land. Here in Oxford everlasting quarrels and squabbles, and lies and slander, and nowhere courage and faith, and no one can speak the truth, and any one who tries to do it brings a perfect hornet's nest about his ears. Can you believe that they have refused an excellent Orientalist, Dr. W. Wright, for the place of Under-Librarian at the Bodleian, because he has dared to affirm that the language of the Phoenician inscriptions is Semitic and not Hamitic, because he doubts that Ham was the father of the Canaanites and denies that Moses wrote the account of his own death? The man is a thorough Christian, is ready to sign the Articles; but it is no good—away with him. And no one moves a finger. Peace at any price! is the watchword. I carried my skin to market, but have been thoroughly beaten, and my friends began to be very much alarmed about me. And then these affairs waste one's time, and destroy all wish for work, so at last I shut myself in, and for weeks saw no one, and heard no one. Happily the Long Vacation will soon begin; if it only lasted the whole year, Oxford would be a real paradise. I have tried my best with the two hymns[1], but they are very difficult to translate, as our words mean so much which was not yet in the old words. The first hymn contains many Manichean thoughts, as, the ray of light which falls from the realm of light into the realm of darkness, and gives the first impetus to creation. And yet I cannot consider the hymn as modern. It belonged to the collection long before the Brâhmanas were written, and at the time of Pânini its syllables were already counted in the sum total of the syllables of the *Rig-veda*. I must stay this summer in England. I must finish some work to satisfy my conscience. If I can get it done early, I may cross the water in September. With hearty thanks for your friendly and unfriendly words, I remain as ever, your truly devoted.'

In June, Max Müller took part as representing Oxford in the examination arranged at Exeter by the late Sir Thomas, then Mr. Acland, for middle class and commercial schools, which was the first practical example of the system of Local Examinations since developed and carried out by our Universities. It was the first public speech in any language Max Müller ever made. His first public speech in German was made eight years later at a Philological Conference at Kiel.

From Exeter he went to Bideford to the Froudes', to get a little rest in fine air before hurrying to London for the annual Indian Civil Service Examination. After finishing up some necessary work in Oxford he started in August for Germany, his mother joining him at Leipzig, where he spent some weeks, seeing his Reading Book (*German Classics*) through the Press. From there he wrote to his friend Kingsley, who was uncle to his future wife:—

LEIPZIG, *August* 10, 1857.

'MY DEAR KINGSLEY,—How I long to be with you at Eversley, but my work here will keep me longer than I expected, though I have little to say in reply to your letter—nothing in fact but "you are quite right." Yet I must write to you to tell you that your clear and decisive words have brought me more comfort than pain; they have driven away a swarm of vain hopes and plans, and the sooner these are scattered the better I can wait and work; and sooner or later all this waiting and working will come to an end, for this life cannot

[1] From the *Rig-veda*, of which a prose translation had been made in Germany for Bunsen.

last for ever, and it will last no longer than we can bear it. I have no right to complain. I have all I wanted—more than I ever hoped for, more than I ever deserved. A disappointment in love is hard to bear because it destroys our faith in ourselves and in everything else; a disappointment in marriage may be a life-long trial, but it need not destroy our faith in our own nature, in the truth of others, or in the wisdom of God. Life may grow more strange and awful every day, but the more strange and awful it grows, the more it reveals to us its truest meaning and reality, and the deepest depth of its divinity. "And God saw everything that He had made, and, behold, it was very good." And so far, I believe, we both agree, and if there are a few words in your letter where we differ, it is better to leave them alone till we smoke our next pipe at Eversley. What you say about my going back to Germany is imaginary. It is as unlikely that I should go to Germany as that you should go to India. But if your duty should ever call you to India, would you like to find yourself fettered by a promise which no man has any right to make?—for His ways are not our ways. All I can say is that after an absence of ten years during the most critical time of life, everything is against my ever returning or settling in Germany. I am not wanted here; other people have taken the places I might have had. You will not easily get rid of me, unless you give me notice to quit. Auf Wiedersehn!'

TO PROFESSOR MAX MÜLLER.

*Translation.* POTSDAM, *August* 28.

'I am much touched, my honoured clever friend, by your amiable desire to see my hoary head once more. My physical powers have been steadily declining for the last nine months, but not my powers of work, nor the mental interest which I take in your creative far-reaching thoughts. I shall stay at home on Tuesday from eleven to two, and gladly expect you. With true friendship, your Vecchio della Montagna,

'A. VON HUMBOLDT.'

FROM CHEVALIER BUNSEN.

*Translation.* CHARLOTTENBURG, *August* 28.

'So there he remains in the centre of Germany a whole month, and lets one hear and see nothing of him. Your last letter was a great delight to me. The snail had there crept out of his shell and spoke to me as the friend; but now "Your Excellency" appears again, so the snail has drawn in his head again. Now, my dear friend, you ought to be thanked for the friendly thought of paying me a visit and writing to me.... That the Oxford Don should ask if I can "afford him a few hours" shows again the English leaven.... What have we not to talk over? The hours belong to the Don's gown, for you know very well that we could in a few hours only figure to ourselves *what* we have to discuss by turns. So come as soon as you can, and stay at least a week here. You will find my house, to be sure, rather lonely....We two old people are here, however, and full of life.... I must tell you with what deep sympathy and melancholy pleasure your touching idyll has filled me. You will easily believe that after the first five minutes I saw you vividly behind the mask. I thank you *very* much for having ordered it to be sent to me. I am very glad that you *have* written it, for I would far rather see you mixing in the life of the present and future, with your innate freshness and energy.'

To this Max Müller replied:—

*Translation.*

'I was glad to hear that you liked *Deutsche Liebe.* The story itself is only a frame. What I wished to make clear to myself and others was, why with the inborn love to our fellow creatures, we could show that love to so very few of them only; why love had to be confined almost entirely to the members of our family, to our parents, our wife, our children, and why any attempt to go beyond generally ended in sorrow. It is so, and we know not why, except again to show us that this life was not meant to be perfect, but only to give us by its very imperfections a faith in and a longing for a better life.'

Early in September Max Müller went to Heidelberg, and the following letter to his mother from Bunsen's tells her of his after proceedings. The visit to Weimar was to attend the inauguration of the great Goethe-Schiller Monument there.

*Translation.* HEIDELBERG, *September* 9.

'How much one can get through in a week, and how fast life runs on from one thing to another. A week ago I was still with you, and here I am in Heidelberg, and ready to rush off to England, and meantime I have seen lots of people, and had a good deal of enjoyment. I suppose you are now in Dresden, where you found so much to do that you are getting over our parting, about which you again made yourself so miserable. If you only knew how you pain me by such excessive grief, you would try and bear more quietly what cannot be helped. Our being so long together this year was quite an unexpected treat, and we ought to thank God that we had such enjoyment. Think how few, even of those who live in Germany, can see each other so often and for so long a time as we do, and then do not spoil the joy of meeting by brooding over the parting. Weimar was more than I expected, and through Brockhaus I made acquaintance with many interesting people—Auerbach, Gerstäcker, Rietschl, Devrient, Andersen and many others, and we met and talked together every night till one or two o'clock. I had no headaches, and all went well. The statues were very fine, and Weimar itself most interesting. I could not pay visits, for theatres, parties, and drives took up the whole day. We saw everything, and very well too. Brockhaus and his pleasant wife stayed till Monday. The Wartburg festival was beautiful and the weather was fine. The representations in the theatre were splendid. I found many old University friends, and it will always be a pleasant memory. Monday I went to Frankfort, and came on here Tuesday. I arrived after tea, and Bunsen had just received an affectionate letter from the King, asking him to go to Berlin and stay with him at the Palace. So I really only saw him yesterday, and to-day he started. I stay till to-morrow, and then go direct to Oxford, for I am longing for my work and quiet. Dr. Meyer is here and Dr. Bernays, so I stayed another day, and have seen Heidelberg again, where we once spent such a happy time together. I am very tired, such incessant excitement is too much. I could not hold out much longer.'

TO THE SAME.

*Translation.* OXFORD, *October* 7.

'Oxford does not feel like home this time, and even my work will not please me. So out of sheer ennui I went last week to Manchester with Thomson to the Exhibition. There was not a bed to be had in any hotel, and so there was nothing for it but to go on to Liverpool and sleep there, and come back next morning early to Manchester. Sir Charles Napier was in the same hotel. The Exhibition was magnificent, but much too much to see in so short a time. We were there from Wednesday to Saturday, and were dead beat when we left. So that pleasure was got through! To-morrow I am going to the country for a few days (to Kingsley's), but take my work with me. I hope to get some riding, which always agrees with me. What you write about Bunsen's *Gott in der Geschichte* delights me.

'Don't trouble yourself about Jacob. He had not a very successful life, and we learn from it that we must not measure God's wisdom in the ruling of human life according to our ideas. Then the idea of a "people of God" is purely Jewish. There is only one people of God, that is all mankind, Jews as well as heathen.... To-day is a day of prayer for India: there is hardly a family that has not friends and relations among the victims, and the feeling throughout England is very great.'

Max Müller undertook two courses of lectures this term, continuing those on the *Nibelungen*, and beginning a course on 'German Literature.'

To Professor Bernays.

*Translation.* 55, St. John Street, *October* 26.

'I suppose you are back at Breslau, and at your work again in the treadmill. It is the same with me in Oxford, and I think with regret of the beautiful summer days that are no more. I feel like Castor and Pollux in one, half day and half night, and I shudder at the thought of the winter in England, and begin already to hope again for the summer in Germany.

'I revel in Meldon's *Mythology*; it has helped me to see so many things more clearly now, especially about the Zeus Monotheism, which nobody has ever yet treated so simply. And what are you doing? I have not yet received your *Aristotelicum*. Keep your heart warm!

'I had finished the above when your kind lines reached me. I see now your heart is quite the same. Yes, if I could have you here! The fresh air would do you much good! In Germany I am useless, here to be sure, too—but the air here is freer and purer. I have not heard from Bunsen. I believe in no improvement from above, it must come from below! The Prince of Prussia (who is Regent) will soon make everything so tedious that people will go to sleep. I have neither heard nor seen anything of Pattison, and therefore know nothing of Scaliger and his regeneration. Farewell, rejoice in life and in human beings, who are far better than we think—they are only ashamed of their good souls.'

Early in November Max Müller tells his mother he has bought a horse, and rides almost every day. His little 'Folly' soon became great friends with its master, and was happily for him a quiet creature, for unless with friends Max Müller was apt to sink into a brown study when riding, and many were the humorous stories he told against himself, and the falls and escapes he had. He parted with his little friend when he married.

To his Mother.

*Translation.* *December* 6, 1857.

'Thirty-four years old. My birthdays here are always quiet and lonely, and when one is as old as I am, one passes willingly over the new step towards the grave without marking it. I often can hardly believe that I am already so old, and you are quite right when you say that I must no longer think of marrying. Well, many have passed through life like me, and if one loses a great deal of happiness by it, I am satisfied with what God has given me. I often long for a larger sphere of usefulness, and my wish to go to India has revived strongly of late. It is quite possible the East India Company may be done away with, and that Government will undertake to rule the country. Whether my *Veda* will be ruined by this I don't know, but I would willingly exchange this work for a few years, for a scientific mission to India. But these are only ideas and we will await quietly what God sends. My little horse "Folly" is a constant pleasure, but it costs a good deal, and like every one else I expect to be bankrupt! I shall stay here for Christmas, though I have many invitations. But I cannot spare the time; if I dawdle away the summer, I must spend the winter in working hard.'

To THE SAME.

*Translation.* OXFORD, *December* 21.

'You need not begin to frighten yourself about India. If I were to find a chance of visiting it, you would be as pleased as me. It is not out of the world, still less beyond God's hand. It would be of the greatest use and interest to me. But you see how difficult it is to discuss any plans with you; you make life so difficult for yourself and for others by such incessant fears, and it is so much easier only to find out and dwell on the good and bright side of things. I have had a very bad cold for above a week and am heartily tired of it. My Christmas will be very quiet and lonely whilst you are all eating your Stolle[1] joyfully. The children no doubt are rejoicing not a little at the prospect of Christmas. I wish one could look forward with delight, as one once did. Now one is only glad when something has passed by and is done with. The book Brockhaus is bringing out for me is finished at last, the extracts from German authors, from the fifth century to Goethe, with translations of the old German things and notes; but it will not be published till Easter. Then you shall have a copy and read Ulfilas and the Minnesinger. It was a hard bit of work, and I am glad to have done with it. Now I am busy on a book on *Indian Religion*, and the *Veda* too is getting on.'

To A FRIEND.

55, ST. JOHN STREET, *Christmas Eve*, 1857.

'As one is getting old and looks forward with fear rather than with hope to what is still in store for us, one learns to appreciate more

[1] Christmas cake.

and more the never-failing pleasure of recalling all the bright and happy days that are gone. Gone they are, but they are not lost. Ever present to our calling and recalling, they assume at last a vividness such as they hardly had when present, and when we poor souls were trembling for every day and hour and minute that was going and ever going and would not, and could not, abide.'

# CHAPTER XI

## 1858–1859

Letters of Philindus. Canterbury. *German Classics*. Fellow of All Souls. Jenny Lind. Birmingham Festival. Correspondent of French Institute. Death of Manuel Johnson. *Ancient Sanskrit Literature*. Marriage. Germany. Life at Oxford. Mother's illness. Correspondent of Turin Academy.

IN the late autumn of 1857, when England was under the influence of the horrors of the Indian Mutiny, a series of papers appeared in the *Times* signed Indophilus and Philindus. It was soon known that they were by Sir Charles Trevelyan and Max Müller respectively. Sir Charles traced the Mutiny solely to the issue of the famous greased cartridges. The first letter by Philindus was entitled 'The neglect of the study of Indian Languages considered as a cause of the Indian Mutiny.' It points out that ignorance of the languages prevented any real intercourse with the natives, and created a feeling of estrangement, mistrust, and contempt on both sides, and mentions that in the examinations for the Indian Civil Service as many marks could be gained for Italian as for Sanskrit or Arabic. In his second letter Indophilus confirmed all that Philindus had said, and he advocated the establishment of an institution in London for the teaching of Oriental languages. In his reply Philindus repeated what he had already said on this subject in 1854, and anticipated the speech made thirty-two years later in the presence of the Prince of Wales, our present King. More letters followed from both Indophilus and Philindus, from Mr. Monier Williams and Professor Syed Abdoolah.

These letters were collected and published together as a small pamphlet, and diligently circulated; but, as is well known, no arrangements were made by Government to assist their candidates for the Civil Service of India in acquiring the various subjects for examinations; and when the East India Company ceased to exist their college at Haileybury, where so many eminent Indian civil servants had been educated, came to an end also, and it was left to the private unaided efforts of the English Universities to provide the special teaching required.

The lectures announced by the Professor for this term were on 'The Principles of Comparative Philology,' and he was also reading *Faust* with a class.

During January Max Müller paid a visit of some days to his friend Dr. Stanley, then Canon of Canterbury, where he met Whewell, Sir John Herschell, and others. He tells his mother, 'We were in all a party of twelve, women as well as men, guests of a young, unmarried man.' He adds that he had seen nothing of the wedding of the Princess Royal, and had always hoped it might bring Bunsen over, but he did not come. Max adds:—

'He has been made Baron without his knowledge or will, and the Prussian nobility may be proud that Bunsen has done them the honour of taking such a title.... Things still look bad in India; and in France they begin to laugh at England—it is only to bring down the Funds, that Morny may do a little business. But it is splendid when one sees how a small country like England can carry on war with India and China, and quarrel with America, Russia, and France, and yet is always cheerful and never loses her head.'

Truly Max Müller loved his adopted country, though he could see her faults as well as her virtues. He had been naturalized in October, 1855.

Bunsen writes in February:—

*Translation.*

'I have read your brilliant article on Welcker in the *Saturday Review* with great delight. In fact everything would give me undisturbed pleasure did I not see (even without your telling me, which however you have done, as a sacred duty between friends) that you are not happy in yourself. Of *one* thing I am convinced, you would be just as little so, *even less*, in Germany, and least of all among the sons of the Brâhmans. If you continue to live as you do now, you would everywhere miss England—perhaps also Oxford, if you went to London.... Unfortunately I have neither read Indophilus, nor

Philindus; please tell me the numbers of the *Times*. . . . I am curious about your German Reading Book. I maintain one thing—you are not happy, and that comes from your bachelor life.'

TO A FRIEND.

55, ST. JOHN STREET, *February* 14.

'I hear you want some translations of the Greek Classics. Oh that I could read some of them with you! They ought not to be read as if they were very wise and learned and unintelligible books, but as if they were written by a man whom we know and like. Those ancients were exactly like our modern poets and philosophers. In their time they were read and criticized by men and women not a whit wiser than we are. It is mere pedantry if, instead of reading and enjoying their writings, we sit down to interpret them, and to look grave and wise over their volumes. If Plato and Aristotle came to stay at our house, most of our young ladies, to say nothing of how shocked they would be by their manners, would converse with them as they do with Maurice, or Kingsley. They would tell them where they could not quite agree with the views of those wise philosophers, they would think now and then that they talked nonsense, and might speak more like other gentlemen, and they would thank them for anything really good and sensible they had to say. The real charm of the Classics is the simplicity with which they say things which in our modern writers would be commonplace. They had nobody to imitate, nor had they to avoid saying what others had said before. There is no effort, nothing far-fetched in their prose and poetry. And then they did not write merely because they wished to publish a book. They generally wrote because they felt they had something really important to say. They wrote with their whole heart and soul, and if we read them carefully we sometimes imagine they knew that they would be read for thousands of years, and that they wrote for mankind rather than for the drawing-rooms of Athens.

'You were right about my article on Welcker in the *Saturday Review*. I had lately written a good deal for that journal, and had just told the editor that for the present I could write no more, because I wanted to finish some other work. Now that I find you read the paper, I shall write again, and I daresay you will find me out, although my horrid German handwriting is changed into decent English print. There was a short time ago an article on German Mystics; I sometimes thought of you whilst I was writing it. I have not yet given up my intention of going to India; I might have had an appointment last year, but I found that my mother, though she wrote she would not dissuade me from going, was so much grieved at the thought of never seeing me again, that I felt I ought not to go as long as she lives. I do not know whether it was right, and yet I cannot bring myself to believe it was wrong.'

To Mrs. Kingsley.

55, St. John Street, *February* 28, 1858.

'I received your kind message and I must thank you for it myself, and tell you that I have been longing to spend a few warm and bright days at Eversley. But the spring will not come, and I am busy and have to lecture, and to write, and cannot get away. As soon as the sun comes back, and as soon as I hear from you or Mr. Kingsley that I may come, I shall be delighted. I want to lay in a new stock of happiness, though what I carried away from you last Christmas is by no means exhausted.

'I had a letter from Bunsen—he tells me he is pouring out his heart about *Hypatia* in a preface. Does Mr. Kingsley know of it? Please to tell him also, that my little horse is the most delightful creature, and quite a pet among the Dons and Donnas of Oxford.'

His mother writes early in March that she had been to a ball, to which Max Müller replies:—

*Translation.*

'There is nothing of that sort for me. Giving lectures and correcting proof-sheets, those are my amusements late and early. Then it is so cold one is quite shrivelled up, and one cannot ride in such weather, and the horse eats his head off and has nothing to do! Froude has been staying with me. I have already told you my salary is raised to £500; I hoped it would be £600, and that is cheap for all the work!'

To a Friend.

55, St. John Street, *March* 7, 1858.

'Your letter written with the accompaniment of Beethoven's *Septette* was all music to me. What is time and space, and earth and life, and all that people call stern reality? While I was reading your letter I was sitting in a quiet corner of your room—watching the dark cedar tree that stretches out its broad branches to bless you and your house, and I listened to every note, and I thought of the happy days when I drank in the same strange melodies as a child, six years old, and my mother told me it was so beautiful, and I believed it because she told me so, and have believed it ever since. And why? Who can tell us the meaning of those sounds? and whence do they come, and whither do they go? I once asked my old music-master who had taught him music, and he told me that he had a master; and then

I went on asking who had taught his master, and he did not understand what I meant, and I remember how his eyes grew bright when I told him, with all the authority of a child, that I was certain that God must have been our first music-master. And now I am thinking what he wrote in my album when I left him in 1836—I was then sent to school at Leipzig. I shall try to translate it for you. "Music, echo of a distant, harmonious world—sign of the angel within us; when the word is speechless, and the eye, and the tear, and when our silent hearts lie lonely behind the bars of our breast, it is thou, Music, through whom they call to each other and mingle their distant sighs." He was a good old man. I hardly know whether he could have written those lines himself, and, as I am writing them down, I think he must have taken them from Jean Paul; but he must have been a true musician whoever wrote them. Poetry is like poverty—the true poet and the truly poor are ashamed to show what they suffer, and what they are longing for. It is not so with music, and you sometimes find men, who would be ashamed to indulge in any poetical sentiment, plunging with their whole soul into the Unknown, the Infinite, the Beautiful, and the Divine, when it appeals to their hardened hearts with the sounds of music. There is a blessing for every one, and even the cold man of the world has somewhere or other his happy valley and his quiet cottage, where he sees his old friends, his old thoughts, his old feelings, which, if they meet him in the drawing-room, he dismisses with a haughty sneer, as if he had never known them. Excuse my wandering. I must say like you—there is the music, it is all that *Septette* of Beethoven, which they are playing in the other room.'

The following letter was sent to Max Müller about this time, from a man who had been long in India, confirming the views advocated by Philindus:—

'There seems to be a greater stir than ever in India about education for the natives, and yet in this country young men who obtain direct commissions in the Company's service are not even obliged to have the slightest knowledge of any vernacular before starting. To such an extent is this carried, that I understand from various pupils who were educated here, that a candidate taking up Hindûstânî is looked upon as rather a fool for his pains. I was extremely glad to see from certain letters in the *Times* that the attention of the future rulers will be directed to this point. The two schemes ought undoubtedly to proceed hand in hand. The poor native ought not to be expected to make every effort to acquire a knowledge of English, without there being also a corresponding effort made by his rulers to acquire the native language.'

To his Mother.

*Translation.* Oxford, *April* 5.

'To-day is Easter Monday, but the Hare has laid no egg for me, as he used to do in the grandfather's garden. Instead of that, I have sat the whole day at work, except that this afternoon I had a visit from Sir Charles Trevelyan, and also saw Lord Macaulay, whose sister Trevelyan married. The Jelfs are here . . . and I dine there on Tuesday, and we shall have some music. A little boy was born at the Thomsons' a few days ago, and one is soon expected at the Kingsleys', or I should have spent Easter there. I have been several times in London for a couple of days. I had to examine. One evening I heard a fine concert in the new St. James's Hall. I have such a bad cold that every limb aches, and yet I have to sit and slave from morning till evening. I have had a great deal of writing about an Oriental Institute in London, to be founded by Government, and then came a change of Ministry, so now we must wait for a new Ministry. My little horse is my best friend. I must spend the summer in my furnace of a room. I am printing an English book on the *Veda*, and that must be finished off, if I am not first finished off myself, as you very truly remark.'

During this year Max Müller became more and more intimate with Dr. Thomson, Provost of Queen's, whose house was always a pleasant change for him from the loneliness and hard work of his own bachelor *ménage*. Mrs. Thomson writes:—

'I know the Archbishop was more devoted to Mr. Max Müller than to any of his Oxford friends, and they met almost daily before his marriage. He retained the same warm affection for Mr. Max Müller to the end of his life, and did so enjoy having him at Bishopthorpe. The Archbishop sympathized in all the difficulties about his marriage, which were confided to him, as Mr. Max Müller had helped him in all the difficulties of his own marriage a few years before.'

At Easter Max Müller's *German Classics* was published, and was welcomed in Germany as warmly as in England. The *Times* reviewed it later in the year most favourably:—

'Unlike all other books of extracts we know, it is compiled with a view of systematizing its contents. The extracts are not thrown together at the capricious suggestion of personal taste, but the Professor has chosen only characteristic specimens, and has so arranged them in their relative sequence that they suggest, as it were, a history of the literature of his country. His brief preface shows the scope of his design, and, brief as it is, is the best History of German Literature, in its relation of social changes, with which we are acquainted. . . . We can accept this as an English class-book, peculiarly adapted for our own special purposes.'

On May 9 Max writes to his mother that he cannot ask her to visit him this year; he is so overwhelmed with work, both in Oxford and elsewhere, that she would have to be much alone. Probably the whole summer must be spent at work, but if he can find time for a week or two in Germany, he comforts her with the assurance that he will go to her. The same letter mentions the death of his old friend Gathy. 'I felt it very much. . . . I had so often seen him of late years; he was a thoroughly brave and honest man. The old friends are gathering on the other side, and he must be happier there than here.'

A very few days after writing the above Max Müller was asked whether he would accept a Fellowship at All Souls if it were offered to him. It was the very thing needed at that time to make his life happier and less lonely; the offer was entirely unexpected, and was accepted with great thankfulness. He often mentioned in later years that, as he entered the College after his election, he said to himself, 'My home for the rest of my life. I shall not leave this till I am carried out.'

### Letter from Sir Robert Herbert.

*March* 3, 1902.

'To Mrs. Max Müller,—Mr. Robarts has told me that you would like to hear from me anything I can tell you about the circumstances connected with your husband's election to a fellowship at All Souls. The story is a very simple one. The person to whom credit is principally due for a step unprecedented at that time—the election of a foreign gentleman to an Oxford fellowship—was the late Henry Coxe, the Librarian of the Bodleian. He and his wife were intimate friends of my family and myself, and I used often to pass a quiet evening with them in Beaumont Street, and meet there Max Müller, for whom Mr. Coxe from the first entertained a warm friendship. I thus became aware that while the status and home afforded by a College fellowship would be an advantage and convenience to your husband, he would, on his part, contribute much honour and pleasure to the College that might secure him as a fellow, and I cordially joined with Mr. Coxe in pressing upon the Fellows of All Souls the advisability of electing him under the special power of doing so conferred by the new statutes. Max Müller could not have failed to find in Oxford a great number of warm friends and admirers, but in the earlier days of his residence there, it must have been a comfort to him to have a *home* in the College which was so proud of him.—Yours very sincerely, 'ROBERT G. M. HERBERT.'

Max Müller's large sitting-room on the ground floor next the Library, in the corner of the great Quad, commanded a beautiful view of the spire of St. Mary's and the dome of the Radcliffe Library, a view that was a constant delight to him, and was always pointed out to his visitors with loving appreciation.

TO DR. ACLAND.

ST. JOHN STREET, *May* 26, 1858.

'MY DEAR ACLAND,—I never thought that anything would happen to me again on which I should be congratulated, but I certainly do appreciate the very kind feeling which prompted the Fellows of All Souls to elect me, and in a dark night even the smallest light is welcome. I am looking forward with great pleasure to living in College, but at present there is no set of rooms where I could put up all my books, &c. I am confident I shall feel quite at home at All Souls for the rest of my life. Wherever our Father leads us, there is our Fatherland.'

TO HIS MOTHER.

*Translation.* ALL SOULS COLLEGE, *June* 7, 1858.

'You will wonder when you see my new address. The bells have been rung again for me in Oxford, for I have, quite unexpectedly, received a fellowship in All Souls College. I have very nice rooms, but I only begin really moving to-morrow, and therefore write to-day, as I shall at first have no time for letters. I had no idea of it, and the thing has excited great surprise. A fortnight ago I was asked if I should have any objection if I were elected, and the next day I was elected. Why they elected me I have no idea: it is a great distinction. What I like best is being free from the trouble of housekeeping. My house will be let; my furniture I bring to my rooms here. The rooms are larger, three of them. But now I can't marry, or receive you as a guest. The Jelfs are here, and are very sorry that I have joined the Monks. Nearly all our fellows belong to the best families in England, several are members of Parliament, some in the Ministry. So you see monkhood is bearable, and I need not have a tonsure! The lectures are nearly over, and in a fortnight I think of going to the seaside.'

FROM THE DEAN OF RIPON.

'MY DEAR MRS. MAX MÜLLER,—You ask me to tell you some of my recollections of your husband in the early days before you were married. I fear they are scanty; but it is pleasant, as he found it, to make an excursion into *Auld Lang Syne*.

'When I went up to Balliol in 1850, he had just begun to give lectures on what was then a new subject, Comparative Philology. I think he had been so immersed in the *Rig-veda* during the two previous years, that his powers as a lecturer had hardly been tested; but his delight in his subject, his clearness of exposition, and his excellent English, not the worse for the slight foreign accent which he always retained, carried us all away. And the ease with which he traced the startling changes of words, such as that which derived the French word *même* from *semet ipsissimum*, came like a series of dissolving views. All such things have become common property long ago, chiefly owing to his very readable books on the science of language and kindred subjects.

'I met him only occasionally during my undergraduate course. Eight years make a great difference at that time of life. But while I was a curate at Claydon I had the happiness to come across his memorable Essay on Comparative Mythology. It was the best counteraction that could be to the narrowness which sometimes besets an earnest pastorate, and carried one into regions before undreamed of both of history and of thought. I was then a fellow of All Souls, and I went back there in 1857 to read under Stanley, who had just become Professor of Ecclesiastical History. It was then that the happy thought occurred to some of our fellows, first, I think, to my old friend Robert Herbert, to invite Max Müller to become a fellow of the College. This was done under the new Ordinance of the Commissioners for giving effect to the Oxford Reform Act of 1854, which allowed us to elect a Professor, a man of literary distinction, to an "Exceptional Fellowship," one which bound him neither to residence, nor to celibacy. He was elected in the beginning of 1858; and, though I was at that time appointed to a College living sixteen miles from Oxford, I saw him every time I drove into the city. I remember especially one such time in the summer of 1858, which (all my parishioners being in the harvest field) I spent in my College rooms, having arranged to meet one of our fellows, Godfrey Lushington, to read German together. We were puzzling over some difficult expressions in Lessing's great "Essay on the Education of Mankind," when Max came to our rescue, and devoted a large part of two days to our benefit. It was delightful to see his enthusiasm in drawing out the thoughts of one of the greatest of his countrymen, and one hardly realized—he was so simple and genial—that one was being taught by one of the leading philologists in Europe.

'The Ordinance under which we elected him demanded, though in language not perfectly clear, that we should choose our fellows according to their merits as shown by the examination; but the old custom still remained of choosing them as one would the members of a social club, and I was one of three who had appealed to the Visitor against this practice. The dispute lasted some five or six years, and I am afraid must have given Max some days of discomfort, though his lot was otherwise enviable. He tried to mediate, and asked, but in vain, that the examiners should report a small list of fit candidates between whom the choice should be made. The decision was eventually given according to our contention: but Max, though mainly on our side, had, I think, what is called a "sneaking kindness" for the old system—had he not been elected by the College as it was?—and maintained that those who, as the *Saturday Review* said, were chosen for "what are vaguely called social considerations," formed a pleasing variety in the monotony of Oxford residents. But though he used to complain that he sometimes suffered from being identified with us, who were spoken of as the Sepoys in allusion to the Indian Mutiny of 1857–8, I am sure he never had an enemy in the College. He was always genial, and had nothing of the mere Don in him. On occasions such as the annual Gaudy on All Souls' Day, he would become the German student again, and join with the somewhat tumultuous merriment of the younger fellows, and be induced to sing "Gaudeamus igitur." If ever there was a cloud upon his brow, it was from a cause unknown to us, and was happily dissipated by the event so full of blessing to you and to him in the following year, 1859. It has always been a dark spot of disappointment to me in the retrospect, that I was prevented by a sharp touch of fever from being present at your wedding.

'Of all that came after that event no one can speak so well as yourself. But I do not like to close this letter without a word expressive of the value that I entertained for his friendship and for his teaching. I never knew him other than a kind and generous friend, and a delightful companion. He would frankly give one of his best on any subject, grave or gay. I remember, when he brought home from Italy the cartoon of the *Carità*, that he asked me to look at it in his library, and to say whose work I thought it to be; and when I said that, though I was not much of a judge, I should have assigned it to Andrea del Sarto, he showed as much pleasure as if it had been the testimony of a connoisseur. But I think that his mind turned more and more to the problems of religion; and it is my belief that his researches and his teaching have done as much as those of any man of his generation to enlarge the horizon of men's views, and to win for Christian faith a truer and a wider basis.

'Believe me, yours sincerely and affectionately,

'W. H. FREMANTLE.'

TO HIS MOTHER.

*Translation.* ALL SOULS COLLEGE, *July* 11.

'When I was in London I made the acquaintance of Jenny Lind. She has a very nice house near Richmond. I called on her twice, and heard the Swedish singers at her house. But she will not sing herself any more, and that is a great mistake. I went too to a great gathering at Harrow; Lord Palmerston was there, and Lord Stratford de Redcliffe, and all the *beau monde* of London, and when my name was mentioned there were great cheers. Then I went to a great whitebait dinner at Greenwich, but all this was very tiring. I went too to a concert at the Crystal Palace, 2,500 people in the chorus and orchestra, and yet it was not powerful enough, unless one was quite near.'

In July Bunsen writes to congratulate:—

*Translation.* CHARLOTTENBERG, *July* 31.

'Nothing could be more agreeable and suitable; it is personally and nationally an honour, and a unique acknowledgement. I can only add the wish that you may enjoy the dignity itself as short a time as possible, and take leave as soon as possible of the Fellow celibates of All Souls. Your career in England wants nothing but this crowning-point. How prosperous and full of results has it been! Without ceasing to be a German you have appropriated all that is excellent and superior in English life, and of that there is so much, and it will last for life.'

For several years Max Müller had been a regular contributor to the *Saturday Review*, and the titles of his articles show the variety of questions that interested him:—The Transactions of the Philological Society, Dialects of Algeria, Chinese Buddhist Pilgrims, Hindûstânî Literature and the King of Oude, The Origin of Goethe's *Faust*, Renan's Essays on the History of Religion, The English Alphabet applied to the Languages of India, German Mystics, Anglo-Indian Phraseology, and Latham's *Celtic Philology*, were among the topics treated by his facile pen. He looked on these writings as a recreation, as a change from Indian Civil Service and Military examinations, from lectures, and from collating and editing the *Rig-veda*. He had already in 1857 begun to put together the materials for his *History of Ancient Sanskrit Literature*, which required considerable research in works which at that time only existed in manuscript. The Bodleian meetings also made constant demands on his time. No wonder that he complains so often of being worn and weary, and longing for rest.

To his Mother.

*Translation.* All Souls, *August* 6.

'I returned yesterday from London, where I had to examine for a whole week from ten till six. My head at last began to buzz, and I am glad that it is over and my holidays at last begin. The summer here is delicious and my monk's life very pleasant. The front view from my windows is beautiful, and I have the whole College to myself, ten servants, &c.; who can want more? I invite my friends to dinner, and nothing is wanting but that you could visit me in my new home, and it is sad that that cannot be. I can only invite ladies for great festivities. Did I tell you that I paid Jenny Lind a visit lately and she sang to me nearly the whole of the *Schöne Müllerin*, and so perfectly? She loves the poems, and she said to me, "I felt I *must* sing them to you." She sang them with so much expression that it was like a real opera; I hardly recognized the songs. Then she sang Schumann and Mendelssohn. It went on from four in the afternoon till one in the night, and then she sent us in her carriage back to London—Benedict, Joachim, and Piatti. Joachim played very well, and Piatti's cello was splendid. In fact it was perfection, and she is a most interesting woman, and when she likes very agreeable. I heard lately from Bunsen . . . he invited me to Heidelberg for his birthday, August 26, but I had to write that I could not come, and I must tell you now, I must stay this summer in England. I have had too many interruptions in my work, and must use the holidays to make the time good. You know how gladly I would go to you, but I should not feel it right, for I am quite well, and do not want rest. I have been riding a great deal, which is always good for me.'

To a friend, to whom he had sent a little novel, very popular just then, *A Lost Love*, he writes :—

All Souls, *September* 10.

'Is there such a thing as a Lost Love? I do not believe it. Nothing that is true and great is ever lost on earth, though its fulfilment may be deferred beyond this short life. Marriage is meant for this life only, but love is eternal, and all the more so, if it does not meet with its fulfilment on earth. If once we know that our lives are in the hands of God, and that nothing can happen to us without His will, we are thankful for the trials which He sends us. Is there any one who loves us more than God? any one who knows better what is for our real good than God? This little artificial and complicated society of ours may sometimes seem to be outside His control, but if we think so, it is our own fault, and we have to suffer for it. We blame our friends, we mistrust ourselves, and all this because our wild hearts will not be quiet in that narrow cage in which they must be kept to prevent mischief.'

To his Mother.

*Translation.* *September* 15.

'I have just lately had a good deal of enjoyment from the Birmingham Festival, where I went to hear the *Elijah* and *Messiah*, &c. It was splendid. I was on a visit to the Minister of Education near Birmingham, and we drove in each day. English country life is so pleasant; nowhere else is there anything like it. Then I spent a couple of days at Rugby with the head master. Will you send me the book of Weber's songs with "Mein Schatz, der ist auf der Wanderschaft"? I have played it to a very dear friend of mine, and she wishes to have it. She is the daughter of Lord Denbigh, where I often go to stay; she sings well, and you would like her.'

Max Müller had carried through his resolution of spending the chief part of Long Vacation in College. He often said later he was looked at with very dubious eyes by the College servants, who were in general completely their own masters in 'the Long,' but were obliged to stay in College if a Fellow was in residence.

It is evident from the following letter that the feeling of soreness between Max Müller and M. Renan had quite passed away. The article translated by M. Renan was the one which originally appeared in the first number of *Oxford Essays*, and was afterwards reprinted in all the editions of *Chips*.

To M. Renan.

All Souls, *October* 27.

'I have looked over the translation of my Comparative Mythology and I think it is excellent. I am extremely obliged to you, and still more to Madame Renan, for the trouble you have taken in making my English language and my German thought palatable to the French public. The corrections I have made bear chiefly on Sanskrit words. . . . In a few passages which I have marked, the chain of the argument seems to me somewhat broken by omitting some of my illustrations. But I leave this entirely to your judgement, as you know how far one may try the patience of the French public.

'I should be glad to have your name on the title-page, as introducing my essay—as you have so kindly done—in the *Revue Germanique*. It might perhaps be as well to add to my name, "Professeur à l'Université d'Oxford" or Fellow of All Souls College at Oxford, only I do not know how the latter can be rendered in French. . . .

'I have received the second edition of your *Grammaire Comparée*, and I have to thank you for it in more than one sense. No doubt we shall always differ on some points in the early history of language, and I shall have to oppose some of your views with all my power. But I feel confident that no difference of opinion with regard to scientific questions will ever lead again to any personal misunderstanding between you and me, and I beg to assure you of my sincere respect and gratitude.'

The lectures this term were on 'The Parts of Speech.' In the Summer Term Max Müller had given a course on 'The Origin and Formation of the French Language,' continuing also his class for reading *Faust*.

To his Mother.

*Translation.* Oxford, *November* 11.

'I had a large dinner of 14 and an evening party the other day. Jenny Lind was here, and would sing nowhere but at my party. It was wonderfully beautiful. You can imagine that people were very anxious for invitations and it all went very well. She came first in the morning to practise a little, then in the evening she sang Mozart's "Batti, batti," Mendelssohn's "Auf Flügel der Gesanges," Swedish songs, Schumann, and Weber's "Mein Schatz, der ist auf der Wanderschaft." She came again the next day and sang Schumann and Schubert: it was a great treat, but really almost exhausting.'

To the Same.

*Translation.* Blenheim Palace, *December* 6.

'You would be surprised to see me sitting here on my birthday, not at All Souls, but on a visit to the Duke of Marlborough. Last week I spent a few days in the country in the house of Lord Lovelace, who married Byron's daughter. It is now inhabited by one of the

Judges, the same who managed the divorce of Lord and Lady Byron, a most interesting old man. Yes, you are right when you say I cannot be grateful enough to God for all the goodness He has shown me, my whole life long. My present position is really, of its kind, quite perfect, and if I only keep well I am thoroughly satisfied. Here I was called away to dinner, which was splendid; we dined in the Rubens room, and opposite me hung Rubens and his wife, Andromeda, and Phillip of Spain. We were twenty-four at dinner. After dinner we wandered about the rooms. There was a splendid Erard in one room, and we had some music; the next day I saw the pictures in the private rooms, which one cannot see otherwise, the gems, the sketches, then more music. The Duchess is musical and very friendly. They asked me to stay another day, but I could not. Two days later I had a party from Blenheim to luncheon—Lord Denbigh's family, &c. It went off very well. The Jelfs are here, and we have a great deal of music.'

TO M. RENAN.

ALL SOULS, *December* 15.

'I have just read your severe remarks on Oriental Studies in England, in one of the recent numbers of the *Débats*. You are partly right, and I was delighted to see how well you perceived the real and true value of the discovery of the *Vedas* for the reconstruction of the annals of the human mind, and the right appreciation of the earliest efforts of man in his search for his true home in God. But how few perceive this importance of ancient Sanskrit literature even now. How few of our best Sanskrit scholars are aware that the stones which they bring to light are the relics of a real temple, and the object of philology is not only to cut stones and collect rubbish, but to find the foundations and ground-plan of that lost Sanctuary. We are all progressing, and the importance of our studies dawns upon us by degrees. To the early Greek refugees, the Greek which they taught in Italy was not the key to a lost civilization, not the lever, as it turned out to be, that was to lift the dead weight of the Middle Ages; it was simply an accomplishment, the mark of a cultivated mind and curiosity. Surely there was something grand in the enthusiasm of the faith with which men like Sir W. Jones and Colebrooke pierced into the jungle of Sanskrit, and where should we be if Wilson had not opened to us many a smooth road into that enchanted forest? However, I know what you mean, only the absence of a bold critical spirit is not to be ascribed to the English nation as a whole, it is the languid temper of the present generation. But then there was a time when England had giants in thought, and Davids in boldness and faith. It will come again, and even now what you take for indolence and cowardice is more truly a feeling of awe at the greatness of the questions which now occupy the best minds in France, in Germany, and in England. You and your friends in Paris do much service by recognizing and patronizing what is good and genuine in the literary life of Germany. You might do the same for England, and thus raise your *Revue Germanique* to a *Revue Teutonique*, including Scandinavia, England, and America. I also read another article of yours, or rather an extract from your forthcoming translation of the Book of Job, with great interest. Might I ask you whether anything has been done to carry your reprint of your translation of my Essay on Mythology through the Press? I sent you the proof-sheets some time ago, but have not heard of it since. I have been very busy, as I am printing a book on the Vedic Age. I hoped it would have been out before now, but I have so many things to read, as I am going on with my work, that it will hardly be published before Easter. In the summer the fourth volume of the *Veda* will be finished, if my health allows me to work hard. As soon as I have brought out my book, I have promised to write several reviews, among the rest one on your *Origine de la langue*, but at present I have not a single moment to spare for anything but the *Veda*.'

Christmas was passed by Max Müller in All Souls—the only Christmas he was destined to pass inside the College walls—and the wish expressed in the following letter was to be fulfilled in a way he little imagined as he wrote it:—

To Miss Grenfell[1].

All Souls, *December* 30.

'I cannot let this old year pass away without once more writing to you. It seems such a long time since I heard from you. If I had followed my inclination you would have received many a letter from me. . . . I felt convinced that even without hearing from you, I might always trust in the continuance of that friendship which has been to me a rich source of blessing for many years. I hear about you now and then from our common friend Mr. Walrond, and it is always a pleasure to listen to the cheerful account he gives of you, and all your party. I am glad you appreciate him, and the longer you know him the more you will find how well he deserves your confidence and esteem. This has been a very important year to me,

[1] The aunt who had educated his future wife.

and I know not whether I should be more thankful for the trials I have had to go through, or for the blessings which God has showered upon me. Much more has been given me than I ever asked for, and I feel as if I had no more to wish for in this life. I have found a home, and a very pleasant home, as you will see when you come to Oxford. I have no cares, and if my health continues there is plenty of work for me to do. It is not such a life as I thought mine would be; you know *what* I have lost. I wish you all a very happy New Year, and I hope that this coming year may sometimes lead us together!'

The early days of the year 1859 brought Max Müller a great distinction; he was made a Corresponding Member of the French Institute, the youngest man ever elected to this honour.

To HIS MOTHER.

*Translation.* ALL SOULS, *January* 23, 1859.

'Your wishes for the New Year have brought me a good beginning. . . . This is really the only distinction that I have always wished for, and I have been not a little pleased at it. It is better than Orders, and I don't think that Tischendorf with all his hangings has been chosen a Corresponding Member of the French Institute. Here in Oxford and London it has been much talked about. It is so peaceful here in the holidays that I cannot make up my mind to go away, though I have a number of invitations, often from people I hardly know. But I prefer sitting quietly at my work, which is getting on. George Bunsen has been with me, and told me many things. Let us hope there will be no rising in Berlin. Then your papers would go down again, but never mind, my Sanskrit papers never go down! My life here is really perfect of its kind, and I say always, things go too well with me.'

To M. RENAN.

ALL SOULS, *January* 3.

'Though I cannot say with Goethe I believe that I am of the religion of Job, yet I thank you most heartily for your *Livre de Job.* Your introduction is excellent, but now and then one feels like a cat stroked the wrong way. I shall hardly be able to resist the temptation of saying something about it in the *Saturday Review,* though I have made a vow not to write any reviews till I have finished my own book. I like very much that little hint you give about Aurora, and your reasons why Hebrew remains so barren in myths. Is it not owing also to the strongly marked radical features of every Semitic word, every one telling its own tale by its three letters, and retaining its appellative power against all equivocation? How can you have pantomimes if every person as soon as he comes on the stage tells you that he is not the Lion, but Smug the Joiner? But the Aryan nations have had their revenge. When language had played all her tricks on them, they let her go, and made themselves a new language, and called it Philosophy, and that language the Semites have never learnt. I was delighted, as I need not tell you, at my election at the "Institut," and I thank you for your kind and active support. I wish I could do it in person, but till July I must slave at Oxford.'

The lectures announced for this term were on 'The Principles of Etymology,' with a catechetical class on German Classics, Max Müller's own work being used as the text-book.

Early in March, Max experienced a great sorrow in the sudden death of Mr. Manuel Johnson, the Radcliffe Observer, one of his earliest friends in Oxford, at whose house when he first arrived in 1848 he met many of the leaders of the High Church party, men of true piety, and many of them really learned, and yet, to the great surprise of the young scholar, almost entirely interested in purely ecclesiastical questions—the validity of Anglican orders, whether gowns or surplices should be worn in the pulpit, whether the candles on the altar should be lighted or not—all trifles that made Max Müller ask Manuel Johnson, 'What has all this to do with true religion?' But though Johnson told Max Müller he 'did not understand,' he remained his faithful friend to the last. Max dined almost every Sunday at the Observatory, and when his mother stayed with him she met with much kindness from Manuel Johnson and his wife. He married late in life, and in his bachelor days the large garden at the Observatory was the constant resort of men like Church, Mozley, Palgrave, Pollen, Burgon, &c. His collection of artistic treasures was a never-failing source of delight, and Max Müller tells us he 'learned much from his Italian engravings and Dutch etchings, which he delighted in showing.'

To Dr. Pauli.

*Translation.* All Souls, *March* 13.

'The sudden death of Johnson has been a great shock. For many years I have not lost any more intimate friend, and one often forgets where one really lives, and what a little step it is which divides us from those who have gone before us. The death of our friends is an earnest warning, and as such, in spite of the sorrow, is rich in blessing. You must have experienced this in the fearful trial God laid on you. I need not say that I shared your sorrow, but I would not intrude on your grief, and did not write, though I knew you were in London. I know from experience that one would rather get through the hard struggles of life in silence and alone, and when one has done so, one can turn again slowly towards life, and to one's friends round one, without having to talk over what is past. Work is a great help and comfort, and I rejoice that you have taken up your great work again. Johnson often spoke of you to me, and especially lately. He would so gladly have seen you here as Professor of Anglo-Saxon. For an Englishman he was wonderfully liberal, and I owe my position in Oxford chiefly to his influence. I shall long miss him. He was always the same, open, hearty and joyous. Well, the sorrows of life, like all other things, pass away, and the larger the number who await us beyond, the easier the parting from those we leave behind. I wish you would come to Oxford . . . but write beforehand, as I am feeling so shaken, I may go to the seaside for change.'

This spring his sister was again in great anxiety about one of her children, and Max Müller always felt his distance from all his own people keenly when they were in sorrow. He writes:—

To HIS MOTHER.

*Translation.* ALL SOULS, *March* 26.

'I often wish I could help in bearing some of your anxieties, for I have little here to make me anxious; however, you would say little pleasure either. But I am satisfied as it is, and thankful for the peace in which my life passes. You have little idea how comfortable the life in College is, and how one lives all day only for oneself and one's work, without being disturbed by anything. I am printing my book on *Ancient Sanskrit Literature*, and hope it will be ready by Whitsuntide. A French translation of my article on Comparative Mythology is just out, by Renan. I suppose I shall have to go to Paris to thank them for my election. I was elected with Lepsius, and am the youngest member.'

He finishes the letter in London, where he was examining. 'I am staying with Walrond, who is still unmarried; so you see there are other people who are as sensible as I am.'

All through this spring Max Müller worked hard at his

*Ancient Sanskrit Literature*, in which he had embodied the Prolegomena to the *Rig-veda*, written ten years before, which had at the time called forth Professor Wilson's wrath. Though, through Bunsen's influence, the East India Company gave it their patronage, and promised the money for its publication, it never was published. The reason for this is explained in the preface to this new work. Ten sheets had been printed, when Max Müller's election to the Professorship of Modern European Languages, and the three courses of lectures each year which this election involved, obliged him to lay aside his general Sanskrit studies, and confine the time not needed by the duties of his Professorship, exclusively to the editing of the text and Commentary of the *Rig-veda.* But though ten years had elapsed since the Prolegomena had been written, Max Müller found that his original views had not been proved erroneous, either by his own later researches, or by the works of other Vedic scholars, and that the greater part of the original manuscript could have been printed as it was. In these ten years many new and young Vedic scholars had arisen, and their works were carefully examined and frequent reference is made to them throughout the book. It is in his preface to this work that Max Müller first mentions a young scholar, Dr. Bühler, then copying and collating Vedic MSS. in London and Oxford. They soon became fast friends, and it was Max Müller who obtained for Dr. Bühler the appointment in India which he filled with such distinction for nearly twenty years. During all that time the friends corresponded on literary questions, and though they often differed, their friendship was close and unbroken. After Dr. Bühler's return from India they met from time to time, and always with a feeling of warm attachment. Max Müller after Dr. Bühler's untimely death in 1898, which affected him deeply, wrote: 'We always exchanged our books and our views on every subject that occupied our interest in Sanskrit scholarship, and though we sometimes differed, we always kept in touch. We agreed thoroughly on one point—that it did not matter *who* was right, but only *what* was right.' *Ancient Sanskrit Literature* was carefully reviewed by the venerable scholar Barthélemy-St.-Hilaire, in five articles in the *Journal des*

*Savants*, that famous periodical, now nearly 250 years old, the contributors to which must all be members of the Institute of France. 'This new work of M. Max Müller,' says the reviewer, 'shows considerable progress in Vedic studies; it answers and explains a number of interesting and doubtful questions, and it traces for Vedic literature a limit which according to our view is definite. It has brought order and light into the huge and confused treasure-house of the primitive monuments of the Brâhmanic religion, and this systematic arrangement rests on a basis which appears well founded.'

'The *History of Ancient Sanskrit Literature* will add greatly to the distinction with which the name of M. Max Müller is already so justly marked. The book of which I am writing is of so high an order that one may well doubt whether any one for a long time to come will surpass, or even equal it.'

Professor H. H. Wilson also wrote an elaborate review of the work, which appeared in the *Edinburgh Review*, October, 1860, being the last thing Professor Wilson ever wrote; in fact the ink of the last words was scarcely dry before the fine old scholar passed away. 'It is not possible,' he says, 'in a brief survey like the present, to render justice to a work every page of which teems with information that no other scholar ever has, or could have, placed before the public.'

A second edition was called for within a year, but so rapid was the progress of Vedic studies at that time, that Max Müller, though often urged to do so, would not publish a third edition, being compelled, after his rejection for the Chair of Sanskrit, to turn his attention mainly to other studies.

### To his Mother.

*Translation.* ALL SOULS, *Easter Sunday*, 1859.

'I am overwhelmed with work, but I have found time to read that book of Schleiermacher of which you wrote to me, and I read it with great interest. It is an important book, more important than his writings. Whether the publication was right it is difficult to say. It is like a *post mortem*. Many would shrink from it, and yet one learns much from it and it may be of use. Men are so made that they seem ashamed of what is best in themselves, and then it is well to have such books to show us that men are all much better than they seem to be. I am now reading *Perthes' Life*, which holds much that is important, but without the poetry of Schleiermacher's surroundings. I can well understand that after reading these books you long for some of the Greek Classics, but it is difficult to enter into the old simple life and thoughts; and to enjoy the beautiful and true as they were then felt and thought of, requires longer and more gradual study. You know Schleiermacher's *Plato*, but it is not easy to enjoy; *Phaedrus* is understandable, also the *Symposium* and *Phaedon*, and these are enough to give you an idea of Plato as a man. I can settle nothing about my summer plans. To begin with, war is sure to break out in Italy, and it may be that powder and shot will be seen on the Rhine.'

It was about this period that the natives of India began to speak of Max Müller as 'Moksha Mûlara,' which was thus explained by one of their Pundits: 'He who by publishing the *Veda* for the first time in a printed form gave (*ra*) the root, (*mûla*) the foundation, the knowledge of final beatitude (*moksha*), he is called Moksha Mûlara.' At the present day this Indianized form of his name is in common use among those who know his works.

To his Mother.

*Translation.* All Souls, *May* 29.

'I am very tired, and yet I have still so much to do before I can get away. Now there are the lectures, and I am printing and writing away at my book. Then I have four examinations before me, and then, please God, I shall start. Here in England things are quiet, but they begin to form volunteer corps. The undergraduates drill and shoot, and we are making ready for whatever comes. My horse costs a lot of money, but not so much as a wife. I have been again in London to hear Jenny Lind and Joachim—beautiful. I sat by the Archbishop of Canterbury. Then I had Deichmann the violinist here, and a party to which Mrs. Gaskell (Mary Barton) came. And so one fights one's way through life, and receives many a black eye! I am very sorry not to have seen old Humboldt again, and indeed for him it was time to rest—he has done his day's work.'

And now, after three years of silence and separation, borne submissively as the will of God, bright prospects suddenly opened, and within a fortnight of the last letter to his mother, Max Müller was asked to Ray Lodge as the future husband of her he had loved for nearly six years. His friend Walrond was engaged to her younger sister, and life appeared one dream of happiness to the two sisters. The day after his arrival at Ray Lodge, Max Müller wrote to her uncle, his friend Charles Kingsley:—

RAY LODGE, *Whit-Sunday*, 1859.

'Can you believe it? I cannot. I knew not that the world contained such happiness. You know what we have suffered, and now think of us, and pray for us to God, that He may help and teach us how to bear such joy and blessing. The past was so dark and awful, and the world now is so happy and bright. We shall meet on Tuesday. I long to see my new dear aunt, my old dear friend Mrs. Kingsley. Oh, this world of God is full of wonders, but the greatest of all wonders is love.'

Baron Bunsen wrote on July 23:—

*Translation.*

'My sons knew too well what delight they would give me by their communication, which has already given us all a foretaste of the delight of your visit with your bride, and meanwhile has brought me your affectionate letter. I have felt all these years what was the matter with you, and I sympathize with your happiness as though it concerned one of my own children. I therefore now, my loved friend, wish you all the more happiness and blessing in the acquisition of the highest of life's prizes, because your love has already shown the right effect and strength, in that you have acquired courage for finishing *at this present time* your difficult and great work on the *Veda*. The work will also give you further refreshment for the future, whilst the editing of the *Veda* still hangs on your hands. Therefore let us all wish you joy most heartily (my wife has received the joyful news in Wildbad), and accept our united thanks beforehand for your kind intention of visiting us shortly with your young wife. By that time we shall all be united here. Beg your bride beforehand to feel friendly towards me and towards us all. You know how highly I esteem her two aunts, though without personal acquaintance with them, and how dear to me is the cultivated, noble, Christian circle in which the whole family moves.'

His devoted mother wrote, on receiving the news of his engagement from her son:—

*Translation.* CARLSBAD, *June* 16, 1859.

'MY DEAR, MY HAPPY MAX,—I write to you a few lines in the greatest excitement of body and mind, so that my most ardent wishes and blessings may reach you even before I seem to be able to take in all the happiness. Yes, I thank God with all my heart for my son, who is the pride and happiness and blessing of my life! I thank God with all my heart for my son, to whom He has given his heart's desire, and I ask God that it may be for His children's blessing!

'A being whom *you* have chosen and whom you have known and loved for such a long time, must be worthy of you, and I will love her with you, as long as I live. My dear, dear Max, if I could but throw my arms round you and press you to my heart! Here I am all alone, so far from you, and I have nobody near who could calm and understand my over-full heart.

'Think what all those who love you so will say to it! And soon you will have a wife, and the happy time of your engagement will be very short, and I am to see you in your great happiness with your wife!

'I cannot write any more, my dear, good Max, the excitement has been too much for me; and you know all I should like to say to you, you know *how* I love you! And for this my love's sake your wife will love me a little! God's richest blessings be on you both! I press you to my full heart in deepest love, and I thank God with you.

'If you can, write to me soon again. You can imagine how much I should like to know everything. Farewell, my dear, good Max, and bring your G. to see me as soon as possible. With truest love,

'Your faithful Mother.'

Extracts from letters written during June and July :—

'A soul to which I cling with my soul. What is it? What is that soul? Who made it? Who sent it here? Who led it on by slow degrees till it should meet that other soul which belonged to it from the very beginning, and longed for it as for its better Self? These are awful mysteries, we cannot look into them without feeling giddy and appalled, and yet we ought to know of them, and then we can throw ourselves into the arms of God like children, utterly helpless and destitute, and yet full of faith in His love and wisdom. "Dies Leben ist doch schön, o Königin."'

'Think of us two in old Oxford again, and now it will be our home; here we shall live together under God's blessing for many years, here we shall grow old together, and from here we shall pass one day into a new and better life. There will be sorrows too waiting for you when you come here, sorrows such as no life is free from. And we shall bear them together, and remember that the same Father who now sends us so much joy, sends us grief also, and all for our real good, though we do not always see it, and though we cannot venture to fathom His wisdom in guiding our steps through this life. If we trust in Him, our life will not have been in vain, and in spite of suffering we shall be more happy than many whose outward life seems so easy and bright.'

To HIS MOTHER.

*Translation.* ALL SOULS, *August* 2.

'This is the last letter I shall write to-night, and it is for you, to thank you for all your love and goodness, and to say that my love for you cannot be lessened or disturbed by any other love: that you know, and I need not say it. And when you see my wife, you will feel how she has given me a new life, and has only increased and raised my love for you and all who are so good to me. I know how you will love her, and I look forward to our life all together with joyous hope. No discord must disturb our happiness, no littlenesses dim our great joy. I will write again from Heidelberg as soon as I can fix the day we shall meet. To-morrow early I start: our wedding is at 11.30. Morier is here; he came all the way from Naples. I call that friendship.'

On August 3 Max Müller was married at Bray Church to Georgina, elder daughter of Riversdale Grenfell and Charlotte Elliot, his wife.

A week was spent at Eversley Rectory, lent by the Kingsleys, a spot that was very dear to both of them. On the Sunday Charles Kingsley came over for his services, and administered the Communion to the newly-married pair, being their guest afterwards at luncheon in his own dining-room. The week was spent in wandering about the lovely moors or beautiful Bramshill, when they were not occupied with the papers of the examinations on which Max Müller had been busy almost up to his wedding-day. Then two or three days were given to Heidelberg, to the fatherly friend whose affection for her husband made a deep impression on the young wife. From there they went on to Dresden, where the meeting with the mother took place, and the three went together to Chemnitz to the sister, and then to Dessau. Later on, Max Müller and his wife secured a fortnight alone in Prague and Saxon Switzerland, where they had what was a most dangerous experience. They had climbed the Papststein, opposite Schandau, one sultry evening, and whilst at the top, a bare rock without any shelter, an appalling thunderstorm suddenly burst over and all round them. The play of the lightning was terrific, and the crash of the thunder such that they could not hear each other speak, and they felt that any moment might be their last. They hurried down, but it was some time before they were off the bare rocks, and then only to find themselves in a thick wood, which was no safe refuge, and thankful they were when the torrents of rain showed that the danger was passing away.

On the return journey to England, Leipzig, Halle, Brussels, and Ghent were visited. At Leipzig, Max Müller and his friend, Victor Carus, met and played together, piano and violin, as in days gone by; and at Halle he had the interest of a long visit to Professor Pott, the eminent philologist. Oxford was reached on October 24, and Max Müller and his wife settled themselves in a small furnished house in New College Lane for a few months, till they could find something more suitable.

Pending a better house, Max had to keep his books and do his work at All Souls.

To his Mother.

*Translation.* Ghent, *October* 20.

'We both long for a little quiet, and I for my work. I have had nothing but pleasure and enjoyment these last months, and I am longing for my usual occupations. The time we spent with you was delightful; how few enjoy such happiness as we had together! Take care of your health, that you may not make us anxious this winter.'

Early in November Max Müller's mother was suddenly taken dangerously ill, and his anxiety was very great. It was happily relieved before November 17, on which day his old friend Theodore Walrond was married at Bray Church to his wife's younger sister. Max Müller and his wife were present, and stayed on a few days. 'They would like to keep us here altogether,' he writes to his mother, 'but that cannot be during the lectures, and I am so happy in my own home.'

The committee of the Athenaeum Club had this year offered to elect Max Müller without a ballot, but as he was just going to be married, he felt he could not afford it at that time. He never joined any London club, as he was not constantly in

London, and used to say £10 a year was too much to pay for a biscuit, or even a glass of wine!

This year being the centenary of Schiller's birth, Max Müller gave a public lecture on Schiller, which was very well attended. 'All Oxford went to hear him,' wrote a friend. This lecture was published as an article on Schiller in the *Times*, and afterwards expanded into a longer paper, published in *Chips*.

Christmas was spent at Ray Lodge with a large family party—Walronds, Froudes, and others; and on December 30 Max Müller tells his mother he had that morning received a diploma from Turin, as Corresponding Member of the Royal Sardinian Academy; and the same day there was a very flattering review in the *Times* of his *Ancient Sanskrit Literature*, of which the first edition was already sold out.

It was during this winter that our King was resident in Oxford, as a Gentleman Commoner of Christ Church. Max Müller was often invited to dine at Frewin Hall, the Prince's residence, and the foundation was then laid of that kindly feeling which the Prince ever after evinced for Max Müller, and to which he alluded in such gracious terms in his speech at the opening of the School of Oriental Studies in 1890, speaking of Max Müller 'as one whom ever since my undergraduate days at the University I have had the advantage and privilege of knowing.'

# CHAPTER XII

## 1860–1861

Mother's illness. Death of Wilson. Move to High Street. Sanskrit election. Birth of first child. Wife's illness. Spring at Ray Lodge. Lectures on 'Science of Language.' Visit from his mother. Death of Prince Consort.

THE early days of this year found Max Müller again in deep anxiety about his mother, who had gone to her daughter at Chemnitz for Christmas, where she was taken suddenly and alarmingly ill, and for a day or two there seemed but small hope that her life would be spared. Her son's anxiety was piteous, so far away from her, and unable to do anything for her, or go to her for fear of exciting her. On February 12 he writes to her:—

*Translation.*

'It was a serious warning, and the years God has added to your life should be all the more valuable and blest. How we suffered with you I need not say. The loss of our parents is the heaviest sorrow we have to bear in life, and nothing can ever blot it out. The separation must come sooner or later, but when it comes something breaks in the heart which can never be the same again.'

To BRYAN HODGSON, ESQ. (formerly Resident in Nepal).

NEW COLLEGE LANE, OXFORD, *February* 6, 1860.

'MY DEAR SIR,—I have to thank you for your valuable papers on the Vayu and Kiranti languages. They arrived here during my absence. I was obliged to stay away from Oxford as my wife was very unwell, and I am only just beginning to resume my work. When I shall be able to go through the results of your immense labours I cannot tell at present. My time is so much taken up with necessary work that I cannot allow myself much leisure for my favourite studies. I have to print text and commentary of the *Rig-veda*, and a second edition of my *History of Ancient Sanskrit Literature*. Then I have to prepare lectures on the Literature of Modern Europe for my Chair here, not to mention a Sanskrit Grammar, which I promised to finish before the summer. Add to all this the duties of a newly-married man, and you will believe me if I tell you that I have but few moments left for following up my researches into the history of the numberless Turanian languages. I am very glad, however, to know that your important labours, though interrupted, were not left incomplete, and I trust you will find leisure in England for writing a *résumé* of all your discoveries in the Himalayan Babel. A linguistic map of that country would be very useful, and no one could do this as well as you. Some day or other I hope to return to those steep regions of philology, and nothing could be a better guide than a physical and ethnological map drawn by you.'

The lectures for this term were called 'Principles of Etymology,' but were really on the English language traced back through Anglo-Saxon to Gothic. They were a very popular course, and though attendance at Professors' lectures was no longer compulsory, Max Müller had a large audience. He had talked over these lectures with his wife, and explained them to her, as they walked together in the beautiful Taplow Woods in the clear winter weather, and on their return to Oxford he dictated the whole course to her. It was like the unfolding of a new world, ever reaching back and back, till lost in the hoary distance, where the forefathers of the European nations still dwelt together with the forefathers of the Persians and Hindus, before the great dispersion west and south.

To Professor Bernays.

*Translation.* New College Lane, *February* 6, 1860.

'Oh yes, a sign of life is always good, and so I thank you, my best friend, for your *Child of Care*. But I should like to know still more how you are, body and soul, and I should also like to know what you think of me and of my happiness. Our missing each other at Heidelberg was a fatality, for I so wished to show you my wife. I really am as happy as a "Child of Care" can be and may be; I often fear the envious Nemesis. What is beautiful is that I have to labour for my bread again, and that also succeeds fairly. I am just printing the second edition of my *History of Ancient Sanskrit Literature*. Have you received it? I sent two copies to Bunsen, one of them was meant for you. The *Veda* proceeds slowly, and other things ripen. Tell me what you are doing and planning. I have not heard from Bunsen for a very long time. George is in London, and I hope to meet him there the day after to-morrow. Nothing new happens here. As a married man I can but tell you one thing, stop being a "single" and become a "double" (*Einsiedler* and *Zweisiedler*). You can find in all women what is worthy of love, and the one who finds it in you is sure to be worthy of your love.

'I am reading *Phaedrus* with my wife, and we often think of you in our readings.'

To the Same.

*Translation.* New College Lane, *March* 29.

'As far as I can see, we have no MS. of the *Historia Sacra* of Sulpicius Severus; something by him about Saint Martin, but nothing else. If I knew that you would come over here, if such a MS. existed, I should write to Simonides[1], but I am afraid nothing will induce you to come over again. It is tiresome that you have not received my *History of Sanskrit Literature*, the more so as it is my fault. Now the edition is out of print and I am printing a second one. My enemies praise the book, and go so far as to say that it did *not* come up to their expectations; what ideas people must have of me! Well, something better is sure to come, when I have come out somewhat from my present bliss. In summer I hope to go to my new house, where I shall arrange my library, and then I look for a calm sea (*Meeresstille*).

'I hope to send you something about Monotheism soon; I do not think you will like it, and therefore perhaps it will bring me a letter. What about your appointment? When you have received that, your double state (*Zweisiedelung*) must certainly assume another shape.

'And what do you think of Humboldt's *Correspondence*? No poetry, but much truth. The old gentleman has sat for his biography to Varnhagen, and has shown himself as Varnhagen could understand him. Unfortunately Varnhagen dies soon after, and the whole matter comes undigested before the public. I am glad to see that Humboldt *on his part* has justified Bunsen, though he has not put a stop to Varnhagen's chattering. But what do the court ladies say? Will there be more of this sort? I have no time for writing; but it will be better when I am in my own house and get all things into order. In faithful friendship, yours, 'M.'

[1] The famous forger of MSS.

To M. Renan.

New College Lane, *March* 27.

'If you think the chapter on the Introduction of Writing likely to interest the larger public, I shall be very happy to see it in the *Revue Germanique*. Boehtlingk has sent me an article of his in answer to my arguments. It does not contain anything to make me change my opinion, or rather to remove the difficulties which I feel myself on the subject. If my article is to be printed in the *Revue Germanique*, it might be civil to mention B.'s objections. I am printing a second edition of my *History of Sanskrit Literature*, and find that all my time is taken up, as I have been appointed Examiner in Indian History and Geography and the Sanskrit language for the Civil Service of India. I have, however, made time to review your *Histoire des Langues Sémitiques*, or rather one chapter of it, on Semitic Monotheism. There were two long articles in print which were to appear in the *Times* at Christmas, but political subjects left no space, and so they had to be postponed till Easter[1]. We both agree and differ, as you will see, and I feel quite relieved after having expressed what I long wished to say on the subject. I am delighted to hear that you are so hard at work, your second volume progressing, and your *Étude sur le Cantique des Cantiques* finished. I have promised to write a review of Barthélemy-St.-Hilaire's researches on Buddhism, for the *Edinburgh Review*, but it will not be out before the autumn, as all the numbers till then are filled up. With sincere regard.'

Max writes to his mother in April that he has at last found a house in High Street, near Magdalen, and that he will move in in July. In all his letters he exhorts her to lead a quiet, comfortable life, and tells her that he always has enough and to spare for her, and that at her age she ought to give herself more comforts. But it was difficult to induce her to do so, after the long years of frugal living, and to the end she saved more of the money her son sent her than she spent.

*Translation.*

'Do not be always thinking how you can spare a few shillings, but enjoy the precious years God has added to your life, with constant gratitude, with quiet and purity of soul, looking more to the heavenly than to the earthly; that gives true joyfulness of soul, if we *every moment* recollect what is eternal, and never quite lose ourselves in the small or even the large cares of life. My love to Auguste and Krug,

[1] Reprinted in *Chips*, Vol. I, first edition.

who nursed you so carefully, whilst I could do nothing to help. May God send His warm sunshine on you, and make your lives as happy as He has made mine, so far beyond all I deserve!'

To M. Renan.

6, New College Lane, *May* 6.

'I have been expecting to hear from you for some time, and I am almost afraid from your silence that you did not quite approve of my review of your work which I sent you at the time of its appearance in the *Times*. The articles have certainly attained their object in England, as I have heard from many quarters. They have drawn general attention to your work, and they have inspired others with the same feelings of respect and admiration for your labours which I sincerely entertain myself. Your works stand too high to be made the object of a merely laudatory review, and I believe that where I have ventured to express a difference of opinion I have done so, not only with that respect which is due to you from everybody, but with the warmest acknowledgement of the value of your researches, even where they did not seem to me completely to confirm the results which you derive from them. I still hope I may be mistaken in my misgivings, but if there should be any expression which could have given you offence, I trust you will tell me openly, and believe beforehand that it was used unintentionally. I am anxious to hear what you think on the main point on which we differ, though in form rather than in substance, and I look forward to your second volume for the full discussion of this question. My hopes of spending part of the summer at Paris have vanished again; my wife is not well, and we shall have to stay quietly at Oxford. Have you seen a volume called *Essays and Reviews?* It would interest you and somewhat surprise you, if you consider that all the writers are clergymen of the Church of England.'

Two days after this letter was written, Professor H. H. Wilson, Boden Professor of Sanskrit at Oxford, died almost suddenly after an operation. It has been already mentioned that his last piece of work was a review of Max Müller's *Ancient Sanskrit Literature*, which was published in the October number of the *Edinburgh*, and was, as the editor says in a note, 'a posthumous testimonial by the first Sanskrit scholar of the age to the erudition and worth of the most eminent of his followers.' When the funeral was over, Max Müller announced himself as a candidate for the vacant Chair, and soon issued his testimonials, which included the names of nearly every Oriental scholar of real eminence in the world. Though the election was not to be before December, the canvass, which was begun at once, occupied nearly the whole year. On May 19 Mr. W. S. W. Vaux, of the British Museum, wrote to Max Müller:—

'On many occasions, and especially the last time (about two months since, in the East India House) when I had the pleasure of seeing him (Professor Wilson), he stated that in his judgement you were the first Sanskrit scholar in Europe. I remarked that I was glad to hear him give so decided an opinion, as I and several others naturally were anxious that his successor at Oxford should be the fittest man we could procure. To this he said, "You will be quite right if your choice should fall on Max Müller."'

The two following letters, from the Bishop of Calcutta and Dr. Pusey, are of interest as showing the good they expected from Max Müller's election to the cause of Christian missions, though Mr. Jowett wrote much about the same time that he could not make up his mind whether Max Müller or his opponent would do most for missions:—

RAVENSWOOD, SIMLA, *July* 13, 1860.

'MY DEAR SIR,—When I heard of the great loss which Sanskrit literature had sustained by the death of Professor Wilson, my thoughts naturally turned to you as his obvious successor, and it will give me great pleasure to hear that the University make an election which is certainly expected and will be approved by every one to whom I have spoken on the subject in this country.

'I feel considerable interest in the matter, because I am sure that it is of the greatest importance for our missionaries to understand Sanskrit, to study the philosophy and sacred books of the Hindus, and to be able to meet the Pundits on their own ground.

'Among the means to this great end, none can be more important than your edition and Professor Wilson's translation of the *Rig-veda.* It would be most fitting in my opinion for a great Christian University to place in its Sanskrit Chair the scholar who has made the Sanskrit scriptures accessible to the Christian missionary.

'I am glad to have this opportunity of thanking you for the clear and satisfactory letter which you wrote to me a year ago, when I consulted you on a theological difficulty which had arisen between two missionaries, as to the translation of some expressions in our Articles into Bengali. Such questions are likely to multiply, and it will be a great point to have the Sanskrit Professorship occupied by one who takes an interest in them, and from thoroughly understanding the Hindu theological terms, is able to give advice on the subject, so that it may express our meaning in a manner which will be at once accurate and will avoid the pantheistic notions which abound in Hindu philosophy, and might by an ignorant translator be transferred to Christian teaching.

'You are at liberty to make any use that you please of this letter.

'With every wish for your success,

'I remain, my dear Sir,

'Yours very sincerely,

'Professor Max Müller. 'G. E. L. CALCUTTA.'

FROM DR. PUSEY.

CHRIST CHURCH, *June* 2, 1860.

'MY DEAR PROFESSOR,—On the first election to the Sanskrit Chair, you will have heard that we were divided before two great names, Professor Wilson, whose first-rate Sanskrit knowledge was in the mouth of every one, and Dr. Mill, who, many of us thought, might fulfil the object of the founder better by giving to the Professorship a direct missionary turn. The same thought would naturally recur to us now, and I have kept myself in suspense since our sudden loss of Professor Wilson. My first impression, however, is my abiding conviction, that we should be best promoting the intentions of the founder by electing yourself, who have already done so much to make us fully acquainted with the religious systems of those whom we wish to win to the Gospel. It is obvious that without this knowledge a missionary must be continually at fault, ignorant alike of the points of contact of which, after the manner of St. Paul, he may avail himself, or of those which present the chief obstacles to the reception of the Gospel in the minds of those whom he would win. I cannot but think then that your labours on the *Vedas*—while they attest your wonderful power in mastering this ancient Sanskrit (and of course of the more modern Sanskrit, through which you had access to the older), and while they evince, as I understand, great philological talent, beyond the knowledge of Sanskrit itself—are the greatest gifts which have been bestowed on those who would win to Christianity the subtle and thoughtful minds of the cultivated Indians. We owe you very much for the past, and we shall ourselves gain greatly by placing you in a position in which you can give your undivided attention to those labours by which we have already so much profited. You know that I have felt it my duty to confine myself to a different class of languages, those which bear directly upon Hebrew. I have written, therefore, on that upon which I am alone competent to write—not your great knowledge of Sanskrit, of which we have such eminent testimony, but of the great value of that special line of study to which you have devoted yourself. Your work will form a new era in the efforts for the conversion of India, and Oxford will have reason to be thankful that, by giving you a home, it will have facilitated a work of such primary and lasting importance for the conversion of India, and which, by enabling us to compare that early false religion with the true, illustrates the more than blessedness of what we enjoy.—Yours very faithfully, E. B. PUSEY.'

The middle of June Max writes to his mother :—

'My time is quite taken up with the election business, and I sometimes wish I had not thought of it. It will absorb my time till December, and if I don't win I shall be very cross! Only think of 4,000 electors, scattered all over England, and each must be written to! In a week the British Association meets here, as in 1847, the first time I made an address in English.'

His old friend Carus came over for the meeting, and stayed with Dr. Acland. Max Müller was far too much occupied to take any part in the discussions, even in opposing the fierce attack of Mr. Crawfurd (the famous Objector-General) on the doctrine of the Aryan race, and the connexion between Hindus and the nations of Europe.

Early in July Max was busy in London examining the candidates for the Indian Civil Service in Sanskrit, Indian History and Geography. On his return to Oxford, the move to the new house, 64, High Street, took place, but his wife was so unwell that he sent her away to her father's, undertaking all the trouble himself.

TO HIS WIFE.

*July*, 1860.

'Surely everything is ordered, and ordered for our true interests. It would be fearful to think that anything, however small in appearance, could happen to us without the will of God. If you admit the idea of chance or unmeaning events anywhere, the whole organization of our life in God is broken to pieces. We are, we don't know where, unless we rest in God, and give Him praise for all things. We must trust in Him, whether He sends us joy or sorrow. If He sends us joy, let us be careful. Happiness is often sent to try us, and is by no means a proof of our having deserved it. Nor is sorrow always a sign of God's displeasure, but frequently, nay always, of His love and compassion. We must each interpret our life as best we can, but we must be sure that its deepest purpose is to bring us back to God through Christ. Death is a condition of our life on earth, it brings the creature back to its Creator. The creature groans at the sight of death, but God will not forsake us at the last, He who has never forsaken us from the first breath of our life on earth. If it be His will, we may live to serve Him here on earth for many happy years to come. If He takes either of us away, His name be praised. We live in the shadow of death, but that shadow should not darken the brightness of our life. It is the shadow of the hand of our God and Father, and the earnest of a higher brighter life hereafter. Our Father in heaven loves us more than any husband can love his wife, or any mother her child. His hand can never hurt us, so let us hope and trust always.'

On his wife's return they settled down to their quiet busy life, feeling for the first time really at home, in their own house, with his books and all their wedding gifts round them. His joyous, happy temperament, and thankfulness for every trifle, made life very bright, notwithstanding the anxiety and hard work connected with the coming election. His little garden was a constant pleasure to Max Müller, and he often worked in it. A flight of steps led to it from his study window, so that he could step out at any moment when tired with work, and enjoy his roses, of which, next to violets and lilies of the valley, he was passionately fond.

It was about this time that Max Müller received an invitation to deliver a course of lectures the following spring at the Royal Institution on Comparative Philology. He at once accepted the invitation, and continued to lecture at the Institution from time to time for above thirty years, his last course there being delivered in March, 1894, on the Vedânta Philosophy. Beyond bringing out the second edition of *Ancient Sanskrit Literature*, writing a very few articles for the *Saturday Review*, and preparing his lectures, Max Müller got through but little literary work this year. The sunshine within the house was a delightful contrast to the weather without, for it had been a summer of almost ceaseless rain, and at the usual time of hay-harvest the hay-fields round Oxford were all flooded.

Max Müller had been kept in constant anxiety about his

mother's health all through the spring and early summer, and at the end of August wrote and offered to pay her a short visit, but she felt hardly well enough for the excitement.

TO HIS MOTHER.

*Translation.* *September* 7.

'I think you are right in being quiet and alone. To see you again, and then to have to leave after a week, would be almost too much for me, how much more for you? Our lives are in the hands of a Father who knows what is best for all of us. Death is painful to the creature, but in God there is no death, no dying; dying belongs to life, and is only a passage to a more perfect world, into which we all go when God calls us. When one's happiness is as perfect as mine is, then the thought of death often frightens one, but even then that is conquered by the feeling and the faith that all is best as it is, and that God loves us more than even a father and mother can love us. It is a beautiful world in which we live, but it is only beautiful, and only really our home, when we feel the nearness of God at each moment, and lean on Him and trust in His love. And so I trust God will spare you to us, as long as it is good for us; and when the hour of parting comes, we know that love never dies, and that God, who bound us so closely together in this life, will bring us together where there is no more parting. . . . I wish you could see us here: our home is charming, and when I remember how I arrived here with one "box," my heart runs over when I see how God has blessed me.'

In September Max Müller and his wife went to Brighton, where he enjoyed the sea-bathing, and renewed his old love of swimming. There were several swimming competitions during their stay, and he always joined the competitors, and was glad to find that he kept up his former power of rapid and strong swimming.

TO PROFESSOR BERNAYS.

*Translation.* 64, HIGH STREET, *October* 21.

'I found your letter on my return, and I write at once to thank you for the beautiful and flattering proof of your friendship. All that comes from you I read with true joy, as far as I can understand it, and I look forward heartily to the fresh feast. Till the middle of December I shall have no leisure. December 7 is the election: whether I am to succeed is doubtful, but I hope I shall, especially as I have lost six months with canvassing. We are all well here; my wife is in good health, our house is all in order, nothing is wanting any more, and I thank God if all remains as it is now. It is true, happiness drives nails into our soul, but all is for the best.

'I hear nothing but sad things about Bunsen. I should grieve to lose that man.

'When will you come to England again? In faithful friendship.'

In the last days of November he heard of the death of his friend and benefactor, Baron Bunsen, who passed away at Bonn, after many months of suffering, so that at first the thought that he was at rest overpowered the sense of loss. But the feeling of loss grew ever stronger as time went on, and a year later Max Müller wrote to M. Renan: 'I miss Bunsen more every day. I feel as if I had lost a limb, and I can hardly believe sometimes that one is never to see him again here below.'

On December 7 the election to the Sanskrit Professorship took place, and Max Müller was rejected. A few days before the election an unknown friend wrote to one of the papers summing up the difference between the candidates, as 'the difference between respectable and honourable proficiency, and the complete and masterful knowledge of the subject possessed by a rare genius and profound scholar, from whose authority on the subjects of Indian philology and philosophy there is no appeal in Europe,' and then, adverting to the objection to Max Müller as not being an Englishman, the same supporter adds:—

'Mr. Max Müller's English is perfect. Many who have not heard the wonderful force and clearness of his public lectures must have read, without knowing it, some of his many contributions to periodical literature. Nothing that I know of—of thought or expression—exists to differentiate Max Müller from the highest type of refined and educated Englishman.

'But the implied charge of un-English religion, and even of irreligion, is at once the most serious, the most gratuitous, and the most cruel. If the country clergy have been persuaded, as has been wittily said, to smell rationalism in the dots over the ü in Mr. Müller's name, I cannot hope to dissipate the detested odour. I can only submit that there is not the slightest particle of ground for the suspicion, not the faintest show for the pretext that Mother Church is in danger. Surely the support and deferential testimonials of the men of highest character and well-known religious opinions in the

University should suffice to dispose of such a vague and ungenerous insinuation. A man's personal character must stand very high, and his theological opinions can afford but little ground for animadversion on either hand, when he unites as his unhesitating supporters Dr. Pusey and Dr. Macbride.'

Dr. Pusey had worked day and night for Max Müller, and when helping to send out the final notices of the election, wrote in his own hand above those he sent: 'Max Müller has already done more for the Gospel in India than any other Sanskrit scholar, by opening to our missionaries their sacred books. His election would enable him to devote himself to that work. He is the first Sanskrit scholar living.'

It was observed by an elector that could the votes have been taken by *weight*, there was no doubt how the matter would have ended. There can be no doubt that it was a keen disappointment to Max Müller, but he lived long enough to trace his almost unique position later in the world of letters, and the influence he was able to exert on religious thought in England, to this very disappointment. Had he been successful, he must have devoted his great powers almost exclusively to Sanskrit, and by doing so would no doubt have remained to the last what Wilson pronounced him to be at the time of his (Wilson's) death, 'The first Sanskrit scholar in Europe.' It was the Chair of Philology, founded some six years later specially for him, his name being mentioned in the statute of foundation, that led him on from the Science of Language to the Sciences of Thought and Religion. As Professor Macdonell says, in his admirable obituary notice in the *Journal of the Royal Asiatic Society*—

'Nothing was known about Comparative Philology when Max Müller came to this country. He introduced and popularized the new science, and soon came to be regarded as its chief exponent. He was, moreover, the first to inaugurate the study of Comparative Mythology in this country. . . . It was not till the latter half of the century that the necessary conditions were at hand for founding a science of religion. Max Müller was there to apply the needful stimulus . . . and to collect the requisite materials in his Sacred Books of the East. Thus there was a great opening in these highly important branches of learning, but no one man could have taken advantage of them . . ., had he not been one of the most talented and versatile scholars of the nineteenth century.'

The following letters were received soon after the election, and were kept together and always treasured by Max Müller:—

FROM HIS FATHER-IN-LAW.

'I know not when I have felt more deeply for the trials of others or had more reason to admire patience and resignation to God's will than in the spirit you have shown, in what I know to be a most severe trial and bitter disappointment. But now that all is over, and I have time to think, I am inclined to believe that with such unscrupulous opponents we could not have won. They had every element of success on their side, but one, and that they disavowed as affecting the claims of the candidates, namely the vast inferiority of one to the other. It must be a bitter disappointment to feel that the path of usefulness you had proposed to follow has been cut from under your feet, . . . but it is God's will, and the time may come when you will see His wisdom in disappointing your hopes and wishes.'

FROM DEAN (THEN CANON) STANLEY.

CHRIST CHURCH, *December* 8.

'You must allow me to write a few words to express what I cannot say. I have never experienced the peculiar trial under which you are suffering, but I believe, from my own bitter disappointment on your behalf, I can feel what it is for you. You will have many consolations. I need not dwell upon them. But *you* must also give *us* the best consolation that we can have, and that is the assurance that we have not been mistaken in the high expectations we had formed of you. You have it still in your power, thank God, to turn your energies from this wretched turmoil to the pursuits which have made your name what it is. You can still show that, although not Boden Professor, you are and will remain the oracle of all who wish to know the secrets of Indian literature and religion. You can still by your writings show what the Christian religion may be to India and the world, as you could not do before, lest you should be suspected of unworthy motives. You can still show us how the Christian scholar and philosopher can put to silence by Christian magnanimity "the ignorance of foolish men." [Can one not hear the beloved little Dean's inimitable chuckle as he penned these words?] You can in this crisis of your life rise to the greatness of the occasion, and make your friends more proud of you, than if they had brought you into the Professorship by a majority of hundreds. "Leave off wrath and let go displeasure; fret not thyself, else shalt thou be moved to do evil." With bitter regrets at not having exerted myself more, with the truest sympathy for you and yours. Ever your sincere friend,

'A. P. STANLEY.'

It was not easy to carry out his friend's advice, for not content with the signal victory they had gained, his opponents brought various utterly unfounded accusations against Max Müller, as that he had inspired an article in his favour which had appeared in the *Times*, and other equally vexing and untrue allegations, which, though triumphantly disproved by men like Dr. Pusey, the Provost of Queen's, Dr. Jacobson, Professor Mountague Bernard, and Mr. Dasent, the editor of the *Times*, were at the time distressing as tokens of personal animosity and malice. To a man of so loving and truthful a character, these attacks were peculiarly painful. His friend Regnier expressed the unanimous feeling of continental scholars in a letter in which he says, 'I kept on declaring, in spite of what any one could say, that your defeat was *impossible*.'

To his mother he wrote, December 16:—

'The last days have been full of disturbance. You will have seen by the papers that I did not get the Sanskrit Professorship. The opposite party made it a political and religious question, and nothing could be done against them. All the best people voted for me, the Professors almost unanimously, but the *vulgus profanum* made the majority. I was sorry, for I would gladly have devoted all my time to Sanskrit, and the income was higher; but we shall manage.'

Of this election Mr. Tuckwell writes:—

'I remember the contest for the Sanskrit Professorship, wherein I voted and, as far as I could, worked for him (Max Müller): an inferior candidate being preferred before him, first because Max was a German and therefore a "Germaniser"; secondly, because a friend of Bunsen must of necessity be heretical; thirdly, because it was unpatriotic to confer an English Chair on any but an Englishman.'

Canon Farrar thus describes this event:—

'Müller himself was made to feel the prejudice in Oxford against any novelty in 1860, when he was passed over for election to the Sanskrit Professorship. It is fair indeed to allow that it was not strictly political or religious opposition that was made to him; but the Englishman's dislike to an adopted son, and the feeling that it was not necessary to go afield to choose the absolutely best man, provided the candidate was respectable. I was of course on Müller's committee; but I soon found that there was no solid ground for hoping for his success; and hardly expected that he would poll so many votes as he did. But in truth Müller's claims were incomparable, as having really performed for early Sanskrit literature that which the Alexandrian scholars of the second century B.C. had performed for Homer, editing the text and reconstructing the antique grammar. Müller himself (this shows his goodness of heart) could not imagine why any other motive could outbalance the sole question as to who was the best candidate. He did not realize the stubborn fixedness of English and Oxford preference for an old Oxford man. Müller felt his disappointment. He was especially grieved with some of his opponent's committee; for he was a man of spirit and sensibility. He could feel the virtue of resentment, but was too noble to display the vice of revenge.'

But all other feelings were swallowed up by the terrible anxiety that fell upon Max Müller very soon after the election. On December 20 his first child, a girl, was born, and for two days his wife lay between life and death, and the doctors gave up all hope of saving her. The horror of that time he never forgot, and six months afterwards, writing to his friend Palgrave, who had lost his father, speaks thus of his experience:—

OXFORD, *July* 8, 1861.

'MY DEAR OLD PALGRAVE,—I should have tried to see you again to-day, but I know from experience that in the presence of great grief I have nothing to say, and for a loss like yours there is no comfort till we can say by ourselves, "Thy will be done." I remember but one time in my whole life when I could not say that, and my trials have been hard at times, harder than I thought I could have borne. But when my wife, whom I had loved for six years without the faintest hope of ever calling her my wife, when she, after one year of a blessed life, was for two days given up as hopeless by the doctors, then I broke down, and I could not say, "Thy will be done." And yet what is the tenure of all our happiness? Are we not altogether at the mercy of God? Would it not be fearful to live for one day unless we knew, and saw, and felt His presence and wisdom and love encompassing us on all sides? If we once feel that, then even death, even the death of those we love best and who love us best, loses much of its terror: it is part and parcel of one great system of which we see but a small portion here, and which without death, without that bridge of which we see here but the first arch, would seem to me a mere mockery. That is why I said to you it is well that human art cannot prolong our life for ever, and in that sentiment I should think we both agree. I have felt much for you, more than I cared to say. We are trained differently, but we are all trained for some good purpose, . . . and the suffering which you have undergone is to me, like deep ploughing, the promise of a rich harvest.'

As soon as his wife was sufficiently recovered, Max Müller took her and his child to Ray Lodge, where they remained until June, he going once a week to Oxford for his lectures there. He joined the Maidenhead Company of the Berkshire Volunteers, to which his father and brothers-in-law already belonged, drilled and marched out regularly, and was soon an excellent marksman; though his drill-sergeant used to complain of his drill, and declare over and over again that 'those gentlemen who think were a difficulty,' as they did not readily become the mere machines which even now is still considered the perfection of a private soldier. Later in the summer, and in subsequent years, he camped out with his company. This he particularly enjoyed, and often in after years laughed over their experiences on the Downs and elsewhere with his kind friend Lord Wantage, who was Colonel of the Berkshire Volunteers.

The agitation about *Essays and Reviews*, which had been going on ever since the publication of the book, reached its high-water mark in this spring, when Canon (afterwards Dean) Stanley's famous article on that work appeared in the April number of *The Edinburgh Review*. Max Müller, knowing many of the contributors to *Essays and Reviews*, had taken a keen interest in the whole affair, and discussed it in many a walk with Canon Stanley; but the following is the only letter found on the subject:—

To Canon Stanley.

Ray Lodge, *April* 17.

'I have not divulged the authorship, but I have just finished the article, and there is but *one* man in England that would have written it. I think that, next to Garibaldi, you are the bravest man in Europe, and the liberty you are fighting for is worth more than the freedom of Italy. I am proud to be mentioned by you in your article and in your preface. As to myself, I try all I can to forget December 7, and I begin to feel that I shall do more, as I am now, than if I were in the easy-chair of Sanskrit. But I am afraid I shall never feel at home in Oxford again, though it was the place I loved most in all the world. I feel very nervous about my lectures in London; I am afraid they won't be interesting to many people. I shall publish them as soon as they are delivered.'

In April began the lectures at the Royal Institution. There are doubtless some still who remember the enthusiastic interest they excited, the lecture-room being more and more crowded as the course went on, whilst Albemarle Street was filled with the carriages of those who attended them. Max Müller was very nervous beforehand, but by the end of his first lecture he felt that he carried his audience with him, and the interested faces of Bishop Thirlwall, the late Duke of Argyll, Dean (then Canon) Stanley, F. D. Maurice, Dean Milman, Faraday, and John Stuart Mill, not to mention many others, were an incentive to him to give of his very best.

An intimate friend who was present at the lectures reported: 'Max Müller was quite self-possessed, his wife proudly humble.' A lady who attended these lectures thus recorded her recollections years afterwards: 'I remember him then as a slight, intellectual, and interesting-looking young man, with a very clear enunciation, and a perfect command of language, and it was amusing to meet him again a few years ago as a square-shouldered, elderly grandfather.'

'These lectures,' says Professor Macdonell in *Man*, February, 1901, 'afterwards published in an extended form, passed through a large number of editions, and soon raised their author to the rank of the standard authority on philology in the estimation of the English public. Though much of what is contained in these lectures is now out of date, there can be no doubt that they not only for the first time aroused general interest in the subject of comparative philology in England, but in their day also exercised a valuable stimulating influence on the work of scholars in the sixties and seventies. Here Max Müller first displayed that power of lucid popular exposition, and of investing a dry subject with abundant interest, which has more than anything else contributed to make his name at least as famous as that of any other scholar of the past century.'

In a most interesting lecture given on December 2, 1900, before the University of Allahabad, by Pundit Satish Chandra Banerjee, these lectures are thus described :—

'Nearly four decades have now rolled away since Max Müller delivered at the Royal Institution in London his "Lectures on the Science of Language," and so much has been done since, and mainly by the learned lecturer himself, to educate the popular consciousness, that it is difficult for us to realize to-day the value and importance of these lectures. As I turn over the pages of these volumes, I come across much that I feel disposed to characterize as the A B C of the science, much that seems scarcely to require the abundance of explanation and illustration with which Max Müller has thought fit to enforce and support it. But we have to remember that when these lectures were first delivered, much of this was new, novel, and startling; it was in fact a new light which was breaking forth upon the dark and then uninviting fields of Comparative Grammar and Philology.'

'It is,' said a contemporary review, 'a fact of no ordinary significance that, in the height of the London season, an enthusiastic audience of both sexes crowded the benches and endured the heat of a popular lecture-room, not to witness the brilliant experiments, or be fascinated by the revelations of a Faraday or an Owen, but to listen to a philosophical exposition of the inner mysteries of language.'

Max Müller has told in *Auld Lang Syne* of several amusing incidents connected with the delivery of his lectures, particularly of the slight estimation in which he was held by Anderson, Faraday's demonstrator, who was so well known to frequenters of the Royal Institution forty years ago, who could not understand a man wanting no gas or experiments, not even a blackboard at first. As soon as the lectures were over, the Max Müllers returned to Oxford. The printing of the lectures began at once, and the book was out by July 9. It passed through fourteen editions, and was rapidly translated into French, German, Italian, Russian, Swedish, and Dutch, and became a most popular book in America. It was chosen by Cardinal Newman as a favourite prize-book for boys.

On July 1 Max Müller had the delight of welcoming his mother to his home, and showing her his child. She remained until the middle of October, thoroughly enjoying her son's pretty house, and going with her children to stay at Ray Lodge, and Rugby, where one of the masters, Mr. Charles Arnold, with his German wife, were old friends of hers from 1856.

The summer passed quietly and happily away, Max Müller preparing the second edition of his *Lectures on Language*, and working at the fourth volume of the *Rig-veda*, which had been delayed for a time—first, by the change of power from the East India Company to the Crown, and the doubt whether Her Majesty's Government would continue the publication of the work, and secondly, by the loss of so many months in 1860 through the Sanskrit election.

The following letter is given as among the first of the long correspondence with Messrs. Longmans, Max Müller's valued publishers, the last letter of which, in his own handwriting, is dated August 25, 1901:—

To William Longman, Esq.

Oxford, *October* 21, 1861.

'I am much pleased to hear of the very rapid sale of my *Lectures*. I hardly expected a second edition, certainly not so soon. Some of the best reviews I believe are still to come, in the *Times*, *Fraser*, *Edinburgh Review*, *Journal des Savants*, &c. You must know best whether it is prudent to make as large an edition as the first. . . . I fully appreciate the advantage of publishing my books with a firm such as yours, and I ascribe not a little of the success of my *Lectures*, as compared with the success of my earlier publications, to the popularity of your house, and your experience and judicious arrangement. So I hope we shall have no difficulty in coming to an equitable arrangement with regard to this, or any other books which I still have *in petto*, and hope to finish if all goes well.'

To Professor Bernays.

*Translation.* 64, High Street, *November* 1.

'Some time ago I sent you a sign of life, i. e. my *Lectures*, and I should much like to hear by letter how you are and what are your plans for your life. I am well, and I should much wish for you the same sunshine which Heaven has bestowed upon me, though a few dark clouds and storms belong to it also.

'How delightful if we could have you here! Germany is beautiful, but England is free, and I know how peculiarly such an atmosphere would agree with you. I have had lately a visit from George Bunsen—a brave fellow—but his father I miss more and more, and I am sure you do too. I have only just read the essay on Bunsen by Abeken, but something much more complete is to be desired. I have just begun to print a second edition of my *Lectures on the Science of Language*, and a very large one indeed. Can you send me, when you have read it, some corrections and additions? But it would have to be by return of post, as I have begun the printing already. I should like to talk to you about some points in it, but letter-paper is not sufficient for spiritual intercourse.

'Nothing new from here. Jowett has not been burnt, and the spark has not caught fire yet. But when it begins to burn, it will burn thoroughly. Pattison has married a young wife, and is now Rector of Lincoln College. Is there anything new to read in Germany? I have only just read Strauss's *Ulrich von Hutten* with great interest.'

To M. Renan.

Oxford, *November* 17.

'I heard the other day of your return from the East, and should have written to you at once to congratulate you and your friends on your safe arrival, if M. Durand, who mentioned your being at Paris, had not told me at the same time that you were in deep affliction [1], and, as far as I could understand him, suffering also yourself from illness. Those afflictions are too sacred to allow any one to intrude on the sufferer, with the expression of even the most sincere sympathy. They bring us face to face with our Father in Heaven, and when we speak and struggle with Him we want to be alone, quite alone. I speak from what I felt myself about a year ago, when my wife was given up by all physicians, and at last restored to me miraculously, I mean through the mercy of God. I have gone through much trouble since I last wrote to you, but yet I feel more like myself again, and begin to see that all was as it ought to be. We both lost a true friend in Bunsen. . . . I had another severe trial in failing to obtain the Chair of Sanskrit at Oxford: calumnious falsehood and vulgar electioneering tactics caused the result, and deprived me of the one sphere where I might have worked with all my heart and soul. However, I have got over that; I dare say it would have made my life too perfect, and disappointments are good discipline. Lastly, I want to send you a book, my *Lectures on the Science of Language*: I gave them in London, and they were well attended. I have now printed them, and am preparing a second and very large edition. I need not

[1] The sister who had educated Renan died at Beyrout of fever.

say I am anxious to have your opinion more than that of any one else. Whether for good or evil, the book has struck root in England, and there is to be a German translation in a very short time. I believe it contains some things that are new, some that are true, and some that will have to be given up as we advance towards the truer knowledge of the mysteries of human speech.'

Kind permission has been given to insert this letter:—

FROM DEAN LIDDELL.

CHRIST CHURCH, OXFORD,
*November* 16, 1861.

'MY DEAR MÜLLER,—Few things, of late, have given me so much satisfaction as reading your *Lectures*, though perhaps I should have had yet more satisfaction if the book had been addressed to readers and not hearers. Will you bear with me if I jot down one or two points which I think require more precision or fullness of statement, in a new edition, which I hope will be (as I am sure it ought to be) wanted soon. It is humiliating to hear that these lectures have been delivered to the heedless ears of Oxford hearers.

'(1) In the last chapter, you use "as an illustration only, not as an explanation," the fact that metals, &c., ring a sound, each with its proper sound.

'How far do you mean the analogy with human speech to go? Do you mean that each attribute denoted by a Root—as ma, ku, &c.—is expressed by that Root *as peculiarly and properly* as gold or silver by their respective ring? or do you mean, generally, that man as naturally expresses each general idea by *some* sound, as gold is betrayed by its peculiar ring, &c.? Has each general idea *its own* sound, or only *a* sound? I am unable to collect from your statements which you intend. For, while your argument seems to imply that each idea has its own proper sound, I cannot but doubt that you really mean to carry the analogy so far. If you do, I think a good deal more is required to prove the statement. If you do not, a few words are needed to guard against such a conclusion.

'(2) Is not the term "Theoretical *Stage*" of science somewhat inaccurate? Theoretical *questions* arise in the infancy of all sciences, and doubtless they cannot be answered till the process of classification is far advanced or even completed. If this is what you mean, I think your general and absolute statements respecting the three stages require modification. I am aware that (p. 20) you admit that "there have been instances" in which theoretical questions have arisen even in the first stage. I have my doubts whether this is not the rule, rather than the exception. Look for instance at the ancient Physics. Look at Smith's and Stewart's Theories of Language, &c.

'(3) I note a few special points that have caught my eye—(p. 21): "I *expect* we shall have to do something else." This, I think, is hardly a classical use of the term "*expect*." It would be impertinent in me to express admiration of the almost uniform precision of your English. ... [Various other small corrections follow.]

'Yours very truly, 'HENRY G. LIDDELL.'

Max Müller's mother left him when the autumn weather set in, and he writes to her:—

*Translation.* 64, HIGH STREET, *November* 20.

'I have not been well enough to write much lately, but have read a good deal, among other books Varnhagen's new work. It is wonderfully interesting, and shows signs of a very noble nature, though weak and cross-grained. He misunderstands many people, and therefore dislikes them—as specially Bunsen. His expressions with regard to him are really infamous, but I don't care for that; words do not make truth, and what he says is not true. One must not mind such false judgement of really noble impulses. As a picture of political and mental efforts, of the stupidity, even madness, of the Government, the book is invaluable. How furious the people in Berlin will be! That the publication has been allowed at all shows the advance made since 1848.'

Early in December, Max Müller received a letter from a gentleman in California, who had read his *Lectures*, urging him to study 'the philological connexion of the Indian languages of Mexico and the Alta California, and thus possibly find a key to trace its ante-Columbian history.' Though Max always felt a keen interest in the North American Indian languages, and when the Mohawk undergraduate Oronhyatakha was in Oxford, prepared a skeleton Mohawk grammar from what he learnt from him, the subject was too remote from his own special line of study, and required far too much time for him to take it up, though he was constantly urging the duty of doing so on American students, and was always very much interested in the publications of the Smithsonian Institute of Washington.

TO HIS WIFE.

OXFORD, *November*, 1861.

'It is so difficult not to grow very fond of this life and all its happiness, but the more we love it the more we suffer, for we know we must lose it, and it must all pass away. Does love pass away too? I cannot believe it. God made us as we are, many, instead of one; Christ died for all of us individually, and such as we are—beings incomplete in themselves, and perfect only through love to God on one side, and through love to man on the other. We want both kinds of love for our very existence, and therefore in a higher and better existence too the love of kindred souls may well exist together with our love of God. We need not love those we love most on earth less in heaven, though we may love all better than we do on earth. After all, love seems only the taking away those unnatural barriers which divide us from our fellow creatures—it is only the restoration of that union which binds us altogether in God, and which has been broken on earth we know not how. In Christ alone that union was preserved, for He loved us *all* with a love warmer than the love of a husband for his wife, or a mother for her child. He gave His life for us, and if we ask ourselves there is hardly a husband or a mother who would really suffer death for his wife or her child. Thus we see that even what seems to us the most perfect love is very far as yet from the perfection of love which drives out the whole self and all that is selfish, and we must try to love more, not to love less, and trust that what is imperfect here is not meant to be destroyed, but to be made perfect hereafter. With God nothing is imperfect; without Him everything is imperfect. We must live and love in God, and then we need not fear: though our life seem chequered and fleeting, we know that there is a home for us in God, and rest for all our troubles in Christ.'

To M. Renan.

Oxford, *November* 30, 1861.

'I was touched when I saw to-day in the *Journal des Debats* your thoughtful and sorrowful lines on the death of our old friend d'Eckstein. I had long been without news from him, and now that he is gone I regret and I reproach myself for not having written to him more frequently. His death reminds me of the happy time in 1846 when I was at Paris attending Burnouf's lectures, and when d'Eckstein helped me and encouraged me, and when I was fighting my way through difficulties which now would seem to me almost insurmountable. And yet I was never so happy as in those days, when sometimes I had to go without a dinner because I could not pay for it, and when I used to copy for d'Eckstein, who paid me for my work in his own generous way. Yes, we have lost many men whom we can hardly afford to spare; we still suffer from Burnouf's death, we shall long miss the presence of our friend Bunsen, but when I think of what we have lost I feel it all the more a duty to live, to work in their spirit, and thus to keep alive, as it were, some small portion of their spirit. I am sure you will feel the same, for you have a great work before you; you are wanted and you will not fail. I should like to hear from you that you are well, in body and mind, and that you do not lose your faith in the work which you have begun, and in the work which is still before you. The revival of learning in the fifteenth century was the dawn of Reformation, and I believe a similar era is approaching to fulfil what the Reformers intended, but which was frustrated by political events. You have an element in France which, if properly advised and directed, might become a most powerful engine for good, as it may be, if left in bad hands, for evil. Germany must follow the example of Italy, and must look not only for political union, but for religious union on high and neutral ground. In England too there is a yearning after real Christianity, though the struggle will be a hard one. It is a time worth living for, and I feel convinced that you will be wanted even for a greater work than that of finishing your *Histoire des Langues Sémitiques*.'

Max Müller and his wife were at Brighton at the time of the Prince Consort's death. Though he had seen but little of the Prince, Max had the truest admiration for his character, and seems to have felt strongly how much the country which misunderstood and misrepresented the noble Prince to the last, really owed him. He had sent his *Lectures* to the Prince as soon as published, and they had been most kindly acknowledged. They were by the bedside of the Prince at the beginning of his illness, as if lately read. Gracious permission has been given to insert the following letter, written nearly twenty years later, when the Queen sent Max Müller the last volume of the *Prince Consort's Life*. The five volumes, each with Max Müller's name written and signed inside by the gracious Sovereign whose subject he was proud to be, will remain a precious heirloom to his children and children's children.

'OXFORD, den 13ten *Mai* 1880.

'EURER MAJESTÄT lege ich meinen tiefgefühlten Dank unterthänigst zu Füssen für den letzten Band des *Life of the Prince Consort* von Sir Th. Martin.

'Der Verfasser hat von neuem seine sichere Kunst, seinen richtigen Takt, sein tiefes Verständniss und seine ehrfurchtsvolle Auffassung der ihm gewordenen Aufgabe herrlich bewährt, und das Geschick, mit dem er die ihm anvertrauten "goldenen Fäden" in sein eigenes Gewebe hineingewebt, so dass Jeder, der Augen hat, sie sieht und fühlt, und sie doch nie die Harmonie des Ganzen stören, beweist die geübte Hand des wahren Meisters.

'Mit ernsten Gefühlen schliesst man das Buch und trennt sich von ihm wie man sich schweren Herzens von einem lieben Grabe trennt. Wie anders hätte die Welt sein können, wie viel Gutes wäre möglich, wie manches Unrecht unmöglich, wenn zwei Augen sich nicht so früh geschlossen! Auf das Warum, das immer und immer wiederkehrt, kann die menschliche Vernunft keine Antwort geben. Nur ein fester Glaube an eine Weisheit und eine Liebe, die Alles übersteigt, was wir Weisheit und Liebe nennen, bringt, wenn auch nicht Trost, doch Ruhe und Frieden auf den einsamen Lebensweg. Was wirklich unser war, das kann keine Macht uns rauben, und nichts auf Erden bleibt uns so sicher als der Besitz vergangenen Glücks.

'Mit wahrer Verehrung habe ich die Ehre zu verbleiben

'Eurer Majestät dankbarer und unterthänigster Diener,

'F. MAX MÜLLER.'

*Translation.* 'OXFORD, *May* 13, 1880. YOUR MAJESTY,—I beg most humbly to offer the expression of my deeply-felt gratitude for the last volume of the *Life of the Prince Consort*, by Sir Theodore Martin. The editor has again nobly proved his sure skill, his true tact, his deep sagacity, and his respectful comprehension of the task committed to him. The dexterity with which, without disturbing the harmony of the whole, he has spun the "golden thread" entrusted to him into his own material, so that every one who has eyes sees and feels it, shows the practised hand of the true master. One closes the book with solemn feelings, and leaves it with a heavy heart as one leaves a loved grave. How different the world might have been, how much good had been possible, if two eyes had not been closed too soon! Human reason can give no answer to the *wherefore* that returns over and over again. Only firm faith in a wisdom and a love that is far above all we call wisdom and love, brings —if not comfort—yet rest and peace on the lonely path of life. What was really ours, no power can take from us, and nothing on earth remains so surely ours as the possession of bygone happiness.—With deep respect, I have the honour to be your Majesty's grateful and most obedient servant, F. MAX MÜLLER.'

### TO HIS MOTHER.

*Translation.* *December* 15.

'What will you say to the death of Prince Albert? He died last night at eleven of gastric fever. This will involve great changes. The Queen can hardly bear the whole burden alone, so there may be a Regency, probably with the Prince of Wales, at first for three months only. It is a fearful loss for the Queen, who has no one who can so help her: and the whole country will long feel his loss. So everything teaches us that our home is not here, but beyond, and that here there is no lasting happiness. How many have gone before us these last years! Would that we were convinced that we must soon follow, and that everything here is but a preparation for what is better!'

TO M. RENAN.

BRIGHTON, *December* 16.

'MY DEAR FRIEND,—I have read your letter with deep interest and sympathy. Such trials as you have had to pass through are not sent without a purpose, and if you say that they have changed your views of life, such a change in a character like yours can only be a change in advance, a firmer faith in those truths which have been revealed to the dim sight of human nature, a stronger will to resist all falsehood and tampering with the truth, and a deeper conviction that we owe our life to Him who has given it, and that we must fight His battle when He calls us to do it. I am not afraid that you could ever desert the post which you have so nobly occupied, and though I am rejoiced to hear that a sphere of honourable activity will be open to you as a successor of Quatremère, I cannot believe that Science alone will ever fill the whole of your heart. I cannot help believing that we are on the eve of great religious and philosophic struggles. There is a longing after true and primitive Christianity in the best spirits of England, France, and Germany, and there is a general desire after an outward union and communion, which is possible only on the basis of that faith which was in Christ as the Son of God, and which is the lifespring of all religion, however different the wordings of formulas and sects. With the restitution of the Papacy to its true function, a great step will have been made. Germany at the time of the Reformation objected to an Italian Pope much more than to the head of a Church. So did England, so to a great extent did France. As soon as the Pope has ceased to be Prince of Rome, a movement will begin in which the true purposes of the Reformers will be realized and through which negative Catholicism, as you call it, will become positive Catholicity. In that movement much will turn on France, and on your Emperor, and that is why I wish to see at his side honest, wise, and learned men. I am staying at Brighton with my wife, who has been very ill, but is now much better. I have just finished my second edition of my *Lectures on the Science of Language*. I should like to know what you think of them. I know we differ, and in my second volume I shall have to fight with you, but I hope and trust that our literary differences will only draw us more closely together. There is that charm about your views and opinions, that they are carved out of marble and not out of plaster. They stand out clearly and firmly and one may grapple with them, but when I read a work of Steinthal's, and even many parts of Humboldt, I feel as if walking through shifting clouds. It may be my fault, there may be much depth of wisdom in all that darkness and vagueness, but I cannot help thinking that there is nothing that cannot be made clear, and bright, and simple, and that obscurity arises in all cases from slovenly thinking and lazy writing. Adieu. Yours with sincere regard.'

To Professor Benfey.

*Translation.* Oxford, *December* 17.

'Though I have put my Oxford address at the head of this letter, I am sitting in reality in Brighton, and from my window I look upon the sea about twenty steps from here. Both of us, I as well as my wife, needed sea-air, and so we hope to enjoy this refreshing atmosphere here till Christmas. Many thanks for your letter. I have also made use of Strabo's remarks about the population of the Caucasus. In a few days a second edition of my *Lectures on Language* will be ready. My chief aim has been reached: the book has been read and has excited great interest in the science of language. It is my conviction that we know nothing really which we cannot teach (I think Aristotle was of the same opinion), and that nothing exists which cannot be clearly and intelligibly expressed. It requires time and trouble indeed, but it is effective, and that is the greatest reward of all work and study.

'The death of Prince Albert is an incalculable loss. It is only now people seem to realize that something good can come even from Germany.'

Christmas was spent at Ray Lodge, quietly, as it was throughout England. The thought of their widowed Queen, and the sad Christmas at Osborne, weighed on all hearts, and the universal mourning, not only in the upper classes, but among servants, tradespeople, and even the poor, showed how the nation was sorrowing with their loved Sovereign.

# CHAPTER XIII

## 1862–1863

**Birth of second child. Exhibition. Stay in London. Ewald. Ranke. Fourth volume of *Rig-veda*. Second course of lectures on Science of Language. Paris. Germany. North Italy. Lectures at Edinburgh. First visit to Windsor.**

ON their return from Ray Lodge to Oxford, Max Müller settled down to work at the *Rig-veda*, determined that the fourth volume should appear this year. In fact, the whole year was one of strenuous work, for a second edition of his *Lectures on Language* came out before the end of January, and a third in May, before the book had been out eleven months, each edition being of 1,250 copies.

Towards the end of January he went to Lord Ashburton's for a couple of days, and from there he writes to his wife:—

THE GRANGE, ALRESFORD, *January* 24, 1862.

'I had a miserable day for travelling, pouring all the time. However, I found all my trains quite right, and arrived at Winchester about one. There I went to Mr. Moberly, one of the masters, and had luncheon. They have a baby five days older than ours, but she cannot run yet. Then we went to Dr. Moberly's, and with him all over the school and cathedral. He explained it all most excellently, but we must go there together. The cathedral is magnificent, but when I have you with me, and sunshine, it will be much more magnificent. . . . At half-past three I started for a nine miles' drive, and arrived here in time for tea. Lady Ashburton seems very pleasant, and he is a perfect English nobleman—I mean what he ought to be. I got your letter this morning, and I hope you got mine. Yes, we are very happy, and I feel as if this life could give us no greater happiness than has been ours these two bright years, and that if we are called away sooner or later we ought to part cheerfully, knowing that this earth could give no more than has been ours, and looking forward to our new home as to a more perfect state, where all that was good and true and unselfish in us will live and expand, and all that was bad and mean will be purified and cast off. So let us work here as long as it is day, but without fearing the night that will lead us to a new and brighter dawn of life. I wish you had been here with me, for it is a delightful place, and very pleasant people. Mrs. Sartoris is *the* Mrs. S. Adelaide Kemble, and she still sings most beautifully. The Bishop of London, too, appeared at dinner, and is staying here. To-night I hear the Bishop of Winchester is expected. The house is full of the most exquisite treasures of art, such pictures! Van Dyck, Titian, Velasquez, Andrea del Sarto, &c. This morning it was bright, and we had a long ride; we started with about twelve horses, and such beauties they all were, and even your old husband had a splendid gallop, but came home quite drenched with rain. We were caught by a pouring shower, and when I came home I had no second coat, and had to appear at luncheon in my Volunteer cape—a splendid figure. Then I found I had not got my grey trousers, but had taken an old pair. However, I contrived to hide them in my cape, and looked a regular night watchman. In the afternoon I sat in my room and read, and now I am looking forward to to-morrow, when I shall have you and the little one again. They have a little one here, eighteen months old, a very nice girl, but no boy coming—and that must be a disappointment with such a place to leave. We have had a very pleasant time, and if they ask us both I shall be very glad to come again.'

On February 21 his second child, another little girl, was born, and he writes to give his mother the good news, adding, 'A little boy would have been nicer, but I am quite as pleased with a little daughter, and girls give less trouble and anxiety than boys.'

To Professor Bernays.

*Translation.* 64 High Street, *February* 23.

'Sooner than I expected I have received from my publisher the prospect of a third edition [of the *Lectures*], and I write therefore to remind you of your kind promise to send me some "corrections and additions"; it would be the more welcome, as a translation into German by Professor C. Böttger in Dessau is to appear at the same time, and the German reviewers have sharper eyes than the English ones. Last week I lived in great disquietude, and the day before yesterday I became father for the second time. Thank God, all passed over happily, but the anxiety and trouble is so great, I feel quite exhausted and ill, and the doctor sent me to bed, but I did not stay there long.

'I had a visit to-day from a Mohawk Indian; he has learnt Latin and Greek, he has come to Oxford to study here, but fancy! he has brought his feather garb with him, but according to the statutes of the University, I am afraid he may not wear it. I found the man very intelligent, and the savages more tolerant than many a civilized man.

'Aufrecht has got the Professorship of Sanskrit in Edinburgh. It was offered to me (£500), but I could not make up my mind to leave Oxford, and I am so glad to know that Aufrecht is now so well provided for. I do not know whether you have ever met him. He is just thinking of publishing a new edition of his *Umbrian and Oscan Inscriptions*.

'Have you read the hyper-sceptic and somewhat arrogant book of Sir Cornewall Lewis, *Historical Survey of Ancient Astronomy?* Lepsius and Mommsen ought to answer him.'

Oronhyatakha, the Mohawk mentioned above, was a most interesting man. Dr. Acland had met him when he was in Canada with the Prince of Wales, and said something which the Indian interpreted as an invitation to Oxford. At all events, early in 1862 he appeared, having been helped in his passage-money by friends. With a wild man's feelings about hospitality, he expected Dr. Acland to receive him in his house, and provide for him. He had been well taught in Canada at a missionary school, and funds were soon collected to enable him to study at Oxford. He used to come regularly to Max Müller, who by dint of much questioning extracted a skeleton grammar of the Mohawk tongue from him. Not that he knew what grammar meant, but by getting him to translate the English equivalents, a student could arrange the grammatical framework. One day, when writing down some declension or conjugation, Max Müller suddenly saw an irregularity, and stopping him, said, 'Why do you say that? It ought to be so-and-so.' The Mohawk looked puzzled at first, and said, 'What you say is the way my old grandmother talked, but we now say as I have told you,' thus showing the rapidity with which an unwritten language may change. Oronhyatakha went on very well in Oxford, but some unfavourable accounts were received of him from some of the missionaries to the Red Indians, and it was thought best to send him back to Canada. He was very unhappy, and the day he came to say good-bye to Max Müller he looked very fierce, and said, 'I buried my tomahawk, but I know where to find it.' He quieted down, however, on arriving in Canada, where he trained as a medical man, and as such has done good work among the settled portion of his own people.

The following letter was written by Max Müller to his old friend Baroness Bunsen, on hearing of the death of her daughter, Baroness Ungern-Sternberg: it shows that in the midst of his own happiness he did not forget to 'weep with those that weep.'

64, High Street, *April* 2.

'I saw in the papers the sad news of the new loss you have suffered, and though I fear almost to intrude on your grief, which is sacred ground, yet I cannot but send you a few words of sympathy to tell you how deeply I share in your affliction. Your husband's death I feel to-day as keenly as when I first heard of it. I feel it as an affliction that has fallen, not on you only, but on all of us; the world is changed since he has left it. Life has lost something of its brightness since those bright eyes and that bright sound of his voice closed. Some part of ourselves is dead in his death. I did not write to you then, because words are such poor things, but I have mourned for him; I always shall, not only as for a friend, but as for a man such as I shall never see again. When I saw the loss of your young, blooming daughter, all the happy days of Carlton Terrace came back like a dream. How perfectly happy your life was then; it was happiness even to watch it. And yet God knows that we want rain and storm as much as sunshine, and He sends us both as seems best to His love and wisdom. When all breaks down, He lifts us up. I have myself suffered deep grief—for three days my wife's life was despaired of. But when we feel quite crushed and forsaken and alone, we then feel the real presence of our truest Friend, who, whether by joys or sorrows, is always calling us to Him, and leading us to that true Home where we shall find Him, and in Him all we loved, with Him all we believed, and through Him all we hoped for and aspired to on earth. Our broken hearts are the truest earnest of everlasting life. May He who alone can send comfort help you to bear the affliction which He has sent. My wife begs me to add the expression of her deep sympathy, and I remain, with sincere regard, yours very truly, 'M. M.'

To his Mother.

*Translation.* Oxford, *April* 6.

'I am hard at work, and am printing my *Veda* and a third edition of my *Lectures*. Our garden is very gay, full of tulips and hyacinths, and is a great amusement to us. I get but little time for reading. I read the Mendelssohn letters with great delight. They are interesting to those who knew the man, and show his great amiability, but the right pith is wanting sometimes. They have been translated into English. I have not yet seen Varnhagen's new volume. The weather here is very bad, and Oxford is surrounded with water.'

To his Wife.

Oxford, *April* 19.

'It is so difficult not to lead a selfish life, placed as we are, with all our duties at home and with hardly any duties to fulfil which are really painful. I feel I ought to work, and do nothing but work, but then I like my work, and though I believe in the end it will answer some good and important purpose, yet whatever I do redounds to my own benefit too. . . . I sometimes think I ought to give more time to you and to society, but I have a feeling that time is so precious, and I have a good work before me, and I should like, with God's assistance, to finish it. It will serve to show the glory of God in the government of the world from the beginning; it will show that there was no portion of mankind ever forsaken by our common Father; and though His ways with the various races of men are wonderful, and at first very perplexing, we must learn from God and not attempt to prescribe to Him how He might better have brought about His mysterious purposes with the sons of men. Well, I feel I ought not to forsake that work; small as it may seem, it will be an important element hereafter for a true appreciation of the history of the world—that great drama in which nothing is without a purpose and a meaning, from the beginning to the end. Much of my work at present is only clearing away rubbish, and would not interest you, but there is a temple underneath, as will appear by-and-by.'

M. Stanislas Julien had persuaded him to send in his *Lectures on Language* in competition for the Prix Volney. On July 29 he received the following letter from M. Flourens, the head of the Commission, announcing his success:—

Institut de France, *July* 28.

'Monsieur,—Permettez-moi de vous annoncer que la Commission du *Prix Volney* a décerné, tout d'une voix, le prix à votre bel ouvrage.

'Le plus ignorant de vos juges, et le plus heureux de votre succès,

'Flourens.'

*Translation.* 'Sir,—Allow me to announce to you that the Commission of the Prix Volney have unanimously adjudged the prize to your beautiful work. The most ignorant of your judges and the most happy at your success,—Flourens.'

It will be remembered this was the second time the prize had been awarded to Max Müller, as author of the best work on language, written in any language during the year.

To his Mother.

*Translation.* Oxford, *May* 29.

'I am very well, though I have so much work. I do not know often how I shall get through it all. I have so many examinations—six to get through in the next two months. It is tedious work, but brings in money. How I wish you could see our garden! The roses and pinks are coming out, and all looks so fresh, and is a great delight to us. The middle of June we think of going to London for a fortnight to see the Exhibition.'

The Kingsleys came to stay with the Max Müllers this year for Commemoration, bringing their eldest daughter. Jenny Lind, who came for one of the concerts, dined one evening at the Max Müllers', and as many people were asked to meet her as the rooms would hold. Deichmann, the violinist, was of the party, and there was also some good amateur singing, but the host and hostess could not ask their distinguished guest to sing. At last, she herself walked to the piano, and sang, accompanied by her husband, five songs by Schumann, one after another. It was very hot weather, and the windows were all open, and High Street filled rapidly at the first sound of the great singer's voice, which rang out into the night, and was heard for a considerable distance. Mr. Tuckwell recalls the scene in his reminiscences:—

'I was his guest sometimes in his pretty house opposite the Magdalen elms, where played Deichmann—

Whose bowing seemed made
For a hand with a jewel—

where Jenny Lind warbled, and Charles Kingsley stammered in impassioned *tête-à-tête*.'

Another reminiscence of Mr. Tuckwell's belongs to this year. Max Müller 'consulted me about two matters in which, strange to say, I was better informed than he—the art of budding roses, and the conduct of marine aquaria. He watched me one day in our garden putting in some buds, and tried his hand, but gave it up presently, saying, "While you are budding a dozen standards, I can earn £5 by writing an article."'

During this year more than one letter passed between Max Müller and his old friend Dr. Patteson, the Missionary Bishop of Melanesia, who had found the *Lectures on Language* a great help to him in studying the many dialects of his scattered diocese.

The Rev. R. H. Codrington writes:—

To Mrs. Max Müller.

St. Richard's Walk, Chichester,
*March* 6, 1901.

. . . 'One thing I very well remember, and that was the Bishop's personal affection for your husband. I don't see that Miss Yonge has mentioned in her *Life* of the Bishop that they met at Dresden when both were young men. The Bishop certainly cherished the memory of those times, and when he talked, as he often used, of the great work of the Professor at Oxford, he used always to speak as a warm friend, not as fellow worker in languages or a learner. He always gave a copy of the *Lectures on the Science of Language* (when he could get one) to men who joined the mission, and he advised us to start with as much knowledge of that book as we could get. For my own part, I am sure that I never should have made any progress in the study of Melanesian languages but for the help and encouragement that I got in that way, and afterwards when on my return for a time to England I was wishing to write something. My own gratitude will never fail. . . . Yours very sincerely,

'R. H. Codrington.'

From Bishop Patteson.

Auckland, N. Z., *May* 30, 1862.

'My dear Müller,—I am very glad to have your book, and more glad still to have a copy of it from you. Edwin Palmer sent me a copy two or three months ago. I have not read it yet, reserving it as a treat for my sea life, which begins again now in about ten days. I wish I could write to you fully about these Melanesian languages. I don't know enough of them to write briefly, and I don't want to take up your time. Gabelentz has sent me his Grammar. I am in communication with him. He is on the right track, and has done a great deal with exceedingly scanty materials.

'The division usually made between Polynesian and Melanesian dialects is an arbitrary one. It is true that east of the Fiji group the Polynesian language is met with in a much purer form than in the

West Pacific, but Fiji is more than half Polynesian; its structure almost wholly so; and the Polynesian element is carried, to my certain knowledge, through all the Banks Islands and all the New Hebrides, and it comes out very clearly in several of the Solomon group; and I found it well developed the other day when I first landed at Ysabel, and found that I could talk somewhat to the people after a short time.

'I believe I might say almost as much of the Santa Cruz Archipelago, but I don't know as much. The Loyalty Islands contain but few affinities with the Polynesian. I don't mean to say that these dialects cannot be classified by one who knows a little of philology; I could prove it to you, if you were here, in five minutes, I am sure; and I am satisfied that if a man had the ability and knowledge of all the dialects, he could reconstruct the original language, or something very near it, just as one puts together a child's puzzle. Practically, till one knows a good many of them, they of course appear to be, and have to be learnt as, separate unconnected languages; the difference of dialect being often very wide.

'What an indication of the jealousy and suspicion of their lives the extraordinary multiplicity of these languages affords! In each generation, for aught I know, they diverge more and more; provincialisms and local words, &c., perpetually introduce new causes of perplexity.

'Well, enough of this; and indeed I have no time to study these languages scientifically, so how can I write about them? I need not tell you that I heartily regret the blunder about the Sanskrit Professorship. From Sir Wm. Martin I have heard something of you; he met you, you may remember, at Oxford. If you can find time to send me a line, I shall be very glad; but I know you are much occupied.

'I am, my dear Müller, very sincerely yours,

'J. C. PATTESON, Missionary Bishop.'

When the Commemoration was over, the Max Müllers spent a fortnight in London, to see the Exhibition. They dined out constantly with their many friends. At a dinner at Mr. William Longman's, a Frenchman who was of the party, and was particularly anxious to make Max Müller's acquaintance, was overheard in the course of the evening to say, 'I did not know a man so learned shall be so very young!'

To MR. WILLIAM LONGMAN.

OXFORD, *July* 27.

'I know that you will be glad to hear that my *Lectures* have just been awarded the Prix Volney by the French Academy. The prize is given for the best work on Comparative Philology, and it is open to all countries. The prize is only 1,200 francs, but it is very pleasant to have got it, and I hope it will help to sell the third edition.'

To his Wife.

London, *July* 7.

'All I can say is that I have heard and read the worst that can be said against our religion—I mean the true original teaching of Christ; and I feel that I am ready in mind, if not in body, to lay down my life for the truth of His teaching. All our difficulties arise from the doctrines of men, not from His doctrine. There is no outward evidence of the truth of His doctrine, but the Spirit of God that is within us. He testifieth to its truth. If it does not, we are not yet disciples of Christ, but we may be hereafter. But more of that later. Be certain of this, that to repress a doubt is to repress the spirit of truth; a doubt well spoken out is generally a doubt solved. Only all this requires great seriousness of mind—it must assume an importance greater than anything else in life, and then we can fight our way through it. God is with us in our struggles.'

To Rev. Charles Kingsley.

*August.*

'Ranke (*The Popes*, &c.) is staying here for a week, and very anxious to make your acquaintance. Could you come here for a day to see him? He dines with us next Saturday, but any other day will do. Next Monday Ewald will be here; he has been here for a fortnight, but comes back all the way from Penrith to see Stanley. If our spare room is occupied (we expect the Walronds), we can always get you a bed close by. I think you would like Ewald—more even than Ranke.'

Ewald's visit has been fully described in the *Autobiography*, and the way he was cross-examined by some of the younger M.A.'s. He was a most lovable old man in private intercourse, though a fiery opponent of anything like political tyranny. His power of work was almost phenomenal: he would spend the whole day at the Bodleian, moving across to the Camera when the great library closed, sometimes returning there again after a late dinner. Canon Farrar records an incident of this visit of Ewald to Oxford:—

'Ranke and Ewald were both in Oxford in the middle of the Long Vacation. I determined to ask them to dinner together, though I dreaded a little friction between them, of Göttingen *versus* Berlin, and of Theology *versus* Modern History. I asked Canon Stanley and

Müller to meet them. It was due to Müller's extreme tact that conversation was kept up and yet friction avoided. Ranke, oddly enough, had his head full of the probable danger to be apprehended in reference to European politics from Servia and Bulgaria (which afterwards proved true), and we could not get him to talk with interest on anything else. Müller showed his cleverness and shrewd common sense by imparting a vein of humour to the conversation, which prevented a painful outburst of disagreement; for Müller had a vein of true humour. It was not sallies of wit, abrupt outbursts of the comic, but a playful fun which flowed like a purling brook, intertwining itself with conversation, and which put crooked spirits in harmony.

'I have already implied that Müller had remarkable powers of conversation: he was always lively and always instructive. His mastery of English, both in voice and pronunciation, and of purity of style in writing, was a marvel. To this ought to be added a pellucid clearness of exposition and description, even in most abstract subjects, which is seen to some extent in his German tracts as well as more conspicuously in his English writings. His syntax was so free from entanglement, and his language so forceful and expressive, that no reader had to halt to ask himself the meaning of what he read.'

It was in the course of the summer that Max Müller received an interesting account from Dr. Martin Haug, director of Sanskrit studies at the College of Poona, of a great assembly of Brahmin Pundits held outside the town, in order to correct their MSS. of the *Rig-veda* by the three first published volumes of his great edition. The Pundits would not touch the books themselves, as the printing made them impure, an idea having got abroad that cows' blood was used in mixing the ink employed. But they sat in solemn conclave for some days, and Max Müller's carefully prepared text was read aloud, and the MSS. corrected by it. 'Their judgement,' says Dr. Haug, 'is to this effect. This edition must be written by a great Pundit versed in the *Vedas* and *Sâstras* (*veda-sâstra sampannm*), the highest title of honour of a learned man in India.' Dr. Haug then speaks of the difficulty of getting trustworthy copies of ancient Sanskrit MSS. 'Not that there are no good MSS. existing, but they are to be found generally in the possession of rich superstitious Brâhmans, who do not admit Europeans to their libraries, and when copies are made for Sahibs, they are made intentionally bad and incomplete. One of my Brâhman friends told me this the other day.'

The following letter is the first of a correspondence which was carried on till within a few months of Mr. Gladstone's death. An ardent Liberal from his University days, Max Müller was a great admirer of Mr. Gladstone, and a member of his Oxford committees till his rejection by the University in 1865. But Max Müller could not follow Mr. Gladstone's Home Rule policy, and was a determined Unionist, a Liberal Unionist, and in the contests in the borough of Oxford voted 'blue' for the last ten years of his life, though his deep respect for Mr. Gladstone's intellectual gifts, and the spell cast by his personality, remained in full force to the last.

TO THE RIGHT HON. W. E. GLADSTONE.

64, HIGH STREET, *September* 7, 1862.

'MY DEAR SIR,—I beg to thank you for your kind letter. It was a true gratification to me to hear that my *Lectures* have attracted your attention, and that on the whole you approved of them. I am fully and painfully aware of the many and doubtful points in them, but I am quite satisfied if I have only succeeded in engaging the interest of a few thoughtful scholars in favour of a science which I feel convinced has still to teach us many important lessons. The sooner my book is superseded by a better one the better. I hope next spring to give a new series of lectures on the same subject, and intend then to enter more fully into the relation between Language and Thought, particularly in ancient times. One of the most important fields where the influence of language on thought—the Tartar's bow, as Bacon calls it—has been at work, is Ancient Mythology, but at the same time nothing is so beset with difficulties as the scientific analysis of mythological names. They belong to a very primitive stratum of language, and are full of anomalies; yet even these anomalies point to laws which determine their formation. Until these laws are discovered, until we can account for every letter, whether radical or formative, in the names of the Arian gods, all guesses at their original conception must be checked. It is almost a truism, but nevertheless a very important truth in the Science of Language, that the first meaning of every word is its etymological meaning. That meaning may grow and change, it may shift to the opposite pole of the compass; yet, if we want to know the first impulse which led to the formation of certain names and notions—of *nomina* or *numina*—the only answer, if any, must be given by etymology. Now as to the name of Ares to which you refer in your letter, I confess that I know nothing at all satisfactory as to its etymology. I cannot find out (1) whether Ἄρης shows any signs of an initial digamma, viz. whether the root from which it is derived began with a semi-vowel or with a vowel; (2) I am puzzled by the accent of Ἄρης, for in adjectives in ης the accent is generally on the last; (3) I am perplexed by the declension, where, as far as I know, no crasis ever takes place in the gen. εος, &c. Till these difficulties are removed, it is impossible to fix on any etymology, or rather, I should say, no etymology can be satisfactory which does not account for all these anomalies. I think it was in your book on Homer that I read the last account of Ares (I have not got it by me to-day), but I have no doubt that you are right in representing Ares as a Thracian god. The coincidence between Aria as the name of Thrace and Ares is therefore curious. But how are the two words to be reconciled? If Ares shows traces of an initial digamma it could not come from the root from which we have Aria; nor could Ares be an adjective or other derivative of Aria. I know of no god named originally from a country, rather are the names of countries derived from the names of gods. But again in this case Ἄρης would never lead to Ἄρια, it would be Ἄρεια. These are nothing but doubts and misgivings, and I have nothing else to say on the subject, but as to ἄρρην its etymology is clear. It has the initial digamma and is identical with the Sanskrit v*ri*shan. Ἀνήρ again is, I believe, the Sanskrit nara or n*ri*, man. In Greek words there is frequently a vowel prefixed to an initial N, D, L, Bh; for instance:—

Sk. nâman, name, ὄνομα.
Sk. nakha, nail, ὄνυξ.
Sk. bhrû, brow, ὀφρύς.
Sk. navan, nine, ἐννέα.
Sk. rudhira, red, ἐρυθρός.
Sk. laghu, light, ἐλαχύς.

I confess I know of no instance where in Greek an α is prefixed to an initial η; it is always ε or ο, but we find α before ς, in

Sk. star, Engl. star, ἀστήρ (stella = sterula).

Whatever therefore may be the etymology of Ares, ἄρρην and ἀνήρ point to two distinct roots, and neither of these would yield a satisfactory explanation of Ares. I should have answered your note before, but I had promised to send the MS. of the fourth volume of my edition of the *Veda* to the Press by Saturday night, and I had to work from morning till evening to keep my promise. I hope you will excuse the delay of my answer, and I only regret that it is so little satisfactory. Believe me to be, my dear sir, your obedient servant and sincere admirer.'

The fourth volume of the *Rig-veda* was now finished. The preface had required long and careful work, as Max Müller had to answer various criticisms on his *Ancient Sanskrit Literature*, and the dates he had there assigned to the Hymns of the *Rig-veda*; Wilson and Whitney agreeing in considering these limits as too narrow, whilst other critics considered them too wide. In his preface therefore Max Müller felt it necessary to enter fully into the question as to whether the age of the Vedic Hymns could be fixed by astronomical evidence—and this led to the further question whether the Indian Nakshatras or divisions of the heavens into twenty-seven equal parts were of Indian origin, or derived from a foreign country; a controversy which had been carried on with some acrimony, Biot the great astronomer claiming to have proved the Chinese origin of the Nakshatras, in which he was supported by Lassen.

The theory which now counts the greatest number of supporters attributes to the Nakshatras a Babylonian origin, whence they spread eastward to both Hindus and Chinese. Max Müller in his preface tried to establish the Indian origin of the Nakshatras, and adds some valuable notes from Professor Donkin and Mr. Main, the Radcliffe Observer, giving the positions of the moon and planets 1424 B.C. All this was reprinted as a separate pamphlet under the title of *Ancient Hindu Astronomy and Chronology*. He further defends himself against various critics who complained that he 'did not enter into all the controverted points, the theories, guesses, doubts, assertions, and counter-assertions of various scholars,' and assures them that he did not shrink from the trouble of examining them, but that he believed it 'to be our duty to learn to distinguish between what is important and what is not. We only retard the discovery of truth by entering into every bypath on the right and on the left. The straight line is always the best, the simplest machinery the most perfect. If we can prove our point without a great apparatus of so-called learning, it is our duty to do so. He sweeps cleanest that makes the least dust.'

Max Müller apologizes for the delay in bringing out this volume in these words:—

'For a time it was doubtful whether the funds necessary for the completion of the *Rig-veda* would be provided. This caused uncertainty and delay. When I resumed my work, my time was no longer my own, and there were more urgent occupations which left me but scant leisure for the prosecution of my Sanskrit studies. Had I been allowed to devote, I do not say the whole, but at least one-half of my time to the study of Sanskrit and the carrying on of my edition of the *Rig-veda*, the present volume would have been published long ago. The MSS. of the Commentary of Sâyana are very inferior for these later portions, the number of passages hopelessly corrupt and imperfect is constantly increasing. There is many a short line in these notes which represents the results of hours, nay of days and weeks of hard work.'

Max Müller again acknowledges the help given him by Dr. Aufrecht, who, though he had long ceased to be his secretary, had been living on in Oxford. The preface contains a warm tribute to the memory of Professor Wilson: 'Wilson had lived through almost the whole history of Sanskrit scholarship, and had taken part in nearly every important work that marked an epoch in the study of Indian literature, history, and religion. Every one of his own works represents a new conquest. He never followed, he was always first.' Finally, in dwelling on the translation of the *Rig-veda*, begun by Wilson, to be carried on by Ballantyne, Max Müller points out the great difficulty of making a thoroughly clear translation of the whole:—

'Some portions, I confess, I consider as hopeless, as likely to resist all attempts at interpretation, but there is no reason to despair. The *Rig-veda* is the most ancient book of the Aryan world. Every Hymn, every verse, every word that can be deciphered in it is a gain. These Hymns represent the lowest stratum in the growth of the human mind that can be reached anywhere by means of contemporaneous literature.'

Max Müller was so thoroughly exhausted by the summer's work, that he found it necessary to get a change before term. He and his wife went for a fortnight to Tenby, which he thoroughly enjoyed, visiting Manorbier, Carew, Pembroke, and other ruins with keen interest, and searching for sea animals for his aquarium in Oxford with the zest of a boy. On their way back a visit was paid to a relative near Swansea, where the large copper-works of his wife's family were inspected with great interest, Max Müller particularly enjoying the part-singing of the men employed at the works, during their dinner hour. He had not heard Welsh singing and voices before, and was much struck with the natural and national turn for music, as a strong contrast to the absence of it in the English labourer and artisan.

To Professor Bernays.

*Translation.* *December* 14.

'I will not let the old year slip past without once more shaking hands with you—as well as it is possible from this great distance. It is so long since I heard from you, or from any of my German friends. I am afraid it may be my fault. I wanted to finish the fourth volume of my *Veda*, and so I could not find time for anything else, nor did I think of anything else. But now I have finished, and I feel like a snake that has just cast her skin, and is now going forth for further prey. In the new Germany I see no sign of life, and I doubt whether we shall live to see what our fathers hoped for, realized. Uhland, one of the last noble, faithful, patriotic men, had been hoping for so long, but he too has been called away without having lived to see the morning dawn. When I think of Bunsen in 1848, and of his sure, prophetic hopes! and he too is gone, and owls sit in the eagle's nest which he had built up here in London. Here in England we possess personal and political freedom, and that is such a blessing—it is like the fresh sea-air, but it is *habeas corpus*, not *habeas animum*. The spiritual struggle proceeds slowly, and the dogged resistance is great, and the passion of persecution would do honour to the sixteenth century. Bishop Colenso appeals to the English mercantile understanding; it makes more impression than all that tastes of mind.

'The book will amuse you. Jowett has somewhat retired, and is at work at his edition of Plato's *Republic*. Stanley fights very bravely; he has just published *Lectures on the Jewish Church*, first series, which produce an effect in England, but will hardly be appreciated in Germany.

'Pattison sits still, says little, but thinks so much. His young wife is a little too young for him, I am afraid, but he is well and of good cheer. To-morrow night there will be some acting at his house in the

College! How is your work getting on, and what are your plans for the future? Shall we meet anywhere next year? I hope to go to Germany next summer, but before that I have to give a course of lectures in London, about the material and spiritual element in Language. My old lectures are appearing now in a German translation, also Italian and French translations are to appear, and I am reproduced in America. I hope the next volume will be an improvement, but whether people will like it is another question.

'How I wish you could see my home here in Oxford! I wish indeed for no better. I have altogether given up having any wishes at all, and I enjoy the most beautiful happiness which life has to offer —a good wife and two healthy children.

'Aufrecht is Professor in Edinburgh, happily married to a pretty, cultured wife with independent means; he writes most happily, and the sunshine has driven away the old clouds of envy and suspicion. In old friendship.'

The Christmas was spent at Ray Lodge, but very quietly, for the awful distress in Lancashire, owing to the 'cotton famine' caused by the American War, weighed on all hearts and all purses. Superfluous luxuries were cut off in almost every household, and except a tiny Christmas tree for the children, there were no presents, all money that could be spared going weekly to the fund for the thousands starving in the North from no fault of their own.

By the middle of January Max Müller was quietly settled again in Oxford, and busy with the preparation of the second course of lectures on 'The Science of Language' for the Royal Institution. His course of lectures this term in Oxford were on 'Bopp's *Comparative Grammar*.' Towards the close of the month he heard that the fourth volume of the *Rig-veda*, the first dedicated to the Queen, had been received at Osborne, and that 'Her Majesty appreciated the learning and erudition that must have been employed in its production, and that it and the three first volumes sent at the same time (beautifully bound in morocco and gold) would form a valuable addition to the Royal Library.' Soon after he heard from his old friend and teacher Professor Brockhaus in Leipzig: 'Your *Lectures on the Science of Language* have, as you know, found many admirers here, and every one is looking forward to your new volume.'

The London lectures were even more crowded than the first course. Max Müller found them more fatiguing, for the course was longer, and he went up and down from Oxford, only sleeping in London if engaged to dine out. Towards the close of the course he delivered a Friday evening lecture on 'The *Vedas*,' to an enormous audience, people sitting on every step of the staircases, and standing in the gangways. This lecture was repeated in substance two years later at Leeds, and will be found in the first edition of *Chips*, Volume I.

To Professor Bernays.

*Translation.* Oxford, *March* 3, 1863.

'What you say about the German translation is just what I feel. I have not wished for a translation, but cannot prevent it being done, and therefore have to leave the rest to the judgement of the publisher. In no case should I undertake to write differently for Germany than for England. My manner of writing may look learned or unlearned, that is the same to me. I know it costs more labour to think out a subject so that it can be clearly stated, than to bring it to light half digested and with all its threads entangled. I work for no class in particular, nor for a definite purpose, and I recognize only one duty which renders our work responsible, i.e. the promoting of truth; and nothing is true which is not perfectly clear. There are some hard nuts hidden in my lectures, the cracking of which has tried the teeth of some obscure scholars; but the honest ones among them will confess this, and will gratefully accept the cleanly peeled kernel. I could have made an immense noise, had I cracked all my hard nuts before the public, and many empty ones might have been mixed up with them without the readers noticing it. But that sort of thing I consider wrong, and I shall never be infected by the aristocratic arrogance of scholars. I can well believe, that if I had written five unreadable volumes instead of one small volume, the sale in Germany would have been more rapid.

'What I have worked out may be good or bad, but each cultivated man, be he an Englishman or a Kaffir, knows what I am driving at and how matters stand. That was not always the case with Bunsen. With all respect for his knowledge, his proofs were not always absolutely convincing, firm or healthy. But I am quite prepared to see my translation abused in Germany; never mind, failure with an honest conscience is better than success with a sacrifice of what one really thinks. If you want to read obscure books about language, read Humboldt, or should you wish to read obscure, superficial books, read Steinthal, &c., &c. How such things can be endured in Germany, I do not understand, and I expect no political or religious freedom till the literary cobwebs are swept away. Now, you will say, "Lion, you have roared effectively!" [*Löwe, gut gebrüllt!*], but I think we understand each other in spite of it all. I have not yet seen Bunsen's *Letters*, but I will try to get them. I sit here toiling away at the *Veda*, and feel heartily tired of the whole business. In faithful love.'

To his Wife.

Oxford, *March* 14.

'I shall live this week like a hermit and try to get on with my lectures. You see, I must work hard, for that is what we are all meant to do, and though it may seem to deprive us of some of the enjoyment of life, it really increases real happiness; it makes one feel that one does not live for nothing, and one enjoys one's holidays with a much stouter heart. I hope our summer will be a very happy one, but till then there is still a good deal of work to be gone through.'

To his Mother.

*Translation.* Oxford, *March*, 1863.

'I live in one perpetual trot, and shall be glad when my lectures in London are over. In the summer I will amuse myself. If I can get away early in June I think of going with G. to Paris; the middle of July I must return for the examination of the Indian civilians, which lasts a fortnight. When that is over we shall go to Germany. But I must have good air, so I think we will meet you in Dresden, and all go together to the Lake of Geneva, for I feel in myself that I want bracing, and Dresden does not do for that. I only grieve that we shall thus see so little of Augusta and Krug. Our great difficulty is about the children. The little one certainly must not go—the doctor forbids it—so the question is about Ada. I don't think I could bear to be so long without her, nor G. either, and yet the long journey is not good at her age. We discuss it every day, and can come to no decision. I can make no fixed plan yet, I am so overpowered with work; but I hope all will be as we wish, and that we may enjoy the summer happily together.'

To Professor Tyndall.

Oxford, *March* 14.

'Accept my best thanks for your kind help in providing me with a most excellent Siren for my lecture yesterday. My audience seemed delighted with it, though I am sorry to say it took up more of my time than I had to spare. I shall have to finish my lecture next Saturday, but I shall not trouble you either for the Siren or for any other experiment, as I must get on with my subject, and cannot afford any more amusements. I am much pleased with Helmholtz's book, and should give a great deal to be able to hear your lectures on "Sound," and to see some of the experiments which, though so well described by Helmholtz, are yet imperfect and unsatisfactory on paper.

'Do you not think that if our scales were properly constructed, all harmonies would be necessarily harmonious, and not inharmonious, as they now are after the 7th?'

Easter was spent at Ray Lodge, with many old friends staying in the house, who all 'enjoyed Müller's music,' says a contemporary Diary.

To his Wife.

*April* 7.

'When I ordered your fly, I found Mrs. —— in great distress: her baby had died on Sunday quite suddenly. I went to see the little child, and it looked so calm and peaceful, and yet that poor mother would have given her very life to have had that little soul back. It was heartrending to see her, and I could give her but little comfort, but it was a solemn sight. What a small line it is that separates us and all that we love here from that life which waits for us, and why should we be so unwilling to go home, for here our home is not, and the great wrench must come, and happy are those who have passed through it. Yet when I looked on that little child that had been playing about but a few days ago, and then thought of our little darlings, I felt it must be fearful to part with them, if one did not feel that a happier life is in store for them than what they would have found here. And with all this misery going on everywhere, one lives on and laughs and takes it all as a matter of course, whereas if one looks into life as it is, one wonders how one can ever forget it again, and ever care again for the littlenesses of which our pleasures and our pride consist here. *Ernst ist das Leben,* so says the German proverb, and very true it is.'

It was at this time that Max Müller first met with Sir George Cox's admirable books on mythology. Sir George seems to have sent him *The Tales of Thebes and Argos*, and the following letter is the beginning of a correspondence on Comparative Mythology, spread over many years. The editor owes these letters to Sir George Cox to the kindness of the Rev. R. W. Rees of Manchester, into whose hands they had passed.

To Rev. G. Cox.

Ray Lodge, *April* 16, 1863.

'Dear Sir,—. . . I was delighted when reading your *Tales*[1], and I feel convinced that in the form in which you have given them these myths are nearer to what they originally were than in any of the works of the mythographer, whether ancient or modern. I never felt so strongly that on the whole the principles of Comparative Mythology are right than when I saw them applied as you have applied them. I do not despair that we shall discover and disentangle many more of the complicated myths of the Aryan nations, though I know but too well that the ground is treacherous and requires great caution. Yours with sincere regard, 'Max Müller.'

The end of April Max Müller went to London as one of the deputation from the University of Oxford, to present the address of congratulation to the Prince of Wales on his marriage. The Prince of Wales graciously promised to honour his *Alma Mater* with his presence at Commemoration, accompanied by the Princess. As is the custom on such occasions, His Royal Highness sent in the names of those whom he desired should receive the honorary degree of D.C.L. Among these appeared the name of Charles Kingsley, one of the Prince's chaplains. At once Dr. Pusey opposed the degree in Council, on the ground that *Hypatia*, Mr. Kingsley's finest work, was *immoral*. Charles Kingsley's friends, among whom may be mentioned Dr. Stanley, Dr. Rolleston, and Max Müller, were very indignant, and the day that the name was finally to be voted on in Council, Dr. Stanley appeared armed with a copy of *Hypatia* borrowed from Max Müller, which still has all the passages marked in it, used by Dr. Stanley in opposing the Professor of Hebrew. But though the name might have been carried in Council, a vote of *non placet* was threatened in the Theatre, in the very presence of the Prince, and to avoid so scandalous a scene, Charles Kingsley's friends withdrew his name. A few days later Max Müller had a letter from Mrs. Kingsley which is given here by permission. In sending it on to his wife, who was away from home, Max says: 'I enclose an excellent letter from Mrs. Kingsley, for which she deserves more than a

[1] *Of Thebes and Argos.*

D.C.L. degree. I am curious to know how the Prince will take it, and I am only afraid that he will never know how badly people behaved.'

FROM MRS. KINGSLEY.

EVERSLEY RECTORY, *Wednesday*.

'MY DEAR MAX,—Charles is away at Whitchurch fishing, so he will not receive your *most kind* letter till to-morrow. I have written by this post to the Rollestons that they may fill up their rooms, merely saying that unavoidable circumstances will keep us at home on June 15, and I do hope they will not think us ungrateful and changeable. I have no doubt there is some wise reason for this great disappointment, and perhaps the great honour under all circumstances which we should have felt it to be, would have been very bad for us. It is so difficult to be perfectly single-minded, even in a little parsonage, that perhaps it is a great blessing to be saved the Theatre of Oxford, which may not be the best soil for the growth of such a virtue; and I am sure I longed too vehemently for the sight of my dear husband in a scarlet gown for it to have done *me* any good. Depend upon us both for not mentioning the subject. It will always be associated with the pleasant and grateful remembrance of *your* kindness, dear Max, and Dr. Stanley's, and I shall try hard to let it obliterate Dr. Pusey and his Christian hatred. Oh! it is a great mercy to live in a parsonage remote from courts and courtiers, and even doctors of divinity. Best love to dearest G. and delicious Ada. Yours ever affectionately,

'F. E. KINGSLEY.'

Early in June the Max Müllers went to Paris, leaving their children at Ray Lodge. Here they passed a delightful month in constant intercourse with many of the most distinguished members of the literary world of Paris, a world that all along kept entirely aloof from the brilliant but evil Court of Louis Napoleon. One evening was spent with the Mohls, Madame Mohl still keeping up on a smaller scale the *Salon* of the earlier part of the century. On this occasion Madame Mohl, who was about to start for her annual visit to London, amused her guests by parading all the bonnets she had provided for her expedition, and trying them on, one after another. Only those who remember Madame Mohl's quaint, almost bizarre, appearance can imagine the droll effect as one by one the smart Parisian bonnets were essayed, and the verdict of her guests, male and female, eagerly expected.

Renan's house too was often visited, with its rooms hung with some of the best portraits by Ary Scheffer, Madame Renan being his niece, daughter of Henri Scheffer, whose fine portrait occupied a conspicuous place. Max Müller attended the meetings at the Institute as a corresponding member, and he and his wife were both present the day that M. Mignet pronounced the *éloge* on Lord Macaulay. It was a fine scene; the hall surmounted by its great dome was well filled by the members of the Institute, all wearing the beautiful *habit brodé* chosen by Richelieu, and ladies in the gayest of summer dresses. Mignet's melodious voice sounded clearly through the vast assemblage, and his words were so distinctly pronounced, they were like words cut out of marble, whilst it was a pleasure to watch each movement of his singularly beautiful mouth. The oration itself was magnificent.

The following letter must be about this date:—

To Rev. F. (now Dean) Farrar.

'My dear Sir,—I am so sorry that we can never meet in peace and exchange views: letters and books are cumbersome ways of mutual explanation, and I do not know how it is that I can never bring myself to believe that people hold different views on matters accessible to scientific treatment, unless for some reason or other they wish to do so. When I read your books I can fully enter into all you mean, and yet I do not feel the least disturbed in my own views. Our real differences refer to facts, and these fortunately are amenable to scientific tests. In my lectures, as you say quite rightly, I have not said half of what I meant to say, perhaps what I ought to have said. It did not seem to me the place for it. But I mean to give another lecture specially on the Antiquity of Language, and then you, or at all events your friends, will be surprised to see how little we differ, although we seem to be diametrically opposed. I could have explained this to you in half an hour of conversation, but I cannot do it by letter, and I shudder at controversy, and have had that horror all my life.'

After three weeks in England for examination work, Max Müller and his wife started for Germany, leaving both of their children behind. They stopped at Bonn to see Baroness Bunsen and Professor Bernays, but Max Müller was again disappointed in making his intimate friend acquainted with his wife, as it was the time of the Black Fast, the fall of

Jerusalem; and Bernays could not go anywhere, and only saw Max Müller for about an hour. After joining his mother at Chemnitz, and taking her and his sister with them to Leipzig and Dessau, the Max Müllers went on to Berlin to see Max's friend Morier, and whilst there were commanded to Potsdam to dine with the Crown Prince and Princess of Prussia. Nothing could exceed the kindness with which they were received, though the visit was shorter than had been intended by the royal hosts, as the Crown Prince had been suddenly summoned to Gastein, where the King and Bismarck were taking the waters. On arriving the guests were driven about the park till the two o'clock dinner. It was intensely hot weather, and the dinner was in the open air. Afterwards the royal children were brought in by their English nurses: Princess Charlotte of Saxe-Meiningen, the present Emperor, and Prince Henry, hardly a year old, to play round the table, and talk to the English guests. The sight of this happy family life made a deep impression on the visitors. A few days later the Crown Princess wrote, through Countess Brühl, to say what pleasure it had been to receive the Max Müllers in her own home. Things at that time were at an unhappy pass in Prussia. Old Professor Bopp mentioned to Max Müller, as a mere *on dit*, something about the Court which had appeared as a fact two months before in the English *Times*, adding, 'It is impossible here to find out the truth'; and in one of the confidential talks that Max had with his Paris friend von Schlötzer when they were alone, for in public it was not safe to talk of politics, von Schlötzer said, 'I would give anything to be English for a day, to know what political freedom means.'

From Berlin, Max Müller and his wife went by Nuremberg and Munich to Leoni on the Starnberger See, taking his mother and his eldest niece with them. Here a delightfully quiet month was passed in a comfortable pension close to the lovely lake, where they bathed and rowed constantly, taking long walks in the beautiful country round. From the higher ground behind the house they could see the snow-covered mountains to the south of the lake. One scene deserves to be recalled. The Vocal Club (*Sänger-Verein*) from Munich came out for the day, and gave an open-air concert on the summit of a hill crowned with pine woods that rose over the lake. It was a picturesque sight, the gay banners, the club members in their many-coloured scarves, and the groups of peasants in their national costumes—the men in high hats, and their coats covered with large silver buttons; the women with their bright petticoats, and black bodices with gold or silver embroidery, with chains and earrings of gold or silver, and small black caps with embroidery to match. The part-singing was beautiful, the voices rich and melodious in themselves, and the expression and light and shade carefully observed. Of course there was plenty of eating and drinking, and at last dancing, but, though all seemed very free and easy, there was no rudeness, nothing objectionable in the gathering.

From Leoni the mother and niece returned to Chemnitz, the Max Müllers going across the Brenner to Italy. It was their first taste of Italy, after which Max had, he tells us, hankered all his life. Venice especially was like a dream realized, though the sight of the Austrian soldiers everywhere roused his indignation. It was found on visiting the Doge's Palace that many of the best pictures were being cleaned. One that he particularly desired to see—*Venezia trionfante*, by Paul Veronese—was not to be seen, and he was lamenting it one day to the old Italian librarian, a true patriot, who, when he found a kindred soul in Max Müller, not only in books but in politics, had many a talk with him on the state of Venice. At his last visit Max Müller said he looked forward to coming again to Italy, adding significantly, 'And then I hope to see *Venezia trionfante!*' At their next visit it was so, but the old librarian had passed away, though he lived long enough to see his beloved city free from the hated foreigner. The travellers returned by Turin and the Italian Lakes, the St. Gothard, where the first snows had fallen, and which they crossed on foot, and rapidly through Switzerland to England.

Max Müller's lectures began as soon as he returned to Oxford, and he was as usual overwhelmed with letters on all subjects.

To Rev. G. Cox.

Oxford, *November* 4.

'I was not at Oxford when Dr. Pusey preached his last sermon. I have not read it, nor have I heard any remarks about it. But I can quite understand the impression which it made on you.

'There are not a few points on which Dr. Pusey's ideas have become perfectly hardened: one cannot reason with him about them, nor is he able himself to handle them. They have become fixed ideas—they do not bend, but threaten to crack.

'With all that, I have a strong personal regard for Dr. Pusey. He is a man of great learning and a vast experience of life, in fact, one of the two or three interesting men at Oxford. Besides that, he has always shown me great kindness, though he knows my opinions, and though in University matters we have had fierce fights together. In spite of that, and though we were hardly on speaking terms at the time of the election for the Sanskrit Professorship, he offered me his help unasked, he sat up day and night (in the literal meaning of the words) writing letters to his friends—whereas my liberal friends, for whom I had worked hard on several occasions, did hardly anything for me, and some of them, on whom I thought I had claims, failed me altogether. Stanley and Pusey were my chief supporters, and the only men who, I believe, felt for me when I failed to obtain that position in which I might have been really useful, and might have been able to finish the work of my life. However, I am not blind to the dangerous consequences of Pusey's teaching. I consider his alliance with the Low Church as a most fatal mistake. But I look at all these things very much *ab extra*; I keep entirely aloof of University politics, and I look more and more to Germany as my real home and the centre which attracts my interests. I shall stay in England to finish the work which brought me here, but I look forward to spending the last years of my life among my old friends in Germany.'

Max Müller had been invited in the spring to deliver two lectures at Edinburgh on 'Language.' He accepted the invitation to lecture, but begged that the lectures might be on 'The Origin of Mythology.' On November 9 he went to Edinburgh to deliver these two lectures at the Philosophical Institution.

To his Wife.

Edinburgh, *November* 10.

'One lecture safely over. I had an immense audience; the place was as full as it could hold. Whether people were pleased or not

I don't know; they applauded and all that, but I think I aimed a little too high. There were all the Professors and learned men, however, and they seemed pleased; also Dr. John Brown, a charming man, of whom I shall see more.'

*November* 11.

'How thankful we ought to be every minute of our existence to Him who gives us all this richly to enjoy! How little one has deserved this happy life, much less than many poor sufferers to whom life is a burden and a hard and bitter trial. But then, how much greater the claims on us; how much more sacred the duty never to trifle, never to waste time and power, never to compromise, but to live in all things, small and great, to the praise and glory of God, to have God always present with us, and to be ready to follow His voice, and His voice only. Has our prosperity taught us to meet adversity when it comes? I often tremble, but then I commit all to God, and I say, "Have mercy upon me, miserable sinner!"

'Let us keep up our constant fight against all that is small, and common, and selfish; let us never lose our faith in the ideal life, in what we ought to be, and in what, with constant prayer to God, we shall be.

'My work here will soon be over. We had a pleasant dinner to-night at Mr. Muir's. I had a drive in the afternoon with Dr. John Brown, a most charming, excellent man, with whom you would have been delighted. He is a good friend of Lady A. Bruce and of Stanley, and he thinks they are worthy of each other. I shall be glad when my lecture to-morrow is over. People are very civil and kind here. Prince Alfred sent me a message to say how sorry he was he could not come to my lectures, but that every one of his evenings had been engaged this week.'

The following description was sent at the time to a connexion of Max Müller's wife in London:—

'I went on Friday night to hear Max Müller on "The Origin of Mythology." It was *most* interesting. I never liked a lecture more. It required close attention, yet was quite clear and intelligible. He seemed to open new worlds, dim, half-revealed, mysterious, and this dimness gave a fascination—wide stretches of thought and conjecture retreating into darkness yet to be explored, when the *Veda*, "still with seven seals upon it," shall be adequately translated.

'His inquiry into the origin of the name of the Supreme Being—alike in Sanskrit, Greek, Latin, and Teutonic—was intensely interesting, and his manner was so reverential on these subjects.

'He looks quite young, and his manner and voice were most pleasant. The hall was crowded.'

TO REV. G. COX.

EDINBURGH, *November* 10.

'Mythology no doubt springs from scattered tales, and to single tales it should be reduced before we attempt to explain it. This is what I thought so particularly happy in your books, that you should have told the tales singly, as they might have been told by any grandmother in any small village of Greece, long before the encyclopaedic treatment of Greek fables began. I have been trying my hand at something of the same kind in German, on the pattern of Grimm's *Märchen*, but I have failed. The story of Oedipus has just been dissected by M. Michel Bréal very cleverly, though I doubt whether people will be convinced by it.

'"Always the Sun, and always the Sun," people exclaim, and yet it is not our fault if the Sun has inspired so many legends and received so many names. And what else do you expect at the bottom of mythology, if not the reflection of heaven and earth in the mind and language of man?'

TO THE SAME.

OXFORD, *November* 29.

'... I cannot bring myself to enter into or to adopt Kuhn's theory of clouds and thunderstorms being at the bottom of all Aryan mythology, a view which I see has just been strongly advocated by Mr. Kelle in his *Indo-European Traditions*. He gives a most incomplete representation of Kuhn's labours. I should have thought that Grote had entirely dispelled the belief that there was any historical substratum in the legends of Troy, or at least any more than in the legends of Charlemagne taking Jerusalem, &c.'

TO HIS MOTHER.

*Translation.* OXFORD, *November* 28.

'I must just tell you we are very well, though we get no rest. Last week a visit from Princess Helena and Princess Louise, to whom I had to show everything; last Wednesday a ball at the Duke of Marlborough's, where G. and I danced in the beautiful library; and to-day a visit from the Crown Prince and Princess of Prussia. They were with Dr. Stanley, and we went there for luncheon, and have been walking about with them till now. To-night a dinner, where we are to meet the Duc d'Aumale and Lord Lawrence, the Viceroy of India. Then next week I am ordered to Windsor to the Queen, then my lectures here—in fact, my head is in a whirl, and I am longing for rest. I am happiest when quiet with my children, who are darlings and thrive so well.'

Just before this letter to his mother, Max Müller was graciously commanded to Windsor for the first time. A day was named for him to go to luncheon: 'The Queen is anxious to see him,' and it was considerately added, 'if the day mentioned is not convenient to him another can be named.'

TO HIS MOTHER.

*Translation.* OXFORD, *December* 11.

'I was with the Queen for three-quarters of an hour, quite alone. Her Majesty received me in Prince Albert's room, and said she had long wished to see me, and hoped it would not be the last time, and then she talked in the most brilliant and interesting way, and spoke German better than I do. The Queen asked me to tell her about my work, spoke a good deal about Bunsen, about Prince Albert, about Schleswig-Holstein, and I could often hardly believe it was the Queen of England talking to me! The Crown Princess was not at Windsor, but sent for me on Tuesday, and we talked for an hour and a half. She too was most charming. The Princess soon returns to Berlin, which cannot be a pleasant place to her at present. She is a very remarkable woman, very liberal, and full of enthusiasm for Germany.'

TO REV. G. COX.

OXFORD, *December* 10.

'The Basque is a most interesting language to study as the type of an agglutinative form of speech, but though it agrees in form most strikingly with the Turanian language, the Finnic more particularly, no one has yet discovered any similarity between the natural elements of the Basque and any other language. How far the Basque was spoken in former days has been shown by Humboldt in his *Essay on the Original Inhabitants of Spain*, before him by Hernas. Michel's derivations of Basque words are copied from earlier writers, mostly theologians, who, in a language such as the Basque, easily found all that they looked for. They are worth nothing. If *year* was called inundation, this is no more than if we call year either spring, or autumn, or winter. But the Basque is a language which, in the hands of an unscrupulous philologist, will be made to say anything.'

On December 21 Max Müller writes to his mother: 'I am very much excited, for I have been commanded to Osborne to give some lectures before the Queen and the Princesses. The days are not fixed, but probably early in January.'

Christmas was spent at Ray Lodge, and then Max Müller went back alone to Oxford to prepare the royal lectures.

To his Wife.

Oxford, *December* 28.

'Here I am at work, and getting on very well, I hope. I dine with Stanley to-night, to hear from him and Lady Augusta what to observe and what to avoid at Osborne. I am sorry to be away from you, but I feel I ought to do my very best, and I can write better when I am here alone and have all my books.'

To his mother he writes, December 30: 'I go to Osborne on the third and stay till the sixth, so you can think of me.'

# CHAPTER XIV

## 1864–1865

Lectures at Osborne. Schleswig-Holstein war. Birth of third child. Member of Royal Irish Academy. Weymouth. Visit of his mother. Lecture at Leeds. Member of Turin Academy. Last visit to Ray Lodge. Sub-Librarianship of Bodleian.

'PROFESSOR MAX MÜLLER had the honour of delivering two lectures last week at Osborne before Her Majesty and the Royal Family, on the Science of Language.' Such was the announcement in the *Court Circular*, and the following letters give the details of this interesting visit:—

To his Wife.

OSBORNE, *January* 5.

'I arrived here all safe. I met the Queen's messenger at Southampton, and we went to Osborne in the *Elfin*, which had brought Prince Alfred over. The crossing took more than an hour, but I did not feel uncomfortable. I sat in the cabin with Prince Leiningen, who commands the vessel, and we had a pleasant chat together in German. I was very tired when I arrived here, and full of cold and headache, so I laid down in my own room, which was warm and cosy, and slept till dinner-time. I dined with the household at eight. I sat between Lady Churchill and Mrs. Ponsonby. All was very pleasant. Sir James Clarke was there, Mr. Ponsonby, Sir Thomas Biddulph, and some more ladies. After dinner we went to the ladies' drawing-room, where a message arrived from the Queen, who wished to see me. So I was conducted into the royal portion of the palace, and in a small boudoir there were the Queen, Princess Hohenlohe, and Princess Helena: afterwards Mrs. Bruce came in. I did my best to talk sense, but oh! my poor head. The Queen was very kind, and thanked me for coming, and said she was looking forward very much to my lectures. The conversation was in German, and you cannot imagine the dignity and graciousness of the Queen when she spoke with great composure of Prince Albert; and the reports spread abroad about her state of health are absolutely absurd. After about twenty minutes the Queen bowed, and I went straight to bed. I feel much better to-day, and hope to get through my lecture without disgrace. I received a message that Princess Helena wished to walk with me in the afternoon. Then at six there is to be the lecture, diagrams and all. Prince Arthur will be there; he was kept a day longer on purpose. The palace is full of beautiful works of art, but I have hardly had time to look at them yet.'

*January* 6.

'My first lecture is over, and from all I can hear it has not been a failure. Yesterday in the afternoon I had a very pleasant walk with Princess Helena and Mrs. Bruce. Princess Helena showed me their private museum, which they keep in a Swiss cottage, full of curious things which have been given them, or which the Princes have collected in their foreign travels. There were the Queen's former playthings, and a kitchen where the Princesses cook and bake, and kitchen gardens, one for each of them, and the Princess Royal every year gets her green peas from her own plot sent to Berlin, and enjoys them greatly. Everything is full of recollections of the Prince, and they all talk about him as if he were still among them. This is thoroughly German, and it always struck me in England how carefully all conversation on those who have gone before us is avoided, and how much of comfort and good influence derived from the memory of those we loved is thereby lost. After we came home from our walk, I had just time to prepare for my lecture, and to get my diagrams mounted. At six all the people assembled in the Council Chamber, and after a time came the Queen and the Princesses. The Queen had not attended a lecture for more than ten years, and everybody was surprised at her appearing. She listened very attentively, and did not knit at all, though her work was brought. After the lecture the Queen conversed with me for a long time, asking many shrewd questions, as did her sister, Princess Hohenlohe. It was then time to dress for dinner, and then to bed. This morning I had an interview with Princess Beatrice, who however was a little shy at first, but became after a time very amusing. She talks English, French, and German.'

*January* 6, 11 p.m.

'Just to finish the account of my visit here, I must tell you that after I had sent my letter to you to-day, the Queen sent for me again to her drawing-room, and brought Princess Beatrice with her to make her read to me in German, English, and French. She did it remarkably well, and the Queen talked to me a good deal about education, and how she taught her children. Afterwards Princess Helena showed me all the family pictures by Winterhalter, and the splendid statues. The Princess, when you know her, reminds you much of the Princess Royal. We walked about for a long time discussing all sorts of things. I had then to prepare for my lecture, to which the Queen came again, but without any work at all. In the evening Lord Granville arrived, and the Queen was very busy. She sent me word she hoped to see me, but afterwards sent to say it was getting too late, and that she was sorry she could not have seen me, and thanked me again. In the evening I had a long talk with Lord Granville, and to-morrow morning I hope to start at 9.30 with Prince Arthur and Sir James Clarke.'

These are the concluding words of the last lecture:—

'When the two last volumes of the *Veda* are published we shall have saved from destruction a work older than the *Iliad*, older than any other literary document of that noble race of mankind to which the greatest nations in the world's history have belonged—a race which after receiving from a Semitic race, from the Jews, its best treasure, its religion, the religion of the Old and New Testaments, is now, with the English in the van, carrying on slowly but irresistibly the conquest of the world by means of commerce, colonization, education, and conversion.'

On Max Müller's return, he heard from Sir Charles Phipps how pleased the Queen had been with the lectures—'of that you must be fully aware'—and Sir Charles added how much he had himself valued the information and instruction communicated, whilst three days later Lady Augusta Stanley forwarded the following extract from a letter from Princess Helena, now Princess Christian of Schleswig-Holstein. Gracious permission has been given to insert it.

'We have had two most interesting and charming lectures from Professor Max Müller. I cannot tell you how much I enjoyed them and value them. Do tell him so when you see him again, and how much I regret not being able to hear any more. I wish there was a possibility of my hearing more at some future time; I hope so—and Mama has not said No! You cannot think how pleasant it was for me to be able to talk to a clever man like Professor M. and one who does not inspire me with fear, as some very learned people do. The subject he treats is one which always interested me *so much*. Ever with much love, your affectionate friend, 'HELENA.'

To Rev. G. Cox.

Oxford, *January* 22.

'. . . When the Rishis first perceived the necessity of one Superior Power is difficult to say. It breaks through here and there, but their religion does not become monotheistic, for this involves the denial of polytheism. It always remains henotheistic, if one may coin such a word. I mean the one single god addressed at the time shares in all the qualities of a supreme being, but soon after another god is addressed equally supreme, and their logic does not in the least revolt at this. The Etruscan names of Greek deities have about the same value as the English names of the Indian deities. I mean they are mere corruptions, partly owing to ignorance, partly to the imperfections of the Etruscan alphabet, which possessed no media, and despised vowels almost as much as the Semitic languages.'

To the Same.

*January* 26.

'. . . Much as I admire M. Bréal's essay on Cacus, I do not the least feel convinced by his explanation of the dualism between Ormuzd and Ahriman, nor by his theory of Persian influences to be discovered in the early portions of the Bible. I am as far from prejudices on this point as M. Bréal, who is a Jew, and who, like most educated Jews, looks upon the books of the Old Testament as much more than inspired—taking inspired in the modern sense of that word—namely, as real, old, historical documents. I should value any such traces of influences received from neighbouring nations by the writers of the Old Testament most highly; but such is the importance from an historical point of view that I shall not feel inclined to build any conclusions on such vague evidence as that brought together by M. Bréal. . . . Any such word as *Asdossodeus*, if it could be discovered in the early books, would be invaluable, but though I do not give up all hope of such discoveries hereafter, I am bound to say that as yet I cannot see them.'

To the Same.

*February* 16.

'I am afraid I have hardly done justice to your book in my review. The fact is, I was overwhelmed with work, and, after a short introduction, I put in a portion of my lectures which I am preparing for the Press. However, I find that my article has at least startled several people who have a tender feeling for Helen and Troy, and I hope they will take to your book and try to get some more information. I may be wrong in my explanation of the relation between Helen and Paris, Saramâ and Pa*n*i, but I cannot help thinking that Helena and Saramâ are the same word.'

The following letter refers first to Mr. Gifford Palgrave, the Arabian traveller, who had just returned from his daring expedition, and then to the Schleswig-Holstein question, which occupied so much of Max Müller's attention during the early part of this year.

To his Wife.

*February* 17.

'After luncheon I went to see the Jesuit, and had a very interesting talk with him about a thousand subjects. I found him clever, well-informed, and devoted to his work; quite unanglicized, however, in all his views, and strangely torn away from all the fibres of his native soil. It is a pleasant contrast to the self-seeking, money-making, place-hunting tendencies, to see a man without any ambition as far as this life is concerned, but evidently full of ambition for another life. I enclose a letter from Delane; so you see I am in for it. I am all in large print, to offer a larger target to the arrows of the enemy.'

Max Müller, both in letters to the *Times* and to friends in England and abroad, upheld the independence of the Duchies: 'They are sovereign and independent states, and are indissolubly united.' He advocated the claims of the house of Augustenburg, and reprobated the high-handed policy of Bismarck, as much as the pretensions of Denmark. In later years he saw that Bismarck's policy with regard to the Duchies was the first link in the chain that led to the unity of Germany. The feeling in England was very strong. Denmark was weak, Prussia and Austria strong; therefore Denmark must be upheld—people forgetting that the Duchies, whose rights were at stake, were still weaker. Max Müller was openly attacked in the papers, and received anonymous letters from Danes in England that were too vile to show to any one; in some his life even was threatened. One old friend assumed in the *Athenæum* that he was the author of a pamphlet, *The Dano-German Conflict and Lord Russell's Proposals of Mediation*, calling it 'an ingenious mystification, the author of which wishes to be supposed to be an Englishman.' The author was an Englishman connected with the Government, and therefore could not give his name. Max Müller always signed his letters, and never masked as an Englishman.

To his Mother.

*Translation.* *March* 4.

'You will have gathered from the papers that I am quite well. I had lately to tell the English something of the truth, and though they don't like to hear it, yet they have taken it well. The common papers abuse me, but they are of little weight, and the leading ones behave civilly, though they answer with the most absurd nonsense. All this takes up my time, that is the worst, and disturbs my work; but one must do one's duty, and now that I am known in England, it fell to my lot to take up the cudgels for the truth on the German side. The affair is still very complicated. Russia, Austria, and Prussia hang together, but with bad intentions. Everything now depends on France, and the Emperor will sell himself to the highest bidder—either to England or Russia. England has plunged deeply, and will hardly come out with a whole skin. Palmerston would like war, but the people, at least in manufacturing towns and the north, are against it. The King of the Belgians arrived to-day.'

To the Same.

*Contemporary Letter.* *March* 4.

'M. has talked of writing to you for some days, as he was afraid you would share the fears of the German papers, which seem to think he must be in prison, or very near it, for his letters to the *Times*. Happily, here any one may speak out his mind freely without fear of any bad consequences. Such certainly is not the case in Berlin now, as we hear from Morier that Herr von Schlötzer has been sent off to Rome for having expressed his feelings against Bismarck too freely. The newspapers are all very angry with M., which proves that they feel the truth of what he says; but every newspaper almost is ultra-Danish, except the local papers of Liverpool and Manchester, and other great places of trade, where the merchants are German in feeling, and entirely opposed to any idea of war. The Queen's life is no easy one at present. Her own feelings entirely German, and her Ministers and people as entirely Danish. She must be happy just now at having old King Leopold with her, as she leans so much on him.'

Max Müller's lectures this term were on 'The Origin of Fables,' and were largely attended.

To his Wife.

Oxford, *March* 30.

'I had a visit to-day from the Schleswig-Holstein architect—a very nice fellow. He came to England on business: is building a grand mansion somewhere near York. He told me many things about the war, &c. He is a man of forty-five, with wife and children, in very good business. He has enrolled himself to fight as soon as the Prussians and Austrians are gone. All his friends, he says, have done the same, and are ready to die rather than submit to the Danes again.

I had a visit from ——, who brought me all sorts of messages from Princess Hohenlohe. However, I told him nothing could be done at present. I also received an address and vote of thanks from Bremen, largely signed.'

Early in April Max Müller heard of the death of his mother's old aunt, Frau Klausnitzer, mother of Emilie, Baroness Stolzenberg. He writes:—

To his Mother.

*Translation.* *April* 5.

'The news of the death of the dear old aunt has affected me very much. She had indeed enjoyed the full measure of human life, and in her old age had a large measure of happiness; but when the moment of parting comes—come as it may—it comes always too soon. I have only had the printed notice, and know nothing of how it was. In your last letter you said she was so well and bright, and then I always thought, "Well, whilst the old aunt is so well and strong my mother has a good spell of life still before her." One only fancies the generations *must* follow each other, till the turn comes for ourselves. Well, for those who have had such a happy old age, and remained strong in mind and body to the last, those who are left can only thank God, and pray for a like end for themselves and for all they love. We accustom ourselves so easily to life as a second nature, and in spite of the graves around us, death remains something unnatural, hard and terrifying. That should not be. An early death is terrifying, but as we grow older our thoughts should accustom themselves to passing away at the end of a long life's journey. All is so beautiful, so good, so wisely ordered, that even death can be nothing hard, nothing disturbing; it all belongs to a great plan, which we do not understand, but of which we know that it is wiser than all wisdom, better than all good, that it cannot be otherwise, cannot be better. In faith we can live, and we can die—can even see those go before us, who came before us, and whom we must follow. All is not according to our will, to our wisdom, but according to a heavenly Will, and those who have once found each other through God's hand will, clinging to His hand, find each other again. Let me soon hear how you are, and submit to God's Will quietly and with resignation.'

All these early months Max Müller was preparing his second volume of *Lectures on Language* for the Press, which had been delayed by his visit to Germany the previous year.

Before, however, they were ready, a fourth edition of the first volume came out, of 1,250 copies like the others. He also wrote a much-admired article on 'The Language and Poetry of Schleswig-Holstein,' with some good translations of Klaus Groth's 'Platt-Deutsch Poems.' This was reprinted in *Chips*, first edition, Volume III.

To Rev. G. Cox.

Oxford, *April* 11.

'If the old generation is uncritically sceptical, the young generation is uncritically credulous. Now the young generation, the rising scholars, to a man, swear in Comparative Philology and Mythology, and the future is theirs. I am afraid as we get older we shall be equally unwilling to change our views and examine our evidence. I hope in that case we may abstain and stand by in silence; but though I hope it, I am not quite certain on that point. Surely, Comparative Mythology is not self-evident; if it were, where would be the pleasure of having dug up some of these old bones? People who make new discoveries ought not to be angry with the world for not accepting them at once! To me, I confess, though it may sound very conceited, there is a pleasure in living in a small University. I am old enough to remember the incredulous wagging of heads when Bopp declared that the infinitive was the dative or some other case of an abstract noun: there is hardly a grammar now where you do not find this. Even now, if you tell people that two only of the ten numerals in Greek and Sanskrit are oxytone, and that this is not by accident, they think you are talking nonsense. Fifty years hence a boy will be plucked who does not know it. Now you know I am myself a great unbeliever in many mythological parallelisms, and I am quite prepared to admit that many of my own comparisons will be knocked over. It is sad that it should be so, but so it is! even old Bopp's *Comparative Grammar* is by this time riddled with shot and crumbling down, but something better has been put in its place. But that the principles I have laid down for the study of Comparative Mythology are sound I am prepared to prove against the world.'

To his Wife.

Oxford, *June* 17.

'Our garden looks so well, and I jump out of window and look at my roses, and then go back to my work. There is to me a beauty and mystery and sanctity about flowers, and when I see them come and go, no one knows whence and whither, I ask, What more miracles do we want? What better, more beautiful, more orderly world could we wish to belong to than that by which we are surrounded and supported on all sides? Where is there a flaw or a fault? Then why should we fear unless the flaws are within us, and we will not see the blessing and the rest which we might enjoy if we only trusted to the Author of all that beauty, order, and wisdom about us? It is a perfect sin not to be happy in this world, and how much of the misery which there is, is the work of men, or could be removed by men, if they would but work together for each other's good. It seems so hopeless to do any good on so small a scale as ours must necessarily be; yet I do not think we do enough, not in proportion to what is given us without any desert.'

Max Müller had very strong feelings about the duty of almsgiving, and considered a tenth of all he had the *least* that should be given away annually. In most years he far exceeded this sum, and even his wife never knew the constant help he gave to poor young students and literary men, both German and English. To his mother and sister he was most generous. He had been a great smoker before his marriage, and indulged in the best cigars, but he gave up smoking *entirely* when he had the expenses of a household to provide for, that his charity purse, as he called it, might not suffer; and it was only in the last twenty years of his life that he took to smoking again, and then only cigarettes, and very few of them each day.

As soon as his book was printed, Max Müller joined his wife and children at Ray Lodge, and on June 22 he writes to his mother that he was expecting the publication of his second volume of *Lectures*, and did not trouble himself as to its reception. 'One does one's best, and one says what one feels is right, and the rest one lets alone. I am not at all sorry that I have spoken out to the English, and if they abuse me, it shows they are ashamed.' And his wife wrote also: 'Max is enjoying his holiday here, for the lectures being off his hands he is giving himself perfect rest and doing nothing but lie in the hayfields or the garden, enjoying the flowers.'

On August 1 Max Müller's third child, a third daughter, was born. In writing to ask his valued friend Dean Stanley to be godfather, he says:—

TO DEAN STANLEY.

*August 2.*

'I always hoped to have you as godfather to my first son, if there should be one. As it seems, however, that there is to be no little Max, I shall wait no longer. I have no doubt that your family of godchildren is a very large one, but as I think you may trust G. and myself that we shall try to bring up our children in the real faith and true discipline of Christ, I hope you will be able to accede to our request, and add this one to many other proofs of real friendship which you have given to both of us. Have you seen Bunsen's *Leben Jesu?* I read it, and wrote to Madame Bunsen asking her to have it published, and translated into English, possibly into French also. I like it, and I think just now it will do good. It contains the soul, which is wanting in Renan's ghost, or rather in his corpse, of Christ. It gives all that is essential in the outward life of Christ, and then throws the burden of believing or disbelieving the divinity of Christ on every one of us, as it was thrown on those who witnessed His real life, who had to break with a religion dear and sacred to themselves, and whose senses and reason must have had to pass through a much more severe struggle than we have to pass through, before they yielded to the voice within, that Christ was the Son of God. I do not know whether you would consider it wise to have your name in any way connected with a translation of Bunsen's work, but I hope it will not be brought out with any appearance of coming from a hostile camp. It should come as a message of peace—as a minimum, a very small minimum, if you like—but with a large margin on every side, which need not remain a blank.'

In writing to tell his mother of the birth of her new grandchild, Max mentions at the end of his letter that 1,000 copies of his *Lectures* had been sold the first day.

TO REV. G. COX.

OXFORD, *August* 5, 1864.

'MY DEAR SIR,—. . . As to annihilation, all I mean is that it is a word without any conceivable meaning, and that it might do some people good to see this clearly. We are—that is enough. What we are does not depend on us; what we shall be, neither. We may conceive the idea of change in form, but not of cessation or destruction of substance. No doubt people mean frequently by annihilation the loss of conscious personality, as distinct from material annihilation. On that point I said nothing, because it would have led me too far out of my own sphere. However, what I feel about it is shortly this. If there is anything real and substantial in our conscious personality, then whatever there is real and substantial in it cannot cease to exist. If on the contrary we mean by conscious personality something that is the result of accidental circumstances, then, no doubt, we must face the idea of such a personality ceasing to be what it now is. I believe, however, that the true source and essence of our personality lies in what is the most real of all real things, and in so far as it is true, it cannot be destroyed. There is a distinction between conscious personality and personal consciousness. A child has personal consciousness; a man who is this or that, a Napoleon or a Talleyrand, has conscious personality. Much of that conscious personality is merely temporary and passes away; but the personal consciousness remains. I do not think that Schleiermacher could have said that the last enemy that would be destroyed in us is the idea of our immortality. What he may have said is, *our* idea of immortality. I should like to see this subject fully and freely discussed. It is no doubt the old controversy between Nominalism and Realism under a new form. We know what stuff words are made of, and it strikes me that those who know the antecedents of words are spared many troubles and difficulties in religious and philosophical struggles.'

The middle of September the whole family party went for change to Weymouth, where they were joined by Max Müller's mother, who returned with them to Oxford and stayed on with them the whole winter.

Politics crop up again towards the close of the year, as the following letter to Morier, Secretary of Legation at Berlin, shows. Morier shared all Max Müller's feelings as to the Duchies:—

OXFORD, *November* 10.

'MY DEAR MORIER,—For the sake of decency, if not from a feeling of personal friendship, I trust the Duchies will soon be handed over to Duke Frederick. If Prussia attempts to swallow the small morsel by itself it will stick in her throat. Hereafter it will go down together with others at one good gulp. I was so sorry not to see you again before you returned to Berlin; we went to Weymouth during September and October; my mother came to me there, and is now staying with us. We are all well, thank God, and if it were not for the dinner-parties this quiet life would be very pleasant. But I am afraid the dinner-parties will drive me sooner or later away from this country to the less hospitable shores of the Spree or Danube. Jowett's salary has again been defeated, this time in Council; it shows how low human nature can sink. It is perfectly disgusting, and I feel ashamed to accept any salary from such a body of men. The matter, however, is not to rest, and a new motion has at once been made. Is there not some great mischief brewing in all these meetings of crowned heads and Ministers? And are you quite certain that there is no mischief hatching as against England? Though John Bull does make a fool of himself now and then, the world would soon go to wrack and ruin without him. Crowned brains are just now very active, and I am sure they all consider England a bull in a china shop. There are certain fellows now very cock-a-hoop, and capable of anything in the way of spite and mischief. Yours ever affectionately.'

Christmas was spent in Oxford for the first time since 1860, and was a regular German Christmas, with a tree for the children, and German *Stolle* (cake) and German dishes. Max Müller, who had not spent Christmas with his mother since 1849, was as happy, and entered into everything with the same zest, as one of his own children. It was never difficult to give him pleasure, for his hard early training made of every little trifle a source of enjoyment and a cause of thankfulness to the Giver of all Good.

Early in 1865 the Max Müllers received the sad news that the family home at Ray Lodge was to be given up and the party there dispersed. The long lease had nearly run out, and the owner would only sell, not let again. Max Müller's father-in-law resolved to settle in London near his younger daughter, and the sister who had lived with him over forty years, bringing up his children, preferred the country, as did Max Müller's brother-in-law, who had hitherto, with his wife and child, lived at Ray Lodge. To the Max Müllers and Walronds it was a great loss; living, as they did, in a town, the country life was a boon to their children, and only a large country house had room for them all to meet together. It was at once resolved to spend as long a time as possible during the summer in the old home.

To LADY AUGUSTA STANLEY.

64, HIGH STREET, OXFORD, *February* 7, 1865.

'DEAR LADY AUGUSTA,—Many thanks for the *Theology of the Nineteenth Century*—and, I hope, of many more centuries to come—which I believe I owe to your kindness. I read it with intense pleasure; it was almost like having a talk with the Dean, or listening to one of his sermons. I do not know the exact date of the Book of Daniel, and this, I am afraid, would be considered heresy by many of the Presidents and Princes; but of this I am certain, that in any century, even in our own, the lions cannot hurt a man who, like Daniel, is a servant of the living God. I hope you and the Dean are quite well. We have been living our quiet and happy life at Oxford. My mother has been with us the whole winter, and the children are well. With *herzliche Grüsse* to the Dean, yours sincerely, 'MAX MÜLLER.'

The following letter touches on the curious legend of the Barnacle Goose, fully detailed in the second volume of Max Müller's *Lectures on Language*, which had excited a good deal of attention not only in England, but on the Continent:—

TO PROFESSOR BENFEY.

*Translation.* 64, HIGH STREET, *February* 26.

'DEAR COLLEAGUE,—. . . I have read the little notice on fishes and birds in *Occident und Orient.* As it is a later addition, it would be most remarkable if the fable had really got into the Eastern fables from the West of Europe. The occurrence of the same legend in different places allows of various explanations, but especially through the passage in Genesis i. 20, to which the priests have often referred, in order to prove that all fowl are of common origin with fishes, and therefore may be eaten on fast-days.

'These commoner legends do not therefore belong to the "myth" treated by me, which does not refer to birds in general, but only to the goose which goes by the special name of Barnacle Goose. This name can be explained, and can be connected with the name barnacle-shell.'

Early in March Max Müller went to Leeds to deliver a lecture on 'The *Vedas*, or the Ancient Sacred Books of the Brâhmans.'

TO HIS WIFE.

LEEDS, *March* 6.

'So you see I found my way after all. It was a wretched day till we got beyond Rugby, and then the sun came out, and the country looked warm and bright. It is quite spring here, and I hope the change will do me good. I found Mr. Hincks waiting for me; he is a clergyman, though I do not know of what denomination yet. He has a nice house, and a wife and two daughters. We had a quiet dinner, and in the evening the intellect of Leeds will assemble here.'

*March* 7.

'We had a very pleasant party last night, chiefly clergy and medical men. The Vicar of Leeds, Dr. Otley, came, though my host is the Unitarian minister of Leeds. I was a little tired, having to talk a great deal. We had a sumptuous supper, and then to bed. This morning we started after breakfast to see the town. Very fine Town-hall, with a statue of the Queen by Noble. Then we explored a wool manufactory, with some beautiful machinery, seeing the whole process from the sheep to the shawls. Then the poor parts of the town, and the Working Men's Club—all very curious, and the weather fine. We dined at three, and in the evening the lecture is to come off. Well, I must do my best. The people are all very civil, but I shall be glad when it is over. Love to mother, and give her this wool, which I saw made.'

The Philosophical Hall at Leeds was packed with a most attentive audience, which included many clergy of the Church of England, and ministers of all the leading nonconformist bodies, for the friendly relations between the Church and Dissent at Leeds, so marked in the days of Dean Hook, still continued in full force. The lecturer concluded by deducing three lessons to be learned from the careful study of the *Vedas* and other Sacred Books of the East. Firstly, that 'most religions were in their most ancient form, or in the minds of their authors, free from many of the blemishes that attach to them in later times. Secondly, that there was hardly any religion which did not contain some truth, sufficient to enable those who sought the Lord to find Him in their hour of need. Thirdly, that we learnt to appreciate better than ever what we really have in our own religion. No one who had not examined patiently and honestly the other religions of the world could know what Christianity really was, or could join with such truth and sincerity in the words of St. Paul, "I am not ashamed of the Gospel of Christ."' The concluding words were quoted thirty-five years later in the sermon preached in Max Müller's parish church the Sunday after his death.

Soon after his return from Leeds, Max Müller's mother, who had been with him since September, returned to Germany. With all her devotion to her son, the quiet, regular life in his house soon wearied her, accustomed as she had been from her earliest days to be actively busy in household affairs; and her deafness prevented her from sharing in the pleasures of society, especially in a foreign country. In summer, when she could be more in the open air and enjoy the beautiful College gardens, she was happier, but the long winter visits were never a success. To her son, the mere feeling that his mother was under his roof was happiness; but she required more variety and amusement than a scholar's house could give her, and it was impossible not to see that she longed for her German home, though she suffered severely when the moment of parting came.

The following letter shows that Max Müller was still occupied with the Schleswig-Holstein question. Mr. Gladstone was at this time Chancellor of the Exchequer:—

To the Right Hon. W. E. Gladstone.

High Street, *April* 2.

'Dear Sir,—I hope to be in London the whole of next week, and should like very much to see you. You will easily guess the subject on which I should wish to speak to you. I have felt throughout that if there is a statesman in England who will form his opinion on the Schleswig-Holstein question, not according to what seems expedient, but according to what is just and right, it is you. There may be reasons however why you might decline to speak to me on that question, but even in that case I hope you will pardon my request.'

This spring Max Müller, who had been elected a Correspondent of the Turin Academy in 1859, was chosen as one of the six Foreign Members of that distinguished society, his colleagues being Cousin, Thiers, Böckh, Mommsen, and Grote.

Before leaving home for the summer, Max Müller found time to write to his old friend Bishop Patteson, in answer to his letter of the year before:—

64, High Street, Oxford, *April* 16, 1865.

'My dear Bishop,—I am so thoroughly ashamed of myself that I was afraid I should never have courage enough to write to you. It has been a weight on my conscience for years, and I doubt whether I shall be able to give you any intelligible reason why I put off writing to you from month to month, and from year to year, till at last I gave it up for very shame. However, the simple truth is this. I have been very busy, and I always hoped I should find time sooner or later to devote special attention to the Melanesian languages. I wished to do so first, and before I troubled you with any inquiries; and then, whenever I began to get ready for the work, I felt that I had other work to do, more necessary, and which my friends expected me to do, and that I must not attempt any new subject before having finished what I had in hand. This is the only intelligible account I can give you of my protracted silence, and now that I have done so, I can only ask that you will forgive me, though I can hardly forgive myself. My thoughts, I can truly tell you, have often been with you and your work. Many times I have envied you your choice of a life's work about which, if once chosen, there can be no doubt that it is right, useful, and pleasing in the sight of God and of men. When I first heard of your departure, I confess I was surprised. I believe I had seen you last at Dresden, revelling in ancient Italian art, and studying Hebrew or Arabic. I thought of you, as I thought of Thomson, as a future Bishop in the midst of the refined society of London, and when I received your first letter, dated somewhere latitude and longitude, I felt for a moment that you had made a mistake, and that the Church at home could ill afford to send men of your stamp as missionaries to mere savages. I do not think so now, and if I compare your lot with that of Thomson, now Archbishop of York, I feel that yours is the higher and the happier of the two.'

OXFORD, *May* 14.

'I had the pleasure of seeing Mr. Codrington, who told me many things about you and your work, full of interest. How different life must seem to you from what it is to us! Everything so clear before you, nothing to cause you any misgivings, work to be done which must be done, a great work without any of the littlenesses which hang about our life in English society. I cannot bring myself to take much interest in all the controversies that are going on in the Church of England, and which to a great extent centre in Oxford. No doubt the points at issue are great, and appeal to our hearts and minds, but the spirit in which they are treated seems to me so very small. How few men on either side give you the impression that they write face to face with God, and not face to face with men and the small powers that be. Surely this was not so in the early centuries, nor again at the time of the Reformation? I have great regard for Stanley, because I know him personally, and know him to be strictly honest to himself, and capable of sacrificing many things he holds most dear for the sake of truth. He takes a warm interest in your work too. I suppose you received some years ago two contributions, one from Stanley, the other from Thomson (Archbishop), which they gave me to forward to you. Stanley was most anxious to send more, but knowing how he spends his money, I would not take more than £10. I still have great faith in the Archbishop of York. Unfortunately his elevation has been very sudden, and there are many who envy him and watch him: that makes him timid, and he hardly dares to be himself. But I feel certain he is averse to persecution, and ready to make every possible allowance for difference of opinion among those who seek honestly for what is true and right. If I may judge as a mere spectator, the danger of the Church lies at present in narrow-minded clamour and partisanship. Newspapers, religious or otherwise, appealing to the masses on points which men of education and special knowledge only can understand, do more harm than any political demagogues. I wish I could send you about twenty persons, both lay and clergy, to work for ten years as missionaries with you, and I feel certain that after the removal of the leaders, the Church would have peace again. But enough of this, for I want to have some space for linguistics. The skeleton grammars you sent me are very valuable, and it is most desirable that all you can write down should be printed. Of course, if the grammatical forms could be more systematized it would be better, but at the same time there is danger in systematizing; and I consider that the most important point which, in the study of languages, can be settled by such languages as yours, and by such only, is the original want of system, the influence of the individual, the family, and the class, in the formation and tradition of speech. The natural state of language is unbounded dialectic variety, but of course in all literary languages that phase is lost to us beyond the hope of recovery. Your own missionary work, the repeating of certain prayers, &c., will artificially arrest the dialectic variety of the native language. I suppose few of your Melanesian friends recollect more than their grandfathers, and therefore it is not likely they should be conscious of changes in their language. But the great variety of local dialects are the best witnesses as to the changeableness of language, and though it would hardly be worth your while to note such things, small peculiarities in the speech of certain families or settlements might throw much light on the process, the most mysterious process, how language changes. This is the great problem on which, in the end, will depend the decision in favour of one or many beginnings of human speech. Literary languages do entirely mislead us, and have misled nearly all scholars on that point. Savage languages alone can show how far languages can change. It would be very important, too, to make observations as to the number of words sufficient for answering all the purposes of a low civilization. How many words does a Melanesian know or use? How many of them convey to him an etymological meaning, i.e. are intelligible to him in their radical intention? Does he use different names for the same thing, or does he call two things by the same name? A language of 1,000 words is more easily changed than a language of 10,000. Out of two synonymes, one is sure to be lost in time, whereas the inconvenience arising from two things being called by the same name is sure to lead to an independent coining of new words. I send you, through Mr. Codrington, a book by Mr. Tylor on *Ancient Civilization*, with a review of mine. It will show you how valuable accurate and trustworthy observations of the habits of savages are for many important inquiries, and it may perhaps induce you to put down in writing the results of your own observations among the ancient strata of mankind cropping out in your islands. I wish I had more time for that kind of work, but I must for the next three or four years give all my time to the finishing of my edition of the *Rig-veda*, the work which originally brought me to England, and which, when finished, will set me free.

'We are hard at work canvassing for Gladstone. I believe he will be returned, and I believe his place would never be contested, if it were not for twenty or thirty idle agitators.'

Early in June the whole family moved to Ray Lodge for their last visit, and stayed there nearly three months, during which time there was a constant succession of family visitors, all wishing to see the last of the house that had been made so pleasant to all members of the large circle of relations. The Walronds were also there with their four children, and the summer months flew by all too fast to the two young wives in the home of their happy childhood and youth. The river was a constant pleasure, Max Müller becoming an expert oarsman, and many were the hours he spent with his wife on the river, under the shadow of the Taplow and Cliveden woods. One long delightful day was spent in a picnic at Medmenham Abbey, with the choir from Bray Church, in which his father-in-law, who had himself a very fine voice, had always taken a keen interest, and the old ruins echoed to many a beautiful glee and chorus. The loved Vicar of Bray drove over with his wife and daughters in the afternoon, in time to come down the river on the barge that held the large party, and, among other singers, Max Müller was persuaded to sing 'O Tannenbaum,' the song that nearly twenty years earlier had amused his friends in 'Billy Russell's' rooms in the Temple, with its imitation of various musical instruments, and which, if report speaks true, was a delight to the 'Monks of All Souls' at their Gaudys for many years.

Drives, too, were taken through Hedsor, Dropmore, the Burnham Beeches, and Windsor Park, and all the other favourite haunts of bygone years. But a sense of regret underlay everything, and Max Müller in his letters of that summer to his mother constantly laments the loss to his children of the grandfather's house and gardens.

Throughout this year there was a frequent exchange of letters with Messrs. Longmans, Max Müller arranging for his friend, Professor Benfey, the publication in England of his *Sanskrit Grammar*, as one of the series of handbooks for Sanskrit which Max Müller was intending to publish. With the thoroughness that he carried into all his work, he made himself master of the details of printing, binding, and publishing, the cost of ink and paper, the proper charges for corrections and advertisements, and he used laughingly to say that the highest compliment he ever received was what Mr. William Longman, half in admiration and half provoked, said of him to Mr. Froude, 'As to your friend Max Müller, he can skin the flints in Paternoster Row!' A second edition of Volume II of the *Lectures* came out this year, and the fifth edition of Volume I.

FROM PROFESSOR HUXLEY.

MUSEUM OF GEOLOGY, JERMYN STREET,
*June* 15, 1865.

'MY DEAR SIR,—I beg your acceptance of the numbers of the *Fortnightly Review* containing my article on Ethnology, which accompanies this note.

'I lost no time on Monday in referring to *Christianity and Mankind*, and the perusal of your chapter on "Ethnology *v.* Phonology" leads me profoundly to regret that I had not been able to avail myself of the aid of so powerful an ally.

'But if you will continue to pull one way, and I the other, I have hopes we shall be able to get Ethnology and Phonology apart in time. Ever, my dear Sir, very faithfully yours, 'T. HUXLEY.'

TO PROFESSOR HUXLEY.

CIVIL SERVICE COMMISSION, *June* 16, 1865.

'MY DEAR SIR,—Accept my best thanks for your article on Ethnology in the *Fortnightly Review.* I shall read it carefully next week, when this examination for the Indian Civil Service is over.

I have 130 candidates to examine in Sanskrit; and six hours of viva voce a day acts like an extinguisher on my reasoning faculties. I hope, however, I shall soon recover, and shall truly rejoice if, after your powerful pleading, Sir Creswell Creswell will grant a divorce to Ethnology and Phonology, two parties that ought never to have been joined together, and whose union has certainly been the cause of a succession of scientific mishaps. Believe me, yours very truly,

'MAX MÜLLER.'

To EDWARD TYLOR, ESQ.

RAY LODGE, *June* 23.

'I am glad to hear you are going to write an article on Wilhelm von Humboldt. Steinthal has made Humboldt far more unintelligible than he is. Humboldt is much more of a poet or seer than an exact philosopher. To attempt to make him what he is not, as Steinthal has done, destroys what he really is. But I confess, to give a faithful, clear, and consistent account of Humboldt's various and sometimes diverging views of language is by no means an easy task, and I am glad you have undertaken it. I was very sorry to have missed you when you were at Oxford. I am still deep in examination papers for the Indian Civil Service. Yours very truly.'

To HIS MOTHER.

*Translation.* RAY LODGE, *July* 16.

'I was lately invited to a luncheon in London to which the Queen of Holland had asked various people she wished to know—Professor Owen, Tennyson, Grote the historian, Lord Houghton, formerly Monckton Milnes and also a poet, the Editor of the *Times*, and my unworthy self. The Queen is very friendly, and very highly educated. She is a daughter of the old King of Wurtemburg, and we talked German together, though she speaks English and French fluently. My second volume of *Lectures* goes off very well, 2,200 copies sold in one year. It is stereotyped in America, and translated into French and Italian. Böttiger gets on slowly [with the German translation] and is not a good translator, but that can't be helped now.'

It was in this summer that Mr. Gladstone stood for the last time for election as a University burgess, and was rejected. The Max Müllers were staying at Claydon House, and from there Max came in to Oxford to record his vote. On his return that evening he brought word of the mishap to the statue of King James over the gateway into the Schools quad. Originally the statue had held a sceptre in the right hand, and a Bible in the left. The tradition in Oxford had always been that the sceptre fell out of James's hand, and was smashed on the pavement, on the day that William III landed at Torbay. Certain it is that, as the voters poured out of the Theatre, the Bible was lying in pieces on the pavement, and was seen by all voters who crossed the Schools quad, coming out of the Theatre. Max Müller was of this number, on his way to his house in High Street. Of course it was considered of great significance by Mr. Gladstone's supporters. Lord Houghton was one of the party at Claydon, and read aloud of an evening Swinburne's *Atalanta in Calydon*, which had not long appeared.

TO THE DEAN OF WESTMINSTER.

RAY LODGE, *July* 19.

'MY DEAR STANLEY,—I was in town yesterday and called at the Deanery; but as I was told you had a bad headache, I did not like to send up my card. When I returned in the evening I found your letter. I shall go to Oxford to-day and be at the station at 3.55. It will be a real pleasure to show Oxford to the Queen of Holland. I liked very much what I saw of her at your house. The only people worth knowing in the world are those who, instead of being Deans or Bishops or Archbishops, &c., are themselves, or try to be, and are proud to be themselves. She hides her crown most gracefully—and crowns, I suppose, are more difficult to hide than mitres, coronets, &c.

'Gladstone is rejected by Oxford, and I grieve to see meanness, narrowness, intolerance, and conceit triumphant once more. I suppose it is right to subscribe to the Bishop of Natal's Fund; I promised to do so, though I cannot subscribe much. I do not think that he understands the language of ancient history—it is a language full of irregularities, and to try to eliminate them all is like eliminating the irregular verbs in Greek. But though I differ from him and his school, I cannot bear to see honest inquiry squashed by the clamour of Demetrius and his craftsmen, and the attempt to starve a man into silence or submission is a discovery which will be a disgrace to the nineteenth century. Ever yours, 'MAX MÜLLER.'

TO E. A. FREEMAN, ESQ.

RAY LODGE, *August* 12.

'MY DEAR FREEMAN,—Could you find time to send me one line if you know any book in English on the English Tell saga? I have got the Swiss books, but I want to know the history of the English tale of Adam Bell, Clym of the Clough, and William of Cloudesley.

I think with you that the myth of Tell or Agamemnon makes the existence of a real Agamemnon probable, but what can the historian do with such probable heroes?'

Max Müller was singularly scrupulous as to inflicting inquiries on his friends, as he suffered himself from letters from all parts of the world, on every imaginable subject. He was most careful to answer all genuine inquiries, but when asked by one lady if football was played in England before the emigration of the Britons (whatever that meant), and by another where to get her horoscope cast, by one gentleman how to find the origin of his name Jones, by another why in learning German he might not say *der* but *das* Pferd, and by an hotel-keeper how to pronounce the word 'schedule,' and whether the term revoke or *renège* should be used at cards, as two gentlemen had laid heavy wagers on these points, he did not feel called on to waste his time in answers. He had a book in which these and other equally foolish letters were pasted, and in which he kept the most amusing of the envelopes addressed to him in every imaginable style.

Among the best of these envelopes are:—

'To the most celebrated and honoured Max Müller.'

'M. le Directeur, Université des Langues, Angleterre,' came straight to him.

'Professor Max Müller, Editor of the Works of the East Indies, General Post Office, London.'

'Max Müller, Ancient Professor of University, England.'

'Mr. Rev. Max Müller.'

'Master Max Müller.'

'To very honourable Knight Max Müller.'

'S[r] Magnificenz Mr. Max Müller, Rector of the University.'

'The Venerable Professor Max Müller.'

'Pundit Max Müller.'

'Mr. Max, Oxford.'

'To the great Linguist Max Müller.'

'To Father Max Müller.'

'The most noblest of the noble, Great Oriental Savant, F. Max Müller.'

'To the Head authority on Language, Oxford.'

But there was one letter which he was fond of showing, though he never knew who were the writers:—

To Professor Max Müller.

*March* 10.

'Sir,—We are a couple of rather wild English girls, who have been trying all our lives to learn something and have not yet succeeded. We have become somewhat dissatisfied lately with our failures, and have made up our minds to master some wonderful language that few girls (or even men) would know. We intended to "go in" for Arabic, but every one says that we should never get over even the alphabet. To take only one or two you mention in your lectures, Persian and Sanskrit are as difficult as Arabic. Zend no one has ever heard of. Prakrit we cannot get the necessary materials for. What are we to do? Every one seems to think we are too fastidious, but all we want is to get hold of an unusual language that is not quite beyond our capabilities. We have at length made up our mind to try and get out of our difficulties by applying to head quarters, and trouble you with our inquiries. We enclose a directed envelope in order to take up as little of your valuable time as possible. We are, yours respectfully, 'Mabel and Ellen.'

The address given was 'Holly, Post Office, Kiln Green, Twyford.'

To this the following answer was sent:—

'Dear Miss Mabel and Miss Ellen,—It is by no means easy to reply to your inquiry. To take up any work in good earnest is a most excellent thing, and I should be the last person to find fault with anybody for fixing on learning a language, even for the mere sake of learning something. Yet it is right that our work should have some useful object beyond the mere pleasure of working. Thus in selecting a language we might look at three ulterior objects—literature, travel, or science of language. Now, as I have no reason to suppose that you want to learn a language that might be useful to you in travelling, or that might furnish promising material for scientific analysis, I will take it for granted that literature would form an object of interest to you in the choice of a language. As it is to be a language which few people in England are likely to know, I should say take Portuguese, if you like Romance, or take Swedish, if you like Teutonic languages. The books for learning these languages are easily procured, and there is a literature both in Swedish and Portuguese very little known in this country, and well deserving the interest of two young ladies. But I am afraid you will consider both Portuguese and Swedish as far too commonplace. Well, in that case, take Siamese. You will have some difficulty in getting grammars and dictionaries, yet, if you are in earnest and apply to Messrs. Williams and Norgate, 14, Henrietta Street, Covent Garden, you will with some little trouble and expense get what you want. There is not a single man in Europe, I believe, who knows Siamese. The French, however, are opening the country, and some of their agents and missionaries have begun to study the language. The alphabet is troublesome, the grammar itself seems easy. There is a vast literature, as yet almost unknown. The King of Siam is a man of literary tastes, a man who reads and writes English, and who would no doubt be delighted to receive, say two or three years hence—for it will take at least that time—a letter written in his own language by two English ladies. With this little glimpse of romance looming in the distance I must close my letter, and beg to remain, with best wishes for perseverance and success, yours faithfully, 'M. M.'

Mabel and Ellen were the daughters of the well-known writer, Mortimer Collins, but they did not learn Swedish, Portuguese, or Siamese!

After another month at Ray Lodge the Max Müllers returned to Oxford, and the Walronds to London, and the old house knew them no more. The weather in September of this year was unusually hot, and evening after evening was spent on the river, not only on the lower river, but the Cherwell, then hardly known even to boating men, was constantly explored nearly to Islip. 'We carried the boat from one river to the other,' says a letter. It was a happy six weeks before term began, and Max Müller, who was working at his *Veda*, without any pressure of other work, greatly enjoyed the quiet—as he tells his mother—alone with his wife and children, and a few intimate friends who were in Oxford.

He gave two public lectures in the October Term on 'Joinville's *Saint Louis*,' which were much appreciated, and formed the nucleus of the article on Joinville in *Chips*, Volume III.

It was in October that Max Müller, finding that his friend the Bodleian Librarian, 'Bodley Coxe,' could not secure the services of any Orientalist for the place of Oriental Sub-

Librarian at the Bodleian, offered himself for the post. As soon as the Vice-Chancellor announced the day on which the 'nomination of Mr. Max Müller to the office of Sub-Librarian, which nomination has received the sanction of the Curators, will be submitted to the House,' disagreeable letters and protests began to appear. One man, signing as 'a Member of Convocation,' made out that Max Müller had an income of at least £1,100 a year from public funds (it was really £700, including his ill-paid work on the *Veda*). This was answered by the Bodleian Librarian, and by a Member of Convocation, in the following letters:—

*November* 4.

'Members of Convocation are respectfully informed that the necessities of the Bodleian Library require at this time an Under-Librarian specially conversant with Oriental Literature. Failing in his endeavour to secure the services of another distinguished Orientalist, the Librarian has been allowed (with the unanimous consent of the Curators) to submit the name of Professor Max Müller to the approval of the House, as one who, together with his Oriental learning, combines a large acquaintance with Modern European Literature, a department of scarcely less importance to the interests of the Library.

'It may be as well to correct three mis-statements which appear in the first of the letters now in circulation:—

1. Professor Müller's salary as Taylorian Professor is £500, not "more than £600."

2. He has resigned the Examinership for the Indian Civil Service.

3. His labours in editing the *Vedas*, so far from being "well paid," entail on him a considerable pecuniary sacrifice.

'H. O. Coxe, Bodley's Librarian.'

*November* 6, 1865.

'The letter of a Member of Convocation contained in the *Standard* of October 30, furnishes us with the keynote to the threatened opposition to Professor Max Müller's appointment as Sub-Librarian to the Bodleian Library.

'As this "distinguished scholar" has been always too much occupied in the duties connected with his Professorship to mix himself up in theological or in political controversies, it is difficult to understand on what grounds he can have rendered himself obnoxious in either of these capacities, except to those who regard every German as a Rationalist, and every member of Gladstone's Committee as a Radical.

'It is to be hoped that Convocation, dismissing all such irrelevant considerations, will leave it, as on former occasions, to the Head Librarian, who has never been suspected of an undue bias towards "Liberalism in politics, or Rationalism in religion," to determine, with the sanction of the Curators, what is most needed with reference to the exigencies of an Establishment for the efficiency of which he is mainly responsible. 'MEMBER OF CONVOCATION.'

Max Müller was elected, and enjoyed the work very much; but the strain of double work was too much, his health broke down under it, and he had to resign the Librarianship after about a year and a half. He of course ceased to be a Curator of the Bodleian (he had been elected in 1856) when he accepted the post of Sub-Librarian.

TO HIS MOTHER.

*Translation.* *November* 1.

'Here people talk of nothing but Palmerston's death. I have never admired the man much. I was introduced to him a couple of years ago; he looked like a dandy, but spoke in a very friendly way. He allowed himself to be more ruled by England than he ruled her. That has its good side, especially here where public opinion is well regulated, but he was entirely wanting in independence and all higher ideas of life. Stanley buried him in Westminster Abbey. I did not go up for it.'

TO DEAN STANLEY.

64, HIGH STREET, *November* 23.

'MY DEAR STANLEY,—Many thanks for the second series of your *Lectures* [1] just received. I shall read them as soon as I find a few quiet days, and they will recall the pleasant time when you were settled here. If you cannot have the man, the next best thing is to have his book, yet it is but a poor substitute. Why did you not put on your titlepage, "Corresponding Member of the Institute of France"? They are rather particular about that in Paris.

'The Convocation for confirming my re-election [2] is fixed for Friday, December 1, at two. Whether there is to be a sulphurous eruption I do not know yet, but I should not be surprised. However, you must not think of coming up. If it is to be, I have no doubt it is meant for good. I have done nothing in the matter, and my rule in life has always been not to struggle against storms that are gathering overhead, but to wait, hoping they may pass, but quite prepared for the drenching if it comes.

'I think I have been treated without that fairness and consideration

[1] *On the Jewish Church.* [2] To his Professorship.

which, as a rule, are generally shown by Englishmen to Englishmen; but though I may have made a mistake in settling in England, and spending here the best years of my life, I shall always be thankful for having passed through this school of life. There are many things I owe to my stay in England and to my English friends, perhaps the most precious things in a man's life—things that cannot be taken away, and that I shall value all the more, if the evening of my life is to be spent in my own country. Ever yours, 'MAX MÜLLER.'

TO THE RIGHT HON. W. E. GLADSTONE.

HIGH STREET, *November* 12, 1865.

'I cannot allow another week to pass without thanking you for your essay on the Providential Position of Greece. I have read it with deep interest, and there are many things which I should like to say about it. But I live just now in the midst of a storm which will very likely drive me away from England [1], and I cannot for the moment concentrate my thoughts on any other subject. I am so glad that you have said many of the things which you have said in your valedictory address. Though no human mind can ever hope to discover or to understand the vestiges of the Creator and Ruler of mankind in the broken strata of history, yet the very search for them comforts and elevates the mind of man, and the sense of our own impotence and ignorance widens and deepens our faith in the Highest Wisdom and Power.

'With many thanks for the honour you have done me in sending me your essay.'

TO HIS WIFE.

OXFORD, *November* 28.

'May God watch over us, and may we never forget how much happiness He has showered upon us! There is something very awful in this life, and it is not right to try to forget it. It is well to be reminded by the trials of others of what may befall us, and what is kept from us only by the love of our Father in heaven, not by any merit of our own.'

Christmas was spent in London at the grandfather's house, but to the sorrow of the two eldest children, who recollected the regular German Christmas of the year before with their grandmother, there was no Christmas tree, the house being too small to give up a room to it.

[1] The opposition threatened to his election as Sub-Librarian on account of his unorthodoxy.

# CHAPTER XV

## 1866–1867

Easter in Paris. *Sanskrit Grammar.* War between Prussia and Austria. Cornwall. 'My Brother.' Gold medal from Duke of Anhalt. Illness. Bournemouth. Letter on Brahma Somâj. Death of niece. 'Parks End' bought. Cure at Ems. *Chips*, Volumes I and II.

BY January 2 the Max Müllers settled quietly again in Oxford, he remaining hard at work till Easter, when the ten days' vacation from the Bodleian was spent in a visit to Paris. The weather was too cold for expeditions, but many pleasant hours were spent with congenial friends—the Mohls, the Regniers, Barthélemy-St.-Hilaire, Stanislas Julien, Michel Bréal, and others. To Max Müller this intercourse and exchange of ideas with friends occupied in work like his own was the greatest refreshment. It was such intercourse he sorely missed in Oxford, where the men who could at all enter into his pursuits were younger than himself, and more like pupils, whilst his older friends, with whom his Oxford career had begun, had almost all moved on to other spheres of work.

To HIS MOTHER.

*Translation.* OXFORD, *April* 16.

'Our time in Paris was very amusing. The only sad thing was the recollection of so many friends whom one knew there, and who are gone. I often thought of Emilie, and of Gathy, and Hagedorn, and of my life in Paris in 1846. That is long ago, and yet I enjoy life as much as I did then, and think the grey hairs are only an outward appearance! . . . I do not believe in war, have never believed in it, but I am curious to see how long men of honour and reasonable men in Germany will submit to such a scandalous government! Now I am busy again with my work, and shall not get away till

August. I have been made an Academician of Turin. There are only seven, and after Thiers and Cousin comes my unworthy self.'

To E. B. Tylor, Esq.

Oxford, *April* 16.

'On my return from Paris I found a copy of the *Quarterly*, and in it your excellent article on the Science of Language. I feel not only personally very much obliged to you, but I believe you have rendered a real service to our common studies by exciting the interest and allaying the fears of that large and important class of Englishmen who are, more or less, led by the *Quarterly Review*. A violent onslaught from that quarter, which was by no means unlikely, might have done serious mischief, and I therefore tender you my thanks both for what you have done, and what you have been the means of preventing. What you say about Prepositions is true. I believe, however, that those which are not predicative like *trans* will turn out to be prenominal, local adverbs pointing to here and there. *Qui vivra verra.* You have managed the Interjectionalists very well. Never did I make a greater mistake than in taking an illustration of the Bow-wow theory from Wedgwood's Dictionary, which happened to be on my table, instead of quoting the same view from a hundred other books! You have put the case very clearly, and I hope no more paper will be wasted on this unprofitable discussion. You attribute too much importance to my phonetic types or typical sounds; they were left as a mere frame, to be filled in by-and-by.'

To the Same.

Oxford, *April* 19.

'Many thanks for your article in the *Fortnightly Review*. I like it very much and agree with every word of it; only that I shall have to write a much more determined defence of the Pooh-pooh and Bow-wow theory than you have done, but of course only after defining the true meaning of these theories. I cannot get over *chagrin*. I do not think it can be merely leather, least of all Eastern leather; but I confess I cannot get at the history of the word. I believe that the chagreen leather is of Eastern origin, but *chagrin* as substantive and adjective, *chagrineux* and *chagriner*—I confess that staggers me. The question is who first used the metaphor, if that is the origin of the word.'

Rumours of war between Austria and Prussia were now rife, and Max Müller wrote to warn his mother not to depend on seeing him and his in Germany in the summer.

To his Mother.

*Translation.* *May* 27.

'We can make no plans for the summer whilst there are these rumours of war. Till now I firmly believed in peace, but now I am afraid the summer will not go by without something happening. I cannot take any interest in these matters, unless it comes to a real popular war. Till now the people have not wished for war, but only the Ministers and the soldiers, and they may eat the broth they have cooked. But how any people can submit to such a way of governing, I cannot comprehend, and am thankful I am not there. I have at last finished my *Sanskrit Grammar*. It came out last week, and it has taken a great load off my conscience.'

In 1864 Max Müller had arranged with Messrs. Longmans to publish a series of handbooks for the study of Sanskrit. In his preface to the first of the series, the first book of the *Hitopadesa*, he explains that these handbooks were intended for two classes of readers: first, for those candidates for the Indian Civil Service who desired not only to acquit themselves well in the examination, but to lay a good foundation for the subsequent study of the spoken vernaculars; and secondly, for a steadily increasing number of scholars who wished to gain an elementary but accurate knowledge of Sanskrit as a key to the study of Comparative Philology. For both these classes the existing works were too diffuse, and only adapted to those who wished to make Sanskrit their lifelong study. Max Müller's handbooks included the first, second, third, and fourth books of the *Hitopadesa*, Benfey's *Sanskrit Dictionary*, and a *Sanskrit Grammar* for beginners by Max Müller. The text of the first book of the *Hitopadesa* was prepared by Dr. Kielhorn, one of the many German Sanskrit scholars for whom Max Müller was instrumental in getting appointments in India.

The Librarian of the India Office, in writing to thank him for the *Hitopadesa*, says, 'It is very obliging of you, in the interest of beginners, to prepare books of this description; that they are very much needed is undeniable—at last it is feasible for a student of ordinary ability to commence the study of Sanskrit without a teacher.'

Max Müller's 'sensible and well-constructed book' was

praised in several reviews, whilst his friend Professor Cowell had from the first welcomed the series as 'an immense help to the student. With such helps as these Sanskrit should be as easily acquired as any other language. The projected series will be invaluable.'

To his Mother.

*Translation.* Oxford, *June* 17.

'I hope that you are safe in Chemnitz, for Dresden is not the place for you. I see that the Prussians have marched into Saxony, and they are very likely to encounter the Austrians in the neighbourhood of Dresden. At Chemnitz, at all events, you are not in the immediate scene of the fighting—you have advice and help from the Krugs. Now that war has really begun things will not quiet down again so very quickly; but in the way war is now conducted, those who live at the very theatre of war will be far less disturbed than in former times. Sooner or later a war between Austria and Prussia was unavoidable, and if it is but decisive, it will lead to what all true Germans have desired for years, a united Germany. Prussia and Austria are merely names, and stand for no more than Anhalt and Reuss. The great thing is that the dualism of Prussia and Austria should be ended. Who conquers, or is conquered, is of little consequence. Germany remains Germany, and cannot be governed, even by a Roman Catholic Emperor, otherwise than she allows herself to be governed. If Prussia wins, she must cease to be Prussia; Austria the same. So wait quietly, no excitement, no partisanship. Bismarck, either with or without his own consent, may become the greatest benefactor of Germany. It is sad that your Austrian investments have fallen again! but don't make yourself miserable about it. How many people are in the same, or even worse, plight! Whatever you want, I can always give. You need have no scruples about it, for if I don't give it to you, I give it to others; and I have for years given away to others far more than I give you. What flows in so richly on me does not belong to me, and I ought to give away a great deal more than I do. So, as I say, don't vex yourself about money. Stay on quietly for the present with the Krugs. We can make no summer plans yet. France and Switzerland are the only places where it would be quiet.... Do not make the times worse than they are by over-anxiety.'

It was in this year that Max Müller made the acquaintance of Mr. John Bellows, the head of the great printing works at Bristol. At first the acquaintance was only by letter, but on meeting they were both much attracted to each other, and a true friendship sprang up which continued to the last, though, being very busy men, they did not meet as often as both desired. In sending his friend's letters to Mrs. Max Müller, Mr. Bellows says:—

'It was in 1866 that I put before Professor Max Müller a plan I had for printing a skeleton dictionary in which travellers and missionaries might record the vocabulary of any particular language, or dialect, they wished to study. He entered heartily into it, and compiled for it a key alphabet for the various sounds that would have to be noted. It so happened that a Scottish firm just then offered me a quantity of paper they had made for Confederate bank-notes during the American War, but which they had failed to run through the blockade at Charleston. As this was very strong and thin, I used it for the *Outline Dictionary*. It answered well, I believe, as the edition all sold. It was really Professor Max Müller's work, however.'

The following letters show how minutely Professor Max Müller entered into the scheme:—

To Mr. John Bellows.

64, High Street, *June* 20.

'I cannot think of anything better than the inverted a to represent the á; we must not have accented letters, otherwise no doubt the Swedish å would be preferable. I do not see quite clearly the principle you follow in giving the various meanings of certain words. The book is meant for Englishmen who must be supposed to know the shades of meaning of each word; besides there is no reason to give them all. Would it not be best to give various meanings only when there is a clearly defined difference, as in Account, 1 narrative, 2 bill, 3 esteem? But why give "coming to the throne" under Accession? If the missionary wants to express that meaning he would put it under Accession, and if he wants to express "an accession to his income" he would place it there likewise, making a note for his own information. Why put casual, and by injury, under Accidental? Does accidental ever mean by injury, except indirectly?'

To the Same.

Oxford, *June* 27.

'There is very little to alter. I should put *v*, bought, all, as a familiar English sound, before the ä of Väter. Also I should put *n* as optional with ñ; in fact I should not have admitted ñ at all if I had not been told that this type is generally to be found in ordinary founts. You know best whether that is so; if not, I should leave it out, and give *n* only. I think a little more care should be taken with the Dictionary.'

To the Same.

*July* 18.

'I received your envelopes and the electro-typed specimens, and am much obliged to you for them. As to your Dictionary, I am afraid there is something wrong in getting the words ready for press. Why should you not take any ordinary Dictionary, and just underline in red the words which you want? I have been collating your proof-sheets with Blackley and Friedländer's *Practical German Dictionary*, just published by Longmans, and I really think it would take less time to underline that, than to collate the proof-sheets, to say nothing of the trouble of making the corrections in the composition. I always think that what is worth doing is worth doing well, and I feel sure that with a little more trouble at first, much trouble afterwards may be avoided.'

Since Max Müller's last letter to his mother great events had taken place in Germany. The rapid advance of the Prussians had been crowned by the great battle of Königgrätz. Austria had given up Venice to France, and the 'Seven Days' War,' as it was called in England, seemed over. The excitement and interest in England were very great.

To his Mother.

*Translation.* Oxford, *July* 8.

'All good Germans have long desired what is now happening. The methods employed might have been better, here and there, but Prussia staked her existence to make Germany united and strong, and though I thoroughly doubt whether the motives were throughout honest and pure, yet I rejoice over the results. Prussia will have a yet harder war to wage, for war with France can hardly be avoided. But in spite of all that, Germany will at last take her right place in Europe, and that she never could have done with the "Bundestag" and thirty princes. Austria will always remain a great power in the East, but in the Protestant North an independent power must be created, be it called Prussia or Germany. I often long now to be back in Germany, though I could be of no use as a soldier. Write to me very often; I am so busy I cannot always write to you, but you have plenty of time, and all you write interests me. Also letters may get lost now, so the more you write the better. Why do not you and Emilie come to England for six or eight weeks? I do not believe that we shall have peace very soon; should it come we might still go to Germany in August and September. Do not worry too much. There is always war, and always will be, like thunder after great heat. I am very sorry for Emilie at Dessau, in the midst of Prussians with her strong Austrian feelings. Where is Adolf, and what has become of Fritz Stockmarr[1]?'

The following letter refers to a communication from Max Müller's old schoolfellow, Karl Elze, of Dessau, a well-known Shakespearian scholar, later on Professor of English Literature at Halle. He wrote to tell his friend that a literary society in Dessau, which for some years had been giving public lectures, had resolved to apply the money so made to the founding of a Wilhelm Müller Prize, to be given each year in the three highest classes of the Dessau Gymnasium (public school) on Wilhelm Müller's birthday.

TO HIS MOTHER.

*Translation.* OXFORD, *July* 16.

'I write whenever I have something to write about, and from the enclosed letter from Elze you will see that we are not quite forgotten in Dessau. I wrote at once to Elze *a beautifully written letter*, to tell him how pleased I was. I at once promised him 100 thalers, and hope later on to give more, so that perhaps in time it may form a Wilhelm Müller Scholarship. So you see there is a bit of good news. One hopes now the war will soon be over; well, the quicker the better. The losses are terrible, but so it has always been, and in no century has Germany been so long at peace as in this. You can well imagine I am no admirer of Bismarck, but I am convinced his policy is the only one to make Germany strong and respected by other nations. What would have become of Germany if France had attacked Hanover, or Saxony, or Hesse, and the jealousy between Prussia and Austria had made all joint action impossible? With Italy united, with the Colossus of Russia and the great mass of France, it was necessary North Germany should be united. Austria was opposed to this union and must therefore suffer, but in spite of all defeats she will always be a great power in the East, and, if she concentrates herself by giving up Italy and Germany, will, one hopes, be strong enough, in spite of Russia, to annex Turkey, and drive the Turks back to Asia. Those are my hopes, but who knows what may come? I expected that Prussia would meet with some great defeat, and that may still happen, and would do Prussia good, as thereby she would become more thoroughly German; but these

[1] Soldier cousins of Max Müller's.

things are not in our hands, and all happens as is for the best. So do not let the grey hairs appear! much worse things have happened in the world than the overthrow of a dynasty. On the whole the world is a very small grain of sand, Europe a small quarter of the world, and Austria a very small part of Europe, and the man one calls from habit Emperor is but a man, not so much better than the thousands who have fallen in Bohemia. I wish I knew how to send you some money—the letters seem to go safely enough. Stay quietly in Chemnitz. It is possible the Prussians may have to retreat, and then Dresden might have to suffer, whilst Chemnitz is off the track. Wish Krug joy for his twenty-five years' doctorate—I shall soon attain a like honour, and yet I cannot feel myself at all old!'

To E. B. Tylor, Esq.

*July* 6.

'Two things have escaped me which perhaps you will help me to catch. I made a note of a passage where the name *Bear*, for the constellation, occurred among a race that could not be suspected of Âryan influences. But I lost my reference. Secondly, I saw a paper by Mr. Edkins on the relation between Chinese, Mongolian, and Tibetan, either in the Ethnological or Anthropological Society; but this too I cannot find again. The finder shall be duly rewarded.'

As the time for his holiday drew near, Max Müller felt more and more unwilling to risk taking his wife and children to Germany in the unsettled state of things; and he was conscious, without any vanity, that he could not travel about entirely unknown, or say what he liked unheeded. He did not wish to be obliged to express any real opinion publicly for either Prussia or Austria, and it seemed wisest to keep out of Germany till things were more settled. Even in his own family party spirit ran very high. His Dessau relatives were all for Prussia, and Max Müller's own feelings were on that side, whereas his cousin Emilie, and, influenced by her, his mother, were violently Austrian.

To his Mother.

*Translation.* Oxford, *August* 5.

'That nothing has come of our plans is very sad. I had gone on hoping we might get to Rügen, but the state of things is too uncertain for travelling, especially with children. It looks more peaceful at this moment, but I do not quite trust it; it is always possible that Austria may venture on another battle. Also the new organization in the north, and the Parliament in Frankfort, are sure to cause local disturbances, and as one can do nothing to help, it is better to stay away, and hope for happier times. . . . One cannot alter matters, and when you think that Babylon and Nineveh, and Athens and Rome, have passed away in the course of time, you cannot wonder so much at the Hapsburg catastrophe. Such things happen now and again, and the world goes on afterwards as before!'

Sir Benjamin Brodie and his family, and Professor Bartholomew Price with his, had gone to St. Ives in Cornwall for the summer, and persuaded the Max Müllers to follow their example. The one difficulty was a house; the few suited to visitors were all taken. At last Lady Brodie found what was really a fisherman's cottage close down to the beach, small and simple, but exquisitely clean, and this was promptly secured. Life at St. Ives was amusingly primitive; the butcher came once a week from Penzance, but every house had its own poultry yard to supply deficiencies. Vegetables and fruit were even more difficult to procure: there was one baker in St. Ives. The town faces north; the part where the visitors lived thirty-six years ago was out of the town proper, which was built on a broad spit of land surrounded, except to the south, by the sea. The town was entirely inhabited by the fishermen, and was almost unapproachable from the smell of stale fish. Behind the cottage which the Max Müllers occupied the land rose to the granite moors, from the top of which there was a wonderful view, south to Penzance and Mount's Bay, and back north to the Bay of St. Ives and the coast towards Perranzabuloe. The smelling town was often braved, for beyond it the spit of land ended in an open meadow, from which one could see on calm days the long swell of the green waters of the Atlantic rolling in with irresistible force, or on stormy days the foaming waves as they dashed and thundered against the cliffs; whilst the sunsets, as seen from this point, were a constant delight. Bathing was carried on from the beach in front of the Max Müllers' cottage, 'Primrose Villa,' the boulders of rock fallen from the cliffs serving as dressing-rooms. At that time of year the moors were one blaze of purple heather and golden gorse—in striking contrast to the grey limestone headlands of the sea-coast. So brilliant was the colouring that, on the first walk to the moors, the eldest child, five and a half years old, who inherited all her father's passion for flowers, gave a cry of rapture as she saw the long stretch of heather and gorse, 'Oh, Daddy, whose garden is this?' Max Müller was delighted with the country, examining the cromlechs and other Celtic remains with keen interest. But his letters shall speak for themselves.

To Mr. Bellows.

St. Ives, *September.*

'I have not been able to see much of Cornwall yet, owing to various reasons: my own health, my wife's health, and the weather. However, we are both well again; and in spite of the weather we have spent three days at the Lizard. Gew Graze, Pigeon Hugo, Kynance, and the coast as far as Cadgewith are full of interest. As soon as the weather settles a little, we mean to go to the Land's End. If possible, we shall do Carnbrea, when I hope to see your friend Mr. Michell, though I am afraid we are not up to descending into the mine. What you say about the accent in Cornish is very true. I did not know about the German miners, and I wonder whether one could find an historical account of them anywhere. The legends and stories of Cornwall are purely German—very little of Cornish left there. The names of places deserve a careful study. Mere etymology will not do it; you want first of all to ascertain their primitive form. As to "Carack luz en kuz[1]," please remember that I am not a Cornish scholar. I consider your argument against the modern form of *kuz*, instead of the Cornish *cuit*, Welsh *coed*, as quite true. So far I go with you, and this seems to me to dispose of the meaning commonly given to "Carack luz en kuz," the hoar rock in the wood. What it really meant I cannot tell; I do not see that you prove the meaning of *bay* for the word *kûz*, or of *holy* for *lûz*, unless you have some further evidence. Mere possibilities will not help much. Nor do I see that you prove that the *Mount* was a burial-place. If you can establish the meaning of *bay* for *kûz* it will be very important, but even to have shown that it could not have meant *wood*, is quite sufficient to guard against the extraordinary conclusions founded on that name. One more question, What is the earliest date for the name "Carack luz en kuz," or of the pilchard song in which it occurs?'

To the Same.

St. Ives, *September* 13.

'The weather is sadly against us here. We saw the Land's End, and walked along the coast to the Logan, with a fearful sea rolling at

[1] An old name for St. Michael's Mount.

our side. It was magnificent. We went down Botollock Mine, which to my mind is as grand as anything I recollect. We have only one more week here. I wish I could stay here longer, it is a delightful neighbourhood and full of interest. Now and then one feels very near the old world. How careless people are about Celtic antiquities; while they send men-of-war to fetch home the lions and bulls of Nineveh, farmers are allowed to pull down cromlechs and caves, and use the stones for pig-styes.'

TO THE SAME.

ST. IVES, *September* 18.

'The fates have been sadly against me during my stay in Cornwall. First I was laid up with cold, &c., and afterwards the weather has been so uncertain that I have only just been able to see what was absolutely necessary. However, in spite of all, I am so delighted with Cornwall, that I am sure to come again, and if I could I should gladly give up Oxford and settle here, in a cottage by the sea-shore, and finish my edition and translation of the *Veda*, which I am afraid I shall never be able to finish at Oxford. The air here is so invigorating, and life so easy, natural, and uninterrupted by society, that one feels up to any amount of work. I tremble when I think of the hurry and flurry of Oxford, and the distraction and lassitude which it entails. . . . The growth of the modern name and legend of *Marazion* is very curious. . . . I wish somebody would take up the history of Cornish names of places. There are so many names of fields, and lanes, and stones, to say nothing of houses and villages, which would yield an ample harvest. . . . I should like to know the meaning of Perran, and St. Perran, and his various aliases. Can it mean "miner" or "smelter"? He seems a saint of Cornish growth, and I expect a saint who never had flesh or bone, as little as his companion, St. Chywiddan, i.e. White house, or Smelting house. Do you happen to know anything about their meaning and origin, beyond what is found in Hunt's *Cornish Tales*?'

So delighted was Max Müller with all he saw and heard in Cornwall—for he was never tired of the tales of Cornish saints, giants, and fairies that he learnt from various Cornish people with whom he came in contact—that he began, almost as soon as he returned to Oxford, to write the paper on 'Cornish Antiquities,' which was published the following year in the *Quarterly*. Another, on the question, 'Were there Jews in Cornwall?' also appeared in a periodical of the next year, and provoked long discussions; whilst a third paper, 'On the Insulation of St. Michael's Mount,' was read before the

Ashmolean Society in Oxford in the autumn of 1867. All three papers were republished in the two first editions of *Chips*.

To Mr. John Bellows.

*September* 29.

'. . . I send you what I have written down about St. Michael's Mount. I wonder whether you will be able to read it, and I want much to know what you think about it before I send it to be printed. I have taken possession of some remarks of yours, to which, however, I would gladly attach your name if you will let me do so. . . . I am in no hurry about printing it. I am pining after St. Ives, and Cornish rocks, and fresh sea-breezes.'

Just after his return to Oxford, Max Müller received intelligence that an impostor, calling himself his brother, was going about in London getting money from those whom he could take in. The story was always the same: he had been robbed on his way over from Germany, and had not enough to pay his ticket to Oxford. As the man or men continued the same fraud for several years, Max Müller at length put a notice in the *Times*, mentioning that he had never had a brother. This stopped the impostor in London after a time, but a few years later the same trick was tried in one of the Australian colonies, and Max received letters from several people who had been duped by him. The imposture continued on and off for quite five years, and there is still a large packet of letters from his victims marked in Max Müller's hand, 'My Brother.'

To his Mother.

*Translation.* *October* 7.

'The Professors in Berlin are wretchedly paid, and whenever I hear of affairs there, I feel I should never be able to fit in there. I am not rich here, but independent. I think I should long ago have been in prison had I stayed in Germany; here in England I can do what I will. People abuse me, but they cannot bite, and everybody barks at his own door.'

To Professor Lepsius.

*Translation.* Oxford, *October* 14.

'. . . The things that happen in Prussia—or shall I say Germany?—occupy one's head and one's heart. What would Bunsen have thought of it all? Many a thing has happened differently to what we should have wished, but that it has happened, and that it has advanced so far, and will advance still more and more, makes it well worth while to have lived to see it come to pass. There will have to be further struggles, but a glorious beginning has been made!'

It was in this autumn that Max Müller received a fine gold medal from his old Duke, Leopold of Dessau, who, knowing that Orders are not worn in England, except at Court, had this medal struck expressly for the student whose career he had watched with interest from his earliest childhood. On the obverse of the medal is the head of the Duke, who was a very handsome man, and on the reverse, within a broad wreath of oak and laurel leaves, the inscription:—

'Für Verdienst um Kunst und Wissenschaft dem Professor Dr. Max Müller, 1866.'

('To Professor Dr. Max Müller, 1866, for services to Art and Science.') It was the first recognition he received, except from learned societies, and was greatly prized, and always kept on his table.

To Mr. John Bellows.

Oxford, *November* 8.

'It is very kind of you to lend me your Cornish Dictionary; I shall take great care of it, and return it as soon as I get my own copy. It seems a very useful book, and carefully put together, only the Sanskrit comparisons are horrible. I wish Mr. Williams would publish his Celtic Grammar, but confine himself to Celtic. I guessed the riddle of the Nine Maidens as soon as I began to read your letter. I saw the stones, and I wish I had known about the missing stone, and where to find it. As to the legend, it would grow up naturally enough. If you once have the nine maidens and turned into stones, the dancing on a Sunday, &c., will come by itself. I think I could match that easily by German legends. You see that even the two pipers were soon added by popular fancy. I wish I could find out whether I am right in supposing that the two pipers, and the two stones that flank the Men-an-tol, point to the equinoctial points, and served to fix the great annual festivals. There are certainly tombs on St. Michael's Mount, and I read an ancient charter which allows people to be buried on the mainland, but still requires the dues to be paid to the Priory. I feel sure an attempt should be made to declare all real antiquities, in Cornwall and elsewhere, national property. I have collected a few cases of vandalism. If you meet with any in your readings, please let me know.'

To the Same.

Oxford, *November* 14.

'You have traced the extracts from the Sikh MSS. beautifully, and before I say more about it, let me ask you where you get that beautiful tracing-paper, and how much it is per quire. Well, there is very little known about the Sikh language. We possess several MSS. of their sacred book, the *Granth*, and of some minor works, all treating of the Sikh religion. The language is the Penjabi as spoken about 1500 A.D., a corruption of Sanskrit, like Hindi and the rest. The alphabet, too, is Devanâgarî, only curiously misapplied. By means of Sanskrit on the one side, and Hindi on the other, one could make out passages here and there, but that was a slow process. So I wrote through a friend of mine to some of the Sikh priests at Umritsir, asking them to write out a Sanskrit translation of some portions of their sacred code. They sent me instead a Hindi and Penjabi translation, and by means of it, and with the help of some friends who are good Hindi scholars, I made out some interesting passages. I have now written again for a literal Sanskrit translation, and when I get it I hope to publish a few specimens of the sacred writings of the Sikhs. Every book that has formed the foundation of a large religious movement ought to be accessible to scholars and theologians. It has taken me twenty years now to bring out the first edition of the sacred book of the Brâhmans, the *Veda*; so I am afraid life is too short to embark on a second undertaking of the same kind—the one representing the oldest, the other the most modern phase of religious thought in India—the one 1,500 years before, the other 1,500 after, our era. I should be very glad some day to see Sir Thomas Phillips's collection; I know it is wonderfully rich. I wish some collector, like him, would rescue what there is still to be rescued of the ancient literature of India. Manuscripts in India, being made of vegetable paper, do not last much longer than 400 years. It was the duty of every rajah to keep a library and a staff of librarians, whose work it was to recopy each manuscript as soon as it began to show signs of decay. As soon as these rajahs were pensioned off, the first retrenchment they made in their establishments was the suppression of these libraries and librarians. They were not even allowed to present their libraries to the East India Company! Well, the result is that at the present moment literary works, which have been preserved for more than a thousand years, are crumbling away. In a few places, where there exists still among the natives an interest in their ancient literature, manuscripts are copied and some of them printed and lithographed. But the great bulk of Sanskrit literature (larger than the literature of Greece) is allowed to perish, whereas a few thousand pounds might preserve all that is worth preserving. If the interest which is now taken in the early history of mankind, in the origin of religions, mythological and philosophical ideas, continues for the next hundred or two hundred years, the Sanskrit MSS. would be valued hereafter, like the Codex Alexandrinus or Sinaiticus. Many of them will be unique. And strange to say the same manuscripts which in the hot and dry climate of India are so perishable are perfectly safe as soon as they are deposited in a European library. But no one takes an interest in these matters, and while people shudder at the supposed vandalism of Omar in destroying the Alexandrian Library, the same unconscious vandalism takes place unheeded under our eyes. I have not forgotten my Cornish articles; but I want to get rid, not only of the Jews, but also of the Saracens. Yours very truly.'

To his Wife.

Oxford, *December* 9.

'Life at —— may be very nice for people who have nothing to do, or think they have nothing to do, and no account to give of their days and hours. But I have not learnt life so. I still have a great work to do, and I often feel that I might have done a great deal more, if I had kept the one object of my life more steadily in view. I sometimes wish you would help me more in doing that, and insist on my working harder at the *Veda* and nothing else. I hope I shall finish that work, and I feel convinced, though I shall not live to see it, that this edition of mine and the translation of the *Veda* will hereafter tell to a great extent on the fate of India, and on the growth of millions of souls in that country. It is the root of their religion, and to show them what that root is, is, I feel sure, the only way of uprooting all that has sprung from it during the last 3,000 years. If those thoughts pass through one's mind, one does grudge the hours and days and weeks that are spent in staying in people's houses, and one feels that with the many blessings showered upon one, one ought to be up and doing what may be God's work.'

To his Mother.

*Translation.* London, *December* 16.

'We stayed from Thursday to Saturday with the Belgian Minister, M. Van de Weyer, who has a beautiful place not far from Taplow. He is a very cultivated man and an experienced statesman, and was a librarian in Holland when the revolution broke out; then he became one of Leopold's Ministers. He married a rich American, and they live in great luxury. We had the same rooms Princess Alice had when she last paid them a long visit. It is very near Windsor and the Queen often drives over to see them.'

The Christmas was spent in London with the grandfather, the last the Max Müllers were to spend away from their own home till their children were grown up.

Max Müller had been far from well whilst in London, and on his return to Oxford was laid up with so severe a bronchial attack, accompanied by great prostration, that his medical attendant and friend, Mr. Symonds, was seriously anxious about him, and took him to London for further advice. He was ordered to leave Oxford at once for a milder climate. The weather was so severe that a journey to the Riviera was thought too great a risk, and just after the middle of January Max with his wife and children settled at Bournemouth, his old friend Professor Cowell undertaking his work as Sub-Librarian at the Bodleian, and occupying his house in Oxford, till it was fit for him to return home. At first he was almost entirely confined to the house, but as the weather improved and he gained strength he was able to enjoy the walks in the sheltered pine woods, which then stretched between the Bourne and Boscombe, or quiet rides with some relatives of his wife living at Bournemouth; and constant talks with one of these relatives, the banker Mr. Glyn, afterwards Lord Wolverton, was a great resource, as he was not fit for any hard mental work, and had been ordered by his doctor to leave his books in Oxford. Both Max Müller and Mr. Glyn were ardent Liberals, and great admirers of Mr. Gladstone, who, as Chancellor of the Exchequer, was in the habit year by year of talking over his Budget with Mr. Glyn, and a favourite point of discussion was whether the nation would accept Mr. Gladstone some day as Prime Minister. Mr. Glyn was in those days inclined to doubt it. One point on which the uncle and nephew disagreed entirely was in their estimation of Louis Napoleon, whom Mr. Glyn admired, as he attributed the commercial prosperity of France to his good government. Max Müller, on the other hand, who had often been in Paris, and knew how the respectable middle class kept entirely aloof of the Government, which they looked on as thoroughly evil, had no admiration for the adventurer.

It was many weeks before Max Müller at all recovered his usual health and strength; and though he began his translation of the *Rig-veda*, of which the prospectus had been published in January, he soon found that he was only up to lighter work, and he began to prepare his articles on Cornwall for the Press. The first, on 'Cornish Antiquities,' had been intended for the *North British Review*. When written he sent it to his friend Mr. Bellows, a Cornishman by birth, for revision, and in his letter mentions that he had a half-promise from a member of Parliament that he would prepare a Bill on the proper preservation of national monuments. It had been a real sorrow to him in Cornwall to see how the interesting Celtic remains were left entirely at the mercy of indifferent landowners and ignorant farmers, who had no scruples in using the fine stones for gateposts and farm buildings; in some cases, as with the ancient wells, pulling them down entirely to build them up in modern style, or as they described it, 'fitty.' Nothing more is to be found about this half-promise in any of the letters, and it was not till about 1873 that Lord Avebury, then Sir John Lubbock, introduced his Ancient Monuments Bill, which was not finally passed till 1882.

The second article, 'Are there Jews in Cornwall?' came out in *Macmillan's Magazine* in the April of this year. The third article, 'On the Insulation of St. Michael's Mount,' was not published till it appeared in the third volume of *Chips from a German Workshop* in 1870.

Before he left Oxford, Max Müller had heard from the Dean of St. Paul's, asking him to furnish a list of books that might be of interest and use to his nephew, Dr. Milman, the new Bishop of Calcutta. On furnishing the list Max Müller forwarded a letter on the Brahma Somâj, or body of pure Theists in India, written to him by Satyendra Nâth Tagore, himself a faithful adherent of the Brahma Somâj, who was the first native to pass the examination for the Indian Civil Service. As Max Müller was intimately acquainted later with Keshub Chunder Sen and Mozoomdar, leaders of the Somâj, and always took the deepest interest in the whole movement, as being, he felt, the real stepping-stone to Christianity in India, the letter is given in the Appendix. It presents the real teaching of the Somâj at that time as explained by a highly educated and enlightened follower.

TO THE DEAN OF ST. PAUL'S.

64, HIGH STREET, OXFORD,
*January*, 1867.

'I enclose a letter from an Indian friend of mine, Satyendra Nâth Tagore, which may possibly interest you, and which, if you like, you may forward to the Bishop. It will give him an insight into the religious aspirations of the best people in India at the present moment. The writer is the grandson of Dwarka Nâth Tagore, whom you may remember in London, some twenty years ago, a very shrewd and amiable man. His grandson came over to pass the Civil Service Examination, and, to the great dismay of the authorities, came out as No. 6. He was about twenty when I knew him in England, and he was then at the head of the so-called Brahma Somâj, which is making very considerable progress among the lower classes in India. The movement began with Râmmohun Roy, and him, too, you may have seen. His idea was to go back to the earliest form of the Indian religion, as preserved in the *Vedas*, and to surround the *Vedas* with all the defences of a revealed book. What he took for the *Veda* was not the original collection, but the more modern philosophical appendices, Upanishads. After his death the movement languished. I remember my young friend telling me: "Râmmohun Roy put us on a wrong track—he was a trimmer. We have entirely broken with the *Veda*." They have certainly put an end to idolatry, they have broken with caste, and they hold the essential points of natural religion. I need not tell you that I find it difficult to meet his arguments, and to remove his doubts with regard to some points of the Christian religion which are his stumbling-blocks. I have not written to him for some time, simply because I feel I cannot grapple with him, and he is not a man to be satisfied with words. I know some other men of a similar character in India—one, a convert, a man more like the martyrs of old than anybody I ever saw. What I feel very deeply when I have to argue with such men, is that the Christianity which conquered the world was very different from our hardened and formularized Christianity, and that the old tree will never bear transplanting into a new soil, though the young seed would probably grow up on Indian soil into as wonderful a tree as anything we have seen as yet in the history of Europe. India wants Apostles enjoying all the freedom of St. Paul; but what would the Elders at Jerusalem say to that?

'Please return Satyendra Nâth Tagore's letter to me when you have done with it.'

TO THE DEAN OF ST. PAUL'S (DR. MILMAN).

STAUNTON HOUSE, BOURNEMOUTH,
*February* 26.

'DEAR MR. DEAN,—I see no objection whatever to Tagore's letter being copied and shown to men who take an interest in the religious future of India, as he says himself I may make any use of it. I am particularly glad that Lord Cranborne should have seen it, if, as you say, he takes an interest in affairs of religion. I have myself the strongest belief in the growth of Christianity in India. There is no country so ripe for Christianity as India, and yet the difficulties seem enormous. The case of Nehemiah Goreh is a most interesting one; it ought to be typical, and yet it seems to be exceptional, and he became a Christian without, nay, in spite of, the missionaries. I have never yet seen a missionary or a civil servant who does not consider himself infinitely superior to any Hindu, and yet this Nehemiah Goreh has suffered more for his Christianity, and of his own free will, than any man I know in England or Germany. Such a man, and many like him, wants sympathy and love, and that is what they never find. Advice, reproof, and a good deal of *de haut en bas* patronizing the natives receive, no doubt, from missionaries, but respectful and loving treatment I doubt whether they ever receive. The idea that a man like Nehemiah Goreh could be in any respect his superior never enters a missionary's mind, yet I confess I felt far more awed by that modest and honest convert than by many a bishop and archbishop. Twelve men such as Nehemiah might do more in India than hundreds of missionaries. I hope my health is getting better. I am not accustomed to be ill, and it makes me very unhappy not to be able to work. My chief complaint is want of strength. I am to stay here till May.'

The end of March brought great sorrow to Max Müller in the news of the death of his sister's eldest daughter, nineteen years of age, after a few days' illness. It may be remembered that she had spent part of the summer of 1863 with the Max Müllers on the Starnberger See. She had grown up into a beautiful girl and was the joy and pride of her parents. Max Müller wished to go at once to his mother and sister, but his doctor would not sanction the journey, and absence again added to his sorrow.

TO HIS MOTHER.

*Translation.* BOURNEMOUTH, *April* 8.

'Auguste's letter has touched me again deeply. May God give her strength to bear this sorrow. I have spent the whole week in great anxiety and grief, and whenever I feel a little better I think I ought to have gone to you. And yet my doctor says I must still take the greatest care, and I feel myself that I only get on slowly, and the smallest change in the weather brings back the swelling and inflammation of the throat, and I might have been more of an anxiety than a help to you.'

It was during this spring that his friend Mr. Bellows brought out the *Outline Dictionary* mentioned earlier in this chapter, to which Max Müller contributed a valuable preface.

TO MR. BELLOWS.

OXFORD, *May* 3.

'I received to-day a dozen copies of the *Outline Dictionary*, and was very much pleased to see the book out. I shall try to make the best use I can of these copies. I shall send one to Lepsius, Berlin Academy; Monsieur Bell, French Academy; Bishop of Melanesia, and the Bishop of New Zealand. The book strikes me as very convenient, just the right shape, and I should think missionaries would be very thankful to have such a book if they knew of it. I begin to feel so much better, now that the weather is mild, and work is again a great delight.'

Through the past winter Max Müller's thoughts had been much occupied by the idea of a possible change in his life. The University authorities at Cambridge had founded a Chair of Sanskrit, and he was doubtful whether he ought or ought not to stand for election. Six years sooner he would have felt no doubt on the question, but he had now turned his attention more to general philology and the problems of mythology. He had lived too for nearly twenty years in Oxford, and both he and his wife were deeply attached to the place, and had many valued friends there. The following letter shows how the matter had been decided for him:—

BOURNEMOUTH, *April* 16, 1867.

'MY DEAR KINGSLEY,—I am not sufficiently up in the Luxemburg question to undertake an article for *Fraser*, but I have written to a friend of mine, an Englishman who knows a good deal about these matters. I hope and trust the matter will be settled peaceably. Germany has enough to do at home, and though I rejoice in a united and strong Germany, I do not like to see the drill-sergeant Government strengthened more than can be helped. The absence of England from the councils of Europe is sadly felt just now. A man must dare to have friends, and dare to have enemies—and so must a people. The natural ally of England is Germany, that is to say, a united, sensibly governed, Protestant, Northern Germany. England and Germany will represent the Teutonic element in Europe, with all that is good and bad in it; and, if united by common objects, they will stand like a breakwater between the Romans and Roman Catholics in the West and South, and the Slavs and Greeks in the East and North. You want a good statesman in whom the country trusts, a man like Pitt or Sir Robert Peel. Gladstone has a foreign policy, but matters must get much worse before people in England will find out what they possess in Gladstone. He ought to retire like Camillus, and wait till greater times call for greater men.

'Cox is a hard-working man. He wants a little sunshine—to throw off the prickles and grow into flower.

'My Cambridge plans are at an end. I had long made up my mind not to stand against Cowell. He has now decided to become a candidate. You could not get a better man. The Master of Trinity, I hear, is favourable to him. Do what you can for him, you may do it safely. Ever yours affectionately.'

The following letter contains the first mention of the work by which perhaps Max Müller became best known to the general public, *Chips from a German Workshop*. On receipt of Mr. Longman's answer he set to work at once on the collection and revision of his articles. The work came out in the autumn, when the fine preface was written. 'It was through the preface to the *Chips* that I first learnt to know and love Max Müller,' wrote one who felt he owed nearly all that was good in him to Max Müller's teaching.

TO W. LONGMAN, ESQ.

BOURNEMOUTH, *April* 20, 1867.

'DEAR SIR,—I have been looking through my essays, and I mean to revise and republish them. The first volume would contain essays on Religion, Mythology, and Traditions.

'Afterwards there would be a second volume on Language and Literature. As a general title I thought of *Chips from a German*

Photo Hills & Saunders, Oxford — Walter L. Colls, Ph. Sc.

7, Norham Gardens, Oxford.

*Workshop.* Would you feel inclined to take these essays on the same terms as the second volume of my *Lectures?* They will be ready for October, I think. Yours very truly, 'M. M.'

On one of the last days of April the Max Müllers returned to Oxford, and the same day they saw the announcement of the sale by auction, in a day or two, of the house Professor Goldwin Smith had built for himself across the Parks—which had already been laid out and planted, and were no longer the bare fields, with the Museum in their midst, of five years before. The house in High Street was damp, cold, and becoming too small, and on finding that 'Parks End,' which was only a bachelor's house, could easily be enlarged, Max Müller resolved to bid for it. It was a bright sunny day when he and his wife first went over their future home, the lilacs were in full bloom, and the little place looked its best. Not a single house then stood to the north of 'Parks End'—on the north side of what is now called Norham Gardens were cultivated fields—the nearest houses were in Park Town, and only two houses existed each side of 'Parks End.' Directly the house was bought plans were made for adding a drawing-room, and what Mr. Goldwin Smith afterwards irreverently called a 'baby-hutch,' and the work was at once begun, as his wife was resolved that Max Müller should leave High Street before the winter set in.

The lectures announced for this term were on the poem of the *Nibelungen*, on which he had lectured sixteen years before.

To his Mother.

*Translation.* 64, High Street, *May* 3.

'You will hardly guess what has kept me from writing sooner. We have bought a house, and I wanted to tell you all about it. . . . You must not be anxious about me. I am really well again: our doctor thinks me much stronger in every way. I have given up the Bodleian, and shall not have so much work. The new house is really very charming, and the children are delighted with it. It is the best built house here in every way; all the chief rooms look south, and as it faces the Parks we can never have any house built in front of us. We must add to it, for it is too small, but we are able to pay the whole out of our savings without borrowing anything. We have had very happy years here, and the children are so strong and healthy; we shall be sorry to leave this house, but we are glad to have a larger and better house, and more out of the town.'

Since her daughter's great sorrow the old mother had resolved to give up her rooms in Dresden and move to Chemnitz, a change which her son had long urged her to make.

To his Mother.

*Translation.* 64, High Street, *May* 19.

'Your rooms in Dresden must look very sad and bare, and whenever I think of poor Auguste my heart is very heavy. It is such a hopeless trial, and one sees nothing to make up for what they have lost. It is well that you have settled to move to Chemnitz, and though you will miss Dresden, few mothers have the comfort of spending their last years with their children and children's children. You can thank God for this, in spite of the many afflictions and trials He has laid on you, and then you will forget the many little disagreeables and misunderstandings which constant living together must bring. I cannot understand why you make yourself so anxious about money. I hope I shall always be able to give you as much as you want. I give away every year a fixed proportion of my income, and if it does not go to you it goes to others. The question is therefore only, whether I give it to you, or to others who perhaps need it less than you do. You should make no difficulty about such matters; there are cares enough in life without making new ones for ourselves.'

On June 9 Max Müller's youngest child and only son was born, and though he had professed to be quite satisfied with his three little girls, his letters show how he rejoiced at the birth of what is called in Germany the 'Stammhalter.'

To his Cousin, Captain von Basedow.

*Translation.* 64, High Street, *June* 30, 1867.

'My dear Adolf,—You will already have heard that at last a little son has appeared here, and I wish to ask you to be one of his godfathers. Both G. and I wish the boy not to be exclusively English, and, like his name Wilhelm Grenfell, so his godfathers should be of both countries. He can then later on choose his own home, and like the old proverb *ubi bene ibi patria.* His other godparents are cousins of G.'s. Of course we should prefer that you should come here yourself, but if that can't be, write if you will accede to our wish, and let me have your answer as soon as possible, as the little heathen is already three weeks old. Here, thank God, all goes on well, but after all the sorrow we have had, we cannot feel very joyful. The last few years have brought many changes, but one must not lose courage. In August I think of going to Germany, and hope I shall find you all well at Dessau. Much love from us both to your wife, your mother, Tante Julie, Rosalia, Berndt and his wife, the Stockmarrs, and any old friends who still remember me. Always in true affection, 'MAX.'

Though very much stronger, it was thought wise for Max Müller to take the waters at Ems this summer, and as soon as his wife could move she and their four children went to stay with the mother-aunt near Maidenhead, and Max started for Ems, where his mother and sister and her husband joined him as his guests; and a happy month was passed together, he doing everything in his power to lighten the cloud of sorrow resting on his sister and Dr. Krug.

TO HIS WIFE.

EMS, *August* 19.

'We have had a beautiful walk this afternoon, and I have often wished you here; you would enjoy it so much, and I should enjoy it all so much with you. And yet what a pleasure it is to see mother so well, at least for her age, and able to enjoy all with us. And those poor Krugs—it is quite sad to see them happy, and always that fearful grief in their hearts. How often one thinks of Marie, and how she would have delighted in seeing all this beautiful scenery, and being with us. . . . Krug speaks so freely about those who are no more; I can only listen, for what can one say? Our view of death is wrong, no doubt, because our view of life is wrong: there is nothing to be feared in this beautiful world of God's own making and ordering. But parting is a wrench, even for a few weeks, and nothing can take away the pang of that long parting with those whom we have truly loved. How one grows together; how you and the children, every one of them, cling to me, and are part and parcel of myself. To lose one of them, even though one may submit to God's will, must tear a wound which can never disappear again, however time may soothe the first agony. We ought to be so grateful. I do not think of *real* happiness God can give more than has been given us: how can one ask for more, or wish for anything? I should like to sit quiet, to rest and be thankful, not to move, lest something should move and fall. I do long for you all, but it was right to give up something of our happiness: the more you give away the more is given you; that seems to me a law of our spiritual life. . . . All send you their best love, and wish you and the children were here; and they say it is so good of you to let me go alone. Krug thinks it will be very good for me here. The evenings are glorious. We have supper in the garden at nine—the river running by, all lighted up, and in the distance lights on the hills, and then the bright stars above. People do enjoy themselves here; there are more than 2,000 here, music everywhere, splendid roses, fine halls—I am sorry to say gambling, too.'

To the Same.

Ems, *August* 27.

'One look up to heaven, and all this dust of the high-road of life vanishes. Yes! one look up to heaven and even that dark shadow of death vanishes. *We* have made the darkness of that shadow ourselves, and our thoughts about death are very ungodly. God has willed it so; there is to be a change, and a change of such magnitude that even if angels were to come down and tell us all about it, we could not understand it, as little as the new-born child would understand what human language could tell about the present life. Think what the birth of a child, of a human soul, is; and when you have felt the utter impossibility of fathoming that mystery, then turn your thoughts upon death, and see in it a new birth, equally unfathomable, but only the continuation of that joyful mystery which we call a birth. It is all God's work; and where is there a flaw or a fault in that wonder of all wonders, God's ever-working work? If people talk of the miseries of life, are they not all man's own work? Would not the carrying out of one single commandment of Christ, "Love one another," change the whole aspect of this world, and sweep away prisons and workhouses, and envying and strife and all the strongholds of the devil? Two thousand years have nearly passed, and people have not yet understood that one single command of Christ, "Love one another." We are as perfect heathens in that one respect as it is possible to be. No! this world might be heaven on earth, if we would but carry out God's work and God's commandments—and so it will be hereafter. We must submit, but we must feel that it is a great blessing to be able to submit, to be able to trust that infinite Love which embraces us on all sides, which speaks to us through every flower and every worm, which always shows us beauty and perfection, which never mars, never destroys, never wastes, never deceives, never mocks. And would that loving Father begin such a work in us, as is now going on, and then destroy it, leave it unfinished? No, what is will be; what really *is* in us will always be; we shall be because we are. Many things which are now will change, many things in us which we take to be our very own will change; but what we really are we shall always be; and if love forms really part of our very life, that love, changed, it may be, purified, sanctified, will be in us and remain with us through that greatest change, which we call death. The pangs of death will be the same for all that, just as the pangs of childbirth seem ordained by God, in order to moderate the exceeding joy that a child is born into the world. And as the pain is forgotten when the child is born, so it will be after death—the joy will be commensurate to the sorrow. The sorrow is but the effort necessary to raise ourselves to that new and higher state of being; and without that supreme effort or agony, the new life that waits for us is beyond our horizon, beyond our conception. It is childish to try to anticipate; we cannot know anything about it; we are meant to be ignorant; and, though we may imagine heaven and hell, even the *Divina Commedia* of a great poet and thinker is but child's play and nothing else. Here, as everywhere else, the purity of Christ's teaching appears. A teacher whose every word is believed is sorely tempted to promise rewards in a future life, and to paint in glowing colours the Jerusalem the Golden that is to receive those who believe in Him. Christ says, "What no eye has seen," and thus shows the truth of His vision, and the honesty in His dealing with His fellow creatures. No illusions, no anticipations, only that certainty, that quiet rest in God, that submissive expectation of the soul, which knows that all is good, all comes from God, all tends towards God. To say more is to deceive ourselves and others. But though we may thus look forward to what is to come, I quite agree with you that it is wrong to look away from this life, or to treat it as an imperfect or contemptible state. This life is as perfect as God would make it, and it is an incredible pride if we are to master and criticize this beautiful work of God. We have spoilt it first, and taken away its very sunshine and warmth—love—and then we complain that it is cold. Poverty is hard to bear, but a cheerful and contented mind does not feel the burden; and how much poverty might be alleviated, if we wished to do it! Illness is hard to bear, but it raises us above the cares of this life; it reconciles us to that parting which must come sooner or later; it makes death easy, which those who are rich and strong dread as the greatest of evils. Unkindness is hard to bear, but it leads us to examine ourselves, to weigh our own motives, to value all the more those loving hearts who return our love, and to look forward to a better time when we shall be known such as we are.'

### To the Same.

Ems, *August* 31.

'We had such a beautiful evening. We drove to a forest between Ems and the Rhine, where we could see the whole neighbourhood, and all the windings of the river about Ehrenbreitstein and Coblentz.

There was a Franciscan monastery with the fourteen stations of the Passion, arranged with such real taste and thought, and at the end a chapel and a beautiful church, all built by the present incumbent, an old man, who is his own architect, and has begged together the funds for the church, which is built in a very old and simple Byzantine style; and the walls and altar and pulpit are covered with crystals and stones and slags found in the neighbourhood, so that the interior is glittering with light. Though the experiment is difficult and apt to degenerate into mere stage effect, there is so much originality and thought about it, that one can enjoy it all, and feel with the old man who spent his life and energy in erecting that sacred place. As we drove home the first line of the new moon was visible, and Jupiter shone in all his beauty.'

To THE SAME.

*September* 2.

'You have no idea how beautiful this valley is—the smooth wooded hills all around, and the river reflecting the undulating landscape, and the beautiful clear sky, and the varying tints and the brilliant stars. Life seems so light and easy here. Then it is very amusing to watch all the strange people from every part of the world—Orientals and Greeks and Wallachians, to say nothing of French, English, Americans, and Jews.

'I had a kind of semi-official application to ask me whether I would not settle in Prussia. They would give me 3,000 thalers (£450), and I need not trouble much about lecturing, either at Berlin or Bonn. I said that for the present I was tied, but that, if I settled in Germany, I should prefer to live independently without taking any office, and make what I wanted by writing. I could not quite make out from whom it came, but Professor Bernays told me the offer was serious, and he is a friend of the Minister of Public Instruction.'

To PROFESSOR BERNAYS.

*Translation.* LUSTGARTEN, EMS, *September*, *Wednesday*.

'I hope to get to Bonn on Friday night, on my return to England, and to stay till Saturday afternoon, and then start straight to London via Cologne. I trust to find you in Bonn, my best friend, for I long to have some spiritual intercourse with you before I leave. I also want to see Brandis. I shall put up at the "Stern"; Morier may be there too. What you mentioned about the German plans the other day has occupied me much, but, as I told you before, it seems to me best to remain in Oxford for a few more years. I do not deny that I should like to spend the evening of life in German air, but I stopped long ago wishing for certain things and making plans; Heaven has so far guided me so mercifully. Hoping to see you soon, ever yours.'

Directly Max Müller returned to England, the move to 'Parks End' began. The roof was already on the new part of the house, which was boarded off from the old part, in which the whole party, tightly packed, spent the winter. When once settled, his wife wrote to a relative :—

PARKS END, *October* 9.

'You can enter into the delight it is to Max to look round and to feel that he has bought this house with his own hard work. I am sure it is a much greater delight than any house left to one could give.'

TO HIS MOTHER.

*Translation.* PARKS END, *October* 9.

'Do not lose heart, but thank God for all that is left you; that is the chief thing, and so I wish you joy of your birthday and of your new home. May God give you many peaceful and happy hours there, and strength to bear whatever He sends. How happy our time was together in the summer, and how seldom does everything succeed so well as our stay in Ems. It is true, the sad recollections were always there as a background; but what life is without such recollections? But we must go on, and comfort comes only when we know whose hand sends the sorrow. I hope, in spite of all your fear and difficulties, that your move is safely over, and that you do not dislike your new home.'

On his own birthday this year, his forty-fourth, he writes to his mother :—

*Translation.* *December* 6.

'Thank you for all your good wishes. I feel always as if there is hardly anything left to wish for. I can only pray God to preserve all I have! The children are all well and bright; the boy grows fast.'

To his sister he writes a few days later :—

*Translation.* *December* 9.

'I often feel how much more happiness has been given me than I deserve; and when I think of all you have lost, I often feel how all that we call our own is only lent us for a short time, and how we cannot, from day to day, call anything ours. This Christmas time will bring you and poor Krug renewed sorrow. But try and remember how much is left you, and do not let the years you yet have together pass in mere sorrow; the years do not come again.'

The allusion in the following letter is to the intention Max Müller had already expressed of dedicating the second volume of *Chips* to Bernays, who was at first too modest to accept it.

To Professor Bernays.

*Translation.* Parks End, *December* 15.

'My dearest Friend,—I had long looked forward to giving you a public recognition of my friendship and gratitude. Though our meetings have not been frequent of late, yet they have left the memory of many beautiful and stimulating hours, and I hope indeed that a lucky star will perhaps once more bring us close to each other for a longer period. What I miss most here in Oxford is stimulating intercourse in literary and scientific circles. That is entirely wanting, especially in my special branch of study. Altogether the Englishman seems to me to have no interest for the "Becoming" or "Growing"; it is all to be tangible and ready made. All dialectic is wanting in the true sense of the word. However, there are deep shadows everywhere, and I do not want to forget the bright sides of English life, and I am afraid that I should find it somewhat difficult to get accustomed again to the rather narrow German trousers. As matters stand now, I feel bound to stay in England as long as my father-in-law is alive; what comes after we will leave to that guidance which so far has led me so beautifully. A house on the Rhine and a Professorship at Bonn would be great attractions later on. Berlin would never tempt me; it requires too many sacrifices to the Non-L——. Here in Oxford, I must say, everything is done to make up for what has been done amiss. I have been relieved from Modern Literature, and they are thinking now of founding for me a Professorship of Comparative Philology, also of raising my salary if possible, and so I hope to get again more time for my own work. I feel very well, thank God, this winter, and I hope to get on famously with my labours for the *Veda*.'

Max Müller found that the change to 'Parks End' gave him more rest and leisure for uninterrupted work. In High Street he had been, as it were, in the gangway, and was liable to constant interruptions. Visitors to Oxford, with half an hour to spare, would drop in unexpectedly, more especially foreigners and Americans, with or without introductions. The distance across the Parks to his house was a barrier to such unexpected invasions, and, though he had more room in his new home to welcome and entertain his friends, his daily life was quieter and more regular.

Among Max Müller's papers there was found a small memorandum, 'Our first luncheon party at "Parks End,"

December, 1867,' with the names of Mr. Jowett, Bob Lowe, Huxley, H. Graham, Rev. W. Rogers.

To the Right Hon. W. E. Gladstone (who was anxious to discuss the law of copyright with Max Müller and Dean Liddell).

Parks End, *December* 30.

'Dear Mr. G.,—I shall be at home to-morrow at 2 p.m., and delighted to hear any news about the Greeks and their schoolmasters, the Phoenicians. If you arrive by the 1.57 up-train, your best plan would be to take a fly at the station, and tell the driver to drive to the house that formerly belonged to Mr. Goldwin Smith. That is the house I now live in, at least one-half of it, for the new half which I have added is not yet habitable. I shall ask the Dean to come to luncheon a little after two to meet you. Dr. Scott is not in Oxford, so far as I know. Yours sincerely.'

Mr. Gladstone's signature heads the long list of distinguished guests that Max Müller had the honour of welcoming to his house during the next thirty years.

# CHAPTER XVI

## 1868–1869

Death of sister. Visit of mother. Letter to Duke of Argyll. LL.D. at Cambridge. Professorship of Comparative Philology. Visits to Frogmore, Fulham, and Gloucester. Isle of Wight. Tennyson. Illness of children. Member of French Institute. *Translations from the Vedic Hymns*, Vol. I. Soden. Kiel. Denmark.

A FEW days after Mr. Gladstone's visit Max Müller wrote to him as follows:—

To THE RIGHT HON. W. E. GLADSTONE.

PARKS END, *January* 5.

'... I do not think that many fresh deities were introduced by the Phoenicians into Greece. The influence they exercised on the Greeks was more like that which the Greek colonists exercised on the Italians. Jupiter was not Zeus, nor Juno Hera, nor Saturnus Kronos. There was a conviction among the Greeks and the Italians that their gods must be the same, and hence any point of similarity was caught at in order to identify different deities. Something of the same kind seems to have taken place when the Phoenicians taught the Greeks their A B C. But while the names of the letters in Greek are simply Phoenician, Alpha, Beta, &c., I do not know of any names of Greek deities that demand a Phoenician etymology. It is true there is no satisfactory etymology of Poseidon, but there are hundreds, nay thousands, of words in Greek, as in English, which have no satisfactory etymology, but which no one would think of deriving from Semitic sources. ... The subject is a very important one, and I expect will excite some interest. ...'

Early in February Max Müller, who had suffered so much the previous year at the loss of his niece, was called on to bear a much heavier sorrow in the death of his only sister. She was ill but a day or two, and the first intimation of any anxiety was the telegram with the news of her death. It was a terrible shock, and Max Müller was quite prostrated by the blow, which seemed all the harder to bear, as his wife had to leave him a day or two later, owing to the alarming illness of her mother-aunt and two of her sister's children.

### To his Mother.

*Translation.* Parks End, *February* 16.

'Poor mother, who would have thought that you must yet bear such a loss, after all the sorrow which God has sent you in your life? And yet it was His will, and He will send the strength to bear it. He has taught us that death is not so terrible as it appears to most men—it is but a separation for a few short days, and then, too, eternity awaits us. For all the sorrow, I can only think, it is well with her; she is spared much, many a heavy burden is taken from her. She had a happy youth, and in spite of many sorrows, in all that makes the true happiness of life, hers was a happy marriage. The children to whom her heart clung are gone before her, and I think she was glad to follow. I have been reading such beautiful hymns of Paul Gerhardt's on Death and Life—you will know them—but in the grief and sorrow God has sent us, one really feels how true, how deep, how beautiful they are. Yet life goes on, and its duties must be carried out. To-morrow I must begin my lectures; I could not do so this week. Try to trust in God, throw your grief on Him; He will help you to bear it. My only thought is how I can get you here as soon as possible. Perhaps you can find some one to travel with you, and I will meet you at Dover. My doctor still says I must not venture on the sea passage. I feel well, and cannot believe the trouble in my throat is of any consequence. Bring your maid with you, shut up your rooms, do everything you can to come soon.'

### To the Same.

*Translation.*

'You must come to me and spend the last years of your life with me. You will find here all those who in life are the nearest to you. Dear Auguste knew, as she closed her eyes, that you would not be left alone in the world. But what will poor Krug do? It goes to my heart when I think of him and all he has suffered this last year. How different life is to what one thought it when young, how all around us falls together till we ourselves fall together. How meaningless and vain everything seems on earth, and how closely the reality of the life beyond approaches us. Many days were beautiful here, but the greater the happiness the more bitter the thought that it all passes away, that nothing remains of earthly happiness but a grateful heart and faith in God, who knows best what is best for us. May God strengthen and keep you. Even with my wife and children life seems so empty to me, and I keep saying, "My dear Auguste!" How delightful it was being together last summer. Oh, God, who could have foreseen this! Write to me as soon as you can, my poor mother. I wish I had you here.'

To his Wife.

Parks End, *February* 24.

'I had a sad, very sad letter from my mother. My thoughts are always with her, and I can hardly bring myself to believe that we have really lost our dear good Auguste. She was my oldest friend and companion, and everything in my early life was connected with her. Now that she is gone, all those pleasant recollections on which one dwells, one hardly knows when, but yet which constantly pass through one's mind, are altogether changed, all life and reality taken out of them; one's own life brought more clearly before one's mind, as what it really is, a short stay in a foreign land. And there is still so much left us, so much to be happy and thankful for; and yet here, too, the thought always rushes across one's brightest hours, it cannot last—it is only for a few years—and then it must be given up. Let us work as long as it is day, let us try to do our duty, and be very thankful for God's blessings which have been showered upon us so richly; but let us learn also always to look beyond and learn to be ready to give up everything, as my poor mother has had to give up almost everything that makes life happy, and yet she can say, "Thy will be done."'

To the Same.

*March* 31.

'It is true that I have plenty of happiness, but great happiness makes one think so often that it cannot last, and that one will have some day to give up all to which one's heart clings so. A few years sooner or later, but the time will come, and come quicker than one expects. Therefore I believe it is right to accustom oneself to the thought that we can none of us escape death, and that all our happiness here is only lent us. But at the same time we can thankfully enjoy all that God gives us, and few have more reason to say this than I.'

As soon as she felt able to travel, his mother came over to her son and stayed through the summer, but preferred returning for the winter to her own rooms in Chemnitz.

The following is one of the first letters of a correspondence with the Duke of Argyll which continued to within a short time of the Duke's death:—

To the Duke of Argyll.

Oxford, *February* 24.

'. . . I only wish I could send a more satisfactory answer, but, as far as I can judge, every attempt at translating the periods of natural growth or structure into the language of definite solar chronology has proved a failure. The history of language opens a vista which makes one feel almost giddy if one tries to see the end of it, but the measuring rod of the chronologist seems to me entirely out of place. Those who have eyes to see will see the immeasurable distance between the first historical appearance of language and the real beginnings of human speech: those who cannot see will oscillate between the wildly large figures of the Buddhists or the wildly small figures of the Rabbis, but they will never lay hold of what by its very nature is indefinite.

'The earliest historical appearance of human language takes place in Egypt. Whatever the date of the earliest hieroglyphic inscription may be, that is the earliest date of Egyptian language. I am not satisfied as yet as to the soundness of Egyptian historical chronology. The Semitic languages make their first historical appearance in the cuneiform inscriptions of Nebuchadnezzar, or, it may be, of some more ancient Babylonian and Assyrian monarchs. In real literature there is nothing Semitic more ancient than the earliest portions of the Old Testament.

'Of Âryan language the first literary relic is the *Veda*. With the evidence now before us, and after a careful consideration of all objections, one may honestly say that the Hymns of the *Veda* could not be more modern than 1200 B.C. I believe they are older, and my belief is chiefly founded on the nature of the Vedic Sanskrit as compared with the Sanskrit of the laws of Manu, the *Mahâbhârata*, &c. I shall just quote one instance. According to all Sanskrit grammars, that language, so rich in other forms, is without any trace of a conjunctive mood. And this is perfectly true if we take into account the ordinary Sanskrit only. But the *Veda* is full of conjunctives, and they are the same conjunctives as those we find in Greek. Greek has a medial form of most verbs, so has Sanskrit. Greek has a first aorist in the medium, so has Sanskrit. That first aorist in Greek is a compound form, ἐτυψάμην, and is formed by an auxiliary verb that yields σα-μην, just as I lov*ed* is formed by an auxiliary verb, viz. by *did*. The Sanskrit aorist is formed by the same auxiliary verb, so that ἐ/δείκ-σα-το is represented by Sanskrit *a/dik-sa-ta*. The conjunctive of the first aorist in Greek takes the personal terminations of the present, and loses the augment. The same in Sanskrit, at least in the Vedic Sanskrit, where corresponding to δείκ-ση-ται we should find *dik-sa-te*.

'If we take this one form, we might call it in one sense almost a work of art, though it is only a product of that art which may be called the art of nature, and which preserves amongst an infinity of possible forms those only that are really good, really adapted for the work they have to do. These conjunctives of the medial aorist exist in Homer and in the *Veda*. They must have existed before Greek was Greek and Sanskrit was Sanskrit, for they are formed out of materials which exist neither in Greek nor in Sanskrit. In the same manner *mais* and *mai* must have been formed before Italian was Italian or French French, for neither of these dialects have the materials out of which *mai* or *mais* could have been formed. But how little should we gain if we argued as some geologists do! It has taken so many centuries before the Latin *magis* dwindled down to *mai* and *mais*, therefore it cannot have taken less time to change the original type of δείκ-ση-ται and *dik-sa-te* into these two forms. It is far better to look at these forms and find out how much even their typical ancestor presupposed, how much wear and tear was necessary before such a compound could become possible as we see fixed in that grammatical system which preceded Sanskrit and Greek. In that compound we have at least four elements. We have the augment, and no language, not even the most ancient, has as yet betrayed the secret as to the material out of which the augment was formed. Secondly, we have the personal termination ται or *te*, clearly a pronoun of the third person, but different from the pronouns of the third person such as we find them in Sanskrit or Greek. Thirdly, an auxiliary verb σα, the Sanskrit *as*, to be, in *as-mi*, ἐσ-μί, &c., which loses its initial vowel as it does in Latin *sum* for *es-um*. This *as* meant originally to breathe (in Sanskrit *as-u*, 'breath'), and before it dwindled down to what we call an auxiliary verb, a mere verbal copula, again how many centuries must have passed? Can we measure them by the distance that divides the Latin *status* from *stato* and *été*? I doubt it, yet we can see deeper and deeper into the shaft from which the ore of human speech is brought, and discover level after level that must have been left behind before the pure metal, and before such amalgamates could have been produced as those which we see in such a conjunctive as *dik-sa-te*. After that amalgamate is formed, and after it has been coined into a definite grammatical token, begins the phonetic decay, the influence, it may be, of diet, climate, and all the rest; and only after all this can we account for the fact that in the Homeric poems we find a form like δείκ-ση-ται, and in the Hymns of the *Veda* a form like *dik-sa-te*.

'In all these considerations the question how a root *dik* came to mean "to show" and nothing else has not been touched upon, though that again can only have been the result of a sifting process of which we can hardly form an adequate idea. If there was proof that it had taken 10,000 years to form out of given radical elements that wonderful system of grammar which was quite finished before Sanskrit became Sanskrit and Greek Greek, I should feel no surprise. Before that date we should still have the formation of roots. What we commonly call the history of language is from the very beginning nothing but a history of decay—the period of youth and growth is past before we know of any language.'

In the month of January, Max Müller had received an invitation from Cambridge to deliver the Rede Lecture in the course of the summer. The Vice-Chancellor, in transmitting the invitation, observed that these lectures were generally scientific rather than literary, but that Mr. Ruskin had been the lecturer of the previous year, adding, 'Your subject, however, is a science, whatever the Royal or any other Institution may say to the contrary.' Max Müller accepted the invitation, and in writing again in April to fix the day, the Vice-Chancellor told him that the University wished to offer him the degree of LL.D. Accordingly, the last week in May, Max Müller and his wife visited Cambridge, where they were the guests of Dr. Thompson, Master of Trinity. Commodore Maury, the American hydrographer, and Dr. W. Wright, the Arabic scholar, received the degree of LL.D. the same day. The Public Orator, Dr. G. W. Clark, thus presented Max Müller:—

'Sequitur deinde Max Müller, Taylorianus apud Oxonienses Professor, qui, cum iuvenis admodum, consiliis et auspicio celeberrimi viri Christiani de Bunsen, se in Britanniam transtulisset, hanc sibi sedem et novam patriam elegit, atque ita profecit ut si loquentem audiveris, non dubites in Anglia natum, si magnitudinem operum respexeris, Germanum esse cognoscas.

'Ad id vero potissimum navavit operam, ut Philologiam doceret, non eam quae circa verborum argutias commoretur, sed illam quae, linguis Teutonicis, Graeca, Latina, Sanscritica, inter se collatis, communem omnium originem exquirat, incunabula gentium recludat, historiam quibusvis annalibus antiquiorem certioremque evolvat.

'Quid multa? cras, ipso audito, quanta facundia difficillimas res expedire possit, omnes iudicaturi estis.'

*Translation.*

'I would next speak of Max Müller, the Taylorian Professor in Oxford, who having while still a youth, with the advice and under the auspices of that illustrious man Christian von Bunsen, come over to Britain, has chosen this land for a new home and country, and has made such progress that, having heard him speak, you think he must have been born in England, whereas, if you consider the importance and quantity of his works, you are quite sure that he must be a German. The work he has devoted himself to especially has been the work of teaching Philology, not that branch of it which is concerned with the niceties and subtleties of words, but that which, by the comparison of the Sanskrit, Greek, Latin, and German languages, investigates their common origin, discovers the cradle of the nations, and unfolds a history more ancient and more certain than that contained in any written annals. What need of further words! To-morrow, when you have heard him speak, you will all be able to judge with what eloquence he can make the most difficult subjects clear and plain.'

The next day Max Müller delivered the Rede Lecture to a very large audience. It will be found in Vol. IV of *Chips*, first edition. In the middle of the lecture, Commodore Maury, who sat behind the lecturer's wife, leant over and said in a loud whisper, 'I must tell you, it's just elegant!'

During the winter months a movement had been going on in Oxford for the foundation of a Chair of Comparative Philology, which was carried out in the May Term, with the proviso in the statute of foundation that Max Müller was to be the first Professor, if he would accept the post. He was deeply gratified by this mark of esteem from the resident members of the University, and it relieved him of the duties of the Chair of Modern Languages, added to his salary, and enabled him to devote all his time and energies to his own line of studies. His inaugural lecture was delivered in the October Term. 'Professor Max Müller,' says a contemporary notice, 'enjoys the high honour—an honour the more signal as he is a foreigner—of occupying the first Professorship ever founded at Oxford by the University Corporation itself; all previous Professorships having been established either by royal benefactions or private announcements.'

Early in June Max Müller paid his first visit to their Royal

Highnesses Prince and Princess Christian, then living at Frogmore. These visits were always a rest and refreshment to him, a delightful contrast to his quiet life of hard work, and the gracious friendly feeling always shown to him and his called forth his lively gratitude to the last.

To his Wife.

Frogmore House, *June* 1.

'I came here in good time last night, though after a long and hot journey. When I arrived at Frogmore the Prince and Princess were just coming back from a walk, and they asked me at once to take a walk with them in the garden, which just now is in great beauty. We passed the Mausoleum, and when we came back sat down and had a long and animated discussion, all in German, though the Prince speaks English very well. We then went in to get ready for dinner, and dined at half-past eight: no one present but the Prince, the Princess, Lady Susan Melville, and myself. One of the servants was in Scotch attire, but no bagpipes[1]. Nothing could be pleasanter. The Princess kindly inquired after you and the children, and is of course wrapped up in her own boy[2], whom I have not yet seen. After dinner, Lady Susan left, and we went up a small staircase to the smoking-room, the Princess sitting down in an armchair and the Prince asking me to smoke. This, however, I could not bring myself to do till the Princess had left. I sat up till nearly twelve with the Prince. He is a true Schleswig-Holsteiner, very quiet but very determined, and very frank. He has fine blue eyes, and is a decidedly handsome man. His photographs do not do him justice.'

To his Children.

Frogmore, *June* 2.

'My dear little Girls,—I have just come back from a beautiful drive through Windsor Forest. We drove in an open carriage—Prince and Princess Christian, Lady Susan Melville, and your daddy. There was a long avenue of rhododendrons all in flower, and we drove through it, and you never saw so many beautiful flowers together. And then the Prince took me to see the house where all the dogs live that belong to the Queen. It was like the Zoological Gardens, but all the animals were different kinds of dogs—greyhounds and deerhounds, like old Oscar, and Teckels, like those mama had at

[1] Bagpipes were a horror to Max Müller.

[2] Prince Christian Victor, who died the day after Max Müller.

Ray Lodge; and some very scarce but valuable dogs, called "mops" in German: there are only three of them left in England, and the Queen takes great care of them. Prince Christian is a German prince, and he married Princess Helena, a daughter of the Queen; and they are very happy together, just like mama and papa, only they are very rich and have a beautiful house and garden; and they have one little boy, a little older than our boykin, and he is a very handsome little fellow, with large blue eyes and rosy cheeks.'

TO PROFESSOR LEPSIUS.

*Translation.* PARKS END, *June* 18.

'MY HONOURED FRIEND,—. . . Bunsen's *Life* has gone straight to my heart, as it has with you. Oh, if we could even in this life forget all that is unessential, all that makes it so hard for us to recognize true greatness and goodness in the character of those with whom this life brings us into contact for a little while! How much we lose by making little things so important, and how rarely do we think highly enough of what is essential and lasting! Bunsen surely was one of the greatest spirits of our times! Where are the greater ones? To have known him, belongs to those things which have bestowed upon my life the greatest value and the greatest charm. I should much like to hear from you where something reliable and trustworthy may be found with regard to Egyptian mythology. Is Bunsen's opinion about a Phoenician origin well founded? Are not there any real Egyptian gods? And can their origin and their development be traced? . . . Some time ago I wrote for the *Times* a notice of Bunsen's *Life*, but until Parliament rises there is not much hope of its appearing; it has been clipped a good deal, and I think a little later on I shall publish it unmutilated.'

TO M. RENAN.

PARKS END, *June* 26.

'MY DEAR FRIEND,—I can truly feel for you in the loss which you have suffered; it will sooner or later come to all of us. But life is different after we have lost our father and mother. I have my mother staying with me, and should enjoy her presence here very much if it were not for the sad cause which brought her here—the death of my only sister, with whom she used to live in Germany. With every one of these losses life seems to become more unreal, there is less and less to live for, to care for; and if one still cares for one's work, it is because it makes one forget life as it is, and life as we thought it was or might be. . . . I hear your new work is nearly finished and I am curious to see what you think of St. Paul. I hope you have seen Jowett's book on the Thessalonians, Galatians, and Romans; it is very good, original, and honest. I am able at last to work again, and I hope my health is quite re-established. I am printing my first translation of the *Rig-veda*; I sent you a specimen the other day, and hope to send you the first volume by September. I am also reprinting my *Chips*, which have just been preached against in Westminster Abbey.'

To the Same.

Parks End, 1868.

'You speak in far too laudatory terms of my own work, and I am afraid it will only raise the bile of certain people. I was amused by what you said about the *Concessions aux Nègres*. You are right to a certain extent, but the same applies to all countries. If you want to carry people along with you, you must begin where you find them, otherwise you run on like an engine without any carriages attached to it. The best proof that I do not concede too much is that the science of religion has been preached against in Westminster Abbey by a real bishop. However, they do not mean to burn me yet, and I hope I shall still convince the Bishop that we heretical Germans are far better Christians than the most orthodox of bishops. I am printing my translation of the *Veda*. I had called it in my preface a *Traduction raisonnée*, if one may use such an expression, and I am glad to find you use that very word in your *Rapports*. I have also finished my edition of the *Prâtisâkhya*, in which I was forestalled by Regnier. His edition is really excellent, and I cannot sufficiently regret that he should have been taken away from Sanskrit. The school of Burnouf will become extinct with him. After carefully examining every line of his *Prâtisâkhya* while printing my own, I am bound to say there is not another Sanskrit scholar living who would have done his work as well as Regnier. It is bad enough that the throne should be usurped, but why Chairs of Sanskrit or Hebrew? However, I am afraid I am talking treason, and with Ewald's[1] example before me I ought to be careful.'

Another pleasant visit paid this year was to the Bishop of London and Mrs. Tait, at Fulham, on one afternoon of which Max Müller and his wife were taken to the Volunteer Camp at Wimbledon, and watched the shooting for the Queen's Prize. Since the Ray Lodge days he had ceased himself to be an active Volunteer.

[1] He had refused in 1867 to take the oath of allegiance to Prussia and was pensioned off.

Soon after this Max Müller made a short visit to Gloucester and its neighbourhood, guided by his friend Mr. Bellows. Of this visit Mr. Bellows writes:—

'When at your house in 1868 I found Professor Max Müller had some thought of visiting the Phillips Library at Cheltenham to examine the Oriental MSS. it contained, and I asked him to come to Gloucester for a few days, when he could do this, besides joining one of our field excursions of the Cotteswold Club to Berkeley Castle, &c.: a little programme that was soon after carried out. I recollect that to impress him the more favourably with our Gloucestershire scenery I told him of an old friend of ours, James Atkins, a well-known botanist, having come to Painswick several years before to spend a fortnight, and that he was so pleased with the Cotswold Hills that he had stayed there ever since.

'Professor Max Müller smiled, and rejoined, "Do you know that that was what happened to me, here at Oxford! *I* came here to spend a fortnight, and I have been here ever since!"

'I first ventured to write to Professor Max Müller on some philological matter—I am not sure what, but I think something about the old Cornish language, about which I wanted to beg his help. When I came to know him personally I was irresistibly attracted by the power of sympathy that was his most striking characteristic, as I am sure others will admit that it was, and the secret of the charm that made him a leader of men. This power of sympathy he possessed in a larger degree than any other person I have ever met, except Count Tolstoi: for greatly as they differed in their other gifts, as well as in their entire environments, Max Müller and Tolstoi were alike in this.

'Even the high attainments Professor Max Müller unquestionably possessed did not so affect those with whom he came in contact as did this force of sympathy, to which he owed his broad-mindedness, and his insight into the essence of religion itself: I will not say of the religions of the East merely, but the general relation of the soul of man to the truth, in which all these are included. I need only refer to his preface to *Chips from a German Workshop* as a noble example of his sympathy for men of widely differing modes of thought. It reads like an expansion of the nineteenth psalm, where the universality of the sunlight and sunheat in the outward creation is shown as the correlative to the uncreated light and power that is unlimited in its operation, by time or space. And now he is gone, and no one will ever again take his place. This very thought is assurance, for it means that he fills a place in another state of existence for which he alone was created.'

One of the visits paid under Mr. Bellows' guidance was to Mr. Bryan Hodgson, who, as Resident at Nepal, had acquired an extensive acquaintance with the tribes and languages of the Himalayan slopes. Mr. Hodgson lived to a great age, and died in 1895. It is from his researches that our knowledge of Northern Buddhism is chiefly derived. He formed a valuable collection of above 300 MSS., a few of which he gave to the Bodleian.

To Mr. Bryan Hodgson

Parks End, *August* 25, 1868.

'My dear Hodgson,—What would I give for your quiet Vihâr at Alderley—your *otium cum dignitate*—doing exactly as you like, reading or writing what you like, without being driven to publish and republish, without lectures, without printer's devils, &c. &c. I can assure you I am sometimes nearly beside myself with all I have to attend to; to say nothing of mere Grihastha matters, which are sometimes troublesome too. However, it cannot be helped, and I only mention it as my excuse for not having written to you before. I have looked at your papers and the drawing, and I think it would be a great pity if those carefully executed sketches were not published. Then as to my lecture (" Stratification of Language ") I cannot think that we differ so much. I have frequently availed myself of lexicographic evidence. But grammatical evidences have, as you know, a different value, and for the object I had in view in my lecture the grammatical structure of language was of the greatest importance.'

In the autumn a new edition of both volumes of the *Lectures on Language* was called for. It was the fifth edition of Vol. I, the second of Vol. II. The new edition of two volumes was of 3,000 copies. At the same time a large second edition of *Chips*, Vols. I and II, was published, and Max Müller found that his writings in this one year had brought in above £1,200.

Except the short visits mentioned, the summer had been spent in work at Oxford, and as soon as his mother returned to Germany, he took his wife and children to Bonchurch, and gave himself up to rest and outdoor life for a fortnight. Long walks were taken with his wife in all directions, and all parts of the beautiful island were explored. One delightful day was given to Carisbrooke, where the rector, Mr. James, an early Oxford friend, received the Max Müllers, showing them the

Castle and the fine Roman villa, which had not been long excavated.

Another expedition, in which their eldest child shared, was to Freshwater, where a night was spent with Mr. and Mrs. Tennyson. The poet was in rather a silent mood till after the ladies withdrew, when, over their pipes, he read out some of his latest poems to Max Müller, his rich deep voice sounding through the house till far into the small hours.

To HIS MOTHER (for her birthday).

*Translation.* BONCHURCH, *October* 9.

'Each birthday, even the happiest, has its sad side. It is a station nearer death; but whilst in youth and the full enjoyment of life this thought seems terrible, it loses much of its terror as one gets older, for the parting from the few whom we leave behind is made up for by the hope of rejoining the many who are gone before us. So, though this birthday must be very sad to you, you must accustom yourself more and more to the thought that here is not our abiding city, that all that we call ours here is only lent, not given us, and that if the sorrow for those we have lost remains the same, we must yet acknowledge with gratitude to God the great blessing of having enjoyed so many years with those whom He gave us as parents, or children, or friends. One forgets so easily the happy years we have had with those who were the nearest to us. Even these years of happiness, however short they may have been, were only given us, we had not deserved them. I know well there is no comfort for this pain of parting; the wound always remains, but one learns to bear the pain, and learns to thank God for what He gave, for the beautiful memories of the past, and the yet more beautiful hope for the future. If a man has lent us anything for several years, and at last takes it back, he expects gratitude, not anger, and if God has more patience with our weakness than men have, yet murmurs and complaints for the life which He measured out to us as is best for us, are not what He expected from us. A spirit of resignation to God's will is the only comfort, the only relief under the trials God lays upon us, and with such a spirit the heaviest as well as the lightest trials of life are not only bearable, but useful, and gratitude to God and peace in life and in death remain untroubled. May this quiet and peaceful resignation beautify and brighten the evening of your life, that is the one wish I have for your sixty-eighth birthday. . . . We were yesterday at Freshwater, where Tennyson has his house, and he invited us (G. and Ada) to stay with him. It was very interesting.'

The following letter was written to the Duke of Argyll soon after his appointment as Secretary of State for India :—

TO THE DUKE OF ARGYLL.

OXFORD, *December* 16.

'. . . As for more than twenty years my principal work has been devoted to the ancient literature of India, I cannot but feel a deep and real sympathy for all that concerns the higher interests of the people of that country. Though I have never been in India, I have many friends there, both among the civilians and among the natives, and I believe I am not mistaken in supposing that the publication in England of the ancient sacred writings of the Brâhmans, which had never been published in India, and other contributions from different European scholars towards a better knowledge of the ancient literature and religion of India, have not been without some effect on the intellectual and religious movement that is going on among the more thoughtful members of Indian society. I have sometimes regretted that I am not an Englishman, and able to help more actively in the great work of educating and improving the natives. But I do rejoice that this great task of governing and benefiting India should have fallen to one who knows the greatness of that task and all its opportunities and responsibilities, who thinks not only of its political and financial bearings, but has a heart to feel for the moral welfare of those millions of human beings that are, more or less directly, committed to his charge.

'India has been conquered once, but India must be conquered again, and that second conquest should be a conquest by education. Much has been done for education of late, but if the funds were tripled and quadrupled, that would hardly be enough.

'The results of the educational work carried on during the last twenty years are palpable everywhere. They are good and bad, as was to be expected. It is easy to find fault with what is called Young Bengal, the product of English ideas grafted on the native mind. But Young Bengal, with all its faults, is full of promise. Its bad features are apparent everywhere, its good qualities are naturally hidden from the eyes of careless observers. . . . India can never be anglicized, but it can be reinvigorated. By encouraging a study of their own ancient literature, as part of their education, a national feeling of pride and self-respect will be reawakened among those who influence the large masses of the people. A new national literature may spring up, impregnated with Western ideas, yet retaining its native spirit and character. The two things hang together. In order to raise the character of the vernaculars, a study of the ancient classical language is absolutely necessary: for from it these modern dialects have branched off, and from it alone can they draw their vital strength and beauty. A new national literature will bring with it a new national life and new moral vigour. As to religion, that will take care of itself. The missionaries have done far more than they themselves seem to be aware of, nay, much of the work which is theirs they would probably disclaim. The Christianity of our nineteenth century will hardly be the Christianity of India. But the ancient religion of India is doomed—and if Christianity does not step in, whose fault will it be?'

The following letter alludes to a little indulgence Max Müller allowed himself more than once. The forests round Dessau are famous for their wild boar, and through his cousin, Baroness Stolzenberg, he was able occasionally to secure one from the ducal forester. The arrival of the first one *entire* made a sensation at the Oxford Railway Station, and a message was sent up that a dead 'Bear' had arrived there for Professor Max Müller. The dinner given to eat the haunch was a great success, and one head of a house was observed to enjoy three helpings.

To his Mother.

*Translation.* Parks End, *December* 20.

'Yesterday we had a large dinner-party, the Vice-Chancellor, &c., and had the haunch of wild boar, which was excellent. We had already lived a week on the boar, which was a very good one, and arrived in good condition. A young man in London who comes here sometimes to work for me brought it in its skin. The skin is being dressed as a mat, the head we have sent to my father-in-law, and the rest we are slowly eating up. It has amused me having it, and brought back old days.'

The first months of 1869 brought great anxiety to Max Müller and his wife. Early in January they went with their two eldest girls to stay with a cousin at Taplow, where, after a few days, their eldest child sickened with scarlet fever. The alarm was very great, as there was a large party of young cousins living in the house, and the whole family moved at once, the mother and her sick child alone remaining isolated on the top floor of a huge country house. Max Müller, who had already returned to Oxford, had the younger children with him, and could not therefore go to his wife and sick child for fear of infection. It was a very severe case, and the eldest child was only slowly recovering when the second little girl developed the terrible illness, and was brought back to be nursed with her sister. Max Müller suffered acutely from the anxiety, which lasted nearly two months, greatly aggravated too by the feeling that they had driven the whole family from their home. Mercifully the infection did not spread. The second child lay for more than a fortnight at death's door. One night, when her case seemed hopeless, the father came to see her, but the lengthy process of disinfection made it impossible for him to repeat the visit, as his lectures had begun. His daily letters were the one support of his wife.

'How little one thinks that these heavy trials and afflictions may come upon us any day. One lives on as if life were to last for ever, and as if we should never part with those who are most dear to us. Life would be intolerable were it otherwise, but how little one is prepared for what life really is.'

*January* 24.

'I am longing to see you and our dear little Ada. I am afraid you do not tell me all, and I cannot tell you how I feel for your solitude in all this fearful anxiety. There is but one help and one comfort in these trials, that is to know by whom they are sent. If one knows that nothing can happen to us without Him, one does not feel quite helpless even under the greatest terrors of this life. I tremble always when I open your letters.'

One ray of sunshine came to brighten this time of gloom, in Max Müller's election as a Foreign Member of the French Institute, the youngest man ever elected. The choice lay between him and Theodor Mommsen, who was some years his senior. In writing to congratulate him, Max Müller's childlike friend, Stanislas Julien, the great Sinologue, says: 'et maintenant vous pouvez porter l'habit brodé'—the beautiful dress invented for the members of the Institute by Richelieu, and which Max Müller, before he was made a Privy Councillor, always wore at Court by the Queen's permission.

To Max Müller.

Paris, 1er *mars*.

'J'ai été heureux, Monsieur, de concourir à votre nomination comme associé étranger de l'Institut. Précisément l'été dernier j'avais lu vos Lectures à la *British Institution* sur la science et la formation du langage, et j'avais été extrêmement frappé de l'élévation, de la profondeur et de l'abondance des idées que vous y avez exposées. Je ne suis pas un juge compétent de vos travaux sur les *Védas*, mais je me félicite d'avoir un peu contribué à vous en fournir les matériaux, et je vous remercie d'en avoir gardé le souvenir. Mon seul regret est de ne vous avoir pas acquis vous-même à la France. C'est une fortune que j'envie un peu à l'Angleterre, tout en lui en faisant mon compliment. Recevez, Monsieur et savant confrère, l'assurance de ma considération la plus distinguée. 'GUIZOT.'

*Translation.*

'I was glad, Monsieur, to contribute to your nomination as a Foreign Member of the Institute. It was only last year that I read your Lectures at the British Institution on the "Science and Formation of Language," and I was very much struck with the elevation, the depth, and the richness of the ideas which you there brought forward. I am not a competent judge of your labours on the *Rig-veda*, but I congratulate myself in having contributed a little in furnishing you with materials for it, and I thank you for remembering this. My one regret is, not to have secured you yourself for France. It is a piece of good fortune for which I envy, though at the same time I congratulate, England. Receive, Monsieur and learned *confrère*, the assurance of my highest esteem. 'GUIZOT.'

TO HIS WIFE.

*February* 14.

'One does not like to think of anything, or feel happy about anything, till this illness of the children is quite over; yet you will see from the enclosed letters that I have felt very happy to-day when I heard that I had been elected one of the eight Foreign Members of the Academy. It has been my ambition, I might almost say my foolish ambition through life, to be some day what I saw Humboldt was, when as a mere boy I first called on him in Paris, a Foreign Member of the French Institute; and now the thing has come to pass, and I do feel very happy about it. Still, what is that till we know that our little Mary is out of danger, and that we may look forward to a happy meeting?'

*March* 15.

'I assure you when I think of what might have been, I seem to have no room for any feeling but that of unceasing thankfulness. "Forget not all His benefits." One ought to keep up the recollection of these great blessings, for daily life is so very apt to wash it away.'

Early in January Max Müller received a pressing invitation from Professor Huxley, who had just been made President of the Ethnological Society, to lecture on the ethnological aspects of Indian Philology.

To Professor Huxley.

Parks End, *January* 8, 1869.

'It is very difficult to say no to such pleading as yours. But I have made a vow to undertake nothing new till what I have now in hand is finished, and it would be dishonest not to keep it. I am truly glad that you have taken the Ethnological Society in hand. I have not followed all the squabbles there seem to have been, but I feel certain that something ought to be done to raise the character of ethnological or anthropological research, and there is no one who can do it as well as you. I shall willingly help you hereafter when I am a little freer, but there are three books in the Press that must be finished first—(1) the first volume of the translation of the *Rig-veda*, (2) the *Prâtisâkhya*, the oldest work on phonetics (this is printed), and (3) the fifth volume of the text of the *Rig-veda*, with the native commentaries. I hope this will all be done before the year is out, but even then I have promised Longman two more volumes of *Chips*.

'I should be so glad if you would come to Oxford from a Saturday to Monday and stay with us. Term begins towards the end of January; if you could let me know a week before, I could then make sure of some friends who would be glad to meet you.'

Among the many young Germans whom Max Müller was able to assist to positions in India few became more distinguished, or have done better work for Sanskrit scholarship, than Dr. Kielhorn, now Professor at Göttingen. The following is one of the many letters that passed between them:—

To Dr. Kielhorn.

*Translation.* Parks End, *January* 10.

'... I am delighted with your photograph, you look so well, and the old Pundit at your side looks a veritable Guru[1] in the true sense of the word. I am glad that the Government is giving a grant for the purchase of MSS. I had already proposed this matter when Lord Elgin was Governor, and advised the Government not to make the matter too public, as that raises the price of MSS. at once. Well, a beginning is made.

'I have finished the *Prâtisâkhya*, and the translation is progressing.

[1] Teacher.

I have sent you and Bühler my second edition of *Chips* through the Government, also to Dr. Wilson.

'Kind regards to Bühler. I have not heard from him for a very long time, but have just received his *Âpastamba*, which gives me much pleasure; it is an old friend of mine. What do you think of a *Corpus Inscriptionum Indicarum?* Could that be done in Bombay? Bhao Dagi is sure to have much material. It ought really to be begun soon.'

### To the Duke of Argyll.

Taplow Court, *January* 14, 1869.

'It is certainly true that the religion of the Hindus, as far as we can gather it from their sacred hymns in the *Veda*, is free from everything that strikes us as degrading in the present state of religion and morality in India. But between the ancient religion of India and the religious worship of the present generation there have been several falls and several rises. Buddhism, in the sixth century before our era, was a reaction against the corruptions that had crept into the ancient religion even at that early time. Then Buddhism, starting with the highest aspirations, degenerated into monasticism and hypocrisy, and a most rigorous form of the old Brâhmanic religion took possession of India, and drove Buddhism out of every corner of the country. Since that time there have been several religious reforms, though of a more local character, and this makes it very difficult to generalize and treat the whole religious life of India as one organic body of religious thought. Yet so much may be said with perfect truth, that if the religion of India could be brought back to that simple form which it exhibits in the *Veda*, a great reform would be achieved. Something would be lost, for some of the later metaphysical speculations on religion, and again the high and pure and almost Christian morality of Buddha, are things not to be found in the *Veda*. But, as far as the popular conceptions of the deity are concerned, the Vedic religion, though childish and crude, is free from all that is so hideous in the later Hindu Pantheon.

'With regard to the inevitable decay of religion, a difference ought to be made between two classes of religion, *national* and *personal*. There are ancient religions, like that of Greece, and that of India too, which grow up like national languages, when it is impossible to speak of individual influences, because all individual influence is determined by the silent and almost unconscious approval or disapproval of the community. In these religions I think we can watch for a time a decided progress, a gradual elimination of what is bad, i.e. what is not acceptable to the national conscience.

'But religions, like Buddhism, Mohammedanism, and Christianity too, belong to a different class. They start with a high ideal conceived by a representative man, representative either of a nation or of the whole of humanity, and that high ideal is hardly ever realized; it has to adapt itself to larger circles and lower levels, and can only be kept from utter degeneration by constant efforts at reform.'

To M. Michel Bréal.

Parks End, *February* 19.

'I knew you would be pleased at the result of the last election, but I was glad all the same to receive your congratulations, and to know that you approve of the choice of that distinguished body, which no doubt before long will count you among its members. To me it is the highest honour that could possibly be bestowed upon me. I believe I may honestly say it has been through life the only object of what you may call a foolish ambition. That I should obtain it so soon I did not expect, and I am afraid my success will secure me many *dipsus*, but I have long learned that no one does us so much service as our *dipsus*, *nos amis les ennemis*, and I do not think my head will be quite turned, as I know too well that "merit is the good opinion which our friends have of us," as Lord Palmerston used to say. I hope I shall have the pleasure of seeing you and making the acquaintance of Madame Bréal before this year is over. As soon as three books of mine which are now in the Press are finished, I hope to present them in person to the Academy. The *Prâtisâkhya* is finished, the first volume of the translation is printed as far as page 224, and there is a third little book printing, which is to be a surprise. I hope when I and my wife come to Paris, we shall find you in the full enjoyment of all the pleasures and treasures of a Grihastha. Many thanks for your *Idées latentes du Langage*, which I read at once with the greatest pleasure, as I do everything you write. You know how to prepare your meats, and do not expect your readers to eat raw flesh. M. Brachet's *Grammar* is out. Now that Parliament is sitting, there is little chance of getting a review, but I shall see what I can do. M. Harris is hard at work translating my *Chips*. There is an Italian translation coming out of my lecture on "Stratification." I need not say that the lecture is quite at your service, if you think a French translation would interest people in France. Schleicher's death is a very great loss to us, more even than Bopp's, who had finished his work.'

Max Müller found that incessant work was the only help in these months of anxiety, and, as is shown in the various letters, he had been far from idle. The first volume of *Translations from the Vedic Hymns* came out in May. His lectures this term were on 'Sanskrit Grammar as a Foundation for Philological Research.' In the following letter to Sir George Cox, he upholds Sanskrit and Comparative Philology as the necessary foundation for a study of Comparative Mythology:—

PARKS END, *March* 3, 1869.

'. . . I should like to see you and talk the matter of Comparative Mythology over with you. I cannot help feeling that you work at this subject under great difficulties, and I sometimes doubt whether you ought to give your principal energies to that subject. I speak to you quite openly, for I believe you would be offended if I did not. The most minute criticism of etymological coincidences seems to me the only safe foundation of Comparative Mythology. When there is no etymological foundation I should not venture to take a step, however clear the material coincidences of character, circumstances, and the general *dénouement* might be. I believe you have done good service by pointing out the necessity of admitting a common origin, even when the evidence of the common nomenclature is wanting, but I doubt whether with those principles it is safe to enter upon the treatment of the whole subject. The dangers are very great, and much harm may be done. And when you come to fables or stories of modern date, the dangers become still greater. Here there is an immense literature to master first, i. e. the historical and purely historical evidence of the migration of fables. When the ground has so far been cleared, there comes the labour of tracing back really old common Âryan stories to their roots, whether mythical or proverbial. If therefore you ask me, I tell you openly, do not make Comparative Mythology the principal work of your life, unless you make up your mind first to study Sanskrit and Comparative Philology. I believe you can do far more real and important work in other fields of research, though I should be very sorry if we were not from time to time to get hints and impetus from you on a subject where you certainly have seen beyond the horizon of other scholars. I am just printing a curious collection of Buddhist stories contained in Buddhaghosha's commentary on the *Dhammapada*, and therefore not later than about A.D. 400.'

Early in April he had all his children safe under his roof again, and it was soon evident that any summer plans must be made with reference to their health. The doctor prescribed a foreign bath, and it was finally settled that after Commemoration the whole family should go to Soden in the Taunus, where Max Müller's mother would join them.

Before leaving home Max Müller heard from his friend Dr. John Muir, from Edinburgh, that he had received the first volume of his *Translations from the Vedic Hymns*, 'in which you show a great deal of minute learning. But if you go into everything in the same elaborate way in future, you will require to live to the age of Methuselah to finish your task. I cannot but express the wish that you had translated more and annotated less; that you had given what the world expected from you, a translation at once scholarlike and elegant, and entering into the spirit of Vedic antiquity, exhibiting in short the results of profound research without much display of the apparatus of learning.' The same complaint was made by many other subscribers, and Max Müller soon found that his plan of translation was far too elaborate. A second volume was published, but not till many years later, as Vol. XLVI of the *Sacred Books of the East*, the volume already published, of which Dr. Muir complains, being reprinted with many additional Hymns as Vol. XXXII of that series, in place of another work of which Max Müller was disappointed. Some idea may be gained of the enormous labour bestowed on this volume of translations from the long list of works on the *Veda* which Max Müller had consulted, and to which he fully admits his indebtedness. The list fills six pages octavo. Max Müller held that the first translators of the *Veda* should be decipherers, 'bound to justify every word of the translation in exactly the same way in which decipherers of hieroglyphic or cuneiform inscriptions justify any step they take.'

In another letter Dr. John Muir expresses the wish that more light should be thrown on Buddha, and trusts that Max Müller intends to write more about him. This wish was fulfilled next year by the translation from the Pâli of Buddha's *Dhammapada*, or Path of Virtue, the book he alludes to in the letter to M. Bréal as 'a surprise.'

To M. Regnier (former tutor to the Comte de Paris, and a distinguished Sanskritist).

Parks End, Oxford, *May* 13, 1869.

'My dear Friend,—It is really very provoking to know that you are in England, and that it is impossible to effect a meeting. I have a lecture every day, and during the Whitsuntide holidays we have friends staying with us, and even if I could leave them for a day, I am kept here because the Archbishop of Canterbury, who is the Visitor of our College (All Souls), will be here from Saturday till Tuesday, and all the Fellows have to be in attendance. I cannot ask you to give me a day as I know how much your presence is valued by your old friends, but if you should by any fortunate chance find yourself free for a day, it would be a great treat to me and my wife to receive you at our house and show you our children, who, I am thankful to say, are either getting stronger or are really quite well again. Sunshine seems to have returned to our house with the spring, and at present there are few clouds to be seen, at least no more than we all want to make the sky really beautiful.

'I shall be busy here till about the end of June, and I hope then to go to Paris, though I am afraid I shall find few of my friends there. My plan was to take lodgings at St. Germain or some other place near Paris, and to settle there for some months with my wife and four children, taking our English nurse and a Swiss *bonne* with us. But this plan has become somewhat doubtful because my mother wishes to spend the summer with us in England, and in that case I should probably go to Paris alone and stay only for a fortnight, and then go to fetch my mother from Germany. Could you or Madame Regnier give us any hint as to where and how to settle ourselves near Paris, if we carry out our original plan?

'I am now printing my last volume (second edition, Sanskrit Grammar), of which I enclose the title. *Prâtisâkhya* and *Rig-veda* (translation) are finished, and I look forward with great pleasure to presenting my "thrins" to the Academy.

'I had a letter from M. Guizot, which I value more than many a *cordon* and *crachat*.'

Shortly before leaving for Germany, Max Müller offered Messrs. Longmans a translation of Coquerel's *Apostles' Creed*, an offer that was rejected, as Mr. Longman did not consider the book sufficiently orthodox. Against this opinion Max Müller protests in the following letter:—

OXFORD, *June* 24.

'MY DEAR LONGMAN,—I am sorry to hear that you think Coquerel's book would not sell, though, if it were of so startling a character as you imagine, I should think that it would excite some interest, and have even a commercial success.

'But allow me to say, that though I should not venture to criticize your judgement as far as the commercial success of the book is concerned, I must protest most strongly against the judgement you have formed of its religious character.

'The book is written in a liberal, but in a deeply religious spirit, teaching men to distinguish between the dead crust and the living kernel of Christianity, and warning them against throwing away what is true, eternal, and divine, because in course of time it has been surrounded and almost hidden by what is conventional, changeable, and human. It is an interpretation and historical vindication of the antiquated, almost unintelligible, and certainly widely misunderstood language of the so-called Apostles' Creed, a document which, I feel sure, no educated man and no clergyman in England would take to be the work of the Apostles. The book is written throughout in the most correct language, and there are passages in it which the most eloquent of our bishops need not be ashamed of in the pulpit.

'I write this, not because I wish you to publish the MS., but because I shall be truly sorry if you think I had offered you a book to publish which would shock people far more than anything you have published.'

To the Dean of Westminster.

Parks End, *June* 29, 1869.

'My dear Stanley,—That book of Jacolliot's[1] is as silly, shallow, impudent a composition as ever I saw. It is sad to think that people can still be taken in with such a book. Would you believe that Gladstone was reading it in the midst of the Irish debate! The book quotes from the *Veda!* The extracts are no more from the *Veda* than from the *Koran*. I felt so disgusted that I could read no more; and then people ask me to review such a book—they might as well ask me to fight a shoe-black!

'What I sent you as a first instalment of the *Veda* is real and old—of course no one will read that! Nor do I care. I meant to write an unreadable book, and I believe I have succeeded.

'But I shall soon send you something that is readable—a collection of Buddha's own sayings. I believe the final struggle between Buddhism and Christianity, whenever that comes to pass, will be a hard one, and will end in a compromise—there is a prophecy! that will have to be tested some thousand years hence—therefore, at all events, it is safe. But I am quite serious, and I know you would not refuse Buddha admittance at Westminster, after you have read his λόγια. How small the Irish Church looks from a more (ex)centric point of view, and that is the real charm and the real blessing of researches into the ancient history of thought and faith; they make one feel happy, quiet, and strong, like Scotch mountain air.'

[1] *La Bible dans l'Inde.*

TO THE RIGHT HON. W. E. GLADSTONE.

PARKS END, *July* 9, 1869.

'DEAR MR. GLADSTONE,—"Do not speak to the man at the helm" may, I suppose, be translated freely into "Do not write to the Prime Minister." If I break this useful rule, it is only for one word of explanation. The volume which I took the liberty to send to you is hardly meant to be read; I know it is perfectly unreadable, except for Sanskrit scholars. It is, in fact, but the underground foundation on which the pillars are to rest which are to support the bridge on which people hereafter may walk across from the nineteenth century after to the nineteenth century before our era. At the same time I may say that the few Vedic Hymns which I have translated, or rather deciphered, in the first volume, are genuine relics of the earliest phase of human thought within our reach. Jacolliot's book, *La Bible dans l'Inde*, which I looked at, is beneath criticism, it is simply untrue. The author has been deceived, has deceived himself, and tries to deceive others. I am sorry that my ticket for Antwerp is taken for next Thursday, and that I shall not be able to avail myself of your kind invitation to breakfast, or to carry off the book which you say is waiting for me.'

The book by Jacolliot, *La Bible dans l'Inde*, alluded to in the letters to Dean Stanley and Mr. Gladstone, was a mere imposture, the author purporting to have found the essential features of the Biblical narrative, the Garden of Eden, Flood, &c., given in the sacred books of the Brâhmans. Max Müller was in London one day during the debates on the Disestablishment of the Irish Church, when he heard a quick footstep behind him, and some one touched him on the shoulder. It was Mr. Gladstone. 'Oh, why,' exclaimed the Prime Minister, 'have you not told us of these wonderful discoveries in India?' and then poured forth, in the middle of St. James's Street, his wonder and admiration of *La Bible dans l'Inde*, which he had been studying, when any less versatile statesman would have been entirely absorbed in his great Irish measure. It took some time, not only in St. James's Street, but by letter, before Mr. Gladstone would give up his belief in Jacolliot's nonsense.

The stay at Soden, dull in some ways, was made interesting to Max Müller by finding an old friend, Professor Hertz, whom he had not seen since they were students together at Leipzig. He was watching over a young daughter dying of decline, and, before they left Soden, Max followed his friend's child to her last resting-place. His deep sympathy was a help and stay to the poor parents, and till he joined his loved child some years later, Professor Hertz often wrote, recalling the time at Soden and the intercourse with the friend of his youth. It was at Soden also that Max Müller first heard from Dr. Appleton, of St. John's College, his plans for starting the *Academy*. Max Müller had taken his whole party for an excursion to the ruins of Cronberg, on one of the hills of the Taunus range, and his children were revelling in the enjoyment of a complete day of holiday with their father, whose incessant work made such a treat a rare one. Dinner in the open air was just over, when Dr. Appleton was seen to descend from the coach running between Soden and Cronberg. He had arrived at Soden to find Max Müller gone out for the day, and, absorbed in his own schemes, did not hesitate to follow him and entirely engross him for the rest of the day, to the dismay of his children. When once started, Max Müller was a constant contributor to the *Academy*, till it changed hands, and entirely altered its character as a literary paper about two years before his death. From Soden the party went to Kiel, where the Platt-Deutsch poet Klaus Groth, with whom Max had formed an intimate friendship during the poet's visit to England a few years before, had secured a delightful apartment for them in one of the pretty villas that line the shores of the beautiful harbour of Kiel. It stood at the entrance to Düsternbrook, a fine beech forest, the trees of which hung over the water of the harbour. The garden of the villa ran down to the water, which is scarcely salt, and has little or no tide. Here a happy six weeks was spent, varied by long day excursions with Klaus Groth and his charming wife to all the most beautiful spots round Kiel. A two days' visit was paid to Plauen and the lakes of Holstein in one direction, whilst in another they visited Husum, 'the grey town on the grey (North) sea,' with its flat coast and dykes as in Holland, to make acquaintance with Theodor Sturm, another Platt-Deutsch poet. Later on, before leaving Kiel, Max Müller and his wife went to Copenhagen, with which they were delighted, enjoying the treasures of the Museum of Northern Antiquities, and the beautiful pictures of native Danish art in the palaces. They also visited Elsinore, and looked across to Sweden; the sea, the day they visited Elsinore, was alive with vessels waiting for a favourable wind to take them through the Sound into the Cattegat. The Max Müllers returned to Kiel by the Belts, and stayed a night at Schleswig to see the cathedral with its wonderful wood carvings of the fifteenth century.

During the stay at Kiel, the German Philological Congress held their annual meeting there, attended by people from all parts of Europe. Mark Pattison, Rector of Lincoln College, was present, M. Jules Oppert from Paris, and many others, and it gave Max Müller an opportunity of meeting many engaged in like studies with himself. He read his paper on Buddhist Nihilism referred to before (p. 192) and made his first speech in German at the farewell banquet.

Many evenings during the visit to Kiel were spent either at Klaus Groth's house, or at Forsteck, an exquisite place belonging to Herr Meyer, a Hamburg merchant, commanding a view of the broadest portion of the great Kieler Bucht, or estuary, where, at the time of the Crimean War, the whole English Baltic Fleet lay for weeks. On these occasions Klaus Groth always read out some of his Platt-Deutsch poems, which, to English ears, are more intelligible read aloud than when read to oneself: the strange spelling misleading the eye. The pleasure of the time at Kiel was greatly added to by the presence of a cousin, Captain, now General, Stockmarr, with his wife and daughter, who joined many of the expeditions. 'We have had many happy hours together,' writes Max to another cousin, whom he tried to draw to Kiel; but at that time the railway communication between Kiel and places on the Baltic shore was too complicated for short visits, especially where children were of the party. It was for this reason that his old friend Dr. Prowe, from Thorn in East Prussia, was unable to comply with Max's earnest wish for a meeting.

Early in October the whole party, including the mother, returned to Oxford, the two eldest children thoroughly restored to health. The lectures announced for this term were a continuation of the course on Sanskrit Grammar. Among the many letters waiting his return was an invitation from the

Khedive of Egypt to be present at the opening of the Suez Canal, but he had to decline the honour, as taking him away too long from his work.

To Professor Benfey.

*Translation.* Parks End, Oxford, *November* 7, 1869.

'Dear Colleague,—Having returned to England some three weeks ago, I had so many letters to answer that I only now find time to thank you for your valuable present. I have, so far, only glanced at your *History of Philology*, but even this glance has shown me how much material you have again accumulated in this work, and how useful and instructive your book is in every way. I hope soon to have time to read it quietly, but I feel I must not delay in sending you my best thanks.

'My path did not lead me, alas! past Göttingen this time, and my hope of meeting you perchance at Kiel, at the Philological Congress, was not fulfilled. . . .

'My first volume of the *Veda* translation has, I hope, reached you, and I should be glad to receive your opinion about it. According to my judgement there is only *one* scientifically justifiable method of interpreting the *Veda*, viz. to settle completely every word which raises the least doubt. The work is slow and laborious, but if it is not done you never come to a conclusion, and the same questions turn up again and again. Of course, for you and me there are certain things which do not need proofs, but we also made our way slowly through all this, therefore, why not save others this trouble? why not cut off, once for all, all unfounded objections at the outset?

'I hope to send you soon a book on Buddha; that makes me think of your review of my *Essays*: accept my best thanks. . . . Alas! I have to get a new edition of my Sanskrit Grammar ready, which I should like to have done with. . . .'

The Christmas was passed in Oxford, a real German Christmas, with a tree, to which a few Germans in Oxford were invited, and at which the various German dishes and sweetmeats, imported by the old mother, bore a conspicuous part.

# CHAPTER XVII

## 1870

Lectures on the Science of Religion. Keshub Chunder Sen. Franco-German War. LL.D. at Edinburgh. Letters to Dean Stanley. To 'the English People.' Work for Sick and Wounded. North Wales. Letters to Dr. Abeken and Mr. Gladstone. *Chips*, Vol. III.

THIS year, that was to be so full of stirring events, opened quietly for Max Müller, who began at once to prepare the lectures he had undertaken to give at the Royal Institution in February and March on the 'Science of Religion.'

To DEAN STANLEY.

*January* 19.

'I return Clark's[1] letter. I quite feel with you that a man like Clark ought not to be satisfied with simply withdrawing; he ought to work and fight, and not look to others to carry a new Reformation. I do not know much of him, but all I do know of him makes me like him very much. His words would carry weight with many people. It might seem bold and imprudent in Temple, but still I think it would be right if, as a Bishop, he answered Clark's letter, and told him publicly that the Old Testament was not originally written in the language of the nineteenth century, but in old, heavy, poetical Oriental phraseology, and that, unless his difficulties extend far beyond the limits indicated by him, he might well continue to read the Ten Commandments, and afterwards preach a sermon, and tell his congregation, if they need to be told, that God never stood on a hill and opened His mouth to tell them in Hebrew what the still small voice had told Moses, and other prophets too, nay, everybody who would but listen to that voice, viz. that there are laws independent of man, nay, in spite of man, yet irresistibly present in the human conscience. . . . Then why not say, "God spake these words and said"? Is our nineteenth-century language so much better, and is it

[1] Public Orator at Cambridge.

altogether free from imagery or idolism? I shall have to say much stronger things in my lectures, and I am not afraid. People know that there are far greater difficulties that must be met—downright atheism among the high and the low. It is so, I assure you, and you probably know it better than I. And then to hear people fight about Colenso's difficulties, as if true religion had anything to do with them, is disheartening. However, let us look to Rome and that hideous[1] performance which passes all mythology, and be thankful. Ever yours.'

The very title of the lectures at the Royal Institution excited opposition and criticism, many people objecting to the possibility of a scientific study of religions. They were, however, very well attended, but Max Müller purposely postponed the publication, hoping to make the lectures more complete, as it had been impossible to deal fully with so vast a subject in the narrow limits of four lectures. They were first published in 1873, and then only slightly enlarged, as Max Müller had found he could not give the necessary time to perfect them; but as they had been pirated in America, he was driven in self-defence to print them in England. The subject was subsequently carried out in his Hibbert and Gifford Lectures.

On March 20 he writes to tell his wife he had been offered the degree of LL.D. at Edinburgh. 'I really ought to take care not to have my head turned with all the honours; there is really nothing left that I care for now, and I sometimes think the course must soon be run and all the work over.'

The visit to Edinburgh had to be postponed to the summer, partly on account of the lectures, partly because his old mother was still with him.

To his Wife.

Frogmore, *March* 31.

'One line to say that I arrived safe. At the station a carriage was waiting for me, but the Prince is in London, and will only be back in time for dinner. I am in my old room again, and all the servants seem to be the same as before, which is a good sign. Love to the mother, and kisses for the children. The Prince has just called me away.'

[1] The Doctrine of the Immaculate Conception of the Virgin.

TO THE SAME.

FROGMORE, *April* 1.

'We have just come back from London, where we had a very interesting luncheon at the Deanery. No one there but Keshub Chunder Sen and the Prince and I. We soon got into a warm discussion, and it was curious to see how we almost made him confess himself a Christian. He will come to Oxford, and then I hope to see more of him. He is not as handsome as Satyendranâth Tagore, but very intelligent and pleasing. Last night we had a dinner-party—the Dean of Windsor and Mrs. Wellesley, Colonel and Mrs. Gordon, who is a sister of Peel, the Fellow of All Souls, and Mr. Ruthven. We used to know him in the Berkshire Volunteers. The Princess is very kind, and asked after you and the children.'

This was Max Müller's first acquaintance with Keshub Chunder Sen, which ripened into real friendship, and they corresponded till the death of the latter in 1884. Unfortunately all Max Müller's letters to Keshub Chunder Sen, touching on the important work of the Brahma Somâj, seem to have been lost or destroyed.

Two public lectures were given at Oxford in the May Term—'On the Origin of Mythology,' and 'On the Migration of Fables.' The latter was repeated on June 3 at the Royal Institution. Max Müller writes to his wife, who was nursing her father:—

DEANERY, WESTMINSTER, *June* 4.

'I believe my lecture ("On the Migration of Fables") went off very well; the place was as full as it could hold. But I lost all heart for it when you were not there. I must go to Oxford to-day, as Keshub Chunder Sen waits for me at the station.

'Dr. Scott has accepted the Deanery of Rochester, and Jowett will be Master of Balliol. I am truly glad, for though it comes late it will make up for many years of disappointment. Few people know what it is to see the work which one could do best taken away from one, and few people make allowance for it, and how it embitters one. I do like to see things come right in the end, though I know they are always right even if we do not see it. I do not think that Jowett's friends have always thought of what he has suffered, and I trust he will have many years to enjoy his Mastership.'

TO PROFESSOR FREEMAN.

*June*, 1870.

'I have read your second and third lectures[1], and I have no remarks to make beyond what I said about your first lecture, that I hope they will be taken to heart. I sometimes wonder that it should be necessary to say these things again and again, but I believe the confusion in the popular mind arises chiefly from a confusion of terminology, using a terminology which was meant for linguistic purposes for historical or physiological work. Let people classify blood as much as they like, only let them use their own bottles for that, and not bottles that were labelled for the purpose of holding languages. I confess to my mind blood is an irrational and ungraspable quantity, but if people like to dabble in it, let them have their sanguinary amusement. I also confess that I consider all historical notices as to race extremely precarious until you come to writers of our own century. Before Caesar no one knew the difference between a Celt and a German, as little as many of our missionaries know the difference between a Hottentot and Bushman, or between a Tatar and Mongolian. Nearly all that is built on the statements of the ancients as to race, is built on sand; it may be very learned, but it will not stand a breath of harsh criticism. One thing I cannot understand. Who has invented the Iberians? I see them of late cropping out here, there, and everywhere. Whoever brought them to England first? It is by no means easy to get a clear idea what the ancients meant by the Iberians in Spain, and whether that name may be used synonymously with Bask. But the historical Iberians or Ebro-people of Spain never came to England, except at the time of the Armada.or thereabouts. And least of all would they explain the black colouring matter among the English, for according to Napier and Prichard the Basks are fair, their eyes blue, grey, bluish, and light brown, never dark brown. Some observations are different, and give us twenty-five brown against twenty-one blue eyes, and this is used as an argument in favour of a theory that the Basks came from two distinct ethnological stems. In some places the people with blonde hair form a decided majority. As to the skulls, the confusion is equally great; see Pruner Bey, *Sur les crânes basques*, 1867. Then what use can the Iberians be in England? People who believe that the Iberians came to England to introduce a dark pigment, will soon believe that the Buddhists came over from India to build Stonehenge.'

And now for nearly a year to come Max Müller's heart and thoughts were to be absorbed by the great Franco-German

[1] 'History of the Cathedral Church of Wells.'

War. When able to fix his attention on his work he went on with the fifth volume of the *Rig-veda*, and was busy in preparing a third volume of *Chips* for the Press, of which an edition of 3,000 was printed; while this year also saw the publication of his translation of the *Dhammapada*.

TO HIS MOTHER.

*Translation.* *July* 17, 1870.

'These last experiences are terrible; one cannot bear to think of it. A murderous attack just because it seems necessary to the Emperor to make himself popular with his army. The feeling in England is strong against France. I do not for a moment doubt the result. Germany may lose some battles, but Germany cannot be killed. The present devil's brood in France will fall after one lost battle. There is perhaps nothing better for the ultimate consolidation of Germany than this war, for no one who speaks German, be he Hanoverian or Saxon, can hold himself aloof. It is the last chance for Austria. If she is great enough to forget the past and to join Prussia against France her future is secured; if she follows Beust's policy now she is done for. Who knows how long this war may last? I should like to live to see the end. The enthusiasm in Germany must be tremendous; all the young Germans in England are leaving, and I would gladly go with them. All my plans are, of course, upset. I hoped to go to Ems in August, and then we might have met, but one cannot think of that now. It is not really necessary, but it did me such good before that I would have used it as a precaution. Now we shall stay quietly here. On August 1 I have to go to Edinburgh to be made an honorary doctor. I put it off once, and cannot do so again. Later on we may go to the sea, but that is uncertain. My assistant, Dr. Thibaut, received a telegraphic despatch to-day, and is already on the way to Rastadt, which of course disturbs my work a good deal.'

The following letter adverts to a scheme that Max Müller had much at heart at one time, but it led to no practical results in England:—

TO WILLIAM LONGMAN, ESQ.

OXFORD, *July* 12.

'What I talked about with Mr. Cox was not a volume of essays, but something very different. I shall try to explain it to you as shortly as I can.

'In Germany the plan has been adopted for some years of publishing a continuous series of lectures and essays, and it seems to have answered well, and gradually to take the place of monthly and quarterly journals.

'In a Monthly or Quarterly you must print many articles which are mere padding; the publisher has to pay for them, and the buyer has to pay for them, though neither one nor the other wants to have them. For instance, if a man wants to have my four lectures on the "Science of Religion" he must pay 10*s*., and then he has to cut them out, and they look untidy.

'Now if there existed a "series of essays," each essay might be sold for 1*s*. or less, and people would then be able to get what they really want. Those who now subscribe to Quarterlies would subscribe to the whole series; those who want the Physical Science only would take those numbers only which treat of Physical Science, &c.

'You would want about six names to represent the different branches of knowledge, who should be responsible for the character of the essays, and give a character to the series. I have spoken to Huxley and others, and find a general concurrence.

'You will probably object that it would be troublesome and expensive as a matter of publishing. But, on the other hand, it gives you a constant means of advertising. The series itself would hardly require more advertising than a Quarterly: you would give a string of titles from time to time.

'I should propose as a title for the series "*Our Time*, a series of essays and lectures, under the editorship of 1, 2, 3, 4, 5, 6." One series in Germany, "Populäre Vorträge," has reached to several hundreds of essays. In France you have something like it in the *Revue des Cours Littéraires*, only that that is published every month, while my plan is to publish whenever there is fresh material.

'I am not a man of business, but I thought that Mr. Cox might act as a general editor, supported by six special editors, whose names would be a guarantee with the public.'

### To the Dean of Westminster.

Parks End, Oxford, *July* 24.

'I send you a copy of my lectures on the "Science of Religion." I do not wish to publish them now, but I had sixteen copies taken, of which yours is one. By-and-by they will form part of a larger work, if life and strength last long enough to enable me to carry out a plan for which all my studies have formed the preparation.

'My heart is too full to say anything about this terrible war. I believe it is a cup that could not pass. France cannot break a united and strong Germany, and the reckless gambler who usurps the throne of France took advantage of this national jealousy to save himself from his inevitable end for a few years longer. But the misery it brings to thousands of happy homes passes all description! This war can only end either in the destruction of Germany, or in a revenge without a parallel in history.'

To the Same.

Parks End, Oxford, *July* 26, 1870.

'I feel by no means quite happy about the "Traité de paix entre la France et la Prusse." If it is genuine, however, then neutrality on the part of England would be criminal. Even Turkey came forward to assist her enemy Greece when it became a question of putting down brigandage. England and Germany hunted down one Corsican—they ought to combine for the same purpose now. You may have watched the feelings of those who lost a husband, a brother, a son, or a friend in the tragedy of Marathon; multiply that feeling by millions, and you may imagine then what the state of Germany must be at the present moment, when every family trembles for the life of those whom they love most, and who are to be mowed down by the French cannon, simply because one great criminal has been driven mad and desperate. War in Germany is different from war in England. It was easy for the Duke of Wellington to preach moderation at Paris. He had to revenge defeat, but no outrages, whilst every German soldier that marches into Paris (and I trust I shall live to see it!) has to revenge the blood of brothers, and tears such as only a mother can shed. I should like to see England, not Russia, as the friend and ally of Germany in this holy war.'

At the end of July Max Müller went to Edinburgh, to receive the degree of LL.D. at the same time as his friend Dr. Acland. The few days' holiday refreshed and cheered him, weighed down as he was by the thought of the war, and all that was at stake for his native country. He wrote to his wife:—

Edinburgh, *July* 31.

'This town is glorious and inspiriting, the true capital of England, far more royal than London. Were I King, I should reside here and leave London to be the great harbour and emporium of the country.'

The following is Professor Macpherson's speech in presenting Max Müller for the degree of LL.D.:—

'I have now to present to you in the name of the Senatus, as one deemed worthy of the same degree, another very eminent Professor in the University of Oxford—Max Müller. I do not think it necessary to mention any of the numerous University honours which he has received, or to give you a catalogue of the great literary and scientific societies that have sought to do themselves honour by enrolling him amongst their members. His name is too well known among us to require such an enumeration. Those who have not had the pleasure of listening to his delightful lectures in this city know him well through his writings. In the University of Oxford he has done more, probably, than any other man to establish the study of modern languages in what used to be considered the throne of the dead languages; and he did so at a period when he was engaged in giving to the world writings which were composed in a language which was dead long before Greek and Latin, I may say, were born. When England was engaged in the Crimean War, it was Max Müller who supplied English ignorance by writing upon the languages of the seat of war. When philologists were beating about, seeking here and there some solution or explanation of the endless facts which had been accumulating for half a century, it was Max Müller who came forward with his Science of Language. And now, when England is agitated with discussions on religious faiths and religious doctrines, Max Müller again steps forward with his Science of Religion, his lectures upon which bear all the impress of his learning and his genius, and breathe a spirit of religious love and toleration, which, if it could be extended to other religious discussions, would take from them the reproach of acrimony which has so often been cast upon them. It is a remarkable circumstance, considering the great stake which Britain has in the East, that it was left to Max Müller to bring in a worthy shape before the world the text of the *Rig-veda*—the value of which is acknowledged by all scholars and by all thinkers throughout the world. As to the manner in which he has done so, a verdict of approval has been pronounced by the scholars of all Europe; and as to his acquaintance with Eastern religious systems, the best testimony to that is the appreciation which his work has received from the Brahmins of India, who revere the name of Max Müller, thank him for his labours, and regard him as the great exponent of their religious doctrines in Europe. With regard to his qualifications for the performance of such a task, I know of no man who could have combined with these qualities the power of generalization which he possesses, the power of detecting truth beneath the accumulations of mythology and beneath the decay of tongues, the power of educing principle and order where apparently there is nothing but confusion and chaos. It is the combination of these qualifications which has enabled him to render such incomparable service to the Science of Comparative Philology and Comparative Mythology, and which has made him conspicuous both as a discoverer and as a presenter in the most interesting and popular form of the results of the labours and discoveries of others. No man has done so much to raise these to the dignity of a science; no man has done so much to popularize topics which formerly were considered fit for discussion only in the closet; and he has done this without departing from the method of severe scientific treatment: he has done it by the charm of the manner in which, in a pure and lucid English which the natives of his adopted country do sincerely envy while they rejoice to read it, he presents an endless array of facts in new and surprising combinations. In a word, his edition of the *Rig-veda*, his lectures upon the "Science of Language," and his lectures upon the "Science of Religion," place him in the very foremost rank of scholars and of thinkers, whether as regards extent of knowledge, or force and originality of speculation.'

Max Müller always felt at Edinburgh, and later at Glasgow, the stimulating influence of intercourse with men ready to talk on the subjects in which they were engaged, and to which they had devoted their lives, and contrasted it with the fear of 'talking shop' that prevails in England. On his return he was again absorbed in the war, and all the work in his house for the sick and wounded.

To his Mother.

*Translation.* *August* 14.

'You can fancy all our thoughts are with Germany, and I wish I were there. Such a triumph of a good cause has seldom been seen in history. Where are Adolf and Fritz[1]? I hope on the Rhine, perhaps already in France. The English are quite amazed at these results, and not quite pleased, but that does not matter. G. collects and works. She has collected already £100, and shrinks from no trouble. Here large collections are being made. That Emilie is still so angry with Germany astonishes me; the heart of every German must beat with joy, and all must be forgotten that recalls the old misery.'

To E. A. Freeman, Esq.

*August* 14.

'I ought to have written to you before, but you may imagine where all my thoughts are just now. Though I never doubted of ultimate

[1] Soldier cousins.

success, I was afraid of reverses in the beginning. Now I expect the war will soon be over, and what I looked forward to for the last eighteen years almost every day as I opened the paper—the downfall of the Empire—has come to pass at last. A more demoralized and demoralizing government than that of Louis Napoleon, history I believe has seldom known. There will be a national bankruptcy too, I have no doubt, and millions of French money will be found in the English funds. Peace will be easy, for Germany wants no conquests, not even Alsace and Lorraine; the land is fine enough, but the people are not worth having. Perhaps France will in future be less eager to guarantee the *status quo* of Germany! Now about the Illyrians; though I do not like to quote my own books, I think I can answer your questions best if for the Illyrians I refer you to a tolerably full account of them in my *Survey of Languages*, second edition, pp. 50–60, and as to the untrustworthiness of classical authorities for ethnological purposes, to a note in my *Lectures on the Science of Language*, Volume I, p. 130.'

TO THE DEAN OF WESTMINSTER.

PARKS END, OXFORD, *August* 23, 1870.

'Yes, these are great days, almost overpowering events. If all goes well, and if the author of this atrocious war is punished, people even in England will believe again that there is a God in history. I tremble for the Crown Prince—the French will fight with fury when they fight *pro aris et focis*, and not for glory and empire. I think we ought on the whole to be satisfied with the state of public feeling in England. Unfortunately Gladstone's mind has taken hold of the idea of neutrality, and squeezed it and defined it till it means abdication of the right of judging between right and wrong, between war and murder. This is a most demoralizing policy, but it cannot be helped now. All liberal and independent thinkers are caught in Gladstone's ministerial net. I wish Goldwin Smith were in England—some such man is wanted just now.

'I do not wonder that there is a feeling of mistrust with regard to Bismarck. In home politics he is as bad as Lord —— would be, if he were Prime Minister. But one may oppose a man as a Minister without despising him, and the same Minister, however self-willed and tyrannical at home, may be the right man as Foreign Minister. I do not love Bismarck, but I feel prepared to defend every step he has taken since 1866 against all comers. He seems to have been *sans reproche*, though no doubt also *sans peur*. If he was a bird of the same feather as Benedetti, why should he have opposed the Emperor if, by merely shutting his eyes, he could have got all he could possibly want for Germany, and at the same time entangle England and France in a war? If Bismarck is to blame in his foreign policy, every German patriot shares his blame. We wanted to be united, and we have had the *naïveté* to think, as the French papers say, that we could arrange our internal affairs without consulting France. If France thinks she has a right to interfere at Rome, at Madrid, and now at Berlin too, she must learn that this cannot be. France has been cruelly treated by the Emperor--how extraordinary that there should be no man to take his place, and to save France!

'We have collected about £120 at Oxford, though nearly everybody is away. My wife has a regular workshop going on all day long, making bandages, &c. &c. Did Lady Augusta receive my book for Princess Louise, or came it too late?'

To THE SAME.

PARKS END, OXFORD, *August* 30.

'... I cannot tell you how this war crushes me. I sometimes feel as if I could bear it no longer and must be off. What savages we are in spite of all these centuries! But surely the Teutonic race is better than the Latin and Slavonic, and the Protestants are better Christians than the Romans; and the German cause is surely thoroughly righteous, and the French thoroughly unrighteous. I always think of the simple soldiers—those who were everything at home, and are nothing in the field of battle—unknown, unnoticed, and probably better and braver than emperors and kings and generals. I cannot get my thoughts away from them.'

On August 29 Max Müller wrote the first of his five letters in the *Times* addressed 'to the English People.' They were reprinted, together with letters from Mommsen, Strauss, and Carlyle, in a small volume, early in 1871, and sold for the good of the Victoria Institute for German Widows and Orphans. The first letter was called forth by a violent attack made by his old and honoured friend, Sir Harry Verney, on the policy of Germany, accusing Bismarck of having been willing to accept Holland, and give up Belgium and Switzerland to France. Such had been more or less Benedetti's scheme, but it is well known now that Bismarck did not listen to these ideas. Max Müller was no admirer of Bismarck, but he felt bound, much as he disliked the unconstitutional proceedings that had marked his internal government, to protest against this attack on his public honour.

To Dr. Abeken (then acting as Bismarck's secretary) [1].

*Translation.* Oxford, *September* 9.

'I send you enclosed cuttings, but doubt whether you will receive them in these chaotic times. If you do receive my letter, it is to tell you that here also a German heart beats full of pride and joy, and often with pain, when it thinks of the friends who have dreamt of this great time of Germany's elevation, but who have not lived to see it realized.'

To his Mother.

*Translation.* *September* 11.

'What great times we live in! though so far away, I can hardly keep myself quiet; one lives on newspapers and telegrams. And then I had so much work that had to be done, that I was at last quite exhausted from excitement and work, and went alone for a week to Brighton. The sea air and bathing did me great good, and I came back on Thursday. G.'s father was here on a visit, so G. could not go with me, though she needs change, and I think in a few days we shall make a little tour together in Wales. You have no idea how hard G. has worked. She will tell you all she has collected. . . . The feeling in Germany must be very sad, in spite of the mighty results, for what terrible sorrow there must be throughout the country! Here in England feelings are much divided. I have fought fiercely in the *Times*, and I think it has told. The best part of the nation is for Germany, but the aristocracy has strong sympathy with France. People are amazed at the gigantic resources of Germany, and the utter moral rottenness of France. Well, in the next few weeks Paris will be won; then our troops will march home. Alsace and Lorraine will be governed militarily, and in France they can then slaughter themselves as they like.'

To Moncure Conway, Esq.

*September* 14.

'My wife has been collecting as much as she could get, and I know from letters received that her collection has done real good to the sufferers in different hospitals. You know that German hospitals are full of French wounded, and I believe if any distinction is made between the French and German wounded in these hospitals, it is in favour of the French. Anyhow, in the presence of death, nationality

[1] Dr. Abeken had been a great friend of Baron Bunsen, at whose house Max Müller had learnt to know and estimate this upright, single-minded man at his right value.

vanishes and humanity takes its place. My wife begs me to say that she will gladly forward any sum however small. She has more appeals than she can respond to. I should pay no attention to newspaper rumours as to what the Germans mean to do with regard to the conditions of peace. The King's behaviour towards the Emperor is mistaken chivalry towards a fallen enemy, nothing more. I think, however, that there ought to be a formal abdication, or a formal decree of a Constituent Assembly transferring the sovereign power from the Emperor to the Provisional Government, or to a President; otherwise it seems impossible to make a treaty of peace. I believe the general opinion in Germany requires no territorial aggrandizement, but the military authorities will probably require a better strategic frontier line, which Germany asked for at the Congress of Vienna, but which she could not obtain then, owing to the intrigues of Austria and Russia. If the inhabitants of that district are devoted to France, and cannot bear the idea of belonging again to Germany, they are free to emigrate. Surely patriotism has made greater sacrifices than this.'

During September Max Müller heard from his old friend Stanislas Julien, the famous Sinologue, in a state of almost childish panic at the approach of the German armies. He had recently lost his wife. Max Müller at once offered him an asylum under his roof; but the old man, though *vivement touché* at his friend's invitation, resolved to stay and guard his precious library and house, on which he had spent large sums, and he went through all the sufferings of the siege. But it undermined his health, and he died about two years later.

TO MONCURE CONWAY, ESQ.

PARKS END, *September* 16, 1870.

'I read your letter with great interest. I believe you are quite right in your estimate of Bismarck, but I think you underrate the capacities of the King. The King is a strange mixture; he was a mere soldier, but he learnt much during his long stay in Bunsen's house. He will never be guilty of such folly as to reinstate Napoleon; but the situation is difficult. Suppose Paris surrendered, which I trust it will do after the first shot, what can the German army do but go into winter quarters in Alsace and Lorraine? There may be a provisional treaty of peace, but it seems to me that, as the Constituent Assembly is convoked, it can be ratified by that Assembly and its delegates only. If the Constituent Assembly should fail, then nothing remains but to convoke the Legislative Assembly and the Senate, both of which still exist both *de jure* and *de facto.* I confess I cannot understand the enthusiasm for the French Republic. A republic is perhaps the most perfect form of government, but also the most difficult. There are good and there are bad republics, and the present French Republic seems to me the most imperfect political organization that can be imagined. I should prefer the Russian or the Chinese régime to the present state of things in France. It seems to me that the enthusiastic admirers of this republic, which has nothing but the name of a republic, exceed in folly the old Legitimists, to whom a King, however foolish and wicked, is a kind of idol to be worshipped with unquestioning devotion. It is very possible that Alsace might recover itself and become German, but I doubt whether it is wise to weaken France at the very moment that Germany becomes so much more powerful. As to making France harmless, that can never be done, and I doubt whether, for the sake of Germany, it is desirable. I hope Moltke will take as little as possible, and Bismarck will make it quite clear that what is taken is taken for strategic purposes only, and not for the sake of aggrandizement, and in order to recover some few millions who formerly were Germans. I hope you will publish your impressions of the war and Bismarck.'

### To the Same.

Parks End, *September* 18, 1870.

'I did not know that the description of the battle of Rezonville in the *Daily News* was yours, and I am glad to hear that we shall have it in a more permanent form in next *Fraser*. I do not expect that anybody will see such fighting again, though, from what I see in the French papers, there will be, I fear, some mad attempt of fighting in and around Paris. The worst effect of Imperialism is that it has stunted a whole generation, and there is hardly one man who towers a head above the mob. They have no statesmen, and Jules Favre himself is reported to have declared that he could not make peace *because his life would not be safe!* Is that statesmanlike or soldierlike? Prévôt Paradol would not have said that! It is fearful to see such a country as France so entirely demoralized, abandoned, ruined; it will take generations to build her up again. Circumstances so exceptional as the present state of France would seem to justify exceptional measures on the part of the other Powers. England will not act alone, and unfortunately there is no cordial feeling between England and the United States. Besides, Mr. Motley is, I suppose, no longer Minister. What I should like to see would be a journey of Mr. Gladstone and Motley to the head quarters of the King of Prussia. They would be able to arrange a peace without a single threat, for Germany is as anxious for peace as France is, and they might lay the foundations of a league between the three Teutonic Powers that would be a guarantee of peace for centuries. France would listen to America, Germany to England, and England and America would be drawn together again by the good work which they would do in common. Bismarck is quite powerful enough to make Germany feel ashamed of any wish of territorial aggrandizement; and all that Moltke wants are the house-door, the bolt and keys of Germany. I shall have to run away from Oxford for a few weeks before term begins, and I hope to be off by Tuesday for North Wales.'

TO THE DEAN OF WESTMINSTER.

CARNARVON, *September* 30, 1870.

'MY DEAR STANLEY,—I was so overdone that I ran away to Wales. We had splendid weather, and enjoyed our rambles immensely. Alas! the English Government is weaker than I expected; they do not seem to perceive that, since the destruction of the Western Empire, nothing like the present events has happened. Germany would be thankful for a little friendly coercion, but what Germany expected was a recognition of the righteousness of her cause, a fact now admitted by France, but not yet by England, except by Lord Russell. This kind of neutrality demoralizes England, and blunts the edge of her moral conscience. I expected something very different from Gladstone.'

The end of September the Max Müllers, both tired out with work for the sick and wounded, spent a delightful fortnight in North Wales, climbing Cader Idris and Snowdon, and exploring each lovely valley.

Scarcely had they settled quietly at home than the work began again, and Max Müller found himself involved on all sides in long correspondence on the subject filling his heart as well as his thoughts.

TO DR. ABEKEN.

*Translation.* PARKS END, OXFORD, *October* 6, 1870.

'DEAR SIR AND FRIEND,— . . . Gladstone is the soul of the Cabinet, a man of slow resolution, but of inflexible will if once the resolution has been made. As far as I know him, he is on our side, not from natural sympathy, but from conviction, from a feeling of right and of duty. He was the only Minister who recognized our right in the Danish question, and who called the Treaty of London a bad continuation of the Vienna treaties. His sympathies are more Latin than Teutonic, as you know, and the commercial prosperity of France had so dazzled him, that he declared hardly a year ago that France would grow to be the Queen of Europe. It will be difficult for him and for many Englishmen to take in the new position of the world calmly and from the right point of view; but he is nearly the only English statesman whose stern uprightness I have never doubted, and who is so entirely guided by noble motives even where he makes mistakes.

'I intend writing to Gladstone, somewhat to this effect:—

'1. The thought of conquest of territory and the acquisition of non-German subjects is foreign to us.

'2. It is a fate which Germany has not brought about, that has brought Alsace and Lorraine into the possession of the German army.

'3. No prince and no statesman in Germany is strong enough to give up again for any price a possession so dearly bought.

'4. The settling of the boundary requires no Congress or diplomatic understanding. It is a purely military question, and in consequence can only be decided by a Military Commission. Germany does not wish for any Frenchmen, nor for one inch of country, only what is indispensable to her future security.

'I am writing this in a great hurry to catch the post.

'Well, once more: do not give any weight to the anti-German outbreaks of the English Press; they come mostly from a French and Old-Danish source.

'The republican sympathies are absurd, and only help us and do no harm. Sir H. Verney has improved, but not enough yet: he is getting old.

'The collections in England are beautiful, larger than for their own patriotic funds after the Crimean War. A recognition on the side of Germany, *especially before the French do so*, would have a good effect, and might be a good occasion of mentioning some useful truths.'

To the Right Hon. W. E. Gladstone.

Parks End, *October* 6, 1870.

'My dear Mr. Gladstone,—If you knew what an effort it has been to me *not* to write to you on some of the events of the last months, you would require no assurance of my readiness to answer, as well as I can, the inquiries contained in your letter of October 4, which I received this morning. I have no hesitation in asserting that the conquest of territory inhabited by people that are not German in national sentiment is an idea repugnant to the German mind. Count Bismarck, whose power arises chiefly from his accurate knowledge of the German character, and who is simply carrying out with the prudence and courage of a statesman what all German patriots have been yearning for during the last fifty years, would never venture on a war of conquest. The tradition that Alsace and Lorraine belonged once to Germany has never been forgotten by the people. German statesmen claimed these provinces in 1815, but Russia supported France in resisting their claim. One of our most popular German poets, Max von Schenkendorf, who died in 1817, wrote:—

> "Doch dort in den Vogesen
> Liegt ein verlornes Gut,
> Da gilt es, deutsches Blut
> Vom Höllenjoch zu lösen."

But an offensive war against France, to recover that "lost patrimony," would have been impossible in Germany.

'Events, however, have happened for which Germany is not responsible. France has attacked Germany with the avowed purpose of annexing German soil. The French army has been beaten back, and the German army, in pursuing the enemy, finds itself in actual possession of Alsace and Lorraine. The sacrifices on the part of Germany have been enormous: there is hardly a German family from the Vistula to the Rhine which is not in mourning. It is a mercy that there have been no German reverses, and that the atrocities of former French invasions have not been repeated. There would have been a feeling of righteous anger and fury before which no stone would have remained upon another at Paris. It is a mercy that this feeling of revenge does not exist. But a new current of national feeling has sprung up in Germany, which rests simply on facts, and which no King, no Minister, would be able to resist. Alsace, they say, is ours, and our sons shall not have died in vain. The thousands and thousands of German hearts that lie buried in Alsace and Lorraine have made that soil German once more. Were Prussia to yield Strassburg and Alsace, she would cease to be Prussia.

'In answer to your first question, therefore, I have no doubt that Count Bismarck did say what M. Jules Favre reported him to have said, that, whether the inhabitants of Alsace hate us or no, we shall hold Alsace for Germany.

'You say "it would surprise you to find that I thought these people could properly be annexed to Germany, if their heart is in France as their country." My answer is this. To conquer a province for the sake of territorial aggrandizement, and to annex people who do not wish to be annexed, would be an outrage of the moral sense of Europe. This is what France intended to do. To hold a hostile province which has been conquered in a defensive war, and with it the people who inhabit that province, is an evil, I grant, but it may be a necessary evil, and it can never be a crime. Anyhow, a culprit who is sent to prison has no right to complain that he is being annexed. I say nothing of the language of Alsace and Lorraine, for the annexation, if it takes place, does not take place on linguistic grounds. I say nothing of the friendly or unfriendly feeling of the people, for the annexation is not advocated on sentimental grounds.

'The annexation is the result of a war forced upon Germany, and the occupation of French territory must be justified on military and strategic grounds. Germany is determined to make herself as safe against France as she can make herself, and no Power in Europe would gainsay her right, nay, her duty, to do what she considers best for her future security.

'The frontier line that is to protect Germany against France can hardly be considered a matter to be settled by a Congress of diplomatists: it can be properly settled by a Military Commission only. Count Bismarck knows perfectly well that a disaffected province is no addition to the strength of a country, but he would probably bow to the judgement of Count Moltke in determining the positions that seem best to secure the safety of Germany. On such points, however, the opinion of military authorities from other countries might justly claim to be heard, and might induce the German strategists to draw the line so as to include as little as possible of purely French soil, and to annex as few as possible of purely French inhabitants. The question of Luxemburg might possibly be reopened and facilitate arrangements in Alsace and Lorraine. I believe that the statements of the hostile feeling pervading all classes of society in Alsace are exaggerated. It is true that I judge from the accounts published by German travellers; but they were published before the war, and when no one thought of annexation. As to accurate statistics, they are to be found in R. Böckh, *Der Deutschen Volkszahl und Sprachgebiet*, Berlin, 1870. The German portion of Alsace comprises half a million inhabitants, that of Lorraine 297,500, of which one-ninth part has become French during the last two centuries. The German inhabitants of Alsace and Lorraine, though they were never considered as the equals of true Frenchmen, have no doubt been greatly humoured by the French Government; and as long as France was "La Grande Nation," and Germany no nation at all, it was easy to rouse a feeling of pride among the Alsacians, not against Germany, which did not exist, but against the petty nationalities of Baden, Hesse, Wurtemberg, Bavaria, &c. In future, when France will be no longer "La Grande Nation," though always "une grande nation," the idea of being a German, and not a Frenchman, will be less intolerable than heretofore.

'And if there are people in the annexed portions of Alsace and

Lorraine who cannot bear the idea of belonging to Germany, surely it is not too much to expect from their patriotism that they should follow the example of thousands of German families which emigrated to Philadelphia when Alsace was annexed to France. When the flower of a nation is ready to die for their country, those who have the option of emigrating from Alsace to France proper are not so greatly to be pitied.

'My great anxiety through all this war has been the unfriendly feeling that is springing up between England and Germany. The whole future of the world seems to me to depend on the friendship of the three Teutonic nations, Germany, England, and America. If Germany is estranged from England, she must become the ally of France and Russia, which would mean another century of imperialism and despotism. Can nothing be done to heal the breach?'

### TO DR. ABEKEN.

*Translation.* *October* 7, 1870.

'... The idea of a Congress is ridiculous, but it is much liked, especially among the diplomatists, though Gladstone does not care for it.... He would like to treat the matter more from a military point of view. A Military Commission would deal with the question in a more technical way, and there would be less talk about France's dishonour, and such-like phrases. Should the question about Luxemburg come up again, it would be a most natural thing to invite the Powers concerned to a Military Conference. Of course I understand nothing of all these matters, and I only speak as a member of the Parliament of "public opinion." The only thing for which I feel useful, and perhaps have been of use, is to keep up the good feeling between England and Germany. If this is also your purpose, please consider me at your service at any time. Ever yours.

'Is there no quicker way to Versailles than via Berlin?'

### TO HIS MOTHER.

*Translation.* *October* 9.

'Though you wish for no congratulations on your birthday, I must still write to you, to comfort you in your loneliness. Many, many who used to meet you on this day with joy, are gone before you, and you miss their presence which you so enjoyed. But they are lost to your sight only, not to your heart, and that which really belonged to you in them, can never be lost to you. Our life here is not our own work, and we know that it is best for us all, just as it is. We ought to bear it, and we must bear it; and the more patiently, yes, the more joyfully we accommodate ourselves to it, the better for us. We must take life as it is, as the way appointed for us, and that must lead to a certain goal. Some go sooner, some later, but we all go the same way, and all find the same place of rest. Impatience, gloom, murmurs, and tears do not help us, do not alter anything, and make the road longer, not shorter. Quiet resignation, thankfulness, and faith help us forwards, and alone make it possible to perform the duties which we all, each in his own sphere, have to fulfil. May God, who has laid many burdens on you, give you the courage to bear them quietly to the end. The darker the night, the brighter the stars in the heavens.

'We have had a delightful time in North Wales, walking everywhere, as if we were as young as ten years ago. I wish Emilie had come to England, as she could not go to Paris; though, if she has no feeling for this wonderful uprising of the German Fatherland, we should not have had much peace together, for I can think of hardly anything else, and G. is more German even than I am. Even for you it must be glorious to have lived to see these great events. The sacrifice is great and terrible, but it has not been in vain. Peace cannot be far off. The French are already becoming reasonable, and should be thankful to have a province like Alsace, only half French and once entirely German, which they can give up without shame; the shame for them is in quite a different direction, not in the punishment, but in the light-hearted folly of which they must now pay the cost.

'We have still a little money by us, if anything special is wanted, and plenty of warm things for the winter. The collections in England have been splendid. Why do the people in Germany abuse England so? They could not expect England to go to war, and that export of arms is nothing. Such snarling is unworthy of Germany.'

### To the Right Hon. W. E. Gladstone.

Parks End, *October* 9.

'Dear Mr. Gladstone,—I wish the French could be made to see that there is no dishonour in taking the punishment which this war has brought on them. If Jules Favre can bring himself to call the war criminal, can he wish the crime to go unpunished, or does he think that such a crime can be atoned for by a mere fine? Jules Favre and all who protested against the war may well say, "Delicta maiorum immeritus lues, Romane," &c., &c.'

### To Mr. Bellows.

Parks End, *October* 11.

'I was glad to hear so promising an account of your little Max. I have a little boy some three years old, and I imagine, just like you, there is nothing like him. I am sorry to hear of the interruption of your Dictionary. I shudder when I think of Paris. I spent some happy years there, and have still several old friends living there, and to think of that town being bombarded! And yet what is the German army to do? and is not every one of the thousands of people that have been killed more precious than the whole of Paris?'

### To Dr. Abeken.

*Translation.* Parks End, Oxford, *October* 11, 1870.

'Dear Sir and Friend,— . . . It is clearer than ever to me, that if you wish for a common understanding with England, you will find it best secured on a military basis. That Germany has a right to secure her position strategically is granted. It remains to demonstrate, (1) that there is no other means to such security but the annexation of Alsace and a part of Lorraine; (2) that the fortresses, which threatened Germany formerly, will not become a menace to France henceforth.

'There are in England also some voices in favour of a *plébiscite* in the parts to be annexed. To me it seems an un-German comedy, which however might be acted in Alsace with good prospect of success, "by desire."

'The French refugees are very numerous in England, and they make mischief in all circles of society. Germany is too great to enter upon a paper war. Also with regard to the export of arms, nothing can be done before Parliament meets.'

### To the Same.

*Translation.* Oxford, Parks End, *October* 25.

'First of all, many thanks for your valuable letter. I had not expected an answer from you, for I know what you have on your shoulders now, but it was a great satisfaction to me to know that I was not mistaken, and that with regard to England our goal is the same. Much might be said with regard to the paths to this goal, but there is no time for that now. Here the situation of things is a very difficult one. Lord Granville is neither a Clarendon nor a Palmerston, but he has the best intentions, and is amiable to everybody. He has many French friends, and of course the French are everywhere in London now. The *Times* is very kind at present. It

has printed a letter of mine to-day, which I enclose. It is meant for England, of course, or I should have used stronger language. The speech of Du Bois-Raymond is much too strong for English readers, and would only rouse ill feelings.

'You know, perhaps, that a French loan has to-day been launched on the English market. You know, of course, also that a German loan would have great success here. Though it does Prussia much credit that she seeks for no foreign loans, yet in so doing she forgoes much of the sympathy which in England, as everywhere else, is felt for one's debtors. Many of the most eager friends of the French are interested in the French funds—*hinc multae lacrymae!* . . .

'If I can be of any help, do make use of me. My influence on the *Times* is, however, *nil*; they only print what suits them. All I can do is to make what I write palatable.'

The second letter to 'the People of England,' in the *Times* of October 22, was in answer to M. Arlès Dufour's appeal to the English nation to save Alsace and Lorraine. The three last letters were answers to 'Scrutator's' letters in the *Times*. It is an open secret now who was the inspirer of 'Scrutator's' letters. 'The hands were the hands of Esau, but the voice was the voice of Jacob;' and before he wrote his last letter Max Müller felt very certain that he 'was called on to withstand in argument one of the most powerful athletes of our time.'

It is impossible now not to see how much of the present ill feeling in Germany against England dates from the year 1870. Without swerving an inch from the position of neutrality rightly observed by the English Government, the justice of the cause for which Germany was fighting, and the reckless wickedness of the French in attacking her, might have been acknowledged by those in power, whereas Mr. Gladstone's preference for the Romance over the Teutonic nations was well known in Germany, and the general apathy, if not antipathy, of the English to the German cause was universally attributed in Germany to his influence.

The third volume of *Chips* came out in the autumn, a very large edition being printed. A second edition of Max Müller's *Sanskrit Grammar* also was brought out. Both were well received. One review states that:—

'Every paper in Mr. Max Müller's third volume of *Chips from a German Workshop* is valuable. Applied to them, the term exhaustive

has really a meaning. Mr. Max Müller always draws from a full cask. He does not write, as so many now do, because he is expected to say something, but because he has something to say. The subject does not make him, he makes the subject. His range, too, is something enormous.'

The *Globe* considered that:—

'A more delightful volume has not been published for a very long time. Bearing marks on almost every page of the profoundest scholarship, it is absolutely free from all taint of that pedantry which is the besetting sin of most German writers.'

Of the *Sanskrit Grammar* a reviewer says:—

'It has been the aim of Mr. Müller to produce a work which should combine the clearness of Bopp with the accuracy of Colebrooke and the native writers whom that great scholar took as his model. In this his success has been so great that the *Sanskrit Grammar for Beginners* is by far the best book that can be put into the hands of a student. In a word, it combines Oriental fullness and accuracy with the European method. It says much, both for the progress of Sanskrit in this country, and for the value of Mr. Müller's own labours, that this admirable Grammar has already reached a second edition.'

To E. A. FREEMAN, ESQ.

*November* 12.

'I thought it possible that my new volume of *Chips* might tempt you to a review. I am not going to write any *captatio benevolentiae*, though I am going to ask a favour. In the two essays "Are there Jews in Cornwall?" and "St. Michael's Mount," I have had to work through a good deal of matter with which no one is so familiar as you, viz. ecclesiastical antiquities. I want very much to know from some competent person whether I am right or wrong. Therefore the favour I ask is this: if you should review my book, would you look at these two essays more particularly, and give me the benefit of your criticism on any points where I may have gone wrong? I meant to have written to you to ask your advice on these essays before they were printed, but I know you are a busy man, and therefore did not wish to take up any of your time. In the essay on "Cornish Antiquities" you will find, I think, that we hold the same opinions on English Ethnology.

'I am quite miserable about Gladstone. England will never have such an opportunity again. Now it is lost, irretrievably lost. With Germany as a friend, the Black Sea question would have been solved amicably, and the German vote in America would have kept the Irish

vote in order, so as to prevent mischief about the *Alabama*. Now the sin is sinned!'

To the Right Hon. W. E. Gladstone.

Parks End, *November* 12, 1870.

'My dear Mr. Gladstone,—I am surprised to hear that my new volume of *Chips from a German Workshop* has not yet reached you. I have written to my publisher, but I hope that by this time the volume may be already in your hands. No doubt the military authorities, who maintain that the south-western frontier of Germany is not secure without taking in part of Alsace and Lorraine, ought to be fully persuaded that they do not deceive themselves and render their line of defence less secure than it is at present. I, of course, know nothing of military science, but I have great confidence in the calm judgement of Moltke. It was for that very reason that I thought a Military Conference the only scheme that could lead to practical results, though, as long as cession of territory was excluded on principle, discussion would have been useless. I am afraid that *now* a conference of military authorities is no longer possible. I have often watched with wonder a pointsman on a crowded railway station, who holds in his hands the fates of thousands, and who by a movement of his hand, hardly perceptible to others, sends one train to the right and the other to the left. . . . I feel as if two trains, both holding dear friends, had just started, though not in the direction in which I hoped they would have gone.'

To E. A. Freeman, Esq.

*November* 27, 1870.

'My dear Freeman,—. . . I want to know whether I am right in declining Dr. Bannister's arguments. Could a man at that time have held land under a Jew? What is the most likely meaning of *le Jeu?* not *le Juif*, surely? I meant Gladstone's Roman and Romance sympathies for France, and his utter inability to appreciate the character of the struggle now going on between Germany and France. He is fully convinced in his heart that every German is a heretic *sive* Protestant, a barbarian, and a villain. He might make a few charitable exceptions in favour of two or three Germans whom he happens to know, and who have had the benefit of a tub, physical and intellectual, in England. Happily the feeling towards England in really influential quarters in Germany is good. Bismarck's papers have never joined in the anti-English barking of the newspapers. The talk about the exportation of arms is silly. I wish the French had bought their arms in Germany. The sooner there is an end of

that kind of international law the better. Let everybody sell what he can, and let everybody capture what he can; everything else is mere deception and hypocrisy. If Gladstone had ever to confess that he was the writer of the article in the *Edinburgh*, it might make mischief, for even Bismarck is only a man. But what the real statesmen in Germany want is an alliance offensive and defensive with England: there is no better way for securing peace in Europe. France and Russia are the disturbers of the peace; but, with the English fleet and the German army as the police of Europe, no cock would dare to crow at Paris, no bear would growl at St. Petersburg. England might have had the alliance of Germany for the asking, and at that very time the writer in the *Edinburgh Review* calls the King of Prussia a hypocrite, Bismarck a villain, and the German people half-civilized brutes!'

To his mother Max Müller writes:—

*Translation.* *November* 29.

'I never said I should like to be a Frenchman, but that I should like to see France strong again, for strong neighbours are good for keeping a country up to the mark, and keep it from arrogance.'

Early in December Max Müller paid the first of several pleasant visits to Hawarden Castle. He woke early in the morning to find a white world, and looking through the window saw Mr. Gladstone making his way alone through the snow to early morning church. He willingly braved the elements later in the day to secure a quiet talk with the Prime Minister.

To his Wife.

Hawarden Castle, *December* 10, 1870.

'I shall not have much time before breakfast, but I just wanted to let you know that here I am, quite safe. A fine large place, full of people. The Bernstorffs are not here; too busy in London. General Burnside was here, dined, and then went off to New York for a week. He is a fine fellow—just like a strong, tall, English general—and he is truly German, and has told Mr. Gladstone some useful truths. Frederick Peel is here and Mr. Haywood, all very pleasant. No talk yet with Mr. Gladstone, except about University matters, but the fight will come, I expect.'

*December* 11.

'There is so much snow that everybody had to stay in. However, Mr. G. and I took a walk through the snow and talked it all over, and I told him that any German statesman who gave up Strassburg

deserved to be hanged, and he shook himself a little, but I think he begins to see that we Germans are not such ogres as he thought. G. is an old friend of Abeken's, but had lost sight of him.'

To Dr. Abeken.

*Translation.* Oxford, Parks End, *December* 13, 1870.

'Dear Friend,—Your letter of December 5 arrived here in good time last Friday, just when I was leaving for Hawarden Castle, where Gladstone had invited me. Count Bernstorff was to be there, but could not get away from London. General Burnside was there, a good ally of the German cause. Above all, however, I must tell you that Mr. Gladstone and Mrs. Gladstone keep your name in friendly and grateful memory; both send their kindest regards to you, and Mr. Gladstone expressed repeatedly how sad, though unavoidable, it was in this earthly existence, that the personal intercourse with men whom we had learnt to love and value highly had to be broken off. It was most fortunate that I could communicate to G. the greater part of your letter; it made a great impression on him. As I told you before, Gladstone's sympathies are by no means for Germany, neither is he familiar with the German language or literature, or the German character or ways; also the French refugees have taken great hold upon him. He distrusts Germany, especially Prussia, and certain unceremonious demonstrations have put him into a bad humour. But he would like to be persuaded, that is clear to me, and if once he perceives the justice of the German claims he is sure to be loyal to his perceptions. The Duc de Grammont has mystified him so much, that Gladstone confessed him to be unreliable. Benedetti's letter in the *Standard* made it easy for me to refute the Duke by means of the Count. If Benedetti keeps his promise of continuing the letters, the only thing remaining of the two cats will be the tails!

'Our conversation dealt chiefly with the provinces to be surrendered. According to G., all our feeling of human dignity is outraged by forcing even one single being to give up his nationality. Of course I could only rejoin that our feelings would be still more outraged by shooting down even one man, and that in order to avoid this alternative, i.e. war, the surrender of certain provinces with their inhabitants has to be taken into consideration. Then followed the question of the real or apparent necessity of the Vosges frontier. I could only reply that this was a question for experts in military and strategic history, and had been discussed continually since 1648, and that friend as well as foe, German as well as Frenchmen, were perfectly at one on this point.

'The question is whether a short representation of this matter, with

which every lieutenant of the Prussian Staff is capable of dealing, would be adequate now. At the close I could only add that at the present juncture of affairs, and in the present mood of the German people and army, a statesman who allows himself to be compelled to surrender Strassburg by threats and not by force would be considered guilty of high treason. G. replied that the greatest mistakes of the statesmen of our century lay in giving greater consideration to the physical than to the moral powers, and that the realization of the German wishes would become a misfortune for Germany. Of course I could only reply that Germany had the right and was in duty bound to decide the question, and that she alone would have to bear the consequences and the responsibility. Many interesting conversations followed, but I do not know whether they are of any interest to you. Gladstone, of course, only spoke for himself, and he remarked several times: "This is *my* opinion. What the Cabinet thinks is quite a different question." He considers the feeling in England not at all unfriendly towards Germany, and I must confess that the German Press seems to me much more hostile than the English. How comes this? In England it is supposed that the German Press says nothing which is not sanctioned by highest authority. This is a general opinion, very difficult to correct. If Germany wishes an understanding with England in the future, both sides must agree to work for it. The opponents of a German-English alliance do not fail to work against it. I told Gladstone clearly that the only sure guarantee for the peace of Europe consisted in combined action between Germany and England, and if the fleet of England and the army of Germany took up again their old fraternal relations no cock in France would crow, no bear in the East would growl. I, of course, remarked in our conversations that he must consider me a *franc-tireur*, as I had never worn a uniform and never would wear one, and that the happiness of two sister nations, in whose union the happiness of mankind consisted, was my earnest wish. There were several members of Parliament present, and also some other influential people, and I had sometimes to maintain a sharp conflict, but "the losses on our side were not important."

'I threw in occasionally a hint that hostile relations between Germany and England would force the former to found a formidable navy, also that the German vote in America had up to the present neutralized the Irish vote. I stayed at Hawarden till last night, and, though I have accomplished nothing, we have certainly parted friends.

'I heard from the German Embassy that a messenger was leaving next Thursday, and that he might take a letter. This gives me an opportunity of sending you a volume, at the end of which you will

find about eighty letters to Bunsen: some of them, I think, might interest you.

'My wife sends her kindest regards. We wish you a bright Christmas, bright through that which alone can give us true joy, i. e. the consciousness of having done our duty and having attained great things. Should you think that the sincere gratitude of one unknown might be welcome to our great *dux* and *auspex*, I ask you, should the opportunity occur, to give expression of my feelings of admiration and gratitude to Count Bismarck; you will do it so much better than I could do it myself.'

Besides several relatives, many of Max Müller's school and University friends were taking active part in the great war, as the following letter to Fontane, the novelist, shows:—

*Translation.* PARKS END, *December* 20, 1870.

'MY DEAR FONTANE,—Nothing for a long time has given me greater pleasure than your letter. I had indeed seen in the papers that you had escaped with a whole skin, but I am glad to hear at first hand that you have returned to Berlin well and strong, and that all goes well with you. The feeling here against Germany is bad, and from pure ignorance; in Germany the feeling seems even worse against England, and from the same cause. It makes one wild, and I have hardly any other thought than how one can help to cure this evil. Help as far as you can!'

TO HIS MOTHER.

*Translation.* OXFORD, *December* 20.

'One gets no rest with this terrible war, and there seems small hope yet of peace. I had a most interesting visit at Gladstone's from December 9–12. It was a great honour, and it is possible it has done some good. He wrote the whole time, so we had to stay in the house, and many were the discussions. Bismarck is much disliked in England: he does mad things, and who knows what enemies he may make. Well, I have done my best, and heard much that was interesting. Also I get some news from Versailles, but that is between us.'

TO PROFESSOR BERNAYS.

*Translation.* PARKS END, *December* 21, 1870.

'MY DEAREST FRIEND,—I feel with you the horrors of this time, and though I am so proud of the heroism of the German nation, I am nevertheless ashamed to think how often the world looked upon the great spiritual victories of the Fatherland with scorn and indifference,

and now is on her knees because we have learnt to aim our bullets with accuracy and skill. However, I trust that the wild beast will soon retire, and that the *spirit* in Germany will attain the upper hand. At all events, Nemesis has arisen with all grandeur, and to have lived to see the fall of Imperialism is a comfort to me. I was somewhat entangled in controversy which was more of an ethical than political nature. My adversary was Gladstone, but we have parted friends. The feeling in England is not good, for many reasons; but it seems to me that the German feeling towards England is still more childish. Till Germany and England recognize that they are sister-nations, there will be no calm in Europe. We all must help to that as far as we can. I have constructed the new volume of my *Chips* with that thought underlying it. . . . Renan is in Paris, Mohl told me, who is in London. London is crowded with Frenchmen, which creates much sympathy with France, especially in Society. Here in Oxford everything is quiet and calm, and I am decorating the Christmas tree for my four children. My work proceeds slowly, for there is hardly any time for anything but for the reading of newspapers. And what are you doing? Pattison is well, always the same.—Always in old friendship, yours.'

### To Professor Klaus Groth.

*Translation.* OXFORD, *December* 22, 1870.

'Your *Quickborn*, received to-day, reminds me of my letter-debts, which I would gladly have paid long ago, but one lives in such a tumult, one can neither read nor write, from the quantities to read in the papers. So, first of all, my thanks for this new sign of life and affection. I shall make my way through it, as it is now vacation. I hope you have received the third volume of my *Chips*, which now and again will remind you of me. I have read your dedication to the Crown Prince with delight, and what you write of Bismarck is cheering and encouraging. Yes, the times are great, but I wish the deluge of blood were over, or the animal in man will become all-powerful, and we shall never come to our senses. However fine and elevating may be the heroic courage of the German nation, killing does not belong to the fine and free arts. God grant an honourable and lasting peace may reward the countless sacrifices made by the nation. For a time I felt alarmed for Kiel and its inhabitants. Your letter, which I translated at once and sent to the *Times*, was never published. The English like deeds and stories of horror, and their taste is for highly-spiced and peppered articles! I hope you need not report the same of Holstein. I have had to fight a good deal in the

English papers. I hope that is now over. I hope you and yours are well, and that the clouds over your happiness are passing away: it grieves me to think that the sunshine is not so bright there as two years ago. But all that belongs to the small evils of life, and one learns, with such terrible evils all round one, to bear the little ones more easily. Shall we meet this year? I hope so, but one dare make no plans. On the whole, it goes well with us; the children are well. I am at times plagued with colds, as lately when Stockhausen was in Oxford, and sang beautifully, and I had to stay in bed! I saw him the next morning: he looked well, and was in splendid voice. To-day some venison and *Marzipan* arrived here, doubtless from Forsteck. Has your wife received the new edition of *Deutsche Liebe?* Now farewell, and may our paths meet in 1871.'

In November of this year Max Müller had been elected a Delegate of the University Press. In July, 1882, he was made a Perpetual Delegate. He resigned in 1896, finding that he could no longer spare the time from his private work and ever-increasing correspondence; partly also from a growing feeling of the great responsibility resting on the Delegates in conducting such an important business, a responsibility which he felt he was not strong enough or young enough to face any longer.

To Matthew Arnold, Esq.

Oxford, *December* 27, 1870.

'My dear Arnold,—I wanted to read your book before writing to thank you for it, and having read it, I can thank you all the more honestly. It requires much courage to write about religious questions, because almost every word you touch is oily and befingered, and it is difficult to handle them without besmutting one's hands. But it is all the more necessary to rescue the old words, to dust them, and rub them clean, and then show them to the world in their original purity and splendour, as you have done. Your justification of St. Paul is most successful, and I expect it will tell more than many learned controversies. You know that the inevitable decay of words forms part of the science of language, and therefore your chapter on the vicissitudes of the Pauline phraseology interests me all the more. It is but a chapter of modern mythology, but a very important one. I send you by book post a copy of some introductory lectures of mine, on the Science of Religion. I have only had sixteen copies struck off, and I send one to you, because if you look at them, you will see at once what my object was in delivering them. It will take several years before I publish what I want to say on the whole subject, but in the meantime I wanted you to know that we are working in the same mine, I on a very low level as yet, you on a high level, but on the whole with the same purpose. There was one expression in your book with which I could not agree. The etymology of words is not a merely fanciful argument; the etymological meaning, if accurately elaborated, is a most important *historical* element. There was a time when the etymological meaning of a word represented what really was to the early framers of language the most striking feature of an object, or the most important characteristic of a new conception. To put an etymology in the place of a definition, is no doubt foolish, but in the history of thought etymology holds a most important place. Plato's chaff is only directed against those who would use etymology instead of a definition; that there could be a historical element in etymology was beyond Plato's horizon. At the same time I do not defend R.'s etymologies. I send you the new edition of *Deutsche Liebe*, because the translation of your poem strikes me as really successful. I was glad to hear that you feel more kindly towards Bunsen; Froude wrote to me to tell me the same. Yours very truly.'

# CHAPTER XVIII

## 1871

King of Burma. Correspondence with Abeken and Gladstone. Taine's Lectures. Peace Festival. Letter from Crown Prince. Death of father-in-law. Ems. Interviews with Emperor and Crown Prince. Dr. Stainer. New edition of *Lectures on Language*.

THE year opened gloomily for France and Germany, and even for many in England, who were watching the great contest with beating hearts. Max Müller found little rest, and the correspondence with Mr. Gladstone and Dr. Abeken at Versailles was actively carried on. January found him preparing a second edition of Volume III of *Chips*, of which the first edition of 3,000 copies was nearly sold out.

Max Müller received about this time a Burmese letter from the Minister for Foreign Affairs at Mandalay, conveying the thanks of Mindoon Min, the enlightened King of Burma, for his translation of the *Dhammapada*, and expressing his great pleasure in hearing of the desire of the learned Professors of Europe and America to know more about the doctrines of Buddha, and ending with a promise to print the three 'Beedaghats[1]' in Pâli, and send copies for distribution to the English Commissioner. If this work was ever begun, it was doubtless stopped by the accession to the throne of the savage Thebaw, and the subsequent conquest and annexation of Burma by the English. It was reserved for King Chulalangkorn, the present enlightened King of Siam, to print the whole Tripitaka.

TO SIR CHARLES MURRAY (Minister at Lisbon).

PARKS END, OXFORD, *January*, 1871.

'MY DEAR SIR,—I should have answered your letter before, but Christmas brings many duties and distractions to a man with a family

[1] Pitakas, the sacred canon of Buddhism.

D d 2

of young children, who at the same time enjoys the privilege of Christmas dinners in College, and has to perform important duties at College meetings. The Warden, to whom I mentioned your letter, told me he would write to you and send me his letter, but he has not done so. I believe his chief object was to remind you of your portrait for our hall.

'Now with regard to "metaphor": that seems to me an inexhaustible subject, and one that can be approached from many points. No single writer could treat it with anything like completeness, and every contribution, however special, would be useful. The array of languages which you can either command or call to your assistance is ample for making a successful attack, and I should think that the library of the Academy at Lisbon would give you the opportunity for verifying any statements for which you do not like to trust to your memory. A book on metaphor, even in English alone, could be made not only very instructive, as revealing the secret working of the national mind, but very amusing, particularly if the languages of the people and their slang expressions are taken into account—a stunner, a fizzer, a brick, &c. I have myself treated the subject of metaphor in its most general aspects in the eighth lecture of my second series, and as you may not have that volume by you, I send you a copy, the Foreign Office having kindly relaxed the extreme rigour of their recent rule against sending anything in the Ambassador's bag. How such a treatise on metaphor should be arranged is more than I could venture to suggest. If it was arranged according to the principal subjects from which metaphors are borrowed, it would become interesting as a study of national character, for "out of the abundance of the heart the mouth speaketh." But any collection carefully made, with reference to authorities, so that it might be used and quoted by subsequent writers, would certainly be well received.

'If at any time my services can be of any use to you in your literary researches, please to command them at all times in the name of the Mallard [1]. Yours faithfully,

'MAX MÜLLER.'

TO DR. ABEKEN.

*Translation.* OXFORD, PARKS END, *January* 3, 1871.

'DEAR FRIEND,—Many thanks for your last letter. I greatly value your full answers to my letters, when your whole time and strength belongs to the sacred cause of the Fatherland, when your heart, your head, and your hands are sure to find little time and rest. If I could only do more here! The desire to do so is not wanting. I have again had an interesting correspondence with Gladstone. I sent him the

[1] The All Souls crest. Sir C. Murray had been a Fellow of the College.

pamphlet by Seidewitz (1867), *Prussia's Rights with regard to Luxemburg*, and as he wrote to me that the last Luxemburg telegrams had made him less hopeful about a better understanding, I communicated to him in English form your opinions with regard to Luxemburg. His answer of December 29 was good. He knew of no answer then to Lord Granville's letter, which had been sent via Berlin, but he admitted that there is no doubt that military urgency might justify, in given circumstances, a Power actually at war in taking into its own hands provisionally the settlement of certain questions, which could only be finally disposed of by a joint authority. The Whigs are very angry at Lord Stanley's famous interpretation of the Luxemburg affair. . . .

'It seems to me it is necessary to think of the future even more than of the present, and I confess that all my hopes of a great future for Europe are based on the alliance of the two great Teutonic sister-nations on the Continent and in the isles. Everything else seems artificial and only temporary; this alone is organic and lasting. But it is indeed a hard task. In England the war has now become a party question: the Tories will make it a reason for their attack on the Government. That is good on the whole; it will lead to a combination of Tories and Radicals, and so the great Liberal party—the support of the Government—will be forced to take up a firm position with regard to foreign policy. Even a change of Government, though not probable at present, would not do any harm, for it would concentrate English power and English opinion. It would be wiser if Germany did not underestimate England's military and naval power, and thus weaken the desire for an English alliance. England's fleet is stronger than ever, her people are strong and patriotic, her credit is the best in the world. (That makes me think the German loan in England ought to have been introduced differently—a better godmother, and a fatter or finer child!)

'My wife sends kindest regards. She is German through and through, and she and my three girls, the youngest only six years old, work indefatigably for the wounded. Henry Acland is doubtful about the German cause, but he was much pleased with your thought about him, and he reciprocates your kind messages.

'I consider Count Bismarck's message to me the greatest reward for the little I have been able to do.'

### To Professor Bernays.

*Translation.* Parks End, *January* 5, 1871.

'I should have answered your last letter before this, if I had not waited to send you a copy of the *Letters on the War*, which arrived to-day at last, and was sent off at once. You will see in them the character of the controversy between me and Gladstone, even without having the letters written by "Scrutator" at hand. I am quite convinced that Gladstone's accomplice has muddled a good deal, for Gladstone, in spite of all his weaknesses, is after all a very fine fellow. One does not become Prime Minister of England without having a very strong back. His sympathies, alas! are altogether Norman, not Saxon, but his feeling for what is right is stronger than all his other feelings. It is not true to say that he could have prevented the war, for, in spite of his great majority, he would have become impossible for his office, had he threatened France, or tried to interfere in the struggle between France and Germany. Now matters stand very differently in England. The war has become a party question: the Tories, with the extreme Liberals, will attack the Ministry on the basis of foreign policy. This will force the powerful Liberal party to a decided and recognized policy, and that is best for us. The German feeling towards England is incomprehensible to me, and the Government does not in the least encourage it. The war-power of England is greater than it has ever been—the fleet is ready to strike, the whole nation is patriotic, and the wealth is colossal. It is worth while to have such an ally, and Germany, conscious of her own greatness, ought to speak as peer to peer, not as a hysterical housewife to a housemaid. Well, we will hope for the best.

'Just think, I have received the warmest thanks from Bismarck from Versailles!'

To his Mother.

*Translation.* *January* 7, 1871.

'I have sent you a little book with my letters on the war. I lately received from Versailles, through Abeken, most grateful thanks from Bismarck. I will copy the letter for you: "First, my thanks for what you have done and are doing for Germany, for our holy cause! This expression of gratitude is not from me alone. I write in the name of Count Bismarck, who spoke to me only yesterday with a full and thankful recognition of your great and influential activity during this time, which he has heard of through the newspapers. He is rejoiced to have such an ally." What can one desire more?'

To the Same.

*Translation.* *January* 15, 1871.

'The news of John's[1] death was a great shock: what misery for his poor mother. . . . The whole land must be full of mourning—even

[1] His cousin, John von Basedow, shot by *franc-tireurs*.

here one cannot enjoy life, when one reads every day of these battles, and one sees no hope of peace. Here in England sympathies are much divided; pity is naturally on the side of France, and Bismarck's policy has alienated many people in England. But, on the whole, all goes well. The screams in the papers signify little: much of it comes from French refugees, who swarm in London. The better classes are inclined to Germany, but not to Bismarck! I am not an admirer of his, highly as I prize the work he has done for Germany, and truly as I recognize that the whole aim of his life has been the welfare of his Fatherland. Such work cannot always be carried out with perfectly clean hands. On the other hand, I cannot agree with the German abuse of the French nation. The French as a nation fight bravely, and show that they are by no means so depraved and perishing as the writers in the German papers think. At all events I hate such hectoring, as if the Germans were the general guardians of morality, and privileged possessors of all virtues. If this war goes on long, all Europe will be a desert, and one must be ashamed of mankind. The wild beasts behave better.'

To the Right Hon. W. E. Gladstone.

*January* 29.

'... As long as one reads the pages of Comte de Gasparin's pamphlet, one seems to live in a pure and bracing atmosphere, one begins to breathe freely, one's heart expands, everything around seems bright and full of hope. But we cannot live on mountain-tops, we must live and work in the low cloudy valleys, and when one is brought again face to face with real life and real men, the heart fails and all hopes vanish. I knew there were such men in France as the writer of this pamphlet. There is the true and noble ring of the old French mettle in all his words and all his thoughts. If a country can still produce such men, it need not despair about its fate. I feel quite ashamed when I see German writers speak of the whole of France as one vast Babylon, implying at the same time that Heaven has granted to us the exclusive privilege of all virtue and godliness. The only pity is that in France the good men withdraw from the front of political life; Gambetta rules, while Gasparin retires to Switzerland.

'Count Gasparin's scheme seems to me quite perfect. It gives in reality far more to Germany than she will get by annexing Alsace and Lorraine. It would be a blessing to Germany, to France, to Europe.

'But can it be? First of all, there is a large and at present very powerful party in Germany, which is no longer accessible to any arguments. We must take men as they are, and we must take nations as they are; and a nation flushed with victory and crushed by grief is not like a nation in its right mind. It is with nations as with individuals. How often do we see a friend rushing into misery, whom we might save if we could hold him by the arm, or make him listen to reason. That fight against the irrational and unconquerable powers of life is the most distressing; yet I do not say that reason should not fight against unreason: I only fear that in this case the fight is hopeless from the beginning.

'Suppose Germany and France placed their fate in the hands of Count Gasparin, what could he do? Could he persuade the Great Powers to guarantee the neutrality of Alsace? Such a guarantee implies a readiness to go to war for the sake of others. If it does not mean that, it means nothing. Does that readiness exist in England? Is there any party in England strong enough to carry such a measure, and to commit the country to such contingencies? Depend upon it, Germany would demand very stringent guarantees, for Lord Stanley's words after the conclusion of the treaty for the neutrality of Luxemburg have been a terrible lesson. I should consider England capable of the most generous and heroic efforts, but from what I see of the temper of the people, and the strange attraction between the most opposite political centres, I have grave doubts as to the possibility of such a guarantee receiving the approval of Parliament.

'Then comes the question about Russia, and whatever the personal character of the present Czar may be, no Russian statesman would help to heal that sore to which he trusts as the best security for the success of the Russian policy of the future.

'Count Gasparin's pamphlet has no doubt been sent to Count Bismarck. If not, I should gladly send it through Dr. Abeken. It is a masterpiece in every sense.

'If Alsace is too small by itself, why not make it a Canton of Switzerland? It would thus join an established political system, and enjoy the traditional prestige of Swiss neutrality. But I have no hope.'

The growth of feeling in England against Germany and for France, was often a sore trial to Max Müller, but he was refreshed from time to time by sympathetic letters from many English friends, and especially from Mr. Goldwin Smith, at that time living at Ithaca in the United States, who took a wide, unprejudiced, historical view of the whole question. He was always for the annexation of Alsace and Lorraine, 'provided a good natural frontier could be formed,' and considered the bombardment of Paris 'a disagreeable necessity'; whilst he asked, in a letter to Max Müller, 'what demon had entered into his countrymen, that when they are delivered by a wonderful display of German heroism, and at vast expense of German blood, from the peril which has always been hanging over them, . . . they, instead of blessing, curse their deliverers?'

To the Right Hon. W. E. Gladstone.

Parks End, *February* 2.

'Before thanking you for your letter, I wrote to Mr. Delane to ask him whether he would allow me to write a review of Count Gasparin's pamphlet, and thus bring his ideas before the English public. I have his reply to-day, and he simply declines. He evidently considers the matter as settled. I have sent the pamphlet to Dr. Abeken. Unfortunately there were some remarks in it which are sure to offend Count Bismarck, particularly where he tells him that by his decision about Alsace he has to prove whether he possesses mere *habileté* or political genius. However, the real difficulty is that even Count Bismarck is not strong enough, supposing he was influenced by the future rather than by the present, to oppose the military party, and I believe the feeling in Germany is so strong that for any statesman now to give up Strassburg would be simply to abdicate. There is a poetry about Strassburg which is stronger than all prose. Nations have their rough-hewn destinies to fulfil; at present I see no help. I just see the morning papers: I do not believe in the conditions of peace; it would be a challenge to Nemesis, and people in Germany have not read history to no purpose. But it is hard to mediate between intoxication and madness.'

To his Mother.

*Translation.* *February* 7.

'The feeling in England is less excited. They must yield to the inevitable. So I have not packed up, but have had to let people know I could live in Germany as well as, if not better than, here! I have not anything to complain of, and continue to have most interesting letters from Gladstone, the Prime Minister. He is a very clever and honourable man, and would willingly do his best, but he has a difficult position.'

The following letter is given by permission, as showing the feeling of an unbiassed historian on the recent events:—

Somerleaze, Wells, Somerset,

*February* 19, 1871.

'My dear Müller,—I have got a wild scheme in my head, in which you may possibly be able to help me. It seems pretty certain that the German troops are to march into Paris. Now that is a thing which does not happen much above once in a thousand years, and a thing for which I have been earnestly longing ever since 976. For the first time in my life, I wish to see a military spectacle. I have said ever since 1851, that, if L. N. Buonaparte was to be guillotined, and they would only send me word, I would come and see the show, in whatever part of the world I might be. And this show will be quite as satisfactory as the other. But is it possible? Is it safe? I do not doubt that you have means of finding out; you doubtless know some of the swells at Versailles or somewhere. If you could give me a lift, I should be deeply obliged. If I could get to see the Emperor's triumph without jeopardizing mine own self, I should greatly enjoy it, and I might make something of it for the public advantage. If I did go, I should like to get Bryce, Pindar, or somebody to come with me.

'I hope you have by this time seen both my *Pall Mall* letters. To my utter amazement, the *Times* has gone and reprinted the second of them. That paper has hitherto made it a fixed rule never to mention me or any writing of mine, or to let my name appear, except at the Mid-Somerset election, when they could not well help it. What does this mean?

'I am sending for the *Academy*, as I see you have been writing in it. Do you altogether forbid me to say "Kikero"?

'Yours very truly, EDWARD A. FREEMAN.'

TO DR. ABEKEN.

*Translation.* PARKS END, *February* 20, 1871.

'DEAR FRIEND,—I enclose the letter of a friend of Germany, Mr. Freeman. I do not know if his name is familiar to you. He is one of the best historians and public men in England—a man like Treitschke, indefatigable with his pen, and always to the point and incisive. He has been faithful to our cause to the end, from solid true conviction. His letter will show you his desire, and I thought it worth while to send it just as it is. You know the English too well to think that a man like Mr. Freeman would keep anything in the background. He is one who has belonged to us from a deep conviction; he keeps himself, however, quite independent, and the only thing it is possible to do for him is a kindness like the one he asks for. We need all the help in England which we can procure by honest means. I often ponder now over the change of affairs at the death of Peter III, and I still hope that we may win the battle of Burkersdorf, though it be only on the diplomatic battle-field, but may we win it before it is too late. Do not underestimate England:

she has only twenty million inhabitants—but they are Englishmen, and they come from Schleswig-Holstein.'

The answer to Mr. Freeman's request was as follows:—

*March* 10, 1871.

'MY DEAR FREEMAN,—I had a letter from my friend at Versailles: he says it was impossible to write, for nothing was settled from hour to hour about the entry, in fact there has been no *entrée triomphale*. It is curious that, in spite of all provocation, my friend—and he reflects Bismarck, I believe, most faithfully—clings to the idea of a friendship between England and Germany as the only safety for the future. Have you seen "Scrutator's" book? I have not, but I heard from a friend this morning that it is simply libellous, and that legal action should be taken. If so, I am certain that Gladstone had nothing to do with it, but that it is ——, *pur et simple*.'

The following letter shows that, amidst all the excitement of the times, Max Müller did not allow his work to flag:—

TO THE RIGHT HON. W. E. GLADSTONE.

PARKS END, *February* 21, 1871.

'You will think me very unreasonable, I am afraid, if just now I trouble you with a question about Homeric Mythology and Religion. I should not venture to do so, did I not think that you or your son could answer my inquiry by a simple Yes or No. The fact is, I am preparing a new edition of my *Lectures on the Science of Language*, and as they are to be stereotyped, I have to revise them carefully once more. When I came to the passage in my Second Series where I had tried in a few lines to explain your view of the origin of Greek Mythology, I did not know what to do. From reading your book I certainly thought that you admitted an early stratum of Jewish thought, on which, by metamorphic and other processes, the religion and mythology of Homer were built up. In a letter which you did me the honour to address to me, you proposed a different theory, or at least you gave me a new insight into your views on the subject. You seem to admit there an independent origin for the religious and mythological opinions of the Greeks and the Jews, and to be satisfied with the admission of a later contact between Aryan and Semitic ideas. Under these circumstances I thought the best plan would be, if you allowed me, to print in a note some extracts from your letter, and I therefore send you the original, that you may look at it once more, and tell me whether you object to my proposal. In either case, whether you say Yes or No, I must request you to return me the letter, for I hope my children will hereafter value it as much as myself.

'PS.—I sent Count Gasparin's pamphlet to Dr. Abeken, but I have not heard from him lately. I am almost afraid my last letters, which I sent through the English Post Office, and not as before through the Prussian courier, may not have reached him. I feel as strongly as ever that Count Gasparin's proposal is the right one, but I cannot believe that at present it is possible. Though I am an extreme Radical in University politics, I was glad that Professor Fawcett's amendment was rejected; it would have weakened our position in the conflict which is coming. But I feel convinced that the sooner the last trace of protection is removed from the study of Theology at Oxford the better. At All Souls our Fellowship Examination is entirely in Modern History and Law, and no clergyman ought to have any chance of being elected; yet out of fifteen fellows elected under the new Statute, four are clerical. They won in a fair and open field.

'M. M.'

FROM DR. ABEKEN.

*Translation.* *February* 21, 1871.

'It is a decisive week on which we have entered. The armistice ends with the end of the week, unless there is a guarantee for peace. It would be a terrible misfortune if war had to begin again; the indignation of our army would be greater than ever. At this moment Thiers is sitting with Prince Bismarck for their first exchange of views in the same *salon* in which, at the beginning of November, he was discussing an armistice. He might *then* have had just the same conditions as now, and what must he feel when he thinks what his country might have been spared, had he or his colleagues then listened to reason! We too should have been spared much, if falsehood and vanity had then been less powerful in France. People tell us to be moderate; they forget what moderation is required if, after our new efforts and sacrifices, we make no harder conditions than we made in November. You say, "Make peace with France and make peace with England." No one can long for it more truly than we. Every alliance is repulsive to us except friendship with England. But the tone of the debates in Parliament, nay, even the tone of the Queen's Speech, which tries to deal equal measure to both sides, and for that very reason deals unequal measure, cannot advance peace and friendship. What might England have done, what misery might England have prevented, if, at the beginning of the war, it had possessed the moral courage to call Good good, Wrong wrong, Right right, Crime criminal! It has turned out well for us that England did not act, now that the world has witnessed this new act in the solemn drama of history. The French sentiments of the people of Alsace and Lorraine prove to me all the more strongly that we are in duty bound to bring back this German race to the German Empire. We have to cure them of a fearful disease, that future generations, though blushing at the disgrace of their forefathers, may grow up to a healthy life. It is inconceivable how, while German language and German morals remained unchanged, the love for the old German Fatherland has become almost extinct. Think of the Protestants of Alsace, of the Evangelical clergy of Alsace! How can they be so blind as not to see that the fate of the Evangelical Church in Alsace depends on their union with Germany, while union with France implies its certain extinction? The Roman Catholics in Germany are not so blind; and their leaders, whose home is not in Germany, but at Rome, do all they can to prevent the union of Alsace with Protestant Germany.'

### To Dr. Abeken.

*Translation.* Parks End, *February* 24, 1871.

'Dear Friend,—I received your letter this morning, and I am indeed glad to hear that the Crown Prince remembers me so kindly. I wrote to him at once, and enclose the letter, asking you to look through it and hand it to the Crown Prince with a copy of the *Letters on the War.* I send the book by post, just as it is; there was no time to have it bound. I have also written to Gladstone, after having received your letter: alas! the Protestant argument has no effect on him. Lord Shaftesbury is the man for that; he has already done something in the matter, but his views are very narrow. Public opinion is getting more moderate in England. The only thing now is to wait—perhaps our enemies may do good service to us.

'I sent you a pamphlet of Count Gasparin. Gladstone is delighted with it, as you may have heard; the spirit of it is good. I could not help telling Gladstone that Russia would never think of helping to heal the wound: many plans for the future are built on the reopening of this wound.

'With regard to Freeman, do what you can; . . . he has a powerful, indefatigable pen, and is German through and through. Could you not persuade old Carlyle to write or to say something very amiable?'

### To the Right Hon. W. E. Gladstone.

Parks End, *February* 27, 1871.

'My dear Mr. Gladstone,—I received your letter this morning, and I look forward with great interest to the short Memorandum to which you refer. I believe there is no scholar occupied with the study of the growth and spreading of religious ideas, who has not had to modify some of his own opinions on the subject during the last ten years. The evidence has become so much larger and richer and deeper, that we are forced, whether we like it or not, to assume a new standpoint in order to command the whole field that is open before us. I sent you the extract from Abeken's letter as it stood, but I marked it *private*, private as it were, even to you, intended for the dispassionate spectator of the grand drama of history, not for the Prime Minister of England. Otherwise I could not have left what Abeken said about Moral Courage without incurring the charge of impertinence. I have told him what I think on the subject, and that it is easy to be wise *post factum*. With the same intention, I sent you his frank confession about the state of feeling in Alsace and Lorraine. I admit it was a surprise to me, and I could quote statements from recent travellers in those provinces that would lead to different conclusions. But before all things it is right that the truth should be known, and I wanted *you* in particular to know it. Lord Granville possesses, no doubt, information on the subject of public feeling in Alsace and Lorraine from independent sources, and he would not quote Abeken against Abeken, in discussing the dangers which this Peace may bring on Europe. The difficulties are doubtless very great, yet blood, language, and religion are three powerful allies in the struggle which will now begin. Yours sincerely.'

TO THE SAME. *February* 28.

'DEAR MR. GLADSTONE,—Accept my best thanks for the Memorandum, of which you sent me a copy. I should be very happy to discuss some points with you in more peaceful times; this Peace is no peace. Yet do not judge the statesmen of Germany too harshly. After the sad experience which they have had of the French, they cannot bring themselves to believe that a people who could not forgive Sadowa, would ever forget Sedan. It is their duty to think, first of all, of the safety of the country committed to their care. They are convinced that war will begin again whatever they do, or at all events they think that the only chance of peace is the hopelessness of a new attack on the part of France.

'As you told me in your letter that a new Bill on Clerical Fellowships would soon be presented to Parliament, I have taken the liberty to send you a few remarks on the subject of Fellowships in general. I have watched their working now for more than twenty-two years, being in fact one of the oldest residents at Oxford, and I confess I should like to see these magnificent resources of the University more usefully applied than they are at present. My remarks on Fellowships in general I should be quite prepared to send to the *Times*, if you thought it could be of any use.'

To M. Renan.

Oxford, *March* 7, 1871.

'I was so pleased to hear that you and Madame Renan had not suffered during the last months, and that you are well enough to resume your work. Let us forget, or let us at least be silent on the past; it has been too horrible. I know you are as strongly French as I am German, but that does not prevent both of us, I think, from feeling deeply the shame and degradation which that war has brought on the race to which we belong as men. We feel ashamed if we are told that our ancestors, our most distant ancestors, were simious; is there one race of animals so savage, so brutal, as man can be? nor does there seem to be any hope of progress or improvement with regard to our ideas respecting war. We all share the guilt of it, we are all ready to take part in it, and we are actually proud of our efficiency in manslaughter. I know of one redeeming feature only in war: it shows that there are some things for which men are ready to die; that there is in man the gift of martyrdom, which I suppose the brutes do not possess; but, apart from that, we must all hide our faces in shame and grief. No doubt the best you and Madame Renan can do, is to go away for a time so as to have complete change. In a few weeks more England will be lovely in the warmth and colours of spring. We shall certainly be at Oxford till June, and my wife asks me to tell you and Madame Renan that she hopes you will come and stay with us at Oxford. There are two rooms at your disposal, you would find plenty of work at the Bodleian Library, and nothing could give her and me greater pleasure than to have you quietly staying here as long as you are able. If you would only let us know a few days before when we may expect you, you will find everything ready for you. I had a letter from M. Taine to-day; I hope the University will invite him to give us a course of lectures. I did not venture to propose you, for, though we are advancing, we advance slowly. He would lecture in French on some period of French Literature. It is not settled yet, but I hope it will succeed.'

To his Mother.

*Translation.* *March* 10.

'One begins to live quietly again, now that peace is made: it was a fearful time, and one keeps thinking, who knows when it may begin again? The joy in Germany must be immense. The Crown Prince sent me word I ought, as an old friend, to have sent him a copy of my *Letters on the War*. I have done so now, and I wrote a beautiful letter too!'

On March 31 Max Müller delivered an evening lecture at the Royal Institution on Mythology, which was, as usual, largely attended. It was some years before this that his friend Lord Strangford wrote: 'Here (in England) there is no school of Philology, and I do not quite hold Max Müller guiltless for not having founded one, instead of going off into Comparative Mythology.'

As the Professorship of Modern European Languages had been abolished when Max Müller accepted the new Chair of Comparative Philology, it was resolved from time to time to invite celebrated foreigners to lecture on some foreign language or literature, and this year the Curators were anxious to secure the services of M. Taine. The following letter gives an account of the scheme, with some hints on lecturing:—

To M. Taine.

OXFORD, *March* 17, 1871.

'I hasten to answer your kind letter as far as I can. First, as to the time. The fact is that our Summer Term is over the first week of June, and very little work is done during the last week. Therefore if you could begin before Whit-Sunday, you would probably have a better audience. Your course of lectures is the first beginning of a new experiment, and everything will depend on your success. Oxford is an extremely difficult place to lecture in, because all audiences are very mixed. You have young students, you have fellows and tutors, you have Professors, and for *your* lectures ladies also, I think. It is difficult to hit where there are so many targets. I do not expect that you will have many young students, and you may therefore aim a little higher. I should lecture as if I were addressing a highly educated lady, not taking much for granted, making everything clear by a full statement of facts, but then drawing out the very best lessons that the facts will yield. For that purpose your philosophers and moralists would be more useful, perhaps, than your dramatists, but I dare say you are right in selecting the latter. My only fear is that the classical dramatic writers are a little too well known, and that they may not prove sufficiently attractive. A picture of the thoughts and manners of the times in which they lived would remedy that defect, and you would know better than anybody else how to place before us the political and intellectual stage on which Racine and Molière were themselves the actors. Lastly, as to the language: it has been decided, not without some opposition, that the lectures should be given in French. But, of course, many of your hearers would have difficulty in following, and therefore a slow and very distinct delivery would be a matter of great consequence. The lectures are open to every member of the University, and the invitation to lecture comes to you from the Vice-Chancellor, in the name of the University. The lectures are delivered at the Taylor Institution, because the funds for paying the Lecturer come out of Sir Robert Taylor's bequest. It is not an easy task which you are undertaking, but I feel very sanguine as to its success. If you want any further information I shall be most happy to give it.'

M. Taine accepted the invitation, and arrived in Oxford soon after the above letter was written.

Though M. Taine was not actually the guest of the Max Müllers, residing in their house, he was constantly with them, and, after he had received the degree of Honorary D.C.L., they gave a very large party, at which they gathered together all the leading spirits in Oxford to meet the distinguished foreigner, who charmed everybody by his easy and agreeable conversation. The next morning the appalling news of some of the worst deeds of the Commune was in the papers, and the brilliant Frenchman was an altered being; he was wounded to the heart by the savage acts of his countrymen, and seemed as if unable to look any one in the face. Happily his lectures were already finished, and he left immediately, deeply commiserated by Max Müller, to whom he acknowledged that it was far worse than the humiliation inflicted by the war with Germany.

To Rev. G. Cox.

'I looked at Gladstone's book *Homeric Synchronism*—it is very disappointing. So great a man, so imperfect a scholar! He has no idea how shaky the ground is on which he takes his stand. The reading of those ethnic names in the hieroglyphic inscriptions varies with every year and with every scholar. I do not blame them: their studies are and must be tentative, and they are working in the right direction. But the use which Gladstone makes of their labours is to me really painful, all the more so because it is cleverly done, and I believe bona fide.'

During the month of April Max Müller accepted the invitation of the committee who were arranging the German

Peace Festival in London, to deliver the address on that occasion. The Festival took place on May 1, and was a brilliant success. The music, the artistic *tableaux vivants*, the expression of deep gratitude, of exultant patriotism, tempered by the thought of all that the victory had cost the Fatherland, can never be forgotten by any of those present. Max Müller's speech throughout struck the right note, and he could feel from the first how he carried his audience with him. The translation, which is given in the Appendix, had the benefit of being corrected by him.

TO HIS MOTHER.

*Translation.* OXFORD, *May* 3.

'My speech will be printed, and I will send you a copy. It has been much discussed in the English papers. It was not an easy task. The audience was a very mixed one. The Ambassador was there, and the republicans, &c. Yes, it went off very well, and I am glad I undertook it. The next day Lord Granville, the Minister for Foreign Affairs, asked me to dinner. To-day I received a most kind letter from the Crown Prince, written by himself. . . . It was very good of him, for doubtless he has many letters to write.'

By gracious permission of His Majesty the German Emperor the letter from the Crown Prince is inserted here:—

BERLIN, 1. *Mai* 1871.

'Ich habe mit aufrichtigem Danke und ganz besonderem Interesse Ihre *Letters on the War* entgegengenommen, welche Sie die Freundlichkeit hatten, mir zu übersenden.

'Mit der einmütigen Hingebung unseres Volkes während der grossen Zeit, die wir durchkämpft, steht in schönem Einklang die patriotische Haltung, welche unsere deutschen Brüder, oft unter den schwierigsten Verhältnissen und mit Opfern aller Art, bewährt, und durch die sie sich für immer einen Anspruch auf die Dankbarkeit des Vaterlandes erworben haben.

'Dass die Erfahrungen, welche die Deutschen in England während unseres ruhmvollen Krieges gemacht, nicht immer erfreulich waren, ist mir freilich bekannt. Gründe der verschiedensten Art kommen zusammen, um eine Verstimmung zu erzeugen, die hüben und drüben von alien einsichtigen und patriotischen Männern gleich schmerzlich empfunden ist.

'Meine feste und zuversichtliche Hoffnung bleibt es aber, dass dieselbe bald jenem herzlichen Einvernehmen wieder Platz machen wird, welches die Natur unserer gegenseitigen Beziehungen und Interessen verlangt. Dieses Ziel wollen wir verfolgen, unbeirrt durch Aufregungen und Eindrücke des Augenblicks, überzeugt, dass es für das Gedeihen beider Länder ebenso heilsam wie für den Frieden Europas unerlässlich ist.

'Sie haben Ihrerseits niemals aufgehört, in diesem Geiste thätig zu sein, und es ist mir deshalb Bedürfniss, Ihnen meine dankbare Anerkennung für Ihr erfolgreiches Wirken hierdurch auszusprechen.

'Ihr wohlgeneigter FRIEDRICH WILHELM, Kronprinz.'

*Translation.* BERLIN, *May* 1, 1871.

'I have received with much interest and sincere thanks your *Letters on the War*, which you so kindly sent to me. The courageous devotion of our people during all the great time of the war is in beautiful harmony with the patriotic feeling which our German brethren everywhere have shown, often under the most difficult circumstances, and which they have proved by sacrifices of all kinds, thus securing for themselves for ever the gratitude of the Fatherland. I know also, only too well, that the experiences of the Germans in England during our glorious war were not always happy ones. Reasons of all kinds combined to produce a discord which makes itself felt as painfully here as in England, by all really discerning and patriotic men.

'My firm and confident hope, however, remains, that this discord will soon give way again to the hearty understanding which is the natural expression of our mutual relations and interests. Let us struggle towards this goal, unhindered by the excitements and impressions of the moment, convinced that this common understanding is as necessary for the development of both countries, as it is indispensable for the peace of Europe.

'You, for your part, have never ceased to act in this spirit, and I therefore feel impelled to give expression to my grateful recognition of your successful efforts. Your well-wisher,

'FREDERICK WILLIAM, Crown Prince.'

The end of May, Max writes to his mother: 'The scenes in Paris are awful, and one thinks what these furies would have done in Germany if they had got there.'

During the latter part of the war Max Müller had carried on an interesting correspondence with the venerable diplomatist Lord Stratford de Redcliffe, whose sympathies were entirely German. It has not been possible to recover Max Müller's letters. Lord Stratford sent him a poem at the close of the war in praise of Germany, which was published in Germany in a collection of poems on the war, and had a large circulation.

Only a month after the Peace Festival Max Müller lost his father-in-law, after a very short illness. As he had already settled to visit Ems again this summer for the waters, he resolved to start as soon as he could, and take his wife for a change, and his little boy with him. They joined his mother at Chemnitz, from which place he wrote to Dr. Abeken, telling him of his plans, and adding, 'From year to year we seem to visit the dead more than the living, and the old happy, beautiful times of meeting do not return.' Shortly before leaving England Max Müller had received a visit from a German, consulting him on the advisability of starting a general subscription among Germans living out of Germany for a monument in commemoration of the war. Max explains his views in the following letter. We know how thoroughly they were realized by the great Germania on the banks of the Rhine.

To Professor Bernays.

*Translation.* Oxford, *June* 12.

'I write by return; Mr. Lang called with a verbal recommendation from Count Bernstorff. I liked the idea, but I told him at once that the impulse must come from Germany. He told me a little while ago that all went well in Germany: a million has been promised in Mayence alone. His plan has the fullest approval from the highest classes. I have not written to him, but to Dr. Heine, who sent me a description of the monument in question; I wrote some encouraging words to him. Let the man work!

'A monument *only* in Berlin is one-sided. I should like to see a German monument on the banks of the German river, protected by a German fortress; and he who does not understand the "German Michael[1]" can hold to the archangel instead. So you see, I think: Let it grow—should it prove to have no substantial foundation it will fade of itself.'

During the stay at Ems the Emperor came there to drink the waters, and Max Müller had the honour of dining with his Imperial Majesty, whom he had last seen in 1849 at Bunsen's house in London, a refugee from the revolution in Berlin. The Emperor was most gracious and cordial, and thanked Max for his letters to the *Times*. But it was the

[1] Nickname for the German soldier.

meeting again with the Crown Prince—'Unser Fritz,' as the troops called him—which gave him the most unfeigned pleasure, and he has described in *Auld Lang Syne* the affectionate welcome accorded him on the occasion, to the surprise of the great officers and officials present. Abeken, too, was at Ems, and the friends met for the last time. The troops were returning from France, and many a regiment turned up the Lahn valley to greet their Emperor and Prince. On these occasions the town supplied refreshments, whilst the visitors subscribed for cigars and waited on the returning heroes.

Max Müller and his wife were among the few admitted to the railway station to see the Crown Prince off for Munich, where he was to hold a great review of the South German troops. The following note to Dr. Abeken alludes to the dinner with the Emperor:—

*Translation.*

'Before I leave Ems I must thank you most heartily once more. I know it is not easy to jump over the magic ring which encircles crowned heads everywhere, but with your support it all went capitally. It will always be for me a "historical moment." I wish the Emperor could read my speech at the London Peace Festival, so that he should know how highly I value the honour which he has bestowed upon me.'

CONTEMPORARY LETTER.

'MONACO,' EMS, *July* 20, 1871.

'I know you will be interested in hearing that Max dined with the Emperor on Monday, at 4.30. Max and the poet Von Redwitz were the only civilians present, and Max the only man without any decoration or order! They were a party of eighteen. The Emperor began by saying to Max: "I know of your great fame as an Oriental scholar: what made you take to that line of study?" Max told him he first heard of Sanskrit as a boy from the Duchess of Dessau, the Emperor's cousin; and they talked about her, and then of his life in England. Everything was so simple, and yet, as they sat at table, Max said, as he listened to the kindly, simple words of the Kaiser, he felt, "Here is a man who hereafter will hold a place second only in German history to Charlemagne." After dinner the Emperor talked to him again, about Bunsen. Max called him "a true German Ambassador." "But not very practical," rejoined the Kaiser. "No," said Max, "but prophetic." "Yes," said the Kaiser, in the most hearty way, "if he had lived, how he would have rejoiced now, how happy he would have been!" Tuesday evening came the Crown Prince. We saw him arrive, looking hardly older than eight years ago; but his countenance, always so good, had gained depth and experience, and he was, indeed, as our friends the Bradleys said, "a noble fellow, the very type of a hero." He sent for Max early yesterday, and he had an hour's intensely interesting talk with him. When Max got there he was told to wait, as some one was with the Prince, but he had hardly sat down in the ante-room, when the door was thrown open, and in came the Prince, both hands stretched out: "But, Maximilianus, why do you wait here? I have no secrets that you cannot hear! Now sit down, put down your hat. *We* asked for you everywhere in England and could not see you; and now I find you here in Ems, and I may take your greetings to my wife, may I not?" Then they plunged into the war, and the Prince openly said how he had hated it; and when Max said something about all he had done, he said: "Oh, no compliments, please; I only did my duty." Then he discussed the union of North and South Germany, and how to unite Catholics and Protestants; and said he feared they were not ready yet for a new Reformation in Bavaria: "It wants more than a mere dogma to effect that, it must spring from the hearts of the people," and he added with deep feeling, "and have we Protestants of the North so much to offer them: have we advanced in religion the last 300 years?" He talked of his very hearty reception everywhere in England, and spoke of various people there with an insight into their characters and opinions that was remarkable. "We dined at Gladstone's, and" (with a knowing laugh) "we talked a great deal about *Art and Literature*." He then told Max how deeply grateful he felt for the efforts he had made to keep up a union in feeling between Germany and England, and added: "You must forgive my not thanking you directly for your letters on the war; and when I did write, I had not time to say half I wished, I have so much to do." He ended by hoping Max would return home in time for both him and the Princess to see him, and added: "It is twenty years since we first met." He left at three o'clock yesterday afternoon. We went to see him off, and he sent for us, coming almost to the door of his room to meet me, and he shook hands in the most hearty way, and as I rose from my curtsy, he said, looking at Boy, "But what then is that?" Max said he was the youngest German sailor, and the Prince shook hands with the small thing; and then talked to me of our visit to Potsdam, and of Oxford, and told me he had my photograph. He talked to us two till the train was ready, when he again shook hands with us both, and went off. I heard Max, as he left, say in German: "Splendid, noble fellow"; and so he is, indeed. He is far handsomer as a man of forty, and, as I said before, there is an earnestness, depth, and grandeur in his face, whilst it has lost none of its bright, genial expression. He is one's ideal of a really noble man. The night he arrived here, one of the hills was illuminated in his honour. It was a most fairy-like scene. At a rocket signal every point in the high hill burst out in bright sheets of Bengal fire, red, white, and green, so that every bush and twig were visible from the base to the summit, and the figures of the men feeding the lights looked like busy gnomes who had created the magical scene.'

Whilst at Ems Max Müller received a note from Dr., afterwards Sir John, Stainer, and later Professor of Music at Oxford, wishing to dedicate his work on *Harmony* to him. The following letters are interesting as showing Max Müller's continued love of music, though he had almost ceased to perform himself, and only took up his playing again later to accompany his children in their singing:—

To Dr. Stainer.

Ems, *July* 2.

'I hardly know what to say, and whether I ought to accept the dedication of your work on *Harmony*. I always feel like a traitor among my musical friends, and quite unworthy of any honourable mention. However, if you think otherwise, I can only say that I shall consider it a great, though most undeserved, honour to have my name connected with your work, and thus to keep a place in the musical annals of Oxford. Some of my happiest recollections date from the years which I spent in the musical atmosphere of Leipzig, when Mendelssohn was there in the full vigour and enjoyment of his genius, and these recollections have often been revived at Oxford when listening to your masterly playing in Magdalen Chapel.'

The dedication is as follows:—

TO PROFESSOR MAX MÜLLER
WHO, THOUGH UNABLE TO DEVOTE HIMSELF
TO THE ART OF MUSIC
OWING TO THE CLAIMS MADE ON HIS TIME
BY OTHER FIELDS OF LABOUR
FORGETS NOT TO ENCOURAGE BY HIS SYMPATHY AND KINDNESS
THOSE WHO ARE PRESSING FORWARD IN ITS PATHS.

To the Same.

*October* 6.

'On my return to Oxford I found your book on my table, and I must thank you once more for your great kindness. I feel ashamed and almost saddened when I read your dedication. There was a time when I thought I should devote the whole of my life to music, and a very happy time it was.

'But new interests carried me away in quite a different direction, and though I tried for a time to keep up my music, I soon found out that music was not a thing to play with, and that one should make up one's mind to be either its priest and minister, or a silent worshipper.

'There is a story of a young clergyman exclaiming, "What is the use of the laity?" I am glad you do not share that feeling with regard to music, but consider mere listeners like myself (and particularly *silent* listeners) an essential element of the musical community.'

On his return to Oxford Max Müller settled down to work, finishing the new edition of his *Lectures on Language*, which were now stereotyped, and getting on with the fifth volume of the *Rig-veda*. His wife was away from home for some time, the mother-aunt being very ill, and requiring some one constantly with her.

To his Wife.

Oxford, *September* 17, 1871.

'Sharing the happiness of other people, entering into their feelings, living life over once more in them and with them, that is all that remains to old people. I suppose it was meant to be so, the principal object of life being the overcoming of self in every sense of the word.

'In fact, as one gets older death seems hardly to make so wide a gulf: a few years more or less, that is all. Meantime, we know in whose hands we all are, that life is very beautiful; but death has its beauty too.'

In the November of this year Max Müller had the gratification of hearing from India that his *Sanskrit Grammar*, of which the second edition had appeared in 1870, was extensively used there. A friend wrote from Benares, 'Your Grammar seems now very near perfection. Your *Hitopadesa* (the first of the handbooks for the study of Sanskrit) is used in the English department of our College, and is valued by the boys, but not much bought—they are too poor.'

To F. Palgrave, Esq.

Parks End, *December* 26, 1871.

'My dear Palgrave,—As a Christmas treat I have been reading Shakespeare's Sonnets—as marvellous as ever, but even more difficult! Now can you tell me (p. 81 of your edition), how do you construe "Will bestow it"? Is it will enrich it, endow it, viz. my wit? Why did you leave out the sonnet—

"A woman's face with nature's own hand painted"?

How do you construe p. 76—

"I will not praise that purpose not to sell"?

These are only a few queries, and they refer to points where I believe I am simply stupid; as to other matters, one might go on asking for ever. On the whole I like Massey—he leaves me freest. Best wishes to you and yours.'

# CHAPTER XIX

## 1872

Memorial to Bishop Patteson. Offer of Professorship at Strassburg. *Rig-veda*, Vol. V. Death of sister-in-law. Strassburg. Baden. Munich. *Life of Stockmar.* Switzerland. Dr. Stanley Select Preacher. Freiligrath's poem.

FROM the moment that it was settled that the University of Strassburg should be reorganized under German auspices, Baron Roggenbach, who was entrusted with the arrangements, endeavoured to attract to it many of the leading German Professors. The Baron had discussed the subject with Max Müller on his return from Ems in 1871, and through the winter the thought of possibly settling in Strassburg as Sanskrit Professor was constantly before him. Max determined to come to no decision before trying how life in Germany really suited him, and therefore only undertook to give a course of lectures at Strassburg in the summer *semester* of 1872.

TO HIS MOTHER.

*Translation.* *January* 1, 1872.

'MY DEAR GOOD MOTHER,—The first letter of the new year must be for you, and may God make it a pleasant year to you—as pleasant as it can be at your age. I hope we shall have a happy meeting this year. I have not yet made any plans for the summer, though I have an idea, if I am well and strong enough, of giving a course of lectures at Strassburg. I have had a very cordial invitation to do so, but I have not yet accepted, for it will give me a good deal of work, and too much work does not pay. It is possible the opening of the University may be postponed till the autumn, and at that time I could not leave Oxford. Well, that is just an idea for the new year. At all events I intend to make an early start from here, and settle somewhere for the summer in Germany with all my belongings. It is not good for the children to travel about, and is also too expensive.

Where do you think we had best go? We had a quiet Christmas. The Meyers sent us venison and a *Marzipan*, and Trübner sent a *Stolle*, so that we had some German Christmas things. Have I told you that Klaus Groth is coming in the spring to Oxford to give three lectures before the University on German literature? He gets £50, and he and his wife will stay with us. I am going this week for a couple of days to Woburn Abbey, the Duke of Bedford's.'

From Woburn Abbey he wrote to his wife:—

*January* 4.

'Here I am in the grand old place. I had a pleasant drive from the station, some seven miles—beautiful sunshine, and the Park looked as green as in summer. Mr. Hastings Russell and his son received me very kindly. We walked about, saw the Park and the Sculpture Gallery and the Chinese Dairy, &c. What an extraordinary nest for one human bird to build himself for his passage through life! When Bunsen was here he told the late Duke, after admiring everything in the way in which he could admire, that he was truly thankful he was not Duke of Bedford. Mr. Russell seemed quite to understand what he meant. I try to keep up my reputation as a historian, but it requires great presence of mind when you are told of every picture: That was the famous Lord A., that was his beautiful daughter-in-law, *the* Duchess of B., and so it goes on—enough to pluck a first-class man. My great difficulty is to find my room [1]. I wander and wander, till at last some kind person takes me in tow. However, here I am, landed safe in my room, and when the dinner bell rings I hope they will send for me!'

In February Max Müller wrote a letter to the *Times* advocating a memorial to his friend Bishop Patteson, whose murder in one of the Melanesian Islands had been mentioned this year in the Queen's Speech. He received letters of thanks from many members of the Bishop's family. 'To have known such a man,' says Max Müller, 'is one of life's greatest blessings. In his life of purity, unselfishness, and devotion to man and faith in a higher world, those who have eyes to see may read the best, the most real *Imitatio Christi*. In his death, following so closely on his prayer for forgiveness for his enemies—"for they know not what they do"—we have witnessed once more a truly Christ-like death.' From this

[1] Max Müller had not the least bump of locality.

time onwards Max Müller felt an interest in the Melanesian Mission above any other.

TO HIS MOTHER.

*Translation.* *March* 3, 1872.

'I should have written sooner, but I have had so much correspondence lately about Strassburg that I had time for nothing else. They have made me all sorts of offers, but I have come to no decision, though I am often drawn towards returning to Germany. The Government offers me 4,000 thalers a year (£600), and will keep the Professorship open for me till Easter, 1873. I have hit on this plan: I will leave this early in May and give a course of lectures in Strassburg, during the Summer Term, on "The Results of Comparative Philology." This binds me in no way, and I can form an idea as to whether I am suited for the work of a German Professor or not. Roggenbach writes I could live near Baden-Baden and go in by train on lecture days. G. and the children will not come till the end of June, so as not to interrupt the children's classes. The lectures end early in August, and I can then make further plans; so as soon as you feel up to it you can come to Strassburg and keep house for me. In the winter I shall in any case return to Oxford, whatever I may ultimately decide on doing. You can fancy how all this has occupied me. I think with an income of 10,000 thalers, of which we need not lay by anything, we could lead a far pleasanter life than we can in England. Naturally, the children are my chief thought, and whether their future would be more successful in Germany than here. But all depends on whether I feel I can be of use, and I can fairly judge that after a term. The weather is so mild that the crocuses and violets are in flower in the garden.'

Hardly had this letter been sent off than Max Müller was taken seriously ill, and for some days typhoid fever was feared. The attack resolved itself into violent neuralgia in the head, and he was for many days in bed, unable to move. At the end of the time he wrote the following letter to his mother. After giving an account of his illness, he continues—

*Translation.*

'Then came the death of Goldstücker[1], which I felt very much—we had worked together so long. So one goes after the other, and one becomes more and more lonely. He really caused his own death: would see no doctor, though begged to do so, and died from the results of a cold. I was better off, for I had no want of careful nursing. So

[1] Whom he knew in Paris and London.

in May I really am going to Strassburg. The money they offer is a good deal for Germany. They tell me it is the highest salary ever offered to a Professor. As I do not know the life at all, it is pleasant to be able to try it before deciding.'

No sooner had the German papers announced that 'Professor Max Müller will *kindly* give a course of lectures during the Summer Term,' than various attacks, some in anger, some in ridicule, began to appear in the French papers. 'We suppose some advances were made to M. Max Müller, but it would have been too great a condescension on his part, too heroic a sacrifice, to exchange the fat (*sic*) endowments of Oxford for (from the English point of view) a very modest Stipendium.' 'It will be a great honour for the Prussians of Strassburg, and it is only bare politeness on their part to announce that M. Max Müller will *kindly* give a course of lectures.' 'Many people in France will be astonished that M. Max Müller, a Foreign Member of our Institute and pupil of Burnouf, should hasten, at the first moment, to deliver German lectures on a soil that we can never cease to consider French!' 'M. Max Müller would have done well if out of regard to France, where he has many friends and admirers, he had waited till the second term, and not associated himself with the inauguration of this University.' The same paper, in mentioning *Deutsche Liebe* as published anonymously, says 'the author perhaps shrank from putting his name to a novelette, or probably was afraid of arousing feelings of retrospective jealousy in the wife he had married in England.' *Deutsche Liebe* came out in 1857, two and a half years before he married. Finally, the article declares that M. Max Müller is determined to aid in the *Germanizing* of Alsace by the lectures he has *kindly* consented to give at the German University.' So sensitive did the French continue, that it was only in the late autumn of 1881 that Max Müller, who was elected in 1869, ventured to take his seat at the French Institute and make his address of admission, which was constantly interrupted in the beginning by the younger members with disagreeable and sneering remarks, till his friends succeeded at last in enforcing silence.

TO DR. KIELHORN.

*Translation.* PARKS END, *April* 6, 1872.

'I did indeed hope that you would make your return journey via England, and that I should be enabled to congratulate you and your future wife in person. So I must do it now at least by letter and in a great hurry. May you be as happy as you deserve to be, and may the Indian years of exile be followed by a happy return to the German home. Write to me soon, when you have arrived in Bombay or Poonah. I have been ill over a month; however, I am better now, and Volume V of the *Rig-veda* is completed, with the exception of the last four pages. I must send it to you to India, also a little keepsake from me for your wedding, which I hoped to have given you in person.

'I have felt Goldstücker's death much; I had known him for such a long time, and small literary differences disappear entirely when we stand at the grave of a dear old friend. I hope to acquire his library for Strassburg. Your old countryman, 'M. M.'

The fifth volume of his great work was now ready. The difficulties of restoring a correct text of Sâyana's Commentary increased with each volume. The MSS. were more and more faulty, probably because the last part had been less studied and used, and therefore the MSS. were not corrected and kept up with the necessary care. No pains had been spared in scouring all India, even the Southern Provinces, for MSS., but in vain. Max Müller says in his preface to Volume V:—

'There is not one doubtful or difficult passage in the whole of this work where I have not myself carefully weighed the evidence of the MSS.; not one where I have not myself verified the exact readings of the MSS., even in those portions which were copied and collated for me by others, except where the originals were out of my reach. I believe I have acknowledged, without stint, whatever assistance I have received from other scholars during the progress of my work. They themselves have assured me that I had said more than they deserved or expected. But, as it has been broadly hinted that for certain portions of Sâyana's Commentary I had parted with my editorial responsibility, I take this opportunity of stating, once for all, that there is no page, no line, no word, no letter, no accent, in the whole of the Commentary for which I am not personally responsible. Nothing was ordered for press that I had not myself carefully examined and revised, and though for certain portions of my edition, as I stated in the preface to each volume, I was relieved of much preliminary labour, the decision in all critical passages, whether for good or evil, always rested with me.'

In this volume is published the first part of the Index Verborum, which was made before Max Müller began the publication of the *Rig-veda* and Sâyana's Commentary, and it was by its help only he was able to make his way through the difficulties of Sâyana. Professor Benfey, of Göttingen, the veteran Sanskrit scholar, on seeing a few proof-sheets of this Index, wrote: 'I see what extraordinary assistance the publication of this Index Verborum will afford to Vedic studies. It will hardly be possible to render you sufficient thanks for it. I in particular expect to derive the greatest help from it for my Vedic Grammar.'

To Canon, now Dean, Farrar.

Parks End, *April* 14, 1872.

'I quite know what it is to be overworked, and how new thoughts take possession of one's brain, and make us for a time forget everything else. You must suffer more than I do in that respect, though I assure you just now, with three books printing in English, and proof-sheets of a French and of a German translation, and lectures every day, I sometimes feel quite bewildered. I shall value the dedication of your Lectures[1] very much, and it is very kind of you to have thought of it. Do not suppose that I am unable to value researches which lead to conclusions different from my own. I know it is my own fault if you think so, for I feel so conscious that I cannot express a difference of opinion without giving offence, that I have given up all criticizing. Were I to criticize ——'s book he would never forgive me, so I leave it alone. There are people who can criticize without offending, but I know I cannot—why I cannot tell. Whenever you print your Lectures I shall be very glad to receive the proof-sheets if you like; but, without having seen it, I shall always consider it an honour to have my name connected with any one of your publications.'

In April the Platt-Deutsch poet Klaus Groth and his wife, with whom the Max Müllers had formed an intimate friendship in 1869 in Kiel, paid a visit to Oxford, where he delivered

[1] *Lectures on the Families of Speech.*

three lectures before the University in German on Platt-Deutsch and its close affinity with English. The genial poet and his charming wife stayed with the Max Müllers, and the visit was keenly enjoyed by both hosts and guests. It was the last time they were to meet. Frau Klaus Groth died a few years later, and after her death the poet remained quietly at Kiel till his death. During their visit Max Müller's sister-in-law, his wife's only sister, to whom Max Müller was warmly attached, was taken alarmingly ill, and though there was a short rally, it was but delusive, and she died May 12, leaving six young children.

To his Mother.

*Translation.* *May* 12, 1872.

'My dear good Mother,—I have just had a telegram from G. that her sister died to-day at two. She had been ill for some time. I am going to London, where G. is, by the next train. One of the boys is here and I must take him to London. It is a terrible sorrow.'

To the Same.

*Translation.* Bonn, *May* 19.

'Only a line to tell you where I am. On Saturday at noon was the funeral, in the same church at Bray where they were married. It was a most affecting scene. That night I started by Dover and Calais for Bonn. To-morrow Roggenbach will meet me here. Wednesday I must give my first lecture.'

His wife remained in England till Max Müller had found a place for her, the children, and his mother. A very few days showed him that Strassburg was impossible for his family: no houses were to be had, and he began looking for one in the neighbourhood. On his way to Strassburg he had been threatened with a terrible misfortune. On arriving at Bonn the large portmanteau containing all his notes and manuscript books, representing the labour of his life, was missing. It had been registered and *plombé* for Bonn in London, together with a smaller one containing clothes. All inquiries at first seemed in vain. The Crown Prince heard of the disaster, and caused a message to be sent to all principal stations (railways in Germany are all Government possessions) that the portmanteau *must* be found. The right effect was produced after a time, and the portmanteau with its contents untouched was returned from somewhere near Hamburg; but no explanation was ever given. Max Müller was nearly ill with anxiety, for the loss would have been irreparable, and really have wrecked his life, as far as his work was concerned; but he never told either his wife or mother at the time all he was going through.

To his Mother.

*Translation.* Strassburg, *May* 22.

'Yes! really in Strassburg—raining, as everywhere. I have found a lodging, but a very small one—two rooms and a very small bed-room. The want of rooms is terrible. Write and say how you are, and whether and when you can come. It can be done, but I cannot promise you much enjoyment till we have a house in the country.'

Max Müller soon found that the life in Strassburg would not do, even for his mother alone, and postponed her arrival. His time at Strassburg was a thorough success, in spite of the discomforts. He found that he could lecture in German without any of the physical fatigue that his English lectures always gave him. He had fifty hearers, the largest class of all, and gave private Sanskrit lessons as well. But what he most enjoyed was the constant intercourse with men, each of whom was a distinguished representative of his own particular line of studies. As there were no arrangements for food in their various lodgings they formed a sort of club at an hotel, and met every day for early dinner and supper. Max Müller made many acquaintances with the rising scholars in Germany who had gathered at Strassburg, as the French papers said, 'to Germanize the French inhabitants.' On June 1 he writes to his wife:—

'No rooms fit for mother; every one is complaining. We are mostly "grass widowers" or bachelors and don't mind. There are no servants. The lectures in themselves are a great pleasure to me, and I see they are liked, but they take a great deal of time. I have to lecture six times a week, and one is not accustomed to that in Oxford, where I only give twenty-four lectures in the whole year!'

Max Müller's inaugural lecture, 'On the Results of Comparative Philology,' has been translated and printed in *Chips*,

Volume IV. It was published by request as soon as delivered, and widely circulated in Germany.

TO PROFESSOR BERNAYS.

*Translation.* STRASSBURG, 4 REGENBOGENGASSE, *May* 31, 1872.

'MY DEAR FRIEND,—I should have written before, but I had to wait a little to see how matters arranged themselves. Up to the present time I like it very much, and I find it much easier and much less of a strain to speak German than English. I have about forty to fifty hearers for Comparative Philology, and ten to twelve for Sanskrit Grammar. Whether this will continue I do not know. What is wanting here is a guiding spirit. We seem to be like a carriage without a driver—it can't go on like this very long. There is an immense deal still to arrange, two Roggenbachs are hardly sufficient for all there is to do. Lodgings are like lake-dwellings (*Pfahlbauten*). I cannot find a house for my family, but I feel quite well notwithstanding. Yes, after four sleepless nights, my portmanteau arrived. It caused me real suffering. My box of books is still on the road.'

TO HIS WIFE.

STRASSBURG, *June* 4, 1872.

'Why is there so much suffering in this world? I cannot think it improves us much, and yet it must have its purpose. All these are questions far too high for us—we are like children, and more than children when we come to think of them. All we know is that when we catch a glimpse of God's handiwork, either in the natural or moral world, it is so wonderfully perfect, so beyond all our measures, that we feel safe, as in a good ship, however rough the sea may be. Whatever we may believe or hope, or wish for, will be far exceeded by that higher Will and Wisdom which supports all, even us little souls.'

STRASSBURG, *June* 6, 1872.

'My work here answers well, and the young men seem to like it. To me it is no effort, and quite a new sensation. I had no idea that the effort of lecturing in English was so great. What takes up my time here is preparing the Lectures, particularly as I have few books, and have to hunt up things wherever I can find them.'

On June 12 Max Müller was commanded to Baden-Baden to dine with the German Empress. He had first seen the Empress some years before at Coblentz, and always considered her to be one of the best educated women he knew.

He thus describes the scene to his wife:—

'I was really overwhelmed with kindness. First the Empress made me a speech in the presence of the whole Court, thanking me for all I had done for Germany in England, and which she said had had more influence than I knew. Then she thanked me for the sacrifice I had made in giving up my summer vacation and rest for the new University of Strassburg, and hoped my example would lead others to do the same. Lastly, she said she knew from her last stay in England what people felt there at the thought of my going away. In fact I was quite overpowered. At dinner I sat opposite to her, and she talked to me a great deal; and after dinner, when all were going away, she called me to her, made me sit down, gave me her hand, and again thanked me most heartily. I stayed half an hour, and we talked of many things. It was very interesting to see and speak with the first German Empress thus face to face.'

To Herr George von Bunsen.

Strassburg, *June* 17, 1872.

'I am still quite alone here, but my wife and children come from England, and my mother from Chemnitz in about a week. I have taken a house in Baden-Baden; I shall lecture here from Tuesday to Friday, and Friday to Tuesday live in Baden-Baden. The lectures are a delight to me. It is a real pleasure to speak without any effort. I cannot think of future plans. For one thing Strassburg is not what it should be. We want not only one, but four Roggenbachs (one for each Faculty, and one for the University) if we are to create something new and great.'

To Professor Bernays.

*Translation.* Strassburg, 4 Regenbogengasse,

*July* 4, 1872.

'My dear Friend,—It is beautiful here, but it is impossible to get to know about anything, so I come to you. I have found a quotation assigned to Aristotle to the following effect: "God, who is One, receives from us names according to the various visions which we come to see." Can you verify this quotation for me, and may it be assigned to Aristotle? Ever faithfully yours.'

The end of June Max Müller's wife and children arrived at Baden-Baden, and were joined the next week by his old mother. A pleasant summer was spent in the pretty villa he had secured there in the Lichtenthaler-Allee on the outskirts of the town, and when the lectures were over at Strassburg, constant excursions were made by the whole party to all the beautiful places in the neighbourhood. His kind old friend Baroness Bunsen and two of her daughters were living at Carlsruhe, and several visits were paid them there. The end of July, Max Müller attended the fourth centenary of the University at Munich as delegate from Oxford. On the day of his arrival, after a long night's journey from Baden, he found the place already crowded; more than 2,000 guests had arrived.

TO HIS WIFE.

MUNICH, *August* 1.

'It is hard work here, but I get through it very well. Yesterday was the reception of all the deputies. I had to speak for England, Holland, and Sweden. It went off very well. In the evening I saw *Lohengrin*, but after two acts the music was too much for me, and I went home. I had telegraphed for my silk gown, hood, and cap, and they have arrived; so to-day, in the public procession, Oxford will be grandly represented. After the procession there will be speeches, dinner, &c.'

*August* 2.

'The amount of festivities one has to go through is great, but I am still afloat. I suppose you see the accounts in the newspapers. During the procession yesterday, my gown, hood, and cap were much admired. We dined in the Odeon, about 400 people. Döllinger presided; on his right and left the two Bavarian Princes, then the Prime Minister, and then I. I was surrounded with stars; I believe I was the only man of the 400 who had not some little star or ribbon. Last night it poured, so I went home; I don't know whether there was a torchlight procession. To-day again festivities from morning till evening.'

The festivities ended with a great *Commers*, or evening gathering, of all the students in one of the Beer Gardens, at which the Bavarian Princes were present, and to which all the delegates, professors, &c., were invited. The total number of guests was 3,377. Dr. Döllinger was then Rector Magnificus. At the opening ceremony, as it was impossible that all the delegates should deliver congratulatory speeches, the assembled delegates elected Professor von Sybel to speak for the German, and Max Müller for the foreign Universities. In his speech Max Müller reminded his hearers that when he was a German student it was highly criminal to believe in a United German Empire; that day he stood before them having just finished a course of lectures at Strassburg, the first University of the United German Empire.

In his reply Dr. Döllinger complimented Max Müller as nobly representing the bond which united the Munich University with the Universities of the whole Teutonic race.

'By education and culture, as by birth, you belong to Germany . . . the splendid task has fallen to you—and I believe it is the first instance in the history of England—of acting as interpreter of German science . . . in that University in which the flower of the English nation receives its education. We look up to Oxford as an elder sister, for she existed centuries before us, and has had a glorious history, such as no German University has had, and our wishes are that Oxford may for ever remain what she has been for centuries, both to England and the world.'

To Dr. Moritz Carrière[1].

*Translation.* Baden-Baden, Schillerstrasse, *August* 4, 1872.

'My dear Friend,—I have returned well satisfied, but also very tired, to Baden-Baden this morning. Many thanks for all your kindness, and for the great pleasure which you procured for me. I had till now no idea of such a festival, and I must send a short description of it to Oxford, to the Vice-Chancellor. My words about Oxford are easily reported, but not the words of warm sympathy which Döllinger uttered in his reply. Do you think that they could be found in print anywhere? I have the gist of his speech clear in my mind, but the *ipsissima verba* would of course produce a far greater impression in Oxford, and coming from Döllinger they are of historical value, and deserve more than an ephemeral existence. . . . My kind regards to Baron von Liebig. Ever yours.'

Early in this year Max Müller had made arrangements with Messrs. Longmans to publish a translation of the *Life of Baron Stockmar*, the intimate friend of King Leopold, the Queen of England, and Prince Albert. It was written by Stockmar's son, and threw a new light on many things connected especially with the life of King Leopold—his first marriage, the death of Princess Charlotte, the offer of the

[1] Philosophical writer and poet—a friend from Berlin University days.

Greek throne, and the final election to Belgium. Max Müller's old friend Morier had been asked to find a translator. The book appeared in the autumn, and a large edition was sold. It had, of course, the advantage throughout of Max Müller's careful superintendence.

To R. B. D. MORIER, ESQ. (Minister at Munich).

BADEN-BADEN, *August* 12, 1872.

'MY DEAR MORIER,—I was very sorry when I was at Munich that you were not there. Everything else was quite perfect, but it took me nearly a week to recover from the feast, both material and intellectual. There were many inquiries for you; I hope you are better by this time. There is nothing so good after a bout of gout as Baden-Baden; the neighbourhood here is most charming, a real Paradise. Now I want to know when we may have the introduction to *Stockmar*. We are getting on well with the translation, and Longman wants to begin printing as soon as possible. Abeken's death is a great loss. He was a faithful friend, the only respectable element in the Pool of Varzin.'

To HERR GEORGE VON BUNSEN
(who was coming to the Black Forest).

BADEN, *August* 21.

'This is delightful—at present we are still tied to this place. We intended going to Switzerland, but our governess has fallen ill in Hanover, and so my wife cannot leave the children. So I hope we shall be able to see much of you. It is so beautiful here, and we three generations, grandmother, mother, and children, enjoy our time here much. . . . Shall we meet at Gernsbach on Friday?'

Early in September Max Müller presented to the University of Strassburg a magnificent gift from the University of Oxford, 650 volumes of the publications of the Clarendon Press, uniformly bound in calf, every volume containing the inscription—

PRESENTED TO
THE LIBRARY OF THE UNIVERSITY OF STRASSBURG
BY THE UNIVERSITY OF OXFORD,
1872.

The books were all ranged in order in one of the halls, where a large company gathered to hear Max Müller's address, in which he gave a sketch of the constitution of the University of Oxford, so totally unlike all foreign Universities, and of its principal institutions, buildings, &c. Later in the month Max Müller and his wife made a short excursion in Switzerland, visiting the Bernese Oberland for the first time. During the stay at Baden Princess Hohenlohe, half-sister of our Queen, died, and Princess Alice (Princess Louis of Hesse) came to Baden to attend the funeral ceremonies. Max Müller had more than one long interview with the Princess. He was much struck by the depth and earnestness of her mind, and her great dignity coupled with a remarkable charm of manner. On his return to England the Princess sent Max Müller the last work by Strauss, *Der alte und der neue Glaube*, as 'Her Royal Highness was persuaded that, quite apart from the question of argument with its contents, either in whole or in part, he would read the work with great interest.'

To his Wife.

Oxford, *November* 4.

'I had a letter from Strassburg. There are more than 400 students, eighty more in the philosophical faculty. I do not know how it is, but I cannot bring myself to write yet. I wait for some hint, for something to happen, which will show me what I ought to do. I have always found a finger-post on my way through the world; I cannot find one just now.'

To the Dean of Westminster.

*November* 17, 1872.

'My dear Stanley,—What I meant was that kings, like Ministers, like members of Parliament, like judges, *et hoc genus omne*, are men, and it is foolish to frame theories according to which they are supposed to be anything else. We do not want friendless or heartless sovereigns, and in a constitutional State the responsibility of the Ministers ought to cover, not only the sovereign in the abstract, but the sovereign as he is, surrounded by wife, children, friends, &c. After all, the sovereign cannot *act* except through responsible Ministers, and would at every crisis have to choose between his Ministers and his friends. The absurdity of certain constitutional theories reached its acme when people complained that Prince Albert acted as the friend and adviser of the Queen. Stockmar is very strong on that point in his *Mémoires*, and I confess his remarks seem to me full of political wisdom. I should not at all be surprised if the book caused a commotion.

'We shall meet at dinner on Saturday at Balliol—to meet Baron Rothschild.

'I have been reading Strauss's last book, and I should like to know what you think of it. I suppose it was sent to you as it was sent to me.

'*Stockmar* will not be out before the 30th, but I hope to give you a copy next Saturday.'

TO THE RIGHT HON. W. E. GLADSTONE.

PARKS END, *November* 23, 1872.

'I have asked my publisher to send you one of the early copies of Baron Stockmar's *Mémoires*. I feel certain you will find the book interesting, and I only hope you may not think the English too German. Though the two languages are so closely related, one hardly ever finds a word in English that will completely render the purport of a German word. Those words which are etymologically and historically the same in German and English are the most treacherous, for they never mean exactly the same in the two languages. One learns here, too, the old lesson that those who differ little are far more apt to misunderstand each other than those who differ *toto coelo*. I have tried in my preface to smooth certain susceptibilities, which no doubt are perfectly justified, but which I should regret to see discussed in public any more than has been done already.'

It will perhaps be remembered that Dean Stanley was this year nominated by Council as one of the Select Preachers. A most determined opposition was started by Mr.—afterwards Dean—Burgon and Dean Goulburn, aided by Mr. Golightly, the champion of the Evangelical party in Oxford. The following letter alludes to this:—

PARKS END, OXFORD, *December* 8, 1872.

'MY DEAR STANLEY,—We *may* win, and that is good—we may be beaten, and perhaps that may be better, in order to open people's eyes to the intolerable intolerance to which Oxford has to submit. *Convocatio delenda est* ought henceforth to be the watchword of all friends of the University.

'For the present we mean to act. Edwin Palmer is very angry; Gathorne Hardy and Mowbray disapprove; Pusey and Liddon abstain. Bernard attended our meeting. Prince Leopold is quite irate! The great question is, can the London lawyers come down to vote? Ever yours full of hope, but very savage,

'MAX MÜLLER.'

The London lawyers, headed by the venerable Sir Stephen Lushington, came down in numbers to vote. Max Müller, who had delivered a lecture at Liverpool the night before, returned to record his vote, much to the dismay of the friends at whose house he was staying, and who were having a large evening party in his honour. Broad Street was nearly filled when the Balliol M.A.'s turned out to support one of the most illustrious and well-loved of their scholars: the great public schools sent up their masters, and the victory was a very complete one. As the numbers were read out Mr. Burgon and Dean Goulburn were seen to wring each other's hands in the area, as if to say 'better luck next time.' When Dean Stanley preached his first sermon, and stood again in the University pulpit after nine years, St. Mary's was densely crowded, every inch of standing room being filled.

The following letter to his mother gives a glimpse of Max Müller with his children. The birthdays of the father and mother were joyfully observed, and as the children grew older they always had some little surprise ready for the day, besides their long-prepared presents.

### To his Mother.

*Translation.* *December* 12.

'I wish you had been here, and especially in the evening, when the children acted for us very prettily. One thing was really very good. You should have seen Ada as Spring, when she recited *Die Herzen auf, die Fenster auf.* She did it with such spirit as quite surprised me. The whole poem *prestissimo,* and really so well done, it could not have been better, and she had arranged and thought it out quite alone. Then they came in dressed up with wigs and coloured eyebrows, Beatrice as a Marquise, Wilhelm as Schneewittchen, so that one could not recognize them. They sang several songs in English and German —in fact the whole was a great success.'

### To the Right Hon. W. E. Gladstone.

*December* 23, 1872.

'I have just been reading your speech at Liverpool. There are some notes in it which delighted my German heart, though I am afraid that much of what you say of the simplicity of German life and love of knowledge for knowledge's sake applies to the past rather than to the present. The dangers of success and prosperity are clearly discernible there, particularly in the large towns, and the two most important elements in the political life of the nation, the Schoolmasters and the Civil Servants (the much-abused but in Germany invaluable Bureaucracy), find it almost impossible to hold their own, and to command the respect which was formerly paid to them. I read with deep interest what you said about Strauss's new book. Not quite a fortnight ago I had wrestled with Strauss before a Liverpool audience, though I did not mention his name. The book in itself seems to me slight, but it acquires great importance as being the last confession of a man such as Strauss. The only strong position in his book is Darwinism, or Revolutionism, which counts as many believers in England as in Germany, if not more. The problems started by Darwin, H. Spencer, Haeckel, &c., are matters of life and death, and they must become the battlefield for the next philosophical campaign. I confess I have no reply to some of their arguments, and I should have liked very much to hear from you with what weapons you think that the victorious progress of their philosophy is to be stopped. It is impossible to decline battle, though no doubt it is fraught with dangers, nor do I see a chance of victory unless many positions which have become untenable are freely surrendered. I am preparing some lectures on the subject for the Royal Institution in March, but I feel far from confident. I am afraid I shall not be able to avail myself of your kind invitation to Hawarden Castle; I have been a martyr to toothache lately, and there is such an accumulation of work that I shall want all my time when I am able to work. Allow me to send you two lectures of mine on German and English University life.

'With the best wishes of the season.'

At the close of this year there was great suffering in North Germany owing to a terrible storm in the Baltic. The sea rose to a fearful height and devastated miles of coast, causing great loss of life and property, especially in the island of Rügen. The poet Freiligrath wrote a beautiful poem, which he called 'Wilhelm Müller, a Spirit Voice,' in which he represented Wilhelm Müller, some of whose best poems had been written from Rügen, as calling on his countrymen to aid the sufferers. The poet's son saw the poem in a paper, and it elicited not only substantial help, but the following letter to the author.

To Herr Ferdinand Freiligrath.

*Translation.* Parks End, Oxford, *December* 25, 1872.

'Dear Sir,—I have only lately seen your beautiful poem in the *Augsburger Zeitung* of December 8, and therefore my thanks come very late. But I must give utterance to what I, as the son of Wilhelm Müller, felt in reading your poem, and I thank you from my heart that you have put in the mouth of a poet, now half-forgotten by the largest portion of the German public, words which most poets would have kept as their own utterance. This has given great delight not only to his son, but to his widow, who is still living, and they both send you their thanks. May the recollection of the too early departed poet, and the love of the German people for the living poet, bring a rich response to your appeal. Fate has hitherto kept us from meeting in England, and it is therefore all the greater satisfaction to me to shake you by the hand, if only in spirit. With true respect,

'Your more than thirty years' admirer,

'Max Müller.'

On December 30 Max Müller writes to his mother:—

*Translation.*

'Stockmar's *Life* came out on November 30 and seems very much liked, and is selling well. The first week 1,900 of the 3,000 copies were sold, and 500 in America. We sent one to the Queen. Prince Leopold complimented G. very prettily on her knowledge of German. He is here as an undergraduate, and came here one day to five o'clock tea. He does not dine out. He is so simple and unaffected.'

Another large edition of the *Lectures on Language* (the seventh) was published this year.

# CHAPTER XX

## 1873–1874

German University finances. Strassburg Professorship declined. Schliemann. Lectures on Darwin's *Philosophy of Language*. Emerson. Veddahs. Cromer. Lecture in Westminster Abbey. Order pour le Mérite. Member of Hungarian Academy. Prince and Princess of Roumania. Oriental Congress. Last volume of *Rig-veda*. American attack on Max Müller.

THE New Year found Max Müller quietly at Oxford, working at the last volume of the *Veda*, and at his *Lectures on Religion*, given in 1870, but never published, and preparing a short course of lectures for the British Institution on Language as the barrier between man and beast, which he called 'On Darwin's *Philosophy of Language*.' This was Prince Leopold's first year at Oxford as an undergraduate. Max Müller saw him constantly, and ever afterwards recalled their intercourse with genuine interest and affection, and he always hoped that the Prince might do much for his country as an enlightened patron of literature and art.

The following letter to Dr. Althaus refers to the dedication to Max Müller of Bulwer's *Coming Race*. The work was published anonymously, and it was only in the obituary notice in the *Times* that the secret of its authorship was disclosed.

OXFORD, *January* 1, 1873.

'Many thanks for Bulwer. Only think, I never knew him, never even saw him, and learnt first after his death, who had written *The Coming Race*. One ought not to be proud of anything, but I was very much delighted.'

To R. B. D. MORIER, ESQ.

OXFORD, *January* 1, 1873.

'MY DEAR OLD FELLOW,—Best wishes for the New Year. I don't know whether you see many English papers; old Stockmar has been reviewed in most of them, and it is very interesting to see how Johannes Bos has looked at him from different points. There was one review in the *Morning Post* more or less official, or Palmerstonian. It might be a good subject for an article in the *Augsburger*, or some other *Zeitung*, to show how the book has been received and partly digested in England. I have had several private letters which show that the book has told in various ways. I hope you observed Gladstone's civilities in his last Glasgow speech (before he came to Strauss). Do you know of anybody who could write such an article? Young Stockmar is not the man to do it; he is evidently put out by the critics, as if it was worth while writing a book to which everybody is to say Amen. Ever yours.'

To Canon, now Dean, Farrar.

*January* 6, 1873.

'Allow me to thank you at once for the copy of your *Lectures on the Families of Speech*, and for your very kind dedication. You say much more than I deserve, and all I can do is to do my best to deserve some part of your good opinion, by what I still hope to do for the Science of Language. At present my hands and my thoughts are full of other work. I am writing lectures on the "Science of Religion," and to know what to say and what not to say in four introductory lectures is no easy matter. In fact, I should gladly retire from my task, if I could, for I hardly feel up to work, and I am not satisfied with what I have written. As soon as I see a little daylight, and find leisure for other work, I shall read your lectures, and after I have done so I hope to write to you again, or, still better, have a talk with you on points on which we differ, and on points on which we agree. In the meantime accept my hearty thanks.'

Mr. Gladstone had addressed some inquiries to Max Müller on the constitution of German Universities, to which the following letter gives an answer:—

Parks End, *January* 12, 1873.

'I have no book at hand where I could find the exact sum allowed to each University by Government, but such books exist, and I have asked George Bunsen at Berlin to send me something like a Blue Book on the subject. The Universities derive their whole income from Government. Even in cases where there are ancient foundations still preserved, the funds or the land must be administered under the cognizance of Government, generally by a Government

Commissioner. The only other source of income consists in the fees paid by the students. These in the case of the principal Professors, who lecture on Anatomy, Church History, or such like indispensable subjects, are considerable. Savigny, being Professor of Law at Berlin, declined the Ministry of Justice, unless his income as Minister could be raised to what his income was as Professor. A class of 400 students would yield a Professor during the two semesters 1,600 louis d'or, and some of the Professors in my time used to give two courses of lectures in each semester. The highest salary now paid to a Professor is only 4,000 thalers, or £600, yet even that is more than the average income of a Professor at Oxford, with the exception of the Theological Chairs. Considering the general income of the country, the sum expended by Government on the Universities is high. The number of Universities is large, each independent Prince wished to have a University, and I believe they will be kept up even now, for they have proved useful centres of intellectual life in every part of Germany. The difficulty to which you allude of teachers examining their own pupils is little felt. The Professor, lecturing to a large class, does not know many of the students personally. The examination is always conducted by a Commission consisting of five or six Professors. Besides, the University degree does not confer any tangible rights. In order to become a lawyer, a clergyman, a physician, a schoolmaster, every candidate has to pass the Government Examination, and with these the Professors, quâ Professors, have nothing to do. It was to me a matter of great interest to compare the working of a German University, such as Strassburg, with what I knew of Oxford. Each country, no doubt, fashions its own Universities, and makes them to supply the real wants of the people. Yet there is much to be learnt from a comparison of the two systems. I shall be very glad to undergo a cross-examination when you are in London again. I believe the time will come when something will have to be done, not only for Ireland, but for England too. Oxford wants new life. Both teaching and learning seem to me to be regarded as a burden, which ought not to be. I send you a few papers which may partly answer your purpose. In the little calendar you will find the statistics of the German Universities, as far as their teaching staff and the number of students are concerned. In the plan of the lectures you see what is done even by so small a University as Strassburg. You can see how almost every Professor has a laboratory, seminary, hospital, or institution, supported by assistants, where he works with his pupils apart from his lectures. These institutions are the real secret of the success achieved by the German Universities. In several cases the students who are admitted to them receive, while they are at work, an exhibition or fellowship. Anyhow, these institutions are the real workshop where the tradition is handed down from generation to generation. The Colleges with their fellowships might be made to answer some such purpose. There are many Professors in Germany who would have spoken like Döllinger on Materialism. What I like in the German Universities is the frankness with which everybody states the convictions at which he has arrived. Strauss's book has been very severely treated in Germany. Yet there is a crisis going on there as in England; something is dying, whether we like it or not. To my mind Mansel's *Bampton Lectures* and the reception they met with were a sign of the times. They seemed to me far more irreligious than Herbert Spencer. They left religion as a mere cry of despair. Frederick Maurice saw the tendency of that school of thought which erects an insurmountable barrier between the finite mind and the infinite, but he could not make himself understood. Mansel and Herbert Spencer seem to me at the present moment to rule at Oxford in the two opposite camps, and I do not wonder that they produce in each much the same results. I spent some interesting hours with Döllinger at Munich. He is a man of great courage in thought and word; but, though he is a strong and vigorous old man, he shrinks from action. He is Erasmus over again; a rougher nature will be wanted to do the rougher work.'

To his Mother.

*Translation.* Oxford, *January* 18, 1873.

'*Stockmar* is selling well. The Queen has thanked me in the kindest manner for the preface. Prince Christian wrote at the Queen's desire, and she expressed herself kindly about the book altogether. . . . I had almost forgotten the Emperor (Napoleon). Let him rest in peace. One must not judge him, but few men have caused so much misery in the world as he. He was always liked in England, so his death has called out a good deal of sympathy. The last years of his life must have been a hard penance.'

To the Same.

*Translation.* *February* 16.

'The Strassburg uncertainty is over. I wrote them word that with all my private work I could only lecture one term in the year, and on account of the other Professors they could not arrange that. I am glad, for I had done my duty, and should have had to make a great pecuniary sacrifice, and it would have taken up too much of my time, and I could not with a good conscience have undertaken more than I offered. My chief thought has been about the children, and whether it would not be better for them to be brought up in Germany. That is often a weight on me, for the arrangements here are very imperfect. One can manage for the girls, but how it will be for Wilhelm, I do not yet see. But time will show. As yet he learns nothing, but is healthy and merry. G. is not very unhappy about Strassburg.'

TO DEAN STANLEY.

OXFORD, *February* 21, 1873.

'I now have lectures in London and Birmingham. As soon as these are over the printing of Volume VI [of the *Rig-veda*] will begin, and then I shall go on with the translation. I found my work so in arrears, that for the present, at least, I have given up a change to Strassburg. I am very sorry, for the life in Strassburg was like a mental sea-bath. I wrote last week to give it up.'

TO HIS MOTHER.

*Translation.* OXFORD, *February* 25.

'Yesterday I dined with Prince Leopold, and he said the Queen had charged him to tell me how pleased she was that I had decided to stay in England. I am writing to Strassburg to found a Stipendium in their University with the 2,000 thalers they paid me last year, for the study of the *Veda*. It will not hurt me, and I am glad not to take any money from them. The people in Strassburg and Berlin have been very friendly over the whole matter; even Bismarck expressed his sorrow at my decision.'

And thus the uncertainty about Strassburg which had hung over the family for above a year came to an end. The Prize founded by Max Müller, and which bears his name, is given every third year for the best dissertation on 'Vedic Literature,' and may be competed for not merely by present students at Strassburg, but by those who have already taken their degree, provided they studied for at least four terms at that University.

It was in this year that Max Müller made the acquaintance of Dr. Schliemann, the famous excavator, at first by correspondence only. From the first, Max Müller took a great interest in Dr. Schliemann's work; the disinterested character of the discoverer appealed to him, though he often found himself unable to follow Dr. Schliemann's deductions, and to the last he used smilingly to say, 'He destroyed Troy for the last time.' In 1875 Dr. Schliemann paid a visit to Oxford, and stayed with Max Müller, who for several years was instrumental in getting Schliemann's papers and articles inserted in the leading newspapers and periodicals. When Dr. Schliemann exhibited his Trojan treasures at the South Kensington Museum, Max Müller spent some time in London helping him to arrange the things—an arduous task, for, as is well known, though he had the scent of a truffle dog for hidden treasures, he had little or no correct archaeological knowledge, and Max Müller found the things from the four different strata which Schliemann considered he had discovered at Troy in wild confusion—though he maintained they were all carefully packed in different cases. One day when Max Müller was busy over a case of the lowest stratum, he found a piece of pottery from the highest. 'Que voulez-vous?' said Schliemann, 'it has tumbled down!' Not long after, in a box of the highest stratum appeared a piece of the rough pottery from the lowest. 'Que voulez-vous?' said the imperturbable Doctor, 'it has tumbled up!' The friends met again at Maloja in 1885. Dr. Schliemann had meantime finished his beautiful house in Athens, in which two bedrooms were called after Max Müller, and many were the pressing invitations to occupy them; but when Max Müller visited Athens in 1893, his kind friend had passed away. He gave Max Müller a good many things from Mycenae, which are now in the Ashmolean Museum, and also a tiny bit of gold from Agamemnon's grave. The correspondence is of too technical a character to be given here; interesting letters from Max Müller on Athene Glaucopis and Hera Boopis, on the Hindu Svastika, and on Jade tools are inserted in Schliemann's *Troja*. Dr. Schliemann also gave Max Müller the valuable Tanagra figures, which his friends will remember in the drawing-room at 7, Norham Gardens.

Max Müller's American friend Mr. Conway was at this time preparing an Anthology culled from the religious books of different sects and beliefs. Hence the following letter. In the sentiments of the latter part most people will agree.

To MONCURE D. CONWAY, ESQ.

PARKS END, *March* 13, 1873.

'I can see no objection to your printing a number of verses from the *Dhammapada*, but as the book is not my own, I think it would be better if you communicated with the publisher, Mr. Trübner. As to lectures, I am at present so overworked that I ought not to make new engagements. I shall have to give three lectures at the Royal Institution, then at Birmingham, and I have my Oxford lectures going on at the same time, so that this is as much as I can safely do. Lastly, a Mythological Society sounds a somewhat ominous name; yet I quite agree with you that it might do good. However, what I should like to see would be a concentration of the different Societies, and the constitution of a London Academy, divided into Sections. So much work and money are now frittered away, and the Transactions and Journals of the numerous Societies have become mere burial-grounds; for who can even cut open their pages? I read with great interest the *Index*, where I occasionally see your name. Does that paper tell in America? and what is or are the really powerful organs of thought in the United States?'

The end of March the three lectures on Mr. Darwin's *Philosophy of Language* were given at the Royal Institution. They were printed in *Fraser's Magazine*, and also a very few copies for presentation, but were never republished in a collected form.

The following letter alludes to the completion this spring of Mr. Bellows' excellent pocket *French Dictionary*, a copy of which Max Müller always took about with him, and he invariably recommended it as the best type of dictionary he knew in any language:—

To MR. BELLOWS.

PARKS END, *April* 2, 1873.

'MY DEAR FRIEND,—Many thanks for your charming Dictionary, which I found here on my return from London. I am too busy just now to do more than admire it, and congratulate you on its successful termination. I know no other pocket Dictionary that could compete with it. Your discoveries at Gloucester are very curious [Roman wall in his own garden], and I hope I shall be able to inspect them some day or other. Just now I am lecturing in London on "Language as the Barrier between Man and Beast," and I have hardly any thought for anything else. In a few weeks I hope I shall be more free again.'

The next letter refers to an interesting article written by Dr. Althaus in one of the magazines on 'The Germans in England.' Max Müller's is the last name in the article.

To Dr. Althaus.

*Translation.* Oxford, *April* 13.

'My dear Doctor,—I do not know how to thank you. I have just read your essay, and indeed I feel it would be superhuman if, after reading what you say, I did not feel as in a sort of champagne mood. I, of course, know best how much too much you have said of me, but even reducing it by half, there remains so much appreciation which I highly value. I have spent many happy and beautiful years in England, and even the little disappointments do not disturb me, and they cannot blur memory's sunny pictures. The only things I long for are my old friends. One feels more and more alone and solitary, and that feeling draws me so often towards Germany with a great longing. I do not know whether you feel the same. When I was young I did not know what *Heimweh* meant; now it increases with every new year.'

It was after the lectures in London that Emerson, who was paying his third and last visit to England, came to Oxford with his daughter as Max Müller's honoured guest. Max was one of Emerson's ardent admirers, and had known and loved his writings from his earliest days in England. On the second day of Mr. Emerson's visit, Prince Leopold lunched at 'Parks End' to meet the old man. It was a brilliant May day, and the whole party sat out in the garden after luncheon, and the hours slipped past in pleasant converse, till Prince Leopold proposed an adjournment to his house, which was near at hand, for five o'clock tea, when he delighted Mr. Emerson by showing him many private photographs of the rooms at Windsor, Osborne, and Balmoral. The next day, after attending Mr. Ruskin's lecture, the Max Müllers and Emersons visited him in his rooms at Corpus, where the scene recorded in *Auld Lang Syne* took place. Mr. Ruskin wrote afterwards to Max Müller to account for it, by saying, 'It chanced that both you and Mr. Emerson happened to say things from which I deeply and entirely dissented, and which reduced me at once to silence.'

TO CHARLES DARWIN, ESQ.

PARKS END, OXFORD, *June* 29, 1873.

'SIR,—In taking the liberty of forwarding to you a copy of my *Lectures*, I feel certain that you will accept my remarks as what they were intended to be—an open statement of the difficulties which a student of language feels when called upon to explain the languages of man, such as he finds them, as the possible development of what has been called the language of animals. The interjectional and mimetic theories of the origin of language are no doubt very attractive and plausible, but if they were more than that, one at least of the great authorities in the science of language—Humboldt, Bopp, Grimm, Burnouf, Curtius, Schleicher, &c.—would have adopted them. However, it matters very little who is right and who is wrong; but it matters a great deal what is right and what is wrong, and as an honest, though it may be unsuccessful, attempt at finding out what is true with regard to the conditions under which human language is possible, I venture to send you my three *Lectures*, trusting that, though I differ from some of your conclusions, you will believe me to be one of your diligent readers and sincere admirers.'

That the *Lectures* did not alter Mr. Darwin's cordial appreciation of Max Müller is shown by the following charming letter, inserted by permission:—

DOWN, BECKENHAM, KENT, *July* 3, 1873.

'DEAR SIR,—I am much obliged for your kind note and present of your *Lectures*. I am extremely glad to have received them from you, and I had intended ordering them. I feel quite sure from what I have read in your works that you would never say anything of an honest adversary to which he would have any just right to object; and as for myself, you have often spoken highly of me, perhaps more highly than I deserve.

'As far as language is concerned, I am not worthy to be your adversary, as I know extremely little about it, and that little learnt from very few books. I should have been glad to have avoided the whole subject, but was compelled to take it up as well as I could. He who is fully convinced, as I am, that man is descended from some lower animal, is almost forced to believe *a priori* that articulate language has been developed from inarticulate cries; and he is therefore hardly a fair judge of the arguments opposed to this belief.

'With cordial respect, I remain, dear Sir,

'Yours very faithfully,

'CHARLES DARWIN.'

F. Max Müller

Aged 50.

From a Medallion by Bruce Joy

The *Lectures* were answered by Mr. Darwin's son, whose article was again replied to by Max Müller in the *Contemporary Review*, called, 'My reply to Mr. Darwin,' which in its turn provoked the violent attack by Professor Whitney on Max Müller described in the next chapter.

During this summer Max Müller sat to Mr. Bruce Joy for a medallion, and later on for a bust, in the *habit brodé* of the French Institute, the clever artist being his guest whilst the work was carried out. Several pleasant and refreshing visits were paid to the Deanery, Westminster, which Lady Augusta Stanley made a second home to many of her husband's old Oxford friends. The Max Müllers also stayed at Sir William Siemens', for the Civil Engineers' *soirée* at the South Kensington Museum, an evening long remembered with pleasure, as spent almost entirely with Charles Kingsley looking at the Vernon collection of pictures, which at that time still hung there.

In July Max Müller went to Germany to bring his mother to England. She had been far from well for some months, and he found her at first unwilling to travel, and thus was kept longer in Germany than he expected.

To his Wife.

*July*, 1873.

'If we do a thing because we think it is our duty, we generally fail; that is the old law which makes slaves of us. The real spring of our life and our work in life must be love—true, deep love—not love of this or that person, or for this or that reason, but deep human love, devotion of soul to soul, love of God realized where alone it can be, in love of those whom He loves. Everything else is weak, and passes away; that love alone supports us, makes life tolerable, binds the present together with the past and future, and is, we may trust, imperishable.'

Whilst at Chemnitz with his mother, Max Müller wrote to tell Professor Benfey that his Index Verborum of the *Rig-veda* was printed. He had prepared it himself before he brought out his first volume of the *Rig-veda* in 1849, and had lately employed a young German to arrange the Index for each one of the six volumes as a whole. It is still of great practical value, as, the references being to hymns and verses and lines, and not to pages, it can be used with any edition of the *Rig-veda*. He also mentions that a new edition of his *Hitopadesa* was called for, and of his *Sanskrit Grammar* in English, 'and yet,' he says, 'I have my hands already quite full.'

The *Lectures on the Science of Religion*, given in 1870, had been published just before Max Müller went to Germany, and were dedicated to Emerson, 'in memory of his visit to Oxford, and in acknowledgement of constant refreshment of head and heart derived from his writings during the last twenty-five years.'

The volume was favourably received, and called out less adverse criticism than it would have done three years before.

'Professor Max Müller,' says one reviewer, 'properly calls the lectures in this volume "An Introduction." They break ground in the little-trodden path of Comparative Theology. He tells us he is convinced that study here will ultimately produce as great a revolution in our ideas of man's past history, and in the relations and character of the various religions of mankind, as study of natural science has produced in our view of the Creation. Researches in the sphere of history, with the help of Comparative Mythology, prove that there are elements in human nature which must have been primal and original, which could never have been developed, which must have been implanted from the beginning—wherever we place that. That man, as a religious being, possesses such an element or disposition, we conceive Mr. Müller himself has gone far to prove. And the more we find, by comparison of the religions of the world, the distinctness and indestructibility, and yet the essential identity of this element under all varieties of forms of development, the more shall we be compelled to accept the fact of the Divine origin of mankind, and, even amid its worst corruptions, of the community of human nature with the Divine, of the finite with the Infinite.'

So little is still known about the Veddahs, that the following letter to Mr. Hartshorne may be of interest:—

OXFORD, *July* 27, 1873.

'DEAR SIR,—I have just returned from Germany, and I am afraid that my answer to your letter of June 23 will hardly reach you in time, before you start again on a new visit to the Veddahs. So much has been said about their peculiarities in language, thought, and manners, that a really trustworthy account of them would certainly be most valuable. How difficult such an account is you must know best by this time. In looking at your list of Veddah words I was struck at once by their Pâli, i.e. secondary Sanskrit character. The question therefore, arises, are those Pâli or Sinhalese words later importations, or is it possible to distinguish between an earlier substratum of Veddah speech and these clearly Aryan words? Or, does the Veddah language take its place simply as a degraded Sinhalese dialect, and the Veddah people as a degraded Sinhalese race, instead of being, as generally supposed, a remnant of a primitive and savage race? This question can be solved scientifically by linguistic evidence only. But the solution is most difficult. We must know what corruptions are possible between Veddah and Sinhalese, between Sinhalese and Elu, between Elu and Pâli, between Pâli and Sanskrit. . . . I have marked on your list of Veddah words many that are clearly of Sinhalese kinship, and these are words which constitute the most necessary portion of a language; for instance, the *pronouns*, words for man, cow, flowers, to cook, to go, &c. &c. Here and there I see a trace of grammatical structure, and you may be certain that there is as much grammar in the Veddah language as in English. You may say, that would not be much, but it presupposes much. No doubt it would be difficult to get an idea of English grammar from a Welsh coal-miner, and your Veddahs have evidently sunk much lower; but with great perseverance something of the grammatical articulation of the language might still be discovered, and has to be discovered, before we can say anything about their origin. I never believe that the Veddah language has no word for *two*. There may be Veddahs who do not count, or who, as philosophers would say, form no syntheses, but that a language which has a word for I and thou, for eye and ear, should have no sign for the dual concept, I shall never believe. More difficult even than the grammar is the religion of a people like the Veddahs. One occasionally sees accounts in the papers of a witness being sworn in an English Court of Law, and if one took his answers about the Deity, about life and death, and right and wrong, as materials on which to build a theory of the Christian religion, one would still be better off, I suppose, than with the best of the Veddahs. And yet these people have a religion, if one only knows how to disinter it. To call "the propitiation of the spirits of deceased ancestors" the most original form of religion is utterly wrong. It takes thousands of years before we arrive at such ideas. The idea of an ancestor involves the idea of relationship; a belief in deceased, but not yet extinct, ancestors implies the germs of a belief in immortality. The idea of a spirit, or of spirits of deceased persons, belongs to the tertiary age of thought, and as to propitiation, that is a concept not yet 3,000 years old. The time has not come yet for a chronology of religious beliefs; what we want are accurate statements of all manifestations which imply a conception of anything beyond what is given to man by his sensuous experience. All this is a work of very great difficulty, and it is because people do not see the difficulty, that we get so much material which is amusing and may fill volumes about Prehistoric Culture, and yet leaves us exactly where we were before. It is difficult when we have to deal with one individual, to say *what he is no more*, and *what he is not yet*; to say the same of a family, a clan, a tribe, a people, is much more difficult. And yet this is what we want to know about the Veddahs, whom many people are so anxious to represent as monkeys and not yet men, but who may be monkeys and men no longer.

'Excuse haste, and believe me,

'Yours very truly,

'F. M. M.'

After Max Müller's return to England with his mother, the whole family went to Cromer, which proved a time of great interest to him, as bringing him into closer contact with many members of the Gurney and Buxton families, with some of whom he had been associated years before through the marriages of his friends Ernest and George von Bunsen. On his return home he devoted himself to work on the sixth and last volume of the *Rig-veda*. He had during this year published the text of the *Rig-veda* in two small octavo volumes, according to the Pada and Samhitâ systems.

But his mind was ere long turned to another subject. His friend Dean Stanley had asked him the year before to give the evening address in Westminster Abbey on Christian Missions. Max Müller had then declined, but the Dean again urged his request this year. It was a bold step on the Dean's part, who had, however, ascertained that it was perfectly legal. He took the opinion on this point of Lord Coleridge, the Lord Chief Justice of England, who replied, 'It is perfectly *legal*, but whether it is *expedient*.' 'I did not ask your opinion on that point,' rejoined the intrepid little Dean. It needed no small courage in Max Müller to accept; but having ascertained from the Dean that it was legal, he now no longer hesitated, feeling it would put him in a position to say things that had long weighed on him. Having once made up his mind, he was perfectly unmoved by the storm it raised, and set about preparing his discourse with his usual tranquil self-possession and power of detaching himself from public opinion.

To R. B. D. Morier, Esq.

*November* 3.

'My dear Morier,—We had our orgie at All Souls last night, and I thought of you when I was presiding as Sub-Warden (the Warden being ill), supported by two noble lords, Lord Devon and Lord Bathurst, and proposing the different healths of the evening. I also thought of Bellum's and all that. Don't you think it is time for me to leave, having reached this exalted pinnacle?'

On December 2 the Max Müllers went to the Deanery at Westminster, and the next day the Lay Sermon was delivered. Charles Kingsley, Theodore Walrond, and Sir Charles Trevelyan dined and attended the service. It was very nervous work, both for the lecturer and many of his hearers, but his voice was clear and carried far, and his earnest, reverent manner impressed the vast congregation from the first moment. To one who for long years had wished that he could have an opportunity of uttering the great truths which were the foundation of his own life, other than that afforded by the Royal Institution, it was a unique moment, and a glance at his quiet, self-possessed face, showed that he was equal to the great task, and stilled all feeling of anxiety.

The next day both the congratulations and vituperations began; the latter made little impression. On his way home Max Müller met Dr. Liddon, who wrung his hand, saying, 'I rejoice from my heart that you have been helping us.' The author of *The Childhood of Religion* wrote:—

'I must thank you for your noble words in the Abbey last week, to which it was my delight to listen. I am sure they will do great good in directing attention to the place each faith has had in the order of this divinely-governed world.'

To the Dean of Westminster.

Parks End, Oxford, *December* 11, 1873.

'My dear Stanley,—So the work is done. I hope it may produce some good effect! I may tell you now that I never felt so nervous in my life before, but I had perfect confidence in you, that you would not have asked me unless you felt it ought to be done, and could be done. All the people I see here seem to acquiesce, but of course I have no opportunity of hearing their real opinion. Ruskin was truly pleased, and I believe would like to lecture himself. I wish the University Sermons could be opened to laymen—there seems to be no reason why they should not. Are you aware that in the Greek Church it is by no means unusual for laymen to occupy the pulpit? I read your sermon to-day—I had hardly heard it in the Abbey, I felt so excited. I like it very much. Did you see the new ending to my lecture? I felt there was something wanting to make the ending less abrupt, and as I am not likely to have another opportunity soon, I thought I might as well say all I had to say. Ever yours.

'I am truly grateful now that you asked me, and glad that I did it.'

### To Professor Klaus Groth.

*Translation.* Oxford, *December* 14, 1873.

'My dear Friend,—It is long since I wrote. You have no idea how my time goes, and the letters I *like* to write have to wait for those I *must* write. I have written to Prince Christian about the Platt-Deutsch Bible: the thing can be done, and I have told him not to consult any one further, but to leave the arrangements entirely to you. One could begin with the New Testament—wait how that succeeds, before the Old Testament is undertaken. Yes, how much has happened again this year, and how little really effected! All has gone well with us. I am often frightened at our happiness. Wife and children well, my mother on a visit to us for the last six months, also far stronger than one dare expect. I certainly was laid up in summer, but am now quite well. I have said farewell to Strassburg with a heavy heart, but I hope wisely. It was not quite what I expected. There was a want of go, of initiative. My idea was that the best powers of Germany would come to this new Byzantium of literature, the Crown Prince at their head, that the Alsatians might be forced to be proud of their country, and that a new mental capital would be founded in Strassburg, as a make-weight to the military metropolis; but the reality, pleasant as it was, was different. Fritz Kraus [1] has thanked *me* for a notice *you* wrote on his Southampton Sonnets. Greetings to all our Kiel friends. . . . I hope your Christmas will be one of undisturbed happiness. Your boys must be growing fast. Shall we soon meet? It does not look like it.'

[1] A young Swiss, who made an excellent translation of Shakespeare's *Sonnets* into German. He was a great invalid, and died of decline in 1881.

To W. Longman, Esq.

Oxford, *December* 15.

'"Why is there so much delay about bringing out the Sermons?" the Dean writes to me from Windsor; but it is not my fault. I ordered my part for press on Wednesday. I look forward to three months' imprisonment with great pleasure. What an amount of work I shall be able to get through, having no dinner-parties, calls, meetings, &c., to interrupt my work!'

Some of the papers had threatened Max Müller with imprisonment for brawling in church, and an Oxford tradesman who had heard of this ran out of his shop one day as he was passing, and, seizing his hand, said, 'Well, sir, when they send you to prison, count on a hot dinner from my table every week.'

To Herr George von Bunsen.

*December* 21.

'... The theological wasps buzz around my ears. It was an exertion indeed, but it was worth while—*fiat experimentum in corpore vili*. There is no going to prison just yet, however—Stanley had a legal opinion from the Lord Chief Justice before he undertook the matter.'

Perhaps the attack that amused Max Müller most was from Mr. Henry Reeve, the editor of the *Edinburgh Review*, who was presumably ignorant of Lord Coleridge's legal opinion, and wrote, 'By the law of England, as I read it, an unordained person who preaches or lectures in a church is guilty of a misdemeanour, punishable with three months' prison, and though Westminster Abbey is so peculiar that it is probable the law could not reach you, I shall always deeply regret that you were induced ... to appear there!'

To Herr George von Bunsen.

*Translation.* Parks End, *December* 25, 1873.

'Many thanks for your letter, and for all the interesting enclosures from friends. I have been very busy lately. The English people have so much time for writing letters, and to explain oneself to three or four different parties is no easy matter. In spite of all, I am nevertheless glad to have followed Stanley's bidding.... Yes, indeed, I thought of your father when I stood in Westminster Abbey—how often the unlikely becomes reality! I send you my lecture, for first

I had to omit some points when I delivered it, and secondly the *Times* omitted some things in reporting it.

'We have had such a happy Christmas; everything was perfect—three generations together—but such happiness fills one with anxiety.

'Alas, the lectures of Pauli[1] have come to nothing; he was proposed *primo loco*, but it was impossible to get a majority in his favour. Then we succeeded in obtaining the votes for Goldwin Smith, who is now paying a visit to Oxford; he however, refused.

'Yes, indeed, the letter from Curtius is very depressing—for the future still more than for the present. And yet it seems unavoidable in Berlin! It is impossible to perform music in a large manufactory. Therefore, I dreamt a dream of Strassburg as a new capital for the new German spirit, but I soon became aware that the wings were wanting, and that they were satisfied with very little.

'Mommsen told me when I met him in Munich that he was ready to leave Berlin at any moment on his own account, and still more on that of his children. At Leipzig there is no Court and all that belongs to Court life; the merchant class in Leipzig is rich and they are patricians, the Professors are poor but highly esteemed: life there is very agreeable. I often feel drawn towards Leipzig—it might become a new Weimar, only grander and of greater national popularity.'

On the last day of the year Max Müller's old friend, Professor Gelzer, the author of several theological works in German, wrote to him from Basle:—

*Translation.*

'My son gave me at Christmas the first part of your *Introduction to the Science of Religion*. I began to read it the next evening, and could not stop till I had finished the second half next morning. How I am longing for the continuation! No work for a long time has so electrified me, and edified my deepest soul. There are passages which flashed on me like lightning, for they found an echo of sympathetic agreement in my thoughts.'

The work of the year 1874 was devoted to the sixth and last volume of the *Rig-veda*. The preparations for the Congress of Orientalists held in London in September, and writing his opening address as President of the Âryan Section, occupied much of Max Müller's time. His mother returned to Germany in March, but throughout the year the Max Müllers

[1] His friends wished him to give a course of historical lectures at Oxford.

had innumerable guests, among them the reigning Prince and Princess of Roumania.

To his Wife (staying near her old home).

*January* 8.

'Our own life is such perfect brightness that I cannot bear the slightest grumble about this or that not being exactly as one likes it. It seems to me so ungrateful to allow one moment to pass that is not full of joy and happiness, and devotion to Him who gives us all this richly to enjoy. The clouds will come, they must come, but they ought never to be of our own making.'

*January* 12, 1874.

'By a grave one learns what life really is—that it is not here but elsewhere; that this is the exile, and there is our home. As we grow older the train of life goes faster and faster, those with whom we travelled together step out from station to station, and our own station, too, will soon be reached.'

To Edward Tylor, Esq.

*January* 14.

'If you have read Whitney's book, would you not write a review of it for the *Academy?* I know Whitney is an opponent of mine, or, I should rather say, he hates me, but that does not matter, and if you think that on any point he is right and I am wrong, I shall not be angry if you say so.'

To his Wife.

*April* 13, 1874.

'The spirit of love and the spirit of truth are the two life-springs of our whole being, or, what is the same, of our whole religion, for whatever we are, or do, or feel, or think, is nothing without the key-note of religion. If we lose that bond which holds us and binds us to a higher world, our life becomes purposeless, joyless; if it holds us and supports us, life becomes perfect, all little cares vanish, and we feel we are working out a great purpose as well as we can, a purpose not our own, not selfish, not self-seeking, but in the truest sense of the word God-serving and God-seeking.

'I shall have more time for my children when the *Veda* is finished. I now always feel, and have felt for years, that every hour when I could work was due to the *Veda*, but I shall feel that no more.'

Max Müller had a great pleasure this spring in a visit to Oxford of his old friend Victor Carus, with his wife and daughters. He was on his way to Edinburgh, where he had undertaken a course of lectures.

TO PROFESSOR CARUS.

*Translation.* *April* 28.

'MY DEAR VICTOR,—Here everything is light and sunny; you ought to have stayed quietly here. It was like old days to have you here. Life spins itself further and further, but the old threads run on through it. The death of Phillips [1] has shocked us all terribly. I was not there, and only heard of the accident the next morning; when I got there he was already dead. There was no suffering, but he died without regaining consciousness. I have just heard from Pauli from Göttingen—always the same. Hearty greetings from us to you all.'

A letter from his old friend and master, Professor Brockhaus, was a great pleasure to him this spring:—

*Translation.* *May*, 1874.

'I heard with great delight that you have been working very hard to finish your *Rig-veda*. It is just thirty years since you first announced your resolution to edit this gigantic work, and now the whole is finished before us. With what delight you must look on the past. You have achieved great things, and your services to this, the richest product of the Indian mind, will gain ever increasing recognition and admiration.'

It was in June of this year that Max Müller received a wholly unexpected honour, the Order pour le Mérite, which may be called the Blue Ribbon of Literature. Soon after, when Max Müller was commanded to dine at Windsor, he wrote to Prince Leopold to ask if he *might* wear his Order, and the wire came back, 'Not *may*, but *must*.'

TO HIS MOTHER.

*Translation.* *June* 7, 1874.

'Have you seen in the papers that they have made me a Knight of the Order pour le Mérite? I cannot understand it. There are but twenty for all Germany. The Knights elect themselves, and the King has only to confirm their choice. Now the Berliners are by no means my best friends; on the contrary, I have had from time to time to disagree sharply with several of their celebrities, and I never once thought of their electing me. Well, it is no ordinary Order, and is the only one that a literary man may wear with pleasure, and so I am really pleased, though I should have been quite happy without any Order. I have not heard direct, only what is in the papers, so

[1] Professor of Geology. He died from falling downstairs at All Souls.

it may not be true after all. It is the one foreign Order I can wear at Court here without special leave.'

To Professor Carus (who was to receive an honorary D.C.L. degree at Commemoration).

*Translation.*

'My dear Victor,—Come on Tuesday, that you may not be tired but have time to rest. We are counting on your coming to us. Won't you bring your wife or a daughter with you? Two rooms are ready—you know that, and we are rejoicing over this unexpected meeting. As to the Order pour le Mérite, it passes my comprehension. I only know as yet what was in the papers. No one in Berlin has written about it. The Berliners do not love me inordinately, and the election is with the Knights. Well, I shall hear more—till then we must "bear the inevitable with resignation."'

To Professor Lepsius.

*Translation.* Parks End, *June* 18.

'My dear and honourable Friend,—I have not yet got over my shock, but the astonishment gives way to mere joy and gratitude. Never for a moment did I think that this honour would be bestowed upon me after having been away so long from the Fatherland[1]; and I can never be grateful enough to those who have not forgotten me on this occasion. I feel again strongly how my heart is drawing me to Germany, and did I still possess such vitality as you do, I should return there to-morrow. Well my slavery is to stop this year; in September, I hope my last volume of the *Rig-veda* will be finished, and who knows what will happen then! I shake your hand most heartily to-day. Am I right to send my official thanks to Ranke? . . . What do you think of another trial for a common alphabet at the Congress? Our paths, as I told you before, do not lie far apart; in short, I am satisfied to express the *fact* of modification, you express the *method* of modification. My system is the more incomplete, by no means, however, excluding the more complete one. It only needs an understanding about the three degrees of modification; I am only afraid there will be no time for it.'

To the Crown Prince.

Parks End, Oxford, *June* 20, 1874.

*Translation.*

'Your Imperial and Royal Highness,—I am almost afraid that I may appear obtrusive, when I venture to express to your Royal

[1] Max Müller was elected one of the twenty German Knights, not as a foreign Knight.

Highness my joy and gratitude at the distinction granted to me by His Majesty the Emperor. But the ardent desire will not give way to conventional constraint, and the reverence which I have had for your Royal Highness for so many years gives me confidence that your Royal Highness will not be offended even should I offend against etiquette.

'I really cannot imagine to whom I owe my gratitude for the great and unexpected honour. His Majesty the Emperor has given me repeated proofs of his gracious kindness, but this, it seems to me, I can only ascribe to the kind intercession of others. It suddenly occurred to me, that the thought of bestowing this distinction upon me might have received its first impulse from your Royal Highness, and, whether I be right or wrong, I could not rest till I had expressed how deeply grateful I feel for this great distinction, and how it inspires me to new life and work.

'I do indeed realize just now, how my heart clings with all its fibres to Germany. The work which brought me to England first of all, and which has kept me incessantly occupied here for twenty-five years, the publishing of the *Veda*, will be finished this summer, and I shall then feel a free man. If I could be of more use in Germany than here, I should like to return to Germany, though I have grown old. I was very happy at Strassburg; it was like an intellectual sea-bath. Only the task appointed me did not seem far-reaching enough. The Alsatians ought to have been made to feel proud of their new Strassburg in spite of themselves, and just one course of lectures did not suffice for that. I had hoped that, as in former times for Bonn, so now for Strassburg, Germany would send her best men, in order to create there a new spiritual Byzantium, a capital of German art, science, and learning. But this was not thought of. Of course I do not mean to assert that the slow and quiet development of circumstances is not perhaps the better one. I soon felt, however, that under these conditions the giving up of my work in England was hardly justified. But now, having finished the work which tied me to England, the old thoughts of home return, and especially the desire to be one of those who fight under the flag of your Royal Highness on the battle-field of the mind. There are sure to be such battles, in fact there are such now, and I am often astonished how little part the people take in the great religious and Church questions of the present time; how the Government seems left to bear all the responsibility, and this makes a healthy and powerful solution of the matter almost an impossibility. And though in England also, material interests absorb a great part of the moral strength, yet in struggles, such as have begun now in Germany, the heart of the whole nation would beat louder and stronger. What good would it do to Germany, to win the whole world and to lose herself, to lose that which has made her great, her earnestness of life, her joy in everything that is truly beautiful, her courage in the search for truth, her faith in something higher than this life? There is much to conquer still, though it may not be Alsace and Lorraine. Great success is exhausting for a while, but it seems time now to think of the future, which, though the past has been great, ought to be still greater.

'With the best wishes for the great future which awaits your Royal Highness, I remain, your Royal Highness' obedient servant.'

On July 1 the following entry stands in his wife's Diary: 'To-day M. finished the MS. of the *Rig-veda*.' The printing had already begun, and was going on apace.

To his Mother.

*Translation.* *August* 2.

'To-day I have been made an Honorary Member of the Hungarian Academy. I don't know how it came about. I, of course, never stirred in the matter, and yet the German literary men are so angry about it. They cannot hide their displeasure, but it does not hurt. The nearer I come to the end of the *Veda*, the more I find there is to do, but it must be ready for the Oriental Congress in September.

'To-morrow is our wedding-day: how fast the time goes, and how much sunshine these fifteen years have brought us, even though the clouds have not been wholly wanting. God will help us further.'

To his Wife (who was at the death-bed of the mother-aunt).

*August* 19, 1874.

'The death of those we love is the last lesson we receive in life—the rest we must learn for ourselves. To me, the older I grow and the nearer I feel that to me too the end must be, the more perfect and beautiful all seems to be; one feels surrounded and supported everywhere by power, wisdom, and love, content to trust and wait, incapable of murmuring, very helpless, very weak, yet strong in that very helplessness, because it teaches us to trust to something not ourselves. Yet parting with those we love is hard—only I fear there is nothing else that would have kept our eyes open to what is beyond this life.'

To M. Renan.

*August* 19.

'My dear Friend and illustrious Colleague,—It is such a long time since I had the pleasure of hearing from you, that I cannot allow an opportunity to pass which may I hope bring us together again. You know that from the fourteenth to the twenty-first of September there will be a large gathering of Oriental scholars in London. I always understood that you would be here at the time, if not for the sake of the Congress, at least for a visit to England, which you had planned last year and postponed to this. Now I hope it may be so, and that we may meet not only in London, but also in Oxford. You know that a visit from you and Madame Renan is a very old promise, and both I and my wife have always looked forward to its fulfilment with great pleasure. We shall, of course, be in London during the actual week of the Congress, but afterwards we return to Oxford, and should be delighted to show you all that is interesting and beautiful both here and in the neighbourhood. Please let me hear what your plans are. If you could be persuaded to join the Congress we should of course consider it a great honour, and you would find among the multitude some scholars whom you would like to meet. My old teacher Brockhaus is coming, also Stenzler, Weber, Windisch, Schrader, Lepsius, Brugsch, and many more; even Pundits from India. Now please consider all this, and let me know your decision. I see that your great work on the Phoenician Expedition is finished, and I congratulate you with all my heart. I can share your feelings, for I have just ordered the last sheet of the *Rig-veda* for press. Twenty-five years of work, and I have now only to print the preface and various readings. The last sheets were printed from copies I had made at Paris, May, 1846, during the bright and happy days when Burnouf lectured at the Collège de France. My wife presents her kind regards to you and Madame Renan, and hopes I shall succeed in persuading you to come. With old and unchanged sentiments of sincere regard.'

In the beginning of September Max Müller had the honour of receiving the reigning Prince and Princess of Roumania under his roof. They wished to see Oxford, and their only free days coincided with some meeting that filled every hotel in Oxford. In a letter to his mother Max Müller speaks of the Princess as very clever, and of the Prince as a man of great courage and determination. 'They have both of them a strong feeling for the duties of their great station, and are full of plans for the good of the people committed to their care.' They met again in London, and a feeling of true esteem and friendship sprang up, which was a source of deep gratification to Max Müller to the last. Only a few days before his death he received the kindest message from the King of Roumania about a little service that he had been able to render to His Majesty.

The Oriental Congress which met in London towards the close of September was a time of great interest and pleasure to Max Müller, who afterwards welcomed to his house in Oxford many old friends—Professor Lepsius and his eldest son, Professor Nöldeke, Dr. Stenzler, Dr. Spiegel, Dr. Gosche, M. Léon Feer, and various distinguished Orientals. The Max Müllers stayed during the Congress with the Kingsleys in their charming old house in the Cloisters at Westminster. Charles Kingsley was in bad health, not having really recovered from the severe illness he had had during his visit to America in the summer. His wife was then perfectly well.

Max Müller was President of the Âryan Section, and in opening the section delivered a striking address on the Importance of Oriental Studies. The Prince of Roumania came up from Hastings to attend it. At the conclusion of the address, Max Müller presented to the Congress the last sheet of the last volume of the *Rig-veda*, with the Commentary of Sâyanâchârya. His old teacher, Professor Brockhaus, was present to witness the completion of his pupil's great work. The address was published in *Chips*, Volume IV. An appreciative article on his work had lately appeared in one of the American papers.

'Professor F. Max Müller is just giving the last touches to his final volume of the *Rig-veda*. The work was begun twenty-five years ago, and was undertaken as a labour of love, for those who at that period were interested in Oriental or Sanskrit studies were few indeed; too few certainly for the German scholar to have anticipated any reward for his labour, except the gratitude of those few, and the consciousness of having given an important contribution to learning. But within that twenty-five years the interest in such studies has quadrupled at least, and thousands now wish to study the *Rig-veda*. I believe there has been some disposition among American students of Sanskrit to criticize Max Müller's work in a disparaging way, but the Hindoo scholars themselves declare that it is the best rendering of their ancient hymns which exists, and such is the growing opinion in England. And how much has he done beside? Those who have only read his *Chips from a German Workshop*, his *Science of Religion*, his *Lectures on Language*, know but the half of his labours, which really have embraced the preparation of a complete set of instrumentalities for the prosecution of Sanskrit studies. Everybody who is engaged in any work of that kind rushes to him, and none are turned empty away. At the same time he has mingled in every important discussion bearing on philology and mythology in both England and Germany, generally carrying the verdict for his point, but always knowing how to yield gracefully to argument, and, moreover, always prompt in recognizing discoveries made by others in directions where he himself had looked without making them. In short, Max Müller is among the most truthful and industrious workers of Europe just now, and he has built up a reputation which few possess.'

To his Mother.

*Translation.* *October* 9.

'We have lately been very much occupied, partly with the Oriental Congress, partly by visits to us and visits we have paid. Happily I had finished my *Veda*, and have only a little to do to the preface, index, &c., which must be finished this week, and then I shall not grudge myself a little freedom. We had Lepsius, father and son, on a visit. Then we went to stay with Mr. Grant Duff, formerly Under-Secretary for India, and with Sir John Lubbock, where we met Darwin, Tyndall, Spencer, and the two Lepsius'. Lectures will soon begin here, and though I have been here through the vacation and worked hard, it has suited me very well. Perhaps I shall take a holiday in winter, if I need it, and a visit to Rome has long been hoped for by us both. My principal work is finished, and I can at last give myself a treat.'

This visit was the only time Max Müller and Darwin met. The conversation turning on apes as the progenitors of man, Max Müller asserted that if speech were left out of consideration, there was a fatal flaw in the line of facts. 'You are a dangerous man,' said Darwin, laughingly.

It was in the November of this year that Bishop Colenso visited Oxford as the guest, first of Max Müller, and then of the Master of Balliol, and was forbidden to preach at Carfax, the City Church, by the Bishop of Oxford.

On November 27 Max Müller writes:—

To his Wife.

'I sent you a line this afternoon after I had seen Colenso. It seems an unwarrantable stretch of authority on the part of the

Bishop, for there is no legal censure of any kind against Colenso. He has simply spoken out and said what every bishop knows or ought to know. I hear there is an attempt to prevent his preaching in Balliol, but in that they will hardly succeed.'

*November* 29.

'Colenso preached an excellent sermon in Balliol Chapel. He dwelt on the natural slowness of all progress in nature, as well as in the world of spirit; that we ought to learn to wait, and not expect to see the kingdom of God on earth, but only to work for it. The chapel was full—his two sons were there, and the whole scene was very touching. The time will come when they will thank Colenso for having shown that the Old Testament is a genuine old book, full of all the contradictions and impossibilities which we have a right to expect in old books, but which we seldom see in books written on purpose. With those who hold that the Song of Solomon was miraculously inspired one cannot agree—it is with them as with those who defend the real material Presence, they have changed the highest truth into most dangerous falsehood. However, let them fight it out; they will never prevail.'

On the same day Max was able to write to his mother:—

*Translation.*

'The last volume of the *Veda* is in the bookbinder's hands—a long piece of work finished. I often hardly believed that I should finish it, but now I feel I have a right to rejoice, and shall often think of it with real delight.'

Many kind congratulations came from old friends who had watched the progress of the work during many years.

The Master of Balliol wrote:—

'I heartily congratulate you on the completion of your great work. I only disagree with one thing in your preface, that you dare to speak of yourself as an old man. We are none of us old until we think that we are.'

TO PROFESSOR ALTHAUS.

*Translation.* *December* 3.

'Many thanks for your letter. Indeed, I had hardly thought it possible that I should be permitted to finish this work, and now that it is finished, something seems to be wanting every day. However, there is plenty of material left for work, and if my strength holds out, the good will to work is never wanting.'

In December Max Müller received the thanks of the

Secretary of State for India in Council for the satisfactory manner in which he had carried out the important work entrusted to him. In his reply to Sir Lewis Malet, Max Müller expressed his pleasure that the work was done, and his gratitude to Her Majesty's Government for having enabled him to finish a task which he thought was worth a life, and for which he had received in France, Italy, and Germany the highest honours which a literary man can aspire to.

'The *Rig-veda*, though for the last 3,000 years it has formed the foundation of the religious life of India, had never before been rendered accessible to the people at large, and its publication will produce, nay, has already produced, in India an effect similar to that which the first printing of the Bible produced on the mind of Europe. Beyond the frontiers of India also, the first edition of the oldest book of the whole Âryan race has not been without its effect, and as long as men value the history of their language, mythology, and religion, I feel confident that this work will hold its place in the permanent library of mankind.'

To Max Müller's surprise and gratification, he received about three months later a letter from Sir Lewis Malet, informing him 'that the Secretary of State for India in Council has sanctioned a grant of money to you, as a special recognition of your services in connexion with the editing and printing of the *Rig-veda*, in addition to the sum received by you as an honorarium, according to the orginal agreement.'

Few but Sanskrit scholars will have read the preface to this sixth and last volume of Max Müller's great work, and some passages are therefore given from it:—

'When I had written the last line of the *Rig-veda* and Sâyana's Commentary, and put down my pen, I felt as if I had parted with an old, old friend. For thirty years scarcely a day has passed on which my thoughts have not dwelt on this work, and for many a day, and many a night too, the old poets of the *Veda*, and still more their orthodox and painstaking expositor, have been my never-failing companions. I am happy, no doubt, that the work is done, and after having seen so many called away in the midst of their labours, I feel deeply grateful that I have been spared to finish the work of my life. But habits established for so long a time are not broken without a wrench, and even now I begin to miss my daily task; I begin to long for some difficult and corrupt passages to grapple with, for some abrupt quotation, or for some obscure allusion to Pânini to trace back to its original source.

'It was in 1845, when attending the lectures of Eugène Burnouf, that my thoughts became fixed on an edition of the *Rig-veda* and its voluminous Commentary. I still see the eager faces of a number of young scholars sitting round the table when Burnouf was lecturing with a vivacity, a keenness, a flow of knowledge, which I have never seen surpassed. . . . I was the youngest of them all, and, though I had published a translation of the *Hitopadesa*, my ideas of Sanskrit literature did nct reach much beyond the Epic Poems and the *Upanishads*. Nothing, I thought, could in beauty of thought or expression exceed the *Upanishads*; I had translated some of them for Schelling. Well do I remember my surprise when I heard Burnouf speak of them as works of small importance, compared with the older portions of the *Veda*. Burnouf was lecturing then on the first book of the *Rig-veda*. He possessed a complete copy of Sâyana's Commentary. After a time Burnouf lent me some of his MSS. and encouraged me to copy them. It was hard work at first . . . and, but for his frank acknowledgement that he too could not always make out Sâyana, I should never have had the courage to persevere. . . . But I worked on till a portion of the work was finished, and after obtaining the patronage of the old East India Company, I was able to publish the first volume in 1849.

'We are now in 1874. Twenty-five years are certainly a long time, and when I saw how some of my friends clamoured at the delay . . . I began to fear I might really be to blame. I therefore made out an account of my stewardship, and the result was as follows: I found that since 1849 there were three years in which I was prevented going on with my work—one year when I was out of health, another when I had to wait for the renewal of the grant, on the extinction of the East India Company, and a third when waiting for a MS. from India, which promised to be if not the original, yet much more ancient than any I had used. During the last twenty-five years I have done other work also. . . . I have not thought that a man ought to live by Sanskrit alone. But after deducting the three years when I could not print, I found to my own surprise that I had published in my two editions of the *Rig-veda*, the large one with, and the small one without Sâyana's Commentary, what amounted to an annual volume of nearly 600 pages octavo, during twenty-five consecutive years. If my friends will also take into account that in that time I published two editions of my *History of Ancient Sanskrit Literature*, two editions of my *Sanskrit Grammar*, the *Prâtisâkhya*, text, translation and notes, and the first volume of my translation of the *Rig-veda*, I think they will admit that I have not been altogether faithless to my first love.'

If we add to this the *Lectures on the Science of Language*, and innumerable lectures and essays on language, mythology, and religion republished in the *Chips*, the total record of work done is not a light one for a man not yet fifty-one!

Max Müller concludes his preface by a few lines in self-defence, which will find an echo in the hearts of most authors:

'I know I have sometimes been blamed for not replying to my critics, but such blame was most unjust. The fact is that I could not possibly do it. When books are reviewed as they now are, not only in England, but in every country in Europe, nay, even in America and India, what are we to do? Many of these reviews never reach me at all, but even if I attempted to read and notice those only which I happen to see, I should have had no time left for anything else. It was not want of respect that made me silent, but simply want of time. I venture to avail myself of this opportunity to explain another apparent neglect on my part, for which I know I have been blamed, if not in public, at least in private. During the last ten years, the number of books sent me from all parts of the world has become so great that I had to give up the attempt to acknowledge them all. When I was a young man it was generally understood that no acknowledgement was expected when a book was sent without a letter; to that rule I have conformed both as a sender and receiver of presentation copies. It is generally said that Humboldt acknowledged all books and answered all letters. . . . Humboldt died before the Penny Post attained its full development. . . . I feel sure that my friends will forgive me if I do not always write, by return of post, that I am looking forward with the greatest pleasure to reading their books. Nothing gives me greater pleasure than reading books written by men with whom I am personally acquainted, but if a friend sends me a book on Comparative Mythology while I am in the midst of work on Sanskrit accentuation, I must put his work aside for a time, and cannot express an opinion till I find leisure to read it carefully. *Soyez raisonnables.*'

Here it is necessary to revert to an extraordinary statement published soon after Max Müller's death in the New York *Nation*, and repeated in other journals. The *Nation* says: 'What Max Müller constantly proclaimed to be his own great work, the edition of the *Rig-veda*, was in reality not his *at all*. . . . A German scholar did the work, and Müller appropriated the credit for it. But even in this case, though the judgement be true, it is harsh. The German scholar was paid for his labour, and did the best he could to circumvent Müller in getting out his *editio prima*. The incident is not altogether creditable to either party.' To those who have read thus far in the *Life of Max Müller*, it will seem almost impossible that a respectable paper could publish so false a statement. Burnouf, Brockhaus, Cowell, and many other Nestors of Sanskrit scholarship watched from 1846 with deep interest the progress of the work, and knew from seeing it how Max Müller had spent years in copying and collating MSS. of the *Rig-veda*, and searching out obscure references in Sâyana's Commentary. The German scholar alluded to is Dr. Aufrecht, for many years Professor of Sanskrit in Edinburgh, and then in Bonn. The passage in the *Nation* is as insulting to him as to Max Müller. Dr. Aufrecht would be the first to acknowledge that the first volume of the *Rig-veda* (the most difficult of all, says Mr. Macdonell, the present excellent Professor of Sanskrit at Oxford) had been published three years before he and Max Müller ever met, and that when he arrived in England to work under Max Müller the second volume was already nearly finished. In the prefaces to the second, third, and fourth volumes Max Müller fully acknowledges his indebtedness to Dr. Aufrecht. For the last two volumes he had the assistance of other younger scholars, and in the prefaces to these volumes he mentions this, and in Volume VI gives the names of Dr. Eggeling, now Professor of Sanskrit at Edinburgh, and Dr. Thibaut, Professor of Sanskrit at Benares, as his helpers. Dr. Kielhorn, Professor of Sanskrit at Göttingen, writes: 'While I was in Oxford (from 1862–65) . . . I have often *seen* Max Müller at work on the *Rig-veda*, and had occasion to consult the index to the text, which he had compiled many years before.' Dr. Eggeling writes: 'From what I saw personally of Max Müller's mode of working, I may say that I always admired the extremely careful and scholarly way in which he dealt with his manuscript materials in constituting his final text.' M. Barthe, writing in April, 1874, says: 'M. Max Müller is, and must always remain, the first editor of the

*Rig-veda.* He was the one man in Europe who had courage enough to enter on this path. It was he who took up the work as it fell from the failing hands of Rosen, and who, extending the design of Rosen, conceived it as worthy to be the principal work of his own life.' Professor Macdonell, after a careful examination, calculates that, if Professor Aufrecht had worked *absolutely alone* at Volumes III and IV, and the end of Volume II, collecting and collating all MSS., &c., he would have done but little over one-third of the work, of which *all* is ascribed to him in the article imposed (no doubt) on the *Nation.* Had there been any truth in the accusation its discovery would not have been left to an anonymous accuser in America, nor its exposure reserved until after Max Müller's death.

A great anxiety fell on the Max Müllers towards the close of the year. Mrs. Kingsley became alarmingly ill, and no hope was given that her life would be spared. Max Müller wrote to his mother:—

*December* 12.

'I meant to write to you to-morrow (Sunday), but a sad duty calls us away. Mrs. Kingsley is very ill, the doctors have given her up, and as she wishes to see G. once again, we shall start very early to-morrow morning for Eversley, and return in the evening. It is a heart disease which has come on suddenly. She herself considers her state as hopeless, so do her husband and children, yet they write with a quiet resignation that astonishes one. There has never been a happier family life, and this sudden end is terrible. It will be a trying day, and I could not let G. go alone. We have not been there together since we spent the first week of our honeymoon there.'

To the Same.

*December* 27.

'We went to Eversley. Mrs. Kingsley spoke quietly to G. about everything, and asked me to play something. Her husband and children were so quiet and self-possessed. I have never seen anything like it. She is a little better, but she might die at any moment. They have had such a happy life together, and it was heart-breaking to see it all.'

As they left Charles Kingsley said to them, 'When I am left alone you will come to me.' His wife lived on, but in little more than a month the Max Müllers returned to Eversley for his funeral.

# CHAPTER XXI

## 1875

Death of Charles Kingsley. Visit to Italy. Windsor. Last visit of mother. *Chips*, Volume IV. The Mumbles. Manchester. Plans for return to Germany. Maximilian Order. Oxford Girls' High School.

FROM the moment that he had written the last line of the last volume of the *Rig-veda*, Max Müller's thoughts again turned longingly to his own country: though he fully realized how hard it would be to break the ties of twenty-seven years that bound him to Oxford, and he also found it very difficult to decide whether England or Germany would offer the best opening for his son, who was then only eight years old. Yet on account of his education it was necessary to come soon to a decision. As he said in one of his letters at this time, he 'waited for some intimation.'

TO PROFESSOR TIELE OF LEYDEN.

*Translation.* *January* 3, 1875.

'DEAR FRIEND,—I should have liked to write to you ere this to thank you for your kind letter and for the essays on the science of language, but my hands were so full that I put off everything which was not absolutely necessary. Shortly after receiving your essay, I got another from Darwin *fils*, inspired, however, by Darwin *père*, which had to be answered by return. It had to be written and printed in a week, an excuse for the many printer's mistakes. I sent you a copy to-day, in which I refer to your essay. It was an opportunity of bringing to light the affair of Whitney & Co., though I detest this sort of thing. I had never before seen the Whitney lectures, and I must confess my astonishment that such a work has been pushed into the foreground by personal efforts. The man takes my lectures, lectures on them and out of them, and then publishes them, and to prove his own originality kicks me. *Voilà tout!* I do not find one single thought in the whole book which is original.

Well, I am little disturbed or troubled by this sort of thing, and without Mr. George Darwin's attack, I should have taken no notice of the book at all. I read the other day that Schiller, when he published the *Horen*, ordered and paid for twelve reviews in the Jena *Journal für Litteratur*. Can such things happen still?

'The serious evil of the tendency of Philosophy and Religion in the present day is that it so neglects the historical side. All feeling for the past is gone, and we have to lend our ear to things which Plato would not have ventured to make his adversaries utter. The more rude, the more original, is everybody's view now. And nothing can be done; we have to work for the few, not for the many; in the end we work best for ourselves alone, leaving the success to circumstances. If we only succeed in finding sufficient competent judges who take an interest in our doings and strivings, we can rest satisfied. I feel convinced that we shall live to see a change and a return to thoroughness in work. I long for Italy, which I have never really seen. My mother is still living at Chemnitz: she did not like England, her lively spirit missed the social intercourse. I hope I may see her this summer.'

To CHARLES DARWIN, ESQ.

TAPLOW, *January* 7.

'I hope in the course of the year to be able to place my whole argument before you. Even if I cannot hope to convince you, I trust at least to be able to show you that there are difficulties connected with the origin of language which deserve careful consideration, which possibly to me may seem greater than to you, but which, I feel sure, you would be the last person to wish to ignore. I can assure you I feel, as strongly as any mere layman in natural history can feel it, the impulsive force of your arguments. If I hesitate in following you in your explanation of the last animal metamorphosis, it is not because I am afraid, but simply because I see certain elements in human nature which would remain unexplained. To ordinary observers these elements may seem infinitesimally small and hardly worth a thought; but *you* know how the infinitesimally small is, after all, what is really important in evolution. You know better than anybody how infinitely great is the difference between man and animal: what I want to know is the first small and hardly perceptible cause of that difference, and I believe I find it in language and what is implied by language.'

During the winter of 1874–5, Prince Leopold had a severe attack of typhoid fever, which called forth the following letter:—

To Robert Collins, Esq.

Parks End, *January* 22, 1875.

'Many a time have I taken the pen to write to you, and always put it down again, fearing that I was only taking up your time, every minute of which must now be so precious. Yet I hope it is not very selfish if I ask you to tell the Prince how deeply I feel for him in his heavy trials, and how I hope and trust that he may soon recover his health. I know how you must be suffering, seeing the Prince suffer so much, he who with his brightness and kindness towards everybody might have enjoyed life so much, and been a source of joy to all around him. I know your strong feelings for the Prince, and I can fully understand them. It was often difficult to remember that he was a young Prince, when one wished to show him how much one appreciated his fine qualities, his power of endurance, his frankness, his uprightness, his sympathy with all that was noble and good, how one really admired him and loved him. Discouraging as the accounts are, it is always right to hope, and I hope most earnestly that our worst fears may not come true.

'I was with the Kingsleys a few weeks ago to say good-bye. I am afraid, while I am writing, he has left us, and she will follow soon. That bright Vicarage of Eversley, where I spent my honeymoon and which I had not seen since, looked very sad when I saw it last, yet what a blessing to be called away together.'

The sad anticipations expressed in the end of this letter to Mr. Collins proved but too true with regard to Charles Kingsley, and the Max Müllers were among the crowd of mourners who attended his funeral. Max Müller has described that solemn and striking scene in his preface to the new edition of Charles Kingsley's *Roman and Teuton.*

To his Mother.

*Translation.* *January* 29, 1875.

'Yesterday I was at Eversley for Kingsley's funeral. It was a very trying day. G. stayed there to help her aunt and the two daughters. Kingsley's was a loving, noble nature, and the feeling for him is very strong. The Queen wrote Mrs. Kingsley a very beautiful autograph letter; the Prince of Wales was represented by an equerry. Stanley read the service. The poor wife never saw her husband again. She is herself very ill of heart disease, and may die at any moment! The composure of the wife and daughters astonishes one: I am only afraid the worst is to come. He is a great loss to me; he has always been a very true friend, and, long as I have known him, we never had a misunderstanding.'

TO HIS WIFE (at Eversley).

OXFORD, *January* 30.

'All one's thoughts dwell on that grave at Eversley, and on the desolate house near it. If we miss him, how must they feel without his inspiriting presence, his constant care and love for all around him! One never thought of anything but life when one saw him and talked to him, for even in his illness there was no diminution in his vigorous activity. It is strange how little we all think of death as the condition of all the happiness which we here enjoy. If we would but learn to value each hour of life, to enjoy it fully, to use it fully, never to spoil a minute by selfishness, then death would never come too soon; it is the wasted hours which are like death in life, and which make life really so short. He was always himself, his very best self. I never heard him say an unkind word, though I have seen him provoked and worried. It is not too late even now to learn from him, to try to be more humble, more forbearing, more courteous, or, what is at the root of all, more loving, for that seemed to me the real secret of his noble life. And how he conquered! Those who would not be present at his marriage were proud to be at his funeral.'

The death of Charles Kingsley left a gap to Max Müller and his wife which was never filled up. The mutual affection had been strong and deep, and though their busy lives kept them from meeting often, the feeling of warm affection never lessened. Max Müller at this time was so entirely overdone and overworked that his doctor ordered complete change, and he resolved to go to Rome, which had been his dream from boyhood.

TO THE DUKE OF ARGYLL.

OXFORD, *January* 29, 1875.

'I should have answered your Grace's letter before, but my thoughts have been of late absorbed by Kingsley's illness and death. I went to his funeral yesterday: it was beautiful—just as he would have wished it. All classes were represented—he knew no classes, and was loved by all. There were his parishioners young and old, soldiers, gipsies, huntsmen and the hounds, officers, deans, bishops, the representative of the Prince of Wales, and many of his old friends. His face in death was sublime: I never saw such a change; all the struggle and worry of his face were gone, and there one saw the perfect, massive features as nature had intended them. There is another light gone out—life darker and poorer—and if one looks round, one sees no one to take his place.

'I am glad to hear that you are preparing for another battle. The question of development must be argued out. I only wish it could be argued without those constant appeals *ad populum*. I confess I am by no means clear in my own mind. There seem to be development and degradation running side by side wherever we touch the history of the world, and what seems improvement from one point of view seems degradation from another. Thus polytheism is an improvement on monotheism, or, as I call it, Henotheism, as long as monotheism represents only a belief in one god, not in the One God. The belief in one god which has not yet passed through the negation of other gods, is as it were a belief in one accidental god, and compared with it, polytheism, or a belief in many single gods, is richer, fuller, more perfect, as enabling man to feel a Divine presence in more and more manifestations, and at last, everywhere. From that last stage the transition into real monotheism is natural, almost inevitable. Now in one sense, Henotheism may seem more perfect than polytheism, for it does not purposely exclude monotheism—monotheism is contained in it, but the One God is not conceived distinctly, till the idea of one god has passed through two negations.

'I look upon primeval revelation as a figment of scholastic theologians, which falls to pieces as soon as we try to grasp and define it. The first suspicion of a something beyond what we see, was the first revelation, and that revelation is continued to the present day, and, we trust, growing more perfect. What I meant by saying that 3,000 years before Agamemnon our forefathers worshipped a Heavenly Father, was this. The name *Dyaus pita*, Ζεὺς πατήρ, Jupiter, *Tiu-s*, occurs in four of the Âryan languages. Therefore it must have existed before Sanskrit was Sanskrit and Greek Greek. The oldest literary Sanskrit carries us back to 1,500 B. C., and it is then so different from Greek that no Greek would have recognized any similarity between his language and that of the *Veda*. I do not think 2,000 or 3,000 years too much to explain that differentiation; the changes are far greater than those which have taken place in 3,000 years between Vedic Sanskrit and Bengali. However, I generally abstain from expressing linguistic time in definite figures, and I cannot recollect the passage where I said 3,000 before Agamemnon.

'I should not say that the worship of Dyaus pita excluded polytheism—the very idea of father led to that of a mother, and so we find in the *Veda*, P*ri*thivî Mata, Earth, the Mother, and Agni, fire, the brother of man.

'I know of no religious expression among the Âryans older than *Dyaus pita.*'

To the Same.

Oxford, *February* 4, 1875.

'The earliest known religious form of the Âryan race is, as nearly as possible, a pure monotheism—yes, that is perfectly true. But it was an undoubting monotheism, in one sense perhaps the happiest monotheism—yet not safe against doubts and negation. Doubt and negation followed, it may be by necessity, and the unconscious, defenceless monotheism gave way to polytheism. That religious form, however, contained within itself the germs of future growth, and by a new negation the polytheistic form gave way again to conscious, determined monotheism. Now, in one sense, the first childlike monotheism may seem more perfect than the second, and polytheism may be treated as a mere degradation. But from another and, it seems to me, a more historical point of view, polytheism makes an advance on unconscious monotheism, because through it alone does man reach the higher monotheism which definitely excludes a return to polytheism.

'Before the earliest expression given by the Âryan nation to their belief in a Heaven-Father, there is no doubt an endless vista of earlier stages. Such words as *Dyaus pita* are like tertiary and metamorphic rocks—we can read in them a long history; but, however far back we may follow the history of linguistic and mental growth among the Âryan nations, nowhere is there any trace, as far as I can see, of what is vaguely called fetichism. It may have been there, but as yet there is no trace of it.

'Among the Jews, I doubt whether the Book of Job, as we have it, is older than the Pentateuch. The arguments on either side are very weak, however. It is possible that the Assyrian monuments may give us earlier phases of Semitic religious thought; but I think it is wise, for the present at least, to wait.

'In religion, as in language and other intellectual manifestations, what is really important is the germ, not the fruit. "A suspicion of something beyond what is seen," springing naturally from a healthy mind, would be far more important in the early ages of mankind than a ready-made catechism. Man has to gain not only his daily bread, but, what is far more important, his thoughts, his words, his faith, in the sweat of his brow. In that sense, I am a thorough Darwinian. Where I differ from Darwin is when he does not see that nothing can become actual but what was potential; that mere environment explains nothing, because what surrounds and determines is as much given as what is surrounded and determined; that both presuppose each other and are meant for each other. Now I take my stand against Darwin on language, because language is the necessary condition of every other mental activity, religion not excluded, and I am able to prove that this indispensable condition of all mental growth is entirely absent in animals. This is my palpable argument.

'There is, however, another argument, based on the nature of all known languages, viz. that they presuppose the faculty of numbering, an argument somewhat Pythagorean, but not therefore the less true.

'Even if it could be proved that man was the lineal descendant of an ape, that would not upset my argument. The ape who could become the ancestor of man, would be a totally different being from the ape that remained for ever the ancestor of apes. That ape would be simply an embryonic man, and we have no ground to be very proud of our own embryonic phases. Yet I quite agree that I see no evidence whatever to force us to admit as real and historical what Darwin has simply proved to be possible and convenient. That man, under all circumstances, was a special creation, we see with our eyes, for every day man is a special creation, different from all other creatures. I grant also that in one sense man may, from the first, have had an intuition or a recollection of the existence of his Maker—but *potentia* only—like every child that is born into this world, never actually, till that intuition could be expressed in words, and such words as *maker* or *existence* are very, very late. We ourselves are still satisfied with the word *father*, as applied to the Deity, yet almost everything that is implied by *father* must be taken out, before the word is fit to convey what we wish it to convey. We mean at least *father*, but we can say no more.

'I look upon the account of Creation as given in Genesis as simply historical, as showing the highest expression that could be given by the Jews at that early time to their conception of the beginning of the world. We have learnt, certainly since Kant, that the knowledge of beginnings is denied to us, that all we can do is to grope back a little way, and then to trust. I think I have a right to accept a special beginning of man, because I cannot account for what he is, if I look upon him as the product of anything else known to me. I require no more a leap for him than for any other creature; I accept him at what I find him from the first dawn of history to the present day. I have no feeling for or against Darwinism, and I always try in approaching these problems to care for nothing that I may care for in my heart. I am certain that we are led; I am certain we ought to follow; I am certain that, even if we go wrong, as long as we do it because we will not resist the power of facts and arguments, we are right. If Darwin's facts were irresistible, I should accept the ape-theory without a murmur, because I should feel that we were meant to accept it. But I feel with you that never was a theory of such importance put forward with a smaller array of powerful arguments than by Darwin. "What is, is best:" these were Kingsley's last words, used no doubt in a purely ethical sense, but applicable nevertheless to all pursuit of truth.'

To Professor Lepsius.

*Translation.* Parks End, *February* 13.

'... I think of going to Rome with my wife on February 23. The doctor prescribes warm air and rest, and so I intend to carry out a long-cherished wish and to convince myself that Rome really exists. I hope the Congress in London has made you feel none the worse; it was too delightful to meet again the dear old well-known faces. Here the whole thing has certainly made a good impression. You will have seen in the papers the death of Charles Kingsley—another cable snapped that tied me here. I was with him a short time before his death. "What is, is best," were his last words to me! And that is an English clergyman! Why have we, in spite of all the great learning, no such men in the Church in Germany?'

Before leaving home, Max Müller was much amused at being asked by Pelligrini to give him an interview, and allow his cartoon to appear in *Vanity Fair*. The day was fixed, and the artist arrived; the conversation during and after luncheon was most brilliant, Pelligrini apparently taking no notes, mental or otherwise, of his host. The next week the admirable cartoon appeared, far less of a caricature than many of his weekly victims, and Jehu Junior's notice was very amusing:—

'Never was there a man with so many learned titles or with so good a claim to them as Max Müller. He is a glorified Dryasdust of the most successful kind. He is the one man who knows everything about every language. He has written libraries, and in order to do so has achieved work which would do credit to Universities. Most of his books are of that high order which nobody will read and most people will never hear of; yet he is known to the many, and indeed is one of the few of those who have trodden the higher and more thorny paths of science whose names command respect even from the vulgar.'

The following letter is not only the first of a long correspondence with Dr. Legge, afterwards Professor of Chinese in Oxford, but contains the first reference to Max Müller's scheme of translations of the *Sacred Books of the East*, which was eventually carried out at the expense of the University of Oxford and the Indian Government.

To Rev. Dr. Legge.

Oxford, *February* 13, 1875.

'It would be the greatest pleasure to me to make your personal acquaintance. I have long wished for an opportunity of being introduced to you, and being able to tell you how much I admire your magnificent edition of the *Chinese Classics*.

'As to the soundness of your work, I have, of course, no right to express an opinion, but I knew when I heard my old friend Stanislas Julien speak of your work in the highest terms, that it must, indeed, be of the highest order to extort such praise from a man not very lavish of praise.

'All I can say for myself is that I wish we had such translations as yours of the other sacred writings of the world.

'I am trying very hard to get a number of scholars together for a translation of these works, but the task is no easy one.'

To his Mother.

*Translation.* *February* 14.

'So I am really going to Rome! In a week I shall give my last lecture, and then we shall start. Of course, till then I have a good deal to do, and I can hardly realize that at my age I shall really see Rome. We shall be away March and April, and, if all goes well, it will be a delightful journey, full of enjoyment. I really want a change, for I have worked very hard lately, and shall see how the *dolce far niente* suits me. I have felt Kingsley's death deeply. He was such a strong man, so full of life, and so really attached to me; and even in his last days he said that we (that is, G. and I) were the dearest to him, after wife and children. So many feel the great loss he is.'

To the Same.

*Translation.* *February* 20.

'We want to see all quietly, and the best of everything; not all the galleries, just to say we have seen them. We already have invitations in Italy from cardinals and dukes down to Garibaldi, but shall not pay any visits of an evening, but rest quietly on the sofa and sleep. A couple of days at Albani and Frascati were better than statues in the Vatican. I am getting too old for that, but never for beautiful nature.

'I have not yet presented the *Veda* to the Queen, for she is still at Osborne. It must wait now till I return.'

Unfortunately Max Müller was really too much overworked when he left England to enjoy Italy as much as he expected. The journey out by Pisa, Siena, and Orvieto, was full of delight, in spite of the constant rain; but hardly had he reached Rome, than he fell ill and was in his room for several days. In spite of this, he managed to see a good deal, but at the cost of great fatigue.

TO HIS MOTHER.

*Translation.* NAPLES, *March* 13.

'We arrived here yesterday. Rome was too much for me. I had no rest. The papers mentioned my name, and one visit followed another. Then the multitude of things new and old to be seen. I could get no sleep. At last the University wanted to give me a banquet, so I settled to come here first for a fortnight's rest, and return to Rome after Easter. We have already seen a great deal, and people were most kind, sending me cards to see things that are generally closed. In the Chambers I made acquaintance with Bonghi, the Minister of Public Instruction, and Sella, Minister of Finance. But I was longing for rest, for my journey was to be a refreshment; instead of that, it was a great effort. Here we are settled at the Hôtel d'Angleterre, in the centre of the bay, with wonderful views over the sea. The camellias are in bloom in the open air, and the leaves are coming out on the trees. The oranges hang on the orange-trees wherever one looks; the weather is mild, not too warm, just what one wants for travelling. We have good accounts of the children, and all would be perfect if we had more rest. One forms exaggerated expectations of Rome, because one has read so much about it, and it is after all unique in its interest. St. Peter's, St. Paul's outside the walls, Sta. Maria Maggiore, impress one immensely; then the old town, with its columns and triumphal arches, just as it was 2,000 years ago. We left the environs till our return, as the season is rather late. We think of staying about here for a fortnight.'

TO PROFESSOR LEPSIUS.

*Translation.* NAPLES, *April* 1.

'... In spite of disagreeable interruptions through illness, we enjoy Italy to the full. For me it is all a new world; it comes just a little too late, it only remains pure enjoyment, which it is impossible to make use of for anything any more. That makes me think of something.

The best collaborators for the translation of the *Sacred Writings of Mankind*, which I have in view, are Germans, so the translations would have to be translated into English. Would not such a work—German—be an undertaking worthy of the Leibniz-Academy? Do think it over: the funds would be of no great importance, and it would sell. The English translation might in that case follow the German original translation. The thought struck me the other day in Sorrento, when I was ill in bed. I should like to hear from you what you think of it; but, as I have already entered into communication with Longmans, I shall have to take a definitive step on my return home.'

On Max Müller's return to Rome, he seemed so much stronger that he fully hoped to be able to attend the banquet which the University wished to give in his honour. But it had to be given up, as he fell ill again. He received the greatest kindness in his illness, the Ministers Bonghi and Sella sitting with him constantly, and a German friend, Baron Hoffmann, owner of the lovely Villa Mattei, brought him fruit and flowers daily. As soon as possible he moved on to Perugia, and thence to Florence. In Florence another banquet was proposed, but gratefully declined. But the students would not be defrauded of seeing the great Âchârya, and so he attended Count de Gubernatis' Sanskrit lecture, when he tells his mother, 'as I entered they all stood up and clapped till I felt quite confused.' One evening he was invited by Count and Countess de Gubernatis to their house. The staircase and entrance were lined by all the students of the Oriental faculty, and he was presented with an album of photographs of the leading Italian Orientalists, with a beautiful portrait of Galileo on the cover, in water-colours. The head student made a suitable speech, to which Max Müller had to reply in French on the spur of the moment.

### To Professor Klaus Groth.

*Translation.* Florence, *April* 17, 1875.

'My dear old Friend,—How often have I wanted to write to you, first in England, then in Italy! I am ashamed, and yet I am not ashamed, for you are one of the few whom I understand, even when I am silent, and I know that you mistrust my silence as little as I should mistrust yours. In most things we are just as we were, and there is not much news to tell you. Last year I worked like a horse to finish my *Veda,* which I have done, thank God, but not without mental and physical fatigue, which would not pass off till my doctor ordered me change of air, which I understood as a journey to Italy. We started the end of February, went along the Corniche to Genoa, then to Pisa, Siena, and Orvieto—which are beautiful. The poems that men can build with a few stones are even more wonderful than the poems built of letters and words. Then we went to Rome. You know how travellers exaggerate, and fill our heads with ideas which we then finish painting. But the worst is that with Rome, in spite of all that, and in spite of certain disillusions, the city amazes one, enchants one, and will not let one go. Its age does not affect me. I am accustomed to greater antiquity in India; the classics no longer make the impression they did thirty years ago; the glories of the Papacy and the Roman Church have no existence for me; but, in spite of all that, the historical reality that the eye sees in every corner satisfies one—the real Forum, the real Arch of Constantine, the real Grave of the Scipios, the real road by which St. Paul approached Rome: and so it goes on, and it strengthens one. In Rome my misfortunes began. I was ill, had to leave, went to Naples—but there I was worse, and to get better went to La Cava, Amalfi, Salerno, Sorrento; it was exquisite, but the power of enjoyment was lacking. My wife took the greatest care of me, and we found a good English doctor. When I was fully recovered, we went again to Rome for a fortnight, and I was hardly three days there before a gastric fever seized me, and I was a prisoner to my room nearly all the time. What is Tantalus compared to this? At last I got over it, and when I had seen the most necessary things, we started home by Perugia, Assisi, and Florence. I shall meet my old mother in Cologne, and take her to Oxford. We have had good news of the children all the time, and shall rejoice when we are with them again. What are your plans, and shall we not soon meet? . . . I send you some letters of Schiller's, which will interest you. I have received some more lately, and think of making them into a pamphlet. Unfortunately I could not get the originals. I have begged to see the originals, and hope to get them. For the rest, all goes on quietly.'

TO PROFESSOR ROLLESTON.

FLORENCE, *April* 24, 1875.

'Oxford has been, and is still, in a state of hibernation; I expect nothing for some years to come. It will wake after a time, but I doubt whether much is gained by disturbing its slumbers for the present. My only comfort at Oxford is that one can work on quietly there, without anybody taking the slightest notice of one. In all other respects I feel that one is perfectly useless there—in fact, that there is less of a real University and University life than there was when I first came, twenty-five years ago. However, the pendulum will swing back, and there is plenty of good material ready among the young men for having again a real University at Oxford; not simply a machine for shooting the examinations, but a machine for getting the world on a step further. Italy is hard at work both in primary and secondary education; the difficulty is the South, which has almost discouraged the North. Priestly rule has done fearful mischief, and I do not know whether it has left more of ignorance and superstition, or of downright recklessness and atheism. However, there is a good leaven at work, and the bad will go down, I believe.

'We have enjoyed our journey, except that I have lost much time by illness—gastric fever. I am better now, and we hope to be back the first week in May.'

To Dean Stanley.

Oxford, *May* 13.

'Our happy flight to Italy is over. I am decidedly better, and a good dose of quiet home-life will soon set me up, I hope. I brought my old mother with me from Germany, so that our little house is full. The last friend of yours we saw was the Duke of Sermoneta. I could not see him at Rome, as I was not up to paying visits, but we met at Florence, where he is staying, and soon to be married to Miss Ellis. He is a delightful man, all the more attractive on account of his helplessness. We also met the Count and Countess of Lingen (Crown Prince and Princess) at Florence, working hard from morning till night—a perfect pair of noble creatures. They spoke much of you. I sat at dinner by Madame Minghetti; do you know her? a most attractive grandmother. In spite of my being confined to my room and unable to go out much, I saw much of the Italians and of the leading statesmen, Sella being evidently their strongest man. Italy is working hard; one can hardly trust one's eyes when one sees Rome without monks and monkeries. They have learnt the German secret, and I expect their schools in a little time will beat the German schools. Soldiers who cannot read and write have to serve *four* years; those who can, three years only. Imagine how that tells on the village schools! The inheritance of priestly rule is fearful: superstition and open atheism divide the population. Love of their country is their chief ennobling power at present. One feels hopeful about Italy; the North will strengthen the South, the South soften the North. That a nation could have lived through such governments as the Papal, the

Neapolitan, and the Austrian, shows what there is in it, and what it may grow into with fresh air and light.

'I was quite overwhelmed with the reception they gave me in the different Universities—banquets, deputations, presents from the students—only I was not up to any efforts of speech-making and eating and drinking, and had to promise to come again. I think one might exchange Oxford for Florence; it combines all the charms of Italy with the bracing air of England. Anyhow, as soon as I can, I shall go there again.

'I wanted to ask your advice. At the time of the extinction of the East India Company, the Queen accepted the dedication of my edition of the *Rig-veda.* The work is now finished, and I should like to present the last volume to the Queen. It is the work of a whole life, at least of thirty years, and I doubt whether there is much life left for hard work now. Whom should I apply to? I have a great dislike to Chamberlains *et hoc genus omne*, and yet I should like the Queen to know that I have now fulfilled the task which brought me to England in 1846! On my return to England I found a letter that Lord Salisbury had proposed that a further grant should be paid to me in recognition of my services in editing the *Rig-veda.* I had no right to expect anything of the kind, and I was very much pleased, particularly as it came from him.

'I have many things I want to talk about with you; when shall we meet? At present I am tunnelling through a whole Mont Cenis of letters and books; oh that my enemies only would write books, and not my friends, who all expect an acknowledgement!'

The following shows the feeling with which the *Rig-veda* was received by enlightened Hindus:—

FROM THE SECRETARY OF THE ADI BRAHMO SOMÂJ.

CALCUTTA, *May* 28, 1875.

'SIR,—Allow me to convey to you the best and most sincere thanks of the Committee of the Adi Brahmo Somâj for your very kind present of your edition of the *Rig-veda,* the sixth volume of which they received the other day. They cannot express to you their sense of the value of your magnificent present.

'The Committee further beg to offer you their hearty congratulations on the completion of the gigantic task which has occupied you for the last quarter of a century. By publishing the *Rig-veda* at a time when Vedic learning has, by some sad fatality, become almost extinct in the land of its birth, you have conferred a boon upon us Hindus, for which we cannot but be eternally grateful.'

The following letter is an acknowledgement of a curious old copy of Sir Walter Raleigh's *History of the World*, from Charles Kingsley's library:—

TO MRS. KINGSLEY.

OXFORD, *June* 25, 1875.

'MY DEAREST AUNT,—Many thanks for the books you sent me. I was very glad to have them, for they are very curious, and then they will always remind me of our dear friend. How often I think of him, though, and of you too. But words break down, and tears are idle tears; what can we do but be silent and trust? After all, life, even the longest, is but a short absence, and we must all learn to wait. Yet I do miss him very much. I cannot brook his loss. I can see no why and wherefore, and we always want something of the kind, whether rightly or wrongly, to settle our mind. With all his illness he was so stout of heart, so full of plans, so happy in his new position. I felt always happy when I thought of him, and now, when my thoughts go their daily round, I often start and say to myself, Ah, why is he gone? There is another cable cut which kept me to England, and I often think I had better return to my own country, for nearly all my old friends are gone. However, our home here is so bright and happy, one shrinks from touching it. We are here three generations living together, my mother, G., and the children—all well, all grateful for every day that comes. You know what such a home is—a blessing that makes us tremble. I shall have to go to Windsor on Monday to see the Queen. I know of whom she will speak to me, and I mean to tell her that she has inherited the royal gift of healing wounds, not by a touch of her royal hand, but by a touch of her own royal heart. I may say so, may I not?'

On June 28 Max Müller was summoned to Windsor to dine and sleep, and present his last volume of the *Rig-veda* to Her Majesty in person. It was on this occasion that he left his luggage behind at Oxford, as described so amusingly in *Auld Lang Syne*.

TO HIS WIFE.

WINDSOR CASTLE, *June* 29.

'Nothing could be kinder than the Queen. She spoke in German, and most beautifully. I had to tell her something about the *Veda*. Then she spoke with deep feeling of Kingsley, and inquired about her and the children. Then we had some conversation about schools and education in Germany and England, and lastly about Tennyson's new play[1]. She had only read the first act—I had read three—but we both agreed we were still waiting for what was to come. Prince and Princess Christian, Princess Beatrice, and Prince Leopold dined. I sat by the Duchess of Roxburghe, a very pleasant and intelligent woman, and Lady Lansdowne. Prince Christian has asked me to stay with him to-day, so I shall not be back before to-morrow afternoon. I am to see the Queen again to-day at three, to give her the book.'

Not long after the Queen, through Prince Leopold, sent the Max Müllers the letter she had received from Mrs. Kingsley on the death of her husband, in answer to Her Majesty's autograph letter. Mrs. Kingsley had the gift of letter-writing, and this letter to her Sovereign was worthy of the writer.

To H.R.H. PRINCE LEOPOLD.

*Translation.* OXFORD, *July* 22, 1875.

'YOUR ROYAL HIGHNESS,—I beg you to express to Her Majesty the Queen, in my name and the name of my wife, our heartfelt gratitude for allowing us to see that beautiful and most touching letter. Yes, so it was! I knew the little paradise of earthly happiness at Eversley, and the warm heart that beat there, a heart that was never closed to the highest or the lowest. I owe much, much to him. He was a friend to me, such as few have been in England. Our views were often far apart, but I never heard an irritable or hard word fall from his lips. One never felt any coldness in him. I saw him till nearly the end. I saw him when he believed that his wife, who was his very life, might die at any moment; saw him in his last illness, when he said, "The shot has gone home." But all that he bore not merely with resignation, but with perfect calmness, with the feeling that it must be so, and not otherwise, in a spirit of which I thought he was incapable. He never knew fear, and as he had often leapt over a fence, he set himself as a brave rider and knight to leap the last fence—Death. I can still hear how he said, "I have never whimpered"; but one saw whence his courage came, and how in everything, great and small, he looked above, how his eyes soared above the little Present to the wide Hereafter.

'His life had not been without clouds and storms. No one knows what demand he made on himself, in mind and body, how many years he had to labour for daily bread. The days of rest came too late, and it is very true what his widow says, he owed the brightest,

[1] *Queen Mary.*

sunniest days in his life to the kindness and the thoughtful care of his Queen. I saw Woolner's bust a few days ago; I hope it will be successful, but it is almost impossible to reproduce in marble so stormy a face as Kingsley's. Ennobled by death, his face was wonderfully reposeful and fine; one saw the ideal of the man, what he should be, what he wished to be. The world knew him only as stammering, helpless, breathless; he lay before one, purified, ennobled, and at rest. We must have not only a marble likeness of him, but a life of him. The description of a life often produces more effect than the life itself. But who shall write it? To write a true life demands the sacrifice of another life. I often felt that, in reading the life of your father. May I keep the letter a few days? My wife is at Taplow, and comes home on Saturday. She was very dear to Kingsley. He often said to me, "Next to my wife and children, I have loved no one so dearly as your wife." The prophecy, "After the Commemoration, the Deluge," seems to be true in Oxford. All the meadows are under water, and as I write it is all dark with thunder-clouds. Your Royal Highness must forgive me for writing in German —German often seems to come more from my heart than English, and I know how easily you speak and understand German.

'I am, with deep respect,

'Your Royal Highness' obedient servant,

'F. MAX MÜLLER.'

It was in the early autumn of this year that His Royal Highness the Prince of Wales (our present King) paid his visit to India. Dean Stanley was most anxious that Max Müller should be one of the suite, but, to the infinite relief of the Max Müllers, jealous John Bull decreed that no 'foreign influence' should accompany His Royal Highness.

TO DEAN STANLEY.

PARKS END, OXFORD, *August* 13, 1875.

'I guessed from your last letter what was going on. I wanted to write to you at once, not to stir in the matter, but I felt it was wrong to interfere. If the offer had been made, I believe I should have gone, unless I could have declined on the score of health. It would have been the greatest sacrifice I could have made at my time of life, giving up half a year of what remains to me of my happy life with my wife and children, but I should have looked upon it as sent, and meant for some good, and I hope and trust I should have done my duty. What good I could have done I hardly know; but we hardly ever know that—good comes from where we least expect it. However, I am grateful, truly grateful. My curiosity to see India is not very great. It is the inner life, not the outward show I care for; and I can see more of the former from reading books, newspapers, and letters, from seeing the men who come to see me here, than from fireworks and Durbars. I know I could have done nothing for the Prince in the way of amusement or anything else, but I believe in India my being with the Prince would here and there have produced a good impression. I can write no more to-day. Many thanks for what you have done. I never told my wife till this morning. I need not tell you what she felt, but she, too, said, "I should have let you go, if some good could have come of it."'

To the Same.

Parks End, Oxford, *August* 22, 1875.

'I am printing at present a volume of essays which is to form the fourth and concluding volume of my *Chips from a German Workshop*. The first was dedicated to Bunsen, the second to Bernays of Bonn, the third to Palgrave, and now I come to ask you whether you would allow me to inscribe your name on the last. It contains chiefly essays on the Science of Language, and also the Westminster Lecture, and with it your Sermon, and a postscript which I should like you to look at before it is struck off. You have been to me during my stay in England *semper idem*, and I know how much I owe you for many kind words spoken to me and of me. You trusted me even when I did not act as you wished, and you made allowance for the difficulties which a foreigner has in always recognizing the right line of action. But it is not only as a tribute of personal friendship that I ask you to accept the dedication of my book, but as a token of my sincere and warmest admiration for the noble fight you have been fighting all your life, through good and evil report, giving heart to others to follow, and securing to your country, after a thirty years' war, an amount of freedom of thought, and with it and through it, of sincerity of faith, such as no one could have dreamt of when I first came to Oxford in 1848. I think my time in England is nearly up. I doubt whether I ought to stay longer. I am only tolerated at Oxford, allowed to help when I am wanted, but never helped myself when I want help. If I had worked in Germany as I have worked for twenty-five years in England, my position would be very different. Here I am nobody in the University; and when I see how I am treated, I really feel sometimes ashamed of myself, not for my own, but for my wife's sake. However, it is my own fault. I would not give up a plan of life which I had made before I knew what life was. In order to carry out my edition of the *Rig-veda*, I had to expatriate myself—it was the only way of getting the work done. But now it is done, and the question is whether I can still be of use in my own country. I sometimes doubt it, but I think I ought to try. How different you must feel after having worked for your country as you have, and seeing the results of your work, and feeling certain of the gratitude of so many for whom you have spent your life.'

To Dr. Rolleston.

*August* 22.

'You Mezzofanti of all passages worth remembering, where is the passage that "the lightning of Jupiter strikes only the highest peaks"? I don't know what to make of Schliemann. I believe he is only giddy. I saw Gladstone for a moment the other day. He seemed hopeful about further diggings at Troy under Schliemann's auspices.'

To the Same.

*August* 27.

'I have just read the poor abstract of your address[1] in the *Times*, and I hope soon to see it and read it *in extenso*. Your faith in skulls reminds me of my old friend Schwabe, at Dessau, whom I see mentioned honourably by one of your presidents. He was a very curious person, whose life ought to be written. Imagine a small town in the central desert of Germany, only discovered when they built a railroad to Leipzig. There he lived in a small house, with a hole in the roof to make his observations. How they laughed at him for registering the spots in the sun! They just tolerated him because he was a kind of wizard—could cure warts and that sort of thing—yet he was a most perfect gentleman, extremely well read in literature, firstrate botanist, &c. Well, now that he is dead, and he must have been past eighty, his measurements begin to tell, and I hope it may be so when you are eighty, and all that, but before *humani aliquid* has happened to you. By-the-by, you great Quotationist, you did not quote Terence rightly. The true meaning was given to that passage for the first time, as far as I know, by the Emperor Max of Germany. In Terence, surely, it only means "I am a great busybody, and every kind of gossip interests me"; but the Emperor gave a new meaning to it, and in that meaning you used it. I mention this because a saturnalian reviewer once abused me for having ascribed a passage from Terence to a German emperor!'

After his mother's return to Germany, Max Müller took his family to the Mumbles, the spit of land which forms the

[1] British Association.

right horn of Swansea Bay, and they thoroughly enjoyed the primitive life of the little bathing-place. Their friends the Story-Maskelynes were staying at the adjoining bay, and many pleasant rambles were undertaken together. Before leaving home, Max Müller had finished the fourth volume of *Chips*, dedicated to Dean Stanley, 'as a token of gratitude and friendship from one who has for many years admired his loyalty to truth, his singleness of purpose, his chivalrous courage, and his unchanging devotion to his friends.' Of this volume, one review says:—

'The first thing one wants to know, in taking up one of Professor Max Müller's remarkable volumes, is how much one can understand; or rather—because his style is as limpid as his brain is clear—how much will be interesting. That his Science of Language will underlie the whole, may be guessed, to begin with: that the superstructure will in some places resemble a fortress, in others a fairy structure of light and graceful design, and in others a great cathedral—all this is well known before the book is opened. Whatever the fourth volume of *Chips from a German Workshop* contains, it is sure to be brimming over with great thoughts, lofty teaching, and the enthusiasm for things high and holy. The learned Professor has pondered over the literature of departed ages till he breathes himself the spirit of wisdom which has actuated the world's greatest men since men began to think, and must needs, perforce, teach whenever he opens his mouth to speak, or takes up his pen to write.'

The English head of one of the native colleges in India wrote of the *Chips*:—

'These volumes, embracing the minor works of Professor Müller, now first collected, comprise the very choicest of his writings. With few exceptions, they pertain directly to India. Most of them are critical; and their criticism is of a higher order than has been even approached by any English scholar that has dealt with the subjects of Hindu antiquity and literature.'

On returning to Oxford, the usual flow of correspondence began again.

To Professor Lepsius.

Parks End, *October* 8.

'. . . I have just finished Eber's *Egyptian Princess*. It is a most remarkable book, as a work of art as well as of history. It has quite astonished me. Whether it will do for England? A mere ordinary translation would not do—it would just ruin the book. It would have to be done by an expert hand, and here and there it would have to be shortened. It is very excellent. Ever yours.'

### To Charles Darwin, Esq.

Oxford, *October* 13.

'Allow me to present you my defence against Professor Whitney's attacks. I think you will see from what I have stated, that Professor Whitney is not an ally whom either you or your son would approve of. I should never have noticed him, had not your son brought him so prominently before the English public. However, even controversy helps sometimes, though not often, to clear away error and bring out truth, and so I hope I have not simply wasted my time in answering Professor Whitney's charges.

'The point at issue between you and me is a very simple one: is that which can pass a certain line in nature the same as that which cannot? It may be, no doubt, and in that case the highest animal would simply be a stunted man. But this seems to me a narrow view of nature, particularly if we consider that everything organic is, after all, much more truly that which it can be, than that which it is. In the higher animals the potential traces of language are smaller than in some of the lower, but even where the phonetic organs are most perfect, there has never been the slightest attempt at language in the true sense of the word. Why should natural science be unwilling to admit this? Why should it not, at all events, leave the question an open question, until some truly scientific evidence has been brought forward, showing at least the potentiality of language in any known animal? "More facts and fewer theories" is what we want, at least in the Science of Language, and it is a misfortune if the collectors of facts are discouraged by being told that facts are useless against theories. I have no prejudice whatever against the faculty of language in animals, it would help to solve many difficulties. All I say is, let us wait, let us look for facts, and let us keep *la carrière ouverte.*'

### To his Mother.

*Translation.* Oxford, *October* 9.

'I hope you have used the money I sent to give yourself a little treat on your birthday. You could give yourself and others many happy hours, if you would, and if instead of dwelling on your own want of health, you thought of the far greater suffering others have to bear. Life must be as it is, and it is for the best without doubt, if we would only look upon it as such. Your health would be much better if you would not excite yourself over trifles. Strong as I am, I should soon be ill if I lived in the constant state of excitement in which you live. As one gets older, one learns to bear many things more quietly, for one feels that life is drawing to its close, and that there is much one cannot change. The lectures here begin soon, and our delightful free time is nearly over. I have to go to Manchester to distribute some prizes and make a speech. One can't refuse everything. Now, my dear mother, enjoy your birthday, and think of the many blessings you have had in life, and remember that we should learn through sorrows, so that we may leave this life without too much regret.'

Max Müller had been invited to present the Diplomas gained by the different schools in Lancashire at the Oxford and Cambridge Local Examinations. For this purpose he visited Manchester, where he was the guest of the Dean, at the end of October. It was a great distinction, and felt to be so by Max Müller, his predecessors having been Lord Derby, Lord Selborne, and other distinguished statesmen. The meeting was held in the Free Trade Hall, the audience numbering over 5,000. The Bishop, the Mayor, and the Members for Manchester were all present. In his address he mentioned the first attempt at examinations inaugurated in 1857 by the late Sir Thomas Acland, at which he had himself assisted. He described the efforts made by his own great-grandfather, the pedagogue Basedow, for elementary and middle-class education in Germany, and ended by advocating State-controlled rather than voluntary schools. This part of his speech called forth strong remonstrances from all Church papers, but it was a point on which he never wavered, though he always felt the necessity of religious, but unsectarian, teaching, such as he had himself been accustomed to as a child.

Max Müller had not long returned from Manchester before he decided that the time had come when he should do wisely to leave Oxford, and return to his own country.

To Dean Stanley.

Parks End, *November* 6.

'I send you a copy of my preface to Kingsley's *Roman and Teuton*, with some alterations here and there.

'I wish I could have seen you and had a quiet talk with you, before deciding on a step which, as you know, I have long contemplated. I hope I have decided rightly, though it was no easy matter to weigh everything. I have now served the University for exactly twenty-five years, and I have at last succeeded in gaining for the new Science of Language a recognized position among the subjects required or allowed in the examinations, and in leaving behind me a number of pupils, any of whom could fill my Chair with credit. As long as the University seemed to approve and appreciate my work, I was willing to stay and work on; and, for the sake of my wife and her friends, I gave up the Professorship offered me at Strassburg, which from a pecuniary point of view was as good as the one I hold here. I mean to go next April, and settle at first at Dresden. I shall have to work hard, as for some time I shall probably be without any official income. But even my wife agrees that I am right, and that I could not stay longer. If life is spared, I feel as if I could still do some work in my quiet retreat in Germany. When the time comes, no doubt it will be a wrench, for I leave many true friends behind, and I feel the sacrifice my wife has to make. I hope it will be for the good of the children. *Nos amis les ennemis* I have found a true saying many a time before—may it be so in this case also! Ever yours affectionately,

'F. Max Müller.

'I wish you could stay with us once more before we go. When shall we hear better news of Lady Augusta?'

To Professor Lepsius.

*Translation.* Oxford, *November* 12.

'. . . I remain here till Easter, then I think of taking a house in Dresden, and the remaining years will be entirely devoted to the *Veda* and to religious philosophy. I have still to print seven volumes of the translation of the *Veda*, not to mention other things, and the *otium cum negotiis* will do me much good. At all events, as Bunsen said, the bird is free! Do not yet mention it, however.'

Though Max Müller had not yet sent in his formal letter of resignation, his own friends and his wife's relatives knew of his determination, and letters of expostulation and regret poured in on all sides. The following is inserted by permission, as representing what all those whose friendship Max Müller most valued, felt and expressed at the time:—

From Rev. Edwin Palmer.

Jerusalem Chamber, *November* 12.

'I must thank you for your kind letter, as I felt that I had been taking a considerable liberty in speaking my mind to you so freely. I can say nothing against a resolution to leave us based on considerations of your own strength, and the time required to finish the main work of your life. The loss to Oxford will be irremediable; but after all that you have done for us, we have certainly no right to complain. To say nothing of the prestige which your residence among us and your consent to be reckoned among our Professors has given us for so many years, I cannot but feel that all of us who have made Philology in any sense a special study, owe to you directly or indirectly all that they know, and indeed the very conception of the Science of Language. I will not attempt to speak of the personal loss to myself. It is quite true that there seemed to exist between us grave differences on some subjects connected with the politics of religion (if I may use that expression), perhaps differences on subjects strictly theological; but, in spite of these, I have always valued your friendship as highly as I have prized your intellectual gifts. Even now I cannot help cherishing a hope that you may reconsider your determination. The void which your absence from Oxford would make is too painful for me to contemplate. Believe me ever, yours affectionately,

'EDWIN PALMER.'

TO HIS MOTHER.

*Translation.* OXFORD, *November* 21.

'My speech at Manchester has excited people a good deal. In England nearly all the national schools are in the hands of the Church. That gives the clergy great influence over the children, and also over the parents, and therefore they do not wish to give them up. They naturally say it is so arranged that the religious instruction may be properly given, but the real reason is that they may maintain their political influence. If they could harm me, or at least do something to injure me, they would do so gladly; but I rejoice in their maledictions, as it shows I have produced some effect. Have you found a house for us, or shall I advertize for one? I have long wished for more leisure and quiet for work, and I cannot get it here, as I am so constantly interrupted by all sorts of people. I am tired of the life here, and we have enough to live independently without my taking any post.'

The following letter shows that *Chips*, Volume IV, was as popular as its three predecessors:—

FROM PROFESSOR HUXLEY.

4, MARLBOROUGH PLACE, *November* 29.

'For a man who does not want to escape paying his creditors, there is a certain inconvenience in having three addresses. I am but rarely in Jermyn Street at this season, but on going there on Saturday I found the volume of *Chips* which you have been kind enough to send me. Accept my best thanks for it. I wish that the English workshops turned out even a few shavings of like character. Yours very truly,

'THOMAS HUXLEY.'

On December 1 Max Müller sent his resignation to the Vice-Chancellor, the Warden of New College; writing also to his own Warden at All Souls to officially announce his determination, as the resignation of his Professorship entailed the loss of his Fellowship. He writes at this time to Dean Stanley: 'I am very tired myself, and hardly able to do anything. It has been a hard struggle, and I only hope I have decided right.' To George von Bunsen he writes: 'Some things that kept me here are more difficult to leave than I thought at first.'

TO HIS MOTHER.

*Translation.* *December* 6, 1875.

'MY DEAR, GOOD MOTHER,—Only a few lines to tell you I have received your two letters, the second to-day for my birthday. Thank God, we are all well, and that is much at my age. Thanks for all your good wishes. Next year will be an important one; pray God that we have decided rightly. It was impossible to put off the decision on account of Wilhelm, who is still young enough to accustom himself to German life. I am very glad that it has come to this. My position here had become often very difficult, and the rest will do me good. I have much work still to do, if my strength lasts, and for this reason I desire to have what time may be left me for my special work. As to money, we must certainly retrench a little, but the children are provided for, and our whole interest is for them. Dresden seems to me the quietest place, and yet with all the advantages of a large city. If we find it too dear there, we must go to a smaller town; but, as I say, we shall have plenty to eat. The lamentations over our leaving are beginning. They have played me some shabby tricks, but now all has changed; but it is too late.'

TO WILLIAM LONGMAN, ESQ.

OXFORD, *December* 8.

'I must tell you that I have sent in my resignation of the Chair of Comparative Philology, and that next year I intend to settle in Germany. I want to have all my time to myself. I have still much work in hand, which I wish if possible to finish, and I could not do it if I stay here.

'I shall leave Oxford and England with a heavy heart, but, as life grows shorter, I felt more and more that I was wasting it in doing work which others could do as well, or even better; while I had to leave undone work which I could do, and ought to do. I shall probably go in April; before that time I hope to have finished my book on *Language as the True Barrier between Man and Beast.*'

No sooner had the announcement of Max Müller's retirement appeared in the papers, than letters poured in from every part of the world, whilst all the chief English papers had leading articles on his work. He was by no means prepared for such an outburst of genuine feeling on all sides, and was deeply touched by it. At the same time letters came from Vienna and many German Universities, from Florence, and even from Bucharest, trying to secure his services.

To H.R.H. THE DUKE OF ALBANY.

PARKS END, OXFORD, *December* 13, 1875.

'SIR,—I was able to say so very little when your Royal Highness gave me that beautiful souvenir, that I must try whether I cannot express my gratitude in better words. The happy hours which I have been allowed to spend with your Royal Highness will always remain among my most cherished recollections of dear old Oxford. I was often afraid that an old German Professor could hardly be a pleasant companion to one so young, so bright, and generally so happy as your Royal Highness. Still, I believe few people could have watched your career at Oxford with deeper interest, and felt for you, both in health and sickness, a truer sympathy than I have. I hope and trust that the dark clouds which surrounded your youth may now have disappeared altogether, though I cannot say that I wish your Royal Highness a perfectly cloudless sky; for, after all, the cloudy sky of England is more beautiful really than the cloudless sky of Italy, and a life without dark shadows is generally a very shallow and useless life. What I hope and wish for you is an active and useful career, and, before all, that physical strength which alone is wanting to enable you to make that excellent and unselfish use of your high position and talents which I know you are determined to make of them, if you can.

'*Fortes creantur fortibus et bonis*. . . .

'The last weeks, when I had finally to decide on my leaving Oxford, have been full of trouble and sorrow to me, and I cannot thank your Royal Highness enough for the unexpected token of your kind feelings towards me: it was like a bright and warm ray of light on a dreary day. No one knows how fond I am of Oxford, and what a sacrifice I make in leaving it and leaving England. But the life of a scholar has its duties, and I must not shrink from them. As Professor I have no sphere of usefulness here. "The young men do not belong to the Professor, nor the Professor to the young men" —that is what Mr. Bonamy Price says in his last pamphlet, and what I have felt for years. As long as the edition of the *Veda* kept me here, I had an excuse for staying at Oxford, though I felt often depressed when I saw how I had to fritter away my time in trying to serve two masters, Sanskrit and the Science of Language.

'But now, when the edition of the *Veda* is finished, and even the *Chips* gathered up, my desire to continue my translation of the *Veda*, and to work out some of the results to which my study of the sacred writings of the ancient world had led me, became stronger and stronger. Yet I felt that I could no longer work as I had done hitherto, and if I had continued to discharge my duties as Professor of Comparative Philology, I should have had to surrender my Sanskrit studies altogether. Were I Professor of Sanskrit at Oxford, nothing would have drawn me away from this, in many respects, delightful place; but, in order to concentrate my powers, and to do something at least before it is too late, I see no choice but to give up my pleasant position here, and retire to some quiet town in Germany. . . .

'The dark cloud has been hanging over my head for the last fifteen years, and as a man who stands under a waterfall is little disturbed by a few rain-drops, the *pudendae iniuriolae* were nothing compared to the weighty considerations which determined my course.

'A rumour (and Oxford is famous for its Common-roomers) says that I have accepted a lucrative position in Germany. It is simply untrue. A lucrative position was offered me in Germany, and I declined it. No one seems able to see that science, too, has its duties, or to believe that a scholar can make a sacrifice for the sake of his work. Now, I believe that the *Veda* is an extremely important book, in fact the only book in Indian literature which is important, not only for India, but for the early history of the whole Âryan race, including Greeks, Romans, and ourselves. It contains the first attempts at expressing religious thought and feeling, and it alone can help us to solve many of the most critical problems in the Science of Religion. The Science of Religion is, in fact, the history of all religions, and when I saw, as quite a young man, the gap in our materials for studying the origin and growth of religious ideas, because no one knew then or could know what the *Veda* was, I determined to devote my life to collecting all the manuscripts that could still be found, and thus to rescue the oldest book of our race from that destruction which would have been inevitable, unless it had been printed. This has now been done. People do not yet see the full importance of the *Veda* in an historical study of religion, and yet I feel convinced that the true solution of many of our theological difficulties—difficulties that will become far more terrible than they are at present—is to be found in the study of the history of all religions. We shall then see what is essential and what is accidental, what is eternal and what is human handiwork; among all the possibilities displayed before us, we shall in the end discover the reality of religion, just as a study of the movements of *all* celestial bodies led in the end to the discovery of a law that supported them all.

'If I stayed at Oxford as Professor of Comparative Philology, I could not hope to finish even my translation of the *Veda*, much less to work out at least a few of the results of thirty years' study. That is why I leave Oxford to settle in some quiet town in Germany, and there to devote myself to the education of my children and to my Sanskrit studies. My friends think me Quixotic, even reckless. I cannot help it. All I can say is, and I know your Royal Highness will agree with me, Life is precious, and we must try to make the best use of it we can.

'I have been proud for years to call myself, while living and working in England, a loyal subject of Her Majesty the Queen. I hope I shall be so still, even when living and working in Germany. While in England I have tried to make my English friends understand and appreciate all that is good and noble in the German character; when in Germany I shall try to make my German friends understand and appreciate what is good and noble in the English character.

'I have sometimes succeeded in England—I hope I may succeed in Germany, for the estrangement between England and Germany is deplorable, and fraught, I fear, with serious danger. Again thanking your Royal Highness for the many proofs of your kindness,

'I have the honour to remain, with sincere gratitude,

'Your Royal Highness's most faithful servant,

'F. MAX MÜLLER.'

In a letter to his mother of December 19, Max Müller says that he longs for rest, rest to work at what really interests him. He also tells her that he has just received the Maximilian Order from Bavaria, and that it is more showy than the Order pour le Mérite, 'but that is the best.' He felt each day that, if freed from his Oxford lectures, he could yet do much good work, for he was true to his first love Sanskrit, and what it had led to, the study of ancient religions, but his lectures in addition were too much for his strength.

To E. Freeman, Esq.

Oxford, *December.*

'As to politics, all I meant to say was that it was dangerous to egg the present Government on to any action in the Eastern Question. Lord Derby is the same as he was at the time of the Cretan insurrection—feelings of humanity are to him, as a politician, mere sentimentality. That Cretan business is the most horrible chapter in modern history. Did you ever read Stillman's book? I tried to review it in the *Times*, but nearly all the really damaging passages were cut out. If Lord Derby thinks he has done something and enough, I believe that is the best thing that could happen just now.

'I look upon myself as a true Anglian. My Sovereign, the reigning Duke of Anhalt, is Duke of Engern. See *Chips*, III, p. 123.'

On December 22 he writes to Dr. Pauli: 'I want at least a couple of years' rest, for I feel rather shaken.'

To C. E. Mathews, Esq.

Oxford, *December* 15.

'Yes, I am going. I feel more and more that I am not wanted at Oxford, and at my time of life one does not like to feel that one is on sufferance only. My old friends are nearly all gone, and the treatment I receive here is not exactly what I like. I want rest in order to finish some work before it is too late. I shall go in April to Germany to look out for a house, and take my family over in June or July.'

Towards the close of the year Max Müller brought out in Germany a little volume of the letters from Schiller to the Duke of Schleswig-Holstein. It was known that many letters had passed between the poet and his generous patron, but it was believed they had been destroyed. His Royal Highness Prince Christian succeeded in discovering part of the correspondence, which he entrusted to Max Müller for publication.

To H.R.H. Prince Leopold.

Parks End, *December* 28, 1875.

'Sir,—The little book containing Schiller's correspondence with the Duke of Schleswig-Holstein (the grandfather of H.R.H. Prince Christian) was only the small end, and as your Royal Highness has accepted it so kindly, I venture to send to-day what indeed will seem the wedge, four stout bundles of *Chips*. I do not ask you to read them, in fact I always feel ashamed when I present any of my books, for it is like asking one's friends to listen for an hour or more to one's uninterrupted talk, it is making oneself a great bore. But what is a poor author to do who wishes, if not to be read, at least to be shelved? Now all I really ask is a place on the shelves of your library. I know I shall be in good company, and if in some idle hour—and no life is tolerable without some idle hours—your Royal Highness should open one of these volumes, perhaps they will remind you of one who, when returned to his native country, will always remember with gratitude the happy years which he spent in the country of his choice, and who has only to think of the great kindness which he received when he least expected it, in order to forget the little unkindnesses which, after all, no one can escape. My friends at Oxford are now doing all they can to keep me here, but I believe I have decided rightly, and I owe it to my enemies that they have helped me to a right decision.

'Florence was very tempting. Vienna, too, held out very attractive offers, but I believe I shall remain faithful to what the Germans somewhat conceitedly call Elb-Florenz, i. e. Dresden. There is one attraction which I have little doubt will sooner or later bring your Royal Highness to Dresden, that is Raphael's Madonna, a picture totally different from all other pictures, and quite worth a journey by itself.

'Your Royal Highness's very faithful servant,

'F. Max Müller.'

We cannot close the memories of this year without adverting to an event in Oxford which was of great interest to the Max Müllers, the foundation and opening of the Girls' Day School by the Public Day School Company. All through this year Max Müller did all he could to promote the scheme, attending all the meetings and taking shares, he having found by experience how unsatisfactory teaching at home by one governess generally is.

His own three girls were among the first twenty-five

scholars with which the school opened, and the other girls were almost all of them their intimate friends. They soon became devoted to their school; the eldest girl was the first Prefect, and among the many reasons that made Max Müller's children feel intensely the idea of leaving Oxford and their loved home the loss of their school was very prominent.

Christmas, the last, as was thought, in the old home, was a sad one, though kept with the usual tree, to which Max Müller always invited all the Germans living in Oxford.

END OF VOL. I

# WORKS

BY THE

# RT. HON. FRIEDRICH MAX MÜLLER.

---

## *COLLECTED WORKS.*

18 Vols. Crown 8vo, 5*s*. each.

VOL. I. NATURAL RELIGION: the Gifford Lectures, 1888.

VOL. II. PHYSICAL RELIGION: the Gifford Lectures, 1890.

VOL. III. ANTHROPOLOGICAL RELIGION: the Gifford Lectures, 1891.

VOL. IV. THEOSOPHY; or, Psychological Religion: the Gifford Lectures, 1892.

## *CHIPS FROM A GERMAN WORKSHOP.*

VOL. V. RECENT ESSAYS AND ADDRESSES.

VOL. VI. BIOGRAPHICAL ESSAYS.

VOL. VII. ESSAYS ON LANGUAGE AND LITERATURE.

VOL. VIII. ESSAYS ON MYTHOLOGY AND FOLK-LORE.

---

VOL. IX. THE ORIGIN AND GROWTH OF RELIGION, as Illustrated by the Religions of India: the Hibbert Lectures, 1878.

VOL. X. BIOGRAPHIES OF WORDS, AND THE HOME OF THE ÂRYAS.

VOLS. XI, XII. THE SCIENCE OF LANGUAGE: Founded on Lectures delivered at the Royal Institution in 1861 and 1863. 2 vols. 10*s*.

VOL. XIII. INDIA: What can it Teach Us?

VOL. XIV. INTRODUCTION TO THE SCIENCE OF RELIGION. Four Lectures, 1870.

VOL. XV. RÂMAK*RI*SH*N*A: his Life and Sayings.

VOL. XVI. THREE LECTURES ON THE VEDÂNTA PHILOSOPHY, 1894.

VOL. XVII. LAST ESSAYS. *First Series.* Essays on Language, Folk-lore, &c.

VOL. XVIII. LAST ESSAYS. *Second Series.* Essays on the Science of Religion.

---

LONGMANS, GREEN, & CO.

LONDON, NEW YORK, AND BOMBAY.

# WORKS

BY THE

# RT. HON. FRIEDRICH MAX MÜLLER.

---


THE SCIENCE OF THOUGHT. 8vo. 21*s*.

CONTRIBUTIONS TO THE SCIENCE OF MYTHOLOGY. 2 vols. 8vo. 32*s*.

THE SIX SYSTEMS OF INDIAN PHILOSOPHY. 8vo. 18*s*.

AULD LANG SYNE. First Series. 8vo. [*Out of print.*

CONTENTS.—Musical Recollections—Literary Recollections—Recollections of Royalties—Beggars.

AULD LANG SYNE. Second Series. *My Indian Friends.* 8vo. 10*s*. 6*d*.

DEUTSCHE LIEBE (GERMAN LOVE): Fragments from the Papers of an Alien. Collected by F. MAX MÜLLER. Translated from the German by G. A. M. Crown 8vo. 5*s*.

MY AUTOBIOGRAPHY. A Fragment. With 6 Portraits. 8vo. 12*s*. 6*d*.

CONTENTS.—Introductory—Childhood at Dessau—School-days at Leipzig—University—Paris—Arrival in England—Early Days at Oxford—Early Friends at Oxford—A Confession.

*HANDBOOKS FOR THE STUDY OF SANSKRIT.*

THE SANSKRIT TEXT OF THE FIRST BOOK OF THE HITOPADE*S*A. 3*s*. 6*d*.

THE SECOND, THIRD AND FOURTH BOOKS OF THE HITOPADE*S*A; containing that Sanskrit Text, with Interlinear Translation. 7*s*. 6*d*.

---

LONGMANS, GREEN, & CO.
LONDON, NEW YORK, AND BOMBAY.

# THE LIFE AND LETTERS
# OF
# THE RIGHT HONOURABLE
# FRIEDRICH MAX MULLER

F. Max Müller

*Aged 74.*

# THE LIFE AND LETTERS
# OF
# THE RIGHT HONOURABLE
# FRIEDRICH MAX MULLER

EDITED BY HIS WIFE

IN TWO VOLUMES
VOL. II

WITH PORTRAITS AND OTHER ILLUSTRATIONS

GYAN

*Published by*

Gyan Publishing House
5, Ansari Road
Daryaganj, New Delhi-110002
Phone: 011-47034999, 9811692060
E-mail: books@gyanbooks.com

*Distribution Network*
gyanbooks.com
India, USA, Canada, UK, Australia, France

**© Publisher**

All rights reserved. No part of this work may be reproduced, stored, adapted, or transmitted in any form or by any means, electronic, mechanical, photocopying, micro-filming, recording or otherwise, or translated in any language, without the prior written permission of the copyright owner and the publisher.

ISBN : 978-81-212-3707-9 (Set)
ISBN : 978-81-212-4846-4 (PB)
First Published, 1903

2nd Impression 2020

*Printed at:* Gyan Press, Delhi.

The book is sold subject to the condition that it shall not, by way of trade or otherwise, be lent, resold, hired out, or otherwise circulated without the prior publisher's written consent.

**The Life and Letters**
**of**
**The Right Honourable Friedrich Max Muller**
Editor by: Mrs. Friedrich Max Muller

# CONTENTS

## CHAPTER XXVII.

### 1884–1885.



## CHAPTER XXVIII.

### 1886–1887.



## CHAPTER XXIX.

### 1888–1889.



## CHAPTER XXX.

### 1890–1891.

### CHAPTER XXXI.

1892–1893.



### CHAPTER XXXII.

1894–1895.



### CHAPTER XXXIII.

1896–1897.



### CHAPTER XXXIV.

1898–1899.



### CHAPTER XXXV.

1900.

## CHAPTER XXXVI.

1900.



## APPENDIX.



## LIST OF ILLUSTRATIONS

# CHAPTER XXII

## 1876

Settles to remain at Oxford. *Sacred Books of the East.* Life at Dresden. Visit to Berlin. Attack by Professor Whitney. Death of eldest daughter.

TIRED and tried by all the kindly lamentations in Oxford, Max Müller and his whole family took refuge on January 1 with his brother-in-law at Taplow, where they spent a pleasant, resting fortnight, though the correspondence with regard to his future plans was carried on actively.

TO HERR GEORGE VON BUNSEN.

*Translation.* TAPLOW, *January* 7, 1876.

'MY DEAR FRIEND,—I must send you a line; but I will tell you *viva voce* why I have finally made up my mind to leave Oxford. Clerical intrigues and petty jealousies, alas! were partly the reason. Now, however, I am grateful to my enemies, for I feel I am on the right path. My happiness I find in my family, in my books and my work—I want no better company, even were I obliged to live among Hottentots.

'But another difficult decision has to be made. I have got an urgent call to Vienna: the Minister makes the most attractive proposals. I answered that I could only accept an independent academical position, so as to publish, in connexion with some erudite friends, an *opus magnum*, the translation of the sacred writings of humanity. They quite agree, and the Minister promises a contribution, should the funds of the Academy prove insufficient, also a high salary, and all the assistance I can desire. So what am I to do? I had mentioned to Lepsius my plan about the *Bibliotheca Sacra*, and he answered that the Berlin Academy *had no money*. Of course I should prefer staying in Prussia, but would it be right to refuse the offer from Vienna? Bismarck sent me formerly amiable messages from Versailles, through Abeken, but he has other things to think of now, and I cannot offer myself. Well, I pursue my path: I have so far always found a sign-post, and I am not afraid. Of course I shall have to present myself in Vienna, and I feel I have to look round there first of all. Hettner told me a great deal about Dresden. Baden is beautiful, but it is easier to hide oneself in a large town than in a small one. In Dresden the Vitzthum-Gymnasium is said to be excellent. Well, let us hope for the best! If you can advise and help me, I know you will do it. In old friendship.'

Just after writing the above, Max Müller received a letter from one of his kindest friends and supporters in Oxford, saying:—

'Here people are ready, in a bewildered way perhaps, to do *anything* to mark their sense of your value, and I believe the knot of the interpretation of the statute will be cut by a proposal from Council that you be treated as a Professor *emeritus*, in consideration of your long and faithful services, i. e. that you be requested to retain your Professorship with a deputy.'

This was followed by other letters, and thus the whole question was reopened, and another month of deep anxiety and uncertainty passed before Max Müller was persuaded to decide finally to stay in Oxford.

To his Mother.

*Translation.* *January* 16, 1876.

'I can get no rest at all; everybody writes to me, and I can come to no decision. I wish if possible to have two years of entire rest, and if I must then go into bondage again, good—if not, all the better. In April, or May, I hope to look about for myself, to find a place that suits me; till then I want to be let alone, and not have to think about the thing at all. All this writing is lost time, and I have still a good deal to work off here, which I cannot do if I am to be always thinking and writing about my plans. Here they offer me the best arrangements, if I will only stay in Oxford. But, as I say, the great thing is not to waste the interregnum.'

Max Müller's mother naturally rejoiced at the idea of having him in his own country, and could not at all enter into his feelings of regret and disturbance, and the correspondence with her at this time fell more into his wife's hands.

TO FRAU HOFRÄTHIN MÜLLER.

*January* 26.

'Max is very tired and poorly: he feels going more than he expected, and then everybody is so kind and full of sorrow, and our friends here are trying all sorts of schemes to prevent Max from leaving. You can have no idea how all this tries him: it is no light matter to leave a place where he has lived and worked twenty-eight years, and then again he feels so entirely uncertain about life in Germany, and whether he can keep free from all public occupation, as he wishes. So you must not wonder if he is "put out": he is not so really, only very anxious as to the future. I am less worried than he is, for I see how he longs for and requires rest, to devote himself to his own Sanskrit work.'

The end of the month, his old friend Professor Gelzer wrote from Basle:—

*Translation.* *January* 29.

'I was very much surprised by the news of your resignation of your Professorship. Whenever I thought of you, it was as our spiritual ambassador in England, as the indispensable representative and pioneer in Britain of German opinions, and cultivation of the highest order. You were in my eyes Bunsen's successor in that grand international or Teutonic mission.'

TO PROFESSOR ALTHAUS.

*Translation.* *January* 30.

'. . . Yes, the bird is free; my enemies—as is so often the case—have done me good service indeed. Of course I took no public notice of such intrigues, and I have longed for years for rest to go on with my own work. It would no doubt have been hard for me to make up my mind to retire, had it not been made so easy for me. Germany is more respected now than in former times, but she is envied also, and that gives a different position to the individual German in England now. And then the theological cliques in Oxford. In short, my position became impossible. I have received capital offers from Germany, but I mean to try whether I am not able to plough my ground without a yoke round me.'

Early in February Max Müller received a letter from Dr. James Martineau on the establishment of a Lectureship for Scientific Theology by the Hibbert Trustees. 'They anxiously desire to know, whether there is any hope that you, to whom we owe the name and the conception of a "Science of Religion," would inaugurate this experiment.'

Though lamenting Max Müller's near departure from England, Dr. Martineau expressed a hope that he 'would come over and help' them. His plans were so unsettled by the vigorous attempts of his Oxford friends to keep him, that Max Müller could only reply that he could make no engagements at the present moment. Afterwards, when he had accepted the arrangement made by the University to relieve him of lecturing and yet keep him in Oxford, Dr. Martineau wrote again that the Trustees would rather await his return in eighteen months, than ask any one else to be their first lecturer. This was accepted, and the lectures 'On the Origin and Growth of Religion' were delivered in the Chapter House at Westminster in the spring of 1878.

To Professor Lepsius.

*Translation.* Oxford, *February* 7.

'... Never have I experienced more true friendship in England than just at the present time. The University—nay, even the Government—offer me everything that can be desired: negotiations are pending. I am hesitating, and under a fortnight no decision can be made. At all events, I intend to take leave for a year or two in order to find a spot where I shall meet with the quiet solitude of the forest for work. I hope to see you soon. How do I deserve the Maximilian Order? or is it on account of the name? *You* discovered my weakness—that was the Order pour le Mérite; but I had not in the least thought of it, and therefore was all the more glad, and shall never forget it!'

To Professor Rolleston.

*February* 8, 1876 (*in bed*).

'Considering all the very peculiar circumstances of the case, I should feel inclined to agree with you that the University should send a representative to the Oriental Congress at St. Petersburg, and pay his expenses. But I confess I have very grave doubts whether the time and money expended on these Congresses produce any adequate results. They are becoming too numerous, and what with jubilees and centenaries, and all the rest, I do not wonder that certain Governments and Universities abroad have declined to countenance these festive gatherings. As long as they were private enterprises, no one had a right to interfere. But now that they are taken up by Governments, and invitations are sent round to all the Universities and scientific societies to send representatives at their expense, the matter assumes a new aspect.

'The Italian Government was severely blamed for not sending representatives to the Centenary of the University of Leyden, but the Minister of Public Instruction declared publicly that, with the large number of Italian Universities, every one of which was expected to send delegates, and with the ever-increasing number of these celebrations, he did not feel justified in spending public money that was wanted for far more useful purposes. I think he was perfectly right, and I believe other countries will soon follow the example of Italy. If I say the circumstances of the Oriental Congress at St. Petersburg are peculiar, it is because I believe it is the first time that the Russian Government has allowed any of these international gatherings; secondly, because the Emperor himself is said to take a personal interest in the matter; thirdly, because a refusal on the part of England or the English Universities might look like an act of national discourtesy; and fourthly, because a refusal to attend on the ground of expense should not come from the wealthiest University in Europe. Unless, however, great care is taken, this grant of money for a delegate to represent the University at the Oriental Congress at St. Petersburg will certainly be turned into a precedent, and the applications for similar grants will be numerous.

'In order to avoid any possible misunderstanding, I may as well tell you (though I have no reason to suppose that the University would ask me to go to St. Petersburg to be present as their representative at the Oriental Congress) that I should not accept an honour which to the outside public might seem an invidious distinction, and which, by those who are better acquainted with the history of Oxford during the last fifteen years, might be misrepresented as an intentional slur on at least one member of our Professoriate. Considering the subjects which are selected for the special consideration of the Congress, I should think that either Sayce or Professor Cheyne would be a very welcome guest at St. Petersburg.'

### To Dr. Stainer.

Oxford, *February* 8.

'I heard to-day that you were gone to Algiers. You are to be envied indeed for escaping this intolerable weather. I have been laid up again and again this winter, and I expect in the end I shall have to give up the battle and go, like you, to some warmer climate. I should like to know how you like Algiers, and what kind of accommodation you find, and whether you really find rest there. I am afraid doctors are right after all, and at my time of life I must learn to obey them, particularly when one finds out what a bad economy it is to be laid up in bed and to be good for nothing. I do not expect you devote himself without interruption to the studies on the Ancient Literature of India which he has hitherto prosecuted with so much success and with so much honour to the University.' As opposition had been threatened, the Dean of Christ Church had prepared and delivered an eloquent speech, which is given in the Appendix. The Dean walked up at once to 'Parks End' to tell Max Müller that the decree had passed, whilst many other friends crowded in, to congratulate themselves and the University, as they said, on their success. Max Müller was deeply touched: he had never realized how much he had won, not only the esteem but the genuine affection of the most distinguished residents in Oxford, and he readily promised, after eighteen months' absence and rest, to return and continue his labours in his English home. Nor did he ever afterwards regret this decision; only once later, under the pressure of great sorrow, his thoughts turned again to Germany, and on that occasion the gracious remonstrance of his Queen influenced him to stay in England.

To his Mother.

*Translation.* *February* 20.

'You will have read in the papers that they have caught me again in Oxford. They took me at my word, and as I said in my letter of resignation that I wanted leisure for my Sanskrit work, they relieved me of all duties, and gave me the means of publishing the books I wanted to bring out, here in Oxford. I hope it is all for the best, though naturally the decision was hard to me.

'I have just received from the King of Italy the Order of the Corona d'Italia (Knight Commander), a great distinction, but I was well satisfied with the Order pour le Mérite.'

To Herr George von Bunsen.

*Translation.* Oxford, *February* 17, 1876.

'I must just send you a couple of lines to tell you of my decision as to my future. Apart from all other considerations, two things pressed upon me: decision as to my boy (Germany or England), and quiet for work for myself. Oxford has now done all I could desire: my income remains the same (the loss of £300 is only apparent), and I have full leisure, and they have given me *carte blanche* for printing my *Bibliotheca Sacra*. In Germany many things were not quite clear, namely, about schools. I would only have taken a Professorship from dire necessity, and then only for Sanskrit. I had, as you rightly guessed, very friendly invitations from Baden and Heidelberg. But after the debate in Convocation last Tuesday, I could hardly decide otherwise than to spend the remaining years of my life here. You will see it all in Wednesday's *Times*. I am quite free for the next year and a half; and I hope to spend half a year in Germany, half a year in Italy, and half a year in France, which will make the children masters of the three languages, and my work will not be hindered. I shall certainly go to Berlin to see my friends and foes. I have always told Lepsius that nothing but a free academical position would have any attraction for me. Whether he really wished to have me is not quite clear to me, and still less clear is it whether the literary atmosphere of Berlin would suit me. Now everything seems clear, and the remaining pathway of life looks cool and sheltered.'

To Dean Stanley[1].

Parks End, Oxford, *February* 21, 1876.

'I can find no words—why should I try? You know what I feel.

'Yes, I have decided to stay—I hope, rightly. I was surprised to see the real kindness of so many people who I thought would care little whether I stayed or went away—of some even who I imagined would be glad if I was gone. —— has behaved very well, though I had spoken to him quite openly, and told him how his best friends had considered his behaviour to me unpardonable. I cannot understand him. Perhaps we make idols of our friends, and if they break, we cannot bear it. What decided me chiefly was the offer of the University Press to print the translations of the Sacred Books of the World. I have good collaborators, and I have now a new object in life. It will quite occupy me for the rest of my life, whatever that may be. When I thought how short that rest might be, I shrank from the effort of moving, and from the sacrifice which I knew it was to my wife, though she never said so. I should have liked spending my last years quietly in Germany; if life had been spared, and an opportunity offered, I imagined I might have done some useful work there, but all that is over now. It has been a great effort and disturbance, and I begin to feel that my doctor is right, and that I want complete rest.

'Pusey preached at St. Mary's yesterday, openly recommending auricular confession to the undergraduates. He spoke of it as a medicine, which doctors might not be able to explain or account for in its effects, but which all patients who had tried it strongly recom-

[1] After Lady Augusta's death.

mended. It seemed to me taking an unfair advantage of the pulpit to advertise the medicine there, but I suppose restrictions would do more harm than good.'

At the same time his wife wrote for him to the mother:—

*February* 27.

'We feel very anxious to know what you feel about M.'s final resolve to stay here, or rather, I ought to say, the determination of his friends here to keep him, to which he has yielded. I can truly say I had nothing to do with it. I was so afraid he might regret it, that at first when the idea was started I was quite against it. I felt we had gone through all the terrible anxiety and sorrow of making up our minds to leave our friends and our home here, and that M., being full of the idea of returning to Germany, would not be happy here. But each day made more clear the wish to keep him, and the warm personal interest taken in the matter quite convinced him that he was really valued and loved here; and as in many ways, by the arrangement made, he is far more independent here than he would be anywhere in Germany if he took a Professorship, he yielded. The strong feeling shown for him has gratified M. very much.'

The Dean of Christ Church and the other Delegates of the Press began at once to make the needful arrangements about the *Sacred Books of the East*, the expense of which was to be defrayed by the University Press and the Indian Government; whilst Max Müller, on his part, opened a correspondence with the proposed translators. As this work was the chief occupation to which the last twenty-five years of Max Müller's life were devoted, some extracts from the prospectus, with the objects and plan of the undertaking, are given:—

'Apart from the interest which the Sacred Books of all religions possess in the eyes of the theologian, and, more particularly, of the missionary, to whom an accurate knowledge of them is as indispensable as a knowledge of the enemy's country is to a general, these works have of late assumed a new importance, as viewed in the character of ancient historical documents. In every country where Sacred Books have been preserved they are the oldest records, and mark the beginning of what may be called documentary, in opposition to purely traditional, history.

'There is nothing more ancient in India than the *Vedas*; and, if we except the *Vedas* and the literature connected with them, there is again no literary work in India which can with certainty be referred to an earlier date than that of the Sacred Canon of the Buddhists. Whatever age we may assign to the various portions of the *Avesta*, there is no book in the Persian language of greater antiquity than the Sacred Books of the followers of Zarathustra. There may have been an extensive ancient literature in China long before Kung-fu-tze and Lao-tze, but among all that was preserved of it, the five King and the four Shoo claim again the highest antiquity. As to the *Koran*, it is known to be the fountain-head both of the religion and of the literature of the Arabs. . . .

'Leaving out of consideration the Jewish and Christian Scriptures, it appears that the only great and original religions which profess to be founded on Sacred Books, and have preserved them in manuscript, are :—

1. The religion of the Brâhmans.
2. The religion of the followers of Buddha.
3. The religion of the followers of Zarathustra.
4. The religion of the followers of Kung-fu-tze.
5. The religion of the followers of Lao-tze.
6. The religion of the followers of Mohammed.

'A desire for a trustworthy translation of the Sacred Books of these six Eastern religions has often been expressed. Several have been translated into English, French, German, or Latin, but in some cases these translations are difficult to procure, in others they are loaded with notes and commentaries, which are intended for students by profession only. Oriental scholars have been blamed for not having as yet supplied a want so generally felt, of a complete, trustworthy, and readable translation of the principal Sacred Books of the Eastern Religions. The reasons, however, why hitherto they have shrunk from such an undertaking are clear enough. The difficulties in many cases of giving complete translations are very great. There is still much work to be done in a critical restoration of the original texts, and in determining the exact meaning of many words and passages. That kind of work is naturally far more attractive to scholars than a mere translation. . . .

'It is clear, therefore, that a translation of the principal Sacred Books of the East can be carried out only at a certain sacrifice. Scholars must leave for a time their own special researches in order to render the general results already obtained accessible to the public at large. . . .

'Lastly, there was the most serious difficulty of all, a difficulty which no scholar could remove, viz. the difficulty of finding the funds necessary for carrying out so large an undertaking. . . .

'No doubt there is much in these old books that is startling by its very simplicity and truth, much that is elevated and elevating, much that is beautiful and sublime; but people who have vague ideas of primeval wisdom and the splendour of Eastern poetry will soon find themselves grievously disappointed. It cannot be too strongly stated, that the chief, and, in many cases, the only interest of the Sacred Books of the East is historical; that much in them is extremely childish, tedious, if not repulsive; and that no one but the historian will be able to understand the important lessons which they teach. It would have been impossible to undertake a translation even of the most important only of the Sacred Books of the East, without the support of an Academy or a University which recognizes the necessity of rendering these works more generally accessible. . . .

'Having been so fortunate as to secure that support, having also received promises of assistance from some of the best Oriental scholars in England and India, I hope I shall be able, after the necessary preparations are completed, to publish about three volumes of translations every year. . . .

'What I contemplate at present, and I am afraid at my time of life even this may seem too sanguine, is no more than a series of twenty-four volumes, the publication of which will probably extend over eight years[1]. . . .

'It will be my endeavour to divide the twenty-four volumes which are contemplated in this series as equally as possible between the six religions. But much must depend on the assistance which I receive from Oriental scholars, and also on the interest and the wishes of the public.'

This work entailed an enormous correspondence, which continued to the last months of Max Müller's life, and, owing to the dilatoriness of one contributor, he did not live to see the completion of the last volume of this great publication.

Over and over again, when all arrangements had been made with a translator, the whole plans for some years to come were upset by illness or death, by constant dilatoriness, by mistakes in calculating the time necessary for the work; or work undertaken and promised by a certain date was suddenly withdrawn; in some cases, after the contract for a work had been signed by the translator, the Press, and the editor, the translator would be seized with scruples as to the suitability of the work he had offered; in other cases

[1] When this first series was finished, a second, of twenty-five volumes, was undertaken.

a demand was made for payment in advance, though the translators had no guarantee to offer that their part of the contract would be fulfilled. As the majority of translators were foreigners, few Englishmen comparatively having that intimate acquaintance with the Sacred Books that was needful, careful revision was necessary by the editor, which revision was often taken in bad part by the translator. In fact, those who watched the work for twenty-four years were often astonished at the patience and tact shown by the editor. He used himself to say that almost the only contributor who never disappointed him was Professor Legge, who was already of advanced age when he contributed the third volume of the series, the *Shû King*. When Professor Legge mentioned a date for the completion of a work, Max Müller knew that by the appointed day the whole MS. would be ready. Many others were *years* behindhand with their promised work.

To Professor Legge.

*March* 10.

'I am so glad you approve of the prospectus. I ought to say that, as a rule, we intend to give translations of complete works only, not extracts. We must have what is tedious and bad as well as what is interesting and good, otherwise we shall be accused of misrepresenting the real character of the Sacred Books—I mean of representing them in too favourable a light. Could you mention the names of the King and Shoo which you consider ought to be included, and then those which you think you would be able to give us as the earliest instalments? You may reckon for China on five or six volumes of 400–450 pages each, to be printed like my *Chips*, the notes being intended to be only such as are absolutely necessary to enable an educated man to understand the translation.'

To his Mother.

*Translation.* *March* 11.

'Dearest Mother,—So you seem quite satisfied with my decision. Decision I can hardly call it. I waited quietly, and things at last took such a form that I could not determine otherwise. I myself would rather have gone to Germany, taken for granted that I could have lived in comfort without taking any position. But I began to doubt that, as in many ways one is spoilt here, and expects more than people in Germany do. Now, as God wills: one hopes all is for the best, if not for me, for the children.'

To R. B. D. Morier, Esq., Minister at Lisbon.

'I went to London, trusting to see you there in all your glory, and when I inquired for you, you were gone. I should have come before, but, alas! we have one enemy in common, I was laid up with gout; I am told I ought to be very proud of so distinguished and statesman-like a malady, but it hurts. I am better now, but I want rest and may have to go to Marienbad. Now where shall we meet before you go to Portugal, completely upsetting the political centre of gravity? Poor Lisbon, what an earthquake there will be! I shall be here till about the end of April; I then go with sack and pack to Germany, and shall probably be away fifteen to eighteen months, spending the winter somewhere south. I am not to go back to the Fatherland altogether, but otherwise I have got all I wanted. After twenty-five years of lecturing I retire to my own work, and there may be life and work in the old hound yet. While I retire an old cripple, you step on the stage in full glory; I was delighted when I heard of it, but I should like to see you once as *Son Excellence le Ministre Plénipotentiaire.* Let me know where that may be, in England or in Germany.'

Before leaving England, Max Müller heard of the illness and death of his old friend Baroness Bunsen at an advanced age.

To Herr G. von Bunsen.

*Translation.* Oxford, *April* 23, 1876.

'My dear Friend,—I have often thought of you. A hard parting may be near you; come when it may, it is a hard parting. We stand then in the front rank, and the next ball strikes us; and then come our successors, and so on, ever so on, who knows whither? Notwithstanding, the great world for which we live seems to me as good as the little world in which we live, and I have never known why faith should fail, when everything, even pain and sorrow, is so wonderfully good and beautiful. Give your dear mother my affectionate love. My mother is still full of life, in spite of much bodily suffering. My wife and children are well, and I often say with Macaulay, "It is scandalous how well all goes with me!"'

To the Same.

*Translation.* Parks End, *April* 27, 1876.

'It may come sooner or later; it is always the hardest parting in life, when she leaves us, who gave us life. It is seldom that we see a more perfect life than your mother's. Now, my dear friend, we must march on bravely till our own time comes. All that we say to console ourselves on the death of those we loved, and who loved us, is hollow and false; the only true thing is rest and silence. We cannot understand, and therefore we must and can *trust*. There can be no mistake, no gap in the world-poem to which we belong; and I believe that those stars which, without their own contrivance, have met, will meet again. How, where, when? God knows this, and that is enough.'

The following letter, referring to the old days of the children's life in Oxford, and their father, finds its fitting place here:—

ASOLO, BICKLEY, KENT, *May* 6, 1901.

'MY DEAR MRS. MAX MÜLLER,—I think the *White Book*[1] is charming, and we are so glad to possess it ourselves; I always used to study the photographs in it, on my father's table, whenever I was up in Oxford. They bring him back so wonderfully, though only the two last are really to me pictures of him as I recall him. Of course, I heard him lecture, and recognized, as every one else did, his extraordinary ability, as well as his personal magnetism; but the memory I have of him will always be chiefly that of the loving father of our dear child-friends, Ada, and Mary, and Beatrice. No doubt you will have quite forgotten the way in which he would join, with bright unfeigned sympathy, in our plays and projects on the happy Saturday half-holiday afternoons we spent together; but we—the children—will never forget it. There was one day when we had prepared a wonderful childish play, and waited longingly in the old schoolroom, in the hope that he would come from his work, and act spectator with *you*, the ever-ready victim! And we were not disappointed; however busy he may have been, the children upstairs were not allowed to know it; when all was ready on the table, which served as the stage, the performers being small, in he came with that kindly expectant smile which, child as I was, cheered me on at once to do my best in the play. It is years ago now, and dear Mary, our heroine, is at rest with him; but I can see, as if it were only yesterday, the smiling sympathy lighting up the beautiful face, as he sat with real enjoyment, taking part all through in the children's pleasure. And another day, when Mary took me to his study that we might offer him some of the toffy we had made ourselves, I remember so well how I feared a hasty refusal, and a command to "run away," such as children so often receive. And then the intense pleasure it was to us to be instead welcomed into his beautiful room, the toffy accepted and praised, and even partaken of before us—which is what children love above all

[1] Prepared for his friends, 1893.

praise—and then the delight of being "shown things," as we called it; his "Penates," the little stone figures that sat round his fireplace, and some old books and pictures.

'And one more little scene I remember well, because it was the first time that a father's intense love for his son ever came home to me, outside my own family. I was having lunch with you, and Wilhelm, quite a little boy, had been at the gymnasium, and so was not with us when we sat down. Suddenly we heard the clear whistle he always gave, even as a tiny boy, and he came in sight from behind the trees, on to the terrace at the back of the house. I can see now the wonderful smile of love that lighted up your husband's face as he saw him, and can hear still the tone in which he cried, "Here comes the boy!"

'These are only childish memories, dating from long ago, but they are very vivid still.

'I shall always be glad that my own boy saw him, and was noticed by him, though only as a baby.

'Ever with much love,

'Yours affectionately,

'H. O'B. Boas.'

The Max Müllers settled themselves in Dresden, in a charming flat taken for them by relatives, and here the children began the regular German school life described in the following letter:—

To Professor Klaus Groth.

*Translation.* Dresden, *May* 29.

'We have been here for about a week, and on German soil I begin to feel quite well again. Wilhelm goes to school; he has to be there by 6.45, and as he has a walk of twenty minutes, we get up at 5 a.m., breakfast at 6 a.m.! The girls leave at 9 a.m. It gives us a nice long day. Now I should like to know whether you think of leaving Kiel for the Whitsun holidays; it would be so nice to meet somewhere. I hope your cares are all gone, so that you may meet the spring with a light heart. Oh! if only it would begin to be warm; here one longs for fires. My wife sends her love to you both, and hopes to see you again soon. Till the middle of June we are sure to be here—we expect a visit from my mother; after that we think of perhaps going to Berlin to see George Bunsen, but our head quarters will be here.'

Max Müller found most congenial society at Dresden, on a quiet easy footing. With Herr von Strauss und Tornay, former Minister at Bückeburg, a great Chinese scholar, Professors Hettner and Gruner at the Museum, Dr. Fleckeisen the Latinist, Count Baudissin, who aided Schlegel in the translation of Shakespeare, and many others, he was in constant and friendly intercourse, and was at once elected an honorary member of the Fourteen Club, a gathering of literary men, and attended their meetings constantly. The Sunday afternoon walks with both parents were a delight to the children, busy all the week at their schools, and Max Müller always found time to be of the party, which he seldom did in Oxford. The Plauensche Grund was a favourite resort, then still in all its natural beauty, unspoilt, as now, by manufactures; Blasewitz, Loschwitz, the Weisse Hirsch, and Pillnitz were constantly visited, and the open-air music at most of these places added to the enjoyment.

The George von Bunsens had invited Max Müller and his wife to stay with them at Berlin.

TO HERR G. VON BUNSEN.

*Translation.* DRESDEN, *June* 3.

'I am so looking forward to our excursion to Berlin. The rest here and the freedom from responsibility are like a mental sea-bath to me, and I do indeed enjoy it to the utmost. I have my house here quite full; we are eight, add to it my mother, my niece, and a maid, that makes eleven. We are comfortably settled here, and my great endeavour is to avoid acquaintances and parties, but it seems impossible. Do you know Hettner? He is an able man; Stockmar's daughter was his first wife. Now a few questions with regard to Berlin. Have I to present myself to the Emperor, Empress, and Crown Prince? The Empress invited me just lately to come to London, and the Crown Princess invited us to dinner in Florence, and it always does my heart good to see the Crown Prince and Princess, a point on which I think we entirely agree. I have to see some of the Professors, but not many: Ranke, Helmholtz, Lepsius, Mommsen, Curtius, and whom else? Then I want to go to the Museum, Picture Gallery, perhaps the Opera, and if worth while, the Parliament. I should like to see Bismarck face to face once, if possible. He sent me some kind messages from Versailles by Abeken; but, of course, I should on no account like to be obtrusive.'

TO THE SAME.

*Translation.* DRESDEN, *June* 12.

'I am looking forward very much to seeing you again. Our dear ones and our friends are cut off right and left, and life seems so lonely at times. . . . Indeed we should like to see *Macbeth*, if possible without great exertion; if not, we shall much enjoy a quiet evening with you. The Eastern Question reminds me of football, Rugby fashion. The pressure from all sides is so even, that the combined mass appears stationary. I should have liked to live to see the development, and I hoped much to greet the Prince of Roumania at Constantinople as President of the United Balkan States.'

The visit to Berlin was of great interest to Max Müller, as he met so many old friends and younger men of literary distinction. He saw for the first time the Meiningen troupe of actors, trained by the Duke of Saxe-Meiningen, who were famous for their acting of Shakespeare, and who, before the days of Sir Henry Irving, had introduced that accuracy in every detail of dress and scenery, which at that time were still almost unknown in England. The day before they left Berlin, the Max Müllers were commanded to Potsdam, and dined *en famille* with the Crown Prince and Princess and their children, seeing more of their family life than in their visit in 1863. After dinner, they drove alone with their royal hosts through the gardens and parks of Potsdam. The next day they went to Dessau to visit their relations. It was the only time that the Duke and Duchess of Anhalt had been in residence during one of their visits, and they expressed a wish to receive the Max Müllers. But here a difficulty arose. No lady, not of noble birth, could be received at the Schloss, according to the etiquette of the little Court, so Max Müller's wife, though presented in England, and therefore received at Court in Berlin and other European capitals, could not be admitted in Dessau. The great difficulty was surmounted by the Duke and Duchess driving out to a country place eight miles off, and there receiving their old friend and his wife.

To Herr George von Bunsen.

*Translation.* Dresden, Bismarckplatz, *June* 28.

'We returned here yesterday. We had to give up staying at Leipzig, because the many dinners and suppers at Dessau had exhausted our powers. I hope that you and your dear wife have quite recovered from the strain which our stay with you must have occasioned. We have both much enjoyed Berlin, but it was rather too much for old people. Old age begins to claim its due, and we have to learn to get old. I really long for sylvan solitude, and that is not to be found in Berlin; here at Dresden, too, there is not much of it, so that we think of going somewhere during the holidays with the children, where there are no human beings, perhaps only an orang-outang—the one in the Aquarium was very beautiful, and has made a great impression on me. And now the first living gorilla is to arrive in Berlin, which provokes great jealousy in England!

'My stay in Berlin seems like a dream; I only just begin to gather myself together and enjoy over again what was so enjoyable. What filled me with the greatest astonishment in Berlin, was that two European Courts have produced and nurtured two such splendid human beings as the Crown Prince and Princess. There must surely be some truth in Darwinism, the survival of the fittest! I only fear they are too good for the rough work of governing. Another thing that struck me was, that the German Professors, in spite of all distractions, continue to work calmly and regularly, and yet spend themselves so little. I could not stand Berlin for one year even.

'I should have liked so to talk over many things with you, things old and new—but where is one to find time for that? You ought to come to Dresden: the journey is so short, and the wheels of life do not rush on here quite so fast. Do think of it!'

### To the Same.

*Translation.* Dresden, *June* 30.

'I cannot form a clear judgement yet about the journey of the Prince of Wales and its consequences. I do not think that in England any tangible results were ever expected from it. He has made a new and agreeable impression through his courteous bearing, he has made some personal friends among the Rajahs—they may, of course, be courtiers only, but in India these sort of people are very important at times. At all events, he has learnt something, if only that very reasonable people are able to worship a cow!'

### To Dean Stanley.

Dresden, *July* 3.

'I am sorry your way does not lead you to Germany. We shall probably stay here for the rest of the summer, and then turn our steps southward. I believe I was right in running away. I have had plenty of rest here, and yet I do not feel quite myself yet. Every little thing excites me and irritates me, which ought not to be. I hope our stay here is useful for the children; they learn German without any effort. Wilhelm goes to school, and enjoys it very much. I travel about seeing old friends. We spent some time with George Bunsen at Berlin. The Crown Prince and Crown Princess were delightful; I can find no fault in either of them. I think of wintering at Lausanne, where the schools are good, and where the children would learn French. But all that is uncertain. My own wish is to go back to Oxford in October, but my doctor tells me to keep away, and enjoy a longer rest. Poor Liddell, I think of him every day, and I fear that he will never recover from that blow[1]. That daughter of his was a most charming, lovable creature, so natural, so beautiful, and he so fond, so proud of her! "Let us die, in order," says a poet in the *Veda*, "that the old may not weep for the young." It was then, as it is now, inscrutable; and I doubt whether we have learnt to be more patient, and to wait our time more cheerfully, than the old worshippers of the Vedic gods.

'We have given up all idea of going to Roumania, but I have promised to visit him at Constantinople. England's policy has made an impression in Germany—people begin to see again that England is a Great Power, more powerful for inflicting injury, and herself invulnerable, than any other. It is well that people should know that: a mistake on that point might prove fatal. The idea that England supports the Porte against her Christian subjects is a popular illusion, and I have no doubt that Lord Derby will come out very well in the forthcoming debate. England has told Russia what she (Russia) shall not do, and that will have been an excellent and really most useful lesson to Russia. I do not like Disraeli's tone, but I am afraid Gladstone would have made a European war inevitable.

'We shall all be glad to have your book[2]; my children know your first volume better than I do. My wife sends you her love. We often speak of you, and much as she longs for England, she often says how deserted it has become during the last few years—how few friends are left, how many are gone.'

During the short summer holidays at the schools, Max Müller took a small house at Schandau in Saxon Switzerland, his mother and Baroness von Stolzenberg and some other relations being there at the same time. The long rambles and expeditions were a great delight to his children, who had never before seen any rocky scenery, and the constant outdoor life was full of enjoyment.

[1] The death of his third daughter. All who knew Edith Liddell will endorse Max Müller's words.

[2] *Lectures on the Jewish Church.*

It was during this summer that the controversy with Professor Whitney, of Yale, which is well known to scholars, reached its culminating point. Professor Whitney had for years attacked Max Müller on various fundamental questions of the Science of Language, and was much irritated that no notice had been taken of these attacks. At length, in 1875, in his *Reply to Mr. Darwin*, Max Müller, as one review put it, 'said a great deal that was severe upon Whitney.' On this, as another review said, 'Professor Whitney, according to his wont, published a violent and utterly indecent attack upon Professor Max Müller. The Oxford combatant replied (*In Self-Defence*) with still greater severity, but with good breeding. The subject is so complex that it is not easy to say if Professor Whitney is alone in the wrong. It is, however, quite clear that he has not the tact and temperance to deal with a polished man of the world like Professor Max Müller, even if the latter were in the wrong.' Mr. Moncure Conway, who knew both Max Müller and Professor Whitney, has kindly sent the following letter on the subject:—

22 East Tenth Street, New York, *May* 7, 1901.

'Dear Mrs. Max Müller,—I send you another letter of Professor Max Müller's, which I found lately among some notes preserved apart by my wife, no doubt on account of its words of sympathy with us on the death of our son Dana fifteen years ago. I felt it—and still feel it—a great privilege to have known the warm and tender heart that was in him. I lamented that Professor Whitney could not have lived for a time at Oxford and really known Professor Max Müller, and indeed told him (Whitney) so when I last saw him.

'Although I am not competent to pass any judgement on the scientific points at issue between Professor Max Müller and Professor Whitney, I felt certain that the sharp language used by the latter was due to his not knowing the character of your husband, partly I fear through the representations of others who could not repress some unconscious jealousy of the honours heaped upon him.

'Before leaving England in 1875 for a few months' visit to America, I had some conversation with Professor Max Müller on the unhappy misunderstanding, which he deplored, and he authorized me and desired me to urge on Professor Whitney the proposal for an arbitration by scholars—naming several who were his (Whitney's) friends, pledging himself to abide by their decision. During the winter, when giving some lectures at New Haven, at which Professor Whitney presided, I was his guest, and I was much disappointed that he did not accept the proposal for arbitration. Why he did not, I was unable to discover, for I do not believe he suspected that he might be in the wrong. I made some notes of his grievances, and they appeared to me such as might fairly be submitted to impartial scholars, but he seemed to think that it would not be honourable in him to so submit them. I fancied he might have engaged with some antagonist of your husband not to do so. At any rate, my attempted intervention in the matter failed, much to my distress. I reported the result to Professor Max Müller, and that was the end of it so far as I was concerned. Your husband never spoke with any bitterness of Professor Whitney, in my hearing, but only said that he did not know what more he could do. I remember, too, his telling me that he held back his article, *In Self-Defence*, for some time because he heard that Professor Whitney was ill. His whole spirit in these conversations was so conciliatory and so free from arrogance, that if I had known of any wrong he had done, I should have felt perfectly free to point it out. He would not have taken any offence, but given it the most candid consideration. I was not intimate with Professor Whitney, but always found him gracious, personally, and very instructive in conversation; and in one of his lectures in Yale College, at which I was able to attend, his sincerity in relating his "grievances" was evident, though just what they were I found it difficult to understand.

'I look forward with eagerness to the work on which you are engaged. I do not believe that any pen but your own can do any real justice to the man; as for the scholar, he is revealed already in his magnificent and monumental works.

'Your old friend,

'MONCURE D. CONWAY.'

As Professor Max Müller's *In Self-Defence* has long been before the public, any one can see that, however severe his words may be, they are not discourteous. Can the same be said of Professor Whitney's expressions, who allowed himself, in writing of Max Müller, to speak of him thus: 'To me he is simply, with all his ability, one of the great humbugs of the century;' 'He has always been rated at full ten times his value as a scholar'?

As Professor Whitney entirely declined the arbitration proposed by Max Müller in *In Self-Defence*, there, as far as Max Müller was concerned, the matter ended. It was a gratification to him to receive about this time from an American an article on the fourth volume of *Chips*, which the author hoped 'might make some amends for the gross injustice you have received from some of your reviewers here.'

A brilliant review in the *Times* of September 25, 1876, on seven of his Sanskrit works, including the six volumes of the *Rig-veda* and the first volume of translation, was also a great pleasure to him. With all his sensitiveness, and his deeply affectionate nature which made him keenly alive to any coldness on the part of friends he loved and trusted, Max Müller was perfectly callous to merely *unfavourable* reviews. He knew that in all his works he did his very best, that he spared neither time nor labour to make them as perfect as he could, and therefore mere fault-finding moved him very little. He could be very wrathful, and righteously wrathful, over misrepresentation and falsehood, but he never allowed himself to use the language that is only too common among scholars in Germany and America; he could be caustic and severe, never abusive.

Mr. St. George Mivart a few years later, in alluding to an argument with Max Müller, wrote: 'The kindness of Professor Max Müller's reply I recognize with pleasure, but without surprise, since those who know him, know him to be as remarkable for his courtesy as for his great learning.'

To Herr G. von Bunsen.

*Translation.* Dresden, *November* 7.

'I congratulate you on your election and your work in Parliament. I come to see more and more what a stranger I have become to the life over here, and how separate I am, with regard to politics, from my friends. I see in Bismarck only what is great, and I cannot forget what he has done. He has had devils to fight, and has sometimes fought them by devils. But are *we* to reproach him for that, *we* for whom he has fought? However, I know the mountains look beautiful from a distance: approach them, and the paths look often dirty and slippery enough.

'If you could come here, that would be nice. Though our house is rather uncomfortable for a married couple, yet with good will it is possible to manage; for a grass widower, however, we could arrange comfortably, and the journey is so short. Who knows how long we may stay here! We like this place so much. I am better, if I take care of myself, and the children thrive beautifully. My old mother is living with us now. How grateful I ought to be!

'I am sorry to have missed Auerbach. I have read the first tale. It is evident he no longer makes a great effort when writing, does not devote himself entirely to his work, but now and then it is like lightning from heaven. No, indeed, I rarely read German papers. I rejoice, however, all the more that the gorilla is alive. I should have liked to see it face to face.'

### To Dean Stanley.

Dresden, Bismarckplatz 10,
*November* 27, 1876.

'I see you are in London again, so I send you a sign of life in the shape of the fourth volume of my *Essays* translated into German. If you have looked at the original, you need not read the translation. There is much fighting in it.

'How I wish you could have come here in the summer! The town and the country are both so beautiful—all so easy to see, and no one to take notice or interfere with one. We had several old friends staying with us, but otherwise lived entirely by ourselves. The rest and quiet were delightful to me, particularly after all the worry at Oxford, and I feel more and more that I should have broken down, had I remained there. We all like the place so much that we cannot move away. We meant to have gone to the Lake of Geneva, but the doctor thinks I am so much better that I may stay here during the winter. The children are all hard at work, Wilhelm doing very well in his German Gymnasium. He has grown to be such a German that he says he wants to stay at his school even when we all go away!

'We have two bishops here, one formerly of Honolulu, Dr. Staley, very bright and intelligent, and, like most missionaries who have had dealings with real heathen, very tolerant to such heathens as myself. Then a Bishop of Rhode Island, a really liberal-minded American bishop, whom you ought to know, Dr. Clark. He has preached some excellent sermons here, and he told me he had preached the same sermon before the assembled bishops of the Pan-Anglican Council. He is much opposed to a new Pan-Anglican, but he represents a small minority in America, I fear.

'Many thanks for your book, which we have been reading out together, enjoying it each in our own way, children and all. I suppose you will go on with your work now, when nothing remains to make life pleasant but work, particularly such work as yours.

'When one reads of all the political excitement in England, it is extraordinary to see the utter apathy in Germany. Bismarck in that respect simply represents the people. They have had enough of fighting, and they will not fight again until they are forced to it. There is not much love for Russia, but I believe there is more for Russia than for England. How that has come to pass I hardly know, but it is so. Russia remained neutral during the Austrian and the French wars—she might have done much mischief to Germany then—and there is a general feeling of gratitude in Germany for that neutrality, whereas a number of German papers have been going on telling the people that England supplied the French with arms, when they had none left to fight with. Then comes the prudential feeling—if Germany were to go against Russia, directly or indirectly, the French would at once embrace the Russians. Germany will be friendly to Russia, and would not mind a war between Russia and Turkey, nor between Russia and England. With all my strong feelings against Disraeli, I think his policy is right, Gladstone's wrong. If Russia really wanted freedom for the Christians, if the Russian people were really to rush in and fight it out till every Turk was driven out of Europe, that would be very different. But Russia is simply bullying, and trying to gain what she can, chiefly an exit for her fleet in the Black Sea. England is strong enough to prevent that. The fact is, England is just now stronger than any other Power in Europe, and Russia would draw back if England took the Dardanelles, and insisted on the Treaty of Paris being respected. What is so extraordinary to me is that the decision of war and peace rests at the present moment with two men, the Russian Emperor and Disraeli. People who decline to be taxed without their consent, submit to being killed without being asked, and without asking any question. Only in America, I believe, war cannot be declared without consulting the Senate; but in England, France, Germany, Russia, Italy, two or three men say war, and the people go and fight like so many wolves and sheep. Savage as it seems, it seems almost as if it could not be otherwise, and that national impulses would be even more dangerous than diplomatic intrigues.'

To M. MICHEL BRÉAL.

DRESDEN, *November* 28.

'I send you to-day the German translation of the fourth volume of my *Essays*. If you will look at the second part of my *Rede Lecture* and the *Criticisms on Curtius' Chronology*, you will see how much we agree with regard to roots and their development. I have gone still further in my lectures on *Darwin's Philosophy of Language*, where I speak of the friction of roots, and I am now hard at work on the same subject. I have just read your article in the *Journal des Savants*; it is quite refreshing to read something independent. I never believed in any Ursprache; it is a *deus ex machina*, an impossibility. I hope soon to hear from M. Darmesteter, whether he can undertake the translation of the *Vendîdâd*. I am afraid the language will prove a difficulty. I feel so well here at Dresden that I cannot make up my mind to move. I am thinking of Geneva, or of some town in France, where my children could speak French; I am thinking most of all of Paris. For you know how fond I am of Paris, and how I have passed there some of the happiest years of my life. But there are always so many *buts*, and this inertia keeps me where I am. I have my three daughters with me, twelve, fourteen, and fifteen years of age, and my boy, nine years old.'

The plan of leaving Dresden in the autumn had been given up, the whole party were too happy in their various occupations, and too comfortable to wish to move, and it was finally settled to stay till Easter. The girls were making good progress with their various masters, the boy was doing well at school, and the parents enjoyed the society and the easy life and beauty of Dresden.

But this happiness was brought to an abrupt and terrible end. The eldest girl, growing to be her parents' friend and help, as she had long been their pride and joy, was taken suddenly ill with meningitis, and in one week was taken from them. They laid her to rest in the beautiful Annen-Kirchhof, the day before her sixteenth birthday. Max Müller never entirely recovered from this loss: the spring, the joy of life was gone. He suffered severely, and it was months before he could at all rouse himself and take up work again. His letters show how deep the wound was.

To Professor Lepsius.

*Translation.* *December* 23.

'How much the sympathy of true friends can soften the deepest heart-sorrow! I should never have believed it, now I know it. Our loss is inconceivable—such a beautiful rich spring was opening before our eyes; a childlike heart, with all the wealth of a woman's goodness. She studied so hard of herself, she learnt to control herself, so that I often felt humiliated myself before her. Her life was full of sunshine, and before the clouds of life could rise on her horizon she passed into a better life. We thank God that He found her worthy to return so young, so unspoilt to her Father's house. She belongs to us now more than before, and what of life is left to me belongs to my child in heaven. My wife is my best support. My old mother is with me, and has had to bear this loss in her old age. Thank your wife from us both, and think of me still with sympathy.'

To his Cousin, Major von Basedow.

*December* 21.

'My dear Adolf,—Your sympathy has been a great comfort to us, and Emma's beautiful wreath lies near Ada's heart. We have suffered very much, but from the first moment we have thanked God that He has taken our dear good child to Himself. She is spared much sorrow in life: she has only known the bright spring, and slept away into a better world. My whole life now belongs to her and her memory, till our long life's journey is over. I should like to have laid her to rest at Dessau, but G. shrank from the effort, and she rests here in a lovely spot. We want now quiet and rest, but I hope we shall meet before we return to England. We stay here till Easter.'

The following letter to Dean Stanley was quoted by him in his sermon to children, preached in Westminster Abbey on Innocents' Day, December, 1876:—

'As soon as her last breath was gone I was able to thank God that He had taken my child into His arms, where she is safe for ever from all the troubles and the sorrows of life. The first chapter of her existence has closed. Who knows what troubles might have been in store for her? But she was found worthy to enter the kingdom of heaven as a little child. Here we have toiled for many years, and been troubled with many questionings, but what is the end of it all? We must learn to become simple again like little children. That is all we have a right to be; for this life was meant to be the childhood of our souls, and the more we try to be what we were meant to be, the better for us. Let us use the powers of our minds with the greatest freedom and love of truth; but let us never forget that we are, as Newton said, "like children playing on the seashore, while the great ocean of truth lies undiscovered before us."'

The sympathy shown on all sides was very deep. The Queen of Saxony sent a kind message to the bereaved parents. The Crown Princess wrote, as did Prince Leopold. The Princess of Roumania ('Carmen Sylva'), whose loss of her only little girl enabled her to speak words of comfort from her own experience, sent the parents many beautiful poems, whilst the letters from friends in England were full of genuine sorrow. The English Chaplain at Dresden, Mr. Gilderdale, and his wife, were a true help and support, and their tender and wise sympathy was never forgotten.

This verse was found among Max Müller's papers:—

'Better so—the world in growing
Might have soiled her with its breath,
Surely God in dearly loving
Gave her, young, His gift of death.'

# CHAPTER XXIII

## 1877–1878

Dresden. Switzerland. Return to Oxford. Letters to Noiré. *Hibbert Lectures.* Graham Bell and the telephone. Malvern. Whitby. Boyton Manor. Publication of *Hibbert Lectures.* Death of Grand Duchess of Hesse.

MAX MÜLLER and his family stayed on quietly in Dresden till April, his old mother with him. He busied himself in the arrangements and correspondence for the *Sacred Books of the East*, though even his work failed to rouse and interest him.

To CHARLES ROBARTS, Esq.

DRESDEN, *January* 1, 1877.

'I knew you would feel with us when you heard of our loss, yet I was glad to have your letter, and the expression of your sympathy. The blow fell upon us so suddenly—our dear Ada was so well and happy, hard at work, growing thoughtful and considerate for others, and she became to both of us a friend and companion, when in not quite a fortnight, an inflammation of the membranes of the brain carried her off, and she fell asleep before our eyes without a struggle. One learns to bear what one must bear, but life is changed, and we ourselves can never be again what we were before. My life has been hitherto so full of sunshine that the sudden change seems more than I can bear. Our life had been so bright and happy here; now all is over, and I long to be back in Oxford. We stay here till Easter, because we can live here in more quiet and solitude than anywhere else; after that our thoughts are homeward. Everything seems so far removed now, and I feel as if I could never care for anything again.'

The kindest letters continued to reach the parents, one of which is given here:—

FROM PROFESSOR KERN.

LEYDEN, *January* 2, 1877.

'MY DEAR SIR,—When after too long a delay I was about to answer your kind letter, and to say that I was willing to accede to your proposal, I got a letter from Boehtlingk, which informed me of the heavy loss you have suffered. I cannot really sit down and write to the scholar, when I am only thinking of the father. Do not think that I will intrude upon the privacy of your sorrow when I express my heartfelt condolence with you at the sad event. Alas! your loss is one of those that throw a lasting shadow on the path of life. There are days in our life when we are apt to acknowledge the truth of the saying that "all is sorrow." Yes, there is truth in it, but it is not *the* truth. It is pitiful indeed to see a young life nipped in its bloom; even the bystanders are moved, and for the parents it is a cause of overwhelming grief. At such occurrences the wise ought not to try to fathom the mysteries of human life and the final destination of man. After raising in the inner recesses of his heart a monument to the sacred memory of the departed one, he should return to the battle of life, where he has to conquer his external and internal foes.'

TO PROFESSOR LEGGE.

DRESDEN, *January* 21, 1877.

'MY DEAR FRIEND,—How long have I wished to thank you for your letter, so full of sympathy, but I had nothing to say but "Yes, yes," to all your comforting words; and yet all strength seemed gone—the heart and the body will not obey. I feel more and more every day how much I have lost.

'I know how happy her lot has been on earth: life must have been a perfect paradise to her, without a suspicion of evil and suffering. I know that she is safe—that is a comfort, almost a relief; but there is the blank, and a wound that can never heal, nay, that I hope will never heal. She suffered very little. She was in the full enjoyment of health till two or three weeks before she was taken from us. No human skill could have saved her—an inflammation of the membranes of the brain acted on the nerves of the heart, which wore itself out, and she slept away without a struggle.'

A new anxiety fell on Max Müller early in February, when his boy caught scarlet fever from a school-fellow, and had it very severely. The following, out of a book of thoughts written at this time, shows how he suffered under this new burden of anxiety:—

'Since yesterday morning W. is ill with scarlet fever. I cannot gather my thoughts—I cannot. I feel after God that He may help; I am dumb before Him. My dear Ada gone, and now God shows me again and makes me feel how we are all in His hand. Oh, God, have mercy upon me, a miserable sinner! "When thou thunderest, then they believe thee," says the old poet in the *Veda*, and is it not so even now? How careless my happy life has been; now Thy terrible thunder, oh God, has roused me. I know Thy will is holy; Thy hand is a Father's hand; help me to bear Thy burden—I cannot.'

The following was written by Max Müller about this time in a friend's album, who had shortly before lost her husband:—

*Translation.*

'There is a large and secret brotherhood in this world, the members of which easily recognize each other, without any visible outward sign. It is the band of mourners. The members of this brotherhood need not necessarily wear mourning; they can even rejoice with the joyful, and they seldom sigh or weep when others see them. But they recognize and understand each other, without uttering a word, like tired wanderers who, climbing a steep mountain, overtake other tired wanderers, and pause, and then silently go on again, knowing that they all hope to see the same glorious sunset high up above. Their countenances reflect a soft moonlight; when they speak, one thinks of the whispering of the leaves of a beech forest after a warm spring shower, and as the rays of the sun light up the drops of dew with a thousand colours, and drink them up from the green grass, a heavenly light seems to shine through the tears of the mourners, to lighten them, and lovingly kiss them away. Almost every one, sooner or later, enters this brotherhood, and those who enter it early may be considered fortunate, for they learn, before it is too late, that *all* which man calls his own is only lent him for a short time, and the ivy of their affections does not cling so deeply and so strongly to the old walls of earthly happiness.

'In friendly remembrance of F. M. M.'

To Charles Robarts, Esq.

Dresden, *April* 8.

'I like to know what is going on at All Souls, at Oxford, in England, though I doubt sometimes whether I shall ever take any part in it again. I cannot recover my spirits nor my strength, and it has been too hard a blow, and I see nothing but anxiety before me. We will bring home a "Désert" like Félicien David, but we all expect something from you worthy of St. Paul's, and the longer you stay away from the turmoil of the city, the better for you, and the better in time, I hope, for us. Do not be in any hurry about answering this. I must stay here till April to finish my lectures. After that, everything is uncertain, but I long for rest and sunshine.

'Oxford is trying to do something to keep me here—it can give me rest, but can it give me sunshine?'

TO PROFESSOR KLAUS GROTH.

*Translation.* *February* 13, 1876.

'I feel rather restless at present, and should have liked to wait with my letter till I could have told you with certainty what has been decided about my future, but everything proceeds slowly here in Oxford. They would like to keep me, but the parties are divided, and hence the delay. To me, either way would be acceptable, and though my heart might draw me to Germany, my head also has a voice in the matter. Should I be offered a post which would allow of sufficient spare time for my own private work, I should not mind staying here; if not, I shall hope to go to Germany, without a yoke of office on my shoulders, only living for my children and for my own work. I have had various offers from Germany, but my dream is rest and perfect independence—political, academical, and social. Well, everything will be decided soon, and I intend leaving for a year or two.... I thought of Dresden, because it is near Chemnitz, and because my old mother has several friends there. The schools are said to be very good there. Ada shows talent for painting, Mary for music, and they can both find good masters there. Kiel draws me much, if only it was not so very distant. I hope, indeed, that we may meet this summer. I shall write to you as soon as I hear anything definite. When my children know German well, we hope all to go to Florence, and then to France; then I have done for them all that is possible, and meanwhile I continue my own work. These are nice soap-bubbles, are they not?—but why not? You had better blow soap-bubbles too; perhaps a favourable wind will bring our bubbles together.

'We are all very well on the whole: my wife is well, thank God; the children flourish; I have the gout!—*horribile dictu*, but it is true! I wish we had better news from you and your wife. It is very cold here: how may it be with you?...'

At last, on February 15, a decree passed Convocation appointing a deputy to lecture in Max Müller's place, and to have half the salary, allowing 'Professor Max Müller to leave this in about a week to try the mountain air of Switzerland. . . . As you may imagine, I have no wish to serve on the University Commission. I find I am much more useful in the second file, loading the guns for others to fire them off. But if I am wanted, I am ready, provided there is a chance of getting a majority of reasonable men on the Committee.'

To Mrs. Kingsley.

Dresden, *April* 14.

'My dearest Aunt,—I send you a letter from the Crown Princess. Please let me have it back by-and-by. We start to-day for Switzerland. You know how heavy our hearts feel. And yet one has to go on, and live and work and smile, and no one knows how all the time our thoughts are elsewhere, and find rest and comfort only in dwelling on one memory, which fills our whole heart. You know all that—you know how one enjoys what people call sorrow, how one longs for silence and solitude, to be alone with those who draw us to another world. We shall find rest where we are going now, I hope. I know G. wants it. What should I have been without her help? I feel so rich, so blessed in her and my three children, but I hardly dare to call anything my own now! Your book[1] has been such a comfort to me. I read it when I could have read nothing else. What a triumph it is! I rejoice in it with you—it is a real resurrection of a man whom the world did not know till they could see him no more. Depend upon it, that book will live long after we are gone. I have long tried to write something about it for the German papers, but I found it so difficult to keep my thoughts together. I can do any amount of drudgery, translation, index-making, &c., but as soon as I attempt to compose, I find I cannot do it. However, I have written an article, and sent it off; people in Germany ought to read the book, and if I attract their attention, that is all I want.

'How often I think of you. There is a communion in sorrow, which binds our hearts together more closely than common joy and happiness. We have had such deep sympathy even from mere strangers, and such sympathy is a help. I did not know it before, but I know it now.'

The party settled at Mollens, a little village on the slopes of the Jura, with the whole range of Mont Blanc in view across the Lake of Geneva. There are many of these villages along the Jura, each with its château, once important houses, now mostly occupied as *pensions*. The châteaux have fine rooms, and the air is superb, but it would be

[1] *Life of Charles Kingsley.*

difficult to find a more primitive life, and more absolute quiet than in these Jura villages. At the back of Mollens rises Mont Tendre, one of the highest points of the Jura range. For the girls the French teaching was excellent, but it was so lonely for his boy, that Max Müller soon sent him to Hofwyl, a famous school near Berne, the head master of which, and his English wife, were old friends of the Max Müllers. Nearly three months were passed in this perfect quiet. Long walks were taken every day, and the wonderful variety of wild flowers were a constant delight and occupation. Above 300 different flowers were found during these three months. Excursions on foot were undertaken to other parts of the Jura, to Le Locle, Le Lieu, Le Pont, and other places where the Huguenots settled on their expulsion from France, and introduced watch-making and other industries. Mont Tendre was ascended more than once, for the sake of the view; the Gemmi was crossed through deep snow, Zermatt and other places opening from the Rhone valley were explored, and Max Müller gradually recovered his usual vigour. He wrote to his mother:—

*Translation.* CHÂTEAU DE MOLLENS, *April.*

'The most rural, retired spot, an old château on a spur of the Jura, three hours from the nearest station, with the hills rising behind the house, and in front, on a fine day, such a view, almost as fine as the famous view from Berne. Mont Blanc just in front, . . . whilst right and left run his snowy companions, and the Lake of Geneva at their foot.

'*April* 19. I was longing for solitude and rest, and I shall find that here. It is said to be very healthy, but is still cold, so that we require fires.'

To R. B. D. MORIER, ESQ.

CHÂTEAU DE MOLLENS, *July* 18.

'I see in the paper that your dear old father has been called to his rest. The longer you have had him, the more you will miss him. Though you have long been away from your father, yet I know how the feeling warms us when we feel chilled in the world, that there is one heart, a father's or a mother's heart, which, whatever the world may say or think of us, loves us with all our faults, and will love us to the end. And what a comfort it must be to you to know how happy and proud your father felt of you, how you were the chief interest that still bound him to this earth. I wonder whether you were with him at the last moment? Well, my dear friend, we stand now in the first line of the battle, and in a few years more our fight will be over too. All we can do is to fight on bravely, as long as we can, though one often longs for rest, and to hear no more of the din of battle.

'I have so often thought of your dear father lately. He was always so kind to me, and when I lost my child, he sent me word to say what he had had to bear, and had been able to bear.

'Switzerland has done me much good—I can sleep again, and the more I work the stronger I feel. We are going away from here in a few days. I want to show my children a little of Switzerland before we return, but in about six weeks I think we shall be back in Oxford.'

After a few days at Hofwyl, where they joined their boy, the Max Müllers settled at Gimmelwald, a little Swiss *pension*, higher up the Lauterbrunnen Valley than Mürren, and much quieter. From this many excursions were made, in which they were joined by friends from Mürren. From Gimmelwald Max wrote to his mother:—

*Translation.* GIMMELWALD, *August* 5.

'Yesterday, at six in the morning, I got a telegram from the Emperor of Brazil in Interlaken, who wished to see me. I went to Interlaken, and had a long conversation with him, all in French. He is a man who has read and thought a great deal, and we agreed in most things. He is now working at Sanskrit, and had much to ask. The Empress was also there; all other visitors were refused. In the afternoon they went on to Berne, and I came back here in the evening. Rest and solitude are doing me good, and I hope to have these even in Oxford. When I sit quietly at my work I feel better, but even here we have seen more people than we wished for. You ask how I like Eber's *Uarda*—very much. It is more of a novel than the *King's Daughter*, but that was historically more interesting, as it treated not only of the Egyptian, but of the Greek and Persian life. The first book was more instructive; this one more artistically perfect.'

A few days were spent at Basle on the way to England, to enable Max Müller to see his old friend Gelzer, the historian, at that time chiefly occupied in writing on religious questions. A few days later Gelzer wrote to Max:—

*Translation.* *August* 16, 1877.

'The short time we were together proved to my entire satisfaction that the presentiment which led me to you was a true inspiration. In intercourse with you I breathed again that same strengthening air that I breathed in my intercourse with Bunsen and others. Your wide views of the world, your living knowledge of England and Germany, your cultivated historical point of view, your religious and ethical disposition, all worked as refreshing dew on my spirit and thoughts.'

TO HIS MOTHER.

*Translation.* OXFORD, *August* 30.

'We have been home since Saturday. What we felt in returning here you can imagine. It was like a second funeral! With every day I miss my child more, and so it will be for one's whole life. I have much to do to get settled again. The children are happy in their old home, but one sees from time to time how they miss their sister. We have seen hardly any one. Most people are still away, so for a time it will be quiet.'

TO MONCURE CONWAY, ESQ. (who had written asking him to lecture for him in London).

OXFORD, *September* 17.

'Thanks for your hearty welcome. I have been back for the last three weeks, trying to feel at home again in my old house, which looks so sad, and strange, and empty. Life to me can never be again what it has been these fifty years of unbroken sunshine, but it may become something better. At present I cannot help you in London. I want rest and quiet, and I have plenty of work. My health is quite restored, better than ever; I never feel tired, and I can sleep again like a child. The translation of the *Sacred Books of the East* progresses well, though I have still much correspondence to carry on to make my collaborators keep step. I am myself continuing my translation of the *Rig-veda*. Here and there there is a gem, but it is strange to see with how little man was satisfied in early days, and, maybe, is even now.'

TO M. RENAN.

OXFORD, *October* 7.

'How many years have passed since I last wrote to you! and now the first thing I do is to ask a favour. That I have the courage to do so will show you that, though we have not exchanged letters of late, you have always remained very near to me. I have read your books, where, after all, a man gives the best that he has, and is, to his friends. Your last book found me in Switzerland. I went through the *Dialogues* with you, and enjoyed your conversation. I only regretted that I could not always see *you* distinctly, and I doubt whether, in these days of monologues, dialogues can do justice to an author. The value of books, however, lies after all in a few salient sentences. I remember one which I read with delight in your *Dialogues*, though I cannot find it now: "Human language, as soon as it tries to reach the supernatural, becomes of necessity mythological"—something like that; you will know the passage I mean. But now comes the favour I meant to ask you. I have been reading of late much of what has been written in modern and ancient times about death, and life after death. I believe that you wrote on that subject when your sister left you, and that you sent what you had written to some of your friends. Would you let me see what you wrote then? I now belong to the same company of mourners: my eldest daughter, sixteen years old, all that a father could desire, and still all my own, left me last year. I know how sacred a thing the grief of our hearts is, and, if you tell me No, I shall fully understand and respect your motives. But many times of late, when I was reading Figuier, or Naville, or Plutarch, or Cicero, I thought of you and what you might have said, and at last I summoned up courage to write to you as I have done. Even if you do not answer at all, I shall know why you remain silent—the heart that knows its own bitterness knows also the bitterness of other hearts.

'We have been back for six weeks; I thought first I should stay a few weeks at Paris on my way back to England, but my heart failed me at the last moment, and we went home direct from Switzerland. I am gradually getting accustomed to my old rooms, and beginning new work. The *Sacred Books of the East* are safe; there are sixteen translators at work, but it will be a year or two before the first volumes appear. I quite share your feelings of admiration for M. Darmesteter. His book on Ormazd and Ahriman is a step, and I am proud to have secured him for the translation of the *Avesta*. Your young Sanskrit scholars too are doing excellent work. The *Upanishads* and the *Vedânta*, if looked into seriously, contain, I believe, the solution of many difficulties which perplex our philosophy. Only it is not enough to translate them, they require the shoulder of a Christophorus to carry them over the channel of two thousand years that runs between the old Vanaprasthas and ourselves.'

To his Mother.

*Translation.* *October 9.*

'I can well believe how you have been living over old days! Fifty years[1] is a long time, and you have had much that has been very hard to bear. But one must learn to bear, and try to understand

[1] Wilhelm Müller died October, 1827.

that it all is as it should be, and that life is best for us as it is. How happy are those who die young, but we who are growing old and grey have the consolation that we shall not be left here, lonely and forsaken, for ever. We must have patience; and then we all cling to life, as long as there are those who love us here. Those who love us there are always ours. Nothing is lost in the world. How it will be we know not, but if we have recognized the working of a Divine wisdom and love here on earth, we can take comfort and wait patiently for that which shall come. So I wish you for your birthday, and for the years to come, quiet and patience. We have many visitors; our friends are very kind, but they don't understand we feel most happy when we are left alone!'

The interview mentioned in the following letter to his wife has been adverted to in an earlier chapter, but it is interesting to see the impression produced at the time:—

*November* 3, 1877.

'I had an interesting visit to-day from Nîlakantha Goreh, the man I often spoke to you about. But how changed! He is one of the Cowley Brothers; has been here for a year and a half, and is going back to India in a few days. Now and then the old spirit seemed to move in him, but he soon relapsed into formulas which he had learnt, and which seemed to satisfy him. He was glad to see me again, but it was sad to see the eagle with broken wings!'

To M. Renan (who had sent him his Memoir of his sister, Henriette Renan).

'Your book arrived to-day, and I sat down at once to read it. I could follow you, feel with you, sorrow with you from beginning to end. One learns, as one grows older, to care more for the great sorrows of life than for its joys. One learns to weep with those who weep, as one learns to laugh with those who laugh. Your sorrow was different from mine, yet at heart it was the same. The love between a father and his young daughter is the same perfect, because unselfish, love as that between a brother and a sister. For fifty years my life had been a constant sunshine, with no clouds but such as are necessary for a beautiful sky. I often said to myself, I could live and work on for two hundred years and never get tired of it. Now all is changed; the very happiness which is left me still in my wife and children makes me tremble, for I know now on what conditions we hold our happiness. One goes on day after day, and one asks, Why that long delay? How happy we should be if we were all called away at sixteen, knowing nothing of life but that it is a garden and a paradise. Truly those who die young are blessed. And shall we find them again such as they left us? Why not? It is really here on earth that those whom we love change, it is here that they die every day; have we not lost the little angel faces as our children first appeared to us when they entered this world? Where are our children of three and four years, with their minds growing like sweet buds? Where are they, such as they were when ten years old, coming to us with their first troubles, their first questions, and convinced that they could all be answered by their father and mother? Where are they, as they first began to judge for themselves, and yet clung to us as their best friends? Where are all those bright joyous faces which we look at when we open our photograph books from year to year? On earth they are lost, but are they not treasured up for another life, where we shall be not only what we are from day to day, never the same to-morrow as we were yesterday, but where we are at once all that we can be—where memory is not different from perception, nor our wills different from our acts? We shall soon know—till then surely we have a right to be what we are, and to cling to our human hopes. The more human they are, the nearer the truth they are likely to be.

'I shall keep your book as a real treasure. Why is it so difficult to say our best things to the world?'

The following letter is among the first of a long and active correspondence carried on with Professor Noiré of Mainz, from now till Noiré's death in 1889. Professor Noiré early lost the beautiful girl to whom he was engaged, and never married. He had written a very severe critique on some of Max Müller's works, which a subsequent perusal of them led him to regret, and he at once wrote to Max Müller acknowledging himself in the wrong. Max, who had not seen the attack, was very much touched by the letter, and a devoted friendship sprang up between them. Noiré was warmly attached to Max Müller's children.

To Professor Noiré.

*Translation.* Oxford, *November* 11.

'It was kind of you to send me your picture: I know you now much better. What are faces for, if not to show us what men are? The words "at the grave of a blessed hope" have touched me deeply. Few would have had the strength to utter such words! My loss was a different one: . . . much remains that belongs to me, my wife and three children, but the feelings of security, the belief in this life are gone. I pack up my luggage and wait for my train. I should still like to finish various things, but I have the feeling that others who are less tired will do it better than I. We are on the right path, and we are further on than we were thirty years ago. But the old ones have to make way for the young ones, and must rejoice if they continue on the same straight road. Work and pleasure in my work is never wanting with me, only the time for it seems so short. I read Carrière's *Order of the Moral World* lately. He is an old friend of mine. You will like Part II. One of these days I mean to take time to study your writings from beginning to end; but I read but slowly. So far I meet with no thoughts which would make me say No. I wonder where we shall differ. You may go farther in regard to Physics and Metaphysics; I seem to take firmer ground in regard to the historical facts of language, but our aim, I think, is the same.'

To the Same.

*Translation.* *November* 18.

'Dear Friend,—For I think I may call you so, for a meeting of spirits and a mutual understanding is a good if not a better foundation for true friendship, than a casual living together or working together in the same place. And nothing binds human beings so closely together—as in our case—as a common sorrow. I thank you for your sympathy, but, believe me, my sorrow is at the same time my best comfort. I should not like to part with it for anything: you know what I mean. My work of course shall not suffer from it; on the contrary, I seem to see much clearer the work pointed out to me, and I throw a great deal overboard to reach the goal all the faster. I have some big tasks in view, tasks which will occupy me for several years to come, and therefore I shun no labour. My *Lectures on Darwin* will, I hope, make a nice volume. . . . I am still searching for the origin of the first concept. I see perfectly what you say about the dualism in the percept of the two arms, eyes, &c., being that of one only. But is reason originally a mere addition? and if so, I ask again, *how* do we add together? *How* do one and one make two, make a pair? I should like to say something in public about your last book, to draw the attention of the English to your work and your philosophical position. . . . But my memory is not quite reliable, and I should like to ask you to give me a clear *résumé* of your work. . . . Let us hold together while life lasts. Hand in hand we may achieve more than each alone by himself. We are much less afraid when we are two together. The chief condition of all spiritual friendship is perfect frankness. There is no better proof of true friendship than sincere reproof, where such reproof is necessary. We are occupied on one great work, and in this consciousness all that is small must necessarily disappear.'

To the Same.

*Translation.* 7, Norham Gardens, Oxford,

*November* 26, 1877.

'Dear Friend,— . . . There is something in the development and perception of language which is like the formation of corals. How I do envy the Greeks their λόγος: how much confusion we might have been spared by such a word as that! I find in your first book what I missed in your last about the origin of language—the foundation, which is far more important than all the later occurrences: whether the materials developed by means of sympathy or mimetic are of little consequence, if only it is clearly realized who is the architect of it all, what he is, and what was his intention. I can well imagine a language rising out of mimetic materials; indeed, I think we have no right whatever to exclude these materials. The great rivers rise from more than one source—language also. Everything depends on how language works out the material, i. e. how it forms its roots. I have reflected much upon that, have sifted and collected much, but it does not please me yet. . . . Our problem is what you have stated most clearly, what do we understand by Reason? where is its origin? whither does Reason tend? Reason springs from the perception of the manifold, and strives for the recognition of the highest Oneness; Nature pursues the inverted process, from the highest Oneness or Unity, acting or acted upon, to the endless manifold. Surely Heaven has been mankind's teacher. Sunrise and sunset preach daily the law of Causality, and in the dawn of the morning we find the first glimmer of Syllogism. The first flush—then the sun appears.'

To Mrs. Kingsley.

Oxford, *December* 13, 1877.

'My dear Aunt,—It is true that time, and the stars, and the sun have little to do with our sorrows, yet you know how these anniversaries bring back the crushing weight, and take away the elevating power of sorrow. How often I think of you when I feel very sad, and hardly know whether to be more grateful for the year that is gone, or for the years that may still be left me to live with those whom I love on earth. Life can never be again what it was before: one never can forget again the uncertainty of the tenure by which we hold here all that we call our own. One sits quiet in a corner, waiting for the next train, and wondering who will leave us next. That we should ever have been so happy on earth as we have been, that is the marvel.

Did not life and happiness seem endless then? and now one only longs that all were over here, and that we were all together again in a safer place. I believe in all our hopes we cannot be human enough. Let us be what we are—men, feel as men, sorrow as men, hope as men. It is true our hopes are human, but what are the doubts and difficulties? Are they not human too? That is what we forget when we try to be very wise. Shall we meet again as we left? Why not? Do we not see in the young girl of sixteen the child of six years, nay, even of six weeks, and love one in the other and all together? We do not know *how* it will be so, but who has a right to say that it *cannot* be so? Let us imagine and hope for the best that, as men, we can conceive, and then rest convinced that it will be a thousand times better. In that hope I live on, and work on, and that, as you know well, is a great help. How I have rejoiced in the success of your book, for your sake as well as for his! A life well lived is, after all, worth living for. I am quite well in health, the children are well, but they too look forward to a saddened Christmas.'

### To Professor Noiré.

*Translation.* 7, Norham Gardens, *December* 17, 1877.

'... "Let bygones be bygones" is a good proverb, which you learn in England. I am hardened, and have been so for years, against all attacks here; they very rarely cause me a sleepless night. When I, the first layman, delivered my address in Westminster Abbey, all the papers barked to such a degree that even my friends began to be anxious. Petitions were sent to bishops and Convocation; I was threatened with a law-suit, and even with six months' imprisonment. In Germany people heaped insults upon me at the same time, saying that, to please the orthodox, I had preached a sermon! What is one to say to all this? The only thing is to know what you want, and then always straight on.... It is important for me to know your opinion as to where my weakness lies with regard to German ideas. Of course I am quite conscious that the English atmosphere leaves its impression on me, and makes its influence felt, though I try to keep free from it; and one's personal foibles and want of clearness must be added to this. We are all *becoming*, I hope, *better*, at all events different from year to year. All my life has been a struggle about religious convictions; I think, even now, I cling to many things still which would find no favour with you. To me religion and philosophy are two dialects of the same language. I speak both, and I think I speak them honestly. We only need to reduce our highest philosophic abstractions etymologically to their origin, and how simple and childlike everything becomes!

'I always think in England you can say everything you like, if you only know how to say it, but I may be mistaken. . . . I must conclude to-day; these are the sad days which take away the elevating consolation of our grief, and which bring back the hard days of remembrance. I work as much as I can, to hide the open grave.'

From the time of his return to Oxford in the early autumn of 1877, Max Müller began to write the lectures he had promised the Hibbert Trustees to deliver early in 1878. The preparing and publication of these lectures, and the translation and printing of the *Upanishads*, Part I, which appeared early in 1879, as Volume I of the *Sacred Books of the East*, occupied Max Müller through the whole year. The spirit in which he worked on is shown in the following letter:—

To his Wife.

*January* 8, 1878.

'I know how much is left us still, but we must learn not to cling too fast to what we think is ours. Nothing is ours on earth, that is what we must learn; and then trust in God, and walk on in faith, but with trembling. It seems hard sometimes for the children that they should have learnt the real lessons of life so early, but it may be good for them to learn the truth and never to forget it again. I had to learn it very late in life, and that made it all the harder. All seemed endless to me before, now I feel at every moment as if the end was near. A few more years and a few more tears, and the work is done. But I do not mean to be idle; on the contrary, I shall try to work with all my might. My work does not separate me from my dear child, she is always with me when I work. I seem to work with her and for her: that is a real help and comfort, nothing else.'

To Professor Noiré.

*Translation.* 7, Norham Gardens, *February* 3, 1878.

'Dear Friend,—I seem really to have nothing to do, and yet I do not seem to get any rest. . . . Here in England we think of nothing now but politics. Gladstone paid a visit here. I ventured to tell him quite humbly that, because we hate the Turks, it did not seem necessary to love the Russians, but one might as well sail up Niagara as meet such a torrent of eloquence. These things make me quite sad. It is, indeed, beautiful when a nation governs itself, and when each and all may say what they think, but with regard to the enemy this seems rather dangerous.

'Gladstone does good, but he does not *know*. He ruins the

Liberal party in England, and the Tories will have a great majority in Parliament.

'I admire the artistic finish of Eber's work. He seems to me amiable and modest, to judge from correspondence I have had with him. Also it does him great credit that, as a Professor, he has the courage to be a man. Do you know Kingsley's *Hypatia?* In spite of all mistakes, it seems to me a most remarkable book, more remarkable than the *Egyptian Princess*, and he was such a good man and faithful friend. I have tried in vain to find out what prominent music connoisseurs admire in Wagner. I have shunned neither time nor trouble, but without results; the swamp in which we find a few lilies is too deep for me.'

TO THE SAME.

*Translation.* *February* 8.

'... You think much too highly of what I have done. I read your books at a time when I had hardly any feelings left for other things. My sorrow had blinded me to all and everything. I stood, as it were, under a waterfall, where, as Jean Paul remarks, we need no shelter from the rain. At another time your remarks might have called forth some sharp rejoinder from me; as it is now, it is difficult for me either to get angry or to rejoice over anything.

'Darwin has given us, in his later editions of the *Origin of Species*, an historical treatise on his mental ancestors. Altogether old Darwin is an honest fellow. The Darwinians are much worse than Darwin himself, and I think the word "Darwinism" ought either to be sharply defined or should be replaced by "evolution-doctrine." Has not the *Bathybius Haeckelii* been long given up by its inventor, Huxley?

'The theory of meteoric stones as life-producers originates from Sir William Thomson; Helmholtz accepted it; after that it was said that it had only been a joke; later on it was taken up again seriously.'

The following letter is an answer to one written by Mr. Freeman from Palermo. Mr. Freeman was deeply interested in the language of Sicily, which he felt historically ought to be Greek with words borrowed from Latin and Arabic, whereas it is Latin with borrowed words.

TO E. FREEMAN, ESQ.

OXFORD, *April* 10.

'The subject on which you write is certainly interesting and very puzzling, but you know a great deal more about it than I do. I only know the present dialect from Pitré's *Fiabe e Novelle*, where there is also a grammar, and at the end a glossary. The Greek and Arabic ingredients are very small and very doubtful, frequently dating from Albanian rather than from Greek. Years ago I read a number of *Greek Charters* published by Trinchers, or some such name, and containing a number of Roman words disguised in Greek. I remember φεοδ = feodum, &c. But before the Norman conquest the literary history of Sicily is to me utterly unknown. My own idea was that Augustus sent large colonies to Sicily, and that from that time the *coloni* spoke Latin. After that they were for a long time bilingual and trilingual in the upper classes, but the influence of the Church would favour the Latin, which maintained itself even where Greek was used for official documents. If there were materials, it would be a chapter of the Science of Language, full of interest, but I believe the materials are wanting. I know that Niebuhr took much interest in the subject, and tried to discover Greek elements in the spoken Sicilian. Bunsen told me of his once being in a boat with Niebuhr with some Sicilian boatmen; there was a storm, and, in order to encourage each other, the rowers suddenly began to sing out "ploï!" Niebuhr was delighted; he asked them what it meant, and they said it was a kind of charm they had learnt from English sailors. No, said Niebuhr, it is Sicilian Greek. No, said Bunsen, it is English, Pull away! Have you been to any of the places, four, I believe, altogether, where they still speak a kind of Arabic? That would be an interesting dialect to analyse. I am just now deep in Sanskrit, having undertaken a course of lectures "On the Origin of Religion," to be delivered in the Chapter House, Westminster. Hard work, but I wanted some hard work. We are just on the eve of our election; Henry Smith comes forward as a candidate. I wish him all success, though I fear "original research" will suffer.'

### To his Mother.

*Translation.* *April* 18.

'My dear, good Mother,—This will reach you on Auguste's birthday. How often I used to pity her that she was called away so early, but now one does not pity her any longer. One pities those who must struggle on here so long. But what is long and what is short? Time goes fast, and we must wait in patience, and employ the time as well as we can. I try to do so. I have plenty of work for my London lectures. I hope they will be a success. The first lecture is to be printed by May 1 in England, Germany, Italy, perhaps in France too. The rest must wait, but all are to be ready by the autumn, so there is plenty to be done. To-day it is quite spring-like here, quite warm already. We went out to pick the flowers (fritillaries) which grow here in the river meadows. How often we went there all together! And then one says constantly to oneself, What a happy dream of life the child dreamt, how much has she been spared! I must for the present go constantly to London, and G. will often go with me, and we shall see friends and relations there, and must begin to get accustomed again to society, hard as it will be. I hope you are well. Spend plenty of money, what is it there for? I should like sometimes to send —— money for her children: how can I do it?'

A short time before delivering his first Hibbert Lecture, Max Müller sent it to a few friends, on whose judgement he relied, for criticism. In every case it was returned with expressions of the highest appreciation, which braced and encouraged him; for the deep sorrow through which he had passed had unnerved him, and though he had, as he knew, done his very best, he mistrusted his own judgement. One friend wrote: 'I have read your lecture with the liveliest pleasure, and very much profit. It is beautiful, so cool, so solid, so wise, so full of humour (these are famous strokes).' Another wrote: 'I do not think it is any peculiar taste of my own which makes me say that the selection and order of topics, the literary form, the tone of feeling, the proportion of original exposition to criticism of others, and the blending of historical with philosophical elements, appear to me altogether admirable in themselves, and for the purpose of the lectureship.' The Westminster Chapter had, at the instance of Dean Stanley, lent the Chapter House at Westminster for the series of seven lectures, but a few days before the first lecture Max Müller received a telegram that 1,400 applications for tickets (which were gratis) had been received, the Chapter House only holding 600. He at once settled to give the same lecture twice, morning and afternoon. One of the leading papers thus described the opening lecture:—

'It was a memorable morning in April, 1878, when Professor Max Müller stood up in the Chapter House of Westminster Abbey to deliver the first of his lectures on "The Origin and Growth of Religion." The place, the lecturer, and the occasion were all alike remarkable. Under the shadow of one of the noblest buildings ever raised by mediaeval Christianity, an Oxford lay Professor came forward to deal with the deepest problems of historical religion in the "dry light" of modern science, and in the name of a trust which was intended by its founder to promote "the unfettered exercise of private judgement in matters of religion." Times change and the generations of men with them, and the crowded audiences which attended Professor Max Müller's lectures showed plainly that the days are past when a scientific treatment of religion could be regarded as either irreverent or heterodox.'

Another said :—

'No person who had the good fortune to be present at these lectures is likely to forget the extraordinary spectacle. The Chapter House was thickly crowded with perhaps the most remarkably eclectic audience ever assembled within that majestic old building. To very many the thought must have occurred, with what astonishment the old monks of Westminster would have looked upon such an audience gathered in their Chapter House for such a purpose.'

It was indeed a varied assembly that met there—dignitaries of the Church, leading Nonconformists, missionaries, and many natives of India, scientific men, fashionable ladies, highly cultivated women like Anna Swanwick, noted free-thinkers, whilst it was reckoned that at least one-tenth of the audience were ordained ministers of the Gospel. After the first lecture a friend wrote to Max Müller :—

'May it not be your high privilege and opportunity now, in the old historic Commons House and Chapter House, to gather together the real Commoners of the vast religious republic (stretching from India to California, from Strauss, Haeckel, and Huxley to Stanley and Emerson) and make a new "chapter" in our religious controversies? If we could only agree on the fundamental point that we are not to look backward 1,878 years for the religious any more than for the scientific *culmination* of humanity, all the rest would be easy.'

Naturally many of the so-called religious and Church papers criticized the lectures unsparingly, but they continued to be thronged to the last, and on every occasion the lecturer could feel that he was in thorough touch with his audience. He wrote to his mother :—

*Translation.* *May* 12, 1878.

'We are living a very disturbed life, and I often long as usual for quiet. The lectures go on well, but it is a great effort; the same lecture twice in the same day. Wednesday we go again to London, and so it will go on for some weeks. People think it is a good change for us. You know it is worse than when one is quietly at home.'

To the Same.

*Translation.* *June* 21, 1878.

'I am very tired from the lectures, and must have some rest. The old body won't go as formerly, and yet new work is always coming in, that one cannot well give up. I must see how a week at Malvern will suit me, and then I shall stay quietly in Oxford, where it is so quiet and pleasant in vacation, unless my doctor sends me to the sea. I have received £300 for my lectures, but settled at once to spend them in memory of Ada, in founding a scholarship at her school[1]. I know that would please her. I must now prepare the lectures for printing—no little work. I think I gained my object in the lectures, but it was a great effort. . . . All the papers one cares for speak warmly in their praise.'

The last words of the last lecture touched a hidden chord in the hearts of many of Max Müller's hearers, and gave expression to the longing of many among them :—

'I hope the time will come when the subterranean area of human religion will be rendered more and more accessible, . . . and that the Science of Religion, which at present is but a desire and a seed, will in time become a fulfilment and a plenteous harvest. When that time of harvest has come, when the deepest foundations of all the religions of the world have been laid free and restored, who knows but that those very foundations may serve once more, like the Catacombs, or like the crypts beneath our old cathedrals, as a place of refuge for those who, to whatever creed they may belong, long for something better, purer, older, and truer than what they can find in the statutable sacrifices, services, and sermons of the days in which their lot on earth has been cast; some who have put away childish things . . . but who cannot part with the childlike faith of their heart? Though leaving much behind of what is worshipped or preached in Hindu temples, in Buddhist vihâras, in Mohammedan mosques, in Jewish synagogues, and Christian churches, each believer may bring down with him into that quiet crypt what he values most :—

'The Hindu, his innate disbelief in this world, his unhesitating belief in another world.

[1] The Ada Scholarship, at the Oxford High School for Girls, for good conduct and proficiency in German.

'The Buddhist, his perception of an eternal law, . . . his gentleness, his piety.

'The Mohammedan, . . . his sobriety.

'The Jew, his clinging . . . to the one God, who loveth righteousness and whose name is I am.

'The Christian, that which is better than all, . . . our love of God, call Him what you like, the infinite, the invisible, the immortal, the Father, the highest self, above all, and through all, and in all, manifested in our love of man, our love of the living, our love of the dead, our living and undying love. That crypt, though as yet but small and dark, is visited even now by those few who shun the noise of many voices, the glare of many lights, the conflict of many opinions. Who knows but that in time it will grow wider and brighter, and that the Crypt of the Past may become the Church of the Future?'

When the book was printed, a friend wrote, in allusion to the touching dedication: 'Never did a brief and lovely existence find a sweeter immortality on earth than that of her whose spirit mingled with her father's, and became enshrined in his finest work.' Professor Noiré wrote: 'Such a wreath was never before laid on the resting-place of a loved one. They are not flowers, they are fruits, golden fruits, the ripest of their time. They will feed the hungry, refresh the thirsty, raise the fainting, and be for future generations a consolation, a glimpse into eternity, into the imperishable.'

The dedication runs thus:—

TO HER, WHOSE DEAR MEMORY
ENCOURAGED, DIRECTED AND SUPPORTED ME
IN WRITING THESE LECTURES, THEY ARE NOW DEDICATED
AS A MEMORIAL OF A FATHER'S LOVE.

After reading the first lecture sent to him in MS., Dr. Liddon wrote:—

'I have read it through, as I need hardly say, with great admiration, and, generally speaking, with complete assent. . . . I, for one, am convinced that in drawing attention to the pathetic interest of struggles after light among the heathen, and to the substantial value of the truths which they attained to, you are doing us a real service. You have the Alexandrians behind you, and the modern Church has too generally forgotten them. . . . And when you say that "Christianity conquered the world without protection," I more than assent.'

Just before going to London to deliver his last lecture,

Max Müller had asked his friends in Oxford to meet Mr. Graham Bell, the inventor of the Bell telephone, which preceded Edison's more perfect instrument. It was the first ever heard in England. A large company gathered together, and intense interest and surprise were felt by every one, even the scientific men present little dreaming of the immense practical importance of the invention, nor the possibility of the almost limitless extension now attained to. Mr. Bell also brought down a microphone, only just invented, and a phonograph. The wire of the telephone was stretched from one end of the garden to the other, and even a whisper was distinctly heard. The wire of the microphone was brought from a room on the second story, and the sound made by a fly crawling along a board in the room upstairs sounded in the garden like the tramp of an elephant. The phonograph was not good, and even one person at a time found it difficult to make out what it repeated. The following week, in London, Max Müller was asked to speak a Sanskrit verse into a better instrument. The scene has been well described by Mr. Moncure Conway:—

'When the phonograph was invented, one of its first appearances was at the house of J. Fletcher Moulton, Q.C. (now M.P.). A fashionable company, among them some eminent men of science and men of letters, gathered round the novelty, and Max Müller was the first called on to utter something in the phonograph. We presently heard issuing from it these sounds: "Agnim î*l*e purohitam ya*gñ*asya devam *ri*tvi*g*am—hotâram ratnadhâtamam." There was a burst of merriment when these queer sounds came from the machine, but a deep silence when Max Müller explained that we had heard words from the oldest hymn in the world, the first (if I remember rightly) in the *Rig-veda*: "Agni I worship; the chief priest of the sacrifice, the divine priest, the invoker, conferring the greatest wealth." And then the young people gathered around the smiling scholar, to learn that the hymns had all passed through thousands of years, in a phonographic way, each generation uttering precisely what was poured into its ear by the preceding generation, until their language died, to be recovered in the West, where for the first time the real meaning of Agni, and the human significance of the hymns, were studied and known. However, I did not hear exactly what the Professor said to the eager inquirers, but stood apart observing the picturesqueness of the scene, and finding in it something symbolical of the whole career of the polite scholar. He had evoked from the oral Sanskrit phonograph the ancient Âryan literature and mythology; the thin metallic voices became real, and cast their poetic spell not merely on the learned, but on fashionable young ladies and gentlemen in drawing-rooms, throughout Europe and America, adding vast estates to their minds, delivering them from the mere pin-hole views of humanity and of the universe, to which our ancestors were limited.'

During Commemoration Max Müller and his wife went to West Malvern, which from this time was a favourite retreat, when he felt overworked, and wished for that quiet which it became increasingly difficult to get in Oxford. The fine air, the long rambles on the hills, the glorious sunsets, for which West Malvern is famous, always refreshed him, and he could return to his life of almost ceaseless labour with renewed vigour. Later on, when his old and valued friend Lady Mary Fielding built herself a house at West Malvern, these visits had a fresh charm added to them.

To Dean Stanley.

Oxford, *July* 2, 1878.

'I am truly sorry for the Roumanians: both the Prince and Princess seemed to me so thoroughly honest, open, trusting, much too good for their place and the people they have to deal with, including Emperors *et hoc genus omne*. No Power could be expected to go to war for Roumania, but England should have protested against what she knows to be an act of fraud and violence. Roumania might have been the Belgium of the East, it may now become another Poland. Russia and Austria want to disintegrate the Roumanian nationality, and then to absorb it. They do not want another nationality between Slaves, Germans, Magyars, and Turks. The people who speak Roumanian in Austria, Russia, and Turkey lean towards the independent Roumanians, and their consolidation might become a danger. Hence the amputation of Bessarabia, and the introduction of a foreign and fermenting element in the Dobrudja. Both will produce results hereafter.

'How little one saw the sadness that fills the world in one's younger days! Now one sees and hears nothing else, and joy and happiness seem all effort and acting. True happiness seems now to lie in undisturbed sadness only. We were at Malvern last week, and on our way back saw both Tewkesbury and Worcester: what grand cathedrals, and splendidly restored!'

To the Same.

7, Norham Gardens, Oxford, *July* 4, 1878.

'I never said that Jingo was derived from Bask; I only said some one, I thought Tylor, had derived it from Bask. Tylor, however, tells me he is innocent. The Bask word is *Tain-coa*; Darrigol says the provincial pronunciation is *Taongoi-coa*, or *Jabe on-goicoa*, and that that would mean "Le bon maître d'en haut."

'My own feeling is that the *living Jingo* is nothing but one of those half-intentional corruptions of a sacred name which people were afraid to pronounce, and yet would pronounce. Thus we have *morbleu* for "mort de Dieu," *parbleu* for "par Dieu," *diantre* for "diable," German *Sapperment* for "Sacrament," *Herrje* for "Herr Jesus." Thus "by the *living Jingo*" was most likely for "by the living Jehovah"—unless somebody knows anything better.'

To his Mother.

*Translation.* *August* 3, 1878.

'We were delighted to get your letter for our wedding-day. The shadows fall thicker and thicker, but even in the shade it is well, often better than in full sunshine. And when the evening comes, one is tired, and ready to sleep! And so all is ordered for us, if we only accommodate ourselves to it quietly. The one thing that grieves me is that you are so often disturbed by such little events in life.'

Plans had been made for a visit to Scotland, but illness detained the Max Müllers, and they finally chose Whitby, chiefly for the sake of being near their friends the Bradleys, with whom long drives and walks over the moors, and expeditions along the coast, made this holiday most enjoyable to old and young.

Mr. Moncure Conway had sent an admirable digest of the *Hibbert Lectures* to an American paper, which called forth the following letter:—

Whitby, *August* 29, 1878.

'Bravo! Bravo! Bravo! that is an excellent abstract, the very marrow from beginning to end. What a pity it could not have been published in an English paper! You know there is no greater satisfaction than to feel and see that one has been really understood, and that one has acted as a successful interpreter between the thoughts of the old Rishis and the most advanced thinkers of the New World. As for the Self, I shall still have much to say; it is all in the *Upanishads*. Emerson did not see further than those old philosophers;

both, I feel convinced, saw the truth. If you could get me a copy of the paper, I should feel grateful. I shall keep it for the present, if I may, and return it to you when you want it. With regard to American publishers, I always think it best to do nothing, though if anything comes of your endeavours I shall be grateful.'

TO HIS MOTHER.

*Translation.* *October* 9, 1878.

'How different was your birthday in old days to now, when so many who used to rejoice with you are gone before us! That is the sorrow of a long life. One is ever more lonely, and lives ever more in the beautiful past than in the present. But one must say to oneself it was to be, and so it is best for us. However old one grows, there is always something to be done and learnt. At all events, one learns to be more indulgent towards others, and to think less and less about oneself. The more love in the heart, the more peace in the life, and that is what I wish for you for the rest of your life's journey.'

TO PROFESSOR BENFEY (on the fiftieth anniversary of his Professorship).

*Translation.* OXFORD, *October* 15, 1878.

'I am not sure whether these lines will reach you in time, but though my congratulations may arrive a day too soon or too late, you will know that they come from my heart, and that I sympathize deeply with the happiness which will be yours at this time. It is rare that a man in full possession of his mental power and strength can look back upon fifty years of a life so rich in labour and success as you are able to do to-day. You know how long I have been one of your pupils and admirers, and the consciousness that I have so often given expression to my admiration for you behind your back, gives me the courage to do so for once publicly and to yourself. Only the other day I came again across your treatise about Medhas, and it made me exclaim, "Nobody comes up to him in the least!" Well, not only on your own account and on account of those belonging to you, but also for our sakes, I wish for many autumns for you still, *s*arada*h*satam! The beauty of our studies is, that they not only occupy the head, but provide much food also for the heart and the inner man. The older we grow, the more do we value the "Wisdom of the Brahmas": and though, in growing old, we do not, like them, go into the forest, still we learn from you that the home also can grow into the forest, and that the true Muni, when his time comes, can fearlessly say: "I will get rid of death as if it were not death, or as if I were immortal."'

Max Müller then tells Professor Benfey that many of his admirers and pupils in England and Germany wished to present him with some token of their esteem, and asks him privately what sort of gift he would prefer. A set of gold dessert dishes were fixed on by the old man, and they were chosen by Max Müller and forwarded to him, together with the long list of subscribers, which included nearly all distinguished men connected with Oriental studies.

To Sir John Lubbock.

Oxford, *November* 19.

'I think you will be interested in the copy of an inscription sent me by Dr. Schliemann. I had written to tell him that all must depend on the inscription which he mentioned as part of his treasure, but I am afraid that nothing will come of what he sent me. Most of it looks to me like mere ornamentation. No doubt one may recognize a *t* and *th* in the cross, and the cross surrounded by a circle, but the inscription of these signs points to an ornamental purpose. In some of the other specimens one recognizes Semitic letters, but not of a very primitive type, an *r*, *s*, *th*, *o*, and on the hone there are a few very fine Phenician letters, only arranged in a way in which Phenician letters were never arranged. All this will not help us much, and I doubt whether there are any more inscriptions. However, the treasure is there, and Dr. Schliemann says its value in pure gold is more than would be found now in many an Imperial palace.'

It has been mentioned that, since the Taylorian Professorship was abolished, the Curators had from time to time invited foreigners, as M. Taine, Klaus Groth, &c., to lecture on foreign literature in some foreign language. This called forth the following letter:—

To M. Renan.

*November* 27.

'You will be surprised at the object of my letter, and will probably look upon it as another sign of the inexplicable in the English character. Well, some of my friends here at Oxford, the very bulwarks of conservatism in politics and religion, have suddenly become possessed by a strong desire to invite Castelar[1] to give them a few lectures at Oxford. I have tried to explain that Castelar will probably not care to lecture in French, while if he lectured in

[1] The republican Spanish orator, statesman, and writer.

Spanish he would have no audience at all. It was all in vain, and I was commissioned to find out whether M. Castelar would be inclined to accept an invitation to lecture, similar to that given to M. Taine, D.C.L. As I do not know M. Castelar personally, and was afraid of asking him directly, I thought I might write to you, to ask whether you could find out privately if M. Castelar, in case he were asked officially, would be likely to accede to such a request. I take it for granted that you know him, and I believe he is at present in Paris. Personally I need hardly say I have a sincere admiration for M. Castelar, and should feel delighted to make the acquaintance of a man who has done so much, and will I believe do much more in the future, but I tell you openly I was a little surprised at my friends' decision to invite him to Oxford, and I think it even possible that there may be some opposition made before the decision can assume an official character. However, if there is one thing which M. Castelar does *not* know, it is fear; and he may possibly think it worth his while to make an effort to place his views and convictions before the future statesmen in England. So if you could help me to reconnoitre the ground before the advance is made, I should feel much obliged. I hope in a few weeks to send you my new volume on the *Origin and Growth of Religion*; there are few men whose opinion I am more anxious to know on what I have had to say on the greatest question of our life, than yours.'

Several interesting letters passed after this between Max Müller and Señor Castelar, who seemed at first willing to undertake the lectures, but found that his duties in the Cortes would prevent him from leaving Spain.

It was towards the close of the year that Max Müller paid the visit to Prince Leopold at Boyton, which is mentioned in *Auld Lang Syne*, when the Prince produced the last bottle of the fine Johannisberg wine which Max Müller had always admired in Oxford, and which the Prince had kept for his visit.

BOYTON MANOR, *November* 30.

'I arrived all right, though it was not easy to find the way. When I came here, the Prince was out shooting, but he soon appeared with Mr. Collins, looking very well. There was a large party in the evening, Lord Bath, Lord Heytesbury, &c. Mrs. Collins is here, and young Campbell, who was with the Prince at Oxford. It is a pretty old house and very comfortably arranged, but he lives here very little, I believe, and it seems a pity he should not be in some place where he could do some good work. I never know why I go away from home. I do not want anything in the whole world: all I want I have at home, and that you know.'

To Dr. Rolleston.

*December* 12.

'I shall have nothing to do with Denominational or Undenominational Halls. Religion, though it does not come from *ligare*, is to bind us together; if it does not do that, it will do nothing else. No, I could not be President of the —— Society; life is short enough as it is.'

At length the *Hibbert Lectures* were published, as the next letters show:—

To M. Renan.

*December* 19.

'I hope you have received my *Hibbert Lectures* by this time. I have said in that book what I have longed to say for many years; you will easily understand what I mean, and what I am striving at, but whether the public at large will, I rather doubt. I could have made three or four large volumes out of the one, but if one wishes to be listened to at all in these days one must concentrate one's thoughts, say only what is essential, and not say everything. In that respect nothing to my mind is more perfect than the Sanskrit Sûtra style, though not without the commentary. I have tried to imitate that to a certain extent, whether successfully I must leave others to judge. Anyhow it will not take up much of your time to read the book, and I shall take it as a true sign of your friendship if you would spare the time, and afterwards tell me just with one word whether what I have seen is land or clouds.'

To Dean Stanley.

Oxford, *December* 7.

'Of course I know that many people will be angry with my *Lectures*. If it were not so, I should not have written them. The more I see of the so-called heathen religions, the more I feel convinced that they contain germs of the highest truth. There is no distinction in kind between them and our own religion. The artificial distinction which *we* have made has not only degraded the old revelation, but has given to our own almost a spectral character. No doubt the man is different from the child, but the child is the man and the man is the child, aye, even the very suckling. We can hardly believe it, yet the fact is there, and so it is in the growth of religion. God does not date from 754 A.U.C.; that is what

I want to teach. St. Augustine taught just the same, "Res ipsa, quae nunc religio Christiana nuncupatur, erat apud antiquos, nec defuit ab initio generis humani, quousque Christus veniret in carnem, unde vera religio, quae iam erat, coepit appellari Christiana" (Retr. I. 13: *Chips*, Preface, Volume I, p. xi).

'I wonder what the Canons would have said, if St. Augustine had preached such doctrines in their Chapter House! But enough of this.'

To his Mother.

*Translation.* *December* 21, 1878.

'We got your card as we came in from skating, so you see it is real winter here. The children have holidays, and Wilhelm and the girls amuse themselves on the ice. I had to skate with them, but it shakes my old bones, and it is high time to give it up. The sad news from Darmstadt[1] came just during the days so full of sad memories to us. One feels more deeply for others when one knows what it is! The poor husband and children, and here the poor mother! She was a lovely, good, and remarkable woman; later on people will have more idea of this. It is but a short time ago she consulted me about a tutor for her son. It is almost unbelievable, and much that is good will perish with her. How imperfect is this life, and how vain the labour of even the best people! My book is out, and there are many who agree with it, but many who oppose it, and that is always the best sign—one knows then that one's shot has told against untruth, and falseness, and envy. I work on quietly, and let them rage till they are weary.'

The following appreciation of the Grand Duchess of Hesse was found among Max Müller's papers:—

'The religious education which the Princess had received was such that, as she grew older, she might indeed have learnt to apprehend more fully the deep meaning of the simple truths she had been taught as a child; but she never would have had to unlearn or to disbelieve anything which she had been led to believe by her father. Another blessing which she carried away from her bright home was that perfect fearlessness which has always been the true reward of pure motives and true faith. How unjust public clamour could be even in a free country, the young Princess had had sad occasion to learn, but she had learnt at the same time the sacredness of the duty never to join in such clamour without a conscientious examination of the facts on which it professed to rest.

'In Germany the very name of Strauss had such a bad sound that it

[1] Death of the Grand Duchess of Hesse.

required no small courage on the part of the Princess to allow him even to be presented to her. Having once admitted him to her society, she felt in duty bound to form an independent opinion of his worth. To many people that would, no doubt, have been a dangerous experiment, and even to her it was, as we know, a painful trial. But she had faith in her faith. As the true child of her father, aye, as a true child of the spirit of St. Paul, she wished to prove everything, and to retain what was best. And she had her reward. Like genuine ore, her faith, though it may have lost some of its slag in the fiery furnace, came out more precious, more bright, more pure. What seemed a loss, became to her a real gain, and in the future no page in her life will probably be read with deeper sympathy, no sacrifice that the Princess has ever made will prove a greater blessing to many sick and wounded in spirit, than her noble courage in facing a danger from which so many shrink, and the triumph of that childlike faith which in the end helped her to bear burdens which seemed almost too heavy to be borne.'

In the visitors' book of this year we find the names of Bishop Staley of Honolulu, Professor Bühler from Bombay, Professor Darmesteter the Zend scholar, Mr. Graham Bell, Mr. Ralston the Russian scholar, the Bishops of Ohio, Colorado, and Shanghai, Turguenieff the novelist, and Herr Abel, the *Times* correspondent in Berlin.

# CHAPTER XXIV

## 1879–1880

Publication of the first volumes of *Sacred Books of the East.* Correspondence with Lady Welby. Renan. Holland. Dessau. Visitors. Japanese pupils. Greek accents. Lowell. Keshub Chunder Sen. Visit of Renan. Speech at Birmingham. 'Shang-ti.'

MAX MÜLLER, ever since his first intercourse with Her Royal Highness the Grand Duchess of Hesse in 1872 at Baden, had the greatest admiration for her character and talents, and we have seen how deeply he mourned over her untimely death.

To H.R.H. PRINCE LEOPOLD.

OXFORD, *February* 5, 1879.

'SIR,—I have thought of your Royal Highness very often during all these weeks, and of those true words of true sorrow in your last letter. I know the time when one first begins to recover from the crushing blow, and when the ordinary duties of life must be fulfilled again. It is the worst of all. One feels that life cannot and ought not to be again as it was, and yet it is. One shudders at the first smile that returns, and one longs for the tears in which wounded nature finds her best relief, but they flow no more.

'The time has not yet come for measuring the loss which not only her nearest relatives and friends, but the world has suffered through the death of your noble sister. You must wonder at the intense feeling of love and admiration with which she inspired all who came near her. To you she was like a great treasure that was your own; to others like a beautiful picture, like some Madonna of Raphael, which seen, it may be once or twice only, leaves a memory of loveliness on one's mind which is a treasure for ever. She was one of those natures in whom one believes at once, of whom one can think nothing but what is good, and by whom one feels certain of never being misunderstood. There was something truly royal in her, in the old sense of the word. Kings and Dukes were in former times leaders of men, leaders against enemies, whatever they might be, claiming the first place in every battle, the place of danger and of honour. That old truly royal spirit was in her, and made her, young as she was, step forward where others would have cowered behind, fearless and as if inspired by an ardent and irresistible love of truth. What is the use of being a King or a Duke if one cannot be a leader, a lover of truth, a champion of the persecuted, and never a slave to prejudice or etiquette? That old truly royal spirit seemed to beam from her eyes and breathe in her words, and made one feel that true chivalry was not yet altogether extinct on earth. I know many men in Germany who expected much from her influence, they hardly knew how and why, but they all trusted her and believed in her.

'I wonder whether the Grand Duke would like to see some letters, written with great freedom and by no courtier? I enclose one, which will show him what his own subjects thought of their Grand Duchess. I have no words of comfort, but I can and do feel the deepest sympathy in his irreparable loss. Trusting that your Royal Highness may not have suffered from these heavy trials and efforts, I remain always,

'Your Royal Highness's very faithful servant,

'F. MAX MÜLLER.'

The following letter makes the first mention of Madame Blavatsky, whose doctrine of Esoteric Buddhism was so contemned later on by Max Müller. It was also the allusions in this letter that led Mr. Malabari, himself a Parsee, to take an interest in Keshub Chunder Sen and the doctrines of the Brahma Somâj. And probably this letter induced Mr. Malabari to have the *Hibbert Lectures* translated into several of the Indian vernaculars.

TO B. MALABARI, ESQ.

OXFORD, *March* 29, 1879.

'I received your letter of March 10 yesterday, and I have at once written to Miss Manning to ask how I could in any way be useful to your young musical friend. I am myself very fond of music, though too old and too busy now to practise. I was a friend of Mendelssohn, and know several musicians in London, and if I can do anything for your friend's son I shall gladly do so.

'I sent you a copy of my *Hibbert Lectures*. These lectures were chiefly written for India. What I wished to do was to show you how much and how little you possess in your own ancient religion. There is a large accumulation of mere rubbish in your religious system: that you know as well as I do, and to an enlightened mind such as yours there can be no offence in my saying this; but beneath that rubbish there are gems. Do not throw those gems away with the rubbish. It is the fate of all religions to form these thick crusts of superstition around them—our own religion forms no exception to that rule—but to those who seek below the surface, in almost all religions there will be a reward. They will find what they seek, and enough to carry them safely through this short life. If you could tell your countrymen something of what I have written in these lectures, it might bear some good fruit. I should like to write a life of Râmmohun Roy. I have many materials for it, but I want more. He was a really great man, much greater than the world imagines, and we here in Europe have to learn from him quite as much as you in India. I have also full faith in Keshub Chunder Sen. I cannot bear to see the unforgiving way in which he has lately been treated. He has made a mistake, no doubt. But even if he had committed a crime, would it be impossible to forgive? Are his judges so immaculate? Do they know the temptations of a man placed in so exceptional a position? He has been too kind, too yielding as a father—he has himself acknowledged that much. That is enough. You will never find immaculate saints on earth: we ought to be grateful when we find an honest man, though he may not be free from human weaknesses.

'I was much amused at your "theosophic Russian countess." If she would learn Pânini while she is in India, she might do more useful work. I know nothing about her or against her. For all we know, she too may be a seeker after truth.'

During March of this year the Crown Prince and Princess of Germany, with their son, the present Emperor, and our present King, spent a long day in Oxford. Max Müller had the honour of receiving them at All Souls, and showing them over his College. He afterwards accompanied Prince William to the river and the barges, and this visit so delighted the Prince that he was anxious to spend one or two terms at Oxford; but it could not be. It was this visit, too, that caused the Prince, when Emperor, to take such an interest in Oxford boating, and, as is well known, he sent his congratulations year after year, through Max Müller, whenever Oxford won the University race.

In April Max was summoned to Germany by the alarming illness of his mother, who was now living at Dessau to be near her relations. He was able to return in about ten days' time, free from anxiety. Knowing how the parting always upset her, he came away without saying good-bye, writing the following letter to be given her when he was gone:—

*Translation.* DESSAU, *April* 26.

'MY DEAR GOOD MOTHER,—My heart was very heavy when I came here, and I go away very much reassured. Even if it is a little time yet before you get up your strength, you will doubtless soon be able to enjoy this lovely spring weather. As long as God wills it, we must learn to bear this life, but when He calls us we willingly close our eyes, for we know it is better for us there than here. When so many whom we loved are gone before us, we follow gladly; and the older we become here, the more one feels that death is a relief. And yet we can thankfully enjoy what is still left us on earth, even if our hearts no longer cling to it as formerly. I am so glad that I came here, and could inspire you with courage to live on. We do not need to say good-bye, for in spirit we are always together, and the miles between do not separate us. I have been so glad to see your home, and what care every one here takes of you. That is such a comfort to me. Take care of yourself, that you may not make us all so anxious again. Greet all at Dessau heartily from me: it is always a delight to be with one's relations who ever remain the same.

'In old love, your

'MAX.'

Early in May Max Müller sent the following letter to the Dean of Christ Church:—

OXFORD, *May* 14, 1879.

'MY DEAR DEAN,—Three volumes of the *Sacred Books of the East* will be ready for publication next week. I believe it was chiefly owing to your exertions, and to the interest taken by Lord Salisbury and Sir H. Maine, that that work could be carried out, and I should much like to dedicate the whole series to that triumvirate. But I shall take no steps before I know what you think about it.

'I know you will tell me openly what you think about this; also whether the wording is sufficiently formal, considering that it is addressed to our Chancellor. I should like to have these three names connected permanently with this undertaking, but I shall be entirely guided by your judgement.'

The dedication runs thus:—

TO
THE RIGHT HONBLE. THE MARQUIS OF SALISBURY, K.G.
CHANCELLOR OF THE UNIVERSITY OF OXFORD
LATELY SECRETARY OF STATE FOR INDIA
SIR HENRY J. S. MAINE, K.C.S.I.
MEMBER OF THE COUNCIL OF INDIA
THE VERY REV. H. G. LIDDELL, D.D.
DEAN OF CHRIST CHURCH
TO WHOSE KIND INTEREST AND EXERTIONS
THIS ATTEMPT TO MAKE KNOWN TO THE ENGLISH PEOPLE
THE SACRED BOOKS OF THE EAST
IS SO LARGELY INDEBTED
I NOW DEDICATE THESE VOLUMES
WITH SINCERE RESPECT AND GRATITUDE
F. MAX MÜLLER.

Lord Salisbury and Sir Henry Maine acceded at once to Max Müller's request, but the Dean hesitated awhile, which called forth another note from his friend, who always felt that it was to Dean Liddell's powerful advocacy he owed the continuance of his life in England.

7, NORHAM GARDENS, *May* 20.

'MY DEAR DEAN,—I should be very sorry if you declined to have your name associated with those of Lord Salisbury and Sir H. Maine in the dedication of the *Sacred Books of the East*. Both Lord Salisbury and Sir H. Maine have accepted the small token of gratitude which I could offer them, and my impression is that you had more to do with starting and carrying the whole matter than either of them. I should be afraid of offending you were I to say more, and I can only repeat my request that you may give me this opportunity of giving expression publicly to some of the sentiments which I have long entertained for you.

'I enclose an uncorrected proof-sheet. It will save you the trouble of writing another note, if you will kindly return it to me soon, with any corrigenda you like.'

It was during this summer that Max Müller made closer acquaintance with Lady Welby, to whom he owed the fine extract from Bishop Beveridge which forms the motto, one may call it, to the *Sacred Books of the East.* It will be found in Volume I of the series. Lady Welby herself stumbled on the passage by accident. Having some spare time one day, she resolved to look through a cupboard containing books that had belonged to her mother-in-law. The first book she drew out was Bishop Beveridge's *Private Thoughts on Religion.* She opened it to see what it might contain, and the passage in question almost at once caught her eye. She copied and sent it to Max Müller as strikingly applicable to his work. But Lady Welby shall tell the story herself:—

'My first interview with Professor Max Müller took place at the Deanery of Westminster. Twelve years afterwards I saw him again at Oxford.

'In the meantime he had brought to a triumphant conclusion the arrangements for his great work on the *Sacred Books of the East.* I had been roused to indignation by the accusations I found taken up by almost every one I knew, that in this signal service to religion he had only wished to discredit Christianity.

'It was after I had found and sent him Bishop Beveridge's prophetic utterance that I saw him at Oxford. I can never forget that picture.

'He was sitting at his writing-table. After a kindly greeting he said, "I was sitting just here when your letter came. It had all the effect upon me of what is called a miracle. Why do we disbelieve in miracle because we are no longer able to associate it with magic? It was a 'bolt out of the blue'; it was exactly what was wanted, and if it had reached me but a few hours later it would have been too late. As it was, I had to wire to the binder to stop work."

'I ought to add that (as appears in one of his letters to me) his sensitive conscience caused him at first to hesitate as to whether Bishop Beveridge would have approved of his words being thus used. But he was afterwards quite convinced that the man who had the courage in those days to write thus would have been equally fearless at all times.

'The ready and sympathetic interest with which for many years he helped and cheered on my humble attempts at inquiry into the conditions and nature of meaning, its changes and developments, are reflected in his letters.

'I can only here repeat my admiration and gratitude to him, whom to know was not merely to admire, but also most warmly to regard, and to whose unfailing kindness I owed so much.

'VICTORIA WELBY.'

### To Lady Welby.

*May* 16.

'Many thanks for those extracts from Bishop Beveridge. I was amazed and delighted on reading them. They came in the very nick of time. I am just publishing three volumes of translations of the *Sacred Books of the East*, and I could not wish for a better—what shall I call it?—motto, figure-head, flag, for these books than the sentences from Beveridge. . . .

'Looking forward to the great pleasure of renewing our acquaintance, I remain, yours sincerely and most gratefully.'

### To the Same.

*June* 1.

'From the pamphlet I send you, you will see that I decided on printing the extract from Bishop Beveridge's *Private Thoughts*. I felt the force of what you said. If two hundred years ago he could express those sentiments in all simplicity and boldness, how much more boldly would he have spoken now, when our knowledge of the so-called heathens is so far more accurate, when we have learnt not to be frightened, but rather to rejoice at every spark of truth that lightened the darkness of our fellow creatures. Perhaps we have also learnt that where those who lived before us saw nothing but light, there is much darkness left, and always will be, so long as we have to see with these poor eyes of ours. If people would only learn that, they would then soon learn the other lesson also which had struck you so much in the words of St. Paul, that charity in thought, word, and deed is more than all creeds and all philosophies. And how easily you discover in life those who have learnt that lesson, who trust everybody, see good in everything, never say an unkind word, and rejoice in helping where they can help. That Church is larger than we think: we have only to enter in ourselves, and we shall find it crowded, and often with those whom we least expected to find there.'

### To M. Renan.

*May* 16.

'I do not know whether you have found time to look at my *Hibbert Lectures*. If you have, I should like to ask you quite privately whether, in case the Trustees should ask you to give a similar course of lectures in London, of course in French, you would feel inclined to do so. I ask the question entirely for my own satisfaction. I feel we must do everything in our power to draw the bonds of international sympathy more closely together, and try to establish a feeling between the small and scattered bodies of truth-loving men in all countries. Hildebrand is at this moment lecturing in London. I hope Castelar will gain some sympathy for the higher aspirations of Spain when he comes to lecture at Oxford in June. His *Hermana de la Caridad* is beautiful. Some lectures from you, though they would rouse great opposition, would in the end do good. They would change a name, an often misunderstood name, into a living man with the English public, and the English public, with all its faults, is after all the salt of the earth. Another question: the *Contemporary Review* wishes to give a number of criticisms on my *Hibbert Lectures* written by men of various and opposite opinions. Would you be inclined to take a part? Your manuscript would be either carefully translated into English or printed in French. Each writer is to take his own special line. Some thoughts from you on the origin of the word Infinite would be truly welcome.'

To Lady Welby.

*June* 18.

'What you say about love superseding faith is perfectly true, and seems to me the keynote of all Christianity. But the world is still far from true Christianity, and whoever is honest towards himself, knows how far away he himself is from the ideal he wishes to reach. One can hardly imagine what this world would be, if we were really what we profess to be, followers of Christ. The first thing we have to learn is that we are not what we profess to be. When we have learnt that, we shall at all events be more forbearing, forgiving, and loving towards others. We shall believe in them, give them credit for good intentions, with which, I hope, not hell, but heaven is paved. But as to our ever being more than nominal Christians, I doubt it.

'I cannot follow you as to love being ever anything but a quality of some one. You may predicate again of what is originally a predicate, you may speak of blue being dark, light, &c. But as little as the blue of the sky is the sky, love is not God. God is full of love, as loving, but if we say God is love, this is only a freedom of language; what we mean is that God cannot be without love, that He is the true self-denying Self. Even that is mere groping in the dark; we hardly know more of what is around and above us than the poor snail in our garden pushing forward its four tentacles, and imagining that it knows where it is when there is nothing to throw it back upon itself.'

The following preface was contributed this year to the first volume of an American work, *The Hundred Greatest Men.* This volume was devoted to Religious Leaders. The work is so little known in England that it seems worth while to give Max Müller's introduction :—

'We live in two worlds: behind the seen is the unseen, around the finite the infinite, above the comprehensible the incomprehensible.

'There have been men who have lived in this world only, who seem to have never felt the real presence of the unseen; and yet they achieved some greatness as rulers of men, as poets, artists, philosophers, and discoverers.

'But the greatest among the great have done their greatest work in moments of self-forgetful ecstasy, in union and communion with a higher world; and when it was done, such was their silent rapture that they started back and could not believe it was their own, their very own: and they ascribed the glory of it to God, by whatever name they called Him in their various utterances, whether Apollo or the Muses, Egeria or the Daimonion.

'And while the greatest among the great thus confessed that they were not of this world only, and that their best work was but in part their own, those whom we reverence as the founders of religions, and who were at once philosophers, poets, and rulers of men, called nothing their own, but professed to teach only either what their fathers had taught before them, or what a far-off Voice had whispered in their ear.

'That highest self-surrender marks the highest point which human greatness can reach, and no ruler, no poet, no artist, no philosopher or discoverer can claim such sway over millions of human hearts as the so-called founders of the ancient religions of the world, whose very names are often unknown to us, and whose glory of countenance no human pencil has ever portrayed.

'The ancient religions were not founded like temples or palaces, they sprang up like sacred groves from the soil of humanity, quickened by the rays of celestial light. In India, Greece, Italy, and Germany not even the names of the earliest prophets are preserved. And if in other countries the forms and features of the authors of their religious faith and worship are still dimly visible amidst the clouds of legend and poetry, all of them, Moses as well as Zoroaster, Confucius,

Buddha, and Mohammed, seem to proclaim with one voice, that their faith was no new faith, but the faith of their fathers; that their wisdom was not their own wisdom, but, like every good and perfect gift, given them from above.

'*Moses* preached the God of his fathers, of Abraham, Isaac, and Jacob, and the laws which he brought down from Mount Sinai were written, he says, with the finger of God.

'*Zoroaster*, whoever he was, believed what the patriarchs had believed before him, and the law which he taught was not what wise men had agreed upon, but what Ahuramazda, the Wise Spirit, had revealed to him, as a friend to a friend.

'*Confucius* resented being called the founder of a new faith. "I am a transmitter," he said, "not a maker. I believe in the ancients and love them."

'Even *Buddha* declared that he had come on the same path on which many had come before him; though he, alone of all religious teachers, knew of no heavenly friend to reveal to him what he, the Enlightened, knew.

'And *Mohammed*, when he first taught Islam, that is, Surrender, only proclaimed anew the old God of the fathers, of Abraham, Ishmael, Isaac, and Jacob; what he wrote was not his own, but the words which Gabriel had spoken to him when showing him "the eternal original of the Koran."

'What should we learn from these prophets who from distant countries and bygone ages all bear the same witness to the same truth?

'We should learn that though religions may be founded and fashioned into strange shapes by the hand of man, religion is one and eternal.

'From the first dawn that ever brightened a human hearth or warmed a human heart, one generation has told another that there is a world beyond the dawn; and the keynotes of all religion—the feeling of the infinite, the bowing down before the incomprehensible, the yearning after the unseen—having once been set to vibrate, have never been altogether drowned in the strange and wild music of religious sects and societies.

'The greatest prophets of the world have been those who at sundry times and in divers manners have proclaimed again and again in the simplest words the simple creed of the fathers, faith in the unseen, reverence for the incomprehensible, awe of the infinite—or, simpler still, love of God, and oneness with the All-father.'

### To Lady Welby.

*July* 25.

'I was away from Oxford when your letter arrived, and now I am in the midst of sorting, destroying, and answering letters previous to our departure for Scheveningen next Monday. You will excuse therefore, I hope, if to-day I only say that I shall always be truly interested in anything you may write to me. Several friends who have opened the first volume of the *Sacred Books of the East* have congratulated me on the happy extract from Bishop Beveridge.

'I wonder whether you would find, what I have found through life, that nothing helps us on so well as some kind of drudgery, some mechanical work to which something can be added every day. When the day is over one feels that *that* at least is done. Extracts from books one reads, carefully arranged under more or less general headings, even a mere index of names, &c., become very useful by-and-by; anyhow they give us regular occupation, which seems to me one of the greatest privileges which men enjoy before women. A collection of passages from the New Testament to show what Christ Himself taught on the great questions which occupy us to-day, or what the Apostles taught, would be valuable still, in spite of all that has been written by theologians by profession. Christ spoke to men, women, and children, not to theologians; and the classification of His sayings should be made, not according to theological technicalities, but according to what makes our own heart beat. . . .'

### To the Same.

*July* 27.

'I send you my volume of the *Upanishads*. I am afraid that the rest of the volume, beyond what I had sent you before, will disappoint you. But we must face the facts. Of one thing I feel very certain, that this translation of the *Sacred Books of the East*, which some of the good people here consider most objectionable, will do a great deal towards lifting Christianity into its high historical position. I look forward to the time when those who objected to my including the Old and New Testaments among the *Sacred Books of the East* will implore me to do so.'

The end of July Max Müller went with his wife and three children to Scheveningen for bathing and sea air; from thence they made excursions to Leyden and Haarlem, whilst the Gallery at the Hague was a constant pleasure. Three or four days were given to Amsterdam and the glorious pictures there, though the dark little rooms at the *Trippen Huis* (the Museum was not then built) prevented real enjoyment of them. On the other hand, the many private collections, where the pictures still hang on the very walls for which they were painted by Rembrandt and the other Dutch artists, gave them the greatest delight. Max Müller had a genuine love of the realistic Dutch School. From Amsterdam the party went on to Dessau to visit his old mother and other relations, and then for a few days to Dresden.

Soon after his return to Oxford, Max Müller received the following letter from a perfectly unknown admirer in New Zealand, who had heard that Max Müller was not always quite strong and up to work. It shows us how his books had made him friends in the most distant corners of the world.

NEW ZEALAND, *June*, 1879.

'Very recently I gave up an employment which injured my health, and yet it would be easier to replace a host like me than to supply *your* place among the workers of this world. Every one beside the University of Oxford has an interest in you, and there is no one who would not join me in wishing to hear of your being away amusing yourself on the Rhine, or in Switzerland, or Italy, instead of over-working yourself at Oxford.'

In October Max Müller went to Birmingham, to lecture at the Midland Institute. His *Lecture on Freedom* was republished in his *Selected Essays*, and is in the new edition of *Chips*.

TO PROFESSOR NOIRÉ.

*Translation.* *October* 25.

'I send you the volume of Kingsley's works which contains my "Farewell." You ought to have known that man; he was so firm, so true, so healthy, through and through. You will no doubt have read his biography. I think I wrote to you about it some time ago. There was to be a German translation of it, but I have never seen it. His book, *Roman and Teuton*, is weak on many points, but you often catch glimpses of the old spirit. He had to work too hard, and so many things had to remain unfinished. *Hypatia* is his great book; also, in another way, *Alton Locke, the Tailor*. At Birmingham I had about 4,000 hearers, and all in full sympathy. I saw there so much machinery, and I wondered why an animal could not invent a machine factory, and why it is still necessary that man should always have to act the part of a mechanical tool. The greatest of all triumphs seems to me the machine which works absolutely alone, and turns out millions of steel pens with which *we* put the world in motion.'

To the Same.

*Translation.* *November* 23.

'We are in the depth of winter here, and one enjoys staying indoors. Christmas comes round again, and that makes me think of the Christmas stories which you sent me. They are prettily told, and may perhaps have a good effect; but I am always sorry for children when they are frightened, and then sooner or later is added the disappointment joined to the feeling of having been duped. Oh, how many stupid experiments we make in bringing up our children!

'I have thought much about the principle attacked by Virchow. I do not mean the evolution principle, the oldest of all human knowledge, but that of caution in teaching new truths. I must confess I have always had the same feeling here that Virchow has. In my lectures I have always fought shy of announcing didactically my own views, or new views of other learned men—*Summa debitur pueris verecundia.* Addressing learned men themselves, I feel I can say anything. They can defend themselves. But, in speaking to students and pupils, I never think it quite honest to communicate to them as a teacher that of which I am personally absolutely convinced, but which other learned men still oppose. I know it is a way to cultivate pupils, but it is not fair to the truth. There is still so much old wine to nourish the young with, that new wine can well be set aside awhile. There is another thing which, ever since my own student days, has been odious to me, when Haupt, for instance, would not only criticize other Professors in the presence of his students, but even insult them. It is cowardly and vulgar to do so, I said to myself; and I think many of the students felt the same. At all events, the impression has remained for life; and I think that, during the twenty-five years of my Professorship, I never mentioned one of the other Professors by name, or ridiculed or abused another in the presence of my hearers. Even had I felt inclined to do so, I should hardly have ventured to do it in the presence of my young students, for I know they would have felt it to be vulgar and cowardly. Of course the evolution theory can by no means be suppressed. To me it seems the oldest theory of the world. All knowledge strives to comprehend the causes and the becoming. True history is only another name for the doctrine of evolution. But to teach that there are four or five beginnings, as

Darwin says, or one beginning, as Haeckel says, or that man descends —historically—from a monkey; all that I could not teach, not even to students, for I know that they would take it very differently from what I meant by it. The true and honest investigator is, in spite of his own convictions, always conscious of the possibility of error. He has always before his eyes the *cum grano salis*. The pupil thinks and feels differently. He takes for granted what I deliver to him, unless I make clear to him that certain opinions are but opinions; and that I, as a teacher, help him honestly and impartially to form an opinion of his own. All this draws me to Virchow, and makes me withdraw from Haeckel. But personally I feel drawn towards Haeckel; there is something strong and open in him, while Virchow is no longer what he was more than thirty years ago, when I knew him. The air of Berlin is bad, and has already corroded much that is good and great.'

To M. Renan.

*December* 4.

'I am truly glad to know that you will come to England next year, to deliver the Hibbert Lectures. We could not have, as yet, a Chair of Comparative Theology in our Universities here, but these Hibbert Lectures, if properly managed, will produce the same effect. You, I hear, will soon have such a Chair at the Collège de France, and that, no doubt, will give a new sanction to a branch of study which has long been looked upon with very unreasonable suspicion. Much, however, will depend upon the first occupant of that Chair. You have often, in France, carried out the excellent principle of founding a Chair as soon as there was a man qualified to fill it. When you had a Champollion, you founded a Chair in Egyptology. But who is to be the first Professor of Comparative Theology? He ought to be a man of mature mind, who has lived through the various phases of religion, and who can understand others because he has learnt to understand himself. He must be an historian, because he ought to be able to sympathize with every effort of religious thought, however perverse and strange it may seem to the outside world. Our science is in its first and empirical stage; what is wanted is a careful collection of facts, from which hereafter inductions will flow by themselves. Our danger consists in the great temptation to make Comparative Theology subservient to the theological theories of the day. Our study requires fearlessness, but it likewise requires skill. Professor Tiele at Leyden is doing excellent work as Professor of Comparative Theology. He treats his subject as an historian, but as an historian who has a heart. He began life as a *pasteur*; he went himself through many mental struggles, and it seems to me that, owing to this, he can treat the struggles of others, be they fetish worshippers or Buddhists, with a discriminating and appreciative sympathy. Would not Réville be pre-eminently qualified for your new Chair, for the same reasons? He too began life as a *pasteur*, but he never sacrificed his freedom of thought. And now that the pulpit has become too narrow for him, he ought to have the broader elbow-room of a professorial Chair. You know, no doubt, his writings, and you are the best judge of his style. To me I confess his style has all the mellow flavour of Lafitte. But even if on this point I should be wrong in my judgement, I cannot be mistaken as to the soundness of his knowledge, the maturity of his thoughts, and the judicial impartiality of his judgements. What a Professor of Comparative Theology ought before all things to be able to do, is to watch and describe the unbroken continuity of thought, which connects the most modern and the most ancient forms of religious thought. The controversy lately carried on between M. de Harlez and M. Darmesteter, with regard to the origin and growth of the Zoroastrian religion and its relation to the Vedic religion, depends entirely on the power of observing the uninterrupted transition from one shade of thought to another. Different as *urbanité* may be from *urbs*, or *sauvage* from *silva*, there is a living nerve which connects the two extremes, and fortunately language is there to prove continuity. We do not say that Jupiter is the sky, but we say without the sky (*dyu*) there would have been no Jupiter. We do not say that the struggle between good and evil in the *Avesta* is the struggle between the light of the blue sky and the thunderstorm, but we do say that the contrast between light and darkness was the first mental germ that developed afterwards into the contrast between good and evil. Accepting the extremest premisses of Materialism or Positivism, to be able to show how, by slow degrees, they lead inevitably to the highest abstractions of religion, morality, and philosophy—that seems to me the chief object of the study of ancient religions. But for that work you require the tact of psychological observation, a mastery of language for rendering the minutest shades of thought, and that wide human sympathy which alone enables the true historian to put old thoughts into new words, old wine into new bottles.

'I do not think it wise to move that the University should confer an honorary degree on you. It was given to Taine, because people did not know his opinions. With you it is different. There would be opposition, controversy, strife, and anger; and for what?'

To his Son.

7, Norham Gardens, Oxford,
*December* 15, 1879.

'My dear Boy,—Your letter made me very happy. It was the best birthday present you could have given me. And I know it made you happy too. Depend upon it, nothing will ever make you so truly happy as the feeling that you have done your best—that you have tried to do your duty, and not so much for your own sake, but for the sake of others. That is a happiness which nothing can take away from us. Even if we fail—and we all must fail sometimes, for there are many good and clever boys and men in the world—but even if we fail, we feel satisfied so long as we can honestly say to ourselves, "I have done my very best." At present, my dear boy, this life may seem very happy to you, but it will not be so always. Young as you are, you have felt what it is to have one, whom we love dearly, taken from us. We do not mourn for her—she is happy, and she has been spared many of the hard struggles of this life. We mourn for ourselves, because we miss her so much, and we know she would have made our life so bright and happy. But we must learn to be ready to give up everything, however dearly we love it, when God bids us to do so. Sooner or later we know we shall have to leave all those whom we love on earth, till we meet again as God's love and wisdom may order it. But what a comfort it is to know that, even when we are gone, we shall not be forgotten, but that our children, in all their trials and troubles, will think of us, and say, as you said when you thought of dear Ada, "We'll do our best, for their sake; we'll never do anything mean, for their sake." Though I am an old man, I often say that to myself when I think of dear Ada, and thus I feel that she is always with me. Learn to do the same, not only now, but for the whole of your life. Think always what those whom you loved and who loved you on earth would think of you, and then you will never go far wrong.'

To Herr von Strauss und Tornay.

*Translation.* Oxford, *December* 16, 1879.

'My honoured Friend,—Only a line to thank you for your *Shi King*, and to congratulate you heartily on the publication of this perfect piece of work. When I see you working on so bravely, I feel ashamed of myself, and take fresh courage. But often when I think of all that has still to be done, I lose all hope, and should like to retire into the forest. To-day is a sad day. You will remember. Three years are gone; three years less to wait.

'I hope you and your dear wife are suffering less from the cold than we are. Only Wilhelm keeps well, and cuts figures on the ice. He is very happy at his school, and to-morrow we expect him for the holidays. With best wishes for a happy Christmas to you and yours, from me and my wife, yours ever.'

### To M. Renan.

*December* 30.

'I have been sharing your fate; I have been in bed with cold, and what is worse, a very troublesome liver. I am better at last, but not quite myself yet. I am glad that you have decided to lecture in London, and I only hope the Trustees will make all proper arrangements. With one or two exceptions, these gentlemen are about as fit as Gambetta for electing a Professor of Comparative Theology. You will have to be very careful, or you will get into hot water in London. With regard to your subject, you ought to consider yourself perfectly free. What I should have liked would have been a description of the first deterioration which the personal teaching of Christ suffered, when percolating through the thoughts and the civil institutions of the Roman world; when it became for the first time of this world, and had to make those concessions which every religion has to make when it wishes to gain majorities. Then to show that we, in our nineteenth century, are no more Christians than Constantine was; that by taking all that is metaphorical for real, and all that is real for metaphorical, we have produced a religion in many respects worse than the old heathen religions; that we are still thousands of years away from the simple teaching of Christ—that might tell, particularly coming from you; but you know best. As to my own Hibbert Lectures, they begin to tell in India; in England people do not understand them. My whole heart is in them, and I do believe them. I shall be glad to know your opinion when the time comes. I see and understand all the complications of the new Chair at the Collège de France; there is in Réville something sound and solid. In his hands the Chair would be safe; others might follow.'

Towards the close of the year Max Müller received an invitation from a society of students at the University of Vienna to give them a course of lectures. The invitation was a great gratification to him, but he was quite unable to comply with the request, and answered as follows:—

*Translation.* OXFORD, *December* 31, 1879.

'HONOURED COLLEAGUES,—Only to-day am I able to answer your welcome and valuable letter, and the reason of the delay is the same, which makes it, alas! impossible for me to accept your kind invitation to give some lectures to the German students in Vienna. I have not been well for some time, and my doctor tells me that if I want to go to Austria, the waters and the quiet walks at Carlsbad would be far better for me than the wine and the brilliant society of the beautiful imperial town. I feel that myself. Not that the wings of the spirit are broken yet; on the contrary, they are stronger than ever. But the wings of the body long for rest, and a flight to Vienna is too much for me now. You happy ones will hardly be able to understand this. You can fly like the young eagles without thought of your wings.

'But let me thank you warmly, for your letter has not only given me pleasure and refreshed me, but has also done me more good than many a spoonful of physic. That you, young German students of Vienna, know my name at all, and that you believe that I might have something worth saying to you which you would like to hear, has certainly surprised me much. When I was as young as you are now, I made up my mind to wander to England, in order to publish, where alone it was possible at that time to publish, the *Rig-veda*, which I consider the oldest literary monument of the whole Âryan family. As we all, as you know, belong to this Âryan or Indo-Germanic family, the *Rig-veda* is, so to speak, our own oldest inheritance, and to make such an inheritance and jewel accessible again to the European scientific world after many thousand years, seemed to me a work worthy the labour, even should its completion occupy my whole life. The work is done, and if you care to visit the Royal and Imperial Library at Vienna, you will find there, at the head of the whole Âryan literature, six massive quarto volumes, my edition of the *Rig-veda*, together with the Sanskrit Commentary; and close to it, perhaps, the work of an Austrian Professor, Professor Ludwig of Prague, whose lately-published German translation of the *Rig-veda* has won for him a place of honour among the best Sanskrit scholars of Europe.

'But this edition of the *Rig-veda*, a complete edition of which did not exist formerly even in India, and many another work of the same kind which I have written for the inner circle of science, form only a sort of substructure of which nobody either sees or hears anything except the architects of special departments. They are like granite blocks, which, buried deep under the surface, lie forgotten, while others continue to build upon them and erect pillars, arches, and bridges which astonish the whole world. It is only in my brief leisure hours that I have been able occasionally to bring to light some of the results of my researches; and that some of my writings have reached as far as Vienna, and have found friends there, is indeed a real and unexpected joy to me. I send you for your library my lately-published *Essays on Comparative Religion.* You may find something in them, which will show you better than a few lectures from me could have done, what is the highest goal of all my work.

'Let me, honoured colleagues, press your hands in spirit and thank you for the pleasure you have given me.

'I remain, with warm sympathy, your sincere friend.'

The year had been a very hospitable one in Max Müller's house. We find among his visitors this year Dr. James Martineau, von Schlötzer, his old friend, Mr. Stillman, the *Times* correspondent, Dr. Kielhorn from India, the Hereditary Grand Duke of Baden, Baron Roggenbach, the Crown Prince of Sweden, and many less-known names.

Two new interests entered into Max Müller's life during the following year. His daughter Mary had now left school, and for her sake there was much more society in the scholar's house than hitherto, and he was brought socially into more general acquaintance with younger members of the University. This year, too, brought him into almost daily intercourse with Bunyiu Nanjio and Kenjiu Kasawara, two Japanese who had been sent by the high priest of their monastery to study Sanskrit in Oxford, the knowledge of the original language of the Sacred Books of the Buddhists having entirely died out in Japan, where they only possessed Japanese translations of Chinese translations of the original Sanskrit. Nanjio had arrived in Oxford early in 1879, and brought an introduction to Professor Max Müller, and Kasawara followed in October; but their knowledge of English was still very imperfect, and it was necessary for them to learn the elements of Sanskrit and perfect their English before they could profit much from Max Müller's instruction. From this time on they read constantly with him, and it was at his instigation that Nanjio caused a search to be made in Japan for original Sanskrit MSS., which ended in the discovery of five texts, one of which was the oldest Sanskrit text (sixth century) which had then been discovered. By Max Müller's advice, Nanjio prepared a complete catalogue of the gigantic Buddhist Canon, which was printed at the University Press, and is of great value to all who study Buddhist literature. Max Müller has given a full account of Nanjio and Kasawara in the new edition of *Chips*, Volume II. Certainly, till Nanjio left England in 1884, they were a great interest in his life. Kasawara had to return to Japan in 1882 in bad health, and leave his work unfinished. He parted with his teacher, for whom he had a very strong feeling of affection, apparently unmoved, and yet he wrote afterwards, 'When I left you the other day, I walked up and down the road, looking at your house, where I had passed the happiest hours of my life.' 'The life of my Buddhist friend,' wrote Max Müller, 'was one of the many devoted yet unfulfilled lives which make us wonder and grieve. . . . He might have been a most useful man on his return to Japan.'

TO M. RENAN.

*January* 15.

'I was truly pleased when I heard of Réville's appointment, though I fear several of my friends at Paris are displeased. I have had some correspondence with the editor of the *Times* about your lectures. Everything in England depends on the *Times*, everybody respects what the *Times* says. I am glad to say that the present editor is personally on our side, and that is of great importance; though it does not follow that the paper itself will not have to make some reserves. The editor has seen you, and talked with you at Florence; he knows your books, and is full of sympathy for you and them. The difficulty in England is that few people read books and form their own opinions; a clamour is raised and everybody joins in it. Now as to your position here, it will be, as you know, a difficult one, because the two strongest parties, the clerical and the materialistic, are opposed to you. I share that misfortune with you, and I hope I always shall. But it was important to have the *Times*, if not as your partisan, at least not as your enemy, and that, so far as I can see, will be the case. The editor is anxious to give a full report of your lectures, as he did with mine, but he says that, in order to do justice to your beautiful French, he cannot allow your translation to be done during the night by some young man from stenographic notes, but he must have your French MS. and give it to be translated by a really competent person. He wishes me to ask you whether you agree to his proposal, and

I believe it is essential to the success of your lectures that some such plan should be adopted.'

### To Bryan Hodgson, Esq.

'I have received two volumes of your *Collected Essays*, for which please accept my best thanks. Many of them are old friends of mine, and I am glad to see them all together and so well got up. How little has been done in that field[1] since you left it, and yet how much is still to be done, and how amply would anybody's labours be rewarded who would follow your example. I suppose you have given away all your Nepalese MSS. I have been reading some of them lately, the *Sukhâvatî-Vyûha*, &c., with two Buddhist priests from Japan, who came here to learn Sanskrit. They are slow, but I expect they will do some good work by-and-by.'

Max Müller had been very poorly all the autumn and early part of the winter, as the following letter shows:—

### To Herr von Strauss und Tornay.

*Translation.* *January* 30.

'I am so terribly in arrears with my letters through my long illness, that I prefer to begin with the last, just received. I am only sorry it does not bring me as good news from you as I am accustomed to receive. Anxiety about those who are dearest is more wearing than anxiety about oneself. It is a real joy to see how bravely you work on. Since October I have been able to do nothing but what was absolutely necessary. A troublesome liver has asserted itself, an illness I have long expected to inherit, and have only kept it at bay so many years by constant exercise and most careful diet.

'The worst is the depression which one cannot subdue. One has no appetite, either physical or mental, and when one hopes it is passing away, the misery begins again. A few days ago I was kept in bed with severe pain, but to-day I feel much better. I tell you all this to explain why I have lain quite fallow, read nothing but novels, and written nothing. I have taken up your *Shi King* several times, but I could not manage it. I wished to write something about your *Essays*, but nothing came of it, and there is a perfect St. Gothard of letters and books in my library, so that I despair of ever driving a tunnel through them. The will is there, and I look forward to the spring. The essay on "Personal Freedom" will appear in the February number of the *Deutsche Rundschau*. The introduction I sent you was

[1] Languages, &c., of Nepal.

not to my *Sacred Books*, but to a great American illustrated work (of little value), *The Hundred Greatest Men of the World*. In a weak moment I undertook the *Founders of Religions*, and had to keep my promise, well or ill. My family are all well. My wife is in London, for a little change; she has been nursing me a long time. Wilhelm is at school a mile from here, and gets on; the two girls are growing up, each in her own way. All seems like *Meeresstille und glückliche Fahrt* (a calm sea, and a good voyage), and yet one never gets any rest.'

The following letters show how constantly Max Müller was appealed to on subjects that were not immediately connected with his own work, or at all events with the work he had on hand at the moment, and how little he shrank from the correspondence involved by such appeals. At the end of January Professor Blackie wrote a private letter to Max Müller from Edinburgh on the teaching and pronunciation of Greek, at the same time publishing in a Scotch paper a long letter to Professor Jebb of Glasgow on the same subject, without having first told Professor Jebb that he was intending to do so. Max Müller wrote back to Professor Blackie:—

*January* 30.

'MY DEAR BLACKIE,—Thanks for your paper. You are perfectly right. The difficulty, however, is to find willing and capable teachers —the boys would learn it fast enough. It was the same with the few simple rules of Latin pronunciation. I know that at one school the boys got on capitally with the new pronunciation: it was the masters who would or could not learn it, and who naturally prevailed. I knew my Greek accents fairly well before I came to England. It was in England, when trying to make myself understood, that my Greek accent-conscience became demoralized. I should not like now to undergo a public examination in Greek accents—I mean those that depend on etymology and usage, and not on general rules. Boys will generally do what is right, if they never hear what is wrong. There is the difficulty. Wishing you all success, I remain yours very truly.'

This letter Professor Blackie immediately asked and got leave to publish. The following letters from Max Müller explain themselves:—

TO PROFESSOR (NOW SIR R.) JEBB.

OXFORD, *February* 5.

'I was answering Professor Blackie's letter to me, and had only glanced at his printed letter to you which he enclosed. (1) I have always thought that accent in Greek, as in Sanskrit, was originally, as its name tells us, by-song, cantilena, or, if you like, change of pitch. That was quite compatible with quantity. (2) Afterwards accent became more strict. Even that was compatible with quantity, and I see no reason why boys should not be taught to say *ἄνθρωπος* without saying *ἄνθροπος.* (3) In Greek poetry stress is surrendered to rhythm. It is sometimes the same in modern music. I heard only last Sunday "apóstolic," instead of "apostólic," in a chanted Choral. Having always defended these three points, I wrote to Professor Blackie that on them I thought he was right. Not having seen what has been written before by you and by him, I could not have expressed any opinion about it. Nor should I like to do so now. Professor Blackie's way of expressing himself is strong. He has used much stronger language about my hallucinations than what appears in his letter to you. . . . When Professor Blackie asked me whether he might publish my note, I wrote to him that he might, for though I did but vaguely recollect what I had written, I hoped my short note contained nothing that could give offence to anybody. I should regret very much if you thought that my remarks referred in any way to you personally; I was thinking simply of the matter under discussion, without any cognizance of who the parties were who defended one or the other view. . . .'

TO THE SAME.

*February* 8.

'I should be very glad if you took no further notice of that short note of mine, which I allowed Professor Blackie to publish. It will lead to a reply from him, and what can be gained by a newspaper controversy on such a point? If, however, you think it necessary to reply, I must ask you to publish the whole of my three points. I have not seen your paper in the publisher's annual, but I gather from the correspondence in the *Scotsman* that there are some points where your views differ from mine. I am in favour of teaching boys to pronounce Greek, ancient as well as modern, according to the accents, only warning them that there is no need to pronounce, for instance, the penultimate short, because the antepenultimate has the acute, and is pronounced by us with stress. This seems to me the point of practical importance for schools. I know the difficulties, but I know what can be done even by *one* determined teacher.

In reading metrical passages the accents must yield, and I know of no evidence that, at the time of Sophocles, the Greeks retained the accents, as stress, in their recitation of poetry. Nor do I think that at that time Greek accent was still cantilena, pure and simple, though it is difficult to be positive on that point, or to determine the time when in Greek the change took place from cantilena to stress.'

To the Same.

*February* 12.

'I am very glad and grateful that you have decided not to notice my letter to Professor Blackie. If you knew how many letters of that kind I have to write, I believe you would make allowance for my not having read the whole controversy to which Professor Blackie's letter referred. I must have expressed myself badly in what I wrote about Greek poetry at the time of Sophocles. What I meant to say was that at his time—so far as I can judge—accent in conversation and prose in general was stress, but that in poetry the stress of rhythm prevailed over the stress of accent, as it does with us sometimes when the time or the beat in music does not agree with the accent or stress of each word sung to it.'

The following letter was written in reply to an inquiry from the Duke of Argyll:—

Oxford, *February* 17, 1880.

'. . . As to sacrifices, I must take a little time to think. The fundamental idea in the earliest Vedic Hymns is simply, Give me something, cattle, children, health and wealth, and I shall give thee something. What? Something that is dear to me, and what therefore you too will like. I like my food, so before I begin to eat, there is a morsel for you. I like my drink, so here is a libation for you. Even when they said they were going to offer to the gods a goat or an ox, that meant generally that they and their friends were going to have a feast in honour of the gods, but the gods received very little. Pigs, sheep, and oxen, *Su-ove-taurilia*, were all eatable animals. The Scythians ate the horse, and therefore they sacrificed it. But however dear a dog or a cat or a bird might be, we seldom hear of their being sacrificed. So the nature of the sacrifices depended much on the nature of the food.

'Another class of sacrifices were those to the Spirits of the Departed. To them was frequently given what had been dear to them in life, and then neither dogs nor horses, neither slaves nor wives were spared. In cases where some of these grand- and great-grandfathers became gods, bloody sacrifices might easily grow up.'

To the Same.

7, Norham Gardens, Oxford, *February* 22, 1880.

'My dear Duke of Argyll,—I do hold that Man was evolved, not however from a beast, but from a child, which actually represents a stage much lower than the highest beast, but potentially a stage out of the reach of any beast.

'I also hold that our so-called Kantian categories are evolved; they are there potentially, but they want the objective world to become actual. What I call the Infinite is that which by its pressure calls forth that form of thought, that category, which Kant would call the category of substantiality. Without that category we should have nothing but predicates: i. e. thought would be impossible. All names of God are predicates, Πρόσωπα, personifications—it does not matter whether they are Sun, Fire, Sky, Enlightener, Warmer, Protector, Dyaus, Ζεύς, Jupiter, Jehovah, Allah, or Father—all are names, some purer, higher, truer than others, but all predicates—and of what? Of that nameless Something which presses on us on all sides, on our senses, on our mind, on our heart, but which from its nature must be nameless—*ein Gott an sich*—Προσωποποιούμενον, but not Πρόσωπον. To say that God is a person, or many persons, represents no doubt a very early, and to us very natural phase of religious thought. But person means so many things. If our body is still felt as our person, God and the gods are black and white as men. But as we surrender one element after the other as not essential to our personality, our body and sex, our senses, our imaginations, our language, our age, such as childhood, manhood, and old age, we at last arrive at that true self of which we may predicate many things, but of which we may in truth only say, "It *is*, and therefore it thinks." The Hindu added a third indefeasible predicate. (1) Sat, (2) Kit, (3) Ânanda = (1) Being, (2) Perceiving and all that flows from it, and (3) Blessed. All the rest are human marks, names, concepts—all true to a certain point; all false, if stretched too far. It always struck me as a wonderful guess at the Divine, when in the *Bhagavad-gîtâ* the Supreme Spirit is made to say: "Even those who worship idols, worship me." St. Paul's "Unknown God" springs from the same source. It was because I wanted a Substance for all Divine ideas that I traced the presence of the Infinite, or the Nameless, or the Unknown, as the antecedent though unconscious *sine quâ non* of all later assertions about it; and I still think that unless we hold to that, we worship εἴδωλα which will be broken some day or other, but that which can never be broken is that of which the εἴδωλον is but the εἴδωλον—the name but a name—and for which I find no better name than the Infinite, or Indefinite, or Indefinable.

'I shall try to put together some of the more important passages about sacrifice in the *Veda*. But sacrifice again means so many things that it is very difficult to put into order what, from its nature, is chaotic, poetic, and free.'

It was at this time that Max Müller made epistolary acquaintance with Mr. Lowell through the letter on 'Jade' given in the *Autobiography*, an acquaintance that ripened into real friendship when Mr. Lowell came to England. Unfortunately none of Max Müller's letters to his brilliant correspondent have been preserved, except the one which follows:—

OXFORD, *February* 3, 1880.

'I have been laid up for some time. I am what ill-natured people in Germany said of Bismarck, *Leber leidend*, and *Leider lebend*, and while that lasts one is fit for nothing. I feel better now, but am always afraid of relapses till this cold weather is over.

'Your remarks about jade are very true. I should have written once more to the *Times*, but I felt jaded, and I was afraid the readers of the *Times* might share that feeling. Otherwise I really felt it due to our troglodyte ancestors to say a few words for their common sense, and not to let people believe that they kept their green jade tools because they reminded them of green fields! Why, the man or the clan who possessed one of those small jade scrapers, or knives, or scissors, was a Rothschild among beggars! You can cut an iron nail with those jade chisels[1], and they show no dent. Diamond only will tell on them. A man who possessed one of those treasures could eat a dozen of oysters and crack ten times as many marrow-bones as his neighbours who had flint knives only, which broke at every blow, and had constantly to be renewed. It was like a Krupp gun compared with old Bess. Of course, any swell or family of swells who possessed such a diploma of nobility would keep it as long as they could keep anything, and, as you say, even when it ceased to be useful, sentiment would protect it, as it protects an old razor, though it has long ceased to be useful. The wonderful fancies about jade begin in the sixteenth century. If you should come across some of the books written by the Court physicians of Charles V and others, the cures which they describe as effected by wearing jade are marvellous. These were men as great as Gull and Paget, only 300 years ago. They describe cases which they watched for ten years and more, and

[1] '*Pace* Sir John Lubbock, for *chisel* has nothing to do with German *kissel*, nor is a *chisel* a survival of a sharpened flint.—M. M.'

give the names of their patients, and describe how the *calculi* passed away in shoals as soon as the patient touched the jade! Are we so much wiser than our fathers?

'I hope the rumour is true that you will soon exchange Madrid for London. What capital use your country makes of that prehistoric institution of Ambassadors lying at Foreign Courts!'

It is needless to give a full account of Max Müller's correspondence with Keshub Chunder Sen, head of the Brahma Somâj of India. He has himself, in his biographical sketch of his friend, printed in *Chips*, Volume II, new edition, entered into the whole controversy of the Kuch Behar marriage and the subsequent split in the Brahma Somâj, and to that the reader is referred. The deeply interesting interview between Keshub Chunder Sen and Dr. Pusey in 1870 will be found there *in extenso*, and the sketch closes with several long and valuable letters that passed between Max Müller and his friend. These are all the letters from Max Müller that have been preserved. During the year 1880 several letters passed between Max Müller and Miss Collet, editor of the *Brahma Year-Book*, who upheld the Sadhârana Somâj, which had separated from the Brahma Somâj.

To Miss Collet.

*February* 29.

'I return the papers with many thanks. I see and appreciate your argument in favour of justice towards the Sadhârana Somâj, but I cannot easily give up a man whom I once trusted. If it is, as you suggest, softening of the brain, has not that poor brain suffered in a noble cause, and is it likely to recover under hard words? However, let us wait and see.'

In February Max Müller read a paper before the Asiatic Society in London on the hitherto unknown Sanskrit text discovered in Japan, a dialogue on Sukhâvatî, or the Paradise of the Buddhists, which was listened to with great interest, and was fully reported at the time in the *Athenæum*. It was one of the texts discovered by the agency of the Buddhist priests mentioned in the beginning of this chapter, an account of whose studies in Oxford was new to the majority of Max Müller's hearers, and attracted great attention.

So long ago as the year 1870 Max Müller had tried to draw the attention of the Colonial Office to the great importance of encouraging missionaries and others living in our more distant colonies in collecting lists of words and preparing papers on the native languages, especially in the various Australian colonies. 'In countries where there are no histories, no traditions, no ancient monuments, language is frequently the only witness of the past, and the only guide by which the historian can discover the origin, the relationship, and the early migration of races.' Lord Kimberley sent copies of Max Müller's letter to the Governors of all the Australian colonies and New Zealand. The Governor of New South Wales, Lord Belmore, speedily replied that his Government had expressed their willingness to obtain the required information in New South Wales, and in November, 1871, Lord Belmore transmitted to the Colonial Office a full report on the Language, Social Laws and Customs, and the Religious and Mythical Traditions of New South Wales. These were sent to Max Müller, who, in returning them, spoke of the valuable information they contained, and urged that as other reports came in, selections from them should be published from time to time:—

'If such a plan had been followed during the last hundred years, many difficulties in the history of the colonies could be cleared up, which now must be left to mere conjecture. Languages that have since become extinct might still be studied. Strange customs and traditions, which now puzzle the ethnologist, might be traced back to an intelligible beginning, and an accurate knowledge of really wild-grown and autochthonic forms of religion would be of the greatest advantage for a comparative study of religions, a branch of inquiry which will become more important with every year.'

He ended by saying that £1,000 yearly would probably cover all expenses of printing, as there would be a certain sale of such reports, both at home and abroad.

The following reply came back:—

'SIR,—I am directed by the Earl of Kimberley to acknowledge your letter of February 7, and to thank you for the remarks you have been good enough to make respecting the collection and publication of reports on native languages and customs in the colonies.

'His Lordship regrets that it is not possible for the Colonial Office to undertake to give effect to your suggestion, but he thinks that possibly the Ethnological Society may be in a position to do so, and your letter will be communicated to that Society.'

In 1874 Max Müller tried again to rouse an interest for these researches in the Colonial Office, and finally in 1880, when he was told that times were very bad at the Treasury, and that the only hope lay in stimulating *private* action and expenditure by an appeal through the papers. This labour Max Müller did not feel called upon to undertake, and the opportunity with Tasmania, where the natives have now died out, has been lost for ever.

To Lady Welby.

*March* 29.

'I put your letter aside for some time, and now that I have read it again, let me begin with the beginning. In the ordinary sense of knowledge, we cannot have any knowledge of God; our very idea of God implies that He is beyond our powers of perception and understanding. Then what can we do? Shut our eyes and be silent? That will not satisfy creatures such as we are. We must speak, but all our words apply to things either perceptible or intelligible. The old Buddhists used to say, the only thing we can say of God is No, No! He is not this, He is not that. Whatever we can see or understand, that He is not. But again I say that kind of self-denial will not satisfy such creatures as we are. What can we do? We can only give the best we have. Now the best we have or know on earth is Love, therefore we say God is Love or loving. Love is entire self-surrender, we can go no further in our conception of what is best. And yet how poor a name it is in comparison of what we want to name. Our idea of love includes, as you say, humility, a looking up and worshipping. Can we say that of God's love? Depend upon it, the best we say is but poor endeavour—it is well we should know it—and yet, if it is the best we have and can give, we need not be ashamed. And we should feel the same as to the language of other religions. Their language may strike us as very imperfect, but at one time or other it was the best they knew. Many old and savage nations saw God in the Dawn, and from what you write I think you can sympathize with them—suffer, so to say, the same language which they suffered. They knew nothing greater and higher in the world, and I believe they were right. And that name for Dawn was sometimes used by them for the feeling of love also; "it dawns" meant "I love." There is some truth in that too, not the whole truth—that we shall never grasp in words—but some spark of it. Wherever I see such sparks, whether in ancient times or in the talk of children around us, I feel my heart warmed. I see the ray of truth, and I shut my eyes to all the darkness and coarseness that often surround the light. We cannot know, we cannot name, the Divine, nor can we understand its ways as manifested in active and human life. We ask why there should be suffering and sin; we cannot answer the question. All we can say is, it was willed to be so. Some help our human understanding may find, however, by simply imagining what would have been our life if the power of doing evil had not been given to us. It seems to me that in that case we, human beings as we are, should never have had a conception of what is meant by good; we should have been like the birds in the air, happier, it may be, but better, no. Or if suffering had always been reserved for the bad, we should all have become the most cunning angels. Often when I am met by a difficulty which seems insoluble, I try that experiment and say, Let us see what would happen if it were otherwise. Still, I confess, there is some suffering on earth which goes beyond all understanding, which even the truest Christian love and charity seems unable to remove or to mitigate. It can teach us one thing only, that we are blind, and that in the darkness of the night we lose our faith in a Dawn which will drive away darkness, fear, and despair. Much, no doubt, could be done even by what is now called Communism, but what in earlier days was called Christianity. And then one wonders whether the world can ever again become truly Christian. I dare not call myself a Christian. I have hardly met ten men in all my life who deserved that name. And again, I say, let us do our best, knowing all the time that our best is a mere nothing. This may answer some of your questions, but many questions must remain unanswered, though we all ask them again and again.'

To M. Renan.

*March* 31.

'I hear from all sides that your lectures will be a great success. I am truly glad; I hope that everything has been well arranged with the *Times*. Mr. Chenery will meet you here at dinner on Saturday. Prince Leopold, the youngest son of the Queen, and a very clever and well-informed man, will come to take tea with you on Monday. I am afraid you will be tired out, but now and then that cannot be helped. Depend upon it, you are doing a great work, which will leave its trace behind. It will be such a pleasure to have you here in a safe and quiet harbour.'

After his Hibbert Lectures were over, M. Renan and his wife came to stay with Max Müller, and at the same time another new friend, Miss Hopekirk, the brilliant pianist. Prince Leopold spent a whole afternoon with the Max Müllers to meet the Renans, with whom his Royal Highness was delighted, as indeed were all who had the chance of meeting the agreeable Frenchman.

To Professor Noiré.

*Translation.* *April* 18.

'... I have had very little time for work here; one visitor followed the other. We went to Brighton, but had to return after a week there to receive Renan in Oxford. He is a very old friend of mine. Before the world knew him, he was known to me. In 1845–6 he was assistant at the Bibliothèque Royale, when I collated my *Veda* manuscripts there. He has had a hard life, and has to thank himself for everything. He is a true-hearted man, a little foggy and sometimes clouded by his language, though the latter certainly produces beautiful colour effects. Here the opinions about him were much divided. Some of my friends refused to meet him at my house. Tyndall and Herbert Spencer they are able to digest here, and yet they go far beyond Renan, who really is a mystical, religious nature. However, all went off well. I have been harshly treated in the papers, but that does not matter; the good cause progresses here also. When Renan left, Professor Elze arrived from Halle; he is a Shakesperian, an old school friend of mine. A few days after Bret Harte announced his visit, and so forth day after day, time flies and work remains undone. I long sometimes to enter a monastery! I hope you and your work succeed better.

'I am very well pleased with the elections here, one can breathe freely again; I myself could never trust Disraeli, though he seems to have been liked by certain gentlemen in Berlin.'

On April 19 Max Müller joined in the greetings sent to Mr. Emerson on the occasion of his seventy-seventh birthday. His letter was as follows:—

7, Norham Gardens, Oxford, *April* 19, 1880.

'The translator of the Upanishads, Moksha Mûlara, sends greetings and best wishes to his American Guru, Amarasûnu, on his seventy-seventh birthday, and encloses an extract from an Upanishad, lately discovered:

'Old age and decay lay hold of the body, the senses, the memory, the mind—never of the Self, the looker on.

'The Self never grows tired—the body grows tired of supporting the Self.

'The Self never grows blind—the windows of the senses become darkened with dust and rain.

'The Self never forgets—the inscriptions on the memory fade, and it is well that much should be forgotten.

'The Self never errs—the many wheels of our own small watches grow rusty, but we look up to the eternal dial in the heavens above, which remains right for ever.

'MAX MÜLLER.'

After Commemoration Max Müller's wife and elder daughter went to Ober-Ammergau for the Passion Play, he being himself too busy to go with them. They returned home by Dessau to see the old mother.

To M. RENAN.

*July* 3, 1880.

'I wished to read your lectures before writing to you and thanking you for them; this I have done at last, and I feel now that nothing could have been better than the intellectual campaign has been from beginning to end. I felt doubtful sometimes how it would succeed; yet I had sufficient faith in the good qualities of the English public to hope that you would be satisfied. I did not expect that all would have gone so well, without a single accident; the right people have praised you, and the right people have abused you, and depend upon it some permanent good has been done. I was delighted to have you and Madame Renan under our roof; I only wish I had seen more of you, and had time for some exchange of thought, but the hurry of life gets worse and worse, and I often long for the days when one could live for oneself, when nobody knew us, when we sat in the Bibliothèque Royale copying and collating manuscripts, and reading one book at a time till it was finished. There is one line in your lectures which I should like to have explained. Can we say even hypothetically, "Si l'infini n'est pas une chimère"? Surely, if there is any reality at all, it is that which is not finite, that which is not visible, that which is not comprehensible. The names which we give to it are chimerical if you like, still they always show "une bonne volonté"; we do our best, we cannot do more, nor can we, such as we are, do altogether without these names. Every generation thinks it has said *le dernier mot*: that is not so; anyhow, we shall never understand the *dernier mot*, unless we try to understand *le premier mot*, and all our labours, yours and mine, seem to be always directed to that end, to represent, in fact, the etymology of religion; but the etymon must be a root, a real root, not an abstraction, still less *une chimère*. I think that is your own feeling, as far as I can see from your works, and I was therefore struck by that sentence, and have been thinking about it for some time. My wife and daughter are still away; they were quite overpowered by the Passion Play of Ober-Ammergau. We have lost far too much of the reality of Christ, and I have always thought that your work has done most good by restoring that reality, so far as it can be, in diametrical opposition to Strauss; and yet a few days ago I was told by a distinguished French theologian, that you had only repeated Strauss. I told him that he was utterly and entirely wrong, and I believe he saw it himself.'

The rest of this Long Vacation, except a short visit to his brother-in-law at Taplow, was spent quietly in Oxford with his wife and children. Daily drives and excursions, picnics on the river, long walks, and lawn-tennis parties, in all of which the father shared, made this an enjoyable summer. There were constant visits, too, from friends both young and old. Max Müller was chiefly occupied through the year with correspondence on the *Sacred Books of the East*, and he gave up much time to his Buddhist pupils. In the autumn he prepared two volumes of *Selected Essays* on Language, Mythology, and Religion, which were published in 1881.

To his mother he writes in September:—

*Translation.*

'Old age begins to make itself felt, things do not go as formerly, and yet there is so much to do. One longs for rest, but one cannot have it here; perhaps it is best as it is. . . . It is not easy to make one's way through life. I often wonder still how I managed it. My life was often a hard battle, and yet I am glad it was; and the little I have done I owe very much to the necessities I had to meet.'

Early in October Max Müller went to Birmingham to be present at the opening of the Mason Science College. In returning thanks for the visitors at the great luncheon, he said:—

'You know that I am not a man of science in the usual, though far too narrow, sense of the word. But, although the science to which

I have devoted the whole of my life, the science of man, is not yet formally represented in this College, depend upon it it will enter in; it is there already, it lurks in every corner, and I trust it will soon fill the whole College with its genial warmth and its quickening impulses. You mean to teach mathematics. Can you teach mathematics without teaching the laws of thought, without telling your pupils something about such men as Thales, Pythagoras, and Euclid, who were ancient Greeks, but who were men of science for all that? You mean to teach physiology and biology, the laws of life and of nature. Are you likely to leave out the very crown of nature, man—to leave nature, like *Hamlet* without the Ghost, a nature without its spirit? A true College of Science could not live if it were to exclude the science of man. Man is the measurer of all things, and what is science but the reflection of the outer world on the mirror of the mind, growing more perfect, more orderly, more definite, more great with every generation? To attempt to study nature without studying man is as impossible as to study light without studying the eye. I have no misgivings, therefore, that the lines on which this College is founded will ever become so narrow as to exclude the science of man, and the science of that which makes man, the science of language, and what is really the same, the science of thought. And where can we study the science of thought, that most wonderful instance of development, except in the languages and literatures of the past? How are we to do justice to our ancestors except by letting them plead their own case in their own language? Literary culture can far better dispense with physical science than physical science with literary culture, though nothing is more satisfactory than a perfect combination of the two. The spirit in which this College has been founded strikes me as a truly liberal spirit—a spirit of faith in the future, a spirit of confidence in youth. Much as I admire the enlightened generosity of the venerable founder of this College, there is nothing I admire more than that one clause in the statutes which states that, with the exception of a few fundamental provisions, the trustees not only may, but must from time to time so change the rules of this institution as to keep it always in harmony with the requirements of the age. We who are growing older ourselves know how difficult it sometimes is for an old man to have faith in youth and confidence in the future. Yet that firm faith in youth, that unshaken confidence in the future, seems to me to form the only safe foundation of all science, and on them, as on a corner-stone, every College of Science ought to be founded. The Professors of a College of Science should not be conservative only, satisfied to hand down the stock of knowledge as they received it, as it were laid up in a napkin. Professors must try to add something, however little it may be, to the talent they have received; they must not be afraid of what is new, but face every new theory boldly, trying to discover what is good and true in it, and what is not. I know this is sometimes difficult. Young men, with their new theories, are sometimes very aggravating. But let us be honest. We ourselves have been young and aggravating too, and yet on the whole we seem to have worked in the right direction. Let us hope, therefore, that the Professors of this College will always be animated by the spirit of its founder; that they will never lose their faith in progress, never bow before the idol of finality. Let them always keep in the statutes of their own mind that one saving clause in the statutes of this College—to keep pace with the progress of the world.'

To his Mother.

*November* 27.

'Last Sunday I stayed at Prince Christian's to meet the young Prince Wilhelm and his bride. I was there from Saturday to Monday, and like both the young people, especially the young Princess. Her sister too was very pleasant, and they all seemed so happy together. In January they are coming to Oxford. Last week the Japanese Minister was here with us, a very interesting man; and next week comes the American Ambassador, Mr. Lowell, a celebrated writer. We get little rest, though we refuse many invitations.'

Towards the close of the year an important correspondence began between Max Müller and Dr. Legge on one side, and the Bishop of Victoria and various missionaries in China on the other, on the translation of the Chinese word 'Shang-ti' by 'God,' in Volume III of the *Sacred Books of the East* by Dr. Legge; the missionaries contending that 'Shang-ti' should be rendered by 'Supreme Ruler' or 'Ruler on High,' not by 'God,' as 'the God of Revelation,' '*Jehovah* of the *Christian* Scriptures'! The letter of expostulation sent to Max Müller was signed by twenty-four missionaries, and transmitted to him by Dr. Burdon, Bishop of Victoria, Hong-Kong. The point in question had been under dispute for 300 years, and the translation, as being used in the *Sacred Books of the East*, appeared to come with authority, whereas the missionaries, headed by Dr. Burdon, contended that the question was still a matter of dispute.

Dr. Legge had written and published a letter to Max Müller, giving at length his reasons for translating 'Shang-ti' by 'God,' and stating that a large number of missionaries in China agreed with him. Dr. Legge was one of those who did not hesitate to say that God has never left Himself without witness to the many millions of the Chinese race; which the narrower spirit of those who condemned Dr. Legge's translation was ready to deny.

In answer to the Bishop of Victoria, Max Müller wrote:—

'Dear Bishop,—I send you enclosed my answer to the letter which you forwarded to me, signed by yourself and a number of Protestant missionaries in China. I should feel truly glad if the explanations I have offered might lead, if not to a solution of our difficulties, at least to a mutual understanding of our motives, and I hope that you and your friends will absolve both Dr. Legge and myself from the charge of unfairness which seems implied in your letter.'

Max Müller's answer enclosed to the Bishop was given in full in the *Times* of December 30, 1880. He says in this letter that in his first article in the *Edinburgh Review*, October, 1851, he had said that it was impossible to find in Chinese a more adequate rendering of 'God' than 'Shang-ti.' The missionaries advocated 'Supreme Ruler' as the fit rendering of 'Shang-ti,' and Max Müller very fitly asks, 'Would this expression have evoked in the minds of Europeans any conception different from that of God?'

The following letter to Dr. Happer, an old missionary in China, gives a summary of the question:—

To Dr. Happer.

*December* 12, 1880.

'A great accumulation of work which I could not put off has hitherto prevented me from answering your letter. Before doing so I naturally wished not only to read your two papers on the proper rendering of "Shang-ti," but to have time for reconsidering the whole question, and more particularly to hear what Professor Legge had to say in defence of his rendering of the Chinese "Shang-ti" by "God."

'Professor Legge, not wishing to wait any longer, has in the meantime published his reply to your paper, and I hope during the Christmas holidays to find some leisure for writing down my own views on the subject. I feel bound, however, to tell you that I am not altogether an impartial judge, for so long ago as 1851 I expressed my decided approval of "Shang-ti" as the right name to be used for God in Chinese.

I did so at the end of an article on "Comparative Philology" in the *Edinburgh Review* (October, 1851), in noticing Sir George Staunton's essay, "An inquiry into the proper mode of rendering the word *God* in translating the Sacred Scriptures into the Chinese Language"; and after maturely reconsidering the question, I still think that, as the nearest equivalent of God, "Shang-ti" is freer from serious objections than any other name in Chinese.

'The question, however, is a much larger one, and affects not only the Chinese, but the translation of almost every volume of the *Sacred Books of the East*. I feel truly grateful therefore to you and your friends for having given me an opportunity of stating my own convictions on that important subject more fully and more freely. In a short letter I can only say that it seems to me that the same spirit which enabled Paul to say at Athens *ὃ οὖν ἀγνοοῦντες εὐσεβεῖτε, τοῦτο ἐγὼ καταγγέλλω ὑμῖν*, should embolden missionaries in China and all over the world to say, "Whom you ignorantly worship, whether Shang-ti or Tien or any other name, Him declare I unto you."'

The following letter from Arinori Mori, at this time Japanese Minister in England, is of interest as giving the view of an enlightened Buddhist on the 'Shang-ti' question. Arinori had been staying with Max Müller, and delighted every one by his bright, joyous manner. It was he who, years before, when Minister in the United States, had rushed into Max Müller's rooms asking him in ten minutes to fix on a state religion for Japan. He was very different now, and with all his high spirits there was an earnestness of purpose about him which inspired his host with a feeling of strong regard.

It will be remembered that, on his return to Japan a year or two later, he was made Minister of Public Instruction, and was murdered in the streets of Tokio by a fanatic of the old conservative school.

JAPANESE LEGATION, LONDON, *November* 22, 1880.

'DEAR PROFESSOR MAX MÜLLER,—I scarcely need to say that my recent visit to Oxford greatly benefited me, and that I immensely enjoyed myself during my stay under your kind care and most hospitable roof.

'I have since read with much interest the copy kindly given me by Dr. Legge of his letter addressed to you on the "term-question" *Shang-ti*. I venture to express that Dr. Legge's translation of the term into *God* is on the whole correct, though in some cases the word

*God*, when rendered by *Shang-ti*, may not be intelligible to the Chinese or any of the Far Eastern peoples, as being used to represent a living, sympathetic Being with all His attributes of love and tenderness. It is true that *Shang-ti* has been regarded as the Supreme Being and the Dispenser of all justice and benevolence, but never as so sympathetic a Being as is held by the Christian faith.'

[See Appendix F, p. 460.]

# CHAPTER XXV

## 1881–1882

Speech at University College, London. Prize Fellowships. Deaths of Carlyle, Stanley, and other friends. Visit to the Hartz and Dessau. Oriental Congress at Berlin. Paris. Speech at French Institute. Kant's *Critique of Pure Reason*. Lectures at Cambridge on India. Death of Dr. Pusey. National Anthem in Sanskrit.

THE whole of this year was one of strenuous work to Max Müller. He had undertaken to make a translation of Kant's *Critique of Pure Reason*, in honour of the centenary of its first publication; he was retranslating Buddha's *Dhammapada* or *Path of Virtue*, from the Pâli; and he prepared with his Buddhist pupils one of the texts from Japan which was published in the Âryan series of the *Anecdota Oxoniensia*, the starting of which undertaking was mainly due to Max Müller's initiative. In addition to this, the editing of the *Sacred Books of the East* was continuous work, involving the reading, and sometimes correcting, of innumerable proof-sheets, besides constant correspondence with scholars offering to take part in the great work, or with others who were dilatory in fulfilling their contracts. As Max Müller was suffering the whole year from what threatened to become scrivener's palsy, he had to dictate almost everything, whether letters or books. Happily, rest and careful treatment warded off the complaint, and he never had any return of it after this year.

To MISS COLLET.

*January* 23.

'I have always admitted that Keshub Chunder Sen has been weak, though I could show you that, after the first step had been taken, he was more helpless than weak. I do not believe that the Hindus do not care for truth; on the contrary, if left to themselves,

I believe (with Col. Sleeman) that they are more truthful than any other nation. Their whole literature from beginning to end is pervaded by reverence for truth. From what I know of Keshub Chunder Sen, I should never suspect him of an untruth.'

In another letter to Miss Collet, Max Müller writes:—

'Yet I have felt that in spite of many whirlpools, eddies, and waterfalls, the main stream was flowing on in the right direction, and that really good work is being done in India, both by Keshub Chunder Sen and by his opponents.'

To the end Max Müller preserved his faith in Keshub Chunder Sen, and did all he could to uphold him and his work against the attacks made on him in India and England.

'Two points only seemed to me of real importance in the teaching of his last years: first, the striving after a universal religion, and the recognition of a common substance in all religions; secondly, the more open recognition of the historical superiority of Christianity as compared with more ancient forms of faith. Keshub Chunder Sen rejoiced in the discovery that, from the first, all religions were but varying forms of one great truth. This was his pearl of great price. To him it changed the whole aspect of the world, and gave a new meaning to his life. That the principle of historical growth or natural evolution applied to religion also, as I had tried to prove in my books on the Science of Religion, was to him the solution of keenly-felt difficulties, a real solace in his own perplexities.'

There is little doubt that it was Keshub Chunder Sen's strong leaning towards Christianity, in which he was before his time, which annoyed the Rationalists in India, and called forth some of the attacks made on him in England.

In the spring of this year Max Müller was asked if he would join 'The Club' if there were a vacancy: 'the most distinguished dining-club in this country,' wrote one of the members; 'it consists of the primates in politics, literature, art, and science.' Max Müller was very much gratified at the wish expressed, but he felt, delightful as it would be, the effort of going to London to attend the ten dinners each session of Parliament would hinder his work too much, and he most reluctantly refused the intended honour.

In February Max Müller attended a great dinner at University College, London, on the occasion of the opening of the north wing, just added to the buildings. Lord Kimberley, as President of the College, was in the chair. It was a large and noble gathering, and among the speakers were Lord Sherbrooke, Professors Henry Smith, Roscoe, and Huxley, Sir F. Leighton, Sir John Lubbock, Sir G. Jessel, and the President of the Royal Society. The toast of the British Universities was proposed by Professor Tyndall, to which Max Müller replied. After assuring his hearers that the majority of people at Oxford had no feelings but those of sincere rejoicing at the rise and growth of what he might call the young Universities, the Universities of the future, he went on to explain a scheme that was then much in his thoughts, for throwing open the 150 Fellowships left in Oxford, after providing for all the wants of tutorial and professorial teaching, to the whole of England. The scheme is fully explained in a paper, extracts from which are given below, which he sent up in March to Professor Tyndall, asking if any of his scientific friends would sign it. It had not, as yet, been shown to any one. The paper is interesting as a scheme that, if carried out, might have put England on a par with France and Germany in the encouragement of scientific and literary research.

'We, the undersigned, beg to submit to the Commissioners of the Universities of Oxford and Cambridge that it would most effectually serve for the promotion of learning, if the so-called Prize Fellowships were thrown open to general competition. It may be desirable to confine other Fellowships, to which tutorial and other College duties are attached, to persons familiar with the spirit of the two Universities, but with regard to Prize Fellowships there seems to be no reason why the field of competition should be limited to candidates brought up at Oxford and Cambridge. The wider the field, the greater would be the value attached to these Fellowships, and the greater also the gain for the two Universities in attracting towards themselves the best talent of the whole country.

'The undersigned would likewise suggest to the Commissioners that these Prize Fellowships should not in future be bestowed without some definite duties being attached to them, and that, as a rule, they should not be tenable for more than five years. . . .

'Holders of Prize Fellowships, if they have done good work during the first five years, should know that they may receive a second Fellowship in addition to the first, both tenable again for five years, and that after ten years, if they have produced some valuable work, and wish to devote themselves entirely to the prosecution of scientific studies, they may look forward to a third Fellowship, and become Professors in the University, under regulations similar to those now proposed by the University Commissioners.

'By thus concentrating the resources which the two Universities possess in their Prize Fellowships (representing, after all deductions are made, an annual sum of about £100,000), the Commissioners might make these Fellowships not only a reward for work done by school-boys and undergraduates, but an incentive to new work. A recognized career would thus be opened to young men of talent, wishing to devote themselves to the prosecution of independent investigations, and to the advancement of sound learning, who, under present circumstances, have either to face years of uncertain adventure, or accept employment detrimental to the scientific character of their work. And the Universities would more truly fulfil their double function of transmitting and enlarging knowledge, by training a class of students really qualified to fill professorial Chairs, and to maintain in the future the high position of English scholarship and learning.'

TO PROFESSOR TYNDALL.

OXFORD, *March* 16.

'I may have made in the paper I sent you the same mistake which I find I made in some others. The sum I want to secure to science is not £10,000 a year, but £100,000 a year. We may put down the Prize Fellowships in each University as at least 150—that leaves a large margin for tutorial and professorial Fellowships.

'300 to 400 Fellowships, each of about £300 a year, gives about £100,000. Is not this worth an effort?'

Professor Tyndall was much interested in Max Müller's scheme, and, though himself ill from overwork, wrote that he thought the statement admirable, and would send it on to those likely to be interested in the subject, whilst he himself would gladly sign it. A few days later Professor Tyndall wrote again: 'I have set your scheme afoot, and I think you will not lack backers.'

TO THE SAME.

*March* 26.

'I was very sorry to hear of your being pulled down. This won't do. Who is to fight, if you give in? I shall get little, if any, support for my proposal here at Oxford. Some people think it high treason. I believe, on the contrary, like many kinds of high treason, it would be a blessing to Oxford, and open a future to English science such as we can hardly imagine as yet. You hardly know what a Crypto-Anglicist I am, and how firmly I believe in the future of England. But really English genius has had no chance, and it is a perfect marvel to me when I see what it has achieved, even when dancing in chains. The waste of power here at Oxford is fearful. I have known dozens of young men who might have done any amount of solid scientific work, and who dwindle away into judges or bishops. What I want is not only a *carrière ouverte*, but a *carrière assurée* for students and scholars. I am afraid we shall not carry this proposal now, but even to have mooted it may do some good hereafter.'

Carlyle had died in the February of this year, and the statue referred to in the following letter was to him. The statue now stands on the Chelsea Embankment, near to Cheyne Row, where Carlyle lived, and is a sitting life-size figure in bronze.

To Professor Tyndall.

Oxford, *May* 4.

'Well done, royally done! taking *royally* in its etymological meaning—*rex* being a leader, a straightforward *director*, the leader of a forlorn hope, the right man, when right (*rectum*) has to be vindicated! Really, when one hears people talk about Carlyle and Disraeli, all landmarks of right and wrong seem to have vanished.

'I have no misgivings about the statue, though the price charged seems rather high. I also should prefer bronze to marble in this climate.

'Froude will be glad to serve on the Committee: he is sure to exert himself. Lowell will help and contribute. We shall have a small committee here, but we want printed papers, &c. The fire must be stirred in the central place.'

To his Son.

*May* 16, 1881.

'"Becoming independent" is one thing, "becoming rich" another. Everybody ought to try hard to make himself independent, but then a man must learn to be independent with little, such as Carlyle was—one of the most independent and honest men I have ever known. Don't forget that I took you once to see him—it is better than to have seen the Pyramids or Niagara.'

Max Müller had the strongest admiration for Carlyle. Soon after his death, he writes:—

'Think of the simplicity and frugality of his life, the nobility of his heart, the sublimity of his purposes. I have known many good and great men. I have never known one so strong and straight, so sturdy and striking as Thomas Carlyle—strong and straight like a pyramid, a mystery to the common crowd of travellers, and certainly not to be measured in its width and breadth, in its height and depth, by the small pocket-rule of "common sense"!'

The translation of the *Dhammapada*, which formed Max Müller's second contribution to the *Sacred Books of the East*, came out, as has been stated, this year, and seems to have been read by his old friend Mrs. Josephine Butler.

To Mrs. Butler.

Oxford, *May* 18.

'Dear Mrs. Butler,—I am glad you appreciate Buddha, like myself. I feel I owe him much. As to a life, we shall never have that: we may know what his various disciples thought of him, but then a picture is never greater than the artist. We shall have to be satisfied with a few stones picked up here and there, and have to build up our own image. I shall send you some more of him, if you like. I expect Froude here in a few days: his son comes to matriculate at Oriel. I am not the least shaken in my belief in Carlyle: he was the greatest and truest man I have ever known, and that will do for me. What a loss Sandwith is[1]! What would England be without its unknown worthies? He too sped through life straight as an arrow, and there are few left like him.'

The following letter shows how completely Max Müller devoted himself to his Buddhist pupils:—

To Mr. Nanjio.

Oxford, *May* 28.

'I had a letter from Lord Granville to-day, informing me that the two MSS. of the *Sukhâvatî-Vyûha* would be sent to me from Paris through the English Ambassador. I expect they will arrive in about a week. Would it not be better now for you and me to stay at Oxford till we have finished the collation of these MSS.? It need not take much time, unless the text should be very different—which, however, I do not expect.

'If we could finish this collation and the printing of the Bodleian Catalogue before going to Paris, it would be well to do so, I think.

[1] Dr. Sandwith was one of the defenders of Kars in 1855, under General Williams.

But tell me really what you like to do, and I shall then see how I can arrange my plans. Though our departure for Paris may be delayed now, yet I am as anxious as ever to go there, and afterwards to Germany, and to take care of you on the journey to Paris and Berlin.

'What shall we put on the title-page?

"Catalogue of Japanese and Chinese Books and Manuscripts, Prepared by Bunyiu Nanjio, Priest of the Monastery, . . . Japan"?'

Just before Commemoration of this year a great sorrow came to Max Müller in the death of his friend Dr. Rolleston. Of all his friends in Oxford, he was the one with whom Max Müller was at this time the most entirely united, and till Dr. Rolleston's illness, which obliged him to leave Oxford for some months, only returning to die in a few days, they were constantly together. In their fearless love of truth, their power of affection, their buoyant natures, their powerful and intuitive grasp of any subject occupying their minds, they had much in common, and for years Max Müller felt the loss in his daily life. To escape Commemoration, for which he had no heart, he went to West Malvern, accompanied by his Japanese priests. It was on this visit that an incident occurred which Max Müller was fond of narrating. Coming home one evening along the ridge of the hills, they stood still to watch one of those glorious sunsets which are so often to be seen from the Malvern range. 'The western sky was like a golden curtain, covering we know not what, when Kasawara said to me, "That is what we call the Eastern Gate of Sukhâvatî, the Land of Bliss." He looked forward to it, and he trusted he should meet there all who had loved him, and whom he had loved, and that he should gaze on the Buddha Amitâbha—the Infinite Light.' A lady who heard Max Müller describe this scene, sent him the following lines:—

'We walked and talked together, and before us
The golden glory of the sunset shone.
Then a great raptured silence brooded o'er us—
The glory glowed with gems—the orb was gone.
Then spoke my friend, with reverent voice and low,
"Yonder! the wondrous Temple's eastern gate!
Within" (he eager gazed) "fain would I go,
Beyond those shining bars my fathers wait."

I hung my head. My Christian eyes had seen
But a grand painting, crimson, green, and gold;
While he, a Buddhist—*by my side*—had been,
Through pearly doors, looking on Light untold.
And now, whene'er I see a glorious sunset sky,
I think—beyond that gate what splendid visions lie.'

To Professor Noiré.

*Translation.* Malvern, *June* 27, 1881.

'My dear Friend,—I have been here for more than a week, enjoying the beautiful fresh air of the Malvern Hills. I longed for rest, for blow after blow had come upon me lately through the deaths of my nearest friends and acquaintances. Bernays was an old friend of mine, of whom I saw much at the Bunsens'. His was a clear mind; he was a splendid Greek scholar, and he was faithfully attached to me. Then, after various other losses, came the death of Professor Rolleston, which was so tragical. You remember him, do you not, and his ethnological museum? He mentioned your name often. . . . Occurrences like his tragic death, and his wife's sad state, are beyond our understanding—we cannot tackle it. It seems something must be out of order to produce such convulsions of life. And so we become poorer and poorer. To-day, again, I hear of the death of a Swiss friend, Fritz Kraus, whom you may remember as the translator of Shakespeare's *Sonnets*—to me a dear friend. And all this is because we grow old, but we cannot help wondering why we ourselves have to remain so long imprisoned here. I try to work as much as I possibly can: that gives me an aim to live for. Kant is difficult, but interests me deeply.'

To B. Malabari, Esq.

*June* 31.

'I was grieved to hear of the death of your child. I know what it is—there are few who do not know that grief. Even in the *Rig-veda* there is a simple prayer, "Let us die in order that the old may not weep for the young." It is a great problem why it should be so, and yet nothing lifts us so much above the cares of this life as love for those who have gone before us, and who are nearer to our hearts now than they were when we could see them every day. To die young is a great blessing—that thought ought to comfort those who are left behind to mourn.'

To Mr. Nanjio.

Oxford, *June* 28, 1881.

'I was glad to hear that you had arrived safely in Oxford, and

I hope your stay at Malvern will have done you some good. I am very anxious that you should acquire a thorough knowledge of Sanskrit, and I am glad to see that you are both making good progress; but there is still much before you, and you will have to work hard. If I sometimes seem impatient, you ought to know that it really arises from my wish to see you get on. You asked me for the meaning of K. M.: it means Knight of the Order of Merit. I have received many orders and ribbons, but that is the one I value most; there are only twenty Knights and they elect themselves, they are not made through the favour of kings or Ministers, but after a Knight has been elected he receives his decoration from the Emperor of Germany. Carlyle, the great historian, who died this year, declined to accept the Grand Cross of the Bath from Lord Beaconsfield, but he accepted the Order pour le Mérite, because it was given him by his peers. All these things no doubt are vanities, but they also produce some good, because scholars all over the world exert themselves to gain that distinction, and thus it encourages them in their work.'

Early in July Max Müller heard of the death of Professor Benfey, Sanskrit Professor at Göttingen, who only the year before had celebrated the Jubilee of his professorship. 'The death of Benfey was a great shock,' he writes; 'he was a wonderful worker.' This was followed by the loss of another Oxford friend, the Librarian of the Bodleian, 'Bodley Coxe,' as his friends loved to call him.

But a far deeper sorrow fell on Max Müller, the shadow from which long rested on him. On July 18 his loved and valued friend Arthur Stanley, Dean of Westminster, died after a very short illness. Max had known him from the time of his own arrival in Oxford in 1848, and had paid him several visits at Canterbury. They had become intimate friends during the years 1856 to 1863, when Stanley was Canon of Christ Church. His marriage and removal to Westminster made no change in their mutual affection. His wife, Lady Augusta, welcomed her husband's friends in the heartiest manner, and the Deanery was a London home to the Max Müllers. 'One could speak to him unreservedly, almost thoughtlessly,' Max writes. 'One knew he believed all one said. . . . It was a treat to speak with him, and to find that he really took one for better than one was—it made one better.' 'I miss Stanley very much. He always remained true to one. After he had once trusted a man, he seldom dropped him again.'

To Professor Noiré.

*Translation.* Oxford, *July* 23.

'I cannot tell you how sad I feel—all strength and joy seems to have left me. How I wish I could have a good cry! Well, we have to pull ourselves together. If I only could get away! On August 6, I hope to go with my wife and children to the Hartz mountains, to meet my old mother, aged 81. . . . On Monday I am going up to London for the funeral. I am afraid of it, but I did not want to miss it. The sympathy all over England is wonderful.'

It had long been settled that the summer should be spent in Germany with his old mother, and she fixed on the Hartz as the place where they would meet and spend the holidays together.

To Lady Welby.

*August* 2.

'I feel very weary. This year has taken away almost all my friends in England and in Germany, and I wonder why I am left. We must not let our friends die, and I trust Stanley will long live among us. I have never known a better man—his very weaknesses arising from the best motives.'

A list exists in Max Müller's writing with not less than twenty-five names of friends who had passed away this year in England and Germany.

The time in the Hartz was a great success; Goslar, Hartzburg, and many other beautiful and interesting spots were visited, including Quedlinburg on the way to Dessau, where a happy week was spent with the relations: the last time they were all to be together. The Max Müllers went on to Dresden, and saw many of their valued friends, and from there Max Müller went to Berlin for the fifth Oriental Congress, and his wife and children returned to England.

To B. Malabari, Esq.

*September* 4.

'I am deeply interested in the effect which my *Hibbert Lectures* will produce in India. When writing them I was often thinking of my friends in your country more than of my audience at Westminster.

The views which I have put forward in these lectures on the origin and on the true nature, character, and value of religion, are the only possible solution of the difficulties which trouble you, or at least all who are honest among you, and which trouble us in Europe. Do not suppose that I say this from any selfish motive. Truth is not mine nor yours: we can only bear witness to it, we cannot make it. All I may truly say of myself is, that I have devoted my whole life to the study of religion and religions, and that the views put forward in my *Hibbert Lectures* are the result of the studies which have not ignored any one of the objections raised against religion whether in England or in India. We must look for that religion which is at the root of all religions, and of which every historical religion is but an imperfect expression. If we once understand why every expression was imperfect, we shall have to bear with every religion—we shall look in each for that with which we can agree, and leave the rest to Brâhmans, Dasturs, and Popes. There is no religion which does not contain some truth, none which contains the whole truth—for religion is the light of truth as reflected in human mirrors—and however pure and spotless your mirror may be, there is none which in reflecting does not deflect the rays of light that fall on it. The first duty which every student of religion has to perform is to make himself acquainted with the books on which each religion claims to be founded. Hence my publication of the *Sacred Books of the East*, i. e. of the world, for all religions come from the East.'

Max Müller was a delegate to the Congress from the University of Oxford, and, as such, delivered an address at the opening meeting, in which he dwelt on the services rendered by Oxford to Oriental learning in the publication of the *Sacred Books of the East* and the *Anecdota Oxoniensia*.

The next day Max Müller gave a detailed account of how he had discovered some Sanskrit texts, hitherto unknown, in Japan, and he showed the fine facsimiles that had been sent him. Professor Weber congratulated Max on his discovery, and, in an able speech, dealt with its great importance for Sanskrit studies.

But much as he enjoyed the Congress, all Max Müller's letters from Berlin are full of expressions of fatigue and his longing for rest. 'You don't know what a beehive it is, not to say wasp-hive!' As much time as he could spare was given to his old friend of early days at Bunsen's, Karl Meyer, who was very ill. They never met again. Lepsius, too, who was to have been president of the Congress, was too ill to take any part in it.

His two Japanese pupils, who had met him at Berlin, accompanied him to Paris. From there he writes, on September 19, to his wife:—

'This place is full of memories, and I walk about often as in a dream—so many gone, so many almost forgotten, till some little thing brings them back to one's memory. It was a hard struggle I had to go through here, and with no definite prospects, risking all on one card. I passed the spot where I remember saying to Schlötzer (it must have been in 1846), "Two things I must get, to be a Member of the French Institute (1869) like Humboldt, and to be a Knight of the Order pour le Mérite" (1874). He shouted! Well, I got both, and he will soon be Prussian Minister at Rome, where Bunsen was. Thus goes the world. But the dream of a reality is often happier than the reality of a dream.'

On September 23 Max Müller took his seat as a Foreign Member of the French Institute, to which he had been elected twelve years before, but his friends had not thought it wise for him to attempt it sooner—the feeling was so strong against all Germans, and even now there was a decided attempt to make it uncomfortable for him; those who had not known him in old days talking loudly when he began his address; but after a time his perfect self-possession, and the interest of his subject (the discovery of the Sanskrit texts in Japan), had their effect. Unfortunately, most of his old friends, who would have given him a cordial reception, were still in the country.

He wrote to his mother:—

*Translation.* PARIS, *September* 27.

'Last Friday I took my seat as a Foreign Member of the French Institute. There was much speechifying, and I had to read a long paper *in French* about the Sanskrit MSS. which I got from Japan. The Japs were there, and, when I mentioned their names, bowed and smiled. All seems to have gone off well. I was elected in 1869, but had never taken my seat. There are only eight Foreign Members.'

TO HIS WIFE.

PARIS, *September* 30.

'My address in the Academy was no joke: since Humboldt no German has spoken there. How different is everything now to 1846, and how many are no longer here! I have seen my old lodging. It is wonderful how well all has gone with me. I began with nothing, and yet have accomplished something. That is the great thing, that one feels one has brought the world a step onwards, finished a little raw work, and carried through a few new ideas. Now may others carry the work still further.'

On his return to Oxford, Max Müller found a letter awaiting him from the Dean of Christ Church, asking if he could be persuaded to offer himself as a candidate for the vacant Bodley Librarianship. It needed little consideration for him to decline such a post. It would have taken all his time, and the great work on which he was embarked, the *Sacred Books of the East*, must have been abandoned. He felt the same about the Wardenship of All Souls, for which some of his friends urged him to stand, and which became vacant this year, by the death of his relative, Dr. Leighton.

Max Müller was appointed a Curator of the Bodleian for the second time towards the close of this year.

To Dr. Tylor.

*November 7.*

'No, the *Wacht am Rhein* was not my father's; it is of later date. The poet seems to have been little known, but he received, I believe, some pension from Government before he died. I believe his name was Müller, if that is a *gnâman*. I wish you would stand for the Bodleian Librarianship, or for part of Rolleston's Professorship.'

On November 9 Max Müller received an invitation from Cambridge to deliver a set of lectures there in the next Lent Term on some Indian subject, with special view to the Indian Civil Service students. The invitation was accepted, and was the origin of the seven lectures entitled, *India—What can it teach us?*

From the time of his return from Paris Max Müller had been printing his translation of Kant, which he had finished in the summer. Many of his friends wondered at his 'wasting his time on a mere translation.' He has fully answered their objections in the noble preface to the translation, where also he mentions his own indebtedness to Kant:—

'While I am looking at the last lines I have written, it may be the last lines that I shall ever write on Kant, the same feeling comes over me which I expressed in the preface to the last volume of my edition of the *Rig-veda* and its ancient Commentary. I feel as if an old friend, with whom I have had many communings during the sunny and during the dark days of life, was taken from me, and I should hear his voice no more. The two friends, the *Rig-veda* and Kant's *Critique of Pure Reason*, may seem very different, and yet my life would have been incomplete without the one, as without the other. The bridge of thoughts and sighs that spans the whole history of the Âryan world has its first arch in the *Vedas*, its last in Kant's *Critique*. While in the *Veda* we may study the childhood, we may study in Kant's *Critique of Pure Reason* the perfect manhood of the Âryan mind.'

A second edition of Max Müller's translation was called for, and was brought out in 1896, with the help of Dr. Adickes, who not only gave Max the benefit of all the important new readings and emendations which he was incorporating into his own standard edition, but also pointed out passages where he felt the exact meaning of Kant's ambiguous style had not been correctly rendered.

To Professor Tyndall.

Oxford, *December* 19.

'I have received an invitation to attend a meeting of the Carlyle Monument Committee on the 22nd. It is almost impossible for me to go to London, nor do I think that I can be of much use. But I am quite decided on one point—we must not allow ourselves to be beaten. If you meet a flock of geese chattering and hissing, the only thing to be done is to walk straight through them. What you have to consider therefore, if there is still a deficiency, is whether some of us should go to Birmingham, Manchester, Liverpool and collect, or whether we should appeal to Germany and America.

'Secondly, we ought to find out for how little a good bronze statue can be produced. I spoke to a first-rate artist at Dresden, who has put up several colossal statues in bronze (he is married to an Englishwoman), and I understood him to say that it could be done for £1,300. Will Mr. Boehm do it for that, and, if not, are we bound to him, and cannot we apply to anybody else?

'I am full of work just now—five proof-sheets a day. However, I hope Kant will be out in January, and then I shall be free again. Just now I feel like a tunnel with three or four trains rushing and foaming against each other.'

In his Christmas letter to his mother he shows how much

his work often weighed upon him. 'We march forwards as long as we can, and when at last "Halt!" is called, we are glad to rest!'

All through the early months of 1882 Max Müller was busy preparing for his lectures on 'India' for Cambridge. Two of them were also to be given at Birmingham, at the Midland Institute.

As a New Year's gift a beautiful paper was sent to him, *Leaders of Modern Thought—F. Max Müller*, giving an account of his life and works, and the spirit that had influenced those works. Some notable extracts follow:—

'We all, as Max Müller has well said, make for ourselves a life-plan; we all belong to an army, and carry a war-plan in our heads, which decides and guides us in the choice of our own march. Here is a scholar who belongs to the noble army of those who fight for the conquest of truth in the battle-field of man's spiritual being, and when he asks himself, what is the right, or at least the most fruitful method in the study of man, he soon becomes convinced that, in order to know what man is, we must, before all things, consider *what man has been and how he has become what he is*. And what has made the poet's son the pride of those in England and Germany who say with Pope, "The proper study of mankind is man"? It is his "godly enthusiasm," the deep, poetic glow, that "infinite susceptivity," and, above all, unflinching loyalty to truth which pervade all his work, and which carry us away with an irresistible charm, so that he has become a veritable ἄναξ ἀνδρῶν!'

After a sketch of Müller's life, the article ends thus:—

'Many are the roads along which the nations have passed on their march to the City of God, and it is to surveying and mapping them out that this great leader of modern thought is devoting the rest of his life, which, let us hope, may be a long one. "To watch the dawn of religious consciousness in mankind must always remain one of the most inspiring and hallowing sights in the whole history of the world; and he whose heart cannot quiver with the first quivering rays of human thought and human faith is unfitted for the study." Yes, brave heart, noble and beautiful words: work on, and God be with thee!

'To him who, on a memorable occasion, asked in stirring tones: "Hab' ich mich je in England als Fremden betrachtet[1]?" let us ever say, No, and we hope you never will!'

[1] 'Have I ever felt myself a stranger in England?'

Though adverse criticism moved him very little, discriminating appreciation of his work was a spur and incentive to his affectionate nature, and cheered him on through many a tough and dry bit of work, whilst each year the solemn feeling deepened that the time left him might be short, and there was 'still so much to do.' He writes in January to his wife:—

'To delight in doing one's work in life, that is what helps one on, though the road is sometimes very stiff and tiring—uphill rather it would seem than downhill, and yet downhill it is.'

To Mr. Nanjio.

*January* 1.

'I was very glad to have your wishes for the New Year, and the two Chinese poems, which I shall keep as a remembrance when you are gone. I hope the work you are doing will bear fruit by-and-by. Though we cannot understand how our deeds ripen, they certainly do ripen, and good work bears good fruit, and bad work bears bad fruit. That is a very old lesson, but there are few better lessons to learn and preach. I have been very busy of late, and have not been able to help you as much as I wished, but I hope we shall now begin again to work in good earnest.'

To B. Malabari, Esq.

Oxford, *January* 29.

'As I told you on a former occasion, my thoughts while writing these lectures [the Hibbert] were with the people of India. I wanted to tell those few at least whom I might hope to reach in English, what the true *historical* value of their ancient religion is, as looked upon, not from an exclusively European or Christian, but from an *historical* point of view. I wished to warn against two dangers, that of undervaluing or despising the ancient national religion, as is done so often by your half-Europeanized youths, and that of overvaluing it, and interpreting it as it was never meant to be interpreted, of which you may see a painful instance in Dayânanda Sarasvatî's labours on the *Veda*. Accept the *Veda* as an ancient *historical* document, containing thoughts in accordance with the character of an ancient and simple-minded race of men, and you will be able to admire it, and to retain some of it, particularly the teaching of the *Upanishads*, even in these modern days. But discover in it "steam-engines and electricity, and European philosophy and morality," and you deprive it of its true character, you destroy its real value, and you break the historical continuity that ought to bind the present to the past. Accept the past as a reality, study it and try to understand it, and you will then have less difficulty in finding the right way towards the future.

'From letters I have received I know that my *Hibbert Lectures* have been read in India. In fact, one of the best reviews of them appeared in the *Theistic Quarterly Review*, published in Calcutta. It was written by Protap Chunder Mozoomdar. But the number of people born in India who can read English, though growing from year to year, is still small, and it was therefore a great satisfaction to me when I heard from you that there was a chance of my lectures being translated into some of the Indian languages.

'Accept now my sincere thanks for all you have done, and for what you still mean to do.'

To Mr. Nanjio.

*February* 8.

'I can assure you it has been a real pleasure to me to have had you and your friend Kasawara as my pupils. I must sometimes have seemed impatient to you, but you know that it was only due to my wishing you to get on more rapidly. I can quite believe that you found Sanskrit very difficult, but you have mastered it now so far, that if you had to leave Oxford, which I hope will not yet be for a while, you will be able to get on by yourself. I always hope that you have some great and useful work before you when you return to Japan. Every one of us must try in his own sphere to be a real Buddha, devoting his life to the good of other people. I know you will do that, and that the work which we have done together will bear some fruit, even after we are called away from this life.'

The following letter contains the first idea of a collected edition of Max Müller's works, though it was many years before the idea was carried out, and the *History of Sanskrit Literature* was never written, if a new work was intended. Nor was a new edition of *Ancient Sanskrit Literature* published, Max Müller feeling he had not time to read up the books written on the subject since 1861.

To C. J. Longman, Esq.

*February* 9.

'I wish very much to be guided by your advice as to a collected edition of my works. I am at work on a course of lectures on Ancient India, to be delivered at Birmingham and at Cambridge; they will grow into a book. And if life lasts I have a final book on the *Logos, Language, and Reason*, on the stocks, which will finish my work. Now you know best what is the right thing to do. The *History of Sanskrit Literature* will take me more than a year to prepare, so we might have the new edition of the *Lectures* at once, and the next volume in the autumn.'

About this time began the correspondence, extending over many years, with Mr. Horatio Hale of Ontario: unfortunately but few of the letters on either side have been preserved.

To Horatio Hale, Esq.

*February* 14.

'It is a great pleasure to me to receive your letter and your paper on *Hiawatha*; that paper is full of instructive hints, particularly as bearing on the state of so-called savages, before they are brought in contact with so-called civilized men. Such evidence is, from the nature of the case, very difficult to obtain, and therefore all the more valuable. To my mind the structure of such a language as the Mohawk is quite sufficient evidence that those who worked out such a work of art were powerful reasoners and accurate classifiers. But it was evidently not in language only that savages had achieved great things, but, as you show, in political organization also and in family laws. I often wonder that so few American scholars work at these Indian Antiquities, as if they were less interesting than Sanskrit or Hebrew, and I hope indeed that you will find time to arrange what you have collected for publication. In many respects savages were much wiser in arranging their passage through life than we are; our struggle for life has become far more savage than theirs was. Still it is very difficult to come to a clear conception of the ascending and descending scales of civilization, and the traces of the fallen angel and the rising ape are curiously mixed together. Language is the greatest puzzle; for if that is to be looked upon as the work of ascending monkeys, we get so near the edge of the glacial period that no gorilla could have lived, much less invented gerunds and supines.'

Early in March Max Müller delivered his two lectures before the Midland Institute at Birmingham, and then returned home to finish the course for Cambridge.

The following shows some of the difficulties with which Max Müller had to contend as editor of the *Sacred Books of the East*. The *Manu* was undertaken by Professor Bühler, and forms Vol. I of Series II = Vol. XXV.

To Professor Bühler.

*Translation.*

*April* 25.

'. . . I received to-day a letter from Burnell, who, after all, is giving up his translation of the *Manu*. He has kept me for six years in uncertainty about it.

'Now before I write about it to others, I should like to ask you first of all whether you will undertake the *Manu*, and, if possible, *before* the *Yâgñavalkya Parâsara?* Jolly wants to publish a text; he has undertaken, besides that, some other *Smritis*, as you see. I should therefore like best a translation from your hand, not only because it would be the best one, but also because you would finish it sooner than anybody else. Jolly is going as Tagore Professor to Calcutta, and his literary work will, I fear, suffer a little. So think about it, and send me a speedy answer. You have, in any circumstances, time till the summer of 1884.'

The hard work was telling on Max Müller, and yet he could give himself no leisure. He seldom worked at this time less than ten hours a day, not counting the time that went in correspondence.

To his Daughter Beatrice (who had spent the winter in Paris).

*April* 18, 1882.

'My dear old Pussy,—I was so pleased with your letter that I want just to write a few lines to you, though Mama will be with you soon. I know you will enjoy your time together at Paris, and you ought by this time to be a capital guide. Yet, as you say, there is no place like home, and no happiness like happiness at home. I want you to do your very best to make our home bright and happy. You know how we love you, and how devoted your mother is to all of you. Young as you are, you know how quick this life passes away, and how suddenly often those whom we love best are taken from us. Therefore let us try not to waste one day or one hour—to think of others more than of ourselves, never to be hasty or harsh. Life has many troubles and sorrows: let us try not to add to them ourselves. You know what I mean, and I know you will do your best to make our home bright and happy. I shall have very hard work before you come home, and hope to get through it without any interruption. Mary will be gone before you come back, so you will have to be Martha, and help Mama as much as you can.

'Ever your loving Father.'

To his Mother.

*Translation.* *April* 19, 1882.

'Here in England my translation of Kant is much discussed, and praised and blamed. I am not at all disturbed by such things, but work on quietly. Next month I go to Cambridge, and have still a good deal to do for my lectures, and am often very tired and languid. We can make no plans for the summer, till I see a little more clearly ahead with my most pressing work. It is often almost too much for me, but one cannot refuse the work when it comes to one.'

Happily he had less call on his time this spring in the way of social duties; his daughters were both away for music and painting lessons, and his son at school.

In April he writes to tell his elder daughter that he had been to London to attend Darwin's funeral in Westminster Abbey:—

*April 27, 1882.*

'Darwin's funeral was a great gathering, though not so great as when Stanley was buried. It was the mourning of the mind in Darwin's case, in Stanley's the mourning of the heart.'

To Professor Bühler.

*Translation.* *April 29.*

'... I have sent, some time ago, a request to the Japanese Government, that my two Buddhists might be sent to India, Nepal, Tibet, and China, in order to look for MSS. They are quite prepared for this now, and, being priests, they hope to get admittance everywhere. But it must all be kept very secret. I am full of hope, though I may not live to see the fulfilment....'

The hope expressed here was never fulfilled. Kasawara died soon after his return to Japan from ill health in this very year; and Bunyiu Nanjio, though sent to India and Corea to look for MSS., has not yet been sent to Tibet.

To his Daughter Mary.

*May 5.*

'I have always been glad that you took to music, and it gives me great pleasure to listen to your playing and think of the time when I was young and enjoyed nothing so much as music. There is also a higher kind of music which we all have to learn, if our life is to be harmonious, beautiful, and useful. There are certain intervals between the young and the old which must be there, which are meant to be there, without which life would be monotonous, but out of these intervals and varieties the true art of life knows how to build up perfect harmonies.... My life is often a life of great effort, and probably will be so to the end,... but when I think of other families, I feel how grateful we all ought to be for our quiet happy home. There lies one great sorrow on us, but even that may be a blessing, by drawing some of our affections away from this life to a better life—of which, it is true, we know nothing, but from which, when we see the wisdom and love that underlie this life, we may hope everything. We are meant to hope and to trust, and that is often much harder than to see and to know. I say again that the greatest of all arts is the art of life, and the best of all music the harmony of spirits. There are many little rules to be learnt for giving harmony and melody to our life, but the thorough bass must be—love.'

In May the lectures began in Cambridge, where Max Müller spent some weeks, being joined after a time by his wife and daughters. The lectures were crowded, and the whole visit was one of great enjoyment and refreshment. Especially delightful to Max Müller was the society of his old friend Professor Cowell, who wrote on his friend's return to Oxford, to tell him how greatly he had enjoyed the lectures, and felt sure they would do good, in creating a new interest in the subject. 'You have helped to stir people up, and set them thinking and inquiring.'

Professor Cowell entirely agreed with Max Müller as to the early age at which Indian civil servants were and are chosen. 'I sometimes fear,' he says, 'that our civilians are selected at too early an age to have developed literary tastes, but your lectures will rouse them, if anything can, to take a real interest in ancient India.'

The following letter refers to this time:—

To Mrs. Max Muller.

Bangalore, *December* 25, 1901.

'I do not know whether you still remember it, but I had the pleasure and privilege of passing a few hours in the company of your late illustrious husband in the middle of May, 1882, at your hospitable residence in Oxford. To you and to your husband it was only one of the numerous visits Indians of all castes and creeds, of all shades and colours, paid to the great Rishi of Oxford, but to me it has been one of the most memorable incidents of my whole life. I still preserve as sacred and valuable relics two or three letters which he kindly wrote to me when I arrived in London. In one . . . he invites me to Cambridge to hear him deliver the series of lectures which have since become famous—*India*. These letters I jealously guard from any mishap or accident. . . . The relations between England and India are becoming closer every day, and no man has contributed so much to bring them nearer in *mind, heart,* and *soul* as your late illustrious husband. To have lost such a friend and companion is a gap that can never be filled up. Allow me to assure you that your sorrows are deeply and sincerely shared by the Hindus. May the New Year bring some new consolation!

'Yours sincerely,

'NISHIKANTA CHATTOPÂDHYÂYA.'

The lecture on the 'Truthfulness of the Hindus' attracted special attention and discussion, both at the time it was delivered, and afterwards when the whole work was published. Max Müller fully entered into the feelings of Thoreau, 'It takes two to speak truth—one to speak, and another to hear.' Of course, the assertion that, never having been in India, he could be no judge of the matter, was made over and over again, both in public print and in private letters. The *Times*, in reviewing the book, stated that 'One of the first lessons which a civil servant has to learn is to distrust native testimony. . . . Perjury is in the Indian air.' It was therefore all the more gratifying to Max Müller to receive a letter from no less an authority than Sir Lewis Pelly, saying that he agreed with nearly every line of that particular lecture. Sir Lewis says: 'Individually I have found among Hindus, Mussulmans, Armenians, and Jews, the most simple and practical good will and fidelity, and in looking back on a long service in India, Persia, and Afghanistan, my sole regret is that, owing partly to ignorance, . . . I did not more thoroughly appreciate my Eastern friends.' Max Müller also heard from a gentleman who had been for many years in a large house of business in Calcutta, who writes: 'I have ever been saying, in an imperfect way, what you say in a perfect and thorough way about our Indian brethren. I found all of them so lovable and honest; and never suffered loss through one of them to the value of a knife.' The Indian *Mirror* reprinted this particular lecture, which was read with warm appreciation in every part of India, and added greatly to the affection felt there for Moksha Mûlara. The lecture called forth innumerable letters, not only from India, many of them couched in quaint language, but also from English and Scotch clerks and employés in many of the great commercial houses throughout India, endorsing Max Müller's views, and speaking with genuine admiration and appreciation of the natives with whom they were in constant contact.

To Professor Bühler.

*Translation.* *June* 8.

'... I am grateful to you that you have relieved me of the anxiety about *Manu*. I have given notice to the Delegates, and as an agreement about *Manu* had been made years ago, it is unnecessary to make another with you, unless you wish for it.... I had become responsible particularly for the Law-Books, and it was unfortunate not to be able to carry out my programme. Sir H. Maine has just read a paper at the Royal Institution on the "Sacred Laws of the Âryas," where he attacks me for having fixed the date of *Manu* at 1300 A.D., and I only said "it did not appear earlier than the *fourth century* A.D." ... My little Buddhists are as accurate as machines: I have only discovered one mistake in their work, and even that seems to me to be a mistake of the printer....

'I always feel the want of time to master the tremendous material on all sides, and work cannot be done so briskly as in former times.'

The following letter is in reply to one from Messrs. Longmans, who were anxious to put their firm more in touch with the school-book trade in India:—

*July* 1.

'I think your plan is excellent, if you can find a really intelligent traveller. The persons responsible for every kind of school in India are the Directors of Education in each Presidency. You see the work they do in the Annual Reports presented to Government. These are to be seen at the India Office. The Universities at Calcutta, and the various Colleges at Bombay, Poona, Madras, Benares, Allahabad, Lahore, &c., are represented by senates and chancellors, but the persons to apply to for information would be the Registrars. There is a publishing department under each Director of Education, and you can see from the published reports how much they spend, and what books they patronize. I believe these book departments have not answered well, and in several cases they are to be discontinued. Dr. Leitner, Registrar of the Punjab University, told me so, and I see from the papers that the Punjab University has just appointed me Honorary President of a Publishing Committee, to be established in connexion with the Oriental College at Woking; what that means

I do not know yet. Anyhow, the question of school-books is being agitated at the present moment, and an able agent might do good service. I ought to tell you that I have long urged the Clarendon Press to establish depots in India. I tell you this that you may not suspect me of serving two masters. If you want any further information, I shall be glad to give it. Letters of introduction to the various Governors would, of course, be useful. I dare say you know Mr. Grant Duff and Lord Reay. I know the Registrar of Bombay, Mr. Peterson, and at Lahore, Dr. Leitner, and at Benares, Dr. Thibaut. The Missionary Schools might also be approached through the Missionary Societies in London.'

To his Mother.

*Translation.* Old Windsor, *July* 9.

'This whole week we have been on the move, and are now paying a visit in the country not far from Windsor and Eton, at Sir Charles Murray's, whom you may remember as English Minister in Dresden. W. comes to-day from Eton, and stays till to-morrow. B. is also here. Our host is a most interesting man, and the house is full of beautiful things. Last Monday we were in London for a great wedding: a cousin of G.'s, a young clergyman, married a daughter of the Duke of Argyll. It was a beautiful wedding. Then we were invited to Harrow, to the Speech Day, and to a party at the Archbishop of Canterbury's, and the great evening party at the Royal Academy. So you see how it goes. I could not stand it long. We stay here till Monday, and then I hope for rest in Oxford. . . . You don't remember how old I am, and that one's old body does not bear as much as formerly. My work, too, does not go as easily as it once did, and yet I have so much to do. New editions of old books, the twelfth of my *Lectures on Language*, and two other books, the *Hibbert Lectures*, and the *Introduction to the Science of Religion*. Then my lectures at Cambridge must be printed. In fact, it is often too much, and I hardly know how the time goes.'

The following was written on this visit in Lady Murray's album by Max Müller:—

The Grange, *July* 10, 1882.

'It is well that there should be here and there a few pure and bright and loving eyes that can only see what is pure and bright and lovely in this world. It is well that there should be here and there a few truly musical souls that can perceive through discords, which jar on other ears, the higher harmonies to which all discords are meant to lead. But for such eyes as discern the perfect in the imperfect, and for such ears as catch the higher harmonies in passing discords, life would seem a confused scrawl—mere noise and tumult. The human soul can lend its own purity, brightness, and loveliness to everything which it sees and hears, and, like the dawn, lift the dark veil of the night and spread its own heavenly splendour over the face of the earth, and light up, and warm, and quicken every heart that comes within its reach.

'F. MAX MÜLLER.'

On returning from this visit, Max decided not to go abroad at all this year, but stay in Oxford at work. His children preferred doing so, and a very happy Long Vacation was spent in their own home. Oxford was by no means deserted, and picnics and lawn-tennis parties and long days on the river made the time fly by to the young people, whilst the busy father worked on in his quiet library, sharing in all their pleasures whenever he could spare the time.

It was in this year that Max Müller was elected a Perpetual Delegate of the Press. He took deep interest in the work, and was assiduous in attending the meetings, till he resigned in 1896.

TO THE RIGHT HON. W. E. GLADSTONE.

7, NORHAM GARDENS, OXFORD, *July* 13, 1883.

'Allow me to thank you for what you said last night about Prince Louis Lucien Buonaparte. I am sorry to hear that the Prince required this assistance. I remember him as a wealthy, independent man, and I know he might have had a great deal more if, by a kind of honourable instinct, he had not kept aloof, as much as possible, from the Napoleonic Court. I was at Oxford when he was made a D.C.L. The Prince has done excellent work. He has been chiefly a collector, but his materials will last and will be consulted long after many of the now popular theories on the Science of Language shall have passed away. I have seldom known a French scholar so hard-working, so persevering, and withal so modest. He ought to be proud in accepting from your hands, and from the English nation, what he was too proud to accept from his Imperial cousins.

'I enclose a short article containing my translation of "God save the Queen" into Sanskrit. I have submitted it to the few remaining native scholars in India, and shall not publish it definitely, before I have received their remarks. I have many friends among educated natives in India, and they speak and write to me, perhaps, more freely than to others. Nothing, I may say, has given me so much confidence in the future of India, as the thorough appreciation of Lord Ripon's sober government by the people of India. I am not thinking so much about the so-called Ilbert Bill, as about the preceding years when I felt very doubtful whether, after the rather Oriental régime of Lord Lytton, Lord Ripon's quiet industry, honesty, and far-seeing statesmanship would be appreciated. I believe there is a strong desire in India that Lord Ripon should remain, and, great as the sacrifice might be, it would, I believe, not be too great for the interests which are at stake. There is, as yet, less commotion in India than there would have been, if those most concerned were not convinced that Lord Ripon will never yield to sentimental, not to say selfish or partisan clamour.

'I wish Mr. Mozoomdar, who is now in England, could have seen you. He is the right hand of Keshub Chunder Sen, and in intellect is far the stronger of the two, though most loyal to his leader, who is over-excited and occasionally strange in his utterances. Still, they are working in the right direction, and it is a pleasure to help them in ploughing, sowing, and watering, though we can never hope to see the harvest.'

To his Mother.

*Translation.* *July* 23, 1882.

'It is an experience that comes to one only late in life, how gladly many people welcome death. I am seeing an old man here, whose mind is still quite vigorous, but he speaks of his death as of a quite ordinary event. And so indeed it is—nothing more ordinary than birth and death. The sad thing is when the old are left, and the young go first. . . . My work grows over my head!'

To Mr. Nanjio.

*July* 23.

'Perhaps when you are in Japan you may be able to publish the Sanskrit text of the *Saddharma-pundarîka*. I shall quite miss you when you are gone, but I hope your stay in Oxford has not been in vain, and that you will help your countrymen forward, though not quite so fast as they seem to be going at present. I still hope to find time to publish the *Sukhâvatî-Vyûha* before you return to Japan, but I want to publish it jointly with you, so as to have your name on the title-page with my own, and I hope to be able to do the same for the *Dharma-Samgraha* with Kasawara, so that there will be a permanent memorial of your stay at Oxford, and of our work during the last three years. If only I had a little more time!'

During the summer the Parsi, Mr. Malabari, who had made himself well known in connexion with the question of infant marriages in India, conceived the plan of getting Max Müller's *Hibbert Lectures* translated into the vernaculars of India. He could not defray the whole expense himself, and hoped to do so by collecting money in the chief cities of India. He was at once encouraged by receiving 1,000 rupees from the enlightened Maharanee of Cossimbazar. He himself undertook the Gujarati translation, and made arrangements for translations into Sanskrit, Bengali, Marathi, Hindi, and Tamil.

One more visit was paid during the vacation, to Max Müller's brother-in-law at Taplow. 'We were forty-two relations in church to-day,' he writes to his mother. Bathing in the Thames was the great amusement during this visit, Max Müller's daughters being expert swimmers and divers.

To Mr. Bellows.

Taplow, *August* 21.

'I am always glad when I hear from you, and I only wish it was oftener. But we seem to be growing more busy with every year, instead of finding more rest. Your business, you say, is large; so is mine, as you will believe when I tell you that at the present moment I have nine volumes passing through the Press—not all my own, yet all entrusted to my care. I hope to find your paper when I return to Oxford. Your study of Barclay's *Apology* might be useful to students of the English language if you were to send your observations on the change of meaning in certain words to Dr. Murray, editor of the great English Dictionary to be published by the University Press. He would be most grateful for them. I hope you and yours are quite well; your little Max must be grown up by this time. My boy is at Eton; my two daughters grown up; my wife well, and I myself as well as, at my time of life, I have any right to expect.'

In September this year Dr. Pusey passed away. In spite of their almost diametrically opposite views on theological questions, Max Müller had long felt the force of Dr. Pusey's character, who, in his turn, showed in many ways his appreciation of his younger colleague's gifts and attainments. The following letter to the editor of the *Times* shows the feeling the two men entertained for each other:—

Oxford, *September* 23, 1882.

'Sir,—You are no doubt quite right in what you say, in your important article of to-day on the future of Hebrew scholarship at

Oxford, that "Dr. Pusey was kept aloof by his theological prepossessions from Ewald and all his school." But it may interest you to hear that, in one sense at least, Dr. Pusey was a pupil of Ewald's. Professor Ewald, the last time he was staying with me at Oxford, told me that when Pusey was studying in Germany, he (Dr. Ewald) acted as his private tutor in Hebrew. When Professor Ewald paid his last visit to Oxford, then an old man, but working twelve hours every day in the Radcliffe Library, and complaining every evening that the Library was not open long enough, he expressed a wish to see Dr. Pusey, and to renew his acquaintance with him. Unfortunately Dr. Pusey was not at Oxford at the time, but when he returned and I told him of Dr. Ewald's wish, a kindly smile played round his lips, and he said he would have been most glad to see him. I did not often trouble him with foreign visitors, but whenever distinguished scholars wished to be introduced to him, he was always ready to receive them, and to receive them with a courteousness peculiarly his own. I shall never forget a long and deeply-interesting conversation which he had with Keshub Chunder Sen. They had a long struggle, but they parted as friends.

'Dr. Pusey, as we all know, could be as intolerant as Athanasius, but, apart from what you call his theological prepossessions, he always retained through life a genuine respect for real scholarship, even for that much derided "original research." He often showed the warmest sympathy for true and earnest students in every field of Oriental philology. He took a deep interest in the discoveries of cuneiform scholars, and fully appreciated their bearing on Hebrew scholarship. He cared to know what the *Veda* and the *Avesta* had to teach us, and he was not afraid of new sciences, such as Comparative Philology and Comparative Mythology. Even when he had no time to study new subjects himself, he was always anxious to hear the latest news.

'Almost the last lines I had from him were meant to express his approval of the *Sacred Books of the East.* No one would have been surprised if the editor of the Library of the Fathers of the Christian Church had objected to this new Library of the Founders and Fathers of all Non-Christian Churches being published by the University Press. Far from it. "*I was very glad,*" he wrote, "*to see the plan of translations in which your name appears. It must be of good service; but the older one grows, the narrower one's little pyramid becomes, if it is not too absurd to speak of a pyramid at all, except to say that in one's old age one has to add only little stones.*"

'Your obedient Servant,

'F. MAX MÜLLER.'

To Horatio Hale, Esq.

*October* 8.

'Yes, I received your letters and the Montreal newspaper, and felt much interested in both. I feel sure that you will be doing a real service to scholars, if you can arouse a truly scientific interest in the study of American languages among your countrymen, but the study must be taken up in a scholarlike spirit. It requires not less, but not more accuracy than Greek and Latin. I wish I had a young army of scholars about me, and could order them about to explore where I know that treasures are to be found, though I am too old to dig for them. If anything I have said to you can help towards stirring up young explorers, please make any use you like of it. I had some correspondence with a gentleman who is preparing a Grammar of the Mohawk language. I sent him what I had collected myself from the mouth of a Mohawk here at Oxford.'

Some time after the Queen had assumed the title of Empress of India, a society was formed in London, called 'The National Anthem for India Fund.' Their object was to collect the best translations of 'God save the Queen' in the various vernaculars of India, so as to spread the knowledge and use of the National Anthem throughout that vast country. The committee numbered among its members many names of distinction, but the most active among them was Canon F. Harford. Rajah Surindro Mohun Tagore, a great authority on Indian music, was applied to for help, with several other distinguished Hindus. Though Sanskrit is no longer a living language, as it still serves as a medium of communication between learned natives of different parts of India, just as Latin was used in Europe in the Middle Ages, it was felt there must be a Sanskrit translation. Max Müller had not been asked to help, but the Sanskrit translation sent in having no rhymes, was to Max Müller's musical ear incapable of being used to the well-known air of the National Anthem. He had himself made a Sanskrit translation, which he submitted to a Pundit at that time in England, and to many of the most learned Sanskrit scholars in Europe. He then sent the perfected translation to his friend Keshub Chunder Sen, with an explanatory letter. Max Müller sent his translation to the London committee, and Canon Harford wrote, 'A thousand thanks for the beautiful Sanskrit, which goes perfectly to the measure of the English words and music,' and he also calls it 'an admirable translation.' His translation was sent to the Queen, who took much interest in the whole project, and it was Max Müller's translation that was, by Her Majesty's special desire, used at the opening of the Colonial and Indian Exhibition in the Albert Hall in 1886, when the second verse of the National Anthem was sung in Sanskrit, notwithstanding the machinations of some of Max Müller's detractors and enviers, who tried to alter the arrangement made by the Queen herself, by saying that it was invidious to choose Sanskrit and leave out Persian and Arabic, also spoken in India. The correspondence still exists, and the animus is very clear. Her Majesty did not agree to the change desired, and therefore Max Müller's translation of the second verse was sung.

To aid the National Anthem Fund a concert was given at Grosvenor House, in which the different translations were sung to the various arrangements of the air by Costa, Cusins, Arne, Rajah S. M. Tagore, Dr. Bull, Turle, Benedict, and Bridge; one of the solos being sung by H.H. Princess Hellan Singh, expressly to show that native ears and voices could accommodate themselves to Western music.

To show how well Max Müller had preserved the rhythm and swing of the tune, we give his Sanskrit translation :—

GOD SAVE THE QUEEN.

1.

| | |
|---|---|
| Râ*gñ*îm prasâdinîm | The Queen, the gracious, |
| Lokapra*n*âdinîm | World-renowned, |
| Pâhî*s*vara | Save, O Lord! |
| Lakshonîprabhâsinîm | In victory brilliant, |
| *S*atrûprahâsinîm | At enemies smiling, |
| Tâ*m* dîrgha*s*âsinîm | Her, long ruling, |
| Pâhî*s*vara | Save, O Lord! |

2.

| | |
|---|---|
| Ehy asmadî*s*vara | Approach, O our Lord, |
| *S*atrûn pratiskira | Enemies scatter, |
| U*kkh*inddhi tân | Make them fall! |
| Ta*kkh*adma nâ*s*aya | Their fraud confound, |
| Mâyâ*sk*a pâ*s*aya | Tricks restrain, |
| Pâhy asmadâ*s*raya | Protect, O thou, our refuge, |
| Sarvâ*ñ* *g*anân | All people! |

3.

| | |
|---|---|
| Tvadratnabhûshitâm | With thy choice gifts adorned, |
| Râ*g*ye *k*iroshitâm | In the kingdom long-dwelling, |
| Pâhî*s*vara | Save, O Lord, |
| Râ*g*yaprapâlinîm | Her, the realm-protecting, |
| Saddharma-*s*âlinîm | By good laws abiding, |
| Tâ*m* stotramâlinîm | Her, with praises wreathed, |
| Pâhî*s*vara. | Save, O Lord! |

The following flattering review of Max Müller's translation appeared in an Indian paper the following year:—

'Professor Max Müller's love of poetry has led him to attempt a Sanskrit translation of "God Save the Queen." For Sanskrit the rendering strikes us as being exceedingly simple and felicitous, though it is not full. Even if the author had not appended his name to the verses, they could only have been ascribed to a poet as well as a scholar possessed of keen musical instincts. The translation, as a whole, is faithful without being servile. Max Müller has brought out the spirit of the Anthem more than its words, and yet its tune or tone approaches the original quite as much as the spirit. Most of the Sanskrit words are exact equivalents of the English, and what is more, some of these are classical Sanskrit taken bodily from the sacred literature of India! No reader of taste can help doing homage to the intellect which can grapple with the knottiest points of grammar, and yet find time to court the most timid of the graces.'

It was always a keen satisfaction to Max Müller, and repaid him for much hard labour, when he heard that his work was appreciated and of real use in India. Such a gratification came to him this year at the Inaugural Convocation of the Punjab University at Lahore, at which the Viceroy, Lord Ripon, was present. In his speech on that occasion Lord Ripon said:—

'I have been very much struck within the last few weeks by reading a remarkable paper, written by one who has a right to speak about Oriental literature: I allude to an article in a late number of the *Contemporary Review* by Professor Max Müller. If I were to speak of Indian Literature, Indian Philosophy, and Indian Science in the language in which Professor Max Müller speaks of them in that essay, doubtless I should be accused of exaggeration and partiality; but no man can bring any such charges against that learned person, who knows better than most people what he is talking about on this matter, and I com-mend to all those who have any doubt about the solidity of Oriental learning and the lessons it has to teach, not to India and to Orientals alone, but to Europeans also, to study the short essay to which I have adverted (cheers). Gentlemen, I thought it worth while just to put down a few words which Professor Max Müller employed in that article in reference to the study of Sanskrit. What does he say? He says: "The study of Sanskrit will open before you"—he was especially addressing young students about to come out to India in the Civil Service—"larger layers of literature, as yet almost unknown and unexplored, and allow you an insight into strata of thought, deeper than any you have known before, and rich in lessons that appeal to the deepest sympathies of the human heart." Gentlemen, I need no other proof of the soundness of the policy pursued in the foundation of this University than is contained in these words of the great Oxford Professor.'

The Viceroy's speech was commented on by most of the Indian papers, from one of which comes the following extract:—

'It is now about nine weeks since we briefly noticed Professor Max Müller's Cambridge Lectures sent us in advance proofs. What we then said has been said again by the *Times of India* this week, said with more clearness and cogency, and to much better purpose. The time is coming for a real, living union between the West and the East, and Max Müller, if his valuable life lasts him, may live to be the officiating high-priest!

'Lord Ripon's reference at Lahore to the value of Max Müller's work is of peculiar importance, not indeed because proceeding from the Viceroy of India, but because it is the deliberate utterance of a scholar and statesman who has thought deeply for himself, and who has acted up to his convictions as few Englishmen of the age have dared to act. There is not a common platform of thought between Professor Max Müller and the Marquis of Ripon; but one of these representatives of different schools is ready to recognize what is best in the public character of the other. It is only when we look for this spirit in India and find it not, that we fully realize the gulf between the intellectual status of Europe and of India. But, as we said above, those who are labouring to fill the gulf have no reason to despair.'

To Professor Noiré.

*Translation.* Oxford, *November* 19, 1882.

'Two books are finished, the third I am still working at. I have had much to disturb me. . . . Family cares are cares of which you know nothing; all that leaves you much freer. One of my Japanese pupils has returned to Japan. Three other Japanese are on their way here, one has arrived already; they all want to learn Sanskrit. Will that seed sprout some day? However, it gives me an insight into human nature, which it is not always easy to obtain. They are the orbits of small planets, but very perfect in their own sphere. I am publishing a large book with one of the Japanese, a full catalogue of the Buddhistic Bible, as they read it in China and Japan. It will be ready this year. I hear so little of Kant here now. The philosophers in England are against him—he does not suit them. However, that cannot be helped, they will have to hear of him. The difficulty lies with the public—if that is lazy, as it is here, how can one expect that they will read Kant? They read Mill and Spencer; that is less weighty and is also called philosophy. Well, we must not expect the impossible. Times get more and more shallow, I do not quite know why.'

### To Lady Welby.

*December* 13.

'Your note is quite right, only instead of saying that *holy* is the same word as *whole* and *hale*, it would be more accurate to say that they are closely connected or derived from the same source.

'Heiland is the Old Saxon Heljand, i.e. the Heal-ing or Healer, he who makes whole, for to *heal* also is derived from the same root.

'Your lines about Shadow and Substance remind me of Plato's parable of the Cave. Do you know it?'

### To Klaus Groth.

*Translation.* *December* 17.

'My dear old Friend,—By chance the *Gegenwart* came into my hands, and with it your last poem, "Min Port." I know your port, and I know how much of what is good and beautiful goes in and out there, and it brought back to me the remembrance of all the beautiful days at Düsternbrook. Well, the past is not passed; it belongs to us more than the present, we feed on it as long as we live—past happiness and past woe. We have just now lived through sad memories again; perhaps we may in time be able to bear it better, but the burden is very heavy still.

'My children have grown up; my boy is fifteen and a half, and bigger than I. He thrives well, and the two girls give me much pleasure; my wife is well, and I—well, I get old and have still much to do, work that will never be finished, others will do it better.

'And how are you and yours? Are there still any old friends left who remember us? What a happy time that was, no discord whatever!

Yes, that is what life would be, if only human beings would let it be. Well, give our love to all, and any who may remember the birds of passage—they are no more as swift as they were, but nevertheless they would dearly like to fly over the sea once more.

'New courage for the New Year; and a Happy Christmas, including the memories of past ones. Ever your faithful.'

# CHAPTER XXVI

## 1883

Death of mother. Stay at Dessau. The McCalls. Summer amusements. Bristol. The Wye. Ilbert Bill. Duffryn. Ramabai. Daughter's marriage.

THE New Year opened on Max Müller and his family quietly at home. It was a year of less incessant literary labour, little being worked at except the *Sacred Books of the East.*

To MONCURE CONWAY, ESQ.

OXFORD, *January* 5.

'I do not like the expression, the Bibles of the World; and I believe I have never used the word Bible except with reference to the books of the Old and New Testament. It sounds to me conceited. We might as well speak of the Vedas, or the Korans of the World. However, I know it is a favourite expression, and has now become so common that it will be difficult to suppress it. I saw the other day that some Buddhists in Japan meant to start what they call a "Bible Society" for printing and distributing portions of the *Tripitaka.* I prefer to speak of "Sacred Books." Strictly speaking, "Sacred Books" are such only as have received some canonical sanction, and form a body of writings to which nothing could be added. They need not be considered of Divine origin or revealed, but they must have been formally recognized as authoritative by a religious body or their representatives. However, you know well that there are many books *sacred* which are not *canonical*, and it was in order not to exclude them from my series that I prefer the title *Sacred Books of the East.* My first series of twenty-four volumes is almost finished; my second series of twenty-four volumes more than filled, and there will be work for many more series after we are gone.

'With best wishes for the New Year.'

TO DR. PROWE.

*Translation.* 7, NORHAM GARDENS, OXFORD, *January* 8, 1883.

'Your letter and your good wishes for the New Year have given me great pleasure; they reminded me of old times, which hardly seem to belong to us any more. How long the ways of life seemed then that lay before us, how short it seems now! Well, we will march on till we hear the call—Halt! What we cannot finish here, others that come after us will do better. I rejoice to hear that your *Copernicus* will soon be completed. I think it will be appreciated in England.

'I have just undertaken a new series of *Sacred Books of the East*, that will remain as a foundation for coming generations.

'I have also completed a volume of Lectures at Cambridge: *India—What can it teach us?* This, I think, will cause much discussion, for I have attributed the whole Sanskrit literature, with the exception of the Vedic, to the year 400 A.D.; for me they are just as interesting at this later date as at the earlier one, but it will be a severe blow to the old Indian pedants!

'We were all very well last year. I felt up to a great deal of work, so that I remained here during all the vacation. My old mother is young in mind, though her body is feeble from great age. I hope to go to Dessau this year and stay there for some time; but it becomes more and more difficult to disentangle oneself from all the threads here.

'Our best congratulations on the engagement of your daughter. The separation is sure to be hard, but, though far from each other, one can remain united in spirit.

'And so, with good luck for the New Year, I am always your old faithful.'

In sending the two following letters to the editor, Mr. Verney wrote: 'Here are two old letters from your dear husband, very characteristic, chiefly because of their kindness, but also from other points of view. The receipt of these letters was a turning-point in my life, and has directed it into the channel of my last seventeen years' work. Constantly I feel the gap which his absence leaves in all sorts of ways. . . . He was one of those men whose personality was the chief influence in his life—even greater, I think, than all his many achievements combined. The combination of young sympathy with mature and masterly work, was never more perfectly shown than in him. This is what gave him his personal influence over others.'

To F. Verney, Esq.

Oxford, *January* 16, 1883.

'My dear Verney,—The Siamese Minister, Prince Prisdang, wishes for an English secretary, adviser, guide, bear-leader, or whatever else you like to call it. He must be a man of business, man of the world, of good family and all that. Lastly, he must be able to speak and write French. The salary is, to begin with, £800 a year. I do not know whether you still find the law a Pool of Bethesda, and would think of applying for such an appointment. It has its interesting sides, for the King of Siam and his two brothers are men of intelligence. One of them is working hard at Oxford. Please send me a line to say what you think of it, and how Mrs. Verney would like it. Kindest messages from all of us, and *do* pay us another visit here, if you can, if only for a Sunday.'

To the Same.

*February* 26.

'I am quite delighted to know that you consider the Siamese scheme likely to succeed. Nothing is so difficult as to find an Englishman who will treat an Oriental as an equal, as a gentleman; if you can do that, you will be surprised what good material there is in them. I may have been fortunate with Orientals, or it may be due to my having always treated them with respect and confidence, but I can honestly say that I have learned to respect and to love several of them. One thing I feel certain about, and that is, that they delight in being trusted, and you as a lawyer know what I mean—that it requires two people to speak the truth. Please come to us, when you can see the young Prince here. I like what I see of him, but I think he wants a freer and larger atmosphere to develop in; he sees very little of Oxford, and wants encouragement. He seems to me to come from a good stock. Kindest messages from all of us.'

To the Right Hon. W. E. Gladstone.

7, Norham Gardens, *January* 18.

'Dear Mr. Gladstone,—I am afraid I am taking a very great liberty in sending you my last book on India. I must confess I have long wished for an opportunity of engaging your interest in behalf of India; I do not mean the mere surface India, with its grotesque religion, its pretty poetry, and its fabulous antiquity, but the real India that is only slowly emerging before our eyes; a whole, almost forgotten act in the great drama of humanity, very different from Greece, from Rome, from modern Europe, and yet not so different that in studying it we cannot feel that *mutato nomine de nobis fabula narratur*. The discovery of that real India, of that new intellectual hemisphere, is to my mind a far greater discovery than that of Vasco de Gama's. It was a misfortune that all the early publications of Sanskrit texts belonged really to the Renaissance of Sanskrit literature. Kâlidâsa's plays, which were supposed to be contemporaneous with Virgil, belong to the sixth century; the Laws of Manu, which Sir William Jones placed 1280 B.C., cannot be older than 300 A.D. But there was an older literature in India, the Vedic and the Buddhistic, which are only now being slowly disinterred, and it is there that we can watch a real growth from the simplest beginnings to the highest concepts which the human mind is capable of, it is there that we can learn what man is, by seeing once more what man has been. As a very old admirer of yours, I should be glad if I could make you look at the work which Sanskrit scholars have lately been doing; but this is only one of many wishes, the fulfilment one may desire, but one hardly expects. In fact, I should not have ventured to say even so much, if I did not know that you have only to put my book aside, and may feel assured that I am not so unreasonable as to expect even a line of acknowledgement from your secretary. The one thing which every one in England wishes for you, is rest, well-earned rest; and asking your pardon for even this short interruption, I remain, with sincere respect,

'Your very old admirer.'

### To Rev. G. Cox.

7, Norham Gardens, Oxford, *February* 13, 1883.

'I have been wanting to write to you from day to day, but from day to day I could not find one quiet hour for a quiet letter, and even now I know I shall be interrupted before I have said half of what I wish to say.

'I am glad that you have looked at my last book. I have tried to make it more complete than my former books, for it may be the last that I can write on that subject. I knew from former conversations that you did not see the true object of the Âtman or Self, and I confess it is difficult to describe it. The beauty of the Hindu system seems to me to lie in this, that it does not anticipate the Âtman, but allows in perfect honesty various stages or *âsramas* leading to it. You remember that fine passage: "All those who worship idols, worship me." The doctrine of the Âtman does not condemn religious mythology; it says, by all means call it Heaven, or Cause, or Father, or Judge—it is all that, but it is more. So you yourself, you are a child, a boy, a man, a woman, a father, a mother, an Englishman, a clergyman, a Christian; wise or foolish, good or bad; but all this has come, has begun, will change, and you are something else, something higher —what? the Self, the Spectator, the Witness, he who could look on while he seemed to be a son or a father, nay, who could see his Self in his fatherhood and childhood, but know himself distinct from all these phases. A man need not go into a cave, because he has found his true Self; he may live and act like everybody else; he is *gîvan-mukta* —"living, but free." All remains just the same, except the sense of unchangeable, imperishable self which lifts him above the phenomenal self. He knows he is wearing clothes, that is all. If a man does not see it, if some of his clothes stick to him like his very skin, if he fears that he might lose his identity by not being a male instead of a female, by not being English instead of German, by not being a child instead of a man, he must wait and work on. Good works lead to quietness of mind, and quietness of mind to true self-knowledge. Is it so very little to be only Self—to be the subject that can resist, i. e. perceive the whole universe, and turn it into his object? Can we wish for more than what we are, lookers-on—resisting what tries to crush us, call it force, or evil, or anything else?

'Well, this is about what an educated Hindu would say, who believed in the *Vedânta*, the end of the *Veda*; but if he heard you say that there is a Father who knows, a Ruler who rules, a Judge who will vindicate righteousness, he would say, Certainly, but there is more, there is a higher concept for all this. Mythology, religion, philosophy, all these are not illusions; they are stages, and right stages, as much as youth and spring are stages to manhood. We all mean the same, but we express it differently, and we are separated by such long periods of growth, that when a Japanese Buddhist speaks to me I cannot understand him, unless I go back for ages, begin with his beginnings, learn his language, i.e. the history of his thoughts. And now I must go to attend Henry Smith's funeral. Much of what he was, or seemed to be, will be hidden in the churchyard; his work will work on, for nothing can be lost; his Self, his Âtman, that is where it always was, before it was incarnate on this atom of a planet, but where mythology ends, language ends, and all we can do is to be silent and to trust.'

The following letter from one of Max Müller's most earnest admirers and friends in India is interesting, as showing the extraordinary memories possessed even to this day by natives of India. It was a point on which Max Müller often dwelt; but his statements occasionally seemed to some of his hearers as if they must be exaggerated. Here we have the same statements at first hand:—

FROM SHANKAR PANDURANG PANDIT.

BOMBAY, *February* 28, 1883.

'Mr. Kane has kindly agreed to take the enclosed photograph to you from me. You will perhaps not recognize me sitting on a chair with a volume of your *editio princeps* of the *Rig-veda*. The most important figure in the group is the blind man who is sitting in front of me, on a stool covered with a panther skin. He was left blind—entirely blind—by a fell attack of small-pox when he was an infant. He is now about thirty-six years old, and lives with and on the kindness and bounty of his brother, a distinguished member of the Bombay Uncovenanted Civil Service. Blind Kesavabhatta, you will be interested to hear, is a most excellent Vaidik. He knows by heart the *whole* of the *Rig-veda Samhitâ*, the *whole* of the *Aitareya Brâhmana*, the *whole* of Pânini's *Ashtâdhyâyî*, and the rest of the *Dasa Granthas*. He can repeat from beginning to end not only the *Samhitâ* text, but also the *Pada-pâtha* and the *Krama-pâtha* too. I have often examined him with your editions of the *Samhitâ* and *Pada* texts in my hands, and found him perfectly accurate in his recitations. He never requires any help to refresh his memory, but is always ready to begin wherever you like. You might tell him to begin at such and such chapter, giving him simply the numerical reference to the passage, and he will at once commence to recite from the passage you have before you in your book. No accent, no letter, no pause, no sound is misplaced, everything is recited in the most correct method. How do you think he managed to master the enormous quantity he can repeat backwards and forwards? His father devised an ingenious plan to educate him. He employed a Vaidik to teach him. He also kept a poor Brahman boy, who was brought up along with Kesavabhatta, and who, after the Vaidik Guru had given his lessons daily, sat down with his manuscript of the *Veda* to learn by heart the same with his blind companion. The latter thus learnt by rote whatever the Guru taught, and whatever his companion read out to him. After about twelve or thirteen years Kesavabhatta became the perfect Vaidik that he now is, and is in his turn a Vaidik teacher! Yours truly,

'SHANKAR PANDURANG PANDIT.'

The following letter was written by Max Müller in reply to a letter from an American clergyman asking his name and influence in aid of the clergyman's efforts to promote Catholicity among all the religions of the world. The letter was read at a 'World's Congress of Religions' held soon after in New York, and which was the forerunner of the far larger 'Parliament' held at Chicago in 1893.

TO THE REV. M. K. SCHERMERHORN.

OXFORD, *March* 6, 1883.

'It is always a great satisfaction to see the budding germs of the seed which one has helped to sow. I wish you all success in your endeavours after a religion of humanity, but success, to be solid, must not be too rapid. The true religion of the future will be the fulfilment of all the religions of the past—the true religion of humanity, that which, in the struggle of history, remains as the indestructible portion of all the so-called false religions of mankind. There never was a false god, nor was there ever really a false religion, unless you call a child a false man. All religions, so far as I know them, had the same purpose; all were links in a chain which connects heaven and earth, and which is held, and always was held, by one and the same hand. All here on earth tends toward right, and truth, and perfection; nothing here on earth can ever be quite right, quite true, quite perfect, not even Christianity—or what is now called Christianity—so long as it excludes all other religions, instead of loving and embracing what is good in each. Nothing, to my mind, can be sadder than reading the Sacred Books of mankind, and yet nothing more encouraging. They are full of rubbish; but among that rubbish there are old stones which the builders of the true Temple of Humanity will not reject—must not reject, if their Temple is to hold all who worship God in spirit, in truth, and in life.'

In this spring Max Müller had the satisfaction of seeing an important work, prepared by his Buddhist pupil Bunyiu Nanjio, published by the University Press at Oxford. It was a catalogue of the Chinese translation of the Buddhist *Tripitaka*, the immense literature which forms the Sacred Canon of the Buddhists in China and Japan, generally called the Northern Buddhists; and later in the year he himself, in collaboration with Mr. Nanjio, brought out in the *Anecdota Oxoniensia* the *Sukhâvatî-Vyûha*, the description of the Land of Bliss.

This year saw the beginning of an acquaintance which soon ripened into intimate friendship with an American family, who came to Oxford and brought introductions to the Max Müllers from Mr. Lowell, at that time American Minister in London. 'They are just such countrywomen as I like to introduce to my English friends,' he wrote. Mrs. McCall and her two daughters spent the whole summer in Oxford, and were joined in the course of it by American friends of their own. For months the McCalls and Max Müllers met daily, and the pleasant, lively intercourse was a special enjoyment to Max Müller, and aided him in recovering from the heavy blow that fell on him in April, a blow which for years he had anticipated with dread.

Early in April, whilst staying at Hastings with his wife and son, he heard of the alarming illness of his old mother, followed immediately by a telegram announcing her death. He started directly for Dessau, and being this year in stronger health, he was not prostrated by grief, as he had been at the time of his sister's death, and those who loved and watched over him could see him go without real anxiety. He arrived in time to see her loved face once more, and, surrounded by every member left of a once large family, he laid her to rest in the vault where his father had been laid fifty-five and a half years previously.

To his Daughter Mary.

Dessau, *April* 18.

'I wish you had been able to see your dear grandmother once more, if only as I saw her, sleeping on flowers, covered with palm-branches, taking with her some faded tokens of her early happiness, unchanged, calm and beautiful. All that is of the earth is then forgotten, all the little failings inherent in human nature vanish from our minds; we only see what was good, unselfish, and loving in that soul, and we think with regret of how much more we might have done to requite that love. How different life might be, if in our daily intercourse and conversation we thought of our friends as lying before us on that last bed of flowers; how differently we should then judge, and how differently we should act. It is curious how forgetful we are of death, how little we think that we are dying daily, and that what we call life is really death, and death the beginning of a higher life. Such a thought should not make our life less bright, but rather more—it should make us feel how unimportant so many things are which we consider all-important: how much we could bear which we think unbearable, if only we thought that to-morrow, either we ourselves or our friends may be taken away, at least for a time. Even you, in your great happiness just now [1], should think of death, should feel that what you call your own is only lent to you, and that all that remains as a real

[1] She was just engaged to be married.

comfort is the good work done in this short journey, the true unselfish love shown to those whom God has given us, has placed near to us, not without a high purpose. Love, which seems so unselfish, may become very selfish, if we are not on our guard. Do not shut your eyes to what is dark in others, but do not dwell on it except so far as it helps to bring out more strongly what is bright in them, lovely and unselfish. The true happiness of true love is self-forgetfulness and trust. I have only a little space left to tell you that a father's and a mother's love is always ready for a child, and that it grows with every year, as I know that my dear mother's love did for me, though I did not always deserve it.'

To his Daughter Beatrice.

Dessau, *April* 23, 1883.

'My dear Beatrice,—I knew that you would feel the death of your dear grandmother, for though you had not seen her often, and could not know much of her, you knew how fond she was of you. We are meant to live in three generations—grandparents, parents, and children; they have each their own purpose, and whensoever we lose one of them we feel that our life is changed.

'As long as my mother lived, I felt that I belonged to her; now I belong to no one, though others belong to me. You have no idea what a rich life hers has been, rich in joys, rich in sorrows, and rich in love and sympathy for others. In her very last letter to me she was full of interest as to your singing. She always hoped you would have a voice like hers. When she was your age she sang at some of the great musical festivals, admired by the best judges. Singing lessons were then paid four *groschen* a lesson—about sixpence, and yet people sang quite as well as now. I am glad to be able to stay here; it does me a great deal of good to be quite alone, and here in my dear mother's old rooms I am surrounded by many memories. It is quite extraordinary to see a number of things which I knew when I was ten years old, just the same now—not chipped or broken, looking almost new, and yet they have travelled from place to place, from Dessau to Leipzig, Chemnitz, Dresden, and back to Dessau. I know how unhappy she was when any accident happened to anything that reminded her of former days. Every letter that I ever wrote to her she had carefully kept. There is nothing in life like a mother's love, though children often do not find it out till it is too late. If you want to be really happy in life, love your mother with all your heart; it is a blessing to feel that you belong to her, and that through her you are connected by an unbroken chain with the highest Source of our being.

'Ever your loving Father.'

The following letter, about the duties of a young Oxford tutor, may be read with interest:—

DESSAU, *May* 12.

'There is plenty of work for a young Oxford tutor to do, and plenty of leisure. Most College duties are such that a man who has taken a First Class requires no further preparation. In giving lectures of a higher character a young man ought not to act simply as a teacher, but as a fellow student. Nothing is more useful to his pupils. But a man ought to reserve some hours every day for really hard work, in order to be able to take a position of his own in the University by-and-by. If he is only to think of making money, he will stunt the whole growth of his mind, and will suffer for it later in life. The career of a scholar is different from that of a lawyer. A scholar cannot lay himself out to make money; if he does, he simply ruins his chances of success. He must be able to work on quietly for years, if he is to achieve anything in the end.'

TO MR. NANJIO.

DESSAU, *April* 12.

'MY DEAR FRIEND,—I thank you for your letter, which I received this morning. I have passed through very sad days; though my dear mother had had a long life (she was eighty-three), yet parting with a mother is one of the saddest events in our life. *We* allow our affections to grow much stronger than *you* do; hence we suffer more, no doubt, but we also enjoy more. It is difficult to give up what we love very much, but "it is better to have loved and lost, than never to have loved at all"! Now that the sharpest pain is over, I settle down here to my work; I have many things to arrange before I can leave this place. I cannot make any plans yet, but as far as I can see, I shall stay here till the middle of June, till term is over, and even then it is very doubtful whether I shall return to Oxford. I am very sorry for this, for there are several books I wanted you to read with me before you return to Japan, particularly the *Yoga* and *Sânkhya Sûtras*, which throw much light on the history of Buddhism. That cannot be now, unless you stay till the end of the year, so that we might meet again and begin work in October. If you like to come to this small quiet town, you could live here and work, and life is not dear here. But perhaps it would be better for you to copy some more MSS. at Paris. Perhaps it is best not to make any plans for the present: in a week or two I shall know better what to do and what to advise; I still feel rather tired and confused.

'I received your proof-sheets to-day, and shall look at them carefully and send them back to you ordered for press.'

TO HORATIO HALE, ESQ.

DESSAU, GERMANY, *April* 12, 1883.

'MY DEAR SIR,—I have to thank you for your kind and considerate letter. I saw at once that —— had failed to understand what I meant, though he himself ought to have been the first to see it. In Greek and Latin we work under the eyes of a large Vigilance Committee; in Mohawk, &c., we must be our own Vigilance Committee. The same applies even to Sanskrit—many things would be impossible in Sanskrit scholarship if we had a strong and well-supported public opinion, as we have for classical studies. However, if your friend sees what is meant, no harm is done: but I have often wondered how it is that, in his capacity of a scholar, a man will often allow himself to say and write things from which, in his capacity as a gentleman, he would shrink instinctively. I am glad to hear of your projects. I feel sure that there is no time to be lost in securing the floating fragments of the great shipwreck of the American languages. When you have stirred up a national interest in it for the North of America, you should try to form a committee for the South. The Emperor of Brazil would be sure to help, provided the work is done by *real scholars*. I had some material lately sent me of a Terra del Fuegian Grammar, which I handed over to Professor Grube, who has just published it in the *Göttinger Gelehrte Anzeigen*. I am just finishing an edition of the *Sukhâvatî-Vyûha*, a description of the Buddhist Paradise, which forms the Bible of the so-called "Pure Land Sect," which counts over ten millions of believers in Japan alone. There are twelve Chinese translations of it, all wrong. They will now have to wait a little longer in Japan for their Revised Version. Yours very truly.'

From Dessau Max Müller went for a day to Dresden. All the old grief of six years before seemed to return. He writes to his wife:—

'I went straight to the Kirchhof. It is the old feeling still. My whole life seemed to me intelligible, but when this blow came, I could not master it, nor can I now. We may still say that all is ordered by Love and Wisdom, but one feels it is a Love and Wisdom which we cannot approach, and *that* has shaken all my old ideas of life. One feels helpless, one cannot even guess. We may understand it all hereafter, yet life is something different from what we thought it was. How different with mother. How natural all seems to be. How well ordained that she should be taken away before the sufferings of extreme old age set in. How willing she was to go, and yet how she enjoyed life to the very last. But dear Ada!—'

We get in the next letter the first idea of a monument to Wilhelm Müller, an idea carried out with such great success eight years later.

To Klaus Groth.

*Translation.* Dessau, *April* 19.

'At present I must quietly stay here, and in a week's time I expect my wife. Should you pass here or near us, on your way to Italy, I should certainly try to see you once more in this life. Now a question in confidence. It has been mentioned to me once or twice, that Dessau is thinking of putting up a monument to my father. Do you think it likely that, even now, subscriptions could still be collected for it in Germany? Do you know how much money is required for a statue? And where can we find the fitting persons for a committee? Could I, as his son, take part in it? Nothing has been done so far, and I should like to ask advice from experts in this matter before anything is done. Would you ask Stockhausen, or Brahms, or who else? Of course there is no hurry.'

To M. Renan.

Dessau, *April* 21.

'I was called away from Oxford by the death of my mother, eighty-three years of age when she died, but as full of life and love as a young girl of eighteen. We have all to pay this debt of deep sorrow for what has been to all of us the greatest happiness in life; but whenever the time comes, the whole of our life seems changed once more, and we know what the next step must be. Another great trial is over, and we must now prepare for the last. If I had not left home at a moment's notice, I should have written to you before, to explain why my last three volumes of my *Sacred Books of the East* were sent to you, with a request to send them to the Académie des Inscriptions. The first series of twenty-four volumes is nearly finished, and when I proposed the second series, *mes amis les ennemis* did all they could to prevent it. They have not succeeded, and the second series will appear, but I shall be glad of an authoritative voice like yours to tell the English public the real purpose of this undertaking. Most of my English critics say "Les Bibles de l'humanité ne sont pas amusantes." Certainly not! they are not amusing; on the contrary, they are the very saddest books to read. But they must be read, they must be meditated on, if we want to know what kind of creature *homo sapiens* is. These Bibles were considered by him as the best he could produce as superhuman and Divine; let that be one lesson. But there is another, and a more cheerful lesson; amid all this *scoria* there are the small grains of gold—be good, be true, be patient, trust—the same everywhere, in the highest and the lowest religions, and these grains are the *quod semper, quod ubique, quod ab omnibus*, which will form the eternal religion of the world. These *Sacred Books of the East* will become in future the foundation of a short but universal religion, they will remain the most instructive archives of the past, studied or consulted when thousands of books of the day are forgotten, and yet my wise friends say *ce n'est pas amusant!* It reflects great credit on the University Press at Oxford, and the Secretary of State for India, that they have not allowed themselves to be frightened by this vulgar clamour; and a few words from you, addressed to the Académie des Inscriptions, on presenting the last three volumes, would be a great help to them and to me. So if you could find time for saying a few weighty words, I should feel truly grateful.'

His wife joined him at Dessau for the month of May, and they had a quiet happy time, living in the mother's old rooms. It was an early season, and the parks and public gardens round Dessau were in their full spring beauty, and the nightingales sang day and night, with a richness of voice hardly ever heard in England.

To Mr. Nanjio.

Dessau, *May* 23.

'I hope you received the *Pall Mall Gazette* with a notice of your Catalogue. I trust I shall find the photograph of the palm-leaf on my return to Oxford. We shall then have it photo-lithographed, and publish it with the other small texts and inscriptions.

'As to a commentary on the Bible, I shall tell you when I return. It is by far the best to read the New Testament without any commentary. It was sent into the world *without* a commentary; it did all the good it could do *without* a commentary; and all the mischief has been done by the commentaries. Therefore I advise you to read the New Testament as it stands, and if you have any difficulties, make a note of them, and I will explain them to you. It is different with the Old Testament. That book requires notes to explain historical difficulties—but read the New Testament first.'

To his Wife.

Dessau, *May*, 1883.

'It is a great change when one loses one's oldest friends; the whole flow of our thoughts has to turn in a new direction, and yet always turns to the old places, and finds they are no longer there. That makes us feel tired and heavy, and there is this constant undercurrent of disappointment, of looking for something which is no more, which does not fall in well with the ordinary current of life. And what a marvel life seems to be, the older we grow! So far from becoming more intelligible, it becomes a greater wonder every day. One stands amazed, and everything seems so small, and the little one can do so very small. One ought not to brood too much, when there is no chance of light, and yet how natural it is that one should brood over life and death, rather than on the little things of life.'

To the Same.

Dessau, *June* 9, 1883.

'It is very sad to break up an old household, and my mind is filled with memories of days long gone by. These sorrows of life are inevitable, but they are hard to bear, for all that. They would be harder still if we did not see their purpose of reminding us that our true life is not here, but that we are here on a voyage that may be calm or stormy, and which is to teach us what all sailors have to learn—courage, perseverance, kindness, and in the end complete trust in a Higher Power.'

To the Same.

Dessau, *June.*

'I shall be glad when I can pack up now and go home. It has been a help to me, living in these rooms and thinking of old times, and of all the love that my mother had for me. Hers had been a very hard life, opening very brightly, and then darkened by early widowhood, deafness, poverty, and many anxieties. Yet she enjoyed her life, and her love and sympathy for others made her forget the burden she had to bear. She had earned her rest. The vault has now been rearranged, the stone put in, the ivy replanted, and so it will remain. I had a very nice letter from Mr. Sahl, the Queen's German Secretary, telling me how much the Queen had felt for me, when she heard of my mother's death.'

Max Müller returned to Oxford by Mainz to see his friend Professor Noiré, and Neuwied, where he stayed at Segenhaus with the Princess Mother to meet the Queen of Roumania.

To his Wife.

Segenhaus, *June*, 1883.

'This place is most charming, the surrounding country perfect, and the people most delightful. There is the old loving Princess Mother, strong and kind and serene. Then there is dear Roggenbach, healthy, true, straightforward. Then the Queen, who has grown immensely —far more than I had any idea of. She has a quite exceptional power of thought and poetry, and will do something really great. She is sometimes quite possessed, yet with all that so womanly, so good, so kind-hearted, that it is a treat to be with her. Alessandri, the Roumanian poet, is very pleasant. Close to Segenhaus is the old Schloss Monrepos, where the Prince resides with his wife, very clever. We dined there to-day in great style, and afterwards had music and reading. They lead an ideal life—all seem so good and kind.'

The 'ideal life' at Segenhaus had a great charm for Max Müller. After breakfast the party separated till early dinner, after which came long walks or drives in the lovely forests, generally with the Prince of Wied in a large brake with six horses. The Prince is an expert whip, but Max Müller occasionally found the pace at which they tore up and down the hills a little trying to the nerves. After supper there was music, reading aloud, and brilliant conversation the whole evening. The quiet mornings were spent by most members of the party in preparation for these delightful evenings. Alessandri would appear with a new poem, the Queen with a new poem or tale, or some song which a Swedish composer, one of the party, had set to music during the afternoon, and which one of the ladies-in-waiting would sing; while the Princess Mother sat by, joining in the talk with her musical voice, and serene expression of face, and deep power of sympathy that seemed to lift those who were privileged to know her into a higher atmosphere, above the common cares and interests of life. The Princess Mother had known deep sorrow, but she had 'the heart at leisure from itself, to soothe and sympathize,' and there are many who owe their physical and moral health to her care and influence. She passed away in March, 1902, after a long illness, and those who had had the privilege of her friendship could only thank God, who had taken His saint to the eternal home, where her heart had long dwelt.

We have spoken of Max Müller's translation into Sanskrit of 'God save the Queen'; on his return to Oxford he received a flattering review of his translation from India.

The Long Vacation was spent in Oxford, and, thanks to their friends the McCalls, was one of the brightest and pleasantest the Max Müllers ever spent, and Max Müller was the centre of all the enjoyment of the time. The following letter from a partaker in the happy social life at 7, Norham Gardens most aptly describes it all:—

HARROW, *April* 26, 1902.

'DEAR MRS. MAX MÜLLER,—I would I could transcribe some of the memories your letter evokes. Golden afternoons on the Cherwell, excursions by road and rail, evenings of music and "candy-pulling": in all these the Professor was our comrade.

'At the time of which I am thinking, some twenty years ago, there was in Oxford a group of young folks who regarded your house as their centre. I know nothing either of the beginning or the end of this little coterie; it was in existence before my time, and continued after I had left Oxford. True, the members changed as residents moved away and generations of undergraduates passed, but its corporate life continued unimpaired, and in all the light-hearted frolic of that rout of young people of both sexes, the Professor took a part.

'Once induce him to quit his books, and he became one of us. How sadly we used to interrupt his work by some of those water-parties, for which he used to set out with an air of resignation and some few groans over a wasted afternoon; then, as the distance between himself and his study increased, his expression would change from resignation to contentment, until when comfortably established in the stern of a boat (for he had a strong objection to toiling at the oar) he would at length assimilate himself with his surroundings and be as frivolous as any of us.

'On such occasions, when sure of his company, he would let himself go in fine flights of nonsense: but these things cannot be written down; enough to say that we were all young—and so was he.

'It was the Professor who showed us how to convert a water-lily into a chibouk by removing part of the yellow centre of the flower and filling it with tobacco which can be smoked through the stem. It works well, but the smoke has, as he remarked, "a botanical flavour." I have never met any one else who knew of this water-party trick.

'Music was a matter of course, in drawing-room, boat, or third-class compartment. Where no accompaniment could be had, we could always raise a glee or German student-song and chorus. In the latter the Professor was our leader and coach, as befitted one who had edited a *Kommers-Buch*.

'Of his musical talent and taste I need say nothing, except that he was a charming accompanist, but an uncompromising critic and a rigorous opponent of trash. But he had a keen appreciation of musical nonsense, provided it were clever nonsense, not that dreary stuff labelled and sold as "comic." I well remember his sitting down at the piano to improvise a fantastic accompaniment to a foolish little ditty which had struck his fancy.

'Ah, well! those were happy days, and the memory of them has set my pen running beyond bounds. I had better stop, and sign myself,

'Yours sincerely,

'B. P. Lascelles.'

Max Müller had been intensely interested in Henry George's books, *Progress and Poverty* and *Social Problems*, and was anxious to see them published and disseminated at a cheap rate.

To Mr. Henry George.

*August* 21.

'I have sent you copies of a second cheap edition of *India—What can it teach us?* Between these they cannot sell less than 50,000 copies in a few months, mainly to people who could not have seen the book in more costly editions. I don't believe in piracy, but this is some compensation. I have spoken to —— about your works, which he expects to print in full. I am anxious to have you popularized as fully as may be, for I know you must exert a powerful and beneficial effect upon thought. To get it into the head of the average man that his race and his creed are not everything, is to melt away bigotry and prejudice and admit larger and nobler views.'

The following letter to his friend Dr. Hosäus, the Ducal Librarian at Dessau, shows that the idea of a monument to Wilhelm Müller was likely to be carried out at last:—

Oxford, *August* 20.

'I rejoice to hear that it seems as if the idea, so often started, and then again forgotten, will at last be realized, and I am indeed grateful to you for taking so warm and active an interest in the plans for carrying it out.'

Dr. Hosäus became secretary of the central committee at Dessau, and spared himself no trouble about the monument.

To Mr. Nanjio (on hearing of Kasawara's death).

Oxford, *September* 21.

'My dear Friend,—I am truly sorry for dear Kasawara, though I long expected it would end so. He might have been so useful, if he had lived. We must try to finish his work and publish at least his *Dharma-Samgraha* as a memorial.

'I hope he received my last letter; I should be so sorry if he had thought that I had forgotten him.

'I go to Bristol on Monday. My lecture will be on Thursday.'

This lecture was on Râmmohun Roy, and was delivered in the Bristol Museum on the fiftieth anniversary of the Rajah's death. It will be remembered that he was buried at Bristol in the Arno's Vale Cemetery. On his tomb are these words: 'A conscientious and steadfast believer in the Unity of the Godhead, he consecrated his life with entire devotion to the worship of the Divine Spirit alone.' As founder of the body of pure Theists in India, Max Müller had a strong feeling of reverence for Râmmohun Roy.

From Bristol Max Müller with his wife and daughters made an excursion up the Wye, and then paid a visit to his friend Lord Aberdare, whose genial and instructive society was always a pleasure to him. They had much in common in literary tastes and political opinions.

On his return to Oxford he found the letter from Lord Ripon given below by permission:—

GOVERNMENT HOUSE, SIMLA, *September* 3, 1883.

'DEAR PROFESSOR MAX MÜLLER,—I hope that you will excuse me for troubling you with a few lines to thank you very much for the able letter which you have addressed to the *Times* in reply to the Report of the Judges of the Calcutta High Court upon the so-called "Ilbert Bill," and also for the very valuable support which you have given to my policy in this country.

'I can assure you that I appreciate very highly the assistance which you have rendered to me. It is a great satisfaction to me to find that the course of policy which I am pursuing meets with your approval. I have need of all the aid which I can receive from England, for I am assailed here with a storm of bitter and unscrupulous hostility, which you, who dwell in a calmer atmosphere, can scarcely realize.

'Believe me,

'Yours faithfully,

'RIPON.'

In giving permission for the use of the above letter, Lord Ripon writes: 'I shall always appreciate most highly the support which he gave at that trying time.'

TO HIS EXCELLENCY THE GOVERNOR-GENERAL OF INDIA.

7, NORHAM GARDENS, OXFORD, *October* 11, 1883.

'It was extremely kind of your Excellency to think of writing to me to express your general approval of the letter which I had sent to the *Times* in answer to the Opinion of the Judges of the High Court of Calcutta. I was afraid the *Times* would go on quoting that Opinion as unanswerable, till people who did not take the trouble to read it would believe that it was so. And yet it contained really very little to enable any one to form an opinion on the main point, namely whether, under present circumstances, it was safe to pass the Bill, or whether it was safe to withdraw it.

'It seems strange that people should entirely forget that those who enjoy the very exceptional privilege of living in India under English rule, must be prepared to submit to certain inconveniences. As a matter of mere sentiment, most people would naturally prefer an English to a native judge. But when, after what had gone before, the extension of the jurisdiction of native judges to criminal cases had become almost a matter of course, one wonders that people should not see how delicately the marvellous structure of English rule in India is poised, and should not hold their breath in discussing measures which those who are responsible for the safety of the Indian Empire have thought it necessary to recommend. Parliament, however, has shown great tact in declining hitherto to discuss the question, and I believe we shall hear little more about it, when the Bill has once become law. I am glad to see that Sir J. Stephen, in his last article in the *Nineteenth Century*, is trying to withdraw gracefully from a false position.

'Thanking you most sincerely for your extreme kindness, I have the honour to remain, my Lord,

'Your Excellency's most obedient servant,

'F. MAX MÜLLER.'

The letter for which Lord Ripon sends his thanks had appeared in the *Times* of August 6. Max Müller ended it by quoting the 'really brave words of the Queen, uttered by Her Majesty when advised by one of the most conservative of English statesmen, the late Lord Derby':—

'And it is our further will that, so far as may be, our subjects of whatever race or creed be freely and impartially admitted to office in our service, the duties of which they may be qualified by their education, ability, and integrity to discharge. We hold ourselves bound to the natives of our Indian territories by the same obligations of duty which bind us to all our other subjects, and these obligations, by the blessing of Almighty God, we shall faithfully and conscientiously fulfil.'

To LADY WELBY.

DUFFRYN, *October* 1.

'I was glad to hear that your book[1] has found so many friends, and that you have had to publish a second edition. Accept my best thanks for your kindness in sending me a copy of it, which I shall find, I hope, on my table when I return to Oxford.

'Losing my Japanese pupil was a great loss to me in every respect. He might have done such good work. Now I feel that so much of the time I gave him is lost. He would have been a kind of submarine cable between Oxford and Tokio, and now it is snapped. With him Nirvâna had become a Paradise, an island with beautiful lakes, trees of gold and silver, steps of emerald and lapis, birds flying about and singing the praises of Buddha Amitâbha—Endless Light—who sits in the centre, while all who believe in him recline on large lotus flowers, lost in contemplation.

'You see human nature will have its way, even with Buddhists. What is most interesting is that this Buddha Amitâbha was once an ordinary mortal, and rose to his supremacy by endless lives devoted to virtue and truth. That supremacy may, in fact, be reached by everybody; only it will take a few *eternities* to reach it. There is a truly human element in all religions and in all philosophies; and it would be very strange if honest thought should not lead every one of us to the truths of Buddhism, or Platonism, or Christianity. The great delight of comparative studies is to find ourselves again in others. I keep to *Self*. The very misunderstanding of the word will often lead to its right appreciation. That appreciation is nowhere so perfect as in the *Vedânta*.'

It was in October of this year that Max Müller made the acquaintance of Pandita Ramabai, who came to stay at his house. He has given a full account of 'the truly heroic Hindu lady, in appearance small, delicate, and timid, but in reality strong and bold as a lioness,' in his *Auld Lang Syne*, Series II. Max Müller wrote to his elder daughter:—

'We had a nice visit from Ramabai, a Brâhman lady, who knows Sanskrit splendidly. She knows books as large as Homer by heart, from beginning to end; speaks Sanskrit correctly, and writes Sanskrit poetry.'

[1] *Links and Clues.*

Ramabai paid the Max Müllers a second visit before she finally left England for America, where she collected sufficient funds to enable her to start a refuge for child-widows in India. She has now 1,950 widows in her different homes. Her *Life of a High-Caste Hindu Woman* is well worth reading.

In November, on the four hundredth anniversary of Luther's birth, the University of Oxford was anxious to mark the event in some way, and the Vice-Chancellor wrote to ask Max Müller to deliver an address in the Sheldonian Theatre. He was, however, far from well just at the time, and had to decline.

To Professor Moritz Carrière.

*Translation.* 7, Norham Gardens, Oxford, *November* 25, 1883.

'My dear and honoured Friend,—It was so good of you to send me your poems; we need poetry, though when we get old we think much more of the underlying thought than of the form that expresses it. Form, words, rhymes, all help our memory, and carry a perfume with them which reminds us of old and forgotten times, but the feeding and strengthening factor is always thought. At least, so it is with me, who have read much poetry, with or without rhymes; what I am most grateful for, and always shall be, is the underlying thought.'

To Mr. Nanjio.

*November* 29.

'My dear Friend,—You may be right, but to me work is really a pleasure and recreation, and if I cannot work it makes me ill. However, I am willing to listen to the advice of my friends, and shall probably go away in the middle of December. On December 12 is my daughter's wedding, which you must see; after that I shall want some rest. I should like to go to Rome myself, but I always catch fever at Rome. You must know your own constitution, and take care of it. If we have finished the translation of the *Sukhâvatî*, take some rest. Finish the *Sanskrit Grammar*: it is easy and useful, and you can do it anywhere. I wish we had a few more students of Sanskrit for Japan. You never know your own religion, unless you study its beginnings in the original books.'

The sixth of December of this year was Max Müller's sixtieth birthday, and many of the German newspapers took notice of the day, and sent him their congratulations and best wishes, and one paper ended by describing his family life as of 'the happiest; in his house in Oxford there reigns that content, that comfort, that, in other countries unattainable, "something," which distinguishes a true English home.'

Towards the close of the year Max Müller's elder surviving daughter was married to Mr. F. C. Conybeare, Fellow and Tutor of University College. In mental power she was the most like her father of all his children, and had she remained unmarried would, no doubt, have been of great assistance to him. But it was not to be.

To Lady Welby.

'A delightful book—how little we know of the untold wealth of the world! In the eyes of the world, who is Amiel? and is he not ten times richer than Lord Overstone? And what beautiful language too—not that I care much about the setting of the jewels, but even jewels can be spoiled by bad settings. Yes, Amiel is delightful, and I have to thank you for two very pleasant evenings from ten to twelve.'

Christmas was spent by Max Müller and his diminished family at West Malvern, for change and rest. Unfortunately the weather was very bad, constant fog hid the beautiful scenery, and it was only the society of their friend Lady Mary Fielding, and the run of her charming house, that made the visit endurable.

To his Daughter Mary.

*December* 24.

'I need not wish you a happy Christmas this year, for I know you have it. Enjoy your happiness while it lasts: you know enough of life to know that sorrows will come, nay, that sorrows are good for us. The beautiful sunsets here, which we watch from our windows, would be nothing without the clouds—and so it is with our own sunset. At present you will not think so, but perhaps you will think of me twenty-five years hence, and understand then what I meant.

'Your loving Father.'

To Mr. Nanjio.

West Malvern, *December* 27.

'My dear Friend,—Your letter was forwarded to me here. I can well understand how distressed you must feel at having lost your father, and that his wish of seeing you once more in this life has remained unfulfilled. However, you must feel comforted by the thought that your father was pleased with you, and that he felt proud of having a son who had done so much good work. I hope he saw your *Catalogue*, for that would have shown him that you had made good use of your long stay in England, away from your parents and friends. This is a very imperfect and uncertain life; we make plans and try to do something really good and useful, and then all our plans are upset by illness or by death! And yet we must not feel discouraged. No good work is ever quite lost; many labourers must be content to sow, others will come to reap the harvest.

'I can quite understand your adopted father's wish to have you back in Japan, and I am not going to dissuade you from it. You have still a year before you, and we may finish some of the work we have in hand. I hope I shall feel better when I return to Oxford, which will be in about a week. The weather is very bad here. I often think of the time when you and Kasawara were staying with me here. We must try to finish Kasawara's *Dharma-Samgraha*—we owe it to him.

'I feel very strongly that, if you wish the study of Sanskrit to be re-established in Japan, you should work hard at a *Sanskrit Grammar*, and a small *Sanskrit-Japanese Dictionary*. If these are published in Japan, the study of Sanskrit will not die, even when you are gone; and I believe it will be a great benefit, if you have in Japan a few learned men, who can study the real history of Buddhism, and distinguish between what is old and what is modern.

'Accept my best wishes for the New Year, and believe that you will always have a true friend in me. Yours very truly.'

# CHAPTER XXVII

## 1884–1885

**Lectures in Birmingham and at the Royal Institution. Stay in London. Death of the Duke of Albany. Tercentenary of the Edinburgh University. Lecture on 'Buddhist Charity.' *Biographical Essays.* Foundation stone of Wilhelm Müller Monument. Hawarden. Social life in the Oxford home. Work at Mainz. The Engadine. Italy. Letter to von Schlötzer.**

To his Cousin, Major von Basedow.

*Translation.* Malvern, *January* 2, 1884.

'Your letter and good wishes found me here on the Malvern Hills. The wedding, and all the business connected with it, had been a great strain on me, and my doctor sent me here for the good air. But we have had little but fog, and are here above the clouds. The past has been a sad year. I have not only lost my mother, but many old friends, and that made me value all the more the time I spent with you and my old Dessau friends and relations. May this year bring you fresh enjoyments and hide old sorrows! Life becomes more earnest and difficult, and it is not easy to keep the wherefore before one's eyes, when one wishes to walk straight on. We expect to go home to-morrow, as on Saturday we are going to Prince Christian's, near Windsor, to stay till Monday. Then I hope to shut myself up snugly for the winter in my room. Of course I have been very much delighted about the monument to my father, but could not help wishing it had come a year earlier, that my mother might have had the pleasure. Hosäus[1] has taken great trouble about it. I have kept myself purposely in the background, and shall continue to do so, as I can work for it far better in the second rank. I have seen one model, but the new one is said to be much better. We must hope for the best.'

The prospect of this monument to his father, the poet Wilhelm Müller, was for years a great delight and interest to

[1] Secretary to the Monument Fund.

Max Müller, and did all honour to the little town, the poet's birthplace, where the idea originated; though, as his son wrote to the secretary, 'Make it quite clear in your prospectus that it is not merely a Dessau-native-place undertaking, but that we appeal to the German nation, and even further, to all true lovers of the arts of poetry and music.' The Greek Government gave the marble to mark their sense of the poet's services rendered to the cause of Greek independence in his *Griechenlieder*, which belong to the classical literature of Germany. The Greeks sent over a block of the beautiful white marble of Pentelicus for the bust, and another of the most delicate tint of grey for the large pedestal. The whole rests on a substructure of very dark red marble. Jenny Lind, Sir Theodore Martin, Sir Robert Morier, Mr. Froude, and others warmly supported the collection in England.

The past year had been one of constant loss to Max Müller, and early in this year he heard of the death of his friend and correspondent Keshub Chunder Sen, on whom he wrote a beautiful obituary notice which was copied in several of the Indian papers:—

'India has lost her greatest son, Keshub Chunder Sen. His was one of the few names known not only most widely among the two hundred and fifty millions who are said to inhabit the vast Indian Empire, but familiar even to European ears. Many of us saw him during his stay in England in 1870, listened to him, admired and loved him, and not a few have ever since remained united with him by the bonds of a real friendship. If we look around for true greatness, not in England or Europe, but in the whole civilized world, and if we try to measure such greatness, not by mere success or popularity, but honestly and, so to say, historically, taking into account the character of the work done, and the spirit in which it was done, few, I believe, would deny that it was given to Keshub Chunder Sen to perform one of the greatest works in our generation, and that he performed it nobly and well. . . . No doubt the controversy between his followers and opponents will continue long after his death. But if we deduct an equal share on both sides—on the side of exaggerated praise as well as on the side of unmerited blame—there remains a sufficient amount of independent contemporary judgement to secure to Keshub Chunder Sen the first place among his fellow countrymen, and a pre-eminent place among the best of mankind.

'As long as there is a religion in India, whatever its name may be, the name of Keshub Chunder Sen will be gratefully remembered, as one who lived and died for the glory of God, for the welfare of mankind, and for the truth, so far as he could see it.'

To PROFESSOR TYNDALL.

OXFORD, *January* 17.

'I shall try again to tempt you and Mrs. Tyndall to pay us a visit at Oxford. Just now I am quite unfit for human society; I drag myself about with lumbago—looking more like one of our gorilla ancestors (*teste* Darwin) than like a rational being. And with all that, I shall have to lecture at Birmingham next Monday! I hope I shall be better for my Friday evening lecture. Do you know Miss S. D. Collet? I only knew her by correspondence, and fondly imagined she was a young lady of twenty. I find out she is as old as I am, and a great invalid. With all that, she is a most excellent lady, a great admirer of Râmmohun Roy. She is collecting materials for a life of the Râjah, &c., and she is very anxious to hear my lecture on Râmmohun Roy—as if I could teach her anything new. Well, the question is, could I have two tickets, and could she and her brother be brought in when there is no crowd? Fond as you are of young ladies, I know you are kind to old ladies too, so if you could help Miss Collet, please do.'

Max Müller gave two lectures in January at the Midland Institute, Birmingham, on 'Religious Reforms in India,' before crowded audiences; and on February 1 he gave the last Friday evening lecture he ever delivered at the Royal Institution, on Râmmohun Roy, mainly founded on the lecture given at Bristol in the previous autumn. After mentioning that, though Râmmohun Roy had clung to the *Veda* as revealed, his great follower Debendranâth Tagore had given up the belief in the Divine inspiration of the *Veda*, the lecturer asked whether 'a kind of heavenly halo is really indispensable in order to secure Eternal Truth an entrance into the heart, and an influence on the acts of man: or whether, as some believe, Truth—Eternal Truth—requires no credentials, but is to rule the world in her own right, nay, is to be welcomed all the more warmly when she appeals to the human heart, unadorned by priestly hands, and clad only in her own simplicity, beauty, and majesty? To Râmmohun Roy the *Veda* was true, because it was Divine; to his followers it was Divine, because it was true. And which of the two showed the greater faith?'

To Miss Byrd McCall.

Oxford, *January* 27.

'My dear Friend, if I may say so,—Many thanks for those American sweets. Sweet presents are very nice, but sweet presence would be nicer! Instead of going to the Land's End, you might have spent the whole of this winter in the more civilized parts of England. We have had hitherto nothing but mild weather; to-day is the first day of east wind and snow. I hope Mrs. McCall has not suffered much from travelling about, instead of settling down in a quiet cosy corner in her town house. I had spun myself in like a silkworm, but, alas! I had to come out at last. I had to lecture at Birmingham last week, have to go there again to-morrow, and on Friday I am to be executed at the Royal Institution in London—all old promises, given in a fit of good nature, which at last have to be fulfilled. B. will take care of me in London. She will escort me to see *Princess Ida*, and Miss Anderson, who is said to be "quite dazzling." In the meantime I have been diverted by another American whom everybody else abuses, Henry George. I wish you would read his last work, *Social Problems*. He must be a good fellow. If his remedy is impossible, that only shows that the case may be hopeless; but that the present state of abject poverty of millions, and the extravagance of a Vanderbilt, cannot be right, I feel as certain as Henry George. I have asked him to come to stay with us to meet the Vice-Chancellor, &c. There will be a good deal of cackle about it, Common-Roomers and all the rest—can't be helped.'

To his Son.

Oxford, *February*, 1884.

'I agree with Mr. Henry George when he describes the present state of society as utterly wrong and unchristian—I mean the excessive poverty on one side, and the excessive wealth on the other. I also think his observations on the growth of towns in America very instructive, and there is nothing to be said against the lesson which he draws, i.e. that *rising* towns should never alienate all their land and never alienate it altogether. A few streets in Chicago, if the land had been reserved, would defray the expenses of the whole municipality. But when he turns round, and says the same mistake has been committed everywhere in Europe, all one can answer is, Yes, but the mistake is beyond remedy; any attempt to nationalize the land would produce civil war. Many things are desirable, but impossible.

Henry George himself is opposed to all violence, and considers property sacred, but he is a fanatic, a man of one idea, and often lays himself open to misinterpretation. I believe he is a good and religious man.

'As to the Hindu Theatre, we have no Sanskrit plays older than about the fifth century A.D. Plays existed before religious performances, also secular representations of episodes of Epic Poetry. In the plays which we possess of Kâlidâsa and others, there are traces of Greek influence, and that is quite natural. Alexander and his successors introduced Greek artisans into India. Actors are specially mentioned. Indian coins show Greek workmanship and inscriptions. Indian astronomy is full of Greek termini-technici. Still the Sanskrit plays have preserved much of their national character, and it is chiefly in the stage arrangements that Greek influence is perceptible.'

Early in March Mr. Henry George came for two nights to Norham Gardens, where a large company were asked to meet him. The next day he held a public meeting, which was very much crowded, and where his views excited great indignation among the younger members of the University; and the scene at last became so disagreeable that Max Müller and his family left before the conclusion of the meeting.

The middle of March the Max Müllers moved to London for two months, and it was whilst they were there that the nation was plunged into grief by the sudden death of the Duke of Albany. To Max Müller, who had seen so much of the Prince at Oxford, and had hoped so much for science, literature, and art from his enlightened patronage, it was a severe blow.

To ROBERT COLLINS, ESQ.

25, PEMBROKE GARDENS, KENSINGTON, W., *March* 29, 1884.

'I must write you a line to say how deeply I feel with you and for you. You had done such a noble work. That young Prince, whom I so well remember when he first came to Oxford, had grown up under your care to be all that you could have desired or hoped for. Everything seemed so bright, so happy, so successful beyond all expectation. And now comes this sudden end, and all seems lost! But it only seems so. How this short life of ours will tell on our next, we cannot know. One thing only we know, that nothing good can ever be lost. And even here on earth that noble work to which you devoted the best part of your life will not be lost. Prince Leopold will remain a proud memory in the Royal Family, a bright example to the nation at large.

'Dear Prince Leopold! I am now an old man, and my memory is very like one of those Roman *columbaria*, full of urns and ashes and dear names. But Prince Leopold will always have his own niche there, as a bright and loving soul, full of the noblest aspirations. You may well place on his beautiful pale head the victor's wreath of laurel which he has so well earned, both by what he has suffered and by what he has achieved; and you may feel, when you look at him for the last time, that your labour has not been in vain.'

Max Müller was a true mourner among the many who obeyed the Queen's commands to attend the touching funeral in St. George's Chapel. Attendance there prevented him from being present at a meeting at Kensington Town Hall on the Ilbert Bill. He wrote to excuse himself:—

*April* 4.

'I have received the Royal command to attend the funeral of the Duke of Albany to-morrow. This, I regret, makes it impossible for me to attend your meeting. I was particularly anxious to be present to congratulate you and all true friends of India, to whatever party they may belong, on the great triumph which you have obtained. Every great triumph is mixed up with some small disappointments, but these can be corrected by-and-by. The essential point is that the fundamental principle on which the Proclamation of the Empress of India rests has been maintained against all quibblings that the honour of England is saved, and the Imperial word has been kept sacred. Do not trust to party, but trust to the great heart of England, or if that sounds too poetical, trust to the good sense of the English people.'

The middle of April Max Müller went to Edinburgh, by invitation from the University, to attend the Tercentenary Festival of its foundation. His wife and daughter accompanied him, and they were the guests of his old friend Professor William Sellar. It was a wonderfully interesting assembly, and Max Müller met many foreign friends and distinguished *confrères*, as Count Saffi, once triumvir in Rome, afterwards teacher of Italian in Oxford, Karl Elze of Halle, a fellow Dessauer, Professor Virchow, Professor Villari of Florence, Georges Perrot, Pasteur, Pressensé, Professor Bunsen of Heidelberg, whom Baron Bunsen used to call 'his golden cousin,' Professor Cremona of Rome, Helmholtz, and many distinguished Americans, not to mention leading representatives of all the Universities and scientific and literary societies of Great Britain. On the day that the honorary degrees were conferred, he, who had received such a degree in 1870, sat with the doctors of the University, wearing his blue doctor's hood. It was a brilliant scene for the spectators. Those who were to receive degrees filled the centre of the large hall, wearing the hoods, caps, and gowns of their respective Universities. They looked like a bed of tulips presenting every imaginable hue, whilst the delegates from many of the European Universities and learned bodies appeared in brilliant-coloured gowns with high birettas to match. There were receptions and entertainments of all sorts, and a very clever dramatized version of the *Fortunes of Nigel* given by the students, who also gave a ball. Max Müller attended nearly all the festivities, except the Students' Symposium on the last night, for which he was too fatigued.

On his return to London he delivered a lecture on 'Buddhist Charity,' the first of a series of lectures on Ancient and Modern Charity [1], the proceeds of which were devoted to the London Association for Befriending Young Servants. The lecture was published in the first volume of the new edition of *Chips*.

Soon after the return to Oxford in the middle of May, the Prince and Princess of Wied visited Oxford to see the city, and consult Max Müller on placing their eldest son at an English school for a year. A suitable school was found, with his help, and the parents were full of gratitude for the counsel and practical aid given them by Max Müller, who threw himself as heartily into the quest as if his own boy were in question. It was this readiness to help on all occasions, no matter what the subject, that from earliest days won him so much esteem and affection.

To the Duke of Argyll.

Oxford, *May* 25, 1884.

'The first thing I did after my return home was to read your book. It carried me on from beginning to end, and I could discover nothing in it of what your Grace called heretical. When I came to the

[1] Organized by the Rev. Brooke Lambert, of Greenwich.

chapters on the origin of religion, I soon perceived that our difference arose from the different points from which we started; your Grace starting from what ought to be, I from the little that is known to be in the oldest documents which we possess. I have tried to put down my thoughts on the subject in the enclosed paper. Before I publish it, I should be glad to know whether I have rightly apprehended and correctly represented your views.'

To the Same.

Oxford, *May* 30, 1884.

'I return my paper with a few answers and explanations to your marginal notes. It seems to me, as I said before, that we do not differ on any essential points, though we approach the subject in a different spirit. My view through life has always been, Let us know as much as there is to be known from history. There is a great deal more to be learnt from that source than we imagine, and the additions to our knowledge of the real historical growth of man, during our lifetime, have been enormous. They are far from being digested yet, and they are certainly more instructive than the mere surface *detritus* which we find among so-called modern savages.

'Your Grace will say that people want to know more; they want to know the beginnings, or the first stages of humanity. I know they do, but they might as well wish to ascend into the Moon. By whom was the first man suckled, and from whom did he learn his language? Was there history before language, &c. &c.? The very absurdity of these questions shows that we are running our heads against a very old and very solid wall. Those who like may do it. I prefer to try to understand the earliest relics which have been left us—mere ruins, it is true—and to form from the character of these ruins some idea of the persons who built them. In the history of religion I try to read the education of the human race, and I have to sympathize with the childishness of the child and with the wanderings of old age, such as you may read in the *Nineteenth Century*, January and March, 1884. You see unity in Nature; I try to see unity, purpose, wisdom in History. I know quite well we may go wrong, and that our little wisdom cannot span the wisdom by which we are surrounded on all sides. But this shows that we were intended to trust, and this trust is the best of all religions. The names may vary—the purpose is everywhere the same.'

Another of Max Müller's early friends passed away this year, Professor Lepsius, the famous Egyptologist, a man of whom Henry de Bunsen wrote, 'Another Colossus of ancient days is gone! What a grand man he was!' Max Müller sent an account of his friend and his work to the *Times*, which he concluded with these words:—

'Taken all in all, Lepsius was the perfect type of a German Professor, devoted to his work, full of ideals, and convinced that there is no higher vocation in life than to preserve and add to the sacred stock of human knowledge, which, though it is seen by the few only, has to be carried, like the Ark of the Covenant, from battle to battle, and kept safe from the hands of the Philistines.'

Bunyiu Nanjio had left England in the spring of this year for Japan, visiting India on his way.

To Mr. Nanjio.

Oxford, *July* 30.

'I should have written to you before, to thank you for your letter, but I waited till I knew that you were settled again in your old home. How happy you must have felt to see your friends and relations again after so many years. And how sad, at the same time, that your dear friend Kasawara was not there to receive you. Let me know how you found all your relations, and how you were received at your monastery. Everything concerning you will interest me, and you must not mind speaking about yourself and your work. I hope you will find an opportunity of making all that you learnt in England useful to your countrymen. I hope you found all the papers and books that belonged to Kasawara safe. Did he ever receive my letters? I have finished the *Sukhâvatî-Vyûha*, and have ordered twenty-five copies to be sent to the Japanese Legation in London to be forwarded to you. I have also worked at Kasawara's *Dharma-Samgraha*, but there is much to be done yet. However, Dr. Wenzel is helping me, and I shall certainly have the book published as a monument of our dear friend. I wait for your translation of the Chinese text about *Sukhâvatî*, which you took with you to revise. And please do not forget *I-tsing!*

'We have been living here very quietly. We have now the Long Vacation, and I have plenty of time for myself. We have all been well, and I feel better than last year. On August 3 we celebrate our Silver Wedding, when we have been married twenty-five years! I hear that Mr. Bendall is going to Nepal, and possibly to Tibet, to look for Sanskrit MSS. Do not forget that at some later time you might do something useful by going to Tibet through China. I do not mean at present, but after some years.

'When you write to me, tell me how you found your wife and your parents. If you have photographs of them, please send me some, also of your temple, or your home. I like to know what your home is like. Try to get some pupils in Sanskrit, and do not forget that a grammar, and dictionary, and reading-book are necessary, to keep up the study of Sanskrit in Japan. I am printing a volume of *Biographical Essays*, which I shall send you when they are finished.'

The only books of his own published this year were another volume of the *Anecdota Oxoniensia*, *The Ancient Palm-Leaves*, which Max Müller had prepared for the press with Mr. Nanjio, and finished after his return to Japan, to which Professor Bühler added an appendix; and a volume of *Biographical Essays*, which, after being many years out of print, formed the second volume of the new edition of *Chips*, published in 1894. In defending himself from the charge of writing about many men whose work in life is but little known, he says, 'Much of the best work in the world is done by those whose names remain unknown, who work because life's greatest bliss is work, and who require no reward beyond the consciousness that they have enlarged the knowledge of mankind, and contributed their share to the final triumph of honesty and truth.' Max Müller sent the book to a valued friend, who in thanking him, wrote, 'Kenjiu Kasawara is most affecting, and makes one look forward to a meeting in that "future state," as we call the great live Eternity which surrounds us all, and which such short careers as his, apparently incomplete to the vulgar eye, would assure one of, if there were no sermons, no Bibles, no priests. The whole book will be a treasure and delight to me.' These *Biographical Essays* were very well received. One review says of them:—

'Professor Max Müller belongs to the elder body of scholars who have devoted their lives to the solution of those world myths out of which religion and history, poetry and art, seem to spring. Whether we agree with or differ from him on the many unsettled questions which surround those thoughts which have not inaptly been termed the daughters of dead myths, it is very useful to us to know what are the views of one who is at once very learned and absolutely truthful.'

In speaking of the essay on Kasawara, another review says:—

'A strange pathos is lent to this memoir by the untimely death of one of these, Professor Max Müller's two pupils, just when about to begin a work in Japan, the issues of which cannot be insignificant. The immense patience, diligence, dutifulness, in that little body, whom many of us may remember to have seen silently gliding about Oxford so short a while ago! The equal patience, kindness, and generosity of the Master, who had unwittingly drawn these children of an alien faith, older than our creed, and outnumbering the Catholic Church itself, across seas and lands to sit at his feet, and spell out, through two languages, their way back to the authentic fountains of their own spiritual force! Is all the effort wasted? Surely here too we may trust the "larger hope."'

To B. Malabari, Esq.

*September* 5, 1884.

'I truly regret all the agitation in India and about India. It will ruin your country. The fault, however, lies not with you, but with the new race of English settlers in India. Unless they are taught how to behave, and kept under control by a strong hand, government in India will become impossible. The Opposition in England, too, is much to be blamed. There are some politicians who would not shrink from saying: "Perish India, if only we can oust Gladstone!" What India wants, and will want for many years to come, is rest and quiet work. What would become of India if there were a second Mutiny, and a successful one, it is fearful to contemplate. You will have civil war, plunder, utter barbarism. But I confess I do not blame the people of India; the whole blame for the present disturbed state falls on the English settlers in India, and on the scheming politicians in England. The India Council too works very badly, because they have neither independence nor responsibility. The present Secretary of State is a very clever man, but he cares chiefly for Parliamentary success. All this agitation about the proper age of candidates for the Indian Civil Service arises from a personal squabble. There can be no doubt that for English boys, to say nothing of Hindus, the age is too low. Let candidates compete from nineteen to twenty-three. If boys of nineteen can beat men of twenty-three, let them go out; they will be the exceptions, and exceptionally strong boys are worth having. What I know for certain is that India loses some of our best men here at Oxford, because they will not cram for an examination at nineteen. The curious result of the present state of things is that the boys who get their appointment at nineteen get tired of it when they are twenty-two, and think that they might have done better by staying in England; while some of our best, when they have taken a first class, would give anything for an appointment to the Indian Civil Service. With regard to your countrymen, I wonder that they care so much for the Indian Civil Service. If I were a Hindu, I should look out for very different work to benefit my countrymen. To tell you the truth, I do not believe in the efficiency of a *mixed* Civil Service. Oil and water will not mix—let the oil be at the top, there is plenty of room for the water beneath.

'You are losing an excellent man in Lord Ripon. If Lord Spencer succeeds, some people in India will find out that he has learnt how to deal with selfish, noisy, and disloyal agitators in Ireland, and that he will govern India for the Indians, and not for interlopers.'

In October, enough money having been collected, the foundation-stone of the monument at Dessau to Wilhelm Müller was laid during a Philological Congress held at Dessau. Max Müller had prepared an address to deliver to the Congress, but as the time drew near he was so unwell, so entirely unfit for the exertion and excitement, that he had to give up the idea of going to Dessau. The stone was laid on October 2, in front of the Gymnasium where Wilhelm Müller had taught, and which his son had attended as a scholar. Some fine choruses composed for the occasion were sung, and a speech was made by Professor Gosche of Halle. The address prepared by Max Müller for the Congress was printed in the *Deutsche Rundschau* of April, 1884, under the title of 'Then and Now.'

'There are moments,' he says, 'when one's life suddenly appears strange to one. One would like to stand still to collect one's thoughts, and as one looks back on the past and forward to the future, one asks oneself in quiet astonishment, what the significance of the wonderful present may be. Such moments are rightly called epochs, for the Greek word *epochê* means originally a halt, a standing still, also reflection and doubt; and then first a period of time in the movement of the stars, in the life of the individual, and lastly, in the history of mankind. I must own this quiet astonishment fills me when I suddenly find myself in my old native place, and in the midst of so many distinguished representatives of German science. Memory, with her dancing forms, rises so powerfully, that it is difficult not to be overwhelmed by her. Everything looks strange and yet so familiar, that I ask myself if the old man who stands before you to-day is the same who was born here sixty years ago, who learnt here first to know and love people, and who, even now, whenever he visits his living and dead friends here, is filled with a sense of home, which he feels nowhere else. But this is not the place or time to speak of myself, and of what I feel when I compare the Now with the Then.'

After presenting the first series of *Sacred Books of the East*, twenty-four volumes, to the Congress, to be placed in the Ducal Library, Max Müller traced the progress of Sanskrit studies from the time he began to work under Brockhaus, to the present time, and he ended by assuring his friends that 'the Now was far better than the Then, and that in reliance on the young students round them, they might feel sure the Future would be better than the Now.'

To H.R.H. PRINCE CHRISTIAN (absent in Germany on family affairs).

*Translation.* OXFORD, *October* 31.

'YOUR ROYAL HIGHNESS,—Many thanks for your kind note and for the offer with regard to the letters of Baggesen and Schiller. Though their correspondence is most interesting to me, I should not like to anticipate the possibility of its being offered to a relation of Baggesen, who probably would have much more time for this work than I. Should there exist any original letters of Schiller's, I should much appreciate some copies for my collection; the work in question, however, I should prefer being entrusted to other hands. . . . The Princess graciously invited my wife and myself last Sunday to Cumberland Lodge.

'I know the feeling of Germany towards England, and especially towards Gladstone. Such phases of feeling come and go, and in our hurried lives they quickly come to the fore and pass away again. In England the German hisses make no impression, because they have no reality. England has from time to time to pass through her crises, and no one can deny that neither her statesmen nor her doctors always prescribe the right remedies. In spite of all this, I consider Gladstone the most experienced, honest, patriotic doctor. When one reads the discussions in Parliament, one might easily fear for England. But they are mere fireworks! The nation is of the good old stock, and woe to him who forgets this! England will never be conquered, not before the last Englishman, the last Scotchman, the last Irishman, aye, the last Irishman, the last Canadian and Newfoundlander, the last Sikh, aye, the last Yankee has fallen. Then, and only then, can Russia rule the world, for then there will be no more decent men. Bismarck knows what England signifies, and that in the whole history of the world no English and Germans have ever crossed swords. No danger threatens Germany from England: though Germany be ever so much in love with her neighbours right and left, John Bull will not be jealous. You see, I am a good Englishman, but also a good German.'

TO PROFESSOR NOIRÉ.

*Translation.* 7, NORHAM GARDENS, *November* 29, 1884.

'... I was hoping to send you a good article about "Savages," but it could not appear in the December number; still you will find something from me in the December *Deutsche Rundschau.* I had to write the little preface for Réville, and so I am often put into harness. The words *C'est magnifique, mais ce n'est pas la guerre,* were used by a French general, who looked on from the distance at the charge of the Light Brigade at Balaclava. I think it was Canrobert. Tell me, why can I not get enthusiastic about the beautiful? To me the beautiful seems so comprehensible, and only the ugly needs explanation. Don't you pay any attention to me, however; in this I feel I am a layman or a heathen.

'I have little rest now; the University occupies me entirely, though I do not lecture. I long so often for rest, for an island, for a monastery, but nothing will come of this, I suppose. And so life slips by and we get old and useless; the best which we might be able to say, remains unsaid. But it must be said, and will be said, though we may not be here any more; younger ones than we will say it, better ones, later ones, who yet could not have any existence without us. Therefore, always on and on, though it may be much slower than in former years.'

TO HER HIGHNESS THE PRINCESS MOTHER OF WIED.

*Translation.* OXFORD, *December* 6.

'YOUR HIGHNESS,—Indeed, that was not the meaning of my letter. I know Baron von Roggenbach is a nomad, and as I had been waiting to receive some business information from him, I thought that my last letter might perhaps be waiting somewhere for him unopened. I always consider it most unmannerly of authors, when they not only pay an uncalled-for visit to their friends, but expect to know by return of post whether the said call was pleasant and agreeable. I thought your Highness might perhaps find something congenial in the *Biographical Essays*, and therefore I ventured to put my book on the table quite unnoticed. A thousand thanks for all the kindness of your Highness's letter. How I should have loved to be again a spectator of the happiness of Segenhaus and Monrepos, but it was not to be!'

To Miss Byrd McCall.

Oxford, *December* 16.

'You would be surprised to see me here quite alone in our house. Mary and Beatrice started yesterday for Rome; Wilhelm and his mother went this morning to St. Leonards. I wanted to be alone, it is sometimes good for me; and so here I am, like a hermit in his cave. You know perhaps that to-day is the saddest day of the year to me, though whenever I think of her, I always feel how much she has been spared. Many thanks for your birthday message and all your kind wishes. I cannot complain at my time of life; though I have lost many old friends, I have found some young ones, and I feel as if I could still do some useful work. If only there were not so many unnecessary troubles in this life! Some troubles there must be, but why should people be silly and perverse, when the straight line is so easy? I have been so much thrown back in my work by all sorts of interruptions, that Italy disappears more and more from my sight. However, I shall not grumble, but work away till my task is finished.'

To the Right Hon. W. E. Gladstone.

7, Norham Gardens, *December* 20, 1884.

'Let me thank you first of all for two very bright and delightful days which I was allowed to pass in your family. But for the *Ate* that made me lay hands on your paper on *Athênê*, mistaking it for some proof-sheets of my own, which, under the title of "The Savage," are to appear in the *Nineteenth Century* next month, they would have been days of unmixed pleasure to me. All I can do is to trust to the *Litae*, and to say once more, Please forgive! The titles of the books which I promised to send you are, *Myths and Songs of the South Pacific*, by the Rev. W. W. Gill; *Savage Life in Polynesia*, by the Rev. W. W. Gill. They give an account of the growth of what may be called popular epic poetry among the Polynesian Islanders. The distance between them and the Greeks is great; still there is a common element. The best account of the collection of epic poems from the mouths of the people in Finland and Lapland, chiefly by Lönnrot, is found in *Kalewala, das National-Epos der Finnen*; *Kalewipoeg, eine estnische Sage*; and Castrèn's *Vorlesungen über finnische Mythologie*. It is a pity that the *Kalewala* has not been translated into English; some portions of it are quite worth it. When we spoke of the accent in Greek, I wished to point out how the coincidences between the Greek and the Vedic accentuation proved the extraordinary continuity of language, in spite of the enormous distance which separates Greek from Sanskrit. In the

Vedic Sanskrit some rational principles can still be discovered which determined the accent; the fundamental principle being that the syllable, which people wished to accentuate logically, was accentuated phonetically in the earliest stages of human speech. That principle was afterwards overlaid by false analogies, by tribal and personal idiosyncrasies, by euphonic and metrical tendencies, &c., but faint traces of it are visible here and there both in Greek and Sanskrit.

'I refer to

| | | | |
|---|---|---|---|
| οἶδα | = | Sanskrit | Véda |
| οἶσθα | = | " | véttha |
| οἶδε | = | " | véda |
| ἴσμεν | = | " | vidmá |
| ἴστε | = | " | vidá |
| ἴσασι | = | " | vihúḥ. |

We cannot explain in Greek why οἶδα should become ἴσμεν. The accent has become stereotyped. In Sanskrit it is still movable. It fell on the terminations in the plural because they were still felt as distinctive modifying elements, and the accent being on the last syllable, the vowel of the first syllable was lightened, or rather was not strengthened, ê became ĭ, oi, ĭ. The only explanation why in German we say, "ich weiss," but "wir wissen," is likewise supplied by the accent in the *Veda*. It will be difficult to explain why the Greeks said:

| | | | |
|---|---|---|---|
| Ζεύς, | = | Sanskrit | Dyaús |
| Διός | = | " | Divás |
| Διί, but | = | " | Diví |
| Δία | = | " | Dívam or Dyâm. |

'In Sanskrit the rule is general that, after monosyllabic bases, the really modifying case terminations have the accent, while the nominative and accusative, the simple subject and object, are not felt in the same way. Does it not seem almost incredible that the only two numerals which in Greek have the accent on the last syllable, viz. ἑπτά and ὀκτώ, should be the only two numerals which in Sanskrit accentuated texts are oxytone? If mere variation of accent can thus be preserved between Athens and Benares, need we wonder at other reminiscences affecting gods and heroes? The facts are there; the difficulty is how to explain them. Lastly, as to my calculations as to the probable number of English-speaking people two hundred years hence (published in 1876 from materials supplied by De Candolle and others), you will find them in a small penny pamphlet of mine, which I forward herewith. How far Bismarck's Colonial policy may vitiate these calculations, it is difficult to tell, but I feel about English and German what I feel about Sanskrit and Greek: wide apart as they seem to be, they draw their life-blood from the same source, and at every great historical crisis their common blood will assert itself.

'Your very sincere admirer.'

To Mr. Nanjio.

*December* 21.

'My dear Friend,—I received your letter of *November* 6 to-day, and I answer it at once. I am glad to hear that you are well, and that you have found a position in your own country where you can make yourself really useful. Since you left, I have not had much time for Buddhism, I am working again at my translation of the *Rig-veda.* I sent you a volume of *Biographical Essays* which by this time has reached you, I hope. You will find something in it about yourself and poor Kasawara. I am sorry to hear that my letters to him are lost. . . . When you have time for work again, the translation of the third Sûtra of *Sukhâvatî*, and of *I-tsing* also, would be useful. Whenever I receive these translations, I shall try to get them published in England.

'You will have to go by-and-by to Tibet, or send some one else to go there, to look for MSS.

'Do not forget to look out for Sanskrit MSS. or inscriptions in Japan, and in Corea too. That poor country seems to be in a very poor state just now. I hope you will enjoy peace in Japan, and not think of conquest: you have plenty to do at home. I wish the European nations would learn that lesson, and not disturb the peace of the East; it is a shameful proceeding, and they are all alike to blame, French, Russians, English.

'I wish you a happy New Year, and a great deal of hard work, for that is the best medicine for this troublesome life.'

To T. Althaus, Esq.

Oxford, *December* 21, 1884.

'Thanks for your notes on Pattison; they contain some very true touches, and bring him visibly back to one's memory. I always considered him the best-read man at Oxford. Anywhere but at Oxford he would have grown into a Lessing. I have just been staying at Hawarden, and to-morrow I go to Hastings to join Wilhelm and my wife. My two daughters are at Rome, and I am the only one here to send you our best wishes for the New Year.'

The new year found Max Müller back in Oxford with only his wife and son; his youngest daughter was in Italy with her married sister. Most of this year's work was devoted to editing the *Sacred Books.* Max Müller also brought out in the *Anecdota Oxoniensia,* with Dr. Wenzel's help, the *Dharma-Samgraha,* an ancient collection of Buddhist technical terms, which had been prepared by his late pupil Kasawara. He wrote a biography of his father, Wilhelm Müller, for the *Allgemeine Deutsche Biographie,* a translation of which was afterwards published in the new edition of *Chips.* He also edited and carefully corrected for press a translation of Scherer's *German Literature,* made by his elder daughter.

To Professor Huxley.

*January* 10.

'You asked me whether the statistics about blue and black eyes and hair in different parts of Germany had been published in the shape of maps. I asked Professor Virchow of Berlin about it, and he writes to say that the maps are nearly, but not quite, ready. If you wish to see them at once, Professor Virchow says he could send a proof; otherwise he would send some copies, as soon as they have been finally revised. He adds, "I wonder whether Mr. Huxley remembers that I once had the honour of sitting by him at a Medical Congress in 1880?" He sends the journal which contains the statistics, which I forward herewith.'

To Professor Noiré.

*Translation.* 7, Norham Gardens, *February* 7, 1885.

'. . . Do read in the *International Journal for Languages* an essay by W. von Humboldt. How much deeper a thinker he was than those of the present day!

'I am working hard on a volume of translations—*Vedic Hymns*; besides that, I am collecting materials for a work on mythology, objective and subjective. I want this work to act as a pioneer for further work of the kind. Oh that I could enter a monastery! Paltry society devours me, and yet it is a sort of duty not to be put entirely aside. Nothing is decided about Italy yet; new claims are constantly rising up, you cannot imagine how many.

'People here are a good deal depressed just now, but that is wholesome for them. The English nation is apt to be arrogant, and is never so great as when she is aware of this. The worst is that she will most likely send her physicians away, instead of attending to her own state, and dieting herself accordingly.

'It was impossible to prevent the fall of Khartoum: the mistake was in letting Gordon go there at all; it was a game of chance, such as a state should never attempt. The petty attacks from Germany are childish, and might in time produce evil consequences. Just as if the world were not large enough for all! The time for founding colonies is past now. The English colonies are no longer colonies, but do exactly what they like. Bismarck is sure to receive his answer, not from London, but from Sydney. *Quanta stultitia regitur mundus!* Well, it does not disturb me; we have to learn to do our work in spite of storms and thunder, and without storms and thunder the tree of humanity can take no firm root.

'How curious that the Schopenhauer Memorial Fund proceeds so slowly! I should have thought that he had numerous adherents now. You ought not to let the matter drop.'

### To Dr. Hosäus.

*Translation.* *February* 8, 1885.

'I hope in the spring to get away from here for some time, though it does not look much like it. New demands on my time are for ever turning up. So one year goes after another, and life draws near its close before one has finished the half of what one wishes to do. I envy you in your quiet, peaceful post at Dessau. Here in Oxford one is disturbed on all sides, and one has but seldom a quiet hour.'

### To the Duke of Argyll.

Oxford, *March* 23, 1885.

'The *Vedic Hymns* give us many glimpses of the life of the people for whom they were composed. It is quite clear that they were a conquering race, entering India from the Punjâb. They called themselves *Âryas*, while the native tribes whom they dispossessed were called by them *An-âryas*, not Âryas, or *Dasyus*, enemies. In my letter to Bunsen, "On the Turanian Languages," published in 1854 in his *Christianity and Mankind*, Vol. III, I pointed out that these indigenous races were black-skinned, and were called *Kravyâd*, eating raw flesh; *anagnitra*, not keeping fire; *a-nâia*, noiseless, &c. These enemies had strongholds, and their wealth consisted chiefly in cattle.

'The Âryan conquerors were agricultural tribes. Their very name Ârya, as I have tried to show (*Encycl. Brit.* s. v. Ârya), meant ploughers, from *ar*, to plough, to ear. Even before the great Âryan separation, agriculture must have been known, for Greek ἄρουρα is the Sanskrit *uruara*. The Âryas in India call themselves Korihti's tribes, and that, too, is derived from *Karih*, to plough.

'The poets of the *Veda* begin to complain that the earth is not large enough for them. Thus *Rig-veda* VI, 47, 20:—

'"O Gods, we have come to a country without meadows; the earth, which is wide, has become narrow."

'The wealth of the Âryas consisted chiefly in cattle, in cows, horses, sheep, and goats, and in men. Corn was cut with sickles, and afterwards threshed. Their settlements were called *urigana*, clearings, *grâma*, villages, while outside the *grâma* was the *aranya*, the thicket or forest. Towns, in our sense, did not exist, though strongholds and camps are mentioned.

'Each family had its house and hearth. Several families seem to have formed a *vis*, vicus, or *grâma*, pagus, and several of such settlements have formed a *gana*, i. e. kin or clan.

'We hear of *vis-patis*, lords of a vis, of *grâma-nis*, leaders of villages, and of kings, *râgan*, who are also called *gopâ ganasya*, shepherd of a clan.

'We even hear of leagues of five *ganas* or clans. Kings were both hereditary and elective. They led the armies, and received booty and tribute. We also hear of public assemblies, *samitis* or *vidathas*, held in a *sabhâ*, a public hall. The king was present. Discussions took place, and likewise social amusements.

'The cultivated land seems to have belonged to the village. Booty in war seems to have constituted the first private property. The possessive pronouns of the third person, *suas*, *suus*, existed before the Âryan separation.'

Early in April Max Müller received a letter from Lord Lytton, in which, after speaking of a translation of the *Mahâbhârata* by Protap Chunder Roy, the former Viceroy of India says, 'Your own enterprise with the *Sacred Books of the East* is colossal. It takes one's breath away. Never was there an *Introducteur des Ambassadeurs* on so vast a scale, nor with such great personages dependent on his good offices.'

To Mr. Bunyiu Nanjio.

*May* 10.

'My dear Friend,—I have waited a long time before answering your last long letter of February 28. I hoped I should be able to send you a copy of Kasawara's *Dharma-Samgraha*, but the printing of the Index has been very slow, and I do not like to wait any longer. Now let me thank you for the seeds, which arrived quite safe. They have been sown and begin to sprout, and I shall often think of you when I see them in full bloom. I am glad to hear that you are actually Professor of Sanskrit, and have a number of pupils. I hope the study of Sanskrit will take root in Japan; you will then have a more intelligent study of Buddhism, and, more particularly, of the history of Buddhism. I hope you will go on with your translation of the third Sûtra of *Sukhâvatî-Vyuha*, and of *I-tsing*; the latter would be very interesting in England, and I should gladly have it published here, and add some notes and a preface. The other text which you sent me may be even older than the palm-leaves of Horiuzi, to judge by the character of the letters. But I can do nothing with it till I get a faithful photograph of it. Perhaps you will be able to have that done for me. And do not forget to look out for other MSS. So many libraries in Japan seem to have been destroyed and dispersed, that old books and MSS. may be scattered about anywhere, possibly also old inscriptions on iron or metal. My family is well, and they all send you kindest greetings. Wilhelm will matriculate in a few days at University College. My two dogs are still alive—you remember Waldmann and Männerl? Your poor countrymen have had a great misfortune in London, their Japanese village being destroyed by fire. I went there before it was burnt, and wished that you had been present. It was very amusing, and I had a cup of tea in a regular Japanese tea-house.

'Now I must finish. I hope that you and yours are very happy together. We often look at your wife's photograph, and always say, "How pretty!"'

TO HORATIO HALE, ESQ.

*May* 18.

'I read your account of Chief Johnson with great interest, but I cannot trust myself to read all the important books which you and others are now publishing about the people and languages of North America. They carry me away from my work, which I have still to finish in quite different latitudes. But I must say that you are doing a great and most delightful work, and if I were young, I believe I should run across to America, and spend some years among these living MSS. What is quite clear to me is the high state of civilization reached by these so-called savages before they came in contact with so-called civilized men; and that, too, is a very important point. I wonder what you will think of my article on the Savage[1]. I hope it may do a little good, but I know others might do it much better.'

[1] *Last Essays*, Series I.

To Herr von Strauss und Tornay.

*Translation.* Oxford, *June* 12, 1885.

'My honoured Friend,—If thoughts were letters, you would often be invaded by me. I have never forgotten your friendly sympathy with my joys and sorrows in Dresden, and shall never do so. But life goes so fast downhill, and I have spun myself in so tightly with many threads in all directions, that I cannot do the half of what I wish to do. You may believe, I often despair of paying all my epistolary debts, and I only wish all my friends would show the same trust in me that you have done. It was a very real pleasure to have your son and grand-daughter here with us. We all like Hedwig very much, and admire her courage, and the amiable way in which she accommodates herself to a foreign life. England is a salt-water bath for the mind, and will have a good effect on her whole life. My son comes up to the University in October. How little one can really do for one's children; how little one can shelter them, and yet how fast they are entwined in our hearts, perhaps more than is right. Well, one's work is always a help and comfort. I have a good deal of trouble with my *Sacred Books of the East*, but the first series will be finished this year—twenty-four volumes—and the second is being arranged for. Work will never be ended; there is much for our successors to accomplish.'

To Lady Welby.

*June* 19, 1885.

'I can see nothing in *Sympneumata*. The world is so simple and transparent, it does not call for such involved and confused language. There may be a grain of gold in it, but what is the use of thinkers and writers if they cannot extract them from the slag? Simplicity is the right stamp of truth and honesty. When I see clouds and vapours, I shut the book. I admire your patience, but I do not possess it.'

To his Daughter Mary.

*June* 28.

'You are quite right in what you say about Noiré. A man who is a good deal ahead of his time ought not to mind being but half understood; unfortunately, Noiré does mind it—he would have his pie and eat it, and hence all his grumbling. But it is strange how slowly people's minds move. That introduction of Noiré's to my translation of Kant is a magnificent piece of work, but no one has found it out; all they say is, that it is too long; the fact being it is as concentrated as Liebig's Extract. However, people will find it out; a few *have* found it out, and the few always become the many—*unfortunately*, as Noiré would say. Of course, to a man of high ideals this world seems very imperfect, and so it ought, if it is ever to become better; but it is equally true that it is as good as it can be, exactly as good as we have made it, exactly as good as we deserve it. If it were otherwise, there would be no Nous in the world, and that there is, even Anaxagoras knew.'

To THE REV. G. COX.

OXFORD, *June*, 1885.

'The Old Testament stands on a higher ethical stage than other sacred books—it certainly does not lose by a comparison with them. I always said so, but people would not believe it. Still, anything to show the truly historical and human character of the Old Testament would be extremely useful in every sense, and would in no wise injure the high character which it possesses . . . it might be done in a review of the *Sacred Books of the East*, showing how the Old Testament is like, and how it is unlike them.'

The following, from the Indian *Echo*, is inserted to show how Max Müller was often misjudged and misrepresented, generally by those who did not know him personally, and many of whom were jealous of his fame and high position in the world of letters :—

'Professor Max Müller has inflicted deserved chastisement on the *Hindu Patriot*, and we are scarcely sorry for it, for our contemporary has brought it upon himself by his wanton disregard of truth, or gross carelessness, in rushing forward to accuse the great Orientalist of one of the most odious things imaginable. It may be remembered that the Professor had delivered, during the days of the Ilbert Bill controversy, a lecture to a Cambridge audience on the "Truthful Character of the Hindus." Quite recently a German translation of Professor Max Müller's Cambridge Lectures on *India—What can it teach us?* was brought out. The *Patriot* alleged that from this translation the particular lecture on the truthful character of the Hindus was omitted or suppressed, *because it was no longer necessary to flatter and cajole the natives of India.* Even if the omission was a fact, the criticism based on it was unworthy of the great reputation of the organ of the greater Zemindars. Our contemporary ostensibly drew his inspiration from information supplied by a *Distinguished Orientalist* to Babu Protap Chunder Roy. Who this informant or informer may be we do not know. But the fact remains that the particular lecture, to which the *Patriot* referred, was not suppressed at all, but duly appeared in its place in the German translation.'

It is only right to state that the *Hindu Patriot* apologized as soon as it found out how it had been misled, but repeated that the statement had been made by 'a distinguished Orientalist . . . as well known and respected in London as the learned Professor himself.'

These attacks became more frequent as time went on, and as the many distinctions bestowed on Max Müller excited the envy of less fortunate contemporaries. It became more and more needful to recollect Byron's lines in *Childe Harold*:—

'He who surpasses or subdues mankind
Must look down on the hate of those below.'

The Summer Term of this year had been again one of constant social intercourse, and the following letter will show the feeling for Max Müller among many of the younger members of the University, whom he gladly received at his house. Some of these may remember the Friday afternoon gatherings in term, the lawn-tennis, the tea on the shady terrace, and Max Müller's bright welcome to all, young and old.

'My dear Mrs. Max Müller,—It is a pleasure to me to do what you ask: my recollection of your husband as I knew him in my undergraduate days is still vivid and delightful, and though I have no claim to speak for others, I may at any rate say that I have found no trace among my contemporaries of an impression at variance with mine.

'I have seldom met any one so entirely different from my imagination of him as Mr. Max Müller. I had pictured a burly, bearded German Professor, carelessly dressed, possibly brusque in manner, certainly of unavoidable learning, the author of all those books. This figure still lies—without its label—in some back cupboard of my mind; the gracious and genial presence of the real man could never be pieced on to it. As to the books, I hardly feel sure which wrote them after all; I never heard anything of them from the true Max Müller. I remember talks on music, dogs, poetry, Hindoo ceremonies, pictures, sweetmeats, and fairy tales: never a professorial or pedantic word. Once only I heard him speak of religion. It was when I was staying with you in August, 1885: I found him in the garden with ——, and he talked to us with great vivacity of Darwin and Haeckel. Presently —— went into the house, and I was left to keep the game up alone. It ended by my host turning upon me, and looking up with that flash through the glasses: "If you say that all is not made by Design, by

Love"—waving an arm towards the Parks—"then you may be in the same house, but you are not in the same world with me." He looked down again; I disclaimed any desire to be in a different world from his, and he beamed with that genial humour which was always hovering about him, even when he pretended to be ruffled. I can see him now, standing at the window, when a picnic day had turned out wet, grumbling, not to us but to the dogs, Waldmann and Männerl, and in a manner most sympathetically dog-like. I see him too, genuinely disturbed over the absence of Männerl, sallying out late at night to find the prodigal, with a lantern; like a figure in one of Richter's charming prints, or Hans Andersen's tales.

'This quaint simplicity, the charm of the perfectly child-like character, always seemed to me the one un-English part of him. It carried with it the power, which we as a nation lack, of entering with ease and sincerity into relations, however sudden and unexpected, with strangers or foreigners. I have been with him, as you know, when visitors of many nationalities and colours were ushered in upon him, but I never saw either him or them for a moment embarrassed; and whether he spoke with an English Prince or with a tramp from Hamburg, his courtesy and shrewd directness were equally ready. It was a great thing for young men to see: I fear we learned to admire rather than to imitate it, but we gained at least a standard of good manners and a touch of the true Humanist tradition.

'Believe me always,

'Yours very sincerely,

'HENRY NEWBOLT.'

In sending this letter to the editor, Mr. Newbolt says, 'It falls short of expressing the full admiration and affection which I personally shall always feel for your husband.'

At the end of July Max Müller went to Mainz to discuss with his friend Professor Noiré a work that was already occupying his mind, *The Science of Thought*. His wife and daughter went to friends in Switzerland, and they all finally joined the married daughter in the Engadine about the middle of August.

TO HIS DAUGHTER BEATRICE.

MAINZ, 7 a.m., *August* 13, 1885.

'MY DEAR BEATRICE,—I am glad to hear from you that you enjoyed your stay with the Blumenthals, in spite of the grasshoppers; I expect you will enjoy the snow mountains even more. It does one good to see those old giants, who have changed so little since the world began, and will be admired by little grasshoppers like ourselves many millions of years hence—always supposing that this little ball of earth will be kept rolling so long. This neighbourhood is tamer, but most lovely; the whole valley of the Rhine and the Moselle are charming: no wonder the Romans preferred them to Rome, and made themselves most comfortable at Cologne, Mainz, Trier, &c. The antiquities they find everywhere are very interesting. I wonder what you would have said to a young Roman lady, with her auburn hair most beautifully and carefully plaited, only she was resting in a stone coffin and all she had with her were a few nicknacks, which probably she had asked her friends to place by her side. Then there was a complete shoemaker's shop, with leather, shoes, all the tools, &c. It is a kind of Pompeii, and every day they find new old things.

'Your loving Father.'

To Miss McCall.

Kursaal Hotel, Maloja, Engadine, *August* 28, 1885.

'My dear Lady Byrd,—Now here comes a most delightful proposal. Supposing your campaign in England is over, and you really sail for America in October, why not fly over here for the last few weeks? You are here most comfortably in forty-eight hours—what is that? This is a heavenly place, really as perfect as Mother Earth could make it; glaciers, snow mountains, lakes, as many and as glorious as your heart can desire; a most comfortable hotel, full of all sorts of pleasant people. Now consider, you really ought not to disappear like a shooting star, but say Good-bye in a more fixed-star-like manner, gliding quickly, gently, aye, reluctantly below the horizon. I could tell you of ever so many charming people who are here. I hope my cousin, the Baronin von Stolzenberg, will also be here soon. Mr. Story, the sculptor, is here, Mr. Mundella, Russian Princesses, even ladies from Philadelphia, Mr. Saunders, and others.

'Now I wonder whether you are capable of a noble resolve: leave all your trunks behind, and, with nothing but a pair of wings, fly over here. I know if you lead the way, your dear sister and kind mother will follow, and when you drive up here with four horses and postilion, I can promise you a hearty welcome from many besides

'Yours very sincerely.'

To Professor Ernst Curtius.

*Translation.* Kursaal, Maloja, Engadine, *August* 28, 1885.

'Dear Friend and Colleague,—Here in the mountains the sad

news of your brother's[1] death reached me; he was an old and faithful friend to me. It is a heavy loss, and, at the same time, a solemn warning to us all. Only a short time ago I read his brisk defence, and rejoiced to be able to give expression to his principles in an article which I was just then writing ("The Lesson of Jupiter") to appear in the next number of the *Nineteenth Century*. Well, he has done much, and much that is great, and, though knowledge will advance, that which he has done will never be forgotten. The counter-stream of the present day is for the most part based on ignorance and mutual misunderstanding. If personal prejudices were left out altogether, the Cause itself would occasion very little difference of opinion. ... It is so everywhere, and quiet, retiring, earnest labour, such as your brother loved, is to be found very rarely now. In vain do I look round for a worthy successor to him, and I am afraid that the gulf between Classical and Comparative Philology will grow wider and wider.

'I can understand how deeply you must feel the loss of such a brother. May you still have many years of vigorous work!

'Ever yours.'

The time passed at the Maloja with congenial friends was a time of unmixed happiness. Among these friends were Mr. Seebohm and his family, Mr. and Mrs. Glazebrook, Mr. and Mrs. Story from Rome, Mr. and Mrs. Wilson, and others. The warm friendship which sprang up with Mr., now Archdeacon, Wilson was a delight to Max Müller through the rest of his life. Long talks, long walks along the beautiful lakes or up the hills, readings out loud by Mr. Wilson and Mr. Story, much music in the large saloon of the hotel, concerts and little dances got up by the young people, made the six weeks fly by. The Max Müllers were among the last to leave, at the end of September, when the roads were already covered with snow, the icicles hung from the trees, and the smaller cascades were all frozen. At the foot of the pass, in sunny Italy, they found themselves in the midst of the grape vintage. All October was spent in Venice, where the Crown Prince and Princess of Germany were staying at the next hotel to the Max Müllers, and with whom they were in daily intercourse. No premonition of illness was then on the noble Prince, yet there was a certain sadness, the joyousness that had marked both Prince and Princess was gone; they seemed

[1] Professor George Curtius.

to feel that their day was passing, and that when they came to the throne a new generation would have sprung up, who had little sympathy with their schemes and desires.

TO ARCHDEACON WILSON.

VENICE, *October* 15, 1885.

'MY DEAR FRIEND,—I can well imagine how busy you are, working for others, not for yourself. I feel quite ashamed at having shaken off my harness so soon, but I do enjoy my leisure, and I do my best not to let it grow into idleness. This is a delightful place, and full of delightful people. Browning is here, Story the sculptor, Layard, &c. The Crown Prince and Princess of Germany left this two days ago. She is very intelligent, and I saw much of her. I showed her your last pamphlet, and she wrote: "Dr. Wilson's pamphlet is excellent, full of truth and good sense, and written in the right spirit. He seems to belong to the few who are *not* silent and need not be, and their words cannot wound or harm." I wish she had more influence in Germany; she would do much good. I also preached Brown's poems to her, and she is anxious to possess *The Doctor*. Could you ask for another copy? Please tell Mr. Brown that Browning is delighted with *The Doctor*, and thinks it quite wrong that it should not be published. I shall see him this afternoon, and shall hear more from him about what he thinks of the poem, but I hear he has spoken enthusiastically about it. I lent him my copy.'

The poems mentioned in the above letter are in the Manx dialect by Mr. Brown, a master at Clifton College. Both *The Doctor* and *Fo'c'sle Yarns* were great favourites with Max Müller. He had been made acquainted with them by Mr. Wilson at Maloja, who, himself a Manxman, read them with the proper pronunciation and intonation. From Venice the Max Müllers went to Bologna, where a long day was spent at Signor Minghetti's, the Minister; and three days were given to Ravenna, and he then settled for November in Florence. Here Max Müller wrote the *Biographies of Words*, and here, too, he found the beautiful sketch of Andrea del Sarto's *Carità*, which, if not the original study, is a very early copy. He published a monograph on this treasure three years later. It is the first portrait of Andrea's wife, and before their marriage about 1515. From Florence Max Müller went alone to Rome to his old friend von

Schlötzer, German Minister to the Vatican, then rejoined his wife and daughter at Siena, and went on by Genoa and Turin to Paris, where his son joined the party as soon as the Oxford vacation began.

TO HIS DAUGHTER MARY.

FLORENCE, *November* 16, 1885.

'I am not sorry to be away during the elections, but I should certainly have voted for Gladstone. I know his foreign policy has been really disastrous, but I cannot help feeling that the Liberal policy is altogether on a higher level, and on a more public-spirited line, than that of the Conservatives. I have perfect trust in a man like Chamberlain; I have none in Lord R. Churchill, or those who use him for their own purposes.'

TO HERR VON SCHLÖTZER.

*Translation.* SIENA, *November*, 1885.

'MY DEAR SCHLÖTZER,—The best thing that happened during our time together in old Rome, seems to me to be Lord Salisbury's toast on an alliance between England and Germany. Whether it was the right time for it, whether Münster's silence meant Yes, or No, are matters for the newspapers; the really important point is, and will be, that a man hitherto so anti-German as Lord Salisbury should have proposed this toast. To speak of an *alliance* between Germany and England is indeed a misnomer. The word applies to alien nations who join for a definite object. Between brother nationalities disputes may arise from time to time; they are generally started by evil-minded neighbours, but when the misunderstandings are once cleared up, the understanding and harmony come of themselves, and alliances, and paragraphs, and clauses, only spoil the natural trust. The terrible and barbarous condition in which we are living can only be ended if Germany and England hold together. We are living like the beasts of prey in prehistoric times. Every man in Europe now is a soldier. It sounds very grand to speak of an armed nation, but the object of human cultivation is security without being eternally ready for war. What should we think of a state in which every one had to carry a revolver in the streets? And what are we to think of Europe when no single state feels itself safe, unless its cannons outnumber those of its neighbour? This must be changed. However much one may now laugh at Metternich, he secured a thirty years' peace for Europe. We shall soon have lived through a thirty years' state of war in Europe. That diplomatic negotiations cannot be carried on in Parliament is now acknowledged by all quiet observers. This impropriety dates from Palmerston's days; before that there was a tacit understanding that the Opposition was not to check the Minister of Foreign Affairs at every step. What has been, may be again. Parliament should have a right to the last word, but to the last, not to daily interference. England is the only land that has not taken to arming the people. Drive England into a corner, and to-morrow every man is a soldier. There may be jealousies between England and her colonies, but if it came to extremities, the colonies would allow no hair of England to be touched. Even India, which was formerly a danger, has shown now that England's enemies are her enemies. Russia may count more millions of subjects than England, but each nation consists of individuals, and can you compare a Russian to an Englishman? I wish they would send you or some other sensible man as ambassador to London. The ambassadors we have had are very clever diplomatists, but they cannot shake off the idea that diplomats must play chess. Come to England, and I will soon show you how things really stand, and what the people really are. So let us hope for better times. The present state of Europe is a disgrace to us all, and history will condemn the second half of the nineteenth century, more strongly than the times of the Huns and Vandals, unless a knight like Charles the Great appears.

'Always yours,

'F. M. M.'

To his Daughter Mary.

Turin, *December* 7.

'Many thanks for your good wishes for my birthday. It was a very quiet day, very different from what they used to be. The weather here is cold, and we have regular English mists. I wish we could have stayed at Maloja. I have never felt so well again. . . . I signed the address for Ruskin, and sent it straight to Dr. Lodge. How strange it is, this craving for recognition, in a man like Ruskin, perfectly unaware that everybody at Oxford will be forgotten when he will be known as the greatest artist in English, and as one of the most honest men of our age. Of course, I do not agree with a great deal of his teaching, but fortunately I can admire men from whom I differ *toto coelo*, so long as I know they are honest in their opinions. The result of the elections seems to me most unfortunate. However, the Liberals will have learnt a lesson, I hope, and Gladstone must try to grow a little younger, and more truly Radical. Have you read my little apostrophe to him in the *Nineteenth Century*?'

After three weeks in Paris, where he was not well enough to enjoy seeing his many French friends, Max Müller and his daughter returned to Oxford, leaving his wife and son in Paris till term began.

To Miss Byrd McCall.

7, Norham Gardens, Oxford, *December* 31, 1885.

'I must not let the year pass by without thanking you and your mother and your sister, "the perfect type of lovely womanhood[1]," for all your good wishes. I do want them indeed, for after we left that delightful place Maloja, all went wrong again, and when we arrived at Paris I felt so far from well, that I went home with Beatrice, leaving Wilhelm and his mother to stay a few weeks longer, as he wants to improve his French. Here, at Oxford, I am better again, and I enjoy the rest. After all, there is a good deal of travail in travelling, at least to an old man—you do not seem to feel it.

'We all enjoyed Maloja so much, and had so many pleasant people staying there, that we shall find it very hard not to go there again next year. What a pity you could not come there: you would have enjoyed it better even than balls and desperate flirtations in England! What will be the end of it, or will there never be an end of it? I am sorry I shall not live long enough to see you a stately matron, very much shocked at the vagaries of those young people. I should like to see that, but alas! it cannot be.

'I went to Rome for a few days only, and saw no one but my old friend Schlötzer, who is now German Minister to the Pope. We talked much about America, and we agreed very much on the subject of American young ladies.

'My very best wishes for 1886 to you and yours. Shall I hear no songs in 1886? Why can what has been, never be again? Yet so it seems. However, whatever befall, believe me,

'Yours very sincerely.'

[1] Ruskin called the elder Miss McCall so.

# CHAPTER XXVIII

## 1886–1887

English Goethe Society. Knighthood declined. Indian Exhibition. Oliver Wendell Holmes. Visit of Prince and Princess Christian. Bishop of Colombo on *Sacred Books of the East*. Death of married daughter. *Science of Thought*. Desire to leave England: Queen's message. Lectures for Oxford Oriental School. Rukhmabai. Jubilee. Visit to Froude. Last interview with Crown Prince at Windsor. Scotland. New edition of *Rig-veda*. Speech at Missionary meeting in St. John's College.

RETURNING home to Oxford, Max Müller found a six months' accumulation of letters, papers, and books to sort and acknowledge, and his wife and son had returned from Paris before the work was finished.

The first part of the following letter refers to Prince Christian Victor, who was coming to Magdalen College as an undergraduate:—

To H.R.H. PRINCE CHRISTIAN.

*Translation.* OXFORD, *February* 2.

'I should say that history and mathematics are useful for all careers. It is all right about the title. At matriculation only the name is mentioned; in the Registers of Magdalen College the full title is given with the addition of "Heir to Norway," which I hope will not involve us in a row with Sweden! I, too, could have wished that the Tories had remained longer at the helm, and especially that they had shown their hand with regard to Ireland. I am convinced that Gladstone is as little likely to make concessions hurtful to England's interests as Lord Salisbury. Gladstone is a thorough Englishman, and who is his equal in experience? His foreign policy was atrocious, I admit. The main reason was the fact that Lord Granville did not oppose him. When one meets Gladstone with determination, he yields. Lord Granville's admiration for him was carried too far. Lord Rosebery may turn out very well, if he will accept advice. He suits Bismarck, who has long been wishing to make amends, and who, in the case of a change of Government, will say, "See how beautifully I have arranged it all: my son and Rosebery will carry out everything, only make him successor." Thus lie the cards, and I see no danger in it. When England and Germany hold together, no man in Europe will get the smallest tract of country. The other dangers are much exaggerated. To restore quiet in Ireland is an affair of administration, not of legislation, while a separation of Ireland from England is simply impossible, and nobody wishes it less than Parnell and Co., whatever the newspapers may say. The great difficulty is the land question; now when America, the colonies, and India enter into competition, land has not much more value in England than in America. It can, as in America, support two people, the farmer and the labourer, not three, farmer, labourer and landlord. When the value of a merchandise falls, the merchants who invested their money in it become bankrupt. I fear land is no exception, and the condition of the landlord is sad enough. If Gladstone is a good financier, he is the right statesman for England now, for everything depends now on how, in deciding the land question, it will be possible to save for each what belongs to him. The sea is stormy, but it is of no avail to rage against the waves, and if a man like Gladstone has the courage to steer the boat in such a storm, safe through the rocks, he deserves the help, it seems to me, of every one who has the well-being of England at heart. Gladstone is a serious man, not very amiable, decidedly no courtier, but when one thinks how easy it is to be a courtier, he may be pardoned. At the present time a Minister must lead, but he must also suffer himself to be led; if not there will be conflicts, as in France, Germany, and Russia. The English people—Ireland excepted—have declared that they will be led by Gladstone, so it is natural that Gladstone should take the reins into his hands in spite of his age. It does not do his old colleagues much credit if they forsake him now. When England's honour is at stake, Tories and Radicals should stand together; how much more Lord Hartington and Lord Granville! Well, in spite of all this, I am not afraid for England. I consider her healthier and stronger than any other land.'

### To Miss Anna Swanwick.

*March* 1.

'I am a great believer in party government, as long as both parties remember that there is something higher than party—the commonwealth. That lesson wants drilling into people's minds now more than ever. For foreign policy both parties ought to be as one—in fact, there ought to be a mixed committee for foreign affairs, possibly for the colonies and India also. All the late mischief is due to England not being able to show a united front, and never maintaining any continuity of policy.

'Therefore any such movement as yours has my fullest sympathy, and if I saw how I could really help, I should gladly join it. But I do not like to give my name, unless I can also give my help; and living as I do in Oxford, I am of no use in London. Besides, as an absentee, one has so often to follow where one does not wish to go, and to lend one's name to measures which one does not altogether approve. But I hope that some movement like the "National Political Union" may succeed, and shall be glad to hear more about it. I most reluctantly gave up the idea of spending another pleasant week with you in London, but I hope we shall meet somewhere before long; I have spent all my holidays, but I think I may get away later during the vacation.

'Believe me,

'Yours very truly,

'F. MAX MÜLLER.'

The allusion in the following letter is to a delightful visit of two days paid by their Royal Highnesses Prince and Princess Christian at 7, Norham Gardens, that they might see something of their son in his undergraduate life.

To H.R.H. PRINCE CHRISTIAN.

*Translation.* *March* 1.

'YOUR ROYAL HIGHNESS,—I have been told repeatedly that it might be desirable that Prince Christian Victor should join the University Volunteer Corps. In Cambridge the joining of the son of the Prince of Wales has given the movement a new impetus, and here such a step is very desirable, as we have only about 300 Volunteers. It is a healthy occupation, and I believe that as soon as the first drills are over, the young Prince would be appointed an officer. I have not said anything to the Prince about it, as I wished first to ascertain whether your Royal Highness would agree. To me it seems desirable all round.

'I hope that the excursion to Oxford has been agreeable to your Royal Highness, and may the discomfort of the narrow limits of a Professor's house prove no hindrance in future.'

It was in this month that steps were taken in London to found an English Goethe Society, and the members were unanimous in trying to induce Max Müller to be their first President.

To Dr. Althaus.

Oxford, *March* 4.

'If I lived in London, nothing would have given me greater pleasure than to act as President of the English Goethe Society. That Society ought to exercise a very powerful influence on English thought, and draw the two nations, the English and the German, very close together through their common sympathy with Goethe, with his works and with his aspirations. As in philosophy we say "Back to Kant!" we shall have to say "Back to Goethe!" in poetry and in all that can help us once more to believe in those high ideals of life which guided and upheld him from his youth to his old age. An English Goethe Society, if properly supported, might do much good both to England and Germany. It would show to the Germans that England has still a warm heart for all that is truly noble; and it would show to the English that Germany can still appreciate those to whom she owes her real and lasting greatness. What the German Shakespeare Society does in Germany, the English Goethe Society ought to do in England. With two such ambassadors as Shakespeare and Goethe, we should soon have a true alliance between Germany and England, an alliance independent of changing cabinets, and firmly founded on mutual respect and love. I feel all this so strongly that I should not have hesitated to break through a rule which I have hitherto followed without exception, not to belong to any Society in London. But the same reasons which have obliged me to decline all but honorary fellowship elsewhere, would make it impossible for me to accept the Presidency of the English Goethe Society, if it were offered me. You want an active President, a man who moves in society, and is on the spot whenever he is wanted. Try to get a man like Lord Acton, Lord Arthur Russell, Mr. Goschen, Mr. Froude—would that Carlyle were still among the living! My lot is cast here—I am growing old, and even a journey to London has become an effort.'

To the Same.

Oxford, *March* 12, 1886.

'I assure you it is no unwillingness on my part that keeps me from accepting the very kind offer to act as President of the Goethe Society. My only doubt is whether I should be able to discharge the duties as they ought to be discharged. Whatever I undertake to do, I like to do as well as I can, and nothing I dislike so much as making a promise, and then having to send an excuse when the time comes. I suffer from recurrent nausea, and when I am in that state I am fit for nothing. So I keep aloof as much as possible from all public duties, and confine myself to my quiet work at home, which I can carry on as well as ever.

'However, to show you that I am willing to serve a good cause whenever I can, I write to ask you whether you would really want no more than, say, two visits to London, and at what time of the year? Also, when would you wish for an Opening Address? Just now I am really smothered with proof-sheets, but after some time I may have a few lucid intervals, and I should then try what I could do. I have some interesting and important materials for such an address; but of that by-and-by. You may tell your friends and colleagues what I have written, but I must reserve my final decision till I hear from you again.'

On March 25, Max Müller was commanded to Windsor to dine and sleep, and present the twenty-four volumes of the *Sacred Books of the East* to Her Majesty in person.

From there he went on for a night to Cumberland Lodge.

To his Wife.

Windsor, *March* 25.

'I have just had a long audience; most delightful—the Queen asking after you and all the Kingsleys. I told her of *Col. Enderby's Wife*. She did not know it, but will send for it. After the audience I received a message to stay till Saturday. Prince and Princess Christian dine here to-night. They will take care of me!'

To the Same.

*March* 26.

'We had a very interesting dinner last night. I sat between Princess Christian and Miss Fitzroy. Princess Christian was next the Queen, so that we could talk together. After dinner the Queen talked to me again very freely. Nothing could be kinder than the Queen. She generally speaks German to me, and shows how much confidence she has in me by speaking very openly about many things. She spoke about Prince Leopold; she was very composed. Dr. Sahl told me how kindly the Queen spoke about me, and wished to show me that she appreciated what I had done by asking me to come to Windsor.'

To W. S. Lilly, Esq.

Oxford, *March* 22.

'Many thanks for your collection of Essays, two volumes full of hard work and honest thought on the highest problems. I always tremble to think what the world would be if somebody were suddenly to solve all these problems as you solve a mathematical problem.

We should all die of *ennui*, and we should have the last note which finished the symphony, and no more. I agree with you that the study of history is our best occupation here, if only to make us humble. When I read Herbert Spencer—a writer without any background—I say on almost every page, "There, he has discovered London again!" And I have the same feeling when reading Comte. Did not Renan say of him that he repeated in bad French what every old woman had been saying for centuries in good French? I like the old writers who say what they have themselves discovered; they may say it in queer words, but the thought is fresh, not yet stale. I have been reading a good deal lately for my last work, which I may or may not be able to finish, the *Science of Thought*; and there I find that with Descartes, Locke, Berkeley, Hume, and Kant, I have all I want—everything else is a *réchauffé* and generally smoked. I have read your Dialogue, and hope to read some of your Historical Essays.'

Early in April Max Müller received the following curious letter from Calcutta, which shows better than anything else the estimation in which he was held in India:—

'INDIA MIRROR' OFFICE, *March* 16.

'A friend of mine, Babu Rakhal Sen, a medical man of this city, on occasion of the Shrad ceremony of his deceased father, made certain gifts to you as the first Sanskrit scholar in Europe. These gifts, consisting of articles usually distributed to the Brâhman Pundits in our country on occasion of a Shrad, have been forwarded to you by my friend. I hope you have received them by this time. He has taken the liberty to make the presents to you, and he hopes that, though very trifling, they may be acceptable to you. He has only endeavoured to render some honour to you, as one occupying a foremost place in the hearts of the Indians for his invaluable services in the cause of Sanskrit learning. The fact of a Hindu having on occasion of his father's Shrad made these gifts to you ought to convince you and our brethren in the West in what high estimation your services are held in this country.

'Yours faithfully,

'NERENDRANÂTH SEN.'

The Shrâddh is the most sacred rite of the Hindu religion. It consists of sacrifices offered to the spirits of the departed; and Hindus who have long learnt to despise idolatry, cling with mysterious awe to the Shrâddh. No stranger is admitted, and only certain classes of Brâhmans can officiate or receive the gifts. These consist in food and presents, varying according to the wealth of the sacrificer.

Max Müller received Shrâddh presents on two other occasions, proving that the Hindus ranked him with their most pious Brahmins. The first present he received was a large finely-shaped brass vase with a Sanskrit inscription, and several yards of thin red silk. Another time a piece of cream-coloured tussore silk was sent, enough for a dress, and lastly a chuddah shawl, with the petition that he would wear it for a time, and great was the amusement of some friends who came in to tea to find Max Müller with the delicate white and orange striped shawl across his shoulders. The sacred thread of the Brahmins was sent with the first of the Shrâddh gifts.

On one of the early days in April, Max Müller received a letter from a friend, stating that the Queen had notified to the Prime Minister her desire to confer some mark of her favour upon him; that Mr. Gladstone suggested Knighthood; and that the Queen, before taking any further steps, was anxious to ascertain privately what Max Müller's feelings were on the subject. Max Müller had never sought for any honour, nor had any of his friends ever done so for him; and the idea that his Sovereign had, of her own gracious thought, wished to confer a *public* mark of her favour on him, touched him very deeply. He had lately been at Windsor, where he was more than ever impressed with a sense of the Queen's great kindness to him. Her Majesty and many members of the Royal Family had for years shown their appreciation of his work; and the sense of their kind feeling, one might even say real friendship for him, was more to him than any public distinction. The one proposed for him by Mr. Gladstone (who, as a literary man himself, was well aware of the position occupied by Max Müller in the literary world of Europe, America, and India) was one he could not accept. France, Germany, Italy, and Bavaria had years before this each conferred on him the highest honours ever bestowed on literary men, more than any other living scholar held at that time in Europe, honours he had never solicited. By the side of these honours the Prime Minister of England, where he had lived and worked for the greatest of her dependencies, India, for thirty-nine years, offered Knighthood. Her Majesty fully appreciated Max Müller's motives in not accepting Knighthood, and her gracious sentiments towards him remained unchanged.

To Professor Huxley.

*April* 16, 1886.

'Zeller is the truest historical philosopher, and there is no salvation in philosophy except through history, as, I suppose, there is none in physiology except through evolution. I am glad I persuaded you to answer the *Dawn of Creation*. It is curious to see how these subjects open like volcanoes periodically. Just a hundred years ago Herder wrote his *Aelteste Urkunde des Menschengeschlechts*, and the world has not grown much wiser since. I have been too busy with uninteresting work lately, but I still hope to find time to write something, not on *Genesis* but on *Genesés*, the various ways in which the human mind has satisfied its cravings after the beginnings of all things. Genesis is no doubt the most sensible, but that will not satisfy our friends.'

To P. le Page Renouf, Esq.

*April* 19.

'I come to torment you—only please do not answer this, if it gives you any trouble. I should like to have a passage—if there is such—in which an old Egyptian expresses a hope that his inscription will be read by people to come, or where he curses those that might injure his writings. I want it to show that the ancients thought of us—that they believed in the destinies of a human race. But, please once more, do not lose any of your time about it. I can imagine how you are driven.'

Of the friendship between Max Müller and Mr. le Page Renouf, Lady Renouf writes:—

'They fully appreciated each other's worth. Both men of learning in so many things followed the same way, observing small, apparently indifferent events in history, from which they deduced what might have led to the formation of different languages. Many years ago I once found them in the Bodleian, Professor Max Müller occupying a chair put for me in one of the dens where my husband worked. They were eagerly discussing from whence Solomon could have received certain apes, in order to trace with what nations he might have been in communication. They were so absorbed that they never discovered my presence, and I listened over an hour to their conversation.'

On May 4 Max Müller was present at the opening of the Colonial and Indian Exhibition by Her Majesty. Mention has been made of the opposition of some of the Committee to the use of a verse of Max's Sanskrit translation of the National Anthem. He had felt strongly how undesirable any change was, after the announcement had been made in the Indian papers that the Sanskrit verse would be used. The following paragraph had been printed in all the leading papers in India, both in the English and in the native vernaculars:—

'As a compliment to India and the Indian visitors who will be present at the opening of the Colonial and Indian Exhibition, the second verse of "God save the Queen" is to be sung in Sanskrit. The translation has been made by Professor Max Müller.'

And it was no mere personal feeling of gratification that filled his mind when he heard from Windsor and London that the Queen had desired that the arrangement she had sanctioned should be carried out.

To Sir Henry Ponsonby.

Oxford, *May* 6.

'I found your letter on my return from London last night. After the kind lines which I received from Mr. F. Knollys, I could not hesitate for one moment to obey the gracious command of his Royal Highness the Prince of Wales to be present at the opening of the Colonial and Indian Exhibition.

'And I feel indeed grateful that I went and witnessed what was not a mere festivity, but an historical event. Behind the gorgeous throne and the simple dignified presence of the Queen, one saw a whole Empire stretching out, such as the world has never known, and an accumulation of thought, labour, power, and wealth that could be matched nowhere else. It is well that England should sometimes be reminded of her real greatness and of her enormous responsibilities.

'But what was even more impressive was the appearance of the Queen among her people, and the touching words which Her Majesty addressed to the Prince of Wales. Many eyes were moist when the Queen spoke with such wonderful composure of the First Exhibition, and the great work which was then planned by the Prince Consort. One felt, in the truest sense of the word, the real presence of that noble spirit who lives on in his works, and whose high and unselfish purposes in life begin to be understood and appreciated more and more, even by those who could not, or would not, understand during his lifetime the Prince's devoted love and enthusiasm for everything English.

'As the Queen's voice sounded through that immense hall, and thrilled through every heart of the thousands who were listening in breathless silence, one perceived the immense power which the Queen possesses, not only as the ruler of the greatest Empire, but as the true guide of all that is noblest in the English character. There is in England an inexhaustible fund of sympathy for all that is good and noble and unselfish, but it must be called out and encouraged. When I left the Albert Hall, I felt as if I had heard, not only musical harmonies, but higher moral harmonies—the return of that old chord in which one note, and that the highest, can never be absent for any length of time, and which called forth so warm a response from all who had the privilege to hear it once more.

'I never like to give trouble, but if you should find an opportunity of telling the Queen how deeply grateful I feel for Her Majesty fulfilling what in my Sanskrit translation I had rendered by "Mâyâs*k*a pâsaya" (verse 2, line 5) I should feel much obliged to you.'

TO GEORGE VON BUNSEN.

OXFORD, *May* 12.

'I confess I feel very ignorant about this Irish question, but it seems to me that people allow themselves to be frightened by words. Ireland cannot be separated from England, nor England from Ireland, but it is quite possible it will be good for both of them to live a little more apart from each other. How that is to be done must be found out by our political doctors, and I confess I trust Gladstone more than Lord Randolph Churchill and Co.'

The Germans in London had persisted in nominating Max Müller as first President of the English Goethe Society, and on May 28 he delivered his inaugural address on Goethe and Carlyle. It is published in the new edition of *Chips*, Vol. III.

TO HIS WIFE.

CLAREMONT, *May* 30.

'The lecture went off very well. It was crammed full. Hatzfeld was not there, but I met many others—Bryce, Seeley, Oscar Browning, Blackie, &c. Here everything looks very bright, though there are sad memories about the place. I have not seen the children yet. Here

I shall have some rest, then Monday the Levee, and then home again, which is best of all. It is quite beautiful here, real summer at last; the Duchess so kind. Dr. MacGregor, preacher to the Queen in Scotland, is staying here, clever and amusing. I heard about all that has been going on. —— says he cannot understand it, because he says Gladstone has been very friendly to me. Well, I can do without it. I should have valued any kindness coming from the Queen, but as it is, I have got more than I ever deserved.'

Early in June Oliver Wendell Holmes, with his daughter Mrs. Sargent, spent some days in Norham Gardens. He charmed everybody by his lively conversation and simplicity of manner. Two large parties were given in his honour, all Oxford desiring to meet the 'Autocrat of the Breakfast-table.' He had already had a brilliant season in London, and towards the end of his visit to Max Müller became so exhausted, that the doctor called in was seriously alarmed, and rigorously excluded all callers for the rest of his visit. He has himself described his time in Oxford in his *Hundred Days in Europe*:—

'We met there, at dinner, Mr. Herkomer, whom we have recently had with us in Boston, and one or two others. In the evening we had music, the Professor playing at the piano, his two daughters, Mrs. Conybeare and her unmarried sister, singing, and a young lady playing the violin. It was a lovely family picture; a pretty house, surrounded by attractive scenery, scholarship, refinement, simple elegance, giving distinction to a home which to us seemed a pattern of all we could wish to see beneath an English roof. It all comes back to me very sweetly, but very tenderly and sadly, for the voice of the elder of the two sisters who sang to us is heard no more on earth, and a deep shadow has fallen over the household we found so bright and cheerful. Everything was done to make me enjoy my visit to Oxford.'

Writing to Mr. Moncure Conway of this visit, Max Müller says: 'I became very fond of Wendell Holmes. I liked his books, and now I love the man—only life seems all over, and nothing remains but some duties to fulfil.'

### To Professor Noiré.

*Translation.* *June* 25.

'We live here in a constant whirl; it makes me feel worn out and tired. All the world comes to Oxford now, and all the world comes to stay with us, and next week we expect Prince and Princess Christian of Schleswig-Holstein. After that I expect some rest. My essay on Goethe and Carlyle I have arranged myself for a German journal. I have only just finished it. . . . I long for rest and work, but I have got so much behindhand lately, that I feel I can make no plans whatever at present; my only thought is how to sit still at home. The political confusions are very engrossing, though I keep away from them as much as possible. I am sorry for Gladstone, he ought to have retired long ago. After all, old age has its limits, which cannot be ignored without evil consequences. He is a political Aristides. Hence all the lacrumae.'

In July Max Müller had the honour of receiving Prince and Princess Christian as his guests for Commemoration. Their Royal Highnesses entered into almost all the gaieties of the week, attending a ball at Magdalen, their son's College, and the Vincent's Club Ball, concerts at Magdalen and New College, the Masonic Fête, the Encaenia and luncheon at All Souls, and ending with a large private picnic at the old Manor House at Water Eaton. It was shortly before this that Mr. Bright had separated from Mr. Gladstone on the Irish question; and knowing that Mr. Bright was to receive an honorary degree at Oxford, the Queen sent him a message, through Princess Christian, to express Her Majesty's pleasure at his staunch adherence to the existing constitution, even at the sacrifice of old and faithful friendship. Mr. Bright came to the Max Müllers to see his Royal Highness, and it was deeply interesting to see how the veteran statesman was gratified and touched by his Sovereign's gracious message.

It was in this year that the Bishop of Colombo wrote to Max Müller with reference to the objectionable character of parts of the *Vinâya* texts, and expressed his regret that the absence of these parts from the English translation, in the *Sacred Books of the East*, had not been more explicitly noted. A violent attack was also made in the *Dawn in India*, stating that 'Max Müller had given a false idea of the real character of some of the Buddhist books, especially of their moral character, and the tendency of their teaching.' Later, in 1895, the Bishop stated that *he* had never meant to insinuate that the translators had intended to conceal what they had omitted to translate.

Max Müller defended himself against the implied imputation of having wilfully deceived the Buddhists as to the moral teaching contained in their Sacred Books, by saying that though the portions omitted were untranslatable, either the originals had been left, or, for the guidance of missionaries, Latin renderings had been given. If Max Müller took any notice of the attack in the *Dawn in India*, which was repeated in the *Home News*, his answer has not been traced. The subject was revived in 1895 by Professor T. M. Lindsay of Edinburgh, who wrote to the papers:—

'The fault I find is that, so far from giving complete translations, Professor Max Müller has omitted large portions without letting his readers know that these have been omitted, and has, in consequence, allowed his readers to misunderstand the more objectionable sides of these religions.'

Dr. Lindsay added that Professor Max Müller's statements seemed to him 'not merely very unsatisfactory, but disingenuous.'

The Bishop of Colombo had written shortly before this a letter to the *Times*, which was followed by a letter from Professor Max Müller saying that he felt 'truly grateful to the Bishop of Colombo for his letter in the *Times*, and for the handsome manner in which he has explained the misunderstanding to which some of his words had given rise.'

Max Müller did not feel called on to answer Professor Lindsay's attack. The Bishop and Max Müller met in 1895, and any little soreness that had been felt was speedily removed in personal intercourse.

### To Professor Noiré.

*Translation.* 7, Norham Gardens, *August* 7, 1886.

'Believe me, it is a great sacrifice to have to give up all travelling plans. I need rest, fresh air, change, and I know I shall have to suffer for it later on. But it cannot be; my duties here require my presence, and it would be wrong to shirk them. I had so looked forward to going through my MS. with you, but that too has to be given up, unless you could come to England. I have to write just what I am writing to you to twenty other friends, whom I hoped to meet at Maloja, and so it cannot be helped, and we have to take life as it comes. There is one advantage, perhaps. I may complete my book a little sooner, all being well. Here it is beginning to be quiet and lonely; only birds of passage appear now and then in order to work here. I am now in the midst of logic, reading Mill and many other books which I have forgotten, and which have to be referred to in order to keep in contact with the public.

'I heard yesterday about Scherer's death. How sad, such a young and active man! I have just finished my Reader, which is to be a pendant to his *History of German Literature*, two volumes. He looked through the last proof-sheets himself. So one is left whilst the bullets strike all round one. I had just lately a letter from Liszt, announcing his visit for next year, and now he too has played his last melody, and is, I suppose, very glad to go to rest. How little seems to remain of a musical artist! All that he has created belongs to the moment only, while the pictorial artist knows that his work will live at least for 500 years. His (Liszt's) compositions do not appeal to me, but his pianoforte playing was astonishing. I heard him for the first time about 1840 at Leipzig, when with Mendelssohn. . . . Well, do take care of yourself, and try to recover strength during your holidays, and shake off your cough before you return to the yoke, and keep in memory your,' &c.

Max Müller's old love of music made the visits of musicians to his house a peculiar pleasure to him. About this time we find in the Visitors' Book the names of Blumenthal, Emil Sauer, Joachim, and Friedländer, for whose new edition of Schubert's songs he wrote the preface.

But a terrible break was to come to the quiet work Max Müller had planned for Long Vacation. On September 3 his married daughter died quite suddenly at the seaside, and was brought home and laid to rest in the beautiful Holywell Cemetery, where so many of Max Müller's friends sleep, and where he himself now rests. Her almost sudden death made a great impression in Oxford, where she was much loved and admired. Adverting to her in his sermon on the first Sunday in the next term, Dean Liddell said, 'One hardly knew which to admire most, her remarkable mental gifts, or the almost ethereal beauty of her person.'

To Sir Henry Acland.

*September* 12.

'I knew what you would feel for me in this new loss. It came so very suddenly. Her life seemed so perfect in every way. How it happened I do not understand, perhaps no one does. Everything was done to revive her, but in vain. I quite understand what you mean by the sweetness of grief; it is but another name for that love which lasts for ever. Old men like you and me may well indulge in it. What is so hard is to think of her poor husband, with this long, empty life before him. My life cannot last much longer: that feeling helps one to bear even a heavy load.'

To Mrs. McCall and her Daughters.

Oxford, *September* 19, 1886.

'My dear Friends,—You will want to know how we are moving on, but there is nothing to say; we sit and look at each other and are silent. The sun rises and sets the same as before, and life goes on with its daily routine of duties. Our health is quite good, the body seems untouched by what affects the soul, and one knows that though we are much poorer, we shall live, and though life cannot be again what it was, it will have to be lived and even to be enjoyed, till a new blow comes to remind us of the conditions of our stay on earth. It is strange how easily we forget those conditions, in spite of all that is going on around us. It is true that death seemed so unnatural. She was so young, so happy, so useful; there were so many old people who ought to have gone before her; still, we have seen the same before. What is heartrending is to see her poor husband, who tries to be so brave, and hardly knows what has happened. My life cannot be long now, but he, with this long and empty life before him, is indeed to be pitied. He is a good deal with us, but I do not know what he means to do. We stay on quietly here, and see as few people as possible. Everybody is so kind—she has been so widely loved and appreciated—but what one likes is to be left quite alone. You know what sorrow is, and how it brings out the old human bond that binds us all together; how we suffer with others far more truly than we rejoice with them. Still there is a time when every one must remain alone with himself, and when he feels that those who are with God are much nearer to him than those who are still in the world, however dear and near they may be to us. It is a help to know that many are suffering with us, and I know it.'

To Sir Robert Collins.

7, Norham Gardens, Oxford, *September* 23, 1886.

'Please give the enclosed letter to the Duchess of Albany. It was so kind of her to write to me. Those who have felt deep sorrow themselves can best feel for others. I know it. I have shared many a sorrow, and even now, under this new blow, it is the misery of that poor husband and the grief of my wife that chokes the heart far more than my own distress. As one grows old, one learns to surrender, and one also feels that those who are with God are often nearer to us than those who are still left to us on earth. But it is hard to see the utter misery of others, and to feel that one cannot help them. Nothing could be more perfect than the happy married life of my daughter. She was so much loved, and, young as she was, she was doing her very best to help others. She was very attractive, yet very earnest, very conscientious, and as true as a silver bell. It was a pleasure to see that such a natural, simple, right, and happy life as theirs was, was possible in our entangled society. But now to see that empty house, and that lonely man in it, is heartrending. I wish I could take him away for a time, but he wants to stay where he is. Perhaps at Christmas we shall move South.

'My wife thanks you for your kind words of sympathy, and I remain always, 'Yours very truly and gratefully.'

To Horatio Hale, Esq.

Oxford, *September* 24.

'I am always very glad to hear from you, and as I am apt to forget answering letters if I do not answer them at once, I sit down to thank you for your paper "On the Origin of Languages." I have read it with much pleasure. I have no faith in Nursery Philology, and have just written on the subject in a book now passing through the Press, *The Science of Thought*. The observers are not scientifically educated, and the children can never be completely isolated. They all have the impression that there is such a thing as speech from seeing and hearing other people. Alphabets have been invented, phonetic alphabets too, by people who saw others write. But the original invention of writing passes through many stages, ideographic, determinative, syllabic, phonetic. So, I believe, it was with speech. As to the date, who can tell! However, 10,000 years will account for many things, even for a common radical period of speech, out of which Âryan, Semitic, and Turanian speech might have developed—for the possibility cannot be questioned, as I tried to show years ago in my letter to Chevalier Bunsen, and again in my *Stratification of Language*. However, there is a wide gap between the possible and the real. I also collected some curious observations on children's languages in my *Lectures on the Science of Language*, which are useful to account for differation, but hardly for invention of speech. I am still able to work, and have always looked on mental work as on bodily exercise—it strengthens, it does not weaken. What has interrupted and prostrated has been sorrow, loss of children and dear friends—that is the penalty we pay for living too long. I hope you have been spared these trials, and that you may long be spared to continue your useful work.

'What a pity it is that your first work, your *Report on the Languages of Australia, &c.*, should be so little accessible! Could you not reprint it in a small form?'

### To Dr. Hosäus.

*Translation.* Oxford, *October* 10, 1886.

'It is a new deep wound, but when one has lived so long, one must get accustomed to such wounds. The happy ones leave us, and we must struggle on till the hour of deliverance strikes for us. I can imagine no more beautiful life or death than my daughter's. She had had all on earth that heart could desire, and in one moment she passed away to the better life. She was most gifted, read Latin and Greek with real enjoyment, spoke German and French like English, and in her last stay in Italy had gone deep into Italian. And with all this she neglected none of her duties, and none miss her here in Oxford more than the poor and the fallen. What the poor husband is to do I cannot think, with a long, empty life before him. To me it is as if the winter of my life had come in earnest, and must soon end it—and that thought helps one to bear much.'

### To Sir Robert Morier.

Oxford, *October* 13.

'One puts off writing and everything else from day to day, but time brings little change. One feels more tired, that is all. It is just ten years ago that I had to go through all this—that was the beginning of autumn; now I feel that the winter has set in, and that all must be over soon. Death seems so natural now, and one feels so willing to go where those who were with us so long have gone before us. She had wonderfully developed: she read Plato with real enjoyment, spoke German and French like English, was deep in Italian, and played really beautifully. With all that, she spent herself for the poor in this place, and the feeling excited by her death was extraordinary, considering how young she was. We received over 300 letters and messages, from the Queen down to little children; and now it is all over, and one has to go on, and work on, and wait till our time comes. I cannot imagine a happier life than hers has been, nor a happier death—it is a mistake to live too long.

'I knew you would feel for us, and sorrow certainly brings out the old bond that binds us all together. That is a help, but still life is changed, and one asks in vain, Why?'

To B. Malabari, Esq.

*October* 26, 1886.

'I hope you do not consider the battle lost. Now seems to me to be the time to resume work with double vigour. In every fight against old-established prejudices, defeat is at first inevitable, but it is invariably the precursor of victory. I do not see that you could have expected more from Government. Government in India is no longer what it was fifty years ago. The motive-power, and therefore the responsibility, is at home, and "at home" means "in a house divided against itself." I begin to believe that Mill, who was so much abused for his defence of the old East India Company, was right after all, and that it was an evil hour for India when it was drawn into the vortex of party government. But, as I say, government in India being what it is, you could not expect more than that advice would be asked all round, and responsibility eschewed.

'Now mind, I am not in favour of paternal government, not even in India. But I hold that Government loses its *raison d'être*, if it does not prevent and punish what is morally wrong, even though the moral wrong has the sanction of religion and tradition. I do not say that infant betrothal or even enforced widowhood are morally wrong, but the consequences flowing from them lead to civil torts, which any Government, deserving that name, ought to prevent.

'That infant marriage has no sanction whatever from either *S*ruti or Sm*ri*ti I told you from the very first, and I see that no Pundit now ventures to gainsay that. Manu wishes a young man to marry when he may become a G*ri*hastha, i.e. when he is about twenty-four years of age. As to the girl, she is to marry when she is fit for it—and that may vary in different climates. But an engagement between infants is never contemplated by any legal authority, much less are the sufferings of widowhood inflicted by *S*ruti or Sm*ri*ti on a girl whose polygamous husband dies before she has even seen him. That argument has been treated with so much learning by your own scholars and lawyers that nothing more need be said on it. The study of Sanskrit, even by so-called Mle*kkh*as like myself, begins to bear fruit. You remember how, in the case of suttee, the Shastris quoted passages from a last sâkhâ of the *Veda*, intended to show that widows should be burnt with their husbands. They actually tampered with a passage from their own sacred *Veda*, and not till I published the passage from the Âsvalâyana Grihasûtras, forbidding widow-burning, would they become silent. With regard to the proper age for marriage, I published the important passages in my *Hibbert Lectures* in 1878, pp. 252–3, and as these lectures were translated under your auspices into most of the modern languages of India, I doubt whether any Shastri *now* will dare to invoke either Sruti or Smriti in support of infant marriage.

'However, the argument derived from Sruti or Smriti may by this time be supposed to be surrendered, and the case stands simply thus: "Infant marriage is a native custom, and we do not want the Government to interfere." I have not a word to say against this argument, provided always that no tort is inflicted on individuals. Government does not deserve the name of Government, if it declares itself unable to protect each individual subject against personal torts, whether sanctioned by custom or not. Now, infant betrothal is a tort—it is a contract made without consent of one of the parties. If therefore that party suffers and wishes to be released from an unjust contract, the Government ought so far to protect him or her. Whether the Government is foreign or native, does not matter. It is *your* Government, so long as you accept it and enjoy all the advantages of it; and to turn round and say that your Government should not prevent and punish iniquity is self-contradictory. Do you not invoke the aid of the Government to stop drunkenness or Thuggee? The Thugs appealed to custom and to their protecting goddess, but the Government did not listen, but did its duty. Now ask any high-minded woman, what is preferable—to be killed in the most expeditious way, once for all, or to marry to a man whom you loathe—and I believe the answer cannot be doubtful. The custom of infant betrothal is unjust, the custom of infant marriage is criminal. In the former case, Government should give every relief that is demanded by the injured party; in the latter, the Government should punish the criminal. But for the unfortunate feeling against Government interference—in many cases a mere excuse of the interested parties—no man worthy of the name of Ârya would tolerate or try to explain away such iniquities. I wish the Government, while declaring its impotence, had at least given expression to the righteous indignation which every Englishman must feel when reading the accounts you have published of infant-brides and infant-widows. That would have been no great risk, and it would at least have given some encouragement to you and those who work with you in continuing your crusade. However, depend on it, justice will be done. Write a short pamphlet, containing nothing but well-known and well-authenticated facts, and send it to the Women of England. They begin to be a power, and they have one splendid quality, they are never beaten. If they once know what is going on in India, tolerated by an English Government, they will tell every candidate for Parliament, "Unless the blot is removed from the escutcheon of England, you shall not be reelected." Women at all events have courage, and when they see what is hideous, they do not wait for orders from home before they say what they think. Secondly, educate your own women, and depend on it, this matter will soon be set right, in spite of temporizing governors or half-hearted reformers among your own countrymen. I know many of my native friends will be very angry with me for writing this. I only wish I could speak to them face to face, and I should soon convince them that I care more for the good name of the true Âryas than they themselves. You know I abstained from writing on this subject for a long time. I felt it was in good hands, and I do not like, nor have I time, to give my opinion on everything But now that apparently you are beaten, I cannot remain silent, and the more my friends in India abuse me, the more proud I shall feel. If they call you ignorant, because you are a Parsi, what will they call me—a mere Mle*kkh*a?'

### To W. S. Lilly, Esq.

Oxford, *November* 22, 1886.

'. . . Materialism, in the most general sense of the word, ought to produce selfishness, and therefore immorality. But as a matter of fact, looking about among my friends and back to what history teaches us, it is not so. Materialists are mostly serious-minded and moral men, whilst the greatest amount of immorality meets us among those who are most orthodox in their religious opinions, most regular in their attendance at church, and most shocked at the opinions of Darwin, Huxley, &c. How is that to be explained? For though I may have stated the facts too broadly, you know no doubt, from your own experience in London, what I mean. A very interesting article might be written on that point, and it would only be fair to write it. Of course one is not at liberty to give illustrations and to say all one does know, but history would supply illustrations, without consulting the Society papers, or the Law Reports.'

### To the Same.

Oxford, *December* 5.

'No, I have been so busy with Roots, that I have not yet been able to read Huxley's article. But I have been thinking a good deal about your thesis that Materialism produces immorality, and I feel more and more convinced that the facts are against you. I believe that in many cases immorality produces Materialism, using that word in a very large sense. Materialism is a welcome refuge for souls troubled by a bad conscience, but as a rule I find the honest Materialist is a serious-minded and conscientious creature. Criminal statistics ought to be studied much more carefully than they are. In Buddhist countries, where religion is atheistic, in the usual sense of the word, morality is wonderfully high. Even now, when India has been infected with many European vices, it stands very high, I believe, in the tables of morality. These things ought to be carefully considered, before we draw large inductions. The *causa mali* must be somewhere else, the *malum* cannot be denied—our society is rotten—but why? I believe it is the *unreality* of all religion which is the principal cause. People read the Psalms every day, and tolerate adultery in their private houses. No religion, and atheism, would be better than that hypocrisy. And that hypocrisy is encouraged by the half-heartedness of all the people, clerical or lay, who write and speak about religion, and who do not believe what they write and say. An honest belief in Karma, such as the Buddhists have and really have, does more good than all the Ten Commandments. So it seems to me, but I confess the recent revelations in London have staggered me, and I am quite prepared for an outburst of indignation which would sweep away certain Dukes from the House of Lords and certain Right Honourables from the Privy Council.

'Our feeling against Matter dates from the Gnostic Schools. Matter in itself is very wonderful; we know very little of it, and yet that very little constitutes the knowledge which we are so very proud of. Matter has been unfairly treated.'

To Moncure Conway, Esq.

Oxford, *December* 13, 1886.

'Your letter has made me very miserable. Yes, I know indeed what it means to look into the open grave of a child: we are much the same again—the heart within us becomes petrified, the joy of life is gone.

'Work is some kind of medicine, and I take as much of it as I can. I hope to bring out a large book, on the *Science of Thought*, next March. I have written it for myself, and I doubt whether many people will read it. . . . I think religious papers should be chiefly historical. They ought to show how we and others have come to be what we are. If we know that, we generally know what we and what they ought to be. History, if properly understood, can take the place of philosophy, and there is so much to be done in the history of religions. If I have any chips likely to suit you, I should send them to you, but my present block is philosophical, not religious.'

The fourteenth edition of the *Lectures on Language* came out this year, and the little monograph on Andrea del Sarto's *Carità*.

After a very quiet Christmas, Max Müller sent his wife and son for change to Hastings, and his daughter went to London, whilst he remained quietly at work in Oxford.

To Professor Legge.

Oxford, *January* 2.

'I do not understand much about Lao-tze, but I can quite believe that what we possess of him may have been written down later than 500 B.C. But that would not affect the canonical character of his book, as little as the uncertain date of certain books of the Old Testament affects its canonicity. I have had a kind of hope that it might be possible to trace Indian influences to Lao-tze. The coincidences between his teaching and that of the Upanishad is great.

'The Tao comes very near to the Rita. But what is possible in one country is possible in another, and as yet I see no historical channels of communication either between the Upanishad and Taoism or between Christianity and Buddhism. We must wait. But there can be no doubt about the usefulness of a scholastic and faithful translation, and I hope you may soon be able to continue your work.'

To Dr. Prowe.

*Translation.* *January* 2.

'Yes, the last year has been a very hard one. But our life cannot last so very much longer, and the happiness that children can give us has been ours. Now we have only two, a son and a daughter. I have tried work as a remedy, and have just finished a thick volume on the *Science of Thought*. It contains much that is old and much that is new; but whether the present-day people will read it or not, I do not know. At all events, one's heart is still for a time, when one's head works, but, alas! it does not last very long. I cannot complain of my state of health; when I can sit quietly at home I feel always well, and my work is progressing, only one's memory is not so trustworthy as it was, and everything has to be verified.

'I think in April, when I have finished everything, we shall leave this for a while, and perhaps go first to Ems and then somewhere else. I wonder whether we shall meet once more in this life? Everything hurries on so fast now; nearly all my friends have preceded me; and life, which looked so long, looks now so very short. *Carpe diem* is all that remains.'

### To Professor Noiré.

*Translation.* *January* 22, 1887.

'At last my book is nearing its end, and I shall be glad indeed to have it off my hands. Then I have to think about writing my lectures on the Science of Thought, and after that I hope to get away. Your remarks are always a pleasure. They are like talking with you. But you know language is always a hindrance to the understanding—no one word has the same meaning for two people. And nothing is more difficult than to represent another's opinion in our own way. Judging by your former remarks, I thought that you tried to derive the demonstrative elements from predicative roots. Others have done the same, and I do not deny the possibility, only I can find no case to *prove* this. You will see I only mention the different view historically without entering upon explanations. You must always put the principal factor in the foreground, especially with Englishmen, and never lean too much either to right or left. I suppose the book will hardly be popular with the English public; well, never mind! *dixi et salvavi animam meam.*

'The matter is behind me now and done with. There is a book on Mythology to follow, and perhaps the preparation of a new edition of *Lectures on the Science of Language*, and then I may be allowed to say, 'Now lettest Thou Thy servant depart in peace."

'The only peace for me is to be found in uninterrupted work, so as to prevent all possibility of brooding. The time will come when all and everything will belong to the past—till then it is best not to look backwards, nor to the right or left, but only forwards.'

### To W. S. Lilly, Esq.

Oxford, *January* 24, 1887.

'My dear Sir,—In the sense in which you take Buddhism it is not Materialism, and I quite agree with what you say. Only so many people call Buddhism, Materialism, though what they mean is, I suppose, disbelief in a personal God. Have the two things anything in common? I do not know.

'Your answer to Huxley is very powerful. Was it he or Tyndall who said he was a materialist before, but an idealist after, a good dinner?

'Huxley writes as he feels at the time, but he is not a close reasoner.

With all that, I have great faith in him, and I think you and he would understand each other. I shall return the article in a few days—there are some passages I want to read again.

'I have had to write about Materialism in the last chapter of my book[1]. It is finished at last, and I wonder what you will say to my representation of Materialism, Spiritualism, and our other difficulties. People will call it *Nominalism* and have done with it, though it is the very opposite of the old Nominalism. It is a book I have written for myself, and I doubt whether it will produce the slightest effect. But I believe in Karma—it is done: that is enough.'

From the time of his gifted daughter's death Max Müller's thoughts often turned again to Germany, but he mentioned it to but few friends, and it was therefore a surprise, but a deep consolation and gratification, when he received the following message from his Sovereign through Princess Christian, by whose gracious permission both the message and Max Müller's answer are given here.

The Queen wrote:—

OSBORNE, *February* 6, 1887.

'I hear with dismay of the possible intention of Prof. Max Müller to leave England and settle in Germany. It would be a most serious loss to the University of Oxford, and to science in this country, where he is of so much use, and is so much looked up to. For his wife and children it would be a terrible blow, for it would rend all the ties of early years, and I am sure neither he nor they would be happy. A short change of scene might be beneficial after his great loss and sorrow, but I should most earnestly deprecate his leaving this country to settle in Germany. His friends will, I am sure, urge and beg him to give this idea up, as I do.'

Max Müller's letter to Princess Christian was as follows:—

*Translation.* OXFORD, *February*, 1887.

'YOUR ROYAL HIGHNESS,—I have been deeply moved by the gracious interest which Her Majesty has condescended to take in my plans. Ever since I came to England I have always felt the deepest reverence for Her Majesty. Though living far from the Court, I heard from my friends, Bunsen, Stockmar, Dr. Meyer, and later on

[1] *Science of Thought.*

Stanley, so much of the innermost sanctuary of the life of the Royal Family, that I always looked upon it as a jewel of the most perfect earthly happiness. The years of mourning which came later, and the insight into the deepest depths of the heart which Her Majesty has accorded us through her books, only heightened the feelings of respect I had cherished so long. I am not speaking of the Queen as the representative of the great power of England, before whom one bows in silent veneration. I speak of her as the noble, good, and heavily chastened woman, who, in spite of all disillusions, has never lost faith in goodness and right, and love to mankind. Words of sympathy from such a heart have moved me more deeply than I can say. I do not know how my thought of spending the evening of my life in Germany has become known. I have only talked about it with my wife and children. My wife quite agreed with me; my children, the two left to me, did not. I had therefore settled to finish up my work here, and leave this in May, and see how it suited us in Germany. After the heavy sorrows I have had here, I often have a feeling as if I must leave Oxford, and place those still left me in a place of safety. And then nearly all my old friends, who received me with open arms when I settled in England, and who made it a second home to me, are gone before me. The new generation knows me not, and jealousy, envy, and intrigues have often of late years embittered my life. I have been silent about this, but I know that my wife and others near to me have felt deeply how unfairly I have been treated, and how in certain quarters trouble has been taken to injure and thwart me in every way. But these smaller trials moved me little, compared to the great sorrow that has fallen on us. But others feel them; I only feel that I must get away; perhaps it is the feeling that I have lived too long. My work made me cling to life, and it is not yet finished. I have, however, just printed a thick volume, *The Science of Thought*. That is the best medicine. But as the invalid after bitter medicine enjoys something sweet from time to time, so have I been refreshed by the gracious words sent me to-day through your Royal Highness. I beg you to express to Her Majesty the Queen, in my name and in the name of my good English wife, our deep gratitude. If anything can make me feel that I am still at home in England, it is the gracious message of Her Majesty.'

Early in March Max Müller's large volume, *The Science of Thought*, was published, and at once called forth a good deal of adverse criticism. In writing to M. Renan, he calls it the last word on a subject that had occupied him all his life, and adds that it runs counter to all that was at the time popular in philosophy.

During the same month Max Müller delivered three lectures at the Royal Institution, on 'The Simplicity of Language, the Identity of Language and Thought, and the Simplicity of Thought,' which are a compendium of his larger work. These lectures were published the following year, and to them the reader is referred. Max Müller's well-known aphorism, 'No thought without language, no language without thought,' is there defended, particularly in a letter to a friend given in the preface; the whole correspondence on Thought without Words, between Mr. F. Galton, Mr. Romanes, the Duke of Argyll, &c., and Max Müller, which appeared in *Nature*, will be found reprinted in the Appendix to that work.

Of the large book one review says:—

> 'His book on *The Science of Thought* is essentially a scientific and closely reasoned work. From beginning to end he seems to have studied plain speaking, and if the terminology, or logic, or if physical science has to be used, it is always handled in a way that shall present the fewest difficulties to the general reader. We rejoice the more over this fact because Professor Max Müller has given us a book which deserves to be very widely and generally read.'

On March 26 a great banquet was held in St. James's Hall by the German teachers in England, in honour of the ninetieth birthday of the old Emperor, and Max Müller was invited to preside. In replying to the toast of his own health, the President expressed his regret that his many occupations in Oxford allowed him to come so seldom to London, and that he therefore had so little social intercourse with his many countrymen in England; for he owned that, long as he had lived in England, German ways and German customs still appealed to his heart. Then directing his speech to the occasion of their meeting, he told his audience that he looked on their old Emperor as the greatest of German teachers, for he had taught them first of all to be diligent. A Frenchman once asked how it was that the Hohenzollerns had been so successful, and was told that the Hohenzollerns were a diligent race. And the old Emperor still worked from morning till night. Then the Emperor had taught them to be modest. He had never looked upon himself as more than a good soldier, and all his great triumphs he attributed to his generals, his Ministers, his people. The third lesson was to be learnt from the Emperor's perfect trust and knightly loyalty to all those who surrounded him. No Minister, and he had had Ministers of all shades of opinion, had ever complained that the Emperor had not treated him with perfect openness and fairness. Lastly, there was one lesson that teachers specially needed, as years went by and the duties of life pressed more heavily, and that was youthful spirits and energy. And from whom better than from the Emperor could they learn to remain young, even with white hair; to remain fresh and energetic, even under the most wearisome work?

Soon after this Max Müller received a letter from a Hindu of high position, telling him that, in honour of the Queen's Jubilee, a special service was to be held in his family temple, and that presents would be made to the learned Pundits present. They were all to receive a large green and white checked shawl, and one would be forwarded to Max Müller, 'not only as a token of the respect and admiration with which we, in common with the whole Hindu community, regard you as a prominent Sanskritist, but also for your genial sympathy with the natives of this land, in every matter connected with their welfare. Unless you are willing to accept it, the service at our family temple will be incomplete.' The offering was willingly accepted, and in the course of the summer a large chuddah shawl was received. A little later in the year Max Müller received another proof of the feeling for him in India, in a letter from a native, telling him that the writer had entrusted his photograph to a 'trained artist, to reproduce it on a new and magnified scale, and make a portrait in oil, therewith to adorn my Ancestral Hall, where all who wish may regale their eyes with the sight of the likeness of a truly great man, a true friend of India: though no canvas which decays or marble which wears are needed to perpetuate the name of a scholar and philanthropist—yea of a *Rishi*, who will be remembered in India as long as Sanskrit learning endures, and a Hindu heart remains that can throb with feelings of gratitude.'

The hope Max Müller had expressed in his letter to Princess Christian of getting away from work for a time had to be given up, as he was appointed examiner in Honours in the new School of Oriental Studies; and there being no one else in Oxford who could prepare the candidates in Vedic Sanskrit, of which the Sanskrit Professor was ignorant, he gave up his plans for going abroad himself, sent his wife, son, and daughter to Wiesbaden, let his house, went into rooms at All Souls, and lectured through the term to the candidates for Honours.

To Mr. Nanjio.

*April* 13.

'So you have actually been in India, to Buddha Gaya and Benares! What a pleasure and interest it must have been to you; only your stay was much too short, and I expect you will soon go again. But why not go by way of China and Tibet, and see what books and MSS. they have at Lassa? We were all in hopes of seeing you again in Oxford: that would have been an unexpected pleasure. Well, I hope it may be so yet, only I am getting very old, and if you want to see me this side of Nirvâna, you must make haste. I suppose you found my last letter at Tokio after your return from India. I wrote to you that the beautiful *crêpe* had arrived, and had been much admired by my wife and daughter.

'I also received the books you sent me. One copy of the translation of my essay on Nirvâna I sent to the British Museum. Your book on the Buddhist sects in Japan is very interesting, and I hope you will go on with your work, in spite of the opposition which you meet with. What you want in Japan is an *historical* study of Buddhism, and of other religions too. Unless you know *how* a thing came to be what it is, you do not know *what* it is. A comparative study of religions is very useful if it gives you the history of these religions. You will find in my *Hibbert Lectures* and in my *Introduction to the Science of Religion* all that is wanted for teaching that subject. The other *Hibbert Lectures* by Le Page Renouf, Rhys Davids, Kuenen, Pfleiderer, and Réville are also very useful. But before we compare, we must thoroughly know what we compare. I therefore still think we ought to publish the translations of the texts considered as canonical in Japan. You will find such a book very useful, but I do not like to publish anything incomplete.'

To Sir Robert Collins.

All Souls, *April* 23.

'I shall have to stay here till the end of June, and act as examiner in the Oriental School. It is a curious sensation, living in a small and decrepit college room, shouting for a servant out of window, dining in hall, and all that. Still every change does one good, at least for a time.

'My wife will be very sorry that she cannot avail herself of the gracious invitation of H.R.H. the Duchess of Albany. If I may come without her, I should enjoy a quiet Sunday at Claremont very much. I am afraid I cannot or ought not to be away on Friday, as my pupils depend on me, but if I might come from Saturday till Monday my conscience need not smite me.'

Among other subjects occupying Max Müller's mind this year, that of Indian infant marriage and enforced widowhood, and particularly the case of Rukhmabai, took a prominent place, and he wrote many forcible letters on the point to the *Times*, at the same time carrying on a large correspondence with people interested in these matters in England, America, and India. His friend Mr. Malabari, of Bombay, had for several years been spending his time, money, and strength on behalf of his young countrywomen. To Max Müller the subject was interesting, not merely from its moral and physical aspect, but in connexion with the ancient Indian laws. On April 17 he wrote to the *Times*:—

'Sir,—I am not going to weary you with all the judicial lore bearing on the question of what is called infant marriage in India. It is accessible now to every one who cares for it. I myself adhere to the statement which I made in my *Hibbert Lectures*, 1878, that Manu wishes a young man to marry when he is about 24 years of age, and a girl when she is fit for marriage; *voilà tout.* But the case of Rukhmabai has really very little to do with Indian law. Let the Indian law be what it is, let public opinion in India sanction the sale and so-called marriage of children of three or four years of age, let those who, like Rukhmabai and others, revolt against this degrading slavery submit to being boycotted or out-casted, but what has the English law to do with such abominations? Why should the English law offer to aid in the restitution of conjugal rights, supposing that conjugal rights exist? We read in no Indian law book that a young girl who refuses to fulfil a contract to which she was no party, or objects to being made a wife by force, should be sent to prison for six months. Whatever the High Court may have decided, the sooner English judges wash their hands of such iniquities the better for the good repute of English law. These are questions which concern Hindoos and Hindoo lawyers. What concerns Englishmen and English lawyers and, more than all, Englishwomen is that the strong arm of the English law should not be rendered infamous in aiding and abetting unnatural atrocities.'

He was careful not to take up Rukhmabai's case with inconsiderate haste, but he felt that use might be made of it to draw general public attention to the miseries of infant marriage, but more especially to the sufferings of the half-million of child-widows, forced to lead a life of degradation and misery, not allowed to remarry, who are treated like lepers, goaded into suicide or infamy, and who have no idea of what happiness in life means. When his friend Ramabai started her homes for child-widows at Poona, Max Müller gave her scheme his warmest support, and aided Mr. Malabari when he arrived in England to draw public attention to the evils of child-marriage. Thoroughly acquainted with native feelings, prejudices, and laws, Max Müller fully recognized the difficulty of the task undertaken by his reforming friends, and founded his hopes for improvement mainly on the spread of education in India, among women as well as men.

Just before the Jubilee festivities Max Müller lost his brother-in-law and friend Theodore Walrond, a man whose ripe judgement and upright character were a guide and help to him in his early Oxford days, whilst his affectionate sympathy had greatly cheered the dark years that preceded Max Müller's marriage.

A week later Max Müller was commanded to Buckingham Palace to present the Jubilee offering of the German colony in England, a large picture of all the living members of the Royal Family. Here he met the Crown Prince, and was greatly distressed at his altered looks, which those who had seen him at a distance in the great Jubilee procession, where he bore himself so gallantly, 'a very perfect knight,' had not noticed. He could hardly speak above a whisper; and, though gracious and cordial as ever, they could have but little conversation.

A fortnight in July was spent by Max Müller and his wife at Salcombe, with his old friend Mr. Froude, who vainly tried to imbue Max with his own love of yachting. It was fiercely hot weather, and though the sea was generally like glass, the heat had all the effect of rough weather, and after a few attempts Max stayed on shore. The country round was explored on foot, or driving, and the old friends enjoyed their time together like school-boys.

On July 16 Max Müller had his last interview with the Crown Prince, whom he had known from the days he spent in Oxford, under his guidance, in the year 1851. He was ordered to dine and sleep at Windsor, to meet the Prince, who had since the Jubilee been at Balmoral, and had returned south, very much benefited by the fine Scotch air. He was able to talk with Max Müller for fully half an hour, till one of the equerries came up and said, 'Your Royal Highness, not another word!' and the friends parted to meet no more. It was on this occasion that Max Müller saw one of the Indian Princes perform his strange homage to the Queen. One of the three Rajahs present, in his full Oriental costume, was standing with his curved sword wrapped up in a magnificent shawl under his left arm. As the Queen approached him, she held out her hand, which the Rajah took, and whilst he held it, he prostrated himself and struck the ground at her feet three times with his forehead, and then sprang lightly up. The whole movement was made with perfect ease and grace, and, strange to say, without causing Her Majesty the least inconvenience, though she found it difficult to repress all signs of astonishment.

To Dr. Hosäus.

Oxford, *July* 20, 1887.

'Though I have given up all hope of seeing the monument to my father with my own eyes, I considered it my bounden duty to wait on the King of Greece yesterday, during his stay in London. The King spoke with the warmest interest about the monument, and assured me that the marble had been chosen, and was ready for sending as soon as the sculptor wants it. I could not naturally expect more, and I think it is now a mere matter of business. I was very sorry that I could be of no use to the Prince of Anhalt during his stay in London. I was away for my health in Devonshire, far from any railroad, and ten hours from London. It would have been a real pleasure and honour to have shown the Prince the beauties of Oxford.'

### To Professor Noiré.

*Translation.* Oxford, *July* 23, 1887.

'I suppose I must have over-exerted myself in the attempt to finish my book, and then there has been so much sad trouble among relations and friends, that I had to lie by and be quiet for a while. I went for a fortnight to my old friend Froude, the historian, on the sea-coast of Devon—beautiful country, beautiful sea, dear people, but the heat was too much. I had to return to go to Windsor to see the Queen and to meet some Indian Rajahs; then to the King of Greece, who had provided the marble for my father's monument; and so forth, from one thing to another, so that one never seems to get any real rest. I mean to try the end of next week what Scotland will do; at all events I shall then be far from all worry. I saw the Crown Prince several times. When I met him the last time, his voice had come back.

'Yes, indeed, the papers attack my book thoroughly, but I come across very little of true understanding, with the exception of Romanes, and he a Darwinian. He writes to tell me that he has been convinced by me, and that means much in these days. The "Spencerians" are furious and insulting, but no answer will be given to them. The ignorance of these people is marvellous. Has nothing been heard in Germany yet? What do you think of an essay about the correspondence I sent to you? I am just reading Taine's book, *De l'Intelligence*. I read it some time ago, but I had quite forgotten it. We approach each other closely with regard to the later development of language. He wrote to me about this, and I ought to have referred to him more clearly in my book. But you cannot think of everything. I do not feel well, but hope for better times.'

### To Monsieur Taine.

Oxford, *July* 27, 1887.

'I cannot understand how it has happened that in my book I have forgotten my best ally. I read your book *De l'Intelligence*, when you presented it to me. I made notes and extracts, but while writing my book these notes escaped my eyes and my memory, because I had lately been reading chiefly English writers. I deplore my stupidity, and I am now reading your book again, and shall take the first opportunity of appealing to your name and authority as completely covering my position, and extending even beyond. My position is that what we call thought or ratiocination is neither more nor less than language *minus* the spoken words—in fact, thought stands to language as memory stands to perception. Of course, if *penser* is used in the case of *sentir*, as Spencer does, then we must have another word, possibly *to reason, raisonner*. No doubt it is difficult for one nation of philosophers to understand another nation of philosophers. It was easier to have an international philosophy when there was an international language, *Latin*. However, I do not despair; nay, I hope that a philosophical study of language will help towards it.

'We are going to Scotland on Friday next, and I have taken your two volumes of *Intelligence* with me.'

August was spent in Scotland with Max Müller's old friend Professor William Sellar, of Edinburgh, and his family. Many expeditions were taken, among others one to Craigenputtock, where they explored Carlyle's house, and looked with special interest at the kitchen where Mrs. Carlyle sat up baking the loaf of bread, on which she wrote the noble letter: 'I remained the only person not asleep in a house in the middle of a desert, my body aching with weariness, my heart aching with a sense of degradation.' Then she thought of Benvenuto Cellini watching his 'Perseus.' 'What is the mighty difference between a statue of Perseus and a loaf of bread, so that each be the thing one's hand has found to do? I cannot express the consolation this germ of an idea spread over my uncongenial life.'

To Moncure Conway, Esq.

Dalry, *August* 11.

'People begin to wonder a little whether there is really something in my book. I had a long controversy with Romanes, and he writes to me that he is now on my side. That does not happen often. Sir James Stephen is writing an article for the *Nineteenth Century*, likewise as a convert, but the Spencerians are fire and fury. Is it true that Whitney's mind is affected? I wrote a reply to his last attack, but I have held it back, because I was told he was in a very critical state. I am very busy, and in addition to all I shall have to bring out a new edition of my *Rig-veda*, six volumes quarto. The first edition took me twenty-five years; I hope the second will not take quite so long.'

The above letter mentions the new work which opened before Max Müller during this year, a second edition of the *Rig-*

*veda.* As early as 1884 he had proposed to the India Office a reprint of Vols. I and II, as Vol. I was out of print, and but few copies of Vol. II were left, whilst constant complaints reached him from India of the difficulty of getting complete copies of the first edition, which could only be purchased at from £20 to £30 instead of £10. Max Müller proposed to add to Vol. I the various readings of Sâyana's Commentary which had been omitted in the first edition of that volume, as well as the more correct readings in the text founded on better manuscripts which he had himself acquired since 1849. The Secretary of State offered to provide funds for Vol. I, but he rejected the idea of reprinting Vol. II as too expensive. Max Müller had to give up the reprinting of Vol. I eventually, as the young English scholar on whose services he reckoned had undertaken other work. Then came an offer from the Mahârâjah of Vijayanagara, the place where Sâyana, the great commentator, was born, to defray the expenses of a reprint of the whole six volumes of Max Müller's edition of the *Rig-veda*, and to pay the salary of an assistant for four years.

Max Müller wrote to the Mahârâjah as follows:—

7, NORHAM GARDENS, OXFORD.

'MOST ILLUSTRIOUS AND MOST GENEROUS MAHÂRÂJAH,—The letter which your Highness addressed to me from Madras has been a source of great satisfaction to me. It proves to me that a patriotic interest in the ancient literature of India is not yet extinct in the hearts of those who used to be its friends and patrons. A nation which cares no longer for its ancient history and its national literature deprives itself of one of the mainstays of its national life. We may be better and wiser than our forefathers, but we owe what we are to what they have done for us. To forget their names and their work shows on a larger scale the same want of piety which the neglect of Shrâddh would betray in our own family. Though yours may be a new dynasty, yet you enjoy the glorious name of the ancient kings of Vijayanagara; and that under your auspices the great Commentary of Sâyana on the *Rig-veda*, which owes its origin to the liberality of King Bukka of Vijayanagara, should now be given to the world again, will remain, I believe, for ever one of the most memorable events in the history of India.

'There ought to be no delay. I am sixty-three years old, and I should like to live to see the work finished.

'I shall of course much desire to dedicate this new edition to your Highness. But as the first edition is dedicated to the Empress of India, I should have first to ask Her Majesty's permission. If there should be any difficulty, we might ask to be allowed to dedicate the work to her in common, you as the patron, I as the workman.

'I am truly pleased that I shall now be enabled to leave behind me a new and complete edition of the *Rig-veda*, a work to which I have dedicated the best years of my life, and which even now has disappeared from the market. As to my other books, I shall make a selection of those which are likely to be of interest to you, and pray your acceptance of them as a small token of my gratitude. I have the honour to be, with sincere regard and gratitude to your Highness,

'Yours very faithfully,

'F. MAX MÜLLER.'

This new edition was intended chiefly for India. The Mahârâjah wished to print the work in India, but this was soon found to be impracticable, and it was printed, like the first edition, at the Oxford University Press. The Mahârâjah concludes one of his first letters to Max Müller thus: 'I wish that some time before long we may have the pleasure of congratulating you on the recognition by the English Government of your great services to India.' The Mahârâjah was a keen sportsman, but not a literary man; and this undertaking, which cost above £4,000, showed a truly patriotic spirit on his part, a proper pride in his country and its ancient sacred book, and an enlightened wish to aid in its preservation. 'Besides,' as he naïvely stated in one of his letters, 'I thought it might be good for my soul.' After some delay, a careful young Sanskritist, Dr. Winternitz, was found, who came to England and devoted himself for four years to the correction of the text, and the reading of proof-sheets, under Max Müller's supervision.

TO B. M. MALABARI, ESQ.

OXFORD, *October* 27, 1887.

'I gather from your last letter that you are not discouraged, and that is everything. Reforms move very slowly, still they move, and what you have done has already borne good fruit. The first thing now is to help Rukhmabai through her troubles, and to get the paragraph about imprisonment cancelled. After that, try to establish schools or refuges for widows. Here you might combine with Ramabai. I suppose she will soon return to India. She has become a Christian, but she is not narrow-minded, and may be made useful. Your idea of founding a Mission of Social Reform with your friend Dagaram Gidumal is excellent. Only do not let people think that by Reform you mean Europeanization. On many points your native customs are excellent, and far better adapted to your country than English customs. I do not know much about great towns, like Calcutta or Bombay, but in your villages and smaller towns the tone of morality seems to me much higher than in Europe, your family life much happier, your criminal statistics much lower. If I can be of any use, you know I am always ready to help. But remember, your countrymen do not like advice from outsiders, and they are quite right in that. Remember also that I am getting old, and my time is much occupied.'

In October Max Müller heard of the death of his old friend from University days at Leipzig and Berlin, Dr. Prowe of Thorn. Little as they could see of each other from the time Max Müller settled in England, the sense of warm friendship never diminished. Of all his University friends, Prowe was the nearest to his own heart, and had formed the most intimate friendship also with his mother and sister. The writer Fontane was now the only one left of those early days.

TO LIEUTENANT PROWE.

*Translation.* OXFORD, *October* 16.

'MY DEAR LIEUTENANT,—It becomes more and more lonely on earth, all one's friends precede one, and one sometimes thinks that one has been forgotten. And though I only saw little of your dear father in later life, I always cherished the feeling, when turning back to the memory of old times, that another still shared with me the joy of the same memories. To become old is to become poor, and few, I think, have lost so much as I have.

'That your father remembered us in the last hours of his life is very precious to me. My mother and my sister were affectionately devoted to him all their lives, and we had such bright and happy hours together, such as never come again in later life. Please express to your honoured mother my deepest sympathy. There is one comfort for old age—one feels so much nearer to the future life than to the present; though we must still wait on patiently, and we know we shall not wait much longer.

'I press your hand in warmest sympathy, and I thank you for your sad but kind lines, which did me good.

'Ever your faithful and sincere.'

Early in November the University Independent Club, at Glasgow, selected Max Müller as their candidate for the Lord Rectorship. It was soon found that the contest would be a very keen one, and that Max Müller would have small prospect of success; his name was therefore withdrawn, and Lord Lytton was elected as the nominee of the University Conservative Club.

To the Secretary of the Glasgow University Independent Club.

Oxford, *November* 9.

'I have highly appreciated the honour of being selected as your non-political candidate for the Rectorship of Glasgow University. You did not lead me to expect that you would be able to succeed on this occasion, but as you thought that a protest, from however small a minority, against the present system of electing your Rector might have a salutary effect in future, I was willing to assist you in a movement which seemed to me both right and politic.

'I am far from thinking that the election of a Rector of your ancient and illustrious University ought not to be considered as a political act. Man is by nature a political animal, and the sooner young men are brought to learn their responsibility as citizens, the better for them and for the commonwealth which they will have to serve hereafter.

'But a political act, in the true sense of the word, requires the putting aside of all private interests and the sacrifice of all partisanship. I can well understand, therefore, that the present moment, when the terror of the caucus has muffled the expression of all independent thought, and the eagerness for power has clouded even the strongest intellects, was ill chosen for the assertion of your principles, and I request you to withdraw my name from the coming contest.'

To Professor Romanes.

Oxford, *November*.

'One line to say how grateful I feel for your review. Of course we differ *toto caelo* as to the nature of language, which you treat as mere expression of impression, i.e. cries, while I hold language, or λόγος, in the true sense, to be a totally different act, beginning with the consciousness of a repeated act; the first generalization possible for man; and then a constant classifying of the individual under the general. We speak of different things, though we use the same word. However, we must learn to agree to differ; we cannot all think the same thoughts, or use the same words. Of course much of our communication consists in expressions, signs, gestures, looks; but animals are the best proof that such communication does not develop into language; at least has not done so hitherto, except in the case of that one animal we call man.'

M. Barthélemy-St.-Hilaire presented a report of Max Müller's *Science of Thought* to the French Institute, and concluded his report thus :—

'C'est beaucoup, dans des études aussi ardues, d'apporter pour sa part des idées originales, qui doivent éveiller l'examen au risque de la contradiction, venant d'un écrivain aussi savant et aussi autorisé.'

To C. J. Longman, Esq.

*December* 1.

'Sir James Stephen's article, which was to appear in the December number of the *Nineteenth Century*, has evidently been crowded out. It was too long, and Sir James objected to cut it into two. As to the *Nation*, it is generally supposed that one line in the *Nation* is better than a column in any other American paper. The last sentence of the review was: "A work in which two of the direst and hardest of studies, Analytic Philology and Mental Philosophy, are made at once lucid and attractive, is an acquisition for which all students of those mysteries have reason to be grateful." The *Nation*, and French Institute, and Sir James Stephen would fairly represent America, France, and England.'

Towards the close of this year, Max Müller, at the request of the Rev. H. J. Bidder, the lately appointed Vicar of St. Giles, the parish in which 7, Norham Gardens is situated, presided at a Missionary Meeting held in the hall of St. John's College. The hall was very full. The subject for discussion was the Christian missionary in his relations to other religions. The speech is so clear an expression of Max Müller's views, with regard to alien (so often wrongly called *false*) religions, that parts are given in the Appendix.

# CHAPTER XXIX

## 1888–1889

Vedic Lectureship. Elected Gifford Lecturer at Glasgow. Death of Emperor William I. Memorial oration. Doctor of Bologna. Death of Emperor Frederick. Colonel Olcott. Lecture at Bradford. First Gifford Lectures. Humble admirers. Lecture at Mansion House. Death of Professor Noiré. Lectures at Sheffield, Leeds, and Toynbee Hall. Speech at Royal Academy Banquet. Daughter's engagement. Lectures at University Extension Meeting. Oriental Congress in Sweden. Order of Polar Star.

HARDLY had the January Term begun, before Max Müller was requested to continue his Vedic lectures and work. The Dean of Christ Church, as he wrote himself, 'most reluctantly' undertook to bring the Vedic difficulties before Max Müller, and ask his help. His reply follows:—

To DEAN LIDDELL.

*January 26.*

'I am now sixty-four years old, and before I answer your question let me tell you what an accumulation of work has fallen on my shoulders.

'1. *The Sacred Books of the East*, with endless correspondence. I have hitherto kept to the three volumes a year, but I broke down last year, and could pass one volume only.

'2. *Translations of Vedic Hymns.* One volume is printed. I am hard at work at the second.

'3. New edition of the *Rig-veda.* I am bound by agreement to pass two sheets a week for press, that is one hundred sheets per annum for four years.

'4. Revising German translation of my *Science of Thought*, two sheets per week.

'5. Rewriting of my *Lectures on the Science of Language*, to be ready before the end of the year.

'6. Threatened new editions of two other books of mine.

'7. There is one more book I want to write before it is too late, *The Science of Mythology*.

'Yet, in spite of all this, I was quite ready to give my lectures on the *Veda* this term. But I had lost nearly four weeks with illness, so that when the young men came to me to ask me to lecture, I told them that really I could not. It gave me real pleasure to work with the selected candidates last year. They were hard-working, bright fellows, and I only wish I could have done more for them. . . . I am quite willing to resume my lectures on Vedic scholarship, but if I do that, I must be allowed to bring out one or two volumes of the *Sacred Books* per annum instead of three. . . . I believe that all that is required for the candidates could be done if I lectured to the more advanced students. I shall always be most happy if I can in any way take part in the work of the University, particularly in the preparation of the young men who are destined for the Civil Service in India. The University would not have me when I was young and worth having. Being old now and not worth having, I cannot *offer* my services, but must wait till I am asked.'

The Dean thought that the Delegates of the Press would agree to rearrange the publication of the *Sacred Books*, and proposed that a Readership in Vedic Sanskrit should be founded, so as to make amends to Max Müller for the £200 he would lose yearly from the *Sacred Books*, if he only brought out one volume a year instead of three. This, having passed Council and Congregation, was thrown out in Convocation at the end of February, to Max Müller's great relief, who found himself able to return to his own quiet pursuits, though he had been willing to put himself into harness again to help the University out of the difficulty they had brought on themselves by the Sanskrit election of 1860.

To Dean Liddell.

7, Norham Gardens, *February* 24.

'No one could have been more pleased with the vote of Convocation than I was. I do not think that those who pressed me behaved quite well, but I am grateful all the same, for I could not have done the work without giving up what at my time of life is, I believe, more important. I have accepted the Gifford Lectures at Glasgow; they will be the outcome of the *Sacred Books of the East*. If I can finish them I shall be satisfied.'

Though Max Müller rejoiced, all those interested in the Oriental School were disappointed at the vote in Convocation. One prominent M.A. wrote: 'This is a great blow. I do not know how the school is to be carried on.' From another, Max Müller heard: 'It never occurred to me that any opposition was possible. I feel that, as a member of Council, I owe you an apology for having been a party to introducing your name into a discussion that has ended so disastrously'; and one member of the Board of Oriental Studies felt so annoyed at the vote that he withdrew at once from the Board.

Early in January several of Max Müller's friends in Edinburgh had urged his election as the first Gifford Lecturer in that University. An old Edinburgh man, Hutchinson Stirling, was chosen, and the following letter was written on the occasion to Professor Lorimer, one of Max Müller's most eager supporters:—

OXFORD, *January* 31.

'Your letter was a great relief to me. Though I had told you how little I thought myself fit for the Gifford Readership, and how overwhelmed with work I was, yet I do not know that I should have been able to resist the temptation of accepting a position which offered so grand an opportunity of saying to the world what one wished to say on the subject of "Natural Religion." Since I wrote to you last, a new work has come to me which I could not decline, a new edition of the *Rig-veda* with Sâyana's Commentary, six volumes quarto, each of 1,000 pages. How I shall ever finish it I do not know, but there are certain things to which one cannot say No, and I am afraid your Readership would have been one of them. I know the man whom you have elected: he is a bona fide student of philosophy, and he will tell you what Natural Religion *would* or *could* or *should* have been. *I* think the time for that is past. We want to know what Natural Religion *has* been; that is enough for any man who knows what history means, and what even a Hegelian will have to admit, if he knows the true secret of Hegel, that the Rational only is the Real, nay what even the Darwinians will have to learn in time, that Natural Selection is in truth Rational Elimination, and that Development means the historical triumph of what is right, or reasonable, or, as they now say, fittest.

'Allow me to thank you for your kind feelings towards me. I should have enjoyed a season at Edinburgh very much.'

As soon as the result of the Edinburgh election was known, Max Müller heard from Principal Caird that the Senate of Glasgow University would like to appoint him to lecture in the autumn of that year, and no sooner had he accepted the proposal to stand than he received by telegram the news of his unanimous election. Meantime a letter was on its way to him from the University of St. Andrews, but arrived too late—he was already elected at Glasgow.

Early this year Max Müller brought out his *Biographies of Words, and The Home of the Âryas.*

'The second part of the book,' says one review, 'is concerned with the discussion as to the home of our Âryan ancestors at the time of their division into the branches of the race which we now recognize. The early philologists were unanimous in selecting Asia as the continent, and there was a general disposition to fix on the mountain ganglion in Asia, the Pamir Steppe, known locally as "the roof of the world." Prof. Müller declines to regard it as possible to determine either the exact locality in which the proto-Âryans lived, or the exact language they spoke, or the date at which they parted company. He thinks that the preponderance of evidence favours an Asiatic rather than a European home for the whole race.'

The Appendix to this work contains several very valuable letters to Max Müller. One is on different plants and animals, others on the original name of Jade, whilst the last is on the question whether it was iron or copper that was known to the proto-Âryans, in addition to gold and silver. These subjects are all treated as throwing light on the home of the Âryas.

On March 9 the old German Emperor died, and Max Müller was asked to deliver the Oration at the great Memorial Meeting held by the Germans in Exeter Hall on March 24. It was a memorable occasion. The hall was hung with black relieved by silver, there was splendid music, the Funeral March from Beethoven's 'Grosse Symphonie,' Siegfried's Tod from the 'Götterdämmerung,' and lastly Wagner's 'Kaiser-Marsch'; and the 'Integer vitae' of Fleming, and Neefe's 'Wie sie so sanft ruh'n,' were exquisitely rendered by the joint choirs of the various German Musical Societies in London. Max Müller's speech was listened to with deepest interest and really breathless attention, and his allusion to the Emperor

Frederick moved all hearts, and many were in tears. Our present King and other members of the Royal Family were present, and the hall was crowded, every one in deep mourning. Max Müller's speech is given in the Appendix.

To Herr G. von Bunsen.

Oxford, *March* 27.

'I am indeed glad to see your writing again. Old age comes with its troubles. I, too, was unwell, but am now better. I could not let the opportunity pass without speaking my mind and my heart. It was an effort, but I could not say No. Yes, the days of '48, where are they, and how much is forgotten! As I was about it, I have written something about the present Emperor for the next *Contemporary Review*. One does what one can, what will come is in other hands. If it were only spring perhaps you would come to us, and we might talk over old times. There are few left with whom one can do so.'

The following letter bears no date, but must have been written to the Crown Prince during his stay at San Remo:—

*Translation.*

'From day to day I have asked myself, Shall I write, or shall I be silent? But I can no longer resist the desire. I was so firmly convinced that all danger was over, and now suddenly this terrible news, "overpowering, hopeless, showing men the power of the gods," these are the words that are always recurring to my mind. And yet not hopeless. No, imperial hero! You have seen greater hopes fulfilled, greater than the greatest kings and emperors. You were willing to lay down your life for that which Germany achieved with you and through you—Königgrätz, and Wörth, and Sedan. Who has such names on his shield? And yet that which was behind the shield, deep in the heart, was greater and finer, and that remains untouched. If we only hold fast the belief that nothing happens but by the will of God, we learn to be still, and can bear everything. The older one grows, the more one feels sure that life here is but a long imprisonment, and one longs for freedom and higher efforts. An imperial crown is a glorious ornament, and difficult to renounce, but how small and insignificant is all in this life, when we raise our eyes above. Gazing up to the Lord of the Universe, all strife is made easy. We speak different tongues when we think of the Highest, but we all mean the same thing. But one thing, as long as there is life there is hope, and a man who not only fills his place in life, but has won it for himself, does not give it up. The Englishman is proud, when it can be said,

"He died in harness!" In one, in two, in five years much can be done, and much hindered, and the German people stand at your side, and will bear no tyranny. I can think of nothing, can do nothing; it is as if the last dream of life were dreamt. On all sides one sees and hears German mourning. Yet it is well, that we can suffer with each other. What can I say to her Imperial Highness, the Crown Princess? That gold shines brightest in the furnace. My wife feels all that I feel.

'In old and true friendship.'

Early in April Max Müller was called on to mourn the loss of another relative and faithful friend, his cousin Emilie, Baroness Stolzenberg, widow of Prince Wilhelm of Dessau, whom she had survived twenty-three years. From his childhood she had been devoted to her little cousin, and after her marriage helped him in many ways, not only with money, but by her kindly support, when other members of the family looked askance at what they thought his unpractical views of life and work. To her he owed the introduction to Bunsen, to whom she wrote about him and his projects, so early as 1844.

To his Daughter Beatrice.

Oxford, *April* 1, 1888.

'My dear Beatrice,—Aunt Emilie's death breaks another link that kept me to this life. From my earliest childhood she loved me dearly, and if anything happened to me, good or evil, my thoughts turned to her. There are few left to whom I feel still tied; I shall leave few behind who love me, but there are many who loved me, and to whom I feel united as closely as ever. Those who are gone before us can be very near to us, and they seem to belong to us altogether.

'Ever your loving Father.'

The following letter was written in reply to one received from the Duke of Argyll on the subject of Max Müller's speech on March 24:—

To the Duke of Argyll.

Torquay, *April* 14, 1888.

'I did not wish to imply that Bunsen advised the King to yield to the Berlin mob. Bunsen, as far as I remember, was not in Berlin at that time. Of course, like everybody else, Bunsen was a little off his balance in February, 1848, and he thought that what happened in 1871 ought to happen in 1848. I believe he exercised an excellent influence on the Prince of Prussia at that time, and his advice has borne good fruit.

'When I spoke of the late Emperor as great, I thought I had made it clear that I spoke of his work, not of his personal gifts. But that was the very lesson I wanted to teach—that a very ordinary lever may be used in history to lift the world out of its old hinges. He had a good horse to ride, and he proved himself a good jockey. In his character, so far as I knew him, there was much to admire. He never was self-indulgent; he was very humble, very industrious, very truthful. How different from Napoléon le Grand! As to Charlemagne, we know very little of his private character—what we know of his family life does not give one a very high idea. But great as the work is which he achieved, it seems to me that a united Germany in the centre of modern Europe is a greater work, and the difficulties were enormous. No doubt, the Emperor had Bismarck's assistance. But Bismarck too is personally—so I am told—a very ordinary mortal; and far less free from human weaknesses than the Emperor. But he too knew how to ride his horse, and a splendid horse it was. In the end it was the German people, and in one sense the German schoolmaster, who really did the work. But that is understood, and when we say that the Emperor won the battle of Sedan, we mean his generals, his officers, his soldiers down to the smallest drummer-boy. I have great faith in the future of Germany. If only England would take a leap and openly join the League of Peace, I do not see how war for some time to come would be possible. Where I admire Bismarck's cleverness is in his allowing so much Home Rule to Saxony, Bavaria, Würtemberg, &c., and yet reserving all imperial interests for the Reichstag. That showed a bold hand and real political genius. I hope that no attempt will be made to simplify matters, as they call it, and to swallow up some of the minor principalities. They are centres of life and very useful, without being dangerous any longer.

'. . . On philosophical questions I should like to write to you more fully than I can at present. It requires an effort to see the inseparableness of language and thought. It has taken me a whole life to perceive it. People imagine that I hold that language and thought are identical. There is no sense in that. No two things can be identical. But they can be inseparable—neither can exist without the other, that is what I mean. We imagine that we can think without words, because we can distinguish between the sound and the meaning. So we can between an orange and its skin, but in *rerum natura* there is no skin without an orange nor an orange without a skin. You were one of the few men in England who I thought would see what I meant. But it requires an effort, and it is only an historical study of language in all its phases that has at last led me to the conviction that the Greeks were right, and that what really makes us men and distinguishes us from the animal, is the Logos, i. e. the gathering, or, as Hobbes said, addition and substraction.'

To the Same.

Oxford, *May* 17, 1888.

'I send you my paper, which will not take up much of your time, and yet, I hope, make my meaning of the oneness of thought and language clearer.

'When we say that we think of a thing, but cannot recollect its name, does not that mean that we think of it under different higher names, but cannot recollect its less special name? If I cannot recollect the name of a flower, I think of it and know it all the time under its more general names, say a kind of anemone, a flower, a growing thing, a visible thing, &c. I know it has a special name of its own, and I may remember that name in German, but cannot recall it in English—perhaps never knew it in English. All this does not prevent my thinking of the special flower under less special names, but to think of it at all, not merely to stare at it or remember its image, I must have names. If that is once admited, much will follow from it—but I shall not have time to work it out.'

To Professor Bühler.

*Translation.* *May* 27.

'... Dr. Winternitz is getting on now much better, and if we go on working together so steadily, it is possible that I may live to see the conclusion of the *Editio Secunda*.

'My lectures at Glasgow on Religious Philosophy are interfering with my work, especially the second volume of the *Rig-veda* translation gets interrupted. Well, I sometimes seem to myself a "maid of all work," for everything is put upon me, though I am no longer young. Happily, however, my health is much better, and work agrees with me. ...'

Early in June the Eighth Centenary of the University of Bologna was celebrated in that city. Max Müller was invited, but was unable to be present. He received the Honorary Degree of Doctor of Philosophy, and sent his thanks to the Rector as follows:—

Oxford, *June* 12.

'Most honoured and illustrious Rector,—I received to-day the Diploma by which the University of Bologna conferred on me the honour of Doctor of Philosophy at the celebration of its eighth centenary.

'Though I deeply regret that I was not able to be present to witness that great historical event, I feel proud indeed that your ancient and world-famed University should have thought of me as worthy of a distinction which can never be rivalled by any other honours.

'A University which has lived and worked 800 years represents one-third of the whole history of Europe.

'If 800 years constitute the life of your University, another 800 years will carry us back to the time of Constantine and the recognition of Christianity as the religion of the Roman Empire, while another 800 years would bring us face to face with Junius Brutus, the founder of the Roman Republic.

'These thrice 800 years constitute the whole growth of that European civilization of which we are now enjoying the fruits, and which no country represents more worthily than Italy, the mother of civil self-government in ancient times, the guardian of religion during the darkest ages, and the nurse of academic learning and enlightenment during the last 800 years.

'To have had my name enrolled amongst those who on so solemn an occasion as the 800th anniversary of the University of Bologna were chosen as not unworthy members of your ancient and illustrious corporation, is a reward far exceeding my deserts, but valued with all the deeper gratitude.

'Please, as Rector of the University of Bologna, to accept my sincere thanks and convey them to my honoured colleagues of the Faculty of Philosophy.

'I have the honour to remain, most illustrious Colleague,

'Yours, with sincere regard and gratitude.'

His deep feeling of anxiety about the Emperor Frederick was telling on Max Müller. He felt unable to attend to his work, and went off alone to West Malvern, where the fine air and more exercise than he could take in Oxford always restored him. There he heard of the Emperor's death, and there he stayed till Commemoration, which was going on at the time of the funeral, was over.

FROM HIS WIFE.

OXFORD, *June*.

'I don't doubt your thoughts, like mine, have been constantly to-day at Potsdam, that palace where we have seen them in their happy private life, where all their children were born, where she has watched over her two dying children, and now over her hero husband. I thought at ten o'clock of the long silent procession winding across the park, where they used to ride daily with their children in happier days, to that beautiful church, with the Rauch statues. I thought of our pleasant drive with them to the Prussian village, our hours with them in Venice, glimpses of them here and elsewhere from time to time, our sight of him at Ems, and all that one has hoped for and from him for years—all ended! What a perfect life it has been, as far as character goes, and who can say what of good he may not have done, in these last months of brave endurance! W. is not going to his club ball to-night. The Emperor was one of the people for whom he had a genuine feeling of respect.'

TO PROFESSOR NOIRÉ.

*Translation.* WEST MALVERN, *June* 16, 1888.

'You see I have followed your advice. I felt so tired, and fled here to the hills. The air here is a continuous refreshment, and the views are beautiful. The formation of the hills is volcanic, and they are covered everywhere with verdure. I have often been here, the last time with my two Japanese friends. One is dead, and the other is working in Japan.

'I received the sad news from Potsdam here. How incomprehensible are these blows of fate—how wonderful the world-symphony must be in which even such discords as this cannot disturb the grand harmony! His death has entirely wiped out my last German dream. I sometimes thought that he might call me back to Germany—it might after all have been too late. I must now be content to stay here. Germany has not many attractions for me now.

'I am reading diligently now. I have read through Pfleiderer's thick volume of *Lectures*, also Teichmüller's *Religious Philosophy*, and am now reading Gruppe's *Greek Worship and Mythology*, important, or at least full of matter. His attack upon me gives me confidence in my own cause. Besides these I read many English books, which have to be read, to be *en rapport* with the majority.

'And how are you? The good will to live means so much. If you were only here, I should make you quite well. I run over the hills like a goat. I am quite alone here from morning till night; loneliness is sometimes very beneficial.'

TO HERR G. VON BUNSEN.

*Translation.* OXFORD, *July* 7.

'MY DEAR FRIEND,—"It was not to be," that says everything, but it is like an earthquake, that overthrows everything. Who could have thought it when you brought the splendid *princeps iuventutis* to Oxford! One must look very high to measure such a fate rightly. . . . My wife and children are paying visits. I sit and toil over the lectures I have to give next winter in Glasgow. Sixteen on Natural Religion. At first it was a great weight on me, now it is like new life. I was so glad to get, through you, a twenty-mark piece with the Emperor Frederick's head. It is very beautiful, and reminds me of him, as I saw him the evening before he left Windsor. He called me one of his oldest friends; since then I have heard nothing from him. I hope you are all well. You will still have plenty to do, for I expect serious conflicts, and the time may come when the liberal party may have to support Bismarck, so keep firm in the saddle. I hope to see Morier soon.'

To G. Romanes, Esq.

*July* 1, 1888.

'Nothing I like better than when I meet a man who differs from me; he always gives me something, and for that I am grateful. Nor am I at all so hopeless as many people, who imagine that two people who differ can never arrive at a mutual understanding. On the contrary, I have been convinced by others and I have convinced others, particularly when we meet face to face. Why do people differ, considering that they all begin with the same love of truth, and are all influenced by the same environment? Well, they often differ, because one is ignorant of facts which the other knows and has specially studied. In that case I am willing to be guided by authority, or at all events to remain silent in the presence of those who know more facts than I do. For instance, if Chinese scholars tell me that they possess books written 4000 B.C., I hold my tongue. But in most cases people differ because they use their words loosely, and because they mix up different subjects instead of treating them one by one. I shall not therefore attempt to answer all your questions, or clear up all the points on which we differ, but take them one by one. You say that because I have proved that all *A* is *B*, I imagine I have proved that all *B* is *A*. You admit that we cannot have concepts without names, but you demur to the conclusion that we cannot have names without concepts. You see at once that you use *names* in two different senses. I speak first of concepts which we cannot have without names, and of such names, without which we cannot have concepts; and of such names only, I state that we cannot have them without concepts. This is a strictly logical inversion, and no more. But now you use the word name in a different sense, not as the *sine qua non* of a concept, but as a sign of something, a sensation, or a percept. Of course you may use name in that sense, but it leads to ambiguity. I know a good deal about the ways of parrots, and I understand the barkings of my dog better than most people. But I keep *name*, considering that it means originally *knowing*, for the signs of concepts. I should never use it for denotative signs or cries. I have shown again and again how even some of these denotative or imitative signs and cries lead a little way—chiefly by poetical metaphor—towards the confines of conceptual language, just as plants encroach on the shore-line of the animal kingdom. But the shore-line is there all the same. Now if we can come to an understanding on this point, if we can agree to use name in one sense and in one sense only, we may afterwards go on to the next point mooted in your letter. You must trust me if I tell you that the great bulk of the Sanskrit language has been derived from conceptual roots; and that words derived from cries, whether bow-wow, or pooh-pooh, or yo-he-ho, are mere outside crust. They may be called language, as we may call whistling language (there is a language consisting entirely of whistles), but we then use the same word in two very different meanings, and we have to pay for it. Language, so far as we can analyse it, begins with conceptual roots—what lies outside these roots could not be called language. How old these roots are no one can ever find out; they are ultimate facts, just as the notes of our scale are ultimate facts for music, though we may say that they are noises rhythmified. *Onomatopoeia* will never lead you to *ὀνόματα*—for that you may trust me, for I should have been delighted if it did. So much for to-day, and simply to show in what sense I say that as we can have no concepts without names, we can have no names without concepts.'

It was in this year that Max Müller signed a protest against the sacrifice of education to examinations, contributing, with several others, an article on the subject to the *Nineteenth Century*. 'Many years ago,' he used to say, 'we wanted examinations for the sake of schools and Universities; now we have schools and Universities solely for the sake of examinations.' He felt that the perpetual examinations at Oxford and Cambridge had destroyed all real joy in study. He also wished to see the examinations conducted by older men, who would try to find out what candidates knew; whereas young men, who are generally appointed as examiners, try to find out what candidates do not know.

To Miss Byrd McCall.

Oxford, *October* 22.

'My wife and daughter are gone to Buxton. In about a fortnight I shall go North, to Bradford, Bishopthorpe, Ripon, and then to Glasgow, where I shall stay till Christmas. I have to give sixteen lectures on Natural Religion, which is a hard task at my time of life. I have not been able to get away from Oxford the whole summer. This is my last work, and it ought to be done as well as possible, gathering up all the threads of my former labours, and showing what their object has been. Work is life to me, and when I am no longer able to work, life will be a heavy burden.'

To B. M. Malabari, Esq.

*October* 24, 1888.

'I am pleased to see that the *Krishna Yajur-veda* has been undertaken by the Theosophical Publication Fund. This text will be useful, and I shall be glad to subscribe to it.

'But it seems to me, considering the higher objects of the Theosophical Society, that you ought to publish a complete and correct edition of the *Upanishads*. The *Upanishads* are, after all, the most important portion of the *Vedas*, for philosophical purposes, and if the Theosophical Society means to do any real good, it must take its stand on the *Upanishads*, and *on nothing else*.

'If you have sufficient funds, you should also publish the Commentaries on the *Upanishads*, but that may be done later. At present, a beautiful and correct edition of the text seems to me almost a duty to be performed by the Theosophical Society.'

To Miss Byrd McCall.

Oxford, *October* 30.

'I wish I could think of some good book for you on Greek art, but Greek art with me belongs to the past. As one grows old, one says "Good-bye" to some old friends—very soon to all. Greek art has always interested me, rather for what it meant to be than for what it was. At first art was meant to express thought and feeling; it often failed, but one liked to see the effort to express something. After a time, the purport of art to express thought or feeling was forgotten; the means became the object, and we get most beautiful copies of nature, true, but nothing behind nature, nothing that speaks and tells us something. So Greek art ceased to interest me, and I am ignorant of recent literature. However, if I should think of a book likely to interest you, I shall send it.

'I am very deep in the waters of despair! Sixteen lectures on Natural Religion is enough to drown anybody!

'I shall go next Monday to Bradford to lecture on 'Savages,' to tell them the worst savages are to be found in Europe.'

It was this year that Max Müller made personal acquaintance with Col. Olcott, one of Madame Blavatsky's ardent supporters, and a genuine believer in Esoteric Buddhism. On his return to India, he wrote: 'I am your debtor for one of the pleasantest days I ever passed, and shall always recall it with great satisfaction. It was indeed an honour to make your acquaintance.' Col. Olcott then pressed Max Müller to consider a suggestion he had made of removing the three images of Buddha, which friends will recollect as always standing on the hearthstone in Max's library, to a nobler place. 'The Buddhists are very sensitive,' he says, 'about such things, and a painful impression would be made upon the mind of any sincere person of that faith, if he should call at your house and see them in your fireplace.' Max Müller endeavoured to comfort Col. Olcott, by assuring him that with the Greeks the hearth was the most sacred spot, and this had induced him to place these Buddhas, which had been taken from the great Temple of Rangoon, in that position.

On his way to Glasgow early in November, Max Müller lectured at Bradford on 'Savages,' staying with Sir Jacob Behrens, a great benefactor of Bradford. His daughter joined him the next day, and together they went to Bishopthorpe to visit his old friend Dr. Thomson, Archbishop of York, where two pleasant days were spent. 'He is overworked,' wrote Max, 'and has no time for anything.' Two days were also spent at Ripon with the Bishop and Mrs. Carpenter.

By the middle of November Max Müller was settled at Glasgow with his wife and daughter, and began his first course of Gifford Lectures on Natural Religion. Everything was done by the various members of the University and many of the citizens to make the stay in their city agreeable to their guest. Soon after the first lecture the student paper *Quiz* announced that

'Proud as we have been of our University, it is no exaggeration to say that additional lustre has been shed upon it by the presence of the Oxford Professor who is now delivering within its precincts the first series of Gifford Lectures. . . . We hear a good deal now and then about the industry and pluck of Scottish students. But at the conclusion of Professor Müller's first lecture there seemed to be only one opinion among his audience, and that was, that in explaining how he had come to devote himself to the study of the sacred literature of the East, and how he hoped by means of the Gifford Lectures to complete and round off the work of his life, he had quite unintentionally taught his hearers a valuable lesson as to the power of industry and perseverance.'

After speaking of the lecturer's style, the writer ends thus: 'He combines at once the boldness and originality of the Germans, and the clear, practical, good sense of the English.'

About 1,400 people were at the first lecture, and the audience settled down into a steady attendance throughout the course of above 1,000, which to an Oxford Professor accustomed to consider fifty a fair number, was a great gratification, and amply repaid the lecturer for all the time and thought bestowed on his work.

A friend wrote to Max Müller at the time:—

'These lectures have given you a reason and opportunity for saying what you had to say on the greatest of all subjects. The longer one lives, the more clearly one sees the terrible mischief done to real genuine religion—I mean piety, the desire to live and work as children of the All-Father—by those who call themselves orthodox; and anything, lecture, book, or sermon, that shows clearly the universality of religious belief, that there *is* one feeling that should bind together all nations, is the best bit of work any one can do. How much you have done already to inculcate this: more than any one now living in England, where religious belief was and is of the narrowest—whether among High Church, Evangelicals, or Dissenters—all alike seeing true faith only in their own little sect, and complacently leaving all others out in the cold.'

Before he left Glasgow a great dinner was given to Max

Müller at the University Club, which was attended by Principal Caird and many of the Professors and leading members of the city. The Scotch are fond of banquets and speeches, and on this occasion there were nine toasts, and as many as eighteen speeches. Max Müller also received a deputation from the University Independent Club, thanking him for having been willing to stand for the office of Lord Rector as the Independent candidate. Under the guidance of some of the younger Professors, he attended various students' meetings, which recalled to him his own German student days, so different to the 'wines' in the Colleges of Oxford and Cambridge.

The lectures were closely followed by a large number of the Glasgow Professors, Dr. Dickson, Professor of Divinity, hearing the whole sixteen. Ministers of every denomination were in the body of the hall, Established, Free Church, Evangelical Union, &c., even Roman Catholic priests. The whole of this course was introductory, and the lectures fell under three divisions, (1) The definition of Natural Religion, (2) The proper method of its treatment, (3) The materials available for its study. On returning from Glasgow just before Christmas, Max Müller began at once to prepare these first lectures on Natural Religion for press. A separate brochure of the introductory lecture had been printed and sent to many friends. The following letter from a man in humble life shows how widely Max Müller's works were known and appreciated. The man was known to the Sellars of Edinburgh, Max Müller's old friends, and had often talked of his books with Professor Sellar. Hence the gift referred to in the letter:—

To Professor Max Müller.

Cab Office, Edinburgh.

'Illustrious Sir,—I wish I could convey to you in adequate language my feelings of gratitude for the distinguished honour you have conferred upon me, in presenting me with a copy of your first lecture. My feelings have been stirred in such a manner that I have not experienced since first I read Dante. You tell the story of your life-work in so fascinating a manner that I feel in the presence and power of, I was going to say, an illustrious personage, embodying philosopher, scholar, teacher, but that does not convey what I feel. You are the Dante of modern scholarship. I am all the poorer to-day in that I missed hearing you when you were lecturing in Edinburgh, but I shall deem it a misfortune indeed if I am not present at your concluding lecture, and witness the ovation that is awaiting you. I am sorry to trouble you for the information, but if you can get conveyed to me the date, hour, and mode of admission to your concluding lecture you will increase the obligations which I already feel.'

Some years before, travelling with his whole family from South Wales, the guard had been very helpful and attentive, and on changing trains Max Müller offered him a tip, without an idea that the man knew him by sight. 'Oh, sir,' said the guard, 'would you send me instead one of your books? I have read some of them.' Needless to say, one was sent off at once to the address the man gave.

To Professor Lorimer.

Oxford, *January* 20, 1889.

'Accept my very best thanks for your letter. I wish I had known that Lord Gifford was a friend of yours. But I assure you I did my best to get information about him, and entirely failed. Mr. —— is about the most reticent man I ever met. I tried all I could to make him speak, but he would not even say "Yes" or "No." However, when I was at Edinburgh for a day I saw Lord Gifford's brother, and though he differs from his brother, he spoke very kindly about him. Then I got some more information from his doctor, and that I have embodied in the reprint of my lecture. If the sheets are not struck off, I shall try, if you do not object, to add something from your letter, but I am afraid it is too late. I have, however, stated that Lord Gifford decidedly gave up his belief in miracles, in the ordinary sense of that word, partly as a judge, on account of want of evidence, partly as a Christian, because they seemed to him in conflict with the exalted spirit of Christ.

'Nothing could have been kinder than my reception at Glasgow. It was hard work having to lecture in the Bute Hall, but I felt that I was in touch with many minds, and that helps. I have been asked to print my lectures as I delivered them, and not to spoil them by learned notes. I have yielded, though rather reluctantly, and I hope the first volume (*Definition, Method, and Materials*) will be out this summer.

'And now allow me to ask you a question. For a busy man like me it is impossible to read books as they appear, and so I have only lately, while writing my lectures, been able to read your *Institution of Law*, which you kindly sent me some years ago. First let me thank you for the kind words you have said about me, and, I may add, about my old friend Bunsen. My object in reading your book was to learn something about the relation of law to religion. I see, however, that you lay the principal stress on the relation between law and ethics, though you secure for ethics a divine basis. What you say about conscience is just the same as I had said in my lectures. But though you rejoice in your Professor of Moral Philosophy not treating conscience as a separate faculty of knowing what is right or wrong, you will see that your colleague, Professor Flint, holds the old view in his *Theism*, i. p. 216.

'What I am anxious to know is whether there is any book which shows how closely religion, I mean outward religion, was connected with law, and how law grew up under the wing of religion. Maine has shown it a little in his *Ancient Law*, and in his article on *International law*, as starting from *Gastfreundschaft* and Ζεὺς ξένιος.

'But I should think the subject must have been treated in fuller detail. Could you refer me to any book not too bulky? In India the case is as clear as possible, but I want evidence from other civilized nations, and not only from savages.'

To the Same.

Oxford, *January* 25, 1889.

'I have just returned from London, and find your letter and your kind present waiting for me. Accept my best thanks for both. My question as to the dependence of law on religion referred to ancient times rather than to mediaeval ages, I might almost say to prehistoric times, at least to a period when the earliest legal terms, such as *fas*, *lex*, *jus*, *spondeo*, &c., were formal and fixed. I am afraid I shall have to be satisfied with indicating what I want to know myself, and what I hope some more competent person will carry out.

'I shall not be able to gather any more information about Lord Gifford for the present. I hope some other lecturer will do fuller justice to his memory. I send you the proof-sheets of my first lecture. Would you kindly return them to me, also a little slip I sent with the first sheet, and on which I had noted down some of your remarks on Lord Gifford?'

To Professor Noiré.

*Translation.* 7, Norham Gardens, *February* 9, 1889.

'My poor dear Friend,—I hear that you feel a little better at Mainz, but that you are still far from well. It is sad to think that everything in life turns out so different from what we expected. But ah, it is difficult to make that thought one's own and to bear calmly all the dissonances, in the hope that in time they must all dissolve into harmony. How I should like to come to you, but what good would that do you? And besides I am so tied here now, as I have used up all my holiday in Glasgow. But my thoughts are with you every day, and I do hope that soon I may hear better news about you. I am printing my Glasgow lectures, which still occupy me much. Other work is not lacking, and yet I feel well, though I am so much older than you are. Well, the chief thing is to keep still, and to feel the desire in oneself to get better. With all good wishes for your recovery.'

In February Max Müller opened the yearly course of University Extension Lectures in London, by a lecture at the Mansion House on 'Some Lessons of Antiquity,' which is published in Vol. I of the new edition of *Chips*. The Egyptian Hall was entirely filled, and the lecture was listened to with great interest; one of the subjects touched on—the relative weight of gold and silver coins in ancient times—calling forth a good deal of criticism in the daily papers, to which Max Müller replied, though declining to enter on the thorny paths of the question of bimetallism, where, as he said, 'wrens make prey, and eagles may not perch.'

This year Max Müller lost his valued friend Professor Noiré of Mainz. It is seldom that it happens to any one so late in life to form so close a friendship as did Max Müller with Professor Noiré. It was perhaps the more strange as the friendship originated (as has been mentioned, ii. p. 37) in Noiré's violent attack on Max Müller's earlier writings. Noiré was alone in the world, entirely without relations, yet a man of the most loving nature. No wonder that his heart was moved on meeting with another equally warm and loving, and far less pessimistic than himself. Max Müller long missed and mourned his friend.

Two lectures were given in March, one at Sheffield and one at Leeds, on the *Sacred Books of the East*. These were almost the last single lectures Max Müller delivered anywhere out of Oxford. He found the effort and excitement more than was good for him, and though constantly pressed in later years to give single lectures in various places, he never again accepted any invitations, except one at Toynbee Hall, in April of this year, when he gave the last Saturday evening lecture for the Winter Term. This was also on the *Sacred Books*. The room was very full, and many were unable to gain admittance. He received an enthusiastic welcome, and hearty wishes were expressed that they might hear him again. But this was the only occasion on which he lectured at Toynbee Hall, though he had felt great interest in the institution from the first.

To Klaus Groth.

*Translation.* 7, Norham Gardens, *May* 2, 1889.

'My congratulations for your seventieth birthday will, I fear, reach you somewhat late, but you will feel all the same the hearty greetings they are meant to convey to you. How I rejoice to hear once more that you are happy and that you have found in your Fatherland the love and appreciation which you so richly deserve. May it be granted to you to enjoy years of quiet and peace in the evening of life! I also approach to the tenth "7" of evil omen, and I long for rest, but do not find it. We are well on the whole, but after such heavy storms as we have experienced one longs for the haven of rest. Work does not decrease, but increases year by year—sometimes it seems almost too much.

'Who knows whether the autumn may not perhaps bring me to Kiel? The King of Sweden has invited me as his guest to the International Oriental Congress at Stockholm, and it will be difficult to say "No" should there be the least possibility of going.

'It is also possible that the monument to my father, in which you have taken such sympathetic interest, may be completed this year, and that of course would take me to Germany.'

A few days after this Max Müller attended the banquet of the Royal Academy, where he had to reply to the toast of Literature. He often said it was one of the greatest ordeals he had ever been called on to pass through, and he used to confess that he came to a pause in the middle of his speech, his attention having been diverted for a moment by a passing incident. The pause could have been but momentary, and he must have recovered his thread in an instant, though to him it had seemed an agony of long duration, for when Browning congratulated him on his brilliant speech, and Max

Müller replied in return, 'But the pause was awful!' 'Páuse?' said Browning, 'I was attending closely, and I remarked none.'

To Doctor (now Sir William) Russell (who was in South America).

Oxford, *May* 12, 1889.

'Where is *Iquique?* I know if I wrote to you *Ubique* it would find you, but where is Iquique? Meanwhile let me congratulate you on your wanderings. I thought of you on the Pyramids, or among the Dervishes, and now, like the seal in the Zoological Gardens, you turn up in the Straits of Magellan. It is too late to ask you to bring a baby from Tierra del Fuego home with you. I have been writing a good deal about these Fuegians lately. Darwin said they were like the Devils in the *Freischütz.* I have now before me a Dictionary of their language containing more than 30,000 words, and remember Shakespeare uses no more than 15,000 words. Then what are these Devils talking about with double that number? I hope you are not taking up your permanent abode among those eloquent savages! If you come home before the Parnell Commission is over, you will find plenty of eloquent savages in London. And what has become of the old Irish fun? not a trace of it during all these dreary weeks. Yes, one little scrap. Henry George lecturing in Ireland, telling them the earth was created for all men, that Adam never paid rent for his acres in Paradise. Shrill voice from a corner of the room, "Sure, but wasn't he evicted then?" We shall stay here till the end of August, and then go to Sweden. I have just finished printing my Gifford Lectures on *Natural Religion*—Religion *au naturel*, they call it—600 pages, and a volume of my new edition of the *Veda*—you remember that in 1848—1,000 pages quarto. Pity the sorrows of a poor scholar! Hard labour for life, that seems to be my sentence.'

In June, the engagement of his only surviving daughter to T. C. Colyer-Fergusson, of Ightham Mote, was a source of great happiness to Max Müller. The early part of Long Vacation was spent at Oxford, varied by short visits to London, Claremont, Highclere, and other places.

To the Princess Mother of Wied.

*Translation.* 7, Norham Gardens, Oxford, *July* 30, 1889.

'Your Highness,—I have just received through Sir Robert Collins your kind invitation to Segenhaus. I cannot think how it happens that either my letters do not reach Herr von Roggenbach, or else he does not answer them. I asked him whether I might perhaps see your Highness at Neuwied about the middle of August, and I begged him to wire to me as soon as possible. Not having received any answer, my wife and I made other plans. But I return to my long-cherished wish. Should my wife and I be able to see your Highness at Segenhaus about the middle of August? also Herr von Roggenbach, and perhaps the Prince and Princess, and possibly even the Queen of Roumania? That would be quite delightful, only might I hear as soon as possible, so as to fix our plans accordingly? We are bound to arrive at Malmö on September 1, in time for the Oriental Congress at Stockholm. And before that date I am due at Berlin and at Dessau. My daughter goes to Scotland to her future parents-in-law, Sir James and Lady Fergusson; my son goes to Schwalbach, after his examination work; so we two old people are alone again, and intend going on a wedding-tour as we did thirty years ago!

'A line or a telegram would fix our plans definitely.'

At the Summer Meeting this year of the University Extension Students, which was the second held in Oxford, Max Müller delivered three lectures in the Sheldonian Theatre on 'Language.' These were published the next year in a small volume, and were republished in America in 1891, with a supplement, 'My Predecessors,' which had appeared in the *Contemporary* in 1888.

TO THE DUKE OF ARGYLL.

OXFORD, *August* 9, 1889.

'Every creative act in language was performed by *one* individual, and, if passively—I mean, driven by outside influences—yet consciously. The unconscious and almost irrational element in the growth of language is due to the acceptance or non-acceptance of individual creations by the majority. The play of this action and reaction does not seem reducible to any rule. By slowly elaborating the rules of language or grammar, the speakers elaborate or bring out the universal laws of thought, and these rule in the realm of thought, just as usages that have been found useful become the laws of a political commonwealth.'

The middle of August Max Müller and his wife left for Sweden, for the eighth Oriental Congress. They spent three days with the Princess Mother of Wied at Monrepos, and went on to Homburg to see the Empress Frederick, and then by Dresden to Dessau, where a pleasant week was spent with the few left of the large family circle whom they had visited there on their honeymoon thirty years before! From Dessau they travelled by Berlin, where Max Müller saw his old friend von Schlötzer for the last time, to Stralsund, one of the most interesting, though to English people least known, of the Baltic towns, with its fine red-brick buildings.

The next day, after a good passage, the travellers reached Malmö in Sweden, where they landed with many other members of the Congress, amidst enthusiastic crowds. Stockholm was reached next morning. The King opened the Congress in person, and welcomed the members in French, and in the evening he received the whole Congress at Dröttningholm, his palace up the Malar. On the return, the river was illuminated for miles. One day was given to Old Upsala, where the University students welcomed the guests, and where Max Müller, standing on the 'Graves of the Gods,' three huge tumuli, gave the students a stirring address. Each morning was spent in the work of the Congress, Max Müller being first President of the Âryan Section. In common with the other King's guests, twelve representatives from twelve different countries, he dined one night with the King, and received from him the Order of the Polar Star, first class, with star. Max Müller himself read a paper at the last working sitting, when he presented the *Sacred Books of the East* to the King as Protector of the eighth Congress. The King closed the first part of the meeting held at Stockholm in a Latin speech, which excited the greatest admiration. The Congress then moved on to Christiania. The whole meeting had been a continued triumph for Max Müller, and a revelation to him of how extensively his books had been read and appreciated. At the stations where the train stopped, people ran along the line, shouting his name, and at Drammen an old clergyman, when he saw him, grasped his hand, saying, 'I have driven in thirty miles just to see you, and tell you all I owe to your books.' Some of the other eminent men who were present could hardly conceal their feelings of jealousy, while the recipient of all this honour, though deeply gratified by the real affection shown for him, remained simple and unaffected throughout, and it required the watchful efforts of many of the members to induce him to show himself at the carriage windows to his ardent admirers On leaving Christiania the great Falls of Trollhattan were visited on the way to Gothenburg, where the final banquet was held, and the members of the Congress separated. The Max Müllers returned by Copenhagen, Bremen, and Flushing.

In spite of the brilliant festivities and the many apparent hindrances to business, Max Müller always maintained that a firmer foundation had been laid at this Congress for future work than at any former meeting.

One amusing incident touching Max Müller only came to light a year or two later. At the final banquet at Stockholm a *menu* was prepared in which all the dishes were described in different Oriental languages by the learned members of the Congress. To Max Müller was assigned the task of describing salmon (*lax*) in Vedic Sanskrit. About a year later a paragraph appeared in a Lahore paper, as follows:—

'Professor Max Müller, who is looked upon as a great Sanskrit scholar by some of our fellow countrymen, and as one who has great respect for the ancient literature of this country, has, it appears, been making fun of the *Vedas* for the delectation of his friends. He has composed what is termed the *Matsya Sûkta*, consisting of six Mantras in praise and honour of Laksha, a species of fish. We will give here a translation of it: "(1) O friends, sing the praises of this wonderful fish, whose name is Laksha, and which is the beloved of the people. (2) When, after having been fed in the sea, and looked after and protected in the rivers, it became hale and strong, it came to us as a guest. (3) May this Laksha, whose praises the poets of this age should sing, as they have been sung by those of old, bring unto us the goddess Lakshami. (4) Come and look at it, how red its flesh is! How pretty it looks, how like silver it shines! (5 and 6) Broth prepared from its flesh is palatable, and worthy of kings, and hence it is that we long for it in this assembly. This beloved fish, which is so pretty that we cannot be satiated by looking at it, is worthy the table of kings." These are the sublime sentiments embodied in the Professor's *Sûkta!* But what, we may ask, can the Professor's object be in composing it? Why, merely to express his contempt of the Vedic teaching. Will this open the eyes of those who are such admirers of the Professor, and who regard him as a great admirer of our past?'

Max Müller's attention was drawn to this paragraph by a Hindu admirer, who took the whole thing as seriously as did the writer in the paper.

*January*, 1891.

'DEAR SIR,—An article has appeared in an Urdu paper, in which, after saying that interested parties have been interpolating the Hindu *Shastras*, the writer accuses you of the same thing, i. e. that you have interpolated certain Mantras in the *Vedas*. Now to us it seems a clear misrepresentation and falsehood, and as this article has been copied by other papers, would you kindly give me the true facts of the case?

'Yours truly,
'S. N. AGNIHOTRIS,
'Minister Diva Somâj.'

To this Max Müller answered :—

OXFORD, *February* 7, 1891.

'DEAR SIR,—I am much obliged to you for sending me the extracts from the *Ârya Gazette*. They are very amusing, but they can hardly have been intended as serious.'

Max Müller then describes the banquet at Stockholm, and how he came to write in praise of the salmon (*lax* in Swedish).

'I confess I was afraid that I might have used grammatical forms not entirely Vedic, or made a mistake in the Vedic, but I did not expect that I should have been accused of an attempt at forging a Vedic Hymn!'

This autumn Max received a letter from a clergyman in Boston, America, asking him whether the word Christos did not mean a *quality* rather than a *person*, whether it was not a *characteristic* passing gradually into a *name*, and whether the word had not been used among the Greeks before the birth of Jesus. The writer adds :—

'I owe more to you than to any other man for establishing me in the sympathies of religion, and helping me to appreciate the breadth of the Christian instructions. I find great help in all your works, and many times have felt a strong impulse to write and tell you of the great services you have rendered. Let me thank you again for what your work has been to me.'

Unfortunately no answer was sent to the above, as the writer contemplated a visit to England, and it was thought that the subject was too vast for a letter. In sending this information to the editor, Mr. Rexford says:—

'I feel more deeply indebted to Max Müller than to any one man for my understanding of religion. He made it sacred by declaring it a universal factum for man, instead of making it artificial by declaring it local and special. More and more I think all the world appreciates the colossal task which he accomplished. It seems a misfortune that he should have been called away from so great a work, but he has taught us all to be submissive.'

To Sir Robert Collins.

Oxford, *October* 18.

'I write to ask you for some advice. When I was at Stockholm the King gave me with his own hand the Polar Star, first class, with star, and expressed a hope that the Queen would allow me to wear it. What ought I to do? I want on no account to ask anything that the Queen would have to refuse, and I know, of course, that in certain official quarters no opportunity would be missed to annoy or injure me. The King told me that the star which he gave me was the highest distinction which could be given in Sweden to men of science. We had a splendid meeting. The King was perfectly charming, and when at last he addressed us all in a Latin speech without any notes, that lasted nearly a quarter of an hour, the Professors were in raptures. He is a very remarkable man, and yet how little the world knows of him!'

The Duchess of Albany herself brought her uncle the King's wish before the Queen, who at once gave her gracious permission to wear the Polar Star at Court. Only a few months before Max Müller's death, the King of Sweden sent him the Grand Cross of the Order. Several friends were by chance at his house, when the Secretary of Legation arrived from London with the decoration, and will remember Max Müller's pleasure at this wholly unexpected honour, and the sad feeling of those present that, shattered as his health was already, there was little hope it could ever be worn. Max Müller was right in his fears expressed to Sir Robert Collins. Red-tape tried to interfere, saying that a *British subject* ought to have no foreign Order. Her Majesty remembered that, when a few years previously she had wished to bestow an English Order on Max Müller, the objection was made that he was a *foreigner*. The present cabal was therefore stopped by the command: 'Max Müller may certainly accept the Order, for, though naturalized, he is still a German.' In sending his 'most humble and sincere thanks for this new mark of Her Majesty's royal favour,' through Sir Henry Ponsonby, Max Müller adds, 'which I appreciate all the more as being, though not by birth, yet by choice, one of Her Majesty's most loyal and devoted subjects.'

A friend, in writing to congratulate him on the distinction, says: 'Every fresh honour paid you causes me to reflect afresh on what I would fain forget, the remissness of our own Government in not recognizing your claims.'

During this autumn the criticisms on Max Müller's first Gifford Lectures on Natural Religion began to appear. One friend, to whom he had sent his book, writes:—

> 'I like the book greatly, and I am glad that you have said what you do. The time had come for saying it, and some of us had kept silence too long. You will of course be attacked, but the time will very soon come when you will be recognized as having done a real service to religion.'

His definition of Religion, as consisting 'in the perception of the infinite under such manifestations as are able to influence the moral character of man,' was questioned and objected to in many quarters. 'This first course,' says Max Müller, 'was purely introductory. It contained an examination of the various definitions of natural religion, and a statement of the objects which it may hope to achieve.' Whilst one critic declared that 'it is by these lectures the author will be longest remembered; they cover the whole field of study with which his name is associated, and they present his conclusions and opinions in their matured form,' another summed up his criticism with the assertion that 'the learned Professor found something good in every religion, *except in Christianity*.'

But neither praise nor blame moved him, and he was strengthened by the conviction that he had done his best in the cause of truth.

Max Müller had postponed his second Gifford Lectures till February, 1890, and the work of this Autumn Term was devoted to finishing them. Being his daughter's last term in her old home, it was also one of constant social intercourse and gaiety, and many farewell visits too were paid to old friends and relations, and the lectures progressed but slowly.

# CHAPTER XXX

## 1890–1891

School of Modern Oriental Studies. Daughter's wedding. Second Gifford Lectures. Malabari and infant marriages. Deal. Queen of Roumania. Birth of first grandchild. Third Gifford Lectures. Attacks on lectures. Christening of grandson. Dr. Leitner's Oriental Congress. Visit of Prince of Naples. British Association at Cardiff. Wildbad. Unveiling of monument to Wilhelm Müller. *Science of Language* rewritten. Resignation of Dean Liddell.

THE first work of this year was connected with the establishment of an Institute, which appealed peculiarly to Max Müller, as filling a gap in our system of education which had weighed heavily on him for more than thirty years. This was the establishment by the Imperial Institute, in connexion with University College and King's College, London, of a School of Modern Oriental Studies. Max Müller was asked to give the Inaugural Address, at the Royal Institution, on January 14. The Prince of Wales, our King, as President of the Imperial Institute, was in the chair. In his address, Max Müller adverted to the efforts he had made more than thirty years previously, at the time of the Crimean War, and then again after the Indian Mutiny, to call attention to this great need in English education; but he had spoken then to deaf ears, notwithstanding the interest which it was known the Prince Consort took in the subject. He acknowledged that the schools and Universities had since then done their best, but entirely without support or aid from Government. Yet, as the speaker said, when Imperial interests are at stake, the country has a right to expect Imperial, that is, concentrated, action, such action as has been taken in Russia, France, Austria, and Germany. The night before Max Müller had written to Sir Frederick Abel, the Chairman of the Committee of Management of the Oriental School:—

To Sir F. Abel.

*January* 13, 1890.

'I hope a beginning has been made. It seems to me absolutely necessary that the sinews of war should be supplied by the Government. If it declines, then nothing remains but to go begging in the City, in Manchester, Birmingham, &c.'

In his speech Max Müller mentioned the number of letters he received from manufacturers and others, asking him to translate advertisements or notices in Oriental papers; and he hoped in future the new School of Oriental Studies would be able to supply such information to every merchant in the British Isles. He then dwelt more particularly on the great benefit it would be to India, if not only officers and civil servants had every facility for acquiring the vernaculars, but merchants, clerks, and employés in general; how the task of government and life in India would be simplified if the governing race were able, by knowledge of their languages, to enter more readily into the thoughts, lives, and aspirations of those they governed. The Prince of Wales, in thanking Max Müller for his 'interesting and eloquent speech,' spoke of him as 'one whom, ever since my undergraduate days at Oxford, I have had the advantage and privilege of knowing.'

Max Müller's speech was keenly appreciated in India, and reviewed in many Indian papers.

The newspapers took up the subject warmly, and the great daily papers, not only in London, but in the provinces, emphasized the importance of the School for practical purposes, and urged the need of Government support; yet, but a few days later, Max Müller heard from the Chairman of the Committee of Management that there was little prospect of receiving any assistance from Government; and thus this subject, of such vital importance to the country, notwithstanding the efforts and interest of the Prince of Wales, was again left to private enterprise.

The Government has never contributed in any way towards the maintenance of the School of Modern Oriental Studies, established by the Imperial Institute authorities. When the School had been organized by the joint action of the Institute, King's College, and University College, and placed under the direction of a committee representing each institution, application was made to the Foreign Office and the War Office to obtain an official recognition of the School, by including in the circulars issued to candidates for Government appointments in Oriental countries the languages taught at it, as optional subjects for the first examinations for such appointments; and, in making this application, it was especially stated that no pecuniary assistance was at that time desired. But this application, although repeated and supported by eminent authorities, was not entertained, and the School has simply continued to this day a struggling existence, supported only by the reputations of the two Colleges, and by a fund furnished by the daughters of the late Colonel Ouseley for the establishment of a few scholarships in Oriental languages.

Max Müller's youngest and only surviving daughter was married on January 30 in Christ Church Cathedral to Thomas Colyer Colyer-Fergusson, of Ightham Mote, Kent. Her happy marriage, his son-in-law's affection, and constant visits to their beautiful old home, were important factors in the happiness of his later years.

As soon as the wedding was over, Max Müller and his wife went to Glasgow, for the second course of Gifford Lectures, on Physical Religion. If the six weeks of their stay in Glasgow were not so entirely filled by social engagements as the first in 1888, they were varied by visits to Thornliebank, Mr. Crum's; Largs, Sir W. Thomson's place on the coast; and to friends at St. Andrews and Edinburgh, besides pleasant day visits to places immediately round Glasgow.

The lectures were again very well attended, even though the audiences were not quite as large as at the first course. This second course was intended to show how different nations had arrived at a belief in many gods in nature, and at last in One God, above all gods; how, in fact, they had conceived and named what Max Müller called the infinite in nature, or that which underlies all that is finite and phenomenal in our experience. Physical religion is the earliest form of human faith, and is based on the phenomena of nature, through which man in his earlier stages of thought endeavoured to account for what lay behind the veil of nature, and created in his own mind the gods of the sky, the fire, and the storm, which concepts, in the development of ages, culminated in our belief in God, the Father. Although traçes of physical religion may be found everywhere and among all races, Max Müller limited his study of its origin and growth to a single country at first, choosing India for the reason that in no other country is physical religion in its simplest form so completely developed as there. Towards the end of the spring, he was elected for a further two years.

Whilst at Glasgow, Max Müller, after a lapse of several years, heard again from his friend Mr. Mozoomdar, who was discouraged in his work by the divisions in the Brahma Somâj since the death of Keshub Chunder Sen. He writes:—

'Much of Keshub's outward work was premature. It will have to be re-embodied and done again. Some one else will have to do it. For myself, it is enough if I can keep the great ideals untainted, and stand firm on the old ground, in spite of the influences that tend to drag us downwards. Perhaps you in Europe, where centres of thought are easily formed, and social sympathies soon organized, cannot conceive the absolute desertion that overtakes truth in the far East.'

To B. M. Malabari, Esq.

*March* 12.

'Your suggestion of a journey to India has gratified me very much, but I have come to the conclusion that at my time of life, and with so much important work still to finish, I must not think of it. It is a great self-denial, doubly difficult, after what you told me, that some of my Indian friends would have been willing to defray my expenses. There would have been no necessity for that, still that such an idea should have been entertained was a great pleasure to me. You are perhaps not aware of the intrigues which some so-called Sanskrit scholars and their friends, old members of the Indian Civil Service, have for years been carrying on against me, as a defender of the Indian character. However, old as I am, I never believe in the success of wickedness; and hitherto it is curious how my enemies have always been, against their will, my greatest benefactors.

'I feel sure you will find the same in your battles for what you consider right. We may be all of us mistaken in what we consider right, but so long as we believe it right, we must fight for it. I have never doubted that early marriage is the greatest impediment in the natural development of a woman's character, and I am equally certain that your stunted wives and mothers are the chief cause of the slow, the very slow social progress in India. You have made rapid progress in everything else, but you do not know yet what light an educated, healthy, and thoughtful wife can spread over every home, whether rich or poor. You deprive your children of the happiest time of their lives, their independent youth, or, at all events, you shorten that period, the happiest in an English girl's life, without any rhyme or reason. I know, of course, all your difficulties, and I never expected you would be able to grapple with some of them so well as you have done. You suffer from your mediaeval traditions, just as we did in Europe. Go back beyond your Middle Ages, go back to your really ancient literature, and you will find there no mothers of twelve years of age, but strong, healthy, educated women, who could even be trusted to choose their husbands. I have nothing to say on the physiological side of the question; but from a psychological point of view, marriage at ten, at twelve, even at fifteen, seems to me the surest means to stunt the natural growth of the mind in its various phases. The law should prevent all that is really noxious to physical health; no individual effort on the part of men of light and leading in India can effect a change in the long-established custom.

'I quite agree with what you say about Ramabai. There you see what an Indian woman *can* be. Most Indian women can talk of nothing but their trinkets, their dresses and their family affairs. With Ramabai you can talk about everything. And what is more important still, you can perfectly trust her—and what a blessing that is! I knew her becoming a Christian would deprive her of many means of usefulness. I quite agreed with her, when she told me "a good Brâhmanî can be a good Christian." But now that she has become a Christian—and I could quite understand her motives—she will have to prove that "a good Christian can be a good Brâhmanî"; and you ought all to help her in her work. If you see her, please tell her we often speak of her, and wish her all success.

'I am very busy, as usual. I have just finished the printing of the first volume of the new edition of the *Rig-veda* and Sâyana. I am printing my *Lectures on Natural Religion*, delivered at Glasgow, and a new edition of my *Lectures on Language*, to say nothing of smaller matters. It is such a pity that one has to do so much mechanical work, which any young man might do quite as well; and there is little time left to do what one can do best. Life in England is so expensive—unnecessarily so. You are much more independent in that respect in India. Still, as long as I can work, I do not complain, and I have through life always been able to make as much as I wanted, and a little more.

'I hope you are in good health and spirits, and that the work in which you have done so much is advancing steadily. Trees do not grow to their full height in a few years. If only they grow, that is enough, even though they who planted and watered them are forgotten, and receive small thanks. *Work done* is the true happiness of life, and you must feel that you have done some good work.'

To the Same.

Oxford, *March* 29, 1890.

'Let me thank you, first of all, for your unflagging interest in the translation of my *Hibbert Lectures*. I hope, like seed scattered broadcast over a field, a grain here and there will bear fruit. We can do little more than to sow. You yourself have done that all your life, and you must know how often some of our best intentions lead to nothing, while others succeed beyond our expectations. I am glad to hear that you are going to allow yourself some rest, and pay us a visit in England. Be sure of a very hearty welcome at my house, whenever you come to Oxford. When you told me that some of your countrymen wished to invite me to India, I was very much pleased. You know how angry the Anglo-Indians are with me for having spoken the truth about India and the Indians. An expression of sympathy therefore from India will show them that, after all, I am not so ignorant of "What India can teach us," as they wish the public in England to believe, and that I have friends in India, though I have never been there in the body.

'I have just received the number of the *Indian Spectator*, containing a review of my *Natural Religion*. I was very much pleased, and have to thank the writer, whoever he is.'

To his Son.

Oxford, *March* 27.

'I do not believe that there has been much of a quarrel between the Emperor and Bismarck. Bismarck is tired; he knew that the Emperor was not in full sympathy with him, and he thought the present moment the most opportune for effecting a transition that otherwise might take place under less favourable circumstances. There have always been two natures in Bismarck—littlenesses on the surface, and great principles at the bottom. No doubt, the littlenesses often predominated, but he was seldom carried away by them. However, we shall see. There will be squabbles in the next Chamber, and the Centre will have a good time of it.'

The Library at Oxford.
(7, Norham Gardens.)

The following letter, which belongs to this date, shows the feeling for Max Müller in Sweden:—

STOCKHOLM, *April* 4, 1890.

'HONOURED SIR,—Count Landberg has asked me to send you a curious article which appeared in the *Vossische Zeitung*. I am glad indeed of the opportunity to tell you at last, what I longed to tell you months ago. In your book, *The Science of Thought*, you develop in your well-known masterly manner the close connexion which exists between word and thought. All who read your fascinating statements, so rich in original ideas, cannot but feel deeply grateful to you. How much more he who has had the honour of receiving the book from the author, from Max Müller himself!

'However, I say much too little when I mention that I count my gratitude by *months*. Thirty years ago, when I was still a mere boy, I *devoured* with delight your *Lectures*, and since then my gratitude has increased every year. You have taught me Sanskrit grammar; guided by your hand, I have gone through the *Hitopadesa* and *Meghadûta*; it is also you who have introduced me to the *Rig-veda*. Your essays, your religious-historical lectures have fascinated *me* as they have fascinated all your readers. And now I have been allowed to see and hear you personally! I shall *boast* of this for all future time. You can imagine how glad we all are to see, from your wife's interesting description of the Congress, that you were both pleased with it, as well as with Scandinavia in general. That you were yourself the most prominent person of the Congress, and that therefore it was chiefly due to you that it received so much attention here, I need hardly mention; this cannot have escaped you. You are indeed not only the *Teacher of the Learned*, but—what is of far greater importance for humanity—you are the *Teacher of the Cultured*.

'In deepest reverence,

'Your faithful disciple,

'E. TEGUES.'

TO HIS SON-IN-LAW, THOMAS C. COLYER-FERGUSSON.

OXFORD, *April* 7, 1890.

'MY DEAR TOM,—I am so glad to hear to-day from B. that in about a fortnight we shall see you again, B. as a demure matron, you as burdened with all the cares and responsibilities of a married man. How you must have enjoyed your time in Italy! I can quite understand your not liking Rome. I was never well there, I don't know why, and as soon as I reached Perugia I was a different being. However, you will enjoy Venice, and I should not be surprised to hear that you could not tear yourself away; just now in spring it must be perfect. We enjoyed our time at Glasgow, but it was hard work both socially and intellectually. They have not re-elected me, and I am not sorry for it. I have plenty of work which I ought to finish. The Scotch papers still go on discussing my lectures. The *Glasgow Herald* had no less than eight letters in one number. Some people would like to burn me, but there seems a strong majority on my side, and there is a wonderful amount of good sense among the people in Scotland.

'Yours always affectionately,

'F. MAX MÜLLER.'

Soon after Max Müller's return to Oxford he received a Sanskrit translation of the English inscription for the statue of the Prince Consort, to be erected in Windsor Park as part of the Women's Jubilee Offering to the Queen. The inscriptions on the pediment of the statue were to be in English, Latin, Gaelic, and Sanskrit. Max Müller was not at first consulted as to the Sanskrit translation, but the secretary, Lieut.-Colonel Tully, who had some knowledge of Sanskrit, felt doubtful as to the rendering sent him, and asked Max Müller's opinion. He at once found that the translation sent was absolutely useless, and concluded his careful analysis in these words: 'The rendering is a poor attempt, in my opinion, by some one with a limited knowledge of Sanskrit and English.' It was curious that he should have so exactly divined the truth, the fact being that one of his opponents had put the matter into the hands of a half-educated native, resolved that Max Müller's name should not be associated with the great monument, a malicious trick that was frustrated by the secretary's conscientious care. Max Müller sent a translation made by himself, which Professor Cowell of Cambridge pronounced to be 'very good,' and he afterwards sent it, with the one submitted to him, to Professor Bhandakar of Poona, one of the most learned of Indian Pundits, who wrote back by return that, among other gross errors, the word used by the first translator for 'Consort' was an absolutely inadmissible word. 'You are certainly to be congratulated,' Bhandakar wrote, 'on having saved our august Queen from a standing insult.' The secretary decided that Max Müller's rendering was the only one of several sent in that could be used. Max

Müller submitted his translation to various other scholars in Europe and India, who suggested a few trifling amendments, and it is his translation into Sanskrit that is on the metal plate which was affixed to the monument in 1895.

To Professor Victor Carus.

*Translation.* Oxford, *April* 11.

'It was a great pleasure to see your well-known writing once more, and to learn that all goes as well with you as one dares to expect at our age. Here too all goes well, but our house has become very empty. Beatrice and her husband are in Venice—may they long enjoy their happy life! They have a house in London, and a lovely old place, Ightham Mote, in Kent. My boy has done with his examinations here, and is preparing for the Diplomatic Service—a precarious career, but what can one do? We, my wife and I, were in Glasgow again in the winter, where I had to deliver the Gifford Lectures. Now we are enjoying the quiet here, and I, the time for work. I have not seen Acland since his return from the Canary Islands.'

In April Mr. Malabari, of Bombay, visited England, hoping to stir up active interest on the questions of infant marriage and the status of Hindu widows. It was a great interest to Max Müller, who had in 1887 shown such concern in the case of Rukhmabai, and also exerted himself to aid Ramabai in her noble work for Hindu widows, to make the personal acquaintance of the energetic reformer, and a close friendship sprang up between the two men, which lasted till Max Müller's death. Mr. Malabari paid his friend a visit at Oxford, and Max Müller gave him good counsel as to his further proceedings, and later in the summer attended a Drawing-room Meeting, to discuss some of the questions relative to the position of women in India. Princess Christian and the Duke of Connaught were present, and Lord Reay was in the chair. Max Müller spoke on the resolution 'that any legal obstacles that still stand in the way of the remarriage of widows should be removed.'

To his Son-in-law, T. C. Colyer-Fergusson.

Oxford, *June* 3, 1890.

'My dear Tom,—Many thanks for your liberal contribution to my father's—your grandfather's—monument. It would be very pleasant if we could all be there to see it unveiled. You would be very much interested and amused in the life of a small capital in Germany, and the country is beautiful. I am very tired. Love to B.

'Ever yours affectionately,

'F. MAX MÜLLER.'

In the course of the summer, whilst staying with his daughter, Max Müller met his old friend 'Billy' Russell, a meeting that called forth the following letter:—

FROM DR. W. RUSSELL.

CARLISLE MANSIONS, *June* 12.

'MY DEAR MAX MÜLLER AND FRIEND,—It was strange to find myself under your daughter's roof-tree, face to face with her father, and "memory through the vale of years" recalling the *eidola* of two young fellows, with all the world before them, light hearts and empty purses! Well, I'm a scribbler still, a worker in the rubbish called daily literature—it should be spelt litter-a-shure—and *you*, the owner of a name to conjure with all over the world, where men know and think. Heaven help us both, Amen!'

TO B. M. MALABARI, ESQ.

7, NORHAM GARDENS, OXFORD, *June* 28, 1890.

'MY DEAR FRIEND,—I saw Princess Christian before I left London. She knew all about you, and is to receive you in a few days.

'But now let me tell you frankly how matters stand. Lord Lansdowne has been written to about the enabling clause. You understand what I mean—a clause enabling a father to keep his daughter till the time has come for her to leave her father's house. That clause will probably be carried by Lord Lansdowne in Council. There ought to be no pressure brought to bear on him. He ought to be allowed to do it himself, spontaneously. Any public demonstration to bring this about would, under present circumstances, do harm. The other question, as to raising the age, is much more serious—is, in fact, a political question, that will have to be fought out openly in India. Whatever Princess Christian may feel on the subject, she could not possibly express an opinion on it in public, or in private, at present. She ought not to be asked to do so.

'I think, therefore, that, however small the enabling clause may seem to be, we ought to be satisfied with getting that carried at present. When that is done, then the agitation ought to begin once more in India.'

TO PROFESSOR KLAUS GROTH.

OXFORD, *July* 25, 1890.

'I thought you might be interested to hear how a thought—which years ago was raised for the first time by you—is now nearing its realization.

'The monument to my father is to be unveiled next spring. We all hope to be in Dessau for that occasion—as many of us, that is to say, as have remained—my son, who is preparing for his examination, and my happily married daughter, my wife, and myself, aged sixty-seven!

'I hope old age is not too heavy a burden on you, though the world has grown very lonely.'

It was a great pleasure to Max Müller to have a long visit from his daughter and her husband during the Long Vacation; and though he was busy writing his third series of *Gifford Lectures* for the coming year, and preparing the second volume for press, he was more inclined to take work easily, and joined in many of the water and other excursions taken in company with the Fearns, a very agreeable American family, spending the summer in Oxford. Mr. Fearn had been American Minister at Athens and Bucharest.

At the third Summer Meeting of the University Extension Students this year, Max Müller delivered the Inaugural Address, a 'Lecture in defence of Lectures,' which was afterwards published in the first volume of the new edition of *Chips*.

In August he went with his daughter to Deal, where he particularly enjoyed the intercourse with Lord Granville at Walmer, and Lord Herschell at Deal, as well as exploring Sandwich, Minster, and many interesting places round. He could always throw himself with zest into these excursions, when not oppressed with too much work. In September the whole party were again settled in Oxford. So hard had Max Müller worked, with his admirable secretary, Dr. Winternitz, at the new edition of the *Rig-veda*, that the first and second volumes were brought out early in October.

The Queen of Roumania had spent the late summer in Wales and Scotland, and had hoped to stay a few days in Oxford; but finding that was impossible, Her Majesty summoned the Max Müllers to London, to spend the last days of her time in England with her. Together they visited the studios of Mr. Watts and Mr. Alma Tadema, and saw the *Bride of Lammermoor* acted at the Lyceum. But the thing that most astonished Max Müller, well as he knew the Queen's versatility of talent, was her reading aloud in English a tragedy, *Meister Manole*, which she had written in German. The Queen was very anxious to have this play acted, and invited Sir Henry Irving and Miss Terry and other friends to hear it. About twenty people were assembled, when it appeared that neither Sir Henry Irving nor Miss Terry could follow German read aloud. 'Then I must read it in English,' said the Queen, adding to Max Müller, 'Sit by me, and help me.' For two hours the Queen translated aloud, without hesitating for a word. Her reading was acting, and she kept her hearers spellbound. On finishing the tragedy, the Queen turned anxiously to the great actor: 'Well, what do you think?' 'Madam,' was the reply, 'such a play requires an Ober-Ammergau audience'; exactly expressing the feelings of all present.

From London the Max Müllers paid a visit to their daughter in her beautiful old home, Ightham Mote, in Kent, the first of many happy days to be spent there.

To MRS. SELLAR (after the death of Professor Sellar).

IGHTHAM MOTE, *October* 24, 1890.

'Many times I have thought of writing to you, but what is one to say! Whenever I thought of you till now, all seemed bright and cheerful with you, and now all is changed. We reckon too little with death, and then when it comes it overwhelms us. We know all the time that our friends must go, and that we must go, but we shut our eyes and enjoy their love and friendship as if life could never end. We should say good-bye to each other every evening,—perhaps the last good-bye would find us then less unprepared.

'Your dear husband's life has been a long one, well filled, and full of much happiness. Who knows but that the few remaining years on which he might have reckoned, would have been years of suffering to him, and to you? One or two more stations, and then we also have come to the end of our journey. Nearly all our cheerful companions are gone, it is difficult to make new friendships, and I assure you, those who have left us are nearer to us, and we nearer to them, than those who are still sitting by our side. We have often been truly happy together: believe me, I feel now truly unhappy with you.'

On Christmas Day, Max Müller's old friend Dr. Thomson, Archbishop of York, passed away. He was associated with some of the brightest and also the saddest days of Max Müller's early life in Oxford, and but two years before, the friends renewed their youth in much pleasant intercourse when Max Müller stayed at Bishopthorpe.

Christmas was spent by Max Müller at Oxford alone with his son; his wife being with her daughter. On December 30 his first grandchild, a boy, was born.

To his Wife.

7, Norham Gardens, *December* 30, 1890.

'You don't know how entirely upset I have been all day: it seemed such a sudden joy, and the suspense and tension had been so long. I quite collapsed with joy. I hope all will go well. I thought I should never see my children's children, and now even that blessing has been granted me! I am tired out.'

Oxford, *December* 31, 1890.

'My dear little Grandson,—I was delighted with your first letter, and I hope I shall receive a great many more, for though I have not seen you yet, I think of you a great deal, and always want to know how you are, and how your dear Mama is. I am glad you like your Grandmama; I like her too, and I know she will be very kind to you, and she will not mind your crying. I don't wonder at your crying; it is a hard world you enter, as you will find out by-and-by. Many people would cry all their lives, if they were not ashamed of it. Besides, you have as yet nothing else to do, and so you are crying "brightly, because you have nothing else to do," isn't that it? Your grandfather is already very proud of you, and perhaps he may live long enough to be really proud of you. Anyhow he hopes you will be a pride to your father and mother; you cannot be anything better. And now when you have cried yourself out, try to sleep, and forget the beginning troubles of your life. Your grandfather is trying to do the same, but he does not always succeed.

'Your loving Grandfather,

'F. Max Müller.'

Early in January, Max Müller started for Glasgow, for his third course of Gifford Lectures, taking London on his way, that he might see his first grandchild. His wife joined him in Glasgow later in the month. This third course, on 'Anthropological Religion,' was intended to show how different nations arrived at a belief in a soul. The first two courses had roused some animosity among the narrower-minded men in Scotland, and this year a violent attack was made on Max Müller's lectures at a meeting of the Established Presbytery of Glasgow, where Mr. Thomson, Minister of Ladywell, moved the motion:—

'Inasmuch as the teaching of Professor Max Müller, the Gifford Lecturer in the University of Glasgow, is subversive of the Christian faith, and fitted to spread pantheistic and infidel views amongst the students and others; the Presbytery appoint a committee to examine the views of Professor Max Müller as set forth in his lectures, and to ascertain the Senate's power in relation to the acceptance of the Gifford bequest and the appointment of a lecturer.'

As an amendment Dr. Watt moved:—

'That the Presbytery express profound regret that teaching of an unsettling character should be given apparently under the sanction of the Senatus of the University, but deem it inexpedient to take any action in the matter.'

Dr. Watt—after saying that it was impossible that any fault could have been found with the first appointment, Professor Max Müller being a man of very great eminence, not only in philology, but also in all branches of modern human learning; and that if fault could have been found with the appointment, voice would have been given to it long before the Professor began his lectures—admitted that possibly it had been a mistake to elect him a second time. Yet, had the Senate said, 'We will not reappoint you,' and if the reason for doing so had been stated, the outcry against them, on the plea that they were repressing freedom of thought, would have been quite as strong as the outcry for giving too much licence.

Dr. Robertson moved, as a further amendment:—

'The Presbytery being advised that the Gifford Lectureship at present held by Professor Max Müller, was founded by Lord Gifford in order that the origin of religions might be discussed on a scientific basis, declare that it is without their province to express an opinion on the wisdom of the founder in constituting the trust, and on the expediency of the University in accepting the trust.'

After further discussion, the clerk having proposed that a vote be taken, a disgraceful scene followed, Mr. Thomson exclaiming, 'Aye, let us see who is for, and who is against, Christ'; an expression he was requested to withdraw. Dr. Robertson's amendment was carried by seventeen votes to five, when Mr. Thomson again exclaimed, 'Only five for Christ,' an expression he had to withdraw. One of the Glasgow papers, commenting on the whole meeting, said:—

'It may be taken as certain that the assertions made to the effect that Mr. Max Müller is a foe to religion in general and to Christianity in particular are altogether unwarranted, and it is conceivable that a serious question may arise as to how far a member of a Presbytery is shielded by his official position from the consequences that sometimes attach to rash statements of this character.'

An even stronger attack on the lectures was made by Monsignor Munro in St. Andrew's (R. C.) Cathedral. His text was from St. Matthew's account of the betrayal of Christ by Judas.

'He meant,' the preacher said, 'to apply that terrible narrative to the subject of his lecture that evening. The Gifford Lectures delivered by Professor Max Müller were nothing less than a crusade against Divine revelation, against Jesus Christ, and against Christianity. The guilt of those who permitted that anti-Christian doctrine in a University founded to defend Christianity, was simply horrible. It was a strange thing that in a Christian University, public feeling should have tolerated the ostentatious publication of infidelity. The pantheism of the lectures made Divine revelation simply impossible; it reduced God to mere nature, and did away with the body and soul as we know them. It was strange that the Professor, who knew so much of other religions, should know so little of the religion which it was his object to overthrow. Judge what Christianity would be in this country in another generation, if teaching was to be tolerated like that of these *blasphemous lectures*. The lectures were the proclamation of atheism under the guise of pantheism. Professor Max Müller was incapable of a philosophical idea, and ignorant of the Christianity he sought to overthrow. His theory uprooted our idea of God, for it repudiated the idea of a personal God.'

The following lines show that such was not the judgement of all his hearers:—

To MAX MÜLLER (on hearing him lecture, February 13, 1891).

'The same as when a youth thy charm I felt,
Illustrious scholar! loving to shed light
Into the caverns of Religious Night,
Where, thro' the ages, men so oft have knelt
Abject before a fetish, wood or stone,
Of their own making: and, most sad to say,
By Magi have been fool'd; their night call'd day;
And their rude concepts vaunted as full-grown
And final! Thou hast shown us wider skies
Than we were wont to see and call Heaven's gate,
Beneath which rose sweet praise and sacrifice
Ere Abraham was; now teachest us to rise
Unto the Universal, scorning fate,
While Truth with lighted torch stands by elate.'

These attacks made no difference to Max Müller's teaching; he only felt it was unfair to have judged him before his final course of lectures. He had long laid Channing's advice to heart: 'Wait not to be backed by numbers. Wait not till you are sure of an echo from a crowd. The fewer the voices on the side of truth, the more distinct and strong must be your own.'

Those who know Max Müller's firm faith in a personal God ruling and directing all things in love and wisdom, and in Christ's own teaching (not, indeed, as shown in the teaching of Roman Catholic priests, or Calvinistic ministers), will hardly believe that such attacks could have been made upon him.

The lectures were again very well attended; the last lecture of the course was crowded. The *Baillie*, a Glasgow paper, wrote thus of this set of lectures:—

'Professor Max Müller's earlier course, like everything that comes from his pen, was both able and interesting. But able and interesting as it was, it was not to be compared, for either of these qualities, with that by which it is being followed. Whether regarded from the scholar's or the philosopher's point of view, the present course is at once wonderfully powerful and wonderfully fascinating. The Professor's amazing stores of knowledge, his keen intellect, and the fervid and almost emotional character of his temperament, are qualifications specially suited for this high and memorable task. In Glasgow the Professor has now become in a measure acclimatized. He finds an abundance of congenial society in University circles at Gilmorehill. Pleasant and unaffected in manner, and simple in tastes, he makes no heavy claim on the ability or attention of the people among whom he passes his days. As a result of his good-nature, the Professor has been trotted out, both publicly and privately, during the present season, now by people of the lion-hunting persuasion, and now by hangers-on of the Young Men's Association species, but the little penances involved by these trottings-out have all been accepted by him in excellent part, and with the best of tempers.'

One of these 'trottings-out' is so characteristic of Max Müller's power of becoming young with the young, that the account of the meeting of a students' club is given from a students' paper:—

'At ten o'clock Professors M'Call Anderson and Max Müller joined the company. Mr. Ramsay was just finishing the present popular song, "His funeral's to-morrow," and at its conclusion the company sang a students' chorus in good style. The chairman then gave the health of the two new arrivals, which was pledged with great enthusiasm. Professor Max Müller, in replying, said: "In Germany, I would say *Commilitones*; in Scotland, I salute you as 'jolly good fellows.' As your chairman has told you, I have known student life in Germany, professorial life in Germany, professorial life at Oxford, but not student life there—in fact, there is no student life at Oxford. I have tasted a little of the professorial life of Glasgow, but this is the first time I have shared its student life, and I feel a student at Leipzig once again. There is never a meeting like this in Oxford."

'Later in the evening Mr. MacLaren sang "Die wacht am Rhein," and Mr. Buchanan "Rhine Wine," at the request of Professor Müller. On their conclusion, he asked the company to join him in singing a song, known in every College in the world—a song that had come down for hundreds of years, the "Gaudeamus igitur." The Professor then took his seat at the piano, and in grand style led the splendid old song, the company joining with the greatest heartiness.'

To Dr. Hosäus.

*January*, 1891.

'It is indeed a blessing to be able to hope that we shall both live to see my father's monument finished. I will gladly say a few words at the unveiling, but the leading part falls to you.'

TO B. M. MALABARI, ESQ.

GLASGOW, *January* 18.

'I was delighted to hear that the first step has been taken. Whatever you may feel yourself, in the eyes of the world, and particularly in England, this will be a great triumph. It would be very bad policy to show ourselves discouraged. On the contrary, the victory is on our side. The principle has been admitted, and may now be acted on, that the limit of the age of consent has nothing to do with religion, but is a matter of public hygiene, for which the Government is responsible. As new light comes in, new measures will have to be taken. I congratulate you on what you have achieved so far, but I feel sure it would be the greatest mistake if you were to show yourself dejected or disheartened.

'Take care of your health—there is no medicine so good as good spirits, and there is still many a fight to fight.'

On Max Müller's return south, he attended the christening of his little grandson at St. George's, Hanover Square; Princess Christian standing sponsor to the child, whom she held at the font, giving him the names of Max Christian Hamilton. Max Müller's old friend Dean Bradley performed the ceremony, and the little fellow was taken from the Dean by his great-great-grandmother, on his father's side, who came to London for the occasion.

In contrast to the attacks made on him in Scotland, Max Müller received just about this time a letter from an almost unknown admirer, recalling a walk 'some few years before, which you permitted me to share with you; ... on that evening my inner self was fed with food that strengthened me, and made me so much the better man to face facts, and live in the Light which lighteth every man, and made me receptive to the incoming of that Life, which by His coming He brought us.'

TO ARCHDEACON WILSON.

OXFORD, *March* 22.

'If you can find time, please read my last lecture, Gifford III, and if you would let me know what you think of it, I should feel grateful. Yes! I know that one or two sentences contain what we had talked and written about at Maloja, happy Maloja! No, my faith in England is not shaken. We must not expect too much, we must not expect all strata of thought to become *one*. Here in Oxford, we shall never get rid of impenetrable Oxford clay, but there is a healthy layer of gravel on the top. I see you are fighting. I have had my fight at Glasgow, but the Professors, with few exceptions, have stood by me. No, I do not despair. In fact, I have no time for it.'

The following letters show how Max Müller was appealed to on every variety of subject:—

OXFORD, *March* 13.

'DEAR SIR,—I cannot enter into details, but if you trust me, you may take it for granted that there is no reason for supposing that the English race represents the lost tribes of Israel.'

OXFORD, *February* 19, 1896.

'DEAR SIR,—I doubt whether the number of Germans pronouncing German in the Hanoverian fashion is known; anyhow, I do not know it. There is no reason to suppose that the South German fashion of pronouncing German is due to the Jews.

'Yours truly,
'F. MAX MÜLLER.'

A good deal of Max Müller's time was taken up this year, as in 1890, by the unfortunate determination of certain members of the eighth Oriental Congress, held at Stockholm in 1889, to upset the arrangements made by the committee of management at Christiania, before the Congress separated. Some members of the Congress, notably Drs. Leitner and Oppert, had taken offence at the arrangements made in Sweden, and succeeded on their return to France and England in gathering round them a body of malcontents, who announced the ninth Congress for September, 1891. It had been proposed in Sweden that Max Müller should be President of the ninth Congress, probably to be held in London. Drs. Leitner and Oppert, both German Jews by birth, declared it was an insult to French scholars to ask them to attend a Congress under the Presidency of Max Müller, quite forgetting that Max Müller was a member of the French Institute and a naturalized Englishman, and that it had been said of him at a former Congress that he was 'Allemand par cœur, Français par honneur, Anglais par demeure,' also that Helmholtz had lately acted as president at some congress held in Paris.

Attempts were made at a compromise, but Dr. Leitner would not agree, and declaring that the meeting at Christiania had departed from the statutes framed in Paris in 1873, as if, as years went on, no alteration was ever to be made in accordance with the demands of the times, he succeeded in gathering an assemblage together in London in September, which he called the ninth Oriental Congress. All German Orientalists held aloof, and Weber wrote a pamphlet against the whole proceeding. Leitner had none of the minutes and regulations of the committee of Christiania, and the beautiful horn presented to the Congress by the King of Sweden, to be held by the President of each Congress till the next meeting, was still in the hands of the Swedish President, and was only passed on the following year to Professor Max Müller. When it was found that Dr. Leitner was determined to carry out his schism, the committee formed at Christiania settled that the real ninth Congress should meet in 1892 in London, and take no further notice of Dr. Leitner. Oxford had been discussed as an alternative place of meeting. All this involved immense correspondence with Oriental scholars throughout Europe and America, and Max Müller often lamented the valuable time thus frittered away.

A new edition of the *Three Lectures on Language* was published this year in America, and it is to this that the following letters allude:—

TO PROFESSOR ROMANES.

OXFORD, *July* 2.

'Here is my defence. I hope you will accept it in the spirit in which it was written, and I do not give up all hope yet that we may come to agree in the end. I believe we both care far more for *what* is right, than for *who* is right.'

Leave has been given to insert the answer:—

OXFORD, *July* 3.

'DEAR PROFESSOR MAX MÜLLER,—Many thanks for your *language*, both as regards the Lectures and the letter. It appears to me, after reading the former, that very little difference remains between us, when once my "misapprehensions" have been subtracted. And my "defence" touching these must be that, as you observe, I am no "master" in philology, and therefore apt to fall into the misunderstandings of an amateur. At the same time, you will doubtless be the first to perceive that it would have been impossible for me to have even attempted a work on the evolution of human thought, without reading the "several books" on language to which you refer. And this much good, at least, may be said to have come from my attempt, that of enabling you to correct erroneous interpretations into which some other of your readers may likewise have fallen. Anyhow, in my eyes, the corrections which you have supplied serve only to enhance the high estimate which I have always held of the value of your work. Of course, I shall notice what you say, should there be a second edition of my book, or if any other suitable occasion should arise.'

To Professor Romanes.

Ightham Mote, *July* 6.

'I must thank you for your letter. It is so painful when personal feelings are mixed up with scientific research. Facts and correct deductions from facts, are all we ought to care for; who discovered them and who made them is of very little consequence. Yet I know from experience that there are but few who would be so completely above all personal feelings as you have shown yourself to be. As you say, the points on which we differ are few and they seem very small, yet I should like some day to reason out some of these questions with you. Of course, I feel the break in evolution between animal and man quite as much as you do. I do not want it or look for it. But I cannot get over this. What is impossible cannot be the same as what is possible. It seems to me we may say that it is impossible for any animal, except man, to attain to language, in its true sense of Logos. At least, it is as impossible as that the sun should rise in the west. It may, of course, but it has never done so, I admit in the abstract that an animal may begin to speak—we see ever so many attempts at communication among animals, and among children, long before the sunrise of language—but I take my stand on the fact that no animal has ever done so. And then I ask why? and I can only answer, because there is something in the human animal which is absent in the brute animal from beginning to end.'

It is a pity that literary differences are not always expressed in the courteous tone of these letters.

To Dr. Hosäus.

Ightham Mote, *July* 8.

'I am delighted to hear that no further difficulties stand in the way of the unveiling of the monument. I certainly hope, please God, to be present. . . . I shall be delighted with any arrangement you make about the festivities. My own family is, as you know, greatly reduced in number, and even of my contemporaries but few are left.'

The Prince of Naples (the present King of Italy) visited Oxford this summer for a few hours, and, by desire of the Prince of Wales, Max Müller acted as his guide. The most important Colleges were visited, and finally All Souls, where the whole party partook of the famous and potent All Souls ale, and inscribed their names in the College visitors' book and in Max Müller's autograph book. The Prince was much amused with the constitution of All Souls, a College without students, and asked whether the monks of All Souls were married, and if their wives might live in College and dine in hall. At the Bodleian, the Prince, who was a keen numismatist, begged to see the collection of coins. The Library had lately acquired some old Italian coins, which the Prince at once proceeded to arrange. He repeatedly expressed his delight with the beauty of Oxford, and showed great interest in everything.

The next event of this year was the Meeting of the British Association at Cardiff, which Max Müller attended, he and his wife being the guests of the Dean of Llandaff. Max Müller, as President of the Anthropological Section, gave an inaugural address on the 'Classification of Mankind by Language or by Blood,' which is published in *Chips*, Vol. I, new edition. He had taken no active part in any meeting of the British Association for forty-four years, since he, as a mere youth, read a paper on 'The Relation of Bengali to the Âryan and Aboriginal Languages of India.' He recalled that meeting, and the belief of those days in Linguistic Ethnology, a science against which he protested even at the time, young as he was, maintaining that there ought to be a complete separation between Philology and Physiology, as sciences, though he acknowledged that the old heresy of Linguistic Ethnology was not entirely extinct even at the present day.

Max Müller and his wife spent a month of quiet enjoyment after this at Wildbad, in the Black Forest. From here he wrote to his old friend Professor Carus:—

WILDBAD, *September* 16.

'MY DEAR VICTOR,—The monument to my father is to be unveiled on September 30. How delightful it would be if you could be present! I hope to be there with my son, daughter, and son-in-law. My grandson is unfortunately too young for travelling. Who knows if we may otherwise meet again in this life?'

At Wildbad they were joined by their son, and they went on together to Dessau, there meeting their daughter and her husband, who, like themselves, had come to attend the unveiling of the monument to Wilhelm Müller, which took place on September 30. The Duke and Duchess of Anhalt, and other members of the Ducal family, were present at the ceremony. In front of the veiled monument a covered stand was erected, occupied by the Ducal party, all the living connexions of Wilhelm Müller, and other invited guests; whilst Max Müller, his son and son-in-law, the deputations from various parts of Germany, the choir, and the speakers at the ceremony, were grouped on each side of the monument. Some fine choruses were well rendered by the choir of the Gymnasium, with military accompaniment, some good speeches were made, and after the monument had been unveiled and handed over by the committee to the care of the town, Max Müller spoke, recalling all the work his father had carried out during his short life of thirty-three years. Then, as the sounds of the Anhalt hymn rose, the deputations, headed by Wilhelm Müller's grandson and the husband of his granddaughter, and two old pupils of the poet, laid wreaths at the foot of the statue, and the interesting ceremony was over. It was followed by a banquet, presided over by Minister von Krosigk, where Max Müller had to respond to the health of himself and his family. Many old friends had come together from a distance, as much to meet Max Müller as to do honour to their popular poet, and many merry old recollections were revived, and old ties reknit.

There was a gala representation of *Iphigenia in Aulis* that evening, at which the Duke and Duchess of Anhalt were present, when the Duke sent for Max Müller and presented him with the Anhalt Order of Albrecht the Bear, first class, with star, the oldest Order in Europe, even older than the Garter.

Soon after his return to England, Max Müller went to Reading to take part in a gathering of the Reading University Extension Association. After a warm eulogy on the system of University Extension Lectures, in which he had from the first been keenly interested, he told his hearers that in his late visit to Germany he had had to answer innumerable questions on the system, which was totally unknown there, and which, as a new departure from the old University lectures, was exciting great attention in Germany. He ended by a word of warning to those attending these lectures:—

'They should not imagine that by attending lectures they have done their duty. Lectures are not meant to stuff and cram the mind. Lectures are meant to excite an appetite for knowledge, and to show how such knowledge may best be acquired. But the actual acquiring of knowledge, the masticating of facts and their healthy digestion, can only be done by each student for himself. There are cramming and stuffing lectures—we know them but too well. They take away all real appetite for knowledge; they produce chronic intellectual dyspepsia. I know from experience how much good a teacher may do by one lecture, aye, by a few words of warning and advice, and I welcome these University Extension lectures as a standing protest against that mere stuffing and cramming, which has wellnigh extinguished all true love of learning among our young men.'

This year Max Müller brought out the final edition of his lectures on language, which he called *The Science of Language*, founded on lectures delivered in 1861 and 1863. The book had been almost rewritten, and yet so much has been done in the study of philology since 1891, that the work is now looked on as antiquated. In reviewing it in 1891, the *Academy* says:—

'We are glad to find that the new edition is not of such a character as to affect the essential identity of the book, which has attained something of the position of a classic.... It has never been superseded as a preliminary survey of the whole subject. ... The grace of style and felicity of illustration have not evaporated in the process of revision.'

To Lady Welby.

*October* 18, 1891.

'I have to finish my fourth volume of *Gifford Lectures* for next January—it will be the last word I have to say, and it is not easy to find out how best to say it, and how to explain in English the unity of the Infinite in nature and the Infinite in man, the true meaning of the "I and My Father are one." After that I shall say no more, for I am getting tired and should like to retire into the forest, if I only knew where to find it.'

To Mrs. Thomson.

Oxford, *November* 14.

'Like everybody else I have been laid up with a wretched cold, otherwise I should have answered your kind lines before. It is sad to think of all that was, and is no more, and yet there is something much more real in memory than one used to think. All is there but what our weak human senses require, and nothing is lost, nothing can be lost except what we knew would vanish one day, but what was the husk only, and not the kernel. I have learnt to live with those who went before us, and they seem more entirely our own than when they were with us in the body. And as long as we have duties to fulfil, so long as there are others who lean on us, and want us, life can be lived a few years longer, it can only be a few years now. . . .

'Ever yours affectionately,

'F. Max Müller.'

In November the Duchess of Albany visited Oxford, to show her two children the place where their father had spent so many happy years. They came to tea in Norham Gardens, and Max Müller, finding that the little Duke had not yet made acquaintance with the famous German child's book *Struwwelpeter*, bought one the next day, and took it with him to the Bodleian Library, where he was engaged to meet the Duchess and show her some of the treasures. After a time, her Royal Highness missed her guide, and he was found in one of the reading recesses with the little Duke on his knee, carefully explaining *Struwwelpeter* to the small boy. It was a curious contrast, the old Professor, the little child, *Struwwelpeter*, amid all the treasures of the Bodleian.

It was at the end of this year that Dr. Liddell, Dean of Christ Church, resigned his Deanery, and he and his family left Oxford; a great loss socially to all Oxford, and especially to the Max Müllers and other families who had been among their more intimate friends. What the loss was to Max Müller he has shown in the article, 'Dean Liddell, as I knew him,' reprinted in the first series of *Last Essays*. From this time, he withdrew almost entirely from participation in University matters, with which he had never much concerned himself; but in those in which he took part, he missed the support and influence of the Dean, from whom he rarely, if ever, differed, and ere long he resigned his place as a Curator of the Bodleian, and, some few years later, as Delegate of the Press.

To W. Lilly, Esq.

*December* 17, 1891.

'I am deep in the Mystics just now: they are my *premier amour*, and I expect they will be my *dernier amour*. They have been through life my protection against all troubles. I only wish people would not call them Mystics; they are as clear as daylight, clearer than the Scholastics with all their systematic arrangements. But will people in England listen to them? Will they not turn up their noses, like Mansell, &c., and say that the Infinite is a negative concept only? . . . I must confess that social and political questions have almost ceased to interest me. I feel so helpless and hopeless before them. I admire those who try to purify the Thames, but I have no shoulders for that kind of work. My favourites of course are the German Mystics, particularly Meister Eckhart and Cardinal Cusanus. Even Thomas Aquinas is permeated by Mysticism—with him too the highest beatitude is the *Visio Dei per consentiam*; that goes beyond Dionysius, who denies the *per essentiam*, does he not? Still, he does not go as far as Eckhart, who is a real Vedântist, and knows the difference between Wesen and Sein.'

To Sir Henry Acland.

Oxford, *December* 21, 1891.

'I have read your letter, and feel, like you, very sad to see Oxford falling away more and more from the ideal which men like Rolleston, Pattison, Stanley, Goldwin Smith, and Henry Smith placed before us. Oxford is becoming a machine, a most successful machine, for enabling a very large number of young men to pass their examinations. To do that under the present system of examinations, either with or without honours, young men have little or no time left for subjects which do not pay in the schools.

'It was the object of Universities to widen and strengthen the minds of young men, before they entered into the narrower grooves of their professional work; now the narrowing and deadening process begins as soon as a boy leaves school. That is, no doubt, a great misfortune, a national misfortune; and its effects begin to be felt in different professions. The present system may produce very fine and sharp blades, it will no longer produce the powerful axe which is wanted to clear a way through the dark future before us. Still, *nil desperandum*.

'With best wishes for the New Year.'

The following alludes to Archdeacon Wilson's noble letter to the *Times*, December 15, appealing in the name of Christian liberty against the 'Declaration on the truth of Holy Scripture,' sent to the *Times* a few days earlier, signed by thirty-eight clergy, advocating the most rigid belief in the verbal inspiration of the Bible:—

To Archdeacon Wilson.

Oxford, *December* 28, 1891.

'I read your letter in the *Times* with very great pleasure. The original manifesto also gave me a better idea and greater hope of the Church of England, considering that thirty-eight only could be found to sign it. I have nothing more to say, beyond what you have said, and I feel so tired out by writing my final course of Gifford Lectures, that I really have no heart to do anything else. My third volume has been printed for some time, but it is not to be out before January 1, when I hope to send you a copy. I expect there will be a strong protest from some quarters, but I am quite prepared for it. I have had to read lately Thomas Aquinas, *et hoc genus omne*, and am surprised at their liberality. They invariably place reason above faith, at least from a subjective point of view. However, my real heroes are what are called the German Mystics, Meister Eckhart, &c. There is nothing mystical in them. It is all as clear as daylight, and very true and beautiful.'

# CHAPTER XXXI

## 1892–1893

Last course of Gifford Lectures. Birth of second grandchild. New edition of *Rig-veda* published. Tercentenary of Trinity College, Dublin. Mr. Froude returns to Oxford. Ninth Oriental Congress. Fourth Gifford Lectures published. Journey to Italy, Greece, and Turkey. Stay at Constantinople. Buda-Pesth. Vienna. Leipzig. Jubilee of Doctor's Degree. Neuwied. Birth of third grandchild. Seventieth birthday.

To Lady Welby.

*January* 5, 1892.

'For all my sins I have been elected President of the next Oriental Congress, and during the last week I have had thirty letters to write to different Rajahs and Mahârâjahs, so what should I give for a little rest! I want to finish my fourth volume of *Gifford Lectures*, and my thoughts are very much where yours are. What is the origin and purpose of a *Sign*, and how is it that we understand a sign in what is Significance? I said long ago that the history of philosophy is the history of our fight against language and all its inevitable misunderstandings. Thence, as Herbert says, true philosophy is definition.

'I think I shall soon elope with myself and hide somewhere in the forest.'

Early in the month the third volume of Gifford Lectures on *Anthropological Religion* came out, the subject being the gradual growth of a belief in something infinite, immortal and divine in man. In his preface Max Müller says:—

'In lecturing on the origin and the growth of religion, my chief object has been to show that a belief in God, in the immortality of the soul, and in a future retribution can be gained, and not only can be, but has been gained by the right exercise of human reason alone, without the assistance of what has been called a special revelation. I have tried to prove this, not, as others have done, by reasoning *à priori* only, but by historical investigation. In doing this, I thought I was simply following in the footsteps of the greatest theologians of our time, and that I was serving the cause of true religion by showing by ample historical evidence, gathered from the Sacred Books of the East, how what St. Paul, what the Fathers of the Church, what mediaeval theologians, and what some of the most learned of modern divines had asserted again and again was most strikingly confirmed by the records of all non-Christian religions which have lately become accessible to us. I could not have believed it possible that, in undertaking this work, I should have exposed myself to attacks from theologians who profess and call themselves Christians, and who yet maintain that worst of all heresies, that, during all the centuries that have elapsed and in all the countries of the world, God has left Himself without a witness, and has revealed Himself to one race only, the Jews of Palestine.'

One reviewer, speaking of the attacks on Max Müller, says: 'The Professor may well be content with expounding what he believes to be the truth with a wealth of learning which few men could rival, and a general sobriety of tone which might be an example to some of his critics; for the rest, we may remind both parties to the controversy of the old motto of another Scottish University, "They say. What say they? Let them say."' One friend, to whom the book was sent, wrote: 'One reason why I value your book is because it is conciliatory, yet firm, and seems likely to help the advance well onward.' The Master of Balliol (Jowett), in writing about this work, spoke of the passage on 'Miracles' at the end of the preface, in which he entirely agreed. 'It was a very bold, and, I think, a very wise thing to make such a statement; it does great service to religion.'

Before the middle of January, the Max Müllers left for Glasgow for the fourth and last course of Gifford Lectures. These were on *Psychological Religion*, giving the history of the various attempts made to define the relation between the infinite in nature and the infinite in man, or the union of the soul with God. The attendance was very large, and this concluding course excited great interest. This time in Glasgow was less filled with social duties, and for the last fortnight Max Müller was alone, his wife having been summoned to her daughter, by the birth of their second grandchild.

TO MADAME BLUMENTHAL.

GLASGOW, *January* 27, 1892.

'I quite sympathize with your indictment against Greek Grammar. But you see language is not made, but grows, and as we accept a gnarled oak-tree, we must accept the Greek language, such as it has grown up. Of course, a language was never meant to be learnt by grammar, but by ear; and the Greek children, who never heard a wrong accent or a wrong tense, never made a mistake. I think that Greek scholars also ought to be satisfied if they know a Greek form when they meet it, and not break their hearts about a solecism, when they attempt to write it. There is, no doubt, reason in all that seems unreasonable in grammar, but the reason is often very unreasonable. False analogy prevails largely, and irregular forms become popular, if used by popular poets. We must not attempt to find a reason for all media—the rules would become as fanciful as the fancy that gave rise to the media in many cases. Anyhow we must not be Pharisees. English and French are quite as bad as Greek. Why do we write *le prix*, but *le pala*is? Why *curieux*, but *mauvai*s, formerly *curieuse, mauvaise*? Voltaire wrote *aprocher*, *soufrir*, *coroux*, *alumer*. Why are unfortunate examinees ploughed, if they write as Voltaire wrote?

'I remember an American Grammar in which it was said that in this language *all* verbs are irregular; I remember a German Grammar in which it was said that the only regular verbs are the irregular. The question is, with whom rests the *norma loquendi*?'

TO MRS. HUMPHRY WARD (on receiving *David Grieve*).

GLASGOW, *February* 2.

'Many thanks for your new novel. I have read it, though I had no cold and no influenza. Looking at the mere workmanship, the mixing of the colours, and the putting them on the canvas, I am perfectly amazed at the mastery you have attained. I am almost afraid I shall be converted to novel-reading in my old age. I used to teach and preach against them like a young Saul. As a matter of fact, tales meant for entertainment form generally the last stages of the literature of the great nations of the world. But there is evidently no escape from them now, and who knows but I shall have to write a religious novel instead of Gifford Lectures? I have no doubt your work will prove a great success, and I can see that there is hard and honest work in it. Still, knowing the feelings of a mother for her first-born, I know you will not feel angry if I feel more deeply interested in *Robert Elsmere* than in *David Grieve*.'

To Professor Maurice Bloomfield, Baltimore (after receiving his *Contributions to the Interpretation of the Veda*).

Oxford, *March* 23, 1892.

'I must answer your very kind letter at once. I feel very guilty, but when you are as old as I am you will, I am sure, have pity on me. I can assure you that if I were to acknowledge all books and papers sent to me, I should simply break down. It is physically impossible. I have always read your papers with real pleasure, because they contained substantial facts, and I always look forward to an opportunity of acknowledging my obligations in public. I should have been delighted to have a translation of the *Atharva-veda* from you for the *Sacred Books of the East*, but, alas! my forty-eight volumes are full, and the Press has lately declined several new offers.'

As time went on, his correspondence weighed more and more heavily on Max Müller, and though he tried to answer some letters through his secretary or his wife, he found such vicarious answers were seldom accepted in good part. People forgot that the eye and hand are not as active at seventy as at thirty; whilst each year added to the mere number of his correspondents and to the multitude of books sent to him on all subjects.

To Professor Estlin Carpenter.

*April* 8.

'Could you, without much trouble, tell me what is the latest date that can safely be assigned to Exodus iii. 14?'

Professor Carpenter having replied that probably Exodus iii. 14 is a late addition to the text, Max Müller wrote thus:—

To the Same.

*April* 11.

'Many thanks for your letter; it was really what I expected and wished for. The very thought struck me as not Jewish, and far too philosophical. Besides, v. 15 contradicts v. 14. But I had another reason. "I am what I am," *Ahmi yat ahmi*, is one of the great names of Ahuramazda, and I could not bring myself to believe that this coincidence was accidental. In Zend the connexion between *Ahuro* and *ah-mi*, "I am," is still felt; it hardly is in *Jehovah* and *hayah!* It seems to me a clear case of Zoroastrian influence on Judaism: what I wanted to know was the chronological limit. The mental influence between the two religions belongs to very different dates, some very early. It seems to me that the reaction against polytheism and the worship of the old Devas, in fact the very origin of the Zoroastrian religion, and the belief in one Supreme God, Ahura-mazda, may have been due to contact with the Jews settled in the cities of India. It is difficult to account for this sudden change without admitting some external impulse. During the second exile the influence seems to come from Mazdaism rather than from Judaism, except in the very latest Pehlevi traditions. We have just published West's translation of the *Dinkard* in the *Sacred Books of the East*. It is very interesting.'

In April, Max Müller received a letter from the Duke of Argyll, on the subject of his third series of Gifford Lectures, *Anthropological Religion*, which the Duke had just read. He replied as follows:—

To the Duke of Argyll.

Oxford, *April* 16, 1892.

'. . . I did not wish to enter on the question of Miracles, because I had little to say that was new; and yet it seemed to me cowardly to avoid the question altogether. What I wanted to say was that Miracles, in their true sense, so far from being impossible, are inevitable; they arise from the distance which always exists between the founders of a religion and their immediate disciples. They spring everywhere from the same source, a deep veneration felt by the great unreasoning masses for those whom they do not understand. Miracles thus receive a new and a more profound meaning. We are relieved from those never-ending discussions as to what is possible, probable, or real, what is rational, irrational, natural, or supernatural. We find ourselves before true *mira*, not small *miracula*. In a world where all is *admirable*, there is no room for small surprises. In a world in which no sparrow can fall to the ground without the Father, where is there room for an extra sparrow? The Greeks have brought themselves to conceive what is ὑπέρμορον; are we to conceive what is ὑπέρθειον? I confess I cannot, though as to denying the physical possibility of miracles, who would do that? My difficulty is to find anything that is *not* a miracle. Thus I take the resurrection, not the ascension, as a fact. Then, people will say, "Christ was *not* really dead." I answer, "If resuscitation excludes the possibility of antecedent death, then He was not." But who is to draw that line? certainly not the centurion who thought that the blood running out of His side proved death, whereas medical authorities say that it proved the contrary. To me what people call a mere trance is quite as miraculous as any other deathlike state. To me it is enough that, in the case of Christ, whatever happened was not without the will of God. That is enough for me, and I dare not ask whether it required any exceptional effort. My belief in Christ's true Divinity is based on my belief in the Logos, and so was the belief of such men as Clement, Origen, and others, who became Christians without surrendering an iota of their philosophical convictions. If only I had more time to read! There it is where the true solution of our difficulties seems to me to lie. I shall try to point out the way in my next volume, but I feel I shall break down—I cannot read what I ought to read. However, I shall try. There is not only Clement and Origen, there is Dionysius the Areopagite, then there is Thomas Aquinas, and last, but by no means least, Meister Eckhart, Tauler, Suso, and all the rest. The Cambridge Neo-Platonists are the last flicker of that ancient light, and all depends on the true meaning of Logos, both word and thought. How much more profoundly these old Platonists conceived the Origin of Species than the Darwinians!'

In the spring of this year, the third and fourth volumes of the new edition of the *Rig-veda*, brought out at the expense of the Mahârâjah of Vijayanagara, were published. These completed the work. In his preface to the first volume, Max Müller alluded to the correspondence that went on during 1884, between himself and the India Office relative to a new edition of the *Rig-veda*, and which has been fully detailed on p. 216. To these statements the India Office demurred, and took the peculiar step of writing to the Delegates of the Press early in 1891, complaining of these statements. Max Müller at once begged that such complaints might be addressed straight to him, that he might have an opportunity of replying personally to the points adverted to in the letter to the Delegates. *This was never done.* These accusations were never addressed directly to Max Müller, and would therefore not be noticed here, had not Professor Boehtlingk in his *Max Müller als Mythen-Dichter* ended his attack by bringing up these charges, saying, on the authority of a former employé of the India Office, that Max Müller's statements were all *pure inventions* (aus der Luft gegriffen). When the third and fourth volumes were ready for publication, Max Müller wrote a letter to the Secretary of State for India, in which he spoke of the charges as 'grave, and most offensive, if not actionable,' but he trusted to be able to prove by 'evidence that cannot be questioned, that every one of these charges is utterly unfounded, and that they reflect great discredit on the persons who invented them.' Who these were, and by what motives they were influenced, was perfectly well known to Max Müller. In his letter to the Secretary of State, he disproves all the charges, and in a letter to Mr. Curzon, then Under-Secretary of State, dated April 9, 1892, agrees not to advert to them in the preface of the last volume, but to let bygones be bygones. In a later letter, he says that he does not ask for an official retractation of the charges, only as they came from the Secretary of State in *Council*, he asks to be set right in the eyes of the Council. He concludes his letter thus:—

'I have either refuted every one of these libellous charges, or I have not. If I have, surely the Members of Council should be informed of it; if I have not, surely I ought to be informed what charges have remained unrefuted. I therefore leave my case with perfect confidence in your hands, being most unwilling to cause a public scandal, either in India or in England, and being most anxious to see those friendly relations re-established between the Indian Government and myself, to whom in the past I have owed so much.'

Unfortunately the matter had become known on the Continent, through a man who did not hesitate to use official information for personal purposes, and who assisted Dr. Boehtlingk's attack, which was widely circulated, whereas Max Müller's refutation was never known.

It was in this year also that the arrangements for the final volumes of the *Sacred Books of the East* were completed, and the number of forty-nine volumes filled up, though Max Müller was occupied with his work as editor to the last.

To Mr. Nanjio.

Oxford, *May* 1.

'I was glad to hear yesterday from your young countryman at Oxford that you were well. I was really afraid that some misfortune might have happened to you during that terrible earthquake. But now that I know where you are, and what you are doing, I write to tell you that we are printing the Sanskrit text of the *Buddha-karita*. I lent your copy to Professor Cowell, who had received another MS. from India, and has restored a very fair text. The book is very important as the oldest life of Buddha, also as the earliest specimen of the Kâvya style in Sanskrit, which we know from Kâlidâsa and others who lived much later. It is not an easy book to read, and I hope Professor Cowell will publish an English translation.

'I have now two grandchildren, a boy and a girl, both flourishing. My son has passed his examination for the Diplomatic Service, which was a great pleasure to me. I myself and my wife are both well.

'If I thought you would read them, I should gladly send you my *Lectures on the Science of Religion*, but I am afraid you might consider me a heretic in Buddhism, and wish to burn me! I wish you would come to our ninth Oriental Congress, to be held in London next September. I shall have to act as President. It will be a brilliant gathering of Oriental scholars, and would interest you very much.'

Professor Whitney had written a violent attack on Max Müller's new edition of the *Science of Language*, and to this the following letter mainly relates:—

To Horatio Hale, Esq.

Oxford, *May* 1.

'No plagiarism, I am sure, is more delightful than that which we all commit on truth. If we succeed in stealing the same good morsel from the larder of Truth we should feel delighted, as I always feel, if others, in their own independent way, arrive at the same results at which I have arrived. We two differ on some points but agree on most, and where we differ I believe an exchange of ideas by word of mouth, and not on paper, would soon make us agree. With regard to Linguistic Ethnology, for instance, all I meant to concede was that though some of the black inhabitants of India learnt to speak an Âryan language, they are ethnologically, or as people say, by blood, different from the Âryas their conquerors. The Celts in Ireland are Celts, though they speak English. More than that I did not mean, and from what happened at the time I believe the people at Cardiff quite understood what I meant. I feel very grateful for what you said about Whitney. I do not know whether you have followed his raids from the first. I thought at first he was honest and sincere, and took the trouble to answer him in a long paper, *In Self-Defence*. In order to put an end to mere squabbling, I proposed to him to choose three judges among his own friends, to submit the points in question to them, and to have done. He showed the better part of valour, and declined the trial on purely whimsical grounds. After that he went on sending me articles, anonymous or signed; in fact, he placed himself outside the pale of literary criticism. As, without losing all self-respect, I could not answer him, I have made it a rule for at least fifteen years never to read his invectives. . . . This is the man who adopts a magisterial tone in all American newspapers. I have always thought him to be exactly what you say, un-American, and I believe my American friends are much too shrewd to be taken in by his discharge of venom. I always think if a naughty boy in the street throws mud at you, it is better not to fight him, but to let the mud dry, and brush it off, or still better, wait till one's friends brush it off for us.'

To M. Renan.

Oxford, *May* 2.

'My dear old Friend,—We are very anxious to have your support, if not your presence, at the next Oriental Congress to be held in London in September. I have to act as President, and an ill-natured report has been spread that French scholars could not attend a Congress presided over by a German. Now I am a German by birth, but I am a naturalized Englishman, and I doubt whether real Frenchmen, real scholars, share the Chauvinism of ——. Lord Reay has asked me to write to you; all we want is your name as a member of the Congress, which entails no more than the ordinary subscription, for which you will receive the transactions of the Congress.'

During Commemoration of this year, the Max Müllers took refuge from the gaieties at Ightham Mote, and then went on to Rugby to their valued friends the Percivals for Speech Day, staying there again a week later on their way to Ireland to attend (by invitation) the Tercentenary of Trinity College, Dublin. There they were the guests of the Lord Mayor. The week was spent in incessant gaieties. On the second day the honorary degrees were conferred, Max Müller being one of the recipients, and being loudly cheered. He was one of the guests chosen to address the students on the last morning of the meeting in Trinity College. The *Irish Times* described his speech as follows:—

'The cheering which marked the appearance of Professor Max Müller at the orators' table was tremendous. This celebrated scholar is a man who rivets the attention of his audience. His style is scholarly and clear; he expresses the results of his study in the simplest of language, and there is not a trace of the pedant in his kindly manner and in his musical voice. He is somewhat above the middle height, is well-built, and his face is one of those strongly-marked, powerful, grey faces which seem to be rough-hewn from granite. His thin hair and bushy whiskers are perfectly white, and, brushed back, they added to the dignity of his highly intellectual face. His pronunciation of English is generally unimpeachable, but at rare intervals a delicately imperfect utterance, corrected almost as soon as spoken, reminded the audience of the celebrated philologist whom they had forgotten in the fluent and forcible speaker of English.'

This fatiguing week was followed by a resting visit to Lord Rosse for three days, after which the Max Müllers made their way by Cork, Glengarriff, and Kenmare, to Killarney, where they stayed with their old friends Professor and Mrs. Butcher, of Edinburgh, exploring, under their guidance, the Lakes, Muckross Abbey, and Ross Castle. The fine scenery was a great delight to Max Müller, whose love of beautiful nature was as vivid at sixty-nine as at twenty-six, when he first visited the Lakes of Cumberland. A day or two were spent at Sir Edward Verner's at Corke Abbey, near Bray, before returning to England.

To C. E. Norton, Esq., of Cambridge, Mass.

Oxford, *July* 29.

'Please accept my late, but very sincere thanks for your welcome and very helpful translation of Dante. I value it all the more, because it shows me that you have kept a place for me in your memory. Life is drawing to an end, the number of friends becomes smaller and smaller, and it is pleasant if our wandering thoughts can dwell with some, and feel that these are still among the living. I ought not to complain, for though I have lost much, much that is most precious has been left to me. I myself go on with my work, though I cannot trust to my memory as much as I did formerly, and must be very careful in verifying everything, not without considerable trouble. I have just finished a second edition of the *Rig-veda*, in four short quarto volumes, and my *Sacred Books of the East* are approaching completion as far as I am concerned. I send you a volume which may interest you more than my ordinary books. You will easily see how I try to solve the problems of Nature, Self, and God, historically, if possible. There is a fourth volume to follow, but I find it almost too hard to finish, and begin to feel my ignorance more and more. At present I am hard at work for the ninth International Congress of Orientalists, to be held in London in September. I have to be President, a great honour, but, like most honours, rather onerous.'

A great pleasure came to Max Müller this year: his old friend Mr. Froude was appointed Regius Professor of Modern History, and though he had not to reside till the Autumn Term, all through the summer he and his daughters came constantly to stay with their relations, first when choosing, and then when furnishing their house. During the two years of Mr. Froude's professorship, the old friends were constantly together, taking long walks, as in long past days (for Mr. Froude, though nearly five years the elder of the two, was singularly active and vigorous), or dropping into each other's houses for tea, sharing their guests, and London or foreign visitors; discussing their work, or politics, or the many interests they had in common. To both it was a renewal of their youth.

TO HIS DAUGHTER BEATRICE.

OXFORD, *August* 2, 1892.

'MY DEAR B.,—Leading such a vagabond life as we do, I quite forgot the first of August and your birthday. But for all that, I wished you many happy returns of the day, now that you are so comfortably settled with so many opportunities of making yourself useful to other people, not only to those who are dearest to you, but to many who are brought in contact with you. We spent some pleasant days with old Sir Harry Verney. The park was swarming with people on Bank Holiday. They had a flower show, athletic sports, and dancing, and everybody seemed supremely happy. Much good, I am sure, is done in that way, and the old man is evidently revered by all the farmers in the neighbourhood. Love to Tom, and a kiss to Maxie and the little girl. How grateful you ought to feel with all that has been given you! May you enjoy it for many years!

'Ever your loving Father.'

In the first days of September, the Max Müllers went to London for the ninth Oriental Congress, which, in spite of all the intrigues, was very successful, thanks chiefly to the exertions of Lord Northbrook, Lord Reay, and others. Knowing that no Congress could hope to rival the one at Stockholm in social brilliancy, the committee wisely endeavoured to make the ninth a real working Congress. On the Monday Max Müller delivered his Inaugural Address as President of the Congress. It gave a sketch of the achievements of Oriental scholarship during the last fifty years, and, as Hofrath Bühler said in his proposal of a vote of thanks, might fill the hearts of Orientalists with just pride. The proposal was seconded by Signor de Gubernatis. The address will be found in the first volume of *Chips*, new edition. One great interest of the meeting was the paper on 'Archaic Greece and the East,' written by Mr. Gladstone. As he could not be present, the paper was read by Max Müller.

One afternoon the President's son-in-law and his wife received the members at their lovely old house, Ightham Mote, near Sevenoaks. On the last day the Congress visited Oxford, the sections being entertained at luncheon in different Colleges, and in the afternoon the whole Congress was received in Wadham Gardens by the President and his wife, Sir William and Lady Hunter, and Professor and Mrs. Clifton. Max Müller returned to London for the final meeting, and there is no doubt that much good work was done during this Congress.

To the Right Honourable W. E. Gladstone.

7, Norham Gardens, *September* 15, 1892.

'It would have given me the greatest pleasure to be allowed to pay another visit to you at Hawarden Castle, but I am just packing my books and papers to spend a few weeks with my children and grandchildren at Westward Ho!, and I feel really so tired after our Oriental Congress as to be quite unfit for society. I considered it a great honour to read your paper at the Congress. It was a very great help to us to have your name among the Presidents of Sections, and I only wish you had been there in person to hear the cheers, and to listen to the debate which followed. The impression left upon those who spoke, myself among the rest, was that there certainly was something behind the restricted use of *ἄναξ ἀνδρῶν*, but that Homer was unaware of anything Phoenician or Egyptian in it. Your explanation took most of us by surprise, but we are getting accustomed to surprises from the East, and I look forward to more surprises to follow. I look upon ἄναξ as a Greek word. We have Ἄνακες, the Dioscuri, then Ἀνάκεια and Ἀνάκειον. Then there is ἀνάκτωρ in Aeschylus, and ἀνακτόριος. Could it be connected with the perfect ἄνωγα, I command? It is possible, but I can say no more. I do not know whether you received a copy of my Presidential Address which I sent to Hawarden, nor do I expect that you will have time to read it. But you would see how I try to find bridges on which Egyptian and Phoenician thought could have travelled from the East to Greece. My best bridge is the Alphabet. Grant that, and all is granted. But I must not take up any more of your time. I hope I shall have the pleasure of seeing you next term, when you are to lecture at Oxford. Unless you have already made arrangements, may I venture to say that it would give us the greatest pleasure if you and Mrs. Gladstone would stay with us, while you are at Oxford. I should consider your visit a very great honour, and I should do everything to secure you rest, and quiet, while preparing and delivering your lecture.'

To recover the fatigues of the Congress, the Max Müllers joined their daughter and her husband and children at Westward Ho!, near Bideford. An expedition was made by Clovelly and Bude to Boscastle, but the trip was spoilt by the rain.

To Dr. Hosäus.

*Translation.* Westward Ho, *October* 2.

'You may feel sure I recollected yesterday the happy days in Dessau, and thought of all those who showed their sympathy by attending the Fêtes. It is seldom that anything that one has wished for so long is brought to so successful an end. I shall never forget all I owe to your untiring energy. It must be a constant satisfaction to you to have the outcome of all your efforts daily before your eyes. Everything has gone as well with us this year, as one could possibly expect at our age. I certainly do not get much rest. When the Oriental Congress was over, I and my wife joined my daughter and son-in-law and two grandchildren here at the sea. I was here years ago with Charles Kingsley, when he was writing *Westward Ho!*, and now I am staying in the bathing-place named after his novel. So life flies by. I am delighted to say that my son entered the Diplomatic Service this year, so that, as far as one can see, his future is settled. It is a fine career, and he takes great interest in his work.'

Early in December Max Müller paid his last visit to Hawarden Castle.

TO HIS WIFE.

HAWARDEN CASTLE, *December* 7, 1892.

'It was a long journey, but the country looked beautiful in the snow. The old man is marvellous ; he looks stronger than ever, and Mrs. Gladstone, too, wonderfully well. The French Ambassador had to leave, so there is only Lady K. staying here. It is certainly interesting to see a man at his age so vigorous, and full of interest for all things. We have not come to Home Rule yet, but I dare say that will come to-morrow.'

On December 15 Max Müller's son left England for his first post as attaché at Constantinople. The parting was a severe trial to his father, and a visit to Claremont, a few days later, was hailed as a welcome change for him.

TO THE RIGHT HONOURABLE W. E. GLADSTONE.

*December* 17.

'The letter and book from Kiel, which were sent to me to Hawarden, contained the answer from Professor Oldenberg, and the number of the *Lüneburg Journal* which I wished you to see. The article contains a chemical analysis of a large number of ancient bronzes, and shows, as far as I can see conclusively, that bronze was gained by accident, that is by smelting ores containing copper and tin. I remember in Cornwall that people speak of the "brown rider on a white horse," when copper is found above tin. The article likewise shows that really pure copper and pure tin are later discoveries, and so is the intentional combination of the two. The article was published in 1865. If you have time to read it during your short holiday abroad, please let me know and I will send it to you.'

TO HIS SON.

*December* 21, 1892.

'I should like to see the Piraeus and the Acropolis, if only for what was there once, and what we can enjoy in Greek literature. A man who has ancestors is called a nobleman, but it is our intellectual ancestors, Plato, Sophocles, &c., that give us true nobility and make us feel our place in the world. Classical education gives us a respect for the past, and without that respect, without that firm ground to stand on, we are like reeds shaken by the wind, like *nouveaux riches* without any heirlooms.'

The first two months of the year 1893 were passed quietly at Oxford, in printing the last series of Gifford Lectures,

*Theosophy or Psychological Religion.* 'Don't be distressed by any comments,' wrote a friend; 'there will be deepest gratitude to you for putting these truths so plainly and so gently.' Max Müller had purposely added the word 'Theosophy' to his title, because

'The venerable name, so well known among early Christian thinkers, as expressing the highest conception of God within the reach of the human mind, has of late been so greatly misappropriated that it was high time to restore it to its proper function. It should be known once for all that one may call oneself a theosophist without . . . believing in any occult sciences and black art.'

In his preface Max Müller again defends the historical method which he had pursued, not only in these four courses of Gifford Lectures, but in all his writings on kindred subjects.

'So long as we look on the history of the human race as something that might or might not have been, we cannot wonder that the student of religion should prefer to form his opinions of the nature of religion, and the laws of its growth, from the masterwork of Thomas Aquinas, the *Summa Sacrae Theologiae*, rather than from the *Sacred Books of the East.* But when we have learnt to recognize in history the realization of a rational purpose, when we have learnt to look upon it as, in the truest sense of the word, a Divine drama, the plot revealed in it ought to assume in the eyes of the philosopher also, a meaning and a value far beyond the speculations of even the most enlightened and logical theologians.'

This last volume was fiercely criticized. The *Academy* considered that it exceeded in interest and information all the preceding volumes. Whilst the *Record* maintained that it was a grave question whether the definition of the Logos could be accepted by the Christian student, another paper declared that they had read nothing better than the particular lectures on the Logos doctrine. The *Inquirer* quoted

'The striking passage . . . in which Mr. Max Müller refers to the difficulty which has been felt by some Christian theologians in fixing the oneness and yet difference between the Son of God and humanity at large. "It was not thought robbery that the Son should be equal with the Father (Phil. ii. 6), but it was thought robbery to make human nature equal with that of the Son. Many were frightened by the thought that the Son of God should thus be degraded to a *mere man.*

Is there not a blasphemy against humanity also, and is it not blasphemous to speak of a *mere man*? What can be the meaning of a *mere man*, if we once have recognized the Divine essence in him, if we once believe that, unless we are of God, we are nothing? If we once allow ourselves to speak of a mere man, others will soon speak of a mere God."'

Another review says:—

'There is, perhaps, no one of the Gifford Lecturers who has endured more vituperative criticism than Professor Max Müller; and yet to the single-minded inquirer after truth his four volumes of *Gifford Lectures* are full of suggestive thought, of fearless criticism, and of reverent study such as should not produce an evil result. Max Müller points out that his plan in framing these lectures was "to show that, given the human mind such as it is, and its environment such as it is, the concept of God and a belief in God would be inevitable." To accomplish this task he set himself to trace the history of religion from the earliest indications of a belief in the supernatural, and was able, as he thinks, triumphantly to show that God had never been without a witness. He traces the influences exerted by Oriental religions upon Christianity with the outspoken frankness that characterizes all his *Gifford Lectures*, and certainly he suggests some very hard problems for his critics to explain upon the theory of a comparatively recent revelation. In his researches he came across many curious maxims and incidents in the oldest Oriental theologies, which strangely anticipated what are deemed distinctive characteristics of the Christian religion. To him these coincidences seemed to prove the truth of Christianity and to make its divine origin more apparent. But it was not so with his critics. They imagined that these striking similarities, so far from proving Christianity, showed it to be an imposture, composed of fragments of earlier beliefs, the outcome of mere human intelligence. The Professor does not spare these purblind zealots. He says, "There survive even now some half-petrified philosophers and theologians who call it heresy to believe that unassisted human reason could ever attain to a concept of, or a belief in, God; who maintain that a special revelation is absolutely necessary for that purpose, but that such a revelation was granted to the human race twice only—once in the Old, and once in the New Testament." This is very bold language, but it is the proper attitude for a Gifford Lecturer to assume. If Professor Müller has stated untruths as facts, or has drawn the wrong inferences, the most fitting reply is to set him right, not simply to abuse him, as if he were a magnified Volney or Voltaire.'

A friend, whose judgement Max Müller valued highly, congratulated him 'on having thus completed so long and laborious a work. The truths expounded are indeed of the first importance. I rejoice that this aspect of religion should have found so powerful and persuasive an interpreter. The ease and freedom of your exposition give us all a lesson in the intelligible treatment of the most abstruse things.'

TO H.R.H. THE DUCHESS OF ALBANY.

7, NORHAM GARDENS, *January* 2, 1893.

'MADAM,—I was much interested to hear that the little I said to your Royal Highness about the *Word*, that is the *Logos*, has found an echo in your thoughts. At present all my work is really concentrated on the origin and the history of that thought. Its deepest roots lie in the most ancient portion of Greek philosophy; there it grows in Plato and Aristotle, and comes to full maturity in Philo. It was adopted by the Greek converts to Christianity, who were steeped in Greek philosophy and yet honestly persuaded of the truth of Christianity, such as it was in the first and second centuries. It is very different now from what it was then! My fourth and last volume of *Gifford Lectures* will be almost entirely devoted to this subject, and will make it possible, I believe, for honest philosophers to be honest Christians. But the work is very hard; I have so much to read, more than I have time and strength for. Still I must do my best before I can take my holidays. In the meantime I should be very glad if you and Mrs. Moreton would look at the first three volumes of my *Gifford Lectures*, which I have taken the liberty to send to you. They are only preparatory, and occasionally, I am afraid, somewhat tedious. But that could not be helped. One has to make bricks before one can build an arch. With the fourth volume as the coping-stone, I hope the arch will prove safe and sound. . . . With many thanks for your Royal Highness's kind wishes for the New Year, which I heartily reciprocate, I have the honour to remain,

'Your Royal Highness's most faithful servant.'

TO THE RIGHT HON. W. E. GLADSTONE.

OXFORD, *January* 9, 1893.

'I send you the paper on Bronze by Dr. Wibel. It has attracted very little attention, but it seems to me extremely valuable, and to remove all difficulties in the most natural way. It is founded, as you will see, on 230 chemical analyses of ancient bronze. It shows that here, as elsewhere, nature suggested the most important discoveries. It was not that people at first learnt to extract copper and tin, and then intentionally mixed the two to produce the harder metal bronze. They could not have done it, it seems, because the extra smelting of pure copper is more difficult than the promiscuous smelting of impure copper and tin ore which produced bronze. It seems to follow that this discovery of bronze could have been made nowhere but in England, where the two ores are found in close propinquity. There are a number of other hints in the paper which I feel sure will interest you, if you can *really* make time to read it.'

To his Son at Constantinople.

*February* 19, 1893.

'From what I saw of M. Waddington, his reasons for resigning seemed to me all far-fetched. Though here he is *plus royaliste que le Roi*, in his heart there is some English feeling, at all events no anti-English feeling. Now my impression is that the French Government wants, by any means, to burst the Triple Alliance, and its *entente* with England. To throw the French upon the German army is a dangerous experiment, and a descent on Italy too would be risky. But to show the teeth to England, or bully it on one of its many vulnerable points, might trouble the waters and enable them to fish. They might then offer almost anything to Russia to excite her ambition, or they might hope to cajole England into a more friendly understanding with France, by offering Egypt or Madagascar, in fact anything that might seem tempting. Now this general policy Waddington as a sensible man would not approve, and would probably decline to have anything to do with it. I feel sure he does not go for the sake of his numismatic studies.'

Soon after this Max Müller dined at the farewell dinner to M. Waddington at the Mansion House, and then with his wife went to Ightham Mote, where they spent the whole of March with their married daughter. Towards the close of the month Max Müller delivered an address at the German Athenaeum in London, 'My Friends in India.' It was published in the *Deutsche Rundschau*, June, 1893, and formed the nucleus of *Auld Lang Syne*, Series II, printed in 1899. Before returning to Oxford, Max Müller writes to his son:—

Ightham, *March* 23.

'We have had a delightful time here: the weather beautiful. I have enjoyed my stay here very much. They all seem so happy here that one trembles. Constantinople must be a lovely place but for the unspeakable Turk. I confess I belong to the bag and baggage party: there is no excuse for these Turanians living in Europe, and keeping the old Byzantine Empire in a state of semi-barbarism.'

This year Max Müller once more received a telegram from the German Emperor, conveying his hearty congratulations to the Oxford crew on their victory after the Boat-race. The telegram, which, with the exception of the concluding sentence, is in German, was as follows:—'By right of my old and never-failing friendship for beautiful Oxford and her brave sons, I again beg you to be the interpreter of my heartiest congratulations to the crew on winning the Boat-race. So enthusiastic a lover of aquatic sports as I am must always rejoice when young men use and cultivate their strength in so rational a way.' (Then in English) 'It was well done from first to last.—WILHELM, I. and R. Berlin.'

TO COLONEL OLCOTT.

OXFORD, *March* 22, 1893.

'I have just been reading Professor Deussen's Address on Vedântism which he delivered at Bombay. That is a true account of Vedântism and of Theosophy, that is what you and your friends have been looking for, that is what you will find, only far more developed, in my last volume of Gifford Lectures, entitled *Theosophy or Psychological Religion*. You should now try to persuade your friends in India to make a new start, i.e. to return to their ancient philosophy in all its purity. I have not forgotten your telling me once that a new religion in order to grow must be *manured*[1]. I do not believe in that. I trust to the pure rain of heaven, and to the light and warmth of the sun, that is, to the vivifying power of truth. Everything else is of evil, particularly in India, where people are so much inclined to believe in what seems miraculous, and not in what is natural. If I have spoken and written against you, I should have done just the same against myself and my best friends, when I saw that they were seeking for the truth but were going on a wrong road to find it. You

[1] '*Comment by Col. Olcott*:—An entire misunderstanding. What I said was that, as young plants had to be manured, so I had noticed that new religions were commonly attended at the beginning by "miracles"—i.e. psychic phenomena, which gave them quickly a grip on the public mind. And the observed wonders were multiplied indefinitely by partisan writers, who thought to thus fertilize them.'

can do much good in India if you will treat the Hindus, not as children, but as men. Wait till you get my *Theosophy*, and then tell me whether that is not what you really wanted for India and for Europe also.

'Once more, you can do a great deal of good if you will help the people in India to discover and recover the treasure of truth in their old Brahma-sophy.'

Not content with all the trouble given before the meeting of the Oriental Congress in 1892, the following letter proves that the same mischievous spirit was still active:—

To B. M. Malabari, Esq.

Oxford, *April* 8.

'If you could see an article which I have just sent to the *Deutsche Rundschau*, on "My Friends in India," you would not think that I or my wife ascribed untruthful articles on the Oriental Congress in your paper to you. Many people, like you and myself, have been puzzled by these London letters, and the only explanation is that money has passed between some one and the writer. You know how many things become intelligible in that way, but I must say I was sorry for it, for your sake and for the sake of the writer.

'In a fortnight I shall go away on a long holiday, and see my son at Constantinople. On the first of September I must be at Leipzig to receive my honorary diploma from my old University, where I took my degree fifty years ago! The Emperor of Germany, as you may have seen in the papers, has just sent me his life-size portrait, magnificently framed, in recognition of my life-long services to ancient Indian literature, and as an acknowledgement for my recent edition of the *Rig-veda*, brought out at the expense of the Mahârâjah of Vijayanagara, and of which the Emperor accepted a copy for his private library. The Queen also accepted a copy.

'I hope you are enjoying some rest, and are satisfied with the progress of the reforms which you started.'

To the Right Hon. W. E. Gladstone.

Oxford, *April* 16, 1893.

'I hope my publishers have by this time sent you a copy of my last volume of Gifford Lectures, *Theosophy or Psychological Religion*. It may seem very irrational on my part, not to say very conceited, to imagine you could find time to look at any book at present. Still there are things more important than Ireland, things that appealed to human hearts before the names of England and

Ireland were known, and that will continue to appeal to human hearts, long after the names of England and Ireland have been forgotten. Some of these eternal questions I have ventured to treat in my volume. I do not think you will find much to interest you, except perhaps the last three or four lectures on the *Word*, or the *Logos*, where I try to show what an immense amount of gratitude we owe to Greece in regard to what we may call Christian Metaphysics. I only wish I had more time to give to this subject, but the time for *contrahere vela* has come, and I have still much in hand that I should like to finish if health remains what it has hitherto been. I assure you I expect no expression of opinion from you, but I should feel glad to think that some evening you have looked at this last book of mine.'

To Mrs. Humphry Ward.

Oxford, *April*, 1893.

'I have asked my publisher to send you a copy of my last volume of *Gifford Lectures*, which I have called *Theosophy*, in order to restore that old name to its legitimate meaning. I wonder what you will say to it! It seems to me to give the solution of all our difficulties. If we can find out why philosophers and men of complete independence like St. Clement and Origen embraced Christianity without sacrificing one iota of their philosophical convictions, we can judge for ourselves whether we can honestly follow their example. I believe that the Anti-Nicene theology and philosophy will supply a rallying-ground for all of us. It is strange that the German reformers should have actually neglected this Anti-Nicene Christianity. They did not see that such expressions as *υἱὸς μονογενής*, filius *unicus*, not *unigenitus*, were of Greek workmanship, that the Logos was the quintessence of all Greek philosophy, bequeathed by the Âryan to the Semitic race, though misunderstood by some of the earliest disciples of Christ. What Philo did to reconcile Greek thought with Jewish faith, sometimes very wildly and fancifully, was achieved by Clement and Origen in reconciling Greek thought with Christian faith. There was no more inducement for Clement to become a Christian than there is for ——, and yet he joined the persecuted Christians bona fides. When he spoke of the Son of God, he meant nothing vulgar or mythological, he used the word in the sense in which Plato had started it.

I was asked to preside at the Religious Congress at Chicago, but have had to decline, and have sent them my book instead as an *irenicon* between philosophy and religion. I send it to you with the same object, for I know how near this conflict is to your heart, and you will see how here too, all we want to solve our difficulties is history, or a knowledge how things came to be what they are.'

To H.R.H. the Duchess of Albany.

7, Norham Gardens, *April* 20, 1893.

'. . . I send to your Royal Highness the last volume of my *Lectures*. It is the key to the whole. I have now said all that was in my mind and heart. Whether the world will understand it, is another question. But I feel certain the truth is there, and that it will be understood some day. I have had to work so hard that, almost for the first time in my life, I feel that I must rest. The springs begin to creak, and the whole carriage jolts. Threescore years and ten is the orthodox limit, and I certainly begin to feel as if *la première jeunesse* was gone!'

Before leaving Oxford at the end of April, Max Müller heard from Colonel Olcott, asking whether he had rightly understood Max Müller to say that there was no such thing as an esoteric interpretation of the Sanskrit *Sâstras*, and that he had exhorted him (Colonel Olcott) not 'to destroy all the good he had done in helping to revive Sanskrit, by pandering to the superstitious credulity of the Hindus, and telling them about phenomena that are impossible, and Mahâtmas who do not exist.' The answer, though written later, is given here:—

To Colonel Olcott.

Constantinople, *June* 10, 1893.

'Dear Colonel Olcott,—I was much pleased to receive your two letters of April 25 and May 11.

'With regard to your letter, I can quite understand your feelings for Madame Blavatsky, particularly after her death, and I have tried to say as little as possible of what might pain her friends. But I felt it my duty to protest against what seemed to me a lowering of a beautiful religion. Her name and prestige were doing real mischief among people who were honestly striving for higher religious views, and who were quite willing to recognize all that was true and beautiful and good in other religions. Madame Blavatsky seems to me to have had the same temperament, but she was either deceived by others or carried away by her own imaginations. There is nothing esoteric in Buddhism. Buddhism is the very opposite of esoteric—it is a religion for the people at large, for the poor, the suffering, the ill-treated. Buddha protests against the very idea of keeping anything secret. There was much more of that esoteric teaching in Brâhmanism. There was the system of caste, which deprived the Sûdras, at least, of many religious privileges. But I do say that, even in Brâhmanism, there is "*no such thing as an esoteric interpretation of the Sâstras.*" The *Sâstras* have but one meaning, and all who had been properly prepared by education had access to them. There are some artificial poems, which are so written as to admit of two interpretations. They are very wonderful, but they have nothing to do with philosophical doctrines. Again there are, as among the Sufis, erotic poems in Sanskrit which are explained as celebrating the love and union between the soul and God. But all this is perfectly well known, there is no mystery about it. Again, it is true that the *Vedânta Sûtras*, for instance, admit of an Advaitic and a Vasishta-advaitic interpretation, and the same applies to the *Upanishads*. But all this is open, and nothing is kept secret from those who have passed through the proper education. Besides, in our time all MSS. are accessible, and the most important *Sâstras* and their commentaries have been printed. Where is there room for esoteric doctrines? No living Pundit or Mahâtma knows more than what is contained in MSS., though I am quite aware that their oral instruction, which they freely extend even to Europeans, is very helpful towards a right understanding of the Sanskrit texts and commentaries.

'You may have seen Mr. Sinnett's answer to my article. It is so childish that I do not know how to answer it. He evidently wishes to step into Madame Blavatsky's place, and to claim for himself the authorship of this whole movement. He and Mrs. Besant are trying to divide the spoils. I believe that Mrs. Besant is honest—at least she was so; as to Mr. Sinnett I have my doubts. A man who can say that the pork of which Buddha died was the *Boar* Avatar of Vishnu is outside the pale. I have always thought that the account of Buddha's death speaks very strongly for the good faith of his disciples. They told the truth, though they must have known that their enemies would make sport of it. Besides, what harm is there in his accepting the gift of Kunda, and what does it matter how the body dies?

'You can really do a good work if you can persuade the people in India, whether Buddhists or Brâhmans, to study their own religion in a reverent spirit, to keep what is good, and discard openly what is effete, antiquated and objectionable. If all religions would do that, we should soon have but *one* religion; and we should no longer call each other unbelievers and Giaurs, and commit atrocities like those in Bulgaria, in which the Christians were quite as bad as the Mohammedans. Nothing can be more useful than publications of the old texts, critically edited, and trustworthy translations. My *Sacred Books of the East* have opened people's eyes in many places. I am sorry to say that I cannot continue the series. Neither the University of Oxford nor the India Office will vote more money. Still, some one will come hereafter and continue the work!

'As to the *Upanishads*, I have the Telugu edition, but the Telugu letters are not familiar to me, and a Devanâgarî reprint would be much more generally useful. I am glad to hear that it is in preparation.

'You can help to forward or retard the good work that has to be done in India. If I can be of any use, I am always willing to help; and, in spite of many disappointments, I have never lost my faith in man, nor in the final victory of truth.'

The end of April the Max Müllers left Oxford, and after some pleasant days with Dean and Mrs. Liddell, at Ascot, and a short visit to Ightham Mote, they started for their long-planned holiday. Stopping at Rheims and Lucerne, they crossed the St. Gothard for the first time since the railroad was completed, to Milan. A day was given to the Certosa, which had formerly been shut to women, and nearly a week was spent in Venice. Sleeping at Ravenna and Ancona, the Max Müllers left Brindisi for Patras. The ship stopped long enough at Corfu to allow them to drive to Canone, and form some idea of the beauty of the island and the luxuriance of the vegetation. The next day, landing early at Patras, they crossed the country to Athens. Max Müller's enthusiastic delight at the first distant view of the Acropolis, rising out of the plain, can never be forgotten. Here a week was spent in the enjoyment of all that is to be seen in Athens, but the weather was too hot, and Max Müller too tired for any expeditions.

To Dr. William Russell.

Athens, *May* 23, 1893.

'Your note of May 2 reached me here. We are on our way to Constantinople, and hope to get some rest there. Our journey has been delightful, but I still feel tired, and Athens, seen for the first time, does not allow much rest. I saw Tricoupi, and also the King. There has been much muddling between the two, and I expect Tricoupi will soon come back. They are in a regular mess financially. You get forty-two drachmas in dirty paper for £1. And yet they say the country is progressing, and can afford to pay its debts!'

Modern Athens, except for its horrible dust, made little impression on Max Müller.

TO HIS DAUGHTER BEATRICE.

ATHENS, *May* 23, 1893.

'MY DEAR BEATRICE,—I must send you a line from Athens and tell you that we are quite well, and that we have enjoyed ourselves very much. This is a place worth seeing when you can. The weather has been splendid. Just now we are back from the harbour of Phaleron, where the French fleet is lying. The sunset was magnificent, and every point you see full of recollections. Yesterday I had an audience of the King, and in the evening we dined at the English Legation to meet Tricoupi the ex-Minister, so the Greek papers declared the English Minister had given a political dinner, and were very angry! To-morrow we shall leave the Piraeus at 7 p.m., and in thirty-six hours we hope to be at Constantinople.

'Ever your loving Father.'

The long quiet day on board, sailing through the Greek Islands, rested Max Müller, who threw off all traces of fatigue the next morning as the vessel neared the Golden Horn, and the Embassy launch appeared, with his son on board. For nearly three months Max Müller revelled in the beauties of Constantinople and the Bosphorus. The Sultan showed great kindness to him, receiving him and his wife and son (after the first Selamlik they attended) in private audience, when he presented Max Müller with the Order of the Medjidieh.

During the whole time of his visit, one of the palace Aides de camp was in attendance on him, so that he was able to see many things not open to the general traveller, amongst others, the Qurban Bairam reception, on the Feast of Sacrifices, when the Sultan having, like every other householder, slain his ram, holds court in the great hall of the Dolmabaghcheh palace, the largest audience-hall in the world. Max Müller dined at the palace, and on the occasion of his presenting the *Sacred Books of the East* to the Sultan, received the Liakat, or Order of Merit, being the first infidel, not in the service of the Sultan, who had received it. He also visited the Sultan's private library and examined the books, but neither there nor in the Seraglio could he discover any trace of Greek MSS., though there is a general impression outside Constantinople that some are still in existence. Broussa was also visited, but the heat was tremendous, and Max Müller was very much exhausted by the excursion; still he was able to enjoy the marvellous beauty of the city, with its countless mosques and *turbehs* or tombs.

To Mr. Nanjio.

Therapia, *July* 2.

'Here I and my wife have been staying for some time, to be near our son. The climate is most beautiful, and the complete rest has done me a great deal of good. We hope to stay here another month, and then go back through Germany, and be at Oxford in October. I had to work very hard to finish my fourth volume of *Gifford Lectures.* I wanted to print my translation of the *Sukhâvatî-Vyûha*, the one which I dictated to you, but I had to put it off as I felt too tired. I hope you will be able to pay one more visit to Oxford; I am now nearly seventy years old, and cannot hope to live much longer, but I feel quite well and hope to do a little more work when I return to Oxford. Kasawara saw how much truth there is in Christianity, and I think it is a serious mistake if followers of different religions always dwell on the points on which they differ; it is far better to try and discover the truths on which different religions agree. On all essential points the best religions of the world agree; there are in each inevitable fictions, and on these they differ. I hope some good may be done at the Chicago Parliament of Religions, but I did not feel strong enough to go there.'

In 1892 Max Müller had made acquaintance with Madame Butenschön, a Swedish lady, a student of Sanskrit, and she then spent some days in Norham Gardens.

To Madame Butenschön.

Therapia, *July* 22, 1893.

'You will be surprised to receive my answer from the East, and not from the West. We have been spending our summer at Constantinople, and on the Bosphorus, and have enjoyed it immensely. I had no idea of the beauty of this part of the world. The climate is simply perfect; for three months, when I opened the windows in the morning, there was the bright sun and the fresh air of the sea. I came here very tired and suffering from neuralgia, and I feel quite restored now, and very sorry to have soon to leave for England.

'I was delighted to receive your letter. I had a feeling, after our pleasant meeting at Oxford, that our orbits would meet again. I am glad to see that you are not discouraged by the difficulties of Sanskrit. You will certainly be rewarded, if you persevere. You have divined what treasures there are in Sanskrit literature, and it is absurd to suppose that a woman's brain could not master the difficulties of a language like Sanskrit. I wish I could send you my last book to St. Moritz, but I have only one copy here, covered with notes. But if you would get it, you would find how fully all your anticipations about the wisdom of India are realized. It is the fourth volume of the *Gifford Lectures*. It contains my last word on the greatest problems of life. I am quite prepared to find that people will not understand it, but I know that there are some who have understood it, and I feel convinced that in the future the old Vedânta philosophy will hold its place of honour by the side of Plato and Spinoza and Eckhart. Perhaps you do not know the latter, but you will know him and love him.'

Leaving Constantinople by Orient express, two days were spent at Buda-Pesth, where, under the guidance of Professor Vambéry, the Max Müllers explored those beautiful towns. They then passed a week in Vienna, which had been very much improved and beautified since Max Müller had visited it nearly forty years previously. Thence the travellers made their way by Dresden to Leipzig, arriving there in time for the seventieth birthday of Max Müller's old friend Professor Carus.

The following letter is an answer to one which gave Max Müller unfeigned pleasure to receive, as it proved to him that his *Gifford Lectures* were penetrating into circles where he had not expected that they would find a welcome:—

To Rev. R. Corbet.

Vienna, *August* 19, 1893.

'A letter like yours is precious indeed, and I must thank you for it, though writing on one's journey from place to place is troublesome, and pen, paper, and ink abominable. I well remember our meeting at Headington Hill many years ago. I hope and trust that other clergymen may find in my *Lectures* what you have found in them. They are the result of a long battle: I have found peace, why should not others? I may be wrong on this or that point, but on the main point, our relation to God and to Christ, history, I believe, will bear me out. We may look forward to new discoveries, throwing light on the early stages of Christianity. I saw some curious fragments of the Gospels (pre-canonical) yesterday in the collection of papyri belonging to the Archduke Rainer. Thanking you heartily for your letter.'

To B. M. Malabari, Esq.

Leipzig, *August* 25.

'Here I am at last at Leipzig, my old University. I received both your letters here, the one with the rough draft of the address on my jubilee, and the other yesterday. I like the address very much—it might have been written by a German Professor, and is quite free from Oriental phraseology. I do not see why Indian reformers should be excluded from signing it. I have all my life been an Indian reformer, though there are some reforms of which I do not approve. I have all my life been a Liberal and a Gladstonian, but I do not approve of Home Rule. I should like to see the names of such men as the Mahârâjah of Vijayanagara, who has been, as you know, very kind to me. But you know best, and I am very grateful for what you have done. I had some most interesting conversations with the Sultan about the *Sacred Books of the East*, and the relation between Christianity and Islam. He is an intelligent, tolerant, and very kind-hearted man.

'I long now to be back in England, and in Oxford among my books. My holiday has done me much good. I hope your health and your good spirits will soon be quite restored. You are much too young to retire from the world—true youth is strong will.'

On September 1, Max Müller celebrated the Jubilee of taking his Degree as Doctor of Philosophy, and received a new diploma from the University of Leipzig. All the Professors were away except Carus and Drobisch, whose lectures Max Müller had attended more than fifty years before, and who was too old to accompany Carus when he presented the new diploma in the name of the University. Telegrams of congratulation came from many people, and various Sanskritists sent their congratulations in the form of Sanskrit slokas. Those from Professor Cowell were rendered into English by their author:—

'Years like a stream flow past nor know return,
Youth fades away,—yet why, loved guru, mourn?
This *râhu*-body has its little day,—
But the bright moon of fame shines on undimmed for aye!'

E. B. Cowell.

Professor Maurice Bloomfield, of Baltimore, wrote: 'You have been in the front rank of those who have liberalized and beautified the thought of the century.' The Bavarian Academy of Sciences sent their congratulations 'to one who for more than forty years had been a Foreign Member of the Academy.'

But what Max Müller valued most, was an address from India from the Pundits, who regretted that there had not been time to collect more signatures. The address runs thus:—

'SIR,—We beg to approach you with our sincere congratulations on your having completed half a century of arduous and important work since you took your Degree at the University of Leipzig. In the midst of the congratulations that will greet you from all parts of the civilized world, we beg you will permit us, who have been your admirers in the far East, to send you this brotherly greeting. Notwithstanding the distance that separates us, we hope that you will welcome this greeting as coming from a land which has been endeared to you by ties of intellectual and spiritual fellowship.

'2. The last half-century has been distinguished by the vigorous and sustained effort of European thought to emancipate itself from the bias caused by the influence of race, nationality, and religion, and to move towards the conception of the essential unity of mankind. This effort has derived a great deal of its momentum from the study of the sacred language of our country and of the literatures and religions of India and other Eastern countries, which European scholars have pursued with wonderful patience and vigour. Among these you have occupied a very prominent place.

'3. By your edition of the *Rig-veda Samhitâ*, with Sâyana's Commentary, you rendered possible an independent study of that unique memorial of the early condition of the whole Âryan race, and not merely of the Indian branch of it; and by your volume of the translation of the hymns to the Maruts, you showed the way how to pursue such studies.

'4. Your series of the *Sacred Books of the East* is calculated to generate and strengthen in the minds of those who read it a conviction that God's ennobling and elevating truth is not the monopoly of any particular race. It unfolds the gradual evolution of religious thought, the different stages of which were developed by different races or by the same race at different times. It has already communicated a strong impetus to the unifying movement alluded to above, and we are glad to observe that the philosophic writers of England have begun to avail themselves of the information therein laid before them.

'5. By your numerous works on comparative philology and comparative mythology, and on the science of language and science of religion, you have materially contributed to the advance of those branches of knowledge.

'6. Though a German by birth, you have obtained such a command over English idiom that the charm of your literary style has enabled you to spread far and wide the knowledge of the results of your labours, and of the labours of your brother scholars in the several departments of knowledge which have engaged your attention and theirs.

'7. It is in this last respect that your services to our country have been of signal value. You have, by publishing in an agreeable form the results of the study of the thought and literature of our country, enabled the people of the countries in which the English language is spoken to understand us, and raised our race in their estimation. And by your works generally, you have made it possible for us, most of whom cannot read German or French, to understand the European methods of study, and enabled a few of us to co-operate with European scholars.

'8. In conclusion, we wish you a long and happy life, and hope and pray that health and strength may be long spared to you to enable you to continue your beneficial and useful labours.'

The following year they sent the address on parchment with many additional signatures. The signatures comprise the best-known names not only of Hindus, but of Mohammedans, Parsis, and of Civil Servants from every Presidency. The sheets containing the signatures were sent in a beautiful silver casket of Indian repoussé work, in the form of a manuscript, having on one side a representation of the sun rising above the Himalaya mountains, with the Ganges flowing from the summit, and at the top the sacred syllable *Om*; on the other side the picture of a sacred bird.

From Leipzig Max Müller and his wife went on to Dessau, and from there he wrote to his son:—

DESSAU, *September* 4.

'I had, among many other telegrams on the 1st, one from the Queen of Roumania, asking us to see her at Wied. The Calices also telegraphed. All went off very well at Leipzig, though there was not a single Professor of the Philosophical Faculty there. Carus had been commissioned to present the new diploma to me. He came in the University carriage, with the bedell, and we made some speeches one to the other. Then we had our Doctorschmaus, and enjoyed ourselves.'

To Dr. Winternitz.

*Translation.* Dessau, *September* 4.

'Thank you heartily for your friendly congratulations on my Jubilee. We have enjoyed our summer on the Bosphorus extremely; there is nothing more beautiful in Europe, and as one can cross over any afternoon in a small boat or caïque to Asia, one is brought nearer to the East than ever before. I have experienced and seen much that was interesting, though nothing Sanskritic. How is Takakusu? He too telegraphed to me. When I return, I should like to work with him on Buddhism, especially the *Mahâyâna*.'

To Professor Weber.

*Translation.* Dessau, *September* 9.

'My dear Weber,—Of all congratulations and letters which September 1 has brought me, your letter of the 4th has, I may say, been the most welcome to me. When we get old, we long for rest and peace, and so I say like you, "Let bygones be bygones!" Our scientific quarrels have not been hurtful to science and learning. We have both tried to show that one is as good as the other, and we have both contributed our part to make Sanskrit philology far more advanced than it was fifty years ago. My warmest thanks therefore for your hearty letter. We both deserve a little rest now. Though I cannot complain of my state of health, yet I cannot work now as I could formerly. And you have well deserved to rest on your laurels after your arduous and pioneering labours. I passed September 1 in Leipzig on my return journey. I saw one of my old examiners, Professor Drobisch, received a new diploma and a *tabula gratulatoria* from the German Oriental Society. Other addresses, among others one from the Pundits in India, await me in Oxford. I hope to return home by the end of September, and then I shall see what can be done with the years that may still remain to me. I have said everything I wish to say in my last volume of the *Gifford Lectures*. More and more I spin myself into the chrysalis of the *Vedânta*—just as it should be.

'We often dwell on the glorious days in Sweden. The evil consequences of it, I hope, have long passed away, and the next Congress at Geneva seems to promise to be a peaceful one.'

From Dessau the Max Müllers went to Neuwied to stay

with the Princess Mother at Segenhaus. Her daughter, the Queen of Roumania, was staying there, recovering from a severe illness. It was during this visit that Max Müller wrote the following lines in the Queen's album:—

'Das Wandern ist des Müllers Lust,
Das Wandern hier auf Erden.
Doch weht ein Hauch durch unsre Brust
Von einem höh'ren Werden.
Vom andern Sein,
Von dem der Schein
Den Sinn uns hier bethöret,
O sehet ein,
Dass Schein, wie Sein,
Dem Einen angehöret.'

Translation for this book:—

'The Miller loves a vagrant life
Through Earth's fair scenes to wander.
But still a whisper stirs the soul
Of higher Life out yonder.
The vision real
Of Life's ideal
Pursues us unabated,
That Life to find,
Let heart and mind
Alike be dedicated.'

MABEL PEACH.

From Wied the travellers turned their steps homewards, Max Müller far stronger and better for his long rest from literary labours.

Many more congratulations awaited Max Müller on his return to England, and amongst others one from the German Athenaeum in London. On October 18 his third grandchild, a second grandson, was born.

To MISS SWANWICK.

7, NORHAM GARDENS, *November* 3.

'It was very kind of you to send me the new edition of your translation of *Faust*. It is one great advantage of getting old, that we can bring out new editions of our works, and mend our ways, if it is necessary. I must congratulate you on being able to remain young in mind.

I try to say with Wendell Holmes, "I am now seventy years young," but how long it will last, who can tell! I enjoyed the whole summer on the Bosphorus immensely. The climate of Oxford is very trying, and all one can do is to lie still and hibernate like a dormouse.'

As President of the Society of Historical Theology in Oxford, Max Müller this year delivered an address on the 'Proper Use of Holy Scripture.' It was published the following year in the first volume of the new edition of *Chips.*

On December 6 he celebrated his seventieth birthday. He had the happiness of having his daughter and her husband and his eldest grandchild with him. Telegrams came from all parts. One, full of kindness and with the expression of a wish for many more *Chips from a German Workshop* in England, came from the German Emperor, and this was followed next day by an announcement from the German Embassy that a colossal bronze bust of the Emperor had arrived as a birthday gift from His Imperial Majesty. The bust was accompanied by the kindest letter. Several learned societies abroad telegraphed their good wishes. An admirer who signed himself 'One who owes to Max Müller's enticing words his first attraction to the study of Ethnology,' sent the following lines:—

'Hermes of varied tongues, nations' bright star,
Be thy years many as thy glories are.'

with a Greek rendering.

The Professors and teachers of German in the Universities and Colleges in England, Scotland, and Ireland, sent him a fine illuminated address.

To Professor Althaus

(who had been instrumental in starting this address).

*Translation.* Oxford, *December* 8.

'Many, many thanks, I cannot say anything but thanks! How small everything which one has done looks now, and how undeserved the praise from so many sides! What pleases one most is praise from those who have long known one, and are attached to one by common interests. I have long known how to value highly your unchanged friendly feelings, though our duties lead us along different paths, and we have been able to meet but seldom. As yet the so-called years of grace have dealt gently with me. May the evening of life be a peaceful one to you and your dear wife! I hope your son is prosperous. That is our greatest blessing in old age.'

To Dr. W. H. Russell.

Oxford, *December* 10, 1893.

'My dearest William, and certainly always William the First; but now tell me how William the Second came to know of my seventieth birthday. You know I don't fib, but I have not the faintest idea how directly or indirectly he came to know it. It was a long telegram, and full of all manner of kind things which would not have done for the *Times*. It is sad how even a man of seventy likes chocolate, though of a different make from that which his grandchild loves. The little man was here on my birthday, and stumped about as if the whole of Oxford belonged to him. Wilhelm III[1], to whom at first I ascribed the imperial telegram, wrote and telegraphed. . . . Who is going to Constantinople, and who to St. Petersburg? Morier[2] was a very old and dear friend from my undergraduate days at Oxford. There are none left now, none to please, none to tease. Well, I hope you will hold out, and fight on, on your stumps, for many years to come. "Years of Grace" they call them in Germany, the years after seventy. Let us hope for the best!'

Christmas was spent in Oxford, his daughter and son-in-law and their three children spending it in the house of the grandparents.

[1] His son. [2] Had died November of this year.

# CHAPTER XXXII

## 1894–1895

Lectures on 'Vedânta Philosophy.' Three months in London. Picture by Watts. British Association in Oxford. New edition of *Chips*. Mundesley. Death of Mr. Froude. Bournemouth. Visitors from all countries. Picture by Herkomer. Dr. Barrows. Visit to Glyn Garth. Dr. Karl Blind. *Sacred Books of the Buddhists*. Centenary of French Institute. Last volumes of *Chips*.

THE presence of the Froudes in Oxford, and the Colyer-Fergussons in his own house, made the year open brightly for Max Müller, even though the loved son was far away.

The following letter from Archdeacon Wilson was a great delight at the time it was received, and permission has been given to insert it here:—

THE VICARAGE, ROCHDALE, *January* 16, 1894.

'MY DEAR FRIEND,—The reading of *Stanley's Life* has brought you much into my mind, especially vol. ii. p. 554. I was at Balliol lodge with him; he was as brilliant as ever; his conversation with Jowett and Lord Lingen was something to be remembered. But as we walked back from Carfax, where he preached, I felt his depression. There was no crowd, but few University men; he felt that he belonged to the past: he gave up this generation.

'And I am almost afraid that you think the same of yourself. Nevertheless it is not so.

'Look at Stanley's work. His spirit does live. His treatment of the Old Testament has revolutionized all teaching of it; and much of what was so new and daring in his mouth is now in every one's mouth. That gentle and sweet spirit has left us. There is none like him. But he did not outlive his work.

'So, if it is not an impertinence in me to say so, I doubt whether you can know or guess how much we all owe to you. Of course, only the mere fragments and epitomes of the results of your work find their way to the masses; but these have found their way, and have done much to transform and deepen the thought of religion. I was preaching last Sunday evening, and quoted from the *Vedas* the saying of Brahma: "Those who honestly worship other gods, involuntarily worship me;" and a working man, as he went out, thanked me for that quotation, and told me he had been reading one of your books. That quotation in a sermon on the Epiphany, and that remark by a weaver, could not have been made but for you.

'Science has discovered much in the Victorian era, but I think that no discovery will bear such lasting fruits as some of yours, and your great edition of the *Sacred Books of the East*.

'So in case the New Year finds you lonely and discouraged, I send you a word of thanks and love from this smoky, foggy town of Rochdale.

'I keep "pegging on." I send you a tract that was published to-day. With all best wishes.

'Ever yours,

'J. M. WILSON.'

TO ARCHDEACON WILSON.

OXFORD, *January* 24.

'I have also been reading *Stanley's Life*, but I want to know a great deal more. In fact, I know a great deal more, but I suppose it could not be published. The second part is much too scrappy: they ought to have given more letters of his, and not extracts only. There were reasons why Stanley was rather disheartened towards the end of his life, yet how well his life was filled, and how much good remains! One must not imagine that one man, during this short life, can change the world, and cart away the rubbish of centuries. All we can do is to cart, and happy those who enjoy the carting. I am glad to say I can still enjoy it, though that cannot last much longer. I enjoyed my stay on the Bosphorus immensely. How I wish you and Mrs. Wilson would stay with us in our quiet house! I have many things I should wish to talk over with you. Any time would suit us. We have had B. and her husband and three children with us all January, and that was very delightful. Now we are quite alone again, and shall be till our boy comes home for his holiday in May. Happy fellow, he is in Egypt just now, basking while we are shivering. I am anxious to know what you think of the last few chapters of my *Theosophy*. Am I right, or am I wrong? If I am wrong, I should be glad to learn, but if I am right then the main difficulty of Christianity is solved, and solved in a way satisfactory both to historians and dogmatists. I have had many letters from Harnack, the Duke of Argyll, and from

Jowett, shortly before his death, but I should like to know what you, as an experienced carter of rubbish, think of it.'

In sending the following letter to the editor, Mr. Boyes-Smith explained that he and a friend had eagerly read the *Gifford Lectures*, and that the last one, on Theosophy, had failed to satisfy them on two points, on which they wrote to Max Müller. The two points were, (1) The argument of the *Lectures* showed how Greek philosophy might well lead to the identification of Jesus with the Logos of Man, but this was a long way short of the Christian belief in Christ as the Logos of God, and they asked if the interval could be bridged. (2) The references in the *Lectures* to the miracles in the life of Jesus seemed to imply that a miracle means a breach of natural laws, which the New Testament does not necessarily assume; and they referred to the wonders of hypnotism, &c. Mr. Boyes-Smith concludes, 'We valued Professor Max Müller's reply, and have kept it carefully since, on account of this new evidence of his fearlessness and consideration, as well as his single-hearted search after truth.'

TO THE REVS. E. BOYES-SMITH AND H. B. COLCHESTER.

*Oxford, February 1, 1894.*

'I should have answered your letter before, but I was immersed in proof-sheets. Please forgive the delay. I was much struck by your letter. I have received many letters on my last book, but none of them hit the weak and yet very critical point on which you write. There is a flaw in my argument, and I have tried in vain to get over it. My position has always been this. There was no external inducement for philosophers like Clement and Origen to embrace Christianity. They lost, they did not gain by their open profession of faith in Christ. Therefore we must admit that they reasoned the step out for themselves honestly. As philosophers they believed in a Supreme Being, and they looked upon the world as His work, His thought and manifestation. In the world all individual objects were perishable, but behind the manifold individuals they had discovered something real, the types, the ideas of things. These ideas were to them not abstract generalizations, but the most real realities, without which the manifold phenomena would be impossible and inconceivable. These ideas were the thoughts or words of the Supreme Being, and they constituted in their entirety the Thought or Logos, or the Son of God; but each single idea or logos also might be called the Word or Son of God. I have not been able to find any passage which makes it clear in which of these two senses the name of Logos or Son of God was assigned by Clement or Origen to Christ. They do not seem to me to have made the difference clear to themselves. Of course the Logos in its entirety would assign to Christ the ideal fullness of the Godhead, while the Logos of manhood, if manifested in Christ, would make Him the ideal man, the perfect man or the realization of the thought of man as conceived by God. If the word was used in the latter sense, other human beings also might aspire to various degrees of Divine Sonship or ideal Manhood; if in the former sense, the fullness of the Divine Logos would dwell in Christ only. I have been hard at work to find passages which would show clearly in which sense the name of Logos was assigned to Christ by the Alexandrian philosophers, and I am still reading, but I am afraid our difficulty was not their difficulty, and after having once given the name, they felt satisfied and their philosophical conscience was appeased. If they could conceive God the Father as a person, they would conceive the Son, the Logos, the first thought of the Universe, before all creation, as a person also, as a power, the Sophia of earlier days. These early thinkers could not entirely shake off their mythological language; everything had to be either masculine or feminine, either man or woman. I should much prefer the explanation that Logos was the logos of man, realized in its original intention once and once only; but I think it will turn out that the Alexandrian philosophers adopted the other view. I think the Urgrund, or the abyss of the Mystics, is the Divine Substance of which Father and Son are the persons. The Urgrund is not personal, as little as the Âtman of the Vedântists. It is shared in common, it forms the essence of both God and Man. Even πνεῦμα is already too much specialized to stand for the Self and the selves. I agree with you that we must allow to Christ great δύναμις in order to account for the effects which are fairly attested. Only I take the manifestation of His δύναμις as facts, not as τέρατα, as they were doubtless taken by the multitudes, and are still. I wish I could have sent you a more satisfactory answer, but this is all I have to say.'

Early in this year Max Müller was made a Doctor of Letters at Lafayette College, Pennsylvania. 'We feel,' wrote President Warfield, 'that you will confer honour on Lafayette College in accepting this degree, and I hope it may be proof of the wide recognition of your services to learning and letters. Please accept our congratulations on the years of honour and fruitful labour God has given you.'

During March Max Müller delivered three lectures at the Royal Institution on the 'Vedânta Philosophy.' The lectures were an attempt to interest an English audience in the philosophy of the leading school of the thinkers of ancient India—the school that appealed most to the mind and heart of the lecturer, so that he could, as the result of his own experience during a long life devoted to the study of many philosophies and many religions, endorse the words of Schopenhauer, 'In the whole world there is no study so beneficial and elevating as that of the Vedânta philosophy, as contained in the *Upanishads*. It has been the solace of my life, it will be the solace of my death.' Max Müller was most anxious to impress on his hearers that there was nothing esoteric in the Vedânta philosophy, that it was open to all; and he closed his last lecture by repeating the Sanskrit line in which a native philosopher formulated the whole teaching of the Vedânta philosophy, which Max Müller translated 'God is true, the world is fleeting, man's soul is God and nothing else.' Then giving the old philosopher's deduction from this teaching, he rendered it, 'What shall it profit a man, if he shall gain the whole world, and lose his own soul?' It was Max Müller's last course at the Royal Institution, where, thirty-three years before, he had delivered his epoch-making lectures on the 'Science of Language.'

Towards the close of March Princess Christian and her daughter, Princess Victoria, stayed for two days in Norham Gardens. The Princess came to Oxford for a meeting in the Sheldonian Theatre of the National Union of Teachers, where her Royal Highness received purses contributed on behalf of the Benevolent Funds of the Union.

After a short visit to Brighton to recover the fatigue of his London lectures, and a good deal of troublesome work connected with the *Sacred Books*, Max Müller and his wife settled for three months in London, where they were joined by their son from Constantinople.

Professor Max Müller was Visitor of Manchester College as well as President of the Society of Historical Research, hence the following letter:—

To Professor Estlin Carpenter.

Hertford Street, *May* 1.

'May I present a copy of my new edition of the *Rig-veda* to the Library of Manchester College, as a slight token of my gratitude, and a remembrance of your unworthy President? Yes, a list of technical Vedânta terms which were inherited by the Buddhists would be very useful. Buddhism is Vedânta popularized, and some of the Vedântists were distinctly called Pra*kh*anns-bauddhas, Cryptobuddhists. Dr. Fairbairn's idea that the later Brâhmanism was influenced by Buddhism would be difficult to prove. It is the other way. Ahimsâ and similar ideas, adopted by the Buddhists, break out again in later Brâhmanism. The older one grows, the more one sees how much there is that ought to be done, but I feel it is time to rest, and trust that all that is really necessary will be done and better done by younger hands.'

To Sir Robert Collins.

Hertford Street, *May* 16.

'I was so glad to hear that the Duchess should really have waded through my *Gifford Lectures*. I have said in them, particularly in the last volume, all that I wished to say on the great questions which concern us all. I hope they may tell in the future even more than they have told now, when most of the theological controversies touch the surface only and leave the depths untouched. My Vedânta Lectures are meant to show how some of the greatest problems which occupy us now, occupied the minds of the earliest philosophers who are known to us. There may have been other philosophers, but they have left nothing behind. I incline more and more to believe that man, instead of being born as the grandchild of an age, was born a philosopher, whether he liked it or not. Who can help being a philosopher and asking "Why?" when he sees a man die, or the sun set? I shall send the little book to her Royal Highness as soon as it is out. Please to thank her, in my name, for the interest she takes in my work. My work is coming to an end. I am just now gathering some more bundles of *Chips from a German Workshop*.'

To B. Malabari, Esq.

Hertford Street, *May* 16.

'I have often thought of you of late, and meant to have written to you about a recent case of a widow committing suicide in order to escape from the miserable life that opened before her after the death of her husband. You may have seen my letter in the *Times*, about three weeks ago. It elicited many expressions of sympathy, and offers of substantial help, if there was any way of bettering the lot of young widows in India. But what can be done? Would the law allow widows to escape from their families, and take refuge in such houses as Ramabai and others have opened for them? You know best whether anything can be done, and what is the right thing to do. Is not a person who is able to contract a marriage able to make a contract with, say, Ramabai, to live at her house and to fit herself for useful work in life? I shall wait to hear from you on the subject, and I am willing to do what I can. Lord Reay is now Under-Secretary of State for India, and he would help us, I think.

'And now let me thank you for all you have done for me. The signatures from Bengal are most valuable, and I shall treasure them with those from Bombay. I am deeply touched by the suggestion of a testimonial. But really the congratulations you have sent me from the most distinguished sons of India are more than I could have expected. If, however, the testimonial should take the form which you suggest, I could only accept it for one of two objects which I have always had at heart. If the sum subscribed is large enough, I should like to see a promising young scholar sent from India to study at Oxford, under my guidance, and to study chiefly the religious literature of India—or, if this would require too large a sum, I should like to assign the proceeds to enable me to publish some more volumes of the *Sacred Books of the East*. My resources have come to an end, and though I have several more important translations to publish, neither the Indian Government nor the University Press at Oxford is willing to expend more money on this undertaking. Forty-eight volumes are provided for. The King of Siam has granted me £600 for three more volumes, and there are three more volumes which I cannot get published, unless I get some help.

'But I say once more, I am more than satisfied by what you and your friends have done already. It shows that my labours have not been in vain, and that I have gained the good will of many people in India. My time will soon be over now, but this Indian Testimonial will remain as a most valuable heirloom in the hands of my children. My son, now Secretary of Embassy at Constantinople, is spending his five months' leave with us. We have taken a house for him in London, and shall stay here till the end of July.'

TO PROFESSOR VICTOR CARUS.

*Translation.* HERTFORD STREET, *June* 12.

'The end is drawing near for both of us, and we must manage what is left as well as we can. I have been very unwell all the winter with cold and neuralgia. But one must learn to grow old, and bear the inevitable with resignation! Otherwise, all goes well with us. We have our two eldest grandchildren with us, and ought to be very thankful, and are so, though one constantly feels it cannot always be so under the changing moon. I wished not to be in Oxford during the British Association; but they have made a point of it, so I have settled to be there, and take part in it. Will you not come to us with Gertrude? I thought we had arranged it all. You would wonder at my life here: dining out or going to the theatre almost every night, and visits all day long, so that I get quite giddy. But one goes on as long as one can. Then I have brought out another book, I suppose the last. Shall we yet meet again on this planet? Well, though the planet rolls on, it remains always the same, and so we will hope. All the old friends go though, and one feels forsaken and forgotten.'

To Madame Butenschön.

Hertford Street, *June* 3.

'I was very glad to receive a sign of life from you, and to learn that you had remained faithful to Sanskrit. I feel sure that you will get something really useful out of it, something to make life interesting and even happy. I send you a copy of my Vedânta Lectures, which will show you what I mean. We are settled for the summer in London, and I have to be idle, and dine out, and all that. My daughter also, and her husband, and her three children, often come to stay with us. I ought to feel very happy, *mais la joie fait peur!*

'I hope you have not quite given up England, and that I may have the pleasure of meeting you once more in this confused world.'

During his stay in London Max Müller heard of the illness and death of his cousin, Major von Basedow, with whom he had grown up as a boy, and to whom, though they met so seldom in later life, he was most warmly attached. The following letters are to his cousin's wife:—

*Translation.* *June* 14, 1894.

'Dear Emma,—I have long been afraid I should have bad news from you about Adolf. We are all coming towards the end, and we can only pray, all of us, for a peaceful parting. May he not have much to suffer! He is my oldest friend, and whenever I think of my childhood, I see him at my side. If he ever thinks of me, press his hand for me. We must all learn to bow to our fate as men, however hard it comes to each one of us. You know where alone help can be found.

'Always your true Cousin.'

*Translation.* *June* 16, 1894.

'DEAR EMMA,—We so willingly forget that we must die, and yet we should learn it every day. I always hoped Adolf would get better; when I saw him last, he certainly looked very ill, but he still had plenty of strength and could do a good deal. The trouble about —— affected him very deeply, and few were more ready to part with life than he was. Well, he has had a rich and happy life. For us old people there is no happiness so great as the happiness of our children, and he had much happiness from his children, even though he could not shield them from all the troubles of life. To me it is as if one of the oldest anchors had parted. He was my earliest friend, and I believe we never had a misunderstanding. Characters such as his become ever rarer. He lived so entirely after the old rule, *Noblesse oblige.* Nothing vulgar or low ever entered his mind. Even want of proper recognition he bore without remonstrance, and he hardly ever uttered a harsh word. We must all learn to mourn in silence. You still have much in your children to bind you to this life. May they be a comfort in your last years! My love to them all. I need not express in words my heartfelt sympathy.

'Ever your truly affectionate.'

The following letter was written in acknowledgement of the beautiful illuminated address from all the German teachers in England, which was sent for Max Müller's seventieth birthday, as mentioned in the last chapter:—

*June*, 1894.

'DEAR FRIENDS AND COLLEAGUES,—I have been much gratified by the friendly sentiments to which, on the occasion of my seventieth birthday, you have given such an artistic expression. The profession which you have chosen in England is often no easy one, but it gives you the opportunity of carrying on quietly great things not only for England but for Germany. As teachers of the German language, and as representatives of German thought, you can draw closer and closer the ties that unite Germany and England, you can encourage in the youth of England sentiments of esteem and love for Germany, you can help to prepare a future in which the people of England, Germany, and America may feel themselves to be brothers, and with united powers carry out in the world's history those high ideals which for years have been in the minds of the best spirits of those three closely related nations.

'Be true to your highest aspirations! You are the sails which must carry our ship of life through rain and storm to our desired haven.

'In true gratitude and respect.'

The three months in London, though tiring, had been greatly enjoyed by Max Müller, who saw something of many old friends from whom he had been separated for years. Among the new acquaintances he made, none was more valued than the venerable painter Watts, who had asked Max Müller to sit to him for one of the portraits for the National Portrait Gallery. Good part of each sitting was spent in conversation, till Mr. Watts would look up, 'Now we must get on a little,' and Max Müller would settle into the right attitude for a short time, and then conversation would break out again. Various short visits were paid to Ightham Mote, and the Colyer-Fergussons stayed several times with the parents in London.

The British Association met in August at Oxford. M. Vambéry and M. van Branteghem stayed for it with Max Müller, who took no active part in the proceedings, merely attending the meetings of the Sections in which he took an interest. He was feeling tired, and soon after the meeting ended was seriously unwell for some days. On his son's return to Constantinople, Max Müller resolved to try sea-air, and he and his wife went to stay with their daughter at Mundesley, on the Norfolk coast. Here a delightful fortnight was spent, and expeditions were taken on the Broads; several of the fine Norfolk churches were seen; a long day was spent at Blickling, where Max Müller was deeply interested in exploring the treasures of the library, especially the famous MS. of the Blickling Homilies, and other rarities. The fine old building and the beautiful gardens delighted him.

Throughout this year Max Müller had been busy in preparing a fresh edition of *Chips*. The first volume was entirely new, and many papers written since the original edition of *Chips* were added in the other three volumes. He asked permission to dedicate the work to the German Emperor, 'as a very small token of deep-felt gratitude and sincere admiration,' and heard in September that the Emperor would consider it as 'a great honour to himself to accept the dedication of so famous a work, and that he heartily thanked Max Müller for this friendly attention.' The Emperor had in the spring of the year composed his *Song to Aegir*, which he asked Max

Müller to translate for an English version, sending him a copy marked in his own handwriting, 'A musical chip for a German workman, with best thanks for translation. Wilhelm, I. R.'

He also received, about this time, his life written in Sanskrit *slokas*, from a Pundit at Jodhpur. He acknowledged it as follows:—

OXFORD, *September* 27, 1894.

'The first thing that I do after my return to Oxford last night is to write to you and to thank you for the kind sentiments which you express towards me, and for the generous appreciation of the little I have been able to do, as a student of Sanskrit literature. Your learned Pundits in India have been very indulgent in their judgement of my work, and I am deeply grateful to them. I have done what I could, often under great difficulties, but I know but too well how little I have done and how little I have deserved all the kind things that have been said and written about me by the scholars of your country. Least of all could I have dreamt that my life and my work should have been made by an Indian poet the subject of a Sanskrit poem, such as you have composed and sent to me. No Sanskrit scholar in England could have written such a poem, least of all myself. We study Sanskrit in order to become acquainted with your literature. Our ambition does not go so far as to attempt to write Sanskrit poems or verse. In that respect we shall always have to yield the palm to your Pundits. I see what a high place you hold in the estimation of the Pundits of Benares, and I consider it indeed a very high and very undeserved honour to have had my praises sung in the language of Kâlidâsa.'

This autumn brought Max Müller another loss in the death of his old friend and connexion, Mr. Froude, after an illness of some months. Shortly before his death Max wrote to his friend:—

OXFORD, *October* 3.

'MY DEAR OLD MAN,—Yes, old we are, but there are few old men who have made such a good fight for it as you have. After all, from the first day of our life, our life is but a constant fight with death. As long as we are young and have the best of it, life seems very pleasant, but after threescore years and ten the old Psalmist is not far wrong. However, there are few men who, after that allotted time, could walk the hours that you could, and now produce another book as you have. I was so pleased to get it, and I am beginning to read it. Many thanks for it. It will be a great treat, for I want to know something more about Erasmus, and I expect to find all that is worth knowing about him in your lectures. But I am not allowed to read much, my eyes are still troublesome—they say it is liver; but I do not see how the liver can jump into my eyes and make me see things crooked and double. You would be pleased to see how respectfully the yappers and yelpers speak of your last book. If you are allowed to read the *Times*, there was an article on the Armada that would interest you.

'I hope you will go on fighting. I do the same, though one feels that, after all, the best of life is gone, and there is little left worth fighting for. Still Aunt Eh seems very happy on her small allowance of vitality. I wish you could come to Oxford.

'Ever yours affectionately.'

Max Müller was always ready to give a warm welcome to any foreigners who joined the University. An American undergraduate thus describes his first visit to Max Müller, to whom he had brought an introduction:—

'I had never seen Max Müller. I tried to recall my earliest knowledge of him, but could not. It seemed to me that every one in America knew about the distinguished Orientalist. Professor Max Müller was in the best of moods, and put everybody at their ease. He is of average height, and well built. He has a high forehead, a genial countenance, and hair almost snow-white. His eyes have lost none of their brilliancy, though he wears glasses. We forgot for the moment that we were chatting with the foremost scholar of the age. That the man so genial and interesting to us had proven equally interesting and entertaining to the highest potentates in the world, and had had all sorts of honours laid at his feet, did not for the moment cross our mind. We were unconsciously as easy as if we were in the house of some intimate friend. I came away with a greater respect and admiration for scholarship. It had, in the person of Professor Max Müller, given me a newer conception of its real meaning. Since that first visit it has been my good fortune to call often at the famous house in Norham Gardens, and I have seen nothing but that which has added to my appreciation of true greatness.'

To his Son.

*November 27.*

'Here in London people still think the Armenian agitators have been exaggerating and making capital out of local disturbance. I should not wonder if they are in Russian pay; but one cannot see any way out of it. The Germans are angry with England in Africa, and England with Germany. That cannot be helped. In Turkey, too, Germany thinks it can keep Russia in good temper by not interfering. All that is natural, and you see the same kind of thing in private life. But at bottom, Germany and England hold together, and the Emperor's will still counts for something there. Here political life is in a regular mess, no leader and no principles.'

Like most men of any note, Max Müller had to submit to be constantly interviewed. One of the most interesting of these interviews was reported at this time in the *Christian Commonwealth*, from which the following extracts are taken. The writer begins with a description of his victim, and then proceeds to more important topics.

'Erect, virile-looking, with face clean-shaven but for light side-whiskers; hair hanging in thick, silvery masses, with here and there a darker streak; alert, bright, smiling, Professor Max Müller, looking pleasantly through his *pince-nez*, cordially greets me, his slight foreign accent adding a charm to his clear pronunciation of the language which has become to him as familiar as his mother-tongue. The Professor, for all his long, laborious years, retains the vigour and vivacity of youth. His manner of speech is rather that of the frolicsome undergraduate than of the typical University Don. He talks in free, colloquial style, showing quite a fondness for certain of our figures of speech. Avoiding the jargon of the schools, his one object is to make his meaning clear to the person with whom he is conversing. "If you don't understand me," he remarked to me more than once, with kindly thoughtfulness, "ask me again."

'Though many may differ from Professor Max Müller's theology, all gladly recognize his deeply religious spirit.

'THE BEST SACRED BOOK.

'Would you say that any one sacred book is superior to all others in the world?'

'It may sound prejudiced, but, taking all in all, I say the New Testament. After that, I should place the Korân, which in its moral teaching is hardly more than a later edition of the New Testament. Then would follow, according to my opinion, the Old Testament, the Southern Buddhist Tripitaka, the Taote-King of Lao-tze, the Kings of Confucius, the Veda, and the Avesta. But this is a very rough classification, and not likely to be accepted by others. There is no doubt, however, that ethical teaching is far more prominent in the Old and New Testaments than in any other sacred book. Therein lies the distinctiveness of the Bible. Other sacred books are generally collections of whatever was remembered of ancient times. For instance, in the *Veda* you get a description of the Flood simply as a deluge; in the Old Testament it takes an ethical meaning, it is a punishment and a reward; there is the difference between the two; and that distinction runs through the whole of the sacred books. There is, of course, plenty of moral teaching in the other sacred books also, but the distinguishing feature of the Old Testament is that the Jews feel themselves the chosen people of God. That idea runs through the whole book. The Jewish people always referred everything that happened to them, whether happiness or misfortune, to a Divine government; it was meant for them; there was a meaning in it; they were made to feel that God was angry or pleased.'

'Revelation.

'How about the Bible revelation?'

'With us things have taken a different shape; we say, not that revelation makes truth, but that truth makes revelation; the sense of truth within us is to us the sense of God; the voice of God is to us the Spirit of Truth. We do not say that the New Testament was handed down from the sky in any miraculous way. The Spirit of Truth speaks, and it is perfectly certain, and more certain than anything else, that is to us inspired.'

The interviewer then questioned him on the Oldest Sacred Book, the Primal Religion, the Origin of Language, and the Revival of Theosophy, and received clear and interesting answers on all of these topics, till he was forced to leave by the arrival of Mr. Takakusu, the Japanese pupil, who is now Professor of Sanskrit in the University of Tokio.

On December 6 Max Müller wrote to his friend, Mr. Malabari:—

'To-day is my seventy-first birthday, and though I have not been very well lately, I still feel as if I could do some more work. I fully expect to see you in England again next summer. You seem an indefatigable traveller, whereas I rejoice in my quiet forest here.'

Some years before this Max Müller had made acquaintance with a very beautiful German girl, in whose fate he ever afterwards took a strong interest. She had married, but not happily, and Max Müller wrote to her from time to time, giving her what counsel he could for the thorny path of duty she had to tread. The following letters are to her :—

*Translation.* OXFORD, *August* 3, 1894.

'To-day is my thirty-fifth wedding-day. I have suffered much, and many wounds inflicted by death bleed as on the first day. And yet, what blessings have been granted me! My daughter, very happily married with three children; my son, a Secretary at the English Embassy in Constantinople, now home on a five months' visit. One trembles at all this happiness. In spite of my age I still have strength for work, and pleasure in it. I send you my answer to the many congratulations I have received. May you have strength to bear the weight of life! One can forgive all as one stands by the bed of death; why not, then, during life?'

*Translation.* OXFORD, *December* 11, 1894.

'As I had no news from you, I said to myself, let us hope all is now arranged; and when one is perfectly happy, one is self-contained and requires no outer world. But alas! it does not seem to be so, and I ask, how is it possible? I can, of course, form no real judgement. I only think that you, as pupil and friend of ——, must have looked deep into earthly life. You know that behind the world of sense, to which we must accommodate ourselves, with all its forms and conventional opinions, our true world really lies, in which alone we can find rest and peace. However beautiful the love and self-sacrifice of a young girl may be, it is almost always a passion in the world of sense—true love lies much deeper. Appearance and beauty with all its mysterious attraction disappears, it must disappear, but as it disappears true love comes first into sight. One does not love the appearance, but the eternal that is in a human being, often as it hides and veils itself from us. Has one but once perceived the eternal, one never loses sight of it again, happen what may. A mother never gives up her child, however troublesome it may be, for mother's love is the most unselfish love; she desires nothing, she only gives. A woman's love should be the same. She should never think of herself, she should forgive everything, trusting to the nobleness in every man, when one only knows how to call it out. But I wish I could help you. I keep thinking how miserable —— would be if he could know how unhappy you are. He thought your future would be such a happy one. But one thing is clear—things cannot stay as they are. Then why wait in indecision? The sacrifice only touches the world of sense. The higher one climbs the smaller grow the human figures, the more trifling seem the earthly sacrifices one has to make. Pride, exaggerated self-respect, and whatever one may call all that, are only of this world, and must be given up where higher interests and higher duties call us. Is there no one who can help you? Resolve firmly, if only for the sake of your children. —— often did things which no one else would have done, and was therefore often called unpractical, and yet I am sure he had many friends and admirers. And we loved him because he was so unpractical. Forgive my freedom: I wish to think of you as happy—as happy as you certainly deserve to be.'

### TO MRS. RADCLIFFE WHITEHEAD (MISS B. MCCALL).

OXFORD, *December* 23, 1894.

'It was very good of you to remember my seventy-first birthday. I had often thought of you, and though I was sorry not to have heard from you, I felt that you were so happy that there was no room left for anything else. And so, of course, it ought to be; otherwise, what is the use of marrying? You seem to live in a perfect paradise; I had no idea of the beauty of California, but I have a very strong idea of the non-beauty of England at this time of year. How could human beings ever have settled here when they came from Italy? and really if this goes on, and we become more and more glacial, I should not be at all surprised if we all migrated to California, to eat peaches and apricots, and bask in the sunshine. We shall soon have a flying machine now, and then, whether invited or not, you will some day see a swallow lighting on your roof and asking for shelter. It is so right that you should be happy, and true happiness consists in making others happy; still, I cannot help grudging you to California. It is so strange to feel that one is not to see those again whom one has learnt to care for; still, I have many such, as you may imagine, and some of them seem to me to belong to me more even than when they were with us. My children are doing very well. W. gives us great pleasure; he enjoys his life, but, as he says, his pleasure is his duty, and he takes to it kindly. You should see B. with her three children and in her beautiful old home, the very picture of peace and plenty. We spent three months in London this year, and what with my young son and his still younger mother, they very nearly made an end of me. I am now slowly recovering from our dissipations, and have not dined out once during the whole term. I lost a very old friend in Froude; he was so well while he was here lecturing, and then the end came very quickly. I have known him ever since 1848, and been with him through all his troubles, when he wrote his *Nemesis of Faith*, and was so poor that he had to sell his books; and now he seems to have left a large fortune. You probably look at American reviews; I sent an article to the *Arena* which will amuse you. It was really a lecture I had been asked to give to the members of an American pilgrimage to England. I have to confess that I am writing this while I ought to be at church, but this time of year it is part of our duty to feel good will towards *men*, and that does not exclude *women*. Old friends need not become cold friends, and you have my warmest wishes for a Merry Christmas and a Happy New Year.

'Yours very sincerely.'

Christmas was spent quietly in Oxford by Max Müller and his wife, and for the New Year they went to their kind and valued friends, Lord and Lady Wantage, at Lockinge.

The early months of 1895 were passed at Oxford, varied by constant short visits to and from his daughter and her husband. Max Müller was already beginning his large work, *Contributions to the Science of Mythology*, and brought out Volumes III and IV of the new edition of *Chips*. There are more frequent notices in his wife's journal of his weariness and want of strength, though his cheerfulness and love of work never flagged, and his friends were hardly aware of the ever-increasing feeling of effort in all he did. He had entirely given up dining out during the two winter terms, as the liability to catch cold, which he had felt from his earliest years in England, increased each year. A friend who spent this winter in Oxford wrote later: 'I close my eyes and think myself back seven years, and there I am at 7, Norham Gardens, the dear rooms; the tea-table; the Professor standing before the fire, with his face all lighted by that smile of wondrous beauty which one felt as well as looked upon; yourself behind the tea-urn, and Dr. Silver (a large Persian) climbing about as his cat-will dictated.'

To B. Malabari, Esq.

Oxford, *January* 8.

'Your beautiful casket has safely arrived [p. 305], as you will see from the enclosed. To have won the good opinion of so many men of light and leading in India is the best reward I could have received for the work of my life. Of course, my work has chiefly been the work of a scholar, but I have tried never to lose sight of the higher objects of scholarship, to make us understand the past in order to understand the present, to make us understand others in order to understand ourselves. Kind and generous as the feeling in England is towards India, there still lurks the old prejudice that, after all, the people of India are strangers, different from ourselves, that allowance must be made for them, and all the rest. Now I have always held that the people of India are not strangers, but are exactly like ourselves, if we only would treat them as such. Their literature, their religion, their customs, are different from ours, but what is essential is the same in both. It may be said that I know the best specimens of Hindu society only, but the best specimens show what a nation is capable of. In literature also, you see, no doubt, the brighter side of a nation; but by all means let us see the bright side wherever we can; the light is there and will conquer in the end, whether in the East or in the West. Reformers like you have the right to disclose the dark sides, and dwell on them: but on one condition only, namely, that like you they work hard to dispel the darkness and to bring in the light. What you have done will not be forgotten, and will bear fruit.'

To his Son.

*January* 8, 1895.

'My article on Agnosticism ought not to be beyond you, considering that you read Plato, and know what he meant by his Ideas. His ideas are the Stoic Logoi, and all conceived as one act of thought from the Logos, the invisible world, the pattern of the visible. These matters are quite simple; the old people two thousand years ago knew them as we know our A B C. Christianity would never have conquered the world, the educated Greek world, without the Greek philosophers of Alexandria, and their philosophical view of Christianity. However, let each man speak his own language, and do his own work.'

Max Müller's old friend Carrière died early in January. They had known each other from their youth, and Max Müller greatly admired his friend's poems, which are hardly known in England. Unfortunately only one of his letters to Carrière has been kept. He writes to another friend: 'All go before me, and I often feel starved and perished with thirst, lost in the desert. Yes! I have a happy home, but the threads that bind me to the outer world are nearly all broken. We old people are happier than ever in our married life, and only tremble at the thought of our great happiness.'

To B. Malabari, Esq.

'I only wish I could rouse more interest and more sympathy for India in England; unfortunately, the only thing that the large public admires in India is the folly of Esoteric Buddhism and Theosophy, falsely so called. What a pity it is that such absurdities, nay, such frauds, should be tolerated! We have had much illness here this winter, and I have lost several friends, Froude among the rest. I myself have hitherto withstood the epidemic, only my eyes have been troublesome now and then, and I feel I must be careful. Still, there is plenty of work I should like to do, if my life is spared.'

At the beginning of the Easter Vacation the Max Müllers went to Bournemouth to take care of their grandchildren, who were recovering from influenza. From there he wrote to his valued friend, Miss Anna Swanwick:—

BOURNEMOUTH, *March* 27.

'It was very good of you, sending me your little book[1]. I read it with very great pleasure. I have seldom read anything where I could say at every page, "How very true!" It is quite a gem, and I am not at all surprised that people who had read it in the *Contemporary Review* wish to possess it. What I always regret when I read a paper like yours, is that so little is done, and can be done, to give it effect. We know what ought to be, but we feel so helpless to carry out what is right. Still, nothing is lost, and at last the flower springs up in the most unexpected places—such as the Parliament of Religions in Chicago, of all places in the world!

'On one point I cannot follow you. I do not believe in what is called Evolution in History. History is the work of individuals; it is not continuous, it advances by fits and starts. To look upon everything as growing and evolving by so-called small and imperceptible degrees, would be to rub out all genius, all impulse, all individuality. When a great work has been achieved, we may look out for its antecedents, and so try to understand it; but that used to be called History or Pragmatic History; it made allowances for free-will, for personal character, for much in men that cannot be explained by formulas. It led to minute and accurate study, instead of lumping things together, and talking of necessary evolution, or so-called Philosophy of History. What we want are facts, minute facts, ever so many facts, which can be classified and thus rendered intelligible; but that is very different from saying that the human race has grown exactly as it ought to grow; that we are evolved from the past, as the future will be evolved from us. I do not think that Goethe was evolved. We are the children of our parents, but not our parents over again. Heredity

[1] *Evolution; or, the Future of Religion.*

is another of those lazy words that save us thinking but teach us nothing.

'Heredity is always right, if we only go back far enough into the realm of ignorance, but surely we are more than heirs. Excuse this little digression, it only refers to the title, not to the body of your book.'

At Bournemouth Max Müller received a letter from the American Press Association, asking him to contribute one of the papers they wished to publish on the reasons for believing or disbelieving the Immortality of the Soul. In response he wrote the article first published in this country in *Last Essays*, Series II, 'Is Man Immortal?'

To Miss Swanwick.

Bournemouth, *April* 1, 1895.

'I must send you one line to say how true an evolutionist I am in your sense of the word. It is so pleasant to agree with others who have thought out the same problems as we ourselves. If you have time to look at an article of mine in the *Nineteenth Century*, "Why I am not an Agnostic," you will see how fully I recognize, in the world of nature and of spirit, the evolution and realization of the *Logos*, the old *Nous*, but not the result of mere natural selection, struggle of life, survival of the fittest, &c. What I am just now working at is to find out in what sense Christ was called the Logos made Flesh. Was it meant for the Logos comprehending all the Logoi in the Divine Mind, or for the Logos of Man, so that he would have been conceived as the ideal man, the realization or incarnation of the Divine idea of Man? I cannot find an answer: even Harnack, to whom I wrote, cannot help me. People then, as now, were carried away by words, and thus made mythology, instead of religion.'

To the Same.

Bournemouth, *April* 5, 1895.

'I should have written to Dr. Martineau, but I begin to learn what time means when a man gets close to ninety. The question which troubles me is whether the author of the Fourth Gospel meant by Logos the fullness of the Logos, or one of the Logoi, namely that of man as the Son of God. I have read Drummond's book on Philo; it is excellent, but of course does not touch on my question. I have waded through several of Philo's treatises myself, and after that had many conversations with Dr. Drummond, who is a most learned and delightful man. But he, too, could not help me. I am just now revising the German translation of the fourth volume of my *Gifford Lectures*, where I have treated the Logos question as well as I could, but nowhere can I find a passage which would answer my question definitely. While I am here I am reading Origen and Hippolytus, both overflowing with thoughts about the Logos, but neither of them answering, nay even asking the question, on which to my mind everything depends in forming a rational idea of Christ as the Logos. If you should see Dr. Martineau, and would sound him on the subject, I should feel grateful. There is time to add something in the German translation.'

TO DR. MARTINEAU.

7, NORHAM GARDENS, *April* 10, 1895.

'Accept my very best thanks for your kind letter, and for the interesting and helpful remarks which it contains. I am afraid you are right, and that it was really the fullness of the Logos which was supposed to have been incarnate in Jesus; that He was, in fact, identified with the Demiurgos or the Second God, the world being the third God in the language of Numenius. I have been hesitating between these explanations: the Philonic, supposing that Philo, if he had known Jesus, had recognized the Logos in Him, as he did in Abraham and others; the Christian, though to me almost unintelligible view, that He was the Demiurgos; and the third, that He was taken as the only realization of the Logos or the idea of manhood, as the Son of God. The last seems to me the sense in which Christ spoke of Himself as the Son of God, as the brother of men, and the only sense in which we can honestly apply to Him the name of Logos, and see in Him the realization of all the possibilities comprehended in the idea of man, as conceived by God. I have tried to digest the materials at hand, and to work out my ideas on the Logos, in the fourth volume of my *Gifford Lectures*, xii–xv. . . . I know the value of your time, and I do not ask you to waste it on my book, but you may find leisure to glance at one or two of my chapters, which will show you what I was striving after, though I am afraid, unsuccessfully. There are curious analogies to the Logos theory in the *Veda*, and these led me on to Philo, Origen, Clement, Hippolytus, &c., in spite of the old warning *ne sutor ultra crepidam*, and I cannot give up the subject yet, though I feel it is high time to *contrahere vela*, if at seventy-one one wishes to keep afloat.

'Yours very truly and gratefully.'

One of the many curious visitors whom Max Müller welcomed to his house was a Red Indian chief, who appeared this year, under the charge of an Englishman; the chief's name was Strong Buffalo. He remained to luncheon, conducted himself with great dignity and self-possession, and Max Müller learnt a good deal from him about the former habits of his tribe. Another visitor was a Jain priest, who had already spent a day with Max Müller at Ightham Mote, and now came to see Oxford. He was a strikingly handsome man, and was dressed entirely in yellow, a pale yellow silk robe and darker yellow turban, and he excited great curiosity as he drove about with his host—in several places they were fairly mobbed. Acquaintance was made with Madame Shimoda, a Japanese lady, sent by the Empress of Japan to study girls' and women's education in England. Madame Shimoda is now Head of the Peeresses' School in Tokio, founded by the Empress. Madame Butenschön also stayed in Norham Gardens this year, getting good advice from Moksha Mûlara Bhatta for her future studies.

In the summer of this year a curious dispute was submitted to Max Müller. The dispute was between two learned Pundits of Wazirâbâd, on the right ceremonial to be observed in the performance of *Srâddha*, the ceremonies at the death of a father. Max Müller was chosen as arbiter by both sides, and requested to describe clearly the ceremonial as enjoined by the *Veda*. The letters to him were written in Hindi and Sanskrit.

This year Max Müller had further evidence of the influence exercised by his works in a quite unknown quarter. Madame de Wagner, living in Rome, wrote to him about a work written by a friend, *Origine de la Pensée et de la Parole*, which was based on Max Müller's works, and leave was asked to make large quotations from his books. Leave was granted, and about two years later, in passing through Rome, Max Müller called on Madame de Wagner, whom he found to be a highly cultivated, clever woman, and then discovered that she was herself the authoress of *La Pensée et la Parole*, at which she was still working. It was a clever analysis of several of his books. Early in 1900 the completed work was sent to him. Max Müller was then slowly recovering from his first severe illness, and could only write, 'Many thanks for your present. To-day I can only say, *Brava! brava!* But I hope to say something more as soon as I can shake off my weakness.' A little later he writes, 'I am very busy and far from well.' Here the correspondence stopped; Madame de Wagner herself passing away not long after her valued correspondent.

To B. Malabari, Esq.

Oxford, *June* 21.

'I have so long wished that you should devote yourself to some other work, besides that which you have been engaged in for so many years. That work is really finished, and though the last measure of the Legislative Council has been a step backward, this can only be *reculer pour mieux sauter*. You may still have to guide the movement, but child-marriages are doomed in India, and child-widows will be under the protection of public opinion, whenever any flagrant case should arise. Now I want you to do something else. There are many Gujarathi books of which we want English translations. You are a master of both languages. Why should you not give us an English translation of Kanga's Gujarathi translation of the *Vendîdâd*? From all I can hear, his work is scholarlike, and would be welcomed by European scholars. The work would be worthy of a man who, like yourself, has proved himself a friend of his country and a true reformer, who knows that no nation should neglect or despise their ancestors, their antiquity, their antecedents, however anxious they may be to improve on what their fathers have done for them. I believe this kind of work would give you a new interest in life, and it would help towards realizing an ideal of which we should never lose sight, a recognition of what is good in every religion, and a building up in the future of a temple in which all believers may join in a common prayer, though retaining what is national in every religion, if only it is not in conflict with the voice of conscience and the commands of reason. I am deeply touched with the expressions of sympathy which continue to reach me from different parts of India in the form of signatures to the address which emanated from you.'

To his Son.

Ightham Mote, *June* 30, 1895.

'I have never liked the aspect of things at Constantinople, and like it less than ever, unless Lord Salisbury is a great deal cleverer than his predecessors. How could anybody believe that Russia and France would help England out of a mess? *into* a mess yes, but never *out* of it. England will have to join the Triple Alliance sooner or later, and sooner would be better than later. The Turkish question must be solved between Turks and Christians. If only the Christians in the Turkish Empire were a better lot, but they seem as corrupt as their rulers, and they imagine that Europe will fight for them, instead of organizing themselves for the fight that is to come.'

This summer Max Müller sat to Professor Herkomer for his picture, done in water-colours in the Professor's own manner of treatment. It was thoroughly successful.

Max Müller had a great pleasure this year in welcoming to his house Frau von Basedow, the widow of his cousin Adolf, with her daughter and second son; the only relatives, except his mother and Baroness Stolzenberg, who had visited him in England. With them excursions were made to Blenheim, Warwick, Kenilworth, and Stratford-on-Avon, and Max Müller took more of a holiday from work than was his wont, and then accompanied his relatives to Ightham Mote. A short visit from his son was also a great happiness.

To Mr. Dharmapâla (a Buddhist).

Oxford, *July* 26.

'Nothing I have desired more than to visit India. But when I was young and able to travel, I was too poor. Now that I am able to bear the expense of so long a journey, my doctor would not sanction my running the risk. So I must be satisfied with India as I have seen it in its literature, and in some of her best sons who have come to see me in England. Dr. Barrows, I hope, will pay me a visit here, before he goes to India. I hope he may be able to arrange another such meeting as you had at Chicago, only with some more really practical and lasting results. England would be the best place for such a meeting. In the meantime you should endeavour to do for Buddhism what the more enlightened students of Christianity have long been doing in the different countries of Europe: you should free your religion from its latter excrescences, and bring it back to its earliest, simplest, and purest form, as taught by Buddha and his immediate disciples. If that is done, you will be surprised to see how little difference there is in essentials between the great religions of the world. And this must be done with perfect honesty. Nothing not quite sincere or truthful should be tolerated. Nothing has injured Buddhism so much in the eyes of scholars and philosophers in Europe as what goes by the name of Esoteric Buddhism. Madame Blavatsky may have been a dear friend to you, but Truth is a dearer friend. I am just printing a translation of the *Gâtakamâlâ* (Sanskrit) which contains some very beautiful passages.'

Dr. Barrows, alluded to in the foregoing letter, had been the chairman of the World's Parliament of Religions in 1893, and visited Oxford this summer on his way to India. This Parliament of Religions had appealed powerfully to Max Müller's imagination, and he had often regretted that he had not shared in the great gathering where hundreds of people from every part of the world had for the first time joined together in prayer to 'Our Father,' bearing witness to the words of the old Hebrew prophet, 'Have we not all one Father; hath not one God created us?' It was therefore a deep interest to Max Müller to see and talk with a man who had not only been present, but had taken so large a share in originating the idea of the great gathering. Dr. Barrows was on his way to India, to see for himself the state of religious belief there.

The following letter is to Mrs. Pauli, who had sent Max Müller the *Life and Letters* of his old friend, Dr. Pauli, which she had prepared and published:—

*Translation.* *September* 7, 1895.

'I must send you a greeting and a word of grateful thanks. Reading the letters has touched me deeply. Recollections that seemed to have long disappeared rose again, and I deplored deeply that our different paths in literature had, in late years, kept us so far from each other. I have been a slave to my work, and have had to give up many things in life to finish that which I wanted to complete. What a rich life, dedicated to friendship, is unfolded in the letters of your dear and noble husband, and how he enjoyed his life, and yet how richly and well he used it! Always just the same as I knew him in Oxford, in 1849. You could not have given a more beautiful picture of him. I am still left behind, as if I had been forgotten; hardly any of the friends of my youth are alive. And yet I must not complain. I have my wife and children, and every cause to be thankful. But one gets weary, and one sits still and waits. But enough of myself. Again, hearty thanks.'

The end of September Max Müller and his wife went to stay with Mrs. Salis Schwabe, at her lovely place, Glyn Garth, in Anglesea. The house is built on the rising ground which bounds the Menai Straits, and gives a fine view of the Welsh mountains opposite; the terraced garden slopes down to the waters of the Straits. Mrs. Salis Schwabe was well known for her great benevolence. She founded a large school for poor children in Naples, and, to enable herself to maintain it, had gradually parted with the splendid pictures by Ary Scheffer, left her by her husband. Among the guests in the house were Dr. Karl Blind and his wife. He and Max Müller were already slightly acquainted, and the meeting was a real pleasure to both. 'In society,' writes Dr. Karl Blind, 'Max Müller easily unbent, comporting himself with as much pleasant joviality as simplicity. At table he was easily disposed to humorous remarks, sometimes with a dash of sarcasm of the milder kind. All possible things in science and politics were discussed at Glyn Garth, and later in Oxford, from questions of ethnology, of language, of history and literature, to German affairs and the condition of Turkey.'

To Doctor Karl Blind.

Oxford, *October* 11, 1895.

'Many thanks for the articles on Notovitch, which I return. I had not seen them. You have effectually disposed of him, but it is impossible to kill him. The editor of the *Nineteenth Century* writes to me that he will bring out another article on Notovitch, and asks me to write a few lines about him, but it is a waste of powder and shot. The days at Glyn Garth were most beautiful, and I was especially glad to make your nearer acquaintance, as our ways had formerly brought us together but seldom. I am hard at work, and have four books in the Press, a new edition of the *Gifford Lectures*, ditto of the *Chips*, a first volume of the *Sacred Books of the Buddhists*, and the *Atharva-veda*, in the *Sacred Books of the East*. At the same time I am writing a big book on Mythology, but who knows whether it will ever be finished! I never get any rest here, and yet I am old enough for rest.'

After Max Müller had completed all the arrangements for the first and second series of the *Sacred Books of the East*, consisting of forty-nine volumes, several offers were made to him of translations of important works, chiefly of Buddhist Texts, which he was most reluctant to leave unpublished. It was a great pleasure to him when the King of Siam came forward and provided the funds for three volumes of Buddhist Texts; and he was able in October of this year to publish the first volume, the *Gâtakamâlâ*, or Birth-Stories, translated by Professor Speyer, of Groningen. In his preface to this volume, as editor, Max Müller, whilst adverting to the great labour and unexpected difficulties he had had to encounter as editor of the *Sacred Books of the East*, expresses his gratitude to the great Oriental scholars of Europe and America for their generous response to his appeal for their aid. 'It has been,' Max Müller says, 'a labour of love, and I shall always feel most grateful to the University of Oxford, and my fellow translators, for having enabled me to realize this long-cherished plan of making the world better acquainted with the Sacred Books of the principal religions of mankind.'

The second volume of the *Sacred Books of the Buddhists* came out after Max Müller's last illness had begun, and when he was already too ill to write a preface. The third volume is now nearly ready.

In October, Max Müller, accompanied by his wife, went to Paris for the Centenary of the Institute of France, of which he was, as will be remembered, a Foreign Member. They were the guests of M. Émile Senart, in his lovely house in the Rue François I, where the large and carefully arranged library excited Max Müller's envy. Though not strong enough to attend all the festivities, it was a great pleasure to him to meet so many old friends from all parts of Europe. This was the last public gathering he attended, and those who met him then will recall his bright spirits, his lively conversation, and keen interest in all the topics broached. The *déjeuners* at his host's house, where distinguished literary men were daily invited to meet the Oxford Professor, were especially enjoyed, as also a dinner given by Comte de Franqueville. The reception at the Élysée proved very interesting, and Max Müller was well enough to join the excursion to Chantilly, where the Duc d'Aumale received his future legatees. Max Müller had a good deal of conversation with the Duke, whom he had often met in England, and on expressing his interest in the beautiful château, with all its treasures of art, and his sense of the Duke's hospitality, the latter replied, laughingly, 'You are the owners, I am only the *concierge*.' At the great public gathering of the five Academies of the Institute, Max Müller, in the *habit brodé*, sat on one of the front benches—those benches on which he used to look with awe, when, as a young man, his patron Burnouf admitted him to a seat at the far end of the hall, to hear a debate or a paper.

'Max Müller is seventy-two years young,' wrote one of the papers at this time, 'for old he is not. White hair, to be sure; but the pink, firm cheeks, the bright eyes, the frank, quick, and animated speech that proves the full as well as active mind; the ready smile that betrays a kindly heart; the utter absence of that severe reserve with which both shallow and pedantic men seek to awe their fellow creatures, and the light humour of his occasional quips, belong to the meridian time, not the afternoon of life.'

The two last volumes of the new edition of *Chips* came out this year, and met with severe criticism from the modern school of anthropologists, those who maintain that humanity emerged slowly from the depths of animal brutality. Max Müller had always maintained that no evidence is older, or can be older than the evidence of language, and felt that the mere collection of myths, except by those who had a full knowledge of the language in which the myths are handed down, was almost always misleading. 'I care,' he says, 'for the establishment of truth, so far as I can see it; I care very little for any personal triumph. The Science of Mythology has a great future before it, not only in the narrow field of mythology, but in the wider spheres of religion and philosophy. I am satisfied with what has been achieved so far, and I know that those who come after me will carry on the work with greater ability, with profounder learning, and with far more eminent success.' 'Yes,' his opponents would say, 'but not on your lines.' It is well known that on the origin of Mythology Mr. Andrew Lang's views were totally opposed to Max Müller's. All the more striking, therefore, was Mr. Lang's testimony in *Longman's Magazine*, November, 1900, to 'the unexampled good-humour, humour, and kindness with which Mr. Max Müller met my "oppositions of science." Had I been an enthusiastic disciple instead of a pertinacious adversary, he could not have been kinder and more genial. He was an example very rare among scholars, who commonly are a race almost as irritable as poets. On the point in which we did not agree he helped to introduce a stricter and more sceptical method in the interrogation of evidence. But it is to his unique qualities as a man that I would give my testimony.'

To Mrs. Bird (his wife's aunt, herself ninety-four years of age).

7, Norham Gardens, *December* 6, 1895.

'My dear Aunt,—It was very kind of you to remember my birthday, the seventy-second! One cannot live through seventy-two years without encountering some of the storms of life, yet, taking all in all, how grateful I ought to be! . . . Whenever the time comes, I may leave this world without much anxiety about those who have been dearest to me in this life. You know what it is to see all one's friends going before us, and how much more one lives with those whom one does not see than with those one sees, and how much of a reality the unseen world becomes. But your life has also been a lesson to all of us never to lose our interest in this life, transient as we know it to be, and never to rest from our labours as long as it is day. Let me thank you for all the kindness you have always shown me, for all the lessons which, unknown to yourself, you have given me, and believe me always,

'Yours affectionately, and with sincere gratitude.'

In the middle of December the Max Müllers went to Wombwell Hall, their son-in-law's place near Gravesend, where a happy Christmas and New Year were spent with their children and children's children.

# CHAPTER XXXIII

## 1896–1897

Torquay. Commander of the Legion of Honour. Doctor of Buda-Pesth. Privy Councillor. 'Coincidences.' Scotland. Spitalhaugh. Armenian Massacres. Rome. Naples. Florence. Venice. *Pferdebürla.* Member of Vienna Academy. Diamond Jubilee. Andrew Lang. King of Siam.

QUITE early in the year Max Müller was able to congratulate his pupil and friend, Mr. Takakusu, now Professor of Sanskrit at Tokio, on the completion of his translation of the *Travels of I-tsing*; a work of great consequence, as settling disputed points in the chronology of Sanskrit literature.

'Your book will show,' he writes, 'what excellent and useful work may be expected from Japanese scholars. If I have gladly given my time and help to you, as formerly to Kasawara and Bunyiu Nanjio, it was not only for the sake of our University, to which you had come to study Buddhist Sanskrit and Pâli, but in the hope that a truly scholarlike study of Buddhism might be revived in Japan, and that your countrymen might in time be enabled to form a more intelligent and historical conception of the great reformer of the ancient religion of India. Religions, like everything else, require reform from time to time. A reformed Buddhism, such as I look forward to, would very considerably reduce the distance which now separates you from other religions, and would help in the distant future to bring about a mutual understanding and kindly feeling between those great religions of the world, in place of the antagonism and the hatred that have hitherto prevailed among the believers in Christ, in Buddha, and Mohammed—a disgrace to humanity, an insult to religion, and a lasting affront to those who came to preach peace on earth, and good will towards men.'

To Rev. R. Corbet.

Wombwell Hall, *January* 15.

'I have only to-day found time to read the pamphlet which you kindly sent me. My mind has been busy in other places, but I always like to be taken home, and I never feel so thoroughly at home as with my friends, the so-called Mystics. Why Mystics? There is no mystery here, all is clear and bright. The mystery begins outside, in the world, the senses, not within. It is a misleading and a harmful name, but it is difficult to find a better. Eckhart, Tauler, &c., called themselves *Die Gottesfreunde*, that was better. So was the Sanskrit *Âtmaved*, self-knowers. If you have time, I wish you would look at the *Vedânta Sûtras*, translated by Thibaut, in the *Sacred Books of the East*. The first volume is published, the second is nearly ready. Of course, there is much Indian outside which has to be removed or pierced, but what remains is very wonderful and very bold. For they also had an objective Deity to deal with, and to find it in themselves, and themselves in it.'

After a month with their children, the Max Müllers settled at home, and the work on Mythology, which was growing into a big book, was taken up again. The whole work was a defence of the philological method of inquiry. Max Müller's point had always been that whatever detritus mythology may carry along with it, its original constituent elements were words and phrases about the most striking phenomena of nature, such as day and night, dawn and evening, sun and moon, sky, earth, and sea, in their various relations to each other and to man. Max Müller's highest object was to discover reason in all the unreason of mythology, and thus to vindicate the character of our ancestors, however distant.

To B. MALABARI, ESQ.

OXFORD, *January* 19.

'Here, in England, we have no time to think at present of anything but foreign politics, Armenia, Transvaal, America. One sometimes wonders where we are. Is it possible that we should allow ourselves to be governed, that is, be driven into murder and rapine, by a few reckless individuals? Politics in America are at a low standard. . . . The President, in order to secure votes, must not shrink from risking a war between America and England, between the most advanced and civilized races, causing murder and misery, not for one or two, but for hundreds of thousands of human beings, destroying what has been built up with the greatest care, and throwing us back into real savagery. So much for republics—and now for monarchies! Has the German Emperor acted with a due sense of his duty to his own people? If England were hot-tempered, we might have had war between England

and Germany; and what that means, no one can imagine. The merits of the case are of no consequence. England may have asked too much in Venezuela, and Englishmen have certainly acted lawlessly in the Transvaal; but should the leaders of men, whether Presidents or Emperors, speak to each other in such language without a moment's thought of what may come from it? If a man strikes a match in a powder magazine, he acts as the President and Emperor have acted. And here we sit, the so-called millions, and we can do nothing to prevent these horrors. And that is the result of our boasted civilization, and of what is called constitutional government. War may be avoided for the present, because Lord Salisbury happens to be a gentleman, but seed has been sown that will produce poison before long. I feel very unhappy when I see all this, and see no way out of it. Political life sinks lower and lower. We are governed by self-seeking, reckless, greedy people. The best people in America are ashamed of their President, but, of course, if one man shouts, the crowd falls in with the shouts, and then come blows, and then comes murder. However, enough of that.

'Tell me how Ramabai is getting on with her quiet work, and what you are doing and mean to do. I feel that I am getting old, and as I have still a few things which I should like to finish, I am working very hard. My *Sacred Books of the East* are not finished yet, and give me much trouble. But my chief work just now is *Comparative Mythology*, which means a great deal more than it seems to mean. It accounts for many cases in which the human mind has misunderstood itself, and could not help it.'

### To Horatio Hale, Esq.

Oxford, *January* 29.

'I have not heard from you for a long time. I suppose we are both growing old, and retire into the forest. I must not complain, though I feel that my work will soon be over. I hope to finish one more big book. A big book is a big mistake, but it has grown and I cannot help it. To-day I write to ask you a favour. I have quoted you as comparing the serious work of scholars with the light work of so-called folk-lorists. You speak of the difficulties of really mastering a foreign language and an ancient literature, to enter into the thoughts of other people, and the easy work of cutting the pages of a book of travels, and marking a few passages. You sent me the paper, and I kept it, and cannot find it now. Can you help me? I hope at the same time to hear that you are still well and vigorous, and will give us some more of your long accumulated treasures.'

To the Right Hon. W. E. Gladstone.

*January* 29.

'It was very kind of you to write to me *propria manu*, and I assure you I know how to appreciate the honour. My last volume of *Gifford Lectures* leads up to what seems to me the highest problem of Christian philosophy as distinct from Christian religion: the *Logos* wrongly translated by the *Word*, in spite of the unfortunate divorce which we have made between Word and Thought. I devoted a big book, *Science of Thought*, to the establishment of the inseparableness of *Word* and *Thought*, and in my last *Gifford Lectures* I drew the practical consequences. Am I right, or am I wrong? and are we to throw away the philosophical foundation on which the Christianity of St. John, and of Clement and the Alexandrian School, was built up? I well remember your growing library; you took me over it yourself during my last delightful visit to Hawarden. Please let me know whether you have Volumes II and III of the *Gifford Lectures*. I know what it is to receive books which one does not want. I had to keep a secretary on purpose for answering letters and acknowledging books; and now that I no longer have a secretary I lose two or three hours every day by useless correspondence. I cannot complain of my health; still, at seventy-two one feels the approach of the end, and I have still several things which I should like to finish. I never dine out, and have long given up paying visits, but if I may, I shall call on you some day when you are in London. I have the two volumes of your edition of Butler, and am looking forward to the third. Certainly Butler has been little noticed in Germany. The time in which he wrote was not a favourable time for philosophy in Germany. There was little of philosophy after Leibniz and before Kant, and the problems which occupied the few original thinkers were connected with the possibility of cognition, and not with practical questions. A new period of philosophical activity began with Kant's *Critique*, 1781, and this again was chiefly concerned with the limits of human cognition. With my best wishes that you may be allowed to finish not only Butler, but the Olympian religion also.'

In February Max Müller's fourth grandchild and third grandson was born.

To Mrs. Whitehead (Miss Byrd McCall), on receiving a photograph of her home in California.

Oxford, *March* 27.

'Yes, that Italian verandah is delightful, and so is the studio, but where is the world? Are we not sent here for a little season, to live in the world, and are trees and hills the world? Socrates used to say, "Trees teach me nothing": his only study was man. I know you must keep a corner to be alone in, or alone with one or two people, but even the old philosophers of India, who spent their whole lives in the forests, and such forests, told their young pupils that they ought to find their forests in their heart, undisturbed by the noise of the world all around them. You know what a quiet forest Oxford is; still, "our ruins are inhabited," and in an hour you are in Hyde Park, and can shake hands with your friends, even on a bicycle, and in a few hours more you are *sur le Boulevard.* I was there only the other day for the Centenary of the Institute, and enjoyed it immensely, though I suffered for it afterwards, but that cannot be helped. We always have to pay for our little happinesses. No doubt this is all very wrong and frivolous for a grandfather with four grandchildren, but we have been very quiet ever since, and shall be till Commemoration is over; then we are thinking of going to Scotland to stay with B., where we shall get refreshed, and see some old friends. For Easter we are due at Torquay to stay with Mr. Norris, the novel writer, whom you may have met at Oxford. And all the time I am writing a very big book on Mythology, which interests me very deeply, but will not amuse many people, though it is full of atrocities in which people delight—if they happen at the present day. W. is doing well at Constantinople, and has just returned from Egypt, Smyrna, Magnesia, and Laodicea . . . I am getting fearfully old! I often pass your old house here, and think of many a happy hour spent there, making toffee and what not.'

In April a visit of ten days to Mr. Norris, the well-known novelist, at Torquay, was a welcome break in Max Müller's hard work, and pleasant days were spent at Dartmouth, Berry Pomeroy, and other places round.

To Professor Bloomfield, Baltimore.

Oxford, *May* 10.

'When one can no longer produce much oneself, one should at all events be able to sympathize with and appreciate the work of others. Your last articles have given me the same pleasure as if I had worked out these questions myself. I sometimes chuckled, and said, "Too good to be true." But true it is for all that; the only question is, do these facts of language admit of any generalization; are they not mere *lusus naturae?* However, even if nature plays and romps, we ought to attend, as you have done. I have been occupied in a very different line, or mine. My book on Mythology, in two volumes, is nearly ready, and yet it is a mere fragment—the subject is so enormous. What can one man, and that an old man, do? However, I hope I shall help to revive the interest of scholars in a subject so much neglected and despised of late. To find reason in unreason is, after all, the best we can do, and we owe it really to the race to which we belong to attempt to show that we are not descended from idiots.'

In May, M. Geoffray, the French Chargé d'Affaires, came to Norham Gardens to present Max Müller with the insignia of Commander of the Legion of Honour, awarded him by the President of the French Republic. The Vice-Chancellor and other leading members of the University dined to meet him. When Max Müller was made a member of the French Institute in 1869, several of his *confrères* told him he should apply for the Legion of Honour. But not only would such a proceeding have been contrary to his principle of never asking for any distinction, but such was his mistrust of Napoleon that he would have felt himself degraded by accepting any honour from him. The feeling with which he received the beautiful decoration from M. Faure, whom he thoroughly respected, was very different. A few days later Max Müller heard that, on the occasion of the Hungarian Millennium, he had received the honorary degree of Doctor of Philosophy at Buda-Pesth.

But a wholly unexpected and far higher distinction was now to come to him. On the morning that the list of Birthday Honours appeared in the *Times*, his wife, who was sitting in the drawing-room, was roused by his coming in suddenly with the *Times* in his hand. 'Don't faint!' he said, as he gave her the paper, with a beaming face. There his English wife, who had for years smarted under the sense that while foreign countries had vied with each other in granting him distinctions, nothing had been given him in the land he had chosen, and where he had worked for nearly fifty years, saw his name, as the only man appointed a Member of the Privy Council. It was exactly the right distinction, placing him at once in his proper position. All day letters and telegrams of congratulation poured in, and he always liked to remember that the first to reach him was from the Controller and employés of the University Press. The following letter is in response to one from his wife's aunt, Mrs. Bird, aged 95:—

OXFORD, *May* 24, 1896.

'MY DEAR AUNT,—It was *very* kind of you to write to me. I said to G., "I feel sure Aunt Eh will be pleased." You are the only one remaining of the old times; all the others who would have been pleased are gone before us. That is the one drop of bitterness in what has been a great pleasure to G. and me. I shall never forget that she married me when I was not a Privy Councillor, though I must confess that, even now, I do not feel at all like a member of H.M.'s Privy Council. I have received many letters of congratulation, from Lord Salisbury, the Prince of Wales, &c., but I value your letter most of all, and shall keep it among my treasures.

'Yours very affectionately.'

TO SIR ROBERT COLLINS.

OXFORD, *May* 23.

'I am really quite upset. I had so little expected anything of the kind, and it is, of course, far too much. However, it shows the Queen's very kind heart. I confess there always was something bitter when I received so many favours from other countries, and nothing from the country of my choice and love. *One* enemy can do more harm than many friends can mend. And while I rejoice over the Queen's gracious sentiments towards me, I feel sad when I think of the many friends who would have rejoiced with me, and who are no more with us. Dean Stanley—he would have danced and wept, he could do that; we shall never see the like of him again—and Pearson (of Sonning), and Morier—they would all have hugged me; and many more—all gone before. If a few years are left to me I shall try to do some right honourable service, but I begin to feel that I cannot work as I used to do, and though I have still much to say, I shall not be able to do it or do it well. Well, we must not grumble, but rather rejoice, and go on. Please to present my dutiful regards to H.R.H. the Duchess. I imagine that some kind words of hers have done me good service.'

One of the letters of congratulation came from the Drill Sergeant of the Berkshire Volunteers, and the answer has been carefully cherished by the old man.

TO SERGEANT CUSS.

OXFORD, *May*.

'Those were bright and happy days when we were being drilled by you, and had our firing practice, and slept under the same tent—six of us—and it was raining all night. You were an excellent sergeant, though you told us, I remember, that "those gentlemen who think are very little use." Well, I believe, for all that, we have been of some use in setting an example; and old and shaky as I am now at seventy-two, I should be ready, at a moment's notice, to join our squad again, and sing

"Then let the French come over,
We'll greet them with three cheers,
And tell them, hey,
They'd better get away
From the Berkshire Volunteers."

'From an old comrade.'

On May 27 Max Müller gave an address before the Royal Society of Literature, on 'Coincidences,' chiefly on the many striking coincidences between Christianity and Buddhism. The address will be found in *Last Essays*, Series I. It called forth a good deal of criticism at the time, and Max Müller had hoped to republish it in a very extended form, and had amassed a good deal of material for the purpose. As the Buddhist Canon was written down a century before the Christian era, it is evident that *if* there were any borrowing, it was by Christianity from Buddhism; though it is possible that the coincidences in teaching may be accounted for by the universality of essential ethics. The Lord Chancellor, who was present, objected greatly to Max Müller's deductions. On the other hand, a venerable clergyman wrote to him: 'Don't despair; you have done a great work in your time, which will bear fruit, if not sooner, some 500 years hence. The progress of truth is very slow—the purchase of blood and sweat, as I suspect you have discovered in spite of your great successes.'

In June the Max Müllers went to Scotland, and after attending Lord Kelvin's jubilee at Glasgow, where they met again nearly all their kind friends of the University, they went to their daughter and son-in-law, who were spending the summer at Spitalhaugh, Sir James Fergusson's place in Peebleshire. The Trossachs were visited, and the Falls of the Clyde, and Hawthornglen, and Roslyn; a long day was spent at Melrose, Abbotsford, and Dryburgh; the Forth Bridge was carefully examined, and many Scotch friends came to stay and make, or renew, acquaintance with Max Müller.

To Herr George von Bunsen.

*Translation.* Spitalhaugh, *June* 25.

'I have been very anxious about you: one grows more and more lonely, and we have known each other for so many years that I felt as if another limb were about to be taken off when I heard what I heard about you. But your own letter is full of the old courage, and we must all accept the warning, when it comes, that the evening of life is meant for rest, for reflection, for retirement. I often say so to myself, and yet I cannot get any rest. There is always some fresh call to work, or what one imagines to be a call, and so I am busy again, printing a large book, let alone other tiresome things. I am busy with a second edition of my translation of Kant's *Critique*, according to the new text which the Berlin Academy is bringing out. The editor, Dr. Adickes, supplies me with the necessary material, and I find a great deal to alter. But even this is not enough; look at the July numbers of the *Fortnightly* and the *Nineteenth Century*, and in each number you will find something that may amuse you. I am staying in Scotland: delicious air and lovely views, besides four grandchildren. My son, too, was with me for a time, so I must not complain; and yet life is no longer easy, one's legs won't carry one as they once did, and one's work does not get on as it used to do. My memory no longer serves me as formerly. I must verify everything, and that worries me. Then I hum "Warte nur, balde!" How I came to be Right Honourable? I have no idea. I had no suspicion till I saw it in the *Times*. Is it the Queen? I don't know. Is it Lord Salisbury? I know nothing. Gladstone offered me knighthood years ago, which I humbly declined. Next week I am to kiss hands. Who would have thought that in 1847? Now, before all things, *fac ut valeas*. *Fac* means much. Keep your true affection for me through the evening of life.

'Ever yours.'

From Scotland Max had to go for a day to Windsor, to kiss hands and be sworn in as a member of Her Majesty's Most Honourable Privy Council. As he knelt before the Queen, she whispered to him in German, 'I am delighted to see you here, Professor!' On his return to Scotland, in writing to Mr. Malabari, he says: 'I was most graciously received by the Queen. I am at present the only non-political P.C., and I am afraid there will be jealousy among scientific people.' On Max Müller's return to Oxford he heard of the death of an old friend, Professor Ernst Curtius, who unearthed the Hermes of Olympia, and he writes to a friend he had seen in Scotland: 'It was so pleasant to meet again—but, oh, what gaps, how many empty places! One has to shake oneself to believe it all. I was rich in friends, I have hardly any left now.'

TO THE RIGHT HON. W. E. GLADSTONE.

OXFORD, *July* 12.

'Please to accept my very sincere thanks for your kindness in sending me your *Subsidiary Studies to Butler's Works.* I am very curious what solution Butler may give for the Great Questions. I am just now revising my translation of Kant's *Critique* for a new edition. It seems to me that the two thinkers are nearer to each other than would at first sight appear. Kant determines the limits of the possibility of human knowledge, and then breaks through the barriers he has himself created, relying on the Categorical Imperative or the Ought which serves as the foundation of his Practical Philosophy. Is not that something like Butler's position? But I shall read Butler, at least I hope so, but, alas! the books which I like to read I cannot, and the books which I do not like to read I must. Kant's text is more corrupt than that of any Greek classic. He lived at Königsberg, and his book was printed at Leipzig, and for half of it he saw no proof-sheets at all. His style is so fearful that one never knows what he may, and what he may not, allow himself to write. If, as translator, one makes his writing to construe, one is blamed; if one gives a faithful rendering, one is blamed also. I send you a copy of the current number of the *Fortnightly Review*, which contains a lecture of mine on "Coincidences." I should feel extremely grateful if you would look at it, and let me know what you think of it. We must come to some decision. To my mind, all these questions, in whatever way they are solved, do not touch the kernel of Christ's teaching. The Logos idea came from an Aryan, the Messiah idea from a Semitic source. Why should not other thoughts that pervaded the atmosphere of Palestine have left their traces in the Christian traditions of the first centuries? How it came about I cannot tell, neither could we tell how Christian ideas could have reached Buddhism in India. The chapter of accidents is long, but hardly long enough for this.'

In July and August Max Müller was at Droitwich, where he found Professor Palgrave, and the two old friends enjoyed being together, as in days long gone by. Max employed himself here in writing most of those papers which, after coming out in *Cosmopolis*, formed the first series of *Auld Lang Syne*.

To the Right Hon. W. E. Gladstone.

Droitwich, *July* 27.

'I always hesitate and hesitate whether I should write to you, and at last I succumb. But if you do not answer, I shall quite understand; I am, in a small way, a fellow sufferer. I cannot answer all the letters I receive, I cannot even read them all, not only because there are so many, but because they are written in so many languages which I do not understand. In spite of all my protests, people will look upon me as a second Mezzofanti—I never was, never wished to be. "Mezzofantiasis" is a very dangerous disease.

'I am sorry that you did not consider the evidence which I put together about the coincidences between Christianity and Buddhism sufficient to enable an intelligent jury—a jury is always intelligent—to give a verdict. However, I must confess that for years I have been very much perplexed myself; and even now, though I cannot resist the impression that there must have been historical contact between the Christian and the Buddhist intellectual atmospheres, I cannot explain how it came about, I cannot point out the exact historical channel through which the communication took place.

'You seem to think that the chapter of accidents is larger than we suppose, and you mention a number of coincidences between the traditions of ancient Greece and other countries—such as Egypt, Assyria, &c. But here we know that there was intellectual commerce between these countries, we know that the Phoenicians brought the Egyptian alphabet to Greece, and we know what influence a schoolmaster may exercise, though he professes to teach only the three R's. And secondly, are not the coincidences such that our common human nature would suffice to account for them? May not Madame Potiphar be matched even in our modern novels and our modern realities? As to speaking animals, they are found everywhere, and it is no wonder. Did not Schopenhauer say that, when he looked at his faithful dog, he was ashamed of mankind? There is a silent eloquence in a dog which many teachers have tried to translate into words, and what applies to dogs applies, I suppose, to Balaam's ass. The animal fable seems a phase through which most nations had to pass.

'I understand what you mean by Logos = Athene. The fundamental idea is the same, though mythologically I should say that the *Sophia* comes nearer to *Athene* than the Logos. Logos is a masculine, a man; and language, after her work is done in the creation of a word, reacts very powerfully on thought. Hence I doubt whether Logos could ever have become Athene, or Athene Logos. Besides, Athene is never creative, is she? Logos seems to me the true answer to Darwin and all his simperings about special acts of creation. I am a great admirer of Darwin, but he had no philosophical education, no Greek background. I knew him personally; he was charming, and very great in his own domain, but his so-called disciples have placed him in a false position, and it will take a long time before the old Logos takes its right place again, instead of a number of purely mechanical pretenders, such as Natural Selection, Survival of the Fittest, Panmixia, &c.—all mythological fictions, no better than the gods of Greece and India!'

To B. MALABARI, ESQ.

DROITWICH, *August* 5.

'I do not deny that the present situation is dangerous, but though people may threaten, they will think twice before they strike a blow at England. I wish there was more English feeling in India, and that it would show itself in words and deeds. What is the use of haggling over the pay of an Indian regiment in Egypt? It is a mere nothing compared with the true interests, the peace and prosperity of India. I can understand Indian patriots who wish to get rid of England altogether, but those who see what that would mean should take to their oar manfully, and pull a good English stroke. You are in the same boat—you can float together, and you would go down together. So it strikes me, though you know that I am generally on the Indian side.'

On returning to Oxford Max Müller had visits from two Indians, Vivekânanda, the Vedântist missionary who afterwards went to America to carry on a propaganda there, and Dharmapâla, the Buddhist teacher. The latter, who is a strikingly handsome man, appeared in his Buddhist yellow dress.

Early in September the Max Müllers were kept in considerable anxiety about their son, during the Armenian massacres. He wrote:—

THERAPIA, *August* 31, 1896.

'I have been more or less in the thick of it, as I had to go to town every day from Thursday to Sunday night. I had to go round to various English domiciles, which had been pillaged, or in which there were Armenians in hiding; and, what with the work, the heat, and the horrible sights I saw on all sides, I was fairly done up last night. On

Friday I paddled about in blood, in pillaged houses and foul back streets the whole morning. I can assure you that going down to town at seven or eight a.m., receiving deputations of terror-stricken British subjects, examining pillaged houses, pulling out Armenians half-dead from fright and hunger, hidden away in the foulest lofts, writing out a report as one steamed back in the launch or *stationnaire*, dining at any hour between nine and ten, and then helping to telegraph home an account of the day's work, was no joke. The experiences of one's friends here would make a volume beside which all tales of piracy and adventure pale. . . . I saw sights which made one's blood run cold: defenceless people clubbed to death, while the police and soldiers looked on inactive; cartloads of dead bodies, shapeless and mangled beyond recognition; then the horrible traces of massacre in the houses I had to visit, blood on the floors and roofs, on the window-sills, where they had thrown the bodies out, all down the staircases, where they had dragged them down; then everything smashed, not a table or chair or desk but was in atoms. What a horrible, fearful thing a human mob is when it is unchained! No pack of wolves would commit so much useless bloodshed.'

The father's quiet work at home was in strange contrast to these awful scenes.

To the Right Hon. W. E. Gladstone.

Oxford, *September* 11.

'It is certainly true, as you say, that Homer looks upon the speaking of animals as a *prodigium*. This is quite different from the animal fable, which Homer does not seem to know at all, though traces of it occur in Hesiod, Archilochus, Simonides, &c. With Homer the speaking of animals is the work of some god; it is Hera that makes Xanthos prophesy. In other cases the god himself assumes for a time an animal form, as Athene, but she does not speak after she has assumed the form of a bird, and even her metamorphosis causes θάμβος. So far there is agreement between the Homeric and the Biblical view. But is not the same idea expressed by the Roman Bos "locutus est"? Such ideas are more or less reasonable, and therefore may spring up everywhere. I quite accept your idea of Athene, but I hold that there was an earlier period in which the gods represented physical phenomena, and Athene represented the light of the morning, the Sanskrit *Ahana*. This view of the gods is as much removed from Homer as the Xoana were from Phidias, but it existed as an historical reality. As to Egyptian and Babylonian deities, they were never anterior to the

Greek names; they were engrafted on Greek rose-trees, but they did not improve them. I read your paper on the *Landmarks* with great interest, but I am much more sceptical as to any contact between the ancient Greeks and Babylonians and Egyptians. We can watch the whole growth of Greek mythology from Greek, or at all events from Âryan soil, and I claim Poseidon as well as the true Aphrodite as entirely Âryan. My first volume on *Mythology* is printed; I hope I shall finish the second before the year is over. It is a subject of absorbing interest, and I only wish I were younger to be able to do full credit to it.'

To Dr. Althaus.

*Translation.* 7, Norham Gardens, *October* 11.

'I was so glad to see your handwriting, and to gather from it that you are hale and strong. I am fairly well for my age (seventy-two), only one thing I need, and that is—rest. New obligations, new editions, new acquaintances, are always cropping up. Since yesterday our house is full of Siamese princes, the brothers of the King, his adjutant, the secretary of the Embassy and his retinue. It is interesting to make the acquaintance of these men. They brought me a complete edition of the *Tripitaka* from Bangkok, as a gift from the King. But of course the hours fly and do not return, and I have still so much on my mind which I should like to talk about, if only I had time and rest for doing so. Well, it is pretty much the same with all of us—poor *aegri mortales!*

'I am glad that you liked my musical recollections. I told some of them to my friend Sir John Stainer, who asked me to write them down, and I did this in a great hurry. I was asked to continue the recollections, but I have no notes, and so I have to depend entirely on my unreliable memory. I have no dates, and our memory alone is no chronicle, but unavoidably lapses into a mixture of poetry and reality, *Dichtung und Wahrheit*. So you see I can but give what lives in my memory. If it should be chronologically inaccurate, I cannot help it. Fortunately, I have my wife to help me. Do you know that George Bunsen is dying? Another tie will be gone; only a few remain. His was a fine nature; he has suffered much, and he was worthy of his father. Ah yes! Where are they? all gone!'

To his Cousin, Berndt von Basedow.

*Translation.* *January* 1, 1897.

'Many thanks for your good wishes for the New Year, which we heartily return. Unfortunately, one does not grow younger, and even I sometimes find work a burden. But I must not complain when one sees what happens to many when they reach their seventy-third year.

On the whole, we have done bravely! We are with B. They are living in his old home, near Gravesend; his property is here, and his tenants like to have him near them. The house is not so interesting as Ightham Mote, but very comfortable. The four children are all well, and a great delight to us. We ourselves have plans, if it gets any colder, for going to Naples, to warm our hands at Vesuvius. It is a long journey, but when we are over there, we shall stay with an American friend, who has a lovely palace, and where we can rest. I begin to find I am getting a little deaf, but that comes with old age, and one must bear it.'

It was whilst staying with his daughter that Max Müller heard of the death of his valued old friend George von Bunsen.

To his Son.

Wombwell Hall, *January* 4.

'I have just had a book on *Schleswig-Holstein*. It is historical, and gives letters from the Emperor and Bismarck; Bismarck, as usual, coming out very badly. What a *fiasco* he has turned out! I never believed in him. I knew how small he had proved himself towards his friends; and as to Sedan and all the rest, he had a splendid horse to ride, and proved himself a good jockey. He played Banco and won, that is all. If he were Chancellor still he would long ago have sent himself to prison, and rightly too. George Bunsen, who died the other day, was a dear friend of mine, and his death has been a great blow to me. He was one of the few of my true friends left. I could always trust him. He was delighted whenever anything good happened to me, and shared all my disappointments. He ought to have distinguished himself far more; but just at the most critical time of life, about twenty-five, his eyes gave way, and he had to rest for several years and take to farming. Afterwards he did much useful work in the Prussian Chamber, and in the Reichsrath, but chiefly on committees, and quietly. Bismarck hated him and all that bore the name of Bunsen, because they would not bend the knee. George, if anything, was too conscientious and too unyielding, if that is possible. A beautiful chapter of my life is closed there.'

The end of January Max Müller and his wife started for Paris and Rome. It was bitterly cold over the Mont Cenis route, and snow fell till Genoa was reached. At Rome a pleasant ten days was spent, seeing many friends and visiting many sights, and Max Müller was able to enjoy all he saw far more than in his first visit twenty-two years before, when he was so constantly ill. He now made personal acquaintance with Madame Wagner, the authoress of *La Pensée et la Parole*; and Count Balzani; Count de Gubernatis; Sir Clare Ford, at the Embassy; Mr. Stillman, the *Times* correspondent; Signor Guidi, an old friend from the days in Stockholm; and Mrs. Otto Siemens, a yet older friend, were amongst those with whom he had constant intercourse. From Rome the Max Müllers went on to Naples, to stay with their friend Major Henry Davis at his lovely place La Floridiana, situated high above the city, on a level with the castle St. Etnas. La Floridiana was built by Ferdinand II (Bomba) for his morganatic wife the Duchess of Floridiana. Whilst in Rome Max Müller had, through his friend Mr. Grissell, Chamberlain to the Pope, asked leave to present the *Sacred Books of the East* to His Holiness, and soon after his arrival at Naples heard through Cardinal Rampolla that 'the Pope would accept the gift with the greatest pleasure, as a most valuable contribution to the Vatican library.'

The house where Max Müller was staying was large and beautiful, a perfect Italian *palazzo*, though with every modern comfort of electric light and warm-air apparatus so judiciously applied as not to spoil the old foreign look of the whole surroundings. The large entrance-hall and broad marble staircase were always lined with palms and flowers in full bloom; whilst in the garden, when he arrived, about 8,000 camellia blooms of all shades hung on the trees. The view from the terrace at the bottom of the garden, across the city and bay to Capri, with Posilippo on the right and the promontory of Sorrento to the left, is one of the most exquisite in Europe, and was a constant delight to Max Müller. Here, on fine days, he would walk up and down, and in wet days in the long library, in earnest talk with his cultivated host. Though the Max Müllers had been in Naples twenty-two years previously, they now had time in their six weeks' visit at La Floridiana to see everything in a much more thorough and leisurely way. They made acquaintance with many of the Italian families, and formed a real friendship with Mr. Rendel and his family, and many pleasant hours were spent at his beautiful place, Maravale, overhanging the sea on the Posilippo promontory.

To the Right Hon. W. E. Gladstone.

La Floridiana, *February* 25.

'I gave orders before I left England for Messrs. Longmans to send you a copy of my two volumes on *Mythology*; whenever they reach you I should be glad if you would glance at them. They do not deal with what you mean by Olympian Religion. They refer to a much lower stratum of Âryan thought, presupposed, no doubt, by Greek Religion and Mythology, but separated from them by intervening strata that defy chronological definition. Compared with that antiquity, the antiquity of Babylon and Egypt shrinks to small proportions, though, in the absence of contemporary events, we shall never be able to determine the date of that Âryan formation which lies far beyond Homer, far beyond the Vedic poets. I have been obliged to take refuge here from the damp and the cold winds of Oxford. The weather here is quite perfect, and I hope you have derived the same benefit from the soft air of Cannes which I have from the sunshine of the Bay of Naples. I see Capri and Vesuvius from my window where I am writing.'

During the Max Müllers' visit, their host's dear old mother, who kept house for her son, and had welcomed his guests with hearty kindness, died after a few hours' illness. They were not allowed to leave, as the rest was so beneficial for Max Müller. Other friends were staying in the house, old friends of the host, Professor and Mrs. Welsch, from Dresden, and with them a warm friendship sprang up.

To his Son.

La Floridiana, *March* 12.

'I am very idle here, but the country is really too beautiful for any work, and I do not feel quite myself yet. Perhaps I never shall, and shall have to learn the lesson of being old, which is not so easy as one thinks.

'Last week we went to Paestum and Amalfi. The three Doric temples in sight of the sea are very imposing, and so full of thought. That is what one learns to admire more and more, not so much what one sees present, but what one sees behind, before such temples to Poseidon could have been conceived. And then one sees how in all the small inlets and bays the sea woos the earth (Poseidon-Demeter); hence, after the temple of Poseidon was built, and evidently a generation later, they built the temple to Demeter. . . . Two books on Rome have interested me very much, Zola's *Rome* and Marion Crawford's *Casa Braccio*, both very powerful, though the former is, as usual, "food for man and beast."'

Many letters reached Max Müller at this time on his work on *Mythology*. One friend wrote:—

'This I hope, that, whatever difference of opinion there may be between you and me, I may follow, at however great a distance, your example as an indefatigable worker. As a writer you are just the same as thirty or forty years ago. Your style, at seventy and more, has lost none of its freshness and spirit, and I enjoy the reading of your youngest work just as much as when I was charmed by the *History of Sanskrit Literature* and the *Chips*.'

On returning to Rome, a long day was spent in going over the Palatine with Signor Barnabei, who was conducting the excavations; and then the Max Müllers joined their friends the Welschs at Frascati, where ten days of great enjoyment were spent in seeing all the beautiful places on the Alban Hills, and in long rambles about the villas of Frascati. Two days, one at Nemi, and another at Tusculum, were days of special interest and delight to Max Müller, as were the two days spent at Tivoli and Hadrian's Villa. He was far stronger than when he left England, and enjoyed himself like a boy. A week was given to Perugia, which included a long interesting day at Assisi, and another week to Florence, and the Max Müllers then joined the Welschs at Venice.

To Major Henry Davis.

Frascati, *April* 4.

'I send this letter to London, where I suppose you have by this time safely arrived. The delightful days of the Floridiana are over, and they have not only left a charming page in my recollections, but have evidently done me a great deal of good. I really begin to feel well again, and ought perhaps to return to Oxford and my work, but Rome and Italy altogether prove too attractive, and I cannot yet make up my mind to return to our inclement climate. I have often thought of you, and wished we could have had a little exchange of thought about Henry Drummond's book. I have been much interested in it, as showing a certain phase of thought which is evidently widely spread and popular. On certain portions of his book, particularly the biological portions, I am no judge, but I suppose he may be trusted there. But when he comes to the Dawn of Mind and the Evolution of Language, he is simply ignorant. He does not see that communication and language are different things, and dwells on the well-known instances of onomatopoeia as if they could explain the origin of conceptual language. Language begins where onomatopoeia ends. There are many instances like tick tick, puff puff, &c., but what have they to do with over 250,000 English words? Whence come our numerals, our propositions? whence such words as tree, sky, sea, &c.? Antennae language is one thing, but Homer's poems are *un autre genre*, and there is no transition from one to the other, even if the earth had been inhabited before the Glacial Period. Why write about things which we do not know? As to his struggle of love, or his Altruism, or Atheism (horrible words), there is some truth in it, but if it affects evolution at all, it can only affect the later evolution of man. Among some races it did not even do this; and, after all, the care for children and the pride in children may be included in the struggle for life, for to have children meant to be strong, meant to be able to defend oneself, nay, love of children involves even now a certain amount of selfishness. To have a quiverful of them meant to be a commander-in-chief, and in the *Veda* a prayer for children is a prayer for strong men, a prayer for strength, without any sentimental background. However, I like that part of his book, but I also understand why scientific men of business like Huxley would have nothing to say to the book. I have written another article on the *Pferdebürla*, and have offered my *peccavi* to his departed spirit, though he would probably strongly object to this dignity. We are enjoying the surroundings of Frascati immensely, only to-day we have had a regular downpour. If it is fine to-morrow, we mean to go to Nemi. Mr. and Mrs. Welsch are here, and we have enjoyed their society very much. I am sorry we shall probably have to part next Thursday. Our own plans are uncertain.

'Yours very truly and gratefully.'

The reference to the *Pferdebürla* in the letter above needs explanation. In the preceding year, Max received many letters on an article which he had written on Celsus in the *Deutsche Rundschau*, in 1895. The most remarkable of these letters was from a German in America, who signed himself 'Pferdebürla,' 'horse-herd,' which Max Müller thought so striking that he wrote a long and careful answer, and printed both that and the letter from the *Pferdebürla* in the November number of the *Deutsche Rundschau*, 1896. This called forth many replies, though none from the *Pferdebürla*. One of these, signed 'Ignotus Agnosticus,' was answered and printed, and the whole grew gradually into a small volume, published early in 1899, called *The Pferdebürla, Questions of the Day, answered by F. Max Müller*. This will soon appear in an English translation.

The pleasure of the time at Venice was added to by the arrival of Max Müller's cousins, the von Basedows, and the whole party witnessed the arrival of the Prince and Princess of Naples, on their first visit to Venice. The royal pair were met at the station by all the noblesse of Venice, in their old state gondolas, with the state liveries, and they escorted the royal *barca* to the Palazzo Reale. The gondolas were coloured in every shade of pink, yellow, blue, and green, picked out in gold or silver, and the *gondoliere* wore the colours of their gondola, with huge black Charles II wigs.

To his Son.

VENICE, *May* 1.

'Things in Italy are not so bright as they look. No doubt the *attentat* has made the King popular for a time, but there is widespread dissatisfaction, the army feels the defeat in Africa, and the taxation is very heavy. Besides, the priests are always at their work, and still hope for a return of the old régime. The state of religion is really worse than pagan; everybody knows it, but nothing happens. There was another ironclad launched here this week, but I expect there will be a financial crash. Money you see none, nothing but paper.'

On the way home, a few days were given to Milan, and from here Max wrote to Mr. Grissell about the *Sacred Books of the East* for the Pope.

MILAN, *May* 11.

'Nothing could have been better arranged than the presentation of the *Sacred Books of the East* to H.H. the Pope. Unfortunately I could not stay at Rome to present the books in person, and to ask for a personal audience. When I wrote to the Vice-Chancellor as Chairman of the Clarendon Press to have a copy of the fifty volumes forwarded to Rome, the Curators of the Press decided to send the present in their own name and in that of the University. This would, of course, give more prestige to the gift, and place the Pope's opinions on the subject in their proper light. The Vice-Chancellor wrote in person to Cardinal Rampolla, and by this time, I doubt not, the books have arrived.

'Accept once more my best thanks for the trouble you have taken. I believe nothing could have been done better, and I am proud to think that my collection will have a place in the Papal Library, and go to the Propaganda with the implied approval of the Pope.'

To Professor Bühler.

*Translation.* 7, Norham Gardens, Oxford, *June* 11, 1897.

'I have just printed a new edition of the *Dhammapada*. There was much *written* in India in the first century B.C., now they actually intend to make Pânini introduce writing. I think above all things we have to cling to facts, the inductions belong to another special branch. It seems remarkable that the introduction of writing should have made so little impression in India. It was surely a greater discovery than that of powder and steam, but it is taken for granted, and Brâhman as inventor of letters is only of secondary consideration. But it was impossible to keep such a light hidden under a bushel, though one cannot deny that there is a pause in India, as well as in Greece, between writing for documents and history, and writing for literature. Here writing would only have dulled the ear. So I still think that we had best cling to the inscriptions which we already possess. We cannot deny that the Senart Inscriptions open out a new channel; but if it leads to Mongolia, we get, after all, only to Semitism again. Had I but time and strength, I should like much to treat the question once again; on the whole there would not be much to change, only a good many things to add, for which we have to thank you. However, one gets old, and it is better to be silent than to commit blunders. The young ones ought to progress as we have done when we were young. But they want courage and perseverance.

'And when are you coming to England? In July the King of Siam is coming; he has taken the house of a cousin of my wife's for ten weeks. He is an intelligent man, and he might collect inscriptions in Suva*m*ad*o*sa. There is anti-Buddhistic strata there, where there is much to be dug out still. I have not yet seen the last manuscripts from near Fayum; they are said to contain much that is new. The finder, Mr. Grenfell, is also a cousin and a very clever man.'

Just after his return, Max Müller was elected a Member of

the Royal Academy of Sciences at Vienna, and to this the following letter refers:—

TO PROFESSOR BÜHLER.

*Translation.* OXFORD, *no date.*

'I have this moment received the telegram signed by you and your colleagues. It was a great joy to receive this great distinction. *Laudari a viris laudatis* does us good, even when we are standing in the last *âsrama.* Please give your colleagues, and as I may proudly add, my colleagues, my warmest thanks. I have only just returned from the South, and I feel Italy has refreshed me bodily and spiritually, but my irritable throat still bids me be careful. How long it may still last, I do not know, but as long as it lasts I shall continue to work. I have just finished your essay on quotations from the *Purânas.* How strong and how tough tradition must have been in India, to preserve such literal fragments! Alas, that no Fayum, which has just produced again such wonderful treasures, can be looked for there! Well, we must be content with tradition, which has nowhere produced such wonders as in India. And yet people still shrink from believing, though they might see it with their own eyes in India, that memory is better than parchment. Again, many thanks to you and those who signed the telegram. I should like best to go at once to Vienna, but I have rested for six months, and I am obliged to take up my work again now.'

TO HIS SON.

WOMBWELL HALL, *June* 13.

'I am so pleased that you and Moritz de Bunsen are together at Constantinople—who could have guessed that fifty years ago? I feel sure you want change, both physically and socially. You live in a rude kind of society, and do not see the finer shades of character with which you will have to deal. There is a diplomacy with the outer world, but there is a diplomacy with our inner world also, to satisfy all interests, to make hostile powers work together, to bring conflicts to a happy issue. For all that, you want to move in a different atmosphere, and more particularly to come in contact with ladies, who are not mere slaves, but, as Browning said, half angel, half bird. You will receive from them what you can afford to give, respect, love, help, as you deserve it. But depend upon it, your ideal of woman can never be too high. You elevate a woman by looking up to her, and with a will you can make everything of her, an angel or a devil.'

The Max Müllers were in London for the Diamond Jubilee,

and Max took charge of his wife and another lady at night, on foot, to see the illuminations, piloting them through the crowds, quite forgetting his seventy-three and a half years.

To Professor Welsch.

*Translation.* Oxford, *June* 28.

'I am much moved by the news of the death of your daughter, and must express my true sympathy in words. It is strange how close death has twice been to us, in so short a time. I had lately often thought of your daughter, and her card has been lying on my writing-table. . . . For such partings there is no comfort unless one truly realizes that it is no parting; those who are gone are nearer to us than the living—all earthly disturbances and differences have ceased. But the wound hurts one, and can be quieted only by perfect stillness.'

Mr. Andrew Lang paid a visit to Norham Gardens this year, and Max Müller and he had some talk on the ethnological and philological explanations of mythology, which Max Müller looked on as allies, not enemies. The visit led to further correspondence:—

To A. Lang, Esq.

Oxford, *July* 3.

'I am always glad if some very ancient thoughts can be discovered among modern savages, but you must excuse my scholar's conscience, if I don't accept even all that Pausanias says, much less what Herr von Wartegg saw. Still, let it all grow against the harvest. Your *Palaeozoic* myths are quite as useful as my Neozoic; the difficulty arises in the Mesozoic stratum. With regard to the passage where you thought my note contradicted the rest, surely you must have found how often my notes are not simply references in support of one view, but *ad notams*, meaning, "Consider, however," &c. They generally came from marginal notes, and are intended to be useful to readers in forming their opinions. I have my own view, but I treat the opinions of others with respect. However, my bastions are there, and I shall be glad to see them tested by any amount of bombarding.'

To the Same.

*July* 8.

'. . . I don't say that I should go to the stake for it, but I am perfectly certain that some good may be got from the study of savages for the elucidation of Âryan myths. I never could find out why I should be thought to be opposed to Agriology, because I was an

Âryologist. *L'un n'empêche pas l'autre.* Still less could I understand why you should have attacked me, or rather my masters, without learning Sanskrit, which is by no means so difficult as people imagine. You must have a rapier to fight a man who has a rapier, otherwise it becomes a row. I did not mean to imply that the buying *mundus* has been kind to me (*Mythology*). I have not even asked Longmans how the book sells. I meant my critics. Even the *Folklore Journal*, from which I expected the wildest counterblast, has been very fair. *Fraser* has never attacked me, and I have always touched my hat to him. He works his mine, I work mine: why should we quarrel?'

The summer brought, as usual, many foreign visitors to Oxford. After the Jubilee came the Bahadur of Khetri, and his son-in-law the Rajah Kumar of Shakpura, on their way to Birmingham. They were in full native dress, and covered with jewels. They were followed by Sri Rajah, a Zemindar of high position, and Mr. Gooneratne, who attended the Jubilee as delegate from Ceylon, and who proved a most agreeable acquaintance.

It was a great interest to Max Müller to attend, with many other friends from Oxford, the gathering at Ascot in honour of the Golden Wedding of Dean and Mrs. Liddell. The old friends never met again. Another interest of Long Vacation was the Summer University Extension Meeting at Oxford, for the opening of which Lord Ripon stayed in Norham Gardens. A considerable number of foreigners came to Oxford to attend the lectures, and the Max Müllers had two afternoon gatherings especially for them, besides small parties of them to luncheon. Max Müller attended the evening gatherings, and though he gave no lecture or address himself, he took more part than he had ever done before in the social pleasures of the meeting.

TO HIS SON.

OXFORD, *September* 3.

'I wonder whether you remember the anniversary of to-day, when dear Mary was taken away from us? Who could tell why? Who could understand it and account for it? And yet we must learn to see a meaning in everything, we must believe that as it was, it was right. No doubt we cannot always see cause and effect, and it is well that we cannot. It is quite true, as you say, that we do not always get our deserts. And yet we must believe that we do—only if we know it, the whole fabric of the world would be destroyed, there would be neither virtue nor vice in the whole world, nothing but calculation. We should avoid the rails laid down by the world, because we should know the engine would be sure to come and mangle us. In this way the world holds together, and it could not in any other way.'

During a visit to Droitwich in September, with his wife and daughter, Max employed himself in preparing *Auld Lang Syne*, Series I, for press. The end of September he had two interviews with the King of Siam, first in Oxford, and two days later at the Mansion House, and was able to tell him that the arrangements for the second volume of the *Sacred Books of the Buddhists* were complete. 'The King,' wrote Max Müller, 'was most delightful. I sat by him, and we had plenty of talk. All went off well.'

The following interview, which was given in a religious paper this year, probably the *Christian World*, is of interest:—

'"My interest in all religions," the Professor remarked, "is chiefly historical; I want to see what has been, in order to understand what is. Our religion is certainly better and purer than others, but in the essential points all religions have something in common. They all start with the belief that there is something beyond, and they are all attempts to reach out to it."

'"Do you distinguish between human guesses and Divine revelation?"

'"I believe in one revelation only—the revelation within us, which is much better than any revelations that come from without. Why should we look for God and listen for His voice outside us only, and not within us? Where is the temple of God, or the true kingdom of God?"

'"The inward voice doesn't give us much information about future life, for instance—does it?"

'"That inward voice never suggested or allowed me the slightest doubt or misgiving about the reality of a future life. If there is continuity in the world everywhere, why should there be a wrench and annihilation only with us? It will be as it has been—that is the lesson we learn from nature: *how* it will be we are not meant to know. There is a very old Greek saying to the effect—to try to know what the gods did not wish to tell us, is not piety. If God wished us to know what is to be, He would tell us. Darwin has shown us that there is continuity from beginning to end."

'"I believe in the continuity of self. If there were an annihilation or complete change of our individual self-consciousness we might become somebody else, but we should not be ourselves. Personally, I have no doubt of the persistence of the individual after death, as we call it. I cannot imagine the very crown and flower of creation being destroyed by its author. I do not say it is impossible; it is not for us to say either yes or no; we have simply to trust, but that trust or faith is implanted in us, and is strengthened by everything around us."'

It is uncertain to which year exactly the following account belongs, but it would probably be this year, when so many Indians visited England.

'One day at tea at Balliol,' writes a friend of Max Müller, 'we met two or three distinguished Indians. One of them said to me, speaking gratefully of Professor Max Müller:—

'"He has done more than any living man to spread the knowledge of English in India. It is difficult for English people to realize the variety of languages in India, and how little one part of India knows the language of another part. But we all want to be able to read our Sacred Books. We now widely study English, in order to read Max Müller; though there have been imitators since, the praise must belong first to Max Müller, who invented and worked out the idea of translating our Sacred Books into English."'

To his Son.

Oxford, *November* 28, 1897.

'You certainly have grown older and more serious. No wonder, considering what you had to go through! You'll understand now my old motto *Das Leben ist ernst* ("Life is earnest"), though that does not prevent us from enjoying what can be enjoyed. I wish you would grow very fond of somebody, or something: that is, after all, the secret of enjoying life; call it a wife, or a hobby, or some passion or other, even a passion for statistics, or something of the kind, but a passion. Otherwise life becomes humdrum. Dressing and washing in the morning, and undressing at night, one gets so tired of it!'

To Mr. Takakusu.

Oxford, *December* 2.

'I am always glad to see the *Hansei Zas-shi*[1], but I wish it con-

[1] An illustrated journal in English.

tained more from you and from Nanjio. I should like to know what you are doing, and how far Sanskrit scholarship is making progress in Japan. It is not enough to acquire knowledge, we must try to make it useful. There are several things to be done, by trying to find out what Sanskrit texts were known and studied by I-tsing and by Hiouen-thsang. I want you to found a school of Sanskrit in Japan, and arouse an interest in genuine Buddhism, particularly Hînayâna. You and Nanjio might do a great deal.

'I have published my *Mythology*, two volumes, and I am now writing a *History of Indian Philosophy*; so, you see, I do not yet give in. I have also published a new edition of my translation of Kant's *Critique of Pure Reason*. I should like to send you a copy, but I do not know how, it is a big book.

'I hope that you and Nanjio are both well, and that you keep up your Sanskrit and work together—two are better than one. I hope I shall stay in England this winter. If Japan were not so far, I should like to spend the winter there. Give my love to Nanjio.'

To his Cousin, Berndt von Basedow.

*Translation.* Wombwell Hall, *December* 23.

'I send you, from here, my best wishes for Christmas and the New Year, and many thanks that you remembered my birthday. I hope we shall yet meet again in this life. Old age indeed, with its difficulties, warns us of his approach. I am an old man of seventy-four. Still, I am fairly well, but I must take care of myself. We are here with B. for Christmas, and her children are our great delight. Only think, father, mother, and the eldest boy Max, are all three just gone out with the foxhounds; so it goes on, one generation after another. Wilhelm was here in the autumn, but had to return to Constantinople; he comes back in the spring, and probably goes to Washington. He longs to leave Turkey, after all the horrors he went through there with the massacres. We shall scarcely get to Washington, that is too far off for an old man. Best wishes to your wife and children. I used to send them to *all* relations in Dessau, but how few are left there! Now take good care of yourself. So courage for another year!'

Max Müller was already hard at work on his last large book, *Six Systems of Indian Philosophy*, and was printing *Auld Lang Syne*, Series I. Though he was by way of resting during his visit to his daughter, his large correspondence alone sufficed to occupy many hours each day. He had for some time given up all work of an evening after dinner, and his wife read a great deal aloud to him. He had never indulged in novel-reading, and now enjoyed hearing Dickens, Thackeray, George Eliot, Lord Lytton, and other standard authors, besides the best novels of the day. Lord Roberts's *Life in India* had been listened to with keen interest; Mrs. Steel's Indian novels, too, were a source of great pleasure; Stanley Weyman's historical tales, Lucas Malet's and Mrs. Humphry Ward's novels, were among those he cared for; and in the very last months of his life Rider Haggard's *Jess* delighted him.

The year before, Mr. N. M. Hennessey, minister of the New Congregational Church, Birmingham, who had long been a student of Max Müller's works, sent him a kind Christmas greeting, which he renewed this year, saying at the same time that he was about to christen his little son 'Max Müller.' 'When he is old enough, I will tell him why he bears the name, why I love it, and how I loved its owner for the books that made me grow.' In sending the following to the editor, Mr. Hennessey wrote: 'The letters are treasures, which I hoard with a miser's love amongst the dearest of the few treasures I have.'

To the Rev. N. M. Hennessey.

Wombwell Hall, *December* 30.

'A kind thought or a kind word and deed always does one good, and I thank you sincerely for your Christmas letter. May your son prosper and never lose touch with a higher world, while making himself useful in this lower world, loving his fellow creatures and loved by them! Though I am an old man now, I am still able to work, and enjoy it more than ever. Just now I am hard at work at a *History of Ancient Indian Philosophy*, six systems, some very strange, some very wonderful. I read in Tennyson's *Life*: "The philosophers of the East had a great fascination for my father, and he felt that the Western religions might learn from them much of spirituality." They might—but will they? People will dally with Esoteric Buddhism, Mahâtmas, and every kind of absurdity, but will they discover in those philosophies some of the many roads that lead towards and converge on truth?'

About this time Max Müller received a letter from Bombay, telling him that a very wealthy native, Mr. Tata, was anxious to devote a large sum of money to enable his countrymen to take advantage of University teaching in England, more especially in physical science. Max Müller consulted his old friend Sir Henry Acland on the matter, who took up the idea warmly, and, notwithstanding his age and failing health, gave himself great trouble in thinking out some plan for giving effect to Mr. Tata's generous ideas.

To Sir Henry Acland.

Wombwell Hall, *December* 31.

'I wonder at your zeal and enterprise. If you really want to begin a new crusade, I know the very man you ought to see. A highly cultivated Hindu, who has £10,000 a year, soon to become £15,000 a year, to be spent entirely on higher education, independent experiment, and research, for the benefit of India. I may know what is desirable for India, he knows what is possible. I gave him some hints, but I have never been an agitator, and am of no use for that kind of work. The money is as yet quite unfettered, and I only hope the man is still in England. He called on me at Oxford some three or four weeks ago. But I cannot even remember his address, being away from Oxford. If you care to see him, let me know, and I will try to get at him, if still in England. The money seemed quite safe, being derived from inhabited land in India. His, or rather my idea was, to get young Hindus to Oxford, to promise them a career in India, give them any amount of laboratories, &c., and employ them for practical purposes, and for becoming centres of life and leading in their own country. Now, if I could get you both together, something might come of it.

'Yours affectionately, and with many good wishes for 1898.'

# CHAPTER XXXIV

## 1898–1899

Death of Dean Liddell. *Auld Lang Syne*, I. Tilak. Collected Works. Death of Professor Bühler. Ems. Death of Fontane. *Râmakrishna's Sayings. Indian Philosophy. Auld Lang Syne*, II. Ems. Beginning of illness. Last visits to Segenhaus, Dessau, and Dresden. Alarm of German doctors. Return to Wombwell and Oxford. Oriental Congress at Rome. Message to Brahma Somâj. Attack at Oxford Diocesan Conference. Gradual convalescence.

THE new year found Max Müller and Sir Henry Acland busy about the proper use of Mr. Tata's money. Mr. Padshah, a friend of Mr. Tata, was in England at this time, and Max Müller and Sir Henry had various visits from him.

To Sir Henry Acland.

*January 2.*

'I think your letter will produce a good effect on the people at Bombay, and also on Mr. Padshah, who seems inclined to listen, though he has not much to say for himself. A good beginning might be made at once, by arranging a course of studies (not lectures only) for Indian students on sanitary matters, with special reference to plague, cholera, &c. Other things will follow, but India must stand in front, and special privileges be given to Indian students. I shall be glad to help, for something will have to be done for other subjects also, if that unfortunate Indian Institute did not stand in the way—bricks *et praeterea nihil!*

'Yours affectionately.'

Later in the year Max writes again to Sir Henry :—

'Padshah called on me again yesterday, and I found him deeply impressed with the Museum, &c. He asked me to write down a scheme as to how to spend Mr. Tata's money. He says that the idea for sanitation is accepted, but he thinks that the Government ought to help, which is not at all likely. I thought an Indian Laboratory would be a possible plan, but, as I told you before, the Indian Institute acts like a red rag. What all the Indians say is, that the rich Oxford University went round with the hat, promising to help Indian students at Oxford, and all the money they subscribed in India was spent in bricks and stuffed animals. That is why they do not want any Indian money to go to Oxford. However, an Indian Laboratory would be a different thing, and I shall certainly try again.'

The money was eventually used in India, as Mr. Tata declined to expend any more Indian money in Oxford.

Hardly had Max Müller settled again at home than he heard of the death of his valued friend, Dean Liddell. In a letter dated January 24, to Prince Christian, he writes: 'The death of Dr. Liddell is a great loss to me. Liddell's influence in Oxford was very valuable. The vulgar were ashamed of themselves before him, and rough natures were dumb in his presence. I have never known a straighter man at Oxford, perfectly trustworthy, simple-minded, and just to everybody. Such men are getting scarce.'

*Auld Lang Syne*, Series I, came out early this year, and had a great success. The whole first edition was sold to the trade before the day of publication, the second was sold out in a short time, and a third was published. This is now out of print. Max Müller was much amused by a letter from a man in America, demanding that every word of German should be translated in the next edition, and the Royalty Recollections entirely left out. 'They will be considered very objectionable here; you will lose the good opinion of every American who reads your book, by your toadying to royalty—it is unmanly. For your own sake, you should cut out all that foolish, child-like, unmanlike toadyism.' To this Max Müller, in writing to the American publisher, says, 'I thought that all were men and brothers in the Great Republic.' The book was well received by all parties. One Church paper called it 'without exaggeration the most delightful book of reminiscences that has ever come into our hands. Another charm of the book, besides its rich variety, is the total absence of *arrière-pensée*. The author has no spites, nor is there a word that could wound the feelings of any.' And the *Times* spoke of the reminiscences as 'genial in tone, full of interest, and recorded in that easy, graceful style which the Professor has long made his own.'

The following letter shows the position taken at this time by Max Müller with regard to Tilak, who had been sent to prison for writing seditious articles at the time that the people of Bombay and Poona were so excited and unsettled by the plague relief measures as to murder a Government servant. Max Müller was blamed in England for advocating mercy, but the release of Tilak had a good effect.

To Sir John Lubbock.

Oxford, *February* 11.

'Many thanks for your letter. My interest in Tilak is certainly that of a Sanskrit scholar, for though I do not agree with the arguments put forward in his *Oñon, or Researches into the Antiquity of the Vedas* (Bombay, 1893), I cannot help feeling sorry that we should lose the benefit of his labours. I sent him my edition of the *Rig-veda*, but I am told now that he is not allowed to read even his Bible and Prayer-book in prison.

'You see, from the wording of our petition, that we do not question the justice of the sentence. Personally, I have wondered for years at the licence allowed to the native Press. But the warning has now been given, and none too soon, though I do not believe that there is any sedition lurking in India at present, not even in the hearts of such men as Tilak. I thought that the Government might possibly like such a petition at the present moment. It seems odd that the murderer was an ignorant fanatic, who could not even read. Such fanatics will always exist in a country like India, but it would be dangerous to identify them with the loyal, or at least contented, population of India.'

The collected edition of Max Müller's works began to appear early this year, a volume each month, and by December the four volumes of *Gifford Lectures*, the *Hibbert Lectures*, *Introduction to the Science of Religion*, *India—What can it teach us?* and four volumes of *Chips*, were published. The collection was continued, and there are now eighteen volumes out. In his preface Max Müller says:—

'This collected edition will serve to place the chief object of all my literary labours in a clear light. During the last fifty years I have never lost sight of the polestar that guided my course from the first. I wanted to show that, with the new materials placed at our disposal during the present century,... it has become possible to discover what may be called historical evolution, in the earliest history of mankind. ... At the present moment it may truly be said that what is meant by evolution, or continuous development, has now been proved to exist in the historical growth of the human mind quite as clearly as in any of the realms of objective nature.... Language, mythology, religion, nay, even philosophy can now be proved to be the outcome of a natural growth, or development, rather than of intentional efforts, or of individual genius.'

To Madame Manacéine (a Russian lady who had called on Max Müller in Oxford).

*Translation.* Oxford, *March* 11.

'My sincere thanks for your kind remembrance, and for your book on *Sleep*—a subject full of interest for me. *Sleep* has spoilt many a sleep for me, when I have meditated upon it so as to find what "Sleep" really is. But, alas! our perception ceases as soon as sleep sets in. All that we are able to do is to search into its conditions, its hindrances and its helps, &c. But what "Sleep" really is, we shall be as little able to discover, as what Life is and what Death is. Your definition of Sleep is *repos de la conscience*. Certainly, it is that, but that is only a sign of it, it is not the thing itself. Who is it that sleeps? Certainly not the self-consciousness, but the *Self* that is conscious. What can be defined of this *Self*? That it is, that it perceives, and nothing besides. This perception, however, is the result of a development. We begin with a deep sleep, without perception; we proceed to a dream sleep; and then awake, with the help of the sunlight, to perception. These seem to me to be the three natural stages—deep sleep = darkness, dream sleep = dusk, morning light = awakening, perception. The outcome of perception is the development of the so-called thinking, formation of logic, word-thoughts, addition and subtraction of these word-thoughts, and so on, to conclusion and judgement. Please excuse this sketchy programme; I can say at least so much for it, that the Indian philosophers use the same terminology.

'I have read your book from beginning to end, though I am deeply occupied with a very different work, but as we sleep so much more than we are awake, I could not put down the book. When we come to think how words, with all their roots and fibres, penetrate the soil of our consciousness, the struggle of a hypnotized person against the *uttered* word seems very natural, it recalls to mind many old nerve vibrations. As every word includes its opposite, i.e. black = not white, straight = not crooked, we need not call to aid Atavistic influences in order to explain bad dreams. In using affirmation we use negation, and these harmonic or inharmonic vibrations sound together in our dreams. It seems to me that we treat our Atavi badly; everything for which we do not feel inclined to pay we put to their account, and what is good we put to our own.'

To his Son.

Oxford, *March* 23.

'You cannot escape from old age, whether it comes slowly or suddenly, but it comes unawares, and you suddenly feel that you cannot walk or jump as you used to do; and even the muscles of the mind don't hold out as they used. Well, so it was meant to be, and it will be pleasant to begin again with new muscles, and to take up new work. After seeing a good deal of life, I still think the greatest satisfaction is work: I do not mean drudgery, but one's own findings out. I am at work again on my *Indian Philosophy*. The plan of bringing out a series of histories of philosophies for different countries has come to an end, but I am glad I did what I did, though rather in a hurry, and I can now work at it again quietly, and make it more complete.'

This letter refers to a scheme started by Professor Knight, of St. Andrews, some three years previously, for which Max Müller began his *History of Indian Philosophy*, but the business part of the plan had not been well considered, and was found impracticable.

To the Rev. C. E. Beeby.

Oxford, *March* 24.

'Though I have not yet been able to finish your book (*Creed and Life*), I do not like to wait any longer before thanking you for having sent it to me, and for having written it. I have read it with great interest and satisfaction, and I hope it may produce an impression on your fellow workers among the clergy of the Church of England. I have seldom felt in such complete agreement with an author, as when reading your sermons. May you have strength to carry on your battle! The harvest is plenteous, but the labourers are few. Stanley's place is not yet filled.'

In sending the above to the editor, Mr. Beeby writes, March, 1901:—

'As you may know, my *Creed and Life* did not receive the welcome he wished for it. On the other hand, I was denounced in no unsparing terms, and prosecution was threatened. Meanwhile, I was treated as a leper by most of my clerical brethren. My faithful band of disciples which centre round my little village church, were greatly encouraged by the generous letter I received from your husband. We felt that his judgement on the subject I had treated was incomparably valuable beyond those of my assailants (I cannot call any of them critics, for in no case was there any attempt to meet me in argument); especially did we appreciate his words, "May you have strength to carry on your battle!" for I was hard pressed, and suffered a good deal. We felt that he knew—who had devoted a lifetime to the steady pursuit of the true—the pain and anxiety involved in making the stand that we were making. It gave us the courage we needed, to come in contact with such a true man, though only by letter, in view of the ignorance and bigotry of the many, and the cowardice and vacillation of others in high position. What a power is the personal character! Professor Max Müller's singlemindedness and integrity will remain a continual inspiration and support to others besides myself, who thank God and take courage from his example.'

To his Son (who had been in Palestine).

Oxford, *April* 9.

'I have had to give up many of these dreams, but somehow one learns to see with the mind and imagination what we cannot see with the eyes: nay, in many cases I believe imagination is truer than what you see. People go to Jerusalem to see the place of some of the miracles, and they do not see the greatest of miracles, that out of that small town, in a small country, there should have risen a light to light the whole world. To learn the lesson of small beginnings is good for everybody, and particularly so for those who are engaged in diplomacy, and who often forget the small factors, and imagine that history is made by large battalions.'

Max Müller had a great shock this year in the death, by drowning, of his friend and fellow labourer, Professor Bühler, of Vienna. He mourned him as a friend, and deeply lamented the loss to Sanskrit studies. 'He was always straightforward, there was nothing mean or selfish in him,' wrote Max Müller. 'He was for many years the very centre of Sanskrit scholarship; he helped us, guided us, and corrected us in our different researches.' Max Müller never ceased to feel his loss. He often consulted him about the *Sacred Books of the East*, even volumes in which Dr. Bühler had no personal concern, and his advice was readily given, and was always valuable and to the point.

During April Max Müller received a letter from a lawyer in Rochester, New York, telling him that a Club of Philology and Language was about to be started in that city, a gentleman having left a large sum for the purpose of publishing works on language. 'In view,' says the writer, 'of the fact that you are the greatest living philologist, we want very much to name our club for you,' and he begs for suggestions for the conduct of the club. Later in the year, the writer reports that the Max Müller Club is making solid progress on the lines that Max Müller had suggested to them, a study of American vernaculars, which we know had long been a subject of great interest to him, though it lay outside his own line of research.

Max Müller had still constant work with the *Sacred Books of the East*; he was also collecting the *Sayings of Râmakrishna*, a Hindu saint, for publication, and he found the enlarged form of the *Six Systems of Indian Philosophy* gave him more labour than he had expected. He was very tired, and went for change to Eastbourne, paying on his way home a pleasant visit to the Frederick Verneys, who then had a delightful place in Burnham Beeches.

To HIS SON.

OXFORD, *June* 3.

'"Life is earnest" is a very old lesson, and we are never too old to learn it. "Life is an art," is Goethe's doctrine, and there is some truth in it also, as long as art does not imply artful or artificial. Huxley used to say the highest end of life is action, not knowledge. There, as you know, I quite differ. First knowledge, then action, and what a lottery action is! The best intentions often fail, and what is done to-day is undone to-morrow. However, we must toil on, and do what every day brings us, and do it as well as we can, and better, if possible, than anybody else.'

To C. J. LONGMAN, ESQ.

OXFORD, *June* 10.

'I have ready a *History of the Six Systems of Indian Philosophy*;

it would make a volume like my *Gifford Lectures*. There is no book on the subject in English, German or French, so this ought to sell. I am ready with *Râmakrishna's Sayings*, but have not received the answer I expect from the Brahmavâdin, so I must wait. The second volume of *Auld Lang Syne*, "My Indian Friends," now appearing in *Cosmopolis*, will be ready by the end of the year. This, too, ought to sell fairly well. At the end of all, I see a separate volume of *Essays on Philosophy and Religion*, looming in the distance. This is not bad for a man of seventy-four, but who knows what may come of it?'

On June 11 Max Müller was at the opening of the buildings of Reading College by the Prince of Wales, and the luncheon given afterwards by Lord Wantage. It was the last public function that he ever attended. He felt increasingly that what strength he had must be kept for his work, and that gatherings of this sort were for younger men. He had had many friends staying with him through the term, and dinner and luncheon parties at home, but he dined out very seldom, and after this term not at all. During Commemoration he went to his grandchildren, whilst their parents were abroad.

This summer Max Müller received from Mysore an earnest entreaty to bring out a cheap edition of the *Rig-veda*, as there was a demand for it and the *Upanishads* in a less expensive form. The writer stated that the old order of things was passing away. The system of committing to memory whole volumes of matter was fast dying out, and the revival of Sanskrit learning, with which no name was more intimately connected than Max Müller's own, had created an ever-increasing demand for printed Sanskrit books. But at his age Max Müller did not feel he could undertake a fourth edition of the *Rig-veda*.

August was spent at Ems.

To the Princess Mother of Wied.

*Translation.* Ems, *August* 11.

'Your Highness,—Alas! I have to say with many regrets that my great wish to see Segenhaus and its dear inhabitants once more in this life cannot be fulfilled. Two things are in the way. Twenty-eight days of bathing, &c., and two monthly return tickets. We have to drink the waters once more on Sunday, and to return straight to Oxford on Monday, where our son expects us, who is on his way from

Constantinople to Washington. At my age one hardly likes to put off one's wishes, but Ems has done us both so much good, that we must return here next year. Of course, plans should not be made at my age, but one feels all the more thankful for every good thing that falls to our lot unexpectedly. I should have liked to see Baron Roggenbach again. We have so many things to say to each other, to lament over so many losses. There are so few to live for now, so few to think of, and to think for. How often, too, my thoughts travel to Roumania, where I hope all is sunny and full of bliss, as it ought to be. I should have liked to show your Highness the pictures of my four grandchildren, to whom we are so deeply attached, and who are a new life to us. My son is well. He has met with a great deal that is interesting in Constantinople, and the little flirtation between England and America is sure to offer much that is interesting and amusing for the quiet observer. I am still at work: what else can one do?

'I remain, with sincere devotion,

'Your Highness's ever faithful.'

To Mrs. Welsch.

Oxford, *September* 26, 1898.

'I have felt the death of Fontane very much. One feels oneself quite forsaken and forgotten. As a young man he was charming, without cares, and thoughtless, and appeared just what he was, without any plan of life, without any reserve. He had to live through many hard days, and at last became a sort of Government hack, but never sank as low as Busch, Bücher, &c. His poetical talent was remarkable, and always kindly. I close my eyes, to live on. And so it goes on, hardly any day without its farewell. And what a happy end was his, just what he deserved! There is something so natural in death. We come and we go, there is no break. Many thanks for the obituary notice; it is full of feeling, but words help but little.'

To Sir William Russell.

Oxford, *October* 4.

'My dear old Friend,—What can one do against the years that rush against us like so many Dervishes? Fight, fight, fight; but even that tires one, and one often longs to lie down and rest. I was so much better when I came back from Ems, quite rejuvenescent, but now the winter comes again and takes all colour out of one. . . . If you wish to be disgusted, read Busch, on Bismarck. I knew Bücher, and he was not the most exalted character, but Busch! one feels ashamed to be a German. I always knew that Bismarck was a brute, but he had the redeeming qualities of a brute, but the reptiles! Surely a man who does a great work may be a very small, a very mean man. And now they are going to erect a monument to B. in the cathedral at Berlin! Oh! the desolation of abomination! Let him who readeth understand!'

To his Niece, Lady Lawrence (on the death of her husband).

Oxford, *October*.

'It is for my own sake, not your sake, that I write. I know but too well that nothing can give us any comfort, when we mourn for one whom we loved, and who for a time has been taken from us. But my thoughts have been so constantly with you, that I want to tell you how deeply I have felt your cruel loss. Nothing can heal a recent wound; it must bleed, and the more it bleeds, the better. I have gone through this agony, as you know, for next to losing a husband, there is the loss of a beloved child. But do we really lose those who are called before us? I feel that they are even nearer to us than when they were with us in life. We must take a larger view. Our life does not end here, if only we can see that our horizon here is but like a curtain that separates us from what is beyond. Those who go before us are beyond our horizon for the present, but we have no right to suppose that they have completely vanished. We cannot see them, that is all. And even that, we know, can last for a short time only. We have lived and done our work in life, before we knew those we loved, and we may have to live the same number of years, separated from them. But nothing can be lost, it depends on ourselves to keep those we loved always near to our thoughts, even though our eyes look in vain for them. The world is larger than this little earth, our thoughts go further than this short life, and if we can but find our home in this larger world, we shall find that this larger home is full of those whom we loved, and who loved us. There is no *chance* in life: a few years more, a few years less, will seem as nothing to us hereafter. With all that, the heart knows its own bitterness, and the wound is hard to bear, and no one can help us. Still, it is a comfort to know that others feel and suffer with us, and I wanted to tell you how deeply I feel for you.'

To Sir Henry Acland.

*November* 23.

'I hope you will go on with your work, to get, if possible, an Institute of Public Health established at Oxford, and then invite Mr. Tata personally to send some young medical students to Oxford. I am not a very sanguine, but I have always been a hopeful man. It is right to sow, though we must not expect every grain to take root and grow.

'Markby is quite right. The natives must be taken into our confidence and allowed to take an oar in our boat. They are men just like ourselves, they are not strange, or suspicious, or untrustworthy, if only they are trusted, and trusted altogether. Nothing is so bad as trusting them half-and-half. They must be made to feel that they are in the same boat with ourselves. They are a cleanly race, more so than we were a hundred years ago; they look upon digging wells, building bathing-places, planting trees, as part of their religion. Even their religion is not so bad as it looks, as I hope to show in a book just finished. I have not much faith in missionaries, medical or otherwise. If we get such men again in India as Râmmohun Roy, or Keshub Chunder Sen, and if we get an Archbishop at Calcutta who knows what Christianity really is, India will be christianized in all that is essential in the twinkling of an eye. On this, too, we must be hopeful, but not too sanguine. Words pierce deeper than swords, and I feel certain that your words may do a great deal of good—old age has its drawbacks, but it has its advantages also.

'Ever yours affectionately.'

In November Max Müller brought out *Râmakrishna, his Life and Sayings*, which had a rapid sale, the third edition coming out the following May. This Indian saint, who died in 1886, had many devoted followers, and from them and from various journals Max Müller collected his Sayings and materials for his life, feeling that attention ought to be drawn in this country to the utterances of men like Râmakrishna, who gather large multitudes round them, and who exercise a powerful influence, not only on philosophers but on large masses of the people. 'A country permeated by such thoughts as were uttered by Râmakrishna cannot possibly be looked upon as a country of ignorant idolaters, to be converted by the same methods which are applicable to the races of Central Africa.'

Though Max Müller no longer dined out, this term had been one of great hospitality at home, and there are constant entries in his wife's Diary of friends staying in the house, of dinners, luncheons, and large afternoon teas; whilst almost every day a friend or two came in about 4.30, knowing they would find a welcome at the tea-table, and Max Müller free at that hour from work and ready for a chat with his visitors.

For several years his Vicar, Mr. Bidder, had been among his most valued and intimate friends, and came in constantly without formality, in the way Max Müller most enjoyed. For his birthday this year, not only his daughter and son-in-law and a grandchild were with him, but his old friend Sir William Russell, and his wife, came down for two or three days.

To Sir William Russell.

7, Norham Gardens, *December* 11.

'Many thanks for your book[1]. That is the very book I wanted you to write, but this is the first volume only, and I hope and trust you will go on with it. One for each war, and one at least for intervening peaceful occupations. I was so glad to have you and your dear wife here for my birthday. One must try to forget it. Really, three-quarters of a century is a very heavy sentence, and there has been no lack of hard labour too. Even now, when most people would rest, I am staggering under a *History of Indian Philosophy*, and I am not at all pleased: there are new books coming over from India which must be read, when I had thought I had finished. When we look at ourselves, and at each other, we hardly seem to be the same creatures we were fifty years ago. However, our friendship remains, and it grows stronger rather than weaker. So, after all, it is not quite winter yet.

'Ever yours affectionately.'

For Christmas Max Müller went to his daughter's, where his son unexpectedly joined the party from Holland—the last time they were all to be together! Other friends were in the house. On Christmas Eve there was a grand tree, on Christmas Day Max Müller had four grandchildren at church with him, and on December 30 there was a children's fancy-dress ball at Wombwell. Into all the amusements he entered with his usual enjoyment.

Among the visitors this year were Miss Ole Bull, who had been long in India, and came to discuss religious reforms with the great Guru; the Siamese Minister; and Miss Umé Tsuda, a Japanese lady; whilst all the winter Max Müller had as a near neighbour Mrs. Nuttall, an American lady, who had studied Mexican antiquities, and whose society was a constant pleasure. They met for the last time in 1900, at Dover, where Mrs. Nuttall came on purpose to see him.

[1] On the Crimean War.

To Mrs. Abeken (on receiving the *Life* of her husband).

*Translation.* Oxford, *January* 2, 1899.

'Please accept my warmest thanks. I must read the book quietly. Even a mere glance at it has interested me deeply. We want such a book just now more than ever, that the world may not believe that the brutalities of the Bismarckian régime have poisoned everything. What a pity that the book has not been translated into English! It will take long for people in England to forget the shamelessness of Busch & Co.'

To the Same.

*Translation.* Oxford, *January* 5.

'I have read the book with the deepest interest, and found nearly everything that I wished to know. How truly the best of his contemporaries loved and valued him! One sees in him the good old German type. You would hardly believe how much that book of Busch's has degraded the whole German nation in the eyes of the world. Brutality and deceit have not hitherto been looked on as characteristic of the German people. The impression will not easily be wiped out. My old friend, Sir Henry Acland, longs to read your book, but says that at eighty-four his German is too rusty. Once more my grateful thanks for the real pleasure your book has given me. You have raised a worthy monument to your dear husband, and one that will last.'

To Sir Robert Collins.

7, Norham Gardens, *January* 4.

'I send you an article of mine on Dean Liddell. Mrs. Liddell asked me to write it, as a kind of forerunner of a biography of the Dean which she is preparing. Perhaps the article may recall happy days to you. But if you come again to reside here with your new charge, you will find Oxford changed, quite a new Oxford. We buried Price yesterday, the last of a generation!

'My boy was here for Christmas; he was presented to the two Queens[1] last night.'

It had been settled that the next Congress of Orientalists should meet at Rome in the autumn of this year, and Max Müller was one of the first to send in his name. 'I write at once,' he says, 'to say that, as I could not come to Italy last year, I certainly hope to see it once more this year, and (D.V.) to be present at your Congress. You may therefore put me down as a member. I look forward with great pleasure to

[1] The Queen of Holland and the Queen Regent.

our meeting, and hope my wife will accompany me.' His adhesion was at once noticed in the Italian papers: 'The President of the Congress in London, the celebrated philologist, philosopher, and mythologist, Max Müller, is one of the first adherents of the Roman Congress.' All through the year Max Müller looked forward to a visit to Rome, and meeting many old friends there, but his illness in the autumn made it impossible.

Many letters passed this year between Max Müller and the Buddhist reformer Dharmapâla, but only one from Max Müller has been obtained:—

To Anagarika Dharmapâla.

Oxford, *January* 17.

'Dear Friend,—I shall always be pleased to belong to a society to which you belong. You have been, and are doing, such good and honest work, that I hope you may be successful in your College at Colombo. Though I am not a Buddhist, I can join in many of your prayers, and I should consider a revival of Buddhist morality a great blessing for the great mass of the people in Ceylon, and India also. But I am a great believer in Âtman, and cannot understand how a religion can do without it. You understand, no doubt, what I mean; there must be a reality somewhere. What is phenomenal always presupposes something that is real. However, these are metaphysical questions, and practical religion may well ignore them. But can real religion do so? I am just now printing a book on the *Six Systems of Indian Philosophy*. I believe a supplementary volume on Buddha's Metaphysics would be very useful. Why do you not undertake it?'

It was in this year, in one of the many interviews to which Max Müller had now to submit, that when he was asked the secret of his success in life, he answered: 'Poverty and hard work. Since I left school at eighteen, I have kept myself with the fingers of my right hand. This is the secret of most men's success in Germany.'

To Sir William Russell (on the death of his son).

Oxford, *January* 27, 1899.

'My very dear old Friend,—No words, but only a touch of the hand, to tell you that I feel for you, and with you. Whatever our reason may say, the heart has its own rights, and it cannot be persuaded and comforted. We know that our children are not immortal, and that the ice on which we skate through life is very thin, yet how natural is the old Vedic prayer, "Oh! let us die in order, that the old may not weep over the young." I know what it is for an old man to weep over the young, and I feel for you with all my heart.'

TO JOHN BELLOWS, ESQ.

OXFORD, *February* 19.

'I see you have lost another old friend; that is what we have to pay for living so long. I stand nearly alone; my young friends, I mean the friends of my youth, *are all gone*, and their place, as you know, is difficult to fill. One begins to feel that one is out of date, and but little in harmony with the young people; still, I feel it a great blessing that I am still able to read and still able to write. I have, even now, two books passing through the Press. I should so much like to have a chat with you. I know you are a busy man, but could not you and Mrs. Bellows spend a Sunday with us? We shall be here for the present, I mean till April, at least, and any time that suits you would suit us, and it would be a real pleasure to have you here.'

Mr. Bellows was too busy to visit Oxford, and the friends never met again.

TO HIS SON.

OXFORD, *March* 22.

'I have just finished Bismarck's *Gedanken und Erinnerungen*. That is a very different work from Busch's disgraceful performance. It is a hard book to read, but worth reading, and one gains a very different idea of the old growler. . . . To look into the cards of a man who makes history is very interesting. Not that the game seems very complicated or to require much genius, but it is well to know how it is played, how it is won, and how it is lost. *Aequam memento rebus in arduis servare mentem* seems to be the outcome of all diplomacy, and of all wisdom, in ordinary life (in German, *Lass dich nicht verblüffen!*). . . . Not that I have changed my mind about Bismarck the man, but about Bismarck the politician.'

A touching letter reached Max Müller this spring, showing how his works had penetrated far and wide. A letter like this seemed ample repayment for his long life of labour. It was from an unknown American in California: 'I have often thought I ought to write and thank you for the help and inspiration I have derived from your life and writings.' After saying that his studies at College had upset the faith received in childhood, he continues: 'I read your *Gifford Lectures*. The last volume brought me to a mountain-top. I could there see to what I had been climbing.' He then ends by saying that he had just lost his wife: 'I want to tell you that your *Deutsche Liebe* lies upon her breast, in accordance with her wish. I want to thank you, on her behalf and my own, for that most beautiful story of spiritual affinity.'

Mention should be made of the constant help Max Müller received in these later years from Dr. Krebs, the Librarian of the Taylor Institution. He said himself that he never appealed to him in vain; whether it was the name of the author of a dictionary, or the name of Cuvier's antagonist in the discussion on evolution, or the origin of the expression, 'Lesen, lesen, seid's gewesen,' or the title of a book with a letter from Heine to Wilhelm Müller, or where to find the saying, 'Denn wer den Besten seiner Zeit genug gethan, der hat gelebt für alle Zeiten,' the help was always readily given.

To the Rev. N. M. Hennessey.

7, Norham Gardens, *April* 3.

'Dear Mr. Hennessey,—Many thanks for your kind thought of me, and for sending me your good wishes for Easter. Considering my age, seventy-six, I cannot complain, but ought to be very thankful. I can still work and enjoy life. How long it will last, who knows? I rather feel in a hurry to say the few things I still have to say. I am just printing an account of the Six Systems of Indian Philosophy, a hard piece of work, but that possibly may do good in showing how carefully the old Indians argued out the same problems which occupied Greek philosophers, and occupy ourselves to the present moment. Then I have another volume of *Auld Lang Syne* in the Press, chiefly on Indian friends. It may be more useful to build ships or to make roads, still it is pleasant to see that even one's books are not quite useless in the world, and it is pleasant to be told so. No doubt, as one nears the end of one's journey, many things that seemed very important formerly, melt away in the distance, and new problems come nearer and nearer; and one learns to look forward, and simply to trust to that wonderful wisdom which is so manifest in every new flower that breaks through the soil. The flowers in church at Easter preach their silent sermons, more impressive than words, though they are only called ornaments.

'I return your Samoan greeting—*Ta-lo-fa* (My love to you).'

To Mr. Takakusu.

Oxford, *May* 12.

'I was glad to learn from your letter of April 10, that all goes well with you, and that you go on with your Sanskrit studies. Yes, you ought certainly to establish a School of Sanskrit in Japan, such, as it seems, existed some centuries ago, only it should be much more broadminded and much more critical. I wish I could have read more Sanskrit books with you, but you know quite enough now to be able to work by yourself, particularly if you have other countrymen of your [own] to work with you.

'I shall be away from Oxford till the end of October, as I have to represent the University at the Oriental Congress at Rome. I hope Japan will be represented too.'

The Lent Term and Easter Vacation had been spent quietly in Oxford, Max Müller working hard in printing his *Six Systems of Indian Philosophy*, and *Auld Lang Syne*, Series II.

About this time Max Müller received from a learned Pundit at Calcutta, Sri Sarat Chandra Sastri, a copy of verses which he had written in his honour in Sanskrit *slokas*. The following is the reply :—

To Sri Sarat Chandra Sastri.

Oxford, *May* 14.

'I must send you just one line to thank you for your excellent *slokas*, though I confess I felt ashamed on reading them, and quite unworthy of your praise. I have done what I could to arouse an interest in the language, literature, and the religions of India, but I have done no more than others, and I know full well how much there is still left to do. I am sorry to say I can no longer work as I used to do, and I feel how much more I ought to have done. Others, I hope, will come after me, and finish what I began. Anyhow, the eyes of people in Europe have been opened to see the treasures of thought that lie buried in Indian literature. You are doing a most valuable service to Buddhist literature by your publications, for we know so little as yet of the Mahâyâna. We want to know its antecedents in Brâhmanic literature, for everything has its antecedent. I wish every success to your valuable work under the auspices of Rai Sarat Chandra Das Bahadur. He has opened a mine in Tibet which yields treasures better than gold.'

In May, Max Müller parted with his son for Washington, and started himself the same day with his wife to Ems.

To his Son.

Ems, *May* 28.

'As one grows old, one feels more and more of how little use one can be to others. It is very easy for old people to give advice, for they see more and know more, but the difficulty is how to make advice acceptable. Though the whole world is built on each generation handing on the results of their experience to the next generation, the next generation takes a long time before it learns that simple truth. All society, civilization, morality, policy, are founded on filial piety, say the Chinese philosophers, and they were not such fools as the Chinese seem to be now. The whole history of the world is one thread, say the Indian philosophers, and we must never let it be broken; it leads us to the beginning of all things, and connects even this present generation with the first man—call him Adam, or any other name, if only you remember that he was the son of God, and is so represented in the first Gospel. Think that out, and it will lead you back, not to a Pithecanthropos, but to the eternal Anthropos, who was conceived by the Father from all eternity.'

The first week at Ems Max Müller was well, and able to take long walks. He had been anxious to show Treves to his wife the year before, but the heat was too great. This year it was cooler, and he spent two days there. The weather suddenly became very hot, and Max Müller returned thoroughly exhausted from the expedition, and for several days was quite ill; after that, for about a fortnight he seemed to rally, and was able to enjoy expeditions up and down the Lahn Valley. But the improvement was of short duration, and though he carried out his plan of visiting the Princess Mother of Wied at Segenhaus, the first signs of jaundice had appeared, and he had to spend the chief part of the visit resting in his room.

From Segenhaus the Max Müllers went to Schwalbach, where it was hoped the fine air would prove efficacious, and many days Max was well enough to enjoy drives in the wooded valleys round; but the heat, which he always enjoyed when well, was too much for him, and he was a good deal exhausted when he arrived at Weimar, where he had all along planned to stay, as his wife had never seen the place which made such an impression on him in 1857. On leaving Weimar the Max Müllers went to Dessau; but the old power of enjoyment was gone, everything was an effort, and it was finally settled that they would go earlier than they intended to Dresden for good medical advice. The last Sunday in Dessau was spent by the Max Müllers alone at Wörlitz, the Duke's beautiful park, about seven miles from Dessau, associated in their minds with many a joyous meeting with those who were gone, for no visit to Dessau was ever paid without a family dinner and gathering at Wörlitz. Their visit now recalled vividly a similar one forty years before, when, on their honeymoon, they escaped from the crowd of relatives, and spent a long happy day alone together at Wörlitz, all their married life before them! More than three weeks were spent in Dresden; where the doctors took a very serious view of Max Müller's case, hardly expecting him to live more than three months. All idea of the visit to Rome was now abandoned, and it was settled to return as soon as possible to England. The Max Müllers were joined in Dresden by their daughter and son-in-law and a friend, who were at Baireuth, and came off at once on hearing the serious opinion of the German doctors. Victor Carus came from Leipzig for two or three days to see Max Müller, and the old friends parted, knowing they should meet no more. The journey was accomplished with very little fatigue to the invalid, who was delighted to find himself under his daughter's roof. The English doctors took a more hopeful view of his case, and he certainly felt himself better. On his return he wrote to his son at Washington:—

WOMBWELL HALL, *September* 8.

'I am afraid they have frightened you more than was necessary. Of course, I am far from well, the doctors take a very gloomy view, but I don't feel so ill as all that. At seventy-six, one must be prepared for everything, and need I tell you I am prepared to go? It would be strange if I were not, with such a long life behind me, and most of it devoted to religious and philosophical questions. What is more natural in life than death? and having lived this long life, so full of light, having been led so kindly by a Fatherly hand through all storms and struggles, why should I be afraid when I have to make the last step? I have finished nearly all my work, and, what is more, I see that it will be carried on by others, by stronger and younger men.

I have never piped much in the market, I gladly left that to others, but I have laid a foundation that will last, and though people don't see the blocks buried in a river, it is on those unseen blocks the bridges rest.'

After a fortnight with his daughter, Max Müller returned to Oxford with her and his wife, who were cheered by an improved account from his doctor. Telegrams were received both from the Queen and the Prince of Wales asking for news, and the Queen telegraphed again a little later.

To his Son.

7, Norham Gardens, *September* 30.

'I feel so altogether under a Higher Power that I wait with perfect equanimity. I know to a young man death has something terrible, not to an old man—it seems so unnatural in youth, so natural in old age. I have had my years of struggle, sometimes of very hard struggle, but I could never look forward to so much real happiness after the heat of the day was over.'

Sir William Hunter was named by the University of Oxford to attend the Oriental Congress in Rome in the place of Max Müller, who had written a letter to the President of the Congress, regretting his inability to be present, as he had so ardently desired for many months. This letter was read at one of the first meetings, and the following report appeared in the *Times*:—

Rome, *October* 10.

'A profound impression was produced in the Oriental Congress yesterday, by a letter from Professor Max Müller, at Oxford. In pathetic but dignified terms the venerable scholar bade farewell to the Congress, on the ground that his illness precluded any hope that he would again take part in its proceedings. He narrated the progress which he had made to bring to completion the translations of the *Sacred Books of the East*, and presented a copy of that magnificent series to the Congress as a testimony of his good will and of the encouragement and help which he had, during many years, received from its members. The communication was received with deep emotion, for the amiable personality of Professor Max Müller, the wide range of his scholarship, and his rare combination of genius with learning, have given him a unique place amongst the Orientalists of Europe.'

Sir William Hunter wrote that not a day passed without Max Müller's name being mentioned in the Congress, or in one or other of its sections, with admiration and love. His presence had been looked forward to with so much pleasure, that to many of the members the Congress seemed incomplete without him. Sir William reported that his beautiful letter produced a genuine outburst of emotion in the Indian Section.

The two books which Max Müller had published just before leaving England, *The Six Systems of Indian Philosophy*, and *Auld Lang Syne*, Series II, 'My Indian Friends,' were beginning to attract attention.

The *Times* thus speaks of them:—

'The serious illness of Professor Max Müller gives to these two books a peculiar interest. In the *Six Systems of Indian Philosophy*, he brings within the compass of some 600 pages the vast area of Sanskrit speculation and ethical thought. His object is not chiefly to restate the mere tenets of each system. His aim is rather to present a comprehensive account of the philosophical activity of the Indian mind, and to show how intimately both the religion and the philosophy of India were "connected with the national character of the inhabitants."

'*Auld Lang Syne* (Second Series) belongs to a widely different sphere of literary effort. It consists of the amiable armchair recollections of a veteran scholar, and is especially devoted to his Indian friends. His Indian acquaintances were not all of his own time, and he introduces us in many charming pages to the great thinkers and reformers of the past, whom in the truest sense he has made his friends. From the Rishis of the *Rig-veda* to the apostles of mediaeval Hinduism and the great theistic teachers of the India of to-day, he makes a procession of noble and venerable figures to pass before our eyes. Happy the man who has gone through life in so goodly a fellowship!'

The book was most warmly greeted in India, and its author received letters from unknown friends all over the Indian empire, expressing their delight and gratitude.

TO SIR WILLIAM RUSSELL.

OXFORD, *October* 30, 1899.

'MY VERY DEAR, POOR FRIEND,—That is really too much for one man, two sons and one grandson! Who can understand it? That an old man like me should be summoned off the stage is natural enough, and I confess it did not surprise me. After all, what difference can one or two years make? The King's private physician at Dresden told my wife that I had only a few weeks, or months to live. Fortunately, I could get home, arrange all my things, and then wait patiently. What puzzled me was my own vitality. I saw the mischief, liver and bile, quite clearly, and that will possibly never be healed; but otherwise I have held my ground, and the doctor thinks I have even made a step forward. I sleep well, I eat well, and feel well. What more can a man desire? I am spoilt like a baby, and since June have done nothing. B. is here to help her mother. Fortunately I could stop Wilhelm coming home from Washington, though he had secured his passage. We all attach ourselves too much, and then comes the time when the barbed arrow has to be taken out, and it hurts. But the young people live on as if nothing could happen to them. They little know. I spend the forenoon in bed, and the afternoon goes, and then I am taken to bed again. This began in June, on my way to Italy. I tried again and again, but at last had to give in at Dresden, and get back to Oxford as well as I could. Here, however, and in London, the doctors gave a less desperate account, and began to feed me up, and for all I know they may be right, though I shall be an invalid for life. Well, I have had my sunshine, and now I must learn to bear rain and mist, and all the rest.'

When Max Müller was at Ems he wrote a long letter to Mozoomdar, the leader of the more liberal portion of the Brahma Somâj, which is of such importance that considerable portions are given here. The matter was very near Max Müller's heart, and as his illness was already beginning when this letter was written, it has something of the nature of a dying message to the Brahma Somâj:—

To P. C. Mozoomdar.

'My dear Friend,—You know for how many years I have watched your efforts to purify the popular religion of India, and thereby to bring it nearer to the purity and perfection of other religions, particularly of Christianity. You know also that I have paid close attention to the endeavours of those who came before you, of men like Râmmohun Roy, Debendranâth Tagore, Keshub Chunder Sen, and others, in whose footsteps you have boldly followed, and whose work you have faithfully carried on, as far as circumstances allowed you to do so. What I have much admired, both in yourself and in your noble predecessors and fellow workers, is the patience and the even temper with which you have prosecuted your religious and social reforms. I know that you have met with many disappointments and many delays, but you have never lost heart and never lost patience. I confess that I have several times felt very unhappy about the mischances that have befallen your good cause; but even when Keshub Chunder Sen was forsaken by a number of his friends and followers, on utterly insufficient grounds, as far as I could judge, and again, when he was taken from us in the very midst of his glorious work, I never lost faith in the final success of his work, though I began to doubt whether I should live to see the full realization of his hopes.

'If you once know what truth is, you also know that truth is in no hurry. Truth is, truth has been, truth will be, whether it is accepted by the whole world or by a small minority only. . . . Your departed friend, Keshub Chunder Sen, had the firm conviction that the way which he and his predecessors had indicated was the only possible way out of the present state of confusion, and out of the misunderstandings that had arisen between him and many of his own countrymen, and likewise out of those which still separated him from his Christian friends and sympathizers.

'Now it seems to me that the first thing you have to do is to try to remove the differences that still exist among yourselves, and to settle how much of your ancient religion you are willing to give up, if not as utterly false, still as antiquated. You have given up a great deal, polytheism, idolatry, and your elaborate sacrificial worship. You have surrendered also, as far as I can judge, the claim of divine revelation which had been so carefully formulated by your ancient theologians in support of the truth of the *Vedas*. These were great sacrifices, for whatever may be thought of your ancient traditions, to give up what we have been taught by our fathers and mothers, requires a very strong conviction, and a very strong will. But though this surrender has brought you much nearer to us, there still remain many minor points on which you differ among yourselves in your various *samâjes* or congregations. Allow me to say that these differences seem to me to have little to do with real religion; still they must be removed, because they prevent united action on your part. . . . If you are once united among yourselves, you need no longer trouble about this or that missionary, whether he come from London, Rome, Geneva, or Moscow. They all profess to bring you the Gospel of Christ. Take then the New Testament and read it for yourselves, and judge for yourselves whether the words of Christ, as contained in it, satisfy you or not.

'I know that you yourself, as well as Râmmohun Roy and Keshub Chunder Sen, have done that. I know one countryman of yours who wrote a searching criticism of the Old and New Testaments, and then joined the Christian Church, as established in England, because there was something in the teaching and life of Christ which he could not withstand. I know this is not an argument, yet it is something to reflect on.

'Christ comes to you as He comes to us in the only trustworthy records preserved of Him in the Gospels. We have not even the right to dictate our interpretation of these Gospels to you, particularly if we consider how differently we interpret them ourselves. If you accept His teachings, as there recorded, you are a Christian. There is no necessity whatever for your being formally received into the membership of one or the other sect of the Christian Church, whether reformed or unreformed. That will only delay the growth of Christianity in India. All that has grown up in the Church after the death of Christ, or the Apostles, does not concern you. You will want, no doubt, some kind of constitution, some government, some Church or Somâj. Have a baptism, or *Upanayana*, if you please, as an outward sign of that new life which baptism signified among the early Christians, and which was well known also to your great teachers of old. Remember, before all things, that you can be followers of Christ, without being Roman Catholics, Anglo-Catholics, or Greek orthodox Catholics, without assuming the names and fashions of Presbyterians, Congregationalists, Unitarians, or any other Dissenters. Keep aloof of all of them, they have proved only stumbling-blocks in the progress of Christianity. Keshub Chunder Sen used to say that, after all, Christ was in many respects an Oriental, and was better understood by Orientals than by Occidentals. Whether this be true or not, you have, at all events, as much right to constitute and regulate your own Church, your own Parishads, your own Samgha, as the Greeks, in their time, had at Alexandria, or the Romans at Rome. You have nothing to do with popes, bishops, priests, ministers, *et hoc genus omne*, unless for some reason or other you wish, besides being Christians, to belong to one of the historical associations also that have sprung up. . . . I do not like to appear sailing under false colours. I am, myself, a devoted member of the English Church, because I think its members enjoy greater freedom and more immunity from priestcraft than those of any other Church. There are, no doubt, many things in that Church also, which still require reformation. But though we are not altogether free from the evils that seem inseparable from the establishment of any priesthood, we have thrown off many of the hideous accretions which nearly took the life out of Christianity during the long night of the dark ages. The real Church, you should remember, before you take any steps towards framing a constitution of your own, consists of the laity alone. It was the laity that appointed its ministers, but these original ministers—such is human nature—have almost invariably become the masters of their masters. The English Church, however, though it has sometimes forgotten the supreme and indefeasible rights of the laity, has never surrendered them formally and altogether; and the highest seat of authority, in matters of faith as well as of public worship, has always remained with the laity and the civil powers, and has never been surrendered formally to the clergy. . . . Try whether you cannot join the Church of England as lay members, but have nothing to do with their ecclesiastical constitutions, and keep aloof from all discussions on so-called orders or their validity. Lay members of the English Church are perfectly free, and I have never repented having joined it. . . .

'Only remember, that there is no reason whatever why you, in forming your own Christian Church, should join any of the European Churches. That idea is what has delayed your progress so long. You have declared in so many words (*New Dispensation*, March 5, 1899): "We regard the words of Jesus Christ as our authority, and consider Him to be our Master." How can any one dare to call men who say this pagans, to be converted like so many Negroes or Hottentots? What keeps these men away from us? They tell us themselves in the same paper: "We cannot accept the teachings of popular Christianity, that is, of the missionaries in India. Their teaching seems to us too anthropomorphic. We are asked to believe in a Deity who does one thing to-day and repents of it to-morrow. He is represented to us as revengeful, changeable, and imperfect. To-day He blesses the children of men; to-morrow He sees their sins, and becomes vindictive, curses them, and seeks their destruction." These may be the teachings of certain missionaries in India, but students of the Bible might easily convince themselves that they are really exaggerations of some of the Jewish views of the Deity, surrounded by a legendary mist. The doctrine of the Atonement also, as preached by certain missionaries, has evidently proved a great stumbling-block to many who felt drawn towards Christ. . . . But surely this, too, is a one-sided and exaggerated view of the Atonement; it is the view of certain theologians, but not of the Gospels. The very name of atonement never occurs in the Gospels, and but once in the New Testament, namely in Romans v. 7, and means there no more than reconciliation.

'You would be surprised if you knew how many honest Christians feel exactly what you feel about the Atonement, and that in this case also, those who compass sea and land to make one proselyte are the very people who prevent you from becoming proselytes, from coming to Christ and to us.

'And if there is nothing that should prevent the Brahmos, with all their objections to certain theologians and missionaries, from coming to us, let us see now whether there is anything that should prevent us from going to them. We read in the same paper: "The Brahmos believe in a perfect and immutable God, whose beneficent purposes in creating man can never be frustrated. If God has created man to be saved, he is doomed to be saved. In virtue of his free will, he may for a time resist the Divine will, but he cannot for ever carry on a war with the infinitely wise and infinitely loving God. The Bible distinctly says: The Lord will not cast off for ever. . . . God, who is unchangeable, and in whom there is not a shadow of turning, loves the sinner, whether he sins, or becomes a saint. The change is in man. Whenever man sins, darkness comes over his soul. He trembles and cannot see the smiling face of God. He discerns only terror and fierceness in His countenance. But whenever he repents and resolves not to disobey, the cloud passes away and the light of the benign face shines upon the sinner, and he finds reconciliation or forgiveness."

'I can see nothing in this view of the Deity that is not Christian, and would be objected to by any *bona fide* Christian. You do not see how near you really are to us, and how it is a mere fiction of your own minds that the preachings and teachings of certain missionaries and bishops could possibly form a barrier between you and Christ. Every religion, nay, every philosophy also, varies according to those who receive it and teach it. Neither missionaries nor bishops even are infallible authorities. Christianity is free to all men, every man has his own Christianity in his own heart, and in the Gospel, as understood by him. Neither the Pope nor the Archbishop of Canterbury is infallible, yet both are Christians; then why not you and your friends? The people of Europe at the time of the Reformation did what you ought to do. When they saw that the old Church of Rome did not teach the pure original Gospel, they protested and became once more true Christians, yielding to no authority but to that of Christ, as preserved in the Gospels. If you think that our various missionaries, reformed or unreformed, do not bring you pure Christianity, why should you hesitate to do what our Reformers did, go back to the Gospels and establish your own Christian Church, and defend it against all comers, whether from East or from West? You are fond of saying that Christ Himself was an Oriental, not an Occidental. Then why not have your own Oriental Christ, your own Oriental Christianity? Only beware from the very first of the leaven of Oriental pharisees. Every religion has been founded by laymen, by men of the people; and every religion has been ruined by priests!

'I have told you already that Keshub Chunder Sen, in intimate conversation, told me that to all intents and purposes he was a disciple of Christ, and when I write to you, and when I think of you, I cannot resist the feeling that you too are a true follower of Christ. . . .

'Tell me some of your chief difficulties that prevent you and your countrymen from openly following Christ. I shall do my best to explain how I and many who agree with me have met them, and solved them. I do not hesitate to say that on some of these points we may have to learn from you more than we can teach you, and I say this honestly, and from personal experience. That too will be a lesson difficult to learn for our bishops and missionaries, but in Christian humility they will have to learn it. From my point of view, India, at least the best part of it, is already converted to Christianity. You want no persuasion to become a follower of Christ. Then make up your mind to act for yourselves. Unite your flock, and put up a few folds to hold them together, and to prevent them from straying. The bridge has been built for you by those who came before you. Step boldly forward, it will not break under you, and you will find many friends to welcome you on the other shore, and among them none more delighted than your old friend and fellow labourer,

'F. MAX MÜLLER.'

This letter remained unanswered for some time, though Mozoomdar published it, with a rejoinder from himself, in some of the Indian papers. The following is part of Mozoomdar's rejoinder:—

'What disconcerts me is the half-expressed contempt which Christian leaders, even of the liberal school, seem to have of the Hindu ideal, and spirituality. When I express my ardent love for Christ and Christianity, they are kindly in sympathy: but the moment I say that Christ and His religion will have to be interpreted in India through Indian antecedents and the Indian medium of thought, I am suspected of trying to bend Christianity down to heathenism. So we must either renounce our national temperament, . . . or renounce Christ, . . . or re-embody our faith and aspirations under a new name, and form, and spirit. We have taken this third course.'

Max Müller's suggestion that the followers of Mozoomdar should call themselves Christians, led to attacks from many different parties. One writer, who signed himself a Hindu, maintained that the early belief in God, as shown in the *Vedas*, was enough to adequately satisfy the craving of the human heart after a high ideal, so as to render recourse to Christian teaching, and change in one's faith, unnecessary and undesirable. The *Duyanodaya* of Bombay, a missionary paper, though not thinking that the Brahmos were as really Christian in their belief as did Max Müller, thought one good would come of the letter. 'Every one hitherto had claimed that Max Müller taught that Hinduism is as good as Christianity, and that it is not important to be a Christian. No one can fairly say so again. He is not satisfied with even the reverence paid to Christ by Brahmos. He appeals to them to openly take the Christian name.'

The *Enquirer*, another missionary paper, also spoke of Max Müller as coming to the aid of the missionaries, and making his own characteristic contribution to mission-work. Yet, in spite of the views of many in India, an attack was made upon him at the Meeting of the Diocesan Conference in Oxford this autumn; made at the very time that all Max Müller's friends were watching with deepest anxiety the struggle that he was making against fatal illness. The attack made on him by the Principal of Pusey House was to the effect that, in his letter to Mr. Mozoomdar, Max Müller urged the members of the Brahma Somâj to call themselves Christians without believing in 'that central doctrine on which the faith and life of the Church was founded.'

Max Müller's valued Vicar replied to the ill-judged attack in a letter to the editor of the *Oxford Times*:—

'Sir,—From your report of the Diocesan Conference, as well as from several independent witnesses, I learn with surprise and pain that my friend and parishioner, Professor Max Müller, was attacked by one of the speakers (the Principal of Pusey House). As one privileged to minister to his closing days, and well acquainted with his religious convictions, I cannot allow the reckless assertion made against Professor Max Müller to go uncontradicted in his own city. The Principal of Pusey House asserted (unless I am misinformed) that the Professor invited the Indian people to declare themselves Christians and to join the Christian Church, at the same time informing them that they could do so without believing in the divinity of our Lord. Of such an assertion I say without hesitation that it is a complete and utter reversal of Professor Max Müller's opinions, and, in particular, of what he wrote last June to one of the leaders of the Brahma Somâj, of which the gist is as follows:—You have been led by

God to recognize in Jesus the Son of God, and to own Him as your Lord and Master; then declare yourselves as what you really are, Christians, and form yourselves into a national Christian Church, without troubling yourselves about the distinctive tenets and quarrels of the contending sects which send their missionaries among you.

'For many years the conversion of the enlightened classes of India has interested the Professor; during the last few months since his illness, it seems to be absorbing more and more of his thoughts, and the letter referred to above and addressed to the Rev. P. C. Mozoomdar, was the very last literary effort which he has been able or perhaps will ever be able to make. It is published in the current journal of the Brahma Somâj, which is now before me, and I venture to quote a few lines of Mozoomdar himself in the same journal in justification of the Professor's attitude in offering him and his followers the right hand of Christian fellowship. "To me the way and the truth is in the supreme personality of the Son of God, who reigns over India, Europe, and the best part of the world, and whom you too" (he is addressing the Brahmos) "have accepted, though you do not know it and do not say it. In the course of a long life (so this noble confession of faith proceeds) in pain and sin and grief and desertion, in loneliness, in injustice and disappointments which have overtaken me, Jesus Christ has given me a strength and rest which nothing else can equal. And in all the great unknown that is in store for the future, nothing can I endure or do except in His Spirit, under His leading. But God is not for Christ, Christ is for God. God only can reveal Christ, and then Christ will reveal God. God is first and last, God is All-in-All." To men who can write thus, have we not the right, nay, are we not bound in duty to say, You have received the like faith with us, you are Christians?'

The weak rejoinder in the paper the following week from the Principal of Pusey House, showed that he had either seen a garbled form of Max Müller's letter to Mozoomdar, or that he had entirely failed to grasp its real meaning. To this letter Mr. Bidder again responded, ending with these words:—

'In taking up the cudgels on behalf of my sick parishioner and his Indian friends, a misgiving seizes me lest, after all, I may seem to have been betrayed into something like an impertinence. If it was excusable to feel some indignation at this gratuitous and undeserved attack upon a good and wise man, perhaps I ought to have remembered that he enjoys a position in the greater world of religious thought—to say nothing of an inward strength and serenity—which place him beyond the reach of attack either from private bigotry or from the Oxford Diocesan Conference.

'Your obedient servant,

'H. J. BIDDER.'

In answer to Max Müller's long letter, Mozoomdar at length wrote: 'A wholesale acceptance of the Christian name by the Brahma Somâj is neither possible nor desirable, within measurable time; it would lead to misconception, which would only do harm. But the acceptance of the Christ spirit, or, as you term it, "the essential religion of Christ," is not only possible, but an actual fact at the present moment. Liberal souls in Christendom will have to rest content with this at least *now*, and let the *name* take care of itself.' This letter had crossed one from Max Müller:—

OXFORD, *November* 3, 1899.

'It seems to me a real marvel that about three weeks ago my illness suddenly gave way, and I begin slowly to mend. Of course I am very weak, but I can read again, and I hope that what remains of my time on earth may not have to be spent in a mere invalid life, of no use to anybody! I have seen some of your Indian papers, and I gather from them that my letter to you, and your own paper, have produced a certain impression. Of course, I have been abused by the Indian papers, and by the journals in England. Let me answer one point in your very kind letter. The name to be adopted by your own reformed Hinduism would be a merely geographical expression. Hinduism as a religion would mean the religion of the Hindus or of India, and thus would comprise every variety of religion practised in India, Durga-worship, Buddhism, Mohammedanism, &c. It would be the name of a mere congeries. You object to anything like Christian, even Christian Brahmos is not satisfactory to you. But surely you owe much to Christ and Christianity, your very movement would not exist without Christianity. One must be above public opinion in these matters, and trust to truth which is stronger than public opinion. However, the name is a small matter. Only I thought that truth and gratitude would declare in favour of Christian Brahmos, or Christian Âryas.

'However, we shall have more important questions to discuss, and I shall require as much courage here in England as I recommend to you in India. Keshub Chunder Sen was a very bold man, and his followers must show the same courage, if they want to carry on his great work. I am too tired to-day, and must not write any more. But if health and strength return, my last years shall be at your service.'

All these months, which the German doctors had pronounced to be his last, Max Müller was slowly mending, and recovering strength. He was able to see many of his friends singly, and enjoy doing so; he drove whenever it was fine; and, though unable to work, he could take an interest in politics and all that was going on, and enjoy the many books, chiefly, it must be owned, novels, that were read out to him. His valued Vicar saw him generally twice a week. Max Müller's greatest pleasure during these months was in constant visits from his daughter or son-in-law, generally bringing one of his grandchildren, and letters from the dearly loved, far-off son. The following letter was sent at this time to Max Müller:—

CALCUTTA, *November* 7, 1899.

'My grandmother, the mother of the late Keshub Chunder Sen, has heard with regret about your illness, and anxiously inquires to know of your health. We, the members of the Sen family, pray to God for your peace and happiness. We are highly indebted to you for what you have done for the elevation of India in the estimation of the enlightened world.'

The following is Max Müller's answer to the inquiries from the venerable mother of Keshub Chunder Sen:—

OXFORD, *November* 27, 1899.

'Please to tell your dear grandmother that I feel much touched by her sympathy. Yes, I have been very ill; but after six months of illness, there has been, quite unexpectedly, a change. I am not allowed to read and write, but I wanted very much to write this line to thank your grandmother for her kind interest. I miss her son very much. He might have done so much good to India, but God knows best why he was taken from us so early, and before his work was finished. But finished it will be, sooner or later, and the fire he has lighted in India will never be extinguished again. He was so kind, so gentle, so good a man too, and his mother ought indeed to be proud to be the mother of such a man.

'With kind regards to her and to you,

'Yours very truly.'

To Professor Deussen, of Kiel.

*Translation.* 7, Norham Gardens, *December* 4, 1899.

'I have received lately many letters and papers from India. The *Vedânta* is working there too, and when I am gone a heavy burden will fall on your shoulders. It will mean not only to make the *Vedânta* intelligible to Europeans, but also to Indians. They possess everything in the *Vedânta*, but they do not know it, and millions of souls have to be taken into account there. The Alexandrian-Christian philosophy is understood by the Indians, but they would like to derive it as self-developed from the *Vedânta*. Well, the thing is not impossible, if only we could find facts. Of course, Alexandria was so close to India and so close to Athens that spiritual intercourse was quite possible. But what good can possibilities do to us? The Syrian Bardesanes had heard something about India, much sooner than the Alexandrians, but, as it seems to me, from ambassadors to Rome from India. I have so far carefully withheld from the idea of Indian influence on Alexandria, but of course the possibility must be faced.

'I should be so glad if you would both come to Oxford at Easter; I hope to be much better by then, at all events I hope to be here. We have a very thorough Alexandrian here, Dr. Aal from Christiania, who has treated the Logos idea. It is curious that what is with the Indians Mâyâ and Avidyâ, appears to the Alexandrians as Sophia or Logos.

'Now I must stop. I enclose something from India, which will show you how the *Vedânta* is beginning to take hold of the Indians. Here in Oxford I have once more been violently attacked as a heretic. Woe to him, who is not a heretic, who does not choose for himself!'

The last birthday was a very happy one. His daughter and son-in-law and two grandsons were with him, and letters and telegrams poured in; lovely flowers were sent from far and near: indeed, Max Müller's library was kept all along like a garden by his kind friends. Though still weak, and leading an invalid life, those who watched him were cheered by daily small signs of improvement, and hope again sprang up in their hearts, that the life, so valuable to so many, might be spared for some years to come.

To Sir William Russell.

7, Norham Gardens, *December* 17, 1899.

'My dear old Friend,—I hope indeed you are getting better. I can say the same of myself, though I never thought that an old machine like my poor body, weakened, for six months, by every kind of trouble, could recuperate as it has done. Even my brain is getting less muddled than it was, and I begin to look around with a certain amount of cheekiness. But it is really a marvel—the only question is, will it last? I wanted to go to London to-morrow, for an important meeting, and felt quite up to it, but my doctor put his veto on it. It is quite clear that he does not consider me so well as I do. I have been most obedient throughout, and now I begin to see that I have my reward. What would have become of us without our wives? I have been so spoilt that I sometimes think I shall go on as an invalid, and be coddled like a baby. This cold weather is against me, but I sometimes drive out and face the north-easter like an old Teuton. That war makes me feel quite miserable. I am afraid our soldiers won't fight under such generals, and no wonder. The war itself seems to me inevitable. It is just like the French and English in India. Out! out!—either you or me. But the English generals ought to have been better prepared, and not an inch of the country should have been left without a strategic survey. I am told they have no maps. I believe any German lieutenant knows more of the distances than General ——. It will cost much blood now, but England won't give in—in fact, cannot. Germany and Russia seem safe for the present, but France is ominous, and the Exhibition alone keeps it quiet.'

# CHAPTER XXXV

## 1900

Hindu prayers for Max Müller. Letters on England's rights in the Transvaal. Dover. Tunbridge Wells. Increase of illness. Visit of a Yogin. Mozoomdar. Last literary work. Death. Letters of sympathy.

THE early days of January were marked by a rapid improvement in Max Müller's health, and by the middle of the month he was able occasionally to take a gentle walk. He liked to drive out of Oxford, and take his walk in better and higher air, and where he was not liable to be met every few steps and stopped by kindly inquiries. He could even have three or four friends at a time to luncheon or tea, besides the single visits which he had so much appreciated from his Vicar, and other intimate friends, during the worst time of his illness. Quite early in the month of January he received the following quaint but touching letter from Madras:—

'When I saw the Professor was seriously ill, tears trickled down my cheeks unconsciously. When I told my friends who are spending the last days of their life with me, and read with me the *Bhagavad-gîtâ* and similar religious books, they were all very much overpowered with grief. Last night, when we were going to our temple as usual, it was suggested to me that we should have some special service performed by the temple priest for his complete restoration. All my friends followed me to the temple, but when we told the priest of our wish he raised various objections. He could not, he said, offer prayers and chant hymns in the name of one who is not a Hindu by birth; if he did so, he would be dismissed from the service, and excommunicated by his caste. We told him that Professor Max Müller, though a European by birth and in garb, was virtually more than a Hindu. When some of my friends offered to pay him ample remuneration, he consented, and when the next day at eleven o'clock at night we came to the temple with cocoanuts, flowers, betel-leaves, nuts, and camphor, which we handed to the priest, he began to chant the Mantras and offer prayers to God for about an hour or so. After everything was done, the priest returned to us some of our gifts, and requested that we should send them to Professor Max Müller.'

Such a service has never been performed before for one who is not a Hindu.

In return for this letter Max Müller sent the writer, L. Vasudivan, his *Six Systems of Hindu Philosophy* with a letter, and Vasudivan writes later to acknowledge its safe arrival: 'Your valuable book is the best book I have ever read. Myself and my friends take great delight in reading it over and over.' On getting Max Müller's letter saying how much better he felt, he ran up to tell his friends, 'and I can't really express the joy we felt on the occasion.' And he then says that they had arranged to offer up prayers for Max Müller at the temple once a month. Later in the month, when a false report of his increased illness appeared in the papers, his Indian friend writes: 'I am sure that the Almighty will not leave my constant prayers for you without effect.'

Another Indian friend wrote from Calcutta: 'I express the fervent hope that God in His infinite grace, even to us the Indian people whom you love, would extend the term of the lease of life which He has just renewed.'

Before long Max Müller was able to undertake a little easy work, for the enforced idleness of his illness had been one of his greatest trials, though borne with that serene resignation and patience which never left him, even under the depressing influence of months of jaundice. Those who tended him never heard a hasty or fretful word, and as one of his faithful servants said after he had passed away, 'It was a privilege to do anything for him.' His mind remained unclouded to the last, and his letters on the Transvaal question, and the three articles on Chinese Religions, showed his old vigour, as well as grace of diction.

The state of feeling in Germany against England, on account of the war in South Africa, was a source of much anxiety to Max Müller, and he wrote several letters on the subject to Prince Christian, who fully shared Max Müller's views as to the mischief caused by the general ignorance in Germany on the rights of the question, an ignorance wilfully fostered by the newspapers.

To Prince Christian.

*Translation.* Oxford, *January* 2.

'Your Royal Highness,—I enclose the cutting from the *Berlin Monday Journal.* The state of public opinion in Germany is very sad, not that it can have any influence with the Government, but it is a pity that newspapers should do so much harm. The Germans do not indeed think of sending any Pomeranians to help Kruger, but the entire misunderstanding of the position of England is very grievous. It was different in the old times, but even England's old friends in Germany are misled. How much I should like to step in, but my bodily strength still fails me. Lying low for six months weakens not only the muscles of the body, but the activity of the mind, and though I never expected a recovery such as mine is, I feel I shall never be again what I was before.

'I hope that you have good news from your son. How much he has already seen of the war, and the people of England will not be unmindful of it. There has never been such a war as this. Who could send an army a distance of 6,000 miles? But all this is forgotten, and England is only abused. Success is the one answer which will be understood.'

To Bunyiu Nanjio (who had sent over a beautiful dress of brocade silk, a pale yellow, with white azaleas on it).

Oxford, *January* 29.

'My dear Friend,—Your silk arrived to-day early. It is most beautiful, only it is much too precious for us, and I know how many calls a Buddhist Bhikshu has; however, I accept it as a sign of your kindness and your remembrance of me. I am now without any pupils, and I often wish I could have some again like you and Kasawara. You two and Takakusu worked well, and I hope you have found new interest in your life, and that you will help towards founding a school of Sanskrit and Pâli in Japan. Your discovery of a work in a 1000 *fasciculi* on the *History of Buddhism in Japan* sounds very astonishing. I placed the matter before the Oriental Congress at Rome, in a letter, as I could not go in person.'

TO PRINCE CHRISTIAN.

*Translation.* OXFORD, *February* 6, 1900.

'Your Royal Highness will see by the enclosed letter from the Editor of the *Deutsche Rundschau*, that I followed your advice and sent him an article on the correctness of the English view as to England's rights, relative to the Transvaal Republic. I had no idea of the sad state of things in Germany, and that no newspaper there ventures to comply with *Audiatur et altera pars*, and listen at least to the other side. I saw from letters of former Anglophil friends, how Leyds and others have taken Germany in, but I certainly did not imagine matters to be quite so bad. I treated the affair historically, from the time of the Vienna Congress to the Treaty of 1884, when England's suzerainty over the Transvaal Republic was accepted by the Boers. I hardly mentioned the present complications; I only referred to the readiness of the *Times* to open her columns to me, when at the time of the Schleswig-Holstein question, and again at the time of the Franco-German War, I wished to publish my opinions which were so unpopular in England. Whatever I write, I sign with my name, and so I did this time, adding: "Strike, but listen!"

'I am indeed astonished. Shall I expose the German Press?'

The article referred to above was the letter which ultimately appeared in the *Deutsche Revue*, after it had been refused by the *Deutsche Rundschau*, to which Max Müller had been a contributor from the first. Professor Mommsen wrote a rejoinder in the same paper, of which a friend said: 'It is very disappointing to see a man of Mommsen's ability spoiling himself by writing on a subject he has never taken the pains to inform himself upon. *He has not even an outline knowledge of the facts.*'

In writing to Prince Christian on February 8, Max Müller says: 'I am quite ready to take the blows on myself which are sure to fall. I know what I am about, and that renders one shot-proof.'

It was a great pleasure to Max Müller to be elected this spring a member of the Berlin Academy, and to receive the information through Professor Weber, who had at one time entertained no friendly feelings for him.

To Professor Weber.

*Translation.* 7, Norham Gardens, *February* 8, 1900.

'Dear Colleague,—Many thanks for your letter, which seemed at first unintelligible. I have deciphered many a handwriting, but try as I would, I did not seem able to read yours! Yet I felt unwilling to tell you so, knowing well how difficult my own handwriting is to read. It was kind of you to tell me so early the news of my election as an Honorary Member of the Academy. I am, of course, very much pleased about it, and I know that I have to thank you for it in many ways.

'It is wonderful how much better I feel. I am not allowed to work yet, and am obliged to stay in bed till eleven o'clock every morning. However, I hope spring will mend all this. I have still to finish so many things, though the chief things are done, and I shall have to content myself with being allowed to look on for a little while longer. Sir W. Hunter is a great loss to me. Dr. Hoernle has shown me the most remarkable MSS. from Turkestan, &c., a new world altogether, but not for me any more. We have to learn, after all, to close our eyes. What a pity that Bühler is no longer here to take the thing in hand!'

The following is the last letter written by Max Müller to his friend Mr. Mozoomdar, again urging on him and his followers to speak out and declare *their real faith*, and their entire separation from modern Hinduism. The appeal has produced no tangible results. Mr. Mozoomdar came to England in the summer, but was at first engaged in London and elsewhere, and when he came to Oxford in the autumn, Max Müller was unable to enter fully into the subject that had so long filled his heart and thoughts.

To Mr. Mozoomdar.

Oxford, *March* 11, 1900.

'My dear Friend,—Though I have long wished to write to you, my health is not yet quite restored, and I must put off many things till I feel stronger. I shall try, however, to . . . remove a false impression which my letter seems to have given you. You ought to know me enough to know that I am not trying to *convert* you and your friends to Christianity. If you are not a Christian, you must not call yourself a Christian. But I confess when I judged from Keshub Chunder Sen's writings, I thought that he was, as you were, more of a Christian than many who call themselves so. And if that is so, then the name of Brahmos or Hindus seemed to me a mere misnomer, and so far not quite honest. When you think of the popular Hinduism of the present day, with its idol-worship, its Pujahs, its temple-service, its caste, its mendicants, surely you do not approve, you rather shrink from them. It is easy enough to come to an understanding with you individually, and with Brahmos who have a philosophical culture. You would admit at once that all these things are not essentials, though they may have some kind of excuse in their historical origin. You want something of that kind for the great masses of uneducated people. All that is true; but what you know to be false and dangerous should be distinctly condemned, and should not be tolerated as part of your religion. Think how much of useless and even dangerous ceremonial the Christians gave up at the time of their Reformation, and I do not deny that some ceremonial, which is nothing but ceremonial, should be given up even now in our Church. But you never have told me what you object to in our Reformed Christianity, nor have you ever clearly formulated what you hold to be essential in your present form of religion. If you would do that, I feel convinced that we should not be so far apart as you imagine. I go even further, and maintain that there are several things in your religion which we might well adopt, and which would render our Christianity more perfect. Religion must always be for the wise *and* the foolish, for the educated and uneducated, and your religious philosophy might teach us many things that are worth knowing and believing. Then may I ask you the question whether you and your friends would consider yourselves bound by "An Appeal" in *Unity and the Minister*, February 18, 1900? You say there that your country cannot do without Christ—that India is Christ's, and Christ is India's. You speak actually of an Indian Church of Christ. Now these words can have one meaning only. You are Christ's, and in that sense you are Christians, without being Roman Catholics, or Anglicans, or Lutherans. I do not want you to join any existing Church or sect, I only wish you to give honour to the name of Christ, to whom you owe the best part of your present religion. If you have more truth to bring into the Christian Church, do so by all means. Tell me what doctrines you wish to profess, and it would not be difficult to tell you whether they are compatible with Christianity or not. But you will have to speak definitely, so that we may understand each other.

'Anyhow, do not suppress any objections you may feel against the Christianity of the English Church. That Church contains, no doubt, good and bad elements, but in no other Christian Church do you enjoy so much liberty. As to myself, no doubt I have been much attacked, but I have never been interfered with. Liddon was my dear friend, so was Stanley. To hold these two men, a Church must be very large, and whatever certain dignitaries may say, it was meant to be so. England, that finds room for so many nationalities and languages, has found room for many forms of religion also, so long as religion is what it ought to be, pure, holy, and tolerant.

'Do not be afraid, do not leave things unsaid which you hold to be true, but which will not be popular in India. There is a great work open to you, a work that must be done, and which may include Brâhmans and Mohammedans as well as Christians. But to do that work well we require perfect sincerity, we require men like Keshub and like yourself.

'I wish I were younger and stronger, but as long as I can I shall fight for religion in the true sense of that word. Religion should unite us, not separate us. It should unite us to God, and unite us in love to our fellow men.'

Throughout March there are constant notices in his wife's diary, proving the real increase of strength, and though in most letters Max Müller complains of inability to work, he carried on a large correspondence, and prepared a second article on England's rights in the Transvaal, in spite of what he says to the contrary in the following letter:—

To Prince Christian.

*Translation.* *March* 29.

'Your Royal Highness,—I see my essay in the *Deutsche Revue* has made an impression. I receive the most *amiable* letters, of which I enclose an example. I was threatened with the "gallows," should I venture to show myself in Germany!

'It is said that the twenty-fifth degree would include the German possessions! Now the Vienna Congress only dealt with Eastern Africa. Western Africa at that time was still no man's land, and even Prussia would not have thanked any one for it in 1814. I have no intention of answering, and only say, what Lady Augusta said of the Dean of Westminster, "Never so well as when he is in hot water!"'

This second article in the *Deutsche Revue* provoked still more angry comments in Germany, comments which proved that his arguments had really struck home. At all events, no counter-arguments were generally attempted, and those advanced by Professor Mommsen were disproved in a short letter of Max Müller's, dated April 29. With Professor Mommsen's consent, the whole correspondence was translated and published in a small pamphlet, and disseminated very largely by the South African Association. It is well to add that this epistolary warfare did not in the least affect the friendly feeling which had existed for long years between Max Müller and Professor Mommsen. So angry was the German public that the Leipzig branch of the Pan-Germanic League (the All-Deutscher Verein) drew up a solemn protest against Max Müller's *apologia* for England. The protest closed with the words, 'You have no longer the right to call yourself a German'; and one newspaper expressed its wish to see 'Max Müller hanging on the same gallows with Chamberlain and Rhodes, and the *Aasvögel* (vultures) picking his wicked bones.' But these vituperations made no impression on him; he only smiled, and felt that the day would come when the eyes of his countrymen would be opened. Yet even after his death, in many of the foreign obituary notices, offensive paragraphs appeared in connexion with this subject, and one of his countrymen in this country did not hesitate to speak of the 'cloud of obloquy which thus suddenly overshadowed his name, and dimmed the lustre of his renown near the end of his laborious life.' If his countrymen allowed themselves to write in this tone, the feeling in the country of his adoption was very different. The Prime Minister wrote that Max Müller's letters formed an excellent statement, and wished him to know how much he had been impressed by them. The Queen accepted a copy; Sir Mountstuart Grant Duff called it a capital pamphlet, adding, 'Mommsen sustains a poor case very poorly.'

So much had Max Müller's health improved that he was able to attend the Easter General Meeting of his College, and was deeply moved by the warm greeting he received as he entered the hall. He was not strong enough to attend the Gaudy dinner at night, and was away at Whitsuntide, so that this was the last gathering of the Fellows at which he was present.

A few days after this, Max Müller heard of the birth of his fifth grandchild, a second granddaughter, and the following week he felt well enough to go to London for the day to see the little creature and its loved mother.

To Prince Christian.

*Translation.* Norham Gardens, *May* 6.

'I have treated Mommsen most indulgently. If one is rude, people think one is hurt. I have always acted on this principle, and with good effect, especially in Germany, where they can be so very boorish!

'My friends in Germany, and their number is small, complain that they cannot obtain my articles, whilst Mommsen's are distributed gratis. That is called fairness!'

A young friend, travelling at this time in Germany, asked for Max Müller's letters at every station where the train stopped between Frankfort and Hamburg, and could not get a single copy, though he found Mommsen's rejoinder everywhere.

On May 9 Max Müller had the honour of receiving King Oscar of Sweden as his guest, and of showing him Christ Church. Merton and Magdalen were visited under other guidance, whilst Max Müller went to All Souls to rest, where he afterwards received His Majesty at luncheon in hall, and showed him the College. The King took tea at Norham Gardens, the Crown Prince of Siam being present to meet him. Nothing could be more genial, even affectionate, than His Majesty's whole manner to Max Müller, so anxious that he should not be fatigued in his still easily-tired condition, and the parting was most hearty.

A few days later, the Max Müllers went to their daughter in London for a short visit, and then on to Dover, where their friends Sir William and Lady Russell had been spending the winter. The old friends met whenever the weather would allow, but during the three weeks of the Max Müllers' stay there was constant rain and fierce, cold winds, bad for invalids, and they hardly saw as much of each other as they had hoped.

Among the friends whom Max Müller had seen go before him during the last few years, none had been more sincerely mourned than Herr George von Bunsen, with whom, of all Baron Bunsen's sons, he had formed in early days in Carlton

Terrace the most intimate friendship. The following letter is to Fräulein Marie von Bunsen, the eldest daughter, who had just written her father's life, which she sent to his old friend:—

*Translation.* GRAND HOTEL, DOVER, *May* 23, 1900.

'DEAR DAUGHTER OF MY FRIEND,—It was good indeed of you to send me the life of your noble and excellent father. I am astonished to see how well you have succeeded, for I must confess I did not consider it an easy task for a daughter to write her father's biography. Yes, indeed, it gives him just as he was. Often I feel quite startled when I think of him, and then suddenly recollect that he is no more here amongst us! I have thought of him often in little and in great things, though we wrote so comparatively seldom.

'Conquered! Was he conquered? He has lived such a beautiful life, and he must have felt how many good seeds he had sown! I knew so little of his good, practical work. He has not written any thick volumes, nor was he ever made a member of the Government; books die, members of Government are forgotten, but a good word spoken at the right moment can never die—it grows and grows, and that is what the Buddhists call *Karman*, which is so often misunderstood.'

TO PROFESSOR MOMMSEN.

*Translation.* TUNBRIDGE WELLS, *June* 13, 1900.

'I enclose the English translation of our correspondence. It is to be circulated by the South African Association, as widely as possible. We are not so far asunder, as you will see. As to the historical position of the Transvaal to England, you are even more emphatic than I am. Therefore, once again, "let us agree to differ," if we do really differ, which I don't quite believe. I am still seeking fresh health and strength, but don't find them, which after my long illness and at my age is natural. If you wish for copies, I can send them, but what pleases in England offends, alas! now in Germany.'

Nearly all June was spent at Tunbridge Wells, where, however, in spite of fine, even hot weather, and the good air, Max Müller did not seem to gain any increase of strength, though he could enjoy the drives in the lovely neighbourhood, and even moderate walks. He had settled to go from Tunbridge Wells for a long summer visit to his children at Ightham Mote, but repairs were going on there which closed the house, and before it was ready to receive the family Max Müller, who had returned to Oxford, was less well, and never left his own home again. It was pathetic how his thoughts this summer turned to Ightham Mote, and he often spoke of his great wish to see it again. But it was not to be.

Even at this time, when those nearest him were anxiously watching each day as it passed, Max Müller impressed strangers as still full of life and interest in everything. Dr. Crüwell, of Vienna, who was working this year in the Bodleian, described Oxford in a German paper, and after speaking of the emptiness of the place in Long Vacation, he says:—

'One person is in Oxford; Max Müller, suffering from illness, has not been able to leave his charming Oxford home. But he keeps it hospitably open for foreign birds of passage, who find their way to Oxford, from all corners of the universe. In his delightful library, bordered by bookshelves and looking on the shady garden, he welcomes the wandering student with that friendly charm which distinguishes this courteous scholar, and helps him with good advice and active kindness. Or he receives us in the garden by the side of his wife, surrounded by friends, imbibing at the same time tea and wisdom. Glad to hear and speak his native language, he asks a great deal about Vienna, which he knows and loves. How young this old man still is! As an evidence of his activity and love of work, he shows me the MS. of a new, far advanced book, which will be of great value to the world, the third volume of his *Memories*, "Old Oxford" (Autobiography). If any hand can reveal the treasures hidden by these old walls, it is his, who at once a poet and a student, has added more than any one else to the knowledge of our times.'

The year previously Max Müller had received from Paris the information that it was intended to hold a Congress on the History of Religions, during the great French Exhibition of this year, and that it was hoped that he, as the founder of this rich branch of studies, would attend. 'The Congress without you would be uncrowned,' wrote M. Réville. In July of this year Max Müller received a letter from M. Réville telling him of the great regret felt by all those who were arranging this International Congress on hearing that there was little chance that his health would allow him to be present. 'The esteem, the admiration, and the gratitude of all specialists in the History of Religions would have acclaimed you, without any possible contest, the President of our first gathering.' M. Réville ends by expressing his own sense of indebtedness to Max Müller for the direction given to his religious views, and in his professorial and scientific career. In August the Secretary, M. Jean Réville, wrote to beg that Max Müller would write the President a letter conveying a message of encouragement to the Congress, and giving them some advice on the method and meaning of the history of religions. This he proceeded to do, as his strength allowed.

To his Son.

Oxford, *July* 21.

'All my friends are going, and here I am still left; though not for long, I should say. You know what I wished from you, but what is the necessity of a name, or a family, or a *Stammhalter?* We must learn to look higher and further than that.'

Among the visitors in July were the Zemindar of Shurmuhamedpuram, the Rajah of Juggarau with his secretary, and the Gaikwar of Baroda; and towards the end of the month one of the Secretaries of the Swedish Legation arrived, bringing the Grand Cross of the Polar Star from the King of Sweden. Max Müller's daughter, a few days later, photographed her father with the Grand Cross and in the *habit brodé* of the French Institute. He was already looking very ill again, and the once tight-fitting uniform brought the wasting effect of his illness painfully before those who were watching over him.

The early part of August was the last period during which Max Müller was able to keep about, and enjoy seeing his friends, and he even wrote at this time an article for the *Forum*, an American journal, on the anti-English feeling among the Germans in America. The article was violently abused in Germany, where the papers seemed unaware that the *Forum* is published in America, and that the article was addressed to the Germans there. The virulent feeling of his countrymen against him was a constant amusement to Max Müller this summer. About the 17th he had a bad attack of shingles, which showed his great weakness, and from this time his strength gradually declined.

On August 7 Max Müller had a visit of unusual interest. Quite early in the morning his wife was told that two Hindus were at the door, and inquiring for Max Müller. She found two strange figures, one dressed in a flowing robe, with his bare feet in slippers, and a turban on his head; the other a much younger man, who could speak a little English. He explained that his companion was a most holy Yogin, by name Agamya Yogindra, from India. They had reached London a few days before, and hastened to Oxford to take counsel with the only man whose name they knew. Max Müller was unable to come downstairs before eleven o'clock, so they went away and returned at that hour. Agamya Yogindra was a genuine Mahâtma, or Yogin, who had mastered all that was to be gained by the ascetic discipline of the East. His position, as a teacher and holy man, was a very high one in India, as was shown by letters that arrived later from Bombay, with anxious inquiries as to the impression he had produced on Max Müller. He is the only saint or Yogin who has ever come to England. Impelled by the pure desire to impart what he believed to be the highest knowledge, he had braved the voyage to this country. 'He had come,' as he told Mr. Bidder later, 'to teach men the subtle enigmas of existence, but England was like a poisonous fruit, fair and attractive to view, but full of deadly juice; there were no good men, no one who wanted to understand knowledge; only in this house have I found a good man and *one who knows*.' In his simple ignorance of the world the Yogin thought that his name and fame must be known in England as in India, and he fully expected to be met at the station in London by admiring crowds. Had it not been for the kindness and sagacity of a porter, the poor man would have been lost. The porter, seeing the Yogin and his *chelah*, or disciple, sitting disconsolately on the bundles that contained their cooking utensils and food, managed to gain some idea of who they were, and took them to a psychical club, the members of which passed them on to Oxford. It had been arranged that Mr. Mozoomdar should spend the day at Norham Gardens, and he arrived not long after the Yogin and Max Müller had begun their discussion on the Vedânta philosophy. The Yogin received Mr. Mozoomdar with great severity. During his few days' stay in London, he had been in communication with Mozoomdar, and had commanded a visit from him at a day and hour, when he was engaged to lecture outside London, and therefore could not go. It was impossible to make the Yogin understand that anything could interfere with a command from himself, the saint, the holy man, and it was evident that Mr. Mozoomdar was in great disgrace, and, what was most curious to observe, he quite accepted the position, and acknowledged the crime of which he had, most unwillingly, been guilty! This gave the bystanders a greater idea than anything else of the position held by Agamya Yogindra in his own country. What follows is in the words of the Rev. J. Estlin Carpenter, who, with Mr. Bidder and Mr. Mozoomdar, was present at the interview:—

'The powerful personality of the teacher at once arrested attention. He was tall and strongly built; and in a face of somewhat unusual breadth the deep-sunk eyes, the wide but firmly closed mouth, the resolute chin, all spoke of long practices of meditation and self-control.

'The interview soon revealed the presence of one well versed in philosophic texts. "He is a first-rate Sanskritist," said Professor Max Müller to me, but the effort of maintaining a conversation, partly in Sanskrit with one who pronounced it in an unfamiliar fashion, and partly in the imperfect English of the Swamy, proved too much for his declining strength, and he was obliged before luncheon to seek a temporary rest. But at table, Max Müller's conversation never flagged; it seemed impossible to me that one so full of life could be in the grip of mortal disease. The Yogin would not sit down to eat with us, and remained in the library. We all joined in friendly talk afterwards over the coffee-table on the garden terrace. I saw the Swamy looking fixedly at his host, almost as one who would read the lines of destiny; I recall my anxiety that the party should not overweary the Professor's endurance; and we separated early, Mr. Bidder taking Babu P. C. Mozoomdar with him, and I leading the Yogin and his follower to my own house.'

Mr. Bidder recalls the parting thus: 'I shall never forget the scene on the garden terrace, when this representative of ancient India took a last farewell of India's friend and champion. "My life is nearly over," said the Professor, "I shall never be able to do any more work;" and the other, placing a hand on either shoulder, and looking long and fixedly into his face, replied, "Yes, I see death has come near you, friend; he has looked you in the face."'

Mr. Estlin Carpenter continues:—

'Professor Max Müller listened carefully to the reports of my subsequent intercourse with the Yogin. He had come to this country, he said, "to teach the subtle apprehension of reality." On that first day, as he sat in my study, he showed me that he could entirely suspend the normal circulation of the blood, and his pulse ceased to beat as I laid my finger on it [1]. But he was very anxious that it should not be supposed that he had come over to this country to excite faith by performing wonders. "These," he said with great earnestness, "are for little people; they are not for the full-grown." In October the Yogin yielded to our advice, and returned to his own country.'

The day after the Yogin's visit, Max Müller heard from Mr. Knowles, editor of the *Nineteenth Century*, that an article he had finished since his return from Tunbridge Wells would be most acceptable for his review. 'It is so absolutely up to date, that I immediately close with your offer.' This was the first of three articles on the 'Religions of China' which came out in September, October, and November of this year, and which are republished in *Last Essays*, Series II. The first was on Confucianism, the second on Tâoism, and the third on Buddhism and Christianity; the proof-sheets of the last Max Müller corrected within a fortnight of his death. In speaking of these articles, all written in the last four months of his life, the *Athenæum* says: 'They are remarkable, if one considers how recently they were written, for they show the grasp which the author retained to the last on the bearing of current events.' The writer in the *Athenæum* concludes his notice in these words:—

'We thus take leave of Max Müller the worker and thinker, in his chosen walk of scholarship surpassed by some few in his own and other countries, but as a scholarly writer second to none in his century. No scholar, perhaps, ever gained by his writings so large a share of

[1] This was afterwards verified for thirty seconds by the late Mr. F. W. Myers and Dr. Hodgson at Cambridge with proper medical aid.

attention from the ordinary public throughout the world, or, like him, succeeded in giving stimulus not merely to "general reading," but also to a far more important work, the gaining of recruits in all countries for studies that still need far more help than they receive.'

In this month the last two letters to his publishers of forty years were written, and show how bravely he was working on, in spite of increasing weakness.

TO C. J. LONGMAN, ESQ.

OXFORD, *August* 16.

'I have been thinking a good deal about the new volume of *Chips*. We might make an independent volume, and not call them *Chips*. It would make a large volume of about 500 pages; or how would it be if we made two small volumes of *Chips?* I see *Râmakrishna* is only 200 pages. Two small volumes of 200 or 250 pages could be sold at 5*s*. each, and be at once incorporated in my complete works. What do you think of that?'

And again:—

*Aug*. 25.

'As soon as I felt a little better I was attacked by a new illness—shingles, if you know what that is? Anyhow, it is most painful, and makes work next to impossible. I see I cannot hope to get my two volumes of Essays ready before Christmas or Easter. What do you think of *Milliaria* as a name? It would require explanation, viz. milestones on my journey. I should give the explanation in the preface.'

The volumes alluded to above were brought out after Max Müller's death, under the title of *Last Essays*.

Though too weak by this time for driving out, Max Müller spent some hours each day on the terrace before his house, reading to himself, chiefly the many journals and periodicals sent him from India.

The following letter to the editor is from the Rev. J. Estlin Carpenter:—

'Before quitting Oxford at the end of August for the Congress of the History of Religions held in Paris, I saw Professor Max Müller for what proved to be the last time. He was full of eagerness about the approaching meeting, and made me the bearer of his greetings to many friends whom he expected to be there. At session after session of the Congress his name never failed to evoke applause, and he was repeatedly cited as the real initiator of the modern comparative study of religions.

'I cannot close without once more expressing the admiration which his genius awakened in me. When I came to Oxford, he at once opened to me the privilege of intercourse with him. He was happy in retaining to the last the freshness of his memory; and as one topic after another arose in his vivacious talk, it was adorned with some vivid reminiscence, or set off with apt suggestion, quickening a younger mind to further inquiry. The habits of industry which he had practised in early life were never abandoned. Nothing but the most punctual and patient labour could have enabled him to keep up the continuous amount of work which he unweariedly performed, and maintain his extensive correspondence with all parts of the world. In the wide fields which he had done so much to open up and explore, it was not possible for him to follow the progress of discovery in every department with equal attention. But in the history of religion he had early found the guiding thread of all his studies. Here was for him the real justification of faith; it was inwoven with an experience which was practically universal. He had the sympathy of the poet, with all the imaginative elements which religious thought calls to its aid, and the clear insight which enabled him to disengage the permanent essence from its varying forms. It was especially in the parallel developments of Indian and European thought that he found certain great harmonies of belief; and it was his delight to show that the springs of trust are for ever inexhaustible, and well up with fresh force in new minds from age to age. This was the secret of his interest in the modern movements of religious life which produced such men as Râmakrishna and Keshub Chunder Sen. Again and again he would read some of the sayings in which the Hindu spirit found striking expression, and his voice trembled with responsive feeling. No other scholar has so successfully interpreted India to the West. Looking at the confidence reposed in him by the multitude of her own learned men, it may also be said that no Western teacher has done so much to interpret India to herself.'

On September 13 Max Müller's daughter came for a short visit, and the dear father dined down for the last time. The next morning he was decidedly worse, and his son was sent for from his post at Washington. And yet, though only able to leave his bed each day for a few hours, he busied himself in correcting by dictation the article on Tâoism for the October number of the *Nineteenth Century*. He also received at this time the proof-sheets of a new French translation of

*Deutsche Liebe*, and finding that the translator had failed to see the true meaning of the extracts from the *Theologia Germanica*, he himself translated them into French, dictating them to his wife.

As late as September 30 there is a notice in his wife's Diary: 'M. busy with me on the German article on Lao-tze.' This was an article for *Die Woche*, a German periodical to which he had contributed several short papers. She recalls vividly the animation with which he dictated, and his clear treatment of a, by no means, easy subject. Ten days later he corrected the article on Buddhism and Christianity for the November number of the *Nineteenth Century*, dictating an entirely new ending to the article.

The loved son arrived on the first of October; the daughter and her husband were already settled in the house. Max Müller was still able to move into another room for a few hours each afternoon, and the mornings were spent in dictating parts of his *Autobiography* to his son. All this time, and to the end, his rooms were like a bower, from presents of the choicest flowers, whilst other friends sent grapes and peaches from their hot-houses, and the feeling of strong interest and affection shown by so many were a constant source of pleasure to him, and called forth his lively gratitude. Those who had the precious task of watching over him, could but thank God that He was calling His faithful servant home so gently—for there was no suffering, only the *malaise* of increasing weakness—and his spirit was indeed entering day by day into living peace. For themselves! 'How often they reproached themselves, for when Death stands at the gate, conscience grows very sensitive regarding any lapses, real or imagined, of duty towards those for whom that dread messenger waits.'

On October 11 the following letter was received from Princess Christian, and permission has been given for its insertion:—

BALMORAL CASTLE, *October* 10.

'DEAREST MRS. MAX MÜLLER,—It does not require any words to tell you of the sorrow which fills my heart, and I am writing to tell you first in my dear mother's name of *her* true sympathy with you, and her distress at the news. She would like to send her kindest remembrance to the dear Professor, and to assure him of her thought of and for him. And *I* would send him my *fond love* and gratitude for all his kindness, all his true friendship, ever since I was a girl. . . .

'Your very affectionate

'HELENA.'

On October 17 Max Müller left his room for the last time. Princess Christian telegraphed to ask if she might come down and see him once more, but Mr. Symonds, his kind medical attendant and friend, forbade the exertion it would entail on him. To the Princess, to whose unfailing kindness he owed many happy hours, he dictated his last letter.

To the end he enjoyed being read to, and took keen interest in the newspapers, and all that concerned the war in South Africa. His valued friend and Vicar, the Rev. H. J. Bidder, was often with him, and a fortnight before he passed away administered the Holy Communion to him, his wife and children. The very day that he left his room for the last time, the British Committee of the Indian National Congress passed a resolution at their meeting: 'That this Committee desires to record its deep concern on account of the illness of Professor Max Müller, the revered friend of India; and, while expressing its admiration and gratitude, earnestly trusts that he will soon be restored to health.' In acknowledging the resolution, his wife wrote to Sir William Wedderburn, chairman of the British Committee, that her husband was deeply touched by it. 'You know,' she wrote, 'how he loves and has worked for India, and the recognition of this love and work has gratified him very much.'

Of these last days Mr. Bidder writes:—

'During the last weeks of his illness it was touching to see how, against much discomfort of body, his spirit would still struggle to assert its wonted brightness and energy. I knew that he always had his daily portion of Scripture and his daily prayers read to him, and when I visited him I made it my aim to let him testify, if only by a few words spoken with difficulty, to the faith which was in him. The future life of the soul was a subject which naturally occupied his thoughts; he felt the difficulties which beset our belief in the immortality of the individual; for the immortal part seems just that which does not belong to ourselves, whilst all that is most distinctly our own is bound up with and conditioned by the temporal and material world. "It is the old question," I said, "of the *principium individuationis*, in which I could never see my way clear." "No, indeed," he replied, "for it is the same question as the origin of the phenomenal world: we cannot explain Creation." I gathered his views to be that the material world was only the temporary instrument and condition for perfecting individual realizations of the universal, whilst at the same time the individual was always striving to overcome his material conditions. "And how," I asked, "about friends and family ties in another world?" "Well," he answered, "of course all that is earthly must perish; but it is not all earthly; it is sometimes what is best and highest in us." On a subsequent visit I returned to the subject by referring to Dr. Martineau's argument to the effect that all the training and discipline of the soul pointed to a continued and progressive existence, though we could not particularize. He was evidently too poorly to enter into any discussion, but I remember he quoted some favourite verses from St. John: "*If it were not so, I would have told you,*" and "*What I do thou knowest not now, but thou shalt know hereafter.*" This was, I think, the day before he received the Holy Communion for the last time, with all his family round him.

'No one can really know the thoughts and beliefs of another, least of all when the thoughts are greater than our own. But there is no mistaking the evidence of a life consistently lived in the presence and the love of God; there is no mistaking the influence which we experience ourselves, of a mind habitually occupied with high thoughts and noble aims. Of such men we may say, whether living or dead, "their citizenship is in heaven."'

The week before the end his brother-in-law with his wife came down to see him. His absolute serenity of mind struck them deeply. 'It is indeed,' said his sister-in-law, as she left the room, 'the peace of God, which passes *all* understanding.' Each night, as his wife repeated a few texts and prayers, he gave some word of earnest, hearty assent. On the night of Saturday, October 27, after repeating his favourite text, 'Thou wilt keep him in perfect peace, whose mind is stayed on Thee: . . . trust ye in the Lord for ever, for in the Lord Jehovah is everlasting strength,' she waited for the usual response, but he only said with a gentle sigh, 'I am *so* tired,' and turned on his side. These were his last words. No one had an idea the end was so near, even his devoted nurses thought he would still last some days, but by early morning he was unconscious, and at half-past eleven, without any struggle or suffering, with those dearest to him watching round, the spirit passed through that gate of death he feared so little, to the immortal life, and the rest he had longed for for many years.

That afternoon telegrams were sent to the Queen at Balmoral, to Princess Christian, and to relations in Germany and England: 'Professor Max Müller passed away peacefully to-day.' Very early the next morning came a touching telegram from the Sovereign whom he so honoured and revered, and who in the last few days had sent more than one message of inquiry and kindly sympathy: 'It is with the truest concern that I learn that your dear and excellent husband passed away to-day. Pray accept my deepest sympathy, and at the same time the expression of my sorrow at the loss of one who was so distinguished a man, and who will be greatly missed. I pray that you may be supported in this hour of overwhelming affliction. V.R.I.'

All day telegrams and messages of love and regret poured in, from the Prince of Wales, Princess Christian, the Emperor of Germany, the Empress Frederick, the King of Sweden, the King of Siam, the Prince and Princess of Wied, the Gaikwar of Baroda, and many, many friends. One of the most beautiful came from the Queen of Roumania (Carmen Sylva): 'The King and I are most deeply affected by the death of our most excellent and beloved friend. We pray God to be your stay and staff in your immeasurable grief and loneliness. May the rays of past blessings light up the hour of darkness. ELISABETH.'

Later in the day came a wire from his friend Mr. Malabari, from Bombay: 'All India mourns with you.'

Scarcely any of his own contemporaries were left to mourn his loss, either among relatives or friends, but the general expressions of sorrow were very striking, and the testimonials in the Press of all countries and in all languages to his influence and the value of his work, showed that though sometimes he might have been envied and misunderstood, his death was felt to have caused a real blank in the world of thought and letters; whilst the expressions of genuine grief from India, both in letters and newspapers, were most touching. Public meetings were held throughout that country, and in innumerable places the native schools were closed for a day. The letters from India were from Parsis, Hindus, Buddhists, Mohammedans, and Jains alike. The letters from Max Müller's Japanese pupils showed deep and genuine sorrow. Professor Takakusu wrote: 'For a week I could give no lectures.' A few typical letters are by permission inserted here.

FROM A LADY OF HIGH POSITION IN GERMANY.

*October* 30.

'Just as I had sent my letter yesterday the sad news came that your beloved Professor's earthly life was past, and that he was called home. Most heartily I grieve with you and yours, and feel for and with you in this sorrow.

'At such a moment one has no right to speak of oneself, and yet I cannot help adding: I sorrow too for the loss of a friend and one to whom I owe much more than he or you can imagine. How am I to say it? He helped me to arrange my thoughts, and brought reason and understanding to my vague feelings, and that helped towards strength, and now I feel the greatest strength is the conviction of life eternal; that nothing is or has been in vain, and that those who have been nearest to us are so still, perhaps all the more near, because this world cannot separate us any more. So I must tell you this as a kind of greeting from him who passed from you to the full light. I am grateful to the Professor for his friendship, and I think you know that. God comfort you and uphold you, and give you peace!'

FROM THE REV. A. BUTLER (late Tutor of Oriel).

14, NORHAM GARDENS, *November* 8.

'I cannot let this week pass, the first week of realization that you, and all those who honoured and in their various ways loved your husband, have yet had, without assuring you of our deep and heartfelt sympathy. He was our last great man at Oxford, and yet it is not so much of his great pre-eminence in knowledge that we are all thinking; it is of his fine character, his loyalty to friends and principles, his charming courtesy, his singular brightness and naturalness, that we feel most strongly.

'As Bidder said on Sunday in his noble sermon, he made one

better, when one talked with him. Even last year, when he was just a little recovering from his first great illness, his composure, his unflagging interest in all good things, his cheerful hopefulness, still remain indelibly in my memory as a type of what we should all be in sickness. And, indeed, I think the mind, so resolute and so calm and steadfast, must have had much to do with that new lease of life that was then accorded to him. What a loss he will be! here, abroad, in India, to all who want encouragement to pursue the student's life; to all who feel the greatness of learning, but seldom carry it out to a conclusion; to crowned heads, to simple learners, to those who wish to know the basis of religion, as well as those who rejoice in its completed work; above all, perhaps, to Englishmen who have to understand and govern their Indian dependencies! From all of these there comes a voice of sorrow, though at the same time they feel that rarely has any life been taken so little prematurely, so literally when its work was done. For myself, I can truly say, that though I did not often like to intrude upon his studies, I have often felt, while passing your house, that sense of something great being there enshrined, which it was good to have known, and an abiding lesson to all lower aims and less devoted industry and energy. We could not all have his great powers, but we could feel inspired by his great example. With all respect and sympathy for your loss and sorrow.

'Yours very sincerely,

'A. G. Butler.'

From the Bishop of Ripon.

'Indeed our hearts are with you. We grieve, for our memories hold so many happy and grateful reminiscences of his kindness. I felt that in speaking to him I could say what I would, and that he would understand. His own frank sincerity provoked—sweetly provoked—sincerity in all. His knowledge, his quickness, his wide intellectual sympathy gave to his sincerity a rich value, so that to meet and to talk with him was a gladness and a strength. I feel that I may at least write thus much to you, for I ever felt that in you both we had true-hearted and kind friends.'

From Archdeacon Wilson.

Rochdale, *November* 2.

'I have purposely waited a few days. You must have been overwhelmed with letters of respect and love for his memory. We all feel alike, and it is of no use trying to say it in different words. But he was such a friend to me that I must say a word of my own. When I first met him in Switzerland, I was a raw and crude man, not a youngster in whom such crudity was excusable, and he was infinitely kind and helpful. I showed him something that I was writing; he gave me advice and suggestions, which turned my brass into gold, and he encouraged me, which was just what I wanted. And so it was always since; with all his great and distinguished friends he found a place in his memory and kindness for me. I shall never cease to honour and love him.'

FROM THE PRESIDENT OF MAGDALEN COLLEGE.

MAGDALEN COLLEGE, *November* 1.

'. . . You know (and I think he knew) something of what I thought of Professor Max Müller years ago before I came to Oxford. I delighted in his books. They were the talk and admiration of my home and friends at Clifton. When I came up, I rushed, I may say, to his lectures, and enjoyed them, and profited by them greatly. Then little by little I came to know him, and found the great man and the distinguished savant, distinguished throughout Europe and the world, honoured and loved by scholars and princes, a most charming and most kindly personality. He accorded me, more and more, a measure of friendship for which I must ever be grateful, and you all gave me the *entrée* of your house and home in a manner which went to make *then* many of the pleasantest hours, and *now* some of the brightest memories of my Oxford life. It is much, a great privilege, especially in a University, to have known such a man, and such a mind. Alas! that Oxford and her sons can have it no more! Others may come, but seldom, very seldom, can come a personality so varied: touching so many points, religion, philosophy, learning, art, men, life and affairs, and yet so gracefully, so harmoniously blended—never can there come just what he was again. What must be his loss to his own home—but that is sacred ground.'

FROM THE BUDDHIST TEACHER, ANAGARIKA DHARMAPÂLA.

CALCUTTA, *November* 29.

'Blessings to you! I was in the holy city of Benares when I received the mournful news of the departure of your beloved husband, the illustrious scholar, from this plane of action to another life in the evolution of existence. So useful a life, indefatigable in the search after truth, one meets only after long intervals. Personally your late husband was kindness personified, and he aided my labours in the cause of eternal truth. When I was yet in my teens I was brought under the influence of his writings, and I have been a reader of his works since 1883.

'In obedience to nature's law, the physical body of the illustrious individuality known as Professor Max Müller has ceased to exist, but his name will continue to exist in influencing future generations. I now offer the deepest sympathy of all Buddhists in your bereavement; and I repeat the noble words of our Lord Buddha, which he uttered 2,489 years ago: "Do not grieve at my passing away, since it is natural to die."'

# CHAPTER XXXVI

## 1900

**Funeral. Judgement of friends. Conclusion.**

MAX MÜLLER was laid to rest on All Saints' Day, November 1, 1900. Early in the morning the coffin was moved to St. Mary's, the University church (as his own parish church, St. Giles's, where he had worshipped for more than thirty years, was too small for the numbers expected), and placed in Adam de Brome's Chapel, where the mourners assembled. As his old friend the Bishop of Oxford was too ill to be present, the service was read by the Vice-Chancellor, a friend of many years, the Vicar of St. Mary's, and his own Vicar. Though no invitations were sent out, the large church was entirely filled, for not only all those who had loved and honoured him in the University and neighbourhood attended, but many friends came from far; representatives from Cambridge, Dublin, and Edinburgh, of which Universities he was an honorary doctor; from the Royal Asiatic Society, the German Athenaeum, the Goethe Society, the Royal Society of Literature, and the University Extension Delegacy; and, being the time of the annual Gaudy at All Souls, a very large proportion of the Fellows of his College were able to be present. The Queen and the Emperor of Germany sent representatives, and the Crown Prince of Siam was present himself. On the coffin lay the wreaths from relatives, from the Emperor, bearing the inscription, 'To my dear Friend,' and from the King of Sweden. The full church, the beautiful music (the volume of sound as the congregation joined in the hymn 'Rock of Ages' produced an effect never to be forgotten), the deep feeling shown by many present,

*Holywell Cemetery Oxford.*

were a meet tribute to him, who had come to Oxford, fifty-two years before, an unknown youth, and who had made himself a name loved as well as honoured in all quarters of the world. Nearly the whole congregation followed on foot to the beautiful Holywell Cemetery, where he was laid to rest not far from the grave of his daughter Mary, his own Vicar reading the prayers at the grave; the ground all round covered with the beautiful flowers sent from far and near. A friend wrote afterwards:—

'The funeral was most beautiful, so quiet and full of dignity. Many of his friends around us in the churchyard were in tears. I dare say you will not have noticed the little bird which sang all through the service, mixing its song with the words of tender consolation. I thought that he would like its song—he who so loved all living, helpless creatures.'

Over the grave his wife has placed a tall Cornish cross of white granite. At the foot of the coping are the words which were his motto through life, 'Wie Gott will'—'As God wills.'

The Sunday following Max Müller's funeral, allusions were made in many churches to the great teacher who had passed away. In his own parish church, where his Vicar preached a noble sermon, in the University pulpit, in Westminster Abbey, and in many other places, it was shown that his memory was indeed cherished with love and respect.

The following letters and notices on Max Müller's life and work enable us to see what effect he produced on his generation. His old friend Canon Farrar, of Durham, has often been quoted in these volumes. He thus sums up his estimate of Max Müller's work:—

'I ask myself, What did he contribute to Oxford life and study? What to Literature? When the lovableness of his personality is unknown, and future students shall know him only by his books, what is likely to be deemed the outline of his varied literary work? What the chief points which he contributed to intellectual improvement?

'First, he was the means of introducing into England, and popularizing, *Comparative Philology*; especially the comparative study of the Âryan family of languages. He carried out that which Bopp had begun in Germany; and in some degree extended it, by studying the influence of early Âryan tongues in unveiling the steps in the organic development of language, and in exhibiting the influence of language in the growth of Mythology. Already the progress of investigation necessitates some modification in matters which he emphasized, but the attention given in England to the study generally is due to his acting as pioneer.

'Secondly, he so showed the importance of Sanskrit that he went far toward making it to be "a third classical language," a *sine qua non* for the knowledge of the *origines* of Greek and of Latin. His books in this line need revision or supplementation; but the originality and suggestiveness in opening up a new range of knowledge are unquestionable.

'Thirdly, earlier in point of time, and closely connected with the last head, is his laborious edition of the *Rig-veda*, the earliest surviving poetry of Sanskrit literature. He collated manuscripts, determined the text, created a canon of the hymns, and explored the antique grammatical forms, which make the basis of a satisfactory translation.

'Fourthly, he introduced into England the science of the *Comparative Study of Religions*. Max Müller opened the subject about thirty years ago in lectures, reprinted at a later time, on the Origin of Religions; wherein I venture, however, to think, he has overestimated the influence of language on thought, in a way which subsequent investigations have modified. He traced the influence of language on early religious thought, in creating, and not merely expressing, religious ideas; in a similar manner to that of Bishop Hampden, in his Bampton Lectures in 1832, in tracing the influence of the Scholastic Philosophy on Christian Theology. But the plan designed by Müller, and partly executed by him, of furnishing a translation of the Sacred Books has no relation to this theory of his, and must remain a classic work for students in generations to come. Though Max Müller treated the subject from the purely scientific point of view, he has offered to the believer in the Hebrew and Greek Scriptures the means of showing, in many respects, their exceptional superiority to the Sacred Books of other religions, not only in degree but in kind. Müller, in his suggestive *Gifford Lectures*, has fully expressed his view of religion; but there is a special value in the theological instruction offered when he is treating of pure literature; the more powerful, because unintended.

'I count it to be a privilege to have known him. While I live, I shall from time to time reperuse some of his books. I revere his memory, and in the language which he used in a brilliant lecture, in 1859, on the centenary of Schiller's birth, I say of him that Max Müller is a writer who excites my love.'

Mr. Andrew Lang's short notice of Max Müller in *Longman's Magazine*, in December, 1900, has already been quoted (see pp. 337, 338). The following letter gives the views of this friendly opponent more fully:—

MARLOES ROAD, KENSINGTON, W., *March* 26, 1902.

'DEAR MRS. MAX MÜLLER,—You kindly permit me to say a few words about Mr. Max Müller, and I am glad to take the opportunity. My own relations with Mr. Max Müller were those of an amateur, or casual inquirer, who ventured, on a single point, to oppose the conclusions of a man eminently learned. We approached the subject, that of the origins of myths, from different quarters, and saw different sides of the shield as in the old apologue. Neither of us was fortunate enough to convert the other, though on other points in the study of early religions we were in agreement, where the majority of inquirers differed, and still differ, from both of us. Such oppositions of opinion must inevitably exist. But what I am anxious to say is, that Mr. Max Müller always met my criticisms, often petulant in manner, and perhaps often unjust, with a good humour and kindness perhaps unexampled in the controversies of the learned and the half-learned. I shall always remember with pleasure certain occasions when Mr. Max Müller turned my own laugh against myself, with victorious humour and good humour. Our little systems have their day, or their hour: as knowledge advances they pass into the history of the efforts of pioneers. But that history would offer reading much more agreeable, if discussions were always conducted (they almost never are) in the genial and humane temper which Mr. Max Müller displayed in dealing with an "opposite" so unworthy as myself.

'It was not often that I had the honour and pleasure of meeting him personally, as I did at St. Andrews, and under your own roof, but these were opportunities which I must always recall as happy hours; and our agreement, on certain important points, became closer, as I learned more, or thought I learned more, of one of the subjects of which he was a master. Even where I, or others in this country, ventured to differ from him, we did, and do, acknowledge him as our teacher and initiator, but for whose guidance we should never have entered the enchanted lands of old religions; while his criticisms of our methods made for sobriety, and exactness, and discrimination.'

One of the best reviews of Max Müller's work and life appeared in the *Open Court*, published at Chicago, from which the following extracts are given by permission:—

'With the death of Friedrich Max Müller, on October 28 of this year, one of the most notable personages of the academic world passed from the stage of history. To the unlearned world at large, he was the personification of philological scholarship,—a scholarship which he knew how to render accessible to his public in inimitably simple and charming style. He was the recipient of more academic honours, orders, titles, royal and imperial favours, perhaps, than any other scholar since Humboldt, and he bore the greatness that was thrust upon him with the grace and dignity of a born aristocrat. Many were the pummellings he received from the hands of his less favoured colleagues; yet their buffets of ink but served to throw his Titanic figure into greater relief, and to afford him an opportunity by his delicate, insidious irony to endear himself still more to his beloved public. Apart from his great and sound contributions to the cause of learning and thought, which none will deny, Max Müller's indisputably greatest service was to have made knowledge agreeable—nay, even fashionable.'

In dwelling on Max Müller's famous doctrine of the Identity of Language and Thought, the writer continues:—

'His definition of thought is, upon the whole, arbitrary and made *pro domo*. The barrier between man and animal is not so impassable as he liked to imagine. But the beauty of style, the wealth and breadth of learning, the controversial skill with which he advocated his doctrine are undeniable, and the controversies to which his zealous championing of his cause led have advanced the cause of truth immeasurably. And this, he avers in an impersonal moment, is his whole concern:

'"You say I shall never live to see it admitted that man cannot reason without words. This does not discourage me. Through the whole of my life I have cared for truth, not for success. And truth is not our own. We may seek truth, serve truth, love truth; but truth takes care of herself, and she inspires her true lovers with the same feeling of perfect trust."

'And again:

'"Scholars come and go and are forgotten, but the road which they have opened remains, other scholars follow in their footsteps, and though some of them retrace their steps, on the whole there is progress. This conviction is our best reward, and gives us that real joy in our work which merely personal motives can never supply."

'As to his personal belief, we may say generally that Professor Max Müller was a Vedântist. He was a believer in the Brâhman doctrine of the *âtman*, or soul-in-itself, the monad soul; he believed in a "thinker of thoughts," a "doer of deeds," a Self within the person, which was the carrier of his personality, and a Self without, which was the carrier of the world, "God, the highest Self"; these two are ultimately the same Self.'

'How deeply these views entered his being is apparent from the following beautiful passage quoted from *Persona* (*Open Court*, Vol. I, p. 505):—

'"We are told that what distinguishes us from all other living beings is that we are personal beings. We are persons, responsible persons, and our very being, our life and immortality, are represented as depending on our personality. We ask what this personality means, and why we are called *personae*: the answers are very ambiguous. Does our personality consist in our being English or German, in our being young or old, male or female, wise or foolish? And if not, what remains when all these distinctions vanish? Is there a higher Ego of which our human ego is but the shadow?

'"Let us remember that *persona* had two meanings, that it meant originally a mask, but that it soon came to be used as the name of the wearer of the mask. We have a right to ask: Does our personality consist in the *persona* we are wearing, in our body, our senses, our language and our reason, our thoughts, or does our true personality lie somewhere else? It may be that at times we so forget ourselves, our true Self, as to imagine that we are Romeo and Juliet, King Lear, or Prince Hamlet. Nor can we doubt that we are responsible each for his own *dramatis persona*, that we are hissed or applauded, punished or rewarded, according as we act the part allotted to us in this earthly drama, badly or well. But the time comes when we awake, when we feel that not only our flesh and our blood, but all that we have been able to feel, to think and to say, was outside our true self; that we were witnesses, not actors; and that before we can go home, we must take off our masks, standing like strangers on a strange stage, and wondering how for so long a time we did not perceive even within ourselves the simple distinction between *persona* and *persona*, between the mask and the wearer. . . ."

'And now the great philologist himself has passed away; his Self also has been merged in the All-Self, creature in Creator. The fullness and purport of his life are such as have been granted to few; his mission has been fulfilled to the utmost; and it was with this consciousness that he departed. As Tacitus said of Agricola, "Let us dwell upon and make our own the history and the picture, not of his person, but of his mind. . . . For all of him that we follow with wonder and love remains and will remain for ever in the minds of men, through the endless flow of ages, as a portion of the past."'

It is a matter of regret that none of Max Müller's letters to his friend Baron Roggenbach (under whose auspices he went to Strassburg in 1872) have been preserved, Baron Roggenbach finding it at one time prudent, for political reasons, to burn *all* papers. The following appreciation of his friend has been furnished by the Baron:—

SEGENHAUS, *June* 4, 1901.

'Now as to the impression your regretted husband made on my mind when first I met him. I must say that never before, and never since, in my life, have I met with a more taking and charming personality than his, with all the gifts nature lavished on him. Though he kept the unique grace of his manner and sympathetic bearing to advanced age, it would be difficult to describe at its full value the effect of his cultivated mind, and his kindly nature open to all high feelings, when combined with the charm of youth.

'He certainly was the representative man of the best result that could be produced by solid German mental training. He had the happy fate of being transplanted with his stock of knowledge and exalted aims to the best soil for the full development of his rare powers—the English soil—and at such an early period of life, that all the blessings of the far advanced free British civilization could exercise its full and lasting influence upon him.

'So he realized in his person, and certainly in his mind, the type of what a close alliance and transfusion of German and British spirit could best produce, and has been a living example of what would be the result for humanity, for civilization and intellectual progress, if both nations would closely unite their best powers, instead of sinking, as they are doing, into the abyss of mutual national hatred, arising from the vile envy of industrial competition and commercial rivalry. In all that really makes the worth and historical value of the German nation, the large views on all human, moral, and religious subjects, the universality of knowledge and science, the courage of unlimited investigation and perfect freedom of thought, he certainly had no equal; but he never would have attained so high a standard, had he not had the good fortune to spend the life he owed to a gifted German family, in the serene atmosphere of English social and political life. Certainly both nations may be equally proud of one who has been an intellectual son of both. I hope the time will come in which the value of such a character as your regretted husband will be judged and recognized in its full value, and that he will be ranged amongst the greatest leaders of civilization for the advancement of humanity. In a certain sense he was too far advanced in his victorious views for the period of recurrent barbarity on which we have entered through the ravaging effects of military glory. But I feel sure that, after this eclipse, the advancement and progress of humanitarian views will set in with new energy, and then the high ideals to which your husband devoted his busy life, will earn for him and his memory new and lasting laurels.

'There are now few friends of his left, to appreciate what they possessed in him, and what they lost by his death. May you succeed in bringing out his picture, as it should be; then he will find new friends in the generation which is springing up, and his memory will be cherished by many more than those who now deeply deplore his loss!'

Dr. Kielhorn, now Professor of Sanskrit at Göttingen, and who spent many years in India, in a post obtained for him by Max Müller, published a paper on his friend's Sanskrit work, from which, by his permission, some extracts are given:—

*Translation.*

'To-day, after a lapse of more than fifty years, we can only realize with an effort the great difficulties which Max Müller had to overcome, before he could publish the first volume of his edition of the *Rig-veda*, a volume which was exclusively his own work. An edition of the text only of the Vedic Hymns would have been useful, and comparatively easy, for this text has been handed down to us for more than two thousand years unaltered. Max Müller determined from the first, and this will always be his great glory, to prepare a critical edition of the Indian Commentary, not of small portions only, chosen at will, but in its entirety. People have disputed warmly as to the value of the native Commentary. But in any case we *must* know the so-called traditional explanation of the Vedic text. When Max Müller began his task there was no perfect lexicon, still less editions of the innumerable texts incessantly quoted by the commentator. *Now*, we possess, besides the great St. Petersburg Dictionary, complete texts of the extensive grammatical literature, and yet every one would confess that it is even now by no means easy to understand Sâyana's Commentary in all parts. Max Müller had these works only in more or less imperfect MSS., he had himself to construct their texts, and to provide at least the most important with indices, before he could even enter on his own special work. It is everywhere acknowledged that he accomplished this task brilliantly. Any one who watched him, as I did, labouring at the *Veda*, knows how conscientiously he worked, and that he was not the man to print a single line of the Commentary, until he had thoroughly conquered its meaning. Did we possess but the first volume of his *Rig-veda*, we must place Max Müller amongst the first Sanskrit scholars of the last century.

'I must mention also two epoch-making works which Max Müller brought out during the publication of the *Rig-veda*: his careful edition of the *Rig-veda Prâtisâkhya*, and his *History of Ancient Sanskrit Literature*, which is not even now superseded by any other work. The enormous amount of this literature, the inaccessibleness of its monuments, and the circumstance that they are so difficult to understand, required long-continued and indefatigable study, united to most uncommon sagacity. We all owe Max Müller a deep debt of gratitude, not only for all he himself brought to light, but for the paths which he opened up for future workers.'

A few short extracts from letters, showing Max Müller's influence on people in very different spheres of life, are subjoined.

The hard-working wife of a parochial clergyman in America writes:—

'I feel almost as if I could burn incense daily to the memory of Professor Max Müller! To me he *lives*, and of late in all my spare time I am reading his books, and learning what it is to think of the greatness of the love of the Eternal One; and more than any of the devotional books I have read, Max Müller's teachings help me to understand what religion means. You know that in the rush and whirl of what is called Church life, one does not reach the highest. In my own little room, with Professor Max Müller I spend all my leisure moments. It is not his memory, but he himself, who in his strong, brave, beautiful life of searching for Truth, now helps me.'

A country clergyman says:—

'I often used to correct the erroneous ideas of people in regard to your husband's faith, for I knew from my long friendship what a good Christian he was. I shall never forget the family prayers in Norham Gardens, and his impressive reading of the Psalms in the (to me, unfamiliar) Bible Version.'

A letter from Madame de Wagner, from Rome, written directly the news of Max Müller's death had been received, ends thus:—

'Yes, dear Friend, he has entered on the true life, which he understood so well even here. I do not feel that we must regret that he is no longer here working for us; his task has been perfectly accomplished: at his age he could hardly have done any fresh work. It is for us to ensure that he has not laboured in vain.'

A Memorial Meeting was held in Columbia University in America, of which Mr. Moncure Conway gives the following account:—

'The large assembly of cultured people was addressed by eminent educators, men occupied with various branches of learning, and the most striking feature of every tribute was its pervading sentiment of personal gratitude to the teacher whose labours had ended. None of the speakers had known Max Müller personally, and only one had seen him, but each had his grateful debt to pay. He had opened for one his field of research; he had stimulated others to their tasks; he had enriched all by his literary and linguistic masterpieces. What are incidental *errata* of a pioneer in unexplored regions compared with the creation of a scholarly race able to correct the mistakes? The master sat at his mighty task, assiduous, unwearied: now his hands are folded on his breast; his case goes to the jury of scholars, and their verdict will everywhere confirm that of the Professor of Philosophy in Columbia University: "In a generation rich in scholars, no one could be called greater than Max Müller."'

The letter which follows, from the Vicar of St. Giles's, forms a fitting close to these notices of Max Müller's life and work:—

To Mrs. Max Müller.

St. John's College, *September*, 1902.

'I shall always count it as the greatest privilege of my life to have known your dear husband, and, above all, to have enjoyed such intimate converse with him upon religious interests. He had the gift of putting any one at their ease; in my own case it was sometimes a few kind words of encouragement on the last Sunday's sermon as we sat together on that terrace of yours; sometimes a searching question which went to the root of the matter; always a free confidence in stating his own convictions, which invited a like confidence in return. Yet his manner was never magisterial or patronizing; it was always rather the case of "iron sharpening iron," and of clearing up our views by mutual discussion. It was only in later years that I learnt the full depth of his religious convictions; but at a much earlier period I had occasion to observe a mystical side to his character, the influence of which, I think, may be traced both in his own religious life, and in his theories upon the nature and history of all religion. It had, indeed, no resemblance to that spurious mysticism which generally stands for what is confused and unintelligible. It was rather the consistent recognition of that "immediate" or "intuitional" element which is the necessary condition in all knowledge, as in all religious belief. The Infinite as a "Besetting God" when we contemplate the world; God as a present reality to the soul; Christ embraced as the very embodiment of God under human conditions; the love of Christ as a constraining power in our lives; the hope and foretaste of reunion with the Divine, enjoyed in the highest exercise of devotion: these characteristics of the true mystic were his, and in all he wrote upon the origin and history of religion we can see his eagerness to discover blind and tentative efforts which pointed in the same direction. On one occasion, when we were talking about Eckhart and Tauler, he told me how he had once contemplated, and even commenced, a translation of some of their sermons. Later in life, when his appointment to the Gifford Lectureship afforded him, as he said, "an opportunity for summing up the whole work of his life," he returned to his old favourites, and treated the German mystics in their proper historical connexion with earlier and kindred seekers after God, from the rise of the Vedânta philosophy to the Alexandrian School and Scotus Erigena. But, meanwhile, all his labours on the meaning and history of the religions of the world had gone to justify his early faith in Christ, and his personal interest in the German mystics.

'In accordance with these convictions and lifelong studies, his message to the world was twofold. On the one hand, it was to vindicate the claims of Natural Religion to be as "the impregnable rock of eternal and universal truth"; and, on the other hand, to show how the religion of Christ fulfils, and only by fulfilling can supersede, all other religions of the world. "No one," he said, in concluding his lecture at Leeds upon the *Vedas*—"no one who has not examined patiently and honestly the other religions of the world can know what Christianity really is, or can join with such truth and sincerity in the words of St. Paul, 'I am not ashamed of the Gospel of Christ.'" It was only a fortnight before he was taken from us that I made bold to remind him of this utterance, finishing the verse of St. Paul. "Yes," he replied, trying to raise his voice, "I remember, and in that I have never wavered." On the other hand, he held that the principal cause of unbelief at the present day was "the neglect of our foundations, the disregard of our own bookless religion, the almost disdain of Natural Religion." To base religion upon the verbal inspiration of a book, upon miracles, or upon ecclesiastical authority, was like trusting for the support of a building to wooden props or scaffolding, with the decay of which the whole building must fall. "Natural Religion," he concludes, "may exist without Revealed Religion; Revealed Religion without Natural Religion is an impossibility."

'These studies naturally gave him a great interest in missionary enterprise, though he would not in every case approve of missionary methods. "While some of our missionaries," he writes, "are delighted when they meet with some of the fundamental doctrines of our own religion expressed almost in the same words by so-called pagans, others seem to imagine it robbery that any truth at all should be found in non-Christian religion." This is why we find him referring so often to the speeches of St. Paul at Lystra and at Athens, which boldly assert that even among the heathen God had not left Himself without a witness, both in the bountiful gifts of Nature and also in that unsatisfied want of the soul within, which prompted them to "seek the Lord, if haply they might feel after Him, and find Him, though He be not far from every one of us." Again and again in his writings we find him pausing, it may be in some noble passage of the *Vedas* or *Upanishads*, or it may be in some traveller's account of rude and savage races, to dwell upon the testimony which they afford to the universal truths of religion and of human nature. . . .

'Although his faith in Christ was so firm, and his acceptance of Him, as indeed the Son of God, was so heartfelt and sincere, it is hardly necessary to say that it was not based upon the miraculous element contained in the Gospels, much less upon any form of ecclesiastical authority. What substratum of fact lay behind the traditional miracles, he was not particular to determine. With his friend, Baron Bunsen, he thought that the Resurrection was probably a temporary resuscitation, and when I argued that this did not afford a *ratio sufficiens* for the effects which followed, he would reply that these were due to the Ascension. This, of course, he did not conceive of as a physical ascent through space, but as a change which came over the Apostles' idea of Christ after His bodily presence had been withdrawn. This change consisted chiefly in their spiritual enlightenment as to the nature of Christ's person and doctrine; and to it he ascribed the Fourth Gospel, which he was constantly reading and quoting, and to which he attached the highest value. "What difference does it make," he would ask, "whether it was written by the son of Zebedee or some other John, if only it reveals to us the Son of God?"

'Similarly, the story of the Nativity he held to be the inevitable form which the belief in the Divine Sonship would assume as soon as that belief became widely spread and popular. But he did not love it the less, and no one could appreciate the holy joy of Christmastide, with its hallowing of motherhood and childhood, with more genuine devotion. . . .

'I was interested myself at this time in the writings of Albert Ritschl. Although he agreed with much that Ritschl contends for as to Christ being the unique source of our knowledge of God, he held fast by the metaphysical speculations which he thought connected Christianity through the Alexandrine school with Plato and even with the Vedânta philosophy. In this connexion he would defend the Athanasian Creed, partly I think in earnest, but partly also perhaps from a playful delight in posing as more orthodox than his Vicar!'

In October, 1901, in laying down his post as Vice-Chancellor, the President of Corpus spoke thus of his old friend:—

'Iisdem fere diebus e vita excessit vir Praehonorabilis Fredericus Max Müller, Collegii Omnium Animarum Socius, per 49 annos, primo linguarum et litterarum Europaearum quoad tempora recentiora, deinde scientiae quam vocant Philologiam Comparativam, in hac Academia Professor, totius orbis litterati decus atque ornamentum, vir omni doctrina, praesertim Orientali et speciatim Sanskritica, eruditus, eaque non solum quoad linguas, sed etiam quoad mores, religiones, historias illarum gentium de quibus scribebat. Nec tantum ob doctrinam eius amplam et variam deflendus est. Erat moribus humanus, sermone facundus, amicitia constans. Itaque fratrem nostrum, morte abuptum, ut sodalem lugemus, ut magistrum desideramus atque veneramur.'

'About the same time' (i.e. as Sir Henry Acland's death), 'there departed from this life the Right Honourable Friedrich Max Müller, Fellow of All Souls College, for forty-nine years a Professor in this University, at first of modern European languages and literature, and then of the science of Comparative Philology—the glory and ornament of the whole world of letters, a man skilled in all learning, but specially in the languages, the manners, the religions, and the histories of the East, of which the Sanskrit language and literature may be particularly specified. Nor was it for his learning only that his friends lamented his loss. In his manners he was kindly and courteous, fluent in conversation, constant in friendship. And so it is that we mourn for our brother, snatched from us by death; as our comrade we miss his presence, and we venerate his memory as our master.'

It may be mentioned here that Max Müller's library, consisting of about 13,000 volumes, besides eighty-one valuable

Sanskrit MSS., and several finely illustrated books, was, in accordance with his wish, sold *en bloc*, and bought by a rich Japanese nobleman, Baron Iwasaki, at the instance of Professor Takakusu, and presented to the University of Tokio, where a hall, to be called the 'Max Müller Library,' is being erected to contain it. Nothing could be more in accordance with his own wishes.

. . . . . . . .

And now these memories must close. An endeavour has been made, imperfectly made, to carry out Max Müller's own definition of a biography, and to show the three lives which he says, in an article on his faithful friend and patron Bunsen, every great and honest man leads: the life which is seen and accepted by the world at large; the second life, seen by a man's most intimate friends; and the third life, seen only by the man himself and by Him who made him; a life of aspiration rather than of fulfilment. The man, the father, the husband has been shown behind the brilliant scholar, the successful man of letters; and glimpses have been given behind the man of his 'angel beholding the face of his Father which is in heaven,' thus teaching us that our greatest men can be our best men, that freedom of thought can exist with true and deep religion. Max Müller's life was an eminently successful life. No doubt he owed much to his natural gifts of mind, to his attractive manners and physical beauty, which won him friends almost at first sight; but he owed still more to his indefatigable industry and indomitable courage, which poverty and hardships could not daunt. In him was literally fulfilled the promise, 'Seest thou a man diligent in his business, that man shall stand before kings.' 'He had little idea through life how he was envied, for the lesson that success breeds envy is one that men of real modesty seldom learn until it is too late.' These are Max Müller's own words of Bunsen, and they may be exactly applied to himself.

Some, in reading these volumes, may think his character is drawn in too bright colours, but only those who lived with him in the close intimacy of daily life can tell what he was. His love never failed; pure, patient, and strong, first to his mother, and then, for forty-seven years, to his wife and children. And is that love dead? No: for he is not dead. As his dear friend Charles Kingsley says: 'Those who die in the fear of God, and the faith of Christ, do not really taste death; to them there is . . . only a change of place, a change of state; they pass at once into some new life, with all their powers, all their feelings unchanged, still the same living, thinking, active beings, which they were here on earth. Rest they may, rest they will, if they need rest. But what is the true rest? Not idleness, but peace of mind. To rest from sin, from sorrow, . . . from care, this is true rest.'

'I know we shall meet again,' wrote Max Müller to Baroness Bunsen after her husband's death, 'for God does not destroy what He has made—nor do souls meet by accident. This life is full of riddles, but Divine riddles have a Divine solution.'

. . . . . . . .

The last chapters of this book have been written under the heavy pressure of new and deep sorrow. The last loved daughter, whose perfect married life was a prominent element in the happiness of Max Müller's last years, has been summoned, after a short illness, to the eternal home, and has joined those 'not lost, but gone before,' and desolation rests on the earthly home where her father passed so many happy hours.

And yet, 'Death is not death, if it gives us to those whom we have loved and lost, for whom we have lived, and for whom we long to live again.'

# APPENDIX

# APPENDIX

## A

### LETTER FROM SATYENDRANÂTH TAGORE

See Vol. I, p. 331.

AHMEDABAD, GUZRAT, *May* 13, 1865.

MY DEAR SIR,—I promised when I had the pleasure of seeing you at Oxford, to send you some information on the tenets and working of the Brâhma Somaj. I am afraid that the materials which I can lay before you are too scanty to be useful or satisfactory. It is this feeling of uncertainty which has deterred me from writing to you so long. Râmmohun Roy, whom the Bengal Theists regard as the great founder of their religion, has left no works from which its distinct tenets could be gathered. The fundamental principle of all his teaching was certainly Monotheism. His liberal views may be witnessed in the trust-deed in regard to a particular building, set apart for worship of the true God in accordance with the principle of the Brâhma Somaj. His was, for the most part, a negative task, that of pulling down the later idolatry of the Purânas. He tried, moreover, to cull out, from the pages of the Koran, the Bible, and the Upanishads, those portions which appeared to him to contain the pure doctrine of Theism. His work called *Precepts of Jesus*, an Arabic work of a controversial character, is constantly dinned into our ears as his best production. His numerous treatises on the Vedas, Upanishads, &c., I think, would bear out my assertion that his leading idea was to establish the doctrine of Monotheism, but that he failed to build up a positive system of religion. The immediate followers of this great Hindu reformer endeavoured, though feebly, to uphold the Vedas, and even some of the later Vedic writings, as Revelation. The earlier Brâhmas seem to have imbibed from their leader an idea that the doctrines of Theism are too pure and sublime to suit the gross ideas of the common people, and that therefore some sort of external authority is necessary to convince them. It was soon felt that the Veda, Vedanta, Upanishads, &c., containing as they do a mass of heterogeneous subjects, philosophical and unphilosophical, could not stand the test of reason in their entirety—that they must either be held to the full, or given up entirely as Revelation. Though the earlier

Brâhmas laid so much stress on the Vedas, yet it does not appear that any Veda scholars rose from among them. More attention, it seems, was from the beginning paid to the Upanishads. The present President and Âchârya[1] of the Brâhma Somaj had his mind first awakened, and his spiritual aspirations fed, by some of the sublime portions of those wild treatises. When he first took them up (he picked up a torn leaf accidentally which excited his curiosity), and began to pore into their pages with an earnestness he never felt before, what struck him most was the complete absence of idolatry in what he read. Many of the Pantheistic doctrines contained in them were easily construed into Monotheism, and the result of the President's studies was a collection of passages from several of the Upanishads, breathing sublime and pure sentiments towards the Supreme Being. This collection is called the Brâhma Dharma, and may be considered as the textbook for the Liturgy and forms of worship of the Brâhmas. It has supplied texts to the Âchârya, when acting as a minister and preacher of the Somaj, for sermons in Bengali which could scarcely be surpassed anywhere in sublimity of thought and vivid representation of spiritual truths. There is another little book in Bengali, prepared by me from his oral lectures, called *Doctrines and tenets of the Brâhma religion.*

A Brâhma, before he can be recognized as such, is called upon to subscribe to a settled form of faith and practice. The cardinal points of his faith are :—

1. In the beginning there was nothing but the one true God. He it was who created the universe.

2. He is the true, the good, and the living God; present in all time, pervading all space, infinite, omnipotent, everlasting.

3. In His worship is our true happiness in this world, and only salvation in the next.

4. Our true worship consists in loving the Lord, and fulfilling the duties He has enjoined.

These are the cardinal points of faith, which every Brâhma binds himself to cherish. As regards his practice, he publicly renounces idolatry, and holds himself to a daily offering of prayer and worship to the one true God. You will perceive that the four doctrinal points, as I have given them, include to the full the doctrine of Immortality. It is written that the soul's true worship of its Maker, dependence on His absolute goodness, and fulfilling of the Law, are the means of its salvation in the world to come. Our solid hope of immortality proceeds from our consciousness of that union with the divine, which has its beginning only in this world, but which is a sure guarantee of the life everlasting and bliss undying which is reserved to the faithful, the very shadow of which supports the soul in her sorrows and trials in this world.

There have been some attempts recently made to establish some sort of ceremonial in accordance with the principles of Brâhmaism.

[1] Keshub Chunder Sen.

The first impetus was given to them by the respected Âchârya of the Somaj on the occasion of his daughter's marriage. It has been for a long time our Âchârya's earnest endeavour to get rid of idolatry in all its branches. He waited till all was ripe for his noble design, and on the occasion of his daughter's marriage he succeeded in striking a deadly blow against idolatry, which has not since dared to show its face in his family. This merely negative step of breaking through idolatry created such a sensation among the Âchârya's relatives, that one and all kept themselves aloof from the wedding. To do away completely with idolatrous portions of the marriage ceremony, mere removal of the idol was not enough; some Mantras used on that occasion, and some other portions of the ceremony, had to be rejected. This improved ceremonial has since been adopted by a few Brâhma families. Not only marriage, but Nama Kurana mourning and other domestic ceremonies, have been invested with a new form.

I need scarcely remark here, that although something has been done to discard idolatry, and to spread the doctrines of pure Theism in Bengal, yet much remains to be accomplished. Some of the leading Brâhmas seem to forget that our religious education cannot go on isolated from our social and moral culture, that all the different parts of our inner life are intimately connected. Duty and good work are the limbs of Brâhmaism, without which faith is lame and powerless. We have the mass of the people to educate and generally to elevate. We have to emancipate our ladies from the darkness of ignorance and the degrading thraldom of the zenana. We have to pull down idolatry and caste, which have enslaved the heart and intellect of millions of our flesh and blood. We have to do all this and more, before we can rear up the superstructure of a pure religion on a sound and durable basis. The social life of a Hindu is thoroughly interwoven with unmeaning forms of religion. The whole system of caste is a monstrous imposition sanctioned by religion. The Brâhmana must put on his sacred thread, which is the badge of his spiritual superiority. All purely social acts have a religious sanction attached to them. A Brâhmana therefore who has renounced with all his heart idolatry and Hindu superstitions, has to exert his moral courage at every step of his life's career. The Brâhmas, as I have already hinted, now admit no book-revelation. They admit, indeed, that there is some manifestation of divine will in all revelations, inasmuch as they are utterances of souls religiously pure and noble. But the great doctrine on which the Brâhmas stand, is internal revelation—revelation to individual souls. As there arise now and then in this world prodigies of intellect, towering above their fellow beings, so there are sent men gifted with religious and moral intuitions in far more than ordinary measure. They are meant as our examples. The great Being who sends to this world individuals strongly stamped with the divine, does not yet cease to inspire the world with His presence and reveal Himself to the prayer of faith. It is to Him only that we are bound to offer our tribute of worship and allegiance. The Brâhmas, however, would not fail to appreciate the beauty of the moral precepts of Christ, or the sense of absolute trust and dependence on Providence, as taught by Mohammed.

In regard to the doctrine of Atonement, the Brâhmas are, I am disposed to think, at variance with some of the Christians. We are told by the missionaries that we are sinners—no religion has ever doubted the fact. Then we are reminded that nothing can save us from our sins but belief in a Christ crucified. The Brâhmas hold that it is God's absolute goodness, from which alone we can hope for our salvation. We cannot undo that which we have done—all we can do is to repent for our past sins and try with all our strength to amend our future. We are not left alone, but if we pray Heaven with an earnest and lowly heart for purity and strength, God will send His blessings to us. Some of these missionaries would turn us out of God's mercy-seat, by frightening us with the awful name of Justice, as if it is something incompatible with His goodness and mercy. If God's mercy and justice will not and cannot save us, the Brâhmas ask, what will? 'Christ's blood,' is the answer. Tell us how? Christ was innocent, and, as you say, perfectly pure. He took upon Himself, it is said, all our sins, and died a torturing death. This was God's dispensation to save sinners. We cannot reconcile this with our idea of God's justice. Kill the innocent to save the guilty, kill him not merely in a physical sense, but throw on him all the sins of all the world, and drown him to death in an ocean of sins, that all sinners might escape! We are landed in this by the ordinary theory of atonement. We have a full faith in immortality, without which religion itself would be unmeaning. The Brâhma believes in a system of rewards and punishments in a future world, and in unending progress of the soul towards perfection and happiness. What the exact nature of that world is to be, no religion has attempted to set forth without falling into fanciful absurdities. The Brâhma, I may remark by the way, is horrified at the idea of eternal hell-fire, with which (the minister of) Christ so often threatens refractory individuals. It is commonly maintained that Brâhmaism or Theism is too theoretical to maintain its ground. The generality of people want something more substantial to stand upon than the vague doctrines of Theism. Whether pure Theism, divested of all false forms and false revelations, which hold such marvellous ascendency in this world, will ever be anywhere dominant, I cannot pretend to say. Many physical improvements, social and moral movements to which the ancients were utter strangers, have taken a start in the modern world, and such an advent may be hoped for in regard to Theism, if it be God's Truth. There are hopeful signs of the spread of Brâhmaism in India, notwithstanding the serious obstacles which obstruct its progress.

## B

## Max Müller's Speech at the Peace Festival, May, 1871

See Vol. I, p. 418.

Ladies and Gentlemen—

'Out of the abundance of the heart the mouth speaketh.' Yes, but the heart may be too full, and one hardly dares to dive into the depths of the soul, and to give utterance to what so powerfully excites and moves us. I feel that I shall not find the right words to-day; but I know that you will understand this and forgive it: for, like my own heart, the hearts of all whom I here address are full, I believe, of overpowering feelings and thoughts, full even to overflowing—full of thankfulness for what has been achieved—full of hope for what has still to be achieved—full of rejoicing as we think of the brave soldiers who, covered with glory, are returning to their homes—full of mourning as we remember those dear to us who are never to return, but whose memory will be sacred to us for ever—full of regret as we recall the men who from the beginning of this century have striven and suffered like martyrs for the deliverance of Germany, who prophetically looked forward to this day of victory, but have not lived to see it—full of joyful pride as we look to the heroes, who through word and deed have completed the great and difficult task of the union and freedom of Germany,—yes, full of enthusiasm as we pronounce the names of our statesmen, our generals, our young Fritz, our old hero-Emperor—but, above and beyond all, full of love for our great and beautiful and noble, and now at last again united and free, Fatherland!

Yes, my German countrymen, Germany has never known greater days; and it is right that we—I mean especially we here in a foreign country—should feel and remember this, and derive strength and comfort from it. The present quickly becomes the past, and even the greatest events look smaller at a distance. Therefore the pictures which have just passed before your eyes were meant to turn the past again into the present, and give new life to it in our remembrance. You have seen how Germania calls her children together to her defence, to guard, to fight for the Rhine. You have seen how she distributes her arms, and how the German host—that is, the German people—pours forth from every city and village of the Fatherland, to guard freedom and honour, and to fight for life or death. '*All Germany stands unanimous in arms*'—that royal word sounded on the second of August as a blast of a trumpet from the old fortress of Mayence, in every palace, in every cottage where beat a German heart. Do you still remember the feelings which then moved our hearts? Not with light, no, with heavy, heavy hearts we saw the dreadful tragedy of war unrolled. We did not believe in rapid victory—we were prepared for a long and hard struggle—we thought of 1806, but we also thought of 1813.

And what gave us our confidence in our army and in our people, and the trust that the just cause must prevail in the end? Four things I have to mention.

First comes German *Courage*; not that wild frenzy which at every disagreeable word grasps the hilt. No, that is not German courage. No people on earth has borne so much as the German. But when not only the independence of a people is curtailed, and its natural development impeded from without—nay, when the old sacred frontiers are invaded, when some fine morning the newly-invented engines of death are tried on the inhabitants of a peaceful city, then the measure is full, patience becomes indignation, indignation wrath unto death—death is better than life under such an outrage. 'The people rose, the storm broke.'

In the second place, I name German *Diligence*. Gentlemen, we have often been abused as a nation of schoolmasters and Professors. I know of no more honourable abuse, and I am firmly convinced that Germany owes much of its great success in war to its hard-working schoolmasters and Professors. The German army is an educated and an intelligent army. Through determined, unbending diligence—through hard, ungrudging work from morning till evening —has our German army become what it is; so that, as in a loom, one touch moves and intertwines a thousand threads, no thread breaks, no pattern fails. Genius is indeed a long patience.

In the third place, I name the German *Sense of Duty*, and in war perfect obedience. When a great work has to be achieved, the individual must sacrifice for a time his personal views and wishes, must stay like a soldier on the battle-field. Gentlemen, people have dared to question the discipline of the German army. Lies have been invented, and when they had been thoroughly refuted, people said, 'There is no smoke without fire.' That is a cowardly proverb. Translate it into German, and you will see how false it is, 'There is no lie without truth.' If such a proverb were believed, the honour of no man would be safe. That in an army of nearly a million there should be some black sheep is not surprising. But before the judgement-seat of history it will appear that in no war has there been so little unnecessary cruelty, in no war has every crime been punished with so much severity, in no war has humanity achieved such triumphs as in the last German war of liberation. We are prouder of these triumphs than of all the triumphs of our arms.

In the fourth place, I mention German *Perseverance*, undauntedness even in misfortune, which is founded on a firm trust in God, and in a Divine Providence. People have not hesitated to scoff at this German trust in God; this faith in the Lord of Hosts. But we keep to our own old German way. Before the battle our army sings with Theodor Körner, 'Father, I call to Thee'; it sings after the battle the old psalm which our Luther has changed into a popular song, 'Our God is a strong tower.'

These four qualities—German Courage, German Diligence, German Sense of Duty, and German Perseverance—have been to us the sure warrants of victory. They pervade the whole army; but I may name for each a living representative.

As representative of German *Courage*, I name Bismarck. His heart never failed him.

As representative of German *Diligence*, I name Moltke. He is the real, true, indefatigable German Professor, and though he can be silent in seven languages, his last lecture will not soon be forgotten by the world.

As representative of German *Sense of Duty*, I name the Crown Prince. No one hates war more than he does; no one has done his duty so faithfully, though often with a heavy heart.

As representative of German *Perseverance*, I name our Emperor. That man has indeed clung to his purpose. At the battle of Jena he was exactly as old as Hannibal when his father made him take his famous oath, and what bitter days has he gone through since! But, undismayed, he has carried on the one work of his life, the raising and strengthening of the German army, till the disgrace of Jena was wiped out on the field of Sedan.

With such irresistible powers Germany began the war and brought it gloriously to an end; and we have to thank the Statesman, the Generals, the Emperor, the German Army, and the 'God who made iron grow,' that we celebrate to-day this happy festival of peace.

We celebrate it in a foreign country;—but is England really a foreign country to us? I confess I hardly ever felt this, not even during this war, when many a dastardly word fell on the English side, and also on the German. I feel that in England I am in a friend's, not in an enemy's country. There are even liberal and rational people, who, during the late war, have judged wrongly of the German nation. Gentlemen, you know that in England a man is worth very little who is not attacked and abused by some party. There are insults of which one ought to be proud, as there is praise of which one ought to be ashamed. Were I to mention the names of those who, from beginning to end, have remained true to the German cause, you would hear names that have the best ring, not only in England, but in the whole world. The kernel of the English people is not against us; the true aristocracy of the country is with us.

And why? Not only because the same blood runs in our veins—not because 'English is, after all, but Old Low-German'—not because the Reformation has its two strongest pillars in Germany and England—no, I can give you a better and a deeper reason. It is so because the Germans and English owe allegiance to the same queen, and recognize the same majesty as their highest authority, and that queen and that majesty is *the Voice of Conscience*. That is the firm ground on which the greatness of England stands immovable, on which the greatness of Germany is being built up.

Gentlemen, the political guidance of Europe belongs in the immediate future to those two so closely related nations; the political guidance of the whole civilized world belongs to the English, the Americans, and the Germans. If these three Teutonic nations hold together, the world will have peace again. But if these three Teutonic nations are divided by suspicion, jealousy, or pride, the furies of war will never be chained in Europe.

Therefore, if this our festival is to be a true peace festival, let us forget from this moment all bitterness; let us do what we can, every one in his own small sphere, in order to maintain mutual respect, and a firm friendship founded on it, between England, Germany, and America. The festival which we celebrate to-day should not be a passing ebullition of joy and gladness, but should receive a higher sanction and confirmation, and become a festival of peace and concord for all times and all people.

The memory of the great days of the years 1870–1 should never fade, but retain its life and vigour, and support in coming generations the same sentiment of patriotism which glows in our hearts to-day—which has brought us together to-day, no longer as North Germans or South Germans, as Protestants or Catholics, as Liberals or Conservatives—no, as brothers, as sons of one Fatherland, as children of one great and beautiful and noble, and now at last again united and free, Germany.

## C

## SPEECH OF DEAN LIDDELL, FEBRUARY 15, 1876

See Vol. II, p. 7.

FROM a letter written by Professor Max Müller, bearing date December 1, 1875, the University learnt, with surprise and regret, that it was the Professor's intention to resign his office at the end of the Academical year. The reasons he gave were that he had served the University as Professor for exactly a quarter of a century; that the chief work of his life had been the publication from MSS. of the text and commentary of the oldest of the sacred books of India; that though this work had been completed, he wished to devote himself to the task of making the hymns of the Brâhmans accessible to general students by translations, together with other work connected with the same object; that he could not undertake to continue this task and at the same time discharge the duties of his professorship.

The purpose of this Decree is to enable him to keep his Chair, and to devote himself to the work in Indian Literature which he proposes to himself; a work not alien from the subject of his Chair; for Sanskrit is the parent of Comparative Philology. I know well the difficulties I have to encounter in bringing this proposal before you. The objections are patent. The difficulties we have to overcome are not so well known. So far as I apprehend them, the objections are of two kinds: first, the objections to the Decree on constitutional grounds, and secondly, objections to the terms of the Decree itself. (1) Now with regard to the objection that we ought to have proceeded by Statute, rather than Decree, I must confess that we are guilty. But then we had no choice in the matter. If any attempt to retain Professor Max Müller was to be made, it must be made at once. He has received several proposals from foreign Governments; and one especially from the Austrian Minister, offering him the Sanskrit Chair lately founded at Vienna, together with an undertaking on the part of the Imperial Academy to publish the Indian translations which he contemplates, and it was necessary to give a prompt answer. This Decree is not intended as a permanent measure. I hope then that the House will not object to pass the Decree, on the distinct understanding that it is only proposed in this form for the purpose of gaining time. (2) But the terms of the Decree are objected to. We are proposing to rob the Chair of Comparative Philology for an indefinite time. As to robbing the Chair, I would ask you to consider this. If the Professor had been unhappily disabled by those calamities enumerated with terrible precision in this as in other Professorial Statutes, he would have had a deputy appointed to do his work at a salary assigned by the Vice-Chancellor, and this might be for an indefinite time. Perhaps also a Professor so disabled might not have been very industrious, might not have conferred honour on the University throughout Europe, America, and India, and yet he might have continued Professor and retained half his salary for a time truly indefinite. But in this case, though the time is undefined rather than indefinite, I hope that no long period may elapse before we may be able to propose a measure terminating this not very satisfactory proposal. I may add that the portion of the salary left to the Professor is not wholly subtracted from the Science of Comparative Philology.

No one, it has been said, who wishes to acquire a thorough knowledge of Greek or Latin, or any other of the Indo-European languages, no one who takes an interest in the philosophy and historical growth of human speech, can, for the future, dispense with some knowledge of the language and ancient literature of India. . . .

I will ask the House to bear with me while I lay before them a brief statement of Professor Max Müller's work. I have collected it from such sources as were open to me, not from the Professor himself. It has made a deep impression on my own mind, and I think it must produce a deep impression on any mind. It appears that more than thirty years ago, Max Müller, then about twenty-three years of age, who had turned his attention to the study of Sanskrit, went to Paris to attend the lectures of the celebrated Eugène Burnouf. At that time he believed firmly in the supreme importance and beauty of the later Sanskrit literature, and was astonished to hear Burnouf disparage these later books as of small value in comparison with the older portion of the *Vedas* and other ancient sacred books. At the time these archaic monuments were unknown, except to Burnouf himself and one or two more scholars. A small beginning had been made in the work of editing them; they remained buried in MS., and in the obscurity of a language which could not be understood by those well versed in the common Sanskrit. Burnouf told him that to enter into the real treasures of Indian Literature, it was necessary to be master of the *Veda* and its voluminous Commentary. Burnouf lent him some of his MSS., and encouraged him to study them. It was hard work, he says, and had not Burnouf told him that he himself was often baffled by the language of the Commentary, he would have relinquished the task of reading them in despair. I remember very well that Professor Gaisford used to advise young Greek scholars to make themselves masters of Homer and the Scholia, and they would then possess the key to all later Greek. But then Homer was printed, and his commentators also. What should we have thought of Gaisford's advice if Homer was still locked up in MSS., if the Commentaries and Scholia were also still in MS., and not a word existed of all that had been done by the great scholars of Germany, France, and England? Who amongst us would have had the courage to say, I will undertake to collate all the MSS. of Homer, to form a reliable text, and will also edit the Commentary of Eustathius in an intelligible text? How many of us *could* have done this? Yet a task like this, only much more difficult, was undertaken with open eyes by the young student at an age when we have only just taken our degree. The text of the *Veda* indeed had already been put into a good condition by learned Indians, but without the Commentary it was, in great part, unintelligible; and the state of the Commentary was such as to daunt the courage of the stoutest scholastic heart. The errors and corruptions are countless; the Commentary abounds in short extracts taken, without reference, from works on all sorts of subjects, grammatical, etymological, philosophical, theological. These extracts are for the most part detached fragments, full of technical phrases, and often absolutely unintelligible by themselves. It was necessary for an editor to hunt up these passages in the authors from which they were taken; very often these works existed only in MS., and they had to be analysed and indexed before they could be used. This Herculean labour was undertaken by the young scholar. He found it necessary to come to England, for the MSS. he must use were in the India House and our own Bodleian. He raised funds by working hard, copying MSS., making translations and the like, for Sanskrit scholars wealthier than himself. By the assistance of his noble countryman, Baron de Bunsen, and encouraged by our own great Professor, Horace Wilson, he began his work. Five years were spent in preparatory labours, and in 1849 his first volume appeared. It was followed at intervals by five other massive quartos; till in

1874, little more than a year ago, he was able to lay down his pen, feeling, as he says, as if he had parted with an old, old friend, on whom his thoughts had been fixed for full thirty years. During these years this absorbing work had not been his only occupation. He published his *History of Sanskrit Literature* in 1859, which, after reaching a second edition, has been now ten years out of print, besides other works bearing on Indian studies, and besides his direct contributions to Comparative Philology, of which the *Lectures on the Science of Language* have been translated into French, German, Italian, Russian, Hungarian, and Swedish. But it is on his great *editio princeps* of the *Veda* and its Commentary that I wish to fix your attention. It is difficult to say whether our wonder and admiration are more excited by the bold ardour with which, as a young man, he undertook such a task; by the steady and courageous perseverance with which he wrought at it for so many long years, or by the genius with which he surmounted all difficulties and erected a monument which may be truly called *aere perennius.* This great work has been printed at our Press, supported by the sagacious liberality of the old East India Company and the new Council of India. The text and its Sanskrit Commentary are in the hands of scholars; and the Professor wishes to devote himself to making these treasures of old Indian lore accessible to the general student, by editing translations with notes and illustrations. This work our Clarendon Press is willing to undertake, so as to secure to Oxford the credit of bringing out books so closely connected with our great Indian Empire.

And shall we allow him to carry his stores of Eastern learning away? Just at the moment when troops of native princes have been paying willing homage to the heir of the British crown, just when it is announced that the Sovereign of our Islands is about to assume the proud title of Empress of India, shall we suffer the groundwork of the old Indian Faith to be translated, not into English, but into German, and published by the munificence of the Austrian Government, who neither have, nor can have, any immediate connexion with India? I have great reason to fear that, unless we embrace the present opportunity, we shall have to submit to this discredit, for discredit I feel it will be. Other Governments have acknowledged Professor Max Müller's great achievements; the French Institute several years ago elected him a Foreign Member, the Royal Academy of Turin paid him the same honour, and made him one of a distinguished six, the others being Cousin, Thiers, Böckh, Mommsen, and Grote. He received the Cross of the Order of Merit from the German Emperor two years ago, along with von Moltke. England has been behindhand. Let Oxford by a unanimous vote to-day do something to repair this backwardness: not for his sake, but for our own, I ask it. Let us keep him if we can, how we can, while we can.

# D

## Missionary Speech, 1887

See Vol. II, p. 220.

I am not going to speak to you to-night about what missionaries have done for the science of language; they have helped us to a much truer and much more elevated knowledge of so-called savage or heathen religions than our fathers ever dreamt of. The question, therefore, which I should like to ask to-night, is this—whether savage religions are really like what savage dialects were represented to be, hardly articulate, brutal, ferocious, fiendish; or whether, hidden beneath the rubbish, they contain some elements of truth and goodness which the missionary may recognize as common ground on which he may build, and on which he should take his stand when first approaching his future converts. The change which has taken place in our view of non-Christian religions is one of the most remarkable features of our age, though, as in the case of many of the newest views of our age, we shall find, I believe, on closer inspection, that after all they are not so new as we imagine. St. Augustine, though he had probably seen and experienced more of the terrible sides of heathen religions than any one else, yet declared his conviction that he never had seen any religion which did not contain some truth.... After a long experience in life, I have been led to divide all my friends, missionaries included, into two classes—those who seem to have eyes for all that is good, and those who seem to have eyes for all that is bad. Well, you all know the men I mean. If you go with them to a concert, they will speak of nothing but the wrong notes. If you go with them to church, the first they tell you is what the preacher ought not to have said. I have been a guide through Oxford for many years, and in watching my friends from every part of the globe I found they fell into two classes, what I call the *bright-eyed* and the *dark-eyed*. The *dark-eyed* tell you that the Oxford buildings are all in rags, that the stone decays and is hideous. They point out incongruities in architectural style, they are scandalized at the attire of the undergraduates coming home in crowds from football, and they wonder whether all University lectures are given in the Parks, because they see undergraduates nowhere else. But there are others, whom I call my *bright-eyed* friends, who admire the effects of light and shade on the crumbling old stones, who read history in the incongruities of architectural style, who approve of the bones and sinews of our athletes, and who express real regret that they could have heard only one of Professor Palgrave's lectures, or one of the Bishop of Ripon's sermons. Now I need not tell you which of these two classes I like best, and I may add that I generally find that the really great artists and scholars and statesmen are bright-eyed, the smaller artists, scholars, and statesmen dark-eyed. I remember so well walking many years ago through the colleges and gardens of Oxford with Professor Rauch, the great German sculptor. He was an old, magnificent, and most beautiful man, and he certainly seemed to have eyes for what was beautiful only. When he looked at the Raphael drawings he stood back in awe, holding his breath. And what was it? Some small child's hand that would have struck no one else's eyes. Over and over again he gazed at an old building, and showed me effects which I had never observed before. All that was commonplace or imperfect seemed hardly to exist for him. We need not wonder, therefore, if missionaries too are dark-eyed and bright-eyed. Some see only the darkness of the night, others the brightness of the stars, even if so dim that ordinary eyes can hardly perceive them. I shall to-night appeal to Dr. Codrington and Mr. Cousins to tell us something, however little it may be, of the bright side, something of what St. Augustine meant when he said that there is no religion which does not contain some truth. They have been so long among heathens that they must have seen more than the mere surface of their religion. They must surely have met some God-fearing men, some pure-minded women, some human creatures to prove that St. Paul was right in saying that God never left Himself without witness, and that St. Peter perceived a great truth when he boldly declared that in every nation he that feareth God and worketh righteousness is accepted with God.

My own acquaintance with non-Christian religions is restricted to what are called in the East book-religions, that is, religions which are founded on some kind of sacred book. When I undertook to publish for the University Press a series of translations of the most important of these sacred books, one of my objects was to assist missionaries. What should we think of a missionary who came to convert us, and who had never read our Bible? No doubt it is but too true that religions are seldom in practice what their Bibles represent them to be, or what they were meant to be by their founders. Yet if we wished our own religion to be judged, we should wish it to be judged by the New Testament. It is but fair, therefore, that we should judge other religions according to the same rule. But, it will be said, you cannot deny that the Hindus are polytheists, that they worship idols. But let us look at their own Bible, at the *Veda*, older than any other book in India. No doubt we find there many names for the Divine, many gods, as we are accustomed to say. But there are also passages in which the oneness of the Deity is clearly asserted. In later writings, too, we find bright sparks of truth. It is true that the Hindus worship idols. But in the *Bhagavad-gîtâ* the Supreme Spirit is introduced as looking with pity on all these helpless childish customs, as saying with the sublimest and almost super-divine unselfishness: 'Even those who worship idols worship me.' Is not this the same thought which St. Paul expressed so powerfully at Athens: 'Whom, therefore, ye ignorantly worship, Him declare I unto you,' and is not this the spirit in which missionaries might and ought to approach every religion? But while for gaining a true and accurate knowledge of any of the great book-religions a study of their recognized sacred books is sufficient, a keener insight, a warmer sympathy, a truly Christian kindness are wanted in our treatment of lower savages and in our judgement of their religion. The lowest of all savages are said to be the Papuas. They are often supposed to be without any religion, any morality, any conscience. Yet these very same Papuas, if they want to know whether what they are going to undertake is right or wrong, squat before their *Karwar*, some hideous stock or stone, clasp the hands over the forehead, and bow repeatedly, at the same time stating their intentions. If they are seized with any nervous feeling during this process it is considered a bad sign, and that project is abandoned for a time; if otherwise, the idol is supposed to approve. Here we have but to translate what they in their helpless language call nervous feeling by our word 'conscience,' and we shall not only understand what they really mean, but confess, perhaps, that it would be well for us if in our own heart the *Karwar* occupied the same prominent place which it occupies in the cottage of every Papua.

## E

## Memorial Oration by Professor Max Müller, March, 1888

See Vol. II, p. 225.

'The German Emperor is gone home.' So spoke his noble son, bowed down with grief; so in deep sorrow speaks the whole German nation. The long and heavy task of his life is finished, the victory won. He had long reached and even exceeded the usual span of human life. What was left for the Emperor still to wish for on earth? After long toil and labour he had a right to rest, and God has called him home to peace with honour.

Therefore, deeply as we sympathize with those who in the Emperor have lost an old and cherished friend, keenly as we all miss the faithful honest eyes which have for so long kept watch over Germany's weal and woe, we feel that mere weak sorrow is out of place at the grave of the German Hero-Emperor. The human heart demands its rights, and the sweet bonds of life cannot be broken without tears. But when the tears are dried, then the voice of lamentation must cease and rise again in new chords of thanksgiving, of firm trust, nay, even of joyful triumph.

Let us speak out boldly! In the whole course of the world's history we shall find no life to compare with the life of the Kaiser Wilhelm. We ourselves stand far too near to the events of the last decades to estimate aright their full importance in the history of the world. We have witnessed great, infinitely great, events.

What does the work which the Emperor achieved really import? What imports a German Empire in the heart of Europe and in the centre of the whole world? Does it only show the success of a clever diplomacy, the restoration of the balance of power in Europe shattered by Napoleon's arrogance? Is the victory of Sedan nothing but a sharp answer to the defeat of Jena?

No; we must look far higher if we are to measure the true importance of these events in the world's history. The struggle of the German nation for its German life, so gloriously ended by the Kaiser Wilhelm, began 2,000 years ago with the first beginnings of European history. It began with the victory of Arminius or Sigfrid in the Teutoburger Forest, it had its first prophet in Tacitus, its numberless martyrs in Grimhilda and Theodoric, for these were their names, and in the German slaves and mercenaries who were buried under the ruins of the Roman Empire. For hundreds, aye, for thousands, of years the storms raged and the waves were tossed hither and thither between the German and Romanic nations, while sometimes one, sometimes the other, overflowed the sacred boundaries which a wise nature had drawn so clearly and visibly between them—the mighty Alps and the free Rhine. In the fifth century the youthful daring of the German hosts triumphed; Germans were lords of Italy and of Gaul. The Western Empire fell, and the German King, Theodoric the Ostrogoth, held at Ravenna in 493 the fate of the whole of Europe in his hands. The Lombard kingdom followed, and still the power was in German hands. Then came Charles the Great, whom Germany, France, and Italy claim as their own, but who was in word and thought a German, and no Roman.

After his death the great nationalities of Europe developed to their full importance—the Franks, soon to become the French, the Romans who became Italians, and the Germans who remained what they were, on German soil, with German spirit and German speech.

The struggle which in earlier centuries had been carried on with the sword was now conducted with the weapons of the spirit. The Romish Papacy threw its net out over France, Spain, and Germany. With every century the quarrels increased which the foreign Roman powers stirred up in Germany, and heavier and heavier became the spiritual pressure of the foreign Roman priesthood in all German countries, till at length, under Charles V, the German mind burst the foreign fetters and succeeded in creating a free Church, though not as yet a free German state.

For, first in the seventeenth century, the Thirty-one Years' War had to be waged against foreign jealousy, and in the eighteenth century the North German nation had to prove its strength in the

Seven Years' War; and then Napoleonic arrogance had to be twice broken down before it was permitted to the German people and the Pomeranian statesman and the Prussian King to fortify anew those sacred boundaries which a wise nature had drawn so clearly and visibly, and to make Germany the guardian of its own Marches, the watch on the Rhine, the watch on the Vistula, the protector of the peace of all Europe.

If we now look down from this high pinnacle over the whole history of the world in order to measure the greatness of the present by the greatness of the past, what do we see? Greater than Arminius, than Theodoric, than Charles the Great, than Frederick Barbarossa, than Gustavus Adolphus—for he, too, was a German—than Frederick the Great, stands the man who has triumphantly closed for ever this struggle of 2,000 years—a man whose home-going we celebrate to-day with heavy yet proud hearts, the Kaiser Wilhelm, the first German Emperor.

And now let us ask what made this man so great? In intellectual gifts his elder brother Friedrich Wilhelm IV was far his superior. But he possessed the strongest sense of duty, and the most noble uprightness, and with that a trust in God—a faith in the inevitable triumph of good and right—which even defeats like Jena and Olmütz, and even ingratitude like that of 1848, could not shake.

I saw him as Prince of Prussia as few people saw him, as he, in 1848, entered the room of the Prussian Minister Bunsen in Carlton Terrace, suddenly and unannounced, a fugitive from his Fatherland, hardly to be recognized by those who had known him as a Prussian officer. Those were indeed the darkest days of his life; but from the first day he was at work. He lived on terms of the most friendly intimacy with Bunsen, and he never forgot how much he then owed to the counsel of this upright but often misjudged statesman. He saw all he could of the first men in England. He knew that the old times in Prussia were over for ever; and, highly as he valued the old Prussia, he quickly recognized it as his duty to fit himself for the active service of the new Prussia. He tried to imbibe the principles of a constitutional Government. He read, he learnt, he worked early and late. It was a hard experience for him to be banished from his own country; to be misunderstood by his own people. His own words describe what he then was, what he then felt, and what he even then hoped. After the first victory near Schleswig he wrote the following lines to one of his comrades:—

'God tries me severely, but with a pure conscience I wait for the day of truth, hoping that I may devote my powers to the new Prussia as I did to the old, though the heart will always be sorrowful over the fall of the old Prussia, the independent Prussia.

'Ever your true friend,

'WILHELM.'

Here you see the future Emperor, here you have the real secret of his future greatness—'*With a pure conscience I wait for the day of truth.*' These are words as if carved in marble, and no more beautiful inscription could be engraved on his tomb than this—'*With a pure conscience I wait for the day of truth.*'

And the day of truth came, as it always will come for all who can wait for it with a pure conscience. He became Regent, he became King, he became Emperor, he became the most revered, the most beloved man of his people, and always he remained the same, faithful to his duties, hard-working from morning till evening, and animated by one thought only—how to make Germany strong and respected, how to secure to the German people peace abroad and peace at home.

After seeing him often as an exile in London, I did not see him again till, in 1871, I was allowed to greet him as Emperor at Ems. There he was, the same man, simple, hard-working, faithful to his duty. While others were enjoying their liberty at Ems, he was attending to his business; and often when I came home late at night, and saw at the window the tall Imperial figure at his desk lighted by the small green lamp, I said to myself, 'That is how the German Imperial Crown was won.'

Yes, we are mourning to-day over the German Emperor; but even now the sounds of sorrow begin to vanish. The lowered flags are raised again, and pride and gratitude re-enter the hearts of the German people that they could call such an Emperor their own.

But we harbour a still deeper sorrow in our hearts. What is more natural than death when our life has lasted 'threescore years and ten, or, by reason of our strength, fourscore years'? It is when we think of the new Emperor, who was once the hope, then the pride, and is now the keenest grief of the German nation, that all thoughts and words fail us. The heart knows its own bitterness. The misfortune is overwhelming, and yet, as the poet says, 'Not hopelessly does man yield to the power of the gods.' The fearless son of a fearless father, the new Emperor will perform the work which Providence has assigned to him. The hero who won the battle of Königgrätz by storm, who never flinched under the shower of bullets at Wörth, who was one of the victors at Sedan—his life has not been in vain. But those who know him best expected still greater deeds, still higher victories from him; and even now they know that whatever his hand finds to do, he does it with all his might. From the depth of our heart we say—'Long live, long live the Emperor Frederick, the darling of the German people; long live the noble Empress Victoria, the darling of the English people; and may the English and the German peoples follow their example, and faithfully hold together in dark, as well as in bright days!'

## F

## TRANSLATION OF THE WORD 'SHANGTI'

*Extracts from letter to Chinese Missionaries.*

See Vol. II, p. 94.

'... THERE are, perhaps, passages in the sacred texts of the Chinese in which Shangti is spoken of in what we should call mythological language; language, in our opinion, inapplicable to the Supreme Ruler of the Universe. But does it follow, therefore, that the Chinese, when they formed the name of Shangti, did not mean the true God, or that the best among them had never had any idea of the true God? You know that there must be in the prayers and creeds of all religions a compromise between the language of the wise and foolish; and that the sacred texts of no nation, not even those of Jews and Christians, are entirely free from childlike, poetical, what are called mythological, expressions.... And if we are not to translate Shangti by God, what are we to do? You would not say that the Chinese alone of all nations on earth had never any name for God at all? You suggest that either the name Shangti should be left untranslated, or that it should have been rendered by Supreme Ruler. If left untranslated, all readers would have taken Shangti for a proper name, such as Jupiter, while Dr. Legge states: "it never became a proper name with the people like Zeus in Greece." If Shangti had been rendered by Supreme Ruler, would it have evoked any conception different to God, the true God? How could missionaries in China, if they are willing to translate Shangti by Supreme Ruler, continue to represent him as a false god, or, at all events, as not quite true?... If we are so hard on the Chinese, and tell them that their word Shangti cannot be used as the name of the true God, because it is used synonymously with T'ien, meaning sky, what shall we say when they point to such verses as "I have sinned against heaven, and in Thy sight"? Do the words of Dante:—

> "Per questo la Scrittura condiscende
> A vostra facultate, e piedi e mano
> Attribuisce a Dio, ed altro intende,"

apply to our Scriptures alone? Should we not apply them in a far more generous spirit to the scriptures of the Chinese, Hindus, &c.?

'Surely the name for God in Chinese or in any other language, unless it is simply intolerable, should be treated with the greatest reverence. Let missionaries slowly and gently cut down the rank growth of mythology that has choked so many of the names of God, but let them be careful lest, in tearing up the roots, they kill the stem on which alone their new grafts can live and thrive. Let them follow in the footsteps of the boldest missionary the world has ever seen, who, at Athens, did not break the altar of the Unknown God, but said, "Whom ye ignorantly worship, Him declare I unto you!"'

# G

## Chronological List of the Right Hon. Professor Max Müller's Works

1844. Hitopadesa, translation.
1847. Meghadûta, translation in verse.
Relation of Bengali to the Aboriginal Languages of India.
1849–73. Rig-veda and Sâyana's Commentary.
1853. Essay on the Turanian Languages.
Essay on Indian Logic.
1854. Proposals for a Uniform Missionary Alphabet.
Languages of the Seat of War.
1856. Essay on Comparative Mythology.
1857. Deutsche Liebe (14th edition, 1901).
Buddhist Pilgrims.
1858. German Classics.
1859. Ancient Sanskrit Literature.
1861. Lectures on the Science of Language, Vol. I (14th edition, 1886).
1862. Ancient Hindu Astronomy.
1864. Lectures on the Science of Language, Vol. II.
1866. Hitopadesa, Text, Notes, &c.
Sanskrit Grammar.
1867-75. Chips from a German Workshop, four vols.
1868. Stratification of Language.
1869. Rig-veda, translation, Vol. I.
Rig-veda Prâtisâkhya.
1870. Dhammapada, translation.
1871. Letters on the War.
1873. Rig-veda in Samhitâ and Pada Texts.
Darwin's Philosophy of Language.
Introduction to Science of Religion.
1875. J. B. Basedow.
Schiller's Briefwechsel.
1876. On Spelling.
1878. Hibbert Lectures.
1879. Upanishads, translation.
1881. Selected Essays.
Kant's Critique, translation.
1882. India—What can it teach us?
1884. Biographical Essays.
1887. Science of Thought.
La Carità of Andrea del Sarto.
1888. Biographies of Words.
Science of Thought, three Lectures.

1888-92. Gifford Lectures, four vols.
1889. Science of Language, three Lectures.
1890-2. Rig-veda, new edition.
1893. Âpastamba Sûtras, translated.
1894. New Edition of Chips, four vols., much altered.
Lectures on the Vedânta Philosophy.
1897. Science of Mythology, two vols.
1898. Auld Lang Syne, Vol. I.
Râmakrishna.
1899. Auld Lang Syne, Vol. II.
Six Systems of Indian Philosophy.
Das Pferdebürla.
1900. Transvaal War.
1901. Posthumous. Autobiography and Last Essays, two vols.

## H

## List of Universities, Colleges, Royal Academies, and Learned Societies which conferred Membership on Professor Max Müller

*Universities:*

Leipzig (M.A. and Ph.D., 1843); Oxford (M.A.); Cambridge (LL.D.); Hon. Doctor in the Universities of Dublin, Edinburgh, Bologna, Buda-Pesth, Princeton, Odessa, Lafayette.

*Colleges:*

All Souls College, Oxford (Fellowship).

*Foreign Associate:*

French Institute, Académie des Inscriptions et Belles-Lettres (8).
Imperial Academy of Vienna.
Royal Academy of Berlin.
Royal Sardinian Academy (6).
Royal Academy of the Lincei, Rome (12).
Royal Bavarian Academy.
Royal Hungarian Academy.
Royal Academy of Belgium.
Royal Irish Academy.
Royal Society of Upsala.
De Maatschappy der Nederlandsche Letterkunde de Leyden.
American Academy of Arts and Sciences.
American Philosophical Society.

*Honorary Membership:*

Royal Academy of Sciences at Amsterdam.
Royal Academy of Roumania.
Royal Batavian Society of Arts and Sciences.
Royal Society of Göttingen.
Royal Society of Literature, London.
Royal Historical Society (Vice-President).
Royal Asiatic Society.
Société Asiatique.
Royal Italian Asiatic Society.
German Oriental Society.
American Oriental Society.
Asiatic Society of Bengal.
Philological Society of Buda-Pesth.
Oriental Society of Peking.
Société de Littérature Finnoise, Helsingfors.
Société Finno-Ougrienne.
Cambridge Philosophical Society.
Syllogos Hellenikos of Constantinople.
Anthropological Institute of Great Britain and Ireland.
Deutsches Hochstift zu Frankfurt.
Philosophical Society of Glasgow.
Literary and Philosophical Society of Liverpool.
Archaeological Society, Moscow.
Litauische Literarische Gesellschaft.
American Philological Society.
Société d'Ethnographie de France.
New Zealand Institute.
Polynesian Society, Wellington.
British Association, Anthropological Section (President, 1891).
International Congress of Orientalists (President of Âryan Section, 1889; President of Congress, 1892).

*Corresponding Membership:*

Royal Academy of Lisbon.
Royal Society of Palermo.
Reale Associazione dei Benemeriti Italiani.

## I

The following letter was sent to the editor after all MS. had gone to press, but as it is so complete a summary of Max Müller's views on Missions, it is inserted:—

TO DR. (SIR HENRY) ACLAND.

PARKS END, *November* 7, 1873.

'MY DEAR ACLAND,—I felt very much tempted to speak last night, yet I am glad I held my peace, for I could not possibly have spoken without giving offence to some of the many people present. It was extraordinary, not extraordinary I ought to say, but it was delightful, to see a man like Sir Bartle Frere, a man accustomed to command and to be obeyed, a ruler of a province as large as many a kingdom, a leading statesman at home, pleading humbly, before an Oxford audience, the cause of Missions. His heart was in it—it was an effort to him, but he did it because he felt it was right. There were several points on which I differed from him, there would probably be many more if we came to enter on details, but I truly admired his manly courage in expressing his convictions as he did. There is this great blessing about Missions, that, however we may differ about theological questions at home, we are all united when it comes to missionary work. We should all rather have a man High, Broad, or Low Church, Roman Catholic, or Unitarian, than to have him not a Christian at all. When we have a real heathen before us—and I have had something to do with a few of them—we think little of Creeds and Articles and Councils, and theories of Inspiration and Miracles; we want him to love—to love God and to love his neighbour for God's sake. I believe that missionary work does quite as much good at home as abroad, if it teaches us to forget the outer crust and to discover the living kernel of Christianity. But I go further—I hold that there is a Divine element in every one of the great religions of the world. I consider it blasphemous to call them the work of the Devil, when they are the work of God, and I hold that there is nowhere any belief in God except as the result of a Divine revelation, the effect of a Divine Spirit working in man. Holding that opinion, I do not wish to see the old religions destroyed. I want to see them reformed, reanimated, resuscitated by contact with Christianity. There is much rubbish in the present form of Brâhmanism, but so there is in the present form of Christianity. Let us try to get rid of the whitewash and the plaster—the work of men, whether Popes, Bishops, or Philosophers—and try to discover the original plan and purpose, whether in Christianity or Hinduism. When we do that, I believe we shall arrive at the deep and only safe and solid foundation of religious belief and a truly religious life—we shall find the true *Quod semper, quod ubique, quod ab omnibus*, in all the religions of mankind. I could not call myself a Christian if I were to believe otherwise—if I were to force myself against all my deepest instincts to believe that the prayers of Christians were the only prayers that God could understand. All religions are mere stammerings, our own as much as that of the Brâhmans; they all have to be translated, and, I have no doubt, they all will be translated, whatever their shortcomings may be.'

# INDEX

# Index

THE END.